AF361583

The Complete Poetry of Percy Bysshe Shelley

To Harriet

Whose is the love that gleaming thro the world
Wards off the poisonous arrow of its scorn?
    Whose is the warm & partial praise
        Virtues most sweet reward?

Whose looks gave grace to the majestic theme
The sacred, free & fearless theme of truth
    Whose form did I gaze fondly on
        And love mankind the more?

Harriet! on thine --- thou wert my purer soul
Thou wert the inspiration to my song
    Thine are these early wilding flowers
        Tho' garlanded by me.

Then twine the withering wreath-buds round thy brow
Its bloom may deck thy pale & faded prime
    Can they survive without thy love
        Their wild & mossy birth?

The Complete Poetry of Percy Bysshe Shelley

VOLUME TWO

EDITED BY

Donald H. Reiman and Neil Fraistat

The Johns Hopkins University Press
BALTIMORE AND LONDON

The Johns Hopkins University Press
2715 North Charles Street
Baltimore, Maryland 21218-4363
www.press.jhu.edu

Library of Congress Cataloging-in-Publication Data
will be found at the end of this book.

A catalog record for this book is available from the British Library.

ISBN 0-8018-7874-8

All of the illustrations in this volume are used with the kind
permission of The Carl H. Pforzheimer Collection of Shelley and
His Circle, The New York Public Library, Astor, Lennox
and Tilden Foundations.

Frontispiece: "To Harriet," the first poem in *The Esdaile Notebook* and,
revised, used as the dedication to *Queen Mab*

For

Hélène Dworzan (Reiman)

For she was beautiful—her beauty made
    The bright world dim, and every thing beside
Seemed like the fleeting image of a shade:

The Witch of Atlas

For

Pamela Wessling

Lamp of Earth! where'er thou movest
Its dim shapes are clad with brightness
And the souls of whom thou lovest
Walk upon the winds with lightness . . .

Prometheus Unbound

Contents of Volume Two

TEXTS

COMMENTARIES

HISTORICAL COLLATIONS

APPENDIXES

Illustrations

Acknowledgments

In publishing this second volume of *The Complete Poetry of Percy Bysshe Shelley* (**CPPBS**), we again take great pleasure in thanking those whose help and support have been crucial to the progress of our work. As with the first volume of **CPPBS,** Volume II has been several years in the making and required extensive travel, staff assistance, and released time from other duties, all of which would have been impossible without the generous support of the National Endowment for the Humanities (NEH, an independent federal agency), the University of Maryland, and the Carl and Lily Pforzheimer Foundation, Inc. At the NEH, we are especially grateful to Margot Backas (who recently retired after many years of distinguished service), Elizabeth Arndt, and Alice Hudgins. At the University of Maryland, we've enjoyed the stalwart support of Dean James Harris, Assistant Dean Michele Eastman, and Chuck Caramello, Chair of the English Department. As always, Irene Sanchez, Business Manager of the English Department, and Petra Hagen, Contract and Grant Administrator in the Office of Research Advancement and Administration, have helped in innumerable ways to keep our financial house in order. Carl H. Pforzheimer III and The Carl and Lily Pforzheimer Foundation, which he heads, have supported the Pforzheimer Research Assistantship at the University of Delaware since Don Reiman's retirement from salaried employment, thereby enabling him to continue his work on both *Shelley and his Circle* and **CPPBS.** Jerry Beasley, Linda Russell, Charles E. Robinson, Bonnie Scott, Mary Richards, and Ellen Pifer at the University of Delaware all helped to make this arrangement work smoothly.

We continue to depend, of course, upon the kindness of strangers and friends alike at research libraries scattered far and wide. We are especially indebted to the proficient and generous staffs of the Library of Congress, the Henry E. Huntington Library, the John Work Garrett Library of Johns Hopkins University, the U.S. National Library of Medicine, the British Library, and the Bodleian Library. At the Bodleian, we once again thank Mary Clapinson, until recently the Keeper of Special Collections and Western Manuscripts, and the entire staff of that department. In particular, the extraordinary bibliographical expertise of Bruce C. Barker-Benfield remains an invaluable source of both information and inspiration. We are beholden as well to Pat Herron and Doug McElrath of the University of Maryland Library, and to Susan Brynteson and Timothy Murray at the University of

Delaware Library. We thank especially Doucet Devin Fischer, Daniel Dibbern, and Elizabeth Denlinger, Don's colleagues in the continuing work on *Shelley and his Circle,* for their unfailing support and to Stephen Wagner, Curator of the Carl H. Pforzheimer Collection of Shelley and His Circle at The New York Public Library, for providing the illustrations from that fountain of Shelleyan scholarship. Susan C. Djabri and Jeremy Knight of the Horsham Museum in Sussex made available their important studies of the Shelley family. We also owe a belated word of public thanks to Theresa M. Kelley for kindly rechecking for us, during our reading of the proofs for Volume I, a bibliographical crux in a rare Shelley edition at the Humanities Research Center, University of Texas at Austin.

We are indeed fortunate in the number of other friends and colleagues who have contributed to our efforts in this volume through their scholarship, consultations, advice, and encouragement: they include Betty T. Bennett, Alan Bewell, James Bieri, Marilyn Butler, Stuart Curran, Morris Eaves, Robert N. Essick, Kevin Gilmartin, Nancy Moore Goslee, Steven E. Jones, William Keach, Jon Klancher, Nigel Leask, J. A. Leo Lemay, Jerome J. McGann, Donald C. Mell, Timothy Morton, Jerrold E. Hogle, Lois Potter, Charles E. Robinson, Orrin N. C. Wang, Susan J. Wolfson, and Carl Woodring.

Special thanks are due to Sally Rogers for her work with PBS's Greek and Latin texts, to Michael Ferber for his help in proofreading the Greek passages, and to Hélène Dworzan (Reiman) for her help with PBS's French texts. Professor David Freeman of Newfoundland used part of a mid-winter holiday in California to provide us with his expert insights into the field of Renaissance emblem books. Timothy Webb shared with us his research on Shelley's and Coleridge's views on Robert Emmet and the United Irishmen. Several helpful correspondents on the NASSR list-serve contributed their knowledge of Mount Snowdon and the myths thereof, the crucial information coming from Bruce Graver and John Cole. Jack Stillinger, with characteristic generosity, reviewed our whole unit on **Queen Mab,** sagely advising us on everything from editorial policy to the content of our Commentary. Nora Crook, who will be joining us as the editor of later volumes of **CPPBS,** provided a brilliantly detailed reading of the entire manuscript to which we are greatly indebted; many of her suggestions are noted in our Commentary.

Great thanks are also due to a *sine qua non* of **CPPBS,** the excellent graduate students serving as our research assistants during the past few years. At the University of Delaware Shiela Pardee, Kainoa Harbottle (who had earlier helped Don read the proofs of Volume I), Jodi Devine, and Noreen Miller each contributed a fruitful year to the work. At the University of Maryland Matthew Bray, Lorna Ellis, and Eleanor Shevlin helped to prepare the various text files for collation with great care and remarkable accuracy, and Melissa J. Sites has served as researcher nonpareil. Most of all, we both are grateful to David Brookshire, the project's superb current research assistant at Maryland, who not only prepared many files for collation but also expended his eyesight, if not his prodigious patience, in formatting the manuscript for the press and checking, revising, and checking again the final digital files that served as the press copy.

The Johns Hopkins University Press has made what might have been an onerous process of production into a creative and collaborative one. We are grateful to James D. Jordan, Wendy Harris, Barbara Lamb, Maura Burnett, Kathleen Szawiola, and latterly Michael Lonegro and Becky Brasington Clark for their help, support, and expertise.

Our greatest thanks, however, go to Anne Whitmore: having survived the editing of the manuscript for Volume I, she has graced yet another volume with what can only be described as her astonishing acuity in both regularizing the style of the whole and also saving us from factual errors and verbal infelicities.

Finally, our thanks go to the friends and family who have continued to share with us this exhilarating, though long and winding, textual road. For friendships that seem only to deepen with each passing year, Neil Fraistat wishes to thank all the usual suspects: Jonathan Auerbach and Marijean Berry, Bonnie Bernstein and Hank Dobin, Stuart Curran, Steve Jones, Len Goldberg, Joan Goldberg and Ted Leinwand, Ivy Goodman and Bob Levine, Sue Lanser, Beth and Bill Loizeaux, Orrin Wang, Joe Wittreich, and Mick and Zara Mangan—to which list should now be added Matt Kirschenbaum and Bill Sherman. Neil is also extremely grateful for the most supportive of families: Louis Fraistat and Felice Lankasky, Terry and Judy Silverlight, Scott and Jennifer Fraistat, and nieces Rachel, Amanda, and Ashley Fraistat—and, most of all, those delightful and irrepressible children, Ann Cleveland Fraistat and Shawn Cleveland Fraistat, who have turned sixteen and twenty years old, respectively, as this volume goes to press. To the dazzling Pam Wessling, who has made all the difference, Neil dedicates his efforts on this volume with deepest love.

Don Reiman's personal list, though curtailed by the passing of some good friends in recent years, has additions as well. Besides his collegial debts to those working on the *Shelley and his Circle* project in New York and to members of the English Department of the University of Delaware and at research libraries, as named above, he is grateful for support and encouragement from his colleagues in the work of the Keats-Shelley Association of America and the Byron Society of America, particularly William T. Buice III, Robert A. Hartley, Alice Levine, Marsha M. Manns, Charles E. Robinson, Robert M. Ryan, Jack Stillinger, and James L. Weil. Ultimately, however, he owes his greatest inspiration to Laurel Reiman Henneman, Charles C. Henneman, and Wyatt and Caspar, their sweet little boys, and to Hélène Dworzan (Reiman), to whom he dedicates his share of this volume with love.

Editorial Overview

In mid-February 1813, Percy Bysshe Shelley (PBS) wrote to his friend and prospective publisher Thomas Hookham, "Queen Mab is finished & transcribed" (*Letters* I, 354), noting that Hookham would receive it along with the collection of early poems that through the vagaries of its history is now known as *The Esdaile Notebook* (*Esd;* see "Principles of Abbreviation and Citation," pp. xxxvii–xxxviii). Although PBS expressed his hope that the two works "should form one volume," neither one was ultimately published by Hookham. For reasons discussed in our Commentary, PBS in 1813 privately issued *Queen Mab* (*QM*)—which became his most influential work during much of the nineteenth century—whereas the poems of *Esd* were not published as a whole until 1964. Volume II of *The Complete Poetry of Percy Bysshe Shelley* (*CPPBS*) for the first time presents these two works together in a single volume, thus fulfilling, some 190 years later, the plan that PBS proposed to Hookham.

As we detail in our Commentary to *Esd,* the fifty-one poems that PBS originally transcribed in the physical Esdaile Notebook (**EN**) show signs of a careful arrangement, both to tell the story of PBS's life with Harriet Westbrook Shelley (HWS) and to trace the development of his thoughts and feelings at least from the time of his conversion experience at Eton in 1810 until he completed *QM,* the first poem in which he assumed a cosmic perspective and (near his twenty-first birthday) articulated his world view, encompassing his conceptions of science, politics, history, religion, society, and individual human relationships. When the two works are read together, *Esd* and *QM* relate to each other in much the way Wordsworth projected the relationship between *The Prelude* and *The Excursion.*

PBS, of course, may well have decided to provide an autobiographical introduction to his first attempt at a philosophical poem without any knowledge of Wordsworth's plans, but it would not be surprising to find that he had stolen a march on Wordsworth, just as John Hamilton Reynolds was later to publish his own satiric version of *Peter Bell* before the appearance of the original that Wordsworth himself had worked on for nearly two decades. The idea of gathering and publishing what PBS called his "Minor [sometimes "minor"] Poems" occurred to him about the turn of the year from 1811 to 1812 while he was sojourning in the Lake District, where he had hoped to meet Wordsworth and where PBS talked with several of that poet's friends, including Robert Southey, who had published a similar collection of short poems at the outset of *his* career (as had Southey's brother-in-law Samuel Taylor Coleridge). Since both William and Dorothy Wordsworth had for years been telling and writing to numerous friends about the progress of Wordsworth's "Poem on my own earlier life" (Wordsworth to Francis Wrangham, January or February 1804) and Wordsworth had read the entire "1805" version of *The Prelude* to Coleridge in January 1807, it is possible that Southey, Robert Lovell (brother-in-law to both Coleridge and Southey), or other associates of Wordsworth whom PBS met during his more than three months in the Keswick area may have alluded to *The Prelude* as an existing poem—though they were likely to have spoken chiefly of Wordsworth's purpose in writing it rather than described its form or contents. For models of those specifics, PBS could have turned to the volumes of miscellaneous early poems by Southey and Coleridge or to Lord Byron's *Poems: Original and Translated* (Newark: S. and J. Ridge, 1808), a volume that he had read, admired, and imitated at least by 1810.

On the other hand, PBS would also have been aware of the attack by the *Edinburgh Review* on Byron's autobiographical *Hours of Idleness* (the revised version of *Poems: Original and Translated*), and when in January 1812 PBS entered into a correspondence with William Godwin, the philosopher whom he then most admired, he was advised not to rush into print with his first blights, just as PBS was to counsel Keats in 1817. To Godwin's initial warning, PBS replied on 26 January 1812: "You regard early authorship detrimental to the cause of general happiness. . . . [but] If any man would determine sincerely and cautiously at *every* period of his life to publish books which should contain the real state of his feelings and opinions, I am willing to suppose that this portraiture of his mind would be worth many metaphysical disquisitions" (**Letters** I, 242). The poems of **Esd** were thus assembled to present just such an autobiographical "portraiture" as prelude to the political, philosophical, and "metaphysical disquisitions" of **QM;** and in order to understand both works better, one needs to keep in mind the *Sturm und Drang* that characterized PBS's life between August 1811 and April 1813.

The Shelleys' Adventures, August 1811–April 1813

Early in August 1811, PBS returned from a visit to Cwm Elan, the Welsh estate of his cousin Thomas Grove, and eloped with Harriet Westbrook (the daughter of a London coffeehouse owner in the fashionable West End), who was a schoolmate of PBS's sisters. Hurrying to Edinburgh, the young couple were married there on 28 or 29 August and then spent about five weeks in "the Athens of the North," much of it in the company of Thomas Jefferson Hogg, PBS's best friend at Oxford, who had been expelled with him from University College in the spring of 1811. As the couple had passed through

York on their way to Scotland, PBS had mailed a note to Hogg, then a legal apprentice in York, asking him to send ten pounds to the Shelleys at Edinburgh (cutting the banknote in half and mailing it in two letters for safety). Instead, Hogg abandoned his work and went north to join them. "My dear friend Hogg that noble being is with me, & will be always" (*Letters* I, 145), PBS declared in the first surviving letter he wrote after his marriage, addressed to Elizabeth Hitchener, a Sussex schoolteacher who had become PBS's epistolary confidante immediately after they met at the home of his uncle Captain John Pilfold at the beginning of June 1811. Short of money, the Shelleys and Hogg then returned to York, where PBS left HWS under Hogg's protection while he went to Sussex in search of funds. When PBS returned, he found that Eliza Westbrook, his wife's older sister, had joined her in York; and Harriet soon told him that during his absence Hogg, "that noble being," had tried to seduce her, using PBS's belief in free love as his primary argument.

After remonstrating with Hogg, PBS fled to the Lake District with HWS and Eliza, planting false clues to discourage Hogg from pursuing them. They rented a cottage in Keswick, where Southey lived, and not far from Greystoke, the northern seat of the Duke of Norfolk, who was the political patron of PBS's father, Timothy Shelley, M.P. Early in December the Shelleys visited the Duke, who tried to arrange a reconciliation between PBS and his father. There they also met William Calvert, a friend of Wordsworth and Southey; and through Calvert PBS soon became an intimate of Southey himself, who—though sympathetic to the Shelleys—condescendingly characterized PBS's ideas as the kind that he had once held in youth but which his greater maturity and wisdom now revealed to be fallacious.

These months and a subsequent period of continued intellectual stimulation, financial struggle, and emotional turmoil that lasted from late 1811 into 1813 are documented in PBS's expansive *Letters* (I, 137ff.), written chiefly to Hogg, Hitchener, Hookham, and Godwin. Additional information appears in a long series of candid letters that HWS wrote to Catherine Nugent, a liberal Irish woman whom the Shelleys met during their first excursion to Dublin. (The letters to Nugent written in 1812 and 1813 appear in footnotes to PBS's *Letters:* I, 283–84, 304–5, 309–10, 320–21, 326–27, 331–32, 349–50, 367–68, 372, 376–77, and 378–79.) PBS's earliest mentions of both *QM* and *Esd* appear in a letter that he wrote to Hitchener about 10 December 1811, saying that he had "in contemplation . . . a Poem" (see Commentary to *QM,* 491–92), to which he added: "I think I shall also make a selection of my younger Poems for publication" (*Letters* I, 201–2). But his first attempts to have his poems printed failed, and though during the following months PBS wrote many poems on the incidents and feelings that he experienced in his travels, it was not until late in 1812 that he began to arrange them, together with others, written chiefly between 1808 and early 1811, in an effort to trace and explain his intellectual and moral development to himself as well as to others.

On 26 December 1811, while still at Keswick, he wrote to Hitchener, "The minor Poems I mentioned you will see soon. They are about to be sent to the Printer's—I think it wrong to publish anything anonymously. I shall annex my name, and a preface in which I shall lay open my intentions as the poems are not wholly useless. 'I sing, and liberty may love the song'" (quotation unidentified; perhaps by PBS?). In a letter written 2 January he added one caveat: "My Poems will make their appearance as soon as I can find a printer"—presumably one willing to postpone payment until PBS reached his majority, when he would be able either to borrow money or to bargain with his father for increased income (*Letters* I, 214, 218). Writing to Hitchener again, in mid-January 1812, PBS expressed optimism about the potential sale of this collection: "All the money I get shall be squeezed out of the rich; the poor cannot understand and wd. not buy my poems, therefore I shall print them expensively" (*Letters* I, 235). And following this remark, he quoted the selected stanzas of *The Devil's Walk* (*DW*) that constitute the letter version of that poem (see *CPPBS* I, 128–29; 281–93), which suggests that he originally intended to include it among his "minor Poems." But by 26 January 1812, he seems to have doubted whether he had yet accumulated enough poetry of a quality that met his standards to justify hasty publication, for he wrote (again to Hitchener): "My Volume of Poetry will I fear be an inferior production, it will be only valuable to philosophical and reflecting minds who love to trace the early state of human feelings and opinions, who can make allowances for some bad versification," even though he had declared earlier in the same letter, when telling Hitchener of his plan to sail to Dublin, "my Poems will be printed there" (*Letters* I, 239). The result of this vacillation and a difficulty he encountered in Dublin was that he did not begin copying his miscellaneous poems into **EN** until late in the year 1812, while living at a hillside villa named Tan-yr-allt, near Tremadoc in Wales. Meanwhile, he decided to initiate some direct political action.

By the end of 1811, the political unrest that had wracked Ireland for decades was stirring again. After the renewed mental illness of King George III forced Parliament to elevate the Prince of Wales (later George IV) to Prince Regent, the Prince continued his father's support of the Tory regime instead of asking the Whigs—the party of his cronies Charles James Fox (died Sept. 1806) and Richard Brinsley Sheridan, who favored Irish self-rule and Catholic Emancipation—to form a new government. Despite warnings from both Southey and Godwin, with whom he began to correspond as soon as Southey informed him that Godwin was still alive, the nineteen-year-old PBS (wise beyond his years but arrogant beyond his wisdom) was determined to help steer the ferment in Ireland into productive, nonviolent channels by personally meeting with and giving advice to leading Irish nationalists and by publishing two prose tracts—*An Address to the Irish People* and *Proposals for an Association of . . . Philanthropists.*

Once in Dublin, PBS arranged for what he then called simply his "Poems" to be printed by John Stockdale (not to be confused with John Joseph Stockdale, the London bookseller who had distributed *Victor and Cazire* and published *St. Irvyne*). John Stockdale of Dublin was a well-known Irish nationalist who in 1797 had established and printed the United Irishmen's periodical *The Press.* According to Mary Pollard (*A Dictionary of Members of the Dublin Book Trade, 1550–1800* [London: Bibliographical Society, 2000], 552–53), not only did he serve time in prison, but while he was there his printshop and presses were destroyed by government agents. Stockdale's two sons, Roger and John, Jr., became active in the firm after 1805. By 1812, though the Stockdales still printed nationalist books and pamphlets and remained friendly with many former United Irish activists, the elder John (or possibly his son) was secretly supplying information on radicals to the British authorities at Dublin Castle (Timothy Webb, "'A Noble Field': Shelley's Irish Expedition . . . ," published in *Robespierre & Co.*, ed. Nadia Minerva [Bologna: Edizione Analisi, 1990], 553–76, 568). Scholars once believed that PBS and John Stockdale quarreled simply about the money that PBS owed the printer for work on "Poems," their evidence being HWS's letters to the Shelleys' Dublin friend Catherine Nugent; but the Stockdales may have been playing a double game, perhaps reporting on PBS's efforts to the British authorities but possibly also protecting the young idealist by frustrating, as much as they could, his attempts to publish writings that might make him subject to prosecution.

When the Shelleys left Dublin the first time (4 April 1812), the manuscript of "Poems" remained in Stockdale's hands; on 4 August 1812, HWS wrote from Lynmouth (then Lymouth), Devon, in reply to Catherine Nugent's apparent offer to read the proofs or help in some other way with the publication of PBS's "Poems": "I thank you in Percy's name for your kind offer of service, tho' at the same time we cannot accept it. The case is this. His printer refuses to go on with his poems until he is paid. Now such a demand is seldom made, as printers are never paid till the profits arising from the sale of the work come in, and Percy agreed with him to this effect, and as long as we staid in Dublin he wore the mask which is now taken off. However, I am in great hope that Mr. Lawless will get them from him. He is coming to London on business and then we shall see him" (*Letters* I, 320). But John Lawless (an Irish nationalist author) failed them, and at the end of a long letter from London in October 1812, HWS wrote to Nugent: "Percy says he wishes you to go to Stockdale's, and get all his manuscript poems and other pieces. I am afraid you will be obliged to use a little manœuvre to get them. In the first place, you can say you wish to look at them, and then you may be able to steal them away from him. I leave it all to you, knowing you will do your best in the way to obtain them . . . " (**Letters** I, 327).

Following this exchange, the Shelleys did not hear from Nugent for some time, perhaps because they were, at this period, without a fixed address, but also possibly because Nugent was not overly charmed by the suggestion that she commit a felony to please her wandering young friends. HWS next wrote to her from Stratford-upon-Avon on 14 November 1812, and after reporting how they had returned Elizabeth Hitchener to Sussex after she had dwelt with them for almost four months and caused dissension in the family ("We are much happier now than all the time she was with us."), she added: "Have you been able to get the poems from Stockdale? If not it cannot be helped, but do pray write to us, for we are quite uneasy at not hearing from you for so long a time. Direct your letters to me at Tanyrallt, near the town of Tremadoc (in Carnarvonshire, North Wales)" (**Letters** I, 331).

PBS's debt to the Stockdales, however, may have involved more than any cost for printing "Poems." E. B. Murray's speculations about the unnamed printer(s) of PBS's Dublin prose publications (see **Prose** I, 338–39) led the editors of *Shelley and his Circle* (*SC*) to determine that Stockdale had probably printed other texts for which PBS owed him money (*SC* IX,195; fn. 25). Since no printer named "I. Eton," as given on the colophon of **Proposals for an Association,** seems to have existed, that name was likely a false imprint (perhaps devised by PBS in honor of his school) to protect the actual printer from prosecution. Moreover, both PBS's **Address to the Irish People** and the broadsheet **Declaration of Rights,** which were also printed in Dublin, not only lack colophons but also share certain misspellings and typographical features with **Proposals,** suggesting that all of these papers were the work of the same printer, the likely candidate being Stockdale. PBS's letters from Dublin indicate, moreover, that he had promised to pay for the printing of John Lawless's *Compendium of the History of Ireland,* which may have increased his debt. If Stockdale had evaded the law by illegally printing PBS's publications sans colophons, he would have been unable to recover PBS's debts to him through legal action and so may have held PBS's poetic manuscripts hostage as the easiest way to persuade the young man to pay his bill.

After the Shelleys left Ireland in April 1812, PBS had unsuccessfully sought to borrow a large sum of money (ostensibly to lease a farm on which to settle down "within a mile" of the Groves' estate at Cwm Elan). He next led his household to Ly(n)mouth, Devon, where Elizabeth Hitchener joined them. There PBS completed **The Devil's Walk** and prose works, which he had printed at Barnstaple, with the results detailed in **CPPBS** I, 281–85. When his Irish servant, Daniel Healey, was arrested for distributing **DW,** the Shelley ménage, which included Hitchener and Eliza Westbrook, fled back to North Wales and eventually settled at Tan-yr-allt, where PBS devoted much of the savage winter of 1812–13 (which destroyed Napoleon's Grand Army in Russia) to completing **QM**. At the same time, he began to arrange his shorter poems and copy them into the lined copybook now known as the Esdaile Notebook. On 17 December 1812 he wrote to Hookham discussing his current writing projects: "I am also preparing a Volume of Minor Poems. Respecting whose publication I shall request your judgement both as publisher & friend. A very obvious question would be.— Will they sell or not?" (**Letters** I, 340). And replying on 2 January 1813 to Hookham's response, he elaborated: "My Poems will I fear little stand the criticism even of friendship.— Some of the later ones have the merit of conveying a meaning in every word, and these all are faithful pictures of my feelings at the time of writing them, but they are in a great measure {abru}pt & obscure. All breathing hatred to government & religion, but I think not too openly for publication.— One fault they are indisputably exempt from, that of being a volume of *fashionable literature.* I doubt not but your friendly hand will clip the wings of my Pegasus considerably" (**Letters** I, 348). On 26 January he could prognosticate to Hookham: "I expect to have Queen Mab, & the other Poems finished by March. Queen Mab will be in ten cantos & contain about 2800 lines. The other poems probably contain as much more. The notes to Q.M. will be long & philosophical" (**Letters** I, 350), and by mid-February, in his final surviving letter written from Tan-yr-allt, he reported: "Queen Mab is finished & transcribed.—I am now preparing the Notes which shall be long & philosophical.—You will receive it with the other poems. I think that the whole should form one volume, but of that we can speak hereafter.—" (**Letters** I, 354).

On 26 February 1813 (a proverbially dark and stormy night), Dan Healey, who had just completed his jail term in Devonshire for distributing **DW** and **Declaration of Rights** (see **CPPBS** I, 283–85), reached Tan-yr-allt, obviously guided there by PBS through correspondence with Mrs. Hooper, his friendly landlady at Ly(n)mouth. Within hours after Healey's arrival, PBS, Healey, and the rest of Shelley's party fled their residence, declaring that they feared for their lives because they had been attacked by a would-be assassin. The so-called "attack at Tanyrallt" is one of the most controversial events in PBS's eventful life. A number of contemporary observers and several later scholars have believed it to be either a hallucination or a ruse staged by PBS (see *SC* IX, 190–217).

After waiting just long enough to borrow additional money from local friends and (by mail) from Hookham, PBS and his party departed Wales for Ireland, leaving behind many unpaid debts to tradesmen in the Tremadoc area (see **Letters** I, 355–58). Soon after arriving in Dublin (about 8 or 9 March), Shelley mailed his "Poem" (**QM**) to Hookham in London, ordering that 250 copies be printed, while adding: "The notes are preparing . . . . I have many other Poems which shall also be sent" (**Letters** I, 361). PBS, it seems, had been unable to complete his "minor Poems" in Wales because he lacked copies of some that John Stockdale was holding for ransom and he had therefore returned to Ireland to recover them. The assumption of scholars familiar with **Esd** has been that PBS succeeded in recovering the manuscripts of the earlier version of his "Poems," probably by paying his debt to the printer with the money that he had recently borrowed to help him flee Wales, which also provided the postage to mail the MS of **QM** to Hookham. But as we analyzed the dating and arrangement of the poems in **Esd,** we came to the conclusion that PBS may have decided upon his sudden flight to Dublin to safeguard his poetic manuscripts when he learned that the elder John Stockdale had died in January 1813 (Pollard, *A Dictionary of . . . the Dublin Book Trade,* 553). As with almost everything involved in PBS's biography, there may be no simple explanation for his behavior (see "Shelley's Arrangement of the Poems" in the Commentary to **Esd,** 323 ff.), and John Stockdale's death presents one new complication.

While in Dublin, PBS invited Hogg to visit him, but when the young lawyer arrived there after a difficult and uncomfortable trip, the Shelleys' friend John Lawless met him and reported that PBS's party had gone to the south of Ireland to view the Lakes of Killarney (and, perhaps, to kiss the Blarney Stone?), another journey that, from lack of evidence, has never been adequately explained. The only contemporary evidence about the trip is PBS's evasive letter of excuse to Hogg (**Letters** I, 364–65), written from Dublin on 31 March when he and HWS (he wrote) had just returned to the capital, the day after Hogg's departure for London (White, *Shelley* I, 286–88; *SC* III, 124–31). Eliza Westbrook and Dan Healey did not return to Dublin but apparently remained behind in the south of Ireland with PBS's books, which they soon seem to have either shipped or accompanied to London—possibly by sea from the port of Cork. Was the excursion to Killarney, then, an impulsive sight-seeing trip to avoid Hogg because HWS did not wish to see her would-be seducer again, or was it a ruse to dispose of contraband, such as remaining copies of PBS's Irish tracts and **Declaration of Rights?** Did Eliza Westbrook and Healey accompany PBS's books to England by sea simply because that trip was less costly than the coach, or to avoid attracting the attention of agents of either English customs officers or the Home Secretary's office, who (as PBS may have feared or been alerted by his Irish friends) might scrutinize his and HWS's luggage? Or did PBS fear that his creditors in either Dublin or Wales might seize his books and papers as collateral if he shipped them from Dublin to London through Holyhead and thus along the coach road through North Wales, where he had recently left so many unpaid debts?

In any case, PBS and HWS (then in the sixth month of her first pregnancy) reached the Westbrook family's London home on or before 5 April 1813 (**Letters** I, 366), and we know from later references that Eliza Westbrook and Dan Healey soon reappeared in London. After this return, PBS's movements and activities lack virtually any contemporary documentation until mid-May and are very sparsely documented during the summer of 1813, when they are known chiefly through his letters about financial matters and in a few laconic entries in Godwin's journal. PBS's surviving letters of May and June 1813 to his father, the Duke of Norfolk, and Thomas Charles Medwin show that the Shelleys had returned to London not only for HWS's care during pregnancy but so that PBS could negotiate a financial settlement with his father before his twenty-first birthday on 4 August 1813, after which he would have the legal power to raise money through loans secured by his status as heir to his grandfather's entailed estates.

Almost no information survives from this period about PBS's writings for two reasons: first, he had little need to correspond with those to whom he was most likely to confide his literary plans—Hogg, Godwin, Hookham, and his new friend Thomas Love Peacock—because he was seeing all of them regularly in London; and, second, it is likely that when *QM* became notorious in 1817 during the chancery court suit (in which PBS tried to gain custody of his children after HWS's death), all parties involved with producing that work are likely to have destroyed any incriminating documents relating to its production and distribution. Not surprisingly then, no further letters by PBS survive from 1813 or 1814 that contain references to *QM, Esd,* or his efforts to publish either. We provide further and more detailed biographical information in the Commentary to *Esd,* where the specifics of PBS's life crucially provide contexts for the poems, but here we must stop to review the editorial principles and procedures that inform this edition.

Editing on Historical Principles

CPPBS presents the poems that PBS intended to publish, according to the groupings he arranged and in the chronological order in which he hoped to issue them. Within each such volume or gathering we place the individual poems, wherever possible, in the order that PBS planned for their publication. Those poems that he released privately to close friends, without attempting publication, are arranged chronologically in separate groupings according to defined periods of his life and, within those groups, in the order that he sent or gave them to friends. We edit these released poems to represent, insofar as the surviving evidence permits, the texts that PBS intended his first reader(s) to see at the time he released them. We correct, according to the principles outlined below, errata in PBS's MSS and first editions, whether or not he is known to have noted them as such, and we attempt to uncover and extirpate errors of the press and later editorial emendations that reflect the judgment of later times and other consciousnesses. Our typical Text will be a critical redaction (sometimes called an "ideal state") of a single version that PBS chose to release to a particular public on a specific occasion. Readers will thus have before them discrete versions that reflect the author's creative thinking about a poetic whole that he intended to release to a historically identifiable audience, rather than a conflation of his judgments at different times, meant for different audiences.

Each released poem, then, will appear in the version in which PBS released it, following his preferred standards of grammar, pointing, and orthography as established by his MSS and published editions. In correcting this base text, we have observed the general principle articulated by Coleridge at the beginning of Chapter 12 of *Biographia Literaria:* "until you understand a writer's ignorance, presume yourself ignorant of his understanding." We have consequently been able to establish the credibility of unusual or doubtful readings in our Text by finding them among the forms and idioms accepted by PBS's contemporaries, as recorded in grammars and dictionaries used during his time, in addition to the *OED* and other scholarly works on the language of his era. In some cases, PBS's supposed errors or eccentricities prove to be merely forms and meanings conventionally correct for a person of his day and class, and we indicate these instances as succinctly as possible. Contemporary editions of the poetry of his peers and predecessors, as well as concordances to their poetry, have also helped us identify the specific sources of some unusual forms, diction, and allusions that he adopted. These sources are sometimes found in the works of writers that PBS is known to have admired during his artistic development, but in other cases our search led to writers and works in whom his interest was formerly a matter of speculation. Aspects of the usage of PBS's time and facets of his intentions are still obscure, and were we to emend without knowledge, we might destroy evidence useful to other readers and researchers in expanding scholarly understanding. Finally, PBS's punctuation was (according to the practice of his time) primarily rhetorical rather than grammatical, and it cannot be modernized without seriously compromising the phrasing and emphases—and, hence, both the metrics and the meaning—of his poems.

In general, therefore, we do not emend the words, orthography, and punctuation of our copy-text unless a reading cannot be justified through historical research or unless we discover strong evidence against it, either from other extant primary authorities or from PBS's own practices in parallel situations. We are willing to accept as much inconsistency in the spelling and punctuation of his texts as PBS did, as we judge from variations in his own MSS and in printed texts derived directly from them. Some variants in spelling may provide evidence of authorship, and sometimes anomalous usage contributes to an understanding of either the nature of the MS underlying the first printed text or the later history of the textual transmission of the work.

We attempt, however, to avoid transmitting obvious errors that PBS elsewhere tried to correct or allowed his amanuenses and printers to correct for him. We have determined over our years of study that he miswrote certain words frequently though not consistently, among them a whole range of words containing *ie* and *ei* (e.g., *thier, feirce, sieze,* and *vermiel*). These were errors that, once discovered, he tried to eliminate from his printed works. In his early MSS and publications there are many omissions or misplacements of the apostrophe for the possessive case—as well as apostrophes added anomalously to simple plurals. We have often emended such solecisms (and noted them as errors) where there seemed to be no possibility of another reading of the sentence that would justify PBS's practice.

In his draft MSS, PBS frequently omitted marks of punctuation, including final stops, quotation marks, and commas within a series of three or more nouns. During the fair-copying or the printing process, he or his amanuenses usually added these conventional marks (which appear in all the volumes published under his supervision during his maturity) but they are sometimes missing from his earliest printed texts. We try to identify and correct all readings that, according to the predominance of the surviving evidence, are erroneous in PBS's terms, not ours. Whenever we emend our copy-text, we signal the change by giving the siglum of the variant at the foot of the page in ***boldface italic*** type (e.g., ***1813***) if the copy-text is a printed source, or simply in **boldface** (e.g., **EN**) if it is a manuscript. In the Commentary we note most such emendations and outline our reasons for making them. Where other responsible editors have emended the text but we do not, we explain why we have refrained from doing so. (After making a point a few times for a particular poem, we let these explanations suffice for analogous cases.) In each specific place where a typographical error, rather than a pattern of idiosyncratic usage, mars the sense—sometimes even in those volumes that PBS himself superintended through the printing process—we emend the text and note our emendation.

Released "Poems" Distinguished from Unreleased "Poetry"

No matter how candid and confessional the poets of the Romantic age might appear when compared with their predecessors, they usually released poetic records of their thoughts and feelings to the world only after they had successfully transmuted those ideas and emotions into artistic forms. When PBS grappled with his material in attempts at composition but failed to resolve the drafts into forms that he considered worthy expressions of his values, he usually abandoned those attempts, though he often recycled images and ideas from such discarded drafts in later poems. Being fully aware of how interesting and how biographically and interpretively revealing these unfinished pieces can be, we include not only such fragments found in other editions but new ones gleaned from the recent work on *The Bodleian Shelley Manuscripts, The Manuscripts of the Younger Romantics, Shelley and his Circle,* and our own researches for **CPPBS.** We edit them, however, not as finished *poems* (as Mary Wollstonecraft Shelley [MWS] and subsequent editors often did), but as fragmentary *poetry*—a distinction that PBS himself makes in **A Defence of Poetry,** based upon one that Coleridge earlier proposed in *Biographia Lit-eraria.* These works in progress, sketches, and bits of poetry should not be analyzed or judged on the same terms as polished works of art. Useful as the unreleased fragments are to students of the poet and his age, such unfinished pieces are not part of PBS's self-presentation to his contemporaries and ought to be edited and studied under different rules.

Instead of placing the unreleased fragments in a chronological order that is factitious (many of them cannot be dated relative to one another or to PBS's public poetry and none has a date of completion or release), we plan to arrange them according to the periodical or edition in which they were first published or—if they appear only in transcriptions of MSS in either *The Bodleian Shelley Manuscripts* or *The Manuscripts of the Younger Romantics: Shelley*—to group them with other poetry found in the same MSS or notebooks in which they survive. Thus, all the fragments and smaller, unpolished poems found in Bodleian MS. Shelley adds. e.7 (which contains the drafts for **Hellas**), except those already published from a later or more finished copy, will appear with the other poetic drafts and fragments found in that notebook (*BSM* XVI, ed. Reiman and Neth). The Text of each fragment will be the latest extant version that appears to have had PBS's approval, but we may sometimes compare those versions, through selective quotation at the foot of the page or in our Commentary, with other versions of the same fragments that were published, in a polished (sometimes corrupted) form after PBS's death.

By the same general principle, we do not treat as independent works preliminary drafts for—or clearly abandoned or rejected fragments of—finished poems, such as the early versions of the **Esdaile** poems found in PBS's letters. When we include these (as in this volume), we either print short examples with the primary collations or label them "Supplements" and place them immediately following the completed, public poems to which they pertain. All such fragments and drafts, like the unreleased poetry in general, will be presented diplomatically to the extent appropriate to each individual case. For some short, undeveloped fragments, all cancellations may be printed along with the uncanceled text. Longer and more substantial independent fragments, such as **The Triumph of Life,** will be given clearer form in hypothesized reading texts, with substantive cancellations and rejected passages presented in collations at the foot of the page or in the Supplements following the poetic fragment.

Like other poets, PBS frequently gave copies of his poems to friends, sometimes using their private reactions to gauge whether the poems were ready to be published. When there exists a later published version (or a later

MS prepared for publication), we may include that public version, while treating the privately released version as a way-station toward the public poem by collating it as an authority that may help reveal typographical errors or explain other apparent anomalies in the public text. Where there exist alternative texts that PBS released to the public, or personal poems that he gave in distinctive versions to different friends, we include critical texts of each of the two or three versions, either as Supplements or as related poems destined for different audiences and perhaps embodying different meanings. By comparing such multiple versions, released at different times or prepared for distinct audiences, readers will be better able to chart PBS's emerging intentions and the means by which he attempted to reach a public or to perfect his artistry, as well as how he varied the theme or tone of a poem, depending upon the circumstances under which he released it and who his intended readers were.

We seek to avoid, however, separating PBS into two Shelleys—the private person whose inner feelings are documented in his unreleased poems and private letters and the public poet who, during a period of great social and ideological upheaval, was struggling against other writers for the hearts and minds of the British establishment and reading public. To this end, our Commentary on the various volumes and groupings and on individual passages and lines link these and other facets of the complex individual whose life and ideas, writings and art, we have studied holistically for many years.

Presentation of Texts and Editorial Apparatus

Although the nature of the surviving textual authorities and histories of particular poems will dictate variations in the general pattern, PBS's poems and their apparatus will normally be arranged as follows: the Text of each book-length poem, multi-poem volume arranged by PBS, or group of separate poems gathered by us will be introduced by a brief headnote that identifies the date, nature, origin, and title of the unit and cites the pages in this volume where the reader can find our editorial Commentary as well as locate the Historical Collations.

So that readers may encounter the living poetry without the weight of scholarly impedimenta, we devote the front of the book to PBS's poetry and footnoted variants from the primary authorities that may warrant textual consideration, follow the Text with our Commentary in the succeeding section, and place the Historical Collations at the end for the use of analytical readers and textual scholars. Readers of the Commentary will, we hope, find useful much of the information gathered there from a number of research libraries, but even scholars who attempt to understand the intricacies of PBS's art and thought and, possibly, to feel an even deeper appreciation of his genius, may gladly return to his poetry in a format that approximates, if it cannot duplicate, the clarity of presentation in which his works appeared to his first readers.

Collation of Primary Authorities

All *verbal* variants and most variants in orthography, punctuation, and format (e.g., stanza numbers and spacing breaks between stanzas or sections of verse) appear in our primary collations, those at the foot of the page containing the poetic Text. The primary authorities that are eligible to be collated at the foot of the page, so long as there is room, include:

1. any MS of the poem in the hand of PBS, all MSS copied from his holographs by those acting as his amanuenses, and corrections to printed texts supplied either in his own hand or in the hand of MWS acting as his amanuensis;

2. all authorized texts of PBS's poems published during his lifetime and MWS's editions of his poems published in 1824, 1839, and 1840 (adding her 1847 editions, when relevant);

3. unauthorized editions that may contain authoritative readings from sources unknown or unavailable to us or that have significantly influenced the textual traditions of a poem (for example, some versions supplied by Thomas Medwin may be possibly derived from contemporary documents now lost, and some pirated editions that MWS used as the base text for *1839* led to errors in her text that were perpetuated by later editors who depended upon hers, thinking that these errors were purposeful emendations by MWS, using lost authorities);

4. the earliest scholarly edition in which a poem was first based on (or significantly corrected from) an authoritative MS.

Historical Collations

The Historical Collations, which precede the Appendix section, trace the history of specific readings through significant editions that, though not always based on primary witnesses, deserve attention because of their influence on subsequent texts and criticism. By recording all verbal variants and significant changes in punctuation and orthography in each historical edition collated in Volume II, we aim to provide scholars with concrete evidence about the conventions employed by different editors, clues to the precedents that each followed, their use of (and attitudes toward) the primary textual authorities, a sense of their relative accuracy or reliability, and the sources of the variants that appear in other, derivative editions and in the work of literary critics.

Although we present the materials relevant to a history of editorial work on PBS, we do not aspire to combine with that a history of typographical practice in England and America during the past two centuries. We therefore often omit from our Historical Collations variants that seem to us purely formal conventions originating with printers or publishers—the length of indentions, the use of full capitals, small capitals, and italic or Gothic type in titles and subtitles of poems—practices subject to the selection of fonts available to the printers and the conventions of the compositorial staff and, more recently, to the preferences of book designers, publishers, and their style manuals. Various editions have signaled the start of a new poem, canto, or poetic paragraph by indenting the first line, or by placing the first word or two in capital letters, or in large and small capitals. Unless there is reason to suppose (e.g., through evidence in PBS's underlying manuscript of the poem in question) that these features indicate in some significant way the author's intention, we have not collated such variants. In our Text, however, we try to follow the practice indicated either by PBS's most polished manuscripts or the printing of the work that we deem most likely to have received his prior instructions and/or his subsequent approval.

In a few cases, where there are doubts about whether the features of a text are authorial, typographical, or editorial, we have collated them to be on the safe side. Forman, the most conservative of our predecessors, announced that he numbered the stanzas of long poems to facilitate reference to specific stanzas and lines. Other editors did also, some using Roman numerals, some Arabic. Since we (like other recent editors) employ line numbers in the margin, we might merely note the differences and skip the detailed collation of these stanza numbers. But we feel that some of PBS's poems (particularly those in ballad stanzas, such as *The Mask of Anarchy*) had their character somewhat altered by the addition of Roman numerals, even in the first edition, published by Leigh Hunt. We therefore collate these features as possible influences upon readers of the poem, especially because later editors (who also employ marginal line numbering) retained the stanza numbers that were originally added simply for ease of reference.

Among the textually or historically important critical editions of PBS's poems that will frequently be cited in the Historical Collations are those edited by Rossetti (*1870, 1878*); Forman (*1876* [pub. 1876–77], *1882,* and *1892F*); Woodberry (*1892W, 1901*); Hutchinson (*1904;* and as revised by Matthews, *1970*); Ingpen and Peck (Julian Edition) I–IV (*1927*); Rogers (*1972*); Reiman and Powers (*1977;* using 3rd issue, pub. 1982) and Reiman and Fraistat (*2002*); Matthews and Everest (*1989*); and Shelley's *Letters,* edited by Frederick L. Jones (appears as *Letters* in our Commentary and as *1964J* in our Collations), as well as some recent critical editions of individual poems and small selections of poetry. For a complete listing of textual authorities collated in this volume, see the list of abbreviations that follows.

PBS's own notes to his public and nonpublic poems, like his prefaces and the other prose published with the poetry, appear with the Texts of the poems, located according to their placement in the copy-text of the volume or poem in question. The prefaces and notes supplied by MWS in her editions of his poetry dated 1824, 1839, 1840, and (where relevant) 1847 are reprinted in appendixes to the volumes to which they pertain, beginning in Volume II.

Our textual and informational notes appear in the second section of this volume as a running Commentary, with footers to identify the specific pages of the Text to which each page of the Commentary refers. An introductory section discusses the history of the composition and publication (or other release) of the poem or collection, its original reception, its textual authorities and transmission, and its place in PBS's intellectual and aesthetic development. Following this introductory section to the collective unit, our Commentary on individual poems, sections, and lines explains and supports the editorial choices made in the Text and points out the implications of the principal deletions, additions, and other revisions by PBS before he either completed or abandoned the work. When citing and quoting particular words from the Text in **CPPBS** of PBS's poem under discussion, we <u>underscore</u> them, rather than using quotation marks, to distinguish references to the Text from variant readings and from quotations from other poets and scholars.

Interspersed with our textual notes are informational notes that provide the reader with basic factual information needed to understand the significance of individual words, passages, or poems. Since this is a scholarly edition, to be used primarily by those who intend to exercise their own critical judgment and who, in many cases, may intend (or be required) to write interpretive essays or books on PBS's poetry, we try not to impose our judgment beyond the demonstrable evidence. We both document the sources of the information presented and indicate the degree of doubt inhering in our inferences—including some broad speculations and hypothetical scenarios—that can be tentatively but usefully drawn from the assembled evidence.

Historical Sources and Perspectives in the Annotation

Our statements about PBS and his immediate circle are based upon more original research than are our statements regarding other contemporary or historical figures and events, for which we often rely on standard authorities. All such research and reference authorities are cited by conventional abbreviations. We also consult other sources, earlier than or contemporary with PBS, to see what meaning and associations the name of a person, event, or book, or of a word or phrase may have evoked in his day and, therefore, what meaning(s) his use of it could have conveyed to his audience within its particular poetic context.

For biographical and historical information we start with the *Annual Register* (*AR*), *Dictionary of National Biography* (*DNB*), and *Encyclopædia Britannica* (*Encyc. Brit.* + copyright date); for the forms and meaning of words in the poems of PBS, we begin with the *Oxford English Dictionary* (*OED*) and three contemporary dictionaries begun in the eighteenth century that went through numerous editions and were popularly known as Bailey's, Johnson's, and Entick's dictionaries. For bibliographical information, we rely on the *National Union Catalogue* (*NUC*), the *New Cambridge Bibliography of English Literature* (*NCBEL*), and the *Nineteenth-Century Short Title Catalogue* (*NSTC*), as well as the Online Computer Library Center's WorldCat and other on-line catalogues. Where a book on which we rely is either unique or especially rare, we identify the library in which it is to be found.

We supplement this research by checking antecedents and allusions to words and phrases in PBS's verse and notes by using the Chadwyck-Healey Literature Online databases (cited as Chadwyck-Healey *LION*), a resource that provides a very comprehensive picture of the usage of words and idioms by eighteenth- and nineteenth-century authors—though we have frequently concluded that PBS probably derived his interest in and understanding of words or phrases from his study of Latin, Shakespeare, Milton, the Bible, or another obvious source to which other writers owed similar debts.

In referring to PBS and the time when he composed a particular poem, we use the adjective *contemporary* generally to refer to events, people, and attitudes of the period between the French Revolution (1789) and the Reform Bills of 1832–33; events before this period we call *historical,* while those after it are termed *modern* or *recent.* In annotating very specific elements in PBS's poetry, the focus of the "contemporary" period shrinks to the years between the time when PBS (b. 1792) would have become aware of the matter under discussion and the date of the poem or event being annotated; conversely, when discussing later editions of his poems and their textual history, we may use *contemporary* in relation, not to PBS himself, but to the editor or the period of textual history under discussion; *contemporary* never refers to our own lives and times—always to those of the people and events being annotated.

Special Features of Volume II

Among the special features worth noting in the Commentary and apparatus of Volume II of **CPPBS** are procedures and information not available in earlier editions of **Esd** and **QM**. During the past half-century, students of PBS have recognized that in such collections as those headed by **Alastor** and

Prometheus Unbound, PBS (like Wordsworth and other contemporaries) gave
thoughtful attention to arranging his poems for artistic and thematic effect,
rather than merely following the chronology of their original inspiration or
composition (see Fraistat, *The Poem and the Book* [1985] and *Poems in Their
Place* [1986]). While studying the poems of the **Esdaile Notebook** for this edi-
tion, we have learned that PBS's critical judgment was also very much in-
volved in sequencing the first fifty-one poems that he copied into **EN**—that
is, the poems that he was ready to release to Hookham for publication along
with **QM.** This finding was somewhat surprising, because his arrangement of
the poems in his earlier volumes, which appeared in Volume I of **CPPBS** (in
some of which he was not primarily a poet but either a political agitator or a
prankster), showed very little artistry in this sense. Because the organization
of **Esd** as a whole and the interrelated groups of poems within it have for so
long gone unnoticed, we devote sustained attention to this issue throughout
our Commentary.

Moreover, although PBS's aesthetic sensitivity doubtless would have ma-
tured naturally as he read more widely and thought more deeply, he was
forced to focus on his art more intensively as he became increasingly isolated
through his expulsion from Oxford and his subsequent radicalization. Esca-
lating conflicts with members of his family and with the British establishment
at large closed the other outlets of expression that he had enjoyed as the
spoiled, free-spending grandson and entailed heir of a baronet and son of a
Member of Parliament. Thus, he was encouraged to focus on his writings—
both poetry and prose—when they suddenly became his primary means of
transmitting his ideas to the world. Recognizing the increased importance
of his literary activities, PBS clearly tried to perfect his compositions, subtly
enhancing his meaning through the complex patternings of sounds—allit-
eration and assonance—that characterize his mature poetry, although his
continuing carelessness in spelling and copying shows that he initially
concentrated his attention on the diction, themes, structures, prosody, and
music of his poems, rather than upon the literal accuracy of their ortho-
graphic transmission.

As one reviewer of the first edition of **Esd** (*1964*) observed, these "early at-
tempts by a poet who later became one of the greatest masters of English
prosody," are "extremely interesting as technical experiments," exhibiting a
wide variety of meter and forms: "in addition to unrhymed and irregularly
rhymed poems . . . and poems in quatrains, there are six sonnets, two poems
in Spenserian stanzas, and poems in at least sixteen other rhymed stanzaic
patterns of from six to twelve lines" (*Modern Language Quarterly,* 26 [July
1965], 341). Nowhere in the rest of PBS's canon does he produce a volume
with such an astonishing range of verse forms. If, as William Wordsworth
later claimed, "Shelley is one of the best *artists* of us all: I mean in workman-
ship of style" (Christopher Wordsworth, *Memoirs of William Wordsworth, Poet-*

Laureate [1851], II, 474), the poems of **Esd** have remained the unacknowledged workshop in which PBS mastered the craft of poetry. Our Commentary, therefore, highlights and closely analyzes the form of each poem in **Esd** and relates PBS's choice of genre and metrical and stanzaic patterns both to the thematic objects of the poems and, insofar as the evidence on the relative dates of composition of the various poems permits, to PBS's development as an artist. We hope, especially because so few of these poems have yet attracted critical attention, that our analyses will provide fruitful avenues for future exploration of them. In addition to our discussion of form in the Commentary, we provide as an Appendix a table, "Poetic Forms in *The Esdaile Notebook*," that gives an overview of the formal elements in the poems and should aid scholars in relating his metrical experiments to one another, as well as lead to the identification of works by other poets that may have served as his models.

For **Queen Mab,** our Commentary attempts to provide a detailed and fully documented account of the philosophical, political, historical, scientific, and literary sources of one of the most intellectually ambitious works PBS was ever to write. In his lengthy notes to the poem (which exceed in word count the verse itself), the young PBS sometimes lifted words, phrases, and ideas verbatim from a range of contemporary and Classical sources in several languages in order to display a commanding but as yet unearned erudition. To promote understanding of his use and intellectual grasp of his sources, we have tried whenever possible to check all of his numerous (and sometimes purposely misleading) citations in the notes against the original editions from which he worked, many of which are extremely rare. In so doing, we have discovered much new information, including passages and ideas from these works that PBS uses but does not cite: For instance, his long erudite note on Philosophical Necessity (**Note 12**) is modeled closely on the (uncited) entry on that subject in Nicholson's *British Encyclopædia*.

Another special feature of the **QM** Commentary is that it contains full translations for all of PBS's numerous and often extensive quotations from Greek, Latin, and French (which appear in our Text proper) and devotes special attention to them. Many of these passages in foreign languages were riddled with errors in *1813.* In order to discover how those errors entered the text and where PBS may have departed from his source, we have tried to determine and locate PBS's original source in every case. The results of these efforts appear both in our Primary Collations and in the Commentary. Such work has revealed, for example, that PBS sometimes intentionally changed his source to make his own point more forcefully, whereas elsewhere his printer—who obviously did not know Greek, Latin, or French and apparently had trouble reading PBS's handwriting—appears to have introduced into the text many errors that PBS failed to correct. For instance, PBS included in **Note 13** an extremely long passage in French from the 1781 edition of Holbach's *Système de la nature,* a rare copy of which is in the Library of Congress). In collating the text of the **QM** note against this copy, we discovered that PBS had interpolated two passages of his own in French, disguised as Holbach's prose, and we were able to draw significant inferences about PBS's command of French and the manner in which this note was prepared for the press.

One other special feature of Volume II ought to be mentioned here. **QM** was the most extensively pirated of all of PBS's works: at least fourteen pirated editions of the poem were published between 1821 and 1839—the year in which MWS was finally able to produce the first authorized complete edition of the poetry—and **QM** also appeared in several larger unauthorized collections of PBS's works during this same period. These piracies, primarily by radical booksellers, have been increasingly recognized by scholars as historically and textually important in their own right, though they have received scant attention from textual editors. In preparing Volume II of **CPPBS** we have, therefore, collated all of the major piracies produced between 1821 and 1839 to map their relations to each other and to trace the textual relationship between these piracies and MWS's editions of 1839 and 1840. Our findings, ~~which contain~~ much new information on this subject, are detailed at length in the section of the Commentary on Textual Transmission and are cited throughout the local notes to textual cruxes. Based on these findings, we have provided complete collations for the two important initial piracies, published in 1821 by William Clark and by William Benbow—which laid the groundwork for all subsequent ones—and two later piracies, published by John Brooks (1829) and by John Ascham (1834), upon which MWS ultimately depended for her text of **QM**. Readings from these editions appear in the Primary Collations.

Although the Commentaries and apparatus in **CPPBS** will always be inflected to address the special nature and issues raised by the poetic work under consideration—as is apparent in the special features of Volume II— our underlying goals remain constant. We try to record, first, the inseminating events and influences that led PBS to compose and arrange his poems. Then we examine his struggle to shape and publish (or otherwise circulate) them to his intended audience; reactions to his poems by their early readers and reviewers; their republication and transmission by relevant unauthorized editors, MWS, and subsequent editors. Finally, we address (as space permits) social and intellectual responses to them by writers, critics, and thinkers that have both reflected and shaped the reactions of other readers during the nearly two centuries since PBS set them afloat, like his beloved paper boats, upon the stream of Time.

Abbreviations

Principles of Abbreviation and Citation

To compress the Commentaries, we often use "PBS," "HWS," and "MWS" in references to Percy Bysshe Shelley, Harriet Westbrook Shelley, and Mary Wollstonecraft Shelley; and we abbreviate the titles of PBS's works and of scholarly sources, but to facilitate comprehension we employ commonsense methods that the reader can either infer or readily learn. In each Commentary to a major section of Texts, a title of a poem by PBS first appears in full, together with its abbreviated form—for example, **Queen Mab** (**QM**) and **Mont Blanc** (**MB**). **Bold italics** distinguish his titles (whether a separately published volume or a smaller work) from those by other writers, which appear in *light italic*. Readers will thus recognize at once a work written by PBS. This rule includes the standard edition of his **Letters,** edited by F. L. Jones, abbreviated thus in bold italics in the Commentary, although the same edition is identified in collations by the siglum *1964J*. The single volume of **Prose** (1993), edited by the late E. B. Murray, is abbreviated **Prose**/EBM. (Until that Oxford edition is completed, we must cite and quote texts of PBS's later prose from a variety of sources.)

Major editions of PBS's poetry that we collate or cite frequently, either in the edition as a whole or in a particular volume, are abbreviated by italicized date codes (e.g., *1989*), as listed below. In collations, the number of a cited volume of a multivolume series or edition may be separated from the abbreviation for the work by a slash, as *SC*/IV or *1927*/VII. Scholarly works to which we refer are usually identified by abbreviated titles, while others to which we refer repeatedly within a particular Commentary are given nonce abbreviations. Modern scholarly books other than critical editions of PBS's writings are cited by author, title (abbreviated, if this can be done without confusion), and year of publication, their publishers and places of publication being accessible through standard bibliographies and catalogues. In general, sources in literary or scholarly periodicals will be cited by author and by date, volume, abbreviated title, and relevant page(s) of the periodical.

Each volume of **CPPBS** will contain its own list of editions of PBS's poetry and reference materials relevant to the Texts and Commentaries therein. When referring to a unique or specific authority—a manuscript (MS—plural, MSS) or an annotated or especially rare printed edition—we identify it by its location, using a code for the institution or collection in which it can be found (e.g., "Bod" for Bodleian Library, Oxford). When both a manuscript and a printed edition of a work are held by a collection and we are referring to the former, we add "MS" to the code (e.g., MS Pfz). Unique textual authorities belonging to individuals or institutions that are not represented in our list of abbreviations will receive nonce codes within the Commentaries that discuss them.

In our transcriptions of MSS, square brackets ([ ]) indicate deletions or illegible characters; angle brackets (< >) represent words missing due to physical damage to the paper. When quoting such transcriptions by other scholars, we sometimes retain or modify their editorial symbols with appropriate explanations.

Abbreviations

LIBRARIES

Berg	Henry W. and Albert A. Berg Collection, New York Public Library
BL	British Library
Bod	Bodleian Library, Oxford University
Cam	Cambridge University Library
Del	University of Delaware Library
Harv	Houghton Library, Harvard University
Htn	Henry E. Huntington Library, San Marino, California
JHU	Johns Hopkins University Libraries
LC	Library of Congress
Md	University of Maryland, College Park
NYPL	New York Public Library
PMgn	Pierpont Morgan Library
Pfz	Carl H. Pforzheimer Collection of Shelley and His Circle, New York Public Library
TCC	Trinity College, Cambridge
TCD	Trinity College, Dublin
TCU	Texas Christian University
Tx	Humanities Research Center, University of Texas at Austin
UCL	University College, London
WSU	Washington State University

MANUSCRIPTS

EN	Esdaile Notebook, at the Pforzheimer Collection, New York Public Library (facsimile in *MYR: Shelley* I)

MS Berg   Letter version of *Esd* #47, at the Berg Collection, New York
               Public Library
MS BLjan, MS BLfeb   Shelley poems in letters to Elizabeth Hitchener
MS ED   Edward Dowden's transcription of the poems in **EN** (the
               next two items)
MS ED-Pfz   Edward Dowden's transcript book containing *Esd* poems
               #1–#32, in the Pforzheimer Collection, New York Public
               Library
MS ED-TCD   Edward Dowden's transcript book containing *Esd* poems
               #33–#58, at Trinity College, Dublin
MS Pfz   Numbers following this symbol refer to the SC numbers in
               Shelley and his Circle, the catalogue of the Pforzheimer
               manuscripts.
MS TCC   Letter version of *Esd* #33, at Trinity College, Cambridge
MS TCU   Letter version of *Esd* #41, at Texas Christian University
MS WSU   Harriet Westbrook Shelley's Commonplace Book, at
               Washington State University

PUBLISHED SOURCES FOR SHELLEY'S POETRY AND NOTES

Alastor   *Alastor; or, The Spirit of Solitude* (also *1816*)
Dæmon   *The Dæmon of the World* (1816)
DW   *The Devil's Walk* (1812)
Esd   *The Esdaile Notebook* (released 1813)
F&V   *Falshood and Vice* (*Esd* #6)
H&L   *Henry and Louisa: a Poem in two parts* (*Esd* #46)
L&C   *Laon and Cythna; or, The Revolution of the Golden City: A
                 Vision of the Nineteenth Century in the Stanza of Spenser*
                 (1817; revised and reissued in 1818 as *The Revolt of Islam*)
Letter to Lord Ellenborough   *A Letter to Lord Ellenborough, Occasioned by
                 the Sentence which He Passed on Mr. D. I. Eaton, As Publisher
                 of the Third Part of Paine's Age of Reason* (*1812.LdEl* in
                 collations)
NA   *The Necessity of Atheism* (*1811.NA* in collations)
Natural Diet   *A Vindication of Natural Diet, being one in a series of notes to
                 Queen Mab, a Philosophical Poem* (1813; *VND* in collations)
PF   *Posthumous Fragments of Margaret Nicholson* (1810)
Prom   *Prometheus Unbound* (1820)
QM   *Queen Mab; A Philosophical Poem: with Notes* (also *1813*)
R&H   *Rosalind and Helen: A Modern Eclogue* (1819)
Refutation   *A Refutation of Deism: in a Dialogue* (1814)
St.Irv   *St. Irvyne; or, The Rosicrucian: A Romance* (1811)
The Voyage   *The Voyage: A Fragment | Devonshire—August 1812* (*Esd* #32)

V&C   *Original Poetry* "by Victor and Cazire" (1810)

VND   *A Vindication of Natural Diet, being one in a series of notes to Queen Mab, a Philosophical Poem* (1813) (except in collations, abbreviated *Natural Diet*)

WJ   *The Wandering Jew; or, The Victim of the Eternal Avenger* (1810)

Z&K   *Zeinab and Kathema* (*Esd* #49)

1781.HOL   Baron D'Holbach. *Système de la nature, ou des loix du monde physique & du monde moral.* London, 1781. (also *Système*)

1811.NA   *The Necessity of Atheism.* Worthing: C. & W. Phillips, 1811. (also *NA*)

1812.LdEl   *A Letter to Lord Ellenborough, Occasioned by the Sentence which He Passed on Mr. D. I. Eaton, As Publisher of the Third Part of Paine's Age of Reason.* Barnstaple: Syle, 1812. (also *Letter to Lord Ellenborough*)

1813   *Queen Mab; A Philosophical Poem: with Notes.* London: Printed by P. B. Shelley, 1813. (also *QM*)

1816   *Alastor; or, The Spirit of Solitude: and Other Poems.* London: Printed for Baldwin, Craddock & Joy and Carpenter & Son, 1816.

1821.BEN   *Queen Mab; A Philosophical Poem.* New York: William Baldwin and Co., 1821 (false imprint; London: William Benbow, 1821).

1821.CLA   *Queen Mab.* London: W. Clark, 1821 (unexpurgated version).

1821.CLAX   *Queen Mab.* London: W. Clark, 1821 (expurgated version).

1824   *Posthumous Poems of Percy Bysshe Shelley* [ed. Mary W. Shelley]. London: John and Henry L. Hunt, 1824.

1829   *The Poetical Works of Coleridge, Shelley, and Keats* [ed. Cyrus Redding]. Paris: A. and W. Galignani, 1829.

1829.BRO   *Queen Mab.* London: John Brooks, 1829.

1834   *Works of Percy Bysshe Shelley, with His Life.* 2 vols. London: John Ascham, 1834.

1839   *The Poetical Works of Percy Bysshe Shelley,* ed. Mrs. Shelley. 4 vols. London: Edward Moxon, 1839.

1840   *The Poetical Works of Percy Bysshe Shelley,* ed. Mrs. Shelley. London: Edward Moxon, 1840 (on printed title page; engraved title page reads: 1839).

1847   *The Poetical Works of Percy Bysshe Shelley,* ed. Mrs. Shelley. 3 vols. London: Edward Moxon & Co., 1847.

1858   Thomas Jefferson Hogg. *The Life of Percy Bysshe Shelley.* 2 vols. London: Moxon, 1858.

1870	*The Poetical Works of Percy Bysshe Shelley,* ed. William Michael Rossetti. 2 vols. London: Moxon, 1870.
1876	*The Poetical Works of Percy Bysshe Shelley,* ed. H[arry] Buxton Forman. 4 vols. London: Reeves & Turner, 1876–77.
1878	*The Poetical Works of Percy Bysshe Shelley,* ed. William Michael Rossetti. 3 vols. London: E. Moxon, Son & Co., 1878.
1880	*The Works of Percy Bysshe Shelley in Verse and Prose,* ed. H[arry] Buxton Forman. 8 vols. London: Reeves & Turner, 1880.
1882	*The Works of Percy Bysshe Shelley,* ed. H[arry] Buxton Forman. 2 vols. London: Reeves & Turner, 1882.
1886	See Dowden, *Life,* below.
1890	*The Poetical Works of Percy Bysshe Shelley,* ed. Edward Dowden. London: Macmillan & Co., 1890.
1892F	*The Poetical Works of Percy Bysshe Shelley,* ed. Harry Buxton Forman. 5 vols. [Aldine Edition] London and New York: George Bell & Sons, 1892.
1892W	*The Complete Poetical Works of Percy Bysshe Shelley,* ed. George Edward Woodberry. Centenary Edition. 4 vols. Boston and New York: Houghton Mifflin, 1892.
1901	*The Complete Poetical Works of Shelley,* ed. George Edward Woodberry. Cambridge Edition. Cambridge, Mass.: Houghton, Mifflin, 1901.
1903	C[harles] D. Locock. *An Examination of the Shelley Manuscripts in the Bodleian Library.* Oxford: Clarendon Press, 1903.
1904	*The Complete Poetical Works of Percy Bysshe Shelley,* ed. Thomas Hutchinson. Oxford: Clarendon Press, 1904. (reset 1905 and 1934 as Oxford Standard Authors Edition; corrected by G. M. Matthews and reset, 1970)
1910K	A. H. Koszul. *La jeunesse de Shelley.* Paris: Bloud & Co., 1910.
1911	*The Poems of Percy Bysshe Shelley,* ed. C[harles] D. Locock. 2 vols. London: Methuen, 1911.
1913	See Medwin *Life,* ed. Forman, below.
1927	*The Complete Works of Percy Bysshe Shelley,* ed. Roger Ingpen and Walter E. Peck. 10 vols. Julian Edition. London: Ernest Benn; New York: Charles Scribner's Sons, 1926–30.
1962BOAS	Louise Schutz Boas. *Harriet Shelley: Five Long Years.* London: Oxford University Press, 1962. (also *Harriet Shelley*)
1964A	*The Esdaile Notebook: A Volume of Early Poems, by Percy Bysshe Shelley. Edited by Kenneth Neill Cameron from the Original*

Manuscript in The Carl H. Pforzheimer Library. New York: Alfred A. Knopf, 1964.

1964B   *The Esdaile Notebook: A Volume of Early Poems, by Percy Bysshe Shelley. Edited by Kenneth Neill Cameron from the Original Manuscript in The Carl H. Pforzheimer Library.* London: Faber and Faber, 1964.

1964J   See **Letters,** below.

1966   *The Esdaile Poems,* ed. Neville Rogers. Oxford: Clarendon Press, 1966.

1967   Neville Rogers. *Shelley at Work: A Critical Inquiry.* 2nd ed. Oxford: Clarendon, 1967.

1968   George David Richards's edition of **QM;** Ph.D. dissertation, Duke University.

1970   *The Complete Poetical Works of Percy Bysshe Shelley,* ed. Thomas Hutchinson, corrected by G. M. Matthews. Oxford Standard Authors Edition. Oxford: Oxford University Press, 1970. (This text, which corrects *1904* locally, is cited as *1970* only where it departs from that parent edition.)

1972   *The Complete Poetical Works of Percy Bysshe Shelley,* ed. Neville Rogers. Volume I, 1802–1813; Volume II, 1814–1817. Oxford: Clarendon Press, 1972 (Vol. I), 1975 (Vol. II).

1977   *Shelley's Poetry and Prose,* ed. Donald H. Reiman and Sharon B. Powers. New York: Norton, 1977 (3rd printing, corrected, 1982).

1989   *The Poems of Shelley,* ed. G. M. Matthews and Kelvin Everest. 2 volumes to date. London: Longman, 1989 and 2000.

2002   *Shelley's Poetry and Prose,* ed. Donald H. Reiman and Neil Fraistat. 2nd ed. New York: Norton, 2002.

BA   *La Belle Assemblée; Or, Bell's Court and Fashionable Magazine. Addressed Particularly to the Ladies* 6 (Jan. 1809): 19–20.

CPPBS I   **The Complete Poetry of Percy Bysshe Shelley.** Volume I, ed. Donald H. Reiman and Neil Fraistat. Baltimore: Johns Hopkins University Press, 2000.

Enq   William Godwin. *The Enquirer: Reflections on Education, Manners, and Literature. In a Series of Essays.* London: G. G. and J. Robinson, 1797. (also *Enquirer*)

GrM   "The Wandering Jew. By Schubart" and signed by "P. W." *The German Museum* 3 (Jan. 1801): 424–26.

SHORT TITLES OF RESEARCH AND REFERENCE WORKS

Abstinence   Joseph Ritson. *An Essay on Abstinence from Animal Food, as a Moral Duty.* London: Richard Phillips, 1802.

Academical Questions   Sir William Drummond. *Academical Questions.* London: Cadell and Davies, 1805.

Antient Metaphysics   James Burnett, Lord Monboddo. *Antient Metaphysics: or, the Science of Universals.* Edinburgh and London: imprint varies, 1779–99.

Anderson, *Legend/WJ*   George Kumler Anderson. *The Legend of the Wandering Jew.* Providence, R.I.: Brown University Press, 1965.

AR   *Annual Register*

BSM   *The Bodleian Shelley Manuscripts,* ed. Donald H. Reiman et al. 23 vols. New York: Garland Publishing, 1986–99.

Byron, *CPW*   *The Complete Poetical Works of Lord Byron,* ed. Jerome J. McGann. 7 vols. Oxford: Clarendon Press, 1980.

Chadwyck-Healey *LION*   Chadwyck-Healey Literature Online databases at <http://lion.chadwyck.com>.

Clairmont, *Journals*   *The Journals of Claire Clairmont, 1814–1827,* ed. Marion Kingston Stocking. Cambridge: Harvard University Press, 1968.

Decline and Fall   Edward Gibbon. *The History of the Decline and Fall of the Roman Empire.* London: T. Cadell and W. Davies, 1813.

DNB   *Dictionary of National Biography*

Dowden, *Life*   Edward Dowden. *The Life of Percy Bysshe Shelley.* 2 vols. London: K. Paul, Trench & Co., 1886.

Ecce Homo   Baron D'Holbach. *Ecce homo!: An Eighteenth Century Life of Jesus: Critical Edition and Revision of George Houston's Translation from the French,* ed. Andrew Hunwick. Berlin: Mouton de Gruyter, 1995.

ELH   *English Literary History*

Encyc. Brit.   *Encyclopædia Britannica* (+ copyright date).

Enquirer   William Godwin. *The Enquirer: Reflections on Education, Manners, and Literature. In a Series of Essays.* London: G. G. and J. Robinson, 1797. (*Enq* in collations)

Enquiry   David Hume. *An Enquiry Concerning Human Understanding.* London: A. Millar, 1748.

ESTC   *English Short Title Catalogue.* London: British Library, 1998 (CD-ROM and on-line editions). (incorporates the *Eighteenth-Century Short-Title Catalogue* [also *ESTC*], available in print)

Evidence of the Imagination   *The Evidence of the Imagination: Studies of Interactions between Life and Art in English Romantic Literature,* ed. Donald H. Reiman, Michael C. Jaye, and Betty T. Bennett. New York: New York University Press, 1978.

The Godwins and the Shelleys   William St. Clair. *The Godwins and the Shelleys: A Biography of a Family.* 1989; rpt., Baltimore: Johns Hopkins University Press, 1991.

Good Sense   *Good Sense: or Natural Ideas, Opposed to Ideas That are Supernatural; Being a Translation from the "Bon Sens" of the Curé Meslier* [i.e., Holbach]. London: Richard Carlile, 1826. (see also *Le bon sens*)

Harriet Shelley   Louise Schutz Boas. *Harriet Shelley: Five Long Years.* London: Oxford University Press, 1962. (*1962BOAS* in collations)

Hogg *Life,* ed. Wolfe   *The Life of Percy Bysshe Shelley as Comprised in* The Life of Shelley *by Thomas Jefferson Hogg,* The Recollections of Shelley & Byron *by Edward John Trelawny,* Memoirs of Shelley *by Thomas Love Peacock,* ed. Humbert Wolfe. 2 vols. London: J. M. Dent, 1933.

Hughes, *Nascent Mind*   A. M. D. Hughes. *The Nascent Mind of Shelley.* Oxford: Clarendon Press, 1947.

Interpreter   *Diderot: Interpreter of Nature,* ed. Jonathan Kemp. London: Lawrence & Wishart, 1937.

Intervals of Inspiration   Donald H. Reiman. *Intervals of Inspiration: The Skeptical Tradition and the Psychology of Romanticism.* Greenwood, Fla.: Penkevill Publishing, 1988.

JEGP   *Journal of English and Germanic Philology*

K-SJ   *Keats-Shelley Journal*

KSMB   *Keats-Shelley Memorial Bulletin*

K-SR   *Keats-Shelley Review*

Le bon sens   Baron D'Holbach. *Le bon sens; ou Idées naturelles opposées aux idées surnaturelles.* London, 1772. (see also *Good Sense*)

Letters   *The Letters of Percy Bysshe Shelley,* ed. Frederick L. Jones. 2 vols. Oxford: Clarendon Press, 1964. (*1964J* in collations)

Letters about Shelley   *Letters about Shelley Exchanged by Three Friends,* ed. R. S. Garnett. London: Hodder and Stoughton, 1917.

LMWS   *The Letters of Mary Wollstonecraft Shelley,* ed. Betty T. Bennett. 3 vols. Baltimore: Johns Hopkins University Press, 1980–88.

Mac-Carthy, *Early Life*   Denis Florence Mac-Carthy. *Shelley's Early Life from Original Sources with Curious Incidents, Letters, and Writings, Now First Published or Collected.* London: John Camden Hotten, 1872.

Medwin *Life,* ed. Forman   *The Life of Percy Bysshe Shelley By Thomas Medwin. A New Edition printed from a copy copiously amended and extended by the Author and left unpublished at his death,*

with an Introduction and Commentary by H. Buxton Forman.
New York: Oxford University Press, 1913.

MLN	*Modern Language Notes*
MLR	*Modern Language Review*
MR	*The Monthly Repository*

MYR: Shelley *The Manuscripts of the Younger Romantics: Percy Bysshe Shelley,*
ed. Donald H. Reiman et al. 9 vols. New York: Garland
Publishing, 1985–96.

Nairs James Henry Lawrence. *The Empire of the Nairs; or The
Rights of Women. An Utopian Romance in Twelve Books.*
London: T. Hookham, 1811.

NCBEL *New Cambridge Bibliography of English Literature,* ed. George
Watson. 4 vols. Cambridge: Cambridge University Press,
1969–71.

Nicholson's William Nicholson. *The British Encyclopedia, or Dictionary of
Arts and Sciences; Comprising an Accurate and Popular View of
the Present Improved State of Human Knowledge.* 6 vols.
London: Longman, Hurst, Rees, & Orme, 1809.

NSTC *Nineteenth-Century Short Title Catalogue.* Cambridge:
Chadwyck-Healey, 1985– (print and CD-ROM editions).

OED *Oxford English Dictionary*

Paine, *Works* *The Life and Works of Thomas Paine,* ed. William M. Van der
Weyde. New Rochelle, N.Y.: Thomas Paine National
Historical Association, 1925.

Paterson's *Roads* [Daniel] Paterson. *Description of the . . . Roads in
England and Wales . . . .* London: Longman et al., 1808
[and various other dates].

Peck, *Shelley* Walter Edwin Peck. *Shelley: His Life and Work.* 2 vols.
Boston and New York: Houghton Mifflin, 1927.

PMLA *Publications of the Modern Language Association*

Poet and Legislator *Shelley: Poet and Legislator of the World,* ed. Betty T.
Bennett and Stuart Curran. Baltimore: Johns Hopkins
University Press, 1996.

Pol. Justice William Godwin. *An Enquiry Concerning Political Justice and
its Influence on General Virtue and Happiness.* 2 vols. 1st ed.
London: G. G. and J. Robinson, 1793. (Citations are first
to book and chapter; followed by volume and page
number.)

Pol. Justice, ed. Priestley William Godwin. *An Enquiry Concerning
Political Justice and its Influence on Morals and Happiness,* ed.
F. E. L. Priestley. 3 vols. Toronto: University of Toronto
Press, 1946. (Photographic facsimile of the third edition
corrected; edited with variant readings of the first and

second editions and with a critical introduction and notes. Citations are first to book and chapter; followed by volume and page number.)

Progrès   Jean Antoine Condorcet. *Esquisse d'un tableau historique des progrès de l'esprit humain* (1795; also published in 1795 as *Outline of an Historical View of the Progress of the Human Mind* [London: J. Johnson]).

Prose/EBM   *The Prose Works of Percy Bysshe Shelley,* ed. E. B. Murray. Oxford: Clarendon Press, 1993. (Only a single volume was published before EBM's death.)

Rees's   Abraham Rees. *The Cyclopædia; or, Universal dictionary of arts, sciences, and literature.* London: Longman, Hurst, Rees, Orme & Brown [etc.], 1803.

Return   John Frank Newton. *The Return to Nature, or, A Defence of the Vegetable Regimen; with Some Account of an Experiment Made During the Last Three or Four Years in the Author's Family.* London: T. Cadell and W. Davies, 1811.

Rights of Woman   Mary Wollstonecraft. *A Vindication of the Rights of Woman.* Cited from *The Works of Mary Wollstonecraft,* ed. Janet Todd and Marilyn Butler. Washington Square: New York University Press, 1989.

Romantic Texts and Contexts   Donald H. Reiman. *Romantic Texts and Contexts.* Columbia: University of Missouri Press, 1987.

RR   *The Romantics Reviewed; Contemporary Reviews of British Romantic Writers.* 9 vols. in 3 parts, A–C. Ed. and introd. Donald H. Reiman. New York: Garland Publishing, 1972.

Ruines   Constantin Volney. *Les ruines, ou méditations sur les révolutions des empires* (1791).

Ruins   Constantin Volney. *A New Translation of Volney's Ruins; or Meditations on the Revolution of Empires* (1802). 2 vols. New York: Garland, 1979.

SC   *Shelley and his Circle: 1773–1822.* Volumes I–IV ed. Kenneth Neill Cameron; V–VI ed. Donald H. Reiman; VII–X ed. Reiman and Doucet Devin Fischer. Cambridge: Harvard University Press, 1961– .

Shelley Concordance   *A Lexical Concordance to the Poetical Works of Percy Bysshe Shelley,* comp. and ed. F. S. Ellis. London: Bernard Quaritch, 1892.

Shelley in England   Roger Ingpen. *Shelley in England: New Facts and Letters from The Shelley-Whitton Papers.* London: Kegan Paul, Trench, Turner & Co., 1917.

Shelley Library   H[arry] Buxton Forman. *The Shelley Library: An Essay in*

Bibliography (1886). Reprint, New York: Haskell House
Publishers, 1971.

Shelley's First Love   Desmond Hawkins. *Shelley's First Love*. London: Kyle
Cathie; Hamden, Conn.: Archon Books, 1992.

Shelley's Venomed Melody   Nora Crook and Derek Guiton. *Shelley's Venomed
Melody*. Cambridge: Cambridge University Press, 1986.

System   Baron D'Holbach. *The System of Nature: or, Laws of the Moral
and Physical World,* trans. H. D. Robinson. Boston: J. P.
Mendum, 1889.

Système   Baron D'Holbach. *Système de la nature, ou des loix du monde
physique & du monde moral*. London, 1781. (*1781.HOL* in
collations)

TI   *Theological Inquirer; or, Polemical Magazine* (1815).

Tokoo, *Concordance*   *A Concordance to the Whole Vocabulary of Percy Bysshe
Shelley's Literary Manuscripts,* ed. Tatsuo Tokoo (electronic
book). Baltimore: Johns Hopkins University Press,
forthcoming.

Trial   Daniel Isaac Eaton. *Trial of Daniel Isaac Eaton*. London:
Eaton, 1812.

UH   Newman Ivey White. *The Unextinguished Hearth: Shelley and
His Contemporary Critics*. Durham, N.C.: Duke University
Press, 1938.

White, *Shelley*   Newman Ivey White. *Shelley*. 2 vols. New York: Alfred A.
Knopf, 1940; London: Secker & Warburg, 1947.

Wise   T[homas] J. Wise. *A Shelley Library*. London: for private
circulation, 1924.

WMW   *The Works of Mary Wollstonecraft,* ed. Janet Todd and
Marilyn Butler. Washington Square: New York University
Press, 1989.

Writings   *The Writings of Thomas Paine,* ed. Moncure Daniel Conway.
4 vols. New York: AMS Press, 1967.

YS   Kenneth Neill Cameron. *The Young Shelley: Genesis of a
Radical*. New York: Macmillan, 1950.

TEXTS

Poems.

—

A sabbath Walk

Sweet are the stilly forest glades:
Imbued with holiest feelings there
I love to linger pensively
And court seclusion's smile
This mountain labyrinth of loveliness
Is sweet to me even when the frost has torn
All save the ivy clinging to the rocks
Like friendship to a friend's adversity!
    Yet in my soul's devotedness
    I love to linger in the wilds
    I have my God, & worship him
    O vulgar souls more ardently
    Than ye the Almighty fiend
    Before whose throne ye kneel

Tis not the soul pervading all
Tis not the fabled cause that framed
The everlasting ribs of heaven

"A sabbath Walk," the second poem in *The Esdaile Notebook,* in PBS's hand

THE ESDAILE NOTEBOOK

Percy Bysshe Shelley (PBS) first tried to release to the public some of the poems in the collection now known as *The Esdaile Notebook (Esd)* during his first visit to Dublin, early in 1812. Then from late in 1812 through mid-1813 he negotiated to have the growing collection that he referred to as "Minor Poems" published by Thomas Hookham, the London bookseller who had become his friend. After the Shelleys returned to London in April 1813, PBS added to the once-blank Notebook (**EN**) the texts of earlier poems, some from copies that he had given to Thomas Jefferson Hogg during the days of their friendship at Oxford and immediately after their expulsion. By the end of the summer of 1813, however, either Hookham had declined to publish the volume or PBS had decided against making it public, perhaps because he was persuaded that to publish these poems would be legally dangerous, but just as likely because he realized that they revealed too much either about the turmoil of his early life or about his growing disaffection from Harriet Westbrook Shelley (HWS). Instead, he added two additional personal sonnets to **EN** and gave the Notebook to HWS as a keepsake of their three eventful years together.

Following PBS's elopement with Mary Wollstonecraft Godwin—later Mary Wollstonecraft Shelley (MWS)—less than a year later, **EN** remained with HWS, who added to it five other poems and fragments from PBS's manuscripts in her possession. After HWS's suicide, it descended through her daughter Ianthe Shelley (later Esdaile) and then to her heirs. Because the Esdaile heirs were reluctant to expose HWS's sad life to public gossip and, possibly, to the unfriendly scrutiny of scholars allied with Sir Percy Florence Shelley and Lady [Jane] Shelley, about two-thirds of the poetry in the Notebook remained unpublished until 1964, when Alfred A. Knopf published Kenneth Neill Cameron's edition, *The Esdaile Notebook: A Volume of Early Poems by Percy Bysshe Shelley.* The history of the Notebook thus explains the role that this collection played—or, rather, failed to play—in the development of PBS's poetic reputation during the first 140 years after his death.

Commentary appears on pages 317–490, Historical Collations on pages 675–790.

Whose is the love that gleaming thro' the world
Wards off the poisonous arrow of its scorn?
Whose is the warm and partial praise,
Virtue's most sweet reward?

Whose looks gave grace to the majestic theme,   5
The sacred, free and fearless theme of truth?
Whose form did I gaze fondly on
And love mankind the more?

Harriet! on thine:—thou wert my purer soul,
Thou wert the inspiration to my song,   10
Thine are these early wilding flowers,
Tho' garlanded by me.

Then twine the withering wreath-buds round thy brow;
Its bloom may deck their pale and faded prime.
Can they survive without thy love   15
Their wild and moody birth?

Text collated with **EN,** *1813, 1964B,* and *SC*/IV.

1 that] that, *1813*
  thro'] thro   **EN** *SC*/IV
        through   *1813*
  world] world,   *1813*
3 and] &   **EN** *SC*/IV
  praise,] praise   **EN** *SC*/IV
4 Virtue's] Virtues   **EN** *SC*/IV
5 Whose] Beneath whose   *1813*
  gave . . . theme,]
      did my reviving soul   *1813*
  theme,] theme   **EN** *SC*/IV
6 The . . . truth?] Riper in truth and
      virtuous daring grow?   *1813*
  and] &   **EN** *SC*/IV
  truth?] truth   **EN** *SC*/IV
7 form did] eyes have   *1813*
  gaze] gazed   *1813*
  on] on,   *1813*
8 love] loved   *1813*
9 thine:—thou] thine.—thou   **EN** *SC*/IV

  soul,] soul   **EN** *SC*/IV
       mind;   *1813*
10 to] of   *1813*
  song,] song   **EN** *SC*/IV
       song;   *1813 1964B*
11 flowers,] flowers   **EN** *SC*/IV
12 Tho'] Though   *1813*
13 twine . . . brow;] press unto thy breast
      this pledge of love,   *1813*
  brow;] brow   **EN** *SC*/IV
14 Its . . . prime.] And know, though time
      may change and years may roll,
      1813
  and] &   **EN** *SC*/IV
  prime.] prime   **EN** *SC*/IV
15 Can . . . love] Each flowret gathered in
      my heart   *1813*
16 Their . . . birth?]
      It consecrates to thine.   *1813*
  and] &   **EN** *SC*/IV

POEMS.

                    A sabbath Walk

       Sweet are the stilly forest glades:
       Imbued with holiest feelings there
       I love to linger pensively
         And court seclusion's smile.
5   This mountain labyrinth of loveliness
       Is sweet to me even when the frost has torn
       All save the ivy clinging to the rocks
       Like friendship to a friend's adversity!
         Yes, in my soul's devotedness
10   I love to linger in the wilds.
       I have my God, and worship him,
       O vulgar souls, more ardently
       Than ye the Almighty fiend
         Before whose throne ye kneel.

15   'Tis not the soul pervading all,
       'Tis not the fabled cause that framed
       The everlasting orbs of Heaven
        And this eternal earth,
       Nor the cold Christians' blood-stain'd King of Kings
20   Whose shrine is in the temple of my heart,—
       'Tis that divinity whose work and self
       Is harmony and wisdom, truth and love,
        Who in the forests' rayless depth

Text collated with **EN,** *1964B,* and *SC*/IV.

4 seclusion's] seclusions **EN** *SC*/IV
  smile.] smile **EN** *SC*/IV
5 labyrinth] labyrith **EN** *SC*/IV
8 friend's] friends **EN** *SC*/IV
9 Yes,] Yes **EN** *SC*/IV
  soul's] souls **EN** *SC*/IV
  devotedness] devotedness, *1964B*
10 wilds.] wilds **EN** *SC*/IV
11 and] & **EN** *SC*/IV
  him,] him **EN** *SC*/IV
12 souls,] souls **EN** *SC*/IV
14 kneel.] kneel **EN** *SC*/IV
15 'Tis] Tis **EN** *SC*/IV
  all,] all **EN** *SC*/IV

16 'Tis] Tis **EN** *SC*/IV
18 earth,] earth **EN** *SC*/IV
19 Christians'] Christians **EN** *SC*/IV
  blood-stain'd]
    blood staind **EN** *SC*/IV
  Kings] Kings, *1964B*
20 shrine] shine **EN** *SC*/IV
  heart,—] heart **EN** *SC*/IV
     heart; *1964B*
21 'Tis] Tis **EN** *SC*/IV
  and] & **EN** *SC*/IV
22 and] & **EN** *SC*/IV
  and] & **EN** *SC*/IV
  love,] love **EN** *SC*/IV
23 forests'] forests **EN** *SC*/IV

And in the cities' wearying glare
In sorrow, solitude and death   25
Accompanies the soul
    Of him who dares be free.

It is a lovely winter's day.
Its brightness speaks of Deity
Such as the good man venerates,   30
    Such as the Poet loves.
Ah! softly o'er the quiet of the scene
A pealing harmony is felt to rise.
The village bells are sweet but they denote
That spirits love by the clock, and are devout   35
    All at a stated hour. The sound
    Is sweet to sense but to the heart
    It tells of worship insincere,
    Creeds half believed, the ear that bends
    To custom, prejudice and fear—   40
    The tongue that's bought to speak,
        The heart that's hired to feel.

But to the man sincerely good
Each day will be a sabbath day
Consigned to thoughts of holiness   45
    And deeds of living love.
The God he serves requires no cringing creed,
No idle prayers, no senseless mummeries,
No gold, no temples and no hireling priests.
The winds, the pineboughs and the waters make   50

---

24 cities'] cities **EN** *SC/IV*
   glare] glare, *1964B*
25 and] & **EN** *SC/IV*
27 free.] free **EN** *SC/IV*
28 winter's] winters **EN** *SC/IV*
30 venerates,]
     venerates **EN** *1964B SC/IV*
31 loves.] loves **EN** *SC/IV*
32 o'er] oer **EN** *SC/IV*
33 rise.] rise **EN** *SC/IV*
35 and] & **EN** *SC/IV*
36 The] the **EN** *SC/IV*
38 insincere,] insincere **EN** *SC/IV*

40 and] & **EN** *SC/IV*
   fear—] fear **EN** *SC/IV*
      fear, *1964B*
41 speak,] speak **EN** *SC/IV*
42 feel.] feel **EN** *SC/IV*
46 living] lving **EN** *SC/IV*
   love.] love **EN** *SC/IV*
48 mummeries,] mummeries **EN** *SC/IV*
49 and] & **EN** *SC/IV*
   priests.] priests **EN** *SC/IV*
50 and] & **EN** *SC/IV*

Its melody. The hearts of all
The beings it pervadeth, form
A temple for its purity;
The wills of those that love the right
55   Are offerings beyond
                Thanksgivings, prayers and gold.

[*Esd #3*]   The Crisis

When we see Despots prosper in their weakness,
When we see Falshood triumph in its folly,
When we see Evil, Tyranny, Corruption
        Grin, grow and fatten—

5   When Virtue toileth thro' a world of sorrow,
When Freedom dwelleth in the deepest dungeon,
When Truth in chains and infamy bewaileth
        O'er a world's ruin—

When Monarchs laugh upon their thrones securely,
10   Mocking the woes which are to them a treasure,
Hear the deep curse, and quench the Mother's hunger
        In her child's murder—

---

51 The] the   **EN** *SC*/IV
52 pervadeth,] pervadeth   *1964B*
53 its] it's   **EN** *SC*/IV
   purity;] purity   **EN** *SC*/IV
56 Thanksgivings,] Thanks givings,   **EN**
              Thanksgiving,
                SC/IV
   and] &   **EN** *SC*/IV

Text collated with **EN,** *1964B*, and *SC*/IV.
1 weakness,] weakness   **EN** *SC*/IV
2 its] it's   **EN** *SC*/IV
  folly,] folly   **EN** *SC*/IV
3 Evil,] Evil   **EN** *SC*/IV
  Tyranny,] Tyrranny,   **EN** *SC*/IV
  Corruption] Corruption,   *1964B*
4 and] &   **EN** *SC*/IV
  fatten—] fatten   **EN** *SC*/IV
        fatten;   *1964B*
stanza break] *omitted*   **EN** *1964B SC*/IV

5 thro'] thro   **EN** *SC*/IV
  sorrow,] sorrow   **EN** *SC*/IV
6 dungeon,] dungeon   **EN** *SC*/IV
7 Truth] Truth,   *1964B*
  and] &   **EN** *SC*/IV
  infamy] infamy,   *1964B*
8 O'er] Oer   **EN** *SC*/IV
  world's] worlds   **EN** *SC*/IV
  ruin—] ruin   **EN** *SC*/IV
     ruin;   *1964B*
stanza break] *omitted*   **EN** *1964B SC*/IV
9 Monarchs] Monarhs   **EN** *SC*/IV
  securely,] securely   **EN** *SC*/IV
10 treasure,] treasure   **EN** *SC*/IV
11 and] &   **EN** *SC*/IV
  Mother's] Mothers   **EN** *SC*/IV
12 murder—] murder   **EN** *SC*/IV
      murder;   *1964B*
stanza break] *omitted*   **EN** *1964B SC*/IV

Then may we hope the consummating hour
Dreadfully, sweetly, swiftly is arriving
When light from Darkness, peace from desolation   15
    Bursts unresisted.

Then mid the gloom of doubt and fear and anguish
The votaries of virtue may raise their eyes to Heaven
And confident watch till the renovating day star
    Gild the horizon.   20

    Passion   *[Esd #4]*
    (to the

Fair are thy berries to the dazzled sight,
Fair is thy chequered stalk of mingling hues,
    And yet thou dost conceal
    A deadly poison there
      Uniting good and ill.   5

Art thou not like a lawyer whose smooth face
Doth promise good, while hiding so much ill?
    Ah! no. The semblance even
    Of goodness lingereth not
      Within that hollow eye.   10

Art thou the tyrant whose unlovely brow
With rare and glittering gems is contrasted?
    No—thou mayst kill the body,

---

14 arriving] arriving, *1964B*

15 desolation] desolation, *1964B*

16 unresisted.] unresisted **EN** *SC*/IV
        unresisted; *1964B*

stanza break] *omitted* **EN** *1964B SC*/IV

17 and] & **EN** *SC*/IV
    and] & **EN** *SC*/IV

19 day star] day-star *1964B*

20 horizon.] horizon **EN** *SC*/IV

Text collated with **EN,** *1964B*, and *SC*/IV.

1 sight,] sight **EN** *SC*/IV

2 hues,] hues **EN** *SC*/IV

5 and] & **EN** *SC*/IV
   ill.] ill **EN** *SC*/IV

7 Doth] Dost **EN** *1964B SC*/IV
   ill?] ill **EN** *SC*/IV

8 The] the **EN** *SC*/IV

10 eye.] eye **EN** *SC*/IV

12 and] & **EN** *SC*/IV
    contrasted?] contrasted **EN** *SC*/IV

13 mayst] mayest *SC*/IV
    body,] body **EN** *SC*/IV

He withers up the soul;
Sweet thou when he is nigh.

Art thou the wretch whose cold and sensual soul
His hard-earned mite tears from the famished hind
Then says that God hath willed
Many to toil and groan
That few may boast at ease?

Art thou the slave whose mercenary sword
Stained with an unoffending brother's blood
Deeper yet shews the spot
Of cowardice, whilst he
Who wears it talks of courage!

Ah no! else while I gaze upon thy bane
I should not feel unmingled with contempt
This awful feeling rise:
As if I stood at night
In some weird ruin's shade.

Thou art like youthful passion's quenchless fire
Which in some unsuspecting bosom glows,
So wild, so beautiful,
Possessing wondrous power
To wither or to warm.

Essence of Virtue blasting virtue's prime,
Bright bud of Truth producing Falshood's fruit,
Freedom's own soul that binds

---

14 soul;] soul   **EN** *SC*/IV

15 nigh.] nigh   **EN** *SC*/IV

16 wretch] wreth   **EN** *SC*/IV

   and] &   **EN** *SC*/IV

17 hard-earned] hard earned   **EN** *SC*/IV

19 and] &   **EN** *SC*/IV

22 brother's] brothers   **EN** *SC*/IV

24 he] the   *1964B*

25 courage!] courage?   *1964B*

30 weird] wierd   **EN** *SC*/IV

   ruin's] ruins   **EN** *SC*/IV

   shade.] shade   **EN** *SC*/IV

31 passion's] passions   **EN** *SC*/IV

32 glows,] glows   **EN** *1964B SC*/IV

33 wild,] wild   **EN** *SC*/IV

   beautiful,] beautiful   **EN** *SC*/IV

35 warm.] warm   **EN** *SC*/IV

36 Virtue] Virtue,   *1964B*

   blasting] blushing   *1964B*

   virtue's] virtues   **EN** *SC*/IV

     virtues'   *1964B*

   prime,] prime   **EN** *SC*/IV

37 Truth] Truth,   *1964B*

   Falshood's] Falshoods   **EN** *SC*/IV

   fruit,] fruit   **EN** *SC*/IV

38 Freedom's] Freedoms   **EN** *SC*/IV

> The human will in chains
>   Indissolubly fast!   40
>
> Prime source of all that's lovely, good and great,
> Debasing man below the meanest brute,
>   Spring of all healing streams,
>   Yet deadlier than the gall
>   Blackening a monarch's heart!   45
>
> Why art thou thus, O Passion? Custom's chains
> Have bound thee from thine Heaven-directed flight
>   Or thou wouldst never thus
>   Bring misery to man,
>   Uniting good and ill.   50

To Harriet   [*Esd #5*]

> Never, O never, shall yonder Sun
>   Thro' my frame its warmth diffuse
> When the heart that beats in its faithful breast
>   Is untrue, fair girl, to thee;
>   Nor the beaming moon   5
>   On its nightly voyage
> Shall visit this spirit with softness again
>   When its soaring hopes
>   And its fluttering fears
> Are untrue—fair girl, to thee!   10

---

40 fast!] fast **EN** *SC/IV*
      fast; *1964B*

41 that's] thats **EN** *SC/IV*
  lovely,] lovely **EN** *SC/IV*
  good] good, *1964B*
  and] & **EN** *SC/IV*
  great,] great **EN** *SC/IV*

42 brute,] brute **EN** *SC/IV*

43 streams,] streams **EN** *SC/IV*

45 monarch's] monarhs **EN** *SC/IV*
  heart!] heart **EN** *SC/IV*
      heart. *1964B*

46 thus,] thus **EN** *SC/IV*
  Custom's] Customs **EN** *SC/IV*

47 Heaven-directed]
  Heaven directed **EN** *SC/IV*

49 man,] man **EN** *SC/IV*

50 and] & **EN** *SC/IV*
  ill.] ill **EN** *SC/IV*

Text collated with **EN**, *1964B*, and *SC/IV*.

1 Never,] Never **EN** *SC/IV*
  O] o **EN** *SC/IV*
  never,] never **EN** *SC/IV*

2 Thro'] Thro **EN** *SC/IV*

4 untrue,] untrue **EN** *SC/IV*
  girl,] girl **EN** *SC/IV*
  thee;] thee **EN** *SC/IV*

7 again] again, *1964B*

10 girl,] girl **EN** *1964B SC/IV*

O Ever while this frail brain has life
Will it thrill to thy love-beaming gaze,
And whilst thine eyes with affection gleam
It will worship the spirit within.
15 And when death comes
To quench their fire
A sorrowful rapture their dimness will shed
As I bind me tight
With thine auburn hair
20 And die as I lived with thee.

[*Esd #6*]   Falshood and Vice
a Dialogue

Whilst Monarchs laughed upon their thrones
To hear a famished nation's groans
And hugged the wealth, wrung from the woe
That makes their eyes and veins o'erflow,
5 Those thrones high built upon the heaps
Of bones where frenzied Famine sleeps,
Where slavery with her scourge of iron
Stained in mankind's unheeded gore,
And war's mad fiends the scene environ
10 Mingling with shrieks a drunken roar,

---

12 love-beaming]   16 fire] fire,   *1964B*
   lovebeaming   **EN** *SC*/IV   20 die] die,   *1964B*
  gaze,] gaze   **EN** *SC*/IV   lived] lived,   *1964B*
14 within.] within   **EN** *SC*/IV   thee.] thee   **EN** *SC*/IV

Text collated with **EN,** *1813, 1964B* and *SC*/IV.
Title. Falshood] Falsehood   *1964B*   5 thrones] thrones,   *1813*
   and] &   **EN** *SC*/IV   6 frenzied] frienzied   **EN** *SC*/IV
1 Monarchs] monarchs   *1813*   Famine] famine   *1813*
  their] thier   **EN** *SC*/IV   sleeps,] sleeps   **EN** *SC*/IV
2 nation's] nations   **EN** *SC*/IV   7 with] wields   *1813*
  groans] groans,   *1813 1964B*   iron] iron,   *1813*
3 wealth,] wealth   *1813*   8 Stained in] Red with   *1813*
4 their] thier   **EN** *SC*/IV   mankind's] mankinds   **EN** *SC*/IV
   its   *1813*   9 war's] wars   **EN** *SC*/IV
  and] &   **EN** *SC*/IV   environ] environ,   *1813*
  veins] viens   **EN** *SC*/IV   10 roar,] roar   **EN** *SC*/IV
  o'erflow,] oerflow   **EN** *SC*/IV
   o'erflow,—   *1813*

There Vice and Falshood took their stand
High raised above the unhappy land.

FALSHOOD

Brother! arise from the dainty fare
  Which thousands have toild and bled to bestow—
A finer feast for thy hungry ear   15
  Is the news that I bring of human woe.

VICE

And secret one, what hast thou done
  To compare in thy tumid pride with me—
I, whose career thro' the blasted year
  Has been marked by ruin and misery?   20

FALSHOOD

What have I done! I've torn the robe
  From baby Truth's unsheltered form
And round the desolated globe
  Worn safely the bewildering charm.
My tyrant-slaves to a dungeon floor   25
  Have bound the dauntless innocent,

---

11 and] & **EN** *SC*/IV
   stand] stand, *1813*
12 land.] land **EN** *SC*/IV
13 Brother!] Brother **EN** *SC*/IV
      Brother, *1964B*
   fare] fare, *1813*
14 toild] toiled *1813*
     toil'd *1964B SC*/IV
   and] & **EN** *SC*/IV
   bestow—] bestow **EN** *SC*/IV
      bestow; *1813*
      bestow, *1964B*
16 woe.] woe **EN** *SC*/IV
17 And] And, *1813*
   done] done, *1813*
18 compare] compare, *1813*
   pride] pride, *1813*
   me—] me **EN** *SC*/IV
     me? *1813*
     me, *1964B*

19 career] career, *1813*
   thro'] thro **EN** *SC*/IV
     through *1813*
   year] year, *1813*
20 marked] tracked *1813*
   ruin] despair *1813*
   and] & **EN** *SC*/IV
   misery?] misery **EN** *SC*/IV
     agony. *1813*
21 done! I've] done!——I have *1813*
22 Truth's] Truths **EN** *SC*/IV
     truth's *1813*
   form] form, *1813*
24 Worn] Borne *1813*
   charm.] charm **EN** *SC*/IV
      charm: *1813*
25 dungeon floor] dungeon-floor *1813*
26 dauntless] fearless *1813*
   innocent,] innocent **EN** *SC*/IV

> And streams of fertilizing gore
> Flow from her bosom's hideous rent
> Which this unfailing dagger gave . . .
30 I dread that blood. No more. This day
> Is ours, tho' her eternal ray
> Must shine upon our grave . . .
> Yet know, proud Vice, had I not given
> To thee the mask I stole from Heaven,
35 Thy shape of ugliness and fear
> Had never gained admission here.

VICE

> And know that had I disdained to toil
> But sate in my noisome cave the while
> And ne'er to these hateful sons of Heaven,
40 GOLD, MONARCHY or MURDER given,
> Hadst thou with all thine art essayed
> One of thy games then to have played,
> With all thine overweening boast,
> Falshood, I tell thee thou had lost!—
45 But wherefore this dispute . . . we tend
> Fraternal to one common end.

---

28 bosom's] bosoms **EN** *SC/IV*
   rent] rent, *1813*
29 gave . . .] gave. *1813*
30 blood. No] blood!—no *1813*
   more. This] more. this **EN** *SC/IV*
      more—this *1813*
31 ours,] ours. **EN** *SC/IV*
      ours *1964B*
   tho'] tho **EN** *SC/IV*
      though *1813*
32 grave . . .] grave. *1813*
      grave . . . . *SC/IV*
33 know,] know **EN** *SC/IV*
   Vice,] Vice **EN** *SC/IV*
34 mask] robe *1813*
   Heaven,] Heaven **EN** *SC/IV*
      heaven, *1813*
35 and] & **EN** *SC/IV*
36 here.] here **EN** *SC/IV*
37 know] know, *1813*
   toil] toil, *1813*

38 noisome] loathsome *1813*
   while] while, *1813*
39 Heaven,] Heaven **EN** *SC/IV*
      heaven, *1813*
40 MONARCHY] MONARCHY, *1813*
   or] and *1813*
   MURDER] MURDER, *1813*
   given,] given **EN** *SC/IV*
      given; *1813*
42 played,] played **EN** *SC/IV*
43 boast,] boast **EN** *1964B SC/IV*
44 Falshood,] Falshood! *1813*
   had] hadst *1813*
45 But] Yet *1813*
   dispute . . . we] dispute?—we *1813*
   tend] tend, *1813*
46 Fraternal] Fraternal, *1813*
   end.] end **EN** *SC/IV*
      end; *1813*

In this cold grave beneath my feet
Will our hopes, our fears and our labours meet.

FALSHOOD

I brought my daughter RELIGION on Earth.
She smothered its sweetest buds in their birth   50
But dreaded Reason's eye severe
So the crocodile slunk off slily in fear
And loosed her bloodhounds from the den—
They started from dreams of slaughtered men
And by the light of her poison eye   55
Did her work o'er the wide Earth frightfully.
The deathy stench of her torches' flare,
Fed with human fat, polluted the air.
The curses, the shrieks, the ceaseless cries
Of the many mingling miseries,   60
As on she trod, ascended high
And trumpeted my Victory!
Brother, tell what thou hast done.

---

47 feet] feet, *1813*
48 fears] fears, *1813*
    and] & **EN** *SC*/IV
    labours] labours, *1813*
    meet.] meet **EN** *SC*/IV
49 daughter] daughter, *1813*
    RELIGION] RELIGION, *1813*
    Earth.] Earth **EN** *SC*/IV
       earth: *1813*
50 its sweetest buds]
    Reason's babes *1813*
    birth] birth; *1813*
51 Reason's] Reasons **EN** *SC*/IV
      their mother's *1813*
    severe] severe,— *1813*
52 fear] fear, *1813*
53 bloodhounds]
    blood hounds **EN** *SC*/IV
    den—] den **EN** *SC*/IV
      den.... *1813*
      den. *1964B*
54 men] men, *1813*

55 And] And, *1813*
    eye] eye, *1813*
56 o'er] oer **EN** *SC*/IV
    Earth] earth *1813*
    frightfully.] frightfully **EN** *SC*/IV
      frightfully: *1813*
57 deathy] dreadful *1813*
    torches'] torches **EN** *SC*/IV
    flare,] flare **EN** *SC*/IV
58 fat,] fat **EN** *SC*/IV
    air.] air **EN** *SC*/IV
      air: *1813*
60 many mingling] many-mingling *1813*
    miseries,] miseries **EN** *SC*/IV
61 trod,] trod **EN** *SC*/IV
62 Victory!] victory!— *1813*
63 Brother,] Brother **EN** *SC*/IV
    done.] done **EN** *SC*/IV

I have extinguished the noonday sun

65   In the carnage smoke of battles won;

Famine, Murder, Hell and Power

Were sated in that joyous hour

Which searchless fate had stampt for me

With the seal of his security.

70   For the bloated Wretch on yonder throne

Commanded the bloody fray to rise;

Like me he joyed at the stifled moan

Wrung from a Nation's miseries,

Whilst the snakes, whose slime *even him* defiled,

75   In extacies of malice smiled . . . .

They thought 'twas theirs!!—but mine the deed:

Theirs is the toil, but mine the meed.

Ten thousand victims madly bleed;

They think that tyrants goad them there

80   With poisonous war to taint the air,

These tyrants on their beds of thorn

---

64 noonday] noon-day *1813*
    sun] sun, *1813*

65 carnage smoke] carnage-smoke *1813*
    won;] won **EN** *SC*/IV
      won: *1813*
      won. *1964B*

66 Famine,] Famine **EN** *SC*/IV
    Murder,] Murder **EN** *SC*/IV
      murder, *1813*
    Hell] hell *1813*
      Hell, *1964B*
    and] & **EN** *SC*/IV
    Power] power *1813*

67 sated] ~~sated~~ **EN** *SC*/IV
      glutted *1813*
    joyous] glorious *1813*

68 stampt] stamped *1813*

69 his] her *1813*
    security.] security **EN** *SC*/IV
      security. *1813*
      security, *1964B*

70 Wretch] wretch *1813*

71 rise;] rise **EN** *SC*/IV
      rise. *1813 1964B*

73 Nation's] Nations **EN** *SC*/IV
      nation's *1813*

miseries,] miseries **EN** *1964B* *SC*/IV
      miseries; *1813*

74 Whilst] While *1813*
    snakes,] snakes **EN** *SC*/IV
    even him] <u>even him</u> **EN** *SC*/IV
      even him *1813*
    defiled,] defiled **EN** *SC*/IV

75 extacies] extasies **EN** *SC*/IV
      ecstacies *1813*
    smiled . . . .] smiled: *1813*
      smiled. . . . *1964B*

76 'twas] twas **EN** *SC*/IV
    theirs!!—but] thiers!!—but **EN**
      theirs,—but *1813*
    deed:] deed **EN** *SC*/IV
      deed! *1813*
      deed. *1964B*

77 meed.] meed **EN** *SC*/IV
      meed— *1813*

78 bleed;] bleed **EN** *SC*/IV
      bleed. *1813 1964B*

79 think] dream *1813*

80 air,] air **EN** *SC*/IV
      air: *1813*

81 tyrants] tyrants, *1813*
    thorn] thorn, *1813*

Swell in their dreams of murderous fame
And with their gains to lift my name
   Restless they plan from night to morn.
I—I do all. Without my aid,   85
Thy daughter, that relentless maid,
Could never o'er a deathbed urge
The fury of her venomed scourge.

FALSHOOD

Brother, well.—The world is ours,
   And whether thou or I have won,   90
The pestilence expectant lowers
   On all beneath yon blasted Sun.
Our joys, our toils, our honors meet
In the milkwhite and wormy winding sheet:
A short-lived joy, unceasing care,   95
Some heartless scraps of godly prayer,
A moody curse and a frenzied sleep
Ere gapes the grave's unclosing deep,
A tyrant's dream, a coward's start,
The ice that clings to a priestly heart,   100

---

82 in their dreams]
   with the thoughts *1813*
   their] thier **EN** *SC*/IV
   fame] fame, *1813*
83 their] thier **EN** *SC*/IV
   name] name. *1813*
84 morn.] morn **EN** *SC*/IV
      morn: *1813*
85 all.] all; *1813*
   Without] without **EN** *1813 SC*/IV
   aid,] aid **EN** *1813 SC*/IV
86 maid,] maid **EN** *SC*/IV
87 o'er] oer **EN** *SC*/IV
   deathbed] death-bed *1813*
88 scourge.] scourge **EN** *SC*/IV
89 Brother,] Brother **EN** *SC*/IV
   well.—The] well.—the **EN** *SC*/IV
      well:—the *1813*
   ours,] ours **EN** *SC*/IV
      ours; *1813*
      ours. *1964B*
90 won,] won **EN** *SC*/IV

92 Sun.] sun. *1813*
93 joys,] joys **EN** *SC*/IV
   toils,] toils **EN** *SC*/IV
94 milkwhite] milk-white *1813*
   and] & **EN** *SC*/IV
   winding sheet:] winding-sheet: *1813*
   sheet:] sheet **EN** *SC*/IV
      sheet. *1964B*
95 short-lived] short lived **EN** *SC*/IV
   joy,] hope, *1813*
   care,] care **EN** *SC*/IV
96 prayer,] prayer **EN** *SC*/IV
97 curse] curse, *1813*
   and] & **EN** *SC*/IV
   frenzied] frienzied **EN** *SC*/IV
98 grave's] graves **EN** *SC*/IV
   deep,] deep **EN** *SC*/IV
99 tyrant's] tyrants **EN** *SC*/IV
   coward's] cowards **EN** *SC*/IV
   start,] start **EN** *SC*/IV
100 heart,] heart **EN** *SC*/IV

A judge's frown, a courtier's smile
Make the great whole for which we toil.
And Brother! Whether thou or I
Have done the work of misery,
105   It little boots.—thy toil and pain
Without my aid were more than vain,
And but for thee I ne'er had sate
The guardian of Heaven's palace gate.

[*Esd #7*]   To the Emperors of Russia and Austria
who eyed the battle of Austerlitz from
the heights whilst Buonaparte was
active in the thickest of the fight

Coward Chiefs! who while the fight
    Rages in the plain below
Hide the shame of your affright
    On yon distant mountain's brow,
5   Does one human feeling creep
Thro' your hearts' remorseless sleep?
On that silence cold and deep
    Does one impulse flow
Such as fires the Patriot's breast,
10   Such as breaks the Hero's rest?

---

101 judge's] judges **EN** *SC*/IV
    courtier's] courtiers **EN** *SC*/IV
    smile] smile, *1813 1964B*
102 toil.] toil **EN** *SC*/IV
        toil; *1813*
103 And] And, *1813*
    Brother!] brother, *1813*
    Whether] whether *1813*
105 boots.—thy] boots: thy *1813*
            boots.—Thy *1964B*
            boots—thy *SC*/IV
    and] & **EN** *SC*/IV
    pain] pain, *1813*
106 aid] aid, *1813*
    vain,] vain **EN** *SC*/IV
        vain; *1813*
107 ne'er] neer **EN** *SC*/IV
108 Heaven's] Heavens **EN** *SC*/IV
        heaven's *1813*

gate.] gate **EN** *SC*/IV

Text collated with **EN**, *1964B*, and *SC*/IV.
Title. and] & **EN** *SC*/IV
    Austerlitz] austrelitz **EN**
            austrtrelitz *SC*/IV
1 who] who, *1964B*
2 below] below, *1964B*
4 mountain's] mountains **EN** *SC*/IV
    brow,] brow **EN** *SC*/IV
6 Thro'] Thro **EN** *SC*/IV
    sleep?] sleep **EN** *1964B SC*/IV
7 and] & **EN** *SC*/IV
    deep] deep? *1964B*
9 Patriot's] Patriots **EN** *SC*/IV
    breast,] breast **EN** *SC*/IV
10 rest?] rest. **EN** *SC*/IV

No, cowards! ye are calm and still,
    Keen frosts that blight the human bud
Each opening petal blight and kill
    And bathe its tenderness in blood.
Ye hear the groans of those who die,   15
Ye hear the whistling death-shots fly,
And when the yells of Victory
    Float o'er the murdered good,
Ye smile secure.—On yonder plain
The game, if lost, begins again.   20

Think ye the restless fiend who haunts
    The tumult of yon gory field,
Whom neither shame nor danger daunts,
    Who dares not fear, who cannot yield,
Will not with Equalizing blow   25
Abase the high, exalt the low,
And in one mighty shock o'erthrow
    The slaves that sceptres wield,
Till from the ruin of the storm
Ariseth Freedom's awful form?   30

Hushed below the battle's jar
    Night rests silent on the Heath,
Silent save where vultures soar
    Above the wounded warrior's death.
How sleep ye now, unfeeling Kings!   35

---

11 No,] No   **EN** *SC*/IV
   and] &   **EN** *SC*/IV
   still,] still   **EN** *SC*/IV
12 bud] bud,   *1964B*
13 and] &   **EN** *SC*/IV
14 blood.] blood   **EN** *SC*/IV
15 die,] die   **EN** *SC*/IV
16 whistling] whilstling   **EN** *SC*/IV
   death-shots] death shots   **EN** *SC*/IV
   fly,] fly   **EN** *SC*/IV
18 o'er] oer   **EN** *SC*/IV
   good,] good   **EN** *1964B SC*/IV
19 secure.—On] secure.—on   **EN** *SC*/IV
20 game,] game   **EN** *SC*/IV
   lost,] lost   **EN** *SC*/IV
   again.] again   **EN** *SC*/IV

22 field,] field   **EN** *SC*/IV
23 daunts,] daunts   **EN** *SC*/IV
24 yield,] yield   **EN** *SC*/IV
26 Abase] Exalt   **EN** *1964B SC*/IV
   exalt] abase   **EN** *1964B SC*/IV
   low,] low   **EN** *SC*/IV
27 o'erthrow] oerthrow   **EN** *SC*/IV
28 wield,] wield   **EN** *1964B SC*/IV
30 Freedom's] Freedoms   **EN** *SC*/IV
   form?] form   **EN** *SC*/IV
31 battle's] battles   **EN** *SC*/IV
32 Heath,] Heath   **EN** *SC*/IV
33 where] when [?where]   *SC*/IV
34 warrior's] warriors   **EN** *SC*/IV
   death.] death   **EN** *SC*/IV
35 now,] now   **EN** *SC*/IV

Peace seldom folds her snowy wings
On poisoned memory's conscience-stings
Which lurk bad hearts beneath:
Nor downy beds procure repose
40 Where crime and terror mingle throes.

Yet may your terrors rest secure.
Thou Northern chief, why startest thou?
Pale Austria, calm those fears. Be sure
The tyrant needs such slaves as you:
45 Think ye the world would bear his sway
Were dastards such as you away?
No! they would pluck his plumage gay
Torn from a nation's woe
And lay him in the oblivious gloom
50 Where Freedom now prepares your tomb.

[*Esd* #8]   To November

O month of gloom whose sullen brow
Bears stamp of storms that lurk beneath,
No care or horror bringest thou
To one who draws his breath
5 Where Zephyrs play and sunbeams shine
Unstained by any fog of thine.

Whilst thou obscurest the face of day
Her radiant eyes can gild the gloom,
Darting a soft and vernal ray
10 On Nature's leafless tomb.

---

37 memory's] memorys **EN** *SC*/IV
38 beneath:] beneath, *1964B*
40 and] & **EN** *SC*/IV
    throes.] throes **EN** *SC*/IV
41 secure.] secure **EN** *SC*/IV
42 Thou] Thou, *1964B*
    chief,] chief **EN** *SC*/IV
    thou?] thou **EN** *SC*/IV
43 Austria,] Austria **EN** *SC*/IV
    Be] be **EN** *SC*/IV
44 you:] you. **EN** *1964B SC*/IV
48 nation's] nations **EN** *SC*/IV

50 tomb.] tomb **EN** *SC*/IV

Text collated with **EN,** *1964B,* and *SC*/IV.
1 gloom] gloom, *1964B*
2 beneath,] beneath **EN** *SC*/IV
5 and] & **EN** *SC*/IV
6 thine.] thine **EN** *SC*/IV
7 obscurest] obscurst **EN** *SC*/IV
8 gloom,] gloom **EN** *SC*/IV
9 and] & **EN** *SC*/IV
10 Nature's] Natures **EN** *SC*/IV
    tomb.] tomb **EN** *SC*/IV

Yes! tho' the landscape's beauties flee
My Harriet makes it spring to me.

Then raise thy fogs, invoke thy storms,
    Thy malice still my soul shall mar,
And whilst thy rage the Heaven deforms   15
      Shall laugh at every care,
And each pure feeling shall combine
To tell its Harriet "I am thine!"

It once was May. The Month of Love
    Did all it could to yield me pleasure,   20
Waking each green and vocal grove
      To a many-mingling measure,
But warmth and peace could not impart
To such a cold and shuddering heart.

Now thou art here—come! do thy worst   25
    To chill the breast that Harriet warms.
I fear me, sullen Month! thou'lt burst
      With envy of her charms
And finding nothing's to be done
Turn to December ere thou'st won.   30

Written on a beautiful day in Spring   *[Esd #9]*

In that strange mental wandering when to live,
To breathe, to be, is undivided joy,

---

11 tho'] tho **EN** *SC/IV*
   landscape's] landscapes **EN** *SC/IV*
12 me.] me **EN** *SC/IV*
13 fogs,] fogs **EN** *SC/IV*
   storms,] storms **EN** *SC/IV*
14 mar,] mar **EN** *SC/IV*
15 thy] the **EN** *SC/IV*
16 care,] care **EN** *SC/IV*
19 May.] May; *1964B*
     May *SC/IV*
   The] the **EN** *1964B SC/IV*
20 pleasure,] pleasure **EN** *SC/IV*
21 and] & **EN** *SC/IV*
22 many-mingling]
   manymingling **EN** *SC/IV*

measure,] measure **EN** *SC/IV*
23 and] & **EN** *SC/IV*
   could] c^d **EN** *SC/IV*
24 and] & **EN** *SC/IV*
   heart.] heart **EN** *SC/IV*
26 warms.] warms **EN** *SC/IV*
27 me,] me **EN** *1964B SC/IV*
   Month!] Month *1964B*
   thou'lt] thoult **EN** *SC/IV*
29 nothing's] nothings **EN** *SC/IV*
30 won.] won! *1964B*

Text collated with **EN,** *1964B*, and *SC/IV*.
1 live,] live **EN** *1964B SC/IV*
2 joy,] joy **EN** *SC/IV*

When the most woe-worn wretch would cease to grieve,
When satiation's self would fail to cloy;

5   When unpercipient of all other things
Than those that press around, the breathing Earth
The gleaming sky and the fresh season's birth,
Sensation all its wondrous rapture brings
And to itself not once the mind recurs—

10   Is it foretaste of Heaven?
So sweet as this the nerves it stirs,
    And mingling in the vital tide
      With gentle motion driven,
  Cheers the sunk spirits, lifts the languid eye,

15   And scattering thro' the frame its influence wide
    Revives the spirits when they droop and die.
The frozen blood with genial beaming warms
And to a gorgeous fly the sluggish worm transforms.

[*Esd* #10]   On leaving London for Wales.

Thou miserable city! where the gloom
  Of penury mingles with the tyrant's pride,
And virtue bends in sorrow o'er the tomb
  Where Freedom's hope and Truth's high Courage died,

5 May floods and vales and mountains me divide
  From all the taints thy wretched walls contain
That life's extremes in desolation wide

---

3 woe-worn] woe worn **EN** *SC*/IV
   would] w.^d **EN**
       w^d *SC*/IV
   grieve,] grieve **EN** *SC*/IV
7 and] & **EN** *SC*/IV
   season's] seasons **EN** *SC*/IV
8 its] it **EN** *SC*/IV
9 recurs—] recurs **EN** *SC*/IV
11 stirs,] stirs **EN** *SC*/IV
13 driven,] driven **EN** *SC*/IV
14 eye,] eye **EN** *SC*/IV
15 thro'] thro **EN** *SC*/IV
16 and] & **EN** *SC*/IV
   die.] die **EN** *SC*/IV

18 transforms.] transforms **EN** *SC*/IV

Text collated with **EN,** *1964B,* and *SC*/IV.
2 tyrant's] tyrants **EN** *SC*/IV
3 o'er] oer **EN** *SC*/IV
4 Freedom's] Freedoms **EN** *SC*/IV
   and] & **EN** *SC*/IV
   Truth's] Truths **EN** *SC*/IV
   died,] died **EN** *SC*/IV
     died. *1964B*
5 and] & **EN** *SC*/IV
   and] & **EN** *SC*/IV
6 contain] contain, *1964B*
7 life's] lifes **EN** *SC*/IV

No more heap horrors on my beating brain,
Nor sting my shuddering heart to sympathy with pain.

With joy I breathe the last and free farewell   10
    That long has quivered on my burdened heart;
My natural sympathies to rapture swell
    As from its day thy cheerless glooms depart,
Nor all the glare thy gayest scenes impart
    Could lure one sigh, could steal one tear from me,   15
Or lull to languishment the wakeful smart
    Which virtue feels for all 'tis forced to see,
Or quench the eternal flame of generous Liberty.

Hail to thee, Cambria, for the unfettered wind
    Which from thy wilds even now methinks I feel   20
Chasing the clouds that roll in wrath behind
    And tightening the soul's laxest nerves to steel!
True! Mountain Liberty alone may heal
    The pain which Custom's obduracies bring,
And he who dares in fancy even to steal   25
    One draught from Snowdon's ever-sacred spring
Blots out the unholiest rede of worldly witnessing.

And shall that soul to selfish peace resigned
    So soon forget the woe its fellows share?
Can Snowdon's Lethe from the freeborn mind   30
    So soon the page of injured penury tear?
Does this fine mass of human passion dare
    To sleep, unhonouring the patriot's fall,

---

8 brain,] brain   **EN** *1964B SC*/IV

9 pain.] pain   **EN** *SC*/IV

  stanza break] *page break*   **EN** *SC*/IV

10 and] &   **EN** *SC*/IV

  free] [?full]   *SC*/IV

    full   *1964B*

11 heart;] heart   **EN** *SC*/IV

    heart,   *1964B*

13 depart,] depart   **EN** *SC*/IV

15 me,] me   **EN** *SC*/IV

17 'tis] tis   **EN** *SC*/IV

  see,] see   **EN** *SC*/IV

18 Liberty.] Liberty   **EN** *SC*/IV

  stanza break] *page break*   **EN** *SC*/IV

19 thee,] thee   **EN** *SC*/IV

  Cambria,] Cambria   **EN** *SC*/IV

22 tightening] tightning   **EN** *SC*/IV

  soul's] souls   **EN** *SC*/IV

  steel!] steel   **EN** *SC*/IV

24 Custom's] Customs   **EN** *SC*/IV

  bring,] bring   **EN** *SC*/IV

26 Snowdon's] Snowdons   **EN** *SC*/IV

  ever-sacred] ever sacred   **EN** *SC*/IV

27 witnessing.] witnessing   **EN** *SC*/IV

30 Snowdon's] Snowdons   **EN** *SC*/IV

33 sleep,] sleep   **EN** *SC*/IV

  patriot's] patriots   **EN** *SC*/IV

  fall,] fall   **EN** *SC*/IV

Or life's sweet load in quietude to bear
35   While millions famish even in Luxury's hall
And Tyranny high-raised stern lowers over all?

No, Cambria! never may thy matchless vales
    A heart so false to hope and virtue shield,
Nor ever may thy spirit-breathing gales
40   Waft freshness to the slaves who dare to yield.
For me! . . . the weapon that I burn to wield
    I seek amid thy rocks to ruin hurled,
That Reason's flag may over Freedom's field,
    Symbol of bloodless victory, wave unfurled—
45 A meteor-sign of love effulgent o'er the world.

Hark to that shriek! my hand had almost clasped
    The dagger that my heart had cast away
When the pert slaves whose wanton power had grasped
    All hope that springs beneath the eye of day
50 Pass before Memory's gaze in long array.
    The storm fleets by and calmer thoughts succeed;
Feelings once more mild reason's voice obey.
    Woe be the tyrant's and the murderer's meed,
But Nature's wound alone should make their Conscience
    bleed.

---

34 life's] lifes **EN** *SC*/IV

35 Luxury's] Luxurys **EN** *SC*/IV

36 high-raised] high raised **EN** *SC*/IV
    lowers] [lowers] **EN** *SC*/IV
    all?] all **EN** *SC*/IV

37 No,] No **EN** *SC*/IV

38 and] & **EN** *SC*/IV
    shield,] shield **EN** *SC*/IV

39 spirit-breathing]
    spirit breathing **EN** *SC*/IV

42 hurled,] hurled **EN** *1964B SC*/IV

43 Reason's] Reasons **EN** *SC*/IV
    Freedom's] Freedoms **EN** *SC*/IV
    field,] field **EN** *SC*/IV

44 victory,] victory **EN** *SC*/IV
    unfurled—] unfurled **EN** *SC*/IV

45 o'er] oer **EN** *SC*/IV

48 slaves] slaves, *1964B*

49 day] day, *1964B*

50 Memory's] Memorys **EN** *SC*/IV
    memory's *1964B*

51 and] & **EN** *SC*/IV
    succeed;] succeed **EN** *SC*/IV
    succeed, *1964B*

52 reason's] reasons **EN** *SC*/IV

53 tyrant's] tyrants **EN** *SC*/IV
    tyrants' *1964B*
    and] & **EN** *SC*/IV
    the] *omitted* *1964B*
    murderer's] murderers **EN** *SC*/IV
    murderers' *1964B*
    meed,] meed **EN** *SC*/IV

54 Nature's] Natures **EN** *SC*/IV
    should] sh.^d **EN**
    sh^d *SC*/IV
    bleed.] bleed **EN** *SC*/IV

Do thou, wild Cambria! calm each struggling thought;
    Cast thy sweet veil of rocks and woods between,
That by the soul to indignation wrought
    Mountains and dells be mingled with the scene.
Let me forever be what I have been,
    But not forever at my needy door   60
Let Misery linger, speechless, pale and lean.
    I am the friend of the unfriended poor;
Let me not madly stain their righteous cause in gore.

No more! the visions fade before my sight
    Which Fancy pictures in the waste of air   65
Like lovely dreams ere morning's chilling light:
    And sad realities alone are there.
Ah! neither woe, nor fear, nor pain can tear
    Their image from the tablet of my soul,
Nor the mad floods of despotism where   70
    Lashed into desperate furiousness they roll,
Nor passion's soothing voice, nor interest's cold control.

A winter's day   *[Esd #11]*

O! wintry day! that mockest spring
    With hopes of the reviving year—
That sheddest softness from thy wing
    And near the cascade's murmuring

---

55 thou,] thou **EN** *SC/*IV
   Cambria!] Cambria **EN** *SC/*IV
      Cambria, *1964B*
   thought;] thought **EN** *SC/*IV
56 and] & **EN** *SC/*IV
   between,] between **EN** *SC/*IV
57 the] thy *SC/*IV
58 and] & **EN** *SC/*IV
   scene.] scene **EN** *SC/*IV
59 been,] been **EN** *SC/*IV
61 speechless,] speechless **EN** *SC/*IV
   and] & **EN** *SC/*IV
   lean.] lean **EN** *SC/*IV
62 poor;] poor **EN** *SC/*IV
63 their] thier **EN** *SC/*IV
   gore.] gore **EN** *SC/*IV
66 morning's] mornings **EN** *SC/*IV

   light:] light, *1964B*
67 there.] there **EN** *SC/*IV
68 woe,] woe **EN** *1964B SC/*IV
   fear,] fear *1964B*
69 Their] Thier **EN** *SC/*IV
   soul,] soul **EN** *SC/*IV
70 despotism] Despotism *1964B*
71 roll,] roll **EN** *SC/*IV
72 passion's] passions **EN** *SC/*IV
   interest's] interests **EN** *SC/*IV
   control.] control **EN** *SC/*IV

Text collated with **EN**, *1964B*, and *SC/*IV.
Title. winter's] winters **EN** *SC/*IV
2 year—] year **EN** *SC/*IV
    year! *1964B*
4 cascade's] cascades **EN** *SC/*IV

5   Awakenest sounds so clear
           That peals of vernal music swing
              Thro' the balm atmosphere:

           Why hast thou given, o year! to May
              A birth so premature,
10   To live one incompleted day
           That the mad whirlwind's sullen sway
              May sweep it from the moor,
           And winter reassume the sway
              That shall so long endure?

15   Art thou like Genius's matin bloom,
              Unwelcome promise of its prime,
           That scattereth its rich perfume
           Around the portals of the tomb,
              Decking the scar of time
20   In mockery of the early doom?

           Art thou like Passion's rapturous dream
              That o'er life's stormy dawn
           Doth dart its wild and flamy beam,
           Yet like a fleeting flash doth seem
25   When many chequered years are gone
           And tell the illusion of its gleam
              Life's blasted springs alone?

           Whate'er thou emblemest, I'll breathe
              Thy transitory sweetness now,
30   And whether Health with roseate wreathe
           May bind mine head, or creeping Death

---

7 Thro'] Thro   **EN** *SC/IV*
  atmosphere:]
    atmosphere.   **EN** *1964B SC/IV*
8 given,] given   **EN** *SC/IV*
  o] O   *1964B SC/IV*
9 premature,] premature   **EN** *SC/IV*
11 whirlwind's] whirlwinds   **EN** *SC/IV*
12 moor,] moor   **EN** *1964B SC/IV*
14 endure?] endure   **EN** *SC/IV*
15 bloom,] bloom   **EN** *1964B SC/IV*
16 prime,] prime   **EN** *1964B SC/IV*

18 tomb,] tomb   **EN** *1964B SC/IV*
20 doom?] doom   **EN** *SC/IV*
21 Passion's] Passions   **EN** *SC/IV*
22 life's] lifes   **EN** *SC/IV*
23 and] &   **EN** *SC/IV*
  beam,] beam   **EN** *1964B SC/IV*
27 Life's] Lifes   **EN** *SC/IV*
  alone?] alone   **EN** *SC/IV*
28 emblemest,] emblemest   **EN** *SC/IV*
29 now,] now   **EN** *SC/IV*

Steal o'er my pulse's flow,
Struggling the wintry winds beneath
I'll love thy vernal glow.

To Liberty   [Esd #12]

O let not Liberty
   Silently perish;
May the groan and the sigh
   Yet the flame cherish
Till the voice to Nature's bursting heart given,   5
   Ascending loud and high,—
   A world's indignant cry—
And startling on his throne
The tyrant grim and lone
Shall beat the deaf vault of Heaven.   10

Say, can the Tyrant's frown
   Daunt those who fear not
Or break the spirits down
   His badge that wear not?
Can chains or death or infamy subdue   15
   The free and fearless soul
   That dreads not their control—
Sees Paradise and Hell,
Sees the Palace and the cell,
Yet bravely dares prefer the good and true?   20

---

32 o'er] oer **EN** *SC*/IV
  pulse's] pulses **EN** *SC*/IV
34 glow.] glow **EN** *SC*/IV

Text collated with **EN,** *1964B,* and *SC*/IV.
2 perish;] perish **EN** *SC*/IV
3 and] & **EN** *SC*/IV
5 Nature's] Natures **EN** *SC*/IV
  given,] given **EN** *SC*/IV
6 and high,—] & high **EN** *SC*/IV
      and high *1964B*
7 world's] worlds **EN** *SC*/IV
  cry—] cry **EN** *SC*/IV
     cry, *1964B*
8 And] And, *1964B*

9 and] & **EN** *SC*/IV
  lone] lone, *1964B*
11 Say,] Say **EN** *SC*/IV
  Tyrant's] Tyrants **EN** *SC*/IV
14 not?] not **EN** *SC*/IV
16 free and] free & **EN**
     pure & *SC*/IV
17 control—] control **EN** *SC*/IV
     control, *1964B*
18 and] & **EN** *SC*/IV
  Hell,] Hell **EN** *SC*/IV
19 and] & **EN** *SC*/IV
  cell,] cell **EN** *SC*/IV
20 and] & **EN** *SC*/IV
  true?] true **EN** *SC*/IV

Regal pomp and pride
 The Patriot falls in scorning,
The spot whereon he died
 Should be the despot's warning:
25 The voice of blood shall on his crimes call down Revenge!
 And the spirits of the brave
 Shall start from every grave
Whilst from her Atlantic throne
Freedom sanctifies the groan
30 That fans the glorious fires of its change.

Monarch! sure employer
 Of vice and want and woe,
Thou Conscienceless destroyer,
 Who and what art thou!—
35 The dark prison house that in the dust shall lie,
The pyramid which guilt
First planned, which man has built,
At whose footstone want and woe
With a ceaseless murmur flow
40 And whose peak attracts the tempests of the sky.

The pyramids shall fall . . . . . .
 And Monarchs! so shall ye!
Thrones shall rust in the hall
 Of forgotten royalty
45 Whilst Virtue, Truth and Peace shall arise
And a Paradise on Earth
From your fall shall date its birth,

---

21 and] &   **EN** *SC*/IV

22 scorning,] scorning   **EN** *SC*/IV

24 despot's] despots   **EN** *SC*/IV
 warning:] warning   **EN** *SC*/IV
  warning.   *1964B*

30 change.] change   **EN** *SC*/IV

32 and] &   **EN** *SC*/IV
 and] &   **EN** *SC*/IV
 woe,] woe   **EN** *SC*/IV

33 Conscienceless]
 conscienceless   *1964B*
 destroyer,] destroyer   **EN** *SC*/IV

34 and] &   **EN** *SC*/IV

35 lie,] lie   **EN** *SC*/IV

37 planned,] planned.   **EN** *SC*/IV
 built,] built   **EN** *SC*/IV
  built;   *1964B*

38 and] &   **EN** *SC*/IV

42 ye!] ye   **EN** *SC*/IV

45 Virtue,] Virtue   **EN** *SC*/IV
 and] &   **EN** *SC*/IV

47 birth,] birth   **EN** *SC*/IV

And human life shall seem
Like a short and happy dream
Ere we wake in the daybeam of the skies.   50

On Robert Emmet's tomb   [*Esd #13*]

May the tempests of Winter that sweep o'er thy tomb
   Disturb not a slumber so sacred as thine;
May the breezes of summer that breathe of perfume
   Waft their balmiest dews to so hallowed a shrine.

May the foot of the tyrant, the coward, the slave   5
   Be palsied with dread where thine ashes repose,
Where that undying shamrock still blooms on thy grave
   Which sprung when the dawnlight of Erin arose.

There oft have I marked the grey gravestones among
   Where thy relics distinguished in lowliness lay   10
The peasant boy pensively lingering long
   And silently weep as he passed away.

And how could he not pause if the blood of his sires
   Ever wakened one generous throb in his heart:
How could he inherit a spark of their fires   15
   If tearless and frigid he dared to depart?

Not the scrolls of a court could emblazon thy fame
   Like the silence that reigns in the palace of thee,
Like the whispers that pass of thy dearly loved name,
   Like the tears of the good, like the groans of the free.   20

---

49 and] & **EN** *SC*/IV

Text collated with **EN,** *1964B,* and *SC*/IV.
Title. Emmet's] Emmets **EN** *SC*/IV
1 o'er] oer **EN** *SC*/IV
2 thine;] thine **EN** *SC*/IV
4 shrine.] shine **EN** *SC*/IV
5 tyrant,] tyrant **EN** *SC*/IV
  coward,] coward **EN** *SC*/IV
  slave] slave, *1964B*
6 repose,] repose **EN** *SC*/IV

9 among] among, *1964B*
10 lay] lay, *1964B*
14 heart:] heart? *1964B*
16 and] & **EN** *SC*/IV
  depart?] depart **EN** *SC*/IV
17 could] c.^{d} **EN**
    c^{d} *SC*/IV
18 thee,] thee X **EN** *SC*/IV
19 name,] name **EN** *SC*/IV
20 free.] free **EN** *SC*/IV

No trump tells thy virtues—the grave where they rest
   With thy dust shall remain unpolluted by fame
Till thy foes, by the world and by fortune caresst,
   Shall pass like a mist from the light of thy name.

25   When the storm cloud that lowers o'er the daybeam is gone,
   Unchanged, unextinguished its lifespring will shine—
When Erin has ceased with their memory to groan,
   She will smile thro' the tears of revival on thine.

[*Esd #14*]   a Tale of Society as it is
                 from facts 1811

        She was an Aged Woman, and the years
        Which she had numbered on her toilsome way
        Had bowed her natural powers to decay.
        She was an Aged Woman, yet the ray
5   Which faintly glimmered thro' the starting tears,
        Pressed from their beds by silent misery,
        Hath soul's imperishable energy.
        She was a cripple, and incapable
        To add one mite to golden luxury,

---

22 fame] fame, *1964B*

23 foes,] foes **EN** *SC*/IV

   and] & **EN** *SC*/IV

   caresst,] carest **EN** *SC*/IV

       caresst *1964B*

24 name.] name **EN** *SC*/IV

25 o'er] oer **EN** *SC*/IV

   gone,] gone **EN** *SC*/IV

26 shine—] shine **EN** *SC*/IV

     shine, *1964B*

27 groan,] groan **EN** *1964B SC*/IV

28 thro'] thro **EN** *SC*/IV

Text collated with **EN,** MS BLjan (lines 1–79), *1964B, 1964J* (lines 1–79), and *SC*/IV.

Title. a . . . 1811] *omitted* BLjan *1964J*

   a] A *SC*/IV

Stanza marker. *none*] 1 BLjan *1964J*

1 Aged] aged BLjan *1964J*

   Woman,] woman, BLjan *1964J*

   and] & **EN** *SC*/IV

3 decay.] decay **EN** BLjan *1964J SC*/IV

4 Aged] aged BLjan *1964J*

   Woman,] Woman **EN** *SC*/IV

      woman. BLjan

      woman, *1964J*

5 thro'] thro **EN** BLjan *1964J SC*/IV

   the] her BLjan *1964J*

   tears,]

     tears **EN** BLjan *1964B 1964J SC*/IV

6 from their beds]

   into light BLjan *1964J*

   misery,]   misery **EN** BLjan *1964B*

      1964J SC/IV

7 soul's] souls **EN** *SC*/IV

   energy.] energy **EN** *SC*/IV

      energy.— BLjan *1964J*

8 cripple,] c<rip>ple BLjan *1964J*

   and] & **EN** *SC*/IV

9 golden] gold-fed BLjan *1964J*

   luxury,] luxury **EN** BLjan *1964J SC*/IV

And therefore did her spirit clearly feel   10
That Poverty—the crime of tainting stain—
Would merge her in its depths never to rise again.

One only son's love had supported her.
She long had struggled with infirmity
Lingering from human lifescenes, for to die   15
When fate has spared to rend some mental tie
Not many wish, and surely fewer dare.
But when the tyrant's bloodhounds forced her Child
For tyrant's power unhallowed arms to wield,
Bend to another's will, become a thing   20
More senseless than the sword of battle field,
Then did she feel keen sorrow's keenest sting,
And many years had past ere comfort they would bring.

For seven years did this poor woman live
In unparticipated solitude: 25
Thou mightst have seen her in the desart rude
Picking the scattered remnants of its wood;

---

10 clearly] dimly   BLjan *1964J*

11 Poverty—the]
    Poverty the   **EN** BLjan *1964J SC*/IV
    stain—] stain   **EN** BLjan *1964J SC*/IV

12 its] its'   BLjan *1964J*
    again.] again   **EN** BLjan *SC*/IV
Stanza marker. *none*] 2   BLjan *1964J*

13 son's] sons   **EN** BLjan *1964J SC*/IV
    her.] her   BLjan *1964J*

15 from] to   BLjan *1964J*
    lifescenes,] life scenes   BLjan *1964J*

16 rend] send   *1964B*

17 Not] <No>t   BLjan
        <?Tha>t   *1964J*
    wish,] wish   BLjan *1964J*
    and] &   **EN** *SC*/IV
    dare.] dare   BLjan *1964J*

18 But] <B>ut   BLjan *1964J*
    tyrant's]
        tyrants   **EN** BLjan *1964J SC*/IV
    her] the   *1964J*
    Child] child   BLjan *1964J*

19 For tyrant's] <?> his cursed   BLjan
           [?With] his cursed
             1964J
    tyrant's] tyrants   **EN** *SC*/IV

wield,] wield   **EN** *SC*/IV
      weild,   BLjan

20 another's] anothers   **EN** *SC*/IV
    will,] will.   **EN** *SC*/IV

21 field,] field   **EN** BLjan *1964J SC*/IV

22 sorrow's] sorrows   **EN** BLjan *1964J*
    SC/IV
    sting,]
      sting   **EN** BLjan *1964B 1964J SC*/IV

23 past] passed   BLjan *1964J*
    would] w.^d   **EN**
        c^d.   BLjan *1964J*
        w^d   *SC*/IV
    bring.] bring   **EN** BLjan *SC*/IV
Stanza marker. *none*] 3   BLjan *1964J*

24 woman] worman   BLjan

25 solitude:]
      solitude   **EN** BLjan *1964J SC*/IV
      solitude.   *1964B*

26 mightst] mighst   BLjan
        might'st   *1964B*
        migh[t]st   *1964J*
    desart] forest   BLjan *1964J*

27 wood;] wood   **EN** BLjan *1964J SC*/IV
      wood.   *1964B*

If human, thou mightst then have learned to grieve.
The gleanings of precarious charity
30   Her scantiness of food did scarce supply;
The proofs of an unspeaking sorrow dwelt
Within her ghastly hollowness of eye:
Each arrow of the Season's change she felt,
Yet still she yearned ere her sad course were run,
35   One only hope it was, once more to see her son.

It was an eve of June, when every star
Spoke peace from Heaven to those on Earth that live.
She rested on the moor . . . . 'twas such an eve
When first her soul began indeed to grieve—
40   Then he was here . . . now he is very far.
The freshness of the balmy evening
A sorrow o'er her weary soul did fling,
Yet not devoid of rapture's mingled tear;
A balm was in the poison of the sting:

---

28 human,]
    human   **EN** BLjan *1964J* SC/IV
    mightst] mighst   **EN** *SC/IV*
        might'st   *1964B*
    then] there   *1964B*
       than   *SC/IV*
    grieve.] grieve   **EN** *SC/IV*
       feel   BLjan *1964J*
30 supply;]
    supply   **EN** BLjan *1964J* SC/IV
32 ghastly] gastly   BLjan
    eye:] eye   BLjan *1964J*
      eye;   *1964B*
33 Season's] Seasons   **EN** *SC/IV*
      seasons   BLjan *1964J*
    felt,] felt   **EN** BLjan *1964J* SC/IV
34 yearned] groans   BLjan *1964J*
    her] yet her   BLjan *1964J*
    sad course] race   BLjan *1964J*
    run,] run   **EN** BLjan *1964J* SC/IV
      run—   *1964B*
35 was, once] was! once   BLjan *1964J*
      was—once   *1964B*
    son.] son   **EN** *SC/IV*
      [?] Son   BLjan
      Son   *1964J*

Stanza marker. *none*] 4 BLjan *1964J*
36 June,] June   BLjan *1964J*
37 to those on Earth that live.]
    x x x x   BLjan *1964J*
    live.] live   **EN** *SC/IV*
38 moor . . . . 'twas] moor. twas   BLjan
      moor. . . 'twas   *1964B*
      moor—twas   *1964J*
39 grieve—]
    grieve   **EN** BLjan *1964J* SC/IV
40 here . . .] here;   BLjan
      here. . .   *1964B*
      here,   *1964J*
    far.] far!   BLjan *1964J*
      far   *SC/IV*
41 freshness] sweetness   BLjan *1964J*
42 o'er] oer   **EN** BLjan *1964J* SC/IV
    weary] aged   BLjan *1964J*
    fling,] fling   **EN** BLjan *1964J* SC/IV
43 rapture's]
    raptures   **EN** BLjan *1964J* SC/IV
    tear;] tear   **EN** BLjan *1964J* SC/IV
44 sting:] sting   **EN** *SC/IV*
    sting!   BLjan *1964J*
    sting.   *1964B*

This aged sufferer for many a year,   45
Had never felt such comfort . . . . she supprest
A sigh, and turning round clasp'd William to her breast.

And tho' his form was wasted by the woe
Which despots on their victims love to wreak—
Tho' his sunk eyeball, and his faded cheek,   50
Of slavery, violence and scorn did speak—
Yet did the aged Woman's bosom glow;
The vital fire seemed reillumed within
By this sweet unexpected welcoming.
O! consummation of the fondest hope   55
That ever soared on Fancy's dauntless wing!
O! tenderness that foundst so sweet a scope!
Prince! who dost swell upon thy mighty sway,
When thou canst feel such love, thou shalt be great as they!

---

45 year,] year BLjan *1964J*
46 such] much BLjan
   comfort . . . . she]
     comfort. she BLjan
     comfort—she *1964J*
47 sigh, and] sigh—and BLjan *1964J*
   and] & **EN** *SC*/IV
   round clasp'd]
     round claspd **EN** *SC*/IV
     round—clasp'd *1964B*
   breast.]
     breast **EN** BLjan *1964J SC*/IV
Stanza marker. *none*] 5 BLjan *1964J*
48 tho'] tho **EN** *SC*/IV
49 despots] tyrants BLjan *1964J*
   victims] Victims BLjan
   wreak—]
     wreak **EN** BLjan *1964J SC*/IV
     wreak, *1964B*
50 Tho'] Tho **EN** *SC*/IV
   and] & **EN** *SC*/IV
   cheek,] cheek **EN** BLjan *1964J SC*/IV
51 slavery,] slavery **EN** *SC*/IV
   violence] violence, *1964B*
   and] & **EN** BLjan *1964J SC*/IV

speak—]
   speak **EN** BLjan *1964J SC*/IV
   speak, *1964B*
52 Woman's] Womans **EN** *SC*/IV
     womans BLjan *1964J*
   glow;] glow **EN** *SC*/IV
     glow! BLjan *1964J*
53 reillumed] re illumed **EN**
54 welcoming.] welcoming BLjan *1964J*
55 O!] Oh BLjan *1964J*
56 Fancy's] Fancys **EN** *SC*/IV
     fancy's BLjan
   dauntless] wildest BLjan *1964J*
   wing!] wing **EN** BLjan *1964J SC*/IV
57 O!] Oh! BLjan
     Oh *1964J*
58 Prince!] Prince BLjan *1964J*
   swell upon]
     pride thee on BLjan *1964J*
   sway,] sway. **EN** *SC*/IV
     sway BLjan *1964B 1964J*
59 love,]
     love **EN** BLjan *1964B 1964J SC*/IV
   great as] ~~blest as~~ great as BLjan
   they!] they **EN** BLjan *1964J SC*/IV
   stanza break] *page break* **EN** *SC*/IV
   Stanza marker. *none*] 6 BLjan *1964J*

60   Her son, compelled, the tyrant's foes had fought,
        Had bled in battle, and the stern control
        That ruled his sinews and coerced his soul
        Utterly poisoned life's unmingled bowl
        And unsubduable evils on him wrought.
65   He was the shadow of the lusty child
        Who, when the time of summer season smiled,
        For her did earn a meal of honesty
        And with affectionate discourse beguiled
        The keen attacks of pain and poverty
70   Till power as envying this, her only joy,
        From her maternal bosom tore the unhappy boy.

        And now cold charity's unwelcome dole
        Was insufficient to support the pair,
        And they would perish rather than would bear
75   The law's stern slavery and the insolent stare
        With which law loves to rend the poor man's soul—
        The bitter scorn, the spirit-sinking noise

---

60 son,] son   BLjan *1964J*
   compelled,]
      compelled   **EN** BLjan *1964J SC*/IV
   tyrant's] tyrants   **EN** *SC*/IV
            country's   BLjan *1964J*
   fought,]
      fought   **EN** BLjan *1964J SC*/IV
61 battle,] battle.   BLjan
   and] &   **EN** BLjan *1964J SC*/IV
62 That] Which   BLjan *1964J*
   and] &   **EN** *SC*/IV
         h^d   BLjan
63 life's] lifes   **EN** *SC*/IV
64 wrought.] wrought   **EN** *SC*/IV
            brought   BLjan *1964J*
66 Who,] Who   **EN** *SC*/IV
   smiled,]
      smiled   **EN** BLjan *1964J SC*/IV
67 For her did earn]
      Did earn for her   BLjan *1964J*
68 beguiled] beguild   BLjan
69 and] &   **EN** *SC*/IV
   poverty] poverty,   BLjan
70 Till] 'Till   BLjan *1964J*
   power] Power   BLjan *1964J*

   this, her] this her   **EN** *SC*/IV
                her this   BLjan *1964J*
   joy,] joy   **EN** BLjan *1964J SC*/IV
71 boy.] boy   **EN** BLjan *1964J SC*/IV
Stanza marker. *none*] 7   BLjan *1964J*
72 charity's] charitys   **EN** *SC*/IV
73 pair,] pair   **EN** *SC*/IV
            Pair   BLjan *1964J*
74 would . . . bear]
      wd perish rather that wd bear   BLjan
      would perish rather than wd. bear
      1964J
75 The . . . slavery]
      The law's stern slavery,   BLjan
      The law's stern slavery,   *1964J*
   law's] laws   **EN** *SC*/IV
   and] &   **EN** *SC*/IV
   the insolent] the insolent   BLjan
76 man's] mans   BLjan *1964J*
   soul—] soul   **EN** BLjan *1964J SC*/IV
            soul,   *1964B*
77 spirit-sinking] spirit sinking   **EN**
      BLjan *1964J SC*/IV

Of heartless mirth which women, men and boys
Wake in this scene of legal misery . . .
Oh! William's spirit rather would rejoice   80
On some wild heath with his dear charge to die.
The death that keenest penury might give
Were sweeter far than cramped by slavery to live.

And they have borne thus long the winter's cold,
The driving sleet, the penetrating rain;   85
It seemeth that their element is pain
And that they never will feel life again,
For is it life to be so deathlike old?—
The sun's kind light feeds every living thing
That spreads its blossoms to the breath of spring,   90
But who feeds thee, unhappy wanderer?
With the fat slaves who from the rich man's board
Lick the fallen crumbs thou scantily dost share
And mutterest for the gift a heartless prayer:
The flow'rs fade not thus. Thou must poorly die.   95
The changeful year feeds them. The tyrant, man, feeds thee.

And is it life that in Youth's blasted morn
Not one of youth's dear raptures are enjoyed—

---

78 women,]
    women   **EN** BLjan *1964J* SC/IV
    and] &   **EN** BLjan *1964J* SC/IV
79 misery . . .]
    misery | x x x x x x — — —   BLjan
    misery | x x x x x x   *1964J*
80 William's] Williams   **EN** SC/IV
81 die.] die   **EN** SC/IV
83 live.] live   **EN** SC/IV
84 borne] born   **EN** SC/IV
    winter's] winters   **EN** SC/IV
    cold,] cold   **EN** SC/IV
85 sleet,] sleet   **EN** SC/IV
    rain;] rain   **EN** SC/IV
87 again,] again   **EN** SC/IV
89 sun's] suns   **EN** SC/IV
    same   *1964B*
90 spring,] spring   **EN** SC/IV
91 thee,] thee   **EN** SC/IV

92 With] With [?Will]   *1964J*
    slaves] slaves,   *1964B*
    man's] mans   **EN** SC/IV
94 prayer:] prayer   **EN** SC/IV
    prayer,   *1964B*
    prayer[?]   *1964J*
95 flow'rs] flowers   *1964B 1964J*
    Thou] thou   **EN** SC/IV
    die.] die   **EN** SC/IV
96 them. The] them. the   **EN** SC/IV
    tyrant,] tyrant   **EN** SC/IV
    man,] man   **EN** SC/IV
    thee.] thee   **EN** SC/IV
97 Youth's] Youths   **EN**
    youth's   *1964B*
    youths   SC/IV
98 youth's] youths   **EN** SC/IV
    enjoyed—] enjoyed   **EN** SC/IV
    enjoyed,   *1964B*
    enjoyed-   *1964J*

All natural bliss with servitude alloyed,
100 The beating heart, the sparkling eye destroyd,
And manhood of its brightest glories shorn,
Debased by rapine, drunkenness and woe,
The foeman's sword, the vulgar tyrant's blow,
Ruined in body and soul till Heaven arrive—
105 His health and peace insultingly laid low,
Without a fear to die or wish to live,
Withered and sapless, miserably poor,
Relinquished for his wounds to beg from door to door?

Seest thou yon humble sod where oziers bind
110 The pillow of the monumentless dead.
There since her thorny pilgrimage is sped
The aged Sufferer rests on the cold bed
Which all who seek or who avoid must find.
O let her sleep! and there at close of eve
115 'Twere holiness in solitude to grieve
And ponder on the wretchedness of Earth.
With joy of melancholy I would leave
A spot that to such deep-felt thoughts gives birth,
And tho' I could not pour the useless prayer
120 Would weep upon the grave and leave a blessing there.

---

99 alloyed,] alloyed **EN** *SC/IV*

100 heart,] heart **EN** *SC/IV*
  eye] eye, *1964B*
  destroyd,] destroyd **EN** *SC/IV*
    destroy'd, *1964B*

101 shorn,] shorn **EN** *1964B SC/IV*

102 rapine,] rapine **EN** *SC/IV*
  and] & **EN** *SC/IV*

103 foeman's] foemans **EN** *SC/IV*
  sword,] sword **EN** *SC/IV*
  blow,] blow **EN** *SC/IV*

104 and] & **EN** *SC/IV*
  arrive—] arrive **EN** *SC/IV*
    arrive, *1964B*

105 and] & **EN** *SC/IV*
  low,] low **EN** *SC/IV*

106 live,] live **EN** *SC/IV*

107 and] & **EN** *SC/IV*
  poor,] poor **EN** *SC/IV*

108 door?] door **EN** *SC/IV*

110 dead.] dead? *1964B*

113 find.] find **EN** *SC/IV*

114 and] & **EN** *SC/IV*

115 'Twere] Twere **EN** *SC/IV*

116 Earth.] Earth **EN** *SC/IV*

118 birth,] birth **EN** *SC/IV*

119 tho'] tho **EN** *SC/IV*

120 and] & **EN** *SC/IV*
  there.] there **EN** *SC/IV*

SUPPLEMENT

Version in Letter to Hitchener, 7 January 1812

1

She was an aged woman, and the years
   Which she had numbered on her toilsome way
   Had bowed her natural powers to decay
   She was an aged woman. yet the ray
Which faintly glimmered thro her starting tears   5
Pressed into light by silent misery
Hath soul's imperishable energy.—
She was a c<rip>ple and incapable
To add one mite to gold-fed luxury
And therefore did her spirit dimly feel   10
That Poverty the crime of tainting stain
Would merge her in its' depths never to rise again

2

One only sons love had supported her
   She long had struggled with infirmity
   Lingering to human life scenes for to die   15
   When fate has spared to rend some mental tie
<No>t many wish and surely fewer dare
<B>ut when the tyrants bloodhounds forced her child
<?> his cursed power unhallowed arms to weild,
Bend to another's will, become a thing   20
   More senseless than the sword of battle field
   Then did she feel keen sorrows keenest sting
   And many years had passed ere comfort they c^d. bring

3

For seven years did this poor woman live
   In unparticipated solitude   25
Thou mighst have seen her in the forest rude
   Picking the scattered remnants of its wood
If human thou mightst then have learned to feel
   The gleanings of precarious charity
   Her scantiness of food did scarce supply   30
The proofs of an unspeaking sorrow dwelt
Within her gastly hollowness of eye
Each arrow of the seasons change she felt
Yet still she groans ere yet her race were run
One only hope it was! once more to see her [?] Son   35

Supplement Version   *[Esd #14]*   39

4

It was an eve of June when every star
Spoke peace from Heaven x x x x
She rested on the moor. twas such an eve
When first her soul began indeed to grieve
40   Then he was here; now he is very far!
The sweetness of the balmy evening
A sorrow oer her aged soul did fling
Yet not devoid of raptures mingled tear
A balm was in the poison of the sting!
45   This aged sufferer for many a year
       Had never felt much comfort. she supprest
       A sigh—and turning round clasp'd William to her breast

5

And tho' his form was wasted by the woe
       Which tyrants on their Victims love to wreak
50   Tho' his sunk eyeball, and his faded cheek
       Of slavery, violence & scorn did speak
Yet did the aged womans bosom glow!
       The vital fire seemed reillumed within
       By this sweet unexpected welcoming
55   Oh consummation of the fondest hope
       That ever soared on fancy's wildest wing
Oh! tenderness that foundst so sweet a scope!
Prince who dost pride thee on thy mighty sway
When thou canst feel such love thou shalt be ~~blest as~~ great as
       they

6

60   Her son compelled the country's foes had fought
       Had bled in battle. & the stern control
       Which ruled his sinews h^d coerced his soul
       Utterly poisoned life's unmingled bowl
And unsubduable evils on him brought
65   He was the shadow of the lusty child
Who, when the time of summer season smiled
Did earn for her a meal of honesty
And with affectionate discourse beguild
The keen attacks of pain and poverty,
70   'Till Power as envying her this only joy
From her maternal bosom tore the unhappy boy

7

And now cold charity's unwelcome dole
   Was insufficient to support the Pair
   And they, <u>wd perish rather than wd bear</u>
   <u>The law's stern slavery</u>, and <u>the insolent</u> stare   75
   With which law loves to rend the poor mans soul
The bitter scorn, the spirit sinking noise
Of heartless mirth which women men & boys
Wake in this scene of legal misery

x   x   x   x   x   x————

The solitary 1810   [*Esd #15*]

Darest thou amid this varied multitude
To live alone, an isolated thing,
To see the busy beings round thee spring
And care for none?—in thy calm solitude,
A flower that scarce breathes in the desart rude   5
   To Zephyr's passing wing?

Not the swarth Pariah in some Indian Grove
Lone, lean and hunted by his brothers' hate,
Hath drunk so deep the cup of bitter fate
As that poor wretch who cannot, cannot love.   10
He bears a load which nothing can remove—
   A killing, withering weight.

He smiles . . . 'tis sorrow's deadliest mockery;
He speaks . . . the cold words flow not from his soul;
He acts like others, drains the genial bowl;   15
Yet, yet he longs altho' he fears to die.

Text collated with **EN**, *1964B*, and *SC*/IV.

4 solitude,] solitude **EN** *SC*/IV
6 Zephyr's] Zephyrs **EN** *SC*/IV
7 Grove] grove **EN** *SC*/IV
8 and] & **EN** *SC*/IV
   hate,] hate **EN** *SC*/IV
10 cannot,] cannot **EN** *SC*/IV
   love.] love **EN** *SC*/IV
11 remove—] remove **EN** *SC*/IV
12 killing,] killing **EN** *SC*/IV
   weight.] weight **EN** *SC*/IV

13 'tis] tis **EN** *SC*/IV
   sorrow's] sorrows **EN** *SC*/IV
   mockery;] mockery **EN** *SC*/IV
14 soul;] soul **EN** *SC*/IV
15 others,] others. **EN** *SC*/IV
   others; *1964B*
   bowl;] bowl **EN** *SC*/IV
16 longs] longs, *1964B*
   altho'] altho **EN** *1964B SC*/IV
   fears] fears, *1964B*
   die.] die **EN** *SC*/IV

He pants to reach what yet he seems to fly,
Dull Life's extremest goal.

[*Esd* #16]

The Monarch's funeral
An Anticipation
1810

The growing gloom of eventide
Has quenched the sunbeam's latest glow
And lowers upon the woe and pride
That blasts the city's peace below.

5

At such an hour how sad the sight
To mark a Monarch's funeral
When the dim shades of awful night
Rest on the coffin's velvet pall;

To see the Gothic Arches shew

10

A varied mass of light and shade,
While to the torches' crimson glow
A vast cathedral is displayed;

To see with what a silence deep
The thousands o'er this death-scene brood,

15

As tho' some wizard's charm did creep
Upon the countless multitude

---

17 fly,] fly **EN** *SC*/IV
18 Life's] Lifes **EN** *SC*/IV
  goal.] goal **EN** *SC*/IV

Text collated with **EN,** *1964B,* and *SC*/IV.
Title. Monarch's] Monarchs **EN** *SC*/IV
1 growing] glowing *1964B*
2 sunbeam's] sunbeams **EN** *SC*/IV
3 and] & **EN** *SC*/IV
4 city's] citys **EN** *SC*/IV
  below.] below **EN** *SC*/IV
5 sight] sight, *1964B*
6 Monarch's] Monarchs **EN** *SC*/IV

8 coffin's] coffins **EN** *SC*/IV
  pall;] pall **EN** *SC*/IV
10 and] & **EN** *SC*/IV
  shade,] shade **EN** *SC*/IV
11 torches'] torches **EN** *SC*/IV
12 displayed;] displayed **EN** *SC*/IV
14 o'er] oer **EN** *SC*/IV
  death-scene]
    death scene **EN** *1964B SC*/IV
  brood,] brood **EN** *1964B SC*/IV
15 tho'] tho **EN** *SC*/IV
  wizard's] wizards **EN** *SC*/IV
16 multitude] multitude; *1964B*

To see this awful pomp of death
    For one frail mass of mouldering clay,
When nobler men the tomb beneath
    Have sunk unwept, unseen away.   20

For who was he, the uncoffined slain,
    That fell in Erin's injured isle
Because his spirit dared disdain
    To light his country's funeral pile?

Shall he not ever live in lays   25
    The warmest that a Muse may sing
Whilst monumental marbles raise
    The fame of a departed King?

May not the Muse's darling theme
    Gather its glorious garland thence   30
Whilst some frail tombstone's Dotard dream
    Fades with a monarch's impotence!

—Yet, 'tis a scene of wondrous awe
    To see a coffined Monarch lay,
That the wide grave's insatiate maw   35
    Be glutted with a regal prey!

Who *now* shall public councils guide?
    Who rack the poor on gold to dine?
Who waste the means of regal pride
    For which a million wretches pine?   40

It is a child of earthly breath,
    A being perishing as he,

---

18 clay,] clay **EN** *1964B SC/*IV

20 unwept,] unwept **EN** *SC/*IV

    away.] away **EN** *SC/*IV

21 he,] he **EN** *SC/*IV

    slain,] slain **EN** *SC/*IV

24 country's] countrys **EN** *SC/*IV

    pile?] pile **EN** *SC/*IV

31 tombstone's] tombstones **EN** *SC/*IV

32 monarch's] monarchs **EN** *SC/*IV

33 —Yet,] —Yes, *1964B SC/*IV

34 lay,] lay **EN** *1964B SC/*IV

35 grave's] graves **EN** *SC/*IV

37 *now*] <u>now</u> **EN** *SC/*IV

38 dine?] dine **EN** *SC/*IV

41 breath,] breath **EN** *SC/*IV

Who throned in yonder pomp of death
Hath now fulfilled his destiny.

45   Now dust to dust restore! . . . O Pride,
          Unmindful of thy fleeting power,
        Whose empty confidence has vied
          With human life's most treacherous hour,

        One moment feel that in the breast
50   With regal crimes and troubles vext
        The pampered Earthworms soon will rest,
          One moment feel . . . . and die the next.

        Yet deem not in the tomb's control
          The vital lamp of life can fail—
55   Deem not that e'er the Patriot's soul
          Is wasted by the withering gale.

        The dross, which forms the *King,* is gone
          And reproductive Earth supplies,
        As senseless as the clay and stone
60   In which the kindred body lies:

        The soul which makes the *Man* doth soar,
          And love alone survives to shed
        All that its tide of bliss can pour
          Of Heaven upon the blessed dead.

65   So shall the Sun forever burn,
          So shall the midnight lightnings die,

---

44 destiny.] destiny **EN** *SC*/IV
45 Pride,] Pride **EN** *SC*/IV
46 power,] power **EN** *SC*/IV
48 hour,] hour **EN** *SC*/IV
50 and] & **EN** *SC*/IV
51 rest,] rest **EN** *SC*/IV
52 feel . . . .] feel . . . *1964B*
    and] & **EN** *SC*/IV
53 tomb's] tombs **EN** *SC*/IV
54 fail—] fail **EN** *SC*/IV
        fail, *1964B*
55 Patriot's] Patriots **EN** *SC*/IV
56 gale.] gale **EN** *SC*/IV

57 dross,] dross **EN** *SC*/IV
    King,] <u>King</u> **EN** *SC*/IV
    gone] gone, *1964B*
58 supplies,] supplies **EN** *SC*/IV
59 and] & **EN** *SC*/IV
60 lies:] lies **EN** *SC*/IV
        lies. *1964B*
61 *Man*] <u>Man</u> **EN** *SC*/IV
    soar,] soar **EN** *1964B SC*/IV
64 dead.] dead **EN** *SC*/IV
65 burn,] burn **EN** *SC*/IV
66 die,] die **EN** *SC*/IV

And joy that glows at Nature's bourn
    Outlive terrestrial misery.

And will the crowd who silent stoop
    Around the lifeless Monarch's bier,   70
A mournful and dejected group,
    Breathe not one sigh, or shed one tear?

Ah! no—'tis wonder, 'tis not woe:
    Even royalists might groan to see
The *Father of the People*, so   75
    Lost in the Sacred Majesty.

To the Republicans of North America   *[Esd #17]*

Brothers! between you and me
    Whirlwinds sweep and billows roar,
Yet in spirit oft I see
    On the wild and winding shore
Freedom's bloodless banner wave,   5
Feel the pulses of the brave
Unextinguished by the grave,
    See them drenched in sacred gore,

---

67 Nature's] Natures **EN** *SC*/IV

68 misery.] misery **EN** *SC*/IV

70 Monarch's] Monarchs **EN** *SC*/IV
   bier,] bier **EN** *SC*/IV

71 and] & **EN** *SC*/IV
   group,] group **EN** *SC*/IV

72 tear?] tear. **EN** *SC*/IV

73 no—'tis] no. 'tis **EN** *SC*/IV
        no. 'Tis   *1964B*
   woe:] woe **EN** *SC*/IV
        woe.   *1964B*

75 *Father . . . People,*]
    Father of the People,   **EN** *SC*/IV
    People,] *People*   *1964B*

76 Majesty.] Majesty **EN** *SC*/IV

Text collated with **EN**, MS BLfeb (lines 1–30, 41–50), *1964B*, *1964J* (lines 1–30, 41–50), and *SC*/IV.

Title. Written . . . 1811]
    omitted BLfeb *1964J*

1 Brothers!] Brothers, BLfeb *1964J*
  and] & **EN** *SC*/IV

2 and] & **EN** *SC*/IV
  roar,] roar **EN** BLfeb *1964J SC*/IV

4 the] thy BLfeb *1964J*
  and] & **EN** *SC*/IV

5 Freedom's]
   Freedoms **EN** BLfeb *1964J SC*/IV
  banner] banners BLfeb *1964J*
  wave,] wave **EN** BLfeb *1964J SC*/IV

6 pulses] pul<ses> BLfeb *1964J*
  brave] brave, *1964B*

7 by] in BLfeb *1964J*
  grave,] grave **EN** BLfeb *1964J SC*/IV

8 gore,] gore **EN** BLfeb *1964J SC*/IV

Catch the patriot's gasping breath
10   Murmuring "Liberty" in death.

Shout aloud! let every slave
 Crouching at corruption's throne
Start into a man and brave
 Racks and chains without a groan!
15   Let the castle's heartless glow
And the hovel's vice and woe
Fade like gaudy flowers that blow,
 Weeds that peep and then are gone,
Whilst from misery's ashes risen
20   Love shall burst the Captive's prison.

Cotopaxi! bid the sound
 Thro' thy sister mountains ring
Till each valley smile around
 At the blissful welcoming.
25   And o! thou stern Ocean-deep
Whose eternal billows sweep
Shores where thousands wake to weep
 Whilst they curse some villain King,

---

9 patriot's] patriots **EN** *SC*/IV
    warriors BLfeb *1964J*
10 "Liberty"] Liberty **EN** BLfeb *1964B*
  1964J SC/IV
 in] or *1964J*
 death.] death BLfeb *1964J*
12 corruption's] corruptions **EN** *SC*/IV
    Corruptions BLfeb
     1964J
13 man] man, *1964B*
 and] & **EN** *SC*/IV
14 and] & **EN** *SC*/IV
 groan!] groan!. **EN** *SC*/IV
    groan BLfeb *1964J*
15 Let] And BLfeb *1964J*
 castle's] castles **EN** *SC*/IV
16 hovel's]
  hovels **EN** BLfeb *1964J SC*/IV
 and] & **EN** *SC*/IV
17 blow,] blow **EN** BLfeb *1964J SC*/IV
18 and] & **EN** BLfeb *1964J SC*/IV

 gone,] gone **EN** BLfeb *1964J SC*/IV
19 misery's]
 miserys **EN** BLfeb *1964J SC*/IV
20 Captive's]
 Captives **EN** BLfeb *1964J SC*/IV
 prison.]
 prison **EN** BLfeb *1964J SC*/IV
24 welcoming.]
 welcoming **EN** BLfeb *1964J SC*/IV
25 o!] oh BLfeb *1964J*
  O! *1964B SC*/IV
 Ocean-deep]
 ocean deep BLfeb *1964J*
 Ocean-deep, *1964B*
26 Whose] Thou, whose BLfeb *1964J*
 eternal] foamy BLfeb *1964J*
28 some] a BLfeb *1964J*
 King,] King **EN** *SC*/IV
  king BLfeb *1964J*

On the winds that fan thy breast
Bear thou news of freedom's rest.	30

Earth's remotest bounds shall start:
	Every despot's bloated cheek,
Pallid as his bloodless heart,
	Frenzy, woe and dread shall speak . . . .
Blood may fertilize the tree	35
Of new bursting Liberty—
Let the guiltiness then be
	On the slaves that ruin wreak,
On the unnatural tyrant-brood
Slow to Peace and swift to blood.	40

Can the daystar dawn of love
	Where the flag of war unfurled
Floats with crimson stain above
	Such a desolated world? . . .
Never! but to vengeance driven	45
When the patriot's spirit shriven
Seeks in death its native Heaven—
	Then to speechless horror hurled

---

30 freedom's]
      freedoms   **EN** BLfeb *1964J SC*/IV
    rest.] rest   BLfeb *1964J*
31 Earth's] Earths   **EN** *SC*/IV
    start:] start   **EN** *SC*/IV
          start, *1964B*
32 despot's] despots   **EN** *SC*/IV
    cheek,] cheek   **EN** *SC*/IV
33 heart,] heart   **EN** *SC*/IV
34 Frenzy,] Frenzy   **EN** *SC*/IV
    and] &   **EN** *SC*/IV
    speak . . . .]
          speak . . .   **EN** *1964B SC*/IV
36 Liberty—] Liberty   **EN** *SC*/IV
          Liberty.   *1964B*
38 wreak,] wreak   **EN** *SC*/IV
39 tyrant-brood] tyrant brood   **EN** *SC*/IV
40 and] &   **EN** *SC*/IV
    blood.] blood   **EN** *SC*/IV

41 the] they   **EN** *SC*/IV
    love] Love   BLfeb *1964J*
44 Such a desolated]
          The fabric of a ruined   BLfeb *1964J*
    world? . . .]
          world . . .   **EN** *1964B SC*/IV
          world   BLfeb *1964J*
46 patriot's]
          patriots   **EN** BLfeb *1964J SC*/IV
    spirit] spirits   BLfeb
47 death] Death   BLfeb *1964J*
    Heaven—]
          Heaven   **EN** BLfeb *1964J SC*/IV
          Heaven,   *1964B*
48 Then] There   BLfeb *1964J*
    speechless horror]
          desolation   BLfeb *1964J*
    hurled] hurled.   *1964B*

50   Widowed Earth may balm the bier
                    Of its memory with a tear.

SUPPLEMENT

Version in Letter to Hitchener, 14 February 1812

Brothers, between you and me
    Whirlwinds sweep and billows roar
Yet in spirit oft I see
    On thy wild and winding shore
5   Freedoms bloodless banners wave
Feel the pul<ses> of the brave
Unextinguished in the grave
    See them drenched in sacred gore
Catch the warriors gasping breath
10   Murmuring Liberty in death

—

Shout aloud! let every slave
    Crouching at Corruptions throne
Start into a man and brave
    Racks and chains without a groan
15   And the castle's heartless glow
And the hovels vice and woe
Fade like gaudy flowers that blow
    Weeds that peep & then are gone
Whilst from miserys ashes risen
20   Love shall burst the Captives prison

—

Cotopaxi! bid the sound
    Thro' thy sister mountains ring
Till each valley smile around
    At the blissful welcoming
25   And oh thou stern ocean deep
Thou, whose foamy billows sweep
Shores where thousands wake to weep
    Whilst they curse a villain king
On the winds that fan thy breast
30   Bear thou news of freedoms rest

---

49 Earth] love   BLfeb *1964J*
   balm the] watch thy   BLfeb *1964J*

50 Of its memory with a] Balm thee with
   its dying   BLfeb *1964J*
   tear.] tear **EN** *1964J SC*/IV

—

41

Can the daystar dawn of Love
   Where the flag of war unfurled
Floats with crimson stain above
   The fabric of a ruined world
Never! but to vengeance driven
When the patriots spirits shriven
Seeks in Death its native Heaven
   There to desolation hurled
Widowed love may watch thy bier
Balm thee with its dying tear.

45

50

Written at Cwm Ellan 1811   *[Esd #18]*

When the peasant hies him home, and the day-planet reposes,
   Pillowed on the azure peaks that bound the western sight,
When each mountain flower its modest petal tremulously closes
   And sombre, shrouded twilight comes to lead her sister Night.
Vestal dark! how dear to me are then thy dews of lightness   5
That bathe my brow so withering, scorched beneath the
   daybeam's brightness:
More dear to me, tho' day be robed in vest of dazzling whiteness,
   Is one folding of the garment dusk that wraps thy form,
     O Night!

With thee I still delight to sit where dizzy Danger slumbers,   9
   Where 'mid the rocks the fitful blast hath wak'd its wildest lay
Till beneath the yellow moonbeam decay the dying numbers,
   And silence, even in fancy's throne, hath seized again the sway.
Again she must resign it, hark! for wildest cadence pouring

Text collated with **EN**, *1964B*, and *SC*/IV.

1 and] & **EN** *SC*/IV
  day-planet]
    day planet **EN** *1964B SC*/IV
  reposes,] reposes **EN** *1964B SC*/IV
2 sight,] sight **EN** *SC*/IV
4 sombre,] sombre **EN** *1964B SC*/IV
  Night.] Night, *1964B*
6 withering,] withering **EN** *1964B SC*/IV
  daybeam's] daybeams **EN** *SC*/IV
  brightness:] brightness **EN** *SC*/IV
    brightness. *1964B*

7 whiteness,] whiteness **EN** *SC*/IV
8 form,] form **EN** *SC*/IV
9 slumbers,] slumbers **EN** *SC*/IV
10 'mid] mid **EN** *SC*/IV
  wak'd] wakd **EN** *SC*/IV
11 numbers,] numbers **EN** *1964B SC*/IV
12 silence,] silence **EN** *SC*/IV
  fancy's] fancys **EN** *SC*/IV
  throne,] throne **EN** *SC*/IV

Far, far amid the viewless glen beneath, the Ellan roaring
Mid tongued woods, and shapeless rocks with moonlight summits
15   soaring
It mingles its magic murmuring with the blast that floats away.

[*Esd #19*]   To Death

Death, where is thy victory!
To triumph whilst I die,
To triumph whilst thine ebon wing
Infolds my shuddering soul,
5   O Death, where is thy sting?
Not when the tides of murder roll,
When Nations groan that Kings may bask in bliss,
Death, couldst thou boast a victory such as this,—
When in his hour
10   Of pomp and power
Thy slave, the mightiest murderer, gave
Mid nature's cries
The sacrifize

---

14 beneath,] beneath **EN** *1964B SC/*IV   and] & **EN** *SC/*IV
15 tongued] tongued [?tangled] **EN**   16 away.] away **EN** *SC/*IV
        [?tangled] *SC/*IV

Text collated with **EN,** MS Pfz120, *SC/*II (1–48), *1964B,* and *SC/*IV.
Title. *omitted* Pfz120 *SC/*II   this,—] this **EN** Pfz120 *SC/*II *SC/*IV
1 Death,] Death **EN** *SC/*IV   this? *1964B*
       Death! Pfz120 *SC/*II   9 hour] hour, Pfz120 *SC/*II
   victory!] Victory! Pfz120 *SC/*II   *No break between lines 9 and 10.*
2 die,] die **EN** Pfz120 *SC/*II *SC/*IV   Pfz120 *SC/*II
3 ebon wing]   10 Of] of Pfz120 *SC/*II
   ~~hand of fate~~ ebon wing Pfz120 *SC/*II   and] & **EN** Pfz120 *SC/*II *SC/*IV
4 Infolds] Enfolds Pfz120 *SC/*II   11 slave,] slave **EN** *SC/*IV
   soul,] soul **EN** Pfz120 *SC/*II *SC/*IV   blow Pfz120 *SC/*II
5 O Death,] Oh! death Pfz120 *SC/*II   murderer,]
         O Death **EN** *SC/*IV   murderer **EN** Pfz120 *SC/*II *SC/*IV
   sting?] sting Pfz120 *SC/*II   12 cries] cries, Pfz120 *SC/*II
6 roll,] roll **EN** Pfz120 *SC/*II *SC/*IV   *No break between lines 12 and 13.*
7 Nations] nations Pfz120 *SC/*II   Pfz120 *SC/*II
   bliss,] bliss **EN** Pfz120 *SC/*II *SC/*IV   13 The] the Pfz120 *SC/*II
8 Death,] Death **EN** *SC/*IV   sacrifize] sacrifice *1964B*
       Death! Pfz120 *SC/*II
   couldst] canst Pfz120 *SC/*II

Of myriads to glut the grave,—
When sunk the tyrant, sensualism's slave, 15
Or Freedom's life-blood streamed upon thy shrine?
Stern despot, couldst thou boast a Victory such as
    mine?—

To know, in dissolution's void
  That Earthly hopes and fears decay,
That every sense but Love, destroyed, 20
  Must perish with its kindred clay,—
    Perish ambition's crown!
    Perish its sceptered sway;
From Death's pale front fade Pride's fastidious frown
In death's damp vault, the lurid fires decay 25
Which Envy lights at heaven-born virtue's beam;
    That all the cares subside
    Which lurk beneath the tide
    Of life's unquiet stream . . . .

---

14 myriads] millions Pfz120 *SC*/II
  grave,—]
    grave **EN** Pfz120 *SC*/II *SC*/IV
      grave, *1964B*
15 tyrant,]
    tyrant **EN** Pfz120 *SC*/II *SC*/IV
  sensualism's]
    desolation's Pfz120 *SC*/II
  slave,] slave **EN** Pfz120 *SC*/II *SC*/IV
16 Freedom's] Freedoms **EN** *SC*/IV
  life-blood]
    life blood **EN** Pfz120 *SC*/II *SC*/IV
  shrine?]
    shrine **EN** Pfz120 *SC*/II *SC*/IV
    shrine, *1964B*
17 despot,] despot **EN** *SC*/IV
      tyrant Pfz120 *SC*/II
  Victory] victory Pfz120 *SC*/II
  mine?—]
    mine **EN** Pfz120 *SC*/II *SC*/IV
    mine? *1964B*
18 know,] know **EN** Pfz120 *SC*/II *SC*/IV
  dissolution's] dissolutions **EN** *SC*/IV
  void] void, *1964B*
19 Earthly hopes and fears decay,]
    mortals ~~hopes & fears~~ bubbles sank
    away Pfz120 *SC*/II

and] & **EN** *SC*/IV
decay,] decay **EN** *SC*/IV
20 sense] thing Pfz120 *SC*/II
    sense, *1964B*
  Love,] Love **EN** Pfz120 *SC*/II *SC*/IV
  destroyed,] destroyed Pfz120 *SC*/II
21 its] it's Pfz120 *SC*/II
  clay,—] clay **EN** Pfz120 *SC*/II *SC*/IV
    clay. *1964B*
22 ambition's] Ambitions Pfz120 *SC*/II
  crown!] crown Pfz120 *SC*/II
23 its] her Pfz120 *SC*/II
  sway;] sway **EN** Pfz120 *SC*/II *SC*/IV
    sway! *1964B*
24 Death's] Deaths **EN** *SC*/IV
  frown] frown. *1964B*
25 death's] Death's Pfz120 *SC*/II
  vault,] vault **EN** Pfz120 *SC*/II *1964B*
    SC/IV
26 Which] That Pfz120 *SC*/II
  heaven-born] heaven born **EN** *SC*/IV
  virtue's] virtues Pfz120 *SC*/II
  beam;] beam[.] **EN**
    beam Pfz120 *SC*/II *1964B*
    SC/IV
29 stream . . . .] stream Pfz120 *SC*/II

30   Yes! this were Victory!
          And on some rock whose dark form glooms the sky
          To stretch these pale limbs when the soul is fled,
          To baffle the lean passions of their prey,
          To sleep within the chambers of the dead!—
35   Oh! not the Wretch around whose dazzling throne
          His countless courtiers mock the words they say,
          Triumphs amid the bud of glory blown,
          As I on Death's last pang and faint expiring groan.

          Tremble, ye Kings whose luxury mocks the woe
40   That props thy column of unnatural state:
              Ye the curses deep tho' low
              From misery's tortured breast that flow
              Shall usher to your fate.—
          Tremble, ye conquerors at whose fell command
45   The War-fiend Riots o'er an happy land—

---

30 Yes!] Yes   Pfz120 *SC*/II
    were] is a   Pfz120
       is   *SC*/II
    Victory!] victory   Pfz120 *SC*/II
31 some] yon   Pfz120 *SC*/II
32 stretch] strech   Pfz120
    fled,] fled   **EN** Pfz120 *SC*/II *SC*/IV
33 their] thier   **EN**
    prey,] prey   **EN** Pfz120 *SC*/II *SC*/IV
34 chambers] palace   Pfz120 *SC*/II
35 Wretch] King   Pfz120 *SC*/II
36 countless courtiers]
    countless countless   Pfz120
    say,] say   **EN** Pfz120 *SC*/II *SC*/IV
37 Triumphs] Triumphs,   *1964B*
    blown,]
      blown   **EN** Pfz120 *SC*/II *SC*/IV
38 I on Death's last pang and]
    I, in this cold bed &   Pfz120 *SC*/II
    Death's] Deaths   **EN** *SC*/IV
    and] &   **EN** *SC*/IV
    groan.]
      groan   **EN** Pfz120 *SC*/II *SC*/IV
    stanza break] *omitted*   *SC*/II
39 Tremble,]
    Tremble   **EN** Pfz120 *SC*/II *SC*/IV
    Kings] proud   Pfz120 *SC*/II

luxury]
    ~~bosoms~~ grandeur   Pfz120 *SC*/II
40 That] Which   Pfz120 *SC*/II
    column] colomn   Pfz120
    state:] state   **EN** Pfz120 *SC*/II *SC*/IV
      state,   *1964B*
41 Ye] Ye,   Pfz120 *SC*/II *1964B*
    curses deep tho']
      plainings faint &   Pfz120 *SC*/II
    deep] deep,   *1964B*
    tho'] tho   **EN** *SC*/IV
    low] low,   *1964B*
42 From] ~~Which~~ From   Pfz120
      ~~Which~~ from   *SC*/II
    misery's] miserys   **EN** *SC*/IV
    breast] ~~breast~~ soul   Pfz120 *SC*/II
    flow] flow,   *1964B*
43 fate.—] fate . .   Pfz120
      fate . .   *SC*/II
44 Tremble,]
    Tremble   **EN** Pfz120 *SC*/II *SC*/IV
    conquerors] conquerors,   *1964B*
45 War-fiend] War fiend   **EN** *SC*/IV
    war-fiend   Pfz120 *SC*/II
    Riots] riots   Pfz120 *SC*/II
    o'er] oer   **EN** Pfz120 *SC*/II *SC*/IV
    an happy] a peaceful   Pfz120 *SC*/II
    land—] land   **EN** Pfz120 *SC*/II *SC*/IV

Ye, desolation's gory throng
Shall bear from victory along
To Death's mysterious strand.
'Twere Hell that Vice no pain should know
But every scene that memory gives   50
Tho' from the selfsame fount might flow
The joy which Virtue aye receives . . .
It is the grave—no conqueror triumphs now;
The wreathes of bay that bound his head
Wither around his fleshless brow.   55
Where is the mockery fled
That fired the tyrant's gaze?
'Tis like the fitful glare that plays
On some dark-rolling thunder cloud,
Plays whilst the thunders roar,   60
But when the storm is past
Fades like the warrior's name.
Death! in thy vault when Kings and peasants lie
Not power's stern rod or fame's most thrilling blasts
Can liberate thy captives from decay.   65
My triumph, their defeat; my joy, their shame.
Welcome then, peaceful Death, I'll sleep with thee—
Mine be thy quiet home, and thine my Victory.

---

46 Ye,] Ye   **EN** *SC/IV*
  desolation's]
    desolations   **EN** Pfz120 *SC/II SC/IV*
48 Death's] Deaths   **EN** *SC/IV*
    that   Pfz120 *SC/II*
  strand.] strand   Pfz120 *SC/II SC/IV*
49 'Twere] Twere   **EN** *SC/IV*
  Hell] well   *1964B*
51 selfsame] self same   **EN**
52 receives . . .] recieves   **EN** *SC/IV*
53 now;] now   **EN** *SC/IV*
55 brow.] brow   **EN** *SC/IV*
57 tyrant's] tyrants   **EN** *SC/IV*
  gaze?] gaze   **EN** *SC/IV*
58 'Tis] Tis   **EN** *SC/IV*
59 cloud,] cloud   **EN** *SC/IV*

60 roar,] roar   **EN** *SC/IV*
62 warrior's] warriors   **EN** *SC/IV*
  name.] name   **EN** *SC/IV*
63 and] &   **EN** *SC/IV*
64 power's] powers   **EN** *SC/IV*
  fame's] fames   **EN** *SC/IV*
65 decay.] decay   **EN** *SC/IV*
66 their] thier   **EN** *SC/IV*
  joy,] joy   **EN** *SC/IV*
  their] thier   **EN** *SC/IV*
  shame.] shame   **EN** *SC/IV*
    shame!   *1964B*
67 then,] then   **EN** *SC/IV*
  thee—] thee   **EN** *SC/IV*
68 and] &   **EN** *SC/IV*

SUPPLEMENT

Version in Hogg Manuscript, ca. 1810

Death! where is thy Victory!
To triumph whilst I die
To triumph whilst thine ~~hand of fate~~ ebon wing
Enfolds my shuddering soul
5   Oh! death where is thy sting
Not when the tides of murder roll
When nations groan that Kings may bask in bliss
Death! canst thou boast a victory such as this
9–10   When in his hour, of pomp & power
      Thy blow the mightiest murderer gave
12–13   Mid nature's cries, the sacrifize
      Of millions to glut the grave
15   When sunk the tyrant desolation's slave
Or Freedom's life blood streamed upon thy shrine
Stern tyrant couldst thou boast a victory such as mine

To know in dissolution's void
      bubbles sank
That mortals ~~hopes & fears~~ away
20   That every thing but Love destroyed
Must perish with it's kindred clay
      Perish Ambitions crown
      Perish her sceptered sway
From Death's pale front fade Pride's fastidious frown
25   In Death's damp vault the lurid fires decay
That Envy lights at heaven-born virtues beam
      That all the cares subside
      Which lurk beneath the tide
      Of life's unquiet stream
30   Yes this is a victory
And on yon rock whose dark form glooms the sky
To strech these pale limbs when the soul is fled
To baffle the lean passions of their prey
To sleep within the palace of the dead!—
35   Oh! not the King around whose dazzling throne
His countless countless mock the words they say
Triumphs amid the bud of glory blown
As I, in this cold bed & faint expiring groan

Tremble ye proud whose ~~bosoms~~ grandeur mocks the woe
40   Which props thy column of unnatural state

Ye, the plainings faint & low
~~Which~~ From misery's tortured ~~breast~~ soul that flow
Shall usher to your fate . .
Tremble ye conquerors at whose fell command
The war-fiend riots oer a peaceful land   45
Ye, desolations gory throng
Shall bear from victory along
To that mysterious strand

"Dark Spirit of the desart rude"   [*Esd #20*]

Dark Spirit of the desart rude
That o'er this awful solitude,
Each tangled and untrodden wood,
Each dark and silent glen below
Where sunlight's gleamings never glow,   5
Whilst jetty, musical and still,
In darkness speeds the mountain rill;
That o'er yon broken peaks sublime,
Wild shapes that mock the scythe of time,
And the pure Ellan's foamy course,   10
Wavest thy wand of magic force—
Art thou yon sooty and fearful fowl
That flaps its wing o'er the leafless oak
That o'er the dismal scene doth scowl
And mocketh music with its croak?   15

I've sought thee where day's beams decay
On the peak of the lonely hill;

Text collated with **EN,** *1964B,* and *SC*/IV.

Title. *no title*] Dark Spirit of the desart
  rude *1964B*

2 o'er] oer **EN** *SC*/IV
 solitude,] solitude **EN** *SC*/IV

3 and] & **EN** *SC*/IV
 wood,] wood. **EN** *SC*/IV

4 and] & **EN** *SC*/IV
 below] below, *1964B*

5 sunlight's] sunlights **EN** *SC*/IV
 glow,] glow **EN** *SC*/IV

6 jetty,] jetty **EN** *SC*/IV
 and] & **EN** *SC*/IV
 still,] still **EN** *SC*/IV

7 rill;] rill **EN** *SC*/IV

8 o'er] oer **EN** *SC*/IV
 sublime,] sublime **EN** *SC*/IV

9 time,] time **EN** *SC*/IV

10 Ellan's] Ellans **EN** *SC*/IV
 course,] course **EN** *SC*/IV

11 force—] force **EN** *SC*/IV
  force; *1964B*

12 and] & **EN** *SC*/IV

13 o'er] oer **EN** *SC*/IV

14 o'er] oer **EN** *SC*/IV

17 hill;] hill **EN** *SC*/IV
  hill, *1964B*

                    I've sought thee where they melt away
                        By the wave of the pebbly rill;
20   I've strained to catch thy murky form
                    Bestride the rapid and gloomy storm:
                    Thy red and sullen eyeball's glare
                    Has shot, in a dream thro' the midnight air
                        But never did thy shape express
25   Such an emphatic gloominess.

                    And where art thou, O thing of gloom? . .
                    On Nature's unreviving tomb
                    Where sapless, blasted and alone
                    She mourns her blooming centuries gone!—
30   From the fresh sod the Violets peep,
                    The buds have burst their frozen sleep,
                        Whilst every green and peopled tree
                    Is alive with Earth's sweet melody.
                        But thou alone art here,
35   Thou desolate Oak, whose scathed head
                    For ages has never trembled,
                    Whose giant trunk dead lichens bind,
                    Moaningly sighing in the wind,
                    With huge loose rocks beneath thee spread—
40   Thou, Thou alone art here!
                        Remote from every living thing,
                    Tree, shrub or grass or flower,
                    Thou seemest of this spot the King

---

18 I've] Ive   **EN** *SC*/IV

19 rill;] rill   **EN** *SC*/IV

20 I've] Ive   **EN** *SC*/IV

21 and] &   **EN** *SC*/IV
   storm:] storm   **EN** *SC*/IV
      storm;   *1964B*

22 and] &   **EN** *SC*/IV
   eyeball's] eyeballs   **EN** *SC*/IV

23 dream] dream,   *1964B*
   thro'] thro   **EN** *SC*/IV

25 gloominess.] gloominess   **EN** *SC*/IV

26 thou,] thou   **EN** *SC*/IV
   gloom? . .] gloom? . . .   *1964B*
      gloom? . . .   *SC*/IV

27 Nature's] Natures   **EN**
     natures   *SC*/IV

28 sapless,] sapless   **EN** *SC*/IV
   and] &   **EN** *SC*/IV

30 peep,] peep   **EN** *SC*/IV

31 their] there   **EN** *SC*/IV
   sleep,] sleep   **EN** *SC*/IV

32 and] &   **EN** *SC*/IV

33 Earth's] Earths   **EN** *SC*/IV

34 here,] here   **EN** *SC*/IV

36 trembled,] trembled   **EN** *SC*/IV

37 bind,] bind   **EN** *1964B SC*/IV

38 wind,] wind   **EN** *SC*/IV

39 spread—] spread   **EN** *SC*/IV
     spread,   *1964B*

41 thing,] thing   **EN** *SC*/IV

42 Tree,] Tree   **EN** *SC*/IV
   flower,] flower   **EN** *SC*/IV

And with a regal power
Suck like that race all sap away 45
And yet upon the spoil decay.

"The pale, the cold and the moony smile" [*Esd* #21]

The pale, the cold and the moony smile
   Which the meteor beam of a stormy night
Sheds on a lonely and seagirt isle
   Till the dawning of morn's undoubted light
Is the taper of life so fickle and wan 5
That flits round our steps till their strength is gone.

Oh! Man, hold thee on with courage of soul
   Thro' the long, long night of thy doubtful way,
And the billows of cloud that around thee roll
   Shall subside in the calm of eternal day: 10
For all in this world we can surely know
Is a little delight and a little woe.

---

46 *And yet upon the spoil*]
   <u>And yet upon the spoil</u> **EN** *SC*/IV
  decay.] <u>decay</u> **EN** *SC*/IV

Text collated with **EN,** *1816, 1964B,* and *SC*/IV.

Title. *no title*] The pale, the cold and the
         moony smile *1964B*
Epigraph. *none*] THERE IS NO WORK,
      NOR DEVICE, NOR
      KNOWLEDGE, NOR
      WISDOM, IN THE GRAVE,
      WHITHER THOU GOEST.
      Ecclesiastes. *1816*
1 The] THE *1816*
  cold] cold, *1816*
  and] & **EN** *SC*/IV
  smile] smile, *1964B*
2 stormy] starless *1816*
3 and] & **EN** *SC*/IV
  seagirt] sea-girt *1816*
  isle] isle, *1816*
4 Till] Ere *1816*
  morn's] morns **EN** *SC*/IV
  light] light, *1816 1964B*
5 taper] flame *1816*
  and] & **EN** *SC*/IV

6 gone.] gone **EN** *SC*/IV
7 Oh! Man,] O man! *1816*
  with] in *1816*
8 Thro'] Thro **EN** *SC*/IV
     Through *1816*
  long,] long **EN** *SC*/IV
  long, long night] stormy shades *1816*
  doubtful] worldly *1816*
  way,] way **EN** *SC*/IV
10 subside] sleep *1816*
  calm] light *1816*
  eternal] a wondrous *1816*
  day:] day **EN** *SC*/IV
     day, *1816 1964B*
11 For . . . know] Where hell and heaven
    shall leave thee free *1816*
12 Is . . . woe.]
    To the universe of destiny. *1816*
  and] & **EN** *SC*/IV
  woe.] woe **EN** *SC*/IV

All we behold, we feel that we know—
    All we perceive, we know that we feel;
15   And the coming of death is a fearful blow
      To a brain unencompassed by nervestrings of steel,
When all that we know, we feel and we see
Shall fleet by like an unreal mystery.

The secret things of the grave are there
20   Where all but this body must surely be,
Tho' the fine-wrought eye and the wondrous ear
      No longer will live to hear or to see
All that is bright and all that is strange
In the gradual path of unending change.

25   Who telleth the tales of unspeaking Death?
      Who lifteth the veil of what is to come?
Who painteth the beings that are beneath
      The wide-stretching realms of the peopled tomb
And uniteth the hopes of what shall be
30   With the fears and the love for that which we see?

---

13 All . . . that]
    This world is the nurse of all   *1816*
    behold,] behold **EN** *SC*/IV
    know—] know **EN** *SC*/IV
        know, *1816*
        know; *1964B*
14 All . . . that]
    This world is the mother of all   *1816*
    perceive,] percieve **EN** *SC*/IV
    feel;] feel **EN** *SC*/IV
        feel, *1816*
16 by nervestrings] with nerves *1816*
    steel,] steel **EN** *SC*/IV
        steel; *1816*
        steel— *1964B*
17 know, we] know, or *1816*
    feel] feel, *1816*
    and] & **EN** *SC*/IV
    and we see] or see, *1816*
18 fleet by] pass *1816*
    mystery.] mystery **EN** *SC*/IV
19 there] there, *1816*
20 body] frame *1816*

be,] be **EN** *SC*/IV
21 Tho'] Tho **EN** *SC*/IV
    Though *1816*
    fine-wrought]
        fine wrought **EN** *SC*/IV
    and] & **EN** *SC*/IV
23 bright] great *1816*
    and] & **EN** *SC*/IV
24 gradual path] boundless realm *1816*
    change.] change **EN** *SC*/IV
25 the tales] a tale *1816*
    Death?] death? *1816*
26 veil] viel **EN** *SC*/IV
    come?] come **EN** *SC*/IV
27 beings] shadows *1816*
28 wide-stretching]
    wide stretching **EN** *SC*/IV
    wide-winding *1816*
    realms] caves *1816*
    tomb] tomb? *1816*
29 And] Or *1816*
30 and] & **EN** *SC*/IV

Death-spurning rocks! here have ye towered since Time
   Sprung from Tradition's mist-encircled height
Which Memory's palsied pinion dreads to climb,
   Awed by the phantoms of its beamless night.
     Death-spurning rocks! Each jagged form   5
     Shall still arrest the passing storm
     Whilst rooted there the aged Oak
     Is shivered by the lightning's stroke.
Years shall fade fast, and centuries roll away—
Ye shall spurn death no more but like your Oak decay.   10

A maniac-sufferer soared with wild intent
   Where Nature formed these wonders. On the way
There is a little spot. Fiends would relent
   Knew they the snares that there for memory lay—
     How many a hope and many a fear   15
     And many a vain and bitter tear—
     Whilst each prophetic feeling wakes
     A brood of mad and venomed snakes
To make the lifesprings of his soul their food,
To twine around his veins and fatten on his blood.   20

To quench his pangs he fled to the wild moor—
One fleeting beam flashed but its gloom to shew:
Turned was the way-worn wanderer from the door

Text collated with **EN,** *1964B,* and *SC/*IV.
Title. *no title*]
     Death-spurning rocks!   *1964B*
1 Death-spurning]
   Death spurning   **EN** *SC/*IV
2 Tradition's] Traditions   **EN** *SC/*IV
  mist-encircled]
   mist encircled   **EN** *SC/*IV
3 Memory's] Memorys   **EN** *SC/*IV
  climb,] climb   **EN** *SC/*IV
4 night.] night   **EN** *SC/*IV
5 Death-spurning]
   Death spurning   **EN** *SC/*IV
  Each] each   *SC/*IV
8 lightning's] lightnings   **EN** *SC/*IV
  stroke.] stroke   **EN** *SC/*IV

9 and] &   **EN** *SC/*IV
  away—] away   **EN** *SC/*IV
10 decay.] decay   **EN** *SC/*IV
14 lay—] lay   **EN** *SC/*IV
15 and] &   **EN** *SC/*IV
16 and] &   **EN** *SC/*IV
  tear—] tear   **EN** *SC/*IV
18 and] &   **EN** *SC/*IV
19 food,] food   **EN** *SC/*IV
20 veins] viens   **EN** *SC/*IV
  and] &   **EN** *SC/*IV
  blood.] blood   **EN** *SC/*IV
21 moor—] moor   **EN** *SC/*IV
   moor.   *1964B*
22 shew:] shew   **EN** *SC/*IV
   shew,   *1964B*
23 way-worn] way worn   **EN** *SC/*IV

Where Pity's self promised to soothe his woe

25   Shall he turn back. The tempest there

Sweeps fiercely thro' the turbid air

Beyond a gulph before that yawns.

The daystar shines, the daybeam dawns.

God! Nature! Chance! remit this misery—

It burns!—why need he live to weep who does not fear

30   to die?

[*Esd #23*]   The Tombs

These are the tombs. O cold and silent Death,

Thy Kingdom and thy subjects here I see.

The record of thy victories

Is graven on every speaking stone

5   That marks what once was man.

These are the tombs. Am I, who sadly gaze

On the corruption and the sculls around,

To sum the mass of loathsomeness,

And to a mound of mouldering flesh

10   Say——"thou wert human life!"

In thee once throbbed the Patriot's beating heart,

In thee once lived the Poet's soaring soul—

The pulse of love, the calm of thought,

---

24 Pity's] Pitys **EN** *SC*/IV

    woe] woe. *1964B*

25 back.] back? *1964B*

    The] the **EN** *SC*/IV

26 thro'] thro **EN** *SC*/IV

27 that] that: **EN**

    yawns.] yawns **EN** *SC*/IV

28 dawns.] dawns **EN** *SC*/IV

29 Chance!] Chance **EN** *SC*/IV

    misery—] misery **EN** *SC*/IV

30 die?] die **EN** *SC*/IV

Text collated with **EN,** *1964B,* and *SC*/IV.

1 and] & **EN** *SC*/IV

    Death,] Death **EN** *SC*/IV

2 and] & **EN** *SC*/IV

    see.] see **EN** *SC*/IV

3 thy] the **EN** *SC*/IV

5 man.] man **EN** *SC*/IV

6 I,] I **EN** *SC*/IV

7 and] & **EN** *SC*/IV

    sculls] skulls *1964B*

    around,] around **EN** *SC*/IV

8 loathsomeness,]

    loathsomeness **EN** *SC*/IV

11 Patriot's] Patriots **EN** *SC*/IV

    heart,] heart **EN** *SC*/IV

12 Poet's] Poets **EN** *SC*/IV

    soul—] soul **EN** *SC*/IV

    soul, *1964B*

13 love,] love. **EN** *SC*/IV

    thought,] thought **EN** *SC*/IV

Courage and charity and truth
And high devotedness—   15

All that could sanctify the meanest deeds,
All that might give a manner and a form
To matter's speechless elements,
To every brute and morbid shape
Of this phantasmal world: 20

That the high sense which from the stern rebuke
Of Erin's victim-patriot's death-soul shone,
When blood and chains defiled the land,
Lives in the torn uprooted heart
His savage murderers burn.   25

Ah, no! else while these tombs before me stand
My soul would hate the coming of its hour,
Nor would the hopes of life and love
Be mingled with those fears of death
That chill the warmest heart.   30

To Harriet   [*Esd #24*]

It is not blasphemy to hope that Heaven
More perfectly will give those nameless joys
Which throb within the pulses of the blood
And sweeten all that bitterness which Earth
Infuses in the heaven-born soul—O Thou   5

---

14 and] &   **EN** *SC/IV*
   and] &   **EN** *SC/IV*
15 devotedness—]
   devotedness   **EN** *SC/IV*
               devotedness;   *1964B*
16 deeds,] deeds   **EN** *SC/IV*
17 and] &   **EN** *SC/IV*
18 elements,] elements   **EN** *SC/IV*
19 every] Every   *SC/IV*
   and] &   **EN** *SC/IV*

22 Erin's] Erins   **EN** *SC/IV*
   victim-patriot's]
      victim patriots   **EN** *SC/IV*
   shone,] shone   **EN** *SC/IV*
23 and] &   **EN** *SC/IV*
   land,] land   **EN** *SC/IV*
25 burn.] burn   **EN** *SC/IV*
26 Ah,] Ah   **EN** *SC/IV*
27 hour,] hour   **EN** *SC/IV*
28 and] &   **EN** *SC/IV*
30 heart.] heart   **EN** *SC/IV*

Text collated with **EN,** *1813* (lines 58–69), *1964B,* and *SC/IV.*
5 Thou] Thou,   *1964B*

            Whose dear love gleamed upon the gloomy path
            Which this lone spirit travelled, drear and cold,
            Yet swiftly leading to those awful limits
            Which mark the bounds of Time and of the space
10   When Time shall be no more: wilt thou not turn
            Those spirit-beaming eyes and look on me,
            Until I be assured that Earth is Heaven
            And Heaven is Earth?—will not thy glowing cheek,
            Glowing with soft suffusion, rest on mine
15   And breathe magnetic sweetness thro' the frame
            Of my corporeal nature, thro' the soul
            Now knit with these fine fibres? I would give
            The longest and the happiest day that fate
            Has marked on my existence, but to feel
20   *One* soul-reviving kiss . . . oh thou most dear,
            'Tis an assurance that this Earth is Heaven
            And Heaven the flower of that untainted seed
            Which springeth here beneath such love as ours.
            Harriet! let death all mortal ties dissolve
25   But ours shall not be mortal—the cold hand
            Of Time may chill the love of Earthly minds
            Half frozen now, the frigid intercourse
            Of common souls lives but a summer's day—
            It dies where it arose upon this Earth:
30   But ours! oh 'tis the stretch of fancy's hope
            To portray its continuance as now,

---

7 and] &   **EN** *SC*/IV

  cold,] cold   **EN** *SC*/IV

9 and] &   **EN** *SC*/IV

11 spirit-beaming] spirit beaming   *SC*/IV

  and] &   **EN** *SC*/IV

13 Earth?—will]

    Earth[?—] will   **EN** *SC*/IV

  cheek,] cheek   **EN** *SC*/IV

14 suffusion,] suffusion   **EN** *SC*/IV

15 thro'] thro   **EN** *SC*/IV

17 fibres?] fibres.   **EN** *SC*/IV

18 and] &   **EN** *SC*/IV

19 existence,] existence   *1964B*

20 *One*] <u>One</u>   **EN** *SC*/IV

  soul-reviving] soul reviving   **EN** *SC*/IV

  oh] oh,   *1964B*

dear,] dear   **EN** *SC*/IV

21 'Tis] Tis   **EN** *SC*/IV

26 minds] minds,   *1964B*

28 souls] souls,   **EN** *SC*/IV

  summer's] summers   **EN** *SC*/IV

  day—] day   **EN** *SC*/IV

    day,   *1964B*

29 dies] dies,   *1964B*

  arose] arose,   *1964B*

  Earth:] Earth   **EN** *SC*/IV

    Earth,   *1964B*

30 'tis] tis   **EN** *SC*/IV

31 its] it's   **EN** *SC*/IV

  now,] now   **EN** *SC*/IV

Warm, tranquil, spirit-healing. Nor when age
Has tempered these wild extacies, and given
A soberer tinge to the luxurious glow
Which blazing on devotion's pinnacle   35
Makes virtuous passion supercede the power
Of reason, nor when life's æstival sun
To deeper manhood shall have ripened me,
Nor when some years have added judgement's store
To all thy woman sweetness, all the fire   40
Which throbs in thine enthusiast heart, not then
Shall holy friendship (for what other name
May love like ours assume?) not even then
Shall custom so corrupt, or the cold forms
Of this desolate world so harden us   45
As when we think of the dear love that binds
Our souls in soft communion, while we know
Each other's thoughts and feelings, can we say
Unblushingly a heartless compliment,
Praise, hate or love with the unthinking world   50
Or dare to cut the unrelaxing nerve
That knits our love to Virtue—can those eyes
Beaming with mildest radiance on my heart
To purify its purity e'er bend
To soothe its vice or consecrate its fears?   55
Never, thou second self! is confidence
So vain in virtue that I learn to doubt
The mirror even of Truth?—Dark Flood of Time!
Roll as it listeth thee. I measure not
By months or moments thy ambiguous course.   60
Another may stand by me on thy brink
And watch the bubble whirled beyond his ken

---

32 spirit-healing.]
   spirit healing.   **EN** *SC*/IV
33 and] &   **EN** *SC*/IV
37 æstival] aestival   *1964B SC*/IV
38 me,] me.   **EN** *SC*/IV
39 Nor] Now   **EN** *SC*/IV
   judgement's] judgements   **EN** *SC*/IV
      judgment's   *1964B*
48 other's] others   **EN** *SC*/IV
   and] &   **EN** *SC*/IV
49 compliment,] compliment   **EN** *SC*/IV

56 Never,] Never   **EN** *SC*/IV
58 The mirror even of Truth?—]
   omitted   *1813*
   Flood] flood   *1813*
   Time!] Time   **EN** *SC*/IV
     time!   *1813*
     Time,   *1964B*
59 thee. I] thee—I   *1813*
60 course.] course   **EN** *SC*/IV
     course;   *1964B*
61 thy] the   *1813*

Which pauses at my feet.—The sense of love,
The thirst for action, and the impassioned thought
65   Prolong my being. If I wake no more
My life more actual living will contain
Than some grey veteran's of the world's cold school
Whose listless hours unprofitably roll,
By one enthusiast feeling unredeemed.
70   Virtue and Love! unbending Fortitude,
Freedom, Devotedness and Purity—
That life my spirit consecrates to you.

[*Esd #25*]   Sonnet: To Harriet
on her birth day, August 1, 1812

O thou, whose radiant eyes and beamy smile
Yet even a sweeter somewhat indexing,
Have known full many an hour of mine to guile
Which else would only bitter memories bring,
5   O ever thus, thus! as on this natal day,
Tho' age's frost may blight those tender eyes,
Destroy that kindling cheek's transparent dyes
And those luxuriant tresses change to grey,
Ever as now with Love and Virtue's glow

---

63 Which] That *1813*
   feet.—The]
     feet—the **EN** *1964B SC*/IV
     feet. The *1813*
   love,] love **EN** *SC*/IV
64 and] & **EN** *SC*/IV
65 being.] being: *1813*
   If] if **EN** *1813 SC*/IV
   more] more, *1813*
67 veteran's] veterans **EN** *SC*/IV
       veterans' *1813*
   world's] worlds **EN** *SC*/IV
   school] school, *1813*
68 roll,] roll **EN** *1964B SC*/IV
70 and] & **EN** *SC*/IV
   Fortitude,] Fortitude **EN** *SC*/IV
71 and] & **EN** *SC*/IV
   Purity—] Purity **EN** *SC*/IV

72 spirit] Spirit *1964B*
   you.] you **EN** *SC*/IV

Text collated with **EN,** *1964B,* and *SC*/IV.
Title. August 1, 1812]
     August 1. 1812 **EN** *SC*/IV
1 thou,] thou **EN** *SC*/IV
   and] & **EN** *SC*/IV
   smile] smile— *1964B*
2 indexing,] indexing **EN** *SC*/IV
      indexing— *1964B*
4 bring,] bring **EN** *SC*/IV
5 thus,] thus **EN** *SC*/IV
   day,] day **EN** *SC*/IV
6 Tho'] Tho **EN** *SC*/IV
   eyes,] eyes **EN** *SC*/IV
7 cheek's] cheeks **EN** *SC*/IV
8 grey,] grey **EN** *SC*/IV
9 and] & **EN** *SC*/IV

May thy unwithering soul not cease to burn.   10
Still may thine heart with those pure thoughts o'erflow
Which force from mine such quick and warm return,
And I must love thee even more than this
Nor doubt that Thou and I part but to meet in bliss.

Sonnet: To a balloon, laden with <u>Knowledge</u>   *[Esd #26]*

Bright ball of flame that thro' the gloom of Even
Silently takest thine etherial way
And with surpassing glory dimm'st each ray
Twinkling amid the dark blue Depths of Heaven,
Unlike the Fire thou bearest, soon shalt thou   5
Fade like a meteor in surrounding gloom,
Whilst that unquencheable is doomed to glow—
A watch light by the patriot's lonely tomb,
A ray of courage to the opprest and poor,
A spark, tho' gleaming on the hovel's hearth,   10
Which thro' the tyrants' gilded domes shall roar,
A beacon in the darkness of the Earth,
A Sun which o'er the renovated scene
Shall dart like truth where Falshood yet has been.

---

10 burn.] burn   **EN** *SC*/IV

11 o'erflow] oer flow   **EN** *SC*/IV

12 and] &   **EN** *SC*/IV

   return,] return   **EN** *SC*/IV

14 and] &   **EN** *SC*/IV

   bliss.] bliss   **EN** *SC*/IV

Text collated with **EN**, *1964B*, and *SC*/IV.

Title. <u>Knowledge</u>] *Knowledge   1964B*

1 thro'] thro   **EN** *SC*/IV

   Even] even   *1964B SC*/IV

3 dimm'st] dimmst   **EN** *1964B SC*/IV

4 Heaven,] Heaven   **EN** *SC*/IV

       Heaven;   *1964B*

5 shalt] shall   **EN** *1964B*

    [?shalt]   *SC*/IV

6 gloom,] gloom   **EN** *SC*/IV

7 that] that,   *1964B*

  unquencheable]

    unquencheable,   *1964B*

    glow—] glow   **EN** *1964B SC*/IV

8 patriot's] patriots   **EN** *SC*/IV

  tomb,] tomb   **EN** *SC*/IV

9 and] &   **EN** *SC*/IV

10 spark,] spark   **EN** *SC*/IV

  hearth,] hearth   **EN** *SC*/IV

11 thro'] thro   **EN** *SC*/IV

  tyrants'] tyrants   **EN** *SC*/IV

  roar,] roar   **EN** *SC*/IV

12 Earth,] Earth   **EN** *SC*/IV

13 o'er] oer   **EN** *SC*/IV

14 truth] Truth   *1964B SC*/IV

  been.] been   **EN** *SC*/IV

[*Esd* #27]   Sonnet: On launching some bottles filled with
<u>Knowledge</u> into the Bristol Channel.

Vessels of Heavenly medicine! may the breeze
    Auspicious waft your dark green forms to shore;
    Safe may ye stern the wide surrounding roar
Of the wild whirlwinds and the raging seas;
5   And oh! if Liberty e'er deigned to stoop
    From yonder lowly throne her crownless brow,
Sure she will breathe around your emerald group
    The fairest breezes of her west that blow.
Yes! she will waft ye to some freeborn soul
10   Whose eyebeam, kindling as it meets your freight,
    Her heaven-born flame on suffering Earth will light
Until Its radiance gleams from pole to pole
And tyrant-hearts with powerless envy burst
To see their night of ignorance dispersed.

[*Esd* #28]   Sonnet: On waiting for a wind
to cross the Bristol Channel from Devonshire to Wales.

Oh! for the South's benign and balmy breeze!
Come gentle spirit! thro' the wide Heaven sweep;
Chase inauspicious Boreas from the seas,
That gloomy tyrant of the unwilling deep.
5   These wilds where Man's profane and tainting hand
Nature's primæval loveliness has marred
And some few souls of the high bliss debarred
(Which else obey her powerful command)

Text collated with **EN,** *1964B,* and *SC*/IV.
Title. <u>Knowledge</u>] *Knowledge   1964B*
1 breeze] breeze,   *1964B*
2 Auspicious] Auspicious,   *1964B*
  shore;] shore   **EN** *SC*/IV
4 and] &   **EN** *SC*/IV
  seas;] seas: *SC*/IV
5 e'er] eer   **EN** *SC*/IV
  deigned] deighned   **EN** *SC*/IV
6 brow,] brow   **EN** *SC*/IV
8 blow.] blow,   **EN** *SC*/IV
10 eyebeam,] eye beam   **EN** *SC*/IV
  freight,] freight   **EN** *SC*/IV
11 heaven-born] heaven born   **EN** *SC*/IV
12 Its] It's   **EN** *SC*/IV

Text collated with **EN,** *1964B,* and *SC*/IV.
1 South's] Souths   **EN** *SC*/IV
  and] &   **EN** *SC*/IV
2 Come] Come,   *1964B*
  spirit!] Spirit!   *1964B SC*/IV
  thro'] thro   **EN** *SC*/IV
  sweep;] sweep   **EN** *SC*/IV
3 seas,] seas   **EN** *SC*/IV
4 deep.] deep   **EN** *SC*/IV
5 and] &   **EN** *SC*/IV
6 primæval] primaeval   *1964B*
  marred] marred,   *1964B*
8 (Which] Which   **EN** *1964B SC*/IV
  command)] command   **EN** *SC*/IV
      command,   *1964B*

I leave without a sigh. Ye mountain piles
That load in grandeur Cambria's emerald vales,   10
Whose sides are fair in cultivation's smiles
Around whose jagged heads the storm cloud sails—
A heart that's all thine own receive in me
With Nature's fervour fraught and calm in purity.

To Harriet   [Esd #29]

Harriet! thy kiss to my soul is dear:
    At evil or pain I would never repine
If to every sigh and to every tear
    Were added a look and a kiss of thine.
Nor is it the look when it glances fire,   5
    Nor the kiss when bathed in the dew of delight,
Nor the throb of the heart when it pants desire
    From the shadows of eve to the morning light,

But the look when a lustre of joy-mingled woe
    Has faintly obscured all its bliss-beaming Heaven,   10
Such a lovely, benign and enrapturing glow
    As sunset can paint on the clouds of even,
And a kiss, which the languish of silent love,
    Tho' eloquent, faints with the toil of expressing,

---

9 Ye] ye **EN** *SC/IV*

10 Cambria's] Cambrias **EN** *SC/IV*
   vales,] vales **EN** *SC/IV*

11 cultivation's] cultivations **EN** *SC/IV*
   smiles] smiles, *1964B*

12 sails—] sails **EN** *SC/IV*

13 that's] thats **EN** *SC/IV*
   receive] [?receive] *SC/IV*
   me] me, *1964B*

14 Nature's] Natures **EN** *SC/IV*
   and] & **EN** *SC/IV*
   purity.] purity [?piety] **EN**
      purity *SC/IV*

Text collated with **EN,** *1964B,* and *SC/IV.*

1 dear:] dear **EN** *SC/IV*
    dear; *1964B*

3 and] & **EN** *SC/IV*

4 and] & **EN** *SC/IV*
   thine.] thine **EN** *SC/IV*

5 fire,] fire **EN** *SC/IV*

6 delight,] delight **EN** *SC/IV*

8 light,] light **EN** *SC/IV*

9 joy-mingled] joy mingled **EN** *SC/IV*

10 bliss-beaming]
    bliss beaming **EN** *SC/IV*
   Heaven,] Heaven **EN** *SC/IV*

11 lovely,] lovely **EN** *SC/IV*
   and] & **EN** *SC/IV*

12 even,] even **EN** *SC/IV*

13 love,] love **EN** *SC/IV*

14 Tho'] Tho **EN**
   The *SC/IV*
   eloquent,] eloquent **EN** *SC/IV*
   expressing,] expressing **EN** *SC/IV*

To Harriet ("Harriet! thy kiss to my soul is dear")   [Esd #29]   67

15   Yet so light, that thou canst not refuse, my dove!
                    To add this one to the debt of caressing.

                Harriet! adieu to all vice and care:
                    Thy love is my Heaven, thy arms are my world;
                While thy kiss and thy look to my soul remain dear
20   I should smile tho' Earth from its base be hurled.
                For a heart as pure and a mind as free
                    As ever gave lover, to thee I give,
                And all that I ask in return from thee
                    Is to love like me and with me to live.

25   This heart that beats for thy love and bliss,
                    Harriet! beats for its country too,
                And it never would thrill with thy look or kiss
                    If it dared to that country's cause be untrue.
                Honor, and wealth and life it spurns,
30   But thy love is a prize it is sure to gain,
                And the heart that with love and virtue burns
                    Will never repine at evil or pain.

[*Esd #30*]   Mary to the Sea-Wind

      I implore thee, I implore thee, softly swelling Breeze,
      Waft swift the sail of my lover to the shore
      That under the shadow of yon darkly-woven trees
      I may meet him, I may meet him to part with him no more.

---

15 refuse,] refuse **EN** *SC*/IV

16 caressing.] caressing **EN** *SC*/IV

17 and] & **EN** *SC*/IV
   care:] care **EN** *SC*/IV
      care. *1964B*

18 world;] world **EN** *SC*/IV

19 and] & **EN** *SC*/IV

20 tho'] tho **EN** *SC*/IV
   hurled.] hurled **EN** *SC*/IV

21 and] & **EN** *SC*/IV

22 lover,] lover **EN** *SC*/IV
   give,] give **EN** *SC*/IV

24 and] & **EN** *SC*/IV
   live.] live **EN** *SC*/IV

25 and] & **EN** *SC*/IV
   bliss,] bliss **EN** *SC*/IV

26 its] it's **EN** *SC*/IV

too,] too **EN** *SC*/IV
   too; *1964B*

28 country's] countrys **EN** *SC*/IV
   untrue.] untrue **EN** *SC*/IV

29 and] & **EN** *SC*/IV
   and] & **EN** *SC*/IV
   spurns,] spurns **EN** *SC*/IV

30 gain,] gain **EN** *SC*/IV

31 and] & **EN** *SC*/IV

32 pain.] pain **EN** *SC*/IV

Text collated with **EN,** *1964B*, and *SC*/IV.

1 thee, I implore thee,]
   thee, I implore thee **EN** *SC*/IV
   Breeze,] Breeze **EN** *SC*/IV

3 darkly-woven] darkly woven **EN** *SC*/IV

4 more.] more **EN** *SC*/IV

For this boon, for this boon, sweet Sea-Wind, will I weave   5
A garland wild of heath flowers to breathe to thee perfume.
Thou wilt kiss them, yet like Henry's thy kisses will but leave
A more heaven-breathing fragrance and sense-enchanting bloom.

And then on Summer evens I will hasten to inhale—
Remembering that thou wert so kind—thy balmy, balmy breath; 10
And when thy tender pinions in the gloom begin to fail
I will catch thee to my bosom ere thou diest on the heath.

I will catch thee to my bosom—and if Henry's oaths are true,
A softer, sweeter grave thou wilt never find than there.
Nor is it, lovely Sea-Wind, nor is it to undo   15
That my arms are so inviting, that my bosom is so fair.

A retrospect of Times of Old   [*Esd #31*]

The mansions of the Kings are tenantless . . . .
Low lie in dust their glory and their shame.
No tongue survives their virtuous Deeds to bless,
No tongue with execration blasts their fame,
But on some ruined pile, where yet the gold*   5

*Gilding yet remains on the cornices of the ruined palace of Persepolis—

---

5 boon, for this boon,]
    boon, for thy boon **EN** *SC*/IV
    Sea-Wind,] Sea Wind **EN** *SC*/IV
6 heath] heatth *SC*/IV
    perfume.] perfume **EN** *SC*/IV
8 heaven-breathing]
    heaven breathing **EN** *SC*/IV
    and] & **EN** *SC*/IV
    sense-enchanting]
    sense enchanting **EN** *SC*/IV
    bloom.] bloom **EN** *SC*/IV
9 inhale—] in hale **EN**
        inhale *SC*/IV
10 kind—thy] kind thy **EN** *SC*/IV
    balmy, balmy]
        balmy balmy **EN** *SC*/IV
    breath;] breath **EN** *SC*/IV
12 heath.] heath **EN** *SC*/IV

13 bosom—and] bosom—& **EN** *SC*/IV
    Henry's] Henrys **EN** *SC*/IV
    true,] true **EN** *SC*/IV
14 softer,] softer **EN** *SC*/IV
    there.] there **EN** *SC*/IV
15 it,] it **EN** *SC*/IV
    Sea-Wind,] Sea Wind, **EN**
        sea wind, *SC*/IV
16 inviting,] inviting **EN** *SC*/IV
    fair.] fair **EN** *SC*/IV

Text collated with **EN,** *1964B,* and *SC*/IV.
2 and] & **EN** *SC*/IV
    shame.] shame **EN** *SC*/IV
3 Deeds] deeds *SC*/IV
    bless,] bless **EN** *SC*/IV
4 fame,] fame **EN** *SC*/IV
5 on] in *1964B*

Casts purple brilliance o'er colossal snow,
Where sapphire eyes in breathing statues glow
And the tainted blast sighs mid the reeds below,
Where grim effigies of the Gods of old
10   In mockery stand of ever-changing men
Their ever-changing worship. Ah how vain!
(Yet baubles aye must please the multitude.)
There Desolation dwells!—Where are the Kings?
Why sleep they now if sleep be not eternal?
15   Cannot Oblivion's silent tauntings call
The kings and heroes from their quietude
Of Death, to snatch the Scrolls from her palsying hand,
To tell the world how mighty once they were.——
They dare not wake . . . thy Victory is here
20   O Death!— Yet I hear unearthly voices cry,
"Death, thou'lt be swallowed up in Victory!"

Yes, Dream of fame! the halls are desolate
Where whitened skeletons of thine heroes lie . . .
Stillness keeps watch before each grass-grown gate
25   Save where amid thy towers the Simoon's sigh
Wakes the lone lyre whose mistress sleeps below
And bids it thrill to notes of awfulness and woe.

There ages since, some Royal Bloodhound crept
When on these pillared piles a midnight lay—

---

6 o'er] oer   **EN** *SC/IV*
  snow,] snow   **EN** *SC/IV*
8 below,] below   **EN** *SC/IV*
10 ever-changing]
   ever changing   **EN** *SC/IV*
  men] men,   *1964B*
11 Their] Thier   **EN** *SC/IV*
  ever-changing]
   ever changing   **EN** *SC/IV*
  worship.] worship   **EN** *SC/IV*
  Ah] ah   **EN** *SC/IV*
   Oh *1964B*
12 multitude.)] multitude)   **EN** *SC/IV*
13 Kings?] Kings   **EN** *SC/IV*
15 Oblivion's] Oblivions   **EN** *SC/IV*
16 and] &   **EN** *SC/IV*
17 Death,] Death   **EN** *1964B SC/IV*
  hand,] hand   **EN** *SC/IV*

18 were.——] were—— —   *SC/IV*
   were——   *1964B*
20 Death!—] Death!—.   *1964B*
  Yet] yet   *SC/IV*
  cry,] cry   **EN** *SC/IV*
21 "Death, thou'lt]
   Death thou wi'lt   **EN** *SC/IV*
  Victory!"] Victory!   **EN** *SC/IV*
24 grass-grown] grass grown   **EN** *SC/IV*
25 Simoon's] Simoons   **EN** *SC/IV*
27 and] &   **EN** *SC/IV*
  woe.] woe   **EN** *SC/IV*
28 There] There,   *1964B*
   Here   *SC/IV*
  since,] since   **EN** *SC/IV*
29 lay—] lay   **EN** *SC/IV*

Which, but from visioned memories, long has fled—   30
To work ambition whilst his brother slept,
And reckless of the peaceful smile that played
Around his dream-fraught features when betrayed—
They told each innocent secret of the day—
Wakened the thoughtless victim, bade him stare   35
Upon the murderous steel . . . The chaste pale glare
Of the midnight moonbeam kissed its glittering blade—
A moment! and its brightness, quenched in blood,
Distained with murder the moon's silver flood.
The blushing moon, wide-gathering vapours shrouded.   40
One moment did he triumph;—but remorse,
Suspicion, anguish, fear, all triumph clouded.
Destruction . . Suicide . . his last resource . . .
Wider yawned the torrent. The moon's stormy flash
Disclosed its black tumultuousness . . . the crash   45
Of rocks and boughs mixed with its roarings hoarse.
A moment! And he dies! Hark to the awful dash!*

*I believe it was only in those early times when Monarchy was in its apprenticeship that its com-
punction for evil deeds was unendurable . . There is no instance upon record parallel to that re-
lated above, but I know that neither men, nor sets of men become vicious but slowly and step by
step, each less difficult than the former.

---

30 Which,] Which **EN** *SC*/IV   fear,] fear **EN** *SC*/IV
 memories,] memories **EN** *SC*/IV   clouded.] clouded **EN** *SC*/IV
 fled—] fled. **EN** *SC*/IV   43 Suicide . . his] suicide . . his   *SC*/IV
31 slept,] slept **EN** *SC*/IV   44 Wider] Wide   *SC*/IV
33 features when]   torrent. The]
  features—when *1964B*   torrent. the **EN** *SC*/IV
 betrayed—]   moon's] moons **EN** *SC*/IV
  betrayed **EN** *1964B SC*/IV 46 and] & **EN** *SC*/IV
34 day—] day **EN** *SC*/IV   hoarse.] hoarse **EN** *SC*/IV
36 The] the **EN** *SC*/IV   47 And] & **EN** *SC*/IV
37 blade—] blade **EN** *SC*/IV   dies!] dies **EN** *SC*/IV
38 and] & **EN** *SC*/IV   Hark] hark **EN** *SC*/IV
 brightness,] brightness **EN** *SC*/IV dash!*] dash! **EN** *SC*/IV
 blood,] blood **EN** *SC*/IV   Footnote. unendurable . .]
39 moon's] moons **EN** *SC*/IV   unendurable . . **EN** *SC*/IV
 flood.] flood **EN** *SC*/IV   parallel] parallell **EN** *SC*/IV
40 moon,] moon **EN** *SC*/IV   neither] niether **EN** *SC*/IV
 shrouded.] shrouded **EN** *SC*/IV men,] men   *SC*/IV
41 remorse,] remorse **EN** *SC*/IV   and] & **EN** *SC*/IV
42 anguish,] anguish **EN** *SC*/IV   former.] former **EN** *SC*/IV

Such were thy works, Ambition, even amid
The darksome times of generations gone,
50   Which the dark veil of viewless hours has hid
The veil of hours forever onward flown.
Swift roll the waves of Time's eternal tide:
The peasant's grave, marked by no tribute stone,
Not less remembered than the gilded bed
55   On which the hero slept! now ever gone,—
Passion and will and power, flesh, heart and brain and bone!

Each trophied bust where gore-emblazoned Victory
In breathing marble shook the ensanguined spear,
Flinging its heavy purple canopy
60   In cold expanse o'er martyred Freedom's bier,
Each gorgeous altar where the victims bled
And grim Gods frowned above their human prey,
Where the high temple echoing to the yell
Of death-pangs, to the long and shuddering groan,
65   Whilst sacred hymns along the aisles did swell
And pitiless priests drowned each discordant moan—
All, all have faded in past time away!
New Gods, like men, changing in ceaseless flow,
Ever at hand as antient ones decay,
70   Heroes, and Kings and laws have plunged the world in woe.

---

48 works,] works **EN** *SC*/IV
   Ambition,] Ambition **EN** *SC*/IV
49 gone,] gone **EN** *SC*/IV
50 veil] viel **EN** *SC*/IV
   hid] hid,— *1964B*
51 veil] viel **EN** *SC*/IV
   flown.] flown **EN** *SC*/IV
52 roll] rolls **EN** *SC*/IV
   tide:] tide **EN** *SC*/IV
53 peasant's] peasants **EN** *SC*/IV
   grave,] grave **EN** *SC*/IV
   stone,] stone **EN** *SC*/IV
54 Not] No *1964B*
55 gone,—] gone **EN** *SC*/IV
56 and] & **EN** *SC*/IV
   and] & **EN** *SC*/IV
   flesh,] flesh **EN** *SC*/IV
   and] & **EN** *SC*/IV

and] & **EN** *SC*/IV
bone!] bone **EN** *SC*/IV
58 spear,] spear **EN** *SC*/IV
60 o'er] oer **EN** *SC*/IV
   Freedom's] Freedoms **EN** *SC*/IV
   bier,] bier **EN** *SC*/IV
62 prey,] prey **EN** *SC*/IV
63 yell] yells *1964B*
64 death-pangs,] death pangs, **EN** *SC*/IV
   and] & **EN** *SC*/IV
   groan,] groan **EN** *SC*/IV
66 moan—] moan **EN** *SC*/IV
67 away!] away **EN** *SC*/IV
68 flow,] flow **EN** *SC*/IV
70 Heroes,] Heroes *1964B*
   and] & **EN** *SC*/IV
   and] & **EN** *SC*/IV
   the] this *1964B*
   woe.] woe **EN** *SC*/IV

Sesostris, Caesar, and Pizarro come!
Thou Moses! and Mahommed,* leave that gloom!
Destroyers! never shall your memory die!
Approach, pale Phantom, to yon mould'ring tomb
Where all thy bones, hopes, crimes and passions lie.   75
And thou, poor peasant, when thou pass't the grave
Where deep enthroned in monumental pride
Sleep low in dust the mighty and the brave,
Where the mad conqueror whose gigantic stride
The Earth was too confined for, doth abide,   80
Housing his bones amid a little clay,
In gratitude to Nature's Spirit bend
And wait in still hope for thy better end.

The Voyage   [*Esd #32*]
A Fragment
Devonshire—August 1812

Quenched is old Ocean's rage;
Each horrent wave that flung
Its neck that writhed beneath the tempest's scourge
Indignant up to Heaven,
Now breathes in its sweet slumber   5

---

*To this innumerable list of legal murderers our own age affords numerous addenda. Frederic of Prussia, Buonaparte, Suwarroff, Wellington and Nelson are the most skilful and notorious scourges of their species of the present day.——

---

71 and] & **EN** *SC*/IV
   come!] come   **EN** *SC*/IV
72 and] & **EN** *SC*/IV
   Mahommed,*]
     Mahommed*   **EN** *SC*/IV
   gloom!] gloom   **EN** *SC*/IV
Footnote. and] & **EN** *SC*/IV
    and] & **EN** *SC*/IV
    day.——] day.—   *1964B*
      day——   *SC*/IV
73 die!] die   **EN** *SC*/IV
74 Approach,] Approach   **EN** *SC*/IV
   Phantom,] Phantom   **EN** *SC*/IV
   mould'ring] mouldring   **EN** *SC*/IV
75 and] & **EN** *SC*/IV
   lie.] lie   **EN** *SC*/IV

76 thou,] thou   **EN** *SC*/IV
   peasant,] peasant   **EN** *SC*/IV
78 and] & **EN** *SC*/IV
   brave,] brave   **EN** *SC*/IV
80 abide,] abide   **EN** *SC*/IV
81 clay,] clay   **EN** *SC*/IV
82 Nature's] Natures   **EN** *SC*/IV
83 end.] end   **EN** *SC*/IV

Text collated with **EN**, *1964B*, and *SC*/IV.
Title. Fragment] Fragment . .   **EN** *SC*/IV
1 Ocean's] Oceans   **EN** *SC*/IV
   rage;] rage   **EN** *SC*/IV
2 horrent] puissant   *1964B*
3 neck] neck,   *1964B*
   tempest's] tempests   **EN** *SC*/IV
4 Heaven,] Heaven   **EN** *SC*/IV

To mingle with the day
A spirit of tranquillity.
Beneath the cloudless sun
The gently swelling main
10   Scatters a thousand colourings
And the wind that wanders vaguely thro' the void,
With the flapping of the Sail, and the dashing at the prow,
And the whistle of the sailor in that shadow of a calm
A ravishing harmony makes.
15   O! why is a rapt soul e'er recalled
From the palaces of visioned bliss
To the cells of real sorrow!

That little vessel's company
Beheld the sight of loveliness—
20   The dark grey rocks that towered
Above the slumbering sea,
And their reflected forms
Deep in its faintly-waving mirror given.
They heard the low breeze sighing
25   The listless sails and ropes among,
They heard the music at the prow,
And the hoarse, distant clash
Sent from yon gloomy caves
Where Earth and Ocean strive for mastery.

30   A mingled mass of feeling
Those human spirits prest
As they heard, and saw, and felt
Some fancied fear, and some real woe
Mixed with those glimpses of heavenly joy
35   That dawned on each passive soul.
Where is the woe that never sees
One joybeam illumine the night of the mind?

Where is the bliss that never feels
One dart from the quiver of earthly pain?
The young and happy spirits now   40
Along the world are voyaging—
Love, friendship, virtue, truth,
Simplicity of sentiment and speech,
        And other sensibilities
Known by no outward name,   45
Some faults that Love forgives,
Some flaws that Friendship shares,
    Hearts passionate and benevolent,
    Alive, and urgent to repair
The errors of their brother heads;   50
    All voyage with them too.

They look to land . . . . they look to Sea;
Bounded one is, and palpable
Even as a noonday scene . .
The other indistinct and dim,   55
Spangled with dizzying sunbeams,
Boundless, untrod by human step,
Like the vague blisses of a midnight dream
    Or Death's immeasurable main,
Whose lovely islands gleam at intervals   60
Upon the Spirit's visioned solitude
Thro' Earth's wide woven and many colour'd veil.

---

39 pain?] pain **EN** *SC*/IV
40 The] Th[e *or* o] **EN**
        Tho' *1964B*
    and] & **EN** *SC*/IV
41 voyaging—] voyaging **EN** *SC*/IV
            voyaging, *1964B*
42 friendship,] friendship **EN** *SC*/IV
    virtue,] virtue **EN** *SC*/IV
    truth,] truth **EN** *SC*/IV
43 and] & **EN** *SC*/IV
    speech,] speech **EN** *SC*/IV
45 name,] name **EN** *SC*/IV
46 forgives,] forgives **EN** *SC*/IV
47 shares,] shares **EN** *SC*/IV
48 and] & **EN** *SC*/IV
    benevolent,] benevolent **EN** *SC*/IV
49 and] & **EN** *SC*/IV
50 heads;] heads— *1964B*

52 Sea;] Sea **EN** *SC*/IV
53 and] & **EN** *SC*/IV
54 scene . .] scene . . *SC*/IV
55 and] & **EN** *SC*/IV
    dim,] dim **EN** *SC*/IV
56 sunbeams,] sunbeams **EN** *SC*/IV
57 step,] step **EN** *SC*/IV
59 Death's] Deaths **EN** *SC*/IV
    main,] main **EN** *SC*/IV
61 Spirit's] Spirits **EN** *SC*/IV
62 Earth's] Earths **EN** *SC*/IV
    and] & **EN** *SC*/IV
    many colour'd]
        many colourd **EN** *SC*/IV
        many-colour'd *1964B*
    veil.] veil **EN** *SC*/IV

                It is a moveless calm.
                The sailor's whistle shrill
65   Speeds clearly thro' the sleeping atmosphere—
                As country curates pray for rain
                When drought has frustrated full long—
                He whistles for a wind
                With just the same success.
70   Two honest souls were they
             And oft had braved in fellowship the storm,
                Till from that fellowship had sprung
                A sense of right and liberty
             Unbending, undismayed, aye they had seen
75   Where danger, death and terror played
                With human lives in the boiling deep,
                And they had seen the scattered spray
             Of the green and jagged mountain-wave
             Hid in the lurid tempest cloud,
80   With lightnings tinging all its fleeting form,
                Rolled o'er their fragile bark.
                A dread and hopeless month
                Had they participated once
                In that diminutive bark:—
85   Their tearless eyes uplifted unto Heaven
                So fruitlessly for aid!
             Their parched mouths oped eager to the shower
             So thin and sleety in that arctic clime.
                Their last hard crust was shared
90   Impartial in equality,
                And in the dreadful night

---

64 sailor's] sailors   **EN** *SC*/IV
65 thro'] thro   **EN** *SC*/IV
   atmosphere—] atmosphere   **EN**
      SC/IV
67 long—] long   **EN** *SC*/IV
69 success.] success   **EN** *SC*/IV
71 storm,] storm   **EN** *SC*/IV
73 and] &   **EN** *SC*/IV
   liberty] liberty.   *1964B*
74 Unbending,] Unbending[.]   **EN**
      Unbending   *SC*/IV
75 danger,] danger   **EN** *SC*/IV
   and] &   **EN** *SC*/IV

78 and] &   **EN** *SC*/IV
79 tempest cloud,] tempest cloud[.]   **EN**
      tempest-cloud,   *1964B*
      tempest cloud   *SC*/IV
80 form,] form   **EN** *SC*/IV
81 o'er] oer   **EN** *SC*/IV
82 and] &   **EN** *SC*/IV
85 Their] Thier   **EN** *SC*/IV
87 Their] Thier   **EN** *SC*/IV
   shower] shower,   *1964B*
88 and] &   **EN** *SC*/IV
   clime.] clime   **EN** *SC*/IV
90 equality,] equality   **EN** *1964B* *SC*/IV

When all had failed . . . even hope,
  Together they had shared the gleam
    Shot from yon lighthouse tower
    Across the waste of waves.   95
And therefore are they brave, free, generous.
For who that had so long fought hand to hand
With famine, toil and hazard, smil'd at Death
When leaning from the bursting billow's height
He stares so ghastly terrible, would waste   100
One needless word for life's contested toys?
Who that had shared his last and nauseous crust
With Famine and a friend, would not divide
A landsman's meal with one who needed it?
Who that could rule the elements and spurn   105
Their fiercest rage, would bow before a slave
Decked in the fleetingness of Earthly power?
Who that had seen the soul of Nature work—
Blind, changeless and eternal in her paths—*
Would shut his eyes and ears, quaking before   110
The bubble of a Bigot's blasphemy?

*It is remarkable that few are more experimentally convinced of the doctrine of necessity than old sailors, who have seen much and various service. The peculiarly engaging and frank generosity of seafaring men probably is an effect of this cause. Those employed in small and ill-equipped trading vessels seem to possess this generosity in a purer degree than those of a King's ship. The habits of subjection and coercion imbued into the latter may suffice to explain the cause of the difference.

---

92 When] Where *1964B*
    failed . . .] failed. . . *SC*/IV
    hope,] hope **EN** *SC*/IV
95 waves.] waves; *1964B*
96 generous.] generous **EN** *SC*/IV
98 and] & **EN** *SC*/IV
    hazard,] hazard. **EN** *SC*/IV
    smil'd] smild **EN** *SC*/IV
99 billow's] billows **EN** *SC*/IV
101 life's] lifes **EN** *SC*/IV
102 and] & **EN** *SC*/IV
103 and] & **EN** *SC*/IV
    would] w.ᵈ **EN**
        wᵈ *SC*/IV
104 landsman's] landsmans **EN** *SC*/IV
    it?] it **EN** *SC*/IV
105 and] & **EN** *SC*/IV
107 power?] power **EN** *SC*/IV

108 work—] work **EN** *SC*/IV
109 and] & **EN** *SC*/IV
    paths—*] paths **EN** *SC*/IV
Footnote. and] & **EN** *SC*/IV
    service.] service **EN** *SC*/IV
    peculiarly]
      peculiarily **EN** *SC*/IV
    engaging]
      engaging, **EN** *SC*/IV
    and] & **EN** *SC*/IV
    and] & **EN** *SC*/IV
    ill-equipped]
      ill equipped **EN** *SC*/IV
    possess] posess **EN** *SC*/IV
    and] & **EN** *SC*/IV
110 and] & **EN** *SC*/IV
111 Bigot's] Bigots **EN** *SC*/IV

The faintly moving prow
Divided Ocean's smoothness languidly.
A landsman there reclined,
115 With lowering close-contracted brow
And mouth updrawn at intervals
As fearful of his fluctuating bent,
His eyes wide-wandering round
In insecure malignity,
120 Rapacious, mean, cruel and cowardly,
Casting upon the loveliness of day
The murkiness of villainy . . .
By other nurses than the battling storm,
Friendship, Equality and Sufferance,
125 His manhood had been cradled,—
Inheritor to all the vice and fear
Which Kings and laws and priests and conquerors spread
On the woe-fertilized world.
Yes! in the dawn of life,
130 When guileless confidence and unthinking love
Dilate all hearts but those
Which servitude or power has cased in steel,
He bound himself to an unhappy woman;
Not of those pure and heavenly links that Love
135 Twines round a feeling to Freedom dear,
But of vile gold, cank'ring the breast it binds,
Corroding and inflaming every thought
Till vain desire, remorse and fear
Envenom all the being.

---

113 Ocean's] Oceans   **EN** *SC*/IV
   languidly.] languidly   **EN** *SC*/IV
114 reclined,] reclined   **EN** *SC*/IV
115 close-contracted]
   close contracted   **EN** *SC*/IV
117 bent,] bent   **EN** *SC*/IV
119 malignity,] malignity   **EN** *SC*/IV
120 and] &   **EN** *SC*/IV
   cowardly,] cowardly   **EN** *SC*/IV
123 storm,] storm   **EN** *SC*/IV
124 and] &   **EN** *SC*/IV
   Sufferance,] Sufferance   **EN** *SC*/IV
125 cradled,—] cradled   **EN** *SC*/IV
126 and] &   **EN** *SC*/IV

127 and] &   **EN** *SC*/IV
   and] &   **EN** *SC*/IV
   and] &   **EN** *SC*/IV
129 life,] life   **EN** *SC*/IV
130 and] &   **EN** *SC*/IV
132 steel,] steel   **EN** *SC*/IV
133 woman;] woman   **EN** *SC*/IV
134 and] &   **EN** *SC*/IV
135 dear,] dear   **EN** *SC*/IV
136 cank'ring] cankring   **EN** *SC*/IV
   binds,] binds   **EN** *SC*/IV
137 and] &   **EN** *SC*/IV
138 and] &   **EN** *SC*/IV
139 being.] being   **EN** *SC*/IV

Yet did this chain, tho' rankling in the soul   140
Not bind the grosser body; he was wont
       All means to try of thriving.
To those above him, the most servile cringe
That ignorance e'er gave to titled Vice
       Was simperingly yielded;   145
To those beneath, the frown which Commerce darts
On cast-off friends, unprofitably poor,
       Was less severe than his.

       There was another too . . .
       One of another mould.   150
He had been cradled in the wildest storm
       Of Passion, and tho' now
The feebler light of worn-out energies
       Shone on his soul, yet ever and anon
       A flash of tempests long past by   155
       Would wake to pristine visions.
Now he was wrapt in a wild, woeful dream.
       Deeply his soul could love,
And as he gazed on the boundless sea
Chequered with sunbeams and with shade,   160
       Alternate to infinity,
       He fell into a dream.

       He dreamed that all he loved
Across the shoreless wastes were voyaging
       By that unpitying landsman piloted,   165
       And that at length they came
       To a black and barren island rock.

---

140 tho'] tho **EN** *SC*/IV   153 worn-out] worn out **EN** *SC*/IV
141 body;] body, **EN** *SC*/IV   156 visions.] visions **EN** *SC*/IV
142 thriving.] thriving **EN** *SC*/IV   157 wild,] wild **EN** *SC*/IV
       striving. *1964B*   dream.] dream **EN** *SC*/IV
145 yielded;] yielded **EN** *SC*/IV   158 love,] love **EN** *SC*/IV
147 cast-off] cast off **EN** *SC*/IV   160 and] & **EN** *SC*/IV
       poor,] poor **EN** *SC*/IV   shade,] shade **EN** *SC*/IV
148 his.] his **EN** *SC*/IV   161 infinity,] infinity **EN** *SC*/IV
       stanza break] *page break* *1964B*   162 dream.] dream **EN** *SC*/IV
149 too . . .] too. . . *SC*/IV   165 piloted,] piloted **EN** *SC*/IV
150 mould.] mould **EN** *SC*/IV   167 and] & **EN** *SC*/IV
152 and] & **EN** *SC*/IV   rock.] rock **EN** *SC*/IV

Barren the isle . . . no egg
Which sea mews leave upon the wildest shore;
170   Barren the isle . . no blade
Of grass, no seaweed, not the vilest thing
For human nutriment . . . .

He struggled with the pitiless landsman there
But nerved tho' his frame with love,
175   Quenchless, despairing love,
It nought availed . . . strong Power
Truth, love and courage vanquished.
A rock was piled upon his feeble breast.
All was subdued, but that
180   Which is immortal, unsubduable.

He still continued dreaming . . . .
The rock upon his bosom quenched not
The frenzy and defiance of his eye,
But the strong and coward landsman laughed to scorn
185   His unprevailing fortitude,
And in security of malice stabbed
One who accompanied his voyagings.
The blood gushed forth, the eye grew dim,
The nerve relaxed, the life was gone.
190   His smile of dastardly revenge
Glared upon dead frame.
Then back the Victim flung his head
In horror insupportable

---

168 isle . . .] isle . . .   *SC/IV*
169 shore;] shore   **EN** *SC/IV*
              shore.   *1964B*
170 isle . .] isle . .   *SC/IV*
172 nutriment . . . .]
          nutriment. . . .   *1964B*
173 there] then   *1964B SC/IV*
174 tho'] tho   **EN** *SC/IV*
176 availed . . .] availed. . .   *1964B SC/IV*
177 and] &   **EN** *SC/IV*
        vanquished.] vanquished   **EN** *SC/IV*
178 breast.] breast   **EN** *SC/IV*
180 unsubduable.]
       unsubduable   **EN** *SC/IV*
      stanza break] *page break*   *1964B*

181 dreaming . . . .]
        dreaming. . . .   **EN** *SC/IV*
183 and] &   **EN** *SC/IV*
      eye,] eye   **EN** *SC/IV*
184 and] &   **EN** *SC/IV*
185 fortitude,] fortitude   **EN** *SC/IV*
187 voyagings.] voyagings   **EN** *SC/IV*
188 forth, the] forth. the   **EN** *SC/IV*
        forth. The   *1964B*
    dim,] dim   **EN** *SC/IV*
189 gone.] gone   **EN** *SC/IV*
191 frame.] frame   **EN** *SC/IV*

Upon the jagged rock whereon he lay,
And human Nature paused awhile   195
   In pity to his woe.

When he awaked to life
She whom he loved was bending over him.
   Haggard her sunken eye . . . .
   Bloodless her quivering lips . . .   200
   She bended to bestow
The burning moisture from her feverish tongue
   To lengthen out his life
   Perhaps till succour came! . .
But more her dear soft eyes in languid love   205
When life's last gleam was flickering in decay
   The waning spark rekindled
And the faint lingering kiss of her withered lips
Mingled a rapture with his misery.
   A bleeding Sister lay   210
   Beside this wretched pair,
And He the dastard of relentless soul
In moody malice lowered over all.

And this is but a dream!
For yonder—see! the port in sight!   215
   The vessel makes towards it!
     The sight of their safety then,
     And the hum of the populous town
Awakened them from a night of horror
   To a day of secure delights.   220

Lo! here a populous Town:
Two dark rocks either side defend,
The quiet water sleeps within
Reflecting every roof and every mast.

---

194 lay,] lay **EN** *SC/IV*
198 him.] him **EN** *SC/IV*
199 eye . . . .] eye. . . . **EN** *SC/IV*
      eye. . . *1964B*
200 lips . . .] lips. . . *1964B SC/IV*
206 life's] lifes **EN** *SC/IV*
209 misery.] misery **EN** *SC/IV*
211 pair,] pair **EN** *SC/IV*

215 sight!] sight **EN** *SC/IV*
220 delights.] delight[s.] **EN**
      delight[s] *SC/IV*
221 Town:] Town **EN** *SC/IV*
222 defend,] defend **EN** *SC/IV*
224 and] & **EN** *SC/IV*
     mast.] mast **EN** *SC/IV*

225   A populous town! it is a den
     Where wolves keep lambs to fatten on their blood.
     'Tis a distempered spot. Should there be one,
     Just, dauntless, rational, he would appear
      A madman to the rest.

230   Yes! smooth-faced tyrants chartered by a Power
     Called King, who in the castellated keep
     Of a far distant land wears out his days
     Of miserable dotage, pace the quay
     And by the magic of that dreadful word,
235   Hated tho' dreadful, shield their impotence,
     Their lies, their murders, and their robberies.
     See, where the sailor absent many years
     With Heaven in his rapture-speaking eyes
     Seeks the low cot where all his wealth reposes,
240   To bring himself for joy, and his small store,
     Hard earned by years of peril and of toil,
     For comfort to his famine-wasted babes.
     Deep in the dark blue Sea the unmoving moon
     Gleams beautifully quiet . . . such a night
245   When the last kiss from Mary's quivering lips
     Unmanned him. To the well-known door he speeds
     His faint hand pauses on the latch . . His heart
     Beats eagerly.—When suddenly the gang
     Dissolves his dream of rapture—no delay!
250   No pity! unexpostulating power
     Deals not in human feelings . . . he is stript
     By those low slaves whose master's names inflict
     Curses more fell than even themselves would give;

---

226 blood.] blood **EN** *SC*/IV

227 'Tis] Tis **EN** *SC*/IV
 Should] should **EN** *SC*/IV
 one,] one **EN** *SC*/IV

229 *stanza break*]
 omitted **EN** *1964B SC*/IV

230 smooth-faced]
 smooth faced **EN** *SC*/IV

234 word,] word **EN** *SC*/IV

236 and] & **EN** *SC*/IV
 their] there **EN** *SC*/IV
 robberies.] robberies **EN** *SC*/IV

237 sailor] sailors **EN** *SC*/IV

239 reposes,] reposes **EN** *SC*/IV

240 and] & **EN** *SC*/IV
 store,] store **EN** *SC*/IV

241 and] & **EN** *SC*/IV
 toil,] toil **EN** *SC*/IV

242 famine-wasted]
 famine wasted **EN** *SC*/IV
 babes.] babes **EN** *SC*/IV

245 Mary's] Marys **EN** *SC*/IV

246 To] to **EN** *SC*/IV
 well-known] well known **EN** *SC*/IV

252 master's] masters **EN** *SC*/IV

The Indian muslins and the Chinese toys,
These for small gain, and those for boundless love, 255
Thus carefully concealed, are torn away;
The very handkerchief his Mary gave
Which in unchanging faithfulness he wore
Rent from his manly neck! his kindling eye
Beamed vengeance, and the tyrant's manacles 260
Shook on his struggling arm; "Where is my Wife?
Where are my Children?"—close beside him stood
A sleek and pampered town's man—"oh! your wife
"Died this time year in the House of Industry—
"Your young ones all are dead, except one brat 265
"Stubborn as you—Parish apprentice now."

They have appropriated human life
And human happiness, but these weigh nought
In the nice balanced Politician's scale,
Who finds that murder is expedient 270
And that vile means can answer glorious ends.
Wide Nature has outstretched her fertile Earth
In commonage to all.—But they have torn
Her dearest offspring from her bleeding breast,
Have disunited Liberty and life, 275
Severed all right from duty, and confused
Virtue with selfishness.—The grass-green hills,
The fertile vallies and the limpid streams,
The beach on the seashore, the sea itself,
The very snow-clad mountain peaks, whose height 280

254 and] & **EN** *SC*/IV
 toys,] toys **EN** *SC*/IV
255 and] & **EN** *SC*/IV
 love,] love **EN** *SC*/IV
256 concealed,] concealed **EN** *SC*/IV
257 handkerchief]
 handcherchief **EN** *SC*/IV
260 and] & **EN** *SC*/IV
263 and] & **EN** *SC*/IV
264 Industry—]
 Industry **EN** *1964B SC*/IV
266 now."] now" **EN** *SC*/IV
 stanza break] *omitted 1964B*
268 happiness,] happiness **EN** *SC*/IV
269 Politician's] Politicians **EN** *SC*/IV
 scale,] scale **EN** *SC*/IV

273 all.—But] all..—but **EN**
 all. .—but *1964B*
 all.—but *SC*/IV
275 and] & **EN** *SC*/IV
 life,] life **EN** *SC*/IV
276 and] & **EN** *SC*/IV
277 selfishness.—The]
 selfishness.——the **EN** *SC*/IV
 grass-green] grassgreen [*crowded at
 edge of paper*] **EN**
 grass green *SC*/IV
 hills,] hills **EN** *SC*/IV
278 streams,] streams **EN** *SC*/IV
279 itself,] itself **EN** *SC*/IV
280 snow-clad] snow clad **EN** *SC*/IV

Forbids all human footstep . . the ravines
Where cataracts have roared ere Monarchs were,
Nature, fair Earth, and Heaven's untainted air
Are all apportioned out . . . some bloated Lord

285   Some priestly pilferer, or some Snake of Law,
Some miserable mockery of a man,
Some slave without a heart, looks over these
And calls them *Mine*—in self-approving pride.
The millionth of the produce of the vale

290   He sets apart for *charity.* Vain fool!
He gives in mercy, while stern Justice cries,
"Be thou as one of them—resign thine hall
Brilliant with murder's trophies, and the board
Loaded with surfeiting viands, and the gems

295   Which millions toil to bring thee.—Get thee hence
And dub thyself a man, then dare to throw
One act of usefulness, one thought of love
Into the balance of thy past misdeeds!"

[*Esd #33*]   A Dialogue—1809

DEATH

Yes! my dagger is drenched with the blood of the brave.
I have sped with Love's wings from the battlefield grave

---

281 footstep . .] footstep. *SC*/IV
282 were,] were **EN** *SC*/IV
283 Nature,] Nature **EN** *SC*/IV
        Nature's *1964B*
    and] & **EN** *SC*/IV
    Heaven's] Heavens **EN** *SC*/IV
285 Law,] Law **EN** *SC*/IV
286 man,] man **EN** *SC*/IV
288 *Mine*—in] <u>Mine</u>—in **EN** *SC*/IV
    self-approving]
      self approving **EN** *SC*/IV

    pride.] pride **EN** *SC*/IV
290 *charity.*] <u>charity.</u> **EN** *SC*/IV
291 cries,] cries **EN** *SC*/IV
292 "Be] Be **EN** *SC*/IV
293 and] & **EN** *SC*/IV
294 and] & **EN** *SC*/IV
295 bring] bring [?buy] **EN**
      buy *SC*/IV
    thee.—Get] thee.—get **EN** *SC*/IV
298 misdeeds!"] misdeeds! **EN** *SC*/IV

Text collated with **EN,** MS TCC (lines 1–10, 13–30, 33–44), *1964B,* and *SC*/IV.
Title. A Dialogue—1809] *omitted* TCC
      A Dialogue | *1809* *1964B*
1 Yes!] —For TCC
  drenched with] bathed in TCC
  brave.] brav **EN** *SC*/IV
      brave TCC

2 have sped with Love's wings]
    come, care-worn tenant of life! TCC
  Love's] Loves **EN** *SC*/IV
  battlefield] battle field **EN** *SC*/IV
      omitted TCC
  grave] gra **EN** *SC*/IV
      grave, *1964B*

Where Ambition is hushed neath the peacegiving sod
And slaves cease to tremble at Tyranny's nod.
I offer a calm habitation to thee, 5
Victim of grief, wilt thou slumber with me?
Drear and damp is my hall, but a mild Judge is there
Who steeps in oblivion the brands of Despair.
Nor a groan of regret, nor a sigh, nor a breath
Dares dispute with grim Silence the empire of Death; 10
Nor the howlings of envy resound thro' the gloom
That shrouds in its mantle the slaves of the tomb.
I offer a calm habitation to thee;
Say, Victim of grief, wilt thou slumber with me?

MORTAL

Mine eyelids are heavy, my soul seeks repose— 15
It longs in thy arms to embosom its woes,
It longs in that realm to deposit its load
Where no longer the scorpions of perfidy goad,
Where the phantoms of Prejudice vanish away
And Bigotry's bloodhounds lose scent of their prey. 20

---

3 Ambition is hushed neath]
   Innocence sleeps 'neath   TCC
peacegiving] peace-giving   TCC
sod] sod,   *1964B*
4 slaves] the good   TCC
nod.] nod   **EN** TCC *SC/IV*
5 thee,] thee   **EN** TCC *SC/IV*
   thee;   *1964B*
6 Victim] Say, victim   TCC
grief,] grief   **EN** TCC *SC/IV*
me?] me,   TCC
7 Drear . . . Judge] Thy mansion is damp,
   cold silence   TCC
and] &   **EN** *SC/IV*
8 Who steeps] But it lulls   TCC
brands] fiends   TCC
Despair.] Despair   **EN** TCC *SC/IV*
9 Nor] Not   TCC
nor] not   TCC
nor] not   TCC
10 Silence] silence   TCC
   Death;] Death   **EN** TCC *SC/IV*

11 thro'] thro   **EN** *SC/IV*
12 tomb.] tomb   **EN** *SC/IV*
13 thee;] thee   **EN** *SC/IV*
   thee . .   TCC
14 Victim] victim   TCC
grief,] grief   **EN** TCC *SC/IV*
me?] me   **EN** *SC/IV*
15 repose—] repose   **EN** TCC *SC/IV*
   repose.   *1964B*
16 arms] cells   TCC
its] its'   TCC
woes,] woes   **EN** TCC *SC/IV*
   woes;   *1964B*
17 that realm] thy cells   TCC
its] its'   TCC
load] load,   TCC *1964B*
18 goad,] goad   **EN** TCC *SC/IV*
19 Prejudice] prejudice   TCC
20 Bigotry's] Bigotrys   **EN** *SC/IV*
bloodhounds] blood-hounds   TCC
   prey.] prey   **EN** TCC *SC/IV*

> Yet tell me, dark Death, when thine Empire is o'er
> What awaits on futurity's mist-circled shore?

DEATH

> Cease, cease, wayward mortal! I dare not unveil
> The shadows that float oer eternity's vale.
> What thinkest thou will wait thee? A *Spirit of Love
> That will hail thy blest advent to mansions above?
> For Love, mortal! gleams thro' the gloom of my sway
> And the clouds that surround me fly fast at its ray.
> Hast thou *loved?*—then depart from these regions of hate

*The author begs to be understood by this expression neither to mean the Creator of the Universe, nor the Christian Deity.—When this little poem was written the line stood thus, "What waits for the good?" but he has altered it on transcription, because however his feelings may love to linger on a future state of Happiness, neither Justice, reason nor passion can reconcile to his belief that the crimes of this life, equally necessary and inevitable as its virtues, should be punished in another:

> "Earth in itself
> "Contains at once the evil and the cure
> "And all sufficing Nature can chastize
> "Those who transgress her law."

---

21 me,] me **EN** TCC *SC*/IV
   Death,] DEath **EN** *SC*/IV
     Death! TCC
   o'er] oer **EN** *SC*/IV
22 futurity's] Futurity's TCC
   mist-circled] mist circled **EN** *SC*/IV
     mist-covered TCC
   shore?] shore **EN** *SC*/IV
23 Cease,] Cease **EN** TCC *SC*/IV
   cease,] cease **EN** TCC *SC*/IV
   mortal! I] mortal I **EN** *SC*/IV
     mortal! . I TCC
   unveil] unviel TCC
24 oer] on *1964B*
   eternity's] eternitys **EN** *SC*/IV
     Eternity's TCC
   vale.] vale TCC
25 What thinkest thou will wait thee?]
   Nought waits for the good but a
   TCC
   A] A* **EN** *SC*/IV
   *Spirit] Spirit **EN** *SC*/IV
     *spirit TCC
   Love] love TCC

Footnote. Deity.—When]
   Deity. When *1964B*
   thus,] thus **EN** *SC*/IV
   Justice,] Justice **EN** *SC*/IV
   life,] life **EN** *SC*/IV
   virtues,] virtues **EN** *SC*/IV
   another:] another **EN** *SC*/IV
   "Contains]
   Contains **EN** *SC*/IV
   and] & **EN** *SC*/IV
   law."] law" **EN**
26 thy] their TCC
   above?] above **EN** TCC *SC*/IV
27 Love,] Love **EN** *SC*/IV
     Love TCC
   mortal!] Mortal! TCC
   thro'] thro **EN** *SC*/IV
   my] my TCC
28 clouds that] shades which TCC
   ray.] ray **EN** TCC *SC*/IV
29 *loved?*—then]
   loved?—then **EN** *SC*/IV
   loved?—then TCC

And in slumber with me quench the arrows of fate   30
That canker and burn in the wounds of a heart
That urges its sorrows with me to depart.
I offer a calm habitation to thee;
Say, Victim of grief, wilt thou slumber with me?

MORTAL

Oh sweet is thy slumber, and sweeter the ray   35
Which after thy night introduces the day!
How soft, how persuasive, self-interest's breath
Tho' it floats to mine ear from the bosom of Death!
I hoped that I quite was forgotten by all,
Yet a lingering friend may be grieved at my fall,   40
And Virtue forbids, tho' I languish to die,
When Departure might heave Virtue's breast with a sigh.
Yet Death! oh! my friend, snatch this form to thy shrine
And I fear, dear destroyer, I shall not repine.

---

30 quench] blunt   TCC
   arrows] arrows'   TCC
31 and] &   **EN** *SC*/IV
32 its] it's   **EN** *SC*/IV
   depart.] depart   **EN** *SC*/IV
33 thee;] thee   **EN** *SC*/IV
      thee,   TCC
34 Say,] Say   TCC
   Victim] victim   TCC *1964B* *SC*/IV
   grief,] grief   **EN** *SC*/IV
35 Oh] Oh!   TCC
   and] &   **EN** *SC*/IV
     oh!   TCC
   sweeter] sweet is   TCC
36 day!] day   **EN** TCC *SC*/IV
37 soft,] soft   **EN** *SC*/IV
     concealed,   TCC
   persuasive,] persuasive   **EN** *SC*/IV
   self-interest's]
     self interest's   **EN** *SC*/IV
38 Tho'] Tho   **EN** *SC*/IV
   Death!] Death   **EN** *SC*/IV
     death   TCC

39 all,] all   **EN** TCC *SC*/IV
40 may] might   TCC
   fall,] fall   **EN** TCC *SC*/IV
41 Virtue] duty   TCC
     virtue   *1964B*
   tho'] tho   **EN** *SC*/IV
   die,] die   **EN** TCC *SC*/IV
42 Departure] departure   TCC
   Virtue's] Virtues   **EN** *SC*/IV
   sigh.] sigh   **EN** *SC*/IV
     sig<h>.   TCC
43 Yet Death! oh!] Oh! death, oh   TCC
   friend,] friend   **EN** TCC *SC*/IV
   shrine] shine   **EN** *SC*/IV
     shr<ine>   TCC
44 fear,] fear   **EN** TCC *SC*/IV
   destroyer,] destroyers   **EN** *SC*/IV
     destroyer   TCC
   repine.] repine   **EN** *SC*/IV
     repine.—   TCC

SUPPLEMENT

Version in Hogg Manuscript, ca. 1810

DEATH

    —For my dagger is bathed in the blood of the brave
    I come, care-worn tenant of life! from the grave
    Where Innocence sleeps 'neath the peace-giving sod
    And the good cease to tremble at Tyranny's nod
5   I offer a calm habitation to thee
    Say, victim of grief wilt thou slumber with me,
    Thy mansion is damp, cold silence is there
    But it lulls in oblivion the fiends of Despair
    Not a groan of regret, not a sigh, not a breath
10   Dares dispute with grim silence the empire of Death

13   I offer a calm habitation to thee . .
    Say, victim of grief wilt thou slumber with me

MORTAL

15   Mine eyelids are heavy, my soul seeks repose
    It longs in thy cells to embosom its' woes
    It longs in thy cells to deposit its' load,
    Where no longer the scorpions of perfidy goad
    Where the phantoms of prejudice vanish away
20   And Bigotry's blood-hounds lose scent of their prey
    Yet tell me dark Death! when thine Empire is o'er
    What awaits on Futurity's mist-covered shore?

DEATH

    Cease cease wayward mortal! . I dare not unviel
    The shadows that float oer Eternity's vale
25   Nought waits for the good but a spirit of love
    That will hail their blest advent to mansions above
    For Love Mortal! gleams thro' the gloom of my sway
    And the shades which surround me fly fast at its ray
    Hast thou loved?—then depart from these regions of hate
30   And in slumber with me blunt the arrows' of fate

33   I offer a calm habitation to thee,
    Say victim of grief, wilt thou slumber with me?

MORTAL

35   Oh! sweet is thy slumber, oh! sweet is the ray
    Which after thy night introduces the day
    How concealed, how persuasive, self-interest's breath

Tho' it floats to mine ear from the bosom of death
I hoped that I quite was forgotten by all
Yet a lingering friend might be grieved at my fall   40
And duty forbids, tho' I languish to die
When departure might heave Virtue's breast with a sig<h>.
Oh! death, oh my friend snatch this form to thy shr<ine>
And I fear dear destroyer I shall not repine.—

1810   [*Esd #34*]

How eloquent are eyes!
Not the rapt Poet's frenzied lay
When the soul's wildest feelings stray
   Can speak so well as they.
   How eloquent are eyes!   5
Not music's most impassioned note
On which love's warmest fervours float
   Like they bid rapture rise.

   Love! look thus again,
That your look may light a waste of years   10
Darting the beam that conquers cares
   Thro' the cold shower of tears!
   Love! look thus again,
That Time the victor as he flies
May pause to gaze upon thine eyes,   15
   A victor then in vain!—

   Yet no! arrest not Time,
For Time, to others dear, we spurn,
When Time shall *be* no more we burn

Text collated with **EN,** MS Pfz166 (lines 33–39), *SC*/II (lines 33–39), *1964B, 1964J* (lines 33–39), and *SC*/IV.

Title. 1810]
  How eloquent are eyes! | *1810 1964B*
2 Poet's] Poets **EN** *SC*/IV
  frenzied] frienzied **EN** *SC*/IV
  lay] lay, *1964B*
3 soul's] souls **EN** *SC*/IV
  stray] stray, *1964B*
4 they.] they **EN** *SC*/IV
6 music's] musics **EN** *SC*/IV
  note] note, *1964B*

7 love's] loves **EN** *SC*/IV
  float] float, *1964B*
8 rise.] rise **EN** *SC*/IV
9 again,] again **EN** *SC*/IV
12 Thro'] Thro **EN** *SC*/IV
13 again,] again **EN** *SC*/IV
15 eyes,] eyes **EN** *SC*/IV
17 Time,] Time **EN** *SC*/IV
18 Time,] Time **EN** *SC*/IV
19 *be*] <u>be</u> **EN** *SC*/IV

20   When Love meets full return.
            Ah no! arrest not Time.
        Fast let him fly on eagle wing,
        Nor pause till Heaven's unfading spring
            Breathes round its holy clime.

25   Yet quench that thrilling gaze
        Which passionate Friendship arms with fire,
        For what will eloquent eyes inspire
            But feverish, false desire?
        Quench then that thrilling gaze
30   For age may freeze the tremulous joy;
        But age can never *love* destroy.
            It lives to better days.

            Age cannot love destroy.
        Can perfidy then blight its flower
35   Even when in most unwary hour
        It blooms in fancy's bower?
            Age cannot love destroy.
        Can slighted vows then rend the shrine
        On which its chastened splendours shine
40   Around a dream of joy?

---

20 return.] return   **EN** *SC*/IV   35 Even] E'en   Pfz166 *SC*/II *1964J*
21 Time.] Time   **EN** *SC*/IV   36 fancy's] fancys   **EN** *SC*/IV
22 wing,] wing   **EN** *SC*/IV   Fancy's   Pfz166 *SC*/II *1964J*
23 Heaven's] Heavens   **EN** *SC*/IV   bower?] bower   Pfz166 *SC*/II *1964J*
24 clime.] clime   **EN** *SC*/IV   37 destroy.] destroy   **EN** Pfz166 *SC*/II
26 fire,] fire   **EN** *SC*/IV   *1964J* *SC*/IV
28 desire?] desire   **EN** *SC*/IV   38 Can slighted vows then]
30 joy;] joy   **EN** *SC*/IV   But Perfidy can   Pfz166 *SC*/II *1964J*
31 *love*] <u>love</u>   **EN** *SC*/IV   shrine] shine   **EN** *SC*/IV
32 days.] days   **EN** *SC*/IV   39 On] In   Pfz166 *SC*/II *1964J*
33 destroy.] destroy   **EN** Pfz166 *SC*/II   chastened]
       1964J *SC*/IV   vermeil   Pfz166 *SC*/II *1964J*
34 Can] But   Pfz166 *SC*/II *1964J*   splendours]
   then blight its]   splendors   Pfz166 *SC*/II *1964J*
      can blast the   Pfz166 *SC*/II *1964J*   40 joy?] joy   **EN** *SC*/IV

Version in Letter to Hogg, 18–19 June 1811

Age cannot love destroy   33
But perfidy can blast the flower
E'en when in most unwary hour   35
It blooms in Fancy's bower
Age cannot love destroy
But Perfidy can rend the shrine
In which its vermeil splendors shine
X   X   X

1810   [*Esd #35*]

Hopes that bud in youthful breasts
Live not thro' the lapse of time:
Love's rose a host of thorns invest
And ungenial is the clime
Where its blossoms blow.   5
Youth says—the purple flowers are mine
That fade the while they glow.

Dear the boon to Fancy given,
Retracted while 'tis granted.

Text collated with **EN**, MS Pfz166 (lines 1–14), *SC/II* (lines 1–14), *1964B*, *1964J* (lines 1–14), and *SC/IV*.

Title. 1810] *omitted* Pfz166 *SC/II 1964J*
     Hopes that bud in youthful
         breasts] *1810 1964B*
1 bud] swell Pfz166 *SC/II 1964J*
2 not] they Pfz166 *SC/II 1964J*
   thro'] thro **EN** *SC/IV*
   lapse] waste Pfz166 *SC/II 1964J*
   time:] time? . . . Pfz166 *SC/II*
     time; *1964B*
     time?— *1964J*
3 a] an Pfz166 *SC/II 1964J*
   invest] invests Pfz166 *SC/II 1964J*
     invest, *1964B*
4 And] Cold Pfz166 *SC/II 1964J*
   clime] clime. **EN** *SC/IV*
5 its] its' Pfz166 *SC/II*
     it's *1964J*

blossoms]
   honours Pfz166 *SC/II 1964J*
blow.]
   blow **EN** Pfz166 *SC/II 1964J SC/IV*
6 says—the] says . . the Pfz166 *SC/II*
7 That fade]
   Which die Pfz166 *SC/II 1964J*
   glow.]
   glow **EN** Pfz166 *SC/II 1964J SC/IV*
8 given,]
   given **EN** Pfz166 *SC/II 1964J SC/IV*
9 while] whilst Pfz166 *SC/II 1964J*
   'tis] tis **EN** *SC/IV*
     it's Pfz166 *SC/II 1964J*
   granted.] granted!—— —— Pfz166
     granted!——— *SC/II*
     granted— *1964J*

1810 ("Hopes that bud in youthful breasts")   *[Esd #35]*   91

10   Sweet the rose that breathes in Heaven
              Altho' on Earth 'tis planted,
              Where its blossoms blow,
          Where by the frosts its leaves are riven
             That fade the while they glow.

15   The pure soul lives that heart within
              Which age cannot remove
          If undefiled by tainting sin,
              A sanctuary of love
             Where its blossoms blow,
20   Where, in this unsullied shrine,
             They fade not while they glow.

SUPPLEMENT
Version in Letter to Hogg,
18–19 June 1811

Hopes that swell in youthful breasts
    Live they thro' the waste of time? . . .
Love's rose an host of thorns invests
    Cold ungenial is the clime
5   Where its' honours blow
Youth says . . the purple flowers are mine
    Which die the while they glow

Dear the boon to Fancy given
    Retracted whilst it's granted! —— ——
10   Sweet the rose which lives in Heaven
    Altho' on Earth 'tis planted
    Where its' honours blow
Where by Earth's slaves the leaves are riven

---

10 that breathes]
     which lives Pfz166 *SC/II 1964J*
11 Altho'] Altho **EN** *SC/IV*
   planted,] planten **EN** *SC/IV*
       planted Pfz166 *SC/II 1964J*
12 its] its' Pfz166 *SC/II*
     it's *1964J*
   blossoms]
    honours Pfz166 *SC/II 1964J*
   blow,]
    blow **EN** Pfz166 *SC/II 1964J SC/IV*

13 Where] While *1964J*
   the frosts its] Earth's slaves the Pfz166
     SC/II 1964J
14 That fade]
    Which die Pfz166 *SC/II 1964J*
   glow.] glow **EN** *SC/IV*
       glow. . . . | *series of four*
         elongated Xs Pfz166
17 sin,] sin **EN** *SC/IV*
     sin,— *1964B*
19 blow,] blow **EN** *SC/IV*
20 shrine,] shrine **EN** *SC/IV*

Which die the while they glow. . . .

X   X   X   X

September 23, 1809   [*Esd #36*]

Moonbeam! leave the shadowy dale
To cool this burning brow—
Moonbeam, why art thou so pale
As thou glidest along the midnight vale
   Where dewy flowrets grow?   5
     Is it to mimic me?
     Ah, that can never be;
     For thy path is bright
     And the clouds are light
That at intervals shadow the star-studded night.   10

Now all is deathy still on Earth,
   Nature's tired frame reposes;
Yet ere the golden morning's birth
   Its radiant gates uncloses,
     Flies forth her balmy breath;   15
     But mine is the midnight of death,

Text collated with **EN,** MS Pfz160, SC/II, 1964B, 1964J, and SC/IV.

Title. September 23, 1809]
    —To The Moonbeam Pfz160
    September 23. 1809 **EN** SC/IV
    To the Moonbeam | September 23.
      1809 *1964B*

1 Moonbeam!]
    Moonbeam, Pfz160 *SC*/II *1964J*
  dale] vale Pfz160 *SC*/II *1964J*

2 cool] bathe Pfz160 *SC*/II *1964J*
  brow—] brow Pfz160 *SC*/II *1964J*

3 Moonbeam,] Moonbeam **EN** *SC*/IV

4 glidest along the midnight] walkest oer
  the dewy Pfz160 *SC*/II *1964J*
  vale] dale Pfz160 *SC*/II *1964J*

5 dewy] humble wild Pfz160 *SC*/II *1964J*
  flowrets] flowers Pfz160 *SC*/II *1964J*
  grow?] glow [?grow] *SC*/IV
    grow Pfz160 *SC*/II *1964J*

7 Ah,] Ah **EN** *SC*/IV
    But Pfz160 *SC*/II *1964J*
  be;] be **EN** Pfz160 *SC*/II *1964J SC*/IV

8 thy path] thine orb Pfz160 *SC*/II *1964J*

10 star-studded] star studded Pfz160
    EN *SC*/II *1964J SC*/IV
  night.] night **EN** Pfz160 *SC*/II
    1964J SC/IV

11 Earth,] Earth **EN** Pfz160 *SC*/II *1964J*
  SC/IV

12 Nature's] Natures **EN** Pfz160 *SC*/II
    1964J SC/IV
  reposes;] reposes Pfz160 *SC*/II *1964J*

13 Yet] And Pfz160 *SC*/II *1964J*
  morning's] mornings **EN** Pfz160
    SC/II *1964J SC*/IV

14 Its] It's Pfz160 *SC*/II *1964J*
  gates] hues Pfz160 *SC*/II *1964J*
  uncloses,] uncloses **EN** *SC*/IV
    discloses Pfz160 *SC*/II *1964J*

15 her] its Pfz160 *SC*/II *1964J*
  breath;] breath **EN** *SC*/IV
    breath, Pfz160 *SC*/II *1964J*

16 death,] death **EN** Pfz160 *SC*/II *1964J*
    SC/IV

September 23, 1809 ("Moonbeam!")   [*Esd #36*]   93

And Nature's morn
To my bosom forlorn
Brings but a gloomier night, implants a deadlier thorn.

20   Wretch! suppress the glare of madness
Struggling in thine haggard eye,
For the keenest throb of sadness,
Pale despair's most sickening sigh,
Is but to mimic me.
25   But that can never be
When the darkness of care
And the death of despair
Seem in my breast but joys to the pangs that rankle there.

SUPPLEMENT

To the Moonbeam in Letter to Hogg, 17 May 1811

—TO THE MOONBEAM

Moonbeam, leave the shadowy vale
To bathe this burning brow
Moonbeam, why art thou so pale
As thou walkest oer the dewy dale
5   Where humble wild flowers grow
Is it to mimic me?
But that can never be
For thine orb is bright
And the clouds are light
10   That at intervals shadow the star studded night

Now all is deathy still on Earth
Natures tired frame reposes

---

17 Nature's] Natures   **EN** Pfz160 *SC*/IV
natures   *SC*/II *1964J*
18 To] to   Pfz160
19 thorn.] thorn   **EN** Pfz160 *SC*/II *1964J*
SC/IV
21 eye,] eye   **EN** Pfz160 *SC*/II *1964J*
SC/IV
22 sadness,] sadness   **EN** Pfz160 *SC*/II
1964J SC/IV
23 despair's] despairs   **EN** Pfz160 *SC*/II
1964J SC/IV

sigh,]
sigh   **EN** Pfz160 *SC*/II *1964J SC*/IV
24 me.] me   Pfz160 *SC*/II *1964J*
25 But that can never] And this must ever
Pfz160 *SC*/II *1964J*
26 darkness] twilight   Pfz160 *SC*/II
1964J
27 death] night   Pfz160 *SC*/II *1964J*
28 rankle] walk   Pfz160 *SC*/II
[?walk]   *1964J*
there.]
there   **EN** Pfz160 *SC*/II *1964J SC*/IV

And ere the golden mornings birth
It's radiant hues discloses
Flies forth its balmy breath, 15
But mine is the midnight of death
And Natures morn
to my bosom forlorn
Brings but a gloomier night, implants a deadlier thorn

Wretch! suppress the glare of madness 20
Struggling in thine haggard eye
For the keenest throb of sadness
Pale despairs most sickening sigh
Is but to mimic me
And this must ever be 25
When the twilight of care
And the night of despair
Seem in my breast but joys to the pangs that walk there

[Poems about Mary]

Advertisement

The few poems immediately following are selected from many written during three weeks of an entrancement caused by hearing Mary's story——I hope that the delicate and discriminating genius of the friend who related it to me will allow the publication of the heart-breaking facts under the title of Leonora.—For myself at that time: nondum, amabam, et amare amabum, quaerebam quid amerem, amans amare.*

Mary died three months before I heard her tale.—

NOVEMBER 1810

---

* Confess. St. Augustin.

Text collated with **EN,** *1964B*, and *SC*/IV.
Title. [Poems about Mary]]
    omitted **EN** *SC*/IV
    Poems to Mary *1964B*
2 Mary's] Marys **EN** *SC*/IV
   story——I] story- —I *SC*/IV
3 and] & **EN** *SC*/IV

4 me] me, **EN** *SC*/IV
   heart-breaking]
    heart breaking **EN** *SC*/IV
5 Leonora.—For] Leonora. —For *SC*/IV
   time:] time **EN** *SC*/IV
   nondum,] nondum **EN** *1964B SC*/IV
   amabum,] amabam, **EN** *1964B SC*/IV
6 amerem,] amarem, **EN** *1964B SC*/IV
   amare.*] amare* **EN** *SC*/IV
Footnote. St.] S^t **EN** *SC*/IV

> Dear girl! thou art wildered by madness,
>   Yet do not look so, sweet.
> I could share in the sigh of thy sadness,
>   Thy woe my soul could meet.

5   I loved a heart sincerely.
>   Yes! dear it was to mine;
> Yet, Mary, I love more dearly
>   One tender look of thine.

> Oh! do not say that Heaven
10   Will frown on errors past;
> Thy faults are all forgiven,
>   Thy Virtues ever last.*

> The cup with death o'erflowing
>   I'll drink, fair girl, to thee.
15 For when the storm is blowing
>   To shelter we may flee.

* This opinion is of all others the most deeply rooted in my conviction. The enquirer will laugh at it as a dream, the Christian will abhor it as a blasphemy.—Mary, who repeatedly attempted suicide, yet was unwilling to die alone.—Nor is it probable that she would, had I instead of my friend been subjected to the trial of sitting a summer's night by her side.—whilst two glasses of poison stood on the table, and she folded me to her tremulous bosom in extasies of friendship and despair!— ~~What are the Romances of Leadenhall Str. to this of real life?~~

Text collated with **EN,** *1964B,* and *SC/IV.*

1 madness,] madness   **EN** *SC/IV*

2 so,] so   **EN** *SC/IV*

  sweet.] sweet   **EN** *SC/IV*

3 sadness,] sadness   **EN** *SC/IV*

4 meet.] meet   **EN** *SC/IV*

6 mine;] mine   **EN** *SC/IV*

7 Yet,] Yet   **EN** *SC/IV*

  Mary,] Mary   **EN** *SC/IV*

8 thine.] thine   **EN** *SC/IV*

10 past;] past   **EN** *SC/IV*

11 forgiven,] forgiven.   **EN** *SC/IV*

12 Virtues] virtues   *SC/IV*

  last.*] last   **EN** *SC/IV*

Footnote. blasphemy.—Mary,]

  blasphemy—Mary,   *1964B*

alone.—Nor]

  alone—Nor   **EN** *SC/IV*

summer's] summers   **EN**

  summer   *1964B SC/IV*

side.—whilst]

  side—whilst   *1964B*

and] &   **EN** *SC/IV*

and] &   **EN** *SC/IV*

13 o'erflowing] oerflowing   **EN** *SC/IV*

14 drink,] drink   **EN** *SC/IV*

  girl,] girl   **EN** *SC/IV*

16 flee.] flee   **EN** *SC/IV*

Thou canst not bear to languish
    In this frail chain of clay,
And I am tired of anguish.
    Love! let us haste away!   20

Like thee, I fear to weather
    Death's darksome wave alone.
We'll take the voyage together.
    Come, Mary! let's begone.

Strange mists my woe efface, love,   25
    And thou art pale in Death . . . .
Give one, one last embrace, love,
    And we resign our breath.

To Mary II   [Esd #38]

Fair one! calm that bursting heart . . . .
    Dares then fate to frown on thee,
Lovely, spotless as thou art?
    Tho' its worst poison lights on me,
        Then dry that tear;   5
        Thou needest not fear
These woes when thy limbs are cold on the bier.

Start not from winter's breathing, dearest,
    Tho' bleak is yonder hill . . .
As perjured love the blast thou fearest   10

---

18 clay,] clay **EN** *SC*/IV

19 anguish.] anguish **EN** *SC*/IV

21 thee,] thee **EN** *SC*/IV

22 Death's] Deaths **EN** *SC*/IV
  alone.] alone **EN**

23 together.] together **EN** *SC*/IV

24 Come,] Come **EN** *SC*/IV
  let's] lets **EN** *SC*/IV
  begone.] begone **EN** *SC*/IV

25 efface,] efface **EN** *SC*/IV
  love,] love **EN** *SC*/IV

26 Death . . . .] Death. . . . *1964B*

27 embrace,] embrace **EN** *SC*/IV
  love,] love **EN** *SC*/IV

28 breath.] breath **EN** *SC*/IV

Text collated with **EN,** *1964B,* and *SC*/IV.

2 thee,] thee **EN** *SC*/IV

3 Lovely,] Lovely **EN** *SC*/IV
  spotless] spotless, *1964B*
  art?] art, *1964B*

4 Tho'] Tho **EN** *SC*/IV
  me,] me **EN** *SC*/IV
   me? *1964B*

5 tear;] tear **EN** *SC*/IV

7 bier.] bier **EN** *SC*/IV

8 winter's] winters **EN** *SC*/IV
  breathing,] breathing **EN** *SC*/IV
  dearest,] dearest **EN** *SC*/IV

9 Tho'] Tho **EN** *SC*/IV

Is not half so deadly chill;
  Like these winds that blow
  No remorse does it know
And colder it strikes than the driving snow.

15 The tomb is damp and dark and low,
  Yet with thee the tomb I do not dread.
There is not a place of frightful woe
  Where with thee I'd refuse to lay my head . . .
  But our souls shall not sleep
20 In the grave damp and deep
But in love and devotion their holy day keep.*

[*Esd* #39]   To Mary III

Mary, Mary! art thou gone
  To sleep in thine earthy cell?
Presses thy breast the death-cold stone?
Pours none the tear, the sob, the groan,
5 Where murdered virtue sleeps alone
  Where its first glory fell?

Mary, Mary, past is past!
  I submit in silence to fate's decree,
Tho' the tear of distraction gushes fast
10 And at night when the lank reeds hiss in the blast
  My spirit mourns in sympathy.

---

* The expression *devotion,* is not used in a religious sense; for which abuse of this lovely word, few have a greater horror than the Author.

11 chill;] chill **EN** *SC*/IV   20 and] & **EN** *SC*/IV
14 snow.] snow **EN** *SC*/IV   21 and] & **EN** *SC*/IV
15 and] & **EN** *SC*/IV   Footnote. *devotion,*] <u>devotion,</u> **EN** *SC*/IV
 and] & **EN** *SC*/IV   sense;] sense, *SC*/IV
 low,] low **EN** *SC*/IV   Author.] Author **EN** *SC*/IV
16 dread.] dread **EN** *SC*/IV

Text collated with **EN,** *1964B,* and *SC*/IV. In the MS, PBS indicates that lines 24 and 25 are to be transposed. The Text reflects this change.

3 death-cold] death cold **EN** *SC*/IV   8 fate's] fates **EN** *SC*/IV
 stone?] stone **EN** *SC*/IV   decree,] decree. **EN** *SC*/IV
4 groan,] groan **EN** *SC*/IV   9 Tho'] Tho **EN** *SC*/IV
6 fell?] fell **EN** *SC*/IV   11 sympathy.] sympathy **EN** *SC*/IV
7 Mary, Mary,] Mary Mary **EN** *SC*/IV

Thou wert more fair in mind than are
    The fabled heavenly train,
But thine was the pang of corroding care,
Thine, cold contempt and lone despair   15
And thwarted love—more hard to bear . . .
And I—wretch!—weep that such they were,
    And I . . . . still drag my chain.

Thou wert but born to weep, to die,
To feel dissolved the dearest tie—   20
Its fragments by the pityless world
Adown the blast of fortune hurl'd
To strive with envy's wreckful storm.
Thou wert but born to weep and die,
Nor could thy ceaseless misery,   25
Nor heavenly virtues aught avail,
Nor taintless innocence prevail
With the world's slaves thy love to spare,
Nor the magic unearthly atmosphere
    That wrapt thine ethereal form.   30

Such, loveliest Mary, was thy fate,
    And such is Virtue's doom . . . .
Contempt, neglect and hatred wait
Where yawns a wide and dreary gate
    To drag its votaries to the tomb.   35

---

13 train,] train **EN** *SC*/IV
14 care,] care **EN** *SC*/IV
15 Thine,] Thine **EN** *SC*/IV
   and] & **EN** *SC*/IV
16 love—more] love more **EN** *SC*/IV
   bear . . .] bear. . . *SC*/IV
17 I—wretch!—weep]
    I wretch! weep **EN** *SC*/IV
   were,] were **EN** *SC*/IV
18 I . . . .] I . . . . *1964B* *SC*/IV
   chain.] chain **EN** *SC*/IV
19 die,] die **EN** *SC*/IV
20 tie—] tie **EN** *SC*/IV
22 hurl'd] hurld **EN** *SC*/IV
23 envy's] envys **EN** *SC*/IV
   storm.] storm **EN** *SC*/IV
24 Thou] 1 Thou **EN** *SC*/IV

and] & **EN** *SC*/IV
die,] die **EN** *SC*/IV
25 Nor] 2 Nor **EN** *SC*/IV
   misery,] misery **EN** *SC*/IV
26 avail,] avail **EN** *SC*/IV
28 spare,] spare **EN** *SC*/IV
30 ethereal] etherial **EN** *SC*/IV
   form.] form **EN** *SC*/IV
31 Such,] Such **EN** *SC*/IV
   Mary,] Mary **EN** *SC*/IV
   fate,] fate **EN** *SC*/IV
32 Virtue's] Virtues **EN** *SC*/IV
   doom . . . .] doom. . . . *SC*/IV
33 Contempt,] Contempt **EN** *SC*/IV
   and] & **EN** *SC*/IV
34 and] & **EN** *SC*/IV
35 tomb.] tomb **EN** *SC*/IV

Sweet flower! that blooms amid the weeds
Where the dank serpent, interest, feeds!

[*Esd #40*]   To the Lover of Mary

Drink the exhaustless moonbeam where its glare
      Wanly lights murdered virtue's funeral
      And tremulous sheds on the corpse-shrouding pall
            A languid, languid flare . . . . .
5   Hide thee, poor Wretch, where yonder baleful yew
      Sheds o'er the clay that now is tenantless—
      Whose spirit once thrilled to thy warm caress—
            Its deadly, deadly dew.
      The moon-ray will not quench thy misery,
10   But the yew's death-drops will bring peace to thee,
      And yonder clay-cold grave thy bridal bed shall be.

      And since the Spirit dear that breathes of Heaven
            Has burst the powerless bondage of its clay
            And soars an Angel to eternal day,
15   Purged of its earthly leaven,
      Thy yearnings now shall bend thee to the tomb,
            Oblivion blot a life without a stain
            And death's cold hand round thy heart's ceaseless pain
                  Enfold its veil of gloom.
20   The wounds shall close of Misery's scorpion goad

---

37 serpent,] serpent **EN** *SC/IV*   misery,] misery **EN** *SC/IV*
     interest,] interest **EN** *SC/IV*   10 yew's] yews **EN** *SC/IV*
     feeds!] feeds **EN** *SC/IV*   death-drops] death drops **EN** *SC/IV*
                                                         thee,] thee **EN** *SC/IV*
Text collated with **EN,** *1964B,* and *SC/IV.*   11 clay-cold] clay cold **EN** *SC/IV*
2 virtue's] virtues **EN** *SC/IV*   be.] be **EN** *SC/IV*
4 languid,] languid **EN** *SC/IV*   14 day,] day **EN** *SC/IV*
     flare . . . . .] flare. . . . . *SC/IV* 15 leaven,] leaven **EN** *SC/IV*
5 thee,] thee **EN** *SC/IV*   16 tomb,] tomb **EN** *SC/IV*
6 o'er] oer **EN** *SC/IV*   17 stain] stain, *1964B*
     tenantless—] tenantless **EN** *SC/IV*   18 death's] deaths **EN** *SC/IV*
7 caress—] caress **EN** *SC/IV*   heart's] hearts **EN** *SC/IV*
8 dew.] dew **EN** *SC/IV*   19 veil] viel **EN** *SC/IV*
9 moon-ray] moon ray **EN** *SC/IV*   gloom.] gloom **EN** *SC/IV*

When Mary greets thee in her blest abode
And worships holy Love, in purity thy God.

O this were joy! and such as none would fear
    To purchase by a life of passing woe,
    For on this earth the sickly flowers that glow   25
      Breathe of perfection there.
Yet live—for others barter thine own bliss,
    And living shew what towering Virtue dares
    To accomplish even in this vale of tears:
      Turn Hell to Paradise,   30
And spurning selfish joy soar high above
The Heaven of Heavens, let ever eternal *love
Despised awhile, thy sense of holier *Virtue prove.

1810   [*Esd #41*]

Dares the Lama, most fleet of the Sons of the Wind,
    The Lion to rouse from his lair?
When the tyger awakes, can the fast-fleeting hind
    Repose trust in his footsteps of air?
No—abandoned it sinks in helpless despair;   5
    The monster transfixes his prey,

* As if they were not synonimous!

---

21 When] When [?Where] **EN**
        [?When] *SC*/IV
22 God.] God **EN** *SC*/IV
23 and] & **EN** *SC*/IV
24 woe,] woe **EN** *SC*/IV
27 bliss,] bliss **EN** *SC*/IV

30 Paradise,] Paradise **EN** *SC*/IV
32 *love] love **EN** *SC*/IV
33 holier] holeir **EN** *SC*/IV
    prove.] prove **EN** *SC*/IV
Footnote. As] as **EN** *SC*/IV

Text collated with **EN**, MS TCU, *1964B*, *1964J*, and *SC*/IV.
Title. 1810] *omitted* TCU
      Dares the Lama | *1810 1964B*
1 Lama,] Lama **EN** *SC*/IV
      lama TCU *1964J*
  Sons] sons TCU *1964J*
  Wind,] Wind **EN** *SC*/IV
      wind TCU *1964J*
2 lair?] scull covered lair TCU *1964J*
3 awakes,] awakes TCU *1964J*
  fast-fleeting]
    fast fleeting **EN** TCU *1964J SC*/IV

4 air?] air TCU *1964J*
5 No—abandoned]
    No!—abandoned TCU *1964J*
  it] he TCU *1964J*
  helpless] a trance of TCU *1964J*
  despair;]
    despair **EN** TCU *1964J SC*/IV
6 prey,] prey **EN** TCU *1964J SC*/IV
    prey; *1964B*

On the sand flows its life-blood away,
And the rocks and the woods to the death-yells reply
Protracting the horrible harmony.

10   Yet the fowl of the desert when danger encroaches
Dares dreadless to perish, defending her brood,
Tho' the fiercest of cloud-piercing tyrants approaches,
Thirsting—aye, thirsting for blood—
And demands, like mankind, his brother for food,
15   Yet more lenient, more gentle, than they;
For hunger, not glory, the prey
Must perish—revenge does not howl o'er the dead,
Nor ambition with fame bind the murderer's head.

Tho' weak as the Lama that bounds on the Mountains
20   And endued not with fast-fleeting footsteps of air,
Yet, yet will I draw from the purest of fountains,

---

7 its] his   TCU *1964J*
  life-blood]
    life blood   **EN** TCU *1964J* SC/IV
  away,] away   TCU *1964J*
8 And the rocks and the]
    Whilst India's rocks to his   TCU *1964J*
  and] &   **EN** SC/IV
  death-yells] death yells   **EN** SC/IV
  reply] reply,   *1964B*
9 harmony.]
    harmony   **EN** TCU *1964J* SC/IV
10 desert] desert   TCU *1964J*
11 Dares] Dare   TCU
  dreadless] fearless   TCU *1964J*
  perish,] perish   TCU *1964J*
  brood,] brood [?blood]   **EN** SC/IV
    brood   TCU *1964J*
12 Tho'] Tho   **EN** TCU *1964J* SC/IV
  cloud-piercing]
    [—?—] cloud-piercing   TCU
  approaches,]
    approaches   **EN** TCU *1964J* SC/IV
13 Thirsting—aye,]
    Thirsting—aye   **EN** SC/IV
  blood—]
    blood   **EN** TCU *1964J* SC/IV
14 demands,]
    demands   **EN** TCU *1964J* SC/IV

mankind,]
  mankind   **EN** TCU *1964J* SC/IV
  food,] food   **EN** TCU *1964J* SC/IV
15 lenient,]
  lenient   **EN** TCU *1964J* SC/IV
  gentle,] gentle   **EN** TCU *1964J* SC/IV
  they;] they   **EN** TCU *1964J* SC/IV
16 hunger,] h<u>un</u>ger,   TCU
    hunger,   1964J
  glory,] glory   **EN** TCU *1964J* SC/IV
17 perish—revenge]
  perish . .   Revenge   TCU
  perish. Revenge   *1964J*
  o'er] oer   **EN** SC/IV
    in   *1964J*
  dead,] dead   **EN** TCU *1964J* SC/IV
18 bind] crown   TCU *1964J*
  head.] head   **EN** TCU *1964J* SC/IV
19 Tho'] Tho   **EN** TCU *1964J* SC/IV
  Mountains] mountains   TCU *1964J*
20 fast-fleeting]
  fast fleeting   **EN** TCU SC/IV
  fa[st] fleeting   *1964J*
  air,] air   **EN** TCU *1964J* SC/IV
21 Yet, yet] Yet yet   TCU *1964J*
  from] fr[om]   *1964J*
  fountains,]
    fountains   **EN** TCU *1964J* SC/IV

Tho' a fiercer than tygers is there,
Tho' more frightful than death it scatters despair,
And its shadow, eclipsing the day,
Spreads the darkness of deepest dismay   25
O'er the withered and withering nations around
And the war-mangled corpses that rot on the ground.

They came to the fountain to draw from its stream
Waves too poisonously lovely for mortals to see;
They basked for awhile in the love-darting beam   30
Then perished—and perished like me,
For in vain from the grasp of Religion I flee:
The most tenderly loved of my soul
Are slaves to its chilling control . . .
It pursues me. It blasts me. Oh! where shall I fly?   35
What remains but to curse it, to curse it and die?

---

22 tygers] ty[gers]   TCU
             ty[ger]   *1964J*
    there,] there   **EN** TCU *1964J* *SC*/IV
23 Tho'] Tho   TCU *1964J*
    frightful] dreadful   TCU *1964J*
    death] Death,   TCU *1964J*
    despair,]
        despair   **EN** TCU *1964J* *SC*/IV
24 And] Tho   TCU *1964J*
    its] its'   TCU
        it's   *1964J*
    shadow,]
        shadow   **EN** TCU *1964J* *SC*/IV
    eclipsing] eclipses   TCU *1964J*
    day,] day   **EN** TCU *1964J* *SC*/IV
25 Spreads] And   TCU *1964J*
26 O'er] Oer   **EN** *SC*/IV
        Spreads   TCU *1964J*
    withered and withering nations]
        influence of soul-chilling terror
            TCU *1964J*
    and] &   **EN** *SC*/IV
27 the war-mangled]
        lowers on the   TCU *1964J*
    ground.]
        ground   **EN** TCU *1964J* *SC*/IV
29 poisonously lovely]
        pure too celestial   TCU *1964J*

see;] see   **EN** TCU *1964J* *SC*/IV
30 basked] bathed   *1964J*
    the love-darting]
        its silvery   TCU *1964J*
31 perished—and]
        perished—&   **EN** *SC*/IV
        perished, &   TCU *1964J*
    me,] me   **EN** TCU *1964J* *SC*/IV
32 Religion] religion   TCU *1964J*
    flee:] flee   **EN** *1964J* *SC*/IV
            fle   TCU
            flee.   *1964B*
34 its] it's   **EN** *SC*/IV
    chilling] hated   TCU *1964J*
    control . . .] control. . .   *1964B* *SC*/IV
                control   TCU *1964J*
35 me. It blasts me. Oh!]
        me, it blasts me! ah   TCU
        me, it blasts me! oh   *1964J*
    It] it   **EN** *SC*/IV
    fly?] fly   **EN** TCU *1964J* *SC*/IV
36 What remains but to curse it, to
        curse it] *underscored in*   TCU
    and die?] & die   **EN** *1964J* *SC*/IV
                <u>& die</u>   TCU

SUPPLEMENT

Version in Letter to Hogg, 20 April 1811

Dares the lama   most fleet of the sons of the wind
   The Lion to rouse from his scull covered lair
When the tyger awakes can the fast fleeting hind
   Repose trust in his footsteps of air
5   No!— abandoned he sinks in a trance of despair
   The monster transfixes his prey
   On the sand flows his life blood away
Whilst India's rocks to his death-yells reply
   Protracting the horrible harmony

10 Yet the fowl of the desert when danger encroaches
   Dare fearless to perish defending her brood
Tho the fiercest of [—?—] cloud-piercing tyrants
    approaches
   Thirsting—aye, thirsting for blood
And demands like mankind his brother for food
15   Yet more lenient more gentle than they
   For h<u>ung</u>er, not glory the prey
Must perish . . Revenge does not howl o'er the dead
Nor ambition with fame crown the murderer's head

Tho weak as the Lama that bounds on the mountains
20   And endued not with fast fleeting footsteps of air
Yet yet will I draw from the purest of fountains
   Tho' a fiercer than ty[gers] is there
Tho more dreadful than Death, it scatters despair
   Tho its' shadow eclipses the day
25   And the darkness of deepest dismay
Spreads the influence of soul-chilling terror around
And lowers on the corpses that rot on the ground

They came to the fountain to draw from its stream
   Waves too pure too celestial for mortals to see
30 They basked for awhile in its silvery beam
   Then perished, & perished like me
For in vain from the grasp of religion I fle
   The most tenderly loved of my soul
   Are slaves to its hated control
35 It pursues me, it blasts me! ah where shall I fly
   <u>What remains but to curse it, to curse it & die</u>

I will kneel at thine altar, will crown thee with bays.
   Whether God, Love or Virtue thou art,
Thou shalt live . . . aye! more long than these perishing lays
   Thou shalt live in this high-beating heart.
Dear love! from its life-strings thou never shalt part,   5
     Tho' Prejudice clanking her chain,
     Tho' Interest groaning in gain,
May tell me thou closest to Heaven the door,
May tell me that thine is the way to be poor.

The victim of merciless tyranny's power   10
   May smile at his chains if with thee;
The most sense-enslaved loiterer in Passion's sweet bower
   Is a wretch if unhallowed by thee.
Thine, thine is the bond that alone binds the free.
     Can the free worship bondage? nay, more,   15
     What they feel not, believe not, adore
What if felt, if believed, if existing must give
To thee to create, to eternize, to live.—

For Religion more keen than the blasts of the North
   Darts its frost thro' the self-palsied soul;   20
Its slaves on the work of destruction go forth;
   The divinest emotions that roll
Submit to the rod of its impious control.
   At the venomous blast of its breath

Text collated with **EN**, *1964B*, and *SC*/IV.

Title. 1809] I will kneel at thine altar |
     1809 *1964B*

1 bays.] bays **EN** *SC*/IV

2 God,] God **EN** *SC*/IV

   art,] art **EN** *SC*/IV

3 live . . .] live . . . *SC*/IV

4 high-beating] high beating **EN** *SC*/IV

   heart.] heart **EN** *SC*/IV

5 life-strings] life strings **EN** *SC*/IV

   shalt] shall **EN** *1964B* *SC*/IV

   part,] part **EN** *SC*/IV

6 Tho'] Tho **EN** *SC*/IV

   chain,] chain **EN** *SC*/IV

7 Tho'] Tho **EN** *SC*/IV

   gain,] gain **EN** *SC*/IV

8 door,] door **EN** *SC*/IV

9 poor.] poor **EN** *SC*/IV

10 tyranny's] tyrannys **EN** *SC*/IV

14 free.] free **EN** *SC*/IV

15 nay,] nay **EN** *SC*/IV

   more,] more **EN** *SC*/IV

16 not,] not **EN** *SC*/IV

   adore] adore— *1964B*

17 felt,] I felt, *SC*/IV

   believed,] believed **EN** *SC*/IV

18 live.—] live— *1964B*

20 soul;] soul **EN** *SC*/IV

21 forth;] forth **EN** *SC*/IV

23 Submit to]
     Submit—to **EN** *1964B* *SC*/IV

   control.] control **EN** *SC*/IV

24 venomous] venemous **EN** *1964B*

   breath] breath, *1964B*

25   Love, concord, lies gasping in death,
             Philanthropy utters a war-drowned cry
             And selfishness, conquering, cries Victory!

             Can we then thus tame, thus impassive behold
               That alone whence our life springs destroyed?
30   Shall Prejudice, Priestcraft, Opinion and Gold—
               Every passion with interest alloyed—
             Where Love ought to reign, fill the desolate void?
               But the Avenger arises, the throne
               Of selfishness totters, its groan
35   Shakes the nations.—It falls, love seizes the sway;
             The sceptre it bears unresisted away.

[*Esd #43*]   Fragment of a Poem,
                          the original idea of which
                     was suggested by the cowardly and infamous
                         bombardment of Copenhagen

                    x x x x x x x x x x x x x x x x x x x

             The ice mountains echo, the Baltic, the Ocean
               Where cold sits enthroned on its solium of snow:
             Even Spitzbergen perceives the terrific commotion.

---

25 concord,] concord   **EN** *SC*/IV   30 Prejudice,] Prejudice   **EN** *SC*/IV
    death,] death   **EN** *SC*/IV   and] &   **EN** *SC*/IV
26 war-drowned]   Gold—] Gold   **EN** *SC*/IV
      war drowned   **EN** *SC*/IV   31 alloyed—] alloyed   **EN** *SC*/IV
27 selfishness,] selfishness   **EN** *SC*/IV 32 reign,] reign   **EN** *SC*/IV
      conquering,] conquering   **EN** *SC*/IV 34 its] it's   **EN** *SC*/IV
28 we] we,   *1964B*   35 nations.—It] nations.—it   **EN** *SC*/IV
    then] then,   *1964B*   sway;] sway   **EN** *SC*/IV
29 destroyed?] destroyed   **EN** *SC*/IV   36 away.] away   **EN** *SC*/IV

Text collated with **EN,** MS Pfz132 (lines 1–14), *SC*/II (lines 1–14), *1964J* (lines 1–14), *1964B,*
and *SC*/IV.

Title.] *omitted*   Pfz132 *SC*/II *1964J*   its] his   Pfz132 *SC*/II *1964J*
        and] &   **EN** *SC*/IV   solium] column   *SC*/II
1 ice mountains]   snow:] snow   Pfz132 *SC*/II *1964J*
     ice-mountains   Pfz132 *SC*/II *1964J*   3 Even] E'en   Pfz132 *SC*/II *1964J*
     echo,] echo.   Pfz132 *SC*/II   perceives] percieves   **EN** *SC*/IV
2 cold] Cold   Pfz132 *SC*/II *1964J*   commotion.] commotion   **EN** Pfz132
     enthroned] enthoned   Pfz132   *SC*/II *1964J* *SC*/IV

The roar floats on the whirlwinds of sleet as they blow,
Blood clots with the streams as half frozen they flow,   5
Lurid flame o'er the cities the meteors of war
And mix their deep gleam with the bright polar glare.

Yes! the arms of Britannia victorious are bearing
Fame, triumph and terror wherever they spread.
Her Lion his crest o'er the nations is rearing,   10
Ruin follows . . . it tramples the dying and dead . . .
But her countrymen fall . . . the bloodreeking bed
Of the battle-slain sends a complaint-breathing sigh;
It is mixed with the shoutings of victory.

I see the lone female. The sun is descending—   15
Dank carnage-smoke sheds an ensanguining glare.

---

4 blow,]
  blow   **EN** Pfz132 *SC*/II *1964J SC*/IV
5 Blood clots with]
  <Bloo>d tinges   Pfz132 *1964J*
  <   >d tinges   *SC*/II
  <Bloo>d tinges   *1964J*
  flow,]
  flow   **EN** Pfz132 *SC*/II *1964J SC*/IV
6 Lurid . . . war] <Th>e meteors of war's
  lurid flame thro' the air   Pfz132
  <   >e meteors of war lurid flame thro'
    the air   *SC*/II
  <Th>e meteors of war lurid flame thro'
    the air   *1964J*
  o'er] oer   **EN** *SC*/IV
7 And] They   Pfz132 *SC*/II *1964J*
  deep] bright   Pfz132 *SC*/II *1964J*
  bright] red   Pfz132 *SC*/II *1964J*
  polar] Polar   Pfz132 *SC*/II
  glare.] glare   **EN** *SC*/IV
      line break followed by series of Xs
        Pfz132 *SC*/II *1964J*
9 Fame,] Fame   **EN** *SC*/IV
  triumph]
    Triumph   Pfz132 *SC*/II *1964J*
  and] &   **EN** Pfz132 *SC*/II *1964J SC*/IV
  terror] Glory   Pfz132 *SC*/II *1964J*
  spread.] spread   **EN** *SC*/IV
        spead   Pfz132 *SC*/II *1964J*
10 o'er]
    oer   **EN** Pfz132 *SC*/II *1964J SC*/IV

rearing,] rearing   **EN** *SC*/IV
        rearing;   Pfz132 *SC*/II *1964J*
11 follows . . .]
    follows!   Pfz132 *SC*/II *1964J*
        follows. . . .   *SC*/IV
    and] &   **EN** Pfz132 *SC*/II *1964J SC*/IV
    dead . . .] dead   Pfz132 *SC*/II *1964J*
        dead. . .   *SC*/IV
12 But her] Thy   Pfz132 *SC*/II *1964J*
    fall . . .] fall,   Pfz132 *SC*/II *1964J*
        fall. . .   *SC*/IV
    bloodreeking] ~~complaint-breathing~~
      ~~sigh~~ blood-reeking   Pfz132 *SC*/II
        blood-reeking   *1964J*
13 battle-slain] battle slain   **EN** *SC*/IV
    complaint-breathing] complaint
      breathing   **EN** Pfz132 *SC*/IV
    sigh;]
      sigh   **EN** Pfz132 *SC*/II *1964J SC*/IV
14 victory.] victory   **EN** *SC*/IV
        Victory!   Pfz132 *SC*/II
        Victory.   *1964J*
15 The] the   *SC*/IV
    descending—]
      descending   **EN** *1964B SC*/IV
16 carnage-smoke]
    carnage smoke   **EN** *SC*/IV
    glare.] glare   **EN** *SC*/IV

Night its shades in the orient earlier is blending
    Yet the light faintly marks a wild maniac's stare.
    She lists to the death shrieks that came on the air,
20   The pride of her heart to her bosom she prest,
    Then sunk on his form in the sleep of the blest.

SUPPLEMENT
Version in Letter to Hogg, 11 January 1811

Yes! the arms of Britannia victorious are bearing
    Fame, Triumph & Glory wherever they spead
[10]   Her Lion his crest oer the nations is rearing;
    Ruin follows! it tramples the dying & dead
5   Thy countrymen fall, the ~~complaint breathing sigh bed~~
                   blood-reeking bed
    Of the battle-slain sends a complaint breathing sigh
[14]   It is mixed with the shoutings of Victory!

Old Ocean to shrieks of Despair is resounding
    It washes the terror-struck nations with gore
10   Wild horror the fear-palsied Earth is astounding
    And murmurs of fate fright the dread-convulsed shore
The Andes in Sympathy start at the roar
    Vast Aetna alarmed leans his flame-glowing brow
    And huge Teneriffe stoops with his pinnacled snow.

15 [1]   The ice-mountains echo. the Baltic, the Ocean
    Where Cold sits enthroned on his solium of snow
E'en Spitzbergen perceives the terrific commotion
    The roar floats on the whirlwinds of sleet as they blow
[5]   <Bloo>d tinges the streams as half frozen they flow
20   <Th>e meteors of war's lurid flame thro' the air
[7]   They mix their bright gleam with the red Polar glare.
    X   X   X   X   X   X   X   X
All are Bretheren,— the African bending
    To the stroke of the hard hearted Englishmans rod

---

18 maniac's] maniacs **EN** *SC/IV*   20 prest,] prest **EN** *SC/IV*
   stare.] stare **EN** *SC/IV*   21 blest.] blest **EN** *SC/IV*
19 shrieks] shieks **EN** *SC/IV*
   air,] air **EN** *SC/IV*

The courtier at Luxury's Palace attending
    The Senator trembling at Tyranny's nod
Each nation wch kneels at the footstool of God
All are Brethren; then banish Distinction afar
Let concord & Love heal the miseries of War.

25

1809   [Esd #44]

On an Icicle that clung to the grass of a grave

O take the pure gem to where Southernly Breezes
    Waft repose to some bosom as faithful as fair,
In which the warm current of love never freezes
    As it circulates freely and shamelessly there,
Which untainted by crime, unpolluted by care,
Might dissolve this dear ice-drop, might bid it arise,
Too pure for these regions, to gleam in the skies.

5

For I found the pure gem when the daybeam returning
    Ineffectual gleams on the snow-spangled plain,
When to others the longed-for arrival of morning
    Brings relief to long night-dreams of soul-racking pain.

10

Text collated with **EN,** MS Pfz129, *SC*/II, *1964B*, and *SC*/IV.

Title. 1809 | On . . . grave]
    omitted Pfz129 *SC*/II
    On an Icicle that clung to the
      grass of a grave | *1809* *1964B*
1 O] Oh! Pfz129 *SC*/II
    Southernly] southernly Pfz129 *SC*/II
    Breezes] breezes Pfz129 *SC*/II
2 fair,] fair **EN** Pfz129 *SC*/II *SC*/IV
3 love] Love Pfz129 *SC*/II
4 circulates freely and shamelessly] rises
    unmingled with selfishness Pfz129
    SC/II
    and] & **EN** *SC*/IV
    there,] there **EN** Pfz129 *SC*/II *SC*/IV
5 Which] Which, *1964B*
    crime,] Pride, Pfz129 *SC*/II
    care,] care **EN** Pfz129 *SC*/II *SC*/IV
6 this] the Pfz129 *SC*/II
    dear] dim Pfz129 *SC*/II *1964B*
      dear [?dim] *SC*/IV

ice-drop,]
  ice drop, **EN** Pfz129 *SC*/II *SC*/IV
  arise,] arise **EN** Pfz129 *SC*/II *SC*/IV
7 skies.] skies **EN** Pfz129 *SC*/II *SC*/IV
8 daybeam] day-beam Pfz129 *SC*/II
9 snow-spangled]
    snow spangled **EN** *SC*/IV
    snow-covered Pfz129 *SC*/II
  plain,] plain **EN** Pfz129 *SC*/II *SC*/IV
10 longed-for] longed for **EN** *SC*/IV
      wished-for Pfz129 *SC*/II
11 long night-dreams]
    long night dreams **EN** *SC*/IV
    long-visions Pfz129
    long visions *SC*/II
    soul-racking] soul racking **EN** Pfz129
     SC/II *SC*/IV
  pain.] pain **EN** Pfz129 *SC*/II *SC*/IV

But regret is an insult. To grieve is in vain.
And why should we grieve that a spirit so fair
Sought Heaven to meet with its kindred there?

15 Yet 'twas some Angel of kindness descending
  To share in the load of Mortality's woe,
Who, over thy lowly-built sepulchre bending,
  Bade sympathy's tenderest tear-drops to flow
And consigned the rich gift to the Sister of Snow;
20 And if Angels can weep, sure I may repine
And shed tear-drops, tho' frozen to ice, on thy shrine.

SUPPLEMENT

Version in Letter to Hogg, 6 January 1811

Oh! take the pure gem to where southernly breezes
  Waft repose to some bosom as faithful as fair
In which the warm current of Love never freezes
  As it rises unmingled with selfishness there
5 Which untainted by Pride, unpolluted by care
  Might dissolve the dim ice drop, might bid it arise
  Too pure for these regions, to gleam in the skies

Or where the stern warrior his country defending
  Dares fearless the dark-rolling battle to pour

---

12 insult. To] insult. to **EN** *SC/IV*
    insult—to Pfz129 *SC/II*
 vain.] vain **EN** Pfz129 *SC/II SC/IV*
13 And] <u>And</u> Say Pfz129 *SC/II*
14 Sought] Seeks Pfz129 *SC/II*
 Heaven] Heaven, *1964B*
 meet] mix Pfz129 *SC/II*
 kindred] Kindred *1964B*
 there?] there **EN** Pfz129 *SC/II SC/IV*
15 Yet] But still Pfz129 *SC/II*
 'twas] twas **EN** *SC/IV*
 Angel] Spirit Pfz129 *SC/II*
16 Mortality's] mortality's Pfz129 *SC/II*
 woe,] woe **EN** Pfz129 *SC/II SC/IV*
17 Who,] Who **EN** Pfz129 *SC/II SC/IV*
 lowly-built] lowly built **EN** Pfz129
  SC/II SC/IV
 bending,]

    bending **EN** Pfz129 *SC/II SC/IV*
18 sympathy's] sympathys **EN** *SC/IV*
 tear-drops] tear drops **EN** *SC/IV*
    tear-drop Pfz129 *SC/II*
19 And . . . Snow;] Not for <u>thee</u> soft
  compassion celestials did know
  Pfz129 *SC/II*
 Snow;] Snow **EN** *SC/IV*
20 And] But Pfz129 *SC/II*
 Angels] <u>Angels</u> Pfz129 *SC/II*
 I] <u>Man</u> Pfz129 *SC/II*
21 And . . . shrine.] May weep in mute
  grief oer thy low laid shrine Pfz129
  SC/II
 tear-drops,] tear drops **EN** *SC/IV*
 tho'] tho **EN** *SC/IV*
 ice,] ice **EN** *SC/IV*
 shrine.] shrine **EN** *SC/IV*

~~Where~~ Or oer the fell corpse of a dread Tyrant bending 10
 Where Patriotism red with his guilt-reeking gore
Plants Liberty's flag on the slave-peopled shore
 With Victory's cry, with the shout of the free
 Let it fly taintless spirit to mingle with thee

For I found the pure gem when the day-beam
 returning 15 [8]
 Ineffectual gleams on the snow-covered plain
When to others the wished-for arrival of morning [10]
 Brings relief to long-visions of soul racking pain
But regret is an insult—to grieve is in vain
<u>And</u> Say why should we grieve that a spirit so fair 20
Seeks Heaven to mix with its kindred there

But still 'twas some Spirit of kindness descending [15]
 To share in the load of mortality's woe
Who over thy lowly built sepulchre bending
 Bade sympathy's tenderest tear-drop to flow 25
Not for <u>thee</u> soft compassion celestials did know
 But if <u>Angels</u> can weep, sure <u>Man</u> may repine [20]
 May weep in mute grief oer thy low laid shrine

And did I then say for the Altar of Glory
 That the earliest the loveliest flowers I'd entwine 30
Tho' with millions of blood-reeking victims 'tis gory
 Tho' the tears of the widow polluted its shrine
Tho' around the orphans, the fatherless pine.
Oh! fame all thy glories I'd yield for a tear
To shed on the grave of an heart so sincere. 35

1808   *[Esd #45]*

Cold are the Blasts when December is howling,
 Chill are the damps on a dying friend's brow,

Text collated with **EN,** MS Pfz114, *SC*/II, *1964B*, and *SC*/IV.

Title. 1808] *omitted* Pfz114 *SC*/II   howling,]
   Cold are the blasts] *1808*   howling **EN** Pfz114 *SC*/II *SC*/IV
    1964B   2 Chill] Cold Pfz114 *SC*/II
1 Cold are the Blasts]   friend's] friends **EN** *SC*/IV
 Cold cold is the blast Pfz114 *SC*/II   mans Pfz114 *SC*/II
            brow,] brow **EN** Pfz114 *SC*/II *SC*/IV

Stern is the Ocean when tempests are rolling,
    Sad is the grave where a brother lies low,
5   But chillier is scorn from the false one that lov'd thee,
    More stern is the sneer from the friend that has proved thee,
    More sad are the tears when these sorrows have moved thee
      That, envenomed by wildest delirium, flow.

    And alas! thou, Louisa, hast felt all this horror! . .
10   Full long the fallen Victim contended with fate
Till—a destitute outcast abandoned to sorrow—
    She sought her babe's food at her ruiner's gate.
Another had charmed the remorseless betrayer;
He turned laughing away from her anguish-fraught prayer,
15   She spoke not, but wringing the rain from her hair,
    Took the rough mountain path, tho' the hour was late.

---

3 is] are   Pfz114 *SC/*II
    Ocean] seas   Pfz114 *SC/*II
    tempests] the wild waves   Pfz114 *SC/*II
    rolling,]
       rolling   **EN** Pfz114 *SC/*II *SC/*IV
4 Sad is] And sad   Pfz114 *SC/*II
    brother] loved one   Pfz114 *SC/*II
    low,] low   **EN** Pfz114 *SC/*II *SC/*IV
5 chillier] colder   Pfz114 *SC/*II
    false one that] being who   Pfz114 *SC/*II
    lov'd] lovd   **EN** *SC/*IV
        loved   Pfz114 *SC/*II *1964B*
    thee,] thee   **EN** Pfz114 *SC/*II *SC/*IV
6 that] who   Pfz114 *SC/*II
    thee,] thee   **EN** Pfz114 *SC/*II *SC/*IV
7 moved] movd   *SC/*IV
    thee] thee,   *1964B*
8 That,] That   **EN** *SC/*IV
    That, . . . delirium,] Which mixed with
      groans, anguish & wild madness
      Pfz114 *SC/*II
    flow.] flow   **EN** *SC/*IV
9 alas! thou,] ah! Poor   Pfz114
        ah! poor   *SC/*II
    thou,] thou   **EN** *SC/*IV
    Louisa,]
      Louisa   **EN** Pfz114 *SC/*II *SC/*IV
    hast] has   Pfz114 *SC/*II
    horror! . .] horror   Pfz114 *SC/*II

10 Victim] victim   Pfz114 *SC/*II
11 Till—a]
    Till a   **EN** Pfz114 *SC/*II *SC/*IV
    outcast] outcase   Pfz114
    sorrow—]
      sorrow   **EN** Pfz114 *SC/*II *SC/*IV
12 babe's] babes   **EN** *SC/*IV
    gate.] gate   **EN** Pfz114 *SC/*II *SC/*IV
13 betrayer;]
    betrayer   **EN** Pfz114 *SC/*II *SC/*IV
14 laughing away]
    callous aside   Pfz114 *SC/*II
    anguish-fraught]
      moans & her   Pfz114 *SC/*II
    prayer,]
      prayer   **EN** Pfz114 *SC/*II *SC/*IV
15 spoke not,]
    said nothing   Pfz114 *SC/*II
    not,] not.   **EN** *SC/*IV
    rain] wet   Pfz114 *SC/*II
    hair,] hair   **EN** Pfz114 *SC/*II *SC/*IV
16 Took] Crossed   Pfz114 *SC/*II
    rough] dark   Pfz114 *SC/*II
    path,] path   **EN** *SC/*IV
      side   Pfz114 *SC/*II
    tho'] tho   **EN** Pfz114 *SC/*II *SC/*IV
    was] it was   Pfz114 *SC/*II
    late.] late   **EN** Pfz114 *SC/*II *SC/*IV

On the cloud-shrouded summit of dark Penmanmawr
    The form of the wasted Louisa reclined,
She shrieked to the ravens loud croaking afar,
    She sighed to the gusts of the wild sweeping wind.—   20
"Ye storms o'er the peak of the lone mountain soaring,
Ye clouds with the thunder-winged tempest-shafts lowering,
Thou wrath of black Heaven, I blame not thy pouring,
    But thee, cruel Henry, I call thee unkind."

Then she wreathed a wild crown from the flow'rs of the mountain,
    And deliriously laughing the heath twigs entwined.   26
She bedewed it with tear-drops, then leaned o'er the fountain
    And cast it a prey to the wild sweeping wind.
"Ah! go," she exclaimed, "where the tempest is yelling.

---

17 On the cloud-shrouded]
   'Twas on the dark   *Pfz*114 *SC*/II
   cloud-shrouded]
     cloud shrouded   **EN** *SC*/IV
   dark] huge   *Pfz*114 *SC*/II
18 The] That the   *Pfz*114 *SC*/II
   reclined,] reclined   **EN** *SC*/IV
19 loud croaking]
     that croaked from   *Pfz*114 *SC*/II
   afar,] afar   **EN** *Pfz*114 *SC*/II *SC*/IV
20 She] And she   *Pfz*114 *SC*/II
   wind.—] wind   *Pfz*114 *SC*/II
21 "Ye] Ye   **EN** *SC*/IV
   "Ye . . . soaring,] I call not yon ~~rocks~~
     clouds where the thunder peals rattle
     *Pfz*114 *SC*/II
   o'er] oer   **EN** *SC*/IV
   soaring,] soaring   **EN** *SC*/IV
22 Ye . . . lowering,] I call not yon rocks
     where the elements battle   *Pfz*114
     SC/II
   thunder-winged]
     thunder winged   **EN** *SC*/IV
   tempest-shafts]
     tempest shafts   **EN** *SC*/IV
   lowering,] lowering   **EN** *SC*/IV
23 Thou . . . pouring,]
     omitted   *Pfz*114 *SC*/II
   pouring,] pouring   **EN** *SC*/IV
24 thee,] thee   **EN** *Pfz*114 *SC*/II *SC*/IV
   cruel] perjured   *Pfz*114 *SC*/II

Henry,]
   Henry   **EN** *Pfz*114 *SC*/II *SC*/IV
   unkind."]
     unkind   **EN** *Pfz*114 *SC*/II *SC*/IV
25 Then] The   *Pfz*114
   a wild crown from the]
     in her hair the wild   *Pfz*114 *SC*/II
   flow'rs] flowrs   **EN** *SC*/IV
      flowers   *Pfz*114 *SC*/II *1964B*
   mountain,]
     mountain   **EN** *Pfz*114 *SC*/II *SC*/IV
26 the heath twigs]
     a garland   *Pfz*114 *SC*/II
   entwined.]
     entwined   **EN** *Pfz*114 *SC*/II *SC*/IV
27 tear-drops,] tear drops.   **EN** *SC*/IV
      tears,   *Pfz*114 *SC*/II
      tear drops,   *1964B*
   leaned] she hung   *Pfz*114 *SC*/II
   o'er] oer   *Pfz*114 *SC*/II
28 And . . . sweeping] And laving it, cast it
     a prey to the   *Pfz*114 *SC*/II
   wind.] wind   **EN** *Pfz*114 *SC*/II *SC*/IV
29 "Ah!] Ah!   **EN** *SC*/IV
   go,"] go   **EN** *SC*/IV
     go"   *Pfz*114 *SC*/II
   exclaimed,]
     exclaimed   **EN** *Pfz*114 *SC*/II *SC*/IV
   "where] where   **EN** *SC*/IV
   yelling.]
     yelling   **EN** *Pfz*114 *SC*/II *SC*/IV

30   'Tis unkind to be cast on the sea that is swelling—
        But I left, a pityless outcast, my dwelling.
            My garments are torn—so they say is my mind."

        Not long lived Louisa.—And over her grave
            Waved the desolate limbs of a storm-blasted yew.
35   Around it no demons or ghosts dare to rave,
            But spirits of love steep her slumbers in dew;
        Then stay thy swift steps mid the dark mountain heather,
        Tho' bleak be the scene and severe be the weather,
        For perfidy, traveller, cannot bereave her
40   Of the tears to the tombs of the innocent due.

SUPPLEMENT
Version in Hogg Manuscript,
Late October or November 1810

        Cold cold is the blast when December is howling
            Cold are the damps on a dying mans brow
        Stern are the seas when the wild waves are rolling
            And sad the grave where a loved one lies low
5   But colder is scorn from the being who loved thee
        More stern is the sneer from the friend who has proved thee
        More sad are the tears when these sorrows have moved thee
            Which mixed with groans, anguish & wild madness flow.

---

30 'Tis] Tis   **EN** *SC/IV*
    swelling—] swelling——   **EN** *SC/IV*
                swelling   Pfz114 *SC/II*
31 left,] left   **EN** Pfz114 *SC/II SC/IV*
    outcast,]
        outcast   **EN** Pfz114 *SC/II SC/IV*
    dwelling.]
        dwelling   **EN** Pfz114 *SC/II SC/IV*
32 torn—so] torn so   Pfz114 *SC/II*
    mind."] mind   **EN** *SC/IV*
        mind"   Pfz114 *SC/II*
33 Louisa.—And] Louisa.—&   **EN** *SC/IV*
            Louisa—but   Pfz114
                SC/II
34 limbs] form   Pfz114 *SC/II*
    storm-blasted]
        storm blasted   **EN** *SC/IV*

yew.] yew   **EN** Pfz114 *SC/II SC/IV*
35 rave,] rave   **EN** Pfz114 *SC/II SC/IV*
36 love] Peace   Pfz114 *SC/II*
    dew;] dew   **EN** Pfz114 *SC/II SC/IV*
37 heather,]
        heather   **EN** Pfz114 *SC/II SC/IV*
38 Tho'] Tho   **EN** Pfz114 *SC/II SC/IV*
    bleak be the scene]
        chill blow the wind   Pfz114 *SC/II*
    and] &   **EN** Pfz114 *SC/II SC/IV*
    weather,] weather   **EN** *SC/IV*
39 perfidy,]
        perfidy   **EN** Pfz114 *SC/II SC/IV*
    traveller,]
        traveller   **EN** Pfz114 *SC/II SC/IV*
40 due.] due   **EN** Pfz114 *SC/II SC/IV*

And ah! Poor Louisa has felt all this horror
    Full long the fallen victim contended with fate   10
Till a destitute outcast abandoned to sorrow
    She sought her babe's food at her ruiner's gate
Another had charmed the remorseless betrayer
He turned callous aside from her moans & her prayer
She said nothing but wringing the wet from her hair   15
    Crossed the dark mountain side tho the hour it was late

'Twas on the dark summit of huge Penmanmawr
    That the form of the wasted Louisa reclined,
She shrieked to the ravens that croaked from afar
    And she sighed to the gusts of the wild sweeping wind   20
          clouds
I call not yon ~~rocks~~ where the thunder peals rattle
I call not yon rocks where the elements battle
    But thee perjured Henry I call thee unkind

Then she wreathed in her hair the wild flowers of the mountain 25
    And deliriously laughing a garland entwined
She bedewed it with tears, then she hung oer the fountain
    And laving it, cast it a prey to the wind
"Ah! go" she exclaimed "where the tempest is yelling
'Tis unkind to be cast on the sea that is swelling   30
But I left a pityless outcast my dwelling
    My garments are torn so they say is my mind"

Not long lived Louisa—but over her grave
    Waved the desolate form of a storm-blasted yew
Around it no demons or ghosts dare to rave   35
    But spirits of Peace steep her slumbers in dew
Then stay thy swift steps mid the dark mountain heather
Tho chill blow the wind & severe be the weather,
For perfidy traveller cannot bereave her
    Of the tears to the tombs of the innocent due   40

Henry and Louisa*
a Poem in two parts

She died for love—and he for glory

THE PARTING
PART THE FIRST.
SCENE — ENGLAND

I

Where are the Heroes? sunk in death they lie.
    What toiled they for? titles and wealth and fame.
But the wide Heaven is now their canopy,
    And legal murderers their loftiest name,
5   Enshrined on brass their glory and their shame
      What tho' torn Peace and martyred Freedom see?
What tho' to most remote posterity
Their names, their selfishness for ay enscrolled,
A shuddering world's blood-boltered eyes behold,
10   Mocking mankind's unbettered misery?

* The stanza of this Poem is radically that of Spencer altho' I suffered myself at the time of writing it to be led into occasional deviations. These defects I do not alter now, being unwilling to offer any outrage to the living portraiture of my own mind; bad as it may be pronounced.

Text collated with **EN,** *1964B*, and *SC*/IV.

Title. 1809 | Henry and Louisa*]
      Henry and Louisa* *1964B*
    and] & **EN** *SC*/IV

Footnote. altho'] altho **EN** *SC*/IV
      unwilling] unwi lling *SC*/IV
      pronounced.]
        prounounced. **EN** *SC*/IV

Subtitle. a Poem | in two parts] *a Poem* |
      in two parts | *1809*   *1964B*

Epigraph. died] dies *SC*/IV
      and] & **EN** *SC*/IV

Heading. First.] *first* *1964B*
      First *SC*/IV

2 and] & **EN** *SC*/IV
   and] & **EN** *SC*/IV
3 canopy,] canopy **EN** *SC*/IV
4 name,] name **EN** *SC*/IV
      name. *1964B*
5 and] & **EN** *SC*/IV
6 tho'] tho **EN** *SC*/IV
   and] & **EN** *SC*/IV
7 tho'] tho **EN** *SC*/IV
8 enscrolled,] enscrolled **EN** *SC*/IV
9 world's] worlds **EN** *SC*/IV
   behold,] behold **EN** *SC*/IV
10 mankind's] mankinds **EN** *SC*/IV
      misery?] misery; **EN** *SC*/IV

Can this perfection give, can valour prove
One wish for others' bliss, one throb of love . . .

II

Yet darest thou boast thyself superior.—Thou!
   Vile worm! whom lovely woman deigns to bless,
And, meanly selfish, bask in glory's glow,   15
   Rending the soul-spun ties of tenderness
Where all desires rise for thine happiness?
   Canst thou boast thus and hope to be forgiven?
Oh! when thou started'st from her last caress,
   From purest love by vulgar Glory driven,   20
Couldst thou have e'er deserved, if thou resigned'st,
   Heaven?

III

IV

---

12 love . . .] love. . . *SC*/IV   19 started'st] startedst **EN** *SC*/IV

14 bless,] bless **EN** *SC*/IV   caress,] caress **EN** *SC*/IV

15 And,] And **EN** *SC*/IV   20 driven,] driven **EN** *SC*/IV

   selfish,] selfish **EN** *SC*/IV   21 e'er] eer **EN** *SC*/IV

   glow,] glow **EN** *SC*/IV   resigned'st,] resignedst **EN** *SC*/IV

16 soul-spun] soul spun **EN** *SC*/IV   Heaven?] Heaven **EN** *SC*/IV

18 and] & **EN** *SC*/IV   *line break followed by series of*

                               dots 1964B

V

And shadowed by affection's purple wing
Bid thee forget how Time's fast footstep sped:
Would die in peace when thou wert mingled with the dead.

VI

25 Had Glory's fire consumed each tender tie
    That links to love the Heaven-aspiring soul?
Could not that voice, quivering in agony,
    That struggling pale resolve that dared control
Passion's wild flood, when wildest it did roll,
30 Could not impassioned tenderness that burst
    Cold prudery's bondage, owning all it felt—
Could not these, warrior, quench thy battle thirst,
Nought this availed thine iron-bound breast to melt,
To make thy footsteps pause where love and freedom dwelt?

VII

35 Yes! every soul-nerve vibrated . . . a space
    Enchained in speechless awe the warrior stood.
Superior reason, Virtue, manner, grace,

---

22 affection's] affections **EN** *SC*/IV
23 Time's] Times **EN** *SC*/IV
24 dead.] dead **EN** *SC*/IV
26 Heaven-aspiring]
   Heaven aspiring **EN** *SC*/IV
   soul?] soul **EN** *SC*/IV
      soul, *1964B*
27 voice,] voice **EN** *SC*/IV
   agony,] agony **EN** *SC*/IV
29 Passion's] Passions **EN** *SC*/IV

flood,] flood *1964B*
31 bondage,] bondage **EN** *SC*/IV
   felt—] felt **EN** *SC*/IV
32 these,] these **EN** *SC*/IV
   thirst,] thirst **EN** *SC*/IV
33 iron-bound] iron bound **EN** *SC*/IV
   melt,] melt **EN** *SC*/IV
34 and] & **EN** *SC*/IV
36 stood.] stood **EN** *SC*/IV
37 grace,] grace **EN** *SC*/IV

Claimed for a space their rights . . . . in varying mood
Before her lovely eyes in thought he stood
Whilst Glory's train flashed on his mental eye   40
   Which wandered wildly where the fight's red flood,
The crash of death, the storm of Victory,
Roll round the hopes of love that only breathe to die.

VIII

Then She exclaimed as love-nerved sense returned,
"Go . . mingle in thy country's battle tide . . .   45
Forget that love's pale torch hath ever burned.
   Until thou meet'est me clothed in Victor-pride
May guardian spirits keep thee . . . far and wide
   O'er the red regions of the day-scorched zone
For glory seek . . but here thou wilt abide—   50
Here in this breast—thou wilt abide alone.
I will thine empire be. My heart shall be thy throne."

IX

When Princes at fair Reason's bidding bend,
   Resigning power for Virtue's fadeless meed,
Or spirits of Heaven to man submission lend,   55
   The debt of gratitude is great indeed;
In vain the heart its thankfulness to prove
   Aye might attempt to do the debt away.
Yet what is this compared to Woman's love,

---

38 rights . . . .] rights . . .   *1964B*

41 fight's] fights   **EN** *SC*/IV
  flood,] flood   **EN** *SC*/IV

42 Victory,] Victory   **EN** *SC*/IV

43 die.] die   **EN** *SC*/IV

44 She] she   *1964B*
  as] as,   *1964B*
  love-nerved] love nerved   **EN** *SC*/IV
      love-nerved,   *1964B*
  returned,] returned.   **EN** *SC*/IV

45 "Go . .] "Go . .   *SC*/IV
  country's] countrys   **EN** *SC*/IV
  tide . . .] tide. . .   *SC*/IV

47 meet'est] meetest   *1964B*

48 thee . . .] thee.   **EN** *SC*/IV
  and] &   **EN** *SC*/IV

49 O'er] Oer   **EN** *SC*/IV
  day-scorched]
    day scorched   **EN** *SC*/IV

50 seek . .] seek . .   *SC*/IV
  abide—] abide   **EN** *SC*/IV
    abide,   *1964B*

51 Here in] Here—in   *1964B*
    Here.in   *SC*/IV
  breast—thou] breast. thou   **EN** *SC*/IV
      breast. Thou   *1964B*
  alone.] alone   **EN** *SC*/IV

52 throne."] throne   **EN** *SC*/IV

53 Reason's] Reasons   **EN** *SC*/IV
  bend,] bend   **EN** *SC*/IV

54 Virtue's] Virtues   **EN** *SC*/IV
  meed,] meed   **EN** *SC*/IV

55 spirits] Spirits   *1964B*
  lend,] lend   **EN** *SC*/IV

56 indeed;] indeed   **EN** *SC*/IV

58 away.] away?   **EN** *SC*/IV

59 love,] love   **EN** *SC*/IV

60   Dear Woman's love, the dawn of Virtue's day,
            The bliss-inspiring beam, the soul-illuming ray?

                                    X
            Then Henry spoke as he checked the rising tear,
                "That I have loved thee and must love for ever
            Heaven is a witness—Heaven to whom are dear
65   The hearts that earthly chances cannot sever,
            Where bloom the flowers that cease to blossom never.
                Religion sanctifies the cause, I go
            To execute its vengeance. Heaven will give
                To me (so whispers hope) to quell the foe.
70   Heaven gives the good to conquer and to live,
            And thou shalt next to God his votive heart receive.

                                    XI
            Say, is not he the Tyrant of the World
                And are not we the injured and the brave?
            Unmoved shall we behold his flag unfurled,
75   Flouting with impious Wing Religion's grave,
            Triumphant gleaming o'er the passive wave,
            Nor raise an arm, nor one short pleasure yield
                The boon of immortality to save?
            Hope is our tempered lance, faith is our shield;
80   Conquest or death for these wait on the gory field.

                                    XII
            Even at that hour when hostile myriads clash
                And terrible death shakes his resistless dart,
            Mingling wild wailings with the battle crash,

---

60 day,] day **EN** *SC*/IV
61 bliss-inspiring]
      bliss inspiring **EN** *SC*/IV
   soul-illuming]
      soul illuming **EN** *SC*/IV
   ray?] ray **EN** *SC*/IV
62 tear,] tear **EN** *SC*/IV
63 and] & **EN** *SC*/IV
65 sever,] sever **EN** *SC*/IV
66 never.] never **EN** *SC*/IV
68 its] it's **EN** *SC*/IV
   vengeance.] vengeance, *SC*/IV
69 foe.] foe **EN** *SC*/IV

70 and] & **EN** *SC*/IV
   live,] live **EN** *SC*/IV
71 shalt next] shalt—next *1964B*
   God his] God—his *1964B*
   receive.] receive **EN** *SC*/IV
73 and] & **EN** *SC*/IV
74 unfurled,] unfurled **EN** *SC*/IV
75 grave,] grave **EN** *SC*/IV
76 o'er] oer **EN** *SC*/IV
   wave,] wave **EN** *SC*/IV
79 shield;] shield **EN** *SC*/IV
80 field.] field **EN** *SC*/IV
82 dart,] dart **EN** *SC*/IV
83 crash,] crash **EN** *SC*/IV

Then thou and Heaven shall share this votive heart.
When from pale dissolution's grasp I start   85
   (If Heaven so wills) even then will I be thine.
Nor can the whelming tomb have power to part
   From all it loves a heart that loves like mine,
From thee . . round whom its hopes, its joys, its fears
   entwine."

XIII

A sicklier tint crept o'er Louisa's cheek   90
   "But thou art dearer far to me than all
That fancy's visions feign, or tongue can speak.
   Yes! may I die, and be that death eternal,
When other thoughts but thee my soul enthrall.
   The joys of Heaven I prize thee far above,   95
Thee, dearest, will my Soul its Saviour call.
My faith is thine . . my faith-gained heaven, thy love;
My Hell, when cruel fates thee from these arms remove.

XIV

Farewell" . . . she spoke. The warrior's war-steeled breast,
   Quivering in feeling's agonized excess,   100
Scarce drew its breath, to sickliness oppressed
   By mingled self-reproach and tenderness;
He dared not speak, but rushed from her caress.
The sunny glades; the little birds of spring
Twittering from every garlanded recess,   105
Returning verdure's joy that seem'd to sing
Whilst woe with stern hand smote his every mental string;

---

84 and] & **EN** *SC*/IV
  heart.] heart **EN** *SC*/IV
85 dissolution's] dissolutions **EN** *SC*/IV
86 thine.] thine **EN** *SC*/IV
88 mine,] mine **EN** *SC*/IV
89 thee . . round] thee——round **SC**/IV
  hopes,] hopes **EN** *SC*/IV
  joys,] joys **EN** *SC*/IV
  entwine."] entwine" **EN** *SC*/IV
90 o'er] oer **EN** *SC*/IV
  cheek . . . .] cheek. . . . **SC**/IV
93 die,] die **EN** *SC*/IV
  and] & **EN** *SC*/IV
  eternal,] eternal **EN** *SC*/IV
94 enthrall.] enthrall **EN** *SC*/IV
95 above,] above **EN** *SC*/IV

96 dearest,] dearest **EN** *SC*/IV
  call.] call **EN** *SC*/IV
97 heaven,] heaven **EN** *SC*/IV
  love;] love **EN** *SC*/IV
98 remove.] remove **EN** *SC*/IV
99 warrior's] warriors **EN** *SC*/IV
  war-steeled] war steeled **EN** *SC*/IV
  breast,] breast **EN** *SC*/IV
100 excess,] excess **EN** *SC*/IV
102 self-reproach]
  self reproach **EN** *SC*/IV
  and] & **EN** *SC*/IV
103 caress.] caress **EN** *SC*/IV
105 recess,] recess **EN** *SC*/IV
106 verdure's] verdures **EN** *SC*/IV
  seem'd] seemd **EN** *SC*/IV

XV

The fragrant dew-mists from the Ivied Thorn
  Whose form o'ershadowed love's most blissful bower,
Where oft would fly the tranquil time of morn,
  Or swifter urge its flight dear evening's hour,
When purple twilight in the East would lower
And the amorous starbeam kiss the loveliest form
That ever bruised a pleasure-fainting flower
  Whose emanative eyebeam, thrilling, warm,
Around her sacred presence shed a rapturing charm;

XVI

Each object so beloved, each varied tone
  Of heavenly feeling that can never die,
Each little throb his heart had ever known
  Impetuous rushed on fainting memory.
Yet not alone for parted extacy,
  To which he now must bid a long adieu,
Started the bitter tear or burst the sigh;
  In all the pangs that, spite concealment, grew
  O'er his Louisa's peace, a deeper soul-pang drew.

XVII

The balmy breath of soul-reviving dawn
  That kissed the bosom of the waveless lake,
Scented with spring-flowers, o'er the level lawn

---

109 o'ershadowed]
    oershadowed **EN** *SC/IV*
  love's] loves **EN** *SC/IV*
  bower,] bower **EN** *SC/IV*
110 morn,] morn **EN** *SC/IV*
111 evening's] evenings **EN** *SC/IV*
  hour,] hower **EN** *SC/IV*
    hour *1964B*
115 eyebeam,] eyebeam **EN** *SC/IV*
  thrilling,] thrilling **EN** *SC/IV*
  warm,] warm **EN** *SC/IV*
118 die,] die **EN** *SC/IV*
119 known] known, *1964B*
120 memory.] memory; **EN** *SC/IV*
121 extacy,] extacy **EN** *SC/IV*

122 adieu,] adieu **EN** *SC/IV*
123 sigh;] sigh **EN** *SC/IV*
124 that,] that **EN** *SC/IV*
  concealment,]
    concealment **EN** *SC/IV*
125 O'er] Oer **EN** *SC/IV*
  Louisa's] Louisas **EN** *SC/IV*
  soul-pang] soul pang **EN** *SC/IV*
  drew.] drew **EN** *SC/IV*
126 soul-reviving]
    soulreviving **EN** *SC/IV*
127 lake,] lake **EN** *SC/IV*
128 spring-flowers,]
    spring-flowers **EN** *SC/IV*
  o'er] oer **EN** *SC/IV*

Struck on his sense, to woe scarce yet awake.
He felt its still reproach, the upland brake   130
Rustled beneath his war-steed's eager prance,
Hastening to Egypt's shore his way to take,
But swifter hastening to dispel the trance
Of grief, he hurried on, smothering the last sad glance.

XVIII

Sweet flower! in dereliction's solitude   135
That scatterest perfume to the unheeding gale
And in the grove's unconscious quietude
Murmurest (thyself scarce conscious) thy sad tale—
Sure it is subject for the Poet's wail,
Tho' faint, that one so worthy to be prized,   140
The fairest flower of the loveliest vale,
To withering Glory should be sacrifized,
That hides his hateful form in Virtue's garb disguised.

XIX

Religion! hated cause of all the woe
That makes the world this wilderness. Thou spring   145
Whence terror, pride, revenge and perfidy flow,
The curses which thy pampered minions bring
On thee shall Virtue's votary fear to fling?
And thou, dear Love! thy tender ties to sever,
To drown in shouts thy bliss-fraught murmuring,   150

---

129 sense,] sense **EN** *SC*/IV
    awake.] awake **EN** *SC*/IV
130 reproach, the]
    reproach,—the *1964B*
131 war-steed's] war steeds **EN** *SC*/IV
    prance,] prance **EN** *SC*/IV
132 Egypt's] Egypts **EN** *SC*/IV
    take,] take **EN** *SC*/IV
134 on,] on **EN** *SC*/IV
    glance.] glance **EN** *SC*/IV
135 dereliction's] derelictions **EN** *SC*/IV
137 grove's] groves **EN** *SC*/IV
138 tale—] tale **EN** *SC*/IV
139 Poet's] Poets **EN** *SC*/IV
    wail,] wail **EN** *SC*/IV

140 Tho'] Tho **EN** *SC*/IV
    prized,] prized **EN** *SC*/IV
141 vale,] vale **EN** *SC*/IV
142 should] sh^d **EN** *SC*/IV
    sacrifized,] sacrifized **EN** *SC*/IV
        sacrificed, *1964B*
143 Virtue's] Virtues **EN** *SC*/IV
    disguised.] disguised **EN** *SC*/IV
146 terror,] terror **EN** *SC*/IV
    and] & **EN** *SC*/IV
    flow,] flow **EN** *SC*/IV
147 curses] curses, *1964B*
    bring] bring, *1964B*
148 Virtue's] Virtues **EN** *SC*/IV
149 thou,] thou **EN** *SC*/IV
150 murmuring,] murmuring **EN** *SC*/IV

Ceaseless shall selfish Prejudice endeavour?
Shall she succeed? . . oh no, whilst I live, never, never!

XX

For by the wrongs that flaming deep
Within this bosom's agony,
155   That dry the source whence others weep,—
I swear that thou shalt die!

Henry and Louisa

THE MEETING

PART SECOND

I

'Tis night . . No planet's brilliance dares to light
The dim and battle-blushing scenery,
Friends mixed with foes urge unremitting fight
160   Beneath War's suffocating canopy,
And, as sulphureous meteors fire the sky,
Fast flash the deathful thunderbolts of War,
Whilst groans unite in frightful harmony
And wakened vultures shrieking from afar
165   Scent their half-murdered prey amid the battle's jar.

II

Now had the Genius of the south, sublime
On mighty Atlas' tempest-cinctured throne,

---

151 endeavour?] endeavour   **EN** *SC*/IV
152 succeed? . . oh] succeed . . oh   **EN**
            succeed?—oh
              1964B
            succeed——oh
              SC/IV
      no,] no   **EN** *SC*/IV
      live,] live   **EN** *SC*/IV
      never!] never   **EN** *SC*/IV
154 agony,] agony   **EN** *SC*/IV
155 dry] day   *SC*/IV
      weep,—] weep   **EN** *SC*/IV
156 shalt] shalt [?shall]   **EN** *SC*/IV
      die!] die   **EN** *SC*/IV
Heading. and] &   **EN** *SC*/IV

157 'Tis] Tis   **EN** *SC*/IV
      night . .] night . .   *SC*/IV
      planet's] planets   **EN** *SC*/IV
158 and] &   **EN** *SC*/IV
      battle-blushing]
        battle blushing   **EN** *SC*/IV
159 Friends] Friends,   *1964B*
      foes] foes,   *1964B*
161 sky,] sky   **EN** *SC*/IV
162 War,] War   **EN** *SC*/IV
165 half-murdered]
      half murdered   **EN** *SC*/IV
      battle's] battles   **EN** *SC*/IV
      jar.] jar   **EN** *SC*/IV
167 tempest-cinctured]
      tempest cinctured   **EN** *SC*/IV
      throne,] throne   **EN** *SC*/IV

Looked over Afric's desolated clime,
Deep wept at slavery's everlasting moan
And his most dear-beloved nation's groan.   170
The Boreal whirlwind's shadowy wings that sweep
    The veined bosom of the northern world
That hears contending thunders on the deep,
    Sees hostile flags on Egypt's strand unfurled,
Brings Egypt's faintest groan to waste and ruin hurled.   175

III

Is this then all that sweeps the midnight sand?
    Tells the wild blast no tales of deeper woe?
Does war alone pollute the unhappy land?
    No—the low fluttering and the hectic glow
Of hope, whose sickly flowret scarce can blow,   180
    Chilled by the ice-blast of intense despair;
Anguish that dries the big tear ere it flow,
And maniac love, that sits by the beacon's glare
With eyes on nothing fixed, dim like a mist-clothed star.

IV

No fear save one could daunt her—Ocean's wave,   185
    Bearing Britannia's hired asassins on
To victory's shame or an unhonored grave,
    Beheld Louisa mid an host alone.

---

168 Afric's] Africs **EN** *SC*/IV
    clime,] clime **EN** *SC*/IV
169 Deep wept] Deep [*written above* Wept]
        Wept [*written through* ?And]
        EN *SC*/IV
    slavery's] slaverys **EN** *SC*/IV
170 dear-beloved]
        dear beloved **EN** *SC*/IV
    nation's] nations **EN** *SC*/IV
    groan.] groan *SC*/IV
171 whirlwind's] whirlwinds **EN** *SC*/IV
173 deep,] deep **EN** *SC*/IV
174 Egypt's] Egypts **EN** *SC*/IV
    unfurled,] unfurled **EN** *SC*/IV
175 Egypt's] Egypts **EN** *SC*/IV
    and] & **EN** *SC*/IV
    hurled.] hurled **EN** *SC*/IV
176 sand?] sand **EN** *SC*/IV
177 woe?] woe. **EN** *SC*/IV

179 low] low, *1964B*
    and] & **EN** *SC*/IV
180 blow,] blow **EN** *SC*/IV
181 ice-blast] ice blast **EN** *SC*/IV
    despair;] despair, *1964B*
182 flow,] flow **EN** *SC*/IV
183 maniac] [m *or* M]aniac **EN**
        Maniac *1964B*
    beacon's] beacons **EN** *SC*/IV
184 mist-clothed]
        mist clothed **EN** *SC*/IV
    star.] star **EN** *SC*/IV
185 wave,] wave **EN** *SC*/IV
186 Britannia's] Britannias **EN** *SC*/IV
187 shame] shame, **EN** *SC*/IV
    grave,] grave **EN** *SC*/IV
188 Louisa] Louisa, *1964B*
    host] host, *1964B*
    alone.] alone **EN** *SC*/IV

The womanly dress that veiled her fair form is gone,
190   Gone is the timid wandering of her eye,
Pale firmness nerved her anguished heart to stone;
        The sense of shame, the flush of modesty,
By stern resolve were quenched or only glowed to die.

V

"Where is my love—my Henry—is he dead?"
195   Half-drowned in smothered anguish wildly burst
From her parched lips—"is my ador'd one dead?
        Knows none my Henry? War! thou source accurst
In whose red flood I see these sands immerst,
        Hast thou quite whelmed compassion's tearful spring
200   Where thy fierce tide rolls to slake Glory's thirst?
        Perhaps thou, Warrior, some kind word dost bring
From my poor Henry's lips when Death its shade did fling."

VI

A tear of pity dimmed the Warrior's gaze.
        "I know him not, sweet maiden, yet the fight
205   That casts on Britain's fame a brighter blaze
        Should spare all yours, if ought I guess aright.
But ah! by yonder flash of sulphurous light
        The dear loved work of battle has begun.
Fame calls her votaries." He fled. The night
210   Had far advanced before the fray was done;
Scarce sunk the roar of war before the rising Sun.

---

190 eye,] eye   **EN** *SC*/IV   199 compassion's]
191 stone;] stone   **EN** *SC*/IV   compassions   **EN** *SC*/IV
192 modesty,] modesty   **EN** *SC*/IV   201 thou,] thou   **EN** *SC*/IV
193 die.] die   **EN** *SC*/IV   Warrior,] Warrior   **EN**
194 love—my] love!—my   **EN** *SC*/IV   warrior   *SC*/IV
   dead?"] dead"   **EN** *SC*/IV   202 fling."] fling   **EN** *SC*/IV
195 Half-drowned]   203 Warrior's] Warriors   **EN** *SC*/IV
   Half drowned   **EN** *SC*/IV   204 not,] not   **EN** *SC*/IV
196 ador'd] adord   **EN** *SC*/IV   fight] fight,   *1964B*
   dead?] dead   **EN** *SC*/IV   205 blaze] blaze,   *1964B*
197 Henry?] Henry.   **EN** *SC*/IV   206 aright.] aright   **EN** *SC*/IV
   accurst] accurst,   *1964B*   207 light] light,   *1964B*
198 flood] blood   *1964B SC*/IV   210 done;] done   **EN** *SC*/IV
   immerst,] immerst   **EN** *SC*/IV   211 Sun.] Sun   **EN** *SC*/IV

VII

But sight of wilder grief where slept the dead
    Was witnessed by the morn's returning glow,
When frantic o'er the waste Louisa sped
    To drink her dying lover's latest vow: 215
Sighed mid her locks the sea-gales as they blew,
    Bearing along faint shrieks of dying men
As if they sympathized with her deep woe.
    Silent she paused a space, and then again
New-nerved by fear and hope sprang wild across the plain.

VIII

See where she stops again! . . . a ruin's shade
    Darkens his fading lineaments, his cheek
On which remorseful pain is deep pourtrayed
    Glares, death-convulsed and ghastly. Utterings break—
Shuddering, unformed—his tongue essays to speak.   225
    There low he lies! poor Henry! where is now
Thy dear, deserted love? Is there no friend
    To bathe with tears that anguish-burning brow,
None comfort in this fearful hour to lend,
When to remorseful grief thy parting spirits bend?   230

IX

Yes! pain had steeped each dying limb in flame
    When, mad with mingled hope and pale dismay,
Fleet as the wild deer his Louisa came,

---

213 glow,] glow **EN** *SC*/IV

214 o'er] oer **EN** *SC*/IV

215 lover's] lovers **EN** *SC*/IV

216 blew,] blew **EN** *SC*/IV

218 woe.] woe **EN** *SC*/IV

219 and] & **EN** *SC*/IV

220 New-nerved] New nerved **EN** *SC*/IV
    and] & **EN** *SC*/IV

221 ruin's] ruins **EN** *SC*/IV

224 Glares,] Glares **EN** *SC*/IV
    death-convulsed]
      death convulsed **EN** *SC*/IV
    and] & **EN** *SC*/IV
    Utterings] utterings **EN** *SC*/IV
    break—] break **EN** *SC*/IV

225 unformed—his]

unformed—; his *1964B*

speak.] speak **EN** *SC*/IV

226 There] Thus *1964B SC*/IV
    where] [w *or* W]here **EN**

227 dear,] dear **EN** *SC*/IV

228 anguish-burning]
    anguish burning **EN** *SC*/IV
    brow,] brow **EN** *SC*/IV

229 lend,] lend **EN** *SC*/IV

230 bend?] bend **EN** *SC*/IV

231 flame] flame, *1964B*

232 When,] When **EN** *SC*/IV
    and] & **EN** *SC*/IV
    dismay,] dismay **EN** *SC*/IV

233 came,] came **EN** *SC*/IV

Nerved by distraction.—A pale tremulous ray
235   Flashed on her eyes from the expiring day.
          Life for a space rushed to his fainting breast.
      The breathing form of love-enlivened clay
          In motionless rapture pale Louisa prest
      And stung by maddening hope in tears her bliss exprest.

                              X

240   Yet was the transport wavering . . . the dew
              Of bodily pain that bathed his pallid brow,
          The pangs that thro' his anguished members flew,
              Tho' half subdued by Love's returning glow,
          Doubt mixed with lingering hope must needs bestow.
245   Then she exclaimed—"Love, I have sought thee far,
          Whence our own Albion's milder sea gales blow
              To this stern scene of fame-aspiring war;
          Thro' waves of danger past thou wert my polar star.

                              XI

          Live then, dear source of life! and let the ray
250   Which lights thy kindling eyebeam softly speak
          That thou hast loved when I was far away—
              Yet thou art pale. Death's hectic lights thy cheek.
              Oh! if one moment fate the chain should break
              Which binds thy soul unchangeably to mine:

---

234 distraction.—A]
      distraction.—a **EN** *SC*/IV
235 day.] day **EN** *SC*/IV
236 breast.] breast **EN** *SC*/IV
237 love-enlivened]
    love enlivened **EN** *SC*/IV
    love-entwined *1964B*
    clay] clay, *1964B*
238 rapture] rapture, *1964B*
239 And] And, *1964B*
    hope] hope, *1964B*
    exprest.] exprest **EN** *SC*/IV
240 wavering . . .] wavering. . . *SC*/IV
242 thro'] thro **EN** *SC*/IV
    flew,] flew **EN** *SC*/IV
243 glow,] glow **EN** *SC*/IV
244 Doubt] Doubt, *1964B*
    hope] hope, *1964B*
    bestow.] bestow **EN** *SC*/IV

245 exclaimed—"Love,]
      exclaimed—"Love **EN** *SC*/IV
    far,] far **EN** *SC*/IV
    far; *1964B*
246 Albion's] Albions **EN**
      Albion *SC*/IV
    blow] blow, *1964B*
247 war;] war **EN** *SC*/IV
248 star.] star **EN** *SC*/IV
249 and] & **EN** *SC*/IV
251 away—] away:— **EN** *SC*/IV
252 Death's] deaths **EN** *SC*/IV
    cheek.] cheek **EN** *SC*/IV
253 should] sh^d **EN** *SC*/IV
254 binds] bind **EN** *SC*/IV
    soul] soul, **EN** *SC*/IV

Another moment's pain fate dare not wreak.   255
    Another moment . . . . . I am ever thine!
Love, turn those eyes on me! ah, death has dimmed their
    shine."

XII

Ceased her voice. The accents mild
    In frightful stillness died away.
More sweet than Memnon's plainings wild   260
    That float upon the morning ray
    Died every sound . . save when
    At distance o'er the plain
Britannia's legions swiftly sweeping,
Glory's ensanguined harvest reaping,   265
    Mowed down the field of men,
And the silent ruins, crumbling nigh,
With echoes low prolonged the cry
Of mingled defeat and victory.

XIII

More low, more faint yet far more dread   270
    Arose the expiring warrior's groan,
Stretched on the sand, his bloody bed,
In agonized death was Henry laid
    But he did not fall alone . . .
Why then that anguished sigh   275
Which seems to tear the vital tie,
Fiercer than death; more fell

---

255 moment's] moments **EN** *SC*/IV
    wreak.] wreak **EN** *SC*/IV
256 moment . . . . .]
    moment *1964B*
    thine!] thine **EN** *SC*/IV
257 Love,] Love **EN** *SC*/IV
    ah,] ah **EN** *SC*/IV
    shine."] shine **EN**
        shine. *SC*/IV
258 The] the **EN** *SC*/IV
259 away.] away **EN** *SC*/IV
260 Memnon's] Memnons **EN** *SC*/IV
262 sound . .] sound . . *SC*/IV
263 o'er] oer **EN** *SC*/IV

264 Britannia's] Britannias **EN** *SC*/IV
    sweeping,] sweeping **EN** *SC*/IV
265 reaping,] reaping **EN** *SC*/IV
266 men,] men **EN** *SC*/IV
267 ruins,] ruins **EN** *SC*/IV
    nigh,] nigh **EN** *SC*/IV
269 and] & **EN** *SC*/IV
270 faint] faint, *1964B*
    dread] dread, *1964B*
271 warrior's] warriors **EN** *SC*/IV
    groan,] groan **EN** *SC*/IV
272 bed,] bed; **EN** *SC*/IV
276 tie,] tie **EN** *SC*/IV
277 death;] death, *1964B*

Than tyranny, contempt or hate?
Why does that breast with horror swell
280   Which ought to triumph over fate?
Why? ask the pallid, griefworn mien
Of poor Louisa, let it speak:
But her firm heart would sooner break
Than doubt the soul where love had been.

XIV

285   Now, now he dies! his parting breath,
The sulphurous gust of battle bears.
The shriek, the groan, the gasp of death,
Unmoved Louisa hears,
And a smile of triumph lights her eye
290   With more than mortal radiancy.—
Sacred to Love a deed is done!—
Gleams thro' battle clouds the Sun,
Gleams it on all that's good and fair
Stretched on the Earth to moulder there.
295   Shall Virtue perish? No;
Superior to Religion's tie,
Emancipate from misery,
Despising self, their souls can know
All the delight love can bestow
300   Where Glory's phantom fades away
Before Affection's purer ray,
Where tyrants cease to wield the rod
And slaves to tremble at their nod.

---

278 hate?] hate   **EN** *SC/IV*
281 pallid,] pallid   **EN** *SC/IV*
　　mien] mein   **EN** *SC/IV*
282 Louisa,] Louisa   **EN** *SC/IV*
284 been.] been   **EN** *SC/IV*
285 breath,] breath   **EN** *SC/IV*
286 bears.] bears   **EN** *SC/IV*
287 shriek,] shrek,   **EN** *SC/IV*
　　death,] death   **EN** *SC/IV*
288 Unmoved] Unmoved,   *1964B*
　　hears,] hears   **EN** *SC/IV*
292 Sun,] Sun   **EN** *SC/IV*
293 and] &   **EN** *SC/IV*

294 there.] there   **EN** *SC/IV*
295 No;] No   **EN** *SC/IV*
296 Religion's] Religions   **EN** *SC/IV*
　　tie,] tie   **EN** *SC/IV*
297 misery,] misery   **EN** *SC/IV*
300 Where] Where [?When]   **EN**
　　　　　　　When *1964B*
　　　　　　　When [?Where]   *SC/IV*
　　Glory's] Glorys   **EN** *SC/IV*
301 ray,] ray   **EN** *SC/IV*
302 Where] When [?Where]   **EN**
303 nod.] nod   **EN** *SC/IV*

There near the stunted palms that shroud
    The spot from which their spirits fled   305
Shall pause the human hounds of blood
    And own a secret dread.
There shall the victor's steel-clad brow,
Tho' flushed by conquest's crimson glow,
    Be changed with inward fear;   310
There stern and steady by long command
The pomp-fed despot's sceptered hand
    Shall shake as if death were near,
Whilst the lone captive in his train
Feels comfort as he shakes his chain.   315

A Translation of   [*Esd #47*]
The Marsellois Hymn

1

Haste to battle, Patriot Band!
    A day of Glory dawns on thee!
Against thy rights is raised an hand:—
    The bloodred hand of tyranny!
See! the ferocious slaves of power   5
Across the wasted country scour
And in thy very arms destroy
The pledges of thy nuptial joy—
    Thine unresisting family!

---

304 There] Then *1964B SC*/IV
307 dread.] dread **EN** *SC*/IV
308 steel-clad] steel clad **EN** *SC*/IV
    brow,] brow **EN** *SC*/IV
309 Tho'] Tho **EN** *SC*/IV
    conquest's] conquests **EN** *SC*/IV
    glow,] glow **EN** *SC*/IV
310 fear;] fear **EN** *SC*/IV

311 There] There, *1964B*
    and] & **EN** *SC*/IV
    command] command, *1964B*
312 pomp-fed] pomp fed **EN** *SC*/IV
    despot's] despots **EN** *SC*/IV
313 near,] near **EN** *SC*/IV
315 chain.] chain **EN** *SC*/IV

Text collated with **EN,** MS Berg (lines 32–40), *1964B, 1964J* (lines 32–40), and *SC*/IV. MS Berg and *1964J* are set in all caps except where indicated.

1 battle,] battle **EN** *SC*/IV
    Band!] Band **EN** *SC*/IV
2 thee!] thee **EN** *SC*/IV

6 scour] scour, *1964B*
8 joy—] joy **EN** *SC*/IV
9 family!] family **EN** *SC*/IV

10   Then citizens, form in battle array,
        For this is the dawn of a glorious day.
        March, march, fearless of danger and toil,
        And the rank gore of tyrants shall water your soil!

2

        What wills the coward, traitorous train
15   Of Kings, whose trade is perfidy?
        For whom is forged this hateful chain,
           For whom prepared this slavery?
        For you. On you their vengeance rests . . .
        What transports ought to thrill your breasts!
20   Frenchmen! this unhallowed train
        To ancient woe would bind again
           Those souls whom valour has made free!
             Chorus &c.

3

        What! shall foreign bands compel
           Us to the laws of tyranny?
25   Shall hired soldiers hope to quell
           The arm upraised for liberty?
        Great God! by these united arms
        Shall despots, their own alarms,
        Pass neath the yoke made for our head!
30   Yea! pomp-fed Kings shall quake with dread—
           These masters of Earth's destiny!
             Chorus &c.

---

10 Then] Then, *1964B*
    citizens,] citizens **EN** *SC*/IV
    array,] array **EN** *SC*/IV
11 day.] day **EN** *SC*/IV
12 and] & **EN** *SC*/IV
    toil,] toil **EN** *SC*/IV
13 your] y^r **EN** *SC*/IV
    soil!] soil **EN** *SC*/IV
14 traitorous] traiterous **EN** *SC*/IV
16 chain,] chain **EN** *SC*/IV

18 On] on **EN** *SC*/IV
20 train] train, *1964B*
22 free!] free **EN** *SC*/IV
24 tyranny?] tyranny **EN** *SC*/IV
25 hope] hopes **EN** *SC*/IV
28 despots,] despots **EN** *SC*/IV
    alarms,] alarms **EN** *SC*/IV
29 head!] head **EN** *SC*/IV
30 dread—] dread **EN** *SC*/IV

4

Tremble, Kings! despised of Man!
Ye traitors to your country,
Tremble! your parricidal plan
At length shall meet its destiny.   35
We all are soldiers fit for fight,
But if we sink in glory's night
Our Mother Earth will give ye new
The brilliant pathway to pursue
That leads to Death or Victory!   40
Chorus &c.

5

Frenchmen! on the guilty brave
Pour your vengeful energy.—
Yet in your triumph, pitying save
The unwilling slaves of tyranny;
But let the gore-stained despots bleed,   45
Be death fell Bouillé's bloodhound-meed;
Chase those unnatural fiends away
Who on their mothers' vitals prey
With more than tyger cruelty!
Chorus &c.

---

32 Tremble,] Tremble **EN** *SC*/IV
     TREMBLE Berg *1964J*
  Kings!] KINGS Berg *1964J*
  Man!] Man **EN** *SC*/IV
33 country,] country **EN** *SC*/IV
    COUNTRY Berg *1964J*
    country— *1964B*
35 destiny.] DESTINY . . . . Berg
    DESTINY. . . . *1964J*
36 fit for fight,] FIT TO *FIGHT* Berg
     FIT TO FIGHT *1964J*
  fight,] fight **EN** *SC*/IV
37 in] I N Berg
  glory's] glorys **EN** *SC*/IV
    GLORYS Berg *1964J*
  night] NIGT Berg
    NIG[H]T *1964J*

38 Earth] EARTH Berg
    EARTH *1964J*
  will give ye] will GIVE ye Berg
     will Give ye *1964J*
40 That] WHICH Berg *1964J*
  to Death or Victory!]
   to Death or Victory **EN** *SC*/IV
   TO *DEATH or VICTORY!* . . Berg
   to *DEATH* or *VICTORY.* *1964J*
43 triumph,] triumph **EN** *SC*/IV
44 tyranny;] tyranny **EN** *SC*/IV
45 gore-stained] gore stained **EN** *SC*/IV
  bleed,] bleed **EN** *SC*/IV
46 Bouillé's] Boullie's **EN** *1964B SC*/IV
  bloodhound-meed;]
   bloodhound-meed **EN** *SC*/IV
48 mothers'] mothers **EN** *1964B SC*/IV
49 cruelty!] cruelty **EN** *SC*/IV

50   Sacred Patriotism! uphold
          The avenging bands who fight with thee;
        And thou, more dear than meaner gold,
          Smile on our efforts, Liberty!
        Where conquest's crimson streamers wave,
55   Haste thou to the happy brave,
        Where at our feet thy dying foes
        See as their failing eyes unclose
          Our glory and thy Victory!

SUPPLEMENT
Stanza Included in Letter to Graham,
ca. 19 June 1811

TREMBLE KINGS DESPISED OF MAN!
    YE TRAITORS TO YOUR COUNTRY
TREMBLE! YOUR PARRICIDAL PLAN
35   AT LENGTH SHALL MEET ITS DESTINY . . . .
WE ALL ARE SOLDIERS FiT TO *FIGHT*
BUT IF WE SINK IN GLORYS NIGT
OUR MOTHER EARTH WIll GIVE ye NEW
THE BRILLIANT PATHWAY TO PURSUE
40   WHICH LEADS TO *DEATH or VICTORY!* . .

[*Esd* #48]   Written in very early youth

    I'll lay me down by the church-yard tree
    And resign me to my destiny;
    I'll bathe my brow with the poison dew
    That falls from yonder deadly yew,
5   And if it steal my soul away
    To bid it wake in realms of day,

---

51 thee;] thee **EN** *SC*/IV
52 thou,] thou **EN** *SC*/IV
    gold,] gold **EN** *SC*/IV
53 efforts,] efforts **EN** *SC*/IV
54 conquest's] conquests **EN** *SC*/IV
    wave,] wave **EN** *SC*/IV
58 and] & **EN** *SC*/IV
    Victory!] Victory **EN** *SC*/IV

Text collated with **EN,** *1964B,* and *SC*/IV.
1 church-yard] church yard **EN** *SC*/IV
2 destiny;] destiny **EN** *SC*/IV
3 I'll] Ill **EN** *SC*/IV
4 yew,] yew **EN** *SC*/IV
5 And] And, *1964B*
    away] away, *1964B*
6 day,] day **EN** *SC*/IV

Spring's sweetest flowers shall never be
So dear to gratitude and me!

Earthborn glory cannot breathe
Within the damp recess of death;   10
Avarice, Envy, Lust, Revenge
Suffer there a fearful change;
All that grandeur ever gave
Moulders in the silent grave.
Oh! that I slept near yonder yew,   15
That this tired frame might moulder too!

Yet Pleasure's folly is not mine,
No votarist I at Glory's shrine;
The sacred gift for which I sigh
Is not to live to feel alone—   20
I only ask to calmly die,
That the tomb might melt this heart of stone
    To love beyond the grave.

Zeinab and Kathema   *[Esd #49]*

Upon the lonely beach Kathema lay;
   Against his folded arm his heart beat fast.
Thro' gathering tears the Sun's departing ray
   In coldness o'er his shuddering spirit past,
And all unfelt the breeze of evening came   5
That fanned with quivering wing his wan cheek's feeble flame.

---

7 Spring's] Springs **EN** *SC*/IV

8 and] & **EN** *SC*/IV

10 death;] death **EN** *SC*/IV

11 Envy,] Envy **EN** *SC*/IV
   Lust,] Lust **EN** *SC*/IV
   Revenge] Revenge, *1964B*

12 change;] change **EN** *SC*/IV

14 grave.] grave **EN** *SC*/IV

15 yew,] yew **EN** *SC*/IV

16 tired] tired [?tried] *SC*/IV

17 mine,] mine **EN** *SC*/IV

18 votarist] votarist, *1964B*
   I] I, *1964B*
   Glory's] Glorys **EN** *SC*/IV
   shrine;] shine **EN** *SC*/IV

20 live] live, *1964B*
   feel] feel, *1964B*

alone—] alone **EN** *SC*/IV
            alone; *1964B*

21 die,] die **EN** *SC*/IV

22 tomb] stomb **EN** *SC*/IV

23 grave.] grave! *1964B*

Text collated with **EN**, *1964B*, and *SC*/IV.

Title. Kathema] Kathemah **EN** *SC*/IV

1 lay;] lay **EN** *SC*/IV

2 fast.] fast **EN** *SC*/IV

3 Thro'] Thro **EN**
   tears] tears, *1964B*
   Sun's] Suns **EN** *SC*/IV

4 o'er] oer **EN** *SC*/IV
   past,] past **EN** *SC*/IV

6 flame.] flame **EN** *SC*/IV

"Oh!" cried the mourner, "could this widowed soul
   "But fly where yonder Sun now speeds to dawn."
He paused—a thousand thoughts began to roll;
10   Like waves they swept in restless tumult on,
Like those fast waves that quick-succeeding beat
Without one lasting shape the beach beneath his feet.

And now the beamless, broad and yellow sphere
   Half sinking lingered on the crimson sea;
15 A shape of darksome distance does appear
    Within its semicircled radiancy.
All sense was gone to his betrothed one—
His eye fell on the form that dimmed the setting sun,—

He thought on his betrothed . . . for his youth
20   With her that was its charm to ripeness grew.
All that was dear in love, or fair in truth
   With her was shared as childhood's moments flew,
And mingled with sweet memories of her
Was life's unveiling morn with all its bliss and care.

25 O wild and lovely Superstition's spell—
   Love for the friend that life and freedom gave;
Youth's growing hopes that watch themselves so well,
   Passion so prompt to blight, so strong to save
And childhood's host of memories combine
30 Her life and love around his being to entwine,

<table>
<tr><td>

7 mourner,] mourner **EN** *SC*/IV

9 roll;] roll **EN** *SC*/IV

10 on,] on **EN** *SC*/IV

12 feet.] feet **EN** *SC*/IV

13 and] & **EN** *SC*/IV

14 Half sinking] Half-sinking *1964B*
   sea;] sea **EN** *SC*/IV

16 radiancy.] radiancy **EN** *SC*/IV

19 betrothed . . .]
    betrothed. . . *1964B SC*/IV

21 truth] truth, *1964B*

22 childhood's] childhoods **EN** *SC*/IV
   flew,] flew **EN** *SC*/IV

24 and] & **EN** *SC*/IV
   care.] care **EN** *SC*/IV
     care— *1964B*

</td><td>

25 O] A *SC*/IV *1964B*
   and] & **EN** *SC*/IV
   Superstition's]
    Superstitions **EN** *SC*/IV
   spell—] spell **EN** *SC*/IV
    spell. *1964B*

26 and] & **EN** *SC*/IV
   gave;] gave, *1964B*

27 Youth's] Youths **EN**
   well,] well **EN** *SC*/IV

28 Passion] Passion, *1964B*
   save] save, *1964B*

29 childhood's] childhoods **EN** *SC*/IV

30 and] & **EN** *SC*/IV
   entwine,] entwine **EN** *SC*/IV
    entwine. *1964B*

</td></tr>
</table>

And to their wishes with its joy-mixed pain.
    Just as the veil of hope began to fall,
The Christian murderers over-ran the plain,
    Ravaging, burning and polluting all.
Zeinab was reft to grace the robbers' land;   35
Each drop of kindred blood stained the invaders' brand.

Yes! they had come their holy book to bring,
    Which God's own son's apostles had compiled
That charity and peace, and love might spring
    Within a world by God's blind ire defiled,   40
But rapine, war and treachery rushed before
Their hosts, and murder dyed Kathema's bower in gore.

Therefore his soul was widowed, and alone
    He stood in the world's wide and drear expanse.
No human ear could shudder at his groan,   45
    No heart could thrill with his unspeaking glance;
One only hope yet lingering dared to burn,
Urging to high emprize and deeds that danger spurn.

The glow has failed on Ocean's western line,
Faded from every moveless cloud above.   50
The moon is up—she that was wont to shine
    And bless thy childish nights of guileless love,

---

31 pain.] pain **EN** *SC*/IV
      pain, *1964B*

33 plain,] plain **EN** *SC*/IV

34 Ravaging,] Ravaging **EN** *SC*/IV
    and] & **EN** *SC*/IV
    all.] all **EN** *SC*/IV

35 Zeinab] Zeniab **EN** *SC*/IV
    robbers'] robbers **EN** *SC*/IV
    land;] land **EN** *SC*/IV

36 invaders'] invaders **EN** *SC*/IV
    brand.] brand **EN** *SC*/IV

37 their] thier **EN**
    bring,] bring **EN** *SC*/IV

39 and] & **EN** *SC*/IV
    peace,] peace *1964B*
    and] & **EN** *SC*/IV

40 God's] Gods **EN** *SC*/IV
    defiled,] defiled **EN** *SC*/IV

41 and] & **EN** *SC*/IV

42 and] & **EN** *SC*/IV
    gore.] gore **EN** *SC*/IV

43 and] & **EN** *SC*/IV

44 and] & **EN** *SC*/IV
    expanse.] expanse **EN** *SC*/IV

45 groan,] groan **EN** *SC*/IV

46 glance;] glance **EN** *SC*/IV

47 burn,] burn **EN** *SC*/IV

48 and] & **EN** *SC*/IV
    spurn.] spurn **EN** *SC*/IV

49 Ocean's] Oceans **EN** *SC*/IV
    line,] line **EN** *SC*/IV

50 above.] above **EN** *SC*/IV

52 love,] love **EN** *SC*/IV

Unhappy one, ere Christian rapine tore
All ties, and stain'd thy hopes in a dear mother's gore.

55   The form that in the setting Sun was seen
            Now in the moonlight slowly nears the shore,
        The white sails gleaming o'er the billows green
            That sparkle into foam its prow before,
        A wanderer of the deep it seems to be,
60   On high adventures bent, and feats of chivalry.

        Then hope and wonder filled the mourner's mind.
            He gazed till vision even began to fail,
        When to the pulses of the evening wind
            A little boat approaching gave its sail,
65   Rode o'er the slow-raised surges near the strand,
        Ran up the beach and gave some stranger men to land.

        "If thou wilt bear me to far England's shore
            Thine is this heap—the Christian's God!"
        The chief with gloating rapture viewed the ore
70   And his pleased avarice gave the willing nod.
        They reach the ship, the fresh'ning breezes rise
        And smooth and fast they speed beneath the moonlight skies.

        What heart e'er felt more ardent longings now?
            What eye than his e'er beamed with riper hope
75   As curbed impatience on his open brow

---

54 ties,] ties;   *SC/IV*
    and] &   **EN** *SC/IV*
    stain'd] staind   **EN** *SC/IV*
    gore.] gore   **EN** *SC/IV*
56 shore,] shore   **EN** *SC/IV*
57 o'er] oer   **EN** *SC/IV*
    billows] billow   *SC/IV*
58 before,] before   **EN** *SC/IV*
59 be,] be   **EN** *SC/IV*
60 and] &   **EN** *SC/IV*
    chivalry.] chivalry   **EN** *SC/IV*
61 and] &   **EN** *SC/IV*
    mourner's] mourners   **EN** *SC/IV*
    mind.] mind   **EN** *SC/IV*
62 fail,] fail   **EN** *SC/IV*
64 sail,] sail   **EN** *SC/IV*

65 o'er] oer   **EN** *SC/IV*
    slow-raised] slow raised   **EN** *SC/IV*
    strand,] strand   **EN** *SC/IV*
66 and] &   **EN** *SC/IV*
    land.] land   **EN** *SC/IV*
67 England's] Englands   **EN** *SC/IV*
68 heap—the] heap the   **EN** *SC/IV*
    Christian's] Christians   **EN** *SC/IV*
    God!"] God"   **EN** *SC/IV*
69 ore] ore,   *1964B*
70 nod.] nod   **EN** *SC/IV*
71 fresh'ning] freshning   **EN** *SC/IV*
72 and] &   **EN** *SC/IV*
    skies.] skies   **EN** *SC/IV*
73 now?] now   **EN** *SC/IV*

There painted fancy's unsuspected scope,
As all that's fair the foreign land appeared
By ever-present love, wonder and hope endeared?

Meanwhile thro' calm and storm, thro' night and day,
   Unvarying in her aim the vessel went   80
As if some inward spirit ruled her way
   And her tense sails were conscious of intent,
Till Albion's cliffs gleamed o'er her plunging bow
And Albion's river-floods bright sparkled round her prow.

Then on the land in joy Kathema leaped   85
   And kissed the soil in which his hopes were sown—
These even now in thought his heart has reaped.
   Elate of body and soul he journeyed on,
And the strange things of a strange land past by
Like motes and shadows prest upon his charmed eye.   90

Yet Albion's changeful skies and chilling wind
   The change from Cashmire's vale might well denote:
There, Heaven and Earth are ever bright and kind;
   Here, blights and storms and damp forever float,
Whilst hearts are more ungenial than the zone—   95
Gross, spiritless, alive to no pangs but their own.

---

76 scope,] scope **EN** *SC*/IV

78 ever-present] ever present **EN** *SC*/IV
    and] & **EN** *SC*/IV
    endeared?] endeared **EN** *SC*/IV

79 thro'] thro **EN** *SC*/IV
    and] & **EN** *SC*/IV
    thro'] thro **EN** *SC*/IV
    and] & **EN** *SC*/IV
    day,] day **EN** *SC*/IV

80 went] went, *1964B*

82 intent,] intent **EN** *SC*/IV

83 Albion's] Albions **EN** *SC*/IV
    o'er] oer **EN** *SC*/IV

84 Albion's] Albions **EN** *SC*/IV
    river-floods] river floods **EN** *SC*/IV
    prow.] prow **EN** *SC*/IV

86 sown—] sown **EN** *SC*/IV

87 reaped.] reaped **EN** *SC*/IV

88 and] & **EN** *SC*/IV
    on,] on **EN** *SC*/IV

90 motes] mites *1964B*
       motes [?mites] *SC*/IV
    and] & **EN** *SC*/IV
    eye.] eye **EN** *SC*/IV

91 Albion's] Albions **EN** *SC*/IV
    and] & **EN** *SC*/IV

92 Cashmire's] Cashmires **EN**
    denote:] denote **EN** *SC*/IV
       denote. *1964B*

93 There,] There **EN** *SC*/IV
    and] & **EN** *SC*/IV
    and] & **EN** *SC*/IV
    kind;] kind **EN** *SC*/IV

94 Here,] Here **EN** *SC*/IV
    and] & **EN** *SC*/IV
    and] & **EN** *SC*/IV
    float,] float **EN** *SC*/IV

95 than] that *SC*/IV
    zone—] zone **EN** *SC*/IV

96 spiritless,] spiritless **EN** *SC*/IV
    own.] own **EN** *SC*/IV

There flowers and fruits are ever fair and ripe;
    Autumn there mingles with the bloom of spring
And forms unpinched by frost or hunger's gripe
100   A natural veil o'er natural spirits fling;
Here, woe on all but wealth has set its foot.
Famine, disease and crime even wealth's proud gates pollute.

Unquiet death and premature decay,
    Youth tottering on the crutches of old age,
105   And ere the noon of manhood's riper day,
    Pangs that no art of medicine can assuage,
Madness and passion ever mingling flames,
And souls that well become such miserable frames—

These are the bribes which Art to man has given
110   To yield his taintless nature to her sway.
So might dark night with meteors tempt fair Heaven
    To blot the sunbeam and forswear the day
Till gleams of baleful light alone might shew
The pestilential mists, the darkness and the woe.

115   Kathema little felt the sleet and wind,
    He little heeded the wide-altered scene;
The flame that lived within his eager mind
    There kindled all the thoughts that once had been.

---

97 There] There, *1964B*
   and] & **EN** *SC/IV*
   and] & **EN** *SC/IV*
   ripe;] ripe **EN** *SC/IV*
98 Autumn] Autumn, *1964B*
   there] there, *1964B*
   spring] spring, *1964B*
99 hunger's] hungers **EN** *SC/IV*
100 veil] viel **EN** *SC/IV*
   o'er] oer **EN** *SC/IV*
   fling;] fling **EN** *SC/IV*
101 foot.] foot **EN** *SC/IV*
102 and] & **EN** *SC/IV*
   wealth's] wealths **EN** *SC/IV*
   pollute.] pollute **EN** *SC/IV*
103 and] & **EN** *SC/IV*
   decay,] decay **EN** *SC/IV*

105 And] And, *1964B*
   manhood's] manhoods **EN** *SC/IV*
   day,] day **EN** *SC/IV*
106 assuage,] assuage **EN** *SC/IV*
107 and] & **EN** *SC/IV*
   flames,] flames **EN** *SC/IV*
108 frames—] frames **EN** *SC/IV*
110 sway.] sway **EN** *SC/IV*
111 dark] dank [?dark] *SC/IV*
   Heaven] Heavn **EN** *SC/IV*
114 and] & **EN** *SC/IV*
   woe.] woe **EN** *SC/IV*
115 and] & **EN** *SC/IV*
   wind,] wind **EN** *SC/IV*
116 wide-altered]
    wide altered **EN** *SC/IV*
   scene;] scene **EN** *SC/IV*
118 been.] been **EN** *SC/IV*

He stood alone in England's varied woe
Safe, mid the flood of crime that round his steps did flow.   120

It was an evening when the bitterest breath
    Of dark December swept the mists along
That the lone wanderer came to a wild heath.
    Courage and hope had staid his nature long;
Now cold, and unappeased hunger spent   125
His strength; sensation failed in total languishment.

When he awaked to life cold horror crept
    Even to his heart, for a damp deathy smell
Had slowly come around him while he slept.
    He started . . . lo! the fitful moonbeams fell   130
Upon a dead and naked female form
That from a gibbet high swung to the sullen storm

And wildly in the wind its dark hair swung,
    Low mingling with the clangor of the chain,
Whilst ravenous birds of prey that on it clung   135
    In the dull ear of night poured their sad strain,
And ghastlily her shapeless visage shone
In the unsteady light, half mouldered thro' the bone.

Then madness seized Kathema, and his mind
    A prophecy of horror filled. He scaled   140
The gibbet which swung slowly in the wind
    High o'er the heath.—Scarcely his strength avail'd

---

119 England's] Englands **EN**
       England s *SC*/IV
  woe] woe, *1964B*
120 Safe,] Safe *1964B*
  flow.] flow **EN** *SC*/IV
123 heath.] heath **EN** *SC*/IV
124 and] & **EN** *SC*/IV
  long;] long **EN** *SC*/IV
125 and] & **EN** *SC*/IV
126 strength;] strength, *1964B*
  languishment.]
    languishment **EN** *SC*/IV
129 slept.] slept **EN** *SC*/IV
130 started . . . lo!] started. . .lo! *SC*/IV

131 and] & **EN** *SC*/IV
132 storm] storm; *1964B*
133 its] it's **EN** *SC*/IV
  swung,] swung **EN** *SC*/IV
134 chain,] chain *SC*/IV
136 strain,] strain **EN** *SC*/IV
138 light,] light **EN** *SC*/IV
  thro'] thro **EN** *SC*/IV
  bone.] bone **EN** *SC*/IV
139 and] & **EN** *SC*/IV
140 He] he **EN** *SC*/IV
142 o'er] oer **EN** *SC*/IV
  heath.—Scarcely]
    heath.—scarcely *SC*/IV

To grasp the chain, when by the moonlight's gleam
His palsied gaze was fixed on Zeinab's altered frame.

145   Yes! in those orbs once bright with life and love
        Now full-fed worms bask in unnatural light;
    That neck on which his eyes were wont to rove
        In rapture, changed by putrefaction's blight,
    Now rusts the ponderous links that creak beneath
150   Its weight, and turns to life the frightful sport of death.

    Then in the moonlight played Kathema's smile
        Calmly.—In peace his spirit seemed to be.
    He paused, even like a man at ease awhile,
    Then spoke—"My love! I will be like to thee,
155   A mouldering carcase or a spirit blest,
    With thee corruption's prey, or Heaven's happy guest."

    He twined the chain around his neck, then leaped
        Forward, in haste to meet the life to come.
    An iron-souled son of Europe might have wept
160   To witness such a noble being's doom
    As on the death-scene Heaven indignant frowned
    And Night in horror drew her veil the deed around.

    For they had torn his Zeinab from her home,
        Her innocent habits were all rudely shriven;
165   And, dragged to live in love's untimely tomb,
        To prostitution, crime and woe was driven.

---

143 moonlight's] moonlights **EN** *SC*/IV
144 Zeinab's] Zeinabs **EN** *SC*/IV
    frame.] frame **EN** *SC*/IV
145 and] & **EN** *SC*/IV
146 light;] light **EN** *SC*/IV
148 putrefaction's]
    putrefactions **EN** *SC*/IV
    blight,] blight **EN** *SC*/IV
150 weight,] weight *1964B*
    and] & **EN** *SC*/IV
    death.] death **EN** *SC*/IV
152 Calmly.—In] Calmly.—in **EN** *SC*/IV
    be.] be **EN** *SC*/IV
153 paused,] paused **EN** *SC*/IV
    awhile,] awhile **EN** *SC*/IV
154 thee,] thee **EN** *SC*/IV

155 blest,] blest **EN** *SC*/IV
156 corruption's] corruptions **EN** *SC*/IV
    Heaven's] Heavens **EN** *SC*/IV
    guest."] guest **EN** *SC*/IV
158 come.] come **EN** *SC*/IV
159 iron-souled] iron souled **EN** *SC*/IV
160 being's] beings **EN** *SC*/IV
161 death-scene] death scene **EN** *SC*/IV
162 deed] dead *1964B SC*/IV
    around.] around **EN** *SC*/IV
163 home,] home **EN** *SC*/IV
164 shriven;] shriven **EN** *SC*/IV
165 And,] And **EN** *SC*/IV
    tomb,] tomb **EN** *SC*/IV
166 and] & **EN** *SC*/IV
    driven.] driven **EN** *SC*/IV

The human race seemed leagued against her weal,
And indignation cased her naked heart in steel.

Therefore against them she waged ruthless war
    With their own arms of bold and bloody crime,—   170
Even like a mild and sweetly-beaming star
    Whose rays were wont to grace the matin-prime
Changed to a comet, horrible and bright,
Which wild careers awhile then sinks in dark-red night.

Thus, like its God, unjust and pityless,   175
    Crimes first are made and then avenged by Man,
For where's the tender heart, whose hope can bless
    Or man's, or God's, unprofitable plan—
A universe of horror and decay,
Gibbets, disease, and wars and hearts as hard as they.   180

The Retrospect.   [Esd #50]
Cwm Elan 1812

To trace Duration's lone career,
To check the chariot of the year
Whose burning wheels forever sweep
The boundaries of oblivion's deep . . . .
To snatch from Time the monster's jaw   5
The children which she just had borne

---

167 weal,] weal **EN** *SC*/IV

168 steel.] steel **EN** *SC*/IV

170 and] & **EN** *SC*/IV
    crime,—] crime **EN** *SC*/IV

171 and] & **EN** *SC*/IV

172 matin-prime]
    matin prime **EN** *SC*/IV

173 comet,] comet **EN** *SC*/IV
    and] & **EN** *SC*/IV
    bright,] bright **EN** *SC*/IV

174 night.] night **EN** *SC*/IV

175 and] & **EN** *SC*/IV
    pityless,] pityless **EN** *SC*/IV

176 and] & **EN** *SC*/IV
    Man,] Man **EN**
        man, *1964B*
        man *SC*/IV

178 plan—] plan **EN** *SC*/IV

179 and] & **EN** *SC*/IV
    decay,] decay **EN** *SC*/IV

180 and] & **EN** *SC*/IV
    wars] wars, *1964B*
    and] & **EN** *SC*/IV
    they.] they **EN** *SC*/IV

Text collated with **EN,** *1964B*, and *SC*/IV.

1 career,] career **EN** *SC*/IV

2 year] year, *1964B*

4 deep . . . .] deep. . . . *1964B SC*/IV

5 Time] Time, *1964B*
    monster's] monsters **EN** *SC*/IV
        monsters, *1964B*

        And, ere entombed within her maw,
        To drag them to the light of morn
        And mark each feature with an eye
10   Of cold and fearless scrutiny . . . .
        It asks a soul not formed to feel,
        An eye of glass, a hand of steel;
        Thoughts that have passed and thoughts that are
        With truth and feeling to compare;
15   A scene which wildered fancy viewed
        In the soul's coldest solitude;
        With that same scene when peaceful love
        Flings rapture's colour o'er the grove,
        When mountain, meadow, wood and stream
20   With unalloying glory gleam
        And to the spirit's ear and eye
        Are unison and harmony.

        The moonlight was my dearer day:—
        Then would I wander far away
25   And lingering on the wild brook's shore
        To hear its unremitting roar,
        Would lose in the ideal flow
        All sense of overwhelming woe;
        Or at the noiseless noon of night
30   Would climb some heathy mountain's height
        And listen to the mystic sound
        That stole in fitful gasps around.
        I joyed to see the streaks of day
        Above the purple peaks decay
35   And watch the latest line of light
        Just mingling with the shades of night;

---

7 And,] And **EN** *SC/IV*
 maw,] maw **EN** *SC/IV*
10 and] & **EN** *SC/IV*
  scrutiny . . . .]
   scrutiny. . . . *1964B SC/IV*
11 feel,] feel **EN** *SC/IV*
12 steel;] steel, *1964B*
13 passed] passed, *1964B*
 and] & **EN** *SC/IV*
 are] are, *1964B*
16 soul's] souls **EN** *SC/IV*
 solitude;] solitude, **EN** *1964B SC/IV*

18 rapture's] raptures **EN** *SC/IV*
 o'er] oer **EN** *SC/IV*
 grove,] grove **EN** *SC/IV*
19 mountain,] mountain **EN** *SC/IV*
 meadow,] meadow **EN** *SC/IV*
 and] & **EN** *SC/IV*
21 spirit's] spirits **EN** *SC/IV*
 and] & **EN** *SC/IV*
26 roar,] roar **EN** *SC/IV*
28 woe;] woe **EN** *SC/IV*
36 night;] night **EN** *SC/IV*

For day with me, was time of woe
When even tears refused to flow;
Then would I stretch my languid frame
Beneath the wild-wood's gloomiest shade   40
And try to quench the ceaseless flame
That on my withered vitals preyed;
Would close mine eyes and dream I were
On some remote and friendless plain,
And long to leave existence there   45
If with it I might leave the pain
That with a finger cold and lean
Wrote madness on my withering mien.

It was not unrequited love
That bade my wildered spirit rove;   50
'Twas not the pride disdaining life,
That with this mortal world at strife
Would yield to the soul's inward sense,
Then groan in human impotence,
And weep, because it is not given   55
To taste on Earth the peace of Heaven;
'Twas not, that in the narrow sphere
Where Nature fixed my wayward fate
There was no friend or kindred dear
Formed to become that spirit's mate,   60
Which searching on tired pinion found
Barren and cold repulse around . . . .
Ah no! yet each one sorrow gave
New graces to the narrow grave:

For broken vows had early quelled   65
The stainless spirit's vestal flame.

---

38 flow;] flow   **EN** *SC/IV*

40 wild-wood's] wild-woods   **EN** *SC/IV*
                 wild-woods'   *1964B*

43 and] &   **EN** *SC/IV*

44 and] &   **EN** *SC/IV*
   plain,] plain   **EN** *SC/IV*

47 and] &   **EN** *SC/IV*

48 mien.] mein   **EN** *SC/IV*

51 pride] pride,   *1964B*
   life,] life   **EN** *SC/IV*

53 soul's] souls   **EN** *SC/IV*
   sense,] sense   **EN** *SC/IV*

56 Heaven;] Heaven.   *1964B*
                Heaven,   *SC/IV*

60 mate,] mate   **EN** *SC/IV*

61 Which] Which,   *1964B*
   pinion] pinion,   *1964B*

62 and] &   **EN** *SC/IV*
   around . . . .]
     around. . . .   *1964B SC/IV*

66 flame.] flame   **EN** *SC/IV*

Yes! whilst the faithful bosom swelled
Then the envenomed arrow came
And apathy's unaltering eye
70   Beamed coldness on the misery;
And early I had learned to scorn
The chains of clay that bound a soul
Panting to seize the wings of morn,
And where its vital fires were born
75   To soar and spurn the cold control
Which the vile slaves of earthly night
Would twine around its struggling flight.
O many were the friends whom fame
Had linked with the unmeaning name
80   Whose magic marked among mankind
The casket of my unknown mind,
Which hidden from the vulgar glare
Imbibed no fleeting radiance there.
My darksome spirit sought. It found
85   A friendless solitude around.—
For who, that might undaunted stand
The saviour of a sinking land,
Would crawl its ruthless tyrant's slave
And fatten upon freedom's grave,
90   Tho' doomed with her to perish, where
The captive clasps abhorred despair.

They could not share the bosom's feeling,
Which passion's every throb revealing
Dared force on the world's notice cold
95   Thoughts of unprofitable mould,
Who bask in Custom's fickle ray,

---

70 misery;] misery, **EN** *SC/*IV

73 morn,] morn **EN** *SC/*IV

74 its] it's **EN** *SC/*IV

75 soar] soar, *1964B*

  and] & **EN** *SC/*IV

77 flight.] flight **EN** *SC/*IV

78 O] O, *1964B*

81 mind,] mind **EN** *SC/*IV

82 Which] Which, *1964B*

  glare] glare, *1964B*

84 It] it **EN** *SC/*IV

87 land,] land[,] **EN**

88 crawl] crawl, *1964B*

tyrant's] tyrants **EN** *SC/*IV

89 freedom's] freedoms **EN** *SC/*IV

  grave,] grave **EN** *SC/*IV

90 perish,] perish *1964B*

92 *They*] <u>They</u> **EN** *SC/*IV

  bosom's] bosoms **EN** *SC/*IV

  feeling,] feeling **EN** *SC/*IV

93 Which] Which, *1964B*

  passion's] passions **EN** *SC/*IV

  revealing] revealing, *1964B*

96 ray,] ray **EN** *SC/*IV

  ray,— *1964B*

Fit sunshine of such wintry day!
They could not in a twilight walk
Weave an impassioned web of talk
Till mysteries the spirit press   100
In wild yet tender awfulness,
Then feel within our narrow sphere
How little yet how great we are!
But they might shine in courtly glare,
Attract the rabble's cheapest stare,   105
And might command where'er they move
A thing that bears the name of love;
They might be learned, witty, gay,
Foremost in fashion's gilt array,
On Fame's emblazoned pages shine,   110
Be princes' friends, but never mine!

Ye jagged peaks that frown sublime,
Mocking the blunted scythe of Time,
Whence I would watch its lustre pale
Steal from the moon o'er yonder vale!   115

Thou rock, whose bosom black and vast
Bared to the stream's unceasing flow,
Ever its giant shade doth cast
On the tumultuous surge below!

Woods, to whose depth retires to die   120
The wounded echo's melody,
And whither this lone spirit bent
The footstep of a wild intent—

Meadows! whose green and spangled breast
These fevered limbs have often pressed   125

---

97 day!] day.   *SC*/IV
98 *They*] They   **EN** *SC*/IV
101 awfulness,] awfulness   **EN** *SC*/IV
104 glare,] glare   **EN** *SC*/IV
108 gay,] gay   **EN** *SC*/IV
109 array,] array   **EN** *SC*/IV
110 Fame's] Fames   **EN** *SC*/IV
     shine,] shine   **EN** *SC*/IV
111 princes'] princes   **EN** *SC*/IV
112 sublime,] sublime   **EN** *SC*/IV
113 Time,] Time   **EN** *SC*/IV

115 o'er] oer   **EN** *SC*/IV
     vale!] vale   **EN** *SC*/IV
116 rock,] rock   **EN** *SC*/IV
     and] &   **EN** *SC*/IV
117 stream's] streams   **EN** *SC*/IV
     flow,] flow   **EN** *SC*/IV
118 its] it's   **EN** *SC*/IV
120 Woods,] Woods   **EN** *SC*/IV
121 melody,] melody   **EN** *SC*/IV
124 whose] Whose   *1964B SC*/IV
     and] &   **EN** *SC*/IV

Until the watchful fiend Despair
Slept in the soothing coolness there!
Have not your varied beauties seen
The sunken eye, the withering mien,
130   Sad traces of the unuttered pain
That froze my heart and burned my brain?

How changed since nature's summer form
Had last the power my grief to charm,
Since last ye soothed my spirit's sadness—
135   Strange chaos of a mingled madness!
Changed!—not the loathsome worm that fed
In the dark mansions of the dead,
Now soaring thro' the fields of air
And gathering purest nectar there,
140   A butterfly whose million hues
The dazzled eye of wonder views,
Long lingering on a work so strange,
Has undergone so bright a change!

How do I feel my happiness?
145   I cannot tell, but they may guess
Whose every gloomy feeling gone,
Friendship and passion feel alone,
Who see mortality's dull clouds
Before affection's murmur fly,
150   Whilst the mild glances of her eye
Pierce the thin veil of flesh that shrouds
The spirit's radiant sanctuary.

O thou! whose virtues latest known,
First in this heart yet claim'st a throne;

---

126 fiend] fiend, *1964B*
    Despair] despair *SC/IV*
        despair, *1964B*
129 mien,] mein, **EN** *SC/IV*
131 and] & **EN** *SC/IV*
    brain?] brain **EN** *SC/IV*
132 nature's] natures **EN** *SC/IV*
133 charm,] charm **EN** *SC/IV*
134 spirit's] spirits **EN** *SC/IV*
    sadness—] sadness **EN** *SC/IV*
137 dead,] dead **EN** *SC/IV*
138 thro'] thro **EN** *SC/IV*

139 there,] there **EN** *SC/IV*
141 views,] views **EN** *SC/IV*
142 strange,] strange **EN** *SC/IV*
146 gone,] gone **EN** *SC/IV*
147 and] & **EN** *SC/IV*
    alone,] alone **EN** *SC/IV*
        alone; *1964B*
148 mortality's] mortalitys **EN** *SC/IV*
152 spirit's] spirits **EN** *SC/IV*
153 known,] known **EN** *SC/IV*
154 claim'st] claimst **EN** *SC/IV*
    throne;] throne **EN** *SC/IV*

Whose downy sceptre still shall share   155
The gentle sway with virtue there;
Thou fair in form and pure in mind,
Whose ardent friendship rivets fast
The flowery band our fates that bind,
Which incorruptible shall last   160
When duty's hard and cold control
Had thawed around the burning soul;
The gloomiest retrospects that bind
With crowns of thorn the bleeding mind,
The prospects of most doubtful hue   165
That rise on Fancy's shuddering view,
Are gilt by the reviving ray
Which thou hast flung upon my day.

The wandering Jew's soliloquy   [Esd #51]

Is it the Eternal Triune, is it He
Who dares arrest the wheels of destiny
And plunge me in this lowest Hell of Hells?
Will not the lightning's blast destroy my frame?
Will not steel drink the blood-life where it swells?   5
No—let me hie where dark Destruction dwells,
To rouse her from her deeply-caverned lair
And, taunting her curst sluggishness to ire,
Light long Oblivion's death-torch at its flame
And calmly mount Annihilation's pyre.   10

Tyrant of Earth! pale misery's jackall thou!
Are there no stores of vengeful violent fate

---

156 there;] there   **EN** *SC*/IV
157 and] &   **EN** *SC*/IV
    mind,] mind   **EN** *SC*/IV
159 bind,] bind   **EN** *SC*/IV
160 Which] Which,   *1964B*
    incorruptible] incorruptible,   *1964B*
161 duty's] dutys   **EN** *SC*/IV
    and] &   **EN** *SC*/IV
162 soul;] soul   **EN** *SC*/IV
164 mind,] mind   **EN** *SC*/IV
166 view,] view   **EN** *SC*/IV
168 day.] day   **EN** *SC*/IV

Text collated with **EN**, *1964B*, and *SC*/IV.
Title. Jew's] Jews   **EN** *SC*/IV
1 Triune,] Triune   **EN** *SC*/IV
4 lightning's] lightnings   **EN** *SC*/IV
6 Destruction]
    destruction   *1964B SC*/IV
    dwells,] dwells   **EN** *SC*/IV
8 And,] And   **EN** *SC*/IV
    ire,] ire   **EN** *SC*/IV
9 Oblivion's] Oblivions   **EN** *SC*/IV
    death-torch] death torch   **EN** *SC*/IV
10 Annihilation's]
    Annihilations   **EN** *SC*/IV
11 misery's] Misery's   *1964B*

Within the magazines of thy fierce hate?
No poison in thy clouds to bathe a brow
15   That lowers on thee with desperate contempt?
Where is the noonday pestilence that slew
The myriad sons of Israel's favoured nation?
Where the destroying minister that flew
Pouring the fiery tide of desolation
20   Upon the leagued Assyrian's attempt?
Where the dark Earthquake demon who ingorged
At thy dread word Korah's unconscious crew?
Or the Angel's two-edged sword of fire that urged
Our primal parents from their bower of bliss
25   (Reared by thine hand) for errors not their own,
By thine omniscient mind foredoomed, foreknown?
Yes! I would court a ruin such as this,
Almighty Tyrant! and give thanks to thee.—
Drink deeply—drain the cup of hate—remit; then I may die.

[*Esd #52*]   To Ianthe. ~~Oct~~ Septr 1813

I love thee, Baby! for thine own sweet sake:
Those azure eyes, that faintly dimpled cheek,
Thy tender frame so eloquently weak,
Love in the sternest heart of hate might wake;
5   But more, when o'er thy fitful slumber bending
Thy mother folds thee to her wakeful heart,
Whilst love and pity in her glances blending,
All that thy passive eyes can feel, impart;
More, when some feeble lineaments of her

---

15 contempt?] contempt   **EN** *SC*/IV
17 Israel's] Israels   **EN** *SC*/IV
22 Korah's] Korahs   **EN** *SC*/IV
   crew?] crew   **EN** *SC*/IV
23 Angel's] Angels   **EN** *SC*/IV
   two-edged] two edged   **EN** *SC*/IV
24 their] thier   **EN** *SC*/IV
25 own,] own   **EN** *SC*/IV
26 omniscient] ~~omniscient~~   **EN** *SC*/IV
   foredoomed,] foredoomed   **EN** *SC*/IV
   foreknown?] foreknown   **EN** *SC*/IV
27 Yes!] yes!   *SC*/IV

this,] this   **EN** *SC*/IV
28 and] &   **EN** *SC*/IV
29 hate—remit;] hate—remit   **EN** *SC*/IV
   die.] die   **EN** *SC*/IV

Text collated with **EN,** *1964B,* and *SC*/IV.
Title. ~~Oct~~ Septr 1813] *Septr 1813*   *1964B*
1 thee,] thee   **EN** *SC*/IV
   sake:] sake;   *1964B*
2 cheek,] cheek   **EN** *SC*/IV
3 weak,] weak   **EN** *SC*/IV
7 and] &   **EN** *SC*/IV

Who bore thy weight beneath her spotless bosom,   10
As with deep love I read thy face, recur,
More dear art thou, O fair and fragile blossom,
Dearest, when most thy tender traits express
The image of thy Mother's loveliness.—

Evening—to Harriet. Sep. 1813   [Esd #53]

O thou bright Sun! beneath the dark blue line
Of western distance that sublime descendest,
And gleaming lovelier as thy beams decline,
Thy million hues to every vapour lendest,
And over cobweb lawn and grove and stream   5
Sheddest the liquid magic of thy light,
Till calm Earth with the parting splendor bright
Shews like the vision of a beauteous dream;
What gazer now with astronomic eye
Could coldly count the spots within thy sphere?   10
Such were thy lover, Harriet, could he fly
The thoughts of all that makes his passion dear,
And turning senseless from thy warm caress,
Pick flaws in our close-woven happiness.
July 31st 1813.

To Harriett   [Esd #54]

Thy look of love has power to calm
The stormiest passion of my Soul
Thy gentle words are drops of balm—
In lifes too bitter bowl.

---

10 bosom,] bosom **EN** *SC*/IV

12 thou,] thou **EN** *SC*/IV

   O] ô **EN** *SC*/IV

   and] & **EN** *SC*/IV

   blossom,] blossom **EN** *SC*/IV

Text collated with **EN**, *1964B*, and *SC*/IV.

3 decline,] decline **EN** *SC*/IV

5 and] & **EN** *SC*/IV

   and] & **EN** *SC*/IV

8 dream;] dream, **EN** *SC*/IV

12 dear,] dear **EN** *SC*/IV

13 And] And, *1964B*

   caress,] caress **EN** *SC*/IV

14 close-woven] close woven **EN** *SC*/IV

   happiness.] happiness **EN** *SC*/IV

Dateline. 31st] 31st: **EN** *SC*/IV

Text collated with **EN**, *1964B*, and *SC*/IV.

2 Soul] Soul; *1964B*

3 balm—] balm **EN** *1964B SC*/IV

4 lifes] life's *1964B*

   bowl.] bowl **EN** *SC*/IV

5   No grief is mine but that alone
           These choicest blessings I have known.

           Harriett! if all who long to live
           In the warm sunshine of thine eye
           That price beyond all pain must give
10   Beneath thy scorn to die
           Then hear thy chosen own too late
           His heart most worthy of thy hate.

           Be thou then one among mankind
           Whose heart is harder not for state—
15   Thou only virtuous gentle kind
           Amid a world of hate
           And by a slight endurance seal
           A fellow beings lasting weal.
                                    Cook's Hotel
           For pale with anguish is his cheek
20   His breath comes fast his eyes are dim
           Thy name is struggling ere he speak,
           Weak is each trembling limb.
           In mercy let him not endure
           The misery of a fatal cure.

25   O trust for once no erring guide
           Bid the remorseless feeling flee

---

6 known.] known   **EN** *SC*/IV
8 eye] eye,   *1964B*
9 give] give,—   *1964B*
10 die] die;   *1964B*
11 own] own,   *1964B*
   late] late,   *1964B*
12 hate.] hate   **EN** *SC*/IV
13 thou] thou,   *1964B*
   then] then,   *1964B*
14 state—] state   **EN** *SC*/IV
15 only] only,   *1964B*
   virtuous] virtuous,   *1964B*
   gentle] gentle,   *1964B*
   kind] kind,   *1964B*
16 hate] hate—   *1964B*

18 beings] being's   *1964B*
   weal.] weal   **EN** *SC*/IV
Comment. *Cook's Hotel*] *appears with the
   dateline at the end of the poem
   in 1964B*
19 cheek] cheek,   *1964B*
20 fast] fast,   *1964B*
   dim] dim;   *1964B*
21 speak,] speak;   *1964B*
          speak   *SC*/IV
22 limb.] limb   *SC*/IV
23 mercy] misery   *SC*/IV
24 cure.] cure   *SC*/IV
25 O] O,   *1964B*
   guide] guide!   *1964B*
26 flee] flee;   *1964B*

Tis malice tis revenge tis pride
Tis any thing but thee.
O deign a nobler pride to prove
And pity if thou canst not love.   30
                    May 1814

                "Full many a mind"   [*Esd #*55]

Full many a mind with radiant genius fraught
Is taught the dark scowl of misery to bear
How many a great soul has often sought
To stem the sad torrent of wild despair

T'would not be Earth's laws were given   5
To stand between Man, God & Heaven
To teach him where to seek & truly find
That lasting comfort peace of mind.
                    Stanmore.   1815

                May 1813: To Harriet . . . .   [*Esd #*56]

Oh Harriet love like mine that glows
What rolling years can e'er destroy

---

27 Tis] 'Tis   *1964B*
     malice] malice,   *1964B*
     tis] 'tis   *1964B*
     revenge] revenge,   *1964B*
     tis] 'tis   *1964B*
     pride] pride,   *1964B*
28 Tis] 'Tis   *1964B*
     thee.] thee   **EN** *SC*/IV
29 O] O,   *1964B*
     prove] prove,   *1964B*
30 love.] love!   *1964B*
          love   *SC*/IV
Dateline. *May 1814*]
          Cook's Hotel May 1814   *1964B*

Text collated with **EN,** *1964B,* and *SC*/IV.
Title. *no title*] Full many a mind   *1964B*

2 bear] bear;   *1964B*
4 despair] despair!   *1964B*
5 T'would] 'T'would   *1964B*
    Earth's] Earths   **EN** *SC*/IV
6 Man,] Man   **EN** *SC*/IV
    &] and   *1964B*
    Heaven] Heaven,   *1964B*
7 &] and   *1964B SC*/IV
8 comfort] comfort,   *1964B*

Text collated with **EN,** *1964B,* and *SC*/IV.
Title. May 1813: To Harriet . . . .]
          To Harriet | *May 1813*   *1964*B
      1813:] 1813   **EN** *SC*/IV
1 Harriet] Harriet,   *1964B*
    glows] glows,   *1964B*
2 destroy] destroy?   *1964B*

Without thee can I tell my woes,
And with thee can I speak my grief?

5   Ah no—past all the futile power
Of words to tell is love like mine.
My love is not the fading flower
That fleets ere it attains its prime
A moment of delight with thee
10   Would pay me for an age of pain

I'll tell not of Rapture and Joy
Which swells thro' the Libertine's frame
That breast must feel bliss with alloy
That is scorched by so selfish a flame

15   It were pleasure to die for my love
It were rapture to sink in the grave
My eternal affection to prove
My ever dear Harriet to save.

Without thee all pleasure were gloom
20   And with thee all sorrow were joy.
Ere I knew thee my Harriet each year
Passed in mournful rotation away
No friend to my bosom was dear
Slow rolled the unvarying day.

25   Shall I wake then those horrors anew
That swelled in my desperate brain

---

3 thee] thee, *1964B*
  woes,] woes? *1964B*
      woes *SC*/IV
4 thee] thee, *1964B*
  grief?] grief **EN** *SC*/IV
5 no—past] no past **EN** *SC*/IV
     no, past *1964B*
6 mine.] mine **EN** *SC*/IV
8 prime] prime; *1964B*
10 pain] pain. *1964B*
12 Libertine's] Libertines **EN** *SC*/IV
  frame] frame; *1964B*

14 flame] flame. *1964B*
15 love] love, *1964B*
17 prove] prove, *1964B*
18 save.] save **EN** *SC*/IV
19 gloom] gloom, *1964B*
20 joy.] joy **EN** *SC*/IV
21 thee] thee, *1964B*
  Harriet] Harriet, *1964B*
22 away] away; *1964B*
23 dear] dear, *1964B*
24 unvarying] unvayrying **EN** *SC*/IV
  day.] day **EN** *SC*/IV

When to death's darkened portals I flew
And sought miseries relief to my pain?

That hour which tears thee from me
Leaves nothing but death and despair   30
And that Harriet never could be
Were thy mind less enchantingly fair.

Tis not for the charms of thy form
Which decay with the swift rolling year
Ah no Heaven expands to my sight   35
For Elysium with Harriet must be.
        Cum Elam
                Adieu my love good night

                "Late was the night"   [*Esd #57*]

Late was the night the moon shone bright
It teinted the wals with a silver light
And threw its wide uncertain beam
Upon its rolling mountains stream

That stream so swift that rushes along   5
Has oft been dyed by the murderes song
It oft has heard the exulting wave
Of one who oft the murderes braved

---

27 death's] deaths   **EN** *SC*/IV
28 miseries] misery's   *1964B*
    pain?] pain   **EN** *SC*/IV
30 despair] despair,   *1964B*
31 that] that,   *1964B*
    Harriet] Harriet,   *1964B*
32 fair.] fair   **EN** *SC*/IV
33 Tis] 'Tis   *1964B*
    form] form,   *1964B*
34 year] year,   *1964B*
            years   *SC*/IV
35 no] no,   *1964B*
36 be.] be   **EN** *SC*/IV
Comment. Cum Elam | Adieu my love
            good night]

            Adieu, my love; good night. |
                Cum Elam   *1964B*
            Elam] Elam)   **EN** *SC*/IV

Text collated with **EN,** *1964B*, and *SC*/IV.
Title. *no title*] Late was the night   *1964B*
1 night] night,   *1964B*
    bright] bright;   *1964B*
2 wals] walls   *1964B*
3 wide] wide,   *1964B*
4 mountains]
        mountain   **EN** *1964B* *SC*/IV
        stream] stream.   *1964B*
6 murderes] murderer's   *1964B*
    song] song;   *1964B*
8 murderes] murderer   *1964B*
    braved] braved.   *1964B*

                    The Alpine summits which raised on high
10   Peacefully frown on the Valley beneath
                    And lift their Huge forms to the Sky
                    Oft have heard the voices of death

                    Now not a murmur floats on the air
                    Save the distant sounds of the torrents tide
15   Not a cloud obscures the moon so fair
                    Not a Shade is seen on the rocks to glide

                    See that fair form that [?] [?]
                    Her garments are tattered her bosom so bare
                    She shrinks from the yawning watery grave
20   And shivering around her enwraps her dark hair

                    Poor Emma has toiled oer many a mile
                    The victim of misery's own sad child
                    Pale is her cheek all trembling awhile
                    She totters & falls on the cold-striken wild.

                                                    1815

---

9 summits] summits,   *1964B*
   which] which,   *1964B*
   high] high,   *1964B*
10 Valley] valley   *SC/IV*
11 Sky] Sky,   *1964B*
12 voices] voice   *1964B*
   death] death.   *1964B*
14 sounds] rounds   *1964B*
   torrents] torrent's   *1964B*
   tide] tide,   *1964B*
15 moon] moors   *1964B SC/IV*
   fair] fair,   *1964B*
16 Shade] shade   **EN** *1964B SC/IV*
   glide] glide.   *1964B*
17 [?] [?]] he can save,   *1964B*
   leans ore   *SC/IV*

18 tattered] tattered,   *1964B*
   bare] bare?   *1964B*
19 grave] grave,   *1964B*
20 And] And,   *1964B*
   shivering] shivering,   *1964B*
   hair] hair.   *1964B*
   stanza break] *omitted*   **EN** *SC/IV*
21 oer] o'er   *1964B*
   mile] mile—   *1964B*
22 victim] victims   *SC/IV*
   child] child.   *1964B*
23 cheek] cheek,   *1964B*
   awhile] awhile,   *1964B*
24 &] and   *1964B*
   cold-striken] [cold-striken]   **EN**
      SC/IV

¹4
Feb^{ry} 28th 1806— To St Irvyne   [*Esd #58*]

Oer thy turrets St Irvyne the winter winds roar
The long grass of thy Towers streams to the blast
Must I never St Irvyne then visit thee more
Are those visions of transient happiness past

When with Harriet I sat on the mouldering height   5
When with Harriet I gazed on the star spangled sky
And the August Moon shone thro' the dimness of night
How swiftly the moments of pleasure fled by.

How swift is a fleeting smile chased by a sigh
This breast this poor sorrow torn breast must confess   10
Oh Harriet, loved Harriet tho' thou art not nigh
Think not thy lover thinks of thee less.

How oft have we roamed thro' the stillness of Eve
Through St Irvyne's old rooms that so fast fade away
That those pleasure winged moments were transient I
    grieve   15
My Soul like those turrets falls fast to decay

Text collated with **EN,** *1964B, 1967* (lines 17-20), and *SC/IV.*

14

Title. Feb^{ry} 28th 1806— To St Irvyne]
      To St Irvyne | *Feb^{ry} 28th 1805*
        1964B
      Feb^{ry} 28th 1805 To St Irvyne
        SC/IV
1 Oer] O'er *1964B*
   turrets] turrets, *1964B*
   St] S^t *SC/IV*
   Irvyne] Irvyne, *1964B*
   roar] roar, *1964B*
2 blast] blast. *1964B*
3 never] never, *1964B*
   St] S^t *SC/IV*
   Irvyne] Irvyne, *1964B*
   more] more? *1964B*
4 past] past— *1964B*

5 height] height, *1964B*
6 star spangled] star-spangled *1964B*
   sky] sky, *1964B*
7 night] night? *1964B*
8 moments] moment *1964B SC/IV*
   by.] by! *1964B*
9 sigh] sigh! *1964B*
10 sorrow torn] sorrow-torn *1964B*
   breast] breast, *1964B*
   confess] confess: *1964B*
11 loved Harriet] loved Harriet, *1964B*
   nigh] nigh, *1964B*
14 St] S^t *SC/IV*
   away] away. *1964B*
15 those] these *1964B*
   pleasure winged]
     pleasure-winged *1964B*
   grieve] grieve; *1964B*
16 decay] decay. *1964B*

My Harriet is fled like a fast fading dream
Which fades ere the vision is fixed on the mind
But has left a firm love & a lasting esteem
20   That my soul to her Soul must eternally bind

When my mouldering bones lie in the cold chilling grave
When my last groans are borne oer Stroods wide Lea
And over my Tomb the chill night tempests rave
Then loved Harriet bestow one poor thought on me.

To H Grove

---

17 fled] fled,   *1967*
    fast fading] fast-fading   *1964B 1967*
    dream] dream,   *1964B 1967*
18 mind] mind,   *1964B 1967*
19 &] and   *1964B 1967*
    esteem] esteem,   *1964B*
20 Soul] soul   *1964B 1967 SC/IV*
    bind] bind.   *1964B 1967*
21 cold] cold,   *1964B 1967*
    grave] grave,   *1964B*

22 oer] o'er   *1964B*
    Stroods] Strood's   **EN** *1964B SC/IV*
    Lea] Lea,   *1964B*
    lea   *SC/IV*
23 night tempests]
    night-tempests   *1964B*
    rave] rave,   *1964B*
24 Then] Then,   *1964B*
    Harriet] Harriet,   *1964B*
    me.] me   **EN** *SC/IV*

QUEEN MAB;

A

PHILOSOPHICAL POEM:

WITH NOTES.

BY

PERCY BYSSHE SHELLEY.

ECRASEZ L'INFAME!
Correspondance de Voltaire.

Avia Pieridum peragro loca, nullius ante
Trita solo ; juvat integros accedere fonteis ;
Atque haurire : juratque novos decerpere flores.
* * * * *
Unde prius nulli velarint tempora musæ.
Primum quod magnis doceo de rebus ; et arctis
Religionum animos nodis exsolvere pergo.
Lucret. lib. iv.

Δος πε ςῶ, καὶ κοσμον κινησω.
Archimedes.

LONDON:

PRINTED BY P. B. SHELLEY,

23, Chapel Street, Grosvenor Square.

1813.

Title page of *Queen Mab* (1813)

QUEEN MAB;

A Philosophical Poem: with Notes.

Although **Queen Mab** (**QM**) has often been dismissed as a juvenile effort, most authorities now agree that it is not only PBS's first major poem but the one most responsible for keeping his reputation alive—however notoriously—between 1824 and 1839, when Sir Timothy Shelley prevented MWS from publishing any of his poetry. Extensively pirated during these years, the poem and its voluminous notes had a wide readership within radical circles of the 1820s and 1830s, becoming important reading for Owenites, Chartists, and various socialist movements of the latter half of the nineteenth century, including Marxists. In addition to representing a major moment of intellectual synthesis and poetic achievement in Shelley's career, **QM** vividly represents its own cultural moment, standing—in the words of Kenneth Neill Cameron—as "a poem of the England of 1812, as typical as the speeches of Burdett or the articles of Cobbett" (*YS*, 240).

QM appeared in only one authorized, although not formally published, edition in PBS's lifetime. Parts of the poem and the notes were published separately in altered form. No pre-print manuscripts of the poem or its notes survive, and there are uncertainties about its date of composition as well as its passage through the press. Our investigation of these issues suggests that the poem itself was composed primarily between April 1812 and February 1813, whereas PBS probably wrote most of the prose notes after completing the poem and may have continued working on them as late as the summer, or even the fall, of 1813—after the printed volume is supposed by scholarly consensus to have emerged from the press. For Commentary see pages 491–670; for Historical Collation see pages 791–836. For the notes concerning **QM** in MWS's 1839 and 1840 editions of PBS's poetical works, see Appendix B, pages 847–57.

QUEEN MAB;

A

PHILOSOPHICAL POEM:
WITH NOTES.

ECRASEZ L'INFAME!

Correspondance de Voltaire.

Avia Pieridum peragro loca, nullius ante
Trita solo; juvat integros accedere fonteis;
Atque haurire: juvatque novos decerpere flores.
    *   *   *   *   *   *
Unde prius nulli velarint tempora musæ.
Primum quod magnis doceo de rebus; et arctis
Religionum animos nodis exsolvere pergo.

Lucret. lib. iv.

Δὸς που στῶ, καὶ κόσμον κινήσω.

Archimedes.

Text collated with *1813*, *1821.CLA* (unexpurgated), *1821.CLAX* (expurgated), *1821.BEN*, *1829.BRO*, *1834*, *1839*, and *1840*. *1821.CLAX* is a subset of *1821.CLA* and appears only to show the expurgated portions of *1821.CLA*. Greek Text in epigraph III collated with *1813*.

Title. MAB;] Mab. *1821.CLA*
        MAB *1829.BRO*
        MAB, *1834*
        MAB. *1839 1840*
Subtitle. A . . . NOTES.] *omitted*
      1821.CLA 1829.BRO 1839 1840
      A . . . POEM:] *omitted* *1834*
      POEM:] Poem. *1821.BEN*
Epigraph I. ECRASEZ . . . *Voltaire.*] *omitted*
      1821.CLA 1821.BEN
      1829.BRO 1834 1839 1840

Epigraph II. Avia . . . *Lucret.* lib. iv.] *omitted*
      1821.CLA 1821.BEN
      1829.BRO 1834 1839 1840
Epigraph III. Δὸς . . *Archimedes.*] *omitted*
      1821.CLA 1821.BEN 1834
      1839 1840
      Δὸς] Δος *1813*
      στῶ,] ςῶ, *1813*
      κόσμον] κοσμον *1813*
      κινήσω.] κινησω. *1813*

TO HARRIET * * * * *

Whose is the love that, gleaming through the world,
Wards off the poisonous arrow of its scorn?
    Whose is the warm and partial praise,
    Virtue's most sweet reward?

5   Beneath whose looks did my reviving soul
Riper in truth and virtuous daring grow?
    Whose eyes have I gazed fondly on,
    And loved mankind the more?

Harriet! on thine:—thou wert my purer mind;
10   Thou wert the inspiration of my song;
    Thine are these early wilding flowers,
    Though garlanded by me.

Then press unto thy breast this pledge of love,
And know, though time may change and years may roll,
15   Each flowret gathered in my heart
    It consecrates to thine.

Dedication. TO HARRIET * * * * * . . .   13 unto] into   *1834 1840*
      thine.] *omitted   1821.CLA*   15 flowret]
      1821.BEN 1839   flow'ret   *1829.BRO 1834 1840*
    TO HARRIET * * * * *]
    TO HARRIET * * * * *.
    1840

QUEEN MAB.

I.

How wonderful is Death,
Death and his brother Sleep!
One, pale as yonder waning moon
With lips of lurid blue;
The other, rosy as the morn   5
When throned on ocean's wave
It blushes o'er the world:
Yet both so passing wonderful!

Hath then the gloomy Power
Whose reign is in the tainted sepulchres   10
Seized on her sinless soul?
Must then that peerless form
Which love and admiration cannot view
Without a beating heart, those azure veins
Which steal like streams along a field of snow,   15
That lovely outline, which is fair
As breathing marble, perish?
Must putrefaction's breath
Leave nothing of this heavenly sight
But loathsomeness and ruin?   20
Spare nothing but a gloomy theme,
On which the lightest heart might moralize?
Or is it only a sweet slumber
Stealing o'er sensation,
Which the breath of roseate morning   25
Chaseth into darkness?
Will Ianthe wake again,
And give that faithful bosom joy
Whose sleepless spirit waits to catch
Light, life and rapture from her smile?   30

Yes! she will wake again,
Although her glowing limbs are motionless,

---

3 moon] moon,   *1839 1840*   rapture] rapture,   *1834 1840*
6 wave] wave,   *1839 1840*   32 motionless,]
27 Ianthe] Iänthe   *1821.BEN*   motionless   *1829.BRO 1834*
30 life]
    life,   *1821.CLA 1821.BEN 1834 1840*

And silent those sweet lips,
Once breathing eloquence,
35   That might have soothed a tyger's rage,
Or thawed the cold heart of a conqueror.
Her dewy eyes are closed,
And on their lids, whose texture fine
Scarce hides the dark blue orbs beneath,
40   The baby Sleep is pillowed:
Her golden tresses shade
The bosom's stainless pride,
Curling like tendrils of the parasite
Around a marble column.

45   Hark! whence that rushing sound?
'Tis like the wondrous strain
That round a lonely ruin swells,
Which, wandering on the echoing shore,
The enthusiast hears at evening:
50   'Tis softer than the west wind's sigh;
'Tis wilder than the unmeasured notes
Of that strange lyre whose strings
The genii of the breezes sweep:
Those lines of rainbow light
55   Are like the moonbeams when they fall
Through some cathedral window, but the teints
Are such as may not find
Comparison on earth.

Behold the chariot of the Fairy Queen!
60   Celestial coursers paw the unyielding air;
Their filmy pennons at her word they furl,
And stop obedient to the reins of light:
These the Queen of spells drew in,
She spread a charm around the spot,
65   And leaning graceful from the etherial car,

---

34 eloquence,] eloquence   *1821.CLA*
    1821.BEN 1839 1840
35 tyger's] tiger's   *1834 1839 1840*
41 shade] shade,   *1821.BEN*
55 moonbeams] moon-beams,
    1821.BEN

63 spells] Spells   *1821.CLA 1821.BEN*
    1839 1840
    in,] in;   *1834*
65 And] And,   *1834*
    etherial] ethereal   *1821.CLA*
    1821.BEN 1834 1839 1840

Long did she gaze, and silently,
        Upon the slumbering maid.

Oh! not the visioned poet in his dreams,
When silvery clouds float through the wildered brain,
When every sight of lovely, wild and grand   70
    Astonishes, enraptures, elevates,
        When fancy at a glance combines
        The wondrous and the beautiful,—
So bright, so fair, so wild a shape
        Hath ever yet beheld,   75
As that which reined the coursers of the air,
    And poured the magic of her gaze
        Upon the maiden's sleep.

        The broad and yellow moon
        Shone dimly through her form—   80
That form of faultless symmetry;
The pearly and pellucid car
        Moved not the moonlight's line:
        'Twas not an earthly pageant:
Those who had looked upon the sight,   85
        Passing all human glory,
        Saw not the yellow moon,
        Saw not the mortal scene,
        Heard not the night-wind's rush,
        Heard not an earthly sound,   90
        Saw but the fairy pageant,
        Heard but the heavenly strains
        That filled the lonely dwelling.

The Fairy's frame was slight, yon fibrous cloud,
That catches but the palest tinge of even,   95

---

70 wild] wild,   *1821.CLA 1821.BEN 1834*
    grand] grand,   *1821.CLA 1821.BEN*
      1834 1839 1840
71 elevates,]
    elevates—   *1821.BEN 1839 1840*
72 fancy] fancy,   *1821.CLA 1821.BEN*
    glance] glance,   *1821.CLA 1821.BEN*
73 wondrous]
    wond'rous   *1821.BEN 1839 1840*

    beautiful,—] beautiful,   *1834*
74 wild] wild,   *1834*
78 maiden's sleep.]
    sleeping maid.   *1821.BEN 1839 1840*
84 pageant:] pageant;   *1821.BEN 1839*
        1840
          pageant.   *1834*
85 looked] look'd   *1839 1840*
94 slight,] slight;   *1834 1839 1840*

And which the straining eye can hardly seize
When melting into eastern twilight's shadow,
Were scarce so thin, so slight; but the fair star
That gems the glittering coronet of morn,
100   Sheds not a light so mild, so powerful,
As that which, bursting from the Fairy's form,
Spread a purpureal halo round the scene,
    Yet with an undulating motion,
    Swayed to her outline gracefully.

105   From her celestial car
        The Fairy Queen descended,
        And thrice she waved her wand
Circled with wreaths of amaranth:
        Her thin and misty form
110   Moved with the moving air,
        And the clear silver tones,
        As thus she spoke, were such
As are unheard by all but gifted ear.

FAIRY.
    Stars! your balmiest influence shed!
115   Elements! your wrath suspend!
    Sleep, Ocean, in the rocky bounds
        That circle thy domain!
Let not a breath be seen to stir
Around yon grass-grown ruin's height,
120   Let even the restless gossamer
        Sleep on the moveless air!
        Soul of Ianthe! thou,
Judged alone worthy of the envied boon,
That waits the good and the sincere; that waits
125   Those who have struggled, and with resolute will
Vanquished earth's pride and meanness, burst the chains,
The icy chains of custom, and have shone

---

98 star] star, *1834*

102 purpureal]
   perpetual *1829.BRO 1834*

103 motion,] motion *1834*

104 *stanza break*] *page break* *1821.CLA*
   omitted *1821.BEN*

107 wand] wand, *1834*

119 height,] height; *1834*

122 Ianthe!] Iänthe! *1821.BEN*

123 boon,] boon *1834 1839 1840*

126 burst] bursts *1821.CLA*

The day-stars of their age;—Soul of Ianthe!
        Awake! arise!

            Sudden arose   130
        Ianthe's Soul; it stood
    All beautiful in naked purity,
    The perfect semblance of its bodily frame.
Instinct with inexpressible beauty and grace,
        Each stain of earthliness   135
    Had passed away, it reassumed
    Its native dignity, and stood
        Immortal amid ruin.

        Upon the couch the body lay
        Wrapt in the depth of slumber: 140
    Its features were fixed and meaningless,
        Yet animal life was there,
    And every organ yet performed
    Its natural functions: 'twas a sight
Of wonder to behold the body and soul.   145
    The self-same lineaments, the same
    Marks of identity were there:
Yet, oh, how different! One aspires to Heaven,
Pants for its sempiternal heritage,
And ever changing, ever rising still,   150
        Wantons in endless being.
The other, for a time the unwilling sport
Of circumstance and passion, struggles on;
Fleets through its sad duration rapidly;
Then like an useless and worn-out machine,   155
    Rots, perishes, and passes.

---

128 Ianthe!] Iänthe! *1821.BEN*

131 Ianthe's] Iänthe's *1821.BEN*
    Soul; it] Soul! It *1834*

133 frame.] frame, *1834*

134 grace,] grace. *1834*

136 away,] away: *1834*
    reassumed] re-assumed *1821.BEN*

139 lay] lay, *1821.BEN 1839 1840*

144 functions:] functions; *1839 1840*

147 identity] identity, *1834*
    there:] there; *1839 1840*

148 oh,] oh *1839 1840*

Heaven,] heaven, *1834 1840*

150 And] And, *1834*
    ever changing,] ever-changing,
      1821.CLA 1821.BEN 1839 1840
    ever rising] ever-rising
      1821.CLA 1821.BEN 1839 1840

154 rapidly;]
    rapidly: *1821.CLA 1821.BEN*

155 Then] Then, *1834*
    an] a *1821.BEN 1834 1839 1840*

156 perishes,] perishes *1839 1840*
    stanza break] *omitted* *1834*

FAIRY.

Spirit! who hast dived so deep;
Spirit! who hast soared so high;
Thou the fearless, thou the mild,
160   Accept the boon thy worth hath earned,
Ascend the car with me.

SPIRIT.

Do I dream? is this new feeling
But a visioned ghost of slumber?
If indeed I am a soul,
165   A free, a disembodied soul,
Speak again to me.

FAIRY.

I am the Fairy MAB: to me 'tis given
The wonders of the human world to keep:
The secrets of the immeasurable past,
170   In the unfailing consciences of men,
Those stern, unflattering chroniclers, I find:
The future, from the causes which arise
In each event, I gather: not the sting
Which retributive memory implants
175   In the hard bosom of the selfish man;
Nor that extatic and exulting throb
Which virtue's votary feels when he sums up
The thoughts and actions of a well-spent day,
Are unforeseen, unregistered by me:
180   And it is yet permitted me, to rend
The veil of mortal frailty, that the spirit
Clothed in its changeless purity, may know
How soonest to accomplish the great end
For which it hath its being, and may taste
185   That peace, which in the end all life will share.

---

158 soared] soar'd   *1839 1840*
161 *stanza break*] omitted   *1834*
162 is] Is   *1821.CLA 1821.BEN 1839 1840*
165 free,] free   *1834*
166 *stanza break*] omitted   *1834*
          page break 1839
168 keep:] keep.   *1839 1840*

171 stern,] stern   *1834*
176 extatic] ecstatic   *1839 1840*
181 spirit] spirit,   *1834 1839 1840*
185 peace,] peace   *1834*
    end] end,   *1839 1840*
    share.] share,   *1821.BEN*

This is the meed of virtue; happy Soul,
        Ascend the car with me!

    The chains of earth's immurement
        Fell from Ianthe's spirit;
They shrank and brake like bandages of straw   190
    Beneath a wakened giant's strength.
        She knew her glorious change,
    And felt in apprehension uncontrolled
        New raptures opening round:
    Each day-dream of her mortal life,   195
    Each frenzied vision of the slumbers
        That closed each well-spent day,
        Seemed now to meet reality.

    The Fairy and the Soul proceeded;
        The silver clouds disparted;   200
And as the car of magic they ascended,
    Again the speechless music swelled,
    Again the coursers of the air
Unfurled their azure pennons, and the Queen
        Shaking the beamy reins   205
        Bade them pursue their way.

        The magic car moved on.
    The night was fair, and countless stars
    Studded heaven's dark blue vault,—
        Just o'er the eastern wave   210
    Peeped the first faint smile of morn:—
        The magic car moved on—
        From the celestial hoofs
The atmosphere in flaming sparkles flew,
        And where the burning wheels   215
Eddied above the mountain's loftiest peak,
        Was traced a line of lightning.
        Now it flew far above a rock,

186 Soul,] soul,   *1821.BEN*

189 Ianthe's] Iänthe's   *1821.BEN*

190 brake] break   *1821.CLA 1821.BEN*

193 uncontrolled]
        uncontrolled,   *1821.BEN*

201 And] And,   *1834*

204 Queen] Queen,   *1839 1840*

205 reins] reins,   *1839 1840*

206 *stanza break*] *page break*   *1829.BRO*
                        omitted   *1834*

211 Peeped] Peep'd   *1839*

215 And] And,   *1834*

The utmost verge of earth,
220   The rival of the Andes, whose dark brow
Lowered o'er the silver sea.

Far, far below the chariot's path,
Calm as a slumbering babe,
Tremendous Ocean lay.
225   The mirror of its stillness shewed
The pale and waning stars,
The chariot's fiery track,
And the grey light of morn
Tinging those fleecy clouds
230   That canopied the dawn.
Seemed it, that the chariot's way
Lay through the midst of an immense concave,
Radiant with million constellations, tinged
With shades of infinite colour,
235   And semicircled with a belt
Flashing incessant meteors.

The magic car moved on.
As they approached their goal
The coursers seemed to gather speed;
240   The sea no longer was distinguished; earth
Appeared a vast and shadowy sphere;
The sun's unclouded orb
Rolled through the black concave;
Its rays of rapid light
245   Parted around the chariot's swifter course,
And fell, like ocean's feathery spray
Dashed from the boiling surge
Before a vessel's prow.

The magic car moved on.
250   Earth's distant orb appeared
The smallest light that twinkles in the heaven;
Whilst round the chariot's way
Innumerable systems rolled,

---

225 shewed] showed *1839 1840*   241 Appeared] Appear'd *1839 1840*
235 semicircled] semi-circled *1821.BEN*   243 concave;] concave: *1821.BEN*
238 goal] goal, *1839 1840*   246 fell,] fell *1834*

And countless spheres diffused
An ever-varying glory.   255
It was a sight of wonder: some
Were horned like the crescent moon;
Some shed a mild and silver beam
Like Hesperus o'er the western sea;
Some dash'd athwart with trains of flame,   260
Like worlds to death and ruin driven;
Some shone like suns, and as the chariot passed,
Eclipsed all other light.

Spirit of Nature! here!
In this interminable wilderness   265
Of worlds, at whose immensity
Even soaring fancy staggers,
Here is thy fitting temple.
Yet not the lightest leaf
That quivers to the passing breeze   270
Is less instinct with thee:
Yet not the meanest worm
That lurks in graves and fattens on the dead
Less shares thy eternal breath.
Spirit of Nature! thou!   275
Imperishable as this scene,
Here is thy fitting temple.

II.

IF solitude hath ever led thy steps
To the wild ocean's echoing shore,
And thou hast lingered there,
Until the sun's broad orb
Seemed resting on the burnished wave,   5
Thou must have marked the lines
Of purple gold, that motionless
Hung o'er the sinking sphere:
Thou must have marked the billowy clouds

---

257 horned] hornèd *1840*   269 lightest] slightest *1839*
259 western] Western *1821.BEN*   277 temple.] temple! *1839 1840*
260 dash'd] dashed *1839 1840*
262 and] and, *1834*   3 there,] there *1834*

10   Edged with intolerable radiancy
                                     Towering like rocks of jet
                                     Crowned with a diamond wreath.
                                     And yet there is a moment,
                                     When the sun's highest point
15   Peeps like a star o'er ocean's western edge,
                   When those far clouds of feathery gold,
                      Shaded with deepest purple, gleam
                      Like islands on a dark blue sea;
                  Then has thy fancy soared above the earth,
20   And furled its wearied wing
                                 Within the Fairy's fane.

                               Yet not the golden islands
                               Gleaming in yon flood of light,
                               Nor the feathery curtains
25   Stretching o'er the sun's bright couch,
                             Nor the burnished ocean waves
                               Paving that gorgeous dome,
                       So fair, so wonderful a sight
                  As Mab's etherial palace could afford.
30   Yet likest evening's vault, that faery Hall!
                  As Heaven, low resting on the wave, it spread
                             Its floors of flashing light,
                               Its vast and azure dome,
                               Its fertile golden islands
35   Floating on a silver sea;
                  Whilst suns their mingling beamings darted
                  Through clouds of circumambient darkness,
                      And pearly battlements around
                      Looked o'er the immense of Heaven.

40   The magic car no longer moved.
                      The Fairy and the Spirit

---

10 radiancy] radiancy,   *1829.BRO 1834*
     1839 1840
26 ocean waves] ocean's waves,
               1821.BEN
           ocean-waves, *1839*
           1840
28 wonderful] wonderful, *1834*
29 etherial] ethereal *1821.CLA*

        1821.BEN 1834 1839 1840
30 faery] fairy *1821.BEN 1839 1840*
        faëry *1834*
39 Looked] Look'd *1839*
  stanza break] *page break* **1813**
      omitted 1821.CLA
        1821.BEN

Entered the Hall of Spells:
            Those golden clouds
        That rolled in glittering billows
        Beneath the azure canopy   45
With the etherial footsteps, trembled not:
        The light and crimson mists,
Floating to strains of thrilling melody
        Through that unearthly dwelling,
Yielded to every movement of the will.   50
Upon their passive swell the Spirit leaned,
And, for the varied bliss that pressed around,
        Used not the glorious privilege
        Of virtue and of wisdom.

        Spirit! the Fairy said,   55
    And pointed to the gorgeous dome,
        This is a wondrous sight
        And mocks all human grandeur;
But, were it virtue's only meed, to dwell
In a celestial palace, all resigned   60
To pleasurable impulses, immured
Within the prison of itself, the will
Of changeless nature would be unfulfilled.
Learn to make others happy. Spirit, come!
This is thine high reward:—the past shall rise;   65
Thou shalt behold the present; I will teach
        The secrets of the future.

    The Fairy and the Spirit
Approached the overhanging battlement.—
        Below lay stretched the universe!   70
        There, far as the remotest line
        That bounds imagination's flight,
            Countless and unending orbs
        In mazy motion intermingled,
        Yet still fulfilled immutably   75

---

42 Entered] Enter'd *1839*   52 pressed] press'd *1839*

43 clouds] clouds, *1834*   57 sight] sight, *1821.BEN 1834*

45 canopy] canopy, *1821.BEN 1839 1840*   59 meed,] meed *1834*

46 etherial] ethereal *1821.CLA*   65 rise;] rise. *1834*

    1821.BEN 1829.BRO 1834 1839 1840   73 orbs] orbs, *1834*

    footsteps,] footsteps *1839 1840*

            Eternal nature's law.
            Above, below, around
            The circling systems formed
          A wilderness of harmony;
80   Each with undeviating aim,
        In eloquent silence, through the depths of space
            Pursued its wondrous way.

            There was a little light
        That twinkled in the misty distance:
85   None but a spirit's eye
            Might ken that rolling orb;
            None but a spirit's eye,
            And in no other place
        But that celestial dwelling, might behold
90   Each action of this earth's inhabitants.
            But matter, space and time
        In those aërial mansions cease to act;
        And all-prevailing wisdom, when it reaps
        The harvest of its excellence, o'erbounds
95   Those obstacles, of which an earthly soul
            Fears to attempt the conquest.

          The Fairy pointed to the earth.
          The Spirit's intellectual eye
          Its kindred beings recognized.
100   The thronging thousands, to a passing view,
          Seemed like an anthill's citizens.
            How wonderful! that even
        The passions, prejudices, interests,
        That sway the meanest being, the weak touch
105   That moves the finest nerve,
            And in one human brain
        Causes the faintest thought, becomes a link
            In the great chain of nature.

---

76 nature's] Nature's   *1839 1840*
77 around] around,   *1821.BEN 1834*
91 space] space,   *1821.CLA 1821.BEN*
    1829.BRO 1834
  time] time,   *1834 1839 1840*

92 aërial] aerial   *1834 1839 1840*
  act;] act: *1829.BRO 1834*
95 obstacles,] obstacles   *1834*
101 anthill's] ant-hill's   *1834 1839 1840*

Behold, the Fairy cried,
Palmyra's ruined palaces!—   110
Behold! where grandeur frowned;
Behold! where pleasure smiled;
What now remains?—the memory
Of senselessness and shame—
What is immortal there?   115
Nothing—it stands to tell
A melancholy tale, to give
An awful warning: soon
Oblivion will steal silently
The remnant of its fame.   120
Monarchs and conquerors there
Proud o'er prostrate millions trod—
The earthquakes of the human race;
Like them, forgotten when the ruin
That marks their shock is past.   125

Beside the eternal Nile,
The Pyramids have risen.
Nile shall pursue his changeless way:
Those pyramids shall fall;
Yea! not a stone shall stand to tell   130
The spot whereon they stood;
Their very scite shall be forgotten,
As is their builder's name!

Behold yon sterile spot;
Where now the wandering Arab's tent   135
Flaps in the desart-blast.
There once old Salem's haughty fane
Reared high to heaven its thousand golden domes,

---

109 cried,] cried.   *1821.CLA*   fall;] fall: *1829.BRO 1834*
110 ruined] ruin'd   *1839 1840*   130 Yea!] Yea,   *1829.BRO 1834*
112 Behold!] Behold   *1834*   132 scite]
121 there] there,   *1821.BEN*   site   *1829.BRO 1834 1839 1840*
123 race;] race,   *1821.BEN*   134 spot;] spot,   *1829.BRO 1834*
    race,—   *1839 1840*   136 desart-blast.] desart blast.   *1821.CLA*
124 them,] them   *1834*   *1821.BEN*
126 Nile,] Nile   *1834 1839 1840*   desart-blast.   *1829.BRO*
128 way:] way;   *1839 1840*   *1839 1840*
129 pyramids]   desart-blast,   *1834*
    Pyramids   *1821.BEN 1839 1840*

And in the blushing face of day
140   Exposed its shameful glory.
Oh! many a widow, many an orphan cursed
The building of that fane; and many a father,
Worn out with toil and slavery, implored
The poor man's God to sweep it from the earth,
145 And spare his children the detested task
Of piling stone on stone, and poisoning
         The choicest days of life,
         To soothe a dotard's vanity.
There an inhuman and uncultured race
150 Howled hideous praises to their Demon-God;
They rushed to war, tore from the mother's womb
The unborn child,—old age and infancy
Promiscuous perished; their victorious arms
Left not a soul to breathe. Oh! they were fiends:
155 But what was he who taught them that the God
Of nature and benevolence had given
A special sanction to the trade of blood?
His name and theirs are fading, and the tales
Of this barbarian nation, which imposture
160 Recites till terror credits, are pursuing
         Itself into forgetfulness.

Where Athens, Rome, and Sparta stood,
There is a moral desart now:
The mean and miserable huts,
165 The yet more wretched palaces,
Contrasted with those antient fanes,
Now crumbling to oblivion;
The long and lonely colonnades,
Through which the ghost of Freedom stalks,
170   Seem like a well-known tune,
Which, in some dear scene we have loved to hear,

---

139 And] And,   *1821.BEN*
    day] day, *1821.BEN*
141 orphan] orphan,   *1834*
144 God] god *1821.BEN*
149 There] Their   *1821.CLA*
150 Demon-God;]
    Demon-God: *1821.BEN*
154 fiends:] fiends! *1834*

155 them] them,   *1821.BEN*
162 Sparta] Sparta,   *1834*
163 desart] desert   *1834 1839 1840*
166 antient] ancient   *1821.CLA*
    1821.BEN 1829.BRO 1834 1839
    1840
168 colonnades,] colonades,   *1821.BEN*

Remembered now in sadness.
But, oh! how much more changed,
How gloomier is the contrast
Of human nature there!   175
Where Socrates expired, a tyrant's slave,
A coward and a fool, spreads death around—
Then, shuddering, meets his own.
Where Cicero and Antoninus lived,
A cowled and hypocritical monk   180
Prays, curses and deceives.

Spirit! ten thousand years
Have scarcely past away,
Since, in the waste where now the savage drinks
His enemy's blood, and aping Europe's sons,   185
Wakes the unholy song of war,
Arose a stately city,
Metropolis of the western continent:
There, now, the mossy column-stone,
Indented by time's unrelaxing grasp,   190
Which once appeared to brave
All, save its country's ruin;
There the wide forest scene,
Rude in the uncultivated loveliness
Of gardens long run wild,   195
Seems, to the unwilling sojourner, whose steps
Chance in that desart has delayed,
Thus to have stood since earth was what it is.
Yet once it was the busiest haunt,
Whither, as to a common centre, flocked   200
Strangers, and ships, and merchandize:
Once peace and freedom blest
The cultivated plain:
But wealth, that curse of man,
Blighted the bud of its prosperity: 205
Virtue and wisdom, truth and liberty,

---

178 shuddering,] shuddering   *1839*   185 and] and,   *1834*
180 cowled and hypocritical]   190 time's] Time's   *1821.BEN*
     hypocritical and cowled   *1821.BEN*   196 Seems,] Seems   *1821.BEN*
181 curses] curses,   *1821.CLA 1821.BEN*   197 desart]
     1829.BRO 1834 1839 1840   desert   *1829.BRO 1834 1839 1840*
183 past] passed   *1840*

Fled, to return not, until man shall know
That they alone can give the bliss
Worthy a soul that claims
210   Its kindred with eternity.

There's not one atom of yon earth
But once was living man;
Nor the minutest drop of rain,
That hangeth in its thinnest cloud,
215   But flowed in human veins:
And from the burning plains
Where Lybian monsters yell,
From the most gloomy glens
Of Greenland's sunless clime,
220   To where the golden fields
Of fertile England spread
Their harvest to the day,
Thou canst not find one spot
Whereon no city stood.

225   How strange is human pride!
I tell thee that those living things,
To whom the fragile blade of grass,
That springeth in the morn
And perisheth ere noon,
230   Is an unbounded world;
I tell thee that those viewless beings,
Whose mansion is the smallest particle
Of the impassive atmosphere,
Think, feel and live like man;
235   That their affections and antipathies,
Like his, produce the laws
Ruling their moral state;
And the minutest throb
That through their frame diffuses
240   The slightest, faintest motion,

---

212 man;] man!   *1821.BEN*
214 cloud,] cloud   *1839*
215 veins:] veins;   *1821.BEN*
230 world;] world: *1821.BEN*

234 feel] feel,   *1821.CLA 1821.BEN 1834*
    live] live,   *1834*
238 throb] throb,   *1834*
240 slightest,] slightest   *1834*

Is fixed and indispensable
As the majestic laws
That rule yon rolling orbs.

The Fairy paused. The Spirit,
In extacy of admiration, felt   245
All knowledge of the past revived; the events
Of old and wondrous times,
Which dim tradition interruptedly
Teaches the credulous vulgar, were unfolded
In just perspective to the view;   250
Yet dim from their infinitude.
The Spirit seemed to stand
High on an isolated pinnacle;
The flood of ages combating below,
The depth of the unbounded universe   255
Above, and all around
Nature's unchanging harmony.

III.

FAIRY! the Spirit said,
And on the Queen of spells
Fixed her etherial eyes,
I thank thee. Thou hast given
A boon which I will not resign, and taught   5
A lesson not to be unlearned. I know
The past, and thence I will essay to glean
A warning for the future, so that man
May profit by his errors, and derive
Experience from his folly: 10
For, when the power of imparting joy
Is equal to the will, the human soul
Requires no other heaven.

---

245 extacy] ecstacy   *1821.BEN 1839 1840*
250 view;] view,   *1834*

2 spells] Spells   *1821.CLA 1821.BEN
1839 1840*

3 etherial] ethereal   *1821.CLA 1821.BEN
1829.BRO 1834 1839 1840*
4 hast] has   *1821.BEN*
10 folly:]   folly; *1834*

Turn thee, surpassing Spirit!
15 Much yet remains unscanned.
Thou knowest how great is man,
Thou knowest his imbecility:
Yet learn thou what he is;
Yet learn the lofty destiny
20 Which restless time prepares
For every living soul.

Behold a gorgeous palace, that, amid
Yon populous city, rears its thousand towers
And seems itself a city. Gloomy troops
25 Of centinels, in stern and silent ranks,
Encompass it around: the dweller there
Cannot be free and happy; hearest thou not
The curses of the fatherless, the groans
Of those who have no friend? He passes on:
30 The King, the wearer of a gilded chain
That binds his soul to abjectness, the fool
Whom courtiers nickname monarch, whilst a slave
Even to the basest appetites—that man
Heeds not the shriek of penury; he smiles
35 At the deep curses which the destitute
Mutter in secret, and a sullen joy
Pervades his bloodless heart when thousands groan
But for those morsels which his wantonness
Wastes in unjoyous revelry, to save
40 All that they love from famine: when he hears
The tale of horror, to some ready-made face
Of hypocritical assent he turns,
Smothering the glow of shame, that, spite of him,
Flushes his bloated cheek.

Now to the meal
45 Of silence, grandeur, and excess, he drags
His palled unwilling appetite. If gold,
Gleaming around, and numerous viands culled

---

20 time] Time *1839 1840*   38 morsels] morsels, *1839*
25 centinels,] sentinels, *1834 1839 1840*   42 assent] assents *1834*
27 happy; hearest] happy. Hearest *1834*   46 gold,] gold *1834*
34 penury;] penury: *1821.BEN*

From every clime, could force the loathing sense
To overcome satiety,—if wealth
The spring it draws from poisons not,—or vice,   50
Unfeeling, stubborn vice, converteth not
Its food to deadliest venom; then that king
Is happy; and the peasant who fulfills
His unforced task, when he returns at even,
And by the blazing faggot meets again   55
Her welcome for whom all his toil is sped,
Tastes not a sweeter meal.

          Behold him now
Stretched on the gorgeous couch; his fevered brain
Reels dizzily awhile: but ah! too soon
The slumber of intemperance subsides,   60
And conscience, that undying serpent, calls
Her venomous brood to their nocturnal task.
Listen! he speaks! oh! mark that frenzied eye—
Oh! mark that deadly visage.

          KING.

          No cessation!
Oh! must this last for ever! Awful death,   65
I wish, yet fear to clasp thee!—Not one moment
Of dreamless sleep! O dear and blessed peace!
Why dost thou shroud thy vestal purity
In penury and dungeons? wherefore lurkest
With danger, death, and solitude; yet shun'st   70
The palace I have built thee? Sacred peace!
Oh visit me but once, but pitying shed
One drop of balm upon my withered soul.

<table>
<tr><td>49 wealth] wealth, 1821.BEN</td><td>69 dungeons?]</td></tr>
<tr><td>50 vice,] vice 1834</td><td>   dungeons! 1821.BEN 1839 1840</td></tr>
<tr><td>52 venom; then] venom,—then 1834</td><td>70 solitude;] solitude: 1839 1840</td></tr>
<tr><td>53 fulfills] fulfils 1821.CLA 1829.BRO</td><td>   shun'st] shunn'st 1821.CLA 1821.BEN</td></tr>
<tr><td>   1834 1839 1840</td><td>   1829.BRO 1834 1839 1840</td></tr>
<tr><td>59 but] But, 1821.CLA 1821.BEN</td><td>71 thee?] thee! 1839 1840</td></tr>
<tr><td>64 No] "No 1821.BEN</td><td>72 but] and 1834 1840</td></tr>
<tr><td>66 wish,] wish 1834 1840</td><td>73 soul.] soul." 1821.BEN</td></tr>
<tr><td>   thee!—Not] thee! Not 1840</td><td></td></tr>
</table>

Vain man! that palace is the virtuous heart,
75 And peace defileth not her snowy robes
In such a shed as thine. Hark! yet he mutters;
His slumbers are but varied agonies,
They prey like scorpions on the springs of life.
There needeth not the hell that bigots frame
80 To punish those who err: earth in itself
Contains at once the evil and the cure;
And all-sufficing nature can chastise
Those who transgress her law,—she only knows
How justly to proportion to the fault
85 The punishment it merits.

                                                Is it strange
That this poor wretch should pride him in his woe?
Take pleasure in his abjectness, and hug
The scorpion that consumes him? Is it strange
That, placed on a conspicuous throne of thorns,
90 Grasping an iron sceptre, and immured
Within a splendid prison, whose stern bounds
Shut him from all that's good or dear on earth,
His soul asserts not its humanity?
That man's mild nature rises not in war
95 Against a king's employ? No—'tis not strange.
He, like the vulgar, thinks, feels, acts and lives
Just as his father did; the unconquered powers
Of precedent and custom interpose
Between a *king* and virtue. Stranger yet,
100 To those who know not nature, nor deduce
The future from the present, it may seem,
That not one slave, who suffers from the crimes
Of this unnatural being; not one wretch,
Whose children famish, and whose nuptial bed
105 Is earth's unpitying bosom, rears an arm
To dash him from his throne!

Speaker. MAB.] *omitted   omnia*
77 agonies,] agonies: *1834*
83 law,—she] law;—she *1834*
95 strange.] strange, *1840*

96 acts] acts,   *1821.BEN 1834*
    lives] lives, *1834*
105 Is] In   *1821.CLA 1821.BEN*

                              Those gilded flies
That, basking in the sunshine of a court,
Fatten on its corruption!—what are they?
—The drones of the community; they feed
On the mechanic's labour: the starved hind   110
For them compels the stubborn glebe to yield
Its unshared harvests; and yon squalid form,
Leaner than fleshless misery, that wastes
A sunless life in the unwholesome mine,
Drags out in labour a protracted death,   115
To glut their grandeur; many faint with toil,
That few may know the cares and woe of sloth.

Whence, thinkest thou, kings and parasites arose?
Whence that unnatural line of drones, who heap
Toil and unvanquishable penury   120
On those who build their palaces, and bring
Their daily bread?—From vice, black loathsome vice;
From rapine, madness, treachery, and wrong;
From all that genders misery, and makes
Of earth this thorny wilderness; from lust,   125
Revenge, and murder. . . . . . And when reason's voice,
Loud as the voice of nature, shall have waked
The nations; and mankind perceive that vice
Is discord, war, and misery; that virtue
Is peace, and happiness and harmony;   130
When man's maturer nature shall disdain
The playthings of its childhood;—kingly glare
Will lose its power to dazzle; its authority
Will silently pass by; the gorgeous throne
Shall stand unnoticed in the regal hall,   135
Fast falling to decay; whilst falsehood's trade

107 That,] That *1840*
108 its] *omitted* *1834*
  corruption!—what]
    corruption, what *1834*
110 labour:] labour; *1840*
117 woe] woes *1821.BEN*
122 vice;] vice, *1839*

126 murder. . . . . . And]
  murder. . . . . And *1829.BRO*
  murder.—And *1839 1840*
128 nations;] nations, *1834*
130 happiness] happiness, *1821.CLA*
    1821.BEN 1834
132 childhood;—kingly]
    childhood; kingly *1834*

Shall be as hateful and unprofitable
As that of truth is now.

                                Where is the fame
Which the vain-glorious mighty of the earth
140   Seek to eternize? Oh! the faintest sound
From time's light footfall, the minutest wave
That swells the flood of ages, whelms in nothing
The unsubstantial bubble. Aye! to-day
Stern is the tyrant's mandate, red the gaze
145   That flashes desolation, strong the arm
That scatters multitudes. To-morrow comes!
That mandate is a thunder-peal that died
In ages past; that gaze, a transient flash
On which the midnight closed, and on that arm
150   The worm has made his meal.

                                  The virtuous man,
Who, great in his humility, as kings
Are little in their grandeur; he who leads
Invincibly a life of resolute good,
And stands amid the silent dungeon-depths
155   More free and fearless than the trembling judge,
Who, clothed in venal power, vainly strove
To bind the impassive spirit;—when he falls,
His mild eye beams benevolence no more:
Withered the hand outstretched but to relieve;
160   Sunk reason's simple eloquence, that rolled
But to appal the guilty. Yes! the grave
Hath quenched that eye, and death's relentless frost
Withered that arm: but the unfading fame
Which virtue hangs upon its votary's tomb;
165   The deathless memory of that man, whom kings
Call to their mind and tremble; the remembrance
With which the happy spirit contemplates

---

141 footfall,] foot-fall, *1840*
143 Aye!] Ay! *1829.BRO 1834*
     to-day] to day *1834*
144 mandate,] mandates, *1834*
150 man,] man *1840*
151 humility,] humility *1834*

157 spirit;—when] spirit; when *1834*
160 eloquence,]
     eloquence *1821.CLA 1821.BEN*
165 man,] man *1834*
166 remembrance] remembrance, *1834*

Its well-spent pilgrimage on earth,
Shall never pass away.

Nature rejects the monarch, not the man;   170
The subject, not the citizen: for kings
And subjects, mutual foes, for ever play
A losing game into each other's hands,
Whose stakes are vice and misery. The man
Of virtuous soul commands not, nor obeys.   175
Power, like a desolating pestilence,
Pollutes whate'er it touches; and obedience,
Bane of all genius, virtue, freedom, truth,
Makes slaves of men, and, of the human frame,
A mechanized automaton.   180

When Nero,
High over flaming Rome, with savage joy
Lowered like a fiend, drank with enraptured ear
The shrieks of agonizing death, beheld
The frightful desolation spread, and felt
A new created sense within his soul   185
Thrill to the sight, and vibrate to the sound;
Thinkest thou his grandeur had not overcome
The force of human kindness? and, when Rome,
With one stern blow, hurled not the tyrant down,
Crushed not the arm red with her dearest blood,   190
Had not submissive abjectness destroyed
Nature's suggestions?

Look on yonder earth:
The golden harvests spring; the unfailing sun
Sheds light and life; the fruits, the flowers, the trees,
Arise in due succession; all things speak   195
Peace, harmony, and love. The universe,
In nature's silent eloquence, declares
That all fulfil the works of love and joy,—

---

171 subject,]
    subject   *1821.CLA 1821.BEN*
179 Makes] Make   *1834*
    and,] and   *1834 1839 1840*
    frame,] frame   *1834 1839 1840*
183 agonizing] agonising   *1839 1840*

185 new created]
    new-created   *1839 1840*
186 sound;] sound,   *1834*
188 and,] and   *1834*
190 arm] arm,   *1839 1840*

All but the outcast man. He fabricates
200   The sword which stabs his peace; he cherisheth
        The snakes that gnaw his heart; he raiseth up
        The tyrant, whose delight is in his woe,
        Whose sport is in his agony. Yon sun,
        Lights it the great alone? Yon silver beams,
205   Sleep they less sweetly on the cottage thatch,
        Than on the dome of kings? Is mother earth
        A step-dame to her numerous sons, who earn
        Her unshared gifts with unremitting toil;
        A mother only to those puling babes
210   Who, nursed in ease and luxury, make men
        The playthings of their babyhood, and mar,
        In self-important childishness, that peace
        Which men alone appreciate?

                Spirit of Nature! no.
215   The pure diffusion of thy essence throbs
            Alike in every human heart.
                    Thou, aye, erectest there
            Thy throne of power unappealable:
            Thou art the judge beneath whose nod
220   Man's brief and frail authority
                Is powerless as the wind
                That passeth idly by.
            Thine the tribunal which surpasseth
                The shew of human justice,
225   As God surpasses man.

                Spirit of Nature! thou
        Life of interminable multitudes;
            Soul of those mighty spheres
        Whose changeless paths thro' Heaven's deep silence lie;
230   Soul of that smallest being,
                The dwelling of whose life

---

199 outcast] outcast,   *1839 1840*
    man.] Man.   *1839 1840*
201 heart;] heart!   *1821.BEN*
205 thatch,] thatch   *1834*
213 *stanza break*]
        page break   **1813** *1821.BEN*
        omitted   1829.BRO 1834

214 no.] no!   *1839 1840*
224 shew] show   *1834 1839 1840*
225 *stanza break*]
        page break   1829.BRO 1839
        omitted 1834
229 thro'] through   *1839 1840*

188   *Queen Mab: A Philosophical Poem*

Is one faint April sun-gleam;—
   Man, like these passive things,
Thy will unconsciously fulfilleth:
   Like theirs, his age of endless peace,   235
     Which time is fast maturing,
      Will swiftly, surely come;
And the unbounded frame, which thou pervadest,
     Will be without a flaw
   Marring its perfect symmetry.   240

IV.

How beautiful this night! the balmiest sigh,
Which vernal zephyrs breathe in evening's ear,
Were discord to the speaking quietude
That wraps this moveless scene. Heaven's ebon vault,
Studded with stars unutterably bright,   5
Through which the moon's unclouded grandeur rolls,
Seems like a canopy which love had spread
To curtain her sleeping world. Yon gentle hills,
Robed in a garment of untrodden snow;
Yon darksome rocks, whence icicles depend,   10
So stainless, that their white and glittering spires
Tinge not the moon's pure beam; yon castled steep,
Whose banner hangeth o'er the time-worn tower
So idly, that rapt fancy deemeth it
A metaphor of peace;—all form a scene   15
Where musing solitude might love to lift
Her soul above this sphere of earthliness;
Where silence undisturbed might watch alone,
So cold, so bright, so still.

       The orb of day,
In southern climes, o'er ocean's waveless field   20
Sinks sweetly smiling: not the faintest breath
Steals o'er the unruffled deep; the clouds of eve

---

235 theirs,] their's, *1821.BEN*
236 Which . . . maturing,] *omitted* *1834*
237 surely] surely, *1840*

1 the] The *1834*
6 Through] Thro' *1834*
7 had] has *1821.BEN 1839 1840*
11 stainless,] stainless *1840*
14 idly,] idly *1834*

Reflect unmoved the lingering beam of day;
And vesper's image on the western main
25   Is beautifully still. To-morrow comes:
Cloud upon cloud, in dark and deepening mass,
Roll o'er the blackened waters; the deep roar
Of distant thunder mutters awfully;
Tempest unfolds its pinion o'er the gloom
30   That shrouds the boiling surge; the pityless fiend,
With all his winds and lightnings, tracks his prey;
The torn deep yawns,—the vessel finds a grave
Beneath its jagged gulf.

                Ah! whence yon glare
That fires the arch of heaven?—that dark red smoke
35   Blotting the silver moon? The stars are quenched
In darkness, and the pure and spangling snow
Gleams faintly through the gloom that gathers round!
Hark to that roar, whose swift and deaf'ning peals
In countless echoes through the mountains ring,
40   Startling pale midnight on her starry throne!
Now swells the intermingling din; the jar
Frequent and frightful of the bursting bomb;
The falling beam, the shriek, the groan, the shout,
The ceaseless clangor, and the rush of men
45   Inebriate with rage:—loud, and more loud
The discord grows; till pale death shuts the scene,
And o'er the conqueror and the conquered draws
His cold and bloody shroud.—Of all the men
Whom day's departing beam saw blooming there,
50   In proud and vigorous health; of all the hearts
That beat with anxious life at sun-set there;
How few survive, how few are beating now!
All is deep silence, like the fearful calm
That slumbers in the storm's portentous pause;

---

30 pityless] pitiless   *1839 1840*   47 conquered] conquer'd   *1839 1840*

34 heaven?—that] heaven!—that *1840*   49 there,] there   *1834 1839 1840*

37 round!] roun *1834*   50 health;] health, *1834*

        round. *1840*   51 there;] there, *1834*

38 deaf'ning] deafening *1821.CLA*   53 is] in *1834*

   1821.BEN 1839 1840   54 storm's] storms   *1821.CLA 1821.BEN*

44 clangor,]   pause;] pause, *1834*

   clangour, *1821.CLA 1821.BEN*

Save when the frantic wail of widowed love   55
Comes shuddering on the blast, or the faint moan
With which some soul bursts from the frame of clay
Wrapt round its struggling powers.

                    The grey morn
Dawns on the mournful scene; the sulphurous smoke
Before the icy wind slow rolls away,   60
And the bright beams of frosty morning dance
Along the spangling snow. There tracks of blood
Even to the forest's depth, and scattered arms,
And lifeless warriors, whose hard lineaments
Death's self could change not, mark the dreadful path   65
Of the outsallying victors: far behind,
Black ashes note where their proud city stood.
Within yon forest is a gloomy glen—
Each tree which guards its darkness from the day,
Waves o'er a warrior's tomb.   70

                I see thee shrink,
Surpassing Spirit!—wert thou human else?
I see a shade of doubt and horror fleet
Across thy stainless features: yet fear not;
This is no unconnected misery,
Nor stands uncaused, and irretrievable.   75
Man's evil nature, that apology
Which kings who rule, and cowards who crouch, set up
For their unnumbered crimes, sheds not the blood
Which desolates the discord-wasted land.
From kings, and priests, and statesmen, war arose,   80
Whose safety is man's deep unbettered woe,
Whose grandeur his debasement. Let the axe
Strike at the root, the poison-tree will fall;
And where its venomed exhalations spread
Ruin, and death, and woe, where millions lay   85
Quenching the serpent's famine, and their bones
Bleaching unburied in the putrid blast,

<table>
<tr><td>63 scattered] scatter'd   1821.CLA</td><td>80 arose,] aros   1834</td></tr>
<tr><td>67 stood.] stood   1834</td><td>81 unbettered] embittered   1834</td></tr>
<tr><td>69 tree] tree,   1834</td><td>82 his] is   1821.BEN</td></tr>
<tr><td>73 not;] not.   1834</td><td>84 And] And,   1834</td></tr>
<tr><td>79 land.] land   1840</td><td></td></tr>
</table>

A garden shall arise, in loveliness
Surpassing fabled Eden.

                              Hath Nature's soul,
That formed this world so beautiful, that spread
Earth's lap with plenty, and life's smallest chord
Strung to unchanging unison, that gave
The happy birds their dwelling in the grove,
That yielded to the wanderers of the deep
The lovely silence of the unfathomed main,
And filled the meanest worm that crawls in dust
With spirit, thought, and love; on Man alone,
Partial in causeless malice, wantonly
Heaped ruin, vice, and slavery; his soul
Blasted with withering curses; placed afar
The meteor-happiness, that shuns his grasp,
But serving on the frightful gulph to glare,
Rent wide beneath his footsteps?

                              Nature!—no!
Kings, priests, and statesmen, blast the human flower
Even in its tender bud; their influence darts
Like subtle poison through the bloodless veins
Of desolate society. The child,
Ere he can lisp his mother's sacred name,
Swells with the unnatural pride of crime, and lifts
His baby-sword even in a hero's mood.
This infant-arm becomes the bloodiest scourge
Of devastated earth; whilst specious names,
Learnt in soft childhood's unsuspecting hour,
Serve as the sophisms with which manhood dims
Bright reason's ray, and sanctifies the sword
Upraised to shed a brother's innocent blood.

---

89 soul,] soul   *1834*

90 That] (That   *1834*

97 love;] love)   *1834*
   alone,] alone   *1840*

101 meteor-happiness,] meteor happiness,
    1821.BEN 1839 1840

102 But] But,   *1834*
   gulph] gulf   *1839 1840*

104 statesmen,] statesmen   *1839 1840*
   flower] flower,   *1839 1840*

111 infant-arm] infant arm   *1829.BRO*
    1834 1839 1840

112 devastated] devasted   *1834*
   names,] names   *1839 1840*

Let priest-led slaves cease to proclaim that man
Inherits vice and misery, when force
And falshood hang even o'er the cradled babe,
Stifling with rudest grasp all natural good.   120

Ah! to the stranger-soul, when first it peeps
From its new tenement, and looks abroad
For happiness and sympathy, how stern
And desolate a tract is this wide world!
How withered all the buds of natural good!   125
No shade, no shelter from the sweeping storms
Of pityless power! On its wretched frame,
Poisoned, perchance, by the disease and woe
Heaped on the wretched parent whence it sprung
By morals, law, and custom, the pure winds   130
Of heaven, that renovate the insect tribes,
May breathe not. The untainting light of day
May visit not its longings. It is bound
Ere it has life: yea, all the chains are forged
Long ere its being: all liberty and love   135
And peace is torn from its defencelessness;
Cursed from its birth, even from its cradle doomed
To abjectness and bondage!

Throughout this varied and eternal world
Soul is the only element, the block   140
That for uncounted ages has remained
The moveless pillar of a mountain's weight
Is active, living spirit. Every grain
Is sentient both in unity and part,
And the minutest atom comprehends   145
A world of loves and hatreds; these beget
Evil and good: hence truth and falsehood spring;

---

119 falshood] falsehood   *1821.CLA*
        1821.BEN 1829.BRO 1834 1839
        1840
126 shelter] shelter,   *1834*
127 pityless] pitiless   *1839 1840*
129 parent] parent,   *1839 1840*
        sprung] sprung,   *1839 1840*

141 remained] remained.   *1813*
        1821.CLA 1829.BRO 1834 1839
        1840
                remained,   *1821.BEN*
143 active,]
        active   *1821.BEN 1834 1839 1840*
147 truth] truth,   *1821.CLA*

Hence will and thought and action, all the germs
Of pain or pleasure, sympathy or hate,
150　That variegate the eternal universe.
Soul is not more polluted than the beams
Of heaven's pure orb, ere round their rapid lines
The taint of earth-born atmospheres arise.

Man is of soul and body, formed for deeds
155　Of high resolve, on fancy's boldest wing
To soar unwearied, fearlessly to turn
The keenest pangs to peacefulness, and taste
The joys which mingled sense and spirit yield.
Or he is formed for abjectness and woe,
160　To grovel on the dunghill of his fears,
To shrink at every sound, to quench the flame
Of natural love in sensualism, to know
That hour as blest when on his worthless days
The frozen hand of death shall set its seal,
165　Yet fear the cure, though hating the disease.
The one is man that shall hereafter be;
The other, man as vice has made him now.

War is the statesman's game, the priest's delight,
The lawyer's jest, the hired assassin's trade,
170　And, to those royal murderers, whose mean thrones
Are bought by crimes of treachery and gore,
The bread they eat, the staff on which they lean.
Guards, garbed in blood-red livery, surround
Their palaces, participate the crimes
175　That force defends, and from a nation's rage
Secure the crown, which all the curses reach
That famine, frenzy, woe and penury breathe.
These are the hired bravos who defend

---

148 will] will,　*1821.CLA 1821.BEN 1839*
　　　1840
　　thought] thought,　*1821.CLA*
　　　1821.BEN 1839 1840
152 heaven's] Heaven's　*1821.BEN*
153 *stanza break*]
　　page break　**1813** *1821.BEN*
　　omitted　*1821.CLA 1829.BRO 1834*

154 formed] form'd　*1839*
155 resolve,] resolve;　*1839 1840*
165 cure,] cure　*1821.BEN*
176 Secure]
　　Secures　**1813** *1821.CLA 1821.BEN*
177 woe] woe,　*1821.CLA 1821.BEN 1834*
　　penury] penury,　*1834*
178 bravos] bravoes　*1839 1840*

The tyrant's throne—the bullies of his fear:
These are the sinks and channels of worst vice,   180
The refuse of society, the dregs
Of all that is most vile: their cold hearts blend
Deceit with sternness, ignorance with pride,
All that is mean and villainous, with rage
Which hopelessness of good, and self-contempt,   185
Alone might kindle; they are decked in wealth,
Honour and power, then are sent abroad
To do their work. The pestilence that stalks
In gloomy triumph through some eastern land
Is less destroying. They cajole with gold,   190
And promises of fame, the thoughtless youth
Already crushed with servitude: he knows
His wretchedness too late, and cherishes
Repentance for his ruin, when his doom
Is sealed in gold and blood!   195
Those too the tyrant serve, who, skilled to snare
The feet of justice in the toils of law,
Stand, ready to oppress the weaker still;
And, right or wrong, will vindicate for gold,
Sneering at public virtue, which beneath   200
Their pityless tread lies torn and trampled, where
Honour sits smiling at the sale of truth.

Then grave and hoary-headed hypocrites,
Without a hope, a passion, or a love,
Who, through a life of luxury and lies,   205
Have crept by flattery to the seats of power,
Support the system whence their honours flow. . . .
They have three words:—well tyrants know their use,
Well pay them for the loan, with usury

---

179 fear:] fear;   *1821.BEN*

181 refuse] refuge   *1839 1840*

184 villainous,]
    villanous,   *1829.BRO 1839 1840*
    villanous   *1834*

185 good,] good   *1834*
   self-contempt,] self-contempt   *1834*

187 Honour] Honour,   *1834*

189 eastern] Eastern   *1839 1840*

196 who,] who   *1821.BEN 1840*

198 Stand,] Stand   *1834*

201 pityless] pitiless   *1839 1840*

203–20 Then . . . power.] *omitted*   *1839*

207 flow. . . .] flow—   *1821.BEN 1840*
              flow. . .   *1829.BRO*

208 words:—well] words: well   *1834*
              words; well   *1840*

210   Torn from a bleeding world!—God, Hell, and Heaven.
       A vengeful, pityless, and almighty fiend,
       Whose mercy is a nick-name for the rage
       Of tameless tygers hungering for blood.
       Hell, a red gulf of everlasting fire,
215   Where poisonous and undying worms prolong
       Eternal misery to those hapless slaves
       Whose life has been a penance for its crimes.
       And Heaven, a meed for those who dare belie
       Their human nature, quake, believe, and cringe
220   Before the mockeries of earthly power.

       These tools the tyrant tempers to his work,
       Wields in his wrath, and as he wills destroys,
       Omnipotent in wickedness: the while
       Youth springs, age moulders, manhood tamely does
225   His bidding, bribed by short-lived joys to lend
       Force to the weakness of his trembling arm.

       They rise, they fall; one generation comes
       Yielding its harvest to destruction's scythe.
       It fades, another blossoms: yet behold!
230   Red glows the tyrant's stamp-mark on its bloom,
       Withering and cankering deep its passive prime.
       He has invented lying words and modes,
       Empty and vain as his own coreless heart;
       Evasive meanings, nothings of much sound,
235   To lure the heedless victim to the toils
       Spread round the valley of its paradise.

       Look to thyself, priest, conqueror, or prince!
       Whether thy trade is falsehood, and thy lusts

---

210 world!—God,]
    world!——— ,   *1821.CLAX*
   world! God,   *1821.BEN*
  Hell,] Hell,   *1821.BEN*
    Hell   *1840*
  Heaven.] Heaven.   *1821.BEN*
211 pityless,] pitiless,   *1840*
  almighty] ———   *1821.CLAX*
    Almighty   *1821.BEN*
  fiend,] Fiend,   *1821.BEN*

213 tygers] tigers   *1834 1840*
222 wills] wills,   *1839 1840*
227 fall;] fall: *1834*
229 blossoms:]
    blossoms,   *1821.CLA 1821.BEN*
   yet] yet,   *1834*
236 *stanza break*] *omitted*   *1821.BEN*

Deep wallow in the earnings of the poor,
With whom thy master was:—or thou delightst   240
In numbering o'er the myriads of thy slain,
All misery weighing nothing in the scale
Against thy short-lived fame: or thou dost load
With cowardice and crime the groaning land,
A pomp-fed king. Look to thy wretched self!   245
Aye, art thou not the veriest slave that e'er
Crawled on the loathing earth? Are not thy days
Days of unsatisfying listlessness?
Dost thou not cry, ere night's long rack is o'er,
When will the morning come? Is not thy youth   250
A vain and feverish dream of sensualism?
Thy manhood blighted with unripe disease?
Are not thy views of unregretted death
Drear, comfortless, and horrible? Thy mind,
Is it not morbid as thy nerveless frame,   255
Incapable of judgment, hope, or love?
And dost thou wish the errors to survive
That bar thee from all sympathies of good,
After the miserable interest
Thou holdst in their protraction? When the grave   260
Has swallowed up thy memory and thyself,
Dost thou desire the bane that poisons earth
To twine its roots around thy coffined clay,
Spring from thy bones, and blossom on thy tomb,
That of its fruit thy babes may eat and die?   265

V.

THUS do the generations of the earth
Go to the grave, and issue from the womb,
Surviving still the imperishable change
That renovates the world; even as the leaves
Which the keen frost-wind of the waning year   5
Has scattered on the forest soil, and heaped

---

240 was:—or] was; or *1834*
   delightst] delight'st *1821.BEN*
    1829.BRO 1834 1839 1840
243 fame:] fame; *1834*
245 king. Look] king—look *1834*
246 Aye,] Ay, *1829.BRO 1834*

254 mind,] mind *1821.CLA 1821.BEN*
260 holdst] hold'st *1821.BEN 1829.BRO*
    1834 1839 1840

6 scattered] scatter'd *1839*

For many seasons there, though long they choke,
Loading with loathsome rottenness the land,
All germs of promise. Yet when the tall trees
From which they fell, shorn of their lovely shapes,
Lie level with the earth to moulder there,
They fertilize the land they long deformed,
Till from the breathing lawn a forest springs
Of youth, integrity, and loveliness,
Like that which gave it life, to spring and die.
Thus suicidal selfishness, that blights
The fairest feelings of the opening heart,
Is destined to decay, whilst from the soil
Shall spring all virtue, all delight, all love,
And judgment cease to wage unnatural war
With passion's unsubduable array.

Twin-sister of religion, selfishness!
Rival in crime and falshood, aping all
The wanton horrors of her bloody play;
Yet frozen, unimpassioned, spiritless,
Shunning the light, and owning not its name—
Compelled, by its deformity, to screen
With flimsy veil of justice and of right,
Its unattractive lineaments, that scare
All, save the brood of ignorance: at once
The cause and the effect of tyranny;
Unblushing, hardened, sensual, and vile;
Dead to all love but of its abjectness,
With heart impassive by more noble powers
Than unshared pleasure, sordid gain, or fame;
Despising its own miserable being,
Which still it longs, yet fears to disenthrall.

9 Yet] Yet,   *1834*

11 earth] earth,   *1821.BEN*

12 deformed,] deform'd,   *1839*

13 springs] springs,   *1821.BEN*

21 *stanza break*] *omitted*   *1839 1840*

22 Twin-sister] Twin-sisters   *1834*
   selfishness!] Selfishness!   *1834*

23 falshood,] falsehood,   *1821.CLA*
   1821.BEN 1829.BRO 1834 1839 1840

26 name—] name   **1813**
   name,   *1821.CLA 1821.BEN*
   name;   *1829.BRO 1834*
   name: *1839 1840*

28 right,] right   *1834*

33 abjectness,] abjectness.   *1821.BEN*

37 longs,] longs   *1834*
   fears] fears,   *1839 1840*
   disenthrall.]
   disenthral.   *1829.BRO 1834*

Hence commerce springs, the venal interchange
Of all that human art or nature yield;
Which wealth should purchase not, but want demand,   40
And natural kindness hasten to supply
From the full fountain of its boundless love,
For ever stifled, drained, and tainted now.
Commerce! beneath whose poison-breathing shade
No solitary virtue dares to spring,   45
But poverty and wealth with equal hand
Scatter their withering curses, and unfold
The doors of premature and violent death,
To pining famine and full-fed disease,
To all that shares the lot of human life,   50
Which poisoned body and soul, scarce drags the chain,
That lengthens as it goes and clanks behind.

Commerce has set the mark of selfishness,
The signet of its all-enslaving power
Upon a shining ore, and called it gold: 55
Before whose image bow the vulgar great,
The vainly rich, the miserable proud,
The mob of peasants, nobles, priests, and kings,
And with blind feelings reverence the power
That grinds them to the dust of misery.   60
But in the temple of their hireling hearts
Gold is a living god, and rules in scorn
All earthly things but virtue.

Since tyrants, by the sale of human life,
Heap luxuries to their sensualism, and fame   65
To their wide-wasting and insatiate pride,
Success has sanctioned to a credulous world
The ruin, the disgrace, the woe of war.
His hosts of blind and unresisting dupes
The despot numbers; from his cabinet   70

---

39 art] heart *1834*
   yield;] yields; *1829.BRO 1834*
44 Commerce!] Commerce, *1821.BEN*
45 spring,] spring; *1839 1840*
48 death,] death *1834*
51 soul,] soul *1834*
   chain,] chain *1834 1839 1840*

52 goes] goes, *1821.BEN 1834*
   stanza break] *page break* *1821.CLA*
      omitted *1821.BEN*
54 power] power, *1839 1840*
55 gold:] gold; *1834*
68 woe] woe, *1834*

These puppets of his schemes he moves at will,
Even as the slaves by force or famine driven,
Beneath a vulgar master, to perform
A task of cold and brutal drudgery;—
75   Hardened to hope, insensible to fear,
Scarce living pullies of a dead machine,
Mere wheels of work and articles of trade,
That grace the proud and noisy pomp of wealth!

The harmony and happiness of man
80   Yields to the wealth of nations; that which lifts
His nature to the heaven of its pride,
Is bartered for the poison of his soul;
The weight that drags to earth his towering hopes,
Blighting all prospect but of selfish gain,
85   Withering all passion but of slavish fear,
Extinguishing all free and generous love
Of enterprize and daring, even the pulse
That fancy kindles in the beating heart
To mingle with sensation, it destroys,—
90   Leaves nothing but the sordid lust of self,
The groveling hope of interest and gold,
Unqualified, unmingled, unredeemed
Even by hypocrisy.

           And statesmen boast
Of wealth! The wordy eloquence that lives
95   After the ruin of their hearts, can gild
The bitter poison of a nation's woe,
Can turn the worship of the servile mob
To their corrupt and glaring idol fame,
From virtue, trampled by its iron tread,
100   Although its dazzling pedestal be raised

---

72 driven,] driven   *1839 1840*

74 drudgery;—] drudgery: *1821.BEN*

76 pullies] pulleys   *1839 1840*

80 Yields]
    Yield   *1829.BRO 1834 1839 1840*

81 pride,] pride   *1834*

87 enterprize] enterprise   *1829.BRO
    1834 1839 1840*
  daring,] daring;   *1834*

89 destroys,—] destroys—   *1821.BEN*

91 groveling]
    grovelling   *1821.BEN 1839 1840*

95 hearts,] hearts   *1834*

96 woe,] woe!   *1821.BEN*

98 idol] idol,   *1839 1840*
  fame,] Fame,   *1839 1840*

99 virtue,] Virtue,   *1839 1840*

Amid the horrors of a limb-strewn field,
With desolated dwellings smoking round.
The man of ease, who, by his warm fire-side,
To deeds of charitable intercourse
And bare fulfilment of the common laws   105
Of decency and prejudice, confines
The struggling nature of his human heart,
Is duped by their cold sophistry; he sheds
A passing tear perchance upon the wreck
Of earthly peace, when near his dwelling's door   110
The frightful waves are driven,—when his son
Is murdered by the tyrant, or religion
Drives his wife raving mad. But the poor man,
Whose life is misery, and fear, and care;
Whom the morn wakens but to fruitless toil;   115
Who ever hears his famished offsprings scream,
Whom their pale mother's uncomplaining gaze
For ever meets, and the proud rich man's eye
Flashing command, and the heart-breaking scene
Of thousands like himself;—he little heeds   120
The rhetoric of tyranny; his hate
Is quenchless as his wrongs; he laughs to scorn
The vain and bitter mockery of words,
Feeling the horror of the tyrant's deeds,
And unrestrained but by the arm of power,   125
That knows and dreads his enmity.

The iron rod of penury still compels
Her wretched slave to bow the knee to wealth,
And poison, with unprofitable toil,
A life too void of solace to confirm   130
The very chains that bind him to his doom.
Nature, impartial in munificence,
Has gifted man with all-subduing will.
Matter, with all its transitory shapes,

---

111 driven,—when]
    driven—when   *1821.BEN*
113 mad. But] mad.—But   *1821.BEN*
116 offsprings]
    offspring's   *1821.BEN 1839 1840*
    offspring   *1829.BRO 1834*
120 himself;—he] himself; he   *1840*
121 tyranny;] tyranny,   *1840*

122 wrongs;] wrongs,   *1839 1840*
125 unrestrained]
    unrestrained,   *1821.CLA*
    1821.BEN
126 *stanza break*] *page break*   *1829.BRO*
    omitted   *1834*
133 will.] will: *1839 1840*

135   Lies subjected and plastic at his feet,
        That, weak from bondage, tremble as they tread.
        How many a rustic Milton has past by,
        Stifling the speechless longings of his heart,
        In unremitting drudgery and care!
140   How many a vulgar Cato has compelled
        His energies, no longer tameless then,
        To mould a pin, or fabricate a nail!
        How many a Newton, to whose passive ken
        Those mighty spheres that gem infinity
145   Were only specks of tinsel, fixed in heaven
        To light the midnights of his native town!

        Yet every heart contains perfection's germ:
        The wisest of the sages of the earth,
        That ever from the stores of reason drew
150   Science and truth, and virtue's dreadless tone,
        Were but a weak and inexperienced boy,
        Proud, sensual, unimpassioned, unimbued
        With pure desire and universal love,
        Compared to that high being, of cloudless brain,
155   Untainted passion, elevated will,
        Which death (who even would linger long in awe
        Within his noble presence, and beneath
        His changeless eyebeam) might alone subdue.
        Him, every slave now dragging through the filth
160   Of some corrupted city his sad life,
        Pining with famine, swoln with luxury,
        Blunting the keenness of his spiritual sense
        With narrow schemings and unworthy cares,
        Or madly rushing through all violent crime,
165   To move the deep stagnation of his soul,—
        Might imitate and equal.

                    But mean lust
        Has bound its chains so tight around the earth,

---

137 past] passed   *1839 1840*   eyebeam),   *1829.BRO 1839*
156 awe] awe,   *1821.BEN*   eye-beam),   *1840*
158 eyebeam)]   165 soul,—] soul—   *1821.BEN*
    eyebeam,)   *1813 1821.CLA*   167 around] about   *1840*

That all within it but the virtuous man
Is venal: gold or fame will surely reach
The price prefixed by selfishness, to all   170
But him of resolute and unchanging will;
Whom, nor the plaudits of a servile crowd,
Nor the vile joys of tainting luxury,
Can bribe to yield his elevated soul
To tyranny or falshood, though they wield   175
With blood-red hand the sceptre of the world.
All things are sold: the very light of heaven
Is venal; earth's unsparing gifts of love,
The smallest and most despicable things
That lurk in the abysses of the deep,   180
All objects of our life, even life itself,
And the poor pittance which the laws allow
Of liberty, the fellowship of man,
Those duties which his heart of human love
Should urge him to perform instinctively,   185
Are bought and sold as in a public mart
Of undisguising selfishness, that sets
On each its price, the stamp-mark of her reign.
Even love is sold; the solace of all woe
Is turned to deadliest agony, old age   190
Shivers in selfish beauty's loathing arms,
And youth's corrupted impulses prepare
A life of horror from the blighting bane
Of commerce; whilst the pestilence that springs
From unenjoying sensualism, has filled   195
All human life with hydra-headed woes.

Falshood demands but gold to pay the pangs
Of outraged conscience; for the slavish priest
Sets no great value on his hireling faith:
A little passing pomp, some servile souls,   200
Whom cowardice itself might safely chain,
Or the spare mite of avarice could bribe

---

169 venal:] venal.   *1834*
    gold] Gold   *1834*
175 falshood,] falsehood,   *1821.CLA*
    1821.BEN 1829.BRO 1834 1839
    1840
178 venal;] venal: *1821.BEN*

194 commerce;] commerce: *1840*
195 sensualism,] sensualism   *1834*
197 Falshood] Falsehood   *1821.CLA*
    1821.BEN 1829.BRO 1834 1839
    1840

To deck the triumph of their languid zeal,
Can make him minister to tyranny.
205 More daring crime requires a loftier meed:
Without a shudder, the slave-soldier lends
His arm to murderous deeds, and steels his heart,
When the dread eloquence of dying men,
Low mingling on the lonely field of fame,
210 Assails that nature, whose applause he sells
For the gross blessings of a patriot mob,
For the vile gratitude of heartless kings,
And for a cold world's good word,—viler still!

There is a nobler glory, which survives
215 Until our being fades, and, solacing
All human care, accompanies its change;
Deserts not virtue in the dungeon's gloom,
And, in the precincts of the palace, guides
Its footsteps through that labyrinth of crime;
220 Imbues his lineaments with dauntlessness,
Even when, from power's avenging hand, he takes
Its sweetest, last and noblest title—death;
—The consciousness of good, which neither gold,
Nor sordid fame, nor hope of heavenly bliss,
225 Can purchase; but a life of resolute good,
Unalterable will, quenchless desire
Of universal happiness, the heart
That beats with it in unison, the brain,
Whose ever wakeful wisdom toils to change
230 Reason's rich stores for its eternal weal.

This commerce of sincerest virtue needs
No mediative signs of selfishness,
No jealous intercourse of wretched gain,

---

205 meed:] meed.   *1834*

206 shudder,] shudder   *1840*

207 heart,] heart   *1821.BEN*

210 nature,] nature   *1834 1840*

211 a] the   *1839 1840*

213 word,—viler]
   word—viler   *1821.BEN*
  stanza break] *page break   1829.BRO*
     omitted   1834

214 glory,] glory   *1840*

216 change;] change: *1821.BEN*

222 last] last,   *1821.CLA 1821.BEN*
    1829.BRO 1834
   noblest] noblest,   *1834*
   title—death;]
    title—death;—   *1829.BRO 1834*

223 —The]
   The   *1821.BEN 1829.BRO 1834*

229 ever wakeful]
   ever-wakeful   *1839 1840*

No balancings of prudence, cold and long;
In just and equal measure all is weighed,   235
One scale contains the sum of human weal,
And one, the good man's heart.

       How vainly seek
The selfish for that happiness denied
To aught but virtue! Blind and hardened, they,
Who hope for peace amid the storms of care,   240
Who covet power they know not how to use,
And sigh for pleasure they refuse to give,—
Madly they frustrate still their own designs;
And, where they hope that quiet to enjoy
Which virtue pictures, bitterness of soul,   245
Pining regrets, and vain repentances,
Disease, disgust, and lassitude, pervade
Their valueless and miserable lives.

But hoary-headed selfishness has felt
Its death-blow, and is tottering to the grave: 250
A brighter morn awaits the human day,
When every transfer of earth's natural gifts
Shall be a commerce of good words and works;
When poverty and wealth, the thirst of fame,
The fear of infamy, disease and woe,   255
War with its million horrors, and fierce hell
Shall live but in the memory of time,
Who, like a penitent libertine, shall start,
Look back, and shudder at his younger years.

VI.

ALL touch, all eye, all ear,
The Spirit felt the Fairy's burning speech.
O'er the thin texture of its frame,

---

234 long;] long. *1834*

235 weighed,] weighed; *1834*

237 one,] one *1834*

239 virtue!] virtue? *1829.BRO 1834*
 they,] they *1834 1839 1840*

242 give,—] give— *1821.BEN*
  give, *1834*
  give:— *1839 1840*

243 designs;] designs: *1821.BEN*

255 disease]
  disease, *1821.CLA 1821.BEN 1834*

256 hell]
  hell, *1829.BRO 1834 1839 1840*

258 libertine,] libertine *1840*

3 frame,] frame *1834*

The varying periods painted changing glows,
5   As on a summer even,
When soul-enfolding music floats around,
     The stainless mirror of the lake
     Re-images the eastern gloom,
Mingling convulsively its purple hues
10   With sunset's burnished gold.

          Then thus the Spirit spoke:
It is a wild and miserable world!
          Thorny, and full of care,
Which every fiend can make his prey at will.
15   O Fairy! in the lapse of years,
          Is there no hope in store?
          Will yon vast suns roll on
Interminably, still illuming
The night of so many wretched souls,
20   And see no hope for them?
Will not the universal Spirit e'er
Revivify this withered limb of Heaven?

          The Fairy calmly smiled
In comfort, and a kindling gleam of hope
25   Suffused the Spirit's lineaments.
Oh! rest thee tranquil; chase those fearful doubts,
Which ne'er could rack an everlasting soul,
That sees the chains which bind it to its doom.
Yes! crime and misery are in yonder earth,
30   Falshood, mistake, and lust;
          But the eternal world
Contains at once the evil and the cure.
Some eminent in virtue shall start up,
          Even in perversest time:
35 The truths of their pure lips, that never die,
Shall bind the scorpion falshood with a wreath

---

4 painted] painted,   *1840*
  glows,] glows;   *1839 1840*
23 Fairy] fairy   *1821.BEN*
26 tranquil;] tranquil: *1821.BEN*

30 Falshood,] Falsehood,   *1821.CLA*
    1821.BEN 1829.BRO 1834 1839 1840
34 time:] time;   *1821.BEN*
36 falshood] falsehood   *1821.CLA*
    1821.BEN 1829.BRO 1834 1839 1840

Of ever-living flame,
Until the monster sting itself to death.

How sweet a scene will earth become!
Of purest spirits, a pure dwelling-place,　　　　40
Symphonious with the planetary spheres;
When man, with changeless nature coalescing,
Will undertake regeneration's work,
When its ungenial poles no longer point
To the red and baleful sun　　　　45
That faintly twinkles there.

Spirit! on yonder earth,
Falshood now triumphs; deadly power
Has fixed its seal upon the lip of truth!
Madness and misery are there!　　　　50
The happiest is most wretched! Yet confide,
Until pure health-drops, from the cup of joy,
Fall like a dew of balm upon the world.
Now, to the scene I shew, in silence turn,
And read the blood-stained charter of all woe,　　　　55
Which nature soon, with recreating hand,
Will blot in mercy from the book of earth.
How bold the flight of passion's wandering wing,
How swift the step of reason's firmer tread,
How calm and sweet the victories of life,　　　　60
How terrorless the triumph of the grave!
How powerless were the mightiest monarch's arm,
Vain his loud threat, and impotent his frown!
How ludicrous the priest's dogmatic roar!
The weight of his exterminating curse,　　　　65
How light! and his affected charity,

---

38 *stanza break*] *page break*　***1813***
　　　omitted　*1821.CLA*
　　　1821.BEN 1829.BRO
　　　1834
41 spheres;]
　　　spheres,　*1821.CLA 1821.BEN*
47 Spirit!] Spirit,　*1839 1840*
48 Falshood] Falsehood　*1821.CLA*
　　1821.BEN 1829.BRO 1834 1839 1840

51 Yet] yet　*1821.CLA 1821.BEN*
　　confide,] confide　*1839 1840*
52 health-drops,]
　　　health-drops　*1821.CLA 1821.BEN*
　　joy,] joy　*1839 1840*
54–238 Now, . . . strength.] *omitted*　*1839*
54 shew,] show,　*1840*
56 recreating] re-creating　*1840*
65 curse,] curse　*1840*

To suit the pressure of the changing times,
What palpable deceit!—but for thy aid,
Religion! but for thee, prolific fiend,
70 Who peoplest earth with demons, hell with men,
And heaven with slaves!

Thou taintest all thou lookest upon!—the stars,
Which on thy cradle beamed so brightly sweet,
Were gods to the distempered playfulness
75 Of thy untutored infancy: the trees,
The grass, the clouds, the mountains, and the sea,
All living things that walk, swim, creep, or fly,
Were gods: the sun had homage, and the moon
Her worshipper. Then thou becamest, a boy,
80 More daring in thy frenzies: every shape,
Monstrous or vast, or beautifully wild,
Which, from sensation's relics, fancy culls;
The spirits of the air, the shuddering ghost,
The genii of the elements, the powers
85 That give a shape to nature's varied works,
Had life and place in the corrupt belief
Of thy blind heart: yet still thy youthful hands
Were pure of human blood. Then manhood gave
Its strength and ardour to thy frenzied brain;
90 Thine eager gaze scanned the stupendous scene,
Whose wonders mocked the knowledge of thy pride:
Their everlasting and unchanging laws
Reproached thine ignorance. Awhile thou stoodst
Baffled and gloomy; then thou didst sum up
95 The elements of all that thou didst know;
The changing seasons, winter's leafless reign,
The budding of the heaven-breathing trees,
The eternal orbs that beautify the night,
The sun-rise, and the setting of the moon,
100 Earthquakes and wars, and poisons and disease,
And all their causes, to an abstract point,

---

69 Religion!] R————!   *1821.CLAX*

72 lookest] look'st   *1840*
  upon!—the] upon!—The   *1834*

79 worshipper.]
  worshiper.   *1829.BRO 1834*
becamest,] becamest   *1834 1840*

82 Which,] Which   *1840*

90 scene,] scene   *1821.CLA 1821.BEN*

93 stoodst]
  stood'st   *1821.BEN 1829.BRO 1834*

101 point,] point   *1840*

Converging, thou didst bend, and called it GOD!
The self-sufficing, the omnipotent,
The merciful, and the avenging God!
Who, prototype of human misrule, sits   105
High in heaven's realm, upon a golden throne,
Even like an earthly king; and whose dread work,
Hell, gapes forever for the unhappy slaves
Of fate, whom he created in his sport,
To triumph in their torments when they fell!   110
Earth heard the name; earth trembled, as the smoke
Of his revenge ascended up to heaven,
Blotting the constellations; and the cries
Of millions, butchered in sweet confidence
And unsuspecting peace, even when the bonds   115
Of safety were confirmed by wordy oaths
Sworn in his dreadful name, rung through the land;
Whilst innocent babes writhed on thy stubborn spear,
And thou didst laugh to hear the mother's shriek
Of maniac gladness, as the sacred steel   120
Felt cold in her torn entrails!

Religion! thou wert then in manhood's prime:
But age crept on: one God would not suffice
For senile puerility; thou framedst
A tale to suit thy dotage, and to glut   125
Thy misery-thirsting soul, that the mad fiend
Thy wickedness had pictured, might afford
A plea for sating the unnatural thirst
For murder, rapine, violence, and crime,
That still consumed thy being, even when   130

---

102 called] call'd *1840*
    it GOD!] it—God! *1821.CLA*
        it—GOD! *1821.BEN*
        it God! *1840*
104 avenging] avenging, *1834*
    God!] GOD! *1829.BRO 1834*
108–10 gapes . . . fell!]
        replaced by dashes 1821.CLAX
108 Hell,] Hell *1821.CLA 1821.BEN*
    forever] for ever *1821.CLA*
        1821.BEN 1834 1840
109 created]
    created, *1821.CLA 1821.BEN*

113 constellations;]
        constellations: *1829.BRO 1834*
114 millions,] millions *1840*
    butchered] butcher'd *1840*
    confidence] confidence, *1821.BEN*
120 gladness,] madness, *1821.BEN*
                gladness *1840*
122 prime:] prime; *1834*
124 framedst] framed'st *1821.BEN*
        1829.BRO 1834
127 pictured,] pictured *1834*

Thou heardst the step of fate;—that flames might light
Thy funeral scene, and the shrill horrent shrieks
Of parents dying on the pile that burned
To light their children to thy paths, the roar
135 Of the encircling flames, the exulting cries
Of thine apostles, loud commingling there,
Might sate thine hungry ear
Even on the bed of death!

But now contempt is mocking thy grey hairs;
140 Thou art descending to the darksome grave,
Unhonored and unpitied, but by those
Whose pride is passing by like thine, and sheds,
Like thine, a glare that fades before the sun
Of truth, and shines but in the dreadful night
145 That long has lowered above the ruined world.

Throughout these infinite orbs of mingling light,
Of which yon earth is one, is wide diffused
A spirit of activity and life,
That knows no term, cessation, or decay;
150 That fades not when the lamp of earthly life,
Extinguished in the dampness of the grave,
Awhile there slumbers, more than when the babe
In the dim newness of its being feels
The impulses of sublunary things,
155 And all is wonder to unpractised sense:
But, active, stedfast, and eternal, still
Guides the fierce whirlwind, in the tempest roars,
Cheers in the day, breathes in the balmy groves,
Strengthens in health, and poisons in disease;
160 And in the storm of change, that ceaselessly
Rolls round the eternal universe, and shakes
Its undecaying battlement, presides,
Apportioning with irresistible law

---

131 heardst]
    heardest *1821.CLA 1821.BEN*
    heard'st *1829.BRO 1834*
  fate;—that] Fate;—that *1821.BEN*
    fate:—that *1829.BRO*
     1834
  light] ligh *1821.CLA*

133 burned] burn'd *1840*
137 thine] thy *1829.BRO 1834 1840*
138 *stanza break*] omitted *1821.BEN*
141 Unhonored] Unhonoured
    1821.CLA 1821.BEN 1840
149 or] nor *1834*

The place each spring of its machine shall fill;
So that, when waves on waves tumultuous heap   165
Confusion to the clouds, and fiercely driven
Heaven's lightnings scorch the uprooted ocean-fords,
Whilst, to the eye of shipwrecked mariner,
Lone sitting on the bare and shuddering rock,
All seems unlinked contingency and chance: 170
No atom of this turbulence fulfils
A vague and unnecessitated task,
Or acts but as it must and ought to act.
Even the minutest molecule of light,
That in an April sunbeam's fleeting glow   175
Fulfills its destined, though invisible work,
The universal Spirit guides; nor less,
When merciless ambition, or mad zeal,
Has led two hosts of dupes to battle-field,
That, blind, they there may dig each other's graves,   180
And call the sad work glory, does it rule
All passions: not a thought, a will, an act,
No working of the tyrant's moody mind,
Nor one misgiving of the slaves who boast
Their servitude, to hide the shame they feel,   185
Nor the events enchaining every will,
That from the depths of unrecorded time
Have drawn all-influencing virtue, pass
Unrecognised, or unforeseen by thee,
Soul of the Universe! eternal spring   190
Of life and death, of happiness and woe,
Of all that chequers the phantasmal scene
That floats before our eyes in wavering light,
Which gleams but on the darkness of our prison,
    Whose chains and massy walls   195
    We feel, but cannot see.

---

165 that,] that   *1821.CLA 1821.BEN*
167 ocean-fords,] ocean fords,   *1840*
170 chance:] chance;   *1834*
175 sunbeam's]
    sun-beam's   *1821.CLA 1821.BEN*
176 Fulfills] Fulfils   *1821.BEN 1829.BRO*
    1834 1840
  destined,] destined   *1834*
177 less,] less   *1821.BEN 1840*

180 other's] others'   *1829.BRO*
  graves,] graves   *1821.BEN 1840*
181 work glory,]
    work—glory,   *1821.CLA 1821.BEN*
189 Unrecognised,]
  Unrecognized,
    1821.CLA 1821.BEN
  Unrecognised   *1834 1840*
196 feel,] feel   *1840*

Spirit of Nature! all-sufficing Power,
Necessity! thou mother of the world!
Unlike the God of human error, thou
200   Requirest no prayers or praises; the caprice
Of man's weak will belongs no more to thee
Than do the changeful passions of his breast
To thy unvarying harmony: the slave,
Whose horrible lusts spread misery o'er the world,
205   And the good man, who lifts, with virtuous pride,
His being, in the sight of happiness,
That springs from his own works; the poison-tree,
Beneath whose shade all life is withered up,
And the fair oak, whose leafy dome affords
210   A temple where the vows of happy love
Are registered, are equal in thy sight:
No love, no hate thou cherishest; revenge
And favoritism, and worst desire of fame
Thou knowest not: all that the wide world contains
215   Are but thy passive instruments, and thou
Regardst them all with an impartial eye,
Whose joy or pain thy nature cannot feel,
    Because thou hast not human sense,
    Because thou art not human mind.

220   Yes! when the sweeping storm of time
Has sung its death-dirge o'er the ruined fanes
And broken altars of the almighty fiend,
Whose name usurps thy honors, and the blood
Through centuries clotted there, has floated down
225   The tainted flood of ages, shalt thou live

---

197 all-sufficing] all sufficing   *1821.BEN*
    Power,] Power.   *1840*
198 Necessity!] NECESSITY!   *1821.BEN*
200 or] nor   *1834*
    praises;] praises: *1821.BEN*
        praises.   *1834*
    the] The   *1834*
205 lifts,] lifts   *1834*
    pride,] pride   *1834*
207 poison-tree,] poison tree,   *1821.BEN*
211 registered,] register'd,   *1840*
    sight:] sight.   *1834*
212 revenge] revenge,   *1834*

213 favoritism,]
    favouritism,   *1829.BRO 1834 1840*
    fame] fame,   *1834 1840*
216 Regardst] Regard'st   *1821.BEN*
    1829.BRO 1834 1840
    eye,] eye   *1840*
222 almighty] Almighty   *1821.BEN*
    fiend,] Fiend,   *1821.BEN*
       fiend   *1834 1840*
223 honors,] honours,   *1821.CLA*
    1821.BEN 1829.BRO 1834 1840
    blood] blood,   *1834*

Unchangeable! A shrine is raised to thee,
    Which, nor the tempest breath of time,
    Nor the interminable flood,
    Over earth's slight pageant rolling,
      Availeth to destroy,— 230
The sensitive extension of the world.
    That wonderous and eternal fane,
Where pain and pleasure, good and evil join,
To do the will of strong necessity,
    And life, in multitudinous shapes, 235
Still pressing forward where no term can be,
    Like hungry and unresting flame
Curls round the eternal columns of its strength.

VII.

I was an infant when my mother went
To see an atheist burned. She took me there:
The dark-robed priests were met around the pile;
The multitude was gazing silently;
And as the culprit passed with dauntless mien, 5
Tempered disdain in his unaltering eye,
Mixed with a quiet smile, shone calmly forth:
The thirsty fire crept round his manly limbs;
His resolute eyes were scorched to blindness soon;
His death-pang rent my heart! the insensate mob 10
Uttered a cry of triumph, and I wept.
Weep not, child! cried my mother, for that man
Has said, There is no God.

---

226 Unchangeable!]
    Unchangeable? *1821.BEN*

227 tempest breath] tempest-breath
    1821.CLA 1821.BEN

228 flood,] flood *1834*

230 destroy,—] destroy— *1821.BEN*

232 wonderous] wondrous *1821.BEN*
    1829.BRO 1834 1840

233 evil] evil, *1834*

    join,] join *1834*

234 necessity,] Necessity, *1821.BEN*

235 life,] life *1840*

1–275 VII. . . . thought.] *omitted* *1839*

2 atheist] Atheist *1821.BEN*

3 pile;] pile, *1821.BEN*

5 And] And, *1834*

10 the] The *1834*

FAIRY.

There is no God!

Nature confirms the faith his death-groan sealed:

15 Let heaven and earth, let man's revolving race,
His ceaseless generations tell their tale;
Let every part depending on the chain
That links it to the whole, point to the hand
That grasps its term! let every seed that falls
20 In silent eloquence unfold its store
Of argument: infinity within,
Infinity without, belie creation;
The exterminable spirit it contains
Is nature's only God; but human pride
25 Is skilful to invent most serious names
To hide its ignorance.

The name of God

Has fenced about all crime with holiness,
Himself the creature of his worshippers,
Whose names and attributes and passions change,
30 Seeva, Buddh, Foh, Jehovah, God, or Lord,
Even with the human dupes who build his shrines,
Still serving o'er the war-polluted world
For desolation's watch-word; whether hosts
Stain his death-blushing chariot wheels, as on
35 Triumphantly they roll, whilst Brahmins raise
A sacred hymn to mingle with the groans;
Or countless partners of his power divide
His tyranny to weakness; or the smoke
Of burning towns, the cries of female helplessness,
40 Unarmed old age, and youth, and infancy,
Horribly massacred, ascend to heaven
In honor of his name; or, last and worst,
Earth groans beneath religion's iron age,

---

14 sealed:] sealed.   *1834*
    seal'd: *1840*
16 generations] generations,   *1834 1840*
19 let] Let   *1834 1840*
  falls] falls,   *1840*
21 argument: infinity]
  argument. Infinity   *1834*
28 worshippers,] worshipers,   *1834*

29 names] names,   *1821.CLA*
  attributes]
  attributes,   *1821.CLA 1821.BEN*
34 chariot wheels,]
  chariot-wheels,   *1821.CLA 1821.BEN*
41 heaven] heaven,   *1821.BEN*
42 honor] honour   *1821.CLA 1821.BEN*
  1829.BRO 1834 1840

And priests dare babble of a God of peace,
Even whilst their hands are red with guiltless blood,   45
Murdering the while, uprooting every germ
Of truth, exterminating, spoiling all,
Making the earth a slaughter-house!

O Spirit! through the sense
By which thy inner nature was apprised   50
Of outward shews, vague dreams have rolled,
And varied reminiscences have waked
Tablets that never fade;
All things have been imprinted there,
The stars, the sea, the earth, the sky,   55
Even the unshapeliest lineaments
Of wild and fleeting visions
Have left a record there
To testify of earth.

These are my empire, for to me is given   60
The wonders of the human world to keep,
And fancy's thin creations to endow
With manner, being, and reality;
Therefore a wondrous phantom, from the dreams
Of human error's dense and purblind faith,   65
I will evoke, to meet thy questioning.
Ahasuerus, rise!

A strange and woe-worn wight
Arose beside the battlement,
And stood unmoving there.   70
His inessential figure cast no shade
Upon the golden floor;
His port and mien bore mark of many years,
And chronicles of untold ancientness
Were legible within his beamless eye: 75

---

47 spoiling] spoiling,   *1834*

48 *stanza break*] *page break*   *1821.CLA*
    omitted   *1821.BEN*

51 shews,] shows,   *1834*
    shows   *1840*
  rolled,] roll'd,   *1840*

53 fade;] fade.   *1834*

54 there,] there;   *1821.BEN*

59 *stanza break*] *page break*   *1829.BRO*
    omitted   *1834*

65 error's] errors   *1821.CLA*

67 Ahasuerus,] Ahasuerus,   *1821.BEN*

75 eye:] eye;   *1834*

Yet his cheek bore the mark of youth;
Freshness and vigor knit his manly frame;
The wisdom of old age was mingled there
With youth's primæval dauntlessness;
80   And inexpressible woe,
Chastened by fearless resignation, gave
An awful grace to his all-speaking brow.

SPIRIT.

Is there a God?

AHASUERUS.

Is there a God!—aye, an almighty God,
85   And vengeful as almighty! Once his voice
Was heard on earth: earth shuddered at the sound;
The fiery-visaged firmament expressed
Abhorrence, and the grave of nature yawned
To swallow all the dauntless and the good
90   That dared to hurl defiance at his throne,
Girt as it was with power. None but slaves
Survived,—cold-blooded slaves, who did the work
Of tyrannous omnipotence; whose souls
No honest indignation ever urged
95   To elevated daring, to one deed
Which gross and sensual self did not pollute.
These slaves built temples for the omnipotent fiend,
Gorgeous and vast: the costly altars smoked
With human blood, and hideous pæans rung
100   Through all the long-drawn aisles. A murderer heard
His voice in Egypt, one whose gifts and arts

---

76 youth;] youth.   *1834*

77 vigor] vigour   *1821.CLA 1821.BEN*
     1829.BRO 1834 1840

81 Chastened] Chasten'd   *1840*

84 God!—aye,]
    God?—aye,   *1821.CLA 1821.BEN*
    God!—ay,   *1829.BRO 1834 1840*

85 almighty! Once]
    almighty!—Once   *1821.BEN*

86 earth: earth] earth:—earth   *1821.BEN*
    shuddered] shudder'd   *1840*
    sound;] sound.   *1834*

87 expressed] express'd   *1840*

88 yawned] yawn'd   *1840*

92 Survived,—cold-blooded]
    Survived—cold-blooded   *1821.BEN*

93 omnipotence;]
    omnipotence: *1821.BEN*

97 omnipotent]
    omnipotent,   *1821.CLA 1821.BEN*
    fiend,] *omitted*   *1821.CLA 1821.BEN*

Had raised him to his eminence in power,
Accomplice of omnipotence in crime,
And confidant of the all-knowing one.
     These were Jehovah's words.   105

From an eternity of idleness
I, God, awoke; in seven days' toil made earth
From nothing; rested, and created man:
I placed him in a paradise, and there
Planted the tree of evil, so that he   110
Might eat and perish, and my soul procure
Wherewith to sate its malice, and to turn,
Even like a heartless conqueror of the earth,
All misery to my fame. The race of men
Chosen to my honor, with impunity   115
May sate the lusts I planted in their heart.
Here I command thee hence to lead them on,
Until, with hardened feet, their conquering troops
Wade on the promised soil through woman's blood,
And make my name be dreaded through the land.   120
Yet ever burning flame and ceaseless woe
Shall be the doom of their eternal souls,
With every soul on this ungrateful earth,
Virtuous or vicious, weak or strong,—even all
Shall perish, to fulfill the blind revenge   125
(Which you, to men, call justice) of their God.

      The murderer's brow
Quivered with horror.

        God omnipotent,
Is there no mercy? must our punishment
Be endless? will long ages roll away,   130
And see no term? Oh! wherefore hast thou made

---

103 omnipotence]

—— —— —— *1821.CLAX*

   Omnipotence *1821.BEN*

108 man:] man. *1834*

114 men] men, *1834*

115 honor,] honour, *1821.CLA*

   1821.BEN 1829.BRO 1834 1840

118 hardened] harden'd *1840*

121 ever burning] ever-burning

   1829.BRO 1834 1840

124 strong,—even]

   strong—even *1821.BEN*

125 fulfill] fulfil *1821.CLA 1821.BEN*

   1829.BRO 1834 1840

128 Quivered] Quiver'd *1840*

In mockery and wrath this evil earth?
Mercy becomes the powerful—be but just:
O God! repent and save.

One way remains:

135   I will beget a son, and he shall bear
The sins of all the world; he shall arise
In an unnoticed corner of the earth,
And there shall die upon a cross, and purge
The universal crime; so that the few
140   On whom my grace descends, those who are marked
As vessels to the honor of their God,
May credit this strange sacrifice, and save
Their souls alive: millions shall live and die,
Who ne'er shall call upon their Saviour's name,
145   But, unredeemed, go to the gaping grave.
Thousands shall deem it an old woman's tale,
Such as the nurses frighten babes withal:
These in a gulph of anguish and of flame
Shall curse their reprobation endlessly,
150   Yet tenfold pangs shall force them to avow,
Even on their beds of torment, where they howl,
My honor, and the justice of their doom.
What then avail their virtuous deeds, their thoughts
Of purity, with radiant genius bright,
155   Or lit with human reason's earthly ray?
Many are called, but few will I elect.
Do thou my bidding, Moses!

Even the murderer's cheek

Was blanched with horror, and his quivering lips
Scarce faintly uttered—O almighty one,
160   I tremble and obey!

O Spirit! centuries have set their seal
On this heart of many wounds, and loaded brain,

---

133 but] *omitted*   *1821.BEN*
134 remains:] remains.   *1834*
140 marked] mark'd   *1840*
141 honor] honour   *1821.CLA 1821.BEN*
    1829.BRO 1834 1840
143 alive: millions] alive. Millions   *1834*
    die,] die   *1834*

147 withal:] withal.   *1834*
148 These] These,   *1821.CLA 1821.BEN*
    gulph] gulf   *1840*
    flame] flame,   *1821.CLA 1821.BEN*
152 honor,] honour,   *1821.CLA*
    1821.BEN 1829.BRO 1834 1840
159 almighty] Almighty   *1829.BRO 1834*

Since the Incarnate came: humbly he came,
Veiling his horrible Godhead in the shape
Of man, scorned by the world, his name unheard,   165
Save by the rabble of his native town,
Even as a parish demagogue. He led
The crowd; he taught them justice, truth, and peace,
In semblance; but he lit within their souls
The quenchless flames of zeal, and blest the sword   170
He brought on earth to satiate with the blood
Of truth and freedom his malignant soul.
At length his mortal frame was led to death.
I stood beside him: on the torturing cross
No pain assailed his unterrestrial sense;   175
And yet he groaned. Indignantly I summed
The massacres and miseries which his name
Had sanctioned in my country, and I cried,
Go! go! in mockery.
A smile of godlike malice reillumined   180
His fading lineaments.—I go, he cried,
But thou shalt wander o'er the unquiet earth
Eternally.————The dampness of the grave
Bathed my imperishable front. I fell,
And long lay tranced upon the charmed soil.   185
When I awoke hell burned within my brain,
Which staggered on its seat; for all around
The mouldering relics of my kindred lay,
Even as the Almighty's ire arrested them,
And in their various attitudes of death   190
My murdered children's mute and eyeless sculls
Glared ghastily upon me.

                   But my soul,
From sight and sense of the polluting woe
Of tyranny, had long learned to prefer

---

163 Incarnate] incarnate   *1821.BEN*
     came: humbly] came. Humbly   *1834*
169 semblance;] semblance: *1821.BEN*
170 blest] bless'd   *1834*
173 At . . . death.] *omitted   1834*
175 sense;] sense,   *1834*
176 Indignantly]
     Indignantly,   *1821.CLA 1821.BEN*

180 reillumined] re-illumined   *1821.CLA
     1829.BRO 1834*
                re-illumed   *1821.BEN*
                reillumed   *1840*
185 charmed] charmèd   *1840*
192 ghastily] ghastly   *1821.BEN 1840*
                ghastlily   *1834*

195   Hell's freedom to the servitude of heaven.
        Therefore I rose, and dauntlessly began
        My lonely and unending pilgrimage,
        Resolved to wage unweariable war
        With my almighty tyrant, and to hurl
200   Defiance at his impotence to harm
        Beyond the curse I bore. The very hand
        That barred my passage to the peaceful grave
        Has crushed the earth to misery, and given
        Its empire to the chosen of his slaves.
205   These have I seen, even from the earliest dawn
        Of weak, unstable and precarious power;
        Then preaching peace, as now they practise war,
        So, when they turned but from the massacre
        Of unoffending infidels, to quench
210   Their thirst for ruin in the very blood
        That flowed in their own veins, and pityless zeal
        Froze every human feeling, as the wife
        Sheathed in her husband's heart the sacred steel,
        Even whilst its hopes were dreaming of her love;
215   And friends to friends, brothers to brothers stood
        Opposed in bloodiest battle-field, and war,
        Scarce satiable by fate's last death-draught waged,
        Drunk from the winepress of the Almighty's wrath;
        Whilst the red cross, in mockery of peace,
220   Pointed to victory! When the fray was done,
        No remnant of the exterminated faith
        Survived to tell its ruin, but the flesh,
        With putrid smoke poisoning the atmosphere,
        That rotted on the half-extinguished pile.

225   Yes! I have seen God's worshippers unsheathe
        The sword of his revenge, when grace descended,

---

205 dawn] dawn,   *1834*

206 unstable] unstable,   *1821.CLA*
  1821.BEN 1834 1840
 precarious] precarious,   *1834*

211 pityless] pitiless   *1840*

214 its] his   *1821.BEN*
 love;] love: *1821.BEN*

215 brothers] brothers,   *1834*
 stood] stood,   *1834*

218 winepress] wine-press   *1821.CLA*
  1821.BEN 1829.BRO 1834 1840

219 cross,] cross   *1821.CLA 1821.BEN*

225 worshippers] worshipers   *1834*
 unsheathe]
  unsheath   *1829.BRO 1834 1840*

226 descended,] descended   *1821.BEN*

Confirming all unnatural impulses,
To sanctify their desolating deeds;
And frantic priests waved the ill-omened cross
O'er the unhappy earth: then shone the sun   230
On showers of gore from the upflashing steel
Of safe assassination, and all crime
Made stingless by the spirits of the Lord,
And blood-red rainbows canopied the land.

Spirit! no year of my eventful being   235
Has passed unstained by crime and misery,
Which flows from God's own faith. I've marked his slaves
With tongues whose lies are venomous, beguile
The insensate mob, and, whilst one hand was red
With murder, feign to stretch the other out   240
For brotherhood and peace; and that they now
Babble of love and mercy, whilst their deeds
Are marked with all the narrowness and crime
That freedom's young arm dare not yet chastise,
Reason may claim our gratitude, who now   245
Establishing the imperishable throne
Of truth, and stubborn virtue, maketh vain
The unprevailing malice of my foe,
Whose bootless rage heaps torments for the brave,
Adds impotent eternities to pain,   250
Whilst keenest disappointment racks his breast
To see the smiles of peace around them play,
To frustrate or to sanctify their doom.

Thus have I stood,—through a wild waste of years
Struggling with whirlwinds of mad agony,   255
Yet peaceful, and serene, and self-enshrined,
Mocking my powerless tyrant's horrible curse
With stubborn and unalterable will,

---

228 sanctify] sanc ify   *1821.BEN*

230 sun] Sun   *1821.CLA 1821.BEN*

234 *stanza break*]
    omitted   1821.CLA 1821.BEN

237 slaves] slaves,   *1840*

239 and,] and   *1821.CLA 1821.BEN*

241 and] and,   *1834 1840*

244 dare] dares   *1834 1840*

chastise,]
    chastise;   *1821.CLA 1821.BEN*

245 now] now,   *1834 1840*

246 imperishable] impe rishable   *1834*

253 frustrate]
    frustrate,   *1821.CLA 1821.BEN*

254 stood,—through]
    stood—through   *1821.BEN*
    of] o   *1821.BEN*

Even as a giant oak, which heaven's fierce flame
260   Had scathed in the wilderness, to stand
A monument of fadeless ruin there;
Yet peacefully and movelessly it braves
The midnight conflict of the wintry storm,
        As in the sun-light's calm it spreads
265   Its worn and withered arms on high
To meet the quiet of a summer's noon.

        The Fairy waved her wand:
            Ahasuerus fled
Fast as the shapes of mingled shade and mist,
270   That lurk in the glens of a twilight grove,
        Flee from the morning beam:
        The matter of which dreams are made
        Not more endowed with actual life
        Than this phantasmal portraiture
275   Of wandering human thought.

VIII.

THE present and the past thou hast beheld:
It was a desolate sight. Now, Spirit, learn
        The secrets of the future.—Time!
Unfold the brooding pinion of thy gloom,
5   Render thou up thy half-devoured babes,
And from the cradles of eternity,
Where millions lie lulled to their portioned sleep
By the deep murmuring stream of passing things,
Tear thou that gloomy shroud.—Spirit, behold
10   Thy glorious destiny!

        Joy to the Spirit came.
Through the wide rent in Time's eternal veil,
Hope was seen beaming through the mists of fear:
        Earth was no longer hell;
15   Love, freedom, health, had given
Their ripeness to the manhood of its prime,

---

2 Now,] Now   *1840*
  learn] learn,   *1840*
12 veil,] veil   *1834*

                    And all its pulses beat
          Symphonious to the planetary spheres:
                  Then dulcet music swelled
          Concordant with the life-strings of the soul;   20
          It throbbed in sweet and languid beatings there,
          Catching new life from transitory death,—
          Like the vague sighings of a wind at even,
          That wakes the wavelets of the slumbering sea
          And dies on the creation of its breath,   25
          And sinks and rises, fails and swells by fits:
                  Was the pure stream of feeling
                  That sprung from these sweet notes,
          And o'er the Spirit's human sympathies
          With mild and gentle motion calmly flowed.   30

                  Joy to the Spirit came,—
              Such joy as when a lover sees
          The chosen of his soul in happiness,
                  And witnesses her peace
          Whose woe to him were bitterer than death,   35
                  Sees her unfaded cheek
          Glow mantling in first luxury of health,
                  Thrills with her lovely eyes,
          Which like two stars amid the heaving main
                  Sparkle through liquid bliss.   40

          Then in her triumph spoke the Fairy Queen:
          I will not call the ghost of ages gone
          To unfold the frightful secrets of its lore;
                  The present now is past,
          And those events that desolate the earth   45
          Have faded from the memory of Time,
          Who dares not give reality to that
          Whose being I annul. To me is given

---

18 spheres:] spheres.   *1821.BEN*

22 death,—] death—   *1821.BEN 1834*

           death.——   *1839*

           death.—   *1840*

24 sea] sea,   *1821.BEN 1829.BRO*

      1834 1839 1840

26 swells] swells,   *1834*

    fits:] fits,   *1829.BRO 1834*

28 sprung] sprang   *1834 1840*

31 came,—] came—   *1821.BEN*

33 happiness,] happiness   *1834*

35 death,] death.   *1821.BEN*

        death;   *1839 1840*

40 *stanza break*] *page break*   *1829.BRO*

        omitted   1834

43 lore;] lore: *1821.BEN*

The wonders of the human world to keep,
50   Space, matter, time, and mind. Futurity
        Exposes now its treasure; let the sight
        Renew and strengthen all thy failing hope.
        O human Spirit! spur thee to the goal
        Where virtue fixes universal peace,
55   And midst the ebb and flow of human things,
        Shew somewhat stable, somewhat certain still,
        A lighthouse o'er the wild of dreary waves.

        The habitable earth is full of bliss;
        Those wastes of frozen billows that were hurled
60   By everlasting snow-storms round the poles,
        Where matter dared not vegetate or live,
        But ceaseless frost round the vast solitude
        Bound its broad zone of stillness, are unloosed;
        And fragrant zephyrs there from spicy isles
65   Ruffle the placid ocean-deep, that rolls
        Its broad, bright surges to the sloping sand,
        Whose roar is wakened into echoings sweet
        To murmur through the heaven-breathing groves
        And melodize with man's blest nature there.

70   Those deserts of immeasurable sand,
        Whose age-collected fervors scarce allowed
        A bird to live, a blade of grass to spring,
        Where the shrill chirp of the green lizard's love
        Broke on the sultry silentness alone,
75   Now teem with countless rills and shady woods,
        Corn-fields and pastures and white cottages;

---

51 treasure;] treasure: *1834*
55 And] And,   *1834 1839 1840*
    midst] 'midst   *1840*
56 Shew] Show   *1834 1839 1840*
    still,] still,—   *1834*
57 lighthouse] light-house   *1839 1840*
    stanza break] *omitted   1821.CLA*
58 bliss;] bliss.   *1834*
61 or] nor   *1834 1839 1840*
65 ocean-deep,]
       ocean-deep   *1821.CLA 1821.BEN*
       ocean deep,   *1829.BRO 1834*

66 broad,] broad   *1834*
67 sweet] sweet,   *1821.BEN*
68 groves] groves,   *1821.BEN 1829.BRO*
       1834 1839 1840
71 fervors] fervours   *1821.CLA 1821.BEN*
       1829.BRO 1834 1839 1840
76 Corn-fields]
       Corn-fields,   *1821.CLA 1821.BEN*
    pastures]
       pastures,   *1821.CLA 1821.BEN*

And where the startled wilderness beheld
A savage conqueror stained in kindred blood,
A tygress sating with the flesh of lambs,
The unnatural famine of her toothless cubs,   80
Whilst shouts and howlings through the desert rang,
Sloping and smooth the daisy-spangled lawn,
Offering sweet incense to the sun-rise, smiles
To see a babe before his mother's door,
   Sharing his morning's meal   85
  With the green and golden basilisk
   That comes to lick his feet.

Those trackless deeps, where many a weary sail
Has seen above the illimitable plain,
Morning on night, and night on morning rise,   90
Whilst still no land to greet the wanderer spread
Its shadowy mountains on the sun-bright sea,
Where the loud roarings of the tempest-waves
So long have mingled with the gusty wind
In melancholy loneliness, and swept   95
The desert of those ocean solitudes,
But vocal to the sea-bird's harrowing shriek,
The bellowing monster, and the rushing storm,
Now to the sweet and many mingling sounds
Of kindliest human impulses respond.   100
Those lonely realms bright garden-isles begem,
With lightsome clouds and shining seas between,
And fertile vallies, resonant with bliss,
Whilst green woods overcanopy the wave,
Which like a toil-worn labourer leaps to shore,   105
To meet the kisses of the flowrets there.

All things are recreated, and the flame
Of consentaneous love inspires all life:

---

77 And] And, *1834*

79 tygress] tigress *1821.BEN 1829.BRO
  1834 1839 1840*
 lambs,] lambs *1839 1840*

81 Whilst]
  While *1829.BRO 1834 1839 1840*
 rang,] rang; *1839 1840*

83 sun-rise,] sunrise, *1829.BRO 1834*

90 morning] morning, *1834*

98 storm,] storm; *1839 1840*

99 many mingling] many-mingling *1834*

103 vallies,] vallies *1821.CLA 1821.BEN
   valleys, *1839 1840*

105 Which] Which, *1834*
 labourer] labourer, *1834*

106 flowrets] flow'rets *1821.BEN*

The fertile bosom of the earth gives suck
110   To myriads, who still grow beneath her care,
        Rewarding her with their pure perfectness:
        The balmy breathings of the wind inhale
        Her virtues, and diffuse them all abroad:
        Health floats amid the gentle atmosphere,
115   Glows in the fruits, and mantles on the stream:
        No storms deform the beaming brow of heaven,
        Nor scatter in the freshness of its pride
        The foliage of the ever verdant trees;
        But fruits are ever ripe, flowers ever fair,
120   And autumn proudly bears her matron grace,
        Kindling a flush on the fair cheek of spring,
        Whose virgin bloom beneath the ruddy fruit
        Reflects its tint and blushes into love.
        The lion now forgets to thirst for blood:
125   There might you see him sporting in the sun
        Beside the dreadless kid; his claws are sheathed,
        His teeth are harmless, custom's force has made
        His nature as the nature of a lamb.
        Like passion's fruit, the nightshade's tempting bane
130   Poisons no more the pleasure it bestows:
        All bitterness is past; the cup of joy
        Unmingled mantles to the goblet's brim,
        And courts the thirsty lips it fled before.

        But chief, ambiguous man, he that can know
135   More misery, and dream more joy than all;
        Whose keen sensations thrill within his breast
        To mingle with a loftier instinct there,
        Lending their power to pleasure and to pain,
        Yet raising, sharpening, and refining each;
140   Who stands amid the ever-varying world,
        The burthen or the glory of the earth;
        He chief perceives the change, his being notes

---

116 storms deform] storm deforms
        1821.CLA 1821.BEN
117 scatter] scatters   *1821.CLA 1821.BEN*
118 ever verdant] ever-verdant   *1821.CLA
        1821.BEN 1829.BRO 1834 1839
        1840*
123 tint] tint,   *1834 1839 1840*

126 dreadless] deadless   *1834*
127 harmless,] harmless;   *1834*
135 joy] joy,   *1834*
139 refining] refining,   *1834*
141 burthen] burthen,   *1829.BRO*
142 change,] change;   *1834 1839 1840*

The gradual renovation, and defines
Each movement of its progress on his mind.
Man, where the gloom of the long polar night   145
Lowers o'er the snow-clad rocks and frozen soil,
Where scarce the hardiest herb that braves the frost
Basks in the moonlight's ineffectual glow,
Shrank with the plants, and darkened with the night;
His chilled and narrow energies, his heart,   150
Insensible to courage, truth, or love,
His stunted stature and imbecile frame,
Marked him for some abortion of the earth,
Fit compeer of the bears that roamed around,
Whose habits and enjoyments were his own: 155
His life a feverish dream of stagnant woe,
Whose meagre wants, but scantily fulfilled,
Apprised him ever of the joyless length
Which his short being's wretchedness had reached;
His death a pang which famine, cold and toil   160
Long on the mind, whilst yet the vital spark
Clung to the body stubbornly, had brought:
All was inflicted here that earth's revenge
Could wreak on the infringers of her law;
One curse alone was spared—the name of God.   165

Nor where the tropics bound the realms of day
With a broad belt of mingling cloud and flame,
Where blue mists through the unmoving atmosphere
Scattered the seeds of pestilence, and fed
Unnatural vegetation, where the land   170
Teemed with all earthquake, tempest and disease,
Was man a nobler being; slavery
Had crushed him to his country's bloodstained dust;

---

157 wants,] wants   *1821.CLA*

160 pang] pang,   *1821.CLA 1821.BEN*
    cold] cold,   *1821.CLA 1821.BEN*
      1829.BRO 1834 1839 1840
    toil] toil,   *1834 1839 1840*

164 law;] law.   *1839*
      stanza break added   *1839*

165 One curse . . . God.] *omitted*   *1839*
    spared—the] spared the   *1821.BEN*

spared—the . . . God.] spared
   —— —— —— —— ——
    1821.CLAX
    God.] G*OD*.   *1821.BEN*

166 Nor] Nor,   *1839 1840*

171 tempest] tempest,   *1821.CLA*
    1821.BEN 1834 1839 1840

172 being; slavery] being. Slavery   *1834*

173 bloodstained] blood-stained
    1821.CLA 1821.BEN 1829.BRO
    1834 1839 1840

Or he was bartered for the fame of power,
175 Which all internal impulses destroying,
Makes human will an article of trade;
Or he was changed with Christians for their gold,
And dragged to distant isles, where to the sound
Of the flesh-mangling scourge, he does the work
180 Of all-polluting luxury and wealth,
Which doubly visits on the tyrants' heads
The long-protracted fulness of their woe;
Or he was led to legal butchery,
To turn to worms beneath that burning sun,
185 Where kings first leagued against the rights of men,
And priests first traded with the name of God.

Even where the milder zone afforded man
A seeming shelter, yet contagion there,
Blighting his being with unnumbered ills,
190 Spread like a quenchless fire; nor truth till late
Availed to arrest its progress, or create
That peace which first in bloodless victory waved
Her snowy standard o'er this favoured clime:
There man was long the train-bearer of slaves,
195 The mimic of surrounding misery,
The jackal of ambition's lion-rage,
The bloodhound of religion's hungry zeal.

Here now the human being stands adorning
This loveliest earth with taintless body and mind;
200 Blest from his birth with all bland impulses,
Which gently in his noble bosom wake
All kindly passions and all pure desires.
Him, still from hope to hope the bliss pursuing,
Which from the exhaustless lore of human weal

---

175 Which] Which,   *1834 1839 1840*
178 where] where,   *1834*
181 tyrants'] tyrant's   *1821.BEN*
184 sun,] sun   *1834 1839 1840*
186 God.] God.   *1821.BEN*
      God,   *1829.BRO 1834*
196 jackal] jackall   *1821.CLA 1821.BEN*
  ambition's] Ambition's   *1821.BEN*
197 bloodhound]
    blood-hound   *1821.BEN*

religion's] Religion's   *1821.BEN*
stanza break] page break   1821.CLA
      omitted   1821.BEN
199 earth] earth,   *1821.CLA 1821.BEN*
  mind;] mind,   *1834*
202 passions] passions,   *1821.BEN*
203 Him,] Him   *1840*
  still] (still   *1840*
204 lore] store   *1821.BEN 1839 1840*

Draws on the virtuous mind, the thoughts that rise   205
In time-destroying infiniteness, gift
With self-enshrined eternity, that mocks
The unprevailing hoariness of age,
And man, once fleeting o'er the transient scene
Swift as an unremembered vision, stands   210
Immortal upon earth: no longer now
He slays the lamb that looks him in the face,
And horribly devours his mangled flesh,
Which still avenging nature's broken law,
Kindled all putrid humours in his frame,   215
All evil passions, and all vain belief,
Hatred, despair, and loathing in his mind,
The germs of misery, death, disease, and crime.
No longer now the winged habitants,
That in the woods their sweet lives sing away,   220
Flee from the form of man; but gather round,
And prune their sunny feathers on the hands
Which little children stretch in friendly sport
Towards these dreadless partners of their play.
All things are void of terror: man has lost   225
His terrible prerogative, and stands
An equal amidst equals: happiness
And science dawn though late upon the earth;
Peace cheers the mind, health renovates the frame;
Disease and pleasure cease to mingle here,   230
Reason and passion cease to combat there;
Whilst each unfettered o'er the earth extend
Their all-subduing energies, and wield
The sceptre of a vast dominion there;
Whilst every shape and mode of matter lends   235
Its force to the omnipotence of mind,

---

205 mind,] mind   *1829.BRO 1834*
             mind)   *1840*
209 scene] scene,   *1821.BEN*
214 Which] Which,   *1834 1839 1840*
     nature's] Nature's   *1821.BEN*
217 loathing] loathing,   *1834*
219 habitants,] inhabitants,   *1821.BEN*
228 dawn] dawn,   *1839 1840*
     late] late,   *1839 1840*
     earth;] earth.   *1834*

229 frame;] frame,   *1821.BEN*
231 there;] there,   *1834*
232 each] each,   *1821.BEN*
     unfettered] unfettered,   *1821.BEN*
     extend] extends   *1829.BRO 1834 1839 1840*
233 Their] Its   *1829.BRO 1834 1839 1840*
     wield] wields   *1829.BRO 1834 1839 1840*

Which from its dark mine drags the gem of truth
To decorate its paradise of peace.

IX.

O HAPPY Earth! reality of Heaven!
To which those restless souls that ceaselessly
Throng through the human universe, aspire;
Thou consummation of all mortal hope!
5   Thou glorious prize of blindly-working will!
Whose rays, diffused throughout all space and time,
Verge to one point and blend forever there:
Of purest spirits thou pure dwelling-place!
Where care and sorrow, impotence and crime,
10   Languor, disease, and ignorance dare not come:
O happy Earth, reality of Heaven!

Genius has seen thee in her passionate dreams,
And dim forebodings of thy loveliness
Haunting the human heart, have there entwined
15   Those rooted hopes of some sweet place of bliss
Where friends and lovers meet to part no more.
Thou art the end of all desire and will,
The product of all action; and the souls
That by the paths of an aspiring change
20   Have reached thy haven of perpetual peace,
There rest from the eternity of toil
That framed the fabric of thy perfectness.

Even Time, the conqueror, fled thee in his fear;
That hoary giant, who, in lonely pride,
25   So long had ruled the world, that nations fell
Beneath his silent footstep. Pyramids,
That for milleniums had withstood the tide

---

2 souls] souls,   *1821.BEN 1834*

6 rays,] rays   *1821.CLA 1821.BEN*

7 point] point,   *1834*

   forever] for ever   *1821.CLA 1821.BEN*

     1829.BRO 1834 1839 1840

10 ignorance] ignorance,   *1821.CLA*

     1821.BEN 1834 1839 1840

   come:] come;   *1821.BEN*

12 dreams,] dreams;   *1839 1840*

13 loveliness]

   loveliness,   *1834 1839 1840*

15 bliss] bliss,   *1839 1840*

18 action;] action: *1821.CLA 1821.BEN*

27 milleniums] millenniums   *1821.CLA*

     1821.BEN 1829.BRO 1839 1840

Of human things, his storm-breath drove in sand
Across that desert where their stones survived
The name of him whose pride had heaped them there.   30
Yon monarch, in his solitary pomp,
Was but the mushroom of a summer day,
That his light-winged footstep pressed to dust:
Time was the king of earth: all things gave way
Before him, but the fixed and virtuous will,   35
The sacred sympathies of soul and sense,
That mocked his fury and prepared his fall.

Yet slow and gradual dawned the morn of love;
Long lay the clouds of darkness o'er the scene,
Till from its native heaven they rolled away: 40
First, crime triumphant o'er all hope careered
Unblushing, undisguising, bold and strong;
Whilst falshood, tricked in virtue's attributes,
Long sanctified all deeds of vice and woe,
Till done by her own venomous sting to death,   45
She left the moral world without a law,
No longer fettering passion's fearless wing,
Nor searing reason with the brand of God.
Then steadily the happy ferment worked;
Reason was free; and wild though passion went   50
Through tangled glens and wood-embosomed meads,
Gathering a garland of the strangest flowers,
Yet like the bee returning to her queen,
She bound the sweetest on her sister's brow,
Who meek and sober kissed the sportive child,   55
No longer trembling at the broken rod.
Mild was the slow necessity of death:

33 dust:] dust.   *1834*

37 *stanza break*] *omitted*   *1821.CLA*
   1821.BEN 1829.BRO 1834

38 love;] love.   *1834*

41 crime] crime,   *1821.CLA 1821.BEN*
   hope] hope,   *1821.CLA 1821.BEN*

42 bold] bold,   *1821.CLA 1821.BEN 1834*

43 falshood,] falsehood,   *1821.CLA*
   1821.BEN 1829.BRO 1834 1839 1840

45 Till] Till,   *1834 1839 1840*

47 wing,] wing.   *1839 1840*

48 Nor . . . God.] *omitted*   *1839 1840*
   God.] ——.   *1821.CLAX*
    God.   *1821.BEN*

50 free;] free: *1829.BRO 1834*
   went] wen   *1834*

53 Yet] Yet,   *1834 1839 1840*

55 Who] Who,   *1821.CLA 1821.BEN*
   sober] sober,   *1821.CLA 1821.BEN*
    1839 1840
   kissed] kiss'd   *1839*

57 death:] death;   *1821.BEN*

The tranquil spirit failed beneath its grasp,
Without a groan, almost without a fear,
60   Calm as a voyager to some distant land,
And full of wonder, full of hope as he.
The deadly germs of languor and disease
Died in the human frame, and purity
Blest with all gifts her earthly worshippers.
65   How vigorous then the athletic form of age!
How clear its open and unwrinkled brow!
Where neither avarice, cunning, pride, or care,
Had stamped the seal of grey deformity
On all the mingling lineaments of time.
70   How lovely the intrepid front of youth!
Which meek-eyed courage decked with freshest grace;
Courage of soul, that dreaded not a name,
And elevated will, that journeyed on
Through life's phantasmal scene in fearlessness,
75   With virtue, love, and pleasure, hand in hand.

Then, that sweet bondage which is freedom's self,
And rivets with sensation's softest tie
The kindred sympathies of human souls,
Needed no fetters of tyrannic law:
80   Those delicate and timid impulses
In nature's primal modesty arose,
And with undoubting confidence disclosed
The growing longings of its dawning love,
Unchecked by dull and selfish chastity,
85   That virtue of the cheaply virtuous,
Who pride themselves in senselessness and frost.
No longer prostitution's venomed bane
Poisoned the springs of happiness and life;
Woman and man, in confidence and love,
90   Equal and free and pure together trod

---

58 grasp,] grasp.   *1839 1840*
61 hope] hope,   *1834*
64 worshippers.] worshipers.   *1829.BRO*
      worshipers: *1834*
67 or] nor   *1821.CLA 1821.BEN*
   1829.BRO 1834 1839 1840
71 Which] With   *1834*
75 *stanza break*] *page break*   *1839*
      omitted   *1840*

76 freedom's] Freedom's   *1821.BEN*
79 law:] law.   *1839 1840*
89 love,] love   *1834*
90 Equal] Equal,   *1821.CLA 1821.BEN*
   free] free,   *1821.CLA 1821.BEN*
   pure] pure,   *1821.CLA 1821.BEN*
    1834 1839 1840

The mountain-paths of virtue, which no more
Were stained with blood from many a pilgrim's feet.

Then, where, through distant ages, long in pride
The palace of the monarch-slave had mocked
Famine's faint groan, and penury's silent tear,   95
A heap of crumbling ruins stood, and threw
Year after year their stones upon the field,
Wakening a lonely echo; and the leaves
Of the old thorn, that on the topmost tower
Usurped the royal ensign's grandeur, shook   100
In the stern storm that swayed the topmost tower
And whispered strange tales in the whirlwind's ear.

Low through the lone cathedral's roofless aisles
The melancholy winds a death-dirge sung:
It were a sight of awfulness to see   105
The works of faith and slavery, so vast,
So sumptuous, yet so perishing withal!
Even as the corpse that rests beneath its wall.
A thousand mourners deck the pomp of death
To-day, the breathing marble glows above   110
To decorate its memory, and tongues
Are busy of its life: to-morrow, worms
In silence and in darkness seize their prey.

Within the massy prison's mouldering courts,
Fearless and free the ruddy children played,   115
Weaving gay chaplets for their innocent brows
With the green ivy and the red wall-flower,
That mock the dungeon's unavailing gloom;
The ponderous chains, and gratings of strong iron,
There rusted amid heaps of broken stone   120
That mingled slowly with their native earth:
There the broad beam of day, which feebly once

---

94 palace] place   *1834*

95 groan,] groan   *1834*

101 tower] tower,   *1834 1839 1840*

102 whispered] whisper'd   *1821.BEN*

   stanza break] *page break   1834 1839*

         omitted   1840

108 corpse] corps   *1834*

110 To-day,] To day,   *1829.BRO*

       To day;   *1834*

112 to-morrow,]

   to-morrow   *1821.CLA 1821.BEN*

115 free] free,   *1834*

120 stone] stone,   *1839 1840*

Lighted the cheek of lean captivity
With a pale and sickly glare, then freely shone
125 On the pure smiles of infant playfulness:
No more the shuddering voice of hoarse despair
Pealed through the echoing vaults, but soothing notes
Of ivy-fingered winds and gladsome birds
And merriment were resonant around.

130 These ruins soon left not a wreck behind:
Their elements, wide scattered o'er the globe,
To happier shapes were moulded, and became
Ministrant to all blissful impulses:
Thus human things were perfected, and earth,
135 Even as a child beneath its mother's love,
Was strengthened in all excellence, and grew
Fairer and nobler with each passing year.

Now Time his dusky pennons o'er the scene
Closes in stedfast darkness, and the past
140 Fades from our charmed sight. My task is done:
Thy lore is learned. Earth's wonders are thine own,
With all the fear and all the hope they bring.
My spells are past: the present now recurs.
Ah me! a pathless wilderness remains
145 Yet unsubdued by man's reclaiming hand.

Yet, human Spirit, bravely hold thy course,
Let virtue teach thee firmly to pursue
The gradual paths of an aspiring change:
For birth and life and death, and that strange state
150 Before the naked soul has found its home,
All tend to perfect happiness, and urge
The restless wheels of being on their way,
Whose flashing spokes, instinct with infinite life,
Bicker and burn to gain their destined goal:
155 For birth but wakes the spirit to the sense

---

129 *stanza break*] *page break*   *1839*
         omitted   1840
137 *stanza break*] *page break*   *1821.CLA*
         omitted   1821.BEN
139 stedfast] steadfast   *1834 1839 1840*

146 Spirit,] Spirit!   *1839 1840*
         course,] course.   *1834*
148 change:] change;   *1834*
149 birth] birth,   *1821.CLA 1821.BEN*
         life] life,   *1821.CLA 1821.BEN*
154 goal:] goal.   *1839 1840*

Of outward shews, whose unexperienced shape
New modes of passion to its frame may lend;
Life is its state of action, and the store
Of all events is aggregated there
That variegate the eternal universe;   160
Death is a gate of dreariness and gloom,
That leads to azure isles and beaming skies
And happy regions of eternal hope.
Therefore, O Spirit! fearlessly bear on:
Though storms may break the primrose on its stalk,   165
Though frosts may blight the freshness of its bloom,
Yet spring's awakening breath will woo the earth,
To feed with kindliest dews its favorite flower,
That blooms in mossy banks and darksome glens,
Lighting the green wood with its sunny smile.   170

Fear not then, Spirit, death's disrobing hand,
So welcome when the tyrant is awake,
So welcome when the bigot's hell-torch burns;
'Tis but the voyage of a darksome hour,
The transient gulph-dream of a startling sleep.   175
Death is no foe to virtue: earth has seen
Love's brightest roses on the scaffold bloom,
Mingling with freedom's fadeless laurels there,
And presaging the truth of visioned bliss.
Are there not hopes within thee, which this scene   180
Of linked and gradual being has confirmed?
Whose stingings bade thy heart look further still,
When to the moonlight walk by Henry led,
Sweetly and sadly thou didst talk of death?
And wilt thou rudely tear them from thy breast,   185
Listening supinely to a bigot's creed,
Or tamely crouching to the tyrant's rod,

---

156 shews,] shows,   *1839 1840*

162 skies] skies,   *1839 1840*

163 And] Of   *1834*

168 favorite] favourite   *1821.CLA*
     1821.BEN 1829.BRO 1834 1839
     1840

170 green wood] greenwood   *1821.CLA*
     1821.BEN 1839 1840
       green-wood   *1829.BRO 1834*

stanza break] *page break   1829.BRO*
                omitted   1834

171 hand,] hand;   *1839 1840*

175 gulph-dream]
       gulf-dream   *1821.BEN 1839 1840*

176 earth] Earth   *1821.CLA 1821.BEN*

183 When] When,   *1834*
     walk] walk,   *1839 1840*

                    Whose iron thongs are red with human gore?
                    Never: but bravely bearing on, thy will
190   Is destined an eternal war to wage
                    With tyranny and falshood, and uproot
                    The germs of misery from the human heart.
                    Thine is the hand whose piety would soothe
                    The thorny pillow of unhappy crime,
195   Whose impotence an easy pardon gains,
                    Watching its wanderings as a friend's disease:
                    Thine is the brow whose mildness would defy
                    Its fiercest rage, and brave its sternest will,
                    When fenced by power and master of the world.
200   Thou art sincere and good; of resolute mind,
                    Free from heart-withering custom's cold control,
                    Of passion lofty, pure and unsubdued.
                    Earth's pride and meanness could not vanquish thee,
                    And therefore art thou worthy of the boon
205   Which thou hast now received: virtue shall keep
                    Thy footsteps in the path that thou hast trod,
                    And many days of beaming hope shall bless
                    Thy spotless life of sweet and sacred love.
                    Go, happy one, and give that bosom joy
210   Whose sleepless spirit waits to catch
                       Light, life and rapture from thy smile.

                       The fairy waves her wand of charm.
                    Speechless with bliss the Spirit mounts the car,
                       That rolled beside the battlement,
215   Bending her beamy eyes in thankfulness.
                       Again the enchanted steeds were yoked,
                       Again the burning wheels inflame
                    The steep descent of heaven's untrodden way.
                       Fast and far the chariot flew:

---

189 will] will,   *1821.CLA*

191 falshood,] falsehood,   *1821.CLA*
    1821.BEN 1829.BRO 1834 1839
    1840

196 wanderings] wanderings,   *1839*

201 control,]
    controul,   *1821.CLA 1821.BEN*

202 pure] pure,   *1834*

209 one,] one!   *1839 1840*
   joy] joy,   *1840*

211 life] life,   *1821.CLA 1821.BEN 1834*
   rapture] rapture,   *1834*

212 fairy] Fairy   *1821.CLA 1821.BEN*
    1839 1840
   charm.] charm,   *1821.BEN*

213 car,] car   *1834*

216 yoked,] yoked   *1829.BRO*

219 flew:] flew;   *1821.BEN*

The vast and fiery globes that rolled   220
        Around the Fairy's palace-gate
Lessened by slow degrees, and soon appeared
Such tiny twinklers as the planet orbs
That there attendant on the solar power
With borrowed light pursued their narrower way.   225

        Earth floated then below:
    The chariot paused a moment there;
        The Spirit then descended:
The restless coursers pawed the ungenial soil,
Snuffed the gross air, and then, their errand done,   230
Unfurled their pinions to the winds of heaven.

    The Body and the Soul united then,
A gentle start convulsed Ianthe's frame:
Her veiny eyelids quietly unclosed;
Moveless awhile the dark blue orbs remained: 235
She looked around in wonder and beheld
Henry, who kneeled in silence by her couch,
Watching her sleep with looks of speechless love,
        And the bright beaming stars
        That through the casement shone.   240

---

223 orbs] orbs,   *1834*   232 then,] then;   *1839 1840*
225 *stanza break*] *omitted   1821.CLA*   233 Ianthe's] Iänthe's   *1821.BEN*
      1821.BEN 1829.BRO 1834   236 wonder] wonder,   *1834 1839 1840*
230 errand] erran d   *1834*

NOTES.

Note 1 (I.242–43)

The sun's unclouded orb
Rolled through the black concave.

BEYOND our atmosphere the sun would appear a rayless orb of fire in the midst of a black concave. The equal diffusion of its light on earth is owing to the refraction of the rays by the atmosphere, and their reflection from other bodies. Light consists either of vibrations propagated through a subtle medium, or of numerous minute particles repelled in all directions from the luminous body. Its velocity greatly exceeds that of any substance with which we are acquainted: observations on the eclipses of Jupiter's satellites have demonstrated that light takes up no more than 8 minutes and 7 seconds in passing from the sun to the earth, a distance of 95,000,000 miles.—Some idea may be gained of the immense distance of the fixed stars, when it is computed that many years would elapse before light could reach this earth from the nearest of them; yet in one year light travels 5,422,400,000,000 miles, which is a distance 5,707,600 times greater than that of the sun from the earth.

Note 2 (I.252–53)

Whilst round the chariot's way
Innumerable systems rolled.

The plurality of worlds,—the indefinite immensity of the universe is a most awful subject of contemplation. He who rightly feels its mystery and

Text collated with *1813*, *1821.CLA* (unexpurgated), *1821.CLAX* (expurgated), *1821.BEN*, *1829.BRO*, *1834*, and *1840*. *1839* omits this note.

1–2 The . . . concave.] *set in italics*   10 8 minutes and 7 seconds] 8' 7"
    1821.BEN 1829.BRO 1834 1839   *omnia*
    1840   11 miles.—] miles.   *1821.CLA 1821.BEN*

Text collated with *1813*, *1821.BEN*, *1821.CLA* (unexpurgated), *1821.CLAX* (expurgated), *1829.BRO*, *1834*, and *1840*. *1839* omits this note.

1–2 Whilst . . . rolled.] *set in italics*   3 worlds,—the]
    1821.BEN 1829.BRO 1834 1840   worlds, the   *1821.CLA 1821.BEN*
        universe is] universe,—is   *1840*

5   grandeur, is in no danger of seduction from the falshoods of religious sys-
tems, or of deifying the principle of the universe. It is impossible to believe
that the Spirit that pervades this infinite machine, begat a son upon the body
of a Jewish woman; or is angered at the consequences of that necessity, which
is a synonime of itself. All that miserable tale of the Devil, and Eve, and an
10   Intercessor, with the childish mummeries of the God of the Jews, is irrecon-
cileable with the knowledge of the stars. The works of his fingers have borne
witness against him.

    The nearest of the fixed stars is inconceivably distant from the earth, and
they are probably proportionably distant from each other. By a calculation of
15   the velocity of light, Syrius is supposed to be at least 54,224,000,000,000
miles from the earth.[1] That which appears only like a thin and silvery cloud
streaking the heaven, is in effect composed of innumerable clusters of suns,
each shining with its own light, and illuminating numbers of planets that re-
volve around them. Millions and millions of suns are ranged around us, all
20   attended by innumerable worlds, yet calm, regular, and harmonious, all
keeping the paths of immutable necessity.

Note 3 (IV.178–79)

These are the hired bravos who defend
The tyrant's throne.

    To employ murder as a means of justice, is an idea which a man of an en-
lightened mind will not dwell upon with pleasure. To march forth in rank

[1] See Nicholson's Encyclopedia, art. Light.

---

5 grandeur,] grandeur   *1834 1840*
  falshoods] falsehoods   *1821.CLA*
    1821.BEN 1829.BRO 1834 1840
7 machine,] machine   *1834 1840*
7–8 begat . . . or]
    omitted   1821.CLAX 1821.BEN
  woman;] woman,   *1834 1840*
8 necessity,] necessity   *1834 1840*
9 synonime] synonyme   *1821.CLA*
    1821.BEN 1840
9–10 and an . . . Jews,]
    omitted   1821.BEN

and . . . Intercessor,]
  is irreconcileable   *1821.CLAX*
10 childish mummeries]
  knowledge   *1821.CLAX*
  God of the] *omitted   1821.CLAX*
11–12 The . . . him.]
    omitted   1821.CLAX 1821.BEN
16 cloud] cloud,   *1834 1840*
Footnote. Encyclopedia,] Encyclopœdia,
    1821.CLA 1821.BEN

Text collated with ***1813,*** *Enq, 1821.BEN, 1821.CLA* (unexpurgated), *1821.CLAX* (expurgated),
1829.BRO, 1834, and *1840. 1839* omits this note.

1–2 These . . . throne.] *set in italics*
    1821.BEN 1829.BRO 1834 1840
1 bravos] bravoes   *1821.CLA 1821.BEN*
2 tyrant's] Tyrant's   *1821.BEN*

3 a] the   *Enq*
  justice,] justice   *1834*
  which] that   *Enq*
  an] *omitted   Enq*

and file, and all the pomp of streamers and trumpets, for the purpose of
shooting at our fellow-men as a mark; to inflict upon them all the variety of
wound and anguish; to leave them weltering in their blood; to wander over
the field of desolation, and count the number of the dying and the dead,—
are employments which in thesis we may maintain to be necessary, but which
no good man will contemplate with gratulation and delight. A battle we sup-
pose is won:—thus truth is established, thus the cause of justice is confirmed!
It surely requires no common sagacity to discern the connection between
this immense heap of calamities and the assertion of truth or the mainte-
nance of justice.

Kings, and ministers of state, the real authors of the calamity, sit unmo-
lested in their cabinet, while those against whom the fury of the storm is di-
rected are, for the most part, persons who have been trepanned into the ser-
vice, or who are dragged unwillingly from their peaceful homes into the field
of battle. A soldier is a man whose business it is to kill those who never of-
fended him, and who are the innocent martyrs of other men's iniquities.
Whatever may become of the abstract question of the justifiableness of war,
it seems impossible that the soldier should not be a depraved and unnatural
being.

To these more serious and momentous considerations it may be proper to
add a recollection of the ridiculousness of the military character. Its first con-
stituent is obedience: a soldier is, of all descriptions of men, the most com-
pletely a machine; yet his profession inevitably teaches him something of
dogmatism, swaggering, and self-consequence: he is like the puppet of a

---

5 and all]
    with all   *Enq 1821.CLA 1821.BEN*
6 a mark;] at a mark,   *Enq*
7 wound] wounds   *Enq*
  anguish;] anguish,   *Enq*
  blood;] blood,   *Enq*
8 dead,—are] dead, are   *Enq*
    dead—are   *1821.BEN*
10 battle] battle,   *Enq*
  suppose] will suppose   *Enq*
11 won:—thus] won. Thus   *Enq*
  established, thus]
    established; thus   *Enq*
    established!—thus   *1821.BEN*
    established;—thus   *1821.CLA*
12 sagacity] sagacity,   *Enq*
  connection] connexion   *1840*
13 calamities]
  calamities,   *Enq 1821.CLA 1821.BEN*

truth] truth,   *Enq 1821.CLA 1821.BEN*
15 Kings,] Kings   *Enq 1821.BEN*
16–17 directed]
    directed,   *Enq 1821.CLA*
    1821.BEN*
22 the] a   *Enq*
24 considerations] considerations,   *Enq*
26 obedience:] obedience.   *Enq*
    obedience;   *1840*
  a] A   *Enq*
  is,] is   *Enq*
  men,] men   *Enq*
27 machine;] machine.   *Enq*
  yet] Yet   *Enq*
28 swaggering,] swaggering   *Enq*
  self-consequence:]
    self-consequence.   *Enq*
  he] He   *Enq*

showman, who, at the very time he is made to strut and swell and display the
30 most farcical airs, we perfectly know cannot assume the most insignificant
gesture, advance either to the right or the left, but as he is moved by his ex-
hibitor.—*Godwin's Enquirer, Essay* v.

I will here subjoin a little poem, so strongly expressive of my abhorrence
of despotism and falshood, that I fear lest it never again may be depictured
35 so vividly. This opportunity is perhaps the only one that ever will occur of res-
cuing it from oblivion.

FALSHOOD AND VICE:

A DIALOGUE.

Whilst monarchs laughed upon their thrones
40   To hear a famished nation's groans,
And hugged the wealth wrung from the woe
That makes its eyes and veins o'erflow,—
Those thrones, high built upon the heaps
Of bones where frenzied famine sleeps,
45   Where slavery wields her scourge of iron,
Red with mankind's unheeded gore,
And war's mad fiends the scene environ,
Mingling with shrieks a drunken roar,
There Vice and Falshood took their stand,
50   High raised above the unhappy land.

FALSHOOD.

Brother! arise from the dainty fare,
Which thousands have toiled and bled to bestow;
A finer feast for thy hungry ear
55   Is the news that I bring of human woe.

---

29 showman,]
    show- [*line break*] man,   *1829.BRO*
    show-man,   *1834 1840*
  strut] strut,   *Enq 1821.BEN 1829.BRO*
    1834
  swell] swell,   *Enq 1821.BEN 1829.BRO*
    1834 1840
31 his] the   *Enq*
  exhibitor.—] exhibitor.   *Enq*
33 poem,] poem   *1821.BEN*
34 falshood,] falsehood,   *1821.CLA*
    1821.BEN 1829.BRO 1834 1840
  never again may]
    may never again   *1821.BEN*

37 VICE:]
    VICE.   *1821.CLA 1821.BEN 1840*
40 nation's] nations   *1821.CLA*
42 o'erflow,—] o'erflow,   *1821.CLA*
    1821.BEN
44 sleeps,] sleeps.   *1821.CLA 1821.BEN*
49 Falshood] Falsehood   *1821.CLA*
    1821.BEN 1829.BRO 1834 1840
50 the] th'   *1834 1840*
52 fare,] fare   *1834 1840*
54 thy] thine   *1821.CLA 1821.BEN*

VICE.

And, secret one, what hast thou done,
To compare, in thy tumid pride, with me?
I, whose career, through the blasted year,
Has been tracked by despair and agony.   60

FALSHOOD.

What have I done!———I have torn the robe
From baby truth's unsheltered form,
And round the desolated globe
Borne safely the bewildering charm: 65
My tyrant-slaves to a dungeon-floor
Have bound the fearless innocent,
And streams of fertilizing gore
Flow from her bosom's hideous rent,
Which this unfailing dagger gave.   70
I dread that blood!—no more—this day
Is ours, though her eternal ray
  Must shine upon our grave.
Yet know, proud Vice, had I not given
To thee the robe I stole from heaven,   75
Thy shape of ugliness and fear
Had never gained admission here.

VICE.

And know, that had I disdained to toil,
But sate in my loathsome cave the while,   80
And ne'er to these hateful sons of heaven,
GOLD, MONARCHY, and MURDER, given;
Hadst thou with all thine art essayed
One of thy games then to have played,
With all thine overweening boast,   85
Falshood! I tell thee thou hadst lost!—
Yet wherefore this dispute?—we tend,
Fraternal, to one common end;

---

57 one,] one! *1840*

58 compare,] compare *1821.BEN*

62 done!———I] done!—I *1821.CLA*
    1821.BEN 1829.BRO
          done?—I *1834 1840*

63 truth's] Truth's *1840*

66 tyrant-slaves] tyrant slaves *1821.BEN*

70 gave. . . . .] gave— *1821.BEN*
    gave . . . *1829.BRO 1840*
    gave. . . *1834*

74 know,] know *1840*

79 that] that, *1834 1840*

81 heaven,] heaven *1834 1840*

82 MURDER,]
    MURDER *1821.CLA 1821.BEN*
    given;] given: *1821.CLA*

86 Falshood!] Falsehood! *1821.CLA*
    1821.BEN 1829.BRO
        Falsehood, *1834 1840*

In this cold grave beneath my feet,
90 Will our hopes, our fears, and our labours, meet.

FALSHOOD.
I brought my daughter, RELIGION, on earth:
She smothered Reason's babes in their birth;
But dreaded their mother's eye severe,—
95 So the crocodile slunk off slily in fear,
And loosed her bloodhounds from the den. . . .
They started from dreams of slaughtered men,
And, by the light of her poison eye,
Did her work o'er the wide earth frightfully:
100 The dreadful stench of her torches' flare,
Fed with human fat, polluted the air:
The curses, the shrieks, the ceaseless cries
Of the many-mingling miseries,
As on she trod, ascended high
105 And trumpeted my victory!—
Brother, tell what thou hast done.

VICE.
I have extinguished the noon-day sun,
In the carnage-smoke of battles won:
110 Famine, murder, hell and power
Were glutted in that glorious hour
Which searchless fate had stamped for me
With the seal of her security. . . . .
For the bloated wretch on yonder throne
115 Commanded the bloody fray to rise.
Like me he joyed at the stifled moan
Wrung from a nation's miseries;
While the snakes, whose slime even him *defiled*,

---

89 feet,] feet   *1834 1840*

90 labours,] labours   *1821.CLA*
 1821.BEN 1829.BRO

92 RELIGION,] ————,   *1821.CLAX*
 earth:] earth;   *1840*

94 severe,—] severe—   *1821.BEN*

96 den. . . .] den. *1821.CLA*
     den—   *1821.BEN*
     den *1829.BRO 1834*
     1840

98 And,] And   *1821.BEN*

99 frightfully:] frightfully;   *1834 1840*

100 torches']
     torches   *1821.CLA 1821.BEN*

101 fat,] fat   *1821.BEN*

103 many-mingling]
     many mingling   *1840*

108 sun,] sun   *1834 1840*

110 hell] hell,   *1821.CLA 1821.BEN 1834*
     1840
     power] power,   *1821.CLA 1821.BEN*
     1834 1840

111 hour] hour,   *1829.BRO 1834 1840*

113 security. . . . .] security—   *1821.BEN*
     security . . . .
     1829.BRO 1834 1840

115 rise.] rise: *1821.CLA 1821.BEN*
     rise—   *1840*

116 me] me,   *1840*

In ecstacies of malice smiled:
They thought 'twas theirs,—but mine the deed! 120
Theirs is the toil, but mine the meed—
Ten thousand victims madly bleed.
They dream that tyrants goad them there
With poisonous war to taint the air:
These tyrants, on their beds of thorn, 125
Swell with the thoughts of murderous fame,
And with their gains to lift my name.
Restless they plan from night to morn:
I—I do all; without my aid
Thy daughter, that relentless maid, 130
Could never o'er a death-bed urge
The fury of her venomed scourge.

FALSHOOD.

Brother, well:—the world is ours;
And whether thou or I have won, 135
The pestilence expectant lowers
On all beneath yon blasted sun.
Our joys, our toils, our honors meet
In the milk-white and wormy winding-sheet:
A short-lived hope, unceasing care, 140
Some heartless scraps of godly prayer,
A moody curse, and a frenzied sleep
Ere gapes the grave's unclosing deep,
A tyrant's dream, a coward's start,
The ice that clings to a priestly heart, 145
A judge's frown, a courtier's smile,
Make the great whole for which we toil;
And, brother, whether thou or I
Have done the work of misery,
It little boots: thy toil and pain, 150
Without my aid, were more than vain;
And but for thee I ne'er had sate
The guardian of heaven's palace gate.

☞

---

119 ecstacies] ecstasies *1821.CLA*
127 name.] name, *1829.BRO 1834 1840*
134 well:—the] well!—the *1840*
138 honors] honours *1821.CLA*
   1821.BEN 1829.BRO
   honours, *1834 1840*
139 winding-sheet:]

winding-sheet; *1834 1840*
143 grave's] graves *1821.CLA 1821.BEN*
  deep,] deep *1834*
145 The] That *1840*
150 thy] the *1821.BEN*
151 aid,] aid *1821.CLA 1821.BEN*
154 ☞] *omitted* *1834 1840*

Note 3 (IV.178–79) 245

Note 4 (V.1–2)

Thus do the generations of the earth
Go to the grave, and issue from the womb.

One generation passeth away and another generation cometh, but the earth abideth for ever. The sun also ariseth and the sun goeth down, and hasteth to his place where he arose. The wind goeth toward the south and turneth about unto the north, it whirleth about continually, and the wind returneth again according to his circuits. All the rivers run into the sea, yet the sea is not full; unto the place whence the rivers come, thither shall they return again.

Ecclesiastes, chap. i.

Note 5 (V.4–6)

Even as the leaves
Which the keen frost-wind of the waning year
Has scattered on the forest soil.

Οἴη περ φύλλων γενεή, τοίη δὲ καί ἀνδρῶν,
Φύλλα τὰ μέν τ᾽ἄνεμος χαμάδις χέει, ἄλλα δὲ θ᾽ ὕλη
Τηλεθόωσα φύει, ἔαρος δ᾽ ἐπιγίγνεται ὥρη·
῞Ως ἀνδρῶν γενεὴ, ἡ μὲν φύει, ἡ δ᾽ ἀπολήγει.

ΙΛΙΑΔ. Ζ᾽. l. 146.

Text collated with *1813, 1821.BEN, 1821.CLA* (unexpurgated), *1821.CLAX* (expurgated), *1829.BRO, 1834, 1839,* and *1840.*

1–2 Thus . . . womb.] *set in italics* *1821.BEN 1829.BRO 1834 1839 1840*

2 grave,] grave *1813 1829.BRO 1834 1839 1840*

3 One] "One *1839 1840*

4 ariseth] ariseth, *1821.BEN*

5 south] south, *1821.BEN 1834 1839 1840*

6 north,] north; *1834 1839 1840*

7 again] again, *1821.CLA 1821.BEN*

9 again.] again." *1839 1840*

10 *Ecclesiastes,*] —*Ecclesiastes,* *1839 1840*

Text collated with *1813, 1821.CLA* (unexpurgated), *1821.CLAX* (expurgated), *1821.BEN, 1829.BRO, 1834, 1839,* and *1840.* Greek Text collated with *1813.*

1–3 Even . . . soil.] *set in italics* *1821.BEN 1829.BRO 1834 1839 1840*

4 γενεή] γενεὴ *1813*
   τοίη δὲ] τοιήδε *1813*

ἀνδρῶν,] ανδρῶν, *1813*

5 δὲ] δέ *1813*

7 ἡ δ᾽] ἠδ᾽ *1813*
   ἀπολήγει.] ἄπολήγει. *1813*

Note 6 (V.58)

The mob of peasants, nobles, priests, and kings.

Suave mari magno turbantibus æquora ventis
E terrâ magnum alterius spectare laborem;
Non quia vexari quemquam 'st jucunda voluptas,
Sed quibus ipse malis careas quia cernere suave'st.   5
Suave etiam belli certamina magna tueri,
Per campos instructa, tua sine parte pericli;
Sed nil dulcius est bene quam munita tenere
Edita doctrina sapientum templa serena;
Despicere unde queas alios, passim que videre   10
Errare atque viam palanteis quærere vitæ;
Certare ingenio; contendere nobilitate;
Nocteis atque dies niti præstante labore
Ad summas emergere opes, rerum que potiri.
O miseras hominum menteis! O pectora cæca!   15

Luc. lib. ii.

Text collated with **1813**, *1821.CLA* (unexpurgated), *1821.CLAX* (expurgated), *1821.BEN*,
1829.BRO, *1834*, *1839*, and *1840*.

1 The . . . kings.] *set in italics*   *1821.BEN*
 1829.BRO 1834 1839 1840

2 Suave]
  Suave,   *1829.BRO 1834 1839 1840*
 ventis] ventis,   *1821.BEN 1829.BRO*
  1834 1839 1840

3 terrâ] terra   *1821.BEN 1839 1840*
 laborem;]
  laborem: *1829.BRO 1834 1839 1840*

4 Non] Non,   *1821.BEN 1829.BRO 1834*
  1839 1840
 'st] est   *1821.BEN*
 jucunda]
  jocunda   *1829.BRO 1834 1839 1840*

5 Sed] Sed,   *1821.BEN 1829.BRO 1834*
  1839 1840
 careas] careas,   *1821.BEN 1829.BRO*
  1834 1839 1840
 suave'st.] suave est.   *1821.BEN*
  1829.BRO 1834
   suave 'st.   *1821.CLA 1839*
  1840

6–7 *These two lines are transposed in*
 1829.BRO 1834 1839 1840

6 tueri,]
  tueri: *1829.BRO 1834 1839 1840*

7 pericli;]
  pericli,   *1829.BRO 1834 1839 1840*

8 est] est,   *1821.BEN 1829.BRO 1834*
  1839 1840
 tenere] tenere,   *1821.BEN 1829.BRO*
  1834 1839 1840

9 doctrina] doctrinâ   *1829.BRO 1834*
 sapientum] sapientum,   *1821.BEN*
  1829.BRO 1834

10 passim que] passimque   *1829.BRO*
  1834 1839 1840

11 Errare] Errare,   *1821.BEN 1829.BRO*
  1834 1839 1840

12 ingenio;] ingenio,   *1821.BEN*
 nobilitate;] nobilitate,   *1829.BRO*
  1834 1839 1840

14 rerum que] rerumque   *1821.BEN*
  1829.BRO 1834 1839 1840

16 *Luc.*]
  Lucret.   *1829.BRO 1834 1839 1840*

Note 7 (V.93–94)

And statesmen boast
Of wealth!

There is no real wealth but the labour of man. Were the mountains of gold and the vallies of silver, the world would not be one grain of corn the richer; no one comfort would be added to the human race. In consequence of our consideration for the precious metals, one man is enabled to heap to himself luxuries at the expence of the necessaries of his neighbour; a system admirably fitted to produce all the varieties of disease and crime, which never fail to characterise the two extremes of opulence and penury. A speculator takes pride to himself as the promoter of his country's prosperity, who employs a number of hands in the manufacture of articles avowedly destitute of use, or subservient only to the unhallowed cravings of luxury and ostentation. The nobleman, who employs the peasants of his neighbourhood in building his palaces, until *"jam pauca aratro jugera, regiœ moles relinquunt,"* flatters himself that he has gained the title of a patriot by yielding to the impulses of vanity. The shew and pomp of courts adduces the same apology for its continuance; and many a fête has been given, many a woman has eclipsed her beauty by her dress, to benefit the labouring poor and to encourage trade. Who does not see that this is a remedy which aggravates, whilst it palliates the countless diseases of society? The poor are set to labour,—for what? Not the food for which they famish: not the blankets for want of which their babes are frozen by the cold of their miserable hovels: not those comforts of civilization without which civilized man is far more miserable than the meanest savage; oppressed as he is by all its insidious evils, within the daily and taunting prospect of its innumerable benefits assiduously exhibited before him:—no; for the pride of power, for the miserable isolation of pride, for the false pleasures of the hundredth part of society. No greater evidence is afforded of the wide extended and radical mistakes of civilized man than this

---

Text collated with **1813**, *1821.CLA* (unexpurgated), *1821.CLAX* (expurgated), *1821.BEN, 1829.BRO, 1834, 1839,* and *1840.*

1–2 And . . . wealth!] *set in italics* *1821.BEN 1829.BRO 1834 1839 1840*

2 wealth!] wealth. *1829.BRO 1834*

3 gold] gold, *1821.CLA 1821.BEN*

4 vallies] valleys *1834 1839 1840*

7 expence] expense *1839 1840*

13 nobleman,] nobleman *1839 1840*

14 *relinquunt,"*] *relinquent,"* *1829.BRO 1834 1839 1840*

16 shew] show *1834 1839 1840*
   adduces] adduce *1839 1840*

17 its] their *1839 1840*
   fête] fete *1821.BEN 1834*

18 poor] poor, *1821.BEN*

19 palliates] palliates, *1834 1839 1840*

20 labour,—for] labour—for *1821.BEN*

22 comforts] comfors *1821.CLA*

23 civilization] civilisation *1839 1840*
   civilized] civilised *1839 1840*

25 assiduously] assidiously *1821.BEN*

28 wide extended]
   wide-extended *1839 1840*
   civilized] civilised *1839 1840*

fact: those arts which are essential to his very being are held in the greatest
contempt; employments are lucrative in an inverse ratio to their usefulness:[1] 30
the jeweller, the toyman, the actor gains fame and wealth by the exercise of
his useless and ridiculous art; whilst the cultivator of the earth, he without
whom society must cease to subsist, struggles through contempt and penury,
and perishes by that famine which, but for his unceasing exertions, would an-
nihilate the rest of mankind. 35

I will not insult common sense by insisting on the doctrine of the natural
equality of man. The question is not concerning its desirableness, but its
practicability: so far as it is practicable, it is desirable. That state of human so-
ciety which approaches nearer to an equal partition of its benefits and evils
should, *cæteris paribus*, be preferred: but so long as we conceive that a wanton 40
expenditure of human labour, not for the necessities, not even for the luxu-
ries of the mass of society, but for the egotism and ostentation of a few of its
members, is defensible on the ground of public justice, so long we neglect to
approximate to the redemption of the human race.

Labour is required for physical, and leisure for moral improvement: from 45
the former of these advantages the rich, and from the latter the poor, by the
inevitable conditions of their respective situations, are precluded. A state
which should combine the advantages of both, would be subjected to the
evils of neither. He that is deficient in firm health, or vigorous intellect, is but
half a man: hence it follows, that, to subject the labouring classes to unnec- 50
essary labour, is wantonly depriving them of any opportunities of intellectual
improvement; and that the rich are heaping up for their own mischief the
disease, lassitude and ennui by which their existence is rendered an intoler-
able burthen.

---

[1] See Rousseau, "De l'Inegalité parmi les Hommes," note 7.

<table>
<tr><td>Footnote 1. "De] De   1834</td><td>48 both,] both   1834 1839 1840</td></tr>
<tr><td>l'Inegalité] l'Inegalite
1821.BEN</td><td>49 intellect,] intellect   1821.BEN</td></tr>
<tr><td>l'Inégalité   1834 1839 1840</td><td>50 man:] man;   1834 1839 1840</td></tr>
<tr><td>31 actor]</td><td>51 depriving] to deprive   1829.BRO
1834 1839 1840</td></tr>
<tr><td>actor,   1829.BRO 1834 1839 1840</td><td>52 improvement;]</td></tr>
<tr><td>34 exertions,] exertion,   1834 1839 1840</td><td>improvement: 1839 1840</td></tr>
<tr><td>38 practicability:]</td><td>mischief] mischief,   1821.BEN 1839</td></tr>
<tr><td>practicability;   1834 1839 1840</td><td>53 lassitude] lassitude,   1821.BEN 1834
1839 1840</td></tr>
<tr><td>40 preferred:]</td><td>ennui] ennui,   1821.BEN</td></tr>
<tr><td>preferred;   1834 1839 1840</td><td>ennui   1821.CLA</td></tr>
<tr><td>41 luxuries] luxuries,   1834 1839 1840</td><td>ennui,   1834 1839 1840</td></tr>
<tr><td>45 moral] moral,   1834</td><td>54 burthen.] burden.   1840</td></tr>
<tr><td>47 conditions]</td><td></td></tr>
<tr><td>condition   1821.CLA 1821.BEN</td><td></td></tr>
</table>

55   English reformers exclaim against sinecures,—but the true pension list is
the rent-roll of the landed proprietors: wealth is a power usurped by the few,
to compel the many to labour for their benefit. The laws which support this
system derive their force from the ignorance and credulity of its victims: they
are the result of a conspiracy of the few against the many, who are themselves
60   obliged to purchase this pre-eminence by the loss of all real comfort.   ☞

The commodities that substantially contribute to the subsistence of the
human species form a very short catalogue: they demand from us but a slen-
der portion of industry. If these only were produced, and sufficiently pro-
duced, the species of man would be continued. If the labour necessarily re-
65   quired to produce them were equitably divided among the poor, and, still
more, if it were equitably divided among all, each man's share of labour
would be light, and his portion of leisure would be ample. There was a time
when this leisure would have been of small comparative value: it is to be
hoped that the time will come, when it will be applied to the most important
70   purposes. Those hours which are not required for the production of the
necessaries of life, may be devoted to the cultivation of the understanding,
the enlarging our stock of knowledge, the refining our taste, and thus open-
ing to us new and more exquisite sources of enjoyment.

    *   *   *   *   *   *   *   *

It was perhaps necessary that a period of monopoly and oppression
75   should subsist, before a period of cultivated equality could subsist. Savages
perhaps would never have been excited to the discovery of truth and the in-
vention of art, but by the narrow motives which such a period affords. But
surely, after the savage state has ceased, and men have set out in the glorious
career of discovery and invention, monopoly and oppression cannot be nec-
80   essary to prevent them from returning to a state of barbarism.—*Godwin's En-
quirer, Essay II. See also Pol. Jus., book VIII. chap.* II.

It is a calculation of this admirable author, that all the conveniences of civ-
ilized life might be produced, if society would divide the labour equally

---

55 sinecures,—but]
    sinecures—but   *1821.BEN*
  pension list]
    pension-list   *1821.CLA 1821.BEN*
69 come,] come   *1840*
70 hours] hours,   *1834 1839 1840*
71 life,] life   *1821.BEN*
72 enlarging] enlargement of   *1829.BRO*
    1834 1839 1840

refining] refinement of   *1829.BRO*
  1834 1839 1840
opening]
  open   *1829.BRO 1834 1839 1840*
75 subsist,] subsist   *1834*
77 But] But,   *1821.CLA 1821.BEN 1834*
  1839 1840
81 *chap.* II.] *chap.* 11.   **1813** *1821.CLA*
  1821.BEN 1829.BRO 1834 1839 1840
82 civilized] civilised   *1839 1840*

among its members, by each individual being employed in labour two hours
during the day.   85

Note 8 (V.112–13)

or religion
Drives his wife raving mad.

I am acquainted with a lady of considerable accomplishments, and the
mother of a numerous family, whom the Christian religion has goaded to in-
curable insanity. A parallel case is, I believe, within the experience of every   5
physician.

Nam jam sæpe homines patriam, carosque parentes
Prodiderunt, vitare Acherusia templa petentes.

Lucretius.

Note 9 (V.189)

Even love is sold.

Not even the intercourse of the sexes is exempt from the despotism of
positive institution. Law pretends even to govern the indisciplinable wan-
derings of passion, to put fetters on the clearest deductions of reason, and,
by appeals to the will, to subdue the involuntary affections of our nature.   5
Love is inevitably consequent upon the perception of loveliness. Love with-
ers under constraint: its very essence is liberty: it is compatible neither with
obedience, jealousy, nor fear: it is there most pure, perfect, and unlimited,
where its votaries live in confidence, equality, and unreserve.

How long then ought the sexual connection to last? what law ought to   10
specify the extent of the grievances which should limit its duration? A hus-

---

Text collated with *1813,* *1821.CLA* (unexpurgated), *1821.CLAX* (expurgated), *1821.BEN,*
1829.BRO, 1834, and *1840. 1839* omits this note.

1–2 or . . . mad.] *set in italics* *1821.BEN*   1 or] Or   *1821.CLA 1821.BEN 1829.BRO*
    1829.BRO 1834 1840   *1834 1840*

Text collated with *1813,* *1821.CLA* (unexpurgated), *1821.CLAX* (expurgated), *1821.BEN,*
1829.BRO, 1834, and *1840. 1839* omits this note.

1 Even . . . sold.] *set in italics* *1821.BEN*
   1829.BRO 1834 1840
4 and,] and   *1821.BEN*
10 connection]
   connexion   *1829.BRO 1834 1840*

band and wife ought to continue so long united as they love each other: any
law which should bind them to cohabitation for one moment after the decay
of their affection, would be a most intolerable tyranny, and the most unwor-
thy of toleration. How odious an usurpation of the right of private judgment
should that law be considered, which should make the ties of friendship in-
dissoluble, in spite of the caprices, the inconstancy, the fallibility, and capac-
ity for improvement of the human mind. And by so much would the fetters
of love be heavier and more unendurable than those of friendship, as love is
more vehement and capricious, more dependent on those delicate peculi-
arities of imagination, and less capable of reduction to the ostensible merits
of the object.

The state of society in which we exist is a mixture of feudal savageness and
imperfect civilization. The narrow and unenlightened morality of the Chris-
tian religion is an aggravation of these evils. It is not even until lately that
mankind have admitted that happiness is the sole end of the science of
ethics, as of all other sciences; and that the fanatical idea of mortifying the
flesh for the love of God has been discarded. I have heard, indeed, an igno-
rant collegian adduce, in favour of Christianity, its hostility to every worldly
feeling![1]

But if happiness be the object of morality, of all human unions and dis-
unions; if the worthiness of every action is to be estimated by the quantity of
pleasurable sensation it is calculated to produce, then the connection of the
sexes is so long sacred as it contributes to the comfort of the parties, and is
naturally dissolved when its evils are greater than its benefits. There is noth-
ing immoral in this separation. Constancy has nothing virtuous in itself, in-

[1] The first Christian emperor made a law by which seduction was punished with death: if the fe-
male pleaded her own consent, she also was punished with death; if the parents endeavoured to
screen the criminals, they were banished and their estates were confiscated; the slaves who
might be accessary were burned alive, or forced to swallow melted lead. The very offspring of
an illegal love were involved in the consequences of the sentence.—*Gibbon's Decline and Fall, &c.*
vol. ii. page 210. See also, for the hatred of the primitive Christians to love and even marriage,
page 269.

13 law] law,   *1834 1840*

15 toleration.] toleration,   *1829.BRO*
     an] a   *1834 1840*

16 considered,] considered   *1834 1840*

17 fallibility,] fallability,   *1829.BRO*

18 mind.] mind?   *1840*

24 civilization.] civilisation.   *1840*

Footnote 1. emperor]
       Emperor   *1829.BRO 1834*
     death:] death;   *1821.CLA*
       1821.BEN
     banished] banished,

       1821.CLA 1821.BEN
     were confiscated;]
       confiscated;   *1834 1840*
       accessary] accessory   *1840*
       love] love,   *1821.CLA*
       1821.BEN 1840

31 But] But,   *1834*
     disunions;] disunions: *1829.BRO*

33 sensation] sensations   *1834*
     produce,] produce;   *1834*
     connection] connexion   *1840*

dependently of the pleasure it confers, and partakes of the temporizing spirit
of vice in proportion as it endures tamely moral defects of magnitude in the
object of its indiscreet choice. Love is free: to promise for ever to love the
same woman, is not less absurd than to promise to believe the same creed: 40
such a vow, in both cases, excludes us from all enquiry. The language of the
votarist is this: The woman I now love may be infinitely inferior to many oth-
ers; the creed I now profess may be a mass of errors and absurdities; but I ex-
clude myself from all future information as to the amiability of the one and
the truth of the other, resolving blindly, and in spite of conviction, to adhere   45
to them. Is this the language of delicacy and reason? Is the love of such a
frigid heart of more worth than its belief?

The present system of constraint does no more, in the majority of in-
stances, than make hypocrites or open enemies. Persons of delicacy and
virtue, unhappily united to one whom they find it impossible to love, spend   50
the loveliest season of their life in unproductive efforts to appear otherwise
than they are, for the sake of the feelings of their partner or the welfare
of their mutual offspring: those of less generosity and refinement openly
avow their disappointment, and linger out the remnant of that union, which
only death can dissolve, in a state of incurable bickering and hostility. The   55
early education of their children takes its colour from the squabbles of the
parents; they are nursed in a systematic school of ill humour, violence, and
falshood. Had they been suffered to part at the moment when indifference
rendered their union irksome, they would have been spared many years of
misery: they would have connected themselves more suitably, and would   60
have found that happiness in the society of more congenial partners which
is for ever denied them by the despotism of marriage. They would have been
separately useful and happy members of society, who, whilst united, were
miserable, and rendered misanthropical by misery. The conviction that wed-
lock is indissoluble holds out the strongest of all temptations to the perverse: 65
they indulge without restraint in acrimony, and all the little tyrannies of do-
mestic life, when they know that their victim is without appeal. If this con-

---

37 temporizing] temporising   *1840*
38 vice] vice,   *1821.BEN*
40 woman,] woman   *1834*
    creed:] creed;   *1821.BEN*
41 enquiry.]
    inquiry.   *1829.BRO 1834 1840*
42 this: The] this: the   *1829.BRO*
44 one] one,   *1821.CLA 1821.BEN*
45 blindly,] blindly   *1834*
    conviction,]
      conviction   *1829.BRO 1834*
46 them.] them.—   *1821.CLA 1821.BEN*

50 one] those   *1829.BRO 1834 1840*
52 partner] partner,   *1840*
56 their children]
    the children   *1834 1840*
57 ill humour,]
    ill-humour,   *1821.CLA 1821.BEN*
58 falshood.] falsehood.   *1821.CLA*
      1821.BEN 1829.BRO 1834 1840
60 misery:] misery;   *1840*
65 indissoluble] indissoluble,   *1840*
    perverse:] perverse;   *1834*

nection were put on a rational basis, each would be assured that habitual ill
temper would terminate in separation, and would check this vicious and
dangerous propensity.

Prostitution is the legitimate offspring of marriage and its accompanying
errors. Women, for no other crime than having followed the dictates of a
natural appetite, are driven with fury from the comforts and sympathies of
society. It is less venial than murder; and the punishment which is inflicted
on her who destroys her child to escape reproach, is lighter than the life of
agony and disease to which the prostitute is irrecoverably doomed. Has a
woman obeyed the impulse of unerring nature;—society declares war
against her, pityless and eternal war: she must be the tame slave, she must
make no reprisals; theirs is the right of persecution, hers the duty of en-
durance. She lives a life of infamy: the loud and bitter laugh of scorn scares
her from all return. She dies of long and lingering disease: yet *she* is in fault,
she is the criminal, *she* the froward and untameable child,—and society, for-
sooth, the pure and virtuous matron, who casts her as an abortion from her
undefiled bosom! Society avenges herself on the criminals of her own crea-
tion; she is employed in anathematizing the vice to-day, which yesterday she
was the most zealous to teach. Thus is formed one tenth of the population of
London: meanwhile the evil is twofold. Young men, excluded by the fanati-
cal idea of chastity from the society of modest and accomplished women, as-
sociate with these vicious and miserable beings, destroying thereby all those
exquisite and delicate sensibilities whose existence cold-hearted worldlings
have denied; annihilating all genuine passion, and debasing that to a selfish
feeling which is the excess of generosity and devotedness. Their body and
mind alike crumble into a hideous wreck of humanity; idiotcy and disease
become perpetuated in their miserable offspring, and distant generations
suffer for the bigotted morality of their forefathers. Chastity is a monkish
and evangelical superstition, a greater foe to natural temperance even than

---

74 murder;] murder: *1840*

77 nature;—society]

    nature,—society   *1834*

    nature?—society   *1840*

78 pityless] pitiless   *1840*

80 infamy:] infamy;   *1821.BEN*

81 disease:] disease;   *1840*

82 child,—and] child—and   *1821.BEN*

      child;—and   *1840*

  society,] society   *1821.BEN*

  forsooth,] forsoosh,   *1829.BRO*

83 matron,] matron   *1840*

85 anathematizing]

    anathematising   *1840*

    to-day,] to-day   *1834*

86 one tenth] one-tenth   *1821.CLA*

    1821.BEN 1829.BRO 1834 1840

89 beings, destroying]

    beings,—destroying   *1840*

90 existence] existence,   *1821.BEN*

    denied;] denied: *1834*

95 bigotted]

    bigoted   *1829.BRO 1834 1840*

unintellectual sensuality; it strikes at the root of all domestic happiness, and consigns more than half of the human race to misery, that some few may monopolize according to law. A system could not well have been devised more studiously hostile to human happiness than marriage.

I conceive that, from the abolition of marriage, the fit and natural arrangement of sexual connection would result. I by no means assert that the intercourse would be promiscuous: on the contrary; it appears, from the relation of parent to child, that this union is generally of long duration, and marked above all others with generosity and self-devotion. But this is a subject which it is perhaps premature to discuss. That which will result from the abolition of marriage, will be natural and right, because choice and change will be exempted from restraint.

In fact, religion and morality, as they now stand, compose a practical code of misery and servitude: the genius of human happiness must tear every leaf from the accursed book of God, ere man can read the inscription on his heart. How would morality, dressed up in stiff stays and finery, start from her own disgusting image, should she look in the mirror of nature! ☞

Note 10 (VI.45–46)

To the red and baleful sun
That faintly twinkles there.

The north polar star, to which the axis of the earth, in its present state of obliquity, points. It is exceedingly probable, from many considerations, that this obliquity will gradually diminish, until the equator coincides with the ecliptic: the nights and days will then become equal on the earth throughout the year, and probably the seasons also. There is no great extravagance in presuming that the progress of the perpendicularity of the poles may be as

---

98 half of] half   *1834 1840*
99 monopolize] monopolise   *1840*
100 marriage.] Marriage.   *1821.BEN*
102 connection] connexion   *1840*
103 contrary;]
    contrary,   *1829.BRO 1834 1840*
    appears,] appears   *1829.BRO 1834*

105 self-devotion.] self devotion.   *1834*
106 it is] it is,   *1821.BEN*
    perhaps] perhaps,   *1821.BEN*
107 marriage,] marriage   *1834*
111 inscription] incription   *1829.BRO*
113 ☞] *omitted*   *1840*

Text collated with *1813*, *1821.CLA* (unexpurgated), *1821.CLAX* (expurgated), *1821.BEN*, *1829.BRO*, *1834*, *1839*, and *1840*.
1–2 To . . . there.] *set in italics*   *1821.BEN*
    1829.BRO 1834 1839 1840

rapid as the progress of intellect; or that there should be a perfect identity
between the moral and physical improvement of the human species. It is cer-
tain that wisdom is not compatible with disease, and that, in the present state
of the climates of the earth, health, in the true and comprehensive sense of
the word, is out of the reach of civilized man. Astronomy teaches us that the
earth is now in its progress, and that the poles are every year becoming more
and more perpendicular to the ecliptic. The strong evidence afforded by the
history of mythology, and geological researches, that some event of this na-
ture has taken place already, affords a strong presumption that this progress
is not merely an oscillation, as has been surmised by some late astronomers.[1]
Bones of animals peculiar to the torrid zone have been found in the north
of Siberia, and on the banks of the river Ohio. Plants have been found in the
fossil state in the interior of Germany, which demand the present climate of
Hindostan for their production.[2] The researches of M. Bailly[3] establish the
existence of a people who inhabited a tract in Tartary 49° north latitude, of
greater antiquity than either the Indians, the Chinese, or the Chaldeans,
from whom these nations derived their sciences and theology. We find, from
the testimony of antient writers, that Britain, Germany and France were
much colder than at present, and that their great rivers were annually frozen
over. Astronomy teaches us also, that since this period the obliquity of the
earth's position has been considerably diminished.

[1] Laplace, Système du Monde.

[2] Cabanis, Rapports du Physique et du Moral de l'Homme, vol. ii. page 406.

[3] Lettres sur les Sciences, à Voltaire. Bailly.

---

11 and that,] and that   *1829.BRO*

13 civilized] civilised   *1839 1840*

16 mythology,]
    mythology   *1834 1839 1840*

18 oscillation,] occillation,   ***1813***

Footnote 1. Système] Systeme   *1821.BEN*
                Système   *1839 1840*

19 animals] animals,   *1821.BEN*

21 Germany,] Germany   *1834*

Footnote 3. à] a   *1821.CLA 1821.BEN*
        Voltaire.] Voltaire.—
            1829.BRO 1834 1839 1840
        Bailly.] *Bailly.*   *1829.BRO*
            1834 1839 1840

23 inhabited]
    inhabit   *1821.CLA 1821.BEN*
  tract]
    tract of land   *1821.CLA 1821.BEN*
  Tartary] Tartary,   *1821.CLA*
    1821.BEN
  49°] 49°.   *1821.BEN*

26 antient] ancient   *1821.CLA 1821.BEN*
    1829.BRO 1834 1839 1840
  Germany] Germany,   *1821.CLA*
    1821.BEN 1829.BRO 1834 1839 1840
  France] France,   *1821.CLA 1821.BEN*
    1829.BRO 1834 1839 1840

27 annually] anuually   ***1813***

28 period] period,   *1821.BEN*

Note 11 (VI.171–73)

No atom of this turbulence fulfils
A vague and unnecessitated task,
Or acts but as it must and ought to act.

Deux exemples serviront à nous rendre plus sensible le principe qui vient
d'être posé; nous emprunterons l'un du physique et l'autre du moral. Dans
un tourbillon de poussière qu'élève un vent impétueux, quelque confus qu'il
paroisse à nos yeux; dans la plus affreuse tempête excitée par des vents op-
posés qui soulèvent les flots, il n'y a pas une seule molécule de poussière ou
d'eau qui soit placée au *hazard*, qui n'ait sa cause suffisante pour occuper le
lieu où elle se trouve, et qui n'agisse rigoureusement de la manière dont elle
doit agir. Un géomètre qui connoîtroit exactement les différentes forces qui
agissent dans ces deux cas, et les propriétés des molécules qui sont mues, dé-
montreroit que d'après des causes données, chaque molécule agit précisé-
ment comme elle doit agir, et ne peut agir autrement qu'elle ne fait.

Dans les convulsions terribles qui agitent quelquefois les sociétés poli-
tiques, et qui produisent souvent le renversement d'un empire, il n'y a pas
une seule action, une seule parole, une seule pensée, une seule volonté, une
seule passion dans les agens qui concourent à la révolution comme destruc-
teurs ou comme victimes, qui ne soit nécessaire, qui n'agisse comme elle doit
agir, qui n'opère infailliblement les effets qu'elle doit opérer, suivant la place

---

Text collated with *1781.HOL* (line 4 to the end), **1813**, *1821.CLA* (unexpurgated), *1821.CLAX*
(expurgated), *1829.BRO*, *1834*, and *1840*. *1839* omits this note.

1–3 No . . . act.]
  set in italics *1829.BRO 1834 1840*
4 Deux] Deux *1781.HOL*
5 posé;] posè; *1821.CLA*
 l'un]
  l'une **1813** *1821.CLA 1829.BRO 1834*
6 poussière] poussiere *1781.HOL*
 qu'élève] qu'éléve *1781.HOL*
  qu'éleve **1813** *1821.CLA*
   1829.BRO 1834 1840
 impétueux,] impetueux, **1813**
  1821.CLA 1829.BRO 1834
7 excitée] excité **1813** *1821.CLA*
  1829.BRO 1834 1840
8 soulèvent] soulevent *1781.HOL*
 molécule] molècule *1821.CLA*
  moléculede *1834*
 poussière] poussiere *1781.HOL*
9 placée] placé **1813** *1821.CLA*
  1829.BRO 1834 1840

hazard,] hasard, *1840*
10 où] oû **1813** *1821.CLA 1829.BRO*
 rigoureusement]
  rigoureussement *1821.CLA*
 manière] maniere *1781.HOL*
11 Un] Une **1813** *1821.CLA 1829.BRO*
  1834
 géomètre] géometre, *1781.HOL*
12 démontreroit] demontreroit **1813**
  1821.CLA 1829.BRO 1834
13 que] que, *1781.HOL*
 données,] donnés, **1813** *1821.CLA*
  1829.BRO 1834
15 Dans] Dans *1781.HOL*
 sociétés] societés *1840*
18 dans] dans, *1834*
20 n'opère] n'opere *1781.HOL*
 infailliblement] infalliblement **1813**
  1821.CLA 1829.BRO 1834 1840
 opérer,] opérer *1840*

Note 11 (VI.171–73) 257

qu'occupent ces agens dans ce tourbillon moral. Cela paroîtroit évident pour une intelligence qui seroit en état de saisir et d'apprécier toutes les actions et réactions des esprits et des corps de ceux qui contribuent à cette révolution.

Systême de la Nature, vol. i. page 44.

Note 12 (VI.198)

Necessity! thou mother of the world!

He who asserts the doctrine of Necessity, means that, contemplating the events which compose the moral and material universe, he beholds only an immense and uninterrupted chain of causes and effects, no one of which could occupy any other place than it does occupy, or acts in any other place than it does act. The idea of necessity is obtained by our experience of the connection between objects, the uniformity of the operations of nature, the constant conjunction of similar events, and the consequent inference of one from the other. Mankind are therefore agreed in the admission of necessity, if they admit that these two circumstances take place in voluntary action. Motive is, to voluntary action in the human mind, what cause is to effect in the material universe. The word liberty, as applied to mind, is analogous to the word chance, as applied to matter: they spring from an ignorance of the certainty of the conjunction of antecedents and consequents.

Every human being is irresistibly impelled to act precisely as he does act: in the eternity which preceded his birth a chain of causes was generated, which, operating under the name of motives, make it impossible that any thought of his mind, or any action of his life, should be otherwise than it is. Were the doctrine of Necessity false, the human mind would no longer be a legitimate object of science; from like causes it would be in vain that we should expect like effects; the strongest motive would no longer be para-

---

22 seroit] sera   *1813 1821.CLA 1829.BRO 1834 1840*

23 réactions] reactions   *1813 1829.BRO* re-actions   *1821.CLA*

révolution.] révolution.—   *1840*

24 *Systême*] Systeme   *1821.CLA 1834* Système   *1829.BRO 1840*

Text collated with *1813*, *1821.CLA* (unexpurgated), *1821.CLAX* (expurgated), *1821.BEN*, *1829.BRO*, *1834*, and *1840*. *1839* omits this note.

1 Necessity! . . . world!] *set in italics*   *1821.BEN 1829.BRO 1834 1840* Necessity!] Necessity,   *1813 1821.BEN 1829.BRO 1834 1840*

2 Necessity,] Necessity   *1834*

5 acts] act   *1821.CLA 1821.BEN 1829.BRO 1834 1840*

9 other.] other.—   *1821.BEN*

13 chance,] chance   *1840* matter:] matter;   *1821.BEN*

16 birth] birth,   *1821.CLA 1821.BEN*

17 which,] which   *1829.BRO*

19 Necessity] necessity   *1821.BEN*

mount over the conduct; all knowledge would be vague and undeterminate;
we could not predict with any certainty that we might not meet as an enemy
tomorrow him with whom we have parted in friendship tonight; the most
probable inducements and the clearest reasonings would lose the invariable   25
influence they possess. The contrary of this is demonstrably the fact. Similar
circumstances produce the same unvariable effects. The precise character
and motives of any man on any occasion being given, the moral philosopher
could predict his actions with as much certainty as the natural philosopher
could predict the effects of the mixture of any particular chemical sub-   30
stances. Why is the aged husbandman more experienced than the young be-
ginner? Because there is a uniform, undeniable necessity in the operations
of the material universe. Why is the old statesman more skilful than the raw
politician? Because, relying on the necessary conjunction of motive and ac-
tion, he proceeds to produce moral effects, by the application of those moral   35
causes which experience has shewn to be effectual. Some actions may be
found to which we can attach no motives, but these are the effects of causes
with which we are unacquainted. Hence the relation which motive bears to
voluntary action is that of cause to effect; nor, placed in this point of view, is
it, or ever has it been the subject of popular or philosophical dispute. None   40
but the few fanatics who are engaged in the herculean task of reconciling the
justice of their God with the misery of man, will longer outrage common
sense by the supposition of an event without a cause, a voluntary action with-
out a motive. History, politics, morals, criticism, all grounds of reasoning, all
principles of science, alike assume the truth of the doctrine of Necessity. No   45
farmer carrying his corn to market doubts the sale of it at the market price.
The master of a manufactory no more doubts that he can purchase the
human labour necessary for his purposes, than that his machinery will act as
they have been accustomed to act.

---

23 certainty]

    certainty,   *1821.CLA 1821.BEN*

24 tomorrow]

    to-morrow,   *1821.CLA 1821.BEN*

    to-morrow   *1840*

  with] from   *1829.BRO 1834 1840*

  tonight;]

    to-night;   *1821.CLA 1821.BEN 1840*

25 inducements]

    inducements,   *1821.BEN*

  reasonings] reasonings,   *1821.BEN*

26 fact.] fact.—   *1821.BEN*

27 the same unvariable]

    unvariably similar   *1829.BRO 1834*

    invariably similar   *1840*

29 certainty] certainty,   *1840*

32 a] an   *1821.CLA 1821.BEN*

    uniform,] uniform   *1834*

33 universe.] universe.—   *1821.BEN*

36 shewn] shown   *1834 1840*

39 action] action,   *1840*

40 or] nor   *1834*

  been] been,   *1840*

41 herculean]

    Herculean   *1821.CLA 1821.BEN*

45 Necessity.] necessity.   *1821.BEN*

48 machinery]

    machines   *1829.BRO 1834 1840*

49 they have] it has   *1821.BEN*

50   But, whilst none have scrupled to admit necessity as influencing matter, many have disputed its dominion over mind. Independently of its militating with the received ideas of the justice of God, it is by no means obvious to a superficial enquiry. When the mind observes its own operations, it feels no connection of motive and action: but as we know "nothing more of causation than the constant conjunction of objects and the consequent inference of one from the other, as we find that these two circumstances are universally allowed to have place in voluntary action, we may be easily led to own that they are subjected to the necessity common to all causes." The actions of the will have a regular conjunction with circumstances and characters; motive is, to voluntary action, what cause is to effect. But the only idea we can form of causation is a constant conjunction of similar objects, and the consequent inference of one from the other: wherever this is the case necessity is clearly established.

The idea of liberty, applied metaphorically to the will, has sprung from a misconception of the meaning of the word power. What is power?—*id quod potest,* that which can produce any given effect. To deny power, is to say that nothing can or has the power to be or act. In the only true sense of the word power, it applies with equal force to the loadstone as to the human will. Do you think these motives, which I shall present, are powerful enough to rouse him? is a question just as common as, Do you think this lever has the power of raising this weight? The advocates of free-will assert that the will has the power of refusing to be determined by the strongest motive: but the strongest motive is that which, overcoming all others, ultimately prevails; this assertion therefore amounts to a denial of the will being ultimately determined by that motive which does determine it, which is absurd. But it is equally certain that a man cannot resist the strongest motive, as that he cannot overcome a physical impossibility.

The doctrine of Necessity tends to introduce a great change into the established notions of morality, and utterly to destroy religion. Reward and punishment must be considered, by the Necessarian, merely as motives which he would employ in order to procure the adoption or abandonment of any given line of conduct. Desert, in the present sense of the word, would no longer have any meaning; and he, who should inflict pain upon another for no better reason than that he deserved it, would only gratify his revenge under pretence of satisfying justice. It is not enough, says the advocate of free-will, that a criminal should be prevented from a repetition of his

---

<table>
<tr><td>50 none have] none has   *1829.BRO 1834*</td><td>55 objects] objects,   *1821.BEN*</td></tr>
<tr><td>51 Independently] Independent   *1840*</td><td>60 we] that we   *1840*</td></tr>
<tr><td>53 enquiry.]</td><td>62 case] case,   *1821.BEN 1834 1840*</td></tr>
<tr><td>   inquiry.   *1829.BRO 1834 1840*</td><td>71 assert] assert,   *1840*</td></tr>
<tr><td>54 but] but,   *1834*</td><td>78 Necessity] necessity   *1821.BEN*</td></tr>
</table>

crime: he should feel pain, and his torments, when justly inflicted, ought precisely to be proportioned to his fault. But utility is morality; that which is incapable of producing happiness is useless; and though the crime of Damiens must be condemned, yet the frightful torments which revenge, under the name of justice, inflicted on this unhappy man, cannot be supposed to have augmented, even at the long run, the stock of pleasurable sensation in the world. At the same time, the doctrine of Necessity does not in the least diminish our disapprobation of vice. The conviction which all feel, that a viper is a poisonous animal, and that a tyger is constrained, by the inevitable condition of his existence, to devour men, does not induce us to avoid them less sedulously, or, even more, to hesitate in destroying them: but he would surely be of a hard heart, who, meeting with a serpent on a desart island, or in a situation where it was incapable of injury, should wantonly deprive it of existence. A Necessarian is inconsequent to his own principles, if he indulges in hatred or contempt; the compassion which he feels for the criminal is unmixed with a desire of injuring him: he looks with an elevated and dreadless composure upon the links of the universal chain as they pass before his eyes; whilst cowardice, curiosity and inconsistency only assail him in proportion to the feebleness and indistinctness with which he has perceived and rejected the delusions of free-will.

Religion is the perception of the relation in which we stand to the principle of the universe. But if the principle of the universe be not an organic being, the model and prototype of man, the relation between it and human beings is absolutely none. Without some insight into its will respecting our actions, religion is nugatory and vain. But will is only a mode of animal mind; moral qualities also are such as only a human being can possess; to attribute them to the principle of the universe, is to annex to it properties incompatible with any possible definition of its nature. It is probable that the word God was originally only an expression denoting the unknown cause of the known events which men perceived in the universe. By the vulgar mistake of a metaphor for a real being, of a word for a thing, it became a man, endowed with human qualities and governing the universe as an earthly monarch governs his kingdom. Their addresses to this imaginary being, indeed, are much

<hr>

87 crime:] crime;   *1840*
   pain,] pain;   *1840*
   and] and,   *1834*
92 long run,] long-run,   *1840*
93 time,] time   *1821.CLA 1821.BEN*
   Necessity] necessity   *1821.BEN*
95 tyger] tiger   *1834 1840*
98 who,] who   *1840*
   desart] desert   *1829.BRO 1834 1840*

104 curiosity] curiosity,   *1821.BEN
   1829.BRO 1834*
   inconsistency] inconsistency,
   1821.BEN 1829.BRO 1834 1840
110 is] are   **1813**
112 possess;] possess!   *1821.BEN*
113 universe,] universe   *1834*
118 qualities] qualities,   *1821.BEN*
   universe] universe,   *1840*

120   in the same style as those of subjects to a king. They acknowledge his benev-
olence, deprecate his anger, and supplicate his favour.

But the doctrine of Necessity teaches us, that in no case could any event
have happened otherwise than it did happen, and that, if God is the author
of good, he is also the author of evil; that, if he is entitled to our gratitude for
125   the one, he is entitled to our hatred for the other; that, admitting the exis-
tence of this hypothetic being, he is also subjected to the dominion of an
immutable necessity. It is plain that the same arguments which prove that
God is the author of food, light, and life, prove him also to be the author of
poison, darkness, and death. The wide-wasting earthquake, the storm, the
130   battle, and the tyranny, are attributable to this hypothetic being in the same
degree as the fairest forms of nature, sunshine, liberty, and peace.

But we are taught, by the doctrine of Necessity, that there is neither good
nor evil in the universe, otherwise than as the events to which we apply these
epithets have relation to our own peculiar mode of being. Still less than with
135   the hypothesis of a God, will the doctrine of Necessity accord with the belief
of a future state of punishment. God made man such as he is, and then
damned him for being so: for to say that God was the author of all good, and
man the author of all evil, is to say that one man made a straight line and a
crooked one, and another man made the incongruity.   ☞

140   A Mahometan story, much to the present purpose, is recorded, wherein
Adam and Moses are introduced disputing before God in the following man-
ner. Thou, says Moses, art Adam, whom God created, and animated with the
breath of life, and caused to be worshipped by the angels, and placed in Par-
adise, from whence mankind have been expelled for thy fault. Whereto
145   Adam answered, Thou art Moses, whom God chose for his apostle, and en-
trusted with his word, by giving thee the tables of the law, and whom he
vouchsafed to admit to discourse with himself. How many years dost thou
find the law was written before I was created? Says Moses, Forty. And dost

---

121 anger,] anger   *1840*
122 Necessity] necessity   *1821.BEN*
123 happen,] happen;   *1840*
125 other;] other: *1821.BEN*
    that,] that   *1840*
129 darkness,] darkness   *1840*
130 the tyranny,] tyranny,   *1821.BEN*
    being] being,   *1840*
132 Necessity,] necessity,   *1821.BEN*
135 God,] God   *1834*
    Necessity] necessity   *1821.BEN*
136 is,] is: *1821.CLAX*
136–37 and . . . so:] *omitted*   *1821.CLAX*
137 for] for,   *1834*

139 ☞] *omitted*   *1821.BEN*
142 Thou,] "Thou,"   *1821.BEN 1840*
    art] "art   *1821.BEN 1840*
    created,] created   *1834*
143 worshipped]
    worshiped   *1829.BRO 1834*
144 fault.] fault."   *1821.BEN 1840*
    Whereto] Whereto,   *1821.BEN*
145 Thou] "Thou   *1821.BEN 1840*
    entrusted]
    intrusted   *1829.BRO 1834*
148 created?] created?"   *1821.BEN 1840*
    Forty.] "Forty."   *1821.BEN 1840*
    And] "And   *1821.BEN 1840*

thou not find, replied Adam, these words therein, And Adam rebelled
against his Lord and transgressed? Which Moses confessing, Dost thou there-   150
fore blame me, continued he, for doing that which God wrote of me that I
should do, forty years before I was created, nay, for what was decreed con-
cerning me fifty thousand years before the creation of heaven and earth?—
Sale's Prelim. Disc. to the Koran, page 164.

Note 13 (VII.13)

There is no God!

This negation must be understood solely to affect a creative Deity. The
hypothesis of a pervading Spirit coeternal with the universe, remains un-
shaken.

A close examination of the validity of the proofs adduced to support any   5
proposition, is the only secure way of attaining truth, on the advantages of
which it is unnecessary to descant: our knowledge of the existence of a Deity
is a subject of such importance, that it cannot be too minutely investigated;
in consequence of this conviction we proceed briefly and impartially to ex-
amine the proofs which have been adduced. It is necessary first to consider   10
the nature of belief.

When a proposition is offered to the mind, it perceives the agreement or

149 find,] find," *1821.BEN 1840*
    these] "these *1821.BEN 1840*
    And] 'And *1829.BRO 1834*
       'and *1840*
150 Lord] Lord, *1821.BEN*
    transgressed?]
      transgressed?" *1821.BEN*
      transgressed?'" *1840*
    Which] Which, *1821.BEN*

Dost] "Dost *1821.BEN 1840*
thou] thou, *1821.BEN*
therefore] therefore, *1821.BEN*
151 me,] me," *1821.BEN 1840*
    for] "for *1821.BEN 1840*
152 created,] created; *1840*
153 earth?—] earth?" *1821.BEN*
    earth? *1821.CLA*
    earth?"— *1840*

Text collated with *1781.HOL* (lines 121–268), *1811.NA* (lines 5–90), **1813**, *1821.CLA* (unex-
purgated), *1821.CLAX* (expurgated), *1821.BEN* (except lines 121–268), *1829.BRO*, *1834*, and
1840. *1839* omits this note.

1 There is no God!] *set in italics*
    1821.BEN 1829.BRO 1834 1840
3 Spirit] Spirit, *1829.BRO 1834 1840*
    coeternal] co-eternal *1821.BEN*
5 close] CLOSE *1811.NA*
6 proposition,] proposition *1834*
    proposition, is] proposition, has ever
      been allowed to be *1811.NA*
    secure] sure *1811.NA*

on] upon *1811.NA*
7 descant:] descant; *1811.NA 1821.BEN*
8 importance,] importance *1811.NA*
    investigated;] investigated. *1834*
9 in] In *1834*
    conviction] conviction, *1811.NA*
      1829.BRO 1834
11 belief.] Belief. *1811.NA*

disagreement of the ideas of which it is composed. A perception of their
agreement is termed *belief.* Many obstacles frequently prevent this perception
from being immediate; these the mind attempts to remove, in order that the
perception may be distinct. The mind is active in the investigation, in order
to perfect the state of perception of the relation which the component ideas
of the proposition bear to each, which is passive: the investigation being con-
fused with the perception, has induced many falsely to imagine that the
mind is active in belief,—that belief is an act of volition,—in consequence of
which it may be regulated by the mind. Pursuing, continuing this mistake,
they have attached a degree of criminality to disbelief; of which, in its nature,
it is incapable: it is equally incapable of merit.

Belief, then, is a passion, the strength of which, like every other passion,
is in precise proportion to the degrees of excitement.

The degrees of excitement are three.

The senses are the sources of all knowledge to the mind; consequently
their evidence claims the strongest assent.

The decision of the mind, founded upon our own experience, derived
from these sources, claims the next degree.

The experience of others, which addresses itself to the former one, occu-
pies the lowest degree.

(A graduated scale, on which should be marked the capabilities of propo-
sitions to approach to the test of the senses, would be a just barometer of the
belief which ought to be attached to them.)

Consequently no testimony can be admitted which is contrary to reason;
reason is founded on the evidence of our senses.

---

14 *belief.*] belief,   *1811.NA*
  Many] many   *1811.NA*
15 immediate;] immediate,   *1811.NA*
  remove,] remove   *1811.NA*
17–18 of . . . each,] *omitted*   *1811.NA*
18 passive:] passive;   *1811.NA 1840*
  investigation]
    investigation,   *1834 1840*
19 perception,] perception   *1811.NA*
20 belief,—that] belief, that   *1811.NA*
        belief—that   *1821.BEN*
  volition,—in] volition, in   *1811.NA*
        volition—in   *1821.BEN*
21 mind.] mind;   *1811.NA*
  Pursuing,] pursuing,   *1811.NA*
  mistake,] mistake   *1811.NA*
22 disbelief;] disbelief   *1811.NA*
        disbelieve;   *1821.BEN*
        disbelief,   *1829.BRO 1834*
  which,] which   *1811.NA*

nature,] nature   *1811.NA*
23 incapable:] incapable;   *1811.NA*
  equally incapable]
    equally so   *1811.NA*
24–25 Belief, . . . excitement.] The
    strength of belief like that of
    every other passion is in
    proportion to the degrees of
    excitement.   *1811.NA*
27 mind;] mind,   *1811.NA*
29 mind,] mind   *1811.NA*
  experience,] experience   *1811.NA*
31 others,] others   *1811.NA*
32 degree.] degree.—   *1811.NA*
33–35 (A . . . them.)] *omitted*   *1811.NA*
34 to the] the   *1829.BRO 1834 1840*
35 them.)] them)   *1834*
36 Consequently] Consequently,   *1840*
  reason;] reason,   *1811.NA*

Every proof may be referred to one of these three divisions: it is to be considered what arguments we receive from each of them, which should convince us of the existence of a Deity.

1st. The evidence of the senses. If the Deity should appear to us, if he should convince our senses of his existence, this revelation would necessarily command belief. Those to whom the Deity has thus appeared have the strongest possible conviction of his existence. But the God of Theologians is incapable of local visibility.

2d. Reason. It is urged that man knows that whatever is, must either have had a beginning, or have existed from all eternity: he also knows, that whatever is not eternal must have had a cause. When this reasoning is applied to the universe, it is necessary to prove that it was created: until that is clearly demonstrated, we may reasonably suppose that it has endured from all eternity. We must prove design before we can infer a designer. The only idea which we can form of causation is derivable from the constant conjunction of objects, and the consequent inference of one from the other. In a case where two propositions are diametrically opposite, the mind believes that which is least incomprehensible;—it is easier to suppose that the universe has existed from all eternity, than to conceive a being beyond its limits capable of creating it: if the mind sinks beneath the weight of one, is it an alleviation to increase the intolerability of the burthen?

The other argument, which is founded on a man's knowledge of his own existence, stands thus. A man knows not only that he now is, but that

---

38 divisions:]
    divisions;   *1811.NA 1821.BEN*
    it . . . considered] we are naturally
    led to consider   *1811.NA*
39 them,] them   *1811.NA*
    which should] to   *1811.NA*
41 senses.] senses.—   *1811.NA*
42 senses] senses,   *1821.CLA 1821.BEN*
    existence,] existence;   *1811.NA*
43 belief.] belief;—   *1811.NA*
    appeared] appeared,   *1811.NA*
44–45 But . . . visibility.] *omitted   1811.NA*
44 Theologians]
    theologians   *1829.BRO 1834*
      1840
46 2d.] Reason claims the 2nd. place,
      1811.NA
      2nd. *1834*
    It] it   *1811.NA*
47 beginning,] beginning   *1811.NA*
    have] *omitted   1811.NA*

eternity:] eternity,   *1811.NA*
    knows,] knows   *1811.NA*
48 cause.] cause.—   *1811.NA*
    When this reasoning]
      Where this   *1811.NA*
49 universe,]
    existence of the universe,   *1811.NA*
    created:] created,   *1811.NA*
50 eternity.] eternity.—   *1811.NA*
51–53 We . . . other.] *omitted   1811.NA*
55 least] less   *1811.NA*
    incomprehensible;—it]
      incomprehensible, it   *1811.NA*
    universe] Universe   *1811.NA*
56 beyond its limits] *omitted   1811.NA*
57 it:] it;   *1811.NA*
58 burthen?] burden?—   *1811.NA*
59 argument,]
    argument   *1811.NA 1821.BEN*
    on] upon   *1811.NA*
60 thus.] thus.—   *1811.NA*

once he was not; consequently there must have been a cause. But our idea of
causation is alone derivable from the constant conjunction of objects and the
consequent inference of one from the other; and, reasoning experimentally,
we can only infer from effects, causes exactly adequate to those effects. But
there certainly is a generative power which is effected by certain instruments:
we cannot prove that it is inherent in these instruments; nor is the contrary
hypothesis capable of demonstration: we admit that the generative power is
incomprehensible; but to suppose that the same effect is produced by an
eternal, omniscient, omnipotent being, leaves the cause in the same obscu-
rity, but renders it more incomprehensible.

3d. Testimony. It is required that testimony should not be contrary to rea-
son. The testimony that the Deity convinces the senses of men of his existence
can only be admitted by us, if our mind considers it less probable that these
men should have been deceived, than that the Deity should have appeared to
them. Our reason can never admit the testimony of men, who not only de-
clare that they were eye-witnesses of miracles, but that the Deity was irrational;
for he commanded that he should be believed, he proposed the highest re-
wards for faith, eternal punishments for disbelief. We can only command vol-
untary actions; belief is not an act of volition; the mind is even passive, or in-
voluntarily active: from this it is evident that we have no sufficient testimony,
or rather that testimony is insufficient to prove the being of a God. It has been

---

61 once he was not;] there was a time
        when he did not exist,   *1811.NA*
    cause.] cause.—   *1811.NA*
61–63 our . . . experimentally,]
        what does this prove?   *1811.NA*
62 objects] objects,   *1821.BEN*
64 effects,] effects   *1811.NA*
    effects.] effects;—   *1811.NA*
65 certain] particular   *1811.NA*
    instruments:] instruments;   *1811.NA*
66 instruments;] instruments,   *1811.NA*
67 demonstration:]
        demonstration;   *1811.NA 1840*
68 incomprehensible;]
        incomprehensible,   *1811.NA*
69 omnipotent] Almighty   *1811.NA*
            omnipotent,   *1840*
    being,] Being,   *1811.NA*
    same] *omitted*   *1811.NA*
71 3d. Testimony.] The 3rd. and last
    degree of assent is claimed by
    Testimony—   *1811.NA*
    3rd. Testimony   *1821.BEN*
        1829.BRO 1834

It] it   *1811.NA*
testimony] it   *1811.NA*
reason.] reason.—   *1811.NA*
72 existence]
        existence,   *1821.CLA 1821.BEN*
74 deceived,] deceived   *1834*
75 them.] them—   *1811.NA*
    Our] our   *1811.NA*
76 miracles,] miracles   *1811.NA*
    irrational; for]
        irrational, for   *1811.NA*
78 disbelief.] disbelief—   *1811.NA*
    We] we   *1811.NA*
79 actions;] actions,   *1811.NA*
    volition;] volition,   *1811.NA*
79–80 or involuntarily active:]
            omitted   *1811.NA*
80 no] not   *1811.NA*
81 insufficient] insufficient,   *1840*
    God.] God,   *1811.NA*
    It has been] we have   *1811.NA*

before shewn that it cannot be deduced from reason. They alone, then, who
have been convinced by the evidence of the senses, can believe it.

Hence it is evident that, having no proofs from either of the three sources
of conviction, the mind *cannot* believe the existence of a creative God: it is   85
also evident, that, as belief is a passion of the mind, no degree of criminality
is attachable to disbelief; and that they only are reprehensible who neglect
to remove the false medium through which their mind views any subject of
discussion. Every reflecting mind must acknowledge that there is no proof
of the existence of a Deity.   90

God is an hypothesis, and, as such, stands in need of proof: the *onus
probandi* rests on the theist. Sir Isaac Newton says: *Hypotheses non fingo, quicquid
enim ex phænomenis non deducitur, hypothesis vocanda est, et hypotheses vel meta
physicæ, vel physicæ, vel qualitatum occultarum, seu mechanicæ, in philosophiâ locum
non habent.* To all proofs of the existence of a creative God apply this valuable   95
rule. We see a variety of bodies possessing a variety of powers: we merely know
their effects; we are in a state of ignorance with respect to their essences and
causes. These Newton calls the phenomena of things; but the pride of philos-
ophy is unwilling to admit its ignorance of their causes. From the phenomena,
which are the objects of our senses, we attempt to infer a cause, which we call   100
God, and gratuitously endow it with all negative and contradictory qualities.

---

82 shewn] shown   *1834 1840*
   reason.] reason,——   *1811.NA*
   They] they   *1811.NA*
   alone, then,] *omitted*   *1811.NA*
83 senses, can]
    senses, they only can   *1811.NA*
84 Hence] From this   *1811.NA*
   that,] that   *1811.NA 1821.BEN*
   either] any   *1811.NA*
85 conviction,] conviction: *1811.NA*
   creative] *omitted*   *1811.NA*
   God:] God,   *1811.NA*
    God;   *1821.BEN*
86 evident,] evident   *1811.NA 1840*
   that,] that   *1811.NA 1821.BEN*
   mind,] mind   *1821.BEN*
87 is attachable] can be attached
    1811.NA
   disbelief;] disbelief,   *1811.NA*
   and that] *omitted*   *1811.NA*
   neglect] willingly neglect   *1811.NA*
88 through] thro'   *1811.NA*
   any] the   *1811.NA*
88–89 subject of discussion.]
    subject.   *1811.NA*

89 acknowledge] allow   *1811.NA*
    acknowledge,   *1840*
90 Deity.] Deity. Q. E. D.   *1811.NA*
91 and,] and   *1821.BEN 1840*
93 *phænomenis*] *phænomenis*   **1813**
    1821.CLA 1821.BEN
    1829.BRO 1834
    phenomenis   *1840*
  deducitur,] *deducitur*   *1840*
  hypotheses] *hypothesis*   **1813** *1821.CLA*
    1821.BEN 1829.BRO 1834 1840
  meta physicæ,] *meta physicæ,*   **1813**
    metaphysicæ,   *1821.CLA*
    1821.BEN
94 *vel physicæ,*] *vel physicæ,*   **1813**
    1821.CLA 1821.BEN
  mechanicæ,] *mechanicæ,*   **1813**
    1821.CLA 1821.BEN
  philosophiâ] *philosophia*   *1821.BEN*
    philosophià
    1821.CLA 1834
96 powers:] powers;   *1840*

From this hypothesis we invent this general name, to conceal our ignorance
of causes and essences. The being called God by no means answers with the
conditions prescribed by Newton; it bears every mark of a veil woven by philo-
sophical conceit, to hide the ignorance of philosophers even from themselves.
They borrow the threads of its texture from the anthropomorphism of the
vulgar. Words have been used by sophists for the same purposes, from the oc-
cult qualities of the peripatetics to the *effluvium* of Boyle and the *crinities* or
nebulæ of Herschel. God is represented as infinite, eternal, incomprehensible;
he is contained under every prædicate in non that the logic of ignorance
could fabricate. Even his worshippers allow that it is impossible to form any
idea of him: they exclaim with the French poet,

> *Pour dire ce qu'il est, il faut être lui-même.* ☞

Lord Bacon says, that "atheism leaves to man reason, philosophy, natural
piety, laws, reputation, and every thing that can serve to conduct him to
virtue; but superstition destroys all these, and erects itself into a tyranny over

---

108 peripatetics] Peripatetics *1840*
109 *nebulæ*] nebulæ **1813** *1821.CLA*
    1821.BEN 1829.BRO 1834 1840
110 prædicate in non] *prædicate in non*
    1821.BEN 1829.BRO 1834 1840
111 fabricate.] fabricate *1834*
   worshippers] worshipers *1834*
112 him:] him; *1840*
113 *Pour*] Poure *1821.BEN*
   Pour . . . lui-même.] set in roman, in
     quotes *1829.BRO 1834*
        set in roman *1840*
    être] etre *1821.BEN*
      étre 1821.CLA
    lui-même.] lut-meme. *1821.BEN*
      lui-mème *1821.CLA*
   ☞] omitted *1821.BEN*
114 "atheism] "Atheism *1829.BRO 1834*
114–19 "atheism . . . life."] "Atheism leaves
    a man to sense, to philosophy,
    to natural piety, to laws, to
    reputation: all which may be
    guides to an outward moral
    virtue, though religion were
    not; but superstition dismounts
    all these, and erecteth an
    absolute monarchy in the minds
    of men: therefore atheism did
    never perturb states; for it
    makes men wary of themselves,
    as looking no farther, and we

see the times inclined to
atheism (as the time of Augustus
Cæsar) were civil times: but
superstition hath been the
confusion of many states, and
bringeth in a new *primum mobile,*
that ravisheth all the spheres of
government." *1821.CLA*
"Atheism leaves a man to sense, to
   philosophy, to natural piety, to
   laws, to reputation; all which
   may be guides to an outward
   moral virtue, though religion
   were not; but superstition
   dismounts all these, and
   erecteth an absolute monarchy
   in the minds of men; therefore
   atheism did never perturb states;
   for it makes men wary of
   themselves, as looking no
   farther, and we see the times
   inclined to atheism (as the time
   of Augustus Cæsar) were civil
   times: but superstition hath
   been the confusion of many
   states, and bringeth in a new
   primum mobile, that ravisheth all
   the spheres of government."
   1821.BEN
115 every thing] everything *1829.BRO*

the understandings of men: hence atheism never disturbs the government,
but renders man more clear-sighted, since he sees nothing beyond the
boundaries of the present life."

Bacon's Moral Essays.   1 2 0

La première théologie de l'homme lui fit d'abord craindre et adorer les
éléments mêmes, des objets matériels et grossiers; il rendit ensuite ses hom-
mages à des agents présidans aux élémens, à des génies inférieurs, à des
héros, ou à des hommes doués de grandes qualités. A force de réfléchir il
crut simplifier les choses en soumettant la nature entière à un seul agent, à   1 2 5
un esprit, à une âme universelle, qui mettoit cette nature et ses parties en
mouvement. En remontant de causes en causes, les mortels ont fini par ne
rien voir; et c'est dans cette obscurité qu'ils ont placé leur Dieu; c'est dans cet
abîme ténébreux que leur imagination inquiète travaille toujours à se fabri-
quer des chimères, qui les affligeront jusqu'à ce que la connoissance de la na-   1 3 0
ture les détrompe des phantômes qu'ils ont toujours si vainement adorés.

Si nous voulons nous rendre compte de nos idées sur la Divinité, nous
serons obligés de convenir que, par le mot *Dieu,* les hommes n'ont jamais pu
désigner que la cause la plus cachée, la plus éloignée, la plus inconnue des
effets qu'ils voyoient: ils ne font usage de ce mot, que lorsque le jeu des   1 3 5
causes naturelles et connues cesse d'être visible pour eux; dès qu'ils perdent

---

117 men:] men;   *1829.BRO 1834*

119 life."] life."—   *1840*

120 *Essays.*] *Essay on Superstition.*
   1821.CLA 1821.BEN

121 première] premiere   *1781.HOL*
   théologie] Théologie   *1781.HOL*

122 éléments] élémens   *1781.HOL 1813*
   1821.CLA 1829.BRO 1834
   mêmes,] même,   *1781.HOL 1813*
   1821.CLA 1829.BRO 1834 1840
   il] ill   *1834*

123 agents] agens   *1781.HOL 1813*
   1821.CLA 1829.BRO 1834
   présidans] présidens   *1813 1821.CLA*
   1829.BRO 1834
   présidents   *1840*
   élémens,] élémens, à des génies
   puissans,   *1781.HOL*
   éléments,   *1840*

124 héros,] héros   *1781.HOL*
   hèros,   *1821.CLA*
   à] á   *1821.CLA*
   doués] douès   *1821.CLA*
   grandes] grands   *1813 1821.CLA*

qualités.] qualitès.   *1821.CLA*

réfléchir] réfléchir,   *1840*

125 entière] entiere   *1781.HOL*

126 un esprit,] une intelligence
   souveraine, à un esprit,   *1781.HOL*
   une] un   *1829.BRO 1834*
   âme] ame   *1781.HOL 1840*
   universelle,] universelle   *1781.HOL*
   universel   *1829.BRO*
   universal,   *1834*

127 de] des   *1813 1821.CLA*

128 voir;] voir,   *1781.HOL*
   cet] cette   *1813 1821.CLA*

130 qui] que   *1813 1821.CLA*
   connoissance]
   connaissance   *1829.BRO 1834*

131 les] less   *1821.CLA*
   phantômes] fantômes   *1840*

133 que,] que   *1781.HOL*
   Dieu,] *Dieu*   *1781.HOL*

135 voyoient:] voyaient: *1829.BRO 1834*
   mot,] mot   *1781.HOL*

136 dès] des   *1834*

Note 13 (VII.13)   269

le fil de ces causes, ou dès que leur esprit ne peut plus en suivre la chaîne, ils tranchent la difficulté, et terminent leurs recherches en appellant Dieu la dernière des causes, c'est-à-dire celle qui est au-delà de toutes les causes
140 qu'ils connoissent; ainsi ils ne font qu'assigner une dénomination vague à une cause ignorée, à laquelle leur paresse ou les bornes de leurs connoissances les forcent de s'arrêter. Toutes les fois qu'on nous dit que Dieu est l'auteur de quelque phénomène, cela signifie qu'on ignore comment un tel phénomène a pu s'opérer par le secours des forces ou des causes que nous
145 connoissons dans la nature. C'est ainsi que le commun des hommes, dont l'ignorance est le partage, attribue à la Divinité non seulement les effets inusités qui les frappent, mais encore les événemens les plus simples, dont les causes sont les plus faciles à connoître pour quiconque a pu les méditer. En un mot, l'homme a toujours respecté les causes inconnues des effets surpre-
150 nans, que son ignorance l'empêchoit de démêler. Ce fut sur les débris de la nature que les hommes éleverent le colosse imaginaire de la Divinité.

Si l'ignorance de la nature donna la naissance aux dieux, la connoissance de la nature est faite pour les détruire. A mesure que l'homme s'instruit, ses forces et ses ressources augmentent avec ses lumières; les sciences, les arts
155 conservateurs, l'industrie, lui fournissent des secours; l'expérience le rassûre ou lui procure des moyens de résister aux efforts de bien des causes qui cessent de l'alarmer dès qu'il les a connues. En un mot, ses terreurs se

---

137 fil] fit **1813** *1821.CLA*

138 la] leur **1813** *1821.CLA 1829.BRO
     1834 1840*
   leurs] leur **1813** *1821.CLA
     1829.BRO 1834 1840*
   appellant] appellent *1821.CLA*
   Dieu] *Dieu 1781.HOL*

139 c'est-à-dire] c'est-à-dire, *1781.HOL*

140 connoissent;]
     connaissent; *1829.BRO 1834*

141 à laquelle] à-laquelle *1829.BRO*
   connoissances]
     connaissances *1829.BRO 1834*

144 s'opérer] s'opèrer *1821.CLA*
   secours] sécours **1813**
        sècours *1821.CLA*

145 connoissons]
     connaissons *1829.BRO 1834*
   nature.] nature.— *1834*

146 le] la **1813** *1821.CLA*
   Divinité] Divinité, *1781.HOL*

147 qui] que **1813** *1821.CLA*
   simples,] simples *1781.HOL*

148 connoître]
     connaître *1829.BRO 1834*

150 l'empêchoit]
     l'empêchait *1829.BRO 1834*
   démêler.] démêler. *1834*
   Ce] En un mot, ce *1781.HOL*
   débris] debus **1813**
        debris *1829.BRO 1834*

151 éleverent] élevèrent **1813** *1821.CLA
     1829.BRO 1834 1840*

152 dieux,] Dieux, *1781.HOL*
   connoissance]
     connaissance *1829.BRO 1834*

153 détruire.] detruire. *1821.CLA*
   mesure] mésure **1813** *1821.CLA*

154 lumières;] lumieres; *1781.HOL*

155 secours;] secours, *1781.HOL*

156 rassûre] rassûre, *1821.CLA*
        rassure *1840*
   bien] biens **1813**

157 mot,] mot *1781.HOL*

dissipent dans la même proportion que son esprit s'éclaire. L'homme instruit cesse d'être superstitieux.

Ce n'est jamais que sur parole que des peuples entiers adorent le Dieu de   160
leurs pères et de leurs prêtres: l'autorité, la confiance, la soumission, et
l'habitude, leur tiennent lieu de conviction et de preuves; ils se prosternent
et prient, parce que leurs pères leur ont appris à se prosterner et prier: mais
pourquoi ceux-ci se sont-ils mis à genoux? C'est que dans les temps éloignés
leurs législateurs et leurs guides leur en ont fait un devoir. "Adorez et croyez,"   165
ont-ils dit, "des dieux que vous ne pouvez comprendre; rapportez-vous en à
notre sagesse profonde; nous en savons plus que vous sur la Divinité." Mais
pourquoi m'en rapporterois-je à vous? C'est que Dieu le veut ainsi, c'est que
Dieu vous punira si vous osez résister. Mais ce Dieu n'est-il donc pas la chose
en question? Cependant les hommes se sont toujours payés de ce cercle vi-   170
cieux; la paresse de leur esprit leur fit trouver plus court de s'en rapporter au
jugement des autres. Toutes les notions religieuses sont fondées uniquement
sur l'autorité; toutes les religions du monde défendent l'examen et ne veu-
lent pas que l'on raisonne; c'est l'autorité qui veut qu'on croie en Dieu; ce
Dieu n'est lui-même fondé que sur l'autorité de quelques hommes qui pré-   175
tendent le connoître, et venir de sa part pour l'annoncer à la terre. Un Dieu
fait par les hommes, a sans doute besoin des hommes pour se faire connoître
aux hommes.

Ne seroit-ce donc que pour des prêtres des inspirés, des métaphysiciens

---

161 pères] peres   *1781.HOL*
   soumission,] soumission   *1781.HOL*
163 pères] peres   *1781.HOL*
   prier:] à prier;   *1781.HOL*
164 temps] tems   *1781.HOL*
   éloignés] éloignés,   *1781.HOL*
165 "Adorez] Adorez   *1829.BRO 1834*
   croyez,"]
     croyez,   *1781.HOL 1829.BRO 1834*
166 "des] des   *1781.HOL 1829.BRO 1834*
   dieux] Dieux   *1781.HOL*
   rapportez-vous en]
     rapportez-vous-en   *1840*
167 Divinité."] Divinité.   *1829.BRO 1834*
   Mais] "Mais   *1821.CLA*
168 rapporterois-je]
     rapporterais-je   *1829.BRO 1834*
   vous?] vous?"   *1821.CLA*
   C'est] "C'est   *1821.CLA*
   ainsi,] ainsi;   *1781.HOL*
169 résister.] résister."   *1821.CLA*
   Mais] "Mais   *1821.CLA*
170 question?] question?"   *1821.CLA*
171 rapporter] rapporte   *1829.BRO 1834*

173 défendent] defendent   ***1813***
   1821.CLA 1829.BRO 1834
   l'examen]
     l'examen,   *1829.BRO 1834 1840*
174 qui] que   *1821.CLA*
   croie] crire   ***1813***
     crut   *1821.CLA*
175 fondé] fonde   ***1813***
176 connoître,] connoître   *1781.HOL*
     connaître,   *1829.BRO*
     1834
   à] a   ***1813*** *1821.CLA*
177 hommes,] hommes   *1834*
   connoître]
     connaître   *1829.BRO 1834*
179 prêtres] prêtres,   *1781.HOL*
   1829.BRO 1834 1840
   métaphysiciens] metaphysiciens
     1813 *1821.CLA*
     1829.BRO
     metaphysiciens,
     1834
     métaphysiciens,
     1840

180   que seroit réservée la conviction de l'existence d'un Dieu, que l'on dit néan-
      moins si nécessaire à tout le genre-humain? Mais trouvons-nous de l'harmo-
      nie entre les opinions théologiques des differens inspirés, ou des penseurs
      répandus sur la terre? Ceux même qui font profession d'adorer le même
      Dieu, sont-ils d'accord sur son compte? Sont-ils contents des preuves que
185   leurs collègues apportent de son existence? Souscrivent-ils unanimement
      aux idées qu'ils présentent sur sa nature, sur sa conduite, sur la façon d'en-
      tendre ses prétendus oracles? Est-il une contrée sur la terre, où la science de
      Dieu se soit réellement perfectionnée? A-t-elle pris quelque part la consis-
      tence et l'uniformité que nous voyons prendre aux connoissances humaines,
190   aux arts les plus futiles, aux métiers les plus méprisés? Les mots *d'esprits, d'im-
      matérialité,* de *création,* de *prédestination,* de *grace;* cette foule de distinctions
      subtiles dont la théologie s'est partout remplie dans quelques pays, ces in-
      ventions si ingénieuses, imaginées par des penseurs qui se sont succédé
      depuis tant de siècles, n'ont fait, helas! qu'embrouiller les choses, et jamais la
195   science la plus nécessaire aux hommes n'a jusqu'ici pu acquérir la moindre
      fixité. Depuis des milliers d'années, ces rêveurs oisifs se sont perpétuelle-
      ment relayés pour méditer la Divinité, pour deviner ses voies cachées, pour

---

180 réservée] reservée *1813* *1821.CLA*
   1829.BRO 1834
  néanmoins] neanmoins *1813*
   1821.CLA 1829.BRO
181 nécessaire] necessaire *1813*
   1821.CLA 1829.BRO 1834
  genre-humain?]
   genre humain? *1840*
182 differens] différens *1781.HOL 1840*
183 répandus] repandus *1813*
  Ceux même] Ceux-mêmes *1834*
  qui] que *1813 1821.CLA*
184 Dieu,] Dieu *1781.HOL*
  contents] contens *1781.HOL*
  que] qui *1829.BRO 1834*
185 collègues] collégues *1781.HOL*
186 présentent] presentent *1813*
   1821.CLA 1829.BRO 1834
187 terre,] terre *1829.BRO 1834*
188 perfectionnée?]
   perfectionné? *1813 1821.CLA*
  consistence] consistance *1840*
189 connoissances]
   connaissances *1829.BRO 1834*
190 méprisés?] meprisés? *1813*
   1821.CLA 1829.BRO 1834

Les] des *1813 1821.CLA 1829.BRO*
  1834
  Des *1840*
 d'esprits,] d'esprit, *1829.BRO 1834*
  1840
192 partout] par-tout *1781.HOL*
  pays,] pays; *1781.HOL*
193 qui] que *1813 1821.CLA*
  succédé] succédés *1813 1821.CLA*
   1829.BRO 1834 1840
194 siècles,] siecles, *1781.HOL*
   siécles, *1840*
  helas!] hélas! *1781.HOL 1840*
  qu'embrouiller]
   qu'embrouilles *1813 1821.CLA*
   qu'embrouillér *1829.BRO*
  choses,] choses; *1781.HOL*
194–95 la science] le science *1813*
   1821.CLA
195 la plus] le plus *1813 1821.CLA*
  nécessaire] necessaire *1813*
   1821.CLA 1829.BRO 1834
196 rêveurs] reveurs *1813 1821.CLA*
   réveurs *1829.BRO 1834 1840*
197 méditer] mediter *1813 1821.CLA*
   1829.BRO 1834
  deviner] déviner *1781.HOL*

inventer des hypotheses propres à développer cette énigme importante. Leur peu de succès n'a point découragé la vanité théologique; toujours on a parlé de Dieu: on s'est égorgé pour lui, et cet être sublime demeure toujours   200 le plus ignoré et le plus discuté.

Les hommes auroient été trop heureux, si, se bornant aux objets visibles qui les intéressent, ils eussent employé à perfectionner leurs sciences réelles, leurs loix, leur morale, leur éducation, la moitié des efforts qu'ils ont mis dans leurs recherches sur la Divinité. Ils auroient été bien plus sages encore,   205 et plus fortunés, s'ils eussent pu consentir à laisser leurs guides désœuvrés se quereller entre eux, et sonder des profondeurs capables de les étourdir, sans se mêler de leurs disputes insensées. Mais il est de l'essence de l'ignorance d'attacher de l'importance à ce qu'elle ne comprend pas. La vanité humaine fait que l'esprit se roidit contre les difficultés. Plus un objet se dérobe à nos   210 yeux, plus nous faisons d'efforts pour le saisir, parce que dès-lors il aiguillone notre orgueil, il excite notre curiosité, il nous paroît intéressant. En combattant pour son Dieu chacun ne combattit en effet que pour les intérêts de sa propre vanité, qui de toutes les passions produites par la mal organisation de la société, est la plus prompte à s'allarmer, et la plus propre à produire de   215 très grandes folies.

Si écartant pour un moment les idées fâcheuses que la théologie nous

---

198 hypotheses] hypothéses   *1829.BRO*
        hypothèses   *1834 1840*
  développer] développe   *1834*
  énigme] enigme   **1813** *1821.CLA*
    1829.BRO 1834
199 succès]
    succés   **1813** *1821.CLA 1829.BRO*
200 Dieu:] Dieu;   *1781.HOL*
  on s'est]
    on s'est disputé, on s'est   *1781.HOL*
202 heureux,] heureux   *1781.HOL*
203 employé] employé,   *1840*
  perfectionner]
    perfectioner   **1813** *1829.BRO 1834*
204 loix,] lois,   *1840*
  éducation,] éducation;   *1781.HOL*
  efforts] efforts,   *1829.BRO*
205 Divinité.] divinité.   *1781.HOL*
  encore,] encore   *1781.HOL*
206 fortunés,] fortunés   *1821.CLA*
207 entre eux,] entr'eux,   *1781.HOL*
210 dérobe]
    derobe   **1813** *1829.BRO 1834*
  nos] nox   *1834*
211 nous] nons   *1781.HOL*

parce que] parceque   *1840*
aiguillone] aiguillonne   *1840*
212 excite] irrite   *1781.HOL*
  paroît] paroit   **1813** *1821.CLA*
    parait   *1829.BRO 1834*
213 Dieu] Dieu,   *1781.HOL 1821.CLA*
214–15 produites . . . société,]
    humaines,   *1781.HOL*
214 produites] produits   **1813** *1821.CLA*
  par la] parla   *1829.BRO*
  mal organisation]
    mal organization   **1813**
      1821.CLA 1829.BRO 1834
    mal-organisation   *1840*
215 société,] societé,   **1813** *1821.CLA*
  à] á   *1834*
  s'allarmer,] s'alarmer,   *1840*
  de] des   **1813** *1821.CLA*
216 très grandes]
    tres grands   **1813** *1821.CLA*
    très-grandes   *1840*
217 Si] Si,   *1834 1840*
  fâcheuses] facheuses   **1813** *1821.CLA*
    1829.BRO 1834

donne d'un Dieu capricieux, dont les décrets partiaux et despotiques déci-
dent du sort des humains, nous ne voulons fixer nos yeux que sur la bonté
prétendue, que tous les hommes, même en tremblant devant ce Dieu, s'ac-
cordent à lui donner; si nous lui supposons le projet qu'on lui prête, de
n'avoir travaillé que pour sa propre gloire, d'exiger les hommages des êtres
intelligens; de ne chercher dans ses œuvres que le bien-être du genre-
humain; comment concilier ses vues et ses dispositions avec l'ignorance vrai-
ment invincible dans laquelle ce Dieu, si glorieux et si bon, laisse la plupart
des hommes sur son compte? Si Dieu veut être connu, chéri, remercié, que
ne se montre-t-il sous des traits favorables à tous ces êtres intelligens dont il
veut être aimé et adoré? Pourquoi ne point se manifester à toute la terre
d'une façon non équivoque, bien plus capable de nous convaincre, que ces
révélations particulieres qui semblent accuser la Divinité d'une partialité
fâcheuse pour quelques-unes de ses créatures? Le tout-puissant n'auroit-il
donc pas des moyens plus convainquans de se montrer aux hommes que ces
métamorphoses ridicules, ces incarnations prétendues, qui nous sont at-
testées par des écrivains si peu d'accord entre eux dans les récits qu'ils en
font? Au lieu de tant de miracles, inventés pour prouver la mission divine de
tant de législateurs, révérés par les différens peuples du monde, le souverain
des esprits ne pouvoit-il pas convaincre tout d'un coup l'esprit humain des
choses qu'il a voulu lui faire connoître? Au lieu de suspendre un soleil dans

---

218 partiaux] partraux   *1813*
        parteaux   *1821.CLA*
220 prétendue,] prétendue   *1840*
   même] méme   *1821.CLA*
   Dieu,] Dieu;   *1781.HOL*
   s'accordent] s'accordant   *1821.CLA*
221 donner;] donner: *1781.HOL*
222 gloire,] gloire;   *1840*
223 intelligens;]
    intelligens,   *1829.BRO 1834*
223–24 genre-humain;] genre humain;
    1821.CLA 1829.BRO 1834 1840
224 vraiment] vraiement   *1781.HOL*
225 invincible] invincible,   *1781.HOL*
   laquelle] lequelle   *1813 1821.CLA*
   plupart] plûpart   *1834*
226 chéri,] cheri,   *1813 1821.CLA*
   1829.BRO 1834
227 tous ces] tousces   *1813*
229 équivoque,] equivoque,   *1829.BRO*
230 particulieres]
    particuliers   *1813 1821.CLA*
    particulières   *1829.BRO 1834 1840*

Divinité] divinité   *1781.HOL*
231 fâcheuse] facheuse   *1813 1821.CLA*
    1829.BRO 1834
   quelques-unes]
    quelqu'uns   *1813 1821.CLA*
    quelques unes   *1829.BRO 1834*
   tout-puissant]
    Tout-puissant   *1834*
    Tout-Puissant   *1840*
232 convainquans]
    convinquans   *1813 1821.CLA*
   aux] ceux   *1813*
   hommes] hommes,   *1781.HOL*
234 entre eux] entr'eux   *1781.HOL*
    1829.BRO 1834
235 miracles,] miracles   *1840*
236 législateurs,] législateurs   *1840*
238 connoître?]
    connaître?   *1829.BRO 1834*

la voûte du firmament; au lieu de répandre sans ordre les étoiles, et les con-
stellations qui remplissent l'espace, n'eût-il pas été plus conforme aux vues   240
d'un Dieu si jaloux de sa gloire et si bien intentionné pour l'homme; d'écrire
d'une façon non sujette à dispute, son nom, ses attributs, ses volontés per-
manentes en caractères ineffaçables, et lisibles également pour tous les habi-
tans de la terre? Personne alors n'auroit pu douter de l'existence d'un Dieu,
de ses volontés claires, de ses intentions visibles. Sous les yeux de ce Dieu si   245
terrible personne n'auroit eu l'audace de violer ses ordonnances; nul mortel
n'eût osé se mettre dans le cas d'attirer sa colère: enfin nul homme n'eût eu
le front d'en imposer en son nom, ou d'interpréter ses volontés suivant ses
propres fantaisies.

En effet, quand même on admettroit l'existence du Dieu théologique, et   250
la réalité des attributs si discordans qu'on lui donne, l'on ne peut en rien
conclure, pour autoriser la conduite ou les cultes qu'on prescrit de lui ren-
dre. La théologie est vraiment *le tonneau des Danaïdes*. A force de qualités con-
tradictoires et d'assertions hazardées, elle a, pour ainsi dire, tellement garoté
son Dieu qu'elle l'a mis dans l'impossibilité d'agir. S'il est infiniment bon   255
qu'elle raison aurions-nous de le craindre? S'il est infiniment sage, de quoi

---

239 répandre]
    repandre   *1813 1821.CLA*
    étoiles,] étoiles   *1781.HOL*
    1829.BRO 1834 1840
240 n'eût-il] n'eut-il   *1813 1821.CLA*
    1829.BRO 1834
    conforme] conformé   *1834*
241 Dieu] Dieu,   *1781.HOL*
    si jaloux] jaloux   *1840*
    bien intentionné]
      bien-intentionné   *1840*
    l'homme;] l'homme,   *1840*
    d'écrire]
      d'ecrire   *1813 1821.CLA 1829.BRO*
242 permanentes] permanentes,
    1821.CLA 1829.BRO 1834 1840
243 caractères] caracteres   *1781.HOL*
    ineffaçables,]
      inéffaçables,   *1781.HOL*
    habitans] habitants   *1813 1821.CLA*
    1829.BRO 1834
244 n'auroit] n'aurait   *1829.BRO 1834*
246 terrible] sensible,   *1781.HOL*
      terrible,   *1821.CLA*
    n'auroit] n'aurait   *1829.BRO 1834*
247 osé … n'eût] *omitted   1840*
    colère:] colere;   *1781.HOL*
    enfin] enfin,   *1829.BRO 1834*

248 d'interpréter]
    d'interprêter   *1781.HOL*
    ses volontés] ces volontés   *1834*
249 fantaisies.]
    phantasies.   *1813 1821.CLA*
250 admettroit] supposeroit   *1781.HOL*
    admetteroit   *1813 1821.CLA*
    admettrait   *1829.BRO 1834*
251 réalité] realité   *1813 1821.CLA*
    1829.BRO 1834
252 autoriser]
    autorizer   *1813 1829.BRO 1834*
253 *le*] le   *1781.HOL*
    Danaïdes.]
      Danaides.   1821.CLA 1834
    qualités] qualities   *1821.CLA*
254 hazardées,] hasardées,   *1840*
    garoté] garroté   *1829.BRO 1834*
      garrotté   *1840*
255 Dieu]
    Dieu,   *1781.HOL 1829.BRO 1834*
    l'a] a   *1813 1821.CLA*
    bon] bon,   *1781.HOL 1829.BRO*
    1834 1840
256 qu'elle] quelle   *1821.CLA 1840*

nous inquiéter sur notre sort? S'il sait tout, pourquoi l'avertir de nos besoins, et le fatiguer de nos prières? S'il est partout, pourquoi lui élever des temples? S'il est maître de tout, pourquoi lui faire des sacrifices et des offrandes? S'il 260 est juste, comment croire qu'il punisse des créatures qu'il a remplies de foiblesses? Si la grace fait tout en elles, quelle raison auroit-il de les récompenser? S'il est tout-puissant, comment l'offenser, comment lui résister? S'il est raisonnable, comment se mettroit-il en colère contre des aveugles, à qui il a laissé la liberté de déraisonner? S'il est immuable, de quel droit prétendri- 265 ons-nous faire changer ses décrets? S'il est inconcevable, pourquoi nous en occuper? S'IL A PARLÉ, POURQUOI L'UNIVERS N'EST-IL PAS CON-VAINCU? Si la connoissance d'un Dieu est la plus nécessaire, pourquoi n'est-elle pas la plus évidente, et la plus claire.

Système de la Nature, London, 1781.

270   The enlightened and benevolent Pliny thus publicly professes himself an atheist:—Quapropter effigiem Dei, formamque quærere, imbecillitatis humanæ reor. Quisquis est Deus (si modo est alius) et quacunque in parte, totus est sensus, totus est visus, totus auditus, totus animæ, totus animi, totus sui. *   *   *   *   *
275 Imperfectæ vero in homine naturæ præcipua solatia ne deum quidem posse omnia. Namque nec sibi potest mortem consciscere, si velit, quod homini dedit optimum in tantis vitae pœnis: nec mortales æternitate donare, aut revocare defunctos; nec facere ut qui vixit non vixerit, qui honores gessit

---

257 inquiéter] inquieter   ***1813** 1821.CLA*
    pourquoi] pourquoir   *1821.CLA*
258 prières?] prieres?   *1781.HOL*
    partout,] par-tout,   *1781.HOL*
259 maître] le maître   *1781.HOL*
    offrandes?] offiandes?   ***1813***
260 remplies] rempli   ***1813** 1821.CLA*
    de] des   *1821.CLA*
    foiblesses?]
        faiblesses?   *1829.BRO 1834*
261 la] sa   *1781.HOL*
    quelle] qu'elle   *1840*
    récompenser?]
        recompenser?   ***1813** 1821.CLA*
262 résister?]
        resister?   ***1813** 1821.CLA 1840*
263 colère] colere   *1781.HOL*
264 déraisonner?] déraisonner!   *1840*
264–65 S'il . . . décrets?] *omitted   1834*

prétendrions-nous] pretendrions-
    nous   ***1813** 1821.CLA 1829.BRO*
265 décrets?] decrets?   ***1813***
266 S'IL] S'il   *1781.HOL*
    A . . . CONVAINCU?]
        set in lowercase   1781.HOL
267 connoissance] connaissance
        1829.BRO 1834 1840
268 évidente,] évidente   *1781.HOL*
    claire.] claire?   *1829.BRO 1834 1840*
269 *Système*] *Systeme   1821.BEN 1834*
        —Système   1840
    Nature,] *Nature.   1821.BEN 1840*
    London, 1781.]
        Seconde Partie.   1821.BEN
277 vitae] vita   ***1813** 1840*
            vitæ   *1821.CLA 1821.BEN*
        1829.BRO 1834

276   *Shelley's Notes to Queen Mab*

non gesserit, nullumque habere in præteritum jus, præterquam oblivionis,
atque (ut facetis quoque argumentis societas hæc cum deo copuletur) ut bis   280
dena viginti non sint, et multa similiter efficere non posse.—Per quæ, decla-
ratur haud dubie, naturæ potentiam id quoque esse, quod Deum vocamus.

Plin. Nat. His. cap. de Deo.

The consistent Newtonian is necessarily an atheist. See *Sir W. Drummond's
Academical Questions, chap.* iii.—Sir W. seems to consider the atheism to which   285
it leads, as a sufficient presumption of the falshood of the system of gravita-
tion: but surely it is more consistent with the good faith of philosophy to ad-
mit a deduction from facts than an hypothesis incapable of proof, although
it might militate with the obstinate preconceptions of the mob. Had this au-
thor, instead of inveighing against the guilt and absurdity of atheism, dem-   290
onstrated its falshood, his conduct would have been more suited to the mod-
esty of the sceptic and the toleration of the philosopher.   ☞

Omnia enim per Dei potentiam facta sunt: imo, quia naturæ potentia
nulla est nisi ipsa Dei potentia, certum est nos eatenus Dei potentiam non in-
telligere, quatenus causas naturales ignoramus; adeoque stulte ad eandem   295
Dei potentiam recurritur, quando rei alicujus, causam naturalem, hoc est, ip-
sam Dei potentiam ignoramus.

Spinosa, Tract. Theologico-Pol. chap. i. *page* 14.

---

280 atque (ut] (atque ut   *1834 1840*
    (ut] ut   ***1813*** *1829.BRO*
    copuletur)] copuletur,)   *1840*
281 viginti] viginta   ***1813*** *1821.CLA*
    1821.BEN 1829.BRO 1834 1840
285 atheism] atheism,   *1840*
286 leads,] leads   *1834*
    falshood] falsehood   *1821.CLA*
    1821.BEN 1829.BRO 1834 1840
288 facts] facts,   *1821.CLA 1821.BEN*
291 falshood,] falsehood,   *1821.CLA*
    1821.BEN 1829.BRO 1834 1840

292 sceptic] sceptic,   *1821.CLA*
    1821.BEN
293 naturæ]
    natura   ***1813*** *1821.CLA 1821.BEN*
294 certum] artem   ***1813***
    autem   *1821.CLA 1821.BEN*
    1829.BRO 1834 1840
    eatenus] catemus   ***1813***
295 quatenus] quatemus   ***1813***
    ignoramus;] ignoramus: *1834*
296 hoc] sive   ***1813*** *1821.CLA 1821.BEN*
    1829.BRO 1834 1840

Note 14 (VII.67)

Ahasuerus, rise!

Ahasuerus the Jew crept forth from the dark cave of Mount Carmel. Near two thousand years have elapsed since he was first goaded by never-ending restlessness to rove the globe from pole to pole. When our Lord was wearied with the burthen of his ponderous cross, and wanted to rest before the door of Ahasuerus, the unfeeling wretch drove him away with brutality. The Saviour of mankind staggered, sinking under the heavy load, but uttered no complaint. An angel of death appeared before Ahasuerus, and exclaimed indignantly, "Barbarian! thou hast denied rest to the Son of Man: be it denied thee also, until he comes to judge the world."

A black demon, let loose from hell upon Ahasuerus, goads him now from country to country: he is denied the consolation which death affords, and precluded from the rest of the peaceful grave.

Ahasuerus crept forth from the dark cave of Mount Carmel—he shook the dust from his beard—and taking up one of the sculls heaped there,

---

Text collated with *1813,* *GrM* (line 2 to the end), *BA* (line 2 to the end), MS Pfz (line 42 to the end), *1821.CLA* (unexpurgated), *1821.CLAX* (expurgated), *1821.BEN, 1829.BRO, 1834, 1840,* and *1858* (line 42 to the end). *1839* omits this note.

1 Ahasuerus, rise!] *set in italics*
    1821.BEN 1829.BRO 1834 1840
2 Ahasuerus] AHASUERUS, *GrM BA*
        "Ahasuerus *1821.BEN*
          1840
  Jew] Jew, *GrM*
    Jew, says the distinguished writer,
      BA
  the dark] a dark *GrM BA*
  Mount] mount *GrM BA*
3 have] are *GrM BA*
  never-ending] ever-encreasing *GrM BA*
4 restlessness]
    restlessness, *1821.CLA 1821.BEN*
  our Lord] Jesus Christ *GrM*
        our blessed Lord *BA*
5 burthen] burden *GrM BA*
  cross,] cross *GrM*
6 brutality.] spiteful brutality: *GrM*
  Saviour] saviour *1840*
6–7 The . . . mankind]
    and the Saviour *GrM*
8 complaint.] complaint.— *GrM*
  An] However, an *GrM*

exclaimed] said *GrM*
indignantly,] indignantly: *GrM BA*
9 "Barbarian!] "barbarian, *GrM*
      "Barbarian, *BA*
  Son] son *GrM BA 1829.BRO 1834*
  Man:] man; *GrM BA*
    Man; *1834 1840*
10 thee] to thee *GrM BA*
  also,] also *GrM BA*
11 A] "A *1840*
  demon,] daemon, *GrM*
    dæmon, *BA*
12 country:] country. *GrM BA*
    country; *1821.CLA*
      1821.BEN 1834
  he] He *GrM BA*
  consolation] sweet consolation *GrM*
14 Ahasuerus] "Ahasuerus *1840*
  the dark] a dark *GrM BA*
  Mount] mount *GrM BA*
  Carmel—he] Carmel; he *GrM BA*
15 beard—and] beard; and *GrM BA*
  sculls] skulls *GrM BA*
  heaped] towered up *GrM*
    heaped up *BA*

hurled it down the eminence: it rebounded from the earth in shivered atoms. This was my father! roared Ahasuerus. Seven more sculls rolled down from rock to rock; while the infuriate Jew, following them with ghastly looks, exclaimed—And these were my wives! He still continued to hurl down scull after scull, roaring in dreadful accents—And these, and these, and these were my children! They *could die;* but I! reprobate wretch, alas! I cannot die! Dreadful beyond conception is the judgment that hangs over me. Jerusalem fell—I crushed the sucking babe, and precipitated myself into the destructive flames. I cursed the Romans—but, alas! alas! the restless curse held me by the hair,—and I could not die!

Rome the giantess fell—I placed myself before the falling statue—she fell, and did not crush me. Nations sprung up and disappeared before me;— but I remained and did not die. From cloud-encircled cliffs did I precipitate

20

25

---

16 eminence:] eminence,   *GrM*
           eminence;   *BA*
   it rebounded]
     that it, hissing, rebounded   *GrM*
   earth . . . atoms.] ground, and was
     shivered to pieces.   *GrM BA*
17 This] "This   *GrM BA 1840*
   father!] father!"   *GrM BA 1840*
   Ahasuerus.] Ahasuerus;   *GrM BA*
   Seven] seven   *GrM BA*
   sculls] skulls   *GrM BA*
18 rock;] rock,   *GrM BA*
   while] whilst   *GrM BA*
   looks,] looks   *1821.CLA*
19 exclaimed—And]
     exclaimed: "and   *GrM BA*
     exclaimed: "And   *BA*
     exclaimed—"And   *1840*
   wives!] wives!"   *GrM BA 1840*
       wives;   *1821.BEN*
   scull] skull   *GrM BA*
20 scull,] skull,   *GrM BA*
   accents—And] accents; "And   *GrM*
          accents:—"And   *BA*
          accents—"And   *1840*
   these] these,   *BA*
21 children!] children.   *GrM BA*
   They *could die;* but]
     They could die!—But   *GrM*
     THEY COULD DIE! but   *BA*
     They *could die;* but,   *1821.CLA*
   I!] I,   *GrM BA*

   alas!] alas,   *GrM BA*
   cannot] *cannot*   *GrM BA*
   die!] die.   *GrM BA*
22 me.] me!   *GrM BA*
23 fell—I] fell. I   *GrM BA*
   sucking babe,]
     sucking-babe,   *1840*
24 Romans—but,]
     Romans; but,   *GrM BA*
   the restless] The restless   *GrM*
25 hair,—and I] hair, and—I   *GrM*
              BA
26 Rome] "Rome   *GrM*
         "Rome,   *BA*
         "'Rome   *1840*
   fell—I] fell; I   *GrM BA*
26–27 statue—she fell, and]
     giantess. She fell; but   *GrM BA*
27 sprung] sprang   *1834 1840*
   up] up,   *GrM BA*
27–28 me;—but] me; but   *GrM BA*
            1840
         me—but   *1821.BEN*
28 I . . . not] *set in italics*   *GrM BA*
   remained]
     remained,   *1821.BEN 1840*
   die.] *die!!*   *GrM BA*
   cloud-encircled]
     cloud-capp'd   *GrM BA*

myself into the ocean; but the foaming billows cast me upon the shore, and
30   the burning arrow of existence pierced my cold heart again. I leaped into
Etna's flaming abyss, and roared with the giants for ten long months, pollut-
ing with my groans the Mount's sulphureous mouth—ah! ten long months.
The volcano fermented, and in a fiery stream of lava cast me up. I lay torn by
the torture-snakes of hell amid the glowing cinders, and yet continued to
35   exist.—A forest was on fire: I darted on wings of fury and despair into the
crackling wood. Fire dropped upon me from the trees, but the flames only
singed my limbs; alas! it could not consume them.—I now mixed with the
butchers of mankind, and plunged in the tempest of the raging battle. I
roared defiance to the infuriate Gaul, defiance to the victorious German; but
40   arrows and spears rebounded in shivers from my body. The Saracen's flam-
ing sword broke upon my scull: balls in vain hissed upon me: the lightnings

---

29 ocean; but] ocean—but   *1821.BEN*
   the foaming] foaming   *GrM*
30 my cold heart] me   *GrM BA*
31 Etna's] Ætna's   *GrM BA*
   flaming] grissly   *GrM*
   roared] there roared   *GrM*
   months,] months   *GrM BA*
   polluting] in accents of despair,
         lashing   *GrM*
      in accents of despair,
         polluting   *BA*
32 Mount's] mount's   *GrM BA 1840*
   mouth—ah!] mouth.—Ha!   *GrM BA*
   months.]
      months!   *GrM BA 1829.BRO 1834*
33 The] the   *BA*
   fermented, and] fermented—and,
     1821.BEN
   lava] lava,   *1821.BEN*
33–34 torn by the torture-snakes]
      convolved with tortures   *GrM*
      amidst tortures   *BA*
34 hell] hell,   *1821.BEN*
   amid] in   *GrM BA*
   and yet] but   *GrM BA*
35 exist.—A] exist. A   *GrM BA 1821.CLA*
     1821.BEN 1834
   fire:] fire.   *GrM*
     fire;   *BA*
   darted] darted,   *1840*

despair] despair,   *1840*
36 wood.] forest.   *GrM*
   trees, but] hair of the trees—but
         GrM
         trees—but   *BA*
   flames] flame   *GrM BA*
36–37 only singed] did only singe   *GrM*
37 limbs; alas!]
     limbs—alas!   *GrM BA 1821.BEN*
   consume them.—I]
     destroy me. I   *GrM BA*
   them.—I] them. I   *1821.BEN*
38 in] into   *GrM BA*
39 Gaul, defiance]
     Gaul—defiance   *1821.BEN*
40–41 The . . . vain] *omitted*   *Pfz 1858*
41 scull: balls] skull. Balls   *GrM BA*
         scull—balls   *1821.BEN*
   in vain] *omitted*   *GrM*
   hissed] hailed   *GrM*
   me: the] me—like peas thrown upon a
         coat of mail. The   *GrM*
      me.—The   *BA*
      me—the   *1821.BEN*
   lightnings] light'nings   *GrM*
         lightenings   *BA*

of battle glared harmless around my loins: in vain did the elephant trample
on me, in vain the iron hoof of the wrathful steed! The mine, big with de-
structive power, burst upon me, and hurled me high in the air—I fell on
heaps of smoking limbs, but was only singed. The giant's steel club re-   45
bounded from my body; the executioner's hand could not strangle me,
the tyger's tooth could not pierce me, nor would the hungry lion in the
circus devour me. I cohabited with poisonous snakes, and pinched the red
crest of the dragon. The serpent stung, but could not destroy me.—The
dragon tormented, but dared not to devour me.—I now provoked the fury   50

---

42 glared] hissed   *GrM*
   around] round   *GrM BA*
   loins: in] loins, as they serpentine
      round the hips of a pointed rock,
      girt with scowling clouds. In
      GrM
          loins. In   *BA*
          loins: in   *1813*
          loins—in   *1821.BEN*
   did] ——did   *1858*
   elephant] Elephant   Pfz
43 on] upon   *GrM BA*
   me, in] me in   Pfz
        me—in   *1821.BEN*
   steed!] steed.   *GrM BA 1858*
       steed   Pfz
   mine,] mine   Pfz
44 power,] powder,   *GrM*
       power   Pfz
   upon] under   *GrM BA 1829.BRO*
     1834 1840
   me,] me   *1858*
   and] &   Pfz
   hurled] hurld   Pfz
   in] into   *GrM BA*
   air—I] air. I   *GrM BA* Pfz *1858*
   on] down upon   *GrM BA* Pfz
      down upon a   *1858*
45 heaps] heap   Pfz *1858*
   smoking] smoaking   *GrM BA*
   limbs,] limbs   Pfz
   but] and   *GrM BA*
   singed.] singd   Pfz
   giant's] Giants   Pfz
   steel club] steel-club   *GrM BA*
46 body;] body.   Pfz *1858*
      body: *1840*
   the] The   Pfz *1858*
   executioner's] executioners   Pfz

me,] me;   *GrM BA 1821.CLA*
   1821.BEN 1858
47 the tyger's . . . pierce me,]
   omitted   Pfz *1858*
   tyger's] tiger's   *GrM BA 1834 1840*
   pierce me,] hurt me;   *GrM BA*
   would] wd   Pfz
   lion] Lion   Pfz
48 circus] Circus   Pfz
   me.] me."   *GrM*
      me   Pfz
      me;   *1858*
   I] "I   *GrM BA*
   snakes,] snakes   Pfz
      snakes;   *1858*
   and] I   Pfz *1858*
   red] dark-red   *GrM*
49 dragon.] dragon;   *GrM BA 1858*
      Dragon   Pfz
   The] the   *GrM BA* Pfz *1858*
   stung,] stung   Pfz *1834*
   could] cd.   Pfz
   destroy] kill   *GrM BA* Pfz *1858*
   me.—The] me; the   *GrM BA 1858*
      me. The   Pfz *1829.BRO*
       1834 1840
      me;—the   *1821.CLA*
       1821.BEN
50 dragon] Dragon   Pfz
   tormented,] tormented   Pfz *1834*
   dared] could   *GrM BA 1858*
      cd.   Pfz
   to] *omitted*   Pfz *1858*
   to devour] destroy   *GrM BA*
   me.—I] me." "I   *GrM*
      me. "I   *BA*
      me. I   Pfz *1821.CLA*
       1821.BEN 1829.BRO 1834
       1858

of tyrants. I said to Nero, Thou art a bloodhound! I said to Christiern, Thou art a bloodhound! I said to Muley Ismail, Thou art a bloodhound!—The tyrants invented cruel torments, but did not kill me.————————Ha! not to be able to die—not to be able to die—not to be permitted to rest after the toils of life—to be doomed to be imprisoned for ever in the clay-formed dungeon—to be for ever clogged with this worthless body, its load of diseases and

51 tyrants.] tyrants;   *GrM BA*
    Tyrants   Pfz
    tyrants: *1821.CLA 1821.BEN*
     1829.BRO 1834 1840
 I said to Nero,] said to Nero,   *GrM*
 Nero,] Nero   Pfz
 Thou] thou   *GrM BA* Pfz
   "Thou   *1858*
 bloodhound!] blood-hound!   *GrM BA*
   bloodhound   Pfz
   bloodhound;"   *1858*
 I said to Christiern,] said to Christiern,
   GrM BA
   said to Christern
   Pfz
   said to Christern,
   1858
 Thou] thou   *GrM BA* Pfz
   "Thou   *1858*
52 bloodhound!] bloodhound;   *GrM*
   blood-hound;   *BA*
   bloodhound,   Pfz
   bloodhound;"   *1858*
 I] *omitted*   *GrM BA* Pfz *1858*
 Muley] Mulei   *GrM BA*
 Ismail,] Ismail   *GrM BA* Pfz
 Thou] thou   *GrM BA* Pfz
   "Thou   *1858*
 bloodhound!—The] bloodhound; the
   GrM
   blood-hound; the
   BA
   blood hound:
    The   Pfz
   bloodhound! The
   1821.BEN 1840
   bloodhound."
    The   *1858*
53 torments,] torments   Pfz

did] cd   Pfz
 could   *1858*
————————Ha! not] —Ha! not
   GrM BA 1834
   Ha! not   Pfz
   Ha! Not   *1858*
54 die—not] die; not   *GrM*
   die! not   *BA*
   die not   Pfz
 die—not . . . die—not]
  die; *not*   *1858*
 die—not] die! not   *GrM 1834*
   die; not   *BA*
   die. not   Pfz
   die, not   *1840*
 to be permitted . . . of] *under-*
    lined   Pfz
    set in italics
    1858
 rest] rest,   *GrM*
55 life—to] life! to   *GrM BA*
   life, to   Pfz
   life; to   *1858*
 to be imprisoned for ever]
  for ever to be imprisoned   Pfz *1858*
 for ever] forever   *1840*
 the clay-formed] the clayformed   *GrM*
   this Clay formed   Pfz
   this clay-formed
   1840
   this *clay-formed*   *1858*
55–56 dungeon—to] dungeon! to   *GrM*
   BA
   Dungen to   Pfz
   dungeon; to   *1858*
56 for ever] forever   Pfz *1840*
 body,] body   Pfz
 its] its'   Pfz
 diseases] Diseases   Pfz
 and] &   Pfz

infirmities—to be condemned to behold for milleniums that yawning monster Sameness, and Time, that hungry hyena, ever bearing children, and ever devouring again her offspring!—Ha! not to be permitted to die! Awful avenger in heaven, hast thou in thine armoury of wrath a punishment more dreadful? then let it thunder upon me, command a hurricane to sweep me down to the foot of Carmel, that I there may lie extended; may pant, and writhe, and die!

This fragment is the translation of part of some German work, whose title I have vainly endeavoured to discover. I picked it up, dirty and torn, some years ago, in Lincoln's-Inn Fields.

60
65

---

57 infirmities—to] infirmities! to   *GrM*
                      infirmities; to   *BA*
                      1858
                      infirmities to   Pfz
   behold] hold   Pfz *1813 1821.CLA*
        1821.BEN 1829.BRO 1834 1840 1858
   milleniums] millenniums   *1821.CLA*
        1821.BEN 1840 1858
   monster] monster,   *GrM BA 1858*
58 Sameness, and] *omitted*   Pfz *1858*
   Sameness,] *Sameness,*   *GrM*
                Sameness   *BA*
                Sameness   *1821.CLA*
                      1821.BEN
   Time,] *Time,*   *GrM BA*
        Time   Pfz
   hungry] lascivious and hungry   *GrM*
   hyena,] hyena   Pfz
        hyæna,   *1834*
   and ever] ever   Pfz *1858*
59 offspring!—] offsprings!   *GrM BA*
                offspring.   Pfz *1858*
   not] Not   *1858*
   Awful] awful   *GrM BA*
60 avenger] avenger,   *GrM*
        Avenger   *1858*
   heaven,] Heaven,   Pfz *1858*
   thou] Thou   *1858*
   thine] thy   *GrM BA*
        Thine   *1858*
   armoury] armory   *GrM BA*

61 dreadful? then] dreadful; then
                GrM BA
        dreadful! Then   Pfz
        dreadful?—then
              1821.BEN
        dreadful? Then   *1858*
   thunder] Thunder   Pfz
   me,] me!   *GrM BA*
        me.   Pfz *1858*
   command] Command   *1858*
   a] an   Pfz
   hurricane] hurricane,   *GrM BA*
62 Carmel,] Carmel   Pfz
   extended;] extended,   *GrM BA 1858*
        extended.   Pfz
        extended: *1821.BEN*
        extended!   *1834*
   may] May   Pfz
        omitted   *GrM*
   pant,] pant   Pfz
63 writhe,] writhe   *GrM* Pfz
   and] &   Pfz
   die!] *die!"*   *GrM BA*
        die   Pfz
        die!" — — — — — — — —
              1821.BEN
        die!'"   *1840*
64–65 This . . . discover.] *omitted*   *GrM BA*
        Pfz *1858*
65–66 I picked . . . Fields.] *omitted*   *GrM*
        BA Pfz *1858*
66 Lincoln's-Inn] Lincoln's-inn
        1829.BRO 1834
   Fields.] Fields   *1813*

Note 14 (VII.67)   283

I will beget a son, and he shall bear
The sins of all the world.

A book is put into our hands when children, called the Bible, the purport
of whose history is briefly this: That God made the earth in six days, and
there planted a delightful garden, in which he placed the first pair of human
beings. In the midst of the garden he planted a tree, whose fruit, although
within their reach, they were forbidden to touch. That the Devil, in the shape
of a snake, persuaded them to eat of this fruit; in consequence of which God
condemned both them and their posterity yet unborn, to satisfy his justice
by their eternal misery. That, four thousand years after these events, (the
human race in the mean while having gone unredeemed to perdition,) God
engendered with the betrothed wife of a carpenter in Judea (whose virginity
was nevertheless uninjured), and begat a Son, whose name was Jesus Christ;
and who was crucified and died, in order that no more men might be de-
voted to hell-fire, he bearing the burthen of his Father's displeasure by
proxy. The book states, in addition, that the soul of whoever disbelieves this
sacrifice will be burned with everlasting fire.

During many ages of misery and darkness this story gained implicit belief;
but at length men arose who suspected that it was a fable and imposture, and
that Jesus Christ, so far from being a God, was only a man like themselves.
But a numerous set of men, who derived and still derive immense emolu-
ments from this opinion, in the shape of a popular belief, told the vulgar,
that, if they did not believe in the Bible, they would be damned to all eter-
nity; and burned, imprisoned, and poisoned all the unbiassed and uncon-
nected enquirers who occasionally arose. They still oppress them, so far as
the people, now become more enlightened, will allow.

Text collated with *1812.LdEl* (lines 46–120), ***1813***, *1821.CLA* (unexpurgated), *1821.CLAX* (ex-purgated), *1821.BEN*, *1829.BRO*, *1834*, and *1840*. *1839* omits this note.

1–2 I . . . world.] *set in italics* *1821.BEN*
    1829.BRO 1834 1840

1 son,] Son, ***1813*** *1821.CLA*
    Son, *1821.BEN 1829.BRO 1834*

5 which] which, *1821.BEN*

9 posterity] posterity, *1821.BEN*
   unborn,] unborn *1821.CLA*

10–16 That, . . . proxy.]
    replaced by dashes *1821.CLAX*

10 events,] events *1840*

11 mean while] meanwhile *1840*

perdition,)] perdition), *1829.BRO*
   1840
    perdition) *1821.BEN*

12 Judea] Judea, *1821.BEN 1834*

13 uninjured),] uninjured) *1821.BEN*
    uninjured,) *1834*

15 burthen] burden *1821.BEN*

16 states,] states *1829.BRO 1834*
   this] his *1821.CLA 1821.BEN*

24 poisoned] poisoned, *1834*

25 enquirers]
    inquirers *1829.BRO 1834 1840*

The belief in all that the Bible contains, is called Christianity. A Roman governor of Judea, at the instances of a priest-led mob, crucified a man called Jesus eighteen centuries ago. He was a man of pure life, who desired to rescue his countrymen from the tyranny of their barbarous and degrading superstitions. The common fate of all who desire to benefit mankind awaited him. The rabble, at the instigation of the priests, demanded his death, although his very judge made public acknowledgment of his innocence. Jesus was sacrificed to the honour of that God with whom he was afterwards confounded. It is of importance, therefore, to distinguish between the pretended character of this being as the Son of God and the Saviour of the world, and his real character as a man, who, for a vain attempt to reform the world, paid the forfeit of his life to that overbearing tyranny which has since so long desolated the universe in his name. Whilst the one is a hypocritical demon, who announces himself as the God of compassion and peace, even whilst he stretches forth his blood-red hand with the sword of discord to waste the earth, having confessedly devised this scheme of desolation from eternity; the other stands in the foremost list of those true heroes, who have died in the glorious martyrdom of liberty, and have braved torture, contempt, and poverty, in the cause of suffering humanity.[1]

The vulgar, ever in extremes, became persuaded that the crucifixion of Jesus was a supernatural event. Testimonies of miracles, so frequent in unenlightened ages, were not wanting to prove that he was something divine. This belief, rolling through the lapse of ages, met with the reveries of Plato and the reasonings of Aristotle, and acquired force and extent, until the divinity of Jesus became a dogma, which to dispute was death, which to doubt was infamy.

---

[1] Since writing this note I have seen reason to suspect, that Jesus was an ambitious man, who aspired to the throne of Judea.

27 contains,] contains   *1834*
28 governor]
    Governor   *1821.CLA 1821.BEN*
    instances] instance   *1821.CLA*
      1821.BEN 1829.BRO 1834
29 Jesus] Jesus,   *1821.BEN*
35 therefore,] therefore   *1821.CLA*
36 being] being,   *1821.CLA 1821.BEN*
    Son] son   *1840*
39 desolated] desolate   *1821.BEN*
    one] one,   *1821.CLAX*
39–40 is . . . demon,]
    replaced by dashes   *1821.CLAX*
40 demon,] dæmon,   *1821.BEN*
    peace,] peace   *1821.CLAX*

40–43 even . . . eternity;]
    omitted   *1821.CLAX*
43 eternity;] eternity,   *1834*
    heroes,] heroes   *1834*
Footnote 1. note] note,   *1821.BEN 1840*
    suspect,] suspect   *1834 1840*
47 event. Testimonies]
    event, and testimonies   *1812.LdEl*
48 wanting] wanting,   *1821.BEN*
49 belief,] belief   *1812.LdEl*
    through] thro'   *1812.LdEl*
49–50 met . . . Aristotle, and]
    omitted   *1812.LdEl*
49 Plato] Plato,   *1821.BEN*
51 death,] death;   *1829.BRO*

Christianity is now the established religion: he who attempts to impugn it, must be contented to behold murderers and traitors take precedence of him
55 in public opinion; though, if his genius be equal to his courage, and assisted by a peculiar coalition of circumstances, future ages may exalt him to a divinity, and persecute others in his name, as he was persecuted in the name of his predecessor in the homage of the world.

The same means that have supported every other popular belief, have
60 supported Christianity. War, imprisonment, assassination, and falshood; deeds of unexampled and incomparable atrocity have made it what it is. The blood shed by the votaries of the God of mercy and peace, since the establishment of his religion, would probably suffice to drown all other sectaries now on the habitable globe. We derive from our ancestors a faith thus fos-
65 tered and supported: we quarrel, persecute, and hate for its maintenance. Even under a government which, whilst it infringes the very right of thought and speech, boasts of permitting the liberty of the press, a man is pilloried and imprisoned because he is a deist, and no one raises his voice in the indignation of outraged humanity. But it is ever a proof that the falshood of a
70 proposition is felt by those who use coercion, not reasoning, to procure its admission; and a dispassionate observer would feel himself more powerfully interested in favour of a man, who, depending on the truth of his opinions, simply stated his reasons for entertaining them, than in that of his aggressor, who, daringly avowing his unwillingness or incapacity to answer them by

---

53 religion:] religion;   *1812.LdEl 1840*
    he] he,   *1834*
    impugn . . . to]
      disprove it must   *1812.LdEl*
55 opinion;] opinion,   *1812.LdEl*
      opinion: *1840*
    though,] tho',   *1812.LdEl*
58 predecessor] predecessor,   *1812.LdEl*
      predecessors   *1834 1840*
59 belief,] belief   *1812.LdEl 1834*
60 assassination,] murder,   *1812.LdEl*
    falshood;] falsehood;   *1812.LdEl*
      1821.CLA 1821.BEN 1829.BRO 1834
      1840
61–64 The blood . . . globe.]
      omitted   *1812.LdEl*
64 faith] belief   *1812.LdEl*
65 supported: we]
      supported.—We   *1812.LdEl*
    hate] hate,   *1829.BRO 1834 1840*
    maintenance.]
      maintenance.—   *1812.LdEl*

66 Even under] Under   *1812.LdEl*
67 press,] press;   *1812.LdEl*
    a man] in a civilized and enlightened
      country, a man   *1812.LdEl*
68 deist,] Deist,   *1812.LdEl 1821.CLA*
      1821.BEN 1834
69 But it] It   *1812.LdEl*
    falshood] falsehood   *1812.LdEl*
      1821.CLA 1821.BEN 1829.BRO 1834
      1840
70 coercion,]
    power and coercion,   *1812.LdEl*
    reasoning,] reasoning and persuasion,
      1812.LdEl
71 admission;] admission.—A   *1812.LdEl*
      admission: *1840*
    and a] *omitted*   *1812.LdEl*
72 favour] favor   *1812.LdEl*
    who,] who   *1812.LdEl 1840*
74 who,] who   *1812.LdEl*
    or incapacity] *omitted*   *1812.LdEl*

argument, proceeded to repress the energies and break the spirit of their   75
promulgator by that torture and imprisonment whose infliction he could
command.

Analogy seems to favour the opinion, that as, like other systems, Chris-
tianity has arisen and augmented, so like them it will decay and perish; that,
as violence, darkness and deceit, not reasoning and persuasion, have pro-   80
cured its admission among mankind, so, when enthusiasm has subsided, and
time, that infallible controverter of false opinions, has involved its pretended
evidences in the darkness of antiquity, it will become obsolete; that Milton's
poem alone will give permanency to the remembrance of its absurdities; and
that men will laugh as heartily at grace, faith, redemption, and original sin,   85
as they now do at the metamorphoses of Jupiter, the miracles of Romish
saints, the efficacy of witchcraft, and the appearance of departed spirits.

Had the Christian religion commenced and continued by the mere force
of reasoning and persuasion, the preceding analogy would be inadmissible.
We should never speculate on the future obsoleteness of a system perfectly   90
conformable to nature and reason: it would endure so long as they endured;
it would be a truth as indisputable as the light of the sun, the criminality of
murder, and other facts, whose evidence, depending on our organization
and relative situations, must remain acknowledged as satisfactory so long as
man is man. It is an incontrovertible fact, the consideration of which ought   95
to repress the hasty conclusions of credulity, or moderate its obstinacy in

---

75 energies] activity,   *1812.LdEl*
        energies,   *1821.BEN*
         1829.BRO
76 promulgator]
    promulgator,   *1812.LdEl 1821.BEN*
78 Analogy . . . to]
    Does not analogy   *1812.LdEl*
    opinion, that] opinion, that,   *1834*
    as, like] as like   *1812.LdEl*
    systems,] systems   *1812.LdEl*
    Christianity] it   *1812.LdEl*
79 that,] that   *1812.LdEl*
80 violence,] violence   *1812.LdEl*
    darkness] *omitted*   *1812.LdEl*
       darkness,   *1821.CLA*
         1821.BEN 1834 1840
    deceit,] falshood,   *1812.LdEl*
81 mankind,] mankind;   *1812.LdEl*
82 opinions,] opinions   *1834*
83 obsolete;] obsolete,   *1812.LdEl*
83–84 that Milton's . . . absurdities;]
     omitted   1812.LdEl
85 laugh] then laugh   *1812.LdEl*

87 saints,] Saints,   *1812.LdEl*
    spirits.] spirits?   *1812.LdEl*
88 Christian] christian   *1812.LdEl*
89 persuasion,] persuasion, by its
    self-evident excellence and fitness,
    1812.LdEl
90 on] upon   *1812.LdEl*
91 reason:] reason.   *1812.LdEl*
      reason;   *1840*
    it] It   *1812.LdEl*
    so] as   *1812.LdEl*
    endured;] endured,   *1812.LdEl*
93 whose evidence,] physical and moral,
    which,   *1812.LdEl*
    organization]
    organization,   *1812.LdEl*
    organisation   *1840*
94 as satisfactory] *omitted*   *1812.LdEl*
    satisfactory]
    satisfactory,   *1821.CLA 1821.BEN*
95 man.] man.—   *1812.LdEl*
96 its] tis   *1829.BRO*

maintaining them, that, had the Jews not been a fanatical race of men, had even the resolution of Pontius Pilate been equal to his candour, the Christian religion never could have prevailed, it could not even have existed: on so feeble a thread hangs the most cherished opinion of a sixth of the human race! When will the vulgar learn humility? When will the pride of ignorance blush at having believed before it could comprehend?

Either the Christian religion is true, or it is false: if true, it comes from God, and its authenticity can admit of doubt and dispute no further than its omnipotent author is willing to allow. Either the power or the goodness of God is called in question, if he leaves those doctrines most essential to the well being of man in doubt and dispute; the only ones which, since their promulgation, have been the subject of unceasing cavil, the cause of irreconcileable hatred. *If God has spoken, why is the universe not convinced?*

There is this passage in the Christian Scriptures: "Those who obey not God, and believe not the Gospel of his Son, shall be punished with everlasting destruction." This is the pivot upon which all religions turn: they all as-

---

97 that,] that   *1812.LdEl*
   fanatical]
      barbarous and fanatical   *1812.LdEl*
98 Christian] christian   *1812.LdEl*
99 existed:] existed.   *1812.LdEl*
99–101 on . . . race!] Man! the very
     existence of whose most
     cherished opinions depends
     from a thread so feeble, arises
     out of a source so equivocal,
     1812.LdEl
101 When . . . humility?]
     learn at least humility;   *1812.LdEl*
101–2 When . . . comprehend?] own at
     least that it is possible for thyself
     also to have been seduced by
     education and circumstance
     into the admission of tenets
     destitute of rational proof, and
     the truth of which has not yet
     been satisfactorily
     demonstrated.   *1812.LdEl*
103 religion] Religion   *1812.LdEl*
   true,] true   *1834*
   false:] false;   *1840*
   false: if] not. If   *1812.LdEl*
105 omnipotent] Omnipotent   *1812.LdEl*
   author] Author   *1812.LdEl*
   allow.] allow;—   *1812.LdEl*

105–6 Either . . . doctrines] If, lastly, its
     truth *cannot* be demonstrated,
     wherefore impotently attempt
     to snatch from God the
     government of his creation, and
     impiously assert that the Spirit
     of Benevolence has left that
     knowledge   *1812.LdEl*
105 power] power,   *1829.BRO*
107 well being]
     well-being   *1821.BEN 1840*
     man] man,   *1812.LdEl*
     in . . . dispute;]
      omitted   *1812.LdEl*
     ones] one   *1812.LdEl*
     their] its   *1812.LdEl*
108 promulgation,]
     promulgation   *1821.CLA*
     have] has   *1812.LdEl*
     irreconcileable]
      irreconcilable   *1821.BEN*
109 hatred.] hatred?—   *1812.LdEl*
     the universe not]
      not the universe   *1812.LdEl*
110–12 There . . . destruction."]
     omitted   *1812.LdEl*
110 Scriptures:] Scriptures:—   *1821.BEN*
112–14 This . . . true.] *omitted*   *1812.LdEl*

sume that it is in our power to believe or not to believe; whereas the mind
can only believe that which it thinks true. A human being can only be sup-
posed accountable for those actions which are influenced by his will. But be-   115
lief is utterly distinct from and unconnected with volition: it is the appre-
hension of the agreement or disagreement of the ideas that compose any
proposition. Belief is a passion, or involuntary operation of the mind, and,
like other passions, its intensity is precisely proportionate to the degrees of
excitement. Volition is essential to merit or demerit. But the Christian reli-   120
gion attaches the highest possible degrees of merit and demerit to that which
is worthy of neither, and which is totally unconnected with the peculiar fac-
ulty of the mind, whose presence is essential to their being.

Christianity was intended to reform the world: had an all-wise Being
planned it, nothing is more improbable than that it should have failed: om-   125
niscience would infallibly have foreseen the inutility of a scheme which ex-
perience demonstrates, to this age, to have been utterly unsuccessful.

Christianity inculcates the necessity of supplicating the Deity. Prayer may
be considered under two points of view;—as an endeavour to change the in-
tentions of God, or as a formal testimony of our obedience. But the former   130
case supposes that the caprices of a limited intelligence can occasionally in-
struct the Creator of the world how to regulate the universe; and the latter,
a certain degree of servility analogous to the loyalty demanded by earthly
tyrants. Obedience indeed is only the pitiful and cowardly egotism of him
who thinks that he can do something better than reason.   135

Christianity, like all other religions, rests upon miracles, prophesies, and
martyrdoms. No religion ever existed, which had not its prophets, its attested
miracles, and, above all, crowds of devotees who would bear patiently the
most horrible tortures to prove its authenticity. It should appear that in no
case can a discriminating mind subscribe to the genuineness of a miracle. A   140
miracle is an infraction of nature's law, by a supernatural cause; by a cause
acting beyond that eternal circle within which all things are included. God
breaks through the law of nature, that he may convince mankind of the truth

113   whereas] whereas,   *1821.BEN*

114–15   A . . . will.] *omitted   1812.LdEl*

115   But] *omitted   1812.LdEl*

    belief] Belief   *1812.LdEl*

116   is] and disbelief are   *1812.LdEl*

    volition:] volition.   *1812.LdEl*

    it is] They are   *1812.LdEl*

118   a passion, or] an   *1812.LdEl*

120   excitement.]

    excitement.—   *1812.LdEl*

120–23   But . . . being.]
    omitted   1812.LdEl

129   view;—as]

    view; as   *1821.CLA   1821.BEN   1840*

133   servility] civility   *1834*

134   Obedience] Obedience,   *1821.BEN*

    indeed] indeed,   *1821.BEN*

136   prophesies,]

    prophecies,   *1821.BEN 1834 1840*

137   existed,] existed   *1834*

138   and,] and   *1840*

141   law,] law   *1834*

142   included.] included.—   *1821.BEN*

of that revelation which, in spite of his precautions, has been, since its intro-
duction, the subject of unceasing schism and cavil.

Miracles resolve themselves into the following question:[2]—Whether it is more probable the laws of nature, hitherto so immutably harmonious, should have undergone violation, or that a man should have told a lie? Whether it is more probable that we are ignorant of the natural cause of an event, or that we know the supernatural one? That, in old times, when the powers of nature were less known than at present, a certain set of men were themselves deceived, or had some hidden motive for deceiving others; or that God begat a son, who, in his legislation, measuring merit by belief, evidenced himself to be totally ignorant of the powers of the human mind—of what is voluntary, and what is the contrary?

We have many instances of men telling lies;—none of an infraction of nature's laws, those laws of whose government alone we have any knowledge or experience. The records of all nations afford innumerable instances of men deceiving others either from vanity or interest, or themselves being deceived by the limitedness of their views and their ignorance of natural causes: but where is the accredited case of God having come upon earth, to give the lie to his own creations? There would be something truly wonderful in the appearance of a ghost; but the assertion of a child that he saw one as he passed through the church-yard is universally admitted to be less miraculous.

But even supposing that a man should raise a dead body to life before our eyes, and on this fact rest his claim to being considered the son of God;—the Humane Society restores drowned persons, and because it makes no mystery of the method it employs, its members are not mistaken for the sons of God. All that we have a right to infer from our ignorance of the cause of any event is that we do not know it: had the Mexicans attended to this simple rule when they heard the cannon of the Spaniards, they would not have considered them as gods: the experiments of modern chemistry would have defied the wisest philosophers of ancient Greece and Rome to have accounted for them on natural principles. An author of strong common sense has observed, that "a miracle is no miracle at second-hand;" he might have added,

---

[2] See Hume's Essay, vol. ii. page 121.

---

144 revelation] revelation, *1840*	164 church-yard]
Footnote 2. Essay,] Essays, *1840*	church-yard, *1821.CLA 1821.BEN*
157 laws, those] laws—those *1821.BEN*	165 our] your *1834 1840*
laws] laws, *1821.BEN*	166 rest] rests *1821.BEN*
160 views] views, *1821.BEN*	son] Son *1821.BEN*
causes:] causes; *1834 1840*	God;—the] God, the *1834*
161 earth,] earth *1840*	167 because] as *1834 1840*
163 ghost;] ghost: *1829.BRO 1834*	168 sons] Sons *1821.BEN*
	170 is] is, *1821.BEN 1840*
	it:] it; *1821.BEN*

that a miracle is no miracle in any case; for until we are acquainted with all natural causes, we have no reason to imagine others.

There remains to be considered another proof of Christianity—Prophecy. A book is written before a certain event, in which this event is foretold; how could the prophet have foreknown it without inspiration? how could he have been inspired without God? The greatest stress is laid on the prophecies of Moses and Hosea on the dispersion of the Jews, and that of Isaiah concerning the coming of the Messiah. The prophecy of Moses is a collection of every possible cursing and blessing; and it is so far from being marvellous that the one of dispersion should have been fulfilled, that it would have been more surprising if, out of all these, none should have taken effect. In Deuteronomy, chap. xxviii, ver. 64, where Moses explicitly foretells the dispersion, he states that they shall there serve gods of wood and stone: "And the Lord shall scatter thee among all people, from the one end of the earth even to the other, *and there thou shalt serve other gods, which neither thou nor thy fathers have known, even gods of wood and stone.*" The Jews are at this day remarkably tenacious of their religion. Moses also declares that they shall be subjected to these curses for disobedience to his ritual: "And it shall come to pass, if thou wilt not hearken unto the voice of the Lord thy God, to observe to do all the commandments and statutes which I command you this day, that all these curses shall come upon thee and overtake thee." Is this the real reason? The third, fourth and fifth chapters of Hosea are a piece of immodest confession. The indelicate type might apply in a hundred senses to a hundred things. The fifty-third chapter of Isaiah is more explicit, yet it does not exceed in clearness the oracles of Delphos. The historical proof, that Moses, Isaiah and Hosea did write when they are said to have written, is far from being clear and circumstantial.

But prophecy requires proof in its character as a miracle; we have no right to suppose that a man foreknew future events from God, until it is demonstrated that he neither could know them by his own exertions, nor that the writings which contain the prediction could possibly have been fabricated after the event pretended to be foretold. It is more probable that writings, pretending to divine inspiration, should have been fabricated after the fulfilment of their pretended prediction, than that they should have really been

180

185

190

195

200

205

---

176 for] for,   *1834*

178 Christianity—Prophecy.]

    Christianity—prophecy.   *1840*

184 blessing;] blessing,   *1840*

187 xxviii,] xxviii.   *1821.CLA 1821.BEN*

    foretells] foretels   *1821.BEN*

193 curses] causes   **1813** *1821.CLA*

    1821.BEN 1829.BRO 1834

194 wilt] will   **1813** *1821.CLA 1829.BRO*

    1834 1840

197 fourth] fourth,   *1821.BEN 1834*

    1840

    fifth] fifth,   *1834*

199 Isaiah] Isaiah,   *1821.BEN 1834*

201 Hosea] Hosea,   *1834*

203 miracle;] miracle: *1834*

210   divinely inspired; when we consider that the latter supposition makes God
       at once the creator of the human mind and ignorant of its primary powers,
       particularly as we have numberless instances of false religions, and forged
       prophesies of things long past, and no accredited case of God having con-
       versed with men directly or indirectly. It is also possible that the description
215   of an event might have foregone its occurrence; but this is far from being a
       legitimate proof of a divine revelation, as many men, not pretending to the
       character of a prophet, have nevertheless, in this sense, prophesied.

       Lord Chesterfield was never yet taken for a prophet, even by a bishop, yet
       he uttered this remarkable prediction: "The despotic government of France
220   is screwed up to the highest pitch; a revolution is fast approaching; that revo-
       lution, I am convinced, will be radical and sanguinary." This appeared in the
       letters of the prophet long before the accomplishment of this wonderful pre-
       diction. Now, have these particulars come to pass, or have they not? If they
       have, how could the Earl have foreknown them without inspiration? If we ad-
225   mit the truth of the Christian religion on testimony such as this, we must ad-
       mit, on the same strength of evidence, that God has affixed the highest re-
       wards to belief, and the eternal tortures of the never-dying worm to disbelief;
       both of which have been demonstrated to be involuntary.

       The last proof of the Christian religion depends on the influence of the
230   Holy Ghost. Theologians divide the influence of the Holy Ghost into its or-
       dinary and extraordinary modes of operation. The latter is supposed to be
       that which inspired the Prophets and Apostles; and the former to be the
       grace of God, which summarily makes known the truth of his revelation, to
       those whose mind is fitted for its reception by a submissive perusal of his
235   word. Persons convinced in this manner, can do any thing but account for
       their conviction, describe the time at which it happened, or the manner in
       which it came upon them. It is supposed to enter the mind by other channels
       than those of the senses, and therefore professes to be superior to reason
       founded on their experience.

240   Admitting, however, the usefulness or possibility of a divine revelation,
       unless we demolish the foundations of all human knowledge, it is requisite
       that our reason should previously demonstrate its genuineness; for, before

---

211 mind] mind,   *1821.BEN*   224 Earl] earl   *1840*
213 prophesies]   232 Prophets] prophets   *1840*
       prophecies   *1821.BEN 1834 1840*   Apostles;] apostles;   *1840*
216 legitimate] egitimate   *1821.BEN*   234 mind] minds   *1829.BRO 1834 1840*
217 prophesied.]   is] are   *1829.BRO 1834 1840*
       prophecied.   *1821.BEN 1834*   235 Persons] Persons,   *1834*
219 prediction: "The]   any thing] anything   *1829.BRO 1840*
       prediction:—"The   *1840*

we extinguish the steady ray of reason and common sense, it is fit that we should discover whether we cannot do without their assistance, whether or no there be any other which may suffice to guide us through the labyrinth of life[3]: for, if a man is to be inspired upon all occasions, if he is to be sure of a thing because he is sure, if the ordinary operations of the spirit are not to be considered very extraordinary modes of demonstration, if enthusiasm is to usurp the place of proof, and madness that of sanity, all reasoning is superfluous. The Mahometan dies fighting for his prophet, the Indian immolates himself at the chariot-wheels of Brahma, the Hottentot worships an insect, the Negro a bunch of feathers, the Mexican sacrifices human victims! Their degree of conviction must certainly be very strong: it cannot arise from conviction, it must from feelings, the reward of their prayers. If each of these should affirm, in opposition to the strongest possible arguments, that inspiration carried internal evidence, I fear their inspired brethren, the orthodox Missionaries, would be so uncharitable as to pronounce them obstinate.

Miracles cannot be received as testimonies of a disputed fact, because all human testimony has ever been insufficient to establish the possibility of miracles. That which is incapable of proof itself, is no proof of any thing else. Prophecy has also been rejected by the test of reason. Those, then, who have been actually inspired, are the only true believers in the Christian religion.

Mox numine viso
Virginei tumuere sinus, innuptaque mater
Arcano stupuit compleri viscera partu
Auctorem peritura suum. Mortalia corda
Artificem texere poli, latuitque sub uno
Pectore, qui totum late complectitur orbem.
Claudian, Carmen Paschale.

Does not so monstrous and disgusting an absurdity carry its own infamy and refutation with itself? ☞

---

[3] See Locke's Essay on the Human Understanding, book iv. chap. xix., on Enthusiasm.

247 because he is sure,] *set in italics* *1840*

251 chariot-wheels]
   chariot wheels *1821.BEN*

257 Missionaries,] missionaries, *1840*

260 That] That, *1834 1840*
   any thing] anything *1840*

265 partu] partu, *1829.BRO 1834 1840*

266 peritura] paritura *1821.CLA*
   1821.BEN 1829.BRO 1834 1840

269 *Claudian,*] *Claudiam,* *1813*
   Claudiani, *1829.BRO*
   1834
   Claudiani *1840*
   Paschale.] *Paschali.* *1813*

270–71 Does . . . ☞] *omitted* *1821.CLAX*

271 ☞] *omitted* *1821.BEN*

> Him, still from hope to hope the bliss pursuing,
> Which from the exhaustless lore of human weal
> Draws on the virtuous mind, the thoughts that rise
> In time-destroying infiniteness, gift
5 > With self-enshrined eternity, &c.

Time is our consciousness of the succession of ideas in our mind. Vivid sensation, of either pain or pleasure, makes the time seem long, as the common phrase is, because it renders us more acutely conscious of our ideas. If a mind be conscious of an hundred ideas during one minute, by the clock, and of two hundred during another, the latter of these spaces would actually occupy so much greater extent in the mind as two exceed one in quantity. If, therefore, the human mind, by any future improvement of its sensibility, should become conscious of an infinite number of ideas in a minute, that minute would be eternity. I do not hence infer that the actual space between the birth and death of a man will ever be prolonged; but that his sensibility is perfectible, and that the number of ideas which his mind is capable of receiving is indefinite. One man is stretched on the rack during twelve hours; another sleeps soundly in his bed: the difference of time perceived by these two persons is immense; one hardly will believe that half an hour has elapsed, the other could credit that centuries had flown during his agony. Thus, the life of a man of virtue and talent, who should die in his thirtieth year, is, with regard to his own feelings, longer than that of a miserable priest-ridden slave, who dreams out a century of dulness. The one has perpetually cultivated his mental faculties, has rendered himself master of his thoughts, can abstract and generalize amid the lethargy of every-day business;—the other can slumber over the brightest moments of his being, and is unable to remember the happiest hour of his life. Perhaps the perishing ephemeron enjoys a longer life than the tortoise.

Text collated with **1813**, *1821.CLA* (unexpurgated), *1821.CLAX* (expurgated), *1821.BEN*, *1829.BRO*, *1834*, *1839*, and *1840*.

1–5 Him, . . . &c.] *set in italics*   *1821.BEN*
      1829.BRO 1834 1839 1840
1 still] (still   *omnia*
2 lore] store   *1839 1840*
3 mind,] mind,)   **1813** *1821.CLA*
      mind)   *1821.BEN 1829.BRO*
      1834 1839 1840
9 an] a   *1834 1839 1840*
   minute,] minute   *1834 1839 1840*
17 indefinite.] indefinite.—   *1821.BEN*

hours;] hours,   *1834 1839 1840*
18 bed:] bed;   *1821.BEN*
19 half an hour]
      half-an-hour   *1839 1840*
21 Thus,] Thus   *1834 1839 1840*
23 dulness.] dullness.   *1829.BRO 1834*
25 generalize] generalise   *1839 1840*
      business;—the]
      business; the   *1821.BEN*

Dark flood of time!
Roll as it listeth thee—I measure not 30
By months or moments thy ambiguous course.
Another may stand by me on the brink
And watch the bubble whirled beyond his ken
That pauses at my feet. The sense of love,
The thirst for action, and the impassioned thought 35
Prolong my being: if I wake no more,
My life more actual living will contain
Than some grey veteran's of the world's cold school,
Whose listless hours unprofitably roll,
By one enthusiast feeling unredeemed. 40

See Godwin's Pol. Jus. vol. i. *page* 411;—
and Condorcet, Esquisse d'un Tableau Historique
des Progrès de l'Esprit Humain, Epoque ix.

Note 17 (VIII.211–12)

No longer now
He slays the lamb that looks him in the face.

I hold that the depravity of the physical and moral nature of man origi-
nated in his unnatural habits of life. The origin of man, like that of the uni-
verse of which he is a part, is enveloped in impenetrable mystery. His gener- 5
ations either had a beginning, or they had not. The weight of evidence in
favour of each of these suppositions seems tolerably equal; and it is perfectly
unimportant to the present argument which is assumed. The language spo-
ken however by the mythology of nearly all religions seems to prove, that at
some distant period man forsook the path of nature, and sacrificed the pu- 10
rity and happiness of his being to unnatural appetites. The date of this event

---

<table>
<tr><td>32 brink] brink,   1834 1839 1840</td><td>veterans   1821.BEN</td></tr>
<tr><td>35 thought]</td><td>41 Jus.] Just.   1834 1839 1840</td></tr>
<tr><td>   thought,   1821.BEN 1834 1839 1840</td><td>43 Progrès] Progress   1821.BEN</td></tr>
<tr><td>38 veteran's] veterans'   1813 1821.CLA</td><td>   Progres   1834</td></tr>
<tr><td>   1829.BRO 1834 1839 1840</td><td>Epoque] époque   1839 1840</td></tr>
</table>

Text collated with **1813**, *VND*, *1821.CLA* (unexpurgated), *1821.CLAX* (expurgated), *1821.BEN*,
1829.BRO, 1834, 1839, and *1840*. Greek Text (lines *407–33*) collated with **1813**.

<table>
<tr><td>1–2 No . . . face.] set in italics   1821.BEN</td><td>8 assumed.] assumed   1840</td></tr>
<tr><td>   1829.BRO 1834 1839 1840</td><td>   spoken]</td></tr>
<tr><td>3 hold] HOLD   VND</td><td>   spoken,   1821.CLA 1821.BEN 1840</td></tr>
<tr><td>5 mystery.] mystery.—   1821.BEN</td><td>9 however]</td></tr>
<tr><td></td><td>   however,   1821.CLA 1821.BEN 1840</td></tr>
<tr><td></td><td>11 event] event,   VND</td></tr>
</table>

seems to have also been that of some great change in the climates of the earth, with which it has an obvious correspondence. The allegory of Adam and Eve eating of the tree of evil, and entailing upon their posterity the wrath of God, and the loss of everlasting life, admits of no other explanation than the disease and crime that have flowed from unnatural diet. Milton was so well aware of this, that he makes Raphael thus exhibit to Adam the consequence of his disobedience.

> —————— Immediately a place
> Before his eyes appeared: sad, noisome, dark:
> A lazar-house it seem'd; wherein were laid
> Numbers of all diseased: all maladies
> Of ghastly spasm, or racking torture, qualms
> Of heart-sick agony, all feverous kinds,
> Convulsions, epilepsies, fierce catarrhs,
> Intestine stone and ulcer, cholic pangs
> Dæmoniac frenzy, moping melancholy,
> And moon-struck madness, pining atrophy,
> Marasmus, and wide-wasting pestilence,
> Dropsies, and asthmas, and joint-racking rheums.

And how many thousands more might not be added to this frightful catalogue!

The story of Prometheus is one likewise which, although universally admitted to be allegorical, has never been satisfactorily explained. Prometheus stole fire from heaven, and was chained for this crime to mount Caucasus, where a vulture continually devoured his liver, that grew to meet its hunger. Hesiod says, that, before the time of Prometheus, mankind were exempt from suffering; that they enjoyed a vigorous youth, and that death, when at length it came, approached like sleep, and gently closed their eyes. Again, so general was this opinion, that Horace, a poet of the Augustan age, writes—

---

13 correspondence.]
    correspondence.— *1821.BEN*
15 God,] God *1834 1839 1840*
    life,] life *1821.CLA*
    explanation] explanation, *VND*
19 place] place, *VND*
20 appeared:]
    appeared, *1829.BRO 1840*
    appear'd, *1834 1839*
    dark:] dark, *1829.BRO 1834 1839*
      dark *1840*
21 seem'd;]
    seem'd, *1829.BRO 1834 1839*
    seemed, *1840*

laid] laid; *1840*
22 diseased:] diseased, *1829.BRO 1834 1839 1840*
23 spasm,] spasm *1834 1839 1840*
26 cholic] colic *1840*
27 Dæmoniac] Demoniac *1839 1840*
31 And] —And *1840*
    thousands] thousand *VND*
33 Prometheus] Prometheus, *VND*
35 mount] Mount *1821.BEN 1839 1840*
36 hunger.] hunger.— *VND*
37 that,] that *VND 1840*
39 Again,] —Again, *VND*

Audax omnia perpeti,
Gens humana ruit per vetitum nefas;
Audax Iapeti genus
Ignem fraude malâ gentibus intulit:
Post ignem ætheriâ domo   45
Subductum, macies et nova febrium
Terris incubuit cohors,
Semotique prius tarda necessitas
Lethi corripuit gradum.

How plain a language is spoken by all this. Prometheus (who represents the   50
human race) effected some great change in the condition of his nature, and
applied fire to culinary purposes; thus inventing an expedient for screening
from his disgust the horrors of the shambles. From this moment his vitals
were devoured by the vulture of disease. It consumed his being in every
shape of its loathsome and infinite variety, inducing the soul-quelling sink-   55
ings of premature and violent death. All vice arose from the ruin of health-
ful innocence. Tyranny, superstition, commerce, and inequality, were then
first known, when reason vainly attempted to guide the wanderings of exac-
erbated passion. I conclude this part of the subject with an extract from
Mr. Newton's Defence of Vegetable Regimen, from whom I have borrowed   60
this interpretation of the fable of Prometheus.

"Making allowance for such transposition of the events of the allegory as
time might produce after the important truths were forgotten, which this
portion of the ancient mythology was intended to transmit, the drift of the
fable seems to be this:—Man at his creation was endowed with the gift of per-   65
petual youth; that is, he was not formed to be a sickly suffering creature as we
now see him, but to enjoy health, and to sink by slow degrees into the bosom
of his parent earth without disease or pain. Prometheus first taught the use

---

42 vetitum] vetetum *VND*
     nefas;] nefas, *VND*
         nefas. *1829.BRO 1834 1839*
          1840
43 genus] genus, *VND*
44 intulit:] intulit, *VND*
       intulit! *1821.BEN*
45 ætheriâ]
     ætheria *1821.BEN 1839 1840*
     domo] domo, *VND*
46 macies et]
     macieset *1813 VND 1821.CLA*
    febrium] febrium, *VND*
47 cohors,] cohors *VND*
48 Semotique] Semotiq *VND*

    necessitas] necessitas, *VND*
49 gradum.] gradum.— *VND*
50 this.] this.— *VND*
      this! *1834 1839 1840*
    Prometheus] Prometheus, *VND*
57 innocence.]
     innocence.— *1834 1839 1840*
60 Mr. Newton's]
     Mr Newland's *1829.BRO*
     Mr. Newland's *1834*
62 allegory] allegory, *VND*
63 produce] produce, *1821.BEN*
    this] the *VND*
64 ancient] antient *VND*

of animal food (primus bovem occidit Prometheus[1]) and of fire, with which
70   to render it more digestible and pleasing to the taste. Jupiter, and the rest of
the gods, foreseeing the consequences of these inventions, were amused or
irritated at the short-sighted devices of the newly-formed creature, and left
him to experience the sad effects of them. Thirst, the necessary concomitant
of a flesh diet," (perhaps of all diet vitiated by culinary preparation,) "en-
75   sued; water was resorted to, and man forfeited the inestimable gift of health
which he had received from heaven: he became diseased, the partaker of a
precarious existence, and no longer descended slowly to his grave."[2]

>But just disease to luxury succeeds,
>And every death its own avenger breeds;
80
>The fury passions from that blood began,
>And turned on man a fiercer savage—man.

Man, and the animals whom he has infected with his society, or depraved
by his dominion, are alone diseased. The wild hog, the mouflon, the bison,
and the wolf, are perfectly exempt from malady, and invariably die either
85   from external violence, or natural old age. But the domestic hog, the sheep,
the cow, and the dog, are subject to an incredible variety of distempers; and,
like the corrupters of their nature, have physicians who thrive upon their
miseries. The supereminence of man is like Satan's, a supereminence of
pain; and the majority of his species, doomed to penury, disease and crime,
90   have reason to curse the untoward event, that by enabling him to commu-
nicate his sensations, raised him above the level of his fellow animals. But
the steps that have been taken are irrevocable. The whole of human science
is comprised in one question:—How can the advantages of intellect and

[1] Plin. Nat. Hist. lib. vii. sect. 57.
[2] Return to Nature. Cadell, 1811.

---

69 food] food, *1821.BEN*
   (primus] (Primus *1840*
71 these inventions,]
   the inventions, *VND*
74 diet,"] diet, *1821.BEN 1839 1840*
  preparation,)]
   preparation) *VND 1821.BEN*
  "ensued;] ensued; *1821.CLA*
   1821.BEN 1839 1840
76 heaven:] heaven; *1821.BEN*
Footnote 2. Return . . . 1811.]
     omitted VND
78 succeeds,] succeeds; *1839 1840*
79 breeds;]
  breeds, *1829.BRO 1839 1840*
  breeds. *1834*

81 savage—man.] savage——Man: *VND*
82 society,] society *1834 1839 1840*
84 die] die, *1821.BEN*
85 violence,] violence *1834 1839 1840*
86 dog,] dog *1821.CLA*
  are] are, *1821.CLA*
88 a] the *1840*
89 pain;] pain, *1821.BEN*
  disease] disease, *VND 1821.BEN*
   1829.BRO 1834 1839 1840
90 that] that, *1834 1839 1840*
91 fellow animals.]
  fellow-animals. *1839 1840*
93 question:—How]
  question: How *1840*

civilization be reconciled with the liberty and pure pleasures of natural life?
How can we take the benefits, and reject the evils of the system, which is now   95
interwoven with all the fibres of our being?—I believe that abstinence from
animal food and spirituous liquors would in a great measure capacitate us
for the solution of this important question.

It is true, that mental and bodily derangement is attributable in part to
other deviations from rectitude and nature than those which concern diet.   100
The mistakes cherished by society respecting the connection of the sexes,
whence the misery and diseases of unsatisfied celibacy, unenjoying prostitu-
tion, and the premature arrival of puberty necessarily spring; the putrid at-
mosphere of crowded cities; the exhalations of chemical processes; the muf-
fling of our bodies in superfluous apparel; the absurd treatment of   105
infants:—all these, and innumerable other causes, contribute their mite to
the mass of human evil.

Comparative anatomy teaches us that man resembles frugivorous animals
in every thing, and carnivorous in nothing; he has neither claws wherewith
to seize his prey, nor distinct and pointed teeth to tear the living fibre. A Man-   110
darin of the first class, with nails two inches long, would probably find them
alone inefficient to hold even a hare. After every subterfuge of gluttony, the
bull must be degraded into the ox, and the ram into the wether, by an un-
natural and inhuman operation, that the flaccid fibre may offer a fainter re-
sistance to rebellious nature. It is only by softening and disguising dead flesh   115
by culinary preparation, that it is rendered susceptible of mastication or di-
gestion; and that the sight of its bloody juices and raw horror does not excite
intolerable loathing and disgust. Let the advocate of animal food force him-
self to a decisive experiment on its fitness, and, as Plutarch recommends, tear
a living lamb with his teeth, and plunging his head into its vitals, slake his   120
thirst with the steaming blood; when fresh from the deed of horror, let him

---

94 civilization] civilization,   *VND*
   civilisation   *1839 1840*
 natural] a natural   *1821.BEN*
95 evils] evils,   *1834 1839 1840*
 system,] system   *1834 1839 1840*
96 being?—I] being? I   *1821.BEN*
97 liquors] liquors,   *VND*
99–107 It is true . . . human evil.]
   omitted   VND
101 connection] connexion   *1839 1840*
103 puberty] puberty,   *1834 1839 1840*
 spring;] spring: *1840*
106 infants:—all] infants;—all   *1834*
  1839 1840
 other] other,   *1834*
 causes,] causes   *1834*

109 every thing,]
  everything,   *1829.BRO 1839 1840*
110 Mandarin] mandarin   *1840*
111 of] "of   *1840*
 class,] class,"   *1840*
 them] them,   *1821.BEN*
112 alone] alone,   *1821.CLA 1821.BEN*
117 horror] horror,   *VND*
118 food] food,   *VND*
119 and, as] and as   *VND*
120 and plunging]
  and, plunging   *1834 1839*
121 horror,] horror   *VND*

revert to the irresistible instincts of nature that would rise in judgment against it, and say, Nature formed me for such work as this. Then, and then only, would he be consistent.

125 Man resembles no carnivorous animal. There is no exception, unless man be one, to the rule of herbivorous animals having cellulated colons.

The orang-outang perfectly resembles man both in the order and number of his teeth. The orang-outang is the most anthropomorphous of the ape tribe, all of which are strictly frugivorous. There is no other species of ani-
130 mals, which live on different food, in which this analogy exists.[3] In many frugivorous animals, the canine teeth are more pointed and distinct than those of man. The resemblance also of the human stomach to that of the orang-outang, is greater than to that of any other animal.

The intestines are also identical with those of herbivorous animals, which
135 present a larger surface for absorption and have ample and cellulated colons. The cæcum also, though short, is larger than that of carnivorous animals; and even here the orang-outang retains its accustomed similarity.

The structure of the human frame then is that of one fitted to a pure vegetable diet, in every essential particular. It is true, that the reluctance to ab-
140 stain from animal food, in those who have been long accustomed to its stimulus, is so great in some persons of weak minds, as to be scarcely overcome; but this is far from bringing any argument in its favour. A lamb, which was fed for some time on flesh by a ship's crew, refused its natural diet at the end of the voyage. There are numerous instances of horses, sheep, oxen, and even
145 wood-pigeons, having been taught to live upon flesh, until they have loathed their natural aliment. Young children evidently prefer pastry, oranges, apples, and other fruit, to the flesh of animals; until, by the gradual depra-

---

[3] Cuvier, Leçons d'Anat. Comp. tom. iii. pages 169, 373, 448, 465, 480. Rees's Cyclopædia, article Man.

---

122 instincts] instinct   *1829.BRO* 1834
    1839 1840

123 then] *omitted   1840*

125 unless] except   *VND*

126 herbivorous] her bivorous   *1834*
    animals,] animals   *VND*

130 which live . . . food,] *omitted   VND*

Footnote 3. Leçons] Lecons   *VND*
    Cyclopædia,] Cyclopœdia,
      1813 *VND 1821.CLA*
      1821.BEN 1829.BRO
      Man.] "Man."   *1839 1840*

132 orang-outang,]
    orang-outang   *1834 1839*

135 absorption] absorption,   *VND*
    1821.BEN 1834 1839 1840

136 colons.] colons.—   *1821.BEN*
    cæcum] cœcum   *VND* ***1813***
    1821.CLA 1821.BEN 1829.BRO 1834

138 frame] frame,   *1821.BEN*
    then] then,   *1821.BEN*

139 diet,] diet   *1840*

142 favour.] favour.—   *VND*

146 natural] accustomed   *VND*
    aliment.] aliment.—   *1821.BEN*

147 fruit,] fruit   *1829.BRO*
    animals;]
    animals,   *1821.CLA 1821.BEN*

vation of the digestive organs, the free use of vegetables has for a time pro-
duced serious inconveniences; *for a time,* I say, since there never was an in-
stance wherein a change from spirituous liquors and animal food to vege-   150
tables and pure water, has failed ultimately to invigorate the body, by
rendering its juices bland and consentaneous, and to restore to the mind
that cheerfulness and elasticity, which not one in fifty possesses on the pres-
ent system. A love of strong liquors is also with difficulty taught to infants. Al-
most every one remembers the wry faces which the first glass of port pro-   155
duced. Unsophisticated instinct is invariably unerring; but to decide on the
fitness of animal food, from the perverted appetites which its constrained
adoption produces, is to make the criminal a judge in his own cause: it is even
worse, it is appealing to the infatuated drunkard in a question of the
salubrity of brandy.   160

What is the cause of morbid action in the animal system? Not the air we
breathe, for our fellow denizens of nature breathe the same uninjured; not
the water we drink, (if remote from the pollutions of man and his inven-
tions,)[4] for the animals drink it too; not the earth we tread upon; not the un-
obscured sight of glorious nature, in the wood, the field, or the expanse of   165

---

[4] The necessity of resorting to some means of purifying water, and the disease which arises from
its adulteration in civilized countries, is sufficiently apparent—See Dr. Lambe's Reports on Can-
cer. I do not assert that the use of water is in itself unnatural, but that the unperverted palate
would swallow no liquid capable of occasioning disease.

---

148 organs,] organs   *1840*
   has] has,   *1821.BEN*
   time] time,   *1821.BEN*
149 *time,*] *time*   *1834 1839 1840*
150 change] change,   *1834 1839 1840*
   food] food,   *VND*
153 elasticity,] elasticity   *1834 1839 1840*
   possesses] possess   *VND*
155 faces] faces,   *VND*
156 but] but,   *1834 1839*
157 food,] food   *1834 1839 1840*
158 in his] of his   *1834 1839 1840*
   cause: it] cause:—it   *VND*
      cause; it   *1821.BEN 1834*
        1839 1840
159 worse, it] worse; it   *1834 1839*
      worse; for it   *1840*
162 fellow denizens]
   fellow-denizens   *1834 1839 1840*
   nature] nature,   *VND*
   uninjured;] uninjured: *1821.BEN*
      uninjured,   *1834*

162–63 not . . . drink,] *omitted*   *1834*
163 drink,] drink   *VND 1821.CLA*
      1821.BEN 1829.BRO 1839 1840
   inventions,)]
    inventions)   *VND 1821.BEN*
Footnote 4. disease] diseases   *1829.BRO*
      1834 1839 1840
     arises] arise   *1829.BRO 1834*
      1839 1840
    civilized]
     civilised   *1839 1840*
    is] are   *1829.BRO 1834 1839*
     1840
    apparent—See]
     apparent.—See   *1821.CLA*
      1821.BEN 1829.BRO
      1834 1839
     apparent. See   *1840*

sky and ocean; nothing that we are or do in common with the undiseased inhabitants of the forest. Something then wherein we differ from them: our habit of altering our food by fire, so that our appetite is no longer a just criterion for the fitness of its gratification. Except in children, there remain no traces of that instinct which determines, in all other animals, what aliment is natural or otherwise; and so perfectly obliterated are they in the reasoning adults of our species, that it has become necessary to urge considerations drawn from comparative anatomy to prove that we are naturally frugivorous.

Crime is madness. Madness is disease. Whenever the cause of disease shall be discovered, the root, from which all vice and misery have so long overshadowed the globe, will lie bare to the axe. All the exertions of man, from that moment, may be considered as tending to the clear profit of his species. No sane mind in a sane body resolves upon a real crime. It is a man of violent passions, blood-shot eyes, and swollen veins, that alone can grasp the knife of murder. The system of a simple diet promises no Utopian advantages. It is no mere reform of legislation, whilst the furious passions and evil propensities of the human heart, in which it had its origin, are still unassuaged. It strikes at the root of all evil, and is an experiment which may be tried with success, not alone by nations, but by small societies, families, and even individuals. In no cases has a return to vegetable diet produced the slightest injury; in most it has been attended with changes undeniably beneficial. Should ever a physician be born with the genius of Locke, I am persuaded that he might trace all bodily and mental derangements to our unnatural habits, as clearly as that philosopher has traced all knowledge to sensation. What prolific sources of disease are not those mineral and vegetable poisons that have been introduced for its extirpation! How many thousands have become murderers and robbers, bigots and domestic tyrants, dissolute and abandoned adventurers, from the use of fermented liquors; who, had they slaked their thirst only with pure water, would have lived but to diffuse the happiness of their own unperverted feelings. How many groundless opin-

---

166 common] common,   *VND*
    undiseased] undeceased   *1821.BEN*
167 forest.] forest;   *1834 1839 1840*
    Something]
      but something   *1834 1839 1840*
    them:] them;   *1834 1839 1840*
169 children,] children   *VND 1821.CLA*
    1821.BEN 1829.BRO 1834
    remain] remains   *1834*
170 instinct] instinct,   *VND*
    determines,] determines   *VND*
    animals,] animals   *VND*

171 otherwise;] otherwise,   *VND*
173 anatomy]
    anatomy,   *1821.CLA 1821.BEN*
175 root,] root   *VND*
176 lie] lay   *VND*
184 success,] success   *1840*
192 bigots] bigots,   *1821.BEN*
193 liquors;] liquors!   *1834 1839 1840*
    who,] who   *1821.CLA 1821.BEN*
194 with pure water,]
    at the mountain stream,   *VND*
195 feelings.] feelings!   *1834 1839 1840*

ions and absurd institutions have not received a general sanction from the
sottishness and intemperance of individuals! Who will assert that, had the
populace of Paris satisfied their hunger at the ever-furnished table of vege-
table nature, they would have lent their brutal suffrage to the proscription-
list of Robespierre? Could a set of men, whose passions were not perverted
by unnatural stimuli, look with coolness on an auto da fé? Is it to be believed
that a being of gentle feelings, rising from his meal of roots, would take de-
light in sports of blood? Was Nero a man of temperate life? could you read
calm health in his cheek, flushed with ungovernable propensities of hatred
for the human race? Did Muley Ismael's pulse beat evenly, was his skin trans-
parent, did his eyes beam with healthfulness, and its invariable concomi-
tants, cheerfulness and benignity? Though history has decided none of these
questions, a child could not hesitate to answer in the negative. Surely the
bile-suffused cheek of Buonaparte, his wrinkled brow, and yellow eye, the
ceaseless inquietude of his nervous system, speak no less plainly the charac-
ter of his unresting ambition than his murders and his victories. It is impos-
sible, had Buonaparte descended from a race of vegetable feeders, that he
could have had either the inclination or the power to ascend the throne of
the Bourbons. The desire of tyranny could scarcely be excited in the indi-
vidual, the power to tyrannize would certainly not be delegated by a society
neither frenzied by inebriation nor rendered impotent and irrational by dis-
ease. Pregnant indeed with inexhaustible calamity is the renunciation of in-
stinct, as it concerns our physical nature; arithmetic cannot enumerate, nor
reason perhaps suspect, the multitudinous sources of disease in civilized life.
Even common water, that apparently innoxious pabulum, when corrupted
by the filth of populous cities, is a deadly and insidious destroyer.[5] Who can

200

205

210

215

220

---

[5] Lambe's Reports on Cancer.

---

196 not] *omitted   1834 1839 1840*
   sanction] sanction,   *VND*
197 intemperance]
   the intemperance   *1834 1839 1840*
   assert] assert,   *VND*
   that,] that   *VND*
198 satisfied] drank at the pure source of
   the Seine, and satisfied   *VND*
201 auto da fé?] *set in italics   1834 1839*
   1840
   auto da fè?   **1813** *VND*
   auto da fè   1821.CLA
   1829.BRO
203 could] Could   *1821.CLA 1821.BEN*
   1829.BRO 1834 1839 1840
206 eyes] eyes,   *1821.BEN*
   concomitants,] concomitants   *VND*

211 ambition] ambition,   *1840*
211–12 impossible, had]
   impossible had   *1821.BEN*
   impossible that had   *VND*
213 have had] have had,   *VND*
215 tyrannize] tyrannise   *1839*
   society] society,   *VND*
216 inebriation] inebriation,   *VND*
   1821.CLA 1821.BEN
217 calamity] calamity,   *VND*
219 civilized] civilised   *1839 1840*
220 pabulum,]
   pabulum,   1821.CLA 1821.BEN
221–29 Who can wonder . . . universal
   sin.] *omitted   1839 1840*

Note 17 (VII.211–12)   303

wonder that all the inducements held out by God himself in the Bible to virtue should have been vainer than a nurse's tale; and that those dogmas, by which he has there excited and justified the most ferocious propensities, should have alone been deemed essential; whilst Christians are in the daily practice of all those habits, which have infected with disease and crime, not only the reprobate sons, but these favoured children of the common Father's love. Omnipotence itself could not save them from the consequences of this original and universal sin.

There is no disease, bodily or mental, which adoption of vegetable diet and pure water has not infallibly mitigated, wherever the experiment has been fairly tried. Debility is gradually converted into strength, disease into healthfulness; madness, in all its hideous variety, from the ravings of the fettered maniac, to the unaccountable irrationalities of ill temper, that make a hell of domestic life, into a calm and considerate evenness of temper, that alone might offer a certain pledge of the future moral reformation of society. On a natural system of diet, old age would be our last and our only malady; the term of our existence would be protracted; we should enjoy life, and no longer preclude others from the enjoyment of it; all sensational delights would be infinitely more exquisite and perfect; the very sense of being would then be a continued pleasure, such as we now feel it in some few and favoured moments of our youth. By all that is sacred in our hopes for the human race, I conjure those who love happiness and truth, to give a fair trial to the vegetable system. Reasoning is surely superfluous on a subject whose merits an experience of six months would set for ever at rest. But it is only among the enlightened and benevolent that so great a sacrifice of appetite and prejudice can be expected, even though its ultimate excellence should not admit of dispute. It is found easier, by the short-sighted victims of disease, to palliate their torments by medicine, than to prevent them by regimen. The vulgar of all ranks are invariably sensual and indocile; yet I cannot but feel myself persuaded, that when the benefits of vegetable diet are math-

---

223 virtue] virtue,   *VND 1821.BEN*

223–25 and that those dogmas, . . .
        essential;] *omitted   1821.CLAX*

223–24 by . . . propensities,]
        apparently favourable to the
        intolerant and angry passions,
        VND

225 Christians] christians   *VND*

226 habits,]
        habits   *1821.CLA 1821.BEN 1834*

227 sons,] sons   *1834*

228 love.] love?   *1834 1839 1840*

231 mitigated,] mitigated   *1821.BEN*

233 healthfulness;] healthfulness,   *1840*
        madness,] madness   *VND 1840*

234 maniac,] maniac   *1834 1839 1840*

239 it; all] it. All   *VND*

240 perfect; the] perfect. The   *VND*

243 truth,] truth   *1834 1839 1840*

244 system.] system!   *1840*
        subject] subject,   *VND*

245 an] and   *1821.BEN*

246 benevolent] benevolent,   *VND*

250 indocile;] in docile;   *1834*

251 persuaded,]
        persuaded   *1834 1839 1840*
        that] that,   *1834 1839 1840*

ematically proved; when it is as clear, that those who live naturally are exempt from premature death, as that nine is not one, the most sottish of mankind will feel a preference towards a long and tranquil, contrasted with a short and painful life. On the average, out of sixty persons, four die in three years. Hopes are entertained that, in April 1814, a statement will be given, that sixty persons, all having lived more than three years on vegetables and pure water, are then *in perfect health.* More than two years have now elapsed; *not one of them has died;* no such example will be found in any sixty persons taken at random. Seventeen persons of all ages (the families of Dr. Lambe and Mr. Newton) have lived for seven years on this diet without a death, and almost without the slightest illness. Surely, when we consider that some of these were infants, and one a martyr to asthma now nearly subdued, we may challenge any seventeen persons taken at random in this city to exhibit a parallel case. Those who may have been excited to question the rectitude of established habits of diet, by these loose remarks, should consult Mr. Newton's luminous and eloquent essay.[6]

When these proofs come fairly before the world, and are clearly seen by all who understand arithmetic, it is scarcely possible that abstinence from aliments demonstrably pernicious should not become universal. In proportion to the number of proselytes, so will be the weight of evidence; and when a thousand persons can be produced, living on vegetables and distilled water, who have to dread no disease but old age, the world will be compelled to regard animal flesh and fermented liquors as slow but certain poisons. The change which would be produced by simpler habits on political economy is sufficiently remarkable. The monopolizing eater of animal flesh would no longer destroy his constitution by devouring an acre at a meal, and many

---

[6] Return to Nature, or Defence of Vegetable Regimen. Cadell, 1811.

253 nine is not one,] one is not nine, *1829.BRO 1834 1839 1840*

255 painful] painful, *1834 1839 1840*
    years.] years, *1821.CLA*

256 Hopes . . . in] In *VND*
    that,] that *1821.CLA 1821.BEN*
    April 14,] April 14 *1813 VND 1821.CLA 1821.BEN 1829.BRO*
    given,] given *1821.CLA 1821.BEN*

260 Dr.] Dr *1829.BRO*

261 Mr.] Mr *1829.BRO*
    diet] diet, *VND*
    death,] death *VND*

262 Surely,] Surely *VND 1840*

263 asthma] asthma, *1829.BRO 1834 1839 1840*

265 Those] Those, *1834 1839 1840*

266 diet,] diet *1834 1839 1840*

267 essay.] essay [*begin new paragraph*] It is from that book, and from the conversation of its excellent and en-lightened author, that I have derived the materials which I here present to the public. *VND*

269 aliments] aliment *1834 1839 1840*

270 universal.] universal.— *1834 1839 1840*

271 evidence;] evidence, *VND*
    and] and, *1834 1839 1840*

272 produced,] produced *VND*

274 liquors] liquors, *VND*
    slow] slow, *VND*

275 economy] economy, *1821.CLA 1821.BEN*

loaves of bread would cease to contribute to gout, madness and apoplexy, in
the shape of a pint of porter, or a dram of gin, when appeasing the long-
protracted famine of the hard-working peasant's hungry babes. The quantity
of nutritious vegetable matter, consumed in fattening the carcase of an ox,
would afford ten times the sustenance, undepraving indeed, and incapable
of generating disease, if gathered immediately from the bosom of the earth.
The most fertile districts of the habitable globe are now actually cultivated
by men for animals, at a delay and waste of aliment absolutely incapable of
calculation. It is only the wealthy that can, to any great degree, even now, in-
dulge the unnatural craving for dead flesh, and they pay for the greater li-
cence of the privilege by subjection to supernumerary diseases. Again, the
spirit of the nation that should take the lead in this great reform, would in-
sensibly become agricultural; commerce, with all its vice, selfishness and cor-
ruption, would gradually decline; more natural habits would produce gen-
tler manners, and the excessive complication of political relations would be
so far simplified, that every individual might feel and understand why he
loved his country, and took a personal interest in its welfare. How would En-
gland, for example, depend on the caprices of foreign rulers, if she con-
tained within herself all the necessaries, and despised whatever they pos-
sessed of the luxuries of life? How could they starve her into compliance with
their views? Of what consequence would it be that they refused to take her
woollen manufactures, when large and fertile tracts of the island ceased to
be allotted to the waste of pasturage? On a natural system of diet, we should
require no spices from India; no wines from Portugal, Spain, France, or
Madeira; none of those multitudinous articles of luxury, for which every
corner of the globe is rifled, and which are the causes of so much individual
rivalship, such calamitous and sanguinary national disputes. In the history
of modern times, the avarice of commercial monopoly, no less than the am-
bition of weak and wicked chiefs, seems to have fomented the universal dis-
cord, to have added stubbornness to the mistakes of cabinets, and indocility
to the infatuation of the people. Let it ever be remembered, that it is the di-
rect influence of commerce to make the interval between the richest and the
poorest man wider and more unconquerable. Let it be remembered, that it
is a foe to every thing of real worth and excellence in the human character.

---

278 madness] madness,   *1821.CLA*
    1821.BEN 1834 1839 1840
280 hard-working]
    hard working   *1821.BEN*
287 licence] license   *1839*
288 privilege]
    privilege,   *1821.CLA 1821.BEN*

289 nation] nation,   *1834 1839 1840*
    take the lead] take lead   *VND*
290 selfishness] selfishness,   *1821.CLA*
    1821.BEN 1834 1839 1840
297 luxuries] luxuries,   *1834 1839*
298 be] be,   *VND*
310 man] man,   *1821.CLA 1821.BEN*
311 every thing]
    everything   *1829.BRO 1839 1840*

The odious and disgusting aristocracy of wealth is built upon the ruins of all
that is good in chivalry or republicanism; and luxury is the forerunner of a
barbarism scarce capable of cure. Is it impossible to realize a state of society,
where all the energies of man shall be directed to the production of his solid
happiness? Certainly, if this advantage (the object of all political specula-
tion) be in any degree attainable, it is attainable only by a community, which
holds out no factitious incentives to the avarice and ambition of the few, and
which is internally organized for the liberty, security and comfort of the
many. None must be entrusted with power (and money is the completest spe-
cies of power) who do not stand pledged to use it exclusively for the general
benefit. But the use of animal flesh and fermented liquors, directly militates
with this equality of the rights of man. The peasant cannot gratify these fash-
ionable cravings without leaving his family to starve. Without disease and
war, those sweeping curtailers of population, pasturage would include a
waste too great to be afforded. The labour requisite to support a family is far
lighter[7] than is usually supposed. The peasantry work, not only for them-
selves, but for the aristocracy, the army, and the manufacturers.

The advantage of a reform in diet is obviously greater than that of any
other. It strikes at the root of the evil. To remedy the abuses of legislation, be-
fore we annihilate the propensities by which they are produced, is to sup-
pose, that by taking away the effect, the cause will cease to operate. But the
efficacy of this system depends entirely on the proselytism of individuals, and
grounds its merits, as a benefit to the community, upon the total change of
the dietetic habits in its members. It proceeds securely from a number of par-

315

320

325

330

335

[7] It has come under the author's experience, that some of the workmen on an embankment in
North Wales, who, in consequence of the inability of the proprietor to pay them, seldom re-
ceived their wages, have supported large families by cultivating small spots of sterile ground by
moonlight. In the notes to Pratt's Poem, "Bread, or the Poor," is an account of an industrious
labourer, who, by working in a small garden, before and after his day's task, attained to an envi-
able state of independence.

---

312 wealth]
    wealth,   *VND 1821.CLA 1821.BEN*
314 realize] realise   *1839 1840*
316 Certainly,] Certainly   *VND*
317 community,]
    community   *1834 1839 1840*
318 holds out no]
    holds no   *1834 1839 1840*
319 organized] organised   *1839 1840*
    security] security,   *1821.CLA*
    1829.BRO 1834 1839 1840
    comfort] comfort,   *1834 1839*

320 entrusted] intrusted   *1829.BRO*
    1834 1839 1840
322 liquors,]
    liquors   *1829.BRO 1834 1839 1840*
Footnote 7. who,] who   *1840*
    Poem,] poem,   *1829.BRO*
    1834 1839 1840
    "Bread,] "Bread   *1840*
328 army,] army   *VND*
329 diet] diet,   *VND*
331–32 suppose, that]
    suppose, that,   *1834 1839 1840*
334 merits,] merits   *VND*

ticular cases to one that is universal, and has this advantage over the contrary
mode, that one error does not invalidate all that has gone before.

Let not too much however be expected from this system. The healthiest
among us is not exempt from hereditary disease. The most symmetrical, ath-
letic, and long-lived, is a being inexpressibly inferior to what he would have
been, had not the unnatural habits of his ancestors accumulated for him a
certain portion of malady and deformity. In the most perfect specimen of civ-
ilized man, something is still found wanting by the physiological critic. Can
a return to nature, then, instantaneously eradicate predispositions that have
been slowly taking root in the silence of innumerable ages?—Indubitably
not. All that I contend for is, that from the moment of the relinquishing all
unnatural habits, no new disease is generated; and that the predisposition to
hereditary maladies gradually perishes, for want of its accustomed supply. In
cases of consumption, cancer, gout, asthma, and scrofula, such is the invari-
able tendency of a diet of vegetables and pure water.

Those who may be induced by these remarks to give the vegetable system
a fair trial, should, in the first place, date the commencement of their prac-
tice from the moment of their conviction. All depends upon breaking
through a pernicious habit resolutely and at once. Dr. Trotter[8] asserts, that
no drunkard was ever reformed by gradually relinquishing his dram. Animal
flesh, in its effects on the human stomach, is analogous to a dram. It is simi-
lar to the kind, though differing in the degree, of its operation. The prose-
lyte to a pure diet must be warned to expect a temporary diminution of mus-
cular strength. The subtraction of a powerful stimulus will suffice to account
for this event. But it is only temporary, and is succeeded by an equable capa-
bility for exertion, far surpassing his former various and fluctuating strength.
Above all, he will acquire an easiness of breathing, by which such exertion is
performed, with a remarkable exemption from that painful and difficult

---

[8] See Trotter on the Nervous Temperament.

---

336 cases] cases, *VND*
338 much] much, *1821.CLA 1840*
    however] however, *1821.CLA 1840*
342 civilized] civilised *1839 1840*
343 wanting] wanting, *VND*
346 that from] that, from *1839 1840*
    the relinquishing] relinquishing
        1829.BRO 1834 1839 1840
348 maladies] maladies, *VND*
    perishes,] perishes *1834 1839 1840*
349 asthma,] asthma *VND*
352 trial,] trial *1834 1839 1840*
    should,]
        should *1821.CLA 1821.BEN*

    practice]
        practice, *1821.CLA 1821.BEN*
354 habit] habit, *VND*
    resolutely]
        resolutely, *1821.CLA 1821.BEN*
    Dr.] Dr *1829.BRO*
356 flesh,] flesh *VND*
    stomach,] stomach *VND*
357 to] in *VND*
358 a pure] pure *1834 1839 1840*
    diet] diet, *VND*
362 such] the same *VND*

panting now felt by almost every one, after hastily climbing an ordinary
mountain. He will be equally capable of bodily exertion, or mental applica-
tion, after as before his simple meal. He will feel none of the narcotic effects
of ordinary diet. Irritability, the direct consequence of exhausting stimuli,
would yield to the power of natural and tranquil impulses. He will no longer
pine under the lethargy of ennui, that unconquerable weariness of life, more
to be dreaded than death itself. He will escape the epidemic madness, which
broods over its own injurious notions of the Deity, and "realizes the hell that
priests and beldams feign." Every man forms as it were his god from his own
character; to the divinity of one of simple habits no offering would be more
acceptable than the happiness of his creatures. He would be incapable of
hating or persecuting others for the love of God. He will find, moreover, a
system of simple diet to be a system of perfect epicurism. He will no longer
be incessantly occupied in blunting and destroying those organs from which
he expects his gratification. The pleasures of taste to be derived from a din-
ner of potatoes, beans, peas, turnips, lettuces, with a dessert of apples, goose-
berries, strawberries, currants, raspberries, and, in winter, oranges, apples
and pears, is far greater than is supposed. Those who wait until they can eat
this plain fare with the sauce of appetite will scarcely join with the hypocriti-
cal sensualist at a lord-mayor's feast, who declaims against the pleasures of
the table. Solomon kept a thousand concubines, and owned in despair that
all was vanity. The man whose happiness is constituted by the society of one
amiable woman, would find some difficulty in sympathizing with the disap-
pointment of this venerable debauchee.

I address myself not only to the young enthusiast, the ardent devotee of
truth and virtue, the pure and passionate moralist, yet unvitiated by the con-
tagion of the world. He will embrace a pure system, from its abstract truth,
its beauty, its simplicity, and its promise of wide-extended benefit; unless cus-
tom has turned poison into food, he will hate the brutal pleasures of the

365

370

375

380

385

390

---

364 one,] one   *1834 1839 1840*
369 ennui,] *ennui,   1821.CLA 1821.BEN*
    life,] life   *1834 1839*
370 to be] *omitted   VND*
    madness,] madness   *1834 1839 1840*
    which] that   *VND*
371 "realizes] "realises   *1839 1840*
373 habits]
    habits,   *VND 1821.CLA 1821.BEN*
377 organs] organs,   *VND*
379 lettuces,] lettice,   *VND*
    dessert] desert   *1821.BEN*
380 and,] and   *VND*
    apples] apples,   *1821.CLA 1821.BEN*
      1829.BRO 1834 1839 1840

382 fare] fare,   *VND*
    appetite] appetite,   *VND*
383 lord-mayor's] lord mayor's   *VND*
385 man] man,   *1834 1839 1840*
386 sympathizing]
    sympathising   *1839 1840*
388 only to the young enthusiast,]
    to the young enthusiast only,
      1839 1840
    enthusiast,] enthusiast: *VND*
389 virtue,] virtue;   *VND*
390 system,] system   *1834 1839 1840*

chace by instinct; it will be a contemplation full of horror and disappoint-
ment to his mind, that beings capable of the gentlest and most admirable
395   sympathies, should take delight in the death-pangs and last convulsions of
dying animals. The elderly man, whose youth has been poisoned by intem-
perance, or who has lived with apparent moderation, and is afflicted with a
variety of painful maladies, would find his account in a beneficial change
produced without the risk of poisonous medicines. The mother, to whom the
400   perpetual restlessness of disease, and unaccountable deaths incident to her
children, are the causes of incurable unhappiness, would on this diet expe-
rience the satisfaction of beholding their perpetual healths and natural play-
fulness.[9] The most valuable lives are daily destroyed by diseases, that it is dan-
gerous to palliate and impossible to cure by medicine. How much longer will
405   man continue to pimp for the gluttony of death, his most insidious, im-
placable, and eternal foe?

[9] See Mr. Newton's book. His children are the most beautiful and healthy creatures it is possible
to conceive; the girls are perfect models for a sculptor; their dispositions are also the most gentle
and conciliating; the judicious treatment, which they experience in other points, may be a cor-
relative cause of this. In the first five years of their life, of 18,000 children that are born, 7,500
die of various diseases; and how many more of those that survive are not rendered miserable by
maladies not immediately mortal? The quality and quantity of a woman's milk are materially in-
jured by the use of dead flesh. In an island near Iceland, where no vegetables are to be got, the
children invariably die of tetanus, before they are three weeks old, and the population is sup-
plied from the main land.—Sir G. Mackenzie's Hist. of Iceland. See also Emile, chap. i. pages
53, 54, 56.

---

393 chace] chase   *1821.CLA 1829.BRO*
        1834 1839 1840
      chaste   *1821.BEN*
394 beings] beings,   *1834 1839 1840*
398 change]
      change,   *1821.CLA 1821.BEN*
399 mother,] mother   *1840*
401 children,] childeren,   *1834*
402 healths] health   *1821.CLA*
      1821.BEN 1829.BRO 1834 1839
      1840
403 diseases,] diseases   *1839 1840*
Footnote 9. Mr.] Mr   *1829.BRO*
      conceive;] conceive: *1840*
      conciliating;]
        conciliating: *1821.BEN*
      treatment,] treatment
        1821.CLA 1821.BEN 1839
        1840
      points,] points   *1839 1840*
      18,000] 18000   *VND*
      diseases;] dieases;   *1834*
        diseases,   *1840*

are not] are   *1821.CLA*
      1821.BEN 1839 1840
mortal?] mortal!   *1839 1840*
milk] milk,   *VND*
island] island,   *1821.CLA*
      1821.BEN
to] t   *VND*
tetanus,]
      tetanus   *1834 1839 1840*
404 palliate]
      palliate,   *1821.BEN 1839 1840*
  cure] cure,   *1839 1840*
406 eternal] eternal,   *1834 1839 1840*
      foe?] foe? [*begin new paragraph*] The
      proselyte to a simple and natural
      diet who desires health, must from
      the moment of his conversion
      attend to these rules—NEVER TAKE
      ANY SUBSTANCE INTO THE STOMACH
      THAT ONCE HAD LIFE. DRINK NO
      LIQUID BUT WATER RESTORED TO
      ITS ORIGINAL PURITY BY
      DISTILLATION.   *VND*

Ἀλλὰ δράκοντας ἀγρίους καλεῖτε καὶ παρδάλεις καὶ λέοντας, αὐτοὶ δὲ μια-
φονεῖτέ εἰς ὠμότητα καταλιπόντες ἐκείνοις οὐδέν. ἐκείνοις μὲν ὁ φόνος τροφή,
ὑμῖν δὲ ὄψον ἐστίν.

*   *   *   *   *   *   *   *   *   *   *   *   *

Ὅτι γὰρ οὐκ ἔστιν ἀνθρώπῳ κατὰ φύσιν τὸ σαρκοφαγεῖν, πρῶτον μὲν ἀπὸ   410
τῶν σωμάτων δηλοῦται τῆς κατασκευῆς. Οὐδὲν γὰρ ἔοικε τὸ ἀνθρώπου σῶμα
τῶν ἐπὶ σαρκοφαγίᾳ γεγονότων, οὐ, χρωπότης χείλους, οὐκ ὀξύτης ὄνυχος οὐ
τραχύτης ὀδόντων πρόσεστιν, οὐ κοιλίας εὐτονία, καὶ πνεύματος θερμότης,
τρέψαι, καὶ κατεργάσασθαι δυνατὴ τὸ βαρὺ καὶ κρεῶδες; ἀλλ' αὐτόθεν ἡ φύσις
τῇ λειότητι τῶν ὀδόντων, καὶ τῇ σμικρότητι τοῦ στόματος, καὶ τῇ μαλακότητι   415
τῆς γλώσσης, καὶ τῇ πρὸς πέψιν ἀμβλύτητι τοῦ πνεύματος, ἐξόμνυται τὴν
σαρκοφαγίαν. Εἰ δὲ λέγεις πεφυκέναι σεαυτὸν ἐπὶ τοιαύτην ἐδωδήν, ὃ βούλει
φαγεῖν, πρῶτον αὐτύς ἀπόκτεινον. ἀλλ' αὐτός, διὰ σεαυτοῦ μὴ χρησάμενος
κοπίδι, μηδὲ τυμπάνῳ μηδὲ πελέκει. ἀλλά ὡς λύκοι, καὶ ἄρκτοι, καὶ λέονες
αὐτοὶ ὡς ἐσθίουσι φονεύουσιν, ἄνελε δήγματι βοῦν, ἢ σώματι σῦν, ἢ ἄρνα ἢ   420
λαγωὸν διάρρηξον, καὶ φάγε προσπεσὼν ἔτι ζῶντος ὡς ἐκεῖνα.

<table>
<tr><td>407 δράκοντας] δρακώντας 1813</td><td>πρὸς] πρός 1813</td></tr>
<tr><td>ἀγρίους] ἀγριούς 1813</td><td>ἀμβλύτητι] ἀμβλύτητι   1813</td></tr>
<tr><td>καλεῖτε] καλεῖτε 1813</td><td>τοῦ] του 1813</td></tr>
<tr><td>παρδάλεις] παρδελέις 1813</td><td>πνεύματος,] πνέυματος, 1813</td></tr>
<tr><td>αὐτοὶ δὲ] αὐτοὶδέ 1813</td><td>ἐξόμνυται] εξόμνυται 1813</td></tr>
<tr><td>408 ὠμότητα] ὠμοτητα 1813</td><td>417 σαρκοφαγίαν.] σαρκοφαγιὰν.   1813</td></tr>
<tr><td>ἐκείνοις] ἐκέινοις 1813</td><td>Εἰ] Ει 1813</td></tr>
<tr><td>ἐκείνοις] ἐκέινοις 1813</td><td>λέγεις] λεγείς 1813</td></tr>
<tr><td>μὲν] μέν 1813</td><td>τοιαύτην] τοιάυτην 1813</td></tr>
<tr><td>τροφή,] τροφὴ, 1813</td><td>ἐδωδήν,] ἐδώδην, 1813</td></tr>
<tr><td>409 ὑμῖν] ἡμῖν 1813</td><td>ὃ] ὅ 1813</td></tr>
<tr><td>410 γὰρ] γάρ 1813</td><td>418 φαγεῖν,] φαγεῖν, 1813</td></tr>
<tr><td>ἀνθρώπῳ] ανθρώπω 1813</td><td>ἀπόκτεινον.] απόκτεινον. 1813</td></tr>
<tr><td>φύσιν] φὺσιν 1813</td><td>αὐτός,] αὐτός, 1813</td></tr>
<tr><td>411 τῶν] των 1813</td><td>419 κοπίδι,] κοπίδη, 1813</td></tr>
<tr><td>σωμάτων] σωμάτων 1813</td><td>μηδὲ] μηδὲ 1813</td></tr>
<tr><td>κατασκευῆς.] κατασκεῦης.   1813</td><td>τυμπάνῳ] τυμπανω 1813</td></tr>
<tr><td>ἀνθρώπου] ἀνθρώπου 1813</td><td>μηδὲ] μηδὲ 1813</td></tr>
<tr><td>412 τῶν] των 1813</td><td>ἀλλά] ἀλλά 1813</td></tr>
<tr><td>ἐπὶ] επι 1813</td><td>λύκοι,] λύκοι, 1813</td></tr>
<tr><td>413 κοιλίας] κοιλίας 1813</td><td>420 αὐτοὶ] αὐτοί 1813</td></tr>
<tr><td>εὐτονία,] ευτονία, 1813</td><td>ἐσθίουσι] ἐσθιούσι 1813</td></tr>
<tr><td>πνεύματος] πνέυματος 1813</td><td>φονεύουσιν,] φὸνευοὺσιν,   1813</td></tr>
<tr><td>θερμότης,] θερμότης, 1813</td><td>ἢ] ἤ 1813</td></tr>
<tr><td>414 τὸ] τό 1813</td><td>ἢ] ἤ 1813</td></tr>
<tr><td>βαρὺ] βαρύ 1813</td><td>ἢ] ἤ 1813</td></tr>
<tr><td>ἀλλ'] ἀλλ' 1813</td><td>421 λαγωὸν] λαγῶον 1813</td></tr>
<tr><td>415 τῶν] των 1813</td><td>φάγε] φάγε 1813</td></tr>
<tr><td>στόματος,] σοματος, 1813</td><td>ζῶντος] ξῶντος 1813</td></tr>
<tr><td>416 γλώσσης,] γλώσσης, 1813</td><td></td></tr>
</table>

*   *   *   *   *   *   *   *   *   *   *   *   *

Ἡμεῖς δὲ οὕτως ἐν τῷ μιαιφόνῳ τρυφῶμεν, ὥστε ὄψον τὸ κρέας προσαγορεύομεν, εἶτα ὄψων πρὸς αὐτὸ τὸ κρέας δεόμεθα, ἀναμιγνύντες ἔλαιον, οἶνον, μέλι, γάρον, ὄξος, ἡδύσμασι Συριακοῖς, Ἀρραβικοῖς, ὥσπερ

425 ὄντως νεκρὸν, ἐνταφιάξοντες. Καὶ γὰρ ὅτως αὐτῶν διαλυθέντων καὶ μαλαχθέντων καὶ τρόπον τινὰ κρευσαπέυντων ἔργον ἐστὶ τὴν πέψιν κρατῆσαι καὶ διακρατηθείσης δὲ δεινὰς βαρύτητας ἐμποιεῖ καὶ νοσώδεις ἀπεψίας.

*   *   *   *   *   *   *   *   *   *   *   *   *

Οὕτω τὸ πρῶτον ἄγριόν τι ζῷον ἐβρώθη καὶ κακοῦργον εἶτα ὄρνις τις ἢ ἰχθὺς εἵλκυστο· καὶ γεύομενον, οὕτο καὶ προμελετῆσαν ἐν ἐκείνοις τὸ νικοῦν ἐπὶ

430 βοῦν ἐργάτην ἦλθε, καὶ τὸ κοσμον πρόβατον καὶ τὸν οἰκουρὸν ἀλεκτρυόνα· καὶ καταμικρὸν οὕτο τὴν ἀπληστίαν τονώσαντες, ἐπίσφαγὰς ἀνθρώπων, καὶ φόνους καὶ πολέμους προῆλθον.

Πλουτ. περι της σαρκοφαγιας.

---

422 Ἡμεῖς] Ἡμεῖς *1813*
   τῷ] τῷ *1813*
   μιαιφόνῳ] μιαιφὄνῳ *1813*
423 προσαγορεύομεν,]
     προσαγορὲυομεν, *1813*
   πρὸς] πρὸς *1813*
   αὐτὸ] ἀυτὸ *1813*
   δεόμεθα,] δέομεθα, *1813*
424 οἶνον,] οἶνον, *1813*
   μέλι,] μέλι, *1813*
   γάρον,] γὰρον, *1813*
   ἡδύσμασι] ἡ δύσμασι *1813*
425 νεκρὸν,] νεκρὸν, *1813*
   ἐνταφιάζοντες.] ἐνταφίαξοντες. *1813*
   αὐτῶν] αὑτων *1813*
   διαλυθέντων] διαλυθέντων *1813*
426 τινὰ] τινὰ *1813*

427 δεινὰς] δεινάς *1813*
   βαρύτητας] βαρύτητας *1813*
   νοσώδεις] νοσῶδεις *1813*
   ἀπεψίας.] απεψιάς. *1813*
428 ζῷον] ξῶον *1813*
   ἢ] ἤ *1813*
   ἰχθὺς] ἰχθύς *1813*
429 εἵλκυστο·] ἔιλκυστο· *1813*
   ἐν] εν *1813*
   ἐκείνοις] ἐκείνοις *1813*
   ἐπὶ] ἐπι *1813*
430 πρόβατον] πρὸβατον *1813*
   οἰκουρὸν] οἰκουρον *1813*
   ἀλεκτρυόνα·] ἀλεκτρὺονα· *1813*
431 ἀπληστίαν] ἀπληστιάν *1813*
   ἀνθρώπων,] ανθρωπων, *1813*
   φόνους] φονους *1813*
432 πολέμους] πολὲμους *1813*

COMMENTARIES

Queen Mab.

BY

PERCY BYSSHE SHELLEY.

London:
PRINTED AND PUBLISHED BY W. CLARK,
201, STRAND.
1821.

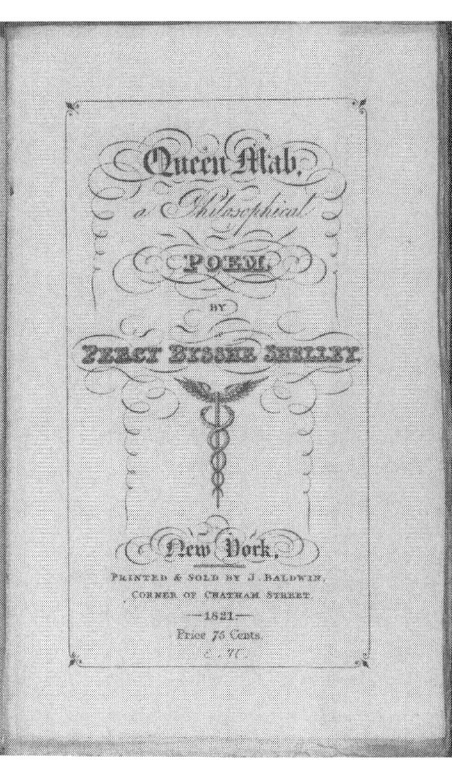

QUEEN MAB,

WITH NOTES.

BY

PERCY BYSSHE SHELLEY.

VERBATIM FROM THE ORIGINAL EDITION.

LONDON:
PRINTED AND PUBLISHED BY
JOHN ASCHAM, 71, CHANCERY LANE, HOLBORN; AND SOLD BY
JAMES PATTIE, 16, HIGH STREET, BLOOMSBURY, AND ALL
BOOKSELLERS IN TOWN AND COUNTRY.
1834.

The Esdaile Notebook

The Esdaile Notebook and Other Textual Authorities

Wherever the dearth of contemporary documentation about PBS's efforts to prepare the *Esdaile* "Poems" for publication leaves gaps in our knowledge, we must utilize the primary evidence provided by the Esdaile Notebook (**EN**), the physical copybook in the Pforzheimer Collection at the New York Public Library (Pfz), that is the major textual authority for our copy-text. **EN**—or simply "the Notebook"—contains the poems and notes to which we refer as *The Esdaile Notebook* or *Esd*. **EN,** originally a blank copybook, is half-bound in red roan and marbled paper boards, the covers of which measure ca. 18.6 × 12.2 centimeters and the leaves of which measure ca. 18.1 × 11.3 cm (= ca. 7.1 × 4.4 inches). Two of its original 140 leaves are now represented only by stubs. Each page is "linear paper," ruled with 22 faint blue horizontal "water-lines" (see E. J. Labarre, *Dictionary and Encyclopaedia of Paper and Papermaking*, 2nd ed. [Amsterdam: Swets & Zeitlinger, 1952], 146, 231) that enabled the user to write in straight lines. More detailed descriptions of the Notebook are found in both Cameron's diplomatic transcription in *SC* IV (924) and Reiman's facsimile in Volume I of *MYR: Shelley* (xxvii–xxviii). Our Commentary also cites not only the published editions of *Esd,* abbreviated by their dates of publication in italics, and the letters and loose MSS that contain other versions of the poems in *Esd* or fragments thereof, identified by the library where each now resides, but also two notebooks in which Edward Dowden transcribed the poems found in **EN,** which we identify by letter abbreviations beginning "MS ED." All these sources are identified and their abbreviations are specified in the lists on pages xxxviii ff., although for clarity when discussing these editions and documents, the names of their transcribers or editors often appear as well.

Late in 1812 and during the first few months of 1813, PBS collected the best of his early short poems in **EN,** arranging them in the order in which he hoped to publish them and planning to use **EN** itself as an intermediate fair copy from which he could later prepare a more polished version of *Esd* for the press, after which **EN** presumably would have served as his safekeeping copy. (He was certainly conscious of his need to retain such a copy to safeguard his writings because of John Stockdale's action in holding hostage his

MS in Dublin as collateral for his debt; see "The Shelleys' Adventures" in the Editorial Overview.)

Kenneth Neill Cameron, while introducing *1964*, suggests a division of the poems in ***Esd*** based on PBS's references to those of more recent date and to "younger" poems. In distinguishing between these two groups (*1964*, 7–17), Cameron relies heavily on the dates that PBS himself affixed when he copied the poems, but since—as Cameron himself mentions (10)—PBS's announced dates of composition are often fictitious (as the redating of his composition of such mature writings such as ***Julian and Maddalo, Peter Bell the Third,*** and ***Hellas*** demonstrates), independent verification of these dates is desirable wherever evidence exists. In the absence of strong external evidence, such as the mention or quotation of the poem in a datable letter or a clear poetic reference in it to a person, place, event, or book that we know PBS could not have been familiar with before a certain date, we exercise caution in dating these poems. Moreover, Cameron's general distinctions by dates of composition and the valiant attempt by Matthews and Everest in *1989* to interfile the individual poems in **EN** chronologically among PBS's other poetry (also of uncertain date) have limited value for studying his artistic development, because whenever each of these poems in ***Esd*** may have been first drafted, we know that PBS (like most poets) almost invariably made substantive changes from his first version while recopying and that he thoroughly revised at least some of them as he gathered, arranged, and copied them for publication from late November or December 1812 into the summer of 1813. So aside from the few poems at the end of **EN** that HWS entered from PBS's earlier drafts in her possession, the poems in the Notebook, whatever the dates of their conception, represent his ideas and feelings and are expressed with the poetic skill and judgment that he possessed by or after November 1812. They are thus roughly contemporaneous with his published text of ***Queen Mab*** (***QM***), although the form in which they survive was not prepared as carefully as the press copy for that poem and their Text is, therefore, less polished and firmly fixed than that of ***QM*** and other poems that PBS fully prepared for the public.

Although the question has been debated, we are convinced that **EN** was not a MS that PBS intended to send to the printer. Cameron strongly supported exactly this view after his intensive study that led to the first comprehensive edition of ***Esd,*** writing there:

. . . in the first place, one would normally send loose sheets rather than a notebook to a printer. Secondly, this particular notebook would have been most unsuitable for a printer. It is comparatively small and nearly every page of writing is crowded, leaving almost no margins, so that a printer would have had little space in which to mark up the copy.

. . . That the poems were not originally copied as a gift for Harriet is indicated by their casual punctuation, lack of apostrophes, and so on, which stand in sharp con-

trast to the two poems which apparently were copied into the book for her—...
namely, a sonnet to Ianthe and one to Harriet, both of which are fully punctuated.
The probability is that the book was originally compiled as a guarantee against loss of
manuscripts. If this was indeed Shelley's motive, the poems must have been
copied ... by about the middle of April 1813 or earlier. (*1964, 24–25*).

Later, however, Cameron changed his mind, reviewing the arguments briefly
in *SC* IV, where he wrote, "the editor now leans toward the ... hypothesis ...
that the Esdaile Notebook was the manuscript sent by Shelley to Hookham
(and returned by Hookham to Shelley). Possibly Shelley did not intend this
volume to go to the printer and if Hookham had accepted the poems would
have had them recopied" (*SC/*IV, 911–12).

Though Cameron's arguments (on both sides of the question) are logical,
he had never examined the bulk of PBS's poetic MSS at the Bodleian Library
and was, therefore, unaware how the poet usually reworked his poems from
rough drafts (often composed in small notebooks) into intermediate fair
copies—often using notebooks reserved for this purpose. During his first re-
copying from his often chaotic drafts, PBS made extensive revisions and not
infrequently left passages unfinished as, Cameron notes, he did in **Henry and
Louisa** in **Esd.** In PBS's later years MWS, Claire Clairmont, and Edward Wil-
liams (all of whom had clearer handwriting than he) served as amanuenses
for many of his major works. PBS would then go over their transcriptions,
make small revisions, sometimes add notes, and fill any gaps that he had left
in the intermediate holograph copy. These transcriptions might be made
either on loose sheets or in larger notebooks, the pages of which he would fi-
nally disbind and renumber for the printer: the former practice is found in
the press copy MSS of **Peter Bell the Third, The Mask of Anarchy,** and **A Defence
of Poetry;** Tatsuo Tokoo has shown that the latter practice was operative in the
press copy of **Laon and Cythna** (**L&C;** see *BSM* VIII, xiii–xiv), and Charles E.
Robinson has found that MWS, working with PBS, also prepared her press
copy of *Frankenstein* in large notebooks that were later disbound (see *MYR:
Shelley* IX, xxxv). In *CPPBS* I, we deduced that the MS from which the two ver-
sions of **The Wandering Jew** (**WJ**) were transcribed for publication in *Edin-
burgh Literary Journal* (1829) and *Fraser's Magazine* (1831) was also in the
form of a bound book (though it was not unusual for owners of MSS and
proof sheets in that period to have them bound for safekeeping). It remains
uncertain whether or not the **WJ** notebook was PBS's intermediate copy, in
which he initially revised the fourth canto when his later press copy was tem-
porarily lost, or whether he recovered and revised that copy before it finally
came into the possession of the Ballantyne brothers (see *CPPBS* I, 189–95).
After checking, disbinding (if necessary), and sending to press the final MS
of his work—whether it was a holograph or a transcription corrected by
him—PBS generally kept his holograph intermediate fair copy as a safe-

keeping copy, in case the MS sent to press should go astray, as had *WJ,* or be held hostage by a printer such as John Stockdale.

EN, in which most of the poems are not only underpunctuated but often so carelessly written as to be all but illegible, was meant to be an intermediate arrangement of poems from various drafts written in different periods of PBS's early life that he revised and assembled *prior* to preparing a polished final copy. If PBS had wished to show **EN** to Hookham, he did not need to *send* it away to London. By the time he finished copying into the Notebook the fifty-one poems that he ultimately planned to publish, he had already returned to London, where he lived a few months before spending some time at Bracknell with Harriet de Boinville and her circle, from which (Godwin's Journal shows), he sporadically returned to the capital. Thus, the poet need not have left **EN** with Hookham for an extended period, but he could instead have carried the Notebook to Hookham's bookshop at 15 Old Bond Street to ascertain whether or not the bookseller wished to publish these poems, either by going over its contents with his friend or leaving it with him one morning and picking it up it later the same day. Unless Hookham or another bookseller showed an interest in publishing the volume, PBS had no reason to polish and retranscribe the nearly three thousand lines of poetry and the notes that it contains.

After the Shelleys returned to England from Dublin, besides seeking money to live on, to pay his debts, and to help Godwin pay down his massive debts, PBS devoted his efforts to completing the notes for *QM* and having that poem printed. During the production of his major poem, PBS seems to have argued with Hookham, the unidentified printer, or both concerning the possible legal consequences of publishing *QM,* for, contrary to the law, the poet ultimately placed his own name as its printer and his father-in-law's address on the colophon. This provided an additional reason why he could not increase the risk of prosecution by publishing *Esd,* an equally seditious collection of very personal poems that could easily be proved to be his.

Reviewing the sequence of events leading up to Hookham's—or perhaps PBS's own—decision not to publish *Esd* thus forces us to conclude that there probably never existed a polished press copy of the poems in **EN.** If one had been executed, it might have been copied principally by HWS, whose handwriting—though idiosyncratic in some respects, as can be seen from her recently identified Commonplace Book (MS WSU)—was more regular than PBS's scrawl. This judgment obviates both Cameron's doubts in *SC* IV about whether **EN** or a second transcription was to serve as press copy and Reiman's argument in the Introduction to the facsimile (*MYR: Shelley* I, xvii–xx) that such a press copy was probably written on loose sheets. We agree, however, with the judgment advanced by Cameron in *1964* and reaffirmed by Reiman in *MYR: Shelley* I that PBS never meant **EN** to serve as printers' copy: it was, rather, first intended as an intermediate fair copy and safekeeping copy of his poems and, later, as a gift to Harriet, once the decision had been made not to publish the "Poems."

Subsequent History of the Notebook and Publication of the Poems in **EN**

EN, the notebook in which these early poems survive, is called the "Esdaile Notebook" because, having remained in HWS's possession when PBS eloped with MWS, it descended to Ianthe Shelley, daughter of HWS and PBS. Ianthe Shelley in 1837 married Edward Jeffries Esdaile, and when she died in 1876 she bequeathed the Notebook to her daughter Eliza Margaret Esdaile, who left it for safekeeping with her brother Charles Edward Jeffries Esdaile. On Eliza Margaret's death in 1930, the Notebook went to her niece Lettice A. Worrell (née Esdaile), who sold it at a Sotheby's auction in London on 2 July 1962. There it was purchased by the Carl and Lily Pforzheimer Foundation on behalf of the Carl H. Pforzheimer Library (Pfz), then a private research library located at 42nd Street and Madison Avenue in New York. The poems in **EN,** expeditiously edited by Kenneth Neill Cameron and the *Shelley and his Circle* staff, first appeared in their entirety as *The Esdaile Notebook: A Volume of Early Poems by Percy Bysshe Shelley* (New York: Alfred A. Knopf, 1964); Faber and Faber in London reset the type and published a slightly revised version of this edition during the following year (also bearing the 1964 copyright date). Although we use this revised London edition (*1964B*) for its corrected details (while weeding out its new errors), when referring to the common history and features of the two versions, we designate both states of the text as simply *1964*.

In a series of tables at the back of *1964* (corrected and extended in *1964B*), Cameron listed the lines found in **Esd** that had been previously published either from **EN** or from other manuscript sources (such as PBS's letters to Thomas Jefferson Hogg). Although Hogg had earlier published in his *Life of Percy Bysshe Shelley* (*1858*) versions of a number of the poems in **Esd** from letters and other manuscripts that PBS had sent or given him, the first record of any of the fifty-eight poems entering the Shelley canon directly from **EN** into a collection of PBS's poetry came later when Rossetti included in his edition of *1870* the first thirteen lines from *"How eloquent are eyes!"* (II, 530), which he says in a note were "extracted by Mr. Garnett from a MS. book" (II, 601), though Hogg had earlier published seven different lines from that poem from the version in PBS's letter to him of 18–19 June 1811 (Hogg, *Life of PBS*, ed. Wolfe I, 398). When in *1876*, Harry Buxton Forman's Library Edition, there appeared nine lines (5–13) of *To Harriet ("It is not blasphemy")* (IV, 359), Forman gave as his authority "Mr. Rossetti from a transcript of Mr. Garnett's, taken from one of the Boscombe MSS." Because there is no MS containing this poem among those known to have been at Boscombe Manor, Richard Garnett, Rossetti, or Forman must have misremembered or obfuscated its actual documentary source.

These references make clear that Garnett, who in addition to his duties at the British Museum acted as an advisor to Sir Percy Florence and Lady Shelley, had also gained access to the Esdaile family's Notebook before 1870. His knowledge of **EN** is confirmed in a letter he wrote to Dowden on 24 December 1883, in which he promises to send Dowden a notebook containing Shelleyan materials, including two sonnets from PBS to HWS of "July and Sept. 1813" that "were given me by a lady, formerly a governess in the Esdaile family, who had copied them from a MS. in Mr. E's possession. She had made no other copies" (*Letters about Shelley*, 87–88). Either through that person or by contacting directly Ianthe Shelley Esdaile's elder son Charles E. J. Esdaile, Garnett had by 1883 received copies of other poems by Shelley.

Later Dowden borrowed **EN** from Charles Esdaile and gained his permission to transcribe it and to publish biographical passages from the poems in his *Life of Percy Bysshe Shelley* (*1886;* see Louise Schutz Boas, "Edward Dowden, the Esdailes, and the Shelleys," *Notes & Queries*, n.s., 210 [May–June 1965], 163–65, 227–31). While the Notebook was in his possession, Dowden transcribed the contents into two copybooks of his own and then lent this transcription to Garnett. In those two copybooks, each man added some marginal notes on the poems. The first of these two transcript books, containing poems #1–#32, is located in the Pforzheimer Collection, New York Public Library (MS ED-Pfz); the second, containing poems #33–#58, which remained with Dowden's papers in the library of Trinity College, Dublin, is here designated MS ED-TCD. In his *Life of Percy Bysshe Shelley*, Dowden quoted for the first time some 379 of the nearly 3,000 poetic lines in **EN** (see Appendix A: Poetic Forms in *The Esdaile Notebook*) to illustrate PBS's activities and moods during his early years. Next, Bertram Dobell included the **EN** text of **The wandering Jew's soliloquy** in an appendix to his edition of PBS's **The Wandering Jew** for the Shelley Society (1887), followed by this note: "I have to thank C. J. E. Esdaile, Esq., for permission to publish the above poem, which now appears in print for the first time." Also in 1887, Forman and T. J. Wise, in the first of their false-imprint limited editions entitled *Poems and Sonnets* (supposedly issued in thirty copies in Philadelphia by "Charles Alfred Seymour"), surreptitiously collected and reprinted the passages of poetry from **EN** that had appeared in Dowden's biography (see Reiman's Introduction to *MYR: Shelley* I, xx–xxi and xxv.) Although this piracy was generally ignored, Dowden's *Life of Percy Bysshe Shelley* (*1886*) had made available to those interested in PBS's writings enough of the contents of the Notebook to whet the curiosity of later scholars.

Dowden himself omitted the poems and fragments from **EN** in his own edition of PBS's poetry for Macmillan (*1890*), explaining there that "Mr. Esdaile, who kindly allowed me to print certain poems of biographical interest in my *Life of Shelley,* has expressed his desire that they should not now be reprinted. It was, as he believes, the wish of Shelley's daughter Ianthe that the poems in this manuscript volume should not be included in an edition of her father's poetical works" (*1890,* xxxvi). The new materials from *1886* were also omitted by Forman from his Aldine Edition (*1892F*), perhaps for copyright reasons. Thus, the American George Edward Woodberry was the first editor to include the poems and fragments that appeared in Dowden's *Life* as part of PBS's poetic œuvre in his Centenary Edition (*1892W*). And even after the appearance of PBS's **Translation of The Marsellois Hymn** in André Koszul's *La jeunesse de Shelley* (*1910K*) and the publication of further poems and fragmentary quotations from **EN** in Neville Rogers's *Shelley at Work* (first edition 1956) and (through Rogers) in Louise Schutz Boas's *Harriet Shelley* (*1962BOAS*), some two-thirds of the poetry in the Notebook still remained unpublished before Cameron's edition of 1964.

Before **EN** was sold at auction, Rogers had been working on an edition of the poems from a photocopy of the Notebook that Oxford University Press had made with Mrs. Worrall's permission. In 1962, Rogers asked Donald H. and Mary W. Reiman to check his transcription of the poems, which they did at Durham, North Carolina, that summer at about the same time that the Notebook was sold at auction. In 1966, two years after Cameron's *editio princeps* appeared, Oxford published Rogers's more modest edition under the title *The Esdaile Poems* (*1966*). That text was later republished, with minor changes, in the first volume of Rogers's ill-fated *Complete Poetical Works of Percy Bysshe Shelley* (*1972*), without the additional evidence that Cameron and his colleagues had meanwhile provided in their diplomatic transcription of **EN** at the end of Volume IV of *Shelley and his Circle* (*SC*). A decade and a half later, Reiman produced a photofacsimile of **EN** as Volume I of *MYR: Shelley* (1985). Finally, in the first volume of the Longman edition of *The Poems of Shelley* (*1989*), G. M. Matthews and Kelvin Everest provided critically edited texts of all the Esdaile poems, collated with other authorities and generously annotated. In keeping with the chronological arrangement of the Longman editions, however, they interspersed them among other early poems, published and unreleased, according to the editors' estimate of each poem's putative date of composition. Nevertheless, in most cases they were obliged to use as their copy-texts the **EN** versions that PBS revised in 1812–13.

Shelley's Arrangement of the Poems

Though students of PBS's mature poetic volumes have demonstrated his skill in structuring them into artistic wholes, the handful of scholars who have seriously studied the poems of *Esd* have given relatively little attention to the aesthetic and rhetorical arrangement of the volume. We, therefore, devote considerable space in our Commentary to PBS's ordering of the poems in **EN,** which he grouped, not primarily by the chronology of their composition, but in a programmatic sequence designed to illustrate his roots, his ideals, and some major influences on the development of his feelings, thought, and art. This analysis appears in detailed discussions of these matters in headnotes to the individual poems or groups of related poems, where we can marshal the existing evidence about the relations among poems gathered in stylistic pairs or thematic clusters. Here, we suggest, the task that PBS set for himself in tracing his early life and thought is exactly the introspective Romantic quest for the origins of a poet's sense of self that Wordsworth, Coleridge, Southey, and Byron (as well as lesser poets, such as Henry Kirke White) had already undertaken in their early poems which PBS is known to have read and admired. As we hope to demonstrate, the commonplace notion that PBS's poems are split between personal introspective poems and objective political and social poems overlooks the strong connections between his aims for their combined effects. Such poems in *Esd* as ***To the Emperors of Russia and Austria . . .*** (#7), ***a Tale of Society as it is . . .*** (#14), and ***Zeinab and Kathema*** (#49) seem to us to have been written, not only to memorialize history or simply tell a tale, but to illustrate the poet's attitudes to such events in the world. Interspersed as they are among poems that reveal his ideals and feelings more directly, these "political poems" serve as parables that illuminate PBS's inner being by narrating his reactions to the social and political events around him.

In the earlier poems found in Volume I of **CPPBS,** PBS had tried to distance himself from such characters as Paulo in ***The Wandering Jew*** and Francis Ravaillac in the ***Epithalamium*** in ***Posthumous Fragments;*** and only modern knowledge of PBS's life, his later poetry, and the Romantic poetic milieu in which such poems were composed enables us to understand the degree to which PBS may have identified with aspects of these potentially unappealing characters. In the period of divided values and shifting sentiments bounded by the French Revolution and at least the end of the French wars in 1815, the Romantic poets, each of whom represented a minority perspective, found it imperative to declare their religious, moral, social, and political ideals and to show how and why they had arrived at their anti-establishment values. They did so by relating their inner feelings of isolation and estrangement from the majority of British society to the corruption and immorality of external social and political institutions and their leaders when measured against the Judeo-Christian and Classical ideals that those leaders claimed to be defending.

The "Minor Poems" that PBS tried to publish as a separate volume in 1813 were probably copied into **EN** in stages. At Tan-yr-allt (a Welsh name meaning, "under the precipice" or "under the wooded hill"), the house overlooking the town of Tremadoc where the Shelley household lived during the winter of 1812–1813, PBS began to copy his shorter poems into the blank note-book that he had purchased in London during his visit there in October–November 1812, but at that time he may have lacked the final texts of at least some of the poems, having left them with John Stockdale in Dublin. He did, however, possess at least rough drafts of most of the poems written while he stayed at Keswick and during his weeks in Dublin early in 1812, those that he wrote in Wales both before his elopement with HWS and after his return from the first Irish expedition, and the poems that he composed while in Devonshire and on the return trip through Wales before settling at Tremadoc.

The poems that PBS had in his possession when he began copying them at the end of 1812 or very early in 1813 are roughly those numbered in this edition *Esdaile* #2–#32. We do not know exactly what poems PBS had left with Stockdale in Dublin during his first visit there, and we cannot be sure that he actually retrieved those manuscripts, for most of the poems that he added to **EN** after the second excursion to Ireland were written before he left Field Place to visit Cwm Elan in 1811, and many other texts are based upon earlier versions that he had either sent or given to Hogg and to which he probably lacked access until he returned to London in April 1813 from that second Irish visit. The MSS he had left with Stockdale may also have been lost or destroyed by the Dublin printer or his sons, or returned to PBS and then destroyed by him because he feared that they were too subversive to be carried safely back through the British customs inspectors. Or possibly, after having spent another year studying poetry and writing many better poems, he concluded that the poems that he had left with Stockdale were (as he had described them to Hitchener on 26 January 1812) "an inferior production" with "some bad versification," being "only valuable to philosophical and reflecting minds" (*Letters* I, 239). It seems likely that PBS also possessed during this period one or more notebooks in which he had drafted some of his youthful poems upon which he eventually drew to add a few additional poems near the end of *Esd* and from which, after he had given **EN** to HWS and less than a year later eloped with Mary Godwin (MWS), HWS copied four of the five poems or fragments that were added to **EN** in her handwriting. This hypothetical notebook or notebooks (now lost) we designate as "Notebook X." (For the evidence concerning Notebook X, see the Commentary on the last five poems in **EN**, i.e., #54–#58.)

PBS arranged his poems in *Esd* to cohere, not on the basis of the chronology of their composition, but through their subject matter, thematic emphases, and stylistic harmony. Not that he gathered all poems of a common nature together in a single sequence, but he created a series of kinship groups of poems, sometimes related by the commonality of the issues they raise or the questions they ask, or at other times brought together to provide a variety of answers to those problems or queries. On the other hand, the contents and arrangement of the poems in **EN** may have been partly dictated by PBS's realization, about the time of the second trip to Ireland, that the Notebook was not a worthy companion to **QM** because it still contained too few poems of which he could be proud. Even so, examination of the structure of **Esd** also suggests that PBS arranged the poems that he initially felt were good enough to represent his early development in an order that makes sense both logically and aesthetically, just as when composing his mature poems he managed to develop aesthetic and thematic cohesion within the confines of complex generic and metrical forms. For example, he first copied into **EN** four poems (**Esd** #2–#5) that he wrote at Keswick in unrhymed lyric lines that show the influence of Southey in themes, metrics, and diction. These poems gave PBS a chance to experiment with and display other aspects of prosody, such as assonance, consonance, and poetic rhetoric unimpeded by the limitations of rhyme. From November 1811 onwards PBS also learned many facets of poetic technique by studying and emulating the subtle excellences in the poetry of Coleridge and Wordsworth—lessons that he illustrates in **Esd** #6 through #15. Then follow two poems treating historical or political issues that are as different as day and night, but each of which modifies the message of the other: first, **The Monarch's funeral** imagines the death of King George III and examines his life from the perspectives of his role as monarch and his nature as a human being, finding (as Byron was later to conclude in *The Vision of Judgment*) that the good qualities of the private man almost balanced his execrable record as King. Then in **To the Republicans of North America** PBS celebrates the uprising in Mexico against colonial oppression from such a distance that the victims of that bloody struggle (unlike George III, the neighbor and patron of Eton College) do not exist for him as individuals. That this juxtaposition of disparate perspectives—human empathy paired with abstract justice—is not accidental can be determined by comparing PBS's similar arrangements of neighboring poems later in **Esd** (e.g., #43 and #44), where the mood and message of each is enlightened by the quite different angle of vision in its companion piece.

    Esd #19–#23, mostly inward-looking poems, cohere in a different kind of thematic relationship. They were written at the Grove family's Welsh estate Cwm Elan in 1811, while PBS felt alone and depressed after the sundering of his engagement to Harriet Grove. The poet, in what we term his Graveyard Group, explores the significance of his life and his deep unhappiness vis-à-vis the depredations of constant change and inevitable death in Nature. Having lost the support and love of Harriet Grove, the one person who, he thought, understood and sympathized with him, PBS turns for comfort to the sublime and the beautiful elements in the surrounding mountain scenery, only to realize that all of Nature is also transient—that even the ancient mountain tops will eventually fall prey to the "scythe of time."

    Immediately after this group, which includes poems entitled or named by their *incipits* **To Death, "Dark Spirit of the desart rude,"** and **The Tombs,** PBS placed a poem, entitled simply *To Harriet* (*Esd* #24), addressed to HWS, his young bride, that provides his tentative answer to the threat of death and oblivion. It begins:

> It is not blasphemy to hope that Heaven
> More perfectly will give those nameless joys
> Which throb within the pulses of the blood
> And sweeten all the bitterness which Earth
> Infuses in the heaven-born soul . . . .

This, the first poem in the collection written in blank verse, is obviously related in form and language to *Tintern Abbey*. Like Wordsworth's poem, *To Harriet ("It is not blasphemy")* centers on the idea that each memory, experience, and anticipation of one's life—the past, as well as the present and future—changes for the better when one shares it with a loving and supportive companion. There follow four sonnets (#25–#28) that commemorate some happy and some uncomfortable moments that PBS and Harriet shared (with her sister and Elizabeth Hitchener) in their crusade to reform British society. Then, in another poem addressed *To Harriet ("Harriet! thy kiss to my soul is dear")*, PBS makes clear that he loves his wife, not primarily for her "fair form," but for their comradeship in the fight against tyranny, injustice, and misery, making this poem the nearest thematic analogue among the works of the English Romantics to the poems that Pablo Neruda addressed to his wife in *Los versos del Capitán* (*The Captain's Verses*, 1953).

Immediately following this biographically important poem, PBS placed *Mary to the Sea-Wind* (#30), a dramatic monologue in the voice of a young woman who asks the sea wind for news of her absent lover. Next he turns to a long critique of the ravages of ambition and war, seen in historical perspective (*A retrospect of Times of Old*); and then *The Voyage*—a long disjointed poem involving experiences from the poet's actual sea journeys, his anxieties as displayed in nightmares, and his social ideology. Though PBS likely salvaged these last two poems from rejected passages originally drafted for *QM*, *The Voyage* (#32) concludes with a passage that seems to relate the unhappy fate of Mary, her sailor husband, and their children in *Esd* #30. Though the sea wind had not harmed them, all fell victim to an unjust social order.

At this point, we believe, PBS had nearly run out of material for his collection of "Poems," except for two that he had set aside for his grand finale— the tragic love story of *Zeinab and Kathema* (#49), with its judgment on British imperialism abroad and social injustice in England, and *The Retrospect* (#50), his finest personal poem thus far, which focuses on the saving grace that HWS brought to him, rescuing his young life from loneliness and despair. But the poems already in the Notebook through *The Voyage* constituted a collection of slightly less than 1,600 lines, well short of his announced goal of having *Esd* match the length of *QM*, or about 2,800 lines of verse, and the best possible source for additional material was Hogg, to whom PBS had given and sent in letters a number of his better early poems. This may have been one reason that PBS maintained a correspondence with his Oxford friend-turned-betrayer and why, in April 1813 (after possibly punishing Hogg by engineering his fruitless trip to Dublin), PBS resumed his association with the pariah immediately after the Shelleys returned to London.

Of the poems that follow *The Voyage,* eight derive from or modify poems that PBS had sent to Hogg in whole or in part between October 1810 and June 1811, while four others—the *[Poems about Mary]* (*Esd* #37–#40)—may have been based on versions that PBS had given Hogg in November 1810 in copies that have not yet been located or are no longer extant. To show readers that these poems are the work of his youth, PBS entitled several of them with the years or precise dates of their composition, dates usually earlier than those he had originally confided to Hogg. Clearly he did not write complex metrical forms extemporaneously, as he had claimed in an attempt to impress his new Oxford acquaintance, although in some cases, when copying or revising a less impressive poem or fragment, he may have dated its composition earlier than it actually was to excuse its imperfections. In either case, had *Esd* been published and Hogg noted PBS's dating of those poems, he would have realized that PBS had lied to him, not only in attributing some of his less artistic poems to Elizabeth Shelley but also in feigning prodigious poetic mastery for himself. By presenting as spontaneous outpourings poems that he had written and polished long beforehand, PBS had so dazzled Hogg with his genius that (if we read the signs correctly) Hogg fell in love with PBS and, while avoiding overt homosexual advances, proceeded throughout the rest of his life to pursue only women who had been close to PBS—Elizabeth Shelley, HWS, MWS, and ultimately Jane Williams.

A few other early poems of less certain textual provenance conclude the collection that PBS arranged for publication, including a long fragment begun in Spenserian stanzas called *Henry and Louisa* (#46), which is one of the more notable anti-war poems in *Esd,* though its story is left half untold—almost in the manner of the first edition of Byron's *The Giaour,* a work (published on 5 June 1813) that PBS may have read before he transcribed the *H&L* fragment into **EN.** Next follows his *Translation of The Marsellois Hymn* (*La Marseillaise*), one stanza of which he had copied about mid-June 1811 into a letter to Edward Fergus Graham (*Letters* I, 107). The earliest poem in the collection, entitled *Written in very early youth* (#48), again evokes the "Graveyard School of Poetry" and shows that young PBS did not need to be jilted by his true love in order to feel very sorry for himself. It suggests that he had been threatening suicide for a long time. Then follow *Zeinab and Kathema* and *The Retrospect: Cwm Elan 1812,* the two poems mentioned above that, it seems likely, PBS had saved for the end of the volume. After he had copied and tallied the line total for *Zeinab and Kathema,* he removed two leaves from the Notebook (folios 78 and 79) and then reduced his tally of lines by forty-eight. We do not know what poetry was written on those missing leaves—not even whether the canceled lines represented one poem or more. At this point—perhaps as a substitution for the forty-eight lines that had occupied the two missing leaves of the Notebook—PBS added one other poem, ***The wandering Jew's soliloquy,*** as the fiftieth and final poem in the volume and (his line counts show) he then returned to a blank leaf left at the very beginning of **EN** and entered the dedication ***To Harriet ("Whose is the love that gleaming thro' the world")*** that he would ultimately revise and transfer to serve as the dedication for ***QM.***

Final Poems in the Notebook

After PBS—or those whom he asked to print and sell this collection—decided not to proceed with the publication of ***Esd,*** he copied into the Notebook two personal sonnets: one, dated September 1813, is addressed to his daughter Ianthe (born 23 June 1813) and the other ***Evening—To Harriet ("O thou bright Sun!"),*** dated at the end "July 31st 1813" but copied (as the subtitle line indicates) in September 1813. These entries strongly suggest that PBS gave the Notebook to Harriet by October of that year as a record of their life together, possibly with the expectation that if she read the poems as a group, she would understand better what he hoped for their union and why.

In commenting on the early poems in Volume I of ***CPPBS,*** we noted that PBS repeatedly expressed doubts or ambivalence about the quality of those apprentice poetic efforts, and many of his comments to Hitchener and Hookham about the "Minor Poems" in **EN** indicate comparable uneasiness. Although a comparable ambivalence is one possible reason for abandoning ***Esd,*** two other possible explanations present themselves. One was PBS's incapacity to subsidize its publication combined with his presumed reluctance to experience another rebuff from booksellers or printers, as well as the risk of legal consequences, after his friend Hookham proved unwilling to be recorded as the publisher of ***QM.*** But possibly more determinative for PBS's decision was the deterioration of his marital relations with HWS, suggested by four poems late in **EN** (#51–#54) and two other poems written to Cornelia Boinville Turner: ***"Thy dewy looks sink in my breast"*** (***CPPBS*** I, 145; 328–29) and ***Stanzas.—April, 1814*** (later published with ***Alastor***). We now believe it possible that, by the time PBS wrote into **EN** the personal sonnet commemorating the birth of his daughter Ianthe, he had lost much of his incentive to publish this group of poems in which he promises to love HWS throughout eternity. On the other hand, PBS spent much time and effort from late in 1811 at Keswick through early 1813 in London writing, revising, and seeking printers and booksellers willing to produce this book on his terms. For this reason, we consider *Esd* to be a volume (something like **Peter Bell the Third** or **Swellfoot the Tyrant**) that PBS would have been happy to see in print if it had appeared when the time was appropriate but which remained unpublished during his lifetime, in part, at least, due to external circumstances beyond his control—that is, insufficient funds and publishing censorship. The revised versions of the poems from *Esd* that PBS published in the **QM** volume and his inclusion of another in the **Alastor** volume were attempts to salvage usable material after he knew that *Esd* could not appear as a whole.

Sometime after PBS's elopement with Mary Godwin (MWS) on 28 July 1814, HWS copied into **EN** five additional poems or poetic fragments. Though at first editors believed that at least some of these poems were composed by HWS herself, G. M. Matthews, in "Who's Little Footsteps? Three Shelley Pieces Re-Addressed" (in *Evidence of the Imagination*) argued that all the poems in HWS's hand were copied from manuscripts by PBS left in her possession and that it was the confusion of some of the drafts from which she worked that prevented her transcriptions from being fully coherent. Because these final five poems were not part of PBS's original plan for *Esd* and are full of mysteries introduced by HWS's insertion of dates and comments, they cannot be explicated and judged with the same rigor we apply to PBS's own shaped volume. We have, therefore, edited them as "unreleased" poems, not intended by the poet for his contemporary public. As such, they still provide additional examples of PBS's early poems that can be useful to biographers and to critics of his development, and, if our analysis is valid, they provide some glimpses into personal moments between PBS and both HWS and Harriet Grove that contribute to PBS's overall purpose for the volume of revealing the course of his early life and thought. One might consider these five poems as a "Supplement" to the volume as a whole.

Harriet Westbrook Shelley's Commonplace Book

During the period in which PBS was collecting and revising his shorter poems and entering them into **EN,** HWS was transcribing poems and fragments of poetry by various other authors into a vellum-bound notebook (originally blank) that now contains poetry by various authors, all copied by HWS except for four short poems in the middle of the MS (folios 17v–18v). This notebook (MS WSU) came to light in the Division of Manuscripts, Archives, and Special Collections of Holland Library at Washington State University, having been acquired from the Shelley scholar Walter E. Peck in 1927, when he taught at Washington State. After we read a detailed account of the Commonplace Book published by F. S. Schwarzbach in *Huntington Library Quarterly* for Winter 1993 (56: 41–55), John Guido, then Director of Special Collections, kindly supplied us with a photocopy of MS WSU. Kainoa

Harbottle then transcribed it and supplemented Schwarzbach's notes and observations with internet research, enabling us to relate its contents to some specific poems by PBS in *Esd.*

HWS copied into MS WSU a variety of short poems, or selections from longer ones, that were, apparently, favorite verses culled from the recent and contemporary poetry that the Shelleys were reading, roughly between June 1811 and 1814. This time line is documented by three dates recorded in MS WSU: "June 22nd, <u>1811</u>," the date given for a poem that appears on folio 15 recto—either the date of the poem's composition or its publication in HWS's source; "June 1812," which is inscribed at the bottom of folio 2 recto—the first page containing quotations—and "Courier 1813" recorded as the newspaper source of a poem transcribed on 16 verso. The date June 1812, corroborated by the inscription "Harriet 1812." in HWS's hand on the flyleaf of the notebook, would suggest that she began copying this poetry in Wales after the Shelleys' first expedition to Ireland or at Ly(n)mouth, North Devonshire, where PBS completed and distributed *The Devil's Walk.* She used this notebook as what is termed a "Commonplace Book"—that is, a "book of literary passages, cogent quotations, occasional thoughts, or other memorabilia" (*Webster's Third New International Dictionary*). Her Commonplace Book, more specialized than most, is devoted almost entirely to quotations of poetry, some by leading poets of the previous century, including Thomson and Burns, but more by such contemporaries as Southey, Amelia Opie, John Wilson ("Christopher North"), Lord Strangford (i.e., Percy Clinton Sydney Smythe, 6th Viscount Strangford and 1st Baron Penshurst, 1780–1855), Bowles, Charlotte Smith, Montgomery, Moore, Kirke White, Richard Cumberland, and Byron. Also included are some poems published anonymously in contemporary periodicals, including (according to HWS's notes) the *Monthly Museum* and the Tory daily newspaper *The Courier.*

Schwarzbach correctly identified many of the poems (though he—lacking access to Chadwyck-Healey's *LION* and similar databases—mislabels a few that we have been able to identify), but several still remain unidentified. While MS WSU exhibits no clear thematic progression, its contents do touch on matters similar to those found in *Esd,* such as intense yet doomed love, bleak but occasionally hope-begetting landscapes (HWS was very interested in poems about winter), and alienated perspectives expressing doubt about both self and society. Additionally, HWS quoted—especially from the middle to the end of the Commonplace Book—poetry that treats women's status in society and the changes needed to improve that. The last three pages of MS WSU contain two poems on the value of women in both the public and the private sphere. As Schwarzbach suggests, the Commonplace Book may serve to measure the peaks and valleys of the couple's love kindling and then dwindling as the years of wandering drew to a close. Considering that the two poets most transcribed in MS WSU are Opie, who dominates the first half, and Byron, who is featured in the latter half, HWS's Commonplace Book can be read as a balance scale that shows how the weight of her attention shifted from one type of poetry to another. Though HWS copied many poems written by women and though several of the others treat themes likely to have been of special interest to her, many are also by poets known to have been favorites of PBS and to have exerted measurable influence on his poetry of these years.

During the period from mid-1811 until their return to London in April 1813, HWS and PBS spent most of their time together and shared their interests in ways that they did not later. PBS soon thereafter became friendly with the circle that included such liberal enthusiasts as John Frank Newton, his wife Cornelia Collins Newton, her sister Harriet Collins de Boinville, and Dr. William Lambe. Thus, we can take HWS's Commonplace Book to be a partial record of the Shelleys' poetic reading during roughly the same period in which PBS planned, wrote, and transcribed the poems of *Esd* into **EN.** In our discussions of individual poems in **EN,** we have tried to keep in mind the contents and tenor of the poems found in MS WSU, examining parallels and possible influences, positive or negative, while remembering that a good deal of PBS's writing reacts to sentiments or ideas that he found in the poems of others, but sometimes because he believed them to be fallacious or harmfully inappropriate. We have not exhausted the interactions between PBS's *Esd* poems and HWS's selected poems and passages, and the sequential arrangement of HWS's choices in the Commonplace Book may be found by other scholars to have its own story to tell.

The Esdaile Notebook Poems #1–#5

In notes to his manuscript transcription of *Esd,* Edward Dowden (who was Southey's biographer as well as Shelley's) commented on the unity of five poems in the Notebook (all in unrhymed lyric stanzas), identifying the classical antecedents of some of PBS's experiments and noting that some of the subject matter and phrasing for those five poems in *Esd* had been directly influenced by Southey's poems. First is the dedicatory poem **To Harriet,** which PBS added later on a leaf that he had left blank for this purpose. Below the heading "Poems" (the tentative title for this proposed volume) he had earlier copied four poems written in stanzas made up of unrhymed lines of varying lengths. **To Harriet (***"Whose is the love"***)**—composed in unrhymed quatrains—was clearly meant to harmonize with those other four unrhymed stanzaic poems. Among them they embody several of the recurring themes in the *Esd* volume. The dedication praises Harriet as the inspiration for a collection of poems that are <u>early wilding flowers</u>, the survival of which depends upon Harriet's sustaining love. Then follow **A sabbath Walk,** which advocates natural piety as an antidote to established religion and conventional religiosity; *The Crisis,* which warns that Britain is being destroyed by political tyranny and corruption; *Passion,* a poem invoking both the power and pleasures and the deleterious effects of what seems to represent both sexual passion and enthusiasm or an excess of emotion separated from reason; and finally another poem *To Harriet* (beginning "Never, O never, shall yonder Sun") in which PBS pledges fealty to his wife to the grave and beyond.

In these five unrhymed poems PBS also asserted his aesthetic agenda through their formal aspects, demonstrating that his muse would not be limited to a few conventional eighteenth-century forms, such as rhymed couplets, debased Miltonic blank verse, either the "false Pindaric" odes as popularized by Abraham Cowley or the more classically correct form of the ode employed by Thomas Gray, or the simple rhymed ballad-stanzas that flourished throughout the latter half of the eighteenth century and which by 1811–13 had become associated with Wordsworth's *Lyrical Ballads.*

To Harriet ("Whose is the love")   [Esd #1]

This Dedication to the *Esd* volume is only one of several poems addressed to Harriet Westbrook Shelley (HWS), whose symbolic importance grows through the first twenty-four poems in **EN.** Up through *The wandering Jew's soliloquy* (*Esd* #51), as Kenneth Neill Cameron observed (*1964,* 27–28), the numbers that PBS jotted to indicate the running counts of poetic lines in **EN** omit *To Harriet* from their totals; but PBS then added to his total those sixteen lines, demonstrating that he inserted the dedicatory poem after he had copied the texts of the fifty poems that were to make up the body of the *Esd* text.

Cameron, Rogers, and Reiman all assumed that after Thomas Hookham declined to publish *Esd,* PBS revised *To Harriet* and transferred it to *Queen Mab* (*QM*), to serve as the dedicatory poem for that volume. But in *1989* Matthews and Everest suggested that *To Harriet* was written first for *QM* and then revised when PBS copied it into *Esd.* They base their conjecture on PBS's early suggestion that he might try to publish *QM* and *Esd* in a single volume and on the assumption that the main text of *QM* was finished by mid-February 1813 and that the notes "were probably complete when printing began three months later" (citing *Letters* I, 368). Our finding that the earliest date on which *QM* was definitely in print was 26 December 1813 (see p. 496) undermines that argument, and this change in chronology—together with the nature of the textual differences between the two versions—reinforces Cameron's original analysis: PBS wrote *To Harriet* for *Esd,* only later transferring the poem to *QM.*

As Dowden noted in his transcription of the poems in the Notebook, *To Harriet* is based on Southey's dedicatory sonnet to his wife, which first appeared in his *Poems* (1797), and was reprinted in 1800 and 1801, and in his three-volume collection of *Minor Poems* (1823) as "To Edith Southey." **Lines 11–12** of ***To Harriet*** closely echo Southey's words, showing that PBS self-consciously composed ***To Harriet*** to serve a similar role for his own "Poems." The verbal changes made in the ***QM*** version of ***To Harriet*** carry the text farther away from Southey's poem. For example, the ***Esd*** version appropriately echoes Southey's reference to his volume of early poems (*Poems*, 4th ed., London: Longman & Rees, 1801) as "wild and simple flowers of poesy" since ***Esd*** was made up of miscellaneous short poems, but this figure does not fit the character of ***QM***, PBS's major philosophical statement about nature and humanity (see note to **lines 13–16** below). Because the version in ***QM*** shows how PBS, in conjunction with the unknown printer, finally decided to punctuate the poem for the public, we have adopted some pointing from ***QM*** where essential punctuation is missing in **EN**. All the *words* in the text and their order come from **EN**.

lines 5–6. In ***QM***, these lines read: "Beneath whose looks did my reviving soul | Riper in truth and virtuous daring grow?" instead of: <u>Whose looks gave grace to the majestic theme,</u> | <u>The sacred, free and fearless theme of truth?</u> (**EN**). Though the language found in the ***Esd*** text might seem appropriate for ***QM*** as well, the comparative nature of <u>Riper</u> and <u>grow</u> in the ***QM*** version are truer to the theme of Godwinian perfectability that PBS articulates in that poem, where instead of static <u>truth</u>, PBS sees an ever-growing understanding of reality as a continuum of "aspiring change" (***QM*** IX.19).

lines 7–8. These lines may hint at PBS's early interest in the Platonic concept of the "Ladder of Love," as delineated in Plato's *Symposium* (210b ff.), a work that he would later translate.

line 9. PBS changed <u>soul</u> to "mind" in ***QM***, a revision that accords with the materialist ideology that appears in parts of ***QM*** but is entirely absent from ***Esd***.

line 10. PBS changed <u>to my song</u> to "of my song" in ***QM***.

lines 11–12. Compare these lines by PBS with lines 10–11 of Southey's dedicatory "Sonnet" to his wife Edith in the version published in *Poems:* "Accept the wreath, Beloved! It is wild | And rudely garlanded; . . . ."

lines 13–16. In ***QM***, this stanza reads: "Then press unto thy breast this pledge of love, | And know, though time may change and years may roll, | Each flowret gathered in my heart | It consecrates to thine." The ***Esd*** text is closer to Southey's poem to his wife ("scorn not thou | The humble offering, where the sad rue weaves | 'Mid gayer flowers its intermingled leaves, | And I have twin'd the myrtle for thy brow."), while the ***QM*** text changes the plural "wreath-buds" of the multiple "Poems" in *Esd* to a single "pledge of love," that is, *QM* ("Each flowret" mentioned in line 15 is in the poet's heart—not his publication). Moreover, the whole tone of the *QM* version changes from a hesitant presentation of unripe and <u>withering</u> poems that may be unable to survive or find acceptance by any but HWS's <u>warm and partial</u> heart. In 1813 PBS was so proud of *QM* that he almost risked sending himself, a printer, and a publisher to jail in order to circulate it. He clearly felt no such confidence in the "Minor Poems" in *Esd,* as the final query in this dedication demonstrates: <u>Can they survive without thy love</u> | <u>Their wild and moody birth?</u> This final stanza anticipates a much later poem, with a negative conclusion based on the same premise. In PBS's *Song* | *On a faded Violet,* the poet laments the withering of a real flower because of the coldness of his beloved—then almost certainly MWS (see *SC* X, 856–86).

A sabbath Walk   [Esd #2]

The absence from the draft of this poem in **EN** of the most basic punctuation customary at the time—the state of several poems copied there—indicates that PBS did not plan to use the Notebook as his final copy for the press. As the primary variants also show, this poem is riddled with words either misspelled or so carelessly written that they seem to be so: see for instance, **lines 5** <u>labyrith</u>; **20** <u>shine</u> (for *shrine*); **46** <u>lving</u>; and **49,** where <u>hireling</u> and <u>priest</u> both seem to lack letters.

On the literary side, the text indicates that when PBS began to transcribe this poem, he had not fully established the form of its unrhymed stanzas. Though these are not quite uniform, they differ from the highly irregular stanzas of **Queen Mab** or Southey's *Thalaba*. The first stanza contains fourteen lines, with the first four lines indented, the next four beginning at the left margin, the next five indented about the same as the first quatrain, and the final line indented about one letter space more than those five. The second stanza has only thirteen lines, with three lines beginning at the left margin, one indented, four more to the margin, then four indented the same depth as is **line 4,** and the final line indented still more. The third stanza contains fifteen lines, with three starting at the left margin, the fourth indented, four more to the margin, then six indented the depth of the first three, and a final line indented farther. The final stanza (like stanza one) has fourteen lines, but these are indented in the general pattern of stanzas two and three. Presumably, by the end of transcribing the poem from his draft, PBS had worked out the desired stanzaic pattern, and if he had copied it again, he might have regularized the length of the four stanzas in the way that we have regularized their indention.

PBS signals the theme of his credo as a proud rebel against religious orthodoxy in its title by beginning <u>sabbath</u> with a lowercase letter, just as conventional Christian poets self-consciously capitalized such sanctified words. The poem was apparently conceived—perhaps even drafted—among <u>forest glades</u> in a <u>mountain labyrinth of loveliness</u>, and this setting suggests that it was written either at Cwm Elan, the Welsh estate of his conventional cousin Thomas Grove (which PBS visited during July and early August 1811, just before his elopement, and again with HWS in June 1812), or during his sojourn at Keswick in the Lake Country from November 1811 through January 1812. Though his defense of "natural piety" (as found in Bacon's essay "Of Superstition") might reflect an argument between PBS and either Thomas Grove or Southey, the Lake Country location obviously fits better because the poem was inspired on a <u>winter's day</u> (**28**).

Dowden's note calls attention to PBS's indebtedness to Southey's early poem "Written on Sunday Morning" (1795), which begins: "Go thou and seek the House of Prayer! I I to the woodlands wend, and there I In lovely Nature see the God of Love," though Cameron's judgment that PBS's "militant anti-clericalism" was "far removed from Southey's mild deism" (*1964, 178–79*) is supported by the evidence adduced in our Commentary to **47–49** below. There seem to be echoes also of Wordsworth and some of Coleridge's conversation poems.

line 1. <u>stilly</u>: This word appears in the 1805 edition of *Entick's New Spelling Dictionary*, alone among the contemporary dictionaries consulted. *Entick's*, like the *OED*, calls it an adverb, and gives the meaning "with stillness, calmly, quietly, silently." But the *OED* not only finds it used adjectivally as early as Middle English, but gives several examples from contemporary poets, including Coleridge ("Eolian Harp," 1795) and another use by PBS (in *St. Irvyne*), while Chadwyck-Healey's *LION* has many examples of adjectival use, including Thomas Moore's song beginning, "Oft, in the stilly night."

lines 4, 18. PBS did not indent these two lines, but we have done so on the analogy of their equivalent lines in the third and fourth stanzas (**31** and **46**).

line 13. The syntax is elliptical: "<u>ye</u> [worship] <u>the Almighty fiend</u> . . . ."

line 19. <u>Christians'</u>] Christians **EN,** Christian's *1989*. PBS probably intended the possessive to be plural, like its antecedents <u>vulgar souls</u> (**12**), <u>ye</u> (**13**) and <u>ye</u> (**14**), in order to distinguish himself as an independent thinker from conventional churchgoers, who follow the herd.

Where this and other long lines of **Esd** exceed the width of the page in **EN,** PBS crowded the final word(s) into the gutter of the Notebook, or inserted them either below or—as in this case—above the line. There was often no room to include end punctuation for such lines.

line 20. shrine: PBS wrote "shine" in **EN;** he also miswrote this word twice in his poem *To Mary who died in this opinion,* transcribed in a letter to Elizabeth Hitchener, where he omits the "r" from both shrine in line 20 and enshrined in line 23 (see *CPPBS* I, 139, 310).

line 24. The cities' wearying glare: PBS initially miswrote the adjective as "wearing" and then careted in the "y" above the line. Having been raised on a rural estate, PBS (like Wordsworth and other contemporaries) remained ambivalent about large cities (see also *Esd* #32, lines 221–22), the glare of which had been steadily increasing (Nora Crook notes) as the use of gaslights had spread from the Lyceum Theater in 1800 to Pall Mall (January 1807) to the founding of the London Light and Coke Company in 1812.

lines 47–49. Although phrases such as cringing creeds, idle prayers, senseless mummeries, and hireling priests may seem clichés to modern readers and might have been staple ideas in anticlerical prose, they appear infrequently in English poetry before 1811. The Chadwyck-Healey *LION* database of British poetry reveals no poetic precedent for PBS's use of cringing creeds. Though the *idea* of hireling priests may have been a commonplace among freethinkers, the phrase itself appears in *LION* only once in a poem possibly available to PBS—John Thelwall's *The Peripatetic* (1793), and idle prayers, though more commonly used, usually appears in contexts in which characters are either praying to pagan gods (as in Dryden's translation of Virgil's *Georgics* and John Gay's beast fable *The Eagle and the Assembly of Animals*) or are themselves unworthy of having their prayers answered. There are Renaissance precedents for the meaning of *mummery* that PBS intends, and William Cowper used the word three times in ecclesiastical contexts: in *The Progress of Error,* Cowper dilates upon the evils of musical entertainments on Sundays and laments, "Oh Italy!—thy sabbaths will be soon | Our sabbaths, closed with mumm'ry and buffoon" (152–53); in *Expostulation,* amid a long passage beginning, "When nations are to perish for their sins, | 'Tis in the church the leprosy begins" (95–96), he pictures the temple (and religion) of the Jews being cleansed by Jesus of "mumm'ries he that dwelt in it disdain'd" (146); and in *The Task,* he berates the clergy for quoting the Greek and Roman classics in their sermons and for "foppish airs | And histrionic mumm'ry, that let down | The pulpit to the level of the stage" (II, 562–64). PBS had written to Hogg on 17 May 1811 that his sister Elizabeth observed religious "mummeries" to win the good opinion of *"the world"* (**Letters** I, 90). The closest literary parallel to his precise phrase senseless mummeries is Byron's description of nineteenth-century conceptions of chivalry as "monstrous mummeries of the middle ages" in his "Addition" to the Preface in the fourth edition of *Childe Harold's Pilgrimage* I–II, published on 14 September 1812 and thus available before PBS copied *A sabbath Walk* into **EN.**

line 52. <u>pervadeth</u> is definitely followed by a comma in **EN**: PBS apparently felt the need to insert this punctuation to emphasize his placement of the cesura late in the line.

line 56. <u>Thanksgivings</u>: The plural "s" is not only clear in **EN** but significant as well, for "Thanksgivings" were religious celebrations proclaimed by the king or the established church, usually to celebrate national military victories. PBS's feelings about such celebrations of "mutual slaughter" must have been akin to Wordsworth's negative feelings about "prayers . . . | Or praises for our country's victories" after he first returned from France (see *The Prelude* [1850 text] X, 288–99).

The Crisis   [Esd #3]

Dowden first identified the form of this poem as "sapphics," that is, the Sapphic stanza associated with the Greek poets Sappho and Alcaeus (seventh–sixth centuries B.C.) and the Latin poets Catullus and Horace (first century B.C.). *Carmen Sæculare* and twenty-five *Odes* in this form made Horace the pre-eminent transmitter of the form to later poets. PBS uses a common English adaptation of the form—the same that Southey employed in "The Widow," subtitled "Sapphics" (1795). PBS learned this form not from Southey, however, but during his Latin school studies: as we noted (**CPPBS** I, 435), his early **Epitaphium**—a Latin translation of lines 117–28 of Gray's *Elegy Written in a Country Churchyard*—was written in Latin Sapphic stanzas, probably based on his study of Horace and Catullus. According to Thomas Medwin, who preserved and published **Epitaphium,** that translation was "probably a school task" from about "1808 or 9," when PBS was at Eton. But even if Southey did not teach PBS the nature of the form, he did provide him a contemporary example in English that may have encouraged him to write original vernacular poetry in the same stanza. In a review of *1964*, Christopher Ricks cited Isaac Watts's *The Day of Judgment* and Cowper's *Lines Written During a Period of Insanity* as earlier English poems in sapphics that invoke doom and retribution (*Guardian*, 23 Oct. 1964; noted by *1989*).

    The Crisis may have been composed at Keswick, as Cameron suggests and as *1989* concurs while citing parallels between the poem and passages in PBS's prose **Address to the Irish People** (written January and issued February 1812). Because PBS's first letters from Dublin express shock at the social and economic conditions of the populace there, his reaction may, however, have triggered the composition of **The Crisis** while in Ireland. The structure of the poem sketches one of the most basic "plots" in PBS's writings: A nation (or all humanity) suffers under tyranny, with everything going rapidly from bad to worse, when, at the situation's nadir, the spirit of Liberty or Hope, or an incarnation thereof, suddenly arises and inspires the downtrodden people to cast off their "mind-forg'd manacles" (Blake, *London*) and overthrow their oppressor, while refraining from becoming oppressors themselves in the new social order. This pattern appears not only in **The Devil's Walk,** elsewhere in **Esd** (e.g., poems #12 and #13), and in his sonnet **England in 1819,** but also in such major efforts as **The Mask of Anarchy, Prometheus Unbound,** and **Œdipus Tyrannus; or, Swellfoot the Tyrant.** In **QM** the Fairy Queen didactically teaches this pattern to Ianthe's soul. **Laon and Cythna (L&C), Hellas,** and **The Cenci** present variations of this plot in which something goes wrong: in both **L&C** and **Hellas,** the empire strikes back, thereby postponing the victory of Good over Evil; in **Cenci,** when Beatrice and her allies adopt the methods and mindset of their oppressor they, like the man whose "iron hand crushed the Tyrants head," become murderers "in his stead" (Blake, *The Grey Monk,* 35–36).

line 2. <u>Falshood</u>: As a young man, PBS preferred this common contemporary spelling, found in dictionaries bearing the names of Bailey (1733), Johnson (1803), and Entick (1805) but replaced by "falsehood" in a pocket Johnson's dated 1826. But the poet's careless spelling and penmanship appear elsewhere in this poem: he wrote <u>Tyrranny</u> for *Tyranny* (**line 3**), <u>Monarhs</u> (for *Monarchs*) and "thier" (**9**). In copying **line 14,** Dowden—either by error or in an attempt to improve the logic of the progression—changed the sequence of adverbs from <u>Dreadfully sweetly swiftly</u> to "Dreadfully swiftly sweetly" (MS ED-Pfz).

lines 19–20. <u>day star</u>: As we noted in the Commentary to **"Why is it said thou canst but live"** (**CPPBS** I, 312), while many poets followed Milton's *Lycidas,* line 168, in using *day star* as a synonym for *sun,* in **"Why is it said," QM,** and two other poems in **Esd** (#17 and #22) PBS uses the phrase to mean, not the sun, but the morning star. Here PBS's intended reference is less clear, but "morning star" may be indicated.

The verb <u>Gild</u> is subjunctive ("star . . . Gilds" being the correct indicative form). PBS thus employs a form suggesting doubt ("may gild"), much as he uses questions at the very end of **Mont Blanc, Ode to the West Wind,** and other poems to alert the reader that, after his attempts to probe "the deep truth" honestly, his affirmations of comfort after litanies of woe are hopeful or provisional, rather than factual or categorical.

Passion | (to the   [Esd #4]

This is one of the earliest poems in which PBS addresses a natural creature and seeks possible analogues for its emblematic qualities in other human or natural experience. A notable later example appears in lines 31–60 of **To a Sky-Lark** (also written in five-line stanzas, but there rhymed). In **Passion,** the unfinished subtitle and, therefore, the identity of the unnamed poisonous plant being addressed in this poem have been the subject of much research and debate. Dowden noted in MS ED-Pfz that PBS may have intended to address the deadly nightshade (*Atropa belladonna*), which is connected with passion in *QM* (VIII.129), although (Dowden notes) PBS certainly would have known that name and written it, had it been his sole focus. Cameron consulted an expert at the New York Botanical Gardens, who concluded that PBS's description of a poisonous plant with <u>Fair</u> . . . <u>berries</u> and a mottled stem "seems best to fit . . . *Arum maculatum* or adder's root" (*1964*, 181), but Nora Crook and Derek Guiton in *Shelley's Venomed Melody* (1986; 137–47), followed by *1989* (I, 189), rejected that identification, arguing that the plant was the woody nightshade or bittersweet, a climbing plant the Latin names of which (*Solanum ducamara* or *Amara dulcis*) also convey the oxymoron "bittersweet." Crook and Guiton further call the poem a conundrum, the subject of which the reader is expected to decipher from the clues in the poem. In mid-November 1811 PBS had poisoned himself by eating the leaves of still another plant, which he calls a "laurel" (*SC* III, 58; **Letters** I, 184), in Crook's current judgment, probably the cherry laurel, or *prunus laurocerasus*. Given these varied possibilities and being unqualified to adjudicate the issue on botanical grounds, we follow the lead of PBS's unfinished subtitle (which may, of course, merely suggest that the poem is set as a conundrum), remaining agnostic on the specific plant to which the poem alludes, while conceding that the strongest arguments are those given in *Shelley's Venomed Melody* in favor of the woody nightshade or bittersweet.

Characteristically, PBS may be melding personal experience with his knowledge of the conventional symbolism of several such beautiful but baneful plants to record his ambivalence toward erotic feelings and behavior—an ambivalence that he also expresses in other poems in **Esd** (e.g., #29) and as late as **The Triumph of Life.** One likely reason that PBS wrote this poem at Keswick late in 1811 (as both *1964* and *1989* note) was his shock at the unbridled passion that triggered Hogg's attempt to seduce HWS at York. In support of this date, Crook and Guiton cite parallels between **Passion** and Southey's *The Holly Tree*, while Matthews and Everest suggest as PBS's models for his unrhymed stanzas two other Southey poems, *To Hymen* and *Written on the First of January,* with Collins's *Ode to Evening* as the precursor of all (*1989* I, 190).

Another possible, though less likely, occasion for this composition occurred about a year later, when PBS and HWS expelled Elizabeth Hitchener from their commune, presumably after a confrontation in which Hitchener "had the artfulness to say" that PBS "was really in love with her and [it] was only his being married that could keep her within bounds now" (HWS to Catherine Nugent, 14 Nov. [1812]; **Letters** I, 331fn). PBS, writing to Hogg on 3 Dec. 1812, called Hitchener "The Brown Demon" and though admitting some responsibility for her poverty and loss of reputation, added (with an exaggeration, as Cameron notes, born of guilt), "She is an artful superficial, ugly hermaphroditical beast of a woman, & my astonishment at my fatuity, inconsistency and bad taste was never so great as after living four months with her as an inmate" (see *SC* III, 109–10, 113–14; ***Letters*** I, 336). Whenever the poem was drafted, this second occasion would have been fresh in PBS's mind when he began to copy poems into **EN** in December 1812, after purchasing the Notebook during the Shelleys' visit to London in October and November 1812, about the same time that he returned Hitchener to her family in Sussex, met William Godwin, and tried unsuccessfully to raise money both for the Tremadoc Embankment project and for himself (see ***Letters*** I, 326n).

lines 6–7. When ***Passion*** was written, Hogg was apprenticed to a York solicitor, in preparation for his legal career. PBS's portrayal of lawyers in ***The Devil's Walk*** (84–87), begun at the same time, was equally negative (***CPPBS*** I, 125, 128–29; 290).

line 7. <u>Doth</u>] Dost **EN,** *1964, 1989:* the subject of this verb is the lawyer's "smooth face" and Rogers's grammatical correction (*1966, 1972*) seems to be in order here.

lines 14–15, 19–20. Each of these lines begins slightly farther to the right than the corresponding lines in other stanzas. Since we find no reason in the meaning to explain this deviation from the pattern of stanzas 1 and 2, we conclude that PBS's copying was imprecise and that his reversion to the pattern he established in the first two stanzas and resumed at the end of the poem establishes his intention to maintain uniformity throughout.

line 16. <u>wretch</u>: appears as "wreth" in **EN,** while another example of PBS's careless copying is "monarhs" for <u>monarch's</u> in **line 45.**

line 17. The word <u>mite</u> is an English translation of *lepton,* the smallest-denomination Greek or Maccabean coin (cf. an English farthing or U.S. penny); for Jesus's lesson of the widow's mites, see Mark 12:42–44. A <u>hind</u> is here a poor agricultural laborer, as in ***QM*** III.110–11.

line 24. <u>he</u> was changed to "the" in *1964B.* The revised English edition of Cameron's first edition of ***Esd*** introduced new errors into the text of this and a few other poems.

line 36. <u>blasting</u>: "blushing" in *1964A* and *1964B* may have been caused by PBS's very difficult handwriting. In **EN,** the word in question might be read as either "blasting" or "blushing." Rogers (*1966*) was the first to give what to us appears to be the correct reading.

lines 36–45. The poet addresses Passion in a series of paradoxical noun phrases that express its antithetical attributes. There is no independent verb in these two stanzas, and since PBS omits punctuation at the ends of both stanzas and the exclamation point was the proper mark of contemporary punctuation when interlocutors were addressed directly, either by name or by attributes, as they are here, we have added exclamation points as the punctuation that he was most likely to have added before publication.

To Harriet ("Never, O never, shall yonder Sun")   [*Esd* #5]

The poet "doth protest too much, methinks." Among the several poems that PBS addressed to HWS in *Esd,* this one is his shrillest. His dedication of the volume *To Harriet,* later recycled for *QM,* urbanely deploys figures earlier used in Southey's dedication of early short poems to *his* wife Edith, and *The Retrospect* (*Esd* #50) owes its structure and some of its language to Wordsworth's *Lines written . . . above Tintern Abbey.* Even most of PBS's political poems of this period contain elements of self-critical skepticism, or limitation, such as the use of the subjunctive of doubt in the final line of *The Crisis* (*Esd* #3). The present poem, on the contrary, is an absolutist declaration, filled with extremes from its opening exclamation, through its invocation of sun and moon to witness the poet's unshaken faithfulness, to his promise that, if Harriet dies first, he will grasp tightly her beloved corpse and cast himself into her grave (as in the graveyard scene in *Hamlet,* or in the later passion of Heathcliff). All this suggests that Harriet had questioned PBS's love for her and either demanded—or wept until she elicited—an oath of fealty.

In *1964* Cameron concludes that, because its unrhymed verses follow Southey's example, the poem was written during the Shelley's stay at Keswick, when PBS's letters to Hogg show him to have been still emotionally wrenched by his friend's betrayal, and that it may reflect "Harriet's jealousy of Hogg." On the other hand, *1989* argues that the imagery of the warm sun (**lines 1–2**) suggests late spring or summer rather than the winter at Keswick as the date of this poem. But an accusation about PBS's excessive friendship for Hogg, who had apparently told HWS that PBS was willing to share everything—including her—with him), might explain the vehemence of his protestations of devotion to his wife, inasmuch as the imagery of the warm sun in this poem may be psychological rather than merely seasonal. Thus, PBS could have written this poem to Harriet just before their elopement, or on their journey to Edinburgh before their marriage, or when he suggested that Elizabeth Hitchener come to live with them (as Matthews and Everest argue in *1989,* dating the poem in late April or early May 1812), or after Hitchener joined them in Devonshire that summer, or (just as likely) late in 1812 when HWS finally demanded that PBS choose between Hitchener and her. But whatever its origin and in spite of its logical structuring and strong rhetorical figures, the poem seems to us to evince excessive emotion and, consequently, may reflect some measure of either coercion or insincerity.

When PBS looked back at this poem after a period of months, he clearly did not share our reaction to it. He placed it here, at a crucial juncture within a poetic volume that repeatedly declares his unconditional love for HWS, to reaffirm the hyperbolic praise of his wife as his highest good and as a necessary antidote to his dark vision of life in a largely hostile society and, possibly, a malevolent universe as well. It thus prefigures similar poems associated with what we call the "Graveyard Group" later in *Esd* (#19–#23).

The two unrhymed stanzas contain ten lines apiece, with an almost identical number of syllables in each—71 in the first stanza and 72 in the second—arranged as follows: 9-7-10-7-5-5-11-5-5-7 and 9-9-9-9-4-4-11-5-5-7. PBS, trained in writing Latin quantitative verse, may have been experimenting with an analogical English form.

line 10. Below the center of this line, PBS drew a horizontal rule like those that appear frequently in his drafts to indicate a stanza break.

line 20. All critical editions (i.e., all editions except *SC* IV, in which appears a literal transcription of **EN,** and the photofacsimile in *MYR: Shelley* I) have added commas after <u>die</u> and after <u>lived</u> to make clear the meaning of <u>as I lived</u>. We agree with these editors' interpretation of the line but do not feel that the commas are necessary to convey PBS's meaning.

Falshood and Vice | a Dialogue   *[Esd #6]*

Falshood and Vice (***F&V***) is modeled on Coleridge's *Fire, Famine, and Slaughter: A War Eclogue,* an attack on the policies of William Pitt's government toward France and Ireland, which first appeared in the *Morning Post* on 8 January 1798. Its date is uncertain, since *Fire, Famine, and Slaughter* was a favorite poem of PBS at least from the time he visited Southey at Keswick until 1816, by which time both PBS and MWS had probably memorized it (see *SC* VII, 1–12). Coleridge's poem is a dialogue in irregularly rhymed verse ultimately indebted to the scenes of the three weird sisters in *Macbeth.* PBS drew upon ***F&V,*** as well as its forerunners by Shakespeare and Coleridge, when he wrote the speeches of the Furies in Act I of ***Prometheus Unbound*** (***Prom***).

Coleridge's poem, with its focused attacks on Pitt underscored by the refrain, "Letters four do form his name," recites the horrors of total war as practiced by both the French revolutionary armies and the British-backed royalists in the Vendée, as well as by Castlereagh during the bloody suppression of the United Irishmen's uprising in 1798 under Wolfe Tone, who after his trial cut his throat with knife or razor because he was to be hanged, rather than shot as a military officer (as his nemesis Castlereagh cut *his* throat to avoid disgrace in 1822). ***F&V,*** written in a loose iambic tetrameter that is varied by the addition of anapestic feet, is less dramatic, less personal, and more abstract than Coleridge's poem, for PBS adds to the ravages of <u>war's mad fiends</u> (**9**) a wide range of moral and intellectual corruptions of church and state in England itself, as when <u>Falshood</u> dresses in the robes of <u>Truth</u>, binds her in a dungeon, and stabs her (**21–29**).

When sending *QM* to press, PBS apparently felt that *F&V* was one of the most impressive poems in *Esd,* for he appended a slightly revised text of it to Note 4 of *QM* (1813, pp. 130–35), introduced by this paragraph: "I will here subjoin a little poem, so strongly expressive of my abhorrence of despotism and falshood that I fear lest it never again be depictured so vividly. This opportunity is perhaps the only one that ever will occur of rescuing it from oblivion" (see *QM* in this volume, pp. 242–45). Verbal variants between PBS's two texts—always involving three words or fewer per line and all recorded in the primary collations below the Text—occur in lines 7, 8, 24, 26, 38, 44, 45, 51, 67, 74, and 95. Both Rogers (*1966* and *1972*) and Matthews and Everest (*1989*) based their texts on the *QM* version; here we provide the *Esd* text found in **EN,** with appropriate changes and supplements to the orthography and punctuation found there, not all of which accord with the text in *QM.*

Title. <u>Falshood</u>: PBS again uses this contemporary spelling; see the Commentary to *Esd* #3, **line 2.**

line 1. <u>their</u>: "thier" in **EN,** where <u>veins</u> in **line 3** appears as "viens." Throughout his life PBS often misspelled words containing "ei" and "ie."

line 2. <u>nation's</u> is given as "nations" in **EN.** PBS's drafts and safe-keeping copies frequently omit apostrophes necessary to form the possessive case or to indicate elisions (see "oerflow" **EN, line 4**). Since these variants appear in the primary collations below the text, we shall comment here chiefly on those where the omission produces ambiguity—as with "wars" in **line 9.**

line 7. <u>with</u> was changed to "wields" in *QM* and adopted also in *1966, 1972,* and *1989.* This, the first of the verbal changes that PBS made in the revised text in *QM,* may correct a copying error in **EN**—though both sense and syntax would also support the use of <u>with</u>.

line 9. <u>war's</u>: "wars" in **EN.** Since "war" is personified, we follow earlier editors in punctuating for the possessive singular, rather than the plural.

line 14. In shortening the word <u>toild</u>, to indicate that it should be pronounced as a monosyllable, PBS omits the conventional apostrophe.

There is no room for punctuation following "bestow"—the final word of one of the long lines in **EN** that runs into the gutter of the Notebook, leaving insufficient space for end punctuation. Modern editors either punctuate according to their understanding of PBS's method, or rely on the pointing in the *QM* version (which may have followed the compositor's preferences), creating a large number of variants. See the Historical Collations.

line 18. tumid: i.e., "swollen"; though the word does not appear in *Shelley Concordance,* he did use it in **Wandering Jew** IV.308 and it was a word used by Milton and by several poets of PBS's time, including Byron in *English Bards and Scotch Reviewers:* "Shall gentle COLERIDGE pass unnoticed here, | To tumid ode, and turgid stanza dear? (2nd edition, 1809; lines 249–50). The direct source of many of these uses may have been such staples of the classical curriculum as Ovid (*Metamorphoses* VIII.396, 495) and Horace (*Satires* I.vii.7).

line 25. The compound noun tyrant-slaves expresses two significant concepts in PBS's social philosophy: first, that tyrants can exist only where the majority either wish to be—or allow themselves to be—thus subjected (cf. Dostoevsky's "Legend of the Grand Inquisitor" in *The Brothers Karamazov*); and second, that unchecked tyrants become slaves of their own self-will. No poetic use of the term appears earlier than this one in Chadwyck-Healey's *LION* database.

lines 41, 44. Hadst and had both seem to be subjunctives: Hadst is a present tense form of second person used to record a contrary-to-fact possibility in the past, while had is a third person form of the past tense, used with thou to express doubt about the result of that action, had it been taken.

line 53. PBS uses bloodhounds (in singular or plural) twice later in **Esd** (#14, line 18; #33, 20), once in **QM** (VIII.197), and in seven later poems, including **L&C, R&H, Mask, The Fugitives,** and **Hellas,** almost always to characterize the minions of tyranny. Byron later applied it memorably in *Don Juan* (IV.858) to characterize a French commander in the Renaissance wars that despoiled Italy, while distinguishing between that man's false fame and Dante's greatness.

line 57. deathy: This word does not appear in contemporary dictionaries, and of the *OED*'s five examples of this variant of "deathly"—three uses as an adjective, two as an adverb—one instance of each comes from the poetry of Southey (1796 and 1826), one of each from PBS (**Witch of Atlas** and **To the Moonbeam** [**Esd** #36]), and one from *Blackwood's Magazine* (1826). Thus, it seems to have been coined by a few writers in the early nineteenth century to avoid what they deemed the awkward pronunciation of *l* between *th* and a following vowel sound.

line 69. In **QM** PBS, evidently reconsidering the gender of fate (**68**), changed his to "her."

line 80. Between this line and line 81 in **EN** appear two parenthetical lines that PBS later canceled, either as extraneous to the central theme of his poem or because the rhyme is unwieldy: ("But hired assassins! 'tis not vice, | 'Tis her sweet sister Cowardice . . .").

line 108. Below this final line, PBS for the first time counted the number of lines that he had completed thus far, recording his line count total as "256." That total does not include the dedication **To Harriet,** but it does include the two canceled lines between **80** and **81,** as well two additional lines, apparently due to miscounting or mis-adding (as he does at the end of **Esd** #51).

To the Emperors of Russia and Austria   [Esd #7]

On 2 December 1805, Napoleon, who had earlier that year crowned himself emperor, defeated at Austerlitz in Moravia the combined armies of Austria and Russia, which were under the nominal command of their rulers, Holy Roman Emperor Francis II (later Francis I of Austria) and Czar Alexander I. Clearly **To the Emperors,** composed in sophisticated ten-line tetrameter stanzas rhymed *ababcccbdd,* was not written when PBS (born 1792) was thirteen years old, and questions arise not only about when the poem was composed but what point PBS intended it to make. Cameron (*1964,* 186) dates the poem relatively early—possibly 1810 or 1811; *1977* suggests that the occasion was agreements in 1813 among Austria, Russia, Prussia, and the British to unite against Napoleon (12); and *1989* declares that "the poem must have been written between October 1809 and January 1811," when PBS was "reading up the earlier campaigns of the war as part of his new enthusiasm for revolutionary France" (I, 138). PBS's reading of French history in 1809–11 would have formed his views on the symbiotic relationship of the able, self-made Napoleon and the incompetent hereditary monarchs (see **19–24** and **43–44**). PBS may also allude to the rapprochement in 1810 of two of the combatants, when Napoleon married Maria Louisa, daughter of the Austrian emperor, in an attempt to legitimate his dynasty by siring a son and heir with an imperial princess. **To the Emperors** probably was not written after news of the disintegration of Napoleon's Grande Armée in Russia reached England in mid-December 1812. Significantly, the only other poem in **Esd** in which PBS employed a ten-line stanza with an identical rhyme scheme was another political poem based on a current event—**To the Republicans of North America** (**Esd** #17), for which there is strong contemporary evidence in his **Letters** dating it in February 1812. The date of the original composition of **To the Emperors** could, then, range between 1809 and mid-1812.

lines 6–7. We have adopted the end punctuation of these lines found in the editions of Rogers (*1966, 1972*) and Matthews and Everest (*1989*), rather than in *1964* and *1977,* moving the question mark from the end of **line 7** to the end of **6,** because both the sense and the symmetry of the passage improve when **lines 5–6** form one sentence and **7–10** another.

line 21. <u>restless fiend</u>: Napoleon.

line 26. <u>Abase the high, exalt the low,</u>: Until Matthews and Everest corrected in *1989* PBS's palpable errors in transcription in this line (citing the biblical parallel at Ezekiel 21:26–27), all earlier editions had followed **EN** in giving the line: "Exalt the high, abase the low,".

lines 35–40. For the sleeplessness of tyrants, see *QM* III.66–73 and our Commentary on that passage (pp. 183, 542).

line 50. Below this line, PBS counted the fifty lines of this poem and entered the new total number of lines copied as "306."

To November   *[Esd #8]*

Although the title of **To November** suggests that it is a companion poem to others in **Esd** about the seasons and weather, this poem is actually a very urbane love poem to HWS and thematically a miniature model of **The Retrospect** (**Esd** #50). Written in stanzas of six lines rhymed *ababcc,* it achieves metrical variety because five lines of each stanza are in iambic tetrameter, while the fourth line is shortened to iambic trimeter.

By the time PBS copied the first batch of poems into the Notebook, he and HWS had been together through two Novembers, 1811 and 1812; previous editors favor the former date of composition. *1989* dates the poem 1 November 1811, partly because **line 25** indicates that November has just arrived, but mainly because the poem contains no hint of the turmoil that followed the revelation by HWS on 30 October (or a day or two later) that Hogg had tried to seduce her while PBS was in Sussex (**Letters** I, 166–67 fn.2; *SC* III, 24 ff.). In *1964* Cameron also found 1811 "the more likely of the two years"; but having edited **Esd** while also editing the letters from PBS to Hogg and writing his essay "Hogg and Harriet: The Keswick Letters" for *SC* (III, 24–34), he understood the problem of dating the poem in early November 1811. He therefore weighed the possibility that this poem might originally have been addressed to Harriet Grove before finally concluding that it was written for HWS about the time of their arrival at Keswick on 6 November 1811 (*1964,* 187). The poem, we believe, could also have been written in 1812, about the time Hitchener was jettisoned during the Shelleys' trip to London, but if one considers the poem as a work of art, rather than a document of biography, there is no necessity to fix a particular date of composition. PBS may have drafted it upon his return to York late in October, planning to present it to HWS on the first of the month, before he learned of Hogg's betrayal. Or he may have written it at Keswick later in November 1811, after his emotions had calmed down and he found that he and his young bride had grown closer as a result of this crisis. One point that favors 1811 over 1812 is the stanza on May and the poet's own <u>cold and shudder-</u>

ing heart, which (as Cameron notes) probably alludes to PBS's unhappy time living at Field Place in virtual isolation from his family (see the Commentary to **lines 19–24**).

Title. Following the title in **EN** is a cross, apparently by PBS, to mark the poem for an unstated reason. Both *MYR: Shelley* I and *1989* suggest that he planned to add a footnote, but we now think this unlikely in a personal poem to his wife containing no facts about which PBS needed to address the public. Instead, the mark may indicate that he once considered using it as the dedication to either *Esd* or *QM*.

line 4. draws: *1966* gives "draw" and *1989*, though having "draws" in the text, indicates that **EN** reads "draw"; this is not the case, for the word concludes with a terminal *s* characteristic of PBS's hand during this period.

line 8. The phrase to gild the gloom was something of a standard poeticism at this period, previously used by, among others, Robert Burns, Anna Letitia Barbauld, Mary Robinson's *Petrarch to Laura*, line 47 (in *Poetical Works*, 1806), and Henry Kirke White's *To Contemplation*, line 110 (in *The Remains of Henry Kirke White*, ed. Southey, 2 vols., London: Vernor, Hood & Sharpe; Longman [et al.], 1807; II, 77).

lines 14–15. To continue the rhyme scheme, PBS introduced two awkward inversions that complicate these lines, which mean: "my soul shall mar [foil] [t]hy [i.e., November's] malice I And whilst thy rage deforms the sky . . . ."

line 18. its Harriet: that is, Heaven's (**15**) Harriet.

line 19. Following May is a dot—possibly a stray ink sputter—that might be accepted as a period, if a comma to mark the cesura were not the more likely and appropriate punctuation here.

lines 19–24. May is the subject of could not impart, while warmth and peace form its compound object (**23**). The allusion to May, recalling PBS's isolation following his expulsion from Oxford, after Hogg capitulated to his family and returned to the North, would support the 1811 dating of the composition. After long negotiations, PBS reached an agreement for an allowance and returned to Field Place in mid-May 1811, but even then he and his father were locked in mutual recriminations, his mother was estranged from him because of a salacious anonymous letter that PBS probably wrote, and his younger sisters merely tolerated him (see *CPPBS* I, 323 or *1964*, 187). Yet the poem's contrast of May with November may be symbolic, rather than literally biographical.

line 30. Below this final line appears PBS's line count: "336."

Written on a beautiful day in Spring   [Esd #9]

In an important exploration of the significance of the poems in **Esd,** David Duff selects **Written on a beautiful day in Spring** to exemplify the entire collection. While explicating it as a juvenile effort, influenced by the poems of Wordsworth, Byron, Southey, and others, he also shows that it demonstrates great promise and illustrates PBS's characteristic themes and poetic techniques ("Shelley's 'Foretaste of Heaven,'" *Wordsworth Circle* 31 [2000]: 149–58). Duff regards the poem as a harbinger of PBS's mature understanding of the major Romantic mode, which is not didactic but rather existential, discovering larger truths as it focuses on the poet's personal experience—here a mood induced by bodily sensations rather than rationalized analysis. He also finds it so revealing of the poet's psychological orientation that he credits it with illuminating much of his poetry, early and late.

To his excellent analysis of this individual poem, Duff adds a few references to other poems in **Esd,** suggesting that **Written . . . in Spring,** composed at Cwm Elan early in 1812, is a companion piece to **The Retrospect (Esd** #50) and that the ultimate cause of PBS's sense of well-being on this spring day has much to do with HWS, whose love has banished the loneliness he felt early in 1811 when he last visited Cwm Elan. Duff's reading fits in with the order of PBS's poems in this section of **Esd,** because as we note above, **To November** is likewise both an analogue of **The Retrospect** and a poem ostensibly about natural phenomena that proves to be about the renewal of PBS's spirits. Given this fact, it is not necessary to assume that this poem was actually written on such a day in spring as the poem describes, which could be a happy moment recollected in tranquility and used as a setting appropriate to its final image of the butterfly (<u>fly</u>) emerging from the chrysalis into which the <u>sluggish worm</u> of the poet's unhappy, isolated state had retreated from what seemed a hostile world.

As Duff notes, the figure of the butterfly focuses the central question as to whether a languid feeling of happiness, untroubled by excessive ratiocination, might be a "foretaste of Heaven." Similar implied quests for a state beyond mortality recur in many poems in **Esd,** especially in what we have designated as the "Graveyard Group" (**Esd** #19–#23), and though PBS often articulates his speculations skeptically, using questions or parables, he clearly seeks an affirmative response to them from his readers and, he hopes, from a spiritual power of the universe.

line 5. Though *percipient* appears in contemporary dictionaries (*Entick's*) and modern ones (*Webster's Third International,* as well as the *OED*), <u>unpercipient</u> cannot be found in either group. PBS's apparent coinage of this word supports Timothy Webb's analysis of PBS's frequent use of negatives—including many original coinages—to express positive conceptions ("The

Unascended Heaven: Negatives in *Prometheus Unbound*," in *Shelley Revalued*, ed. K. Everest [Leicester University Press, 1983], 37–62; reprinted in part in *2002*, 694–711).

line 9. <u>recurs—</u>: As in *"Sweet Star!"* (*CPPBS* I, 144; 322–26), the early lines of this poem contain no unsubordinated verb, requiring that the sentence continue through the next line (**10**), where PBS concludes this periodic sentence with a question in which the pronoun <u>it</u> serves as an appositive to the substantive subject <u>mental wandering</u> in **line 1**. Since "recurs" (**EN**) provides no help to the reader, all editors have added punctuation ("recurs—" *1966, 1972;* "recurs," *1989)*, but in one sense, PBS's unpunctuated form serves to reinforce function: his wandering syntax, embodied in regular iambic verses of varied length and ending in solid rhymes that are to a certain degree unpredictable, tends to evoke the state of harmonious reverie that the poem explores. For another early poem in which PBS reflects upon creative indolence, see *"Why is it said thou canst but live"* (*CPPBS* I, 139–40; 310–13).

line 18. Below this final line appears "354," PBS's line count, which did not usually include the titles of poems.

On leaving London for Wales.   [Esd #10]

Having begun with four unrhymed poems (and later adding the unrhymed dedication **To Harriet**), PBS followed with a series of rhymed poems, no two in the same exact form, before introducing one in the Spenserian stanza, then generally regarded as the most challenging of all set forms for multi-stanza works. Edward Bysshe, in his 438-page *The Art of English Poetry* (1702), wrote at the beginning of his discussion of poems written in rhymed stanzas of nine to eleven lines in the 1705 edition:

Spencer has compos'd his *Fairy Queen* in stanzas of 9 Verses, where the 1st rhymes to the 3d, the 2d to the 4th 5th and 7th; and the 6th to the two last. But this Stanza is very difficult to maintain, and the unlucky choice of it reduc'd him often to the necessity of making use of many exploded Words; nor has he, I think, been follow'd in it by any of the Moderns; whose 6 first Verses of the Stanzas that consist of 9, are generally in Rhymes that follow one another [i.e., couplets], and the three last a Triplet . . . . (33)

In the eighteenth century James Thomson and James Beattie each took up Bysshe's challenge by writing substantial poems in Spenserians: Thomson's *The Castle of Indolence* (1748), consists of two books of 77 and 79 stanzas respectively, or 1,404 lines, while Beattie's *The Minstrel*, issued in two books each of 62 stanzas, totals 1,116 lines (1771, 1774). Both authors prefaced their poems with a defense of the Spenserian stanza. The elder Romantics were influenced by Thomson and Beattie. Though later they eschewed this form as too representative of the prior age, Wordsworth not only published *The Female Vagrant* in *Lyrical Ballads* but in 1802 wrote endearing sketches of Coleridge and himself in eight Spenserians entitled *Stanzas Written in My Pocket-Copy of Thomson's "Castle of Indolence"* (not published until 1815 but possibly in Southey's possession when PBS visited Keswick).

PBS was familiar with Beattie's *Minstrel* as well as with Thomson (see E. H. King, "Beattie and Shelley" in *English Studies* 61 [August 1980]: 338–53). And inasmuch as PBS had ancestors whose family name was Bysshe (see Susan Cabell Djabri et al., *The Shelleys of Field Place* [Horsham Museum Society, 2000], 35–36), he is likely to have read Edward Bysshe's popular treatise, which had been republished in at least 1708, 1710, 1714, 1718, 1724, 1725, 1737, and 1762. If PBS did so, he would almost certainly have felt challenged to attempt the Spenserian stanza form there judged to be so difficult, just as he later began to write in *terza rima*. In any case, he had earlier undertaken the form in a longer narrative poem, **Henry and Louisa** (**Esd** #46), and he succeeded better in **On leaving London for Wales,** which is exactly the length of Wordsworth's *Stanzas . . . "Castle of Indolence."* Two other contemporary influences on PBS's choice of the form may have been Henry Kirke White's *The Christiad,* a fragmentary attempt at an epic in Spenserian stanzas, left incomplete by White's death at the age of twenty-one but included in Southey's edition of White's *Remains* of 1807 (II, 173–91), and Byron's *Childe Harold's Pilgrimage* I–II, which had initially appeared in March 1812 and the fourth edition of which (containing the "Addition to the Preface" mentioned in the Commentary to **Esd** #2, lines 47–49) was published on 14 September 1812, shortly before PBS and his party returned to London to seek financial support for the Tremadoc Embankment and to pay his own growing debts. Thus, PBS could have read *Childe Harold* before "leaving London for Wales" in mid-November. PBS's diction, like his stanza form, is in the high style, as seen in such phrases as <u>Custom's obduracies</u> (**24**), <u>Snowdon's Lethe</u> (**30**), and <u>injured penury</u> (**31**). (On more general influences of Spenser and his eighteenth-century followers throughout PBS's career, see Greg Kucich, *Keats, Shelley and Romantic Spenserianism* [Pennsylvania State UP, 1991].)

lines 1–15. This diatribe on London resembles PBS's later picture of that city as "Hell" in **Peter Bell the Third.**

line 10. In Dowden's transcription (MS ED-Pfz), he had doubts whether the penultimate word in this line was <u>free</u> or "full" (the reading of Cameron, Rogers, and Matthews and Everest), but eventually chose <u>free</u>, with which reading Garnett agreed, as do we.

line 19. <u>Cambria</u>: the poetic name for Wales.

line 23. <u>True! Mountain Liberty</u>: Both Dowden (*Life of PBS*) and Rogers (*1966, 1972*) alter the punctuation and orthography in **EN** to read, "True

mountain Liberty"; but PBS's exclamation point was apparently intended to
show his emphatic agreement with Milton's characterization of "the moun-
tain-nymph, sweet Liberty" (*L'Allegro* 36), a sentiment that Southey re-
inforced, as *1989* notes, in his evocation of "The hope of mountain liberty"
in *Madoc* (XII.51–57) and Wordsworth also did in his sonnet on the "Subju-
gation of Switzerland": "Two voices are there; one is of the sea, | One is of the
mountains; . . . | They were thy chosen music, Liberty" (1807).

line 26. <u>Snowdon's ever-sacred spring</u> and <u>Snowdon's Lethe</u> (**line 43**): The
allusions here probably derive from PBS's recollection of myths relating to
Mount Snowdon from an earlier reading of Thomas Pennant's *Tours in Wales,*
first published in 1778 and 1781, and reprinted with supplementary notes
in three octavo volumes, June 1810, by a consortium of booksellers headed
by Wilkie and Robinson, who about the same time published PBS's **Zastrozzi**
after agreeing to do so sometime in July 1809 (*SC* IX, 59–66). In his section
on Snowdonia, Pennant tells the story of the first encounter between King El-
phin and the bard Taliesin (their history forms the core of Peacock's novel
The Misfortunes of Elphin of 1829), giving an English translation of Taliesin's
poem *Elphin's Consolation,* which tells how much better it is to be given a bard
than material sustenance (II, 316–19). In reference to the many lakes high
in Snowdonian massif, Pennant writes, "The quantity of water which flows
from the lakes of *Snowdonia,* is very considerable; . . . collectively they would
exceed the waters of the *Thames,* before it meets the flux of the ocean" (II,
339), and a few pages later he notes: "*Snowdon* was held as sacred by the
antient *Britons,* as *Parnassus* was by the *Greeks,* and *Ida* by the *Cretans.* It is still
said, that whosoever slept upon *Snowdon,* would wake inspired, as much as if
he had taken a nap on the hill of *Apollo*" (II, 343–44).

line 27. This line (Dowden noted in MS ED-Pfz) was added later with a
newly sharpened quill.

   <u>rede of worldly witnessing</u>,: that is, worldly advice or counsel; <u>rede</u>, com-
mon as a noun and a verb in Old and Middle English, survived as a poeticism
in modern English, including thirteen appearances in *The Faerie Queene* and
a notable appearance in *Hamlet* (I.iii.51).

line 36. The syntax of this line would be clearer if PBS had placed a comma
after <u>high-raised</u>, showing that both the compound adjective and <u>stern</u> mod-
ify <u>Tyranny</u>.

   <u>lowers over all</u>: These words are cramped downward into the Notebook's
gutter; <u>lowers</u> is the reading agreed to by MS ED-Pfz, *1964, 1989,* and us, but
Dowden transcribed <u>over</u> as "on."

line 41. The <u>weapon that</u> PBS <u>burned</u> <u>to wield</u> was the picture of the true
state of society in **QM,** which he had begun to compose in Devonshire and
was completing during the winter at Tremadoc.

line 48. <u>pert</u>: here used in senses of *OED* III.4, "saucy, cheeky," or III.5, "audacious, presumptuous." The word is clearly written, but Dowden—perhaps finding the reading unShelleyan (it does not appear in the old *Shelley Concordance* and appears just this once in Tatsuo Tokoo's unpublished Concordance)—jotted down "past" and "great" as other possibilities.

lines 43–45. <u>Reason's flag</u> should become a sign in the sky (<u>meteor-sign</u>, **45**) of <u>love</u> luminous (<u>effulgent</u> as defined by *Entick's Dictionary*) for all the world to see. PBS may have in mind (and be here revising) the account of the Emperor Constantine seeing the cross in the sky and conquering under *that* sign.

line 49. <u>the eye of day</u>: This standard poeticism for the sun appears in Milton's *O Nightingale,* line 5; Pope's *One Thousand Seven Hundred and Thirty Eight. Dialogue II,* 222; Southey's *Curse of Kehama,* 17, and *Madoc in Wales,* I.v.954; and three times each in Barbauld's and Mary Robinson's poems.

lines 53–54. The poet, his anger against injustice under control, now wishes that <u>Woe</u>, the appropriate <u>meed</u> (reward, recompense) of the tyrant and the murderer (each a generic singular, we believe), should be administered, not by his own violence but by <u>Nature</u> through each malefactor's <u>Conscience</u>.

lines 55–58. <u>the soul</u>: In **EN** <u>the</u> is blotted but legible and <u>soul</u> here definitely pertains to the poet, not to Cambria, which is asked to allow his <u>soul</u> to mingle a <u>scene</u> of <u>rocks</u>, <u>woods</u>, <u>Mountains and dells</u> to <u>calm</u> his <u>thought</u> and to dampen the indignation he feels because of his experiences in London.

line 60. <u>my needy door</u>: This phrase is something of a Freudian slip, if PBS intends to suggest his own charity to the poor, for he was at this period also borrowing money, soliciting gifts, and purchasing even necessities upon credit (see *SC* IX, 185–207).

lines 64 ff. The final stanza, describing the poet's loss of vision, sets a pattern that was to recur in later poems written in the same high style, notably ***Ode to Liberty.***

line 67. <u>sad realities</u>: a common phrase of the time that PBS would repeat memorably in his Dedication to ***The Cenci.***

line 72. Below this final line, PBS entered his line count, but the third digit is overwritten and smeared, rendering his intention difficult to determine: 426 is the correct total.

A winter's day   [*Esd #11*]

A key to both the theme and the genre of this poem appears in the words, <u>Whate'er thou emblemest</u> (**28**), for this poem—like ***To a Sky-lark*** and other poems by PBS and his fellow Romantics—might be considered a "word-emblem" as described by specialists on Renaissance emblem books (see Peter M. Daly, *Literature in the Light of the Emblem* [Toronto: U of Toronto P, 1979], 102), though it uses natural description, rather than a biblical or patristic quotation to set the subject. In the *Emblemes* of Francis Quarles (1635), the emblem itself consists of an engraving that illustrates a paradox or "conceit" articulated by a verbal motto and an extended *explicatio*, but some Renaissance poets achieved similar effects by embodying the emblem itself in words, as in John Donne's poems *A Valediction: of my name, in the window*, or *The Flea*. Sometimes, as in these examples, the poem's title takes the place of the "motto," while the development of the rest of the poem explicates the paradoxes and possible significations of the creature, object, occasion, or action described in the "emblem." The emblematic poem, as written by Donne and others in the late sixteenth and early seventeenth centuries, seems to have arisen during an intellectual and emotional crisis similar to that faced by the Romantics: both groups attempted to read natural phenomena, which in each era had gained authority through advances in natural science, as clues to spiritual ideas and entities that seemed more distant as fideism waned in their respective cultures (see Josef Lederer, "John Donne and the Emblematic Practice," *Review of English Studies* 22: 182 ff. [July 1946]; on the question of whether PBS knew Donne's poetry see *SC* VI, 911–15). On the relationship of PBS's poem to emblem books proper, David Freeman of Memorial University of Newfoundland, a specialist on emblem books who kindly read and critiqued this commentary, noted several differences, pointing out that Shelley's "beautiful and sombre poem" has "emotional resonances and subtle evocations unknown to the comparatively minor emblem poets of earlier times," who produced "a controlled and restricted form. While his poem suggests an emblematic structure, Shelley gives his romantic imagination free reign" (personal communication, 23 December 2002).

As *1964* and *1989* agree, **A winter's day** was written either at Keswick in the winter of 1811–12 or at Tan-yr-allt late in 1812. The poem's strong Wordsworthian flavor (demonstrated by Duff in "Shelley's 'Foretaste of Heaven,'" 149–58) weighs in favor of the earlier date, while PBS was sojourning in the Lake Country. Its first stanza describes a springlike day in the midst of winter that leads the poet to speculate in the three remaining stanzas on its emblematic significance: Does the surprisingly fine day portend a betrayal by nature, in which the <u>year</u> (**8**) turns control of the weather back to <u>winter</u> (**13**)? If so, does this betrayal emblematize the destruction of youthful <u>Genius</u> (**15**)—perhaps as exemplified by Thomas Chatterton or by Henry Kirke White, whose poems were edited after his death by Southey in 1807 and excerpts from one of which HWS copied into her Commonplace Book (folio 13 recto) from *To a Friend in Distress* (*Remains of Henry Kirke White* II, 115–16)? Or does it most resemble the fatal power of <u>Passion's rapturous</u>

dream (**21**), as explicated in **Passion** (**Esd** #4, another such poem likely written at Keswick)? In the final stanza, the poet casts a skeptical eye on his own emblematic speculations and, according with another recurring theme in PBS's personal poems (e.g., **Euganean Hills**, **Stanzas written in Dejection**, and **To Jane: The Invitation**), he elects to enjoy the day's transitory sweetness now without overtheorizing about it—a motif found also in such early lyrics by Wordsworth as *To My Sister* ("It is the first mild day of March") and *The Tables Turned.*

A winter's day exhibits a complex seven-line stanza in iambic tetrameters rhymed *abaabab*. PBS may have experienced difficulty in completing the subsequent stanzas with just two rhymes in each. In the second stanza he apparently resorts to *rime riche* by repeating the rhyme word sway (though this repetition could be a copying error; see note below). The third stanza contains just six lines, rhymed *abaaba*, a gap that PBS recognized, for in **EN** he left space for a seventh line. Although we have not identified an exact model for this stanza form, PBS may simply have modified slightly either rime royal, the traditional seven-line stanza in iambic *pentameter* rhymed *ababbcc* that was used by Chaucer, Shakespeare, and Wordsworth (e.g., in *Resolution and Independence*), or else the stanza found in Mark Akenside's *Ode: To the Cuckow* (beginning, "O rustic herald of the Spring!"), which has seven-line stanzas in iambic tetrameter, rhyming *ababccb*.

line 1. O!: This first exclamation point indicates heightened emotion, whereas those following day! and year! (**line 8**) simply signal the vocative case of direct address, according to the conventions of punctuation during the period.

line 7. Though the *OED* does not record the use of balm as an adjective, here as in **Wandering Jew** I.14 (see **CPPBS** I, 44 and 210), it conveys the idea of fragrant and soothing ("balmy").

line 10. incompleted: *Bailey's Dictionary* (1733) and a pocket dictionary "compiled from Dr. Johnson" (1803) both list *incomplete* but not *uncomplete* as an adjective, and *Entick's New Spelling Dictionary* (1805) lists both *incomplete* and *uncomplete.* PBS likely used the participial form here to give the line an extra syllable.

lines 11 and 13. PBS repeats the rhyme word sway—but this repetition could signal either an eye-skip error while copying, or a simple mistranscription at the end of **line 11** for what he may have intended as *spray*.

lines 15–16. The promise of the matin (early morning) flowering of Genius is Unwelcome, presumably because "the good die young," as Wordsworth wrote in lines from *The Excursion* that PBS later used as the epigraph for **Alastor.**

line 19. <u>Decking the scar of time</u>: The blooms of Genius (**15**)—that is, the poems or writings of the talented youth—both perfume the entrance to his tomb and cover (deck) the ravages of time by keeping fresh the dead youth's memory. This stanza prefigures ***Adonais.***

line 23. The word <u>flamy</u>, though not found in contemporary dictionaries and rare in modern literature, was a recognized adjective during PBS's lifetime: the *OED* cites examples from Sidney's *Arcadia,* Pope's *Iliad,* Hannah More, Southey's *Thalaba* (1801), and Cary's translation of the *Paradiso.* It also appears in Pope's four-book *Dunciad* of 1742 (III.254). PBS's use of <u>flamy</u> to alliterate with <u>fleeting flash</u> in **24** might be regarded as an example of youthful poetic excess.

lines 26–27. After comparing the deceptively warm day to illusive youthful passion, PBS inverts the syntax—and tortures the grammar—in the final two lines of the stanza in order to maintain his complex rhyme scheme. The apparent meaning is that <u>Life's blasted springs alone</u> record, or may make known, the illusiveness of passion (<u>tells</u>, the verb, may be subjunctive, or it may have been made singular before he had determined its precise subject in the following line). In this context <u>life's springs</u> might seem to be a reference to the deleterious effects of venereal disease, especially if compared only with ***QM*** IX.87–88: "No longer prostitution's venomed bane | Poisoned the springs of happiness and life" (see page 543). But the use of similar language at ***QM*** III.78 ("They prey like scorpions on the springs of life."), spoken by the Fairy Mab as she shows Ianthe a monarch who is unable to sleep because he is tortured by mental anxieties, provides another likely parallel, and the general use of the phrase "springs of life" by PBS's predecessors and contemporaries (it appears no fewer than 127 times in the poetry on Chadwyk-Healey's *LION* database and was a favorite of such religious poets as Isaac Watts) referred not to <u>blasted</u> procreative organs, but to the roots of spiritual well-being.

line 31. <u>mine head</u>: Contemporary usage prescribed that *mine* be substituted for *my* (and *thine* for *thy*) before a vowel that the poet did not wish to elide, and such substitutions before *head* and other words beginning with *h* are very frequent in Shakespeare's plays, three typical examples being "mine host" (*Merry Wives* I.i.140), "mine heart" (*Measure for Measure* IV.iii.151), and "mine honor" (*Tempest* II.i.317), and recur frequently and perhaps consistently in PBS's poetry. The regularity of this form suggests that the aspirate was often dropped in polite society (as well as by "Cockneys") in reading poetry and, perhaps, in conversation during the Romantic period.

line 34. PBS's running line count appears below this final line of the poem: 461.

To Liberty   [Esd #12]

By insisting that Liberty should not <u>Silently perish</u>, PBS demonstrates his fears that just such a thing may happen, and his hyperoptimistic final stanza may be seen as underlining his doubts as much as refuting them. Young PBS was greatly discouraged by his first excursion to Dublin and the failure of his well-intentioned effort to influence Irish politics, and Cameron (*1964,* 195) dates the poem in the general period of his retreat to Wales (ca. March 1812) on the basis of images and phrases that **To Liberty** shares with **QM**. Although such evidence lacks precision (since PBS tended to repeat over a period of years good phrases coined by both himself and others), we also guess that **To Liberty** may have been written a little later than the following poem inspired by Robert Emmet. That poem asserts the ultimate victory of the spirit of Liberty in more limited terms but escapes the desperate tone displayed in the first two stanzas here.

PBS embodies this vision in intricate ten-line stanzas, the basic rhyme scheme being *ababCddeeC,* where small letters indicate lines containing two or three stresses and capital letters mark lines with either four, five, or six stresses. In the first stanza, he reduced the number of rhymes by having **lines 6** and **7** rhyme with **1** and **3**. In Edward Dowden's note accompanying his transcription of this poem in MS ED-Pfz, he finds it influenced by Scott and Campbell, but does not specify what poems or aspects of their work he has in mind. Crook calls our attention to the affinity of PBS's meter to the first two stanzas of Fitz-Eustace's "Song" in *Marmion* (III.x–xi).

line 16. <u>free</u>: was read as "pure" in *SC* IV and *1989.* Though the word in **EN** is difficult to decipher, we believe that <u>free</u> is the correct reading. Both printings of *1964* read "free," but Cameron or his staff at Pfz changed the reading to "pure" in *SC* IV (perhaps after noting that Dowden's transcription gives "pure") and *1989* followed this change by those who had direct access to **EN.**

line 18. As PBS began to copy this line, his eye skipped to **line 20,** causing him to write <u>Yet bravely</u>. When he realized his mistake, he partially erased those words, and—indenting the line farther—copied the text of **18,** with <u>Sees Paradise</u> superimposed upon the erasure.

lines 28–29. By representing <u>Freedom</u> upon an <u>Atlantic throne</u>, PBS suggests that the young American republic—perhaps seconded by current revolutions in New Spain—might be the new home of Liberty, then banished from the British Isles. This sentiment foreshadows his lines in a late Semi-Chorus of **Hellas:** "Let Freedom and Peace flee far | To a sunnier strand, | And follow Love's folding star | To the Evening-land!" (lines 1027–30).

lines 31–34. The rhythm of these lines (<u>Monarch! sure employer</u> | <u>Of vice and want and woe,</u> | <u>Thou Conscienceless destroyer,</u> | <u>Who and what art</u>

thou!—) parallels that of the first four lines of most stanzas in **To a Sky-Lark**, but in **Sky-Lark** the fifth (final) line of each stanza is an Alexandrine (iambic hexameter) instead of the largely pentameter fifth and tenth lines of these stanzas.

line 38. <u>footstone</u>: though not listed in *OED*, the word in this context must refer to any stone forming part of the lowest, foundational level of the pyramid.

lines 41–50. The fall of <u>Monarchs</u> and even of the <u>pyramids</u> and other monuments built to glorify them was a conventional motif, found (among other places) in Blair's *The Grave*, Volney's *Ruins of Empire*, and Peacock's *Palmyra*, that PBS treated both in **QM** (e.g., II.126–33) and in **Ozymandias.** In **To Liberty,** however, PBS adds to his vision of the frustration of the arrogant powerful an anticipated bliss for the righteous that is a double delight: a millennial <u>Paradise on Earth</u>, followed by an awakening into an apparently supernal Heaven. Whether PBS viewed his words as likely truth or mythic encouragement, he expressed a similar hope in **QM:** "Death is a gate of dreariness and gloom, | That leads to azure isles and beaming skies | And happy regions of eternal hope" (IX.161–63), though this perspective may be at odds with another central theme of **QM** (e.g., III.11–13), the creation of a personal Heaven by the liberated human mind.

line 50. Below this final line of the poem appears "511," PBS's line count to this point in the Notebook (as usual, excluding the dedicatory poem **To Harriet,** not yet composed).

On Robert Emmet's tomb   [Esd #13]

The subject of this poem captured the imaginations of several leading Romantic poets. For most modern historians, on the other hand, the attempt of Robert Emmet (1778–1803) to revive the struggle of the United Irishmen for independence from England in 1803 seems merely a minor anecdote of Irish history. In *The Making of Modern Ireland* (1966), for example, J. C. Beckett mentions the incident in part of one sentence in a paragraph discussing nationalist activity after the Act of Union between Great Britain and Ireland (1800; effective 1801): "there was neither leadership nor organization for a revolutionary movement: when Robert Emmet tried to revive the United Irish spirit for a new rising in 1803 his efforts ended in a scuffle in a Dublin street" (285). The article on Emmet in *Encyclopædia Britannica* (1973) describes his botched attempt on 23 July 1803 to attack Dublin Castle with about 160 men, giving as its only result the murder of the Chief Justice of Ireland, Lord Kilwarden (Arthur Wolfe), and his nephew, whose carriage the patriots happened to meet on their way toward Dublin Castle. After Emmet escaped that scene, he was captured because he insisted on remaining near the home of his beloved Sarah Curran (daughter of Godwin's good friend John Philpot Curran) and was executed on 20 September 1803. The short piece concludes, however, on another note: "High minded, with gallant courage, yet without discretion or common prudence, Emmet has been for generations one of the most romantic heroes of Irish lost causes," citing two of Thomas Moore's tributes to him: *"She is far from the land where her young hero sleeps"* and *"Oh! breathe not his name."*

According to Helen Landreth, however, the case of Emmet is much more complex, for her archival researches in Dublin uncovered correspondence between two Dublin Castle officials (possibly prompted by William Pitt himself) who sent agents to Paris specifically to urge Emmet to return to Ireland in order to enmesh him in the 1803 uprising. When he did return, they surrounded him with spies who egged him on in order to make an example of him and all Irish patriots who might attempt to free the country from the English by force. Landreth estimates that after the British authorities crushed the 1803 uprising, they arrested at least 3,000 activists from all over Ireland, hanging a number of them on the basis of information gathered by such spies and *agents provocateurs.* As Landreth wrote in her Foreword, however, "Looking back on his life, it seems inevitable that Robert Emmet should have become the symbol of Irish nationalism, but not in the way his enemies intended. The very height of Emmet's idealism saved him. . . . He struck a note so pure, so selfless, so lofty, that all the finer qualities of his fellow-countrymen responded to it, and in spite of the untruths told about him his name became immortal" (*The Pursuit of Robert Emmet* [New York: McGraw-Hill, 1948], xii).

Emmet remains a heroic figure also because the eloquence with which he responded to the court at the end of his trial struck a responsive chord in a number of contemporary poets, including Moore, Coleridge, and Southey. PBS may have known Southey's poem, *Written Immediately after Reading the Speech of Robert Emmet, on His Trial and Conviction for High Treason: Sept. 1803* (Southey, *Poetical Works* [1838], II, 245–47), which versifies the sentiments that Coleridge, with whom Southey then shared a house, expressed in a letter of 1 October 1803 (Coleridge, *Letters,* ed. Griggs, II, 999–1003; see also Timothy Webb, "Coleridge and Robert Emmet," *Irish Studies* 8 [2000], 303–24). Southey's and Coleridge's earlier interest in Emmet parallels PBS's feelings when he met Southey at Keswick in 1811–12, just before PBS's first Irish expedition. PBS, however, takes his verse form—quatrains in anapestic tetrameter—from Moore's *"Oh! breathe not his name,"* though Moore's two stanzas rhyme *aabb,* while PBS's seven rhyme *abab.*

The poems of Southey, Moore, and PBS all allude to Emmet's justly famous "speech from the dock." When Lord Norbury, the new Chief Justice, after finding Emmet guilty, asked if he had anything to say before sentence

was pronounced, Emmet (whose father had been physician to the Lord Lieu-
tenant of Ireland) began his reply with signs of respect for the prosecutor
and judge. But his rhetoric became increasingly inflammatory as the court
interrupted him at least seven times and eventually tried to silence his at-
tempt to describe his motives and defend his character from the imputation
that he was merely a self-serving agent of Napoleon and French imperialism.
After Norbury in one of these interruptions alluded to the murder of the
Lord Chief Justice and his nephew, Emmet (according to some reports of his
words) responded: "if it were possible to collect all the innocent blood that
you have shed in your unhallowed ministry, in one great reservoir, Your
Lordship might swim in it."

Most of Emmet's speech (often embellished by his admirers) similarly as-
serted the purity of his motives and appealed to the judgment of God, the
noble dead, and posterity: "If the spirits of the illustrious dead participate in
the concerns and cares of those who are dear to them in this transitory life—
oh, ever dear and venerated shade of my departed father, look down with
scrutiny upon the conduct of your suffering son; and see if I have even for a
moment deviated from those principles of morality and patriotism which it
was your care to instill into my youthful mind, and for which I am now to of-
fer up my life!" But his final words (even as they appeared in an officially
sanctioned shorthand account signed by the counsel both "for the crown"
and "for the prisoner") were what caught the imagination of each of the
poets named above:

I am now going to my cold and silent grave. I have but one request—Let no Epitaph
be upon my tomb—no man can write my Epitaph—I am not permitted to vindicate
my character.—No man now dare vindicate my character. When my country takes her
place amongst the nations of the earth, then and then only can my character be vin-
dicated: then only may my epitaph be written—I am done.

(*The Trial, of Robert Emmet, Esq. For High Treason . . . on the 19th. Day
of September, 1803* [Dublin: Holmes & Charles, 1803], 56)

After Emmet was hanged and then beheaded according to Lord Nor-
bury's sentence, his head was carried off by an artist named George Petrie,
who made a death mask of him; while Petrie did so, the headless corpse dis-
appeared from Newgate Gaol (Landreth, *Pursuit*, 352–53). Going beyond
the various possible sites of Emmet's burial discussed in R. R. Madden's *Life
and Times of Robert Emmet* (1857), on which *1964* relied, and Madden's *The
United Irishmen; their Lives and Times* (1846), *1989*'s source, Landreth enu-
merates the many places in Dublin that "claim the honor of holding Emmet's
body," including the graveyards of St. Michan's, St. Peter's, the vaults of St.
Ann's, and a "quiet little burying-ground . . . at Glasnevin, made famous by
its association with Dean Swift"; she reports that "when investigations were
made at these places . . . nothing was found to confirm the rumours." On the

other hand, when the vault in St. Paul's Church, King Street, Dublin, of the family of Dr. Edward Trevor (in Emmet's time the "medical attendant and deputy governor of Kilmainham gaol" and one of the interrogators of the political prisoners) "was opened" in 1904, though "[t]he Parish Registry had entries for only four bodies for this vault," it contained the "remains of five . . . . One, enclosed in a thin penal shell, was the headless skeleton of a young man about Emmet's build" (Landreth, *Pursuit*, 53). PBS, however, who must have relied on the rumors of his day, may have visited any or all of the earlier claimant churchyards, for if the ruling authorities did hide the body to prevent it from becoming a patriotic relic, they would not have shared their secret with the young English radical.

line 4. <u>shrine.</u>: the word is again misspelled "shine" in **EN,** as we noted regarding *Esd* #2, lines 20 and 23.

line 7. The tradition that St. Patrick chose the lowly <u>shamrock</u>, with its three leaflets, to symbolize the Trinity and employed it to drive all the snakes from Ireland into the sea made it a symbol of Catholic Ireland and its later nationalist movements. According to the *Encyclopædia Britannica, shamrock* refers not to a single plant but "to several plants of the pea family," including wood sorrel, white clover, suckling clover, and black medic (the first and the second of these are the plants displayed as "shamrocks" on St. Patrick's Day in the U.K. and U.S.A., respectively). These perennials are also <u>undying</u> in the sense that they retain their color throughout mild winters.

line 8. <u>dawnlight</u>: This word appears neither in the *OED* nor any of the early dictionaries we have consulted, and the only previous examples in Chadwyck-Healey's *LION* that PBS was likely to have seen were by Mary Robinson, who used the word in her novel *Walsingham* (1797; IV, Chap. 8) and in three poems in her *Poetical Works* (1806)—*The Poor Singing Dame* (line 58), *The Lascar* (Part 2, line 106); and *Golfre. A Gothic Swiss Tale* (Part I, line 80).

lines 9–12. In this poem PBS distorts the syntax and diction, as many classically trained poets did, to maintain his rhyme scheme: <u>among</u> has been transposed from its proper place (after <u>marked</u>) to serve as the first rhyme; the second rhyme, <u>lay</u>, seems to be a substitution for "lie" (the <u>oft</u> in **9** indicating that Emmet's <u>relics</u>—presumably his bones—habitually or continually lie <u>among</u> the <u>grey gravestones</u>). The <u>silently</u> weeping <u>peasant boy</u> whom the poet observes resembles the youth at the end of Gray's *Elegy Written in a Country Church-yard* (PBS's schoolboy translation into Latin of the final Epitaph of which appears in *CPPBS* I, 435–36).

line 12. In *1966* and *1972* this line, which is perfectly legible in **EN,** unaccountably appears within wide-angle brackets, as though the text had suffered damage.

line 18. As Dowden notes, PBS wrote an "X" following this line, and both *1964* and *1989* suggest that he may have planned to write a footnote. A more likely explanation is that PBS marked the solecism at the end of the line, where he wrote <u>the palace of thee</u> instead of "the palace of thine" simply because he needed a rhyme for <u>free</u> (**20**). Perhaps he intended to revise the stanza to remove this blemish.

line 23. <u>caresst</u> appears as "carest" in **EN** and *SC* IV and as "caressed" in *1966*, *1972*, and *1989*. Here PBS's MS indicates that the word (rhymed with <u>rest</u>) should be pronounced as two syllables, with its final consonant unvoiced; we, like *1964*, have doubled the *s* to make clear that the verb is *to caress* rather than *to care*.

lines 25–26. <u>lifespring</u>: As noted for **A winter's day,** lines 26–27, PBS conceived of the "springs of life" as a spiritual as well as a physical concept, here comparing Emmet's spirit to a <u>daybeam</u> temporarily obscured by a <u>storm cloud</u> but <u>unextinguished</u> (like the hearth in **Ode to the West Wind**).

line 28. Below this final line appears **PBS**'s line count of 540, which includes the title of **Emmet's tomb** as well as its 28 poetic lines but still does not include the dedicatory poem **To Harriet.**

a Tale of Society as it is | from facts *1811*   *[Esd # 14]*

This poem, drafted at Keswick, may be PBS's most direct attempt to imitate the Wordsworthian manner by paralleling the elder poet's tales of the poor, old, abandoned, or outcast in such poems as *The Old Cumberland Beggar, The Female Vagrant,* and *The Last of the Flock* (all in *Lyrical Ballads*), or *The Sailor's Mother* and *The Affliction of Margaret* (in *Poems; in Two Volumes,* 1807). PBS included a draft of the first 78 lines of **a Tale of Society** in a letter (in the British Library) to Hitchener of 7 January 1812 (collated as BLjan), in which—after alluding to his desire to meet Coleridge and Wordsworth—he introduced the verse thus: "I now send you some Poetry—the subject is not fictitious; it is the overflowing of the mind this morning. The facts are real; that recorded in the last fragment of a stanza literally true.— The poor man said:—None of my family ever came *to parish,* and I wd. starve first. I am a poor man but I could never hold my head up after that." After copying out his draft of six stanzas and eight lines of the seventh, PBS added, "Adieu my dearest friend. Think of the Poetry which I have inserted as a picture of my feelings not a specimen of my art" (**Letters** I, 223–26). Yet, while *1964* echoes PBS in describing **a Tale of Society** as a "tale of 'humble' life told in deliberately unadorned style," its meter and stanzaic form exhibit a higher level of art than PBS had attempted previously, and its diction and tone stamp it as Shelleyan, rather than Wordsworthian.

The basic form of *a Tale of Society* is a very complicated stanza of twelve lines, the first eleven in iambic pentameter while the final line is an Alexandrine (hexameter), with an interlocking rhyme scheme *abbbaccdcdeE*—a stanza form that may be called super-Spenserian. To extend the *Tale* in this form stretched PBS's capacity to the breaking point (not surprisingly, if he wrote it as rapidly as he claims): in the letter version he left blank the last half of **line 37** and employed many words that he later revised. Even in its final version in **EN** two of its ten stanzas are irregular: the second one has only eleven lines, using just four repeated rhymes (*abbbaccdcdD*), while the eighth stanza has thirteen lines, with its ninth line completely unrhymed (see the Commentary to **line 92**). PBS's effort to relate a story of humble life in a sophisticated stanza form was, in itself, neither unique nor unlike Wordsworth, who had in the 1790s written his *Salisbury Plain* in 61 Spenserian stanzas, which he expanded to 92 stanzas in the poem's revised form, *Adventures on Salisbury Plain*—the poem that first impressed Coleridge with the scope of Wordsworth's genius (see *The Salisbury Plain Poems of William Wordsworth*, ed. Stephen Gill [Ithaca: Cornell UP, 1975]). PBS would have known a thirty-stanza section of this poem entitled *The Female Vagrant* from *Lyrical Ballads,* just as from *Poems* (1807) he would have known *The Affliction of Margaret* in seven-line stanzas rhymed *ababccc* and *Resolution and Independence* (originally *The Leech-gatherer*) in rime royal. The features that most distinguish PBS's manner from that of Wordsworth are his diction and tone, as Reiman argued in an essay that contrasts the temperaments of the two poets as "pastoral" and "Gothic," stating that "Shelley's language displays a nervous tension and impassioned diction that remind one at times of Coleridge rather than Wordsworth at his best or most characteristic" (see *Romantic Texts and Contexts,* 345–53).

Title. <u>Society as it is</u> clearly echoes *Things as They Are*—a phrase that received its political origin in Richard Price's famous address at the Old Jewry in 1789 but was made a permanent part of literary history as the original title (later the subtitle) of Godwin's novel now generally known as *Caleb Williams,* which PBS greatly admired. (See PBS's evaluation of Godwin's various writings in his letter to Elizabeth Hitchener of 26 November 1811; ***Letters*** I, 195.) This title prepares the reader for the Godwinian ideas and phrasing scattered throughout the poem, as in the description of the life of a soldier (**lines 18–21**) or of the poor who awake <u>in this scene of legal misery</u> (**79**).

line 15. <u>lifescenes</u>: PBS here either coins or chooses another rare compound word like *footstone* (***Esd*** #12, line 38), *lifespring* (***Esd*** #13, line 26), and *daystar* (***Esd*** #17, line 41 and #22, line 28). Since he had studied German by this date (see Leland Phelps's argument, cited in ***CPPBS*** I, 433), he may have been influenced by the utility of the numerous compound words in that language.

lines 18–23. For PBS's denunciation of the impressment of the poor into the military, see *QM* IV.190–95 and Commentary; for his views on the soldiers' machinelike obedience to authority, see his Note 3 to *QM,* which includes a long quotation from Godwin's *Enquirer.*

line 25. In unparticipated solitude: In this line PBS again displays his interest in words with the prefixes *in-* and *un-* but this word also appeared in the works of several of his older contemporaries, including Godwin's *Fleetwood* (1805) II, Book XX, page 295, and Kirke White's poem *Time,* in which God is said to be "Invincible, and throned | In unparticipated might" (*Remains* [1807], II, 167). By using the six-syllable word, PBS managed to write a regular iambic pentameter line in just three words, in that respect outdoing not only Kirke White (who adds "Behold" to conclude his line), but even Shakespeare's famed line "The multitudinous seas incarnadine" (*Macbeth* II.ii.59).

line 28. then: Previous editions give this word as "there"; but often in **EN,** as in PBS's other MSS, these two words appear to be virtually identical. The sense of the verse seems to be: after the reader had witnessed the poor widow searching for firewood in the bleak desart rude, then the reader (If human: read "humane") might have learned to grieve through empathy with the widow's sufferings.

line 86. It seemeth that their element is pain: As *1989* points out, PBS later has Prometheus, amid *his* sufferings, declare to the Furies: "Pain is my element, as hate is thine" (***Prom*** I.477); 1989 also identifies a possible source for the image from Southey: "The pious soul hath fram'd unto itself | A second nature, to exist in pain | As in its own allotted element" (*The Curse of Kehama* [London: Longman, Hurst, Rees, Orme, and Brown, 1810], pp. 137–38; = Book XIII, tenth verse paragraph, lines 7–9).

lines 92–96. When PBS reached this point, he was struggling to maintain the difficult stanzaic form that he had chosen. **Line 92** is the only unrhymed line in the poem and gives this stanza thirteen lines instead of the normal twelve, but PBS apparently retained the supernumerary line specifically to indict the clergy of the Established Church (fat slaves), as he was later to do at greater length in his fragmentary **Ballad** beginning, ***"Young Parson Richards stood at his gate"*** (in the larger Harvard Shelley Notebook; *MYR* V,150–55).

In **93–96** the syntax becomes muddled, partly due to the lack of appropriate punctuation in **EN:** Lick is an imperative addressed to the unhappy wanderer (**91**), while thou dost share and mutterest serve a clause dependent upon crumbs, for which the missing introductory relative pronoun (*which* or *that*) is understood. The final two lines of the stanza (**95–96**) contrast the condition of the poor in England to that of the flowers, which, earlier fed by the <u>sun's kind light</u> (**89**) are now fed by the <u>changeful year</u>, just as the aged mother and her sick son <u>must poorly die</u> because they are at the mercy of <u>the tyrant, man</u>. The stanza thus not only presents a beneficent natural world corrupted by human society under the heel of monarchy and established religion but even denies Jesus's message in the Sermon on the Mount that God, who clothes the lilies of the field and feeds the birds of the air, will care for human beings as well (Matthew 6:25–33; Luke 12:22–31).

line 109. "Osier or Ozier . . . a tree of the willow kind" (*Entick's Dictionary*, 1805). Though rarely used by PBS's contemporaries, the term does appear in Erasmus Darwin's *Botanic Garden* (1799), Part II, Canto IV, page 155.

line 120. Below this line PBS has given "661" as the tally of lines completed, in this case adding one line for the poem's title to the 120 lines in the poem itself.

Supplement: Version in Letter to Hitchener, 7 January 1812

This supplement for ***Esd*** #14, ***a Tale of Society,*** comes from PBS's letter to Elizabeth Hitchener dated 7 January 1812 (***Letters*** I, 224–26), the first of two poems that PBS is known to have sent to Hitchener and later included in ***Esd.*** The poetic text was reproduced in photofacsimile in *MYR: Shelley* VIII, 43–49, with a diplomatic transcription, from the manuscript in the British Library (BLjan). Our transcription differs slightly from that in *MYR*, correcting a few of the indentions and readings of the MS.

    "She was an aged woman" is forty-two lines shorter than ***a Tale of Society,*** lacking the last three stanzas of the poem in ***Esd,*** which reach beyond the story of the <u>aged woman</u> and her son William to generalize on the sufferings of the poor. In the final stanza of the ***Esd,*** at the unmarked grave of the <u>aged sufferer</u>, the poet himself appears, caught up in the <u>joy of melancholy</u>, to weep and bless the spot. All the Godwinian sentiments of those stanzas are missing from the Letter Version, though whether or not PBS had composed the conclusion by the time he wrote to Hitchener, he lacked space in his long and crowded letter to copy the whole of it.

line 8. Wear along the letter's fold line has damaged the word "c<rip>ple," leading someone (not PBS) to write the word "cripple" just below the damaged word and then draw a separating line (that rises up towards **line 8** just beneath the end of the original "c<rip>ple") between the clarifying insertion and **line 9.**

line 16. "mental": *MYR* transcribes the word as "mortal"; however, both in MS BLjan and in **EN,** the word is clearly "mental" (more clearly so in BLjan than in the Notebook).

line 18. "her child": PBS seems to have first written "her" but then superimposes <u>the</u> upon it—"the" is also the reading from the Notebook. In *MYR*, the transcript appears as "her/the child" (VIII, 47).

line 19. "weild": Here PBS's typical misspelling of an *ie* word is left uncorrected. The word "field" in **line 21** is also miswritten, with the third letter almost looking like an *i* rather than an *e*, while the second letter is clearly a dotted *i*.

line 26. "forest rude" in BLjan becomes <u>desart rude</u> in **EN,** probably to emphasize both the difficulty of the <u>Aged Woman</u>'s search for <u>wood</u> (**line 27**) and her <u>unparticipated</u> isolation; <u>desart</u> refers primarily to an absence of other people, not a lack of vegetation. Note his use of "desart rude" also in the first line of *Esd* #20.

line 35. PBS canceled a word before "Son," which begins with a long *s*.

line 37. PBS placed four *X*s after the first half of the line because, unlike some earlier poems that he had sent to Hogg under the pretense that they were recent, spontaneous compositions, ***"She was an aged woman"*** probably was really unfinished and in process when he copied this part for Hitchener.

line 47. <u>A sigh, & turning round claspd William to her breast</u> **EN.** The rather sudden appearance of <u>William</u> is awkward in the Letter and Notebook versions and in other critical texts. The problem here illustrates how PBS's experiments in *Esd* with very complex and strict poetic forms sometimes cramped his narratives and expositions, though the skill he gained with versification through these exercises prepared him for greater achievements later.

line 59. "great as they": appears below the canceled ~~blest as~~ at the very bottom of the first page of the MS (see *MYR: Shelley* VIII, 46).

line 64. brought] wrought **EN.**

line 67. PBS first wrote "Did" with a lowercase *d* but then wrote the capital *D* over it.

The solitary *1810* [Esd #15]

This poem was first published in *1870* by W. M. Rossetti, who had received it from Richard Garnett, *his* source perhaps being the woman, "formerly a governess in the Esdaile family," who (as Garnett wrote to Dowden on 24 December 1883) also gave Garnett "Two sonnets addressed by Shelley to Harriet in July and Sept. 1813" (i.e., *Esd* #52 and #53) that she had copied "from a MS. in Mr. E[sdaile]'s possession" (*Letters about Shelley,* 87–88). Though brief, the poem again displays PBS's command of metrics and rhymes in carefully wrought stanzas rhymed *abbaab*, consisting of five lines of iambic pentameter and a line of iambic trimeter.

The poem articulates a persistent theme in Romantic literature: the psychic danger inherent in isolation from human society. PBS's immediate model here may be Wordsworth's *Lines Left upon a Seat in a Yew-Tree*, the third poem in *Lyrical Ballads* (1798), which moralizes upon the wasted life of a talented but disillusioned visionary who withdrew from society and, after spending "many a morbid hour" nourishing "a morbid pleasure" by "tracing here an emblem of his own unfruitful life" (27–29), "died, leaving this seat his only monument" (43). PBS's need for community and fear of isolation are obvious not only from **The Wandering Jew** and from other poems in **Esd,** but as well from such later works as **Alastor,** the essay **On Love,** and **Athanase: A Fragment.** And he wrote on this theme partly to remind himself to be more accepting of the limitations of other people and to reach out to them—for, as Wordsworth wrote, "pride, | Howe'er disguised in its own majesty, | Is littleness" and "he, who feels contempt | For any living thing, hath faculties | Which he has never used" (*Yew-Tree*, lines 41–50 *passim*). PBS's poems and passages dealing with the theme of loneliness and isolation are often framed as admonitions of this kind, as in his comments on Maddalo/Byron both in the Preface and the text of **Julian and Maddalo:** "The sense that he was greater than his kind | Had struck, methinks, his eagle spirit blind" (50–51).

In their notes to **The solitary,** both *1964* and *1989* focus on biographical issues and the date of composition, trying to determine when in late 1810 or early 1811 (see note on title) PBS would have felt it necessary to lecture an unnamed isolate (whom they presume to be himself) to write such a poem. Cameron focuses on PBS's holiday at home from Oxford over Christmas and New Year's, 1810–11, Matthews and Everest on his early days at Oxford in October 1810. There is more contemporary evidence to support the former position, including a long series of lonely and embittered letters that PBS wrote to Hogg over that vacation, while the latter case depends chiefly on Hogg's highly colored retrospective memories (and distortions) of events decades earlier. Although **The solitary** could have been written in either period (after PBS had learned that his engagement to Harriet Grove had been broken off), we believe that the persistence of the theme through a good portion of PBS's career obviates the need for such precise dating. In **Esd, The solitary** appears as one of many poems that explore various attitudes toward life and potential ways for the protagonist (clearly representing PBS) to find a calling that can make his life meaningful for himself, for those he loves, and, ideally, for human beings generally.

Title and date. As *1964* notes, PBS first wrote the date (which is separated from the title and was apparently written later, with a blunted quill) as "1811"; he then added a loop to the final digit, turning it into <u>1810</u>.

line 4. <u>calm solitude</u>: Here as so often in PBS's writings, <u>calm</u> connotes a lack of empathetic feeling for others.

line 7. <u>Pariah in some Indian Grove</u>: <u>Pariah</u> appears in none of our four abridged dictionaries dated 1733, 1803, 1805, and 1826, and the earliest example of the figurative meaning of *pariah* as a shunned outcast (*OED* 3) is from a PBS letter of 1819. Therefore, this—PBS's sole use of *pariah* found in Tokoo's *Concordance*—likely comes from current books on the East, perhaps including works by Sir William Jones, Southey's poems, Volney's *Ruins of Empire,* (Chapter 20 [see *1989* I, 144]), or other poems and novels with oriental themes. Mary Shelley, Crook notes, used the word in her novel *The Fortunes of Perkin Warbeck* (1830) in reference to a character belonging to "a Pariah race" because of his treachery; and according to the *LION* database, both Shelleys were ahead of their time in using *pariah,* for the word appears not to have come into general use until the second half of the nineteenth century.

line 16. <u>Yet, yet he longs altho' he fears to die.</u> The line lacks internal punctuation in **EN,** but <u>altho' he fears</u> should probably read as though it were set off by parentheses, commas, or dashes.

The Monarch's funeral | *An Anticipation* | *1810*   [*Esd #16*]

Though the subject of this poem may have been suggested by Southey's *The Pauper's Funeral* (1796), assuming that PBS had found and read Southey's early effort before 1810, the two poems have nothing more in common than their antithetical titles. PBS almost certainly revised his poem after his search for the grave of Robert Emmet early in 1812, as indicated by his reference in **21–24** to <u>the uncoffined slain,</u> | <u>That fell in Erin's injured isle</u>, and he may have added or changed the title then. ***The Monarch's funeral,*** in predominantly iambic tetrameter quatrains rhymed *abab,* proves to be something of a dialogue or debate between two perspectives on the subjects in its title: one view emphasizes the natural human sorrow at the fact of death, while the other focuses on the monarch's role in human society. The sadness associated with any death and especially that of a public figure whose loss causes national mourning (**1–18**) is suddenly undermined in **lines 19–32** by the memory of nobler persons, more worthy of public grief (as in PBS's prose ***Address to the People on the Death of the Princess Charlotte*** of 1817). But in **33** a dash denoting a pause and the word <u>Yet</u> return the poem to its opening theme of the sadness at the death of anyone, a sorrow partly relieved by the poet's thought that after <u>the dross, which forms the *King* is gone</u> (**57**), the essence of his humanity will remain. In the final quatrain, the poet, in an act of discovery, realizes that the <u>royalists might groan</u> at the monarch's death because they finally understand what they lost, not when he died, but when his humanity as the *Father of the People* was swallowed up in the <u>Sacred Majesty</u> of his social role as king (**73–76**).

PBS's attitude toward King George III, whose mental health had been so precarious for many years that his son had to be named Regent in February 1811, was shaped in part not only by gossip from PBS's mentor Dr. James Lind, one of the mad king's physicians, but also by actual encounters between Eton students and the King at nearby Windsor Castle. George III was the patron of the school, and Etonians communicated directly with him during annual ceremonies celebrating the monarch's birthday on 4 June. In an essay entitled "Shelley in 1810," Reiman discusses the discovery that during PBS's last spring term at Eton he and two friends planned to absent themselves on that date in 1810, thereby boycotting these royal festivities (see *SC* IX, 77–90). By dating **The Monarch's funeral** "1810," PBS may have been relating it to that symbolic act of protest, whether or not he and his companions actually carried it out.

line 1. <u>The growing gloom</u>: PBS first wrote "glowing" before changing the *l* into a tall *r*.

line 33. —<u>Yet,</u>] —Yes, *1964, SC/IV, 1989*. PBS's *t* lacks a modern cross but has a downward stroke characteristic of his terminal *t*'s of this early period. For the significance of this changed reading, first introduced in *1966*, see the introductory Commentary on this poem's structure.

To the Republicans of North America   [Esd #17]

This poem displays PBS's increasingly skillful artistry, marshaled in the same ten-line stanza in tetrameter rhymed *ababcccbdd* that he used in **To the Emperors** (**Esd** #7). Presumably he wrote **To the Republicans of North America** soon after his arrival in Dublin, where on 14 February 1812 he wrote to Elizabeth Hitchener: "Have you heard, a new republic is set up in Mexico. I have just written the following short tribute to its success." Below this sentence, PBS copied four stanzas (all but the fourth stanza of the finished poem) into his letter and followed that with the ten-line fragmentary poem beginning **"Bear witness Erin!"** (**Letters** I, 253; on the latter poem, see **CPPBS** I, 145; 326–27). On 10 March 1812, he wrote again to Hitchener: "[The] Republic of Mexico proceeds & extends. I have seen American papers, but have not had time to read them . .—I only know that the spirit of Republicanism extends in South America, and that the prevailing opinion is that there will soon be no province which will recognize the ancient dynasty of Spain.—" (**Letters** I, 272).

Cameron (in *1964*) outlined problems relating to the poem, including the textual crux in its title, where PBS seems first to have addressed his poem to the <u>Republicans</u> of "New Spain." Perhaps his uncertainty about which

Spanish colony in the New World that name applied led him to revise the title to address those in <u>North America</u> (i.e., the Mexican revolutionaries). About the same time a group of aristocrats in the northern provinces of Peru (now Equador) were carrying on a similar, though less successful effort to achieve home rule. News about the Mexican Revolution and uprisings in Venezuela, Argentina, and other regions of Latin America appeared regularly in British newspapers and magazines at least as early as 1810. For example, the monthly *Scots Magazine and Edinburgh Literary Miscellany*, which had a regular section entitled "Historical Affairs," included accounts of such events in Latin America. In its August 1810 issue, it notes "that a disposition prevails on that great Continent, to shake off its dependence on the mother country. The example of the Caracas has been followed by several other provinces, whose object appears clearly to be the establishments of their own independence" (618). In September 1810, the *Scots Magazine* contained a letter from the British government, apparently circulated among the Spanish possessions in America, promising British support for any revolutions by their people against the French-dominated regime in Spain: "The great object which his Majesty has in view from the first moment when intelligence was received in this country of the glorious resistance of the Spanish nation, against the tyranny and usurpation of France, was to assist by every means in his power this great effort of a brave, loyal, and high spirited people, and to secure, if possible, the independence of the Spanish monarchy in all parts of the world" (701). The December 1810 issue of the *Scots Magazine,* apparently in response to interest in Latin American politics, included a long excerpt from *"Humboldt's Travels"* entitled "Account of the Character and present Condition of the different Classes of Inhabitants in Mexico, or New Spain" (916–20), which depicts all races and classes in the colonies as oppressed people, waiting to be liberated, while the April and June 1811 issues included excerpts from Southey's *History of Brazil.* PBS, who could have found in such contemporary periodicals both current events and the history of the American colonies of Spain and Portugal, would also have been able to use the British support of independence for the possession of Napoleon-dominated Spain as a way to praise popular uprisings in general without falling afoul of the legal authorities in Ireland and England.

The uprising in Peru was in the vicinity of Cotopaxi, the highest active volcano in the world, which would also have been known to PBS from the writings of the contemporary German scientist-adventurer Freiherr (Count) Alexander von Humboldt, whose magisterial *Voyages aux régions équinoxiales du nouveau continent, fait en 1799–1804* (Paris: F. Schoell, 1805; the first in a 28-volume series entitled *Voyage de Humboldt et Bonpland*) describes in detail his ascents in 1803 of nearby Pichincha, Chimborazo, and two other volcanos (in what is now Equador), as well as his unsuccessful attempt to be the first European to ascend Cotopaxi from the valley at its foot (9,000 feet above sea level) to its summit (19,347 feet high). In a contemporary letter to his brother, Humboldt observed, after viewing the destruction throughout the vicinity of Quito caused by major eruptions and earthquakes of 1797, "the whole of the more elevated portion of the province is one vast volcano" and "the so-called mountains of the Cotopaxi and Pichincha are but small peaks, the craters of which constitute the emission tubes (chimneys) of the vast subterranean fires" (*Life of Alexander von Humboldt,* ed. Karl Bruhns; translated by J. and C. Lassell [London: Longmans, Green, & Co., 1873], I, 305). Did PBS invoke Cotopaxi instead of Popocatepetl and Ixtacihuatl, the volcanoes overlooking Mexico City, because he confused its location, because he was unable to recall those difficult names, or simply because they did not fit the meter of his poem? Or perhaps he was purposely using Cotopaxi, the tallest of these volcanic peaks, to universalize his message by alluding to uprisings throughout Latin America, just as the later *Ode to Naples* invokes a series of active volcanos in the Mediterranean region to symbolize the spread of revolutionary ferment in the entire area (see G. M. Matthews, "A Volcano's Voice in Shelley," *ELH* 24 [1957]: 191–228; condensed version in *2002,* 550–68).

The Mexican Revolution itself, proclaimed by Father Miguel Hidalgo y Costilla at the small mountain town of Dolores on 16 September 1810, was— after a series of bloody rebel victories in the provinces west of Mexico City— blunted at the Battle of Calderon in mid-January 1811. Hidalgo and the rebellion's other principal leaders were betrayed and captured in March 1811. Most were tried and executed in April, but Hidalgo, because he was a priest, had to be defrocked by the ecclesiastical authorities before he was executed on 31 July 1811. The revolution continued, however, with popular support among both the indigenous peoples and the Mexican-born population of European descent, who had been misruled and exploited for generations by governors sent over by the Spanish crown who had siphoned off the wealth of the country for their own profit and the glory of the motherland (see H. H. Bancroft's *History of Mexico,* IV; in his *Works* [San Francisco, 1886], XII, 96 ff.).

A basic source of PBS's knowledge of the history of New Spain was likely William Robertson's classic *History of America* (1777; reprinted in the eighteenth century and in 1800–1801, 1808, 1809, 1811, and 1812), which recounts the entire conquest (and oppression) of the native Mexican and Peruvian peoples by the Spaniards. PBS ordered a copy of this work from Clio Rickman on 24 December 1812 (*Letters* I, 343–45). Though Rickman may never have filled that order (which requested a large number of expensive books on credit), PBS was probably already familiar with the works of Robertson, for most literate people of this period read the great Scottish historian (e.g., Keats read Robertson in 1818–19) and PBS later alludes to key anecdotes found in the *History of America.*

The fourth stanza (**lines 31–40**) was not in the earlier version that he sent to Elizabeth Hitchener (see below). If he had written it by the time he wrote that letter, he omitted it because he either lacked room for it or had misgivings about its violent imagery. (He could never be sure who might be reading his mail, either in transit or over Hitchener's shoulder.) That stanza in **Esd** expands upon the theme of Nature's <u>curse</u> on <u>a villain king</u>, expressing fear that, as in the French Revolution, "<u>Blood may fertilize the tree</u> | <u>Of new bursting Liberty</u>" (**lines 35–36**), while hoping that the <u>guiltiness</u> for any violence will be upon the <u>slaves</u> of the <u>tyrant-brood</u>, thereby shifting the poem from a call to arms on the part of "patriots" to a hope that, as he was later to write in **Mask of Anarchy,** the people should attempt to overcome force with active but peaceful resistance and moral suasion, such as Gandhi and others since have shown to be practicable against all but the most ruthless sociopaths.

line 1. <u>Brothers!</u>: As the references in the *Shelley Concordance* indicate, there are just a few instances in PBS's poems where he refers to comrades-in-a-cause as "brothers"—and some of these occur in a pejorative context, as in **Falshood and Vice** (**Esd** #6) and **Laon and Cythna** X.vi.2 (line 3839). The two positive uses closest to the present one appear at **L&C** VI.ix.1 (line 2407) and **Prom** (I.578). Rather, for most of the positive occasions he employs *brethren,* which, the *OED* explains, became in the seventeenth century a "special plural" used "in reference to spiritual, ecclesiastical, or professional relationship."

line 27. <u>thousands wake to weep</u>: The phrase "wake to weep" is common in PBS's poetry, with variants appearing, for example, in **L&C** III.xxvii.9 (line 1350) and XI.ix.4 (line 4300), **R&H** 775, **Prom** I.736 ("wake in sorrow"), *"The flower that smiles today"* 21, **Hellas** 20, and **Triumph** 334 and 430, with the phrase usually applying to the poet or his surrogates, rather than to oppressed thousands. Antecedent usages by poets that PBS read are few (Byron's *Song* beginning "Breeze of the Night!" though written in 1808, remained unpublished till 1898): leaving Mary Robinson's *The Sorrows of Memory,* 75—"When in the grave this heart shall sleep, | No soothing dream will bless thy slumber, | For thou perchance may'st wake to weep, | And with remorse my sorrows number!" (Robinson, *Poetical Works* [1806] II, 261) —and Henry Kirke White's *Childhood,* the first poem in his *Remains,* ed. Southey [1807], I, 286: "Yes, Childhood, thee no rankling woes pursue, | No forms of future ill salute thy view, | No pangs repentant bid thee wake to weep, | But Halcyon peace protects thy downy sleep" (Part 2, lines 23–26). Since both Byron (who like White was from Nottinghamshire) and PBS read Krike White's *Remains* soon after its publication, the last words of Byron's *Song* about Miss Campbell, a mistress whom he had just discarded or was about to discard (see Byron, *Poetical Works* I, 215 and 390) and PBS's use of

<u>wake to weep</u> in this poem may both derive from Kirke White's precocious phrase-making.

lines 35–36. PBS's image of the blood of tyrants fertilizing the Tree of Liberty had precedents, *1964* notes, in a letter by Thomas Jefferson (13 November 1787) and a speech by Barère de Vieuzac during the trial of Louis XVI in the French National Convention (1792).

line 41. <u>Can the daystar dawn of love</u>: <u>dawn</u> here is a verb (as *1989* notes), its subject being <u>the daystar</u> . . . <u>of love</u> (here, Venus as the morning star).

Supplement: Version in Letter to Hitchener, 14 February 1812

The Supplement for **To the Republicans of North America** appears in PBS's letter written to Elizabeth Hitchener on 14 February 1812 (MS BLfeb; *MYR: Shelley* VIII, 63–66; *Letters* I, 250–55), which includes **lines 1–30** and **41–45**— the first three stanzas and the fifth stanza of the *Esd* text. For discussion of the context of this letter as well as the poem, see above. PBS revised very little in these four stanzas when he transcribed the poem into **EN,** though a small change from "banners" to <u>banner</u> in *Esd* may signify either PBS's fear that "Freedom's bloodless banners" were becoming fewer or his hope that Freedom, if achieved without bloodshed, would be a unifying rather than a divisive force among nations.

line 6. "pul<ses>": Part of the word is illegible due to a crease in the MS.

line 27. Although the word "shores" seems fairly legible in the MS, someone other than PBS has underlined the word in pencil and written another "shores" next to it.

Written at Cwm Ellan 1811   [Esd #18]

That one of PBS's goals in composing and arranging the poems of *Esd* was to illustrate his virtuosity in different English meters and stanza forms is demonstrated again in this poem, which derives from one of two obsolete verse forms—either "fourteeners" (heptameter couplets) or "poulter's measure." The latter form—used by Sir Thomas Wyatt, Henry Howard, Earl of Surrey, Sir Philip Sidney, Fulke Greville, and other sixteenth-century poets and considered old-fashioned by the time of Shakespeare's maturity—is defined as "rhyming couplets made up of a line of iambic hexameter followed by a line of iambic heptameter," the term deriving from the old poultrymen's practice of giving twelve eggs for the first dozen but fourteen for the second (see Sara deFord and Clarida Harriss Lott, *Forms of Verse* [1971], 341). But here as elsewhere, PBS adapts the form to make his task more difficult, using an eight-line stanza rhymed *ababcccb*, rather than the easier couplets. By the second stanza he regularized his lines to iambic heptameters, with fifteen syllables for lines ending in double (feminine) rhymes, fourteen syllables for those with masculine rhymes.

Both subject and theme of **Written at Cwm Ellan** involve PBS's oft-stated preference for night over day (cf. **The Retrospect—Esd** #50, lines 23–40). His mature poem that most nearly resembles and best fulfills the poet's conception is **To Night,** beginning "Swiftly walk o'er the western wave | Spirit of Night!" Although **To Night** is arranged in varied short lyric lines, its rhythms resemble those of **Written at Cwm Ellan;** the greater effect of the later poem suggests that PBS's choice of heptameter lines may be partly responsible for the comparative inferiority of this youthful effort. He seems to have recognized the limitations of the poem when copying it into **EN** in 1812–13, for by adding 1811 to the poem's title, he indicated not only that it was written before his elopement with Harriet (the event that according to a recurrent theme in **Esd,** guaranteed his happiness) but also that the poem dated from his poetic apprenticeship, before he had composed the previous poems in the collection that he regarded more highly.

The Grove family's estate in Wales (its Welsh name was usually spelled Cwm Elan) was near Rhayder (Rhaydergwy, according to *Paterson's Roads,* 1808), in Radnorshire (now Powys), the junction of the two main roads between London and Aberystwyth, one from London to Rhayder via Oxford, Gloucester, and Hereford (181 miles), and the other—the mail-coach road—through Oxford and Worcester (178 miles). In 1792, the year of PBS's birth, his uncle Thomas Grove had bought almost 11,000 acres of "worthless land," upon which he developed both a rural estate with "a neat and elegant mansion" and a profitable lead mine (Desmond Hawkins, *Shelley's First Love,* 92). The Rev. William Lisle Bowles (whom Coleridge praised in *Biographia Literaria* and against whom Byron later debated the nature of poetry), the clergyman in a village near the Groves' Wiltshire estate, visited their Welsh retreat in September 1798 and soon afterwards published a poetic tribute to the place in a slim volume entitled *Coombe Ellen*—a detailed (351-line) loco-descriptive account of the scenery of the place, written chiefly in blank verse, with moralizing passages consonant with Bowles's profession. Whether or not PBS had recently read that poem (a copy of which would certainly have been in the library of the estate it celebrated), these stanzas on "Cwm Ellan" and their companion poems **"Dark Spirit of the desart rude"** (**Esd** #20) and **"Death-spurning rocks"** (#22) reply to Bowles's poem, much as **Mont Blanc** answers Coleridge's *Hymn before Sunrise.* Where Bowles had praised God for the natural beauties and sublime vistas of the place, PBS imagines its *genius loci* to be a Gothicized spirit of the sublime filled with dizzy Danger (9) that presided over the scene like a **"Dark spirit"** that he views either as a demonic power or, at best, a force totally indifferent to human beings and their fate.

line 10. ’mid the rocks: Though we add punctuation sparingly to **EN,** our copy-text, we attempt to follow PBS’s lead by adding apostrophes in all the places analogous to those where he has done so in the Notebook. Here he placed the apostrophe before ’mid, though it is the first instance he did so in the poems of *Esd* (compare Mid in **line 15** of the present poem), just as published texts of the day commonly used the apostrophe before this abbreviated form of the adverb *amid* to distinguish it from the adjective. That anomaly provokes us to ask why he did so. Did PBS add the apostrophe here to signal that ’mid, rather than Where, should receive the first metrical stress in this line? Did he simply wish to emphasize that a change to the unabbreviated *amid* would harm the meter of the line?

line 16. Below this final line appears PBS’s line count: “821” (which still omits the dedicatory poem *To Harriet*).

To Death   [Esd #19]

In the second volume of *SC* (1961), Cameron transcribed and discussed a manuscript containing a forty-five-line version of this poem that PBS gave to Hogg at Oxford in November or December 1810 (*SC* II, 641–45), remarking that there was another version of the poem in **EN** (which the Pforzheimer Library did not purchase until the middle of the year after *SC* I and II appeared). Cameron’s informative commentary focused on one of the central scholarly issues raised by the placement of *To Death* in **EN**—namely, the provenance and occasions of the poems that PBS gave to Thomas Jefferson Hogg, either in separate manuscripts or in the texts of the letters that PBS wrote to him. Of these, the Pforzheimer manuscript that contains nearly two-thirds of *To Death* (the text of which we reproduce as a Supplement to the *Esd* Text) was the earliest poetry that PBS gave to his new friend after writing *“Oh wretched mortal”* into Hogg’s notebook on what may have been the first night of their acquaintance at University College (see *CPPBS* I, 138, 305–7).

As noted in our introductory account of the biographical background and the history of the growth of the *Esd* collection, not until after the Shelleys returned to London in 1813 after their second visit to Ireland was PBS able to borrow back the bulk of the poetry that he had shared with Hogg during and immediately after their time at Oxford. Soon after PBS returned to London in April 1813 and looked up Hogg, whom he had not seen since the night before the Shelleys left London to return to Wales in November 1812 (having avoided Hogg’s visit to Dublin), PBS was probably able to recover the texts of most of the poems that he had given or mailed to Hogg between October 1810 and June 1811.

In this poem PBS addresses Death as a potentate or demigod, using the form of an irregular ("false Pindaric") ode, a genre that began its popularity with Abraham Cowley's *Pindarique Odes* (1656), was used notably by Dryden in *Alexander's Feast* and by Gray in *The Bard,* and was successfully revived in Coleridge's *Dejection: An Ode* and Wordsworth's *Ode: Intimations of Immortality* (see Stuart Curran, *Poetic Form and British Romanticism* [New York: Oxford UP, 1986], 63–84). The imagery of **To Death** is fundamentally biblical, with PBS taking **lines 1** and **5** from St. Paul (I Corinthians 15:55)—lines that also appear both in the Christian burial service and as the final lines of *The Dying Christian to His Soul,* Pope's reply to *De anima* by the pagan Emperor Hadrian, which Pope also translated (see *The Poems of Alexander Pope,* ed. John Butt [New Haven: Yale UP, 1963], 116–17). PBS in turn was responding to those two poems, and he imitates them again (though hardly in the terse, epigrammatic style of Hadrian and Pope) later in this collection in **A Dialogue** between Death and a Mortal (**Esd** #33), which he dates 1809.

To Death thus foreshadows crucial issues and imagery that permeate not only **Esd** but **Adonais,** and like that masterpiece it provides a detailed refutation of the power of death to subdue the poet. Here he asserts that Death can bring no sting to the dying or victory to the awful abstraction so long as *life* is filled with such horrors as <u>Thy slave, the mightiest murderer</u> who in spite of <u>nature's cries</u> sends <u>myriads to glut the grave</u> (**11–14**). PBS may have thought of Napoleon as the current representative <u>tyrant, sensualism's slave</u> (see the list in his third note to **A retrospect of Times of Old, Esd** #31), though Cameron, before seeing **EN,** assumed that George III was intended. In the second strophe, the poet (like Prometheus in Act I of **Prom**), declares that even <u>on some rock whose dark form glooms the sky,</u> he would gladly <u>stretch these pale limbs when the soul is fled,</u> | <u>To baffle the lean passions of their prey,</u> thereby, though in an inanimate state, being better off than <u>the Wretch around whose dazzling throne</u> | <u>His countless courtiers mock the words they say</u> (**31–36**; compare **Ozymandias**). PBS would later portray the state of the dead poet Keats as preferable to that of his corrupted, albeit living, reviewer, a "noteless blot on a remembered name!" (**Adonais** 327).

Title. The fragmentary text in *SC* II (MS Pfz 120) lacks a title, as well as the final lines of **Esd** #19.

line 13. <u>sacrifize</u>: PBS presumably spelled the word thus to indicate that the sibilant is to be voiced to rhyme perfectly with <u>cries</u>.

lines 18–30. The subject of this long periodic sentence is the infinitive <u>To know</u>, which PBS has set off by a comma, since the verb of this periodic main clause is the subjunctive <u>were</u>, followed by <u>Victory!</u> in **line 30.**

lines 20–21. These lines affirming the immortality of <u>Love</u>, though implied in several earlier poems, are here given as a declaration of metaphysical truth. But this statement, like that articulated by Demogorgon in **Prom**

(II.iv.119–20), may be an exercise in mythmaking. For discussion of some less optimistic views of love found in PBS's prose and late poetry, see *SC* VI, 633–47.

line 24. <u>From Death's pale front fade Pride's fastidious frown</u>: that is, just as in the previous lines <u>ambition's crown</u> and <u>its sceptered sway</u>, <u>must perish</u> (**21–23**), so ultimately even Death's pride in its conquests should <u>fade</u> (subjunctive) from the white forehead (<u>front</u>) of Death's skull.

line 39. <u>Kings whose luxury mocks the woe</u>: The word <u>mocks</u> can be read as a variation on its use in **To Mary who died in this opinion** (see **CPPBS** I, 139, 309), here meaning both "ignores" and "defies," prefiguring <u>mockery</u> in **line 56.**

line 45. <u>an happy</u>: another instance where PBS uses <u>an</u> rather than *a* before an *h* that is usually now aspirated.

line 46. The comma following <u>Ye</u> indicates that the pronoun for <u>conquerors</u> in (**42**) is the direct object of <u>Shall bear</u> (**47**).

lines 49–52. Though the syntax seems murky here, the poet deems that it would be <u>Hell</u> to find that <u>Vice</u> suffered <u>no pain</u> except (<u>But</u>) its <u>memory</u> of its evil past (sadists might enjoy recollecting their evil deeds), even <u>Tho' joy</u> might flow to <u>Virtue</u> from the <u>selfsame</u> source (i.e., the memory of past deeds). The following lines suggest that only complete annihilation in the grave can, therefore, provide true justice, a conclusion similar to that suggested by George Crabbe in his comparisons between the lot of the poor and the rich in *The Village:* "And each in all the kindred vices trace, | Of a poor, blind, bewilder'd, erring race: | Who, a short time in varied fortune past, | Die, and are equal in the dust at last." (Bk. II, lines 97–100).

line 66. <u>their</u> . . . <u>their</u>: both misspelled "thier" in **EN.**

lines 67–68. <u>Welcome then, peaceful Death, I'll sleep with thee— | Mine be thy quiet home, and thine my Victory.</u>: This final heroic couplet reads like an epigram adapted or translated from an earlier (perhaps classical) one, but if so its source has eluded us.

Below **line 68** is PBS's line count to this point in the Notebook: 889.

Supplement: Version in Hogg Manuscript, ca. 1810

To Death is the first poem included in **EN** for which we have an earlier version of which PBS gave a copy to Hogg—this one during their early days at Oxford in 1810. For our discussion of the provenance of Pfz 120 (*SC* II, 641–45), as well as the themes of the poem, see the Commentary above. Almost all of the changes made to Pfz 120 when it was added to **EN** relate to word choice or line breaks, featuring PBS's myriad synonyms for <u>tyrant</u>, which appear in support of the poem's theme that Death is the great equalizer. By breaking **lines 9–11** into **lines 9–13** in *Esd* #19, PBS created memorable dimeter lines, varying the normal reading tempo to emphasize plodding despotism's <u>pomp and power</u>. The addition of **lines 49–68** to *Esd* #19 completes the theme outlined in the Supplement version, ending with an image more specific and macabre than simply "that mysterious strand" of the Supplement, in which the tyrant's "wreathes of bay . . . Wither around his fleshless brow" (**54–55**). The seemingly paradoxical conclusion in **EN** situates the speaker comfortably in the grave with "peaceful Death" as his companion (**line 67**), while praising Death's victory over tyranny with the certainty that "not power's stern rod or fame's most thrilling blasts | Can liberate thy captives from decay" (**64–65**).

line 16. PBS's <u>shrine</u> appears to be written "shine" in Pfz 120, as it often is in **EN**.

       bubbles sank
line 19. ~~hopes and fears~~: PBS underscored the canceled phrase after canceling it, signaling that he planned to return to his original wording, as he in fact did in *Esd* #19, where "hopes and fears" is the reading.

line 36. In Pfz 120, PBS apparently miscopied the phrase "countless courtiers," instead repeating the first word so that the MS reads "countless countless." (Though *SC* II argues that the *l* is merely a long *i*, what would have to be an *r* also looks like an *n*.)

line 42. "~~Which~~ From": *SC* II (643) does not transcribe PBS's capitalization of "From," although the letter appears clearly to be a capital *F*.

"Dark Spirit of the desart rude"   [Esd #20]

"Dark Spirit" is composed in tetrameters with rhymes that, as the meaning requires, vacillate between couplets and irregular patterns (like the rhymes in ***Wandering Jew,*** though here they evidence greater assurance and precision). This subordination of form to meaning signals that this poem is no formal exercise but arises from an idea, feeling, or experience personally important to PBS. In *1964* Cameron (followed by *1966*) dated this poem in the late summer of 1811, when PBS visited Wales before eloping with HWS. But the editors of *1989*, noting that both Cameron and Rogers had dated it "on the grounds of its gloom and loneliness," argue that the mention of reviving spring flora in **lines 30–33** suggests that the poem was composed about 20 April 1812, when the Shelleys returned to Radnorshire and lived for a short time at Nangwilt, near Cwm Elan, while PBS tried unsuccessfully to borrow money to lease that property and when HWS's illness added to PBS's bad mood over the failure of the Irish expedition and his indecision about how next to promote the reform of Great Britain. But *"Dark Spirit"* is less closely bound to a particular time and place than these critics might think: It resonates with metaphysical inquiry and speculation on a theme central to the Romantics, for whom the bloodletting of the French Revolution and its aftermath had destroyed their illusions about the inevitability of Enlightenment meliorism. Just as PBS had challenged the clichés of Christian theology while under the direction of his relatives and his teachers at Eton and Oxford, so once he had embarked on his Quixotic quest to reform the opinions of all the English and Irish to a faith in human reason and natural emotions, he began to doubt that this was, indeed, the best of all possible worlds, with guaranteed salvation for those who "first follow Nature." In this mood, spring and dawn, autumn and nightfall are not just seasonal or diurnal events, but symbols of a cyclical pattern of nature and, perhaps, of the all-but-inevitable waxing and waning of human liberty, social justice, and poetic optimism.

"Dark Spirit," though set in springtime, explores the possibility that the tutelary spirit of the Elan Valley—and, by extension, untamed Nature in general, or the Power that governs natural creation—is malevolent rather than benevolent. Like *Written at Cwm Ellan* (*Esd* #18), this poem challenges William Lisle Bowles's assumption that the sublime terrors of the untamed wilderness were the totally good gifts of a beneficent God. Instead, PBS looks for a <u>Dark Spirit</u> of this place in traditional symbols of ill-fortune and devastation, such as <u>yon sooty and fearful fowl</u>, like one of the many ravens that, according to a later book, frequented the area (see *1989* I, 219), flapping <u>its wing o'er the leafless oak</u> (**12–13**). The second verse-paragraph (**16–25**) tells how the poet (like the one in *Alastor* or *Hymn to Intellectual Beauty*) had sought the supernatural power in dark and eerie places, only to discover that the natural wilderness seemed to <u>express</u> an <u>emphatic gloominess</u>.

The final verse-paragraph begins with the repeated question and its answer: The symbolic embodiment of the <u>Dark Spirit</u> is the <u>leafless oak</u> (**13**), which <u>sapless, blasted and alone, mourns her blooming centuries gone!—</u> (**26–29**). Though spring revives the perennial <u>Violets</u> and <u>frozen buds</u>, the <u>desolate Oak</u> with its lightning-<u>scathed head</u> represents the individual, as opposed to the species, which does *not* revive with seasonal cycles. As the anonymous late Latin poet, perhaps of the period of Hadrian, laments in *Pervigilium Veneris* (i.e., *"Vigil on the eve of a spring festival honoring Venus"*) and was echoed by poets through the centuries, down to the Romantics, T. S. Eliot, and Allen Tate: "O when shall I be like the swallow?"

Earlier a giant oak tree appeared in PBS's poetry bearing a very different significance: In the fourth canto of *The Wandering Jew* (*WJ*), "the branches of an oak, | . . . riven by the lightning's stroke" save the life of Vittorio just as he is about to fall "Into the ocean's yawning womb" (IV, 140–45). And in the translation from Schubart's German poem that provided PBS's conception of the Wandering Jew as one persecuted by a malicious deity and unable to die, Ahasuerus complains that "[t]he lightning . . . blasted me; and like the scattered [*or* shattered] oak, which remains a monument of faded grandeur, and outlives the other monarchs of the forest, doomed me to live for ever" (footnote to *WJ* III, 196; *CPPBS* I, 66 and 78; 200 and 222–23). In *"Dark Spirit,"* however, the keystone of PBS's sequence of poems exploring the role of death in humanity's quest for meaning, the <u>scathed Oak</u> seems to become a symbol, not of extended life, but of the inevitable destruction of even the superior individual. PBS's perception may have been altered by a passage in Bowles's *Coombe Ellen* that describes just such a tree (possibly the same one, if its decaying trunk could have survived from 1798 to 1811 or 1812):

> Upon the adverse bank, wither'd, and stript
> Of all its pleasant leaves, a scathed oak
> Hangs desolate; once sov'reign of the scene,
> Perhaps, proud of its beauty and its strength,
> And branching its broad arms along the glen:
> O speaks it no remonstrance to the heart?
>
> (pp. 7–8; lines 54–59)

Bowles's pedestrian lines may have called PBS's attention to the oak and, when he realized that Bowles had described the same, or a similar, lifeless trunk a decade earlier, his conception of the great tree may have changed. Perhaps this discovery caused PBS to make a crucial revision in **line 35,** so that **34–36** read: <u>But thou alone art here,</u> | <u>Thou desolate Oak, whose scathed head</u> | <u>For ages has never trembled</u> [i.e., it no longer has leaves to tremble in the wind]. Having concluded, however, that this embodiment of the <u>Dark Spirit</u> is not really a potent force of evil, but an *absence* of life, the poet's tone changes from metaphysical awe to political satire as he notes that the carcass of the tree, though lifeless, has like the <u>King</u> in *The Monarch's funeral* (*Esd* #16) decayed even after sucking up nutriments meant for others. The poem concludes with another epigram (**43–46**), the last line of which is underscored—perhaps indicating that it is quoted or paraphrased from another source, as yet unidentified. Thus, while the issues first raised in *"Dark Spirit"* prefigure the great questions raised in *Mont Blanc,* the present poem, though begun in the high style of the sublime, concludes in epigrammatic lines that change the poem's tone and may preview that of the last seven stanzas of *Peter Bell the Third,* Part Fourth (especially lines 353–63), which also feature a dead tree, not as a symbol of life and death, but as the analogue of a corrupt patron of writers.

line 6. <u>jetty</u>: black.

line 11. <u>Wavest thy wand</u>: Here are the delayed verb and the object of the dependent noun clause beginning at **2;** the main verb addressing the <u>Spirit</u> follows in **line 12.**

line 23. <u>Has shot,</u>: PBS placed a comma after this verb to make clear that it belongs with <u>glare</u> (**22**), rather than with what follows.

line 31. PBS's misspelling of <u>their</u> as "there" in **EN** shows that he composed, or in this case copied by ear, rather than by eye.

line 33. **EN** indicates that PBS first wrote "Is alive with Nature's awe," then erased "Nature's awe" by smearing the wet ink with his finger, and wrote <u>Earth's sweet</u> over the smear before concluding the line with <u>melody.</u>

line 35. <u>Thou desolate Oak</u>: PBS first wrote "Thou desolate rock" but changed "rock" to <u>Oak</u> after the page was completed, for the wet ink from this change blotted onto the facing page when he turned the page or closed the Notebook. This crucial change may have been made, therefore, after PBS read (or recalled) Bowles's account of the "scathed oak" quoted above.

line 46. PBS indicated his wish to italicize this line by underscoring it; beneath it appears "935," his running line count.

"The pale, the cold and the moony smile"   *[Esd #21]*

This poem, of unknown date, is the only one in *Esd* that PBS published after *QM,* for he included it as the fourth of the eleven "Other Poems" published with *Alastor* in *1816.* There the text was heavily revised, as indicated in the primary variants to the *Esd* version of the text. (The significance of these changes for the poem's new context will be discussed in *CPPBS* III.) PBS may have selected this poem out of those in *Esd* simply because he failed to keep copies of most of the works in that collection, and *perhaps* "moony smile" had been drafted in a notebook in his possession after he separated from HWS. But even if PBS had copies of a number of the poems in *Esd* after he eloped with Mary Godwin (MWS), there are artistic and thematic reasons why *"moony smile"* was more compatible with the new poems he wrote for *1816* than are many others in *Esd.*

In *1816,* as in *Esd,* this poem lacks a separate title (though in both *1966* and *1972* Rogers gave the poem the fanciful title "Reality"), but in *1816,* it is headed by an epigraph from the biblical book Ecclesiastes: "THERE IS NO WORK, NOR DEVICE, NOR KNOWLEDGE, NOR WISDOM, IN THE GRAVE, WHITHER THOU GOEST." While examining the interrelations of the twelve poems in PBS's *Alastor* volume of 1816, Fraistat pointed out that this, one of the first six poems in the volume, fulfilled Earl R. Wasserman's description of the central theme of *1816* as "man's transience and nature's inconstancy," a feeling that could have led PBS to reject life and seek meaning in death (Fraistat, "Shelley's *Alastor* Collection," *K-SJ*, 33 [1984]: 181). The arrangement of *"moony smile"* and its companion poems in the "Graveyard Group" in *Esd* (#19 through #23) supports both that reading and Fraistat's insight that the final six poems in *Alastor* change the tone to a more positive view of life by the end of that volume, thus following the pattern that characterizes Edward Young's *Night Thoughts,* in which the poet's thoughts move from "The Complaint" to "The Consolation."

Besides being thematically harmonious with the other five poems that open *1816*, *"moony smile"* is far more closely related to the *Alastor* volume artistically than are the other poems in *Esd*—even those of the "Graveyard Group." First, unlike some of PBS's experiments with long lines and complex rhyme schemes (e.g., the "super-Spenserian" stanzas of *a Tale of Society,* #14, or the hexameters of *Written at Cwm Ellan 1811,* #18), its form—six-line stanzas of basically anapestic four-stress lines, rhymed *ababcc*—does not call attention to itself, nor does it contain such technical problems that occasionally overshadow or distort PBS's meaning in those more challenging verse forms when the young poet's virtuosity failed him. Second, many of the poems on death in *Esd* are occasional in nature, involving such personal experiences as PBS's search for Robert Emmet's grave in Dublin (#13), his prospective musings about the death of King George III (#16), or his encounter with a particular lightning-shattered oak tree on his kinsman's Welsh estate (#21). Contrastingly, *"moony smile"* attains the same abstract and generalized philosophical style as *Alastor, "O! there are spirits of the air,"* and the two final poems in *1816* that derive from revised sections of *QM,* making the disquisition on death in *"moony smile"* perhaps more harmonious with the other poems in *1816* than any other poem in *Esd* might be.

In **EN** PBS indented the lines of verse irregularly in all but the first stanza, though the rhyme scheme remains the same (*ababcc*) throughout all five stanzas. We have regularized the indentions in accordance with those in the *Alastor* volume.

lines 1–6. The main elements of this sentence read: <u>taper of life Is</u> (**5**) <u>the moony smile</u> (**1**) of a <u>meteor beam</u> (**2**). Whether, as *1989* queries, the <u>meteor beam</u> (**2**) is a lightning flash, the aurora borealis, or an *ignis fatuus,* PBS has explicated its significance by identifying its qualities as <u>pale</u>, <u>cold</u>, and <u>moony</u>, consistent with his symbolism (e.g., in *Epipsychidion*) of the moon in contrast to the sun. Here he states that <u>the taper of life</u> (**5**) is analogous to analytic reason, rather than the synthesizing imagination present in <u>morn's undoubted light</u> (**4**).

line 16. <u>nervestrings</u>: Like <u>body</u> in **line 20** (and "eyeballs" in *"Dark Spirit,"* line **22**), this word is not only part of the Gothic diction for what Keats termed "wormy circumstance" (*Isabella,* 385) but also suggests a materialist ontology. In revising the poem for *1816*, PBS changed <u>nervestrings</u> to "nerves" and <u>body</u> (**20**) to "frame," suggesting that he became disillusioned with the materialist position sometime between 1814 and 1816. He later declared materialism to be "a seducing system to young and superficial minds" that he abandoned because it did not accord with human nature, which "disclaim[s] alliance with transience and decay" (***On Life;*** *Shelley's Poetry and Prose/*2 [2002], p. 506). As we indicate in the Commentary to the poems of the Graveyard Group that follow, PBS shows himself in this sequence (likely drafted at different times, but placed in a climactic order when he arranged the poems of ***Esd***) to be groping toward his rejection of dogmatic materialism, a change of perspective completed when he adopted the skeptical idealism of the later Platonic Academy and of Hume, as revived by Sir William Drummond in *Academical Questions* (1805), a work to which Peacock may have introduced him, perhaps in the spring or summer of 1813, for PBS mentions Drummond in Note **13** to ***QM***.

lines 19–24. Whereas the first stanza states unequivocally that the <u>taper of life</u> is transient, the final two stanzas cast doubt on our knowledge of what follows life, suggesting that rational certainties overlook mysteries beyond our ken. Among the <u>secret things of the grave</u> (**19**) where everything besides <u>this body must surely be</u>, there is, or may be, a place for the part of life that is non-body, where <u>All that is bright and all that is strange</u> will follow a <u>gradual path of unending change</u>, even though our eyes and ears will not be able to witness it. (**Line 24** may suggest why the *Purgatorio* was PBS's favorite part of Dante's *Divina Commedia*.)

lines 25–30. The final stanza consists of a series of questions that seem not rhetorical, but simply unanswerable. Perhaps based on Chapter 38 of the Book of Job (*1989* I, 427), in which God answers Job by pointing out human limitations and ignorance, it drives home the point that life's transient flickering is surrounded by darkness, and there are—or at least may be—more things in Heaven and Earth than are to be found in a rationalist philosophy.

line 26. <u>lifteth the veil</u>: an early instance of the figure of the veil between life and death that PBS uses frequently in such later poems as ***Sonnet: "Lift not the painted veil."***

line 30. Below this line, PBS wrote his line count: "965."

"Death-spurning rocks!"   *[Esd #22]*

When the poet had confronted the wilderness around Cwm Elan in ***"Dark Spirit"*** (***Esd*** #20), he concluded that all aspects of natural creation were subject to the ravages of "Fate, Time, Occasion, Chance, and Change" (***Prom*** II.iv.119) except the rugged Welsh mountains—"yon broken peaks sublime, | Wild shapes that mock [i.e., defy] the scythe of time" (8–9). But in ***"Death-spurning rocks!"*** he announces that even they are not exempt from the <u>Dark Spirit</u> symbolized by the lightning-shattered oak tree: <u>Ye shall spurn death no more but like your Oak decay</u> (**10**). PBS's early awareness of the Gershwin brothers' dictum that "In time the Rockies may crumble, Gibralter may tumble— | They're only made of clay" marks the culmination of the Graveyard Group in ***Esd*** that collectively explores the issue of the death and destruction of human individuals, their artifacts, their created memorials, and even the natural settings that nurture them: To PBS, at the moment he wrote this poem, all things beneath the moon seemed to him transient and destined for total destruction—and, in fact, the whole Elan Valley has since been drowned under the reservoir system of the city of Birmingham (see "The Elan Valley dams from Shelley to the Dambusters" on the website of the Powys Digital History Project). After PBS perceived the threat of this slow apocalypse, he sought to discover some means by which individual human beings could hope to preserve their personal aspirations and humane moral values.

Following this confrontation with nihilism in the first stanza, the second stanza relates the rejection of a symbolic <u>maniac-sufferer</u> (**11**)—a <u>way-worn wanderer</u> who is turned away <u>from the door</u> | <u>Where Pity's self promised to soothe his woe</u> (**23–24**). Although *1989* compares PBS's posture here to that of the protagonist in Goethe's *Sorrows of Young Werther,* which PBS had read by June 1811, the poet had earlier portrayed such a "maniac" in his ***Fragment ("Yes! All is past—swift time has fled away"),*** the fourth poem in ***Posthumous Fragments*** (***CPPBS*** I, 35, 100), and he later portrayed other maniac-sufferers (e.g., in ***Julian and Maddalo***) who, like this one, seem to be largely self-portraits.

Having found little comfort in the processes of natural Necessity, the poet's pain and despair are so great that, as he gazes across the <u>gulph</u> of the grave <u>that yawns</u> before him (**27**), he asks rhetorically whether death might not be preferable to life: <u>why need he live to weep who does not fear to die?</u> (**30**). After facing the implications of a despair that erases any hope of ulti-mate meaning for human life, PBS here—and in ***The Tombs,*** which follows— seems to have rejected the philosophical materialism that brought him to this impasse. Instead, he looks forward to the dawning of a new <u>daystar</u> beyond the <u>gulph</u> of death. Then, in the poems of ***Esd*** that follow ***The Tombs,*** he rebuilds hope for a meaningful life through the inspiration of a new lov-ing relationship. Just as Harriet Grove (or possibly PBS's mother or his sister Elizabeth; see *1989*) was a likely human embodiment of <u>Pity's self</u> who ear-lier turned him from her door, he chooses HWS to support the renewal of his commitment to the betterment of mankind, first articulated at Eton in ***"I will kneel at thine altar"*** (***Esd*** #42) and later recounted more circumstantially in ***Hymn to Intellectual Beauty*** and the Dedication to ***Laon and Cythna.*** To give purpose to his life in the face of its tribulations and the apparent finality of death, he resolves to be true to his best self by seeking the good of other human beings, his spirit being supported by the love and sympathy of his partner, HWS. In *The Retrospect* (*Esd* #50), the penultimate poem in *Esd,* he asserts that, because of the support of his young wife, Nature has regained its potency and value and he can once again address the Welsh mountains as immortals: "Ye jagged peaks that frown sublime, | Mocking the blunted scythe of Time" (112–13).

PBS certainly wrote *"Death-spurning rocks!"* at Cwm Elan, probably while visiting Thomas Grove there in August 1811 after Harriet Grove or her family had terminated his engagement to her, as Cameron argued (*1964,* 211 ff.), against the opinions of Dowden and Garnett, whose notes in MS ED-Pfz favored 1812. *"Death-spurning rocks!"* shows PBS to be completely isolated, and at least in his poetic expressions, suicidal, which he had not appeared to be after his elopement so long as he and HWS retained their affectionate relationship. The rhyme scheme and meter of the ten-line stanzas in *"Death-spurning rocks!"* support the case for the earlier date, for the prosodic elements of this poem are simpler than the more ambitious stanzaic forms that PBS developed in his experiments of 1812–13. Though he seems to be reaching toward the complexities of the super-Spenserian stanzas of *a Tale of Society* of early 1812, the first four lines of each stanza here are pentameters (settling into fairly regular iambs by stanza two), rhymed *abab,* followed by two tetrameter couplets, and concluded by a couplet consisting of a pentameter line rhymed with an Alexandrine.

line 20. <u>veins</u> was misspelled "viens" in **EN**.

line 22. <u>One fleeting beam flashed but its gloom to shew</u>: This reference to the <u>fleeting beam</u> may provide a clearer picture of the "meteor beam" in line 2 of *"moony smile"* (*Esd* #21). The antecedent of <u>its</u> is <u>the wild moor</u> (**21**), rendering the sense of this line thus: a <u>fleeting beam</u> of light <u>flashed</u>, only to render the <u>gloom</u> of the <u>moor</u> even darker by contrast. Compare *Hymn,* lines 44–45, where the poet says that the spirit of Intellectual Beauty provides "nourishment" to "human thought" as does "darkness to a dying flame!" Similar images of transient lights being enhanced by the contrasting effects of darkness also appear in his later poems.

Here, as often in PBS's poetry, <u>but</u> means "only" or "except." He rhymes <u>shew</u> with <u>woe</u> (**24**), confirming that "shew" and "show" were not (as in Spenser's time) pronounced differently; PBS may have used these alternative spellings to distinguish the verb from the noun.

lines 23–25. The <u>way-worn wanderer</u> (presumably the poet) was <u>turned</u> away by a person (evoked as <u>Pity's self</u>) who had <u>promised</u> to comfort him if he would <u>turn back</u>. A biographical reading suggests that Harriet Grove had rejected him even after he had appealed to her (by letter, if not in person), saying that he would renounce his radical or anti-clerical opinions, or whatever else stood between them, if she would only <u>soothe his woe</u>. As he <u>fled to the wild moor</u> (**21**), he experienced an epiphany: He did not need to bear <u>this misery</u>, if he did <u>not fear to die</u>.

line 30. No line count follows this poem.

The Tombs   *[Esd #23]*

When sequencing his poems in **EN,** PBS placed this poem at the end of the Graveyard Group to mark the point in the volume at which (as in Young's *Night Thoughts*) *The Complaint* begins to turn into *The Consolation.* As both Cameron (*1964,* 215–16) and Matthews and Everest (*1989* I, 202) observe, this poem was likely written in Dublin between February and April 1812, at about the same time he wrote **On Robert Emmet's tomb** (**Esd** #13)—another sign (if one is still required) that he arranged the poems neither chronologically, according to their periods of composition, nor randomly. Freeing himself from what in **A Defence of Poetry** he was to call "the accident of surrounding impressions," he positioned his poems to tell the story of his inner life from the time of his conversion experience at Eton in the spring of 1810 till mid-1813 and to emphasize HWS's significance for that history. Ten poems earlier, he had asserted the value of Emmet's sacrifice and declared that once the "storm cloud" of tyranny passed, the "daybeam" of Emmet's nobility would shine forth. Here PBS, having explored the dark night of his soul in the Graveyard Group, uses a companion poem that alludes strongly to Emmet (<u>Erin's victim-patriot</u>, **22**) to declare that, though PBS's imagination had been shaken, he would not <u>sum</u> . . . <u>human life</u> as merely <u>a mound of mouldering flesh</u> (**6–10**) as long as there were those such as Emmet who were willing to give their lives in the noble fight for human liberty.

Having followed **Esd**'s first five unrhymed poems with seventeen intricately rhymed ones, PBS places at this point a poem in unrhymed five-line stanzas, each of which has two pentameter lines followed by three tetrameters.

line 7. <u>sculls</u> **EN.** *OED* recognizes "scull" as an alternate spelling of *skull* from the sixteenth through the nineteenth centuries; more specifically, our dictionaries of 1733, 1803, and 1805 list both spellings, but by 1826, only "skull" appears. Since the influence of Norse invaders had given Scottish and north-English dialects many more words using *sk* than southern English (e.g., *skiff* vs. *ship*), one may speculate that the dominance of Scots in the printing and publishing trades in the late eighteenth and early nineteenth centuries played some part in tipping the scales in favor of the *sk* spelling.

line 10. Quotation marks appear in **EN** before and after <u>thou wert human life!</u> The additional quotation marks placed by various editors before <u>In</u> (**11**) and <u>All</u> (**16**) and after <u>world.</u> (**20**) have no authority from PBS's holograph, even though **lines 11–20** seem to continue the poet's lament.

line 20. For <u>this phantasmal world</u>, see Commentary for *QM* IX.74.

lines 24–25. PBS here seems to imply that the English and their Irish accomplices burned Emmet's heart—perhaps a synecdoche for his missing corpse (see Commentary to *Esd* #13), and rumors to that effect may have been circulating in Dublin at the time. Historical and literary precedents that PBS may have known are cited in *1989* (I, 204).

line 26. <u>Ah, no! else</u>: These three words transform the message of this poem from fear of death to <u>the hopes of life and love</u> (**28**).

line 30. Below this line is PBS's line count: "1025."

To Harriet ("It is not blasphemy to hope")   *[Esd #24]*

This ***To Harriet*** was the first poem destined for publication that PBS wrote entirely in blank verse. In 1817, when PBS wrote his Preface to ***Laon and Cythna,*** he indicated that he was hesitant to attempt "the blank verse of Shakespeare and Milton" because it afforded "no shelter for mediocrity: you must either succeed or fail" (paragraph eight). ***To Harriet*** illustrates the problem that he confronted and suggests that his experience in attempting blank verse here may have contributed to his awareness of its aesthetic difficulties. Dowden's notes to his transcription emphasize the Wordsworthian elements in the poem, especially the influence of *Tintern Abbey,* and observe that PBS would have passed the ruin mentioned in Wordsworth's title on the Shelleys' trip down the River Wye to Chepstow, while on their way to Lymouth (now Lynmouth), Devon. That is where both Dowden and Cameron (*1964*) place the composition of ***To Harriet;*** Cameron suggests the time as the summer of 1812, but *1989* argues for November or December 1812, during the Shelleys' stay at Tremadoc (I, 261). We find the evidence favoring either of those two dates inconclusive. Though the poem follows the theme of *Tintern Abbey* and overtly echoes its diction (in **lines 2–3, 16,** and **34**), PBS had already written for HWS ***The Retrospect*** (#50), a much finer poem based on the structure and theme of *Tintern Abbey,* while sojourning in Radnorshire, before that trip down the Wye, and there is no reason that PBS would forget the diction or tone of Wordsworth's finest early-published poem in blank verse before the end of 1812, if ever.

PBS's first effort in blank verse is technically less impressive than many of his earlier experiments with complex verse forms in *Esd.* Thematically, however, it is central among his attempts to establish a foundation for a new millennial social order in which <u>this Earth is Heaven</u> (**21**), and, therefore, he placed it immediately after the group of negative poems about the supreme power of Death over mortal achievements, using it to introduce his basis for renewed hopes for human destiny. Though this poem, like its counterpart *To Harriet ("Never, O never"; Esd* #5), sounds shrill, the tone in this case seems not to result from either insincerity or its contrary—a fanaticism for ideal love in the abstract—but from PBS's near-despair caused by his cumulative reverses during the previous two years. His self-image was further eroded by his failure to make a positive impact on the political situations in Dublin and in Devonshire. By the middle of 1812, his vision of a renovated social fabric depended even more upon his relationship with HWS. Yet, objective observers all recognize how great a burden such demands might be for an insecure seventeen-year-old girl. Either when PBS tried to bring Elizabeth Hitchener into their family community at Ly(n)mouth, by the end of their stay at Tremadoc, or at least by the time the Shelleys returned to London in 1813, Harriet's enthusiasm for their itinerant life as indigent apostles of Liberty had waned. Once back home, she may have tried to distance herself from the role in which her emotionally needy husband had cast her, and the word <u>blasphemy</u> in **line 1** of *To Harriet* may suggest to some that the poem was provoked by HWS's complaints to PBS about his penchant for idolizing her as his personal goddess.

Because *To Harriet* derives from some such crisis of faith, it not only closely echoes Wordsworth's *Tintern Abbey* in places but also parallels in tone and language several later poems in which PBS articulated his core needs and beliefs. For example **lines 13–17** prefigure PBS's poem to Jane Williams entitled *The Magnetic Lady to Her Patient* (now classified among the poems of 1822, though it cannot be dated precisely because there is no known draft of this poem: see *BSM* XII, xxix and 141), and the metaphor in which <u>common</u> (i.e., insensitive) <u>souls</u> are likened to ephemerids or May-flies (**28–29**) reappears (reshaped to new contexts) in *Sensitive-Plant* (II.49), *Witch of Atlas* (9), and most closely in the twenty-ninth stanza of *Adonais* (253–61). **Lines 32 ff.**, which foresee the maturing of the poet and his beloved through their later years, show PBS's acceptance of lessons about the stages of life that he found in the poetry of Wordsworth (as well as the private admonitions of Southey and Godwin), and the passage previews similar ones in *Hymn to Intellectual Beauty* (final stanza) and in *West Wind* (47–51, 57–61).

The closest parallel with PBS's thought in *To Harriet* is his note to *QM* VIII.203–7, in which (as Dowden first observed) he quotes **lines 58–69** of *To Harriet.* If our redating of the *QM* Notes is correct, PBS copied *To Harriet* in **EN** considerably earlier than he wrote the note to *QM* VIII. In *To Harriet* PBS also grapples with the difficult conception of the relationship between Time and Eternity, which (Cameron notes; *1964,* 220) he was to treat later at the beginning of Act IV of ***Prometheus Unbound***—especially IV. 9–20. PBS's desire that HWS <u>turn</u> her <u>spirit-beaming eyes</u> on him (**10–13**) both prefigures the passage in Act IV of ***Prom*** in which The Moon compares her attraction for The Earth to "the Polar Paradise | Magnet-like, of lovers' eyes" (IV.465–66) and (Nora Crook observes) may be PBS's first allusion to "animal magnetism," described in "letter" 51 of Southey's *Letters from England,* which (according to Medwin) PBS read in 1811 (Crook and Guiton, *Shelley's Venomed Melody,* 246, n. 59).

In spite of PBS's inveterate myth-making, his characteristic intellectual skepticism often led him, in ***To Harriet*** as elsewhere, to frame his ideals and hopes as questions, rather than declarations. Employing another technique common in his poetry, PBS describes his idealized visions—here involving the potentialities of connubial love—in long complex sentences, but when recording his descent from a visionary state to the recognition of cold realities, he tightens the reins of his imagination to write shorter, simpler clauses and sentences.

lines 5–13. Dowden noted that these lines had previously been published from Richard Garnett's "transcript of a Boscombe MS"—that is, from the archive of MSS collected at Boscombe Manor, the home of PBS's son Sir Percy Florence Shelley at Bournemouth. But since later scholars have not located such lines in those former Boscombe MSS (now reunited at the Bodleian Library), Garnett more likely received them (as *1989* suggests) from the same governess in the Esdaile family who also gave him texts of two sonnets from **EN** (see *Letters about Shelley,* 87–88).

lines 6–7. While PBS's image of himself as a <u>lone spirit</u> traveling on a <u>gloomy path</u>, <u>cold and drear</u>, suggests the Wandering Jew, maniacs, and other pitiable outcasts who served as his surrogates in earlier writings, the whole passage from **5** to **13** foreshadows the visionaries of ***Alastor, Epipsychidion,*** and ***Adonais,*** who have something important to offer the world besides their isolated suffering. This change suggests that PBS was beginning to recognize the value of his vocation as a poet.

line 13. <u>Earth?—will</u>: The marks in **EN** after <u>Earth</u> are puzzling: they seem to be a period followed by a dash, above which is what looks like an inverted horseshoe or the top loop of a question mark—thus suggesting our pointing.

lines 17–23. One argument advanced by *1989* for dating ***To Harriet*** at Tremadoc in November–December 1812, rather than at Devonshire during the summer, centers on **lines 22–23,** in which PBS uses the imagery of an <u>untainted seed | Which springeth here beneath such love as ours.</u> Matthews and Everest take this to signal PBS's "awareness of Harriet's pregnancy" (*1989* I, 261), an argument that would gain support from there being nine cantos of **QM,** matching the months of human gestation, if Edward Young's *Night-Thoughts* had not already established a pattern of nine-book philosophical or religious poems (which Blake also planned to imitate in *Vala*). But in the context of the full sentence involving **lines 17–23,** the result of *One* soul-reviving kiss is <u>an assurance that this Earth is Heaven</u> | <u>And Heaven the flower of that untainted seed</u> | <u>Which springeth here beneath such love as ours</u>. In other words, the fruit of their *spiritual* union will be, not a child, but <u>Heaven</u>, imagery equally possible whether or not PBS knew that HWS was pregnant.

line 19. PBS's comma after <u>existence</u> marks the line's cesura.

line 26. The *c* in <u>chill</u>, larger than usual, was superimposed on another letter, probably *f.*

lines 32–55. PBS loved to write long periodic sentences, and this one is difficult to follow, although its general thought is partly clarified by its affinity for lines 26–33 of *Tintern Abbey:* when PBS and Harriet mature, their ideals will bond and will protect them from becoming slaves to <u>the cold forms</u> | <u>Of this desolate world</u> (**44–45**)—what he was later to term "the contagion of the world's slow stain" (**Adonais** 356). This passage both praises Harriet's future potential and hints at a current conflict lying just beneath the surface of the young couple's relationship.

line 37. <u>æstival sun</u>: summer sun.

line 41. <u>enthusiast heart</u>: See Commentary to **QM** I.49.

lines 58–69. <u>Dark Flood of Time</u> . . . <u>unredeemed</u>: These dramatic lines reappear in PBS's note to **QM** VIII, 203–7, where he presumably quoted them after he had abandoned his hope of publishing **Esd** to save them, like **Falshood and Vice** (**Esd** # 6), for posterity. Because the text in **EN** required emendation, we have here repunctuated the lines to reflect PBS's preferences when he saw the passage of **QM** through the press. On the subjective and relative nature of time, see PBS's Note 16 to **QM** and our Commentary on it.

line 72. Below this line, PBS recorded the line count as 1100. As our Commentary suggests, the poems in the sequence on death crescendo toward a climactic vision, and PBS may have planned **To Harriet,** which ends with this rounded line count, to mark the end of one major section of his "minor Poems."

Sonnet: To Harriet | on her birth day, August 1, 1812   *[Esd #25]*

PBS wrote some sonnets while carrying out his propaganda campaign in Devonshire in the summer of 1812. After reaching the natural stopping place of 1,100 lines of verse in **EN,** he copied these sonnets into the Notebook to link the previous poems, which reflect his contrasting feelings during his two visits to Cwm Elan, in 1811 and 1812, with the poems that follow. After *To Harriet ("It is not blasphemy")*, he copied the sonnet that he wrote to celebrate his wife's seventeenth birthday. (Though Louise Schutz Boas gives only HWS's christening date of 27 August 1795 in *Harriet Shelley* (4), a fold-out plate, "Pedigree to Show the descent of Percy Bysshe Shelley," at the end of Ingpen, *Shelley in England* provides her date of birth as 1 August 1795.)

Aside from translations of a few classical epigrams, PBS's sonnets are among the shortest of his completed poems that survive. Those that he wrote in England primarily follow the example of Wordsworth, who published some of the finest of his 535 sonnets in *Poems: in Two Volumes* (1807), the first volume of which contains—besides the "Prefatory Sonnet" beginning *"Nuns fret not at their Convent's narrow room"*—forty-six others in two groups, one group on personal and the other on political themes. As Lee M. Johnson demonstrates in *Wordsworth and the Sonnet* [Anglistica, XIX; Copenhagen: Rosenkilde & Bagger, 1973], 174–83), most of Wordsworth's sonnets were precisely crafted in the Petrarchan or Italian form, with an octave rhymed *abbaabba* that describes a scene or situation, followed by a sestet rhymed *cdecde* or *cdcdcd* that comments on it. Wordsworth almost invariably limited his deviations from this ideal to: (1) introducing a new rhyme in lines 6 and 7; (2) allowing the thought of the octave to spill over into the ninth line (thus varying the location of the *volta*, or turn in the thought); or (3) varying the position of the second or third rhymes in the sestet. Other poets had followed the example of Shakespeare, whose sonnets, written in iambic pentameter usually consist of three quatrains rhymed *ababcdcdefefgg*. PBS wrote far too few sonnets either to achieve technical mastery of the form or to support critical generalizations, but in 1812 he seems to have been less inclined to follow a preestablished ideal than to bend the form, either to express his meaning or as experiments with the form itself. PBS's **Sonnet: To Harriet** is quite irregular: it rhymes *ababcddcefefgG*, thus beginning and ending in the manner of a Shakespearian sonnet, places the *volta* at the end of **line 10,** and lengthens the final line to iambic hexameter (an Alexandrine).

The chief novelty of this poem appears not, however, in its form but in its message. After mentioning some of HWS's visible charms—which comments by Peacock and by PBS's sister Hellen (HWS's school friend [see *1989*]) indicate were considerable—and alluding to <u>even sweeter</u> ones that these superficial beauties <u>index</u> (i.e., point to), PBS foresees that the ravages of time will someday dim her eyes and erase her cheeks' color. Still, he hopes, <u>ever thus</u> . . . <u>may</u> she retain <u>Love and Virtue's glow</u> in her <u>unwithering soul,</u> thereby making his love even stronger and fitting both of them for an eternal <u>bliss</u>. The *topos* of praising young women by imagining them as more precious when they are old is a very rare one. W. B. Yeats's *When You Are Old* (published 1892), inspired by young Maud Gonne, might seem at first to be one analogue. But Pierre de Ronsard's sonnet beginning *"Quand vous serez bien vielle"* (1578), the accepted basis of Yeats's poem, does not involve this theme but two quite different ones: first, that the poet's words will give immortality to his beloved's beauty and, second, that since her charms will fade, the lovers ought to seize the day. Scholars have, in fact, documented Ronsard's "antagonism towards neo-Platonic love doctrines" and his parody of those who claim that the soul can transcend the body (Malcolm Quainton, *Ronsard's Ordered Chaos* [U of Manchester P, 1980], 179–86).

A contemporary parallel to and likely influence on PBS's poem is *"Believe me, if all those endearing young charms,"* a very popular song by Thomas Moore that appeared in the second part of the Powers brothers' publication of his *Irish Melodies* (1808). PBS read and admired Moore's early poetry, and from HWS's Commonplace Book we find direct evidence that he knew Moore's *Irish Melodies* in 1812, for on folio 11 verso of that manuscript HWS has copied down "On Music from the Irish melodies by T. More Esq." (which begins, "When thro' life unblest we rove"); HWS's misspelling of Moore's name suggests that she may be writing down the poem either from a text read to her by her sister or PBS, or from PBS's recitation of the poem from memory. Thus, though neither the form nor the language of PBS's sonnet resembles that of Moore's *"Believe me"* and though PBS's awareness of Wordsworth's perspective on the stages of life and his own speculations about the future of his relationship with HWS (see **Esd** # 29) might have led him to the theme independently, it seems likely that Moore's song about love surviving the inevitable loss of "endearing young charms" provided the basic concept through which PBS here expresses his thoughts and feelings.

line 5. <u>thus, thus!</u>: After the first <u>thus</u> PBS first wrote "as on," then canceled the phrase and wrote the second <u>thus!</u> before writing "as on" again. Since the meter does not require the extra emphatic <u>thus!</u> (which gives it six metrical stresses), PBS intended to reinforce the point that HWS's <u>soul</u> was especially vibrant and <u>unwithering</u> (**10**) on this particular day.

line 7. <u>dyes</u>: PBS accidentally wrote the verb *dies* and then corrected to the noun by overwriting the second and third letters with a *y*.

Sonnet: To a balloon, laden with <u>Knowledge</u>   *[Esd #26]*

This sonnet's form, somewhat more regular than that of the previous poem, is closer to the English, or Shakespearian, form. It consists of a single breathless sentence in regular iambic pentameter, rhymed *abbacdcdefefgg*. Though there is no *volta* in the Petrarchan sense, there is a break at the end of **line 7**; following the main clause, which contrasts the temporary brightness of the balloon lit by the sinking sun with <u>the Fire</u> of <u>Knowledge</u> that it bears to its lucky finders, the final half of the poem contains five parallel appositive phrases, each one or two lines long, that address that <u>unquenchable</u> wisdom as <u>A watch light</u> guarding the <u>patriot's lonely tomb</u>, <u>A ray of courage</u>, and so forth.

We have no contemporary information to confirm the idea expressed in this sonnet, written in August 1812, that PBS used a hot-air balloon to disseminate political propaganda, but he may actually have done so. We know that he learned the principles of launching such balloons (high technology in the early nineteenth century) from lectures given at Eton by Adam Walker (see *1989* I, 239). Hogg recounted that even while they were students at Oxford PBS told him, "Why are we so ignorant of the interior of Africa?—why do we not despatch intrepid aeronauts to cross it in every direction, and survey the whole peninsula in a few weeks? The shadow of the first balloon, which a vertical sun would project precisely underneath it, as it glided silently over that hitherto unhappy country, would virtually emancipate every slave and would annihilate slavery forever" (Hogg, *Life,* ed. Wolfe I, 63; Chap. 3). If PBS did send up a toy balloon in Devon, he could have attached to it one or more of his "seditious" political printings, such as ***Declaration of Rights*** and ***The Devil's Walk,*** which—as the Commentary to the following poem mentions—he launched into the Bristol Channel sealed in old wine bottles (***CPPBS*** I, 284–85).

line 1. <u>Even</u>: In spite of the reading "even" found in other texts, it seems to be capitalized in **EN,** perhaps to identify it as a noun, rather than adjective, adverb, or verb.

line 3. <u>dimmst</u> is spelled as a monosyllable. Had PBS printed the poem, he might have added an apostrophe before the *s.*

line 5. <u>shalt</u>: shall **EN** Dowden wrote "shalt" above PBS's <u>shall</u> to correct the grammatical error of using a third person verb form with <u>thou</u>. Though the grammatical anomaly may suggest that PBS felt uncomfortable using the intimate second person familiar form to address a balloon, he probably simply failed to cross the final riser to form the "t."

line 7. <u>doomed</u>: i.e., destined or fated

line 11. We have made <u>tyrants'</u> a plural possessive to match <u>domes</u>. Although one tyrant can own more than one <u>gilded</u> dome, we believe that PBS meant to contrast the <u>lonely</u> patriot (**8**) with a multiplicity of tyrants in the world.

line 14. In this context, <u>yet</u> carries its basic temporal meaning of "until now" with its sometimes implicit "contrast to a future or subsequent state"; one contemporary example in *OED* comes from the fourth stanza of Wordsworth's *To the Cuckoo:* "Thrice welcome, Darling of the Spring! | Even yet thou art to me | No bird; but an invisible Thing, | A voice, a mystery." (*Poems* [1807], II, 58)—lines that PBS kept in mind at least till he wrote **To a Sky-Lark.**

Sonnet: On launching some bottles filled with <u>Knowledge</u> into the Bristol Channel.   [Esd #27]

Though we lack direct information on PBS's experiments with balloons in Devonshire, evidence concerning his launching of the bottles of this companion sonnet appears in a letter sent in August 1812 by Henry Drake, Town Clerk of Barnstaple, to Lord Sidmouth (the Home Secretary) reporting that PBS had been seen launching bottles into the Bristol Channel, and when one was retrieved, it was found to contain "a seditious Paper"—**The Devil's Walk**—while another such bottle reached the port of Milford Haven in Wales (see **CPPBS** I, 283–85). As Mrs. Blackmore, the adopted daughter of PBS's landlady at Ly(n)mouth later recalled, PBS also sometimes sealed up and launched little boxes containing his publications (see *1964*, 221–23; *1989* I, 238).

The sonnet form here is notably imprecise. Though it is written in pentameter lines, the rhyme scheme reads *abbacdcdeffegg* and includes such off-rhymes as <u>brow</u> with <u>blow</u> and <u>freight</u> with <u>light</u>.

line 3. <u>stern</u>: Previous editors give the word as "stem," but PBS here uses another nautical verb, meaning "to propel a boat stern foremost" (*OED* 2), that better describes the way a wine-bottle floats, as its thick, heavier bottom (the part affected by the sea currents) moves ahead of its narrower neck, which extends above the water level.

line 7. The <u>dark green</u> (2) bottles float out into the Bristol Channel, an arm of the Irish Sea, like a miniature armada, powered by <u>breezes</u> from the <u>west</u> (8).

Sonnet: On waiting for a wind to cross the Bristol Channel from Devonshire to Wales.   [Esd #28]

About 28 August, a few days after the arrest of Dan Healey, their Irish servant, for distributing PBS's "seditious Papers" in person rather than by bottle, box, or balloon, the Shelleys' party left Ly(n)mouth, Devon, just one jump ahead of the officials from Barnstaple. Unable to hire a fishing boat to carry them directly from Ly(n)mouth northward to Wales because the wind was unfavorable, they then went to Ilfracombe, a nearby seaside village to the west, from which, according to *Paterson's Roads* (see *1964*, 223), there was twice-a-week packet boat service to Swansea, Wales. Thus, we calculate that this sonnet was inspired and probably drafted 28 or 29 August 1812.

PBS's description of <u>Boreas</u>, the north wind, as the <u>gloomy tyrant of the unwilling deep</u> (**4**) sets the scene for *Prometheus Unbound* III.ii, at the end of which Ocean, no longer ruled by tyrannical winds after learning of Jupiter's downfall, ends his conversation with Apollo to complete the transformation of "the unpastured sea," which is still "hung'ring for calm." The mythology in both poems derives, of course, from ancient Greek poetry, especially *The Odyssey*.

Formally, this sonnet is as irregular as the previous ones, rhyming *ababcd-dcefefgG* and once again ending in an Alexandrine. Its publishing history illustrates one of the problems in the public awareness of the poems in *Esd.* To simplify the case, Dowden, in keeping with his promise to the Esdaile family to quote in his *Life of Percy Bysshe Shelley* (*1886*) only those poems or parts of poems necessary to illuminate PBS's life, worked into his narrative just four full lines (**6–8, 10**) and three partial lines (**1, 5, 9**) of *Esd* #28, while mentioning in a footnote that he was quoting from an "unprinted sonnet" (I, 298–99). Since the part of **line 1** he quoted ("the south's benign and balmy breeze") was given within quotation marks, rather than blocked, as were the sonnet's other lines, later editors—unsure whether it was part of the sonnet or prose from another source—reprinted only the remainder, to which they gave various titles—"Fragment of a Sonnet: Farewell to North Devon" (Woodberry, *1892W* IV, 333); "Farewell to North Devon" (Hutchinson, *1904,* 977); and "Sonnet written before leaving Lynmough for Ilfracombe" (Roger Ingpen, *1927* III, 110), though in his last endnote to that volume Ingpen gave it still another title, "Sonnet on waiting to cross the Bristol Channel from Devonshire" (III, 323).

Title. Having mentioned the Bristol Channel in the title of the previous poem, PBS at first left out the word <u>Bristol</u> here, but then—to avoid confusion with the better known English Channel—he careted in <u>Bristol</u> above the line.

line 14. Previous editors all read the last word of the poem as <u>purity</u>, even though, as with many of the carelessly written words in **EN,** it is ambiguous and equally readable as "piety"—also appropriate for the sound and sense of the line. With the word <u>Nature's</u> in the same line, "piety" recalls Wordsworth's use of "natural piety" at the end of "My heart leaps up" in Volume II of *Poems* (1807) and prefigures PBS's use of that phrase in *Alastor* (**3**). PBS (and perhaps Wordsworth?) had also encountered the phrase and its significance as a moral alternative to theism in Bacon's "Of Superstition" (on this influence, see our Commentary on PBS's *QM,* Note 13, lines 128–34). But though PBS may have intended his text here to read "piety," the visual evidence in **EN** is not strong enough to warrant our changing the received reading, especially since of the eleven occurrences of *purity* in the *Shelley Concordance* five are in *QM* and *purity* occurs at least four other times in *Esd* (*Sabbath*

Walk 53; *To Harriet (. . . Blasphemy)* 54 and 71; and *To the Lover of Mary* 21 (not counting this likely one).

line 14. Below this line PBS wrote "1156," thereby adding to his tally the lines of the four sonnets in the group.

To Harriet ("Harriet! thy kiss to my soul is dear")   *[Esd #29]*

There is no external evidence from which to date this poem, but since PBS explains to HWS (as he did also in *Esd* #25, his sonnet to her on her birthday) that the quality of her character or soul is more important to him than her beauty or sexual attractions, it may have been written about the same time, perhaps as another birthday offering. Though her kiss and her heart, when it pants desire from eve to . . . morning (**6–8**), are dear to his soul, he loves her even more when she expresses in her looks a lustre of joy-mingled woe (**9**). In the third stanza, PBS reaffirms his affection for his young wife by employing such metaphors of love-to-excess as he might have learned from Shakespeare's *Romeo and Juliet,* but he—who was later to characterize himself through the persona of the Maniac in *Julian and Maddalo* "as a nerve o'er which do creep | The else unfelt oppressions of this earth" (449–50)—also describes his heart as one that beats for its country as well as for his wife (**25–26**), and he ends this poem with an assurance that his heart, if she emulates him, can burn with love and virtue and will, therefore, never repine at evil or pain (**30–32**). In **line 2** he had used the same verb, telling HWS that he would never repine ("fret, grieve, murmur, or grumble") if she showed the same degree of feeling (signaled by a look and a kiss) for the sighs and tears of others as she lavishes on him (**3–4**).

Though in a poem as rhetorical as this one it is difficult to measure the level of sincerity in the poet's voice, PBS's clear statement that he would love HWS more if she were more philanthropic and less centered in self (and on him) suggests one cause, quite apart from any intellectual disparity between them, for the deterioration of their marriage (see also the Commentary to *Esd* #51–#53). Cameron suggested that differences between PBS and HWS may have arisen because Eliza Westbrook feared that their political activities in Devon were exposing them to legal dangers, and he judged that this poem *To Harriet* might mark the beginning of PBS's deep hatred of Eliza (*1964,* 224–25).

The poem consists of eight-line stanzas, rhymed *ababcdcd,* in flexible anapestic tetrameter, one of the most basic forms in English prosody, which seems to merge the four-stress line of Anglo-Saxon poetry with the ballad stanza quatrain rhymed *abab.* Here again, when PBS wrote a personal poem that he intended to convey a clear message, he generally eschewed the artistic complications of intricate forms.

line 4. <u>a look</u>: As PBS was writing these words, a blob of ink (from a faulty pen nib or a tipped ink well) marred the words and he smeared the ink (perhaps with a pen-wiping cloth) to dry it. He then rewrote <u>look</u> beyond the ink smear, leaving the still-legible <u>a</u> smeared but obviously still part of the poem.

line 32. Below the poem's final line, PBS recorded his line count: "1188."

Mary to the Sea-Wind   [Esd #30]

In this poem, for which (as for ***Esd*** #29) we lack any firm date of composition, PBS assumes a character clearly distinguishable from his own persona to write a dramatic lyric in the voice of a woman. In ***Mary to the Sea-Wind*** a young wife or sweetheart apostrophizes the sea-wind, seeking knowledge of her beloved's whereabouts and asking the wind to bring her Henry home again. PBS had begun his poetic career by writing poems of this ventriloquistic type. His ***Original Poetry by Victor and Cazire*** features both lyrics and narratives ostensibly in the voices of medieval knights, as well as contemporary Italian, German, and Irish speakers; ***The Wandering Jew*** contains long passages of dramatic speech by its small cast of characters, and a bardic narrator like those in Scott's narrative poetry; and ***Posthumous Fragments of Margaret Nicholson,*** supposedly written by the insane washerwoman who had tried to assassinate King George III, includes dramatic lyrics in the voices of the regicides Charlotte "Corday" and "Francis" Ravaillac, along with less clearly defined personae as an Irish nationalist and a madman. In analyzing these and other poems in Volume I of ***CPPBS,*** we attributed PBS's attempts to distance his poetic persona from his existential self partly to his uncertainty about the quality of his poems and partly to his need to hide his identity in order to avoid ridicule or prosecution. But, based on the number of subterfuges PBS adopted in his real-life dealings with friends and creditors alike, we now realize that the poet was also an actor manqué who delighted in playing roles and hoodwinking others for fun and profit. Our study of the early poems lends support to those scholars who have argued that, at least in the works he sent to press, PBS was much more a dramatic poet than is usually recognized—though he gave a large proportion of his ventriloquized words not to human characters but to such mythological or nonhuman beings as Queen Mab, a Cloud, a Sky-lark, Prometheus, Asia, Demogorgon, the Spirits of the Hours, Apollo, Pan, the Witch of Atlas, the shade of Rousseau, and their ilk. ***Mary to the Sea-Wind*** may be seen, then, as a small step in PBS's transformation from a confessional poet into a mythological dramatist. (Nora Crook has observed to us that PBS was reading some works by Mary Wollstonecraft as early as 1812 and may, therefore, have had in mind her *Letters from Norway* when he composed this poem.)

    Mary to the Sea-Wind—composed in quatrains rhymed *abab,* with lines of variable length, but all scannable as anapestic tetrameters—appears in **EN** shortly after the sonnets that invoke the winds to disseminate "Knowledge" through sky and sea (and to aid the flight of the purveyors of that knowledge) and shortly before *The Voyage* (#32), a long narration about a sea crossing. This continues his arrangement of the poems of *Esd* in sequences designed to create what Fraistat has called a "contexture" that enhances the collection as a whole beyond the merit of its individual parts (see *The Poem and the Book* [U of North Carolina P, 1985], 3 ff.). More specifically, Mary's address to the sea-wind, seeking news of her absent lover, seems to anticipate the passage in *The Voyage* in which an unnamed sailor returns home, only to find that his wife, Mary, has died since he began his voyage to the Orient (lines 237–66). The poems are not presented as companion pieces, but a leitmotif found in one poem reappears in the other, which, though not contiguous, is close enough for the reader to sense their relationship.

line 7. "but" altered to <u>yet</u> in **EN**.

line 11. <u>And when</u> written upon "That" (canceled by smearing the wet ink).

line 15. <u>undo</u>: i.e., betray.

line 16. Below this line is a line count that, though difficult to read, is 1204.

A retrospect of Times of Old   [Esd #31]

Of the nine primarily military poems in *Esd,* only *A retrospect of Times of Old* treats generically the issues of ambition and conquest within a long historical perspective. (A good recent study of PBS's views of these subjects throughout his career is Michael Ferber's "Shelley and 'the Disastrous Fame of Conquerors,'" *K-SJ* 51 [2002]:145–73.) This irregularly rhymed, iambic pentameter poem takes readers once again into the ruins of empires and preaches about <u>Desolation</u> (**13**) and <u>Death</u> (**20**) as the great levelers. The whole poem reads, in fact, like an excerpt that PBS had drafted for **QM** before he settled on its form as unrhymed-lyric cum blank-verse, and liked well enough to give it a place among his "minor Poems." (This hypothesis accords with the views in *1964* and *1989*, both of which date the poem in the summer of 1812 in Devonshire, where PBS began to work on **QM** in earnest.) Its theme thus both derives from Volney's *Les Ruines* and Peacock's *Palmyra* (see *1964*, 227–28) and prefigures *Ozymandias.* The outlines of the meditation are clear enough, from the fratricide and suicide (**28–47**) that, as *1989*'s excellent note on the passage shows, conflate various possible source stories into a unified myth of the fruits of <u>Ambition</u> (**48**). But the crucial point of the poem is found in PBS's third and final note—keyed to **line 72**—in which he concludes his list of <u>legal murderers</u> of his <u>own age</u> with the names of <u>Wellington and Nelson</u>, who epitomized the military successes of his own nation.

That the source from which PBS took *A retrospect* was an unfinished draft (into the copying of which he put little creative effort) can be seen in his numerous careless errors of transcription and his all but illegible penmanship. Like *The Voyage* (#32), PBS probably included this poem in *Esd* partly to enhance its size, though *A retrospect* is more coherent and perhaps more closely linked thematically to the volume as a whole than is *The Voyage.*

lines 9–11. For PBS's extended attack on contemporary religions, see the beginning of *QM* VII and the Commentary to *QM* VII.30.

line 18. PBS originally wrote "this world" but overwrote the "is" with a large "e" to produce the world.

line 21. "Death . . . swallowed up in Victory!: PBS adapts his line from St. Paul's first Letter to the Corinthians 15:54, the verse preceding, "O death, where is thy sting?" which appears in both *To Death* (#19) and *A Dialogue* (#33).

To maintain the iambic pentameter line, he changed his original "thou wi'lt" to thou'lt by crossing out the "wi" with a small horizontal stroke. Similarly, in the following line (**22**), he canceled the phrase "brilliant piles" by smearing the half-dry ink and then superimposing Dream of fame on the smear.

line 25. Simoon is one Western transliteration of an Arabic word "*semum,* meaning poison" (*OED*); it denominates "a hot, dry suffocating sand-wind" sweeping across desiccated areas of the Middle East and North Africa. The word appears sporadically in poetry of the period, including Book II of Southey's *Thalaba,* with a long footnote on the word and its referent (1801; Vol. I, 100–101) and in the first edition of Byron's *The Giaour, A Fragment of a Turkish Tale* (published by John Murray on 5 June 1813), where Byron uses "Simoom" (44 lines into the first edition; page 3, penultimate line) to describe the title character—"He came, he went, like the Simoom"—and keys to the word this note at the bottom of the page: "The blast of the desert, fatal to every thing living, and often alluded to in eastern poetry." Both Southey and Byron, however, use the more common English spelling "Simoom," while PBS spells the word *simoon* in four poetic uses of it (the others appear in *BSM* XIII, 105 and 107, and *BSM* XVI, 91). Since *semoun* and *simoun* were the preferred French spellings, a French source or one deriving from that language seems likely.

That the wind produces music in a lone lyre—an aeolian harp, which *1989* says was perhaps suggested from Erasmus Darwin's account of the "gigantic statue of Memnon in his temple at Thebes" with "a lyre in his hands" (*The Botanic Garden,* Part I, additional Note 8: "Memnon's Lyre," which glosses Canto I.183–88 of Darwin's poem). This statue was said to "sound when the rising sun shone upon it every morning at dawn." Since the early morning sun, rather than wind, initiates the music, PBS's use of the figure here and elsewhere in *Esd,* as well as in *Alastor* (42–44)—may derive from the account of this statue by Darwin or by James Montgomery in his poem *The Battle of Alexandria* (on which, see Commentary to **Henry and Louisa,** #46), rather than only from Coleridge's *The Aeolian Harp* (first published 1796) or PBS's first-hand knowledge of wind harps, then common in country houses. Darwin's anecdote from Herodotus that "[T]he statue of Memnon was overthrown by Cambyses and sawed in half to discover its internal structure" is also relevant to the negative view of conquerors expressed by PBS in this poem.

line 28. Previous editions and transcriptions read <u>There</u> as "Here." Several analogues have been suggested for the story of royal fratricide narrated in **lines 28–47** (see *1964,* 228–29; *1989* I, 242), including *Hamlet* and the story of the Persian emperor Cambyses (Kanbujiya II, son of Cyrus the Great; d. 522 B.C.). Herodotus in his *History* (III, Chaps. 28–68) tells how Cambyses conquered Egypt, Libya, Cyrene, and northern Ethiopia, but how in the madness of unbridled power he not only mistreated the Egyptians, but also ordered his brother's murder, married two of his sisters (killing one), and— like Nero and Caligula—slaughtered various friends and advisors. Since Cambyses delegated the killing of his brother to another person, PBS's allusion here is syncretic, embodying elements from many historical and literary sources (e.g., *Hamlet*) in which ambition leads to crime and tyranny becomes anarchy. This incident itself, as the poet says in **30,** <u>long has fled</u> . . . from all but <u>visioned</u> (i.e., imaginative) <u>memories</u>.

line 32. <u>reckless of</u>: unheeding of, not considering.

line 34. <u>They told each innocent secret of the day—</u>: This line seems to record the subject of the victim's dream that brings to his face the <u>peaceful smile</u> (**32**) just before he is murdered. If PBS was copying from a rough draft originally intended for **QM,** he may have misplaced this line, possibly because it was inserted out of its proper order in the draft, or because it was an uncanceled line amid others that PBS had intended to discard.

line 36. As Dowden notes in MS ED-Pfz, <u>steel</u> is written so carelessly that it looks like *shell.*

line 51. PBS superimposed <u>flown</u> upon another word—possibly "glow." In the next line (**52**) he changed "rolls" to <u>roll</u> after writing its plural subject, <u>waves</u>.

line 54. PBS originally wrote "Nor" and then superimposed a *t* on the *r;* in the next line (**55**) he changed a comma following <u>hero slept</u> to an exclamation point.

line 61. PBS began to write "bloody altar" but changed his mind and wrote <u>gorgeous</u> over "bloo" (presumably to avoid having "bloody" and "bled" in the same line).

line 66. PBS miswrote <u>drowned</u> and then revised the word.

line 70. <u>the world</u> can also be read as "this world" (as in *1964*). PBS had difficulty writing in the notebook's gutter, and his cramped orthography makes it difficult to establish a definitive reading.

line 71. According to Herodotus (II, chap. 102 ff.), <u>Sesostris</u>, an early "king of Egypt," conquered much of the eastern Mediterranean world, leaving inscriptions throughout Syria, Asia Minor, and as far as Thrace. Early in the twentieth century Sesostris was sometimes identified with Ramses II, the pharaoh of the Exodus, but more recent authorities identify him with earlier pharaohs of the twelfth dynasty in the Middle Kingdom, perhaps Sensuret I (1971–1928 B.C.), a conqueror of Nubia and developer of mines and quarries; Sensuret III (1878–1843 B.C.), whose prosperous and well-governed Egypt conquered Nubia, Palestine, and the "sand-dwellers"; or a legendary conflation of these rulers. Egyptians revered the memory of Sesostris even more after the Assyrians and the Persians had conquered Egypt.

Francisco <u>Pizzaro</u> (ca. 1474–1541) was the Spanish *conquistador* who—with 180 men, 27 horses, and great courage, cunning, and cruelty—conquered the Inca empire, then battled with his lieutenant Diego de Almagro and executed him, only to be assassinated by Almagro's followers. PBS would have known his story in detail from Robertson's *History of America* (for which see *To the Republicans*, #17, Commentary).

At the end of **line 71** PBS originally placed a small "x" as the key for his third and final footnote but then erased it by smearing the wet ink and placing a more prominent star after <u>Mahommed</u> in **line 72**.

line 72. In *QM* PBS expatiates on <u>Moses</u> as "a murderer" and "Accomplice of omnipotence in crime" (Canto VII.100–104 and Commentary) and on <u>Mohammed</u> and Moslems as participants in the "slaughter house" produced by religion (see Commentary to VII.48). PBS's note to this line, in which he provides contemporary <u>addenda</u> to the <u>list of legal murderers</u> of past history, shows how strongly his hatred of war overrode his patriotic nationalism. Among the <u>notorious scourges of their species</u> that he singles out there, some had earlier been demonized in England: Frederick II ("the Great") of Prussia (1712–86), instigator of several wars that ravaged central Europe; Napoleon <u>Buonaparte</u>; and <u>Suwarroff</u> (i.e., Russian Field Marshall Count Aleksandr Vasilievich Suvorov, 1729–1800), whose illustrious but bloody career included victories during the Russo-Turkish War of 1787–91, notably the siege of Ismail (depicted by Byron in *Don Juan*), which cost the lives of

10,000 Russians and 20,000 Turks; the suppression of the Polish uprising of 1794 under Kosciuszko, during which Suvorov's troops slaughtered 23,000 men and women after overrunning the Polish troops at Praga; and victories over the French Revolutionary armies in Italy in 1799. To these ravagers, PBS adds the Duke of Wellington, then steadily gaining praise (from Southey, among others) for his victories in the Peninsular Campaign, and Horatio, Viscount Nelson, the hero of the British naval victories of the Nile (1798) and Copenhagen (1801; see *Esd* #39) and the martyr-hero of Trafalgar (1805), where the British fleet ended Napoleon's dream of invading England. See the Commentary on ***Fragment . . . bombardment of Copenhagen*** and ***Henry and Louisa*** (*Esd* #43 and #46).

line 83. PBS's line count follows: "1287."

Footnote 2. In the second sentence, PBS first copied "upon record that"; then realizing that his eye had skipped ahead, he erased "that" by smearing the ink and proceeded with "parallell" (the spelling of which we have regularized).

The Voyage | A Fragment | Devonshire—August 1812   [Esd #32]

Although PBS's heading designates ***The Voyage***—originally titled "The Journey" (partially erased)—as having been composed in Devonshire, *1989* says that it could have been "during or immediately after S.'s passage from Ilfracombe . . . on August 31" (I, 247). Earlier, Cameron, in the fullest account of the poem, posited that PBS's headline on the place of composition is accurate and that this account of the end of a lengthy and troubled sea-crossing probably reflects PBS's first recorded sea voyages in early February 1812, when the Shelleys sailed from what PBS described to Hitchener as "the miserable manufacturing Town" of Whitehaven, Cumberland (*Letters* I, 248), to the Isle of Man and thence to Ireland. During the second journey, the small ship in which PBS, HWS, and Eliza Westbrook sailed from the Isle of Man was driven north of Ireland by a storm, delaying their arrival after what PBS wrote to Godwin was "a most tedious journey of sea and land" (*Letters* I, 250, 258). As Cameron suggests (*1964*, 232–33), memories of this experience, combined with those of their similarly difficult return voyage from Dublin to Holyhead, which took thirty-six hours in contrary wind and rain, without any food (see HWS to Catherine Nugent; *Letters* I, 283–84n), could have provided the emotionally charged memories to elicit PBS's passionate account found in ***The Voyage***.

Descriptions of realistic events on shipboard and during the landing are interrupted by symbolic passages about human life as a sea voyage (**lines 40–62**) and by a long passage (**149–213**) that relates a phantasmagoric nightmare experienced by a young Shelleyan idealist who is one of the passengers aboard, part of which (**176–80**) anticipates the opening of *Prom,* Act I. At the end of the passage, the Shelleyan persona dreams that he has awakened to find that <u>She whom he loved</u> is leaning over him and, though she herself has <u>Haggard . . . eye</u> and <u>Bloodless . . . lips</u>, she gives him <u>The burning moisture from her feverish tongue</u> | <u>To lengthen out his life</u>. Then he dreams that <u>A bleeding Sister lay</u> | <u>Beside this wretched pair</u> (**198–211**), over whom hulked a <u>pitiless landsman</u> with whom the idealist had struggled earlier in the dream. (This dream prefigures, in part, Laon's feverish nightmare at the opening of Canto III of *L&C.*)

If we accept *1989*'s idea that PBS composed this poem at the very end of his expedition in Devonshire and the speculations in *1964* that he may originally have intended to make it part of *QM* (see below), we can conjecture that the nightmare exhibits the unspoken anxieties and doubts that found release in the idealist's dreams. PBS may have sought to convince others— or, perhaps, himself—that he, as well as his servant Dan Healey (then beginning to serve a six-month sentence in the Barnstaple jail), was making sacrifices to achieve political reform. PBS, always very interested in his dreams, could have drafted this poem based on nightmares that reflected his earlier voyages and were stimulated during the last week of August by the anxieties aroused as his party sought to flee Devonshire by sea before the local authorities could catch up with them. If so, he may have added accounts of the crew and other passengers both to provide a realistic context for the visionary parts and to disguise the confessional revelation of his ambivalent feelings for HWS and Eliza Westbrook, much as he later encased his outcries against MWS within the dramatized dialogues that frame those complaints in *Julian and Maddalo.*

PBS presumably intended his praise of sailors in *The Voyage* to show that he, an idealistic aristocratic reformer, had empathy with common people. The passage on the two sailors, trained by hard experience to share things and to take the rough events of life in their stride, may reflect his admiration for the everyday courage of seamen whom he observed during the terrible storm on the trip to Dublin, but he also makes use of their attitude to confirm the Godwinian doctrine of Necessity, which he propounds in *QM* (see his note to *The Voyage,* **109**). The passages contrasting those two sailors (**70–111**) with the villainous "Landsman" engaged in commercial pursuits (**112–48**) are routine social ideology, probably making use of characters encountered on the various voyages to and from Dublin. This was the one <u>populous Town</u> that he had visited of which it could reasonably have been said that there <u>wolves keep lambs</u> (**221–26**) and that it was ruled by <u>smooth-faced tyrants chartered</u> by a <u>King</u> in <u>a far distant land</u> (**230–32**)—that is, the English monarchy and oligarchy at Windsor and in London. At Dublin PBS probably witnessed for the first time passengers and sailors alike being accosted by customs agents searching for contraband. (His luggage was searched and some pamphlets printed in Dublin were seized after the return voyage.) In *The Voyage* the victim of these officials is another young sailor, returning after years in the China trade, who brings home a few trinkets for his family only to have them seized as he is strip-searched and manacled. After learning that his wife Mary is dead (cf. *Mary to the Sea-Wind, Esd* #30) and that his sole surviving child has been farmed out as an apprentice by parish officials (**221–66**), he may then be (Cameron surmised) pressed into the king's navy. (On the politics of the impressment of seamen, see Daniel James Ennis, *Enter the Press-Gang: Naval Impressment in Eighteenth-Century British Literature* [Newark: U of Delaware P, 2002].) The poem concludes with an invective on corrupt or insensitive governmental and, implicitly, ecclesiastical officials who become an added burden on those whom it is their responsibility to help.

The greatest problem facing readers of *The Voyage* may not be to ascertain its date or which parts of it are fictional, anecdotal, or based on PBS's personal observations and dreams but to decide why he included in *Esd* this disjointed poem, containing few thoughts and feelings that are not better expressed elsewhere in the collection. His transcription of it is filled with errors and ambiguously written words, as well as interpretive problems, suggesting that he was bored by the process of copying it (as Dowden's transcription suggests that *he* was). Perhaps PBS's overriding motive for undertaking what seems to have been a distasteful task was his discovery that, just as had happened when he sent to press the copy for earlier collections of poems, he did not have enough material to fill a book of the length that he had promised. On 26 January 1813 he wrote to Hookham: "Queen Mab will be in ten cantos & contain about 2800 lines. The other poems [i.e., *Esd*] probably contain as much more" (*Letters* I, 350). But if he then tabulated the length of the poems already copied, he must have begun searching among his papers for other poetic drafts, which if revised could swell the projected volume to its intended size. *The Voyage,* with its 298 lines, bolstered the total of lines transcribed to 1588. But to approach his goal of 2800 lines, PBS needed to retrieve an additional cache of earlier poems and fragment-poems after the Shelleys' return to London in April 1813. Ultimately, when he completed his original plan for the volume with fifty poems and added his dedicatory poem *To Harriet ("Whose is the love"),* the collection contained, according to his calculations, 2822 lines of verse, or almost precisely the total that he had promised Hookham. (Our tally finds the total number of lines, including the dedicatory poem but not the poem titles, to be 2772 lines, the difference being due partly to PBS's errors in arithmetic and partly to his counting as present about two and a half Spenserian stanzas in *Henry and Louisa* that he ultimately left blank. (For these calculations, see Appendix A.)

The source of the material from which **The Voyage** was created almost certainly included a rejected portion of PBS's drafts for **QM**, which he recycled to bolster the "minor Poems." Cameron provided the clue to its origin when he "suspect[ed]" that the lines from **230** to the end of the fragment originally constituted "a separate poem" in "a different verse form," connected by "a rather tacked-on" bridge; the ship, he notes, reaches "port in the morning (lines 215–20), but when the press gang seizes the sailor . . . it is night" (**243–44**; see *1964*, 231). According to our analysis, the verse form of the opening 220 lines and the short bridge that Cameron identified (**221–29**) can be characterized as the irregular unrhymed verse found in the lyrical sections of **QM**, whereas **lines 230–98** are written in the blank verse that PBS employed in **QM** for narratives, as well as moral and philosophical reflections. As *1964* also points out, PBS's subtitle of **The Voyage** <u>August 1812</u> ties this poem directly to the completion of the first stage of **QM**, of which PBS sent to Hookham on 18 August "by way of specimen all that I have written" of the "little poem begun since" his "arrival in England" after his first Irish expedition (**Letters** I, 324). August 1812 may thus indicate the time that PBS decided that the lines in question did not belong in **QM**. He probably revised and copied them into **EN** some months later, either during his second visit to Ireland, or after his return to London.

line 2. <u>Each</u>: the "E" is superimposed upon an "I"—likely an eye-skip error, since **3** begins with <u>In</u>.

 <u>horrent</u>: This adjective, common in the period, derives from the Latin *horrens*. Though it can mean "horrible," *Entick's Dictionary* (1805) gives alternative meanings of "rough, sharp, standing up" (or "bristling" *1989*) that also apply to waves in dangerous storms; compare PBS's use of the word at **QM** VI.132.

line 37. <u>joybeam</u>: Apparently PBS's coinage and used by him just this once, this word is not found in Chadwyck-Healey *LION*, contemporary dictionaries, the *OED*, or the *Shelley Concordance*.

line 40. <u>The young</u>: the last letter of <u>The</u> is muddled with extra ink; *1964* reads "Tho'" but there is no apostrophe and considering the context, we believe <u>The</u> to be the more likely reading.

 <u>now</u>: superimposed on another word—"?here" or "?know"—canceled by smearing ink.

line 50. The <u>heads</u> of the young voyagers are <u>brothers</u> of their <u>hearts</u> (**48**).

line 62. <u>many colour'd veil</u>: This key Shelleyan image, well known through PBS's use of it in his sonnet beginning "Lift not the painted veil" as well through related allusions to veils and rainbows at key points in other works from **Alastor** to **Triumph of Life,** expresses the disparity between earthly phenomena, as viewed through the refraction of light by the Earth's atmosphere, and the pure white light of the sun, which figures ultimate truth seen from beyond this distorting medium. As S. R. Swaminathan points out in his *Vedanta and Shelley* (Salzburg: University of Salzburg, 1997), the idea that the material world is an illusory panorama shielding humanity from the true spiritual nature of things may derive from the Hindu concept of *maya* (or illusion), which PBS would have encountered in his reading of works by Sir William Jones, Edward Moor's *The Hindu Pantheon* (London: J. Johnson, 1810), or Sydney Owenson's *The Missionary* (3 vols., London: J. J. Stockdale, 1811), which impressed PBS in June 1811 (*Letters* I, 101, 107).

Throughout **Esd,** PBS irregularly places hyphens between the elements of compound adjectives and nouns. The facsimile in *MYR: Shelley* I provides the raw information about his actual practice; our Text (which embodies the suggestions of earlier editors) adds a number of hyphens, though this issue requires further study of PBS's practice in his published poems.

lines 85, 87. In both these lines, PBS misspelled the first word as *Thier.*

line 109. PBS's description of necessity as <u>Blind, changeless and eternal in her paths</u> and his accompanying footnote (which suggests that the lives of sailors led them to accept the doctrine of Necessity and that sailors on small, private ships were more generous than those who served on the <u>King's ships</u>) echo his treatment of Necessity in both the poetry of **QM** and its excursive footnote on Necessity; see the Holbachian hymns to the "Spirit of Nature" ending Cantos I and II of **QM,** as well as PBS's Note 12 and the related Commentary.

lines 114–17. In the received text (which we follow), the <u>mouth</u> of the despised <u>landsman</u> is said to be <u>updrawn at intervals</u> | <u>As fearful of his fluctuating bent</u>: taken at face value, this simply means that he seems not to trust his own mercurial nature. But to us (as to Edward Dowden) the word <u>bent</u> might as easily be read as <u>tent</u>, because at this period PBS often crossed his initial letter *t* with a loop coming down the left side of the riser from its top and then crossing it and continuing in a single stroke to form the next letter (*e* in this case), with the resulting letter *t* in some cases resembling an initial *b*. If PBS did mean to write *tent,* he was creating an interesting metaphor in which the land-lubber observes the fluttering sails above him and shows his fear that the canvas "tent" is about to collapse on him.

line 130. <u>guileless</u>: PBS after miswriting "guiless" wrote *le* upon *ss* and then rewrote <u>ss</u>.

line 131. <u>hearts</u>: PBS originally wrote "hand" (or "hands") and then changed it to <u>hearts</u>.

line 139. <u>Envenom all</u>: **EN** reads "Envenom ~~of~~ all".

line 142. <u>thriving</u>: The change to "striving" in *1964B* from the clearly correct reading in *1964A* was likely a typographical error when the text was reset for the London edition.

line 146. For the background to PBS's general attack on <u>Commerce</u>, see the Commentary for *QM* V.38.

line 156. There is some question whether <u>visions</u> might really be "vision" but the effective difference to the poetry or meaning between these alternatives is negligible.

line 167. PBS originally wrote <u>black and</u> "fruitless" before canceling this adjective by smearing the ink and inscribing <u>barren</u> upon the cancel-smear.

line 173. PBS originally wrote <u>He</u> immediately below **172**; then, deciding that a stanza break was needed, he canceled the word and reentered the text in the line space below.

line 191. <u>upon dead frame</u>: The editorial efforts to improve PBS's grammar or meter here in *1966* ("upon [the] dead frame") and *1989* ("upon [a] dead frame") seem to us superfluous.

line 201. <u>bended</u>: *Entick's Dictionary* gives "bended" and "bent" as alternative forms for both the preterite and participle; PBS here used the disyllabic form to fill the meter and, possibly, to distinguish it from his use of *bent* as a noun in **117**.

line 208. <u>withered lips</u>: The final words of this long line are cramped and contorted in the gutter of the Notebook.

line 225. <u>town!</u>: This word is written over a canceled word—possibly "den" (the final word in the revised line).

line 230. We have emended the text in **EN** by inserting a line break before this to mark the change (discussed in the final paragraph of the introductory commentary to **The Voyage**) from the narrative section in unrhymed, irregular (i.e., Southeyan) stanzas and the concluding juridical blank verse.

line 264. <u>House of Industry</u>: This is the "workhouse" of the contemporary English welfare system, where paupers were confined and made to work for subsistence of food and shelter. Frank Crompton points out in *Workhouse Children* (Gloucestershire: Sutton Publishing, 1997) that prior to the 1834 Poor Law Amendment Act, paupers who became <u>Parish apprentice</u>[s] (**266**) often suffered because the Old Poor Law lacked any central administration, placing the duty of monitoring the welfare of the apprentices on individual parishes.

In this nightmarish poem, PBS surely imagined the worst for the young child of the returning sailor—perhaps even a fate such as that depicted by

George Crabbe for the apprentices of Peter Grimes in Letter 22 of *The Borough* (1810; Crabbe, *Life and Poems* [London: John Murray, 1834], IV, 37–53). Although there is no record that PBS read Crabbe, since *The Borough* went through three editions in 1810, two in 1812, and another in 1813, there is a distinct possibility that while PBS was at Keswick planning, or in Ireland, Devonshire, and North Wales campaigning, to help the oppressed he may have encountered some of Crabbe's poems of quiet desperation—at least in excerpts in one of the (at least fifteen) reviews *The Borough* received.

line 277. grass-green: Running out of space at the right-hand margin of the paper (after marking an extravagantly long dash), PBS pressed grassgreen together as a single word, though he seems to have tried to keep them separated. We supply a hyphen.

line 283. PBS canceled what appears to be an "H" before writing Nature over it. We follow *1966* and *1989* by inserting a comma between Nature and fair Earth; *1964* changed the word to "Nature's" instead, which, though not based on physical evidence, could be accurate if PBS (like Thomas Love Peacock) had learned from Welsh bardic poetry to love Triads.

lines 291–98. The final speech, uttered by the voice of Justice, resembles those voiced by "indignant Earth" in lines 147 ff. of **Mask of Anarchy** and by Demogorgon at the end of **Prom.** In **295,** the correct reading in **EN** is bring thee.— rather than "buy thee" (cf. Keats's *Isabella*, 105–20). In **292** we (like Dowden) question whether one of them— should not read "one of these—."

The Hogg Manuscripts

Following **A retrospect** and **The Voyage** (#31 and #32), which seem to have been spin-offs from the composition of **QM**, are four poems (#33–#40) that seem thematically related to *[Poems about Mary]*. The first of these, entitled **A Dialogue,** is a debate between Death and a Mortal (#33) that explores whether suicide is an appropriate cure for human unhappiness, concluding that to commit suicide would be unfair if one leaves behind a friend who needs support. The next three poems recapitulate the course of PBS's emotional life from mid-1809 to October 1810, beginning with the height of his romantic feelings for Harriet Grove (#34 and #35) through the beginning of his strained relations with her (#36) and into his comradeship with Hogg, who told him the moving story of "Mary" that parallels his own saga of "boy meets girl, boy loses girl" in a more tragic key. PBS's Advertisement to *[Poems about Mary]*, the footnote for **To Mary I,** and the poem **To the Lover of Mary** together suggest that PBS felt, early in his acquaintance with Hogg, that his new friend lacked sensitivity and empathy for others. For example, PBS's letter to Hogg of 8 May 1811 suggests that the character of Mary in Hogg's novel pleased him far more than did Hogg's heroine Leonora (*Letters* I, 77). Incidentally, the poems that immediately follow *The Voyage* provide a message about his prior disillusionment with Harriet Grove, his sister Elizabeth, and Hogg that parallels his message in *To Harriet ("It is not blasphemy")* (*Esd* #24), in which PBS anatomizes his relationship with his wife and urges HWS to become a person who can empathize with the pain of others and is willing to sacrifice self to alleviate their sufferings.

Apart from such thematic relationships among the poems following *The Voyage* that may have led PBS to wish to cluster them together, there is a more practical commonality linking them. If, as we believe, PBS was seeking additional poetry to fill out "Minor Poems" when he returned to London in 1813, he knew one person there who could be especially helpful to him.

From the beginning of PBS's residence at University College, Oxford, until he and HWS fled York after he learned of Hogg's betrayal, PBS had shared his poetry with Hogg. To this point he had transcribed into **EN** just one poem that he is known to have given to Hogg—namely *To Death ("Death! where is thy victory")* (*Esd* #19). The likely reason why he had not included more was that he did not possess his latest copies of the other poems; even if he had with him one or more of his notebooks containing drafts of his early poetry, he may have given away all of his polished fair copies to various friends, such as Harriet Grove, Edward Fergus Graham, and Hogg.

Clearly relations between PBS and Hogg had been badly strained by Hogg's attempted seduction of HWS at York in September 1811. Yet, according to Hogg's account, during the Shelleys' visit to London in late October–November 1812 to return Elizabeth Hitchener, meet Godwin, raise money for the Tremadoc project, and sign a lease for Tan-yr-allt, PBS sought out Hogg at his lodgings and invited him to dine the next day at the Shelleys' hotel. But after Hogg spent that evening with the Shelleys, during which (according to his own report) he scoffed at pamphlets on Robert Emmet and Irish liberty (see Hogg, *Life*, ed. Wolfe, Chap. 19; I, 366–67; *1858* II, 165–71), the Shelleys left London without seeing him again. On this, the only occasion when the Shelleys were in London with Elizabeth Hitchener, Hogg called on them again; but Harriet was unavailable because she "had a headache" and PBS was away on business, leaving Hogg to experience only an uncomfortable walk between the two Elizas—Westbrook and Hitchener. (Hogg misplaces this walk late in Chapter 23 after his visit to Ireland and PBS's return therefrom in 1813 [see *Life*, ed. Wolfe, Chap. 23, II, 55–57; *1858* II, 366–69], long after Hitchener was out of the picture.)

Ostensibly, the Shelleys' feelings toward Hogg had mellowed by December 1812, for by the time of PBS's second letter to Hogg from Tan-yr-allt, both PBS and HWS were corresponding with him and PBS mentioned that Hogg might visit the Shelleys there (**Letters** I, 345–47). But in March 1813, when Hogg accepted PBS's invitation to meet them in Dublin and traveled there at great discomfort and expense, they left the city before his arrival and returned only after he had run out of money and vacation time and was forced to return to England. Hogg's sardonic account of this episode occupies Chapters 21 and 22 of his *Life of Percy Bysshe Shelley* (ed. Wolfe [*1933*] I, 392–415; *1858* II, 217–57). Either HWS's continuing hostility toward Hogg had persuaded PBS to leave Dublin before his arrival there or PBS's renewed friendliness was merely feigned (see pp. xxiv–xxv).

As soon as the Shelleys returned to London in 1813, however, PBS again called on Hogg at his chambers and invited him to visit the Shelleys' lodgings. By this time PBS may have copied into **EN** everything up through *The Voyage,* therewith exhausting the usable salvage from **QM.** So it would have been natural for him to ask Hogg to lend him the manuscripts and letters in his possession containing early poems by PBS. Such a scenario explains why twelve out of the first thirteen poems that follow *The Voyage* relate to manuscripts that PBS had probably given Hogg between October 1810 and mid-1811. At Oxford, PBS had given Hogg an untitled and undated version of *A Dialogue* (**Esd** #33), the first of these twelve poems; we discuss this early version, a Supplement to the text in **EN,** below.

A Dialogue—1809   [Esd #33]

At the head of *A Dialogue* in **EN,** PBS carefully designated it as having been written in 1809, suggesting that it (like other poems that he gave to Hogg) had been composed earlier and merely updated and copied by PBS at Oxford to impress his new friend. The poem's verse form—anapestic tetrameter couplets—accords with that used in other early poems of PBS, all strongly influenced by Scott's narratives, that he had employed in **V&C** (e.g., **Revenge** and **"Ghosts of the Dead"**; **CPPBS** I, 28–30, 110), **WJ,** and the poems in **St.Irv.** Its theme—that death may be preferable to the outrages committed by the scorpions of perfidy, phantoms of prejudice, and Bigotry's bloodhounds (**18–20**)—is one that tended to surface when PBS hit a particularly low point in his mood-swings; but the Mortal in the *Dialogue* ends by refraining from suicide, lest a lingering friend may be grieved at my fall. Considering PBS's treatment of the sad death of "Mary" in *Esd* poems #37–#40, this dissuasion from suicide in *A Dialogue* might be read as a message to Hogg about the seriousness of the topic. In form, diction, and tone, however, *A Dialogue* seems more likely to be a poetic exercise than a contemplation of suicide, and it may have been written, like *To Death,* as an answer to the Emperor Hadrian's *De anima,* a poem that young Byron had translated and Pope had answered in an epigram of his own (see Commentary on *Esd* #19), suggesting that it was a standard student exercise in the classical curricula of the era.

A Dialogue was probably written before PBS felt the full impact of Harriet Grove's rejection of him. Even if Cameron is correct in saying that he gave this poem to Hogg with four other literary manuscripts after the Christmas holidays of 1810–11 (*1964*, 235–37), all of these poems may have been written before he entered college and simply retrieved at Field Place and revised during that vacation to impress his friend. (The editors of *1989* conjecture a date of January to April 1811 but provide no evidence to support their modification of Cameron's suggestion.) In 1813, after recovering his MS of *A Dialogue* from Hogg, PBS made additional changes in the text, added the title, and wrote the footnote with its quotation of parts of *QM* III.80–83, taken from this passage:

> There needeth not the hell that bigots frame
> To punish those who err: earth in itself
> Contains at once the evil and the cure;
> And all-sufficing nature can chastise
> Those who transgress her law,—she only knows
> How justly to proportion to the fault
> The punishment it merits.
>
> (*Queen Mab* III.79–85)

In this and other revisions made to the text found in the copy given to Hogg (MS TCC), PBS's version in *Esd* may have been altered by the doctrines he expounds in *QM* (see Commentary below to lines 2–3 of the Supplement).

A Dialogue differs in genre from *Falshood and Vice: a Dialogue* (*Esd* #6), which is not a balanced skeptical debate between various points of view but is a conversation between co-conspirators, much like the Witches' scenes in *Macbeth*. The genre of the philosophical dialogue that PBS emulates here (as did Pope) was used by the Platonic Academy (which became the main school of Skepticism in antiquity) and by such later Skeptics as Cicero, Hume, and Sir William Drummond, to undercut dogmatisms (see C. E. Pulos, *The Deep Truth* (Lincoln: U of Nebraska P, 1954) and Chapter 1 of Reiman, *Intervals of Inspiration*). PBS used this form not only in his prose pamphlet *A Refutation of Deism* (1814) but in such poetic dialogues as the debate between *Julian and Maddalo* and the competing *Song of Apollo* and *Song of Pan* (see Earl R. Wasserman, *Shelley: A Critical Reading* [Johns Hopkins UP, 1971], 46–66).

The theme of contemplating death with equanimity—though developed skeptically here—reappears in PBS's later poems, including more than once in the *Alastor* volume as well as in *Rosalind and Helen, Stanzas—written in Dejection,* and *Adonais,* where in stanzas 39 ff. his tone crescendoes to a peak of celebration. Nevertheless, that PBS could contemplate death with equanimity from 1809 through 1821 shows that he was either uncertain of its merits or was in no great hurry to enjoy its benefits.

lines 11–12. Among numerous errors in the texts by PBS that Hogg pub-
lished in Chapter 5 of his *Life* (ed. Wolfe I, 124; *1858* I, 197–98), he omitted
these two lines, as well as **lines 31–32** of *A Dialogue,* omissions repeated in all
editions until *1964.*

line 41. Though *1989* uses **EN** as its copy-text for *A Dialogue,* it here emends
Virtue to "duty" (TCC) on the grounds that to repeat Virtue's in **line 42** "is
weak and seems inadvertent" (*1989* I, 163).

Supplement: Version in Hogg Manuscript, ca. 1810

The Supplement version of the poem in its entirety appears in the undated
MS that PBS gave to Hogg and which Hogg, in turn, gave to Dawson Turner
in 1834 and is now at Trinity College, Cambridge (MS TCC), part of a be-
quest by Turner's daughter. A facsimile and transcript of it were published in
MYR: Shelley (VIII, ed. Reiman and Michael O'Neill [1997], 29–35). This
poem was included in Hogg's *Life,* together with the letter that Hogg sent to
Dawson Turner (ed. Wolfe I, 123–24; *1858* I, 197–98) claiming the work to
be an example of PBS's early poetry from 1810.

line 1. PBS drops the dominant consonance of the line by changing
"bathed" to drenched in the first line of *A Dialogue.* Upon reflection, PBS
may have decided that the three accented *b* sounds ("bathed," "blood," and
"brave") made Death sound too bouncy.

line 2. PBS included what appears to be an exclamation mark following life
(which looks a bit like a period with an apostrophe hovering over it), most
likely signifying direct address, a convention of the punctuation at the time.
The exclamation marks in **lines 21** and **23** provide other examples.

lines 2–3. PBS's scattered yet substantial changes from the TCC version of
the poem to the one that appeared in **EN** alter the tone of the entire poem.
As Cameron noted, PBS's revisions there shift the focus of the poet's reaction
to death from "a personal, philosophical reference to a social, anti-war ref-
erence" (*1964*, 237). By inverting Death's role in *Esd* #33 to a bringer of
peace to Ambition (*Esd,* **line 3**) rather than to "Innocence," PBS renders
problematical what had been a simple black-and-white dichotomy, making
Death declare himself equally a refuge for all unhappy human beings of
whatever moral character.

line 7. PBS underlined the "len" of "silence," perhaps to mark either a shift-
ing of the metrical stress to the second syllable or to emphasize the entire
word.

lines 7–8. In revising, PBS changed the focus from "Thy mansion" (i.e., the
grave of the Mortal) to Death's (my) hall and the Judge there who steeps in

<u>oblivion the brands of Despair</u> (***Esd*** #33). PBS takes a fairly trite couplet and transforms it with a very visceral and consistent image.

lines 8–9. PBS spaced words irregularly here and elsewhere in MS TCC (about seven inches wide; see *MYR: Shelley* VIII, 29, 32–34). The larger spaces may show how the words should be grouped in reading to achieve his intended rhythms.

line 10. Because "of Death" did not fit on the width of the page, PBS wrote the phrase at the right-hand margin, just beneath "empire."

line 13. Following "thee" are what appear to be two periods, though one may be a simple fleck of ink.

line 14. Both here and at the end of **line 34** PBS omitted question marks that would not fit on the right-hand edge of the page. In both lines the word "me" is also severely cramped at the edge.

lines 16–17. The apostrophes after "its" in both lines appear in the MS as represented in our text.

line 22. The question mark would not fit at the end of this line (the last on this page of MS TCC) but is written at the bottom right-hand corner, directly beneath "shore."

line 23. After "mortal" there are an exclamation mark and then a period, the mark itself signaling Death's direct address to the Mortal, while the period may signify that the reader is to pause longer than usual between the words "mortal!" and "I" (i.e., longer than the reader would between "Mortal!" and "gleams" in **line 27,** where the exclamation mark is not followed by a period).

"unviel": Again PBS misspells a word that involves an *ei* or *ie*.

line 26. "above": This word appears below the line, due to the space constraint on the page.

line 27. PBS underlines just the *v* of "Love" and the *m* of "my." Was he indicating stress patterns or marking his use of the consonants in the line in an effort to improve its aural effects?

lines 42–43. The letters that appear to be missing in the facsimile edition are present but hidden from view by the binding frame in which the MS is mounted for protection.

line 44. The bottom of the verso page of the MS is rather blotchy—becoming progressively more so from **line 39** to the bottom of the page, either from show-through of ink from the recto side or from blotting of whatever MS was laid upon it while the ink was still wet. This makes the last line, especially in the middle, somewhat difficult to read. This could be why *MYR: Shelley* (VIII,

34–35) represents "destroyer" as having a capital *D*, though the facsimile itself appears to have a lower case *d* that is slightly smudged.

1810 ("How eloquent are eyes!")   [*Esd* #34]

In heading both this and the next poem (beginning *"Hopes that bud in youthful breasts"*) with the date, *1810,* rather than verbal titles, PBS indicated that they were to be considered youthful efforts (not to be confused with his mature work of ages nineteen to twenty-one) and that they are companion pieces—both, apparently, on the question "Can love last?" Both Dowden in his transcription and Cameron (*1964*) observed that in PBS's letter to Hogg of 18–19 June 1811 *Sweet star!* was followed by fragments of these two poems (see the Supplements to our texts and Cameron's analysis in *SC* II, 813–15). That conflation of fragments from the two *1810* poems was transmitted to the public by Hogg in *Life* and only partially corrected by Garnett, who gave Rossetti a text of the first thirteen lines of *"How eloquent"*—perhaps copied, as *1989* plausibly suggests (I, 91), by the former governess in the Esdaile household who had provided Garnett with copies of what he referred to as "two sonnets addressed by Shelley to Harriet in July and September 1813" (*Letters about Shelley,* 87–88). PBS's letter introduces *Sweet star!* (published in *CPPBS* I, 144; Commentary, 322–26) and the fragments of *Esd* #34 and #35 with this sentence: "I transcribe for you a strange melange of maddened stuff which I wrote by the midnight moon last night" (*Letters* I, 107). Perhaps he had written *Sweet star!* "last night" as he claimed, but he added the other two fragments and tried to confuse Hogg about their origin to present himself once again as a more prolific and spontaneous poet than he actually was, by representing as extemporaneous effusions poetry that he had composed and polished earlier.

Both *1964* and *1989* deduce that *"How eloquent are eyes!"* and *"Hopes that bud in youthful breasts"* (*1989* I, 90–94) were originally written for Harriet *Grove* (not HWS), perhaps during or shortly after their time together in April and May 1810 (on which see Hawkins, *Shelley's First Love,* 29–41). When seen as a product of PBS's chiefly epistolary romance with Harriet Grove, the originating impulse for *1810 ("How eloquent are eyes!")* becomes clearer: the poem articulates the sublimated passions of unconsummated youthful love, in which <u>eyes</u> become the symbol of other personal attributes (such as the "fair form" that appears several times in his poems to HWS after she became his wife) that he could not yet mention to Grove under the etiquette of the day. The poem virtually pants with <u>the soul's wildest feelings</u> (**3**) and <u>love's warmest fervours</u> (**7**), but the mingling of souls that it describes takes place, not in his beloved's bed, but in the poet's imagination. This beautiful lyric of youthful desire expresses a seemingly unbridled passion that has actually been tamed by the art of poetic form—here eight-line stanzas of iambic trimeter and tetrameter (3-4-4-3-3-4-4-3), rhymed *abbbacca*, with the fifth line of each stanza repeating the first line of that stanza—subtly varied in the third and fourth stanzas. PBS's apprenticeship here served him well when he composed such masterpieces of sublimated desire as **To Constantia** and **Epipsychidion.**

line 10. <u>waste of years</u>: This phrase, which appears also in **QM** VII.254 and three times in PBS's later poetry, became a cliché among English poetasters of a slightly later period, but it appeared in just a few poems before 1813, including Byron's lines, "Yet all this giddy waste of years, | This tiresome round of palling pleasures" (*To ——— ["Oh! Had my fate been join'd with thine"]*, 25–26; Byron, *CPW* I, 49), which first appeared in *Hours of Idleness* and was reprinted in *Poems, Original and Translated* (1808, 165–67). In **CPPBS** I (269, 274–75) we established that PBS probably knew or owned this volume as early as 1810, and HWS copied Byron's *The Tear* from the same volume into her Commonplace Book (folios 26 recto to 27 verso).

line 17. In **EN,** this line is not indented as are the first lines of the other stanzas.

line 23. <u>Heaven's unfading spring</u>: Although this exact phrase does not occur in Chadwyck-Healey's *LION*, there are many occurrences in poetry of the English Romantic period of similar phrases beginning "Heaven's unfading" but followed by such words as "bow" (i.e., rainbow), "bowers," "clime," "loveliness," "mercy," and "spheres"; among these, "bowers" wins the plurality, perhaps because it echoes the idea of "amaranthus," the unfading flower of Heaven that PBS invokes elsewhere (see the following Commentary). PBS's phrase <u>unfading spring</u>, unlike almost all contemporary parallels, combines the idea of immortality with a clearly temporal concept drawn from the mutable seasonal cycle, thereby embodying both his hopes and his doubts in a characteristically skeptical manner.

line 38. <u>shrine</u>: Here, as in **Esd** #2 and #13, PBS miswrites "shine" where he intends "shrine."

line 40. Following this line, PBS's line count for the poems transcribed thus far is 1677.

Supplement: Version in Letter to Hogg, 18–19 June 1811

Here we have transcribed the portion of PBS's letter to Hogg from 18–19 June 1811 (Pfz 166; *SC* II, 811; **Letters** I, 106–8) that included a fragment which would eventually become the last stanza (**lines 33–40**) of **1810 ("How eloquent are eyes!")**. This fragment appears in the letter as the last of a series of fragments and is written directly after the Supplement for **Esd** #35, **1810**

*(**"Hopes that swell in youthful breasts"**),* which follows the poetic fragment
"Sweet star!" (see *CPPBS* I, 144, 322–26). PBS's inverts this order when he
transcribes and completes the poem in **EN.** Our transcript beginning "Age
cannot love destroy" does not exactly duplicate the indentions that appear in
the transcription from *Shelley and his Circle* (*SC* II, 811, lines 53–59), because
here we attempt to follow more literally what appear to be the indentions of
the MS itself.

The most significant difference between this fragment and *Esd* #34 is ap-
parent in the fragment's lack of punctuation. This seemingly insignificant
difference becomes critical to PBS's transformation of this brief beginning
into its fully Shelleyan form when he modifies all of the fragment's definite
statements into uncertainties—that is, by changing "But" in line 2 to <u>Can</u> in
Esd #34, **line 34** and adding a question mark at **36** (the question mark fol-
lowing **line 40** is an editorial addition). This makes *1810 ("How eloquent are
eyes!")* a bit more hopeful than the Supplement fragment by questioning if
the powers of <u>Perfidy</u> really are stronger than the powers of <u>Age</u> (a superior-
ity that the Supplement assumes as a given). PBS's further shift, by including
"slighted vows" with <u>Perfidy</u> after the stanza's repetition of "Age cannot love
destroy" (*Esd* #34, **line 38**), shows that PBS revised the poem for inclusion in
Esd after he had experienced specific instances of what may <u>love destroy</u> that
provided better examples than the abstraction <u>Perfidy</u>.

line 34. PBS here left extra space between "perfidy" and the remainder of
the line, as he sometimes spaced other early MSS, perhaps to suggest the
line's rhythm.

line 39. Following this line PBS marked three large *X*s, to separate the text
of the poem from the prose of the letter (which begins immediately after this
poem).

1810 ("Hopes that bud in youthful breasts")   *[Esd #35]*

This poem is composed of generally iambic tetrameter and trimeter lines,
arranged in seven-line stanzas (4-3-4-3-3-4-3) rhymed *ababcbc*, of which the
lines with the *c*-rhymes are repeated in each stanza, with a single crucial vari-
ation in the final line of the poem. *Esd* #34, which has thematic similarities
to this poem, also has repeated lines, and PBS shows that the two poems are
related by entitling both poems with the same year of composition and plac-
ing them together in the Notebook, as he had quoted from both in his 1811
letter to Hogg. At first these companion pieces seem meant to express op-
posing views on the question of whether love can endure, for whereas *"How
eloquent"* exclaims that neither <u>Time</u> nor <u>When Time shall be no more</u> can
change the love between the poet and Harriet Grove (lines 17–24), *"Hopes
that bud"* seems to take issue with such idealism, replying that <u>Love's rose</u> is

besieged (<u>invested</u>) by <u>a host of thorns</u> and that Youth is deceived by its <u>purple flowers</u> . . . | <u>That fade the while they glow</u> (**3–7**). But after a transition in the next stanza, using a metaphor of love as <u>the rose that breathes in Heaven</u> | <u>Altho' on Earth 'tis planted</u> (**10–11**), PBS clarifies his thought in the final stanza by distinguishing a <u>pure soul</u> that lives within the mortal <u>heart</u> and that, if <u>undefiled by tainting sin</u>, can keep love <u>unsullied</u>—apparently forever.

In an earlier poem, PBS had foreshadowed this concept of earthly existence as a garden nursery from which healthy flowers of love may be transplanted to Heaven and there blossom eternally—something of a horticultural forerunner of Keats's more biblical concept of earthly life as a "vale of soul-making." PBS alludes to the amaranthus, a flower named with a Greek adjective meaning unfading or everlasting, in **Song (*"How stern are the woes"*)**, a lyric that he wrote for Harriet Grove and first released in a letter to Edward Fergus Graham in mid-September 1810 (***Letters*** I, 16) before publishing it in **St. Irv:** "Heaven will save | The spirit . . . in its amaranth bower" (see **CPPBS** I, 115–16 and 275–78). In **QM**, Mab's magic wand is circled by "wreaths of amaranth" (I.108), though in the poem as a whole, PBS—or, more precisely, Ianthe after she has been catechized by Mab—denies the need for personal immortality (**QM** III.11–13). And since the conception of potential immortality for the righteous found in these poems of 1810 contradicts at least that stage of Ianthe's lessons in **QM**, PBS may have identified these poems in **Esd** as having been written in 1810 partly to show that he is not being inconsistent about his current beliefs, though in his youth he held a belief, however unorthodox, in an afterlife. (See his comments to Hitchener about **To Mary who died in this opinion** in his letter of 23 November 1811 [**Letters** I, 190] and our analysis of them in **CPPBS** I, 307–10.) But, as the *Shelley Concordance* indicates, PBS also used *amaranth* in crucial places in poems published later— as an adjective in **Rosalind and Helen** (line 1308) and as a noun in **Prom** (II.iv.61), using its etymology and traditional associations to suggest immortality of an unspecified kind.

PBS's line count at the end of this poem in **EN** is 1693.

Supplement: Version in Letter to Hogg, 18–19 June 1811

PBS's letter to Hogg from 18–19 June 1811 (Pfz 166, *SC* II, 809–12; **Letters** I, 106–8) includes the first fourteen lines of **1810 (*"Hopes that bud in youthful breasts"*)** (**Esd** #35), which follow the fragment of **"Sweet star! which gleaming oer the darksome scene"** and precede the Supplement to **Esd** #34 (see **CPPBS** I, 144, 322–26). This fragment consists of what would become the first fourteen lines of **1810 (*"Hopes that bud in youthful breasts"*)**, the final stanza of which suggests a positive ending, the hope that a "pure soul lives" where "age cannot remove" a "sanctuary of love" (**lines 15–18**). PBS's revisions of this fragment in **EN** are, again, as subtle as adjustments in punctuation and syntax: what he originally wrote as a question in the letter version ("Hopes that swell in youthful breasts | Live they thro' the waste of time? . . .") became in *Esd* a statement (<u>Hopes that bud in youthful breasts | Live not thro' the lapse of time</u>). Therefore, while PBS's doubts about the temporality of ordinary love had grown from a question to a certainty, the final version of the poem adds hope for a future state, with continuity for special lovers (*Esd* #35, **line 16**).

line 2. "thro'": This word appears to be "this" in a facsimile of the MS, but *SC* notes that Hogg had misread the line as "Leave they this" rather than "Live they thro'"—likely because the *o*, which is admittedly unclear, has a dot above it "which is apparently accidental or was carelessly added later but which Hogg took as a dot for an *i*" (*SC* II, 812). Taking into consideration the reading in **EN,** which is definitely <u>thro</u>, we believe that to be the more likely reading.

line 6. "Youth says . . the": PBS clearly placed two periods following the word "says," as if to indicate a pause double the length of a normal period. The version that appears in **EN** confirms this idea, since PBS there wrote <u>Youth says—the</u>.

line 9. "granted!—— ——": PBS here marked a long pause with two dashes, though a lack of ink makes the second appear to be two smaller dashes. In **EN** PBS substituted a period for the dashes.

line 13. PBS revised the letter version's "Where by Earth's slaves the leaves are riven" to <u>Where by the frosts its leaves are riven</u> in **EN.** The fragment concludes with a political image that PBS later felt detracted from the central theme of his poem, which centers upon love that is decidedly private, rather than public.

"Where" is difficult to read in MS Pfz because it is written through "~~Youth~~", which PBS apparently miscopied from **line 6.**

line 14. PBS added the four elongated *X*s beneath this line to separate it from the fragment that immediately follows: the Supplement to *Esd* #34 (see our Commentary above).

September 23, 1809
("*Moonbeam! leave the shadowy dale*")   [*Esd #36*]

Having entitled the two previous poems by the year of their composition, PBS names *September 23, 1809* more explicitly by month, day, and year. Yet, as *1964* and *1989* point out, PBS had previously sent the Supplement version of this poem to Hogg in a letter dated 17 May 1811, with the comment,

"Here is raphsody [*sic*]" (*SC* II, 791; ***Letters*** I, 91), that is, an irregular, miscellaneous composition and produced spontaneously or extemporaneously. In actuality, ***"Moonbeam! leave the shadowy dale"*** is a complex metrical experiment. It begins with a ten-line stanza made up of trimeter and tetrameter lines rhymed *abaabccddd;* the second and third stanzas transmute into nine-line variants lacking the third *a*-rhyme (*ababccddd*), and having a final line of hexameter that is not a pure Alexandrine, inasmuch as it is not in regular iambic measure but includes a variety of metrical feet, determined by the accent of the individual words and the emphases elicited by the meaning of the words within their syntactical structure.

Though in *1964* Cameron rightly points out the importance of the long final line in PBS's later poetry, the long lines in the example he cites (***Prom*** IV.141–46) are simply anapestic tetrameters. Here PBS wrote lyric stanzas that contain lines varying from trimeters to hexameters, as he later did in poems that return the form to its Greek origins in **Ode to Liberty, Ode to Naples,** and some choruses of **Hellas** (e.g., 940–47, 973–1007). After analyzing within this poetry the subtle variations of metrical *stress,* verbal *accent,* and rhetorical *emphasis* (on the interaction of which, see Reiman, *Shelley's "The Triumph of Life"* [Urbana: U of Illinois P, 1965], 89–93), one may say of PBS's poetry in this vein what Coleridge said of Donne's versification: "To read Dryden, Pope &c, you need only count syllables; but to read Donne you must measure *Time,* & discover the *Time* of Each word by the Sense & Passion" (Coleridge, *Marginalia,* II, ed. George Whalley [London and Princeton, 1984], 216). Such poetry is hard to scan and virtually impossible to read well aloud without rehearsal. PBS's use of these forms suggests that his lyrical models were from the *lieder* tradition (with which he and the musician Edward Fergus Graham had early experimented), as the complex stanzas followed the formal bardic tradition, deriving ultimately from Pindar but best exemplified in formal English poetry by the odes of Dryden and, especially, Thomas Gray, whose poems strongly influenced PBS from childhood.

To confirm that PBS's date/title <u>September 23, 1809</u> was accurate, Matthews and Everest established that there was "a full moon, with showers" on 24 September (*1989* I, 9). Reading the poem as an outburst caused by rejected love, they follow Cameron (*1964*) in citing September 1809 as a period of dwindling recorded correspondence between PBS and Harriet Grove. Though her diary indicates some diminution of the flow of what had been almost daily letters between the Shelley and Grove families during July and August, *The Grove Diaries,* edited by Desmond Hawkins (Newark: U of Delaware P, 1995), also shows that—besides mentioning several letters between Harriet Grove and either PBS or his sister Elizabeth—Harriet canceled to illegibility no fewer than thirty-three lines in her diary entries between 4 and 19 September, including one entire entry of nine lines. Since virtually all such cancellations in her diaries for 1809–10 that have been deciphered mention PBS, the correspondence between Harriet and him may not so much have diminished as deepened into subjects that she found intriguing enough to record at the time but later perceived as so embarrassing that she obliterated them completely. Perhaps this was the period in which PBS wrote and sent her the two preceding poems denominated here as simply *1810,* beginning *"How eloquent are eyes!"* and *"Hopes that bud in youthful breasts,"* to which she may have replied in a manner that, for one reason or another, left the young night-walking poet with a <u>burning brow</u> (**2**) and with a <u>bosom forlorn</u> (**18**). PBS may ask the moonbeam to <u>cool</u> his <u>burning brow</u> not because Harriet was rejecting him, but because their long-distance romance had heated their imaginations so much that he was driven to <u>the death of despair</u> (**27**) simply by not being able to see his beloved.

But for all we know, his unhappy mood may have derived from some other shock of adolescence, such as a dispute with his father or becoming aware of what he believed to be his mother's illicit relationship with Graham (see *SC* IX, 147–68). Or—and this was the chief subject of his letter to Hogg of 17 May 1811 into which he copied the poem's earlier version—his sister Elizabeth's refusal to ally herself publicly with his anti-Christian position may have triggered a mood so dark that it led him to declare that no other <u>Wretch</u> with a <u>glare of madness</u> in his <u>haggard eye</u> had endured such <u>sadness</u> and <u>despair</u> (**20–27**).

At the end of the poem, PBS's line count is 1723, adding two more lines than are actually present, probably because he forgot that the second and third stanzas contained one less line than the first stanza.

line 11. <u>deathy</u>: See the Commentary to *Falshood and Vice* (*Esd* #6) line 57.

Supplement: To the Moonbeam in Letter to Hogg, 17 May 1811

PBS copied the early version of this poem into his letter to Hogg dated 17 May 1811 (*SC* II, 790–91; *Letters* I, 91), the first part of which letter is taken up with PBS's disgust that his sister Elizabeth, though believing none of the doctrines of Christianity, declared herself a Christian so as not to lose what PBS termed "The opinion of the world" (*SC* II, 790). Clearly the poem, which he entitled in the letter "—To the Moonbeam," had been written earlier—eight months earlier, according to the date/title in **EN.** PBS does not tell Hogg that he just dashed the poem off, though immediately after copying it he writes, "Here is raphsody [*sic*]", implying that it was a spontaneous effusion.

PBS made few revisions to the version he sent to Hogg as he transferred it into *Esd,* but his dozen or so substitutions of words transformed a competent poem into a very beautiful one. The letter version's bluntly alliterative line 2 ("To bathe this burning brow") was improved by the substitution of <u>cool</u> for "bathe" and for the same reason he changed the letter version's "dewy dale" (4) to <u>midnight vale</u>, while having the moonlight <u>glide</u> instead of "walk" over the <u>vale</u> and in the next line changing "humble wild flowers" (5) to <u>dewy flowrets</u> in **EN**. Similar changes of single words in lines 8, 26, 27, and 28 show the growth of the poet's artistry in accomplishing the minute shadings of both sound and meaning without altering the rhyme scheme, structure, or basic thought of the poem.

[Poems about Mary]   [Esd #37–#40]

PBS's four poems in *Esd* relating to "Mary" appear without a general title but are preceded by an <u>Advertisement</u> (i.e., preface). Modern editors have entitled them "Poems *to* Mary," but although the first three are addressed to Mary by her unnamed "Lover," the last poem is addressed by the poet, not to Mary but to that Lover, in a tone suggesting that PBS was judging the Lover-persona harshly for the sentiments expressed in the first three poems of the group. We prefer, therefore, to call the group *[Poems about Mary].* In the <u>Advertisement</u> to this integral group, PBS claims to have written <u>many</u> poems <u>during three weeks of an entrancement caused by hearing Mary's story</u>, but the texts of just five such poems survive—these four in *Esd* and another that PBS sent to Elizabeth Hitchener in his letter of 23 November 1811, introducing it as *To Mary who died in this opinion* (*CPPBS* I, 138–39). When Cameron published these four *Esd* poems for the first time (*1964*: texts, 115–22; commentary, 242–48), he gathered most of the available information about their origins. To those facts, we added in *CPPBS* I (307) the name of the real "Mary" from contemporary letters written by and to Thomas Jefferson Hogg's father John Hogg, of Norton in County Durham, which B. C. Barker-Benfield described and quoted from in *Bodleian Library Record* XIV (Oct. 1991, 14).

During Hogg's summer vacation in 1810, his family feared that he had become infatuated with a "Miss Dillon," whose "history" (wrote one of his father's friends on 2 October 1810) "is a kind of romance." Apparently she was a young woman of lower social standing or questionable reputation, and his family feared that the young man might elope with her. On 5 October a clergyman friend of the family proposed that Miss Dillon be conveyed from Norton to the seaside town of Hartlepool, to keep her out of the way until the young man returned to Oxford. Whether Miss Dillon, who (Hogg apparently told PBS) had a deep faith in immortality, actually did take her own life is something that awaits further research in the local diaries, newspapers, and records of deaths, burials, and coroner's inquests in County Durham. Now we know only that in late October or early November 1810, soon after PBS and Hogg met in the dining hall at University College and became constant companions, Hogg told him the sad tale of "Mary," who had been persecuted by others because of her past history or her association with Hogg and had committed suicide. In a letter to Hogg of 1 April 1811, PBS alludes to Mary in a way suggesting that Hogg also told her story in his unpublished novel *Leonora,* in which she was, apparently, a subordinate character destroyed, perhaps, by the protagonist Leonora (see *SC* II, 770; **Letters** I, 77 and fn. 4). Although in his <u>Advertisement</u> PBS praises <u>the delicate and discriminating</u> <u>genius</u> of the unnamed <u>friend who related</u> the story to him, after one reads his poem ***To the Lover of Mary,*** it is difficult to be sure how sincere this praise of Hogg was meant to be.

Mary's history not only inspired PBS to write these poems, but it may even have had a profound impact on his own life: PBS eloped with HWS—a young woman of lower social standing and wealth than he, who was persecuted by her schoolmates for her friendship with the young "atheist" recently expelled from Oxford (see *SC* II, 759–62; **Letters** I, 76)—and "suicide was with her a favorite theme," or so he told Hitchener in a letter written on 28 October 1811 to explain that such a threat brought him back to London and, together with HWS's confession of love for him, led to their elopement. Thus, PBS's first marriage may have been triggered partly by the unhappy conclusion of Hogg's tale, whether or not the story was factual. The history of Hogg's "Mary" may also figure in the life and art of MWS, for PBS suggested a double suicide with Mary Godwin to persuade her to elope with him. Then, following HWS's suicide, Mary (according to Claire Clairmont's later report) threatened to kill herself if PBS would not marry her. These two episodes, Crook points out, MWS drew upon for Chapter 10 of her novella *Mathilda.*

Scholars have presumed that PBS gave Hogg copies of his poems concerning Mary's story late in 1810, but no such manuscript versions survive, as they do for the other poems that Hogg received during the same period—*Esd* numbers 19, 33, 34, 35, 36 preceding these poems and numbers 41, 43, 44, and 45 following them. Perhaps Hogg considered the ***[Poems about*** ***Mary]*** too personal even in 1813 to return to PBS for possible publication—especially if either his story about "Mary" was not founded on fact, or he objected to PBS's treatment of it. Inasmuch as PBS had access to the text of ***To*** ***Mary who died in this opinion*** at Keswick in November 1811 when he sent it to Hitchener, he may still have had in his possession at least drafts of the other poems of the group from which he could reconstruct or modify them for ***Esd*** (as he later recreated ***Mont Blanc*** from its draft). But whether PBS composed the texts of these four "Mary" poems in ***Esd*** under the influence of deep emotion when he first heard her story or reconceived them after a lapse of nearly two years, he used the occasion to sharpen his poetic skills, for all four poems display a variety of carefully chosen line lengths, rhyme schemes, and meters.

In his <u>Advertisement</u>, PBS characterizes himself <u>at that time</u> by quoting in Latin from *The Confessions of St. Augustine* (III.i) a passage that may be translated: "Not yet did I love, yet I was in love with loving. . . . I sought what I might love, loving to love." This is the same quotation that he would later use as the epigraph of **Alastor** and copy into a notebook of which he used only five pages before giving it to Claire Clairmont in mid-August 1814 in France, during the elopement journey of PBS, MWS, and Clairmont (after which she reversed the notebook and continued her journal in it; Clairmont, *Journals,* 61 and fn. 31).

To Mary I   [Esd # 37]

The first poem is very regular, with all seven quatrains being rhymed *abab* and, more remarkably, with all twenty-eight lines being composed in basically iambic trimeter, varied only in the number and occasional placement of extra unstressed syllables (making it the only all-trimeter poem in **Esd**). Though the rapidity of the short lines reinforces the thematic action articulated in **line 20:** <u>Love! let us haste away!</u>, it may undercut the character of the speaker, whose brisk proposal that he and Mary take poison together (<u>For when the storm is blowing</u> | <u>To shelter we may flee</u> [**15–16**]) makes his life-and-death proposal seem too unconsidered and precipitous, given the permanence of its consequences. On the other hand, these qualities may contribute to the psychological verisimilitude of the teenage protagonists contemplating suicide, especially as PBS viewed them in retrospect, after Hogg's attempt to seduce HWS.

PBS's footnote (for which there is no asterisk or other marker in the text of the poem in **EN**) most likely refers to **lines 9–12,** in our numbering. His speculations regarding the afterlife indicate a preference for, if not a firm belief in, universal salvation. The note's canceled reference to the <u>Romances of Leadenhall Str.</u> alludes to the street where the Minerva Press, founded by John Lane (?1745–1814), was famous for publishing lurid popular romances, both Gothics and tear-jerkers, from 1773 to 1820—all of which are listed and analyzed by type and authorship in Dorothy Blakey's *The Minerva Press: 1790–1820* (London: Bibliographical Society and Oxford UP, 1939).

PBS's line count at the end of this poem: "1751."

To Mary II   [Esd #38]

Each of this poem's three stanzas contains seven lines, with a variable number of stresses, rhymed *ababccc.* The first six lines of each stanza are basically iambic, while the seventh lines feature anapests. Again the speaker is the Lover of Mary, addressing her on the utility of suicide, much as in *A Dialogue* "Death" tries to lure the "Mortal." The Lover promises Mary that <u>our souls shall not sleep</u> | <u>In the grave damp and deep</u> (**19–20**), thereby restating, if only to deny, the orthodox Anglican belief that the dead, instead of going to Heaven or Hell immediately, rest each in a grave ("earthy cell" in *To Mary III,* line 2) to await the angelic trumpet that will announce the Last Judgment (see PBS's early use of this doctrine in ***CPPBS*** I, 185–86 and 226–27). The speaker here assures Mary that she and he will immediately enter a new existence in which they can express their love and devotion to each other.

PBS's note disclaiming the religious associations of the word <u>devotion</u> in the final line would imply that the author of the poem and the persona of the Lover who addresses this poem to Mary were one and the same. Since this is clearly not the case, the note must have been added as PBS, then preparing ***QM*** for the press and writing notes for it, considered how his earlier hopes for some form of immortality (a longing that recurs frequently in ***Esd***) conflicted with the Enlightenment materialism pervading parts of ***QM,*** particularly its Notes. Perhaps one reason that he abandoned his plan to publish ***Esd*** with ***QM*** was that he found it hard to reconcile the two perspectives. In his later writings, however, PBS—like Wordsworth, Coleridge, and even Godwin before him—rejected the sterile rationalism of the *philosophes* and, with the aid of Academic Skepticism, made room for the possibility that his earlier hopes might be realized (see fifth paragraph of ***On Life*** in *2002,* 506–7).

lines 8–14. In this stanza *1989* finds echoes of "two Shakesperean dirges": *Cymbeline* IV.ii.258–60 (beginning "Fear no more the heat o' th' sun, | Nor the furious winter's rages") and *As You Like It* II.vii.174–93 (beginning, "Blow, blow, thou winter wind").

Following the poem is PBS's line count: "1772."

To Mary III   *[Esd #39]*

Having persuaded Mary that death holds nothing for them to fear, her shocked suitor now finds that she has gone on without him. The confusion of his response is reinforced by five irregular stanzas of six, five, seven, twelve, and seven lines respectively, each with a different rhyme scheme and again featuring tetrameter and trimeter lines, as in ballad stanzas or the "common measure" of hymn texts. Surprisingly, after having assured her in ***To Mary II*** that following death they would not "sleep | In the grave," he now asks whether she has gone <u>To sleep in [her] earthy cell?</u>—the very condition that in line 19–20 of ***To Mary II*** he denied would occur. Having washed his hands of complicity in Mary's death, he finds peace of mind in resignation: <u>I submit in silence to fate's decree</u> | <u>Tho'. . . My spirit mourns in sympathy</u> (7–11). In the next two stanzas the Lover speaks of Mary as having been <u>more fair in mind</u> than angels, as <u>born to weep, to die</u> (**19**), but in the final one, he concludes that <u>such is Virtue's doom,</u> the natural fate of such a <u>Sweet flower! that blooms amid the weeds</u> | <u>Where the dank serpent, interest, feeds!</u>

line 7. <u>Mary, Mary, past is past!</u> Crook notes that this line echoes stanza 9 of Gottfried August Bürger's *Lenore* (*O Mutter, Mutter! Hin ist hin!* | *Verloren ist* *verloren!*), a poem in which the grave is also the bridal bed. An illustrated translation of this poem made a powerful impression on PBS early in life (see Medwin, *Life* 45–46).

line 10. lank reeds: In both the New York and London editions of *1964* and in *SC* IV Cameron read the phrase this way, but *1989* gives the adjective as "rank," while collating Cameron's reading as "dank." The word clearly begins with an *l*, and the meaning of lank in this instance would be (according to contemporary dictionaries) "slender," "limber," "hanging down."

line 13. The fabled heavenly train presumably refers to the angels that surround God's throne.

lines 23–24. As Dowden notes in his transcription, PBS, while copying, accidentally skipped **line 23,** adding it below **line 24,** and then added "2" to the left of the upper line (Thou wert but born to weep and die,) and "1" before the lower one (To strive with envy's wreckful storm). All editors have followed PBS's direction.

The *OED* has two entries for *wreckful,* the first of which, meaning "vengeful," it declares "obsolete," and the last example of it is dated 1610; but a related word, *wreakful* (in a separate entry) carried that meaning into the mideighteenth century. The 1805 edition of *Entick's Dictionary* (used by PBS in his youth) gives *wreakful* only (not listing *wreckful*), and defines it as "revengeful, malicious, very angry." In 1810 Walter Scott wrote of "all the wreckful storms that cloud the brow of War" (*Lady of the Lake* V.i.9), which the *OED* gives as an example of the other meaning of *wreckful,* "causing shipwreck, ruin, or disaster; dangerous, destructive." PBS (whose orthography in **EN** allows the word to be read as either *wreakful* or *wreckful*) may have taken the word *wreckful* from Scott, while intending its meaning to be that of the (differently spelled) word in *Entick's Dictionary.* Whether PBS here meant "envy's *malicious* storms" or "envy's *destructive* storms" seems moot in this context.

line 37. interest: that is, self-interest, as in "financial interest"; the opposite of "disinterestedness." Below this line is PBS's line count for the texts transcribed: "1809."

To the Lover of Mary   *[Esd #40]*

Did **PBS,** the creator of these poems recording the sentiments of Mary's Lover in three dramatic monologues, approve and identify with that persona whose rationalizations he recorded? Or did he intend the dramatic monologues of the Lover to paint the self-portrait of a flawed character who recommends suicide to the young woman whom he says he loves but, when she follows his advice, first views her fate with horror and then decides that the act was predetermined by her virtue, leaving him with no responsibility for her tragic death? To make his judgment clear, PBS added a final poem in his authorial voice, addressed to the implied speaker in the three poems "To Mary."

The speaker of *To the Lover of Mary* does not assign the blame for Mary's death (murdered virtue's funeral, **2**) to such abstractions as Fate and "interest" but commands the Lover (poor Wretch) to hide himself under a churchyard yew tree, where its poisonous death-drops can bring peace to thee when the grave thy bridal bed shall be (**10–11**). In the second of three identically crafted eleven-line stanzas of this ode (rhymed *abbacddceee*), PBS's persona praises the Spirit of Mary, who now soars an Angel (**12–14**), but he condemns Mary's Lover to be overpowered by yearnings that shall drive him to the tomb, where Oblivion will blot a life without a stain (**16–17**). These lines suggest that, whereas Mary's societal sins have been swept away in the next world and her good qualities immortalized in this world by PBS's poems, her unnamed Lover—who prudentially refrained from being stained by the sin of suicide—will be swallowed by Oblivion, a fate PBS later assigned to the *Quarterly* reviewer of Keats, a "nameless blot on a remembered name!" (*Adonais* 327).

PBS's line count, 1831, follows the second stanza of this poem but is erased, indicating (as *1989* notes) that the third stanza was an afterthought. In the final stanza, as in *Adonais,* the poet commands the guilty Lover to live so that (unlike the reviewer) he can hope for redemption if for others he must barter [his] own bliss I And living shew what towering Virtue dares (**27–28**). Thus, whereas the poems of the Graveyard Group in *Esd* (#19–#23) paint the futility and frustration of isolated persons who seek comfort, reputation, or immortality only for themselves, the poems in the "Recovery Sequence" from *To Harriet ("It is not blasphemy")* through the *[Poems about Mary]* emphasize in a variety of situations how those who are willing to seek their happiness by loving and devoting themselves to others (love being, according to PBS's footnote, synonimous with Virtue) can create an internalized psychic paradise that may translate into everlasting happiness in a future state of being.

line 19. PBS changed "vail" to "viel"; we have corrected this to veil.

line 22. Following this line, PBS added to his previous line count of "1809" and marked down "1831" but then canceled it, giving no line count after the third stanza.

line 24. passing: i.e., "surpassing" as an adjective.

PBS not only dates, but also entitles this poem *1810*. But earlier he had sent a fair copy of it to Hogg in a letter dated 20 April 1811 (misdated 28 April by Hogg in his *Life of PBS;* date corrected, *SC* II, 757), followed by this claim: "There it is—a mad effusion of this morning.—" The poem in *Esd* entitled *1810 ("Dares the Lama")* and the letter-version (now in the W. Luther Lewis Collection, Texas Christian University—**MS TCU**), which provides the Supplement text, share a complicated and hyper-regular metrical form with the next poem, *1809 ("I will kneel at thine altar")*. Each poem consists of four stanzas of nine lines, rhymed *ababbccdd*, in anapestic tetrameter and trimeter, arranged thus: *4-3-4-3-4-3-3-4-4*. PBS's dressing of these two adjacent poems with complementary themes as identical twins certifies that he had labored over their composition for an extended period and that neither was, in fact, "a mad effusion of this morning."

In *Poems about Mary*, PBS lectured Hogg on moral behavior and possibly planned—by pointing out the identity of the "Lover of Mary" to those who knew the authorship of "Leonora"—to censure him publicly. As PBS wrote to Hogg directly in a series of letters in November 1811, after he learned of Hogg's attempted seduction of HWS (see *SC* III, 24–60) and as he later informed the public in a review of Hogg's pseudonymous male-sexual-fantasy romance entitled *Memoirs of Prince Alexy Haimatoff* (London: T. Hookham, Jr., and E. T. Hookham, 1813), PBS judged that his erstwhile friend lacked moral sensitivity in dealing with women. (For PBS's review, see *Critical Review*, 4th Series, VI [December 1814], 566–74; *Prose*/EBM, 140–46, 390–92.) By ostentatiously redating most of the poems in **EN** that he had sent to Hogg during the height of their friendship, PBS not only emphasized his precocity but also revealed to Hogg how he had fooled him about the composition of the poems that he had given him earlier.

The new date-title for *1810 ("Dares the Lama most fleet")* probably means that he wrote it before going to Oxford—as *1989* observes, "The theme of persecution by conventional Christianity links the poem with *WJ*, and it is rhythmically akin to the poems of [early] 1810 influenced by Scott's 'Hellvellyn'" (*1989* I, 160–61). In **EN** this *1810* is followed by *1809 ("I will kneel at thine altar")*, likely written during his final year at Eton, by his *Fragment . . . bombardment of Copenhagen*, declaring it to be the work of his sister, and *1809 ("O take the pure gem")*—both of which he had given Hogg longer versions of early in their acquaintance in 1810, and *1808 ("Cold are the blasts")*, first published in *Original Poetry by Victor and Cazire* (*V&C*), which, though printed during the summer of 1810, PBS apparently never showed to Hogg.

Once PBS recovered these earlier poems, he revised and arranged them so that *1810 ("Dares the Lama")* appears among the *Esd* poems where its lament on the destruction of innocent beauty by religious bigotry provides an appropriately generalized commentary on the tragic result of such bigotry detailed in ***Poems about Mary.*** Here his metaphors for bigotry's victims are the <u>lama</u> (alternate spelling of llama throughout the nineteenth century) and the <u>hind</u> (a female deer), which are hunted by such predators as <u>the lion</u> (glossed by *1989* as puma or mountain lion) and <u>tyger</u> respectively (**lines 1–9**). Even as a defenseless <u>fowl of the desert</u> will die to defend her <u>brood</u> when a <u>cloud-piercing tyrant</u> (i.e., bird of prey) swoops down to seize a <u>brother</u> bird <u>for food</u>, so the poet declares that he will fearlessly defend his unorthodox ideas (**10–18**). Following the logic of his analogies—drawn, perhaps, from Pliny's *Natural History* (where it is stated that few birds will eat others of their own species) and, in the case the <u>lama</u>, probably from Humboldt's *Travels*—PBS declares in the third stanza that he will <u>draw from the purest of fountains</u>, even if the result proves to be <u>more frightful than death</u> and brings him to deep <u>despair</u>. The meaning of this crucial passage may seem ambiguous ideologically, if not grammatically, but it can be explicated in the light of PBS's later poetry. The grammatical antecedent of the pronoun <u>it</u> which <u>scatters despair</u> in **line 23** is a [creature, entity] <u>fiercer than tygers</u> (22) that haunts the pure <u>fountain</u>, waiting for prey, while <u>its shadow Spreads darkness</u>, <u>eclipsing the day</u> (24–25, reordered). The surface meaning, then, is that religion is the unnamed but deadly creature that lies in wait to pounce upon truth-seekers coming to drink from the <u>purest of fountains</u> of knowledge; this identification is supported by PBS's use of this metaphor in ***The Triumph of Life,*** where the speaker sees chained to Life's chariot "Gregory and John and men divine [i.e., the popes] | Who rose like shadows between Man and god | Till that eclipse, still hanging under Heaven, | Was worshipped by the world . . . | For the true Sun it quenched—" (lines 288–92). Later in ***The Triumph,*** the decayed spirit of Rousseau describes his youthful encounter with "a shape all light," who responds to the young truth-seeker's demand for the meaning of life—"Shew whence I came, and where I am, and why" (398)—by telling him to quench his thirst (400) from "a chrystal glass | Mantling with bright Nepenthe" (described earlier at 358–59). When Rousseau does so, the drink destroys his innocence by showing him the inner meaning of the pageant of life. In another mood, PBS described the Witch of Atlas as playing malicious pranks on mortals by granting them visions of moral order and of immortality; and in a still darker mode he warned humans not to lift the veil, painted with superficial beauty, that screens mortals from life's dark secrets. Even in this poem the truth-seeking speaker suggests that by approaching the <u>purest of fountains</u>, where he knows that the thought-police are constantly lurking, he may be condemning himself to face despair, either from persecution by those who refuse to face the truth, or from his awareness that the <u>fountain</u> has <u>Waves too *poisonously* lovely for mortals to see</u> (**28–29,** emphasis added; note the sharp change in diction here from the earlier letter-version in line 29 of the Supplement).

    1810 ("Dares the Lama") raises issues about the pursuit of "the deep truth" in a cruder form than do PBS's later treatments of the theme in **Alastor, Mont Blanc, Prom,** and the final chorus in **Hellas.** But here, in spite of the poet's strong statement that he is morally obligated, at whatever cost, to expand his knowledge of life's meaning (or lack thereof) to the limits of his ability, the text of this poem broadens the issue: Are there people—as is suggested by Marlow's "true lie" in Conrad's *Heart of Darkness* and by Ivan's "Legend of the Grand Inquisitor" in Dostoevsky's *The Brothers Karamazov*—for whom a vision of "the deep truth" would be corrupting, rather than liberating? The fourth stanza of *1810 ("Dares the Lama"),* describing the poet's personal efforts to flee <u>from the grasp of Religion</u>, thus suggests that PBS sensed (at least at some subliminal level) that a quest for ideal love or Intellectual Beauty could be as harmful to the individual quester as the eclipsing darkness of "superstition" was to the bloodstained societies of Christendom, Islam, or pagandom.

PBS's stance in *"Dares the Lama"* somewhat resembles that of Søren Kierkegaard (1813–55). Like the Danish father of Christian existentialism, PBS rejected the conventional religiosity of his social class and time, but young PBS's views were more conflicted than those in Kierkegaard's master-pieces *Either/Or* and *Fear and Trembling* (both 1843), for he sought to recon-cile his personal needs and experience with the ideas of three major tradi-tions: the life and teachings of Christ as taught by the Church of England (see Robert M. Ryan, *The Romantic Reformation* [1997], pp. 193 ff.); the dog-matic anti-clericalism and materialistic atheism of the French Enlighten-ment tradition, as in Holbach, Volney, Paine, and Godwin's *Political Justice;* and the Skepticism found in Hume's writings, Godwin's *Enquirer,* and Sir William Drummond's *Academical Questions*. Ultimately, PBS was to cast his lot with Skepticism because it best protected his hopes for the triumph of moral and spiritual values and for the immortality that, as the poems in **Esd** testify, he had craved from an early age.

line 1. The phrase <u>Sons of the Wind</u> comes from James MacPherson's *The Poems of Ossian,* of which PBS owned a two-volume edition dated 1807 (now in Pfz) that he inscribed in 1810. The searchable *LION* edition is in two vol-umes, 1805, in which such phrases as "sons of the sea," "sons of the rock," of "mighty Cormac," and the like appear frequently in the first volume of *The Poems of Ossian,* while "son of the wind" or "sons of the wind" (often preceded by the adjective "feeble") appears six times in *Fingal. An Epic Poem* (e.g., at I.428–30). But PBS seemingly reverses the meaning of Fingal's contemptu-ous phrase to compliment the peaceful <u>Lama</u>, rather than its predators, un-less this phrase identifies the <u>Lama</u> as a symbol of the herd of <u>slaves</u> (**34**) who kowtow before the <u>Lions</u> and <u>tygers</u> of royal or ecclesiastical authority.

line 8. <u>And the rocks and the woods to the death-yells reply,</u>: The earlier ver-sion given to Hogg reads: "Whilst India's rocks to his death-yells reply" (MS TCU; **Letters** I, 73). In revising this line for **Esd,** PBS universalized the poem's theme of bigotry's victims by shifting its setting from a specific location to an unstated one.

lines 24–27. This passage, about a <u>shadow, eclipsing the day</u> where <u>war-mangled corpses . . . rot on the ground</u>, echoes Montgomery's lines in *The Ocean* on "the pestilent Upas, the hydra of trees," which read: "The birds on the wing, and the flowers in their beds, | Are slain by its venomous breath, | That darkens the noon-day with death, | And pale ghosts of Travellers around, | While their mouldering skeletons whiten the ground" (*The Wanderer of Switzerland*, 163–64). PBS later used similar language at the end of **Peter Bell the Third**.

lines 33–34. Cameron argues (*1964*, 250) that when PBS wrote the poem in 1810, the phrase <u>most tenderly loved</u> referred to Harriet Grove, but when he copied it into the letter for Hogg, it applied to his sister Elizabeth, who also pulled back from his anti-religious stance, and *1989* (I, 161) supports these identifications. To view the poem's focus as fixed upon two individuals detracts from its sweeping theme, which maintains universal implications until the sudden use of first-person pronouns in lines 31 ff. *1989* (I, 152) quotes a letter to Hogg from 3 January 1811 in reference to **lines 22–25** of *1809 ("I will kneel at thine altar")* (*Esd* #42), in which PBS voices similar feelings: "I swear that never will I forgive Christianity! it is the only point on which I allow myself to encourage revenge . . . . I am convinced too that it is of great disservice of society that it encourages prejudice which strikes at the root of the dearest the tenderest of its ties" (*Letters* I, 35). As Dante and Milton did, PBS universalizes his personal pain, here caused by a religiosity that induces its adherents to turn against those by whom they are <u>most tenderly loved</u>.

line 36. <u>curse it and die</u>: PBS concludes the poem by invoking the Book of Job. When Job's sufferings have reached their peak, his wife scolds him for not accepting his fate: "Dost thou still retain thine integrity? curse God, and die" (Job 2:9), to which Job replies, "Shall we accept good from God, and not trouble?" PBS reinterprets the exchange, rejecting passivity in the face of the evils plaguing humanity. As he also wrote to Hogg on 3 January 1811, "I wish I *were* the Antichrist, that it were *mine* to crush the Demon, to hurl him to his native Hell never to rise again—I expect to gratify some of this insatiable feeling in Poetry" (*Letters* I, 35). Note that PBS's statement in the letter inverts *Paradise Lost* I.330, just as his poem does the Book of Job.

Supplement: Version in Letter to Hogg, 20 April 1811

PBS included this version of *"Dares the Lama, most fleet"* in a letter to Hogg dated 20 April 1811, the MS of which now resides in the W. Luther Lewis Collection at Texas Christian University (MS TCU); it was described and transcribed by Lyle H. Kendall, Jr., in *A Descriptive Catalogue of the W. L. Lewis Collection, Part One: Manuscripts, Inscriptions, Art* ([Fort Worth]: Texas Christian University, 1970), 94–97, and reproduced in photofacsimile, transcribed, and annotated in *MYR: Shelley* VIII, 19–28. Basing our text on the last transcript, we have readjusted the lengths of a few blank spaces found in the MS.

line 1. "Dares the lama   most fleet": We reproduce here the extra space between "lama" and "most" in PBS's letter to Hogg because it may signify the pause that we represent with a comma in *Esd* #41. No comma appears in this line in **EN,** but there may be a similar space, though it is difficult to detect: this line is particularly cramped due to the smaller dimension of the pages in **EN** than in PBS's letter paper. (See *MYR: Shelley* I, 122, and our Commentary to Supplement, line 28, below.)

line 12. "fiercest of [——?——] cloud-piercing tyrants": PBS obliterated a word by drawing a thick line through it and then smearing the wet ink. The canceled word may be *cloud* miswritten (*MYR: Shelley* VIII, 26), for there appears to be a canceled hyphen following the blotted word.

line 16. PBS underlined the *ung* of <u>hunger</u>, perhaps indicating that this syllable is to receive emphasis.

line 17. "Must perish . . Revenge": Here in the letter text PBS used two periods to signify the lengthened pause for which he later inserted a dash in **EN.** This sort of pause also occurs in his letter immediately following the poem: "There it is . . a mad effusion of this morning . ."

line 22. "ty[gers] is": This line, at the very bottom of the page, was damaged by the seal tear when the letter was opened. A sliver of the descender of the *g* and most of "is" remain legible.

lines 26–27. "Spreads the influence of soul-chilling terror around | And lowers on the corpses that rot on the ground": PBS adds specificity to these images in the letter to Hogg by changing the lines to read in *Esd:* <u>O'er the withered and withering nations around</u> | <u>And the war-mangled corpses that rot on the ground</u>.

line 28. "They came   to the fountain   to draw from its stream": Our text of the Supplement reproduces spacing similar to that in the first line of the version in the letter to Hogg; here PBS seems less concerned with a pause necessitating specific grammatical markings than with the rhythm of the line.

line 29. "Waves too pure too celestial" (TCU) becomes in **EN:** <u>Waves too poisonously lovely</u>; this shift in diction emphasizes the pain experienced by the speaker after he viewed unadorned Truth, but it may also cast doubt on the value of an enlightenment that leads simultaneously to the suffering of those who achieve it. An analogue to this thought appears where PBS alludes to himself in *Adonais* as one who had "gazed on Nature's naked loveliness, / Actæon-like, and now he fled astray" pursued by "his own thoughts . . . like raging hounds" (stanza 31).

line 35. "ah where": We reproduce these as separate words, although in MS TCU they appear almost as one, with the end of the *ah* carrying over into a barely legible "where" (almost illegible, with the letters *ere* appearing as a short squiggle).

1809 ("I will kneel at thine altar")   [Esd #42]

As we noted above, *1810 ("Dares the Lama")* is, in prosodic form, an identical twin to this poem, also consisting of four stanzas, each with nine lines in anapestic tetrameter and trimeter (4-3-4-3-4-3-3-4-4), rhymed *ababbccdd*. Thematically the poems are also paired. In *"Dares the Lama"* PBS excoriates religion as a baneful influence on the human mind and society, leading to the persecution of the individuals who seek the highest humane values. In this companion poem, *1809 ("I will kneel at thine altar"),* he declares his own commitment to worship selflessly a <u>God, Love or Virtue</u> that contrasts with the <u>Prejudice</u> and <u>Interest</u> that he believed to be the essence of the established, orthodox, and conventional religion practiced in his social stratum.

While noting that *1809 ("I will kneel at thine altar")* is the first poem to describe PBS's conversion experience at school that he later featured in *Hymn to Intellectual Beauty* and the Dedication to *Laon and Cythna,* Cameron finds the title/date *1809* troublesome because in later poems PBS indicates that the experience in the schoolyard took place in May, and Cameron judges May 1809 to be too early for PBS to have read Godwin's *Enquiry concerning Political Justice* (*1964,* 250 ff.). Believing that those interpreting allegorical—and biographical—poetry of the Romantic era need not take too literally either the specific year (which PBS might have pushed back to show his precocity) or the month of May (a standard poeticism for Youth), Reiman discusses *1809 ("I will kneel at thine altar")* in an essay based partly on notes in PBS's pocket diary for 1810 (*SC* IX, 67–90). In an entry for 19 February 1810, immediately after he noted the publication of *Zastrozzi* and a week before he began work on *The Wandering Jew,* PBS wrote "Resolutions made." A cross-reference from that 19 February entry to another entry in the diary's space for 4 June indicates that PBS and two school companions at Eton had agreed in advance to absent themselves from the celebration of the birthday of King George III on 4 June 1810. In this context, Reiman dates the poem between Christmas of 1809 and May or June 1810 (*SC* IX, 81–86) and finds PBS's later accounts of the same conversion experience consonant with the premise that it was sometime during his last school year at Eton that PBS vowed to worship <u>Love or Virtue</u>, rather than <u>Prejudice, Priestcraft, Opinion and Gold</u> (**line 30**).

As *1989* points out, the act of homage to an unseen deity such as PBS promises at the outset of this poem was a common ritual during ceremonies early in the French Revolution (e.g., the Festival of the Federation, 14 July 1790, and the Festival of Reason, 10 November 1793), and Volney represents such a ceremony in Chapter 17 of *Ruins of Empire*—as PBS was to do in Canto V of *L&C*. The point of such public events was to reassure the people who, after the churches were stripped of their authority, missed the pageantry and the recognition of a higher Power, and to serve as a gesture by the leaders of the Revolution that they were not godless self-worshipers. PBS's poem is likewise calculated to inform the world that his denial of the rights and rites of the established church did not signify an atheism lacking moral controls, because he felt a sense of awe in the face of ideals, values, and powers greater than his ego and was determined to sacrifice his self-interest to a higher Good.

lines 3–4. These lines are notable in attributing longer life to the poet's high-beating heart than to his perishing lays, another sign that PBS wrote the poem early, before he had gained confidence in poetry as the medium through which he might make his mark in the world.

lines 14–18. In **EN** PBS did not supply enough punctuation to make his intention clear, this entire stanza being punctuated with only a semicolon at the end of **line 11,** a question mark after bondage in the middle of **15,** commas after feel not (**16**) and felt (**17**), and a decisive period and dash at the end of the stanza (**18**). Besides these marks, directly below free at the end of **14** (which runs into the gutter) there is a large dot of ink that may be PBS's period to end that line. But to make sense of the stanza as a whole, the reader needs to know where the stops are in **lines 15–16** and how to interpret the word What at the beginning of **17,** which is different from the What that begins **16.** As we have punctuated these lines—accepting all of PBS's given pointing and adding only where necessary—they read:

> Thine, thine is the bond alone binds the free.
>   Can the free worship bondage? nay, more,   15
>   What they feel not, believe not, adore
> What if felt, if believed, if existing must give
> To thee to create, to eternize, to live.—

Cameron (*1964,* 125) points the way by adding minimal punctuation. On the other hand, Matthews and Everest in *1989* (I, 151)—assuming that the thoughts from the end of **line 15** to the end of the stanza are parallel in structure to the query in **15**—added a question mark at the end of **16** and changed PBS's period at the end of the stanza to another question mark, thereby (in our opinion) making PBS say something trite instead of what we believe is a profound statement about the need of human beings, when they cannot accept a dead orthodoxy, to make a leap of faith in existential commitment to the greatest Good that they can imagine.

PBS's problem was to compress this complex meaning within the tightly controlled meter and rhyme scheme that he had chosen. To complete the rhymes in **15–18** he had to curtail and invert the syntax to express this complicated thought: "Is it possible for the free not only to worship bondage but, what is more, adore What (i.e., "that which") if they really felt and believed in—and if, in fact, it really exists—they must (i.e., would then feel naturally obligated to) give their allegiance To thee (i.e., to the religious, creative, spiritual Power itself, rather than to any narrow sectarian definition of it) in order to create (i.e., to use their full creative powers), to eternize (a verb found in *Entick's Dictionary* as a variant form of "eternalize," meaning "to immortalize"), to live (in the fullest sense of that verb). What PBS begins as a rhetorical question thus ends as a declaration of faith in the power of the spirit that he invokes to lift human existence to a new level of meaning. As Nora Crook observed in correspondence, "Shelley . . . is appropriating the Christian paradox that God's service is perfect freedom," a paradox that she also identifies in *QM:* "that sweet bondage which is freedom's self" (IX.76).

lines 33–36. After excoriating Religion as a venomous blast (venemous in **EN** being a misspelling according to authorities both contemporary and modern) and lamenting at the end of the third stanza that selfishness, conquering, cries Victory!, PBS ends the poem by expressing confidence that Hope can create out of the wreckage an Avenger capable of overthrowing the throne | Of selfishness. This differs from Demogorgon's admonition at the end of ***Prom:*** "To love, to bear, to hope, till Hope creates | From its own wreck the thing it contemplates" (IV.573–74), for PBS had not yet worked through his sense of isolation and persecution, writing in this spirit to Hogg on 20 December 1810: "I swear on the altar of perjured love to revenge myself on the hated cause [Christianity] of the effect [Harriet Grove's withdrawal from their engagement] which *even now* I can scarcely help deploring.—" (*Letters* I, 27). But, as he wrote in Note 2 to ***Hellas,*** his final completed major work, PBS usually believed, "it is the province of the poet to attach himself to those ideas which exalt and ennoble humanity" (*2002, 462*), therein providing an explanation for his persistence in encouraging the downtrodden children of light with words of hope and revival at the ends of works ranging from ***Devil's Walk, Laon and Cythna,*** and ***Mask of Anarchy*** to ***Prom,*** and ***Hellas*** itself, which ends, after the Janizaries at Istanbul cry "Victory!" with a Chorus of slaves contemplating the return of "The world's great age" (***Hellas*** 1060 ff.).

Fragment of a Poem, | *the original idea of which was suggested by the cowardly and infamous bombardment of Copenhagen*   *[Esd #43]*

PBS originally sent a different fragmentary version of this poem to Hogg in a letter he wrote from Field Place on 11 January 1811, calling it the work of "Eliza," at a time when he was trying to ignite a relationship between Hogg and his sister Elizabeth Shelley. In *SC* II (700–705) Cameron discussed it as probably the work of Elizabeth Shelley but noted that it might be by PBS because of its appearance in **EN** (about which he then knew only from the Julian Edition [*1927*] III, 316–17, and VIII, 40–41n). In *1964* (255–56) Cameron acknowledged that PBS was indeed the author of the fragmentary poem—or at least all of it except possibly the final stanza of the letter version, which is set off by a row of *X*s. The letter version (see its text in *Esd* #43, Supplement) consists of four stanzas, two of which do not appear in *Esd;* one of the three stanzas in *Esd* is absent from the letter to Hogg, while those two stanzas that are common to both versions are in a different order. This complex relationship between the two texts of *Fragment . . . bombardment of Copenhagen* is analyzed below in our Commentary to the Supplement.

Why did PBS wish to publish the truncated and revised version in *Esd* at all, and why does it differ so much from the version sent to Hogg in 1811? First, PBS wished to specify the charge that he made in his final footnote to *A retrospect of Times of Old* (*Esd* # 31) that Horatio Nelson was one of the contemporary "legal murderers," and he chose to revise his fragment and make it part of *Esd* just when Robert Southey published his laudatory *Life of Nelson;* it became Southey's best-received work and has been republished frequently (including in a 1990 edition in the series "Classics of Naval Literature" published by the U.S. Naval Institute at Annapolis, Maryland). Though almost all Britons applauded Nelson's victories over Napoleon's fleets at the Nile and Trafalgar, the British bombardment of the capital of the neutral Danes on 2 April 1801, which caused many civilian casualties, was not directed against the French enemy but was an exercise in geopolitical power. When Russia, Sweden, and Denmark entered into a league of armed neutrality, the leaders of the British military decided that it was in their national interest to seize or destroy the Danish fleet, so that it could not fall into French hands. The Danes, when thus threatened, moved their ships as close to the city as possible to give them added protection from the guns of the city's fortresses and land-based artillery, and the devastation to the city and its civilian population was, therefore, considerable. For this reason, many informed Britons came to consider the entire enterprise to have been a lawless act. The British "victory" was so politically ineffectual, in fact, that it drove Denmark from armed neutrality into friendship with France, and the British navy had to bombard Copenhagen again in 1807, two years after Nelson's death at Trafalgar, this time stirring up open anti-government

feelings in England. PBS's fragment, which generalizes the two bombard-
ments into one, attempts to fuel the anger of the British public over the
recent brutal attack and discredit Nelson's earlier (and similarly bloody) tri-
umph.

According to contemporary accounts as well as modern research, Nelson
himself acted with courage and resourcefulness in winning the battle in
1801 despite the misjudgment of his commanding officer, stationed in the
rear, who shortly before the Danes accepted Nelson's offer of a truce leading
to the surrender of their fleet, signaled for a British withdrawal (a flag signal
that Nelson pretended not to see, placing his telescope to his blind eye). Nel-
son also behaved with humanity and courtesy after the battle, winning the
admiration of Danish military officers. Indeed, the only British officer who
behaved egregiously both in the battle and afterwards was William Bligh,
later captain of the *Bounty*. (For a detailed modern account of the battle in
its context, based upon British and Danish archival sources, see *The Great
Gamble* by Dudley Pope [London: Weidenfeld & Nicholson, 1972].) But for
PBS, the heavy destruction and many civilian casualties in the city of Copen-
hagen did not deserve praise or honors such as Nelson received. Southey
had begun to write his *Life of Nelson* in 1810 and sent some finished chapters
to press by August 1812. He and PBS may, therefore, have discussed the
battle during their time together at Keswick in early 1812. But Southey did
not receive copies of his printed book until 9 July 1813. If Southey's reverent
treatment of Nelson's actions at Copenhagen did provide PBS's motive for
resurrecting what seem to be scattered stanzas of an uncompleted poem, the
Fragment may not have been transcribed into **EN** until after that date, pro-
viding a possible time-marker for his progress in copying the poems of ***Esd***
into the Notebook.

The four-stanza letter version of the poem is cosmic in scope, imagining
that the rampant and armed British <u>Lion</u> (an image that appears in a
crowned shield as the watermark in the paper upon which PBS wrote his let-
ter to Hogg containing the Supplement version) was <u>victorious</u> in the inter-
est of <u>Britannia</u>—a female figure armed, like Athena, with helmet, shield,
and spear (or trident) that is featured in the watermarks of the other letter
paper that PBS used regularly at Field Place throughout 1810–12. (For these
watermarks, see the illustrations in Plate 28, facing p. 659 in *SC* II.) Though
the first stanza may thus have been inspired by PBS's musings about a war-
like watermark in the paper upon which he was writing his letter to Hogg, he
was not the first English poet to say that the casual use of British naval power
during the balance-of-power struggle against Napoleon was wreaking havoc
around the world. When James Montgomery in *The Ocean* turned his eyes
upon Europe, he saw "the war-tempested flood | All foaming, and panting
with blood; | The panic-struck Ocean in agony roars, | Rebounds from the
battle, and flies to his shores." There follows this stanza:

> For Britannia is wielding her trident to-day,
> Consuming her foes in her ire,
> And hurling her thunder with absolute sway
> From her wave-ruling chariots of fire:
> —She triumphs;—the winds and the waters conspire
> To spread her invincible name;
> The universe rings with her fame;
> —But the cries of the fatherless mix with her praise,
> And the tears of the widow are shed on her bays!
>
> (*The Wanderer in Switzerland*, 167–68)

This stanza provides an outline for PBS's central themes, and like *The Ocean,* PBS's fragment in its earliest form expands its range of vision far beyond Denmark and the Baltic Sea. In the second stanza of the letter version, the "terror-struck nations" that border "Old Ocean" set off the eruption of volcanoes around the world (see Commentary to Supplement, below), similar to the upheavals that PBS imagines in **To the Republicans of North America** (**Esd** #17). These geologic disturbances, like convulsions of the earth that PBS later describes in Act I of **Prom** and in other poems, symbolize the capacity of destructive human hatred and the ferocity of war to cast a blight on the harmony of Nature.

In its **Esd** version, **Fragment . . . bombardment of Copenhagen** consists of three seven-line stanzas of anapestic tetrameter, rhymed *ababbcc*—exactly the same form as that of the poem that follows it. For implications of this pairing, see our analysis in the Commentary to **1809: On an Icicle that clung to the grass of a grave** (**Esd** #44). It is interesting that of the first three volumes of miscellaneous poems that PBS assembled for publication—**V&C, Posthumous Fragments of Margaret Nicholson,** and **Esd**—each contains one or more poems entitled "Fragment," as well as others that have incomplete lines or are palpably incomplete. This pattern continues in both **Alastor . . . and Other Poems** and **Prometheus Unbound . . . with Other Poems.** Of his publications containing more than the title poem, only the **Rosalind and Helen** volume (with three additional poems, selected by Charles Ollier) and **Hellas,** to which PBS added at the last minute his intricate stanzas **Written on Hearing the News of the Death of Napoleon,** lack any poetic fragments. We suspect that, along with his highly polished odes and other complex metrical achievements, he purposely introduced a little disorder as part of his skeptical gesture, to signal his readers that he did not think of poetic truth as something cut and dried.

line 2. <u>solium of snow</u>: The *OED*'s only recorded example before 1810 of the word *solium*—which means, in this case, "throne"—appeared in Southey's edition of *The Remains of Henry Kirke White* (1807), in White's fragmentary epic *The Christiad. A Divine Poem* (II, 179), where Satan appears in an early scene (I.xii), seated on a throne of ice. We would suspect that PBS had read

White, simply from this use of *solium,* but there is confirmatory evidence in quotations from another of White's poems, *To a Friend in Distress,* in HWS's Commonplace Book (see Commentary to **Esd** #10).

line 3. <u>Spitzbergen</u>: an uninhabited island in the Arctic Ocean north of Norway and east of Greenland. During the eighteenth and nineteenth centuries, though claimed by Denmark, it provided a summer base for whaling ships from several nations.

Supplement: Version in Letter to Hogg, 11 January 1811

Our transcription of the poetic fragment in PBS's letter to Hogg dated 11 January 1811, now in the Pforzheimer Collection, reproduces the complexities of Pfz 132, while changing or commenting on a few doubtful words in the transcription in *Shelley and his Circle* (*SC* II, 701–2; see also **Letters** I, 41–43). Both the first and the third stanzas of Pfz 132 remain largely intact (though their order is inverted) in **Esd,** but the Supplement's second stanza, which focuses on additional geographic "murmurs" of nature's sympathetic turmoil, is omitted. The new stanza that appears in **Esd** ignores the hopefulness of the Supplement's fourth stanza (also omitted), replacing it with a tragic personal moment: the death of a woman caused by grief as she cradles her slain child (or perhaps lover). If the fourth stanza of the Supplement was by Elizabeth Shelley, that would be enough to motivate its omission, but as our examination of the relationship of **Fragment . . . bombardment of Copenhagen** with its matching poem, **Esd** #44 will suggest, even if PBS wrote that final stanza (with the separating row of Xs merely marking an omission of other stanzas in the copy), he still had good reason to omit it when he arranged his poems in **Esd.**

line 5. "fall": This reading appears in *SC* II, yet the MS is unclear, and the word can also be read as "pale," which would fit the context of the line. However, since **Esd** clearly reads <u>fall</u> (**line 12**), we defer to this reading.

lines 5–6. The mistake that leads PBS to write "blood-reeking bed" below **line 5** likely resulted from an eye-skip while copying from his draft that caused him to write "complaint breathing" (the compound adjective from line 6), in **line 5** at first and then to cancel and replace it.

lines 8–14. Ultimately the "terror-struck nations" that border "Old Ocean" cause "Earth" to be "fear-palsied" as they convulse the "shore" with "dread" and as volcanoes in the "Andes," the Canary Islands (both described by Alexander von Humboldt in his *Travels*), and classic Aetna in Sicily all erupt in sympathy.

line 14. The towering volcano "Teneriffe" (spelled variously in English reference books of PBS's time; now Tenerife), the largest of the Canary Islands, was both climbed and described by Alexander von Humbolt and mentioned in the translation of Schubart's poem on the Wandering Jew that influenced PBS's conception of that mythic figure (see note to *QM* VII.67 and references there).

line 16. solium] column *1961* While *SC*'s transcription of the MS notes that "column" is only a "probable reading" (*SC* II, 703), <u>solium</u> (the reading in the corresponding line in *Esd* #43, line 2) is the correct one. For PBS's source of the word *solium,* see above.

line 20. "war's": Here we correct (but not silently, as *SC* does) PBS's strange shortening of "wars" to "was"; PBS often scrunched his *r*'s when he copied hastily, but here the concluding letter looks like a character between an *r* and an *s.*

line 21. Following this line in MS Pfz 132 are eight large *X* marks (*SC* II transcribes seven of them), used as a separator between the final two stanzas—marking either a lacuna in the text PBS copied or the separation of PBS's stanzas from one by his sister Elizabeth (see Commentary to *Esd* version).

line 26. "footstool of God": This idea appears in the Bible, both the Old and New Testaments: Isaiah 66:1, "Thus saith the Lord, The heaven *is* my throne, and the earth *is* my footstool"; and Acts 7:48–49 (in the testimony of Stephen, just before he is martyred), "the most High dwelleth not in temples made with hands; as saith the prophet, | Heaven *is* my throne, and earth *is* my footstool . . . ."

line 28. "heal": This corrected transcription of the word (given as "hear" in *SC* II) changes considerably the tone of the last line, which now reads: "Let concord & Love heal the miseries of War." This stanza gives the letter version a hopefulness not found either in the first three stanzas of the Supplement or in the three-stanza *Esd* text. Though PBS often ended his major poems on a similarly hopeful note (as the Commentary to *Esd* #42 documents), if he wrote this stanza, he omitted it from *Esd* #43 because his intention was to darken Nelson's heroic reputation by focusing on the sufferings of innocent victims of his aggressive mode of warfare.

1809 | On an Icicle that clung to the grass of a grave   [Esd #44]

PBS paired with the *Fragment . . . bombardment of Copenhagen* (*Esd* #43) this poem, which he had also sent to Hogg in 1811, untitled in the letter version but in **EN** named *1809: On an Icicle that clung to the grass of a grave.* In its original form, this poem—like *Fragment . . . bombardment of Copenhagen*—was longer (five stanzas), but when PBS adapted it for *Esd,* he removed two stanzas that deal with the evils that war inflicts on loving individuals, thereby changing its thematic focus, which is central to ***Fragment . . . bombardment of Copenhagen*** (as well as to ***Henry and Louisa; Esd*** #46). In thus pruning the longer versions of this pair of poems sent to Hogg in 1811, PBS separated the two messages originally embodied in both poems—the evil that war wreaks on both the bodies and souls of men and women. But he then placed the revised poems side by side, dressed as twins, so that readers would not miss the relationship between the two themes. The resulting poems each consist of three seven-line stanzas in anapestic tetrameter rhymed *ababbcc.*

Beyond their poetic form, the most obvious likenesses between ***1809: On an Icicle*** and ***Fragment . . . bombardment of Copenhagen*** are that both speak of the North and cold weather and deal with death. Whereas in the final stanza of ***Fragment . . . bombardment of Copenhagen*** a "lone female," casualty of British balance-of-power politics, clasps the body of her lover or child to her breast and then herself pitches forward "in the sleep of the blest," the opening stanza of ***On an Icicle*** takes place at a graveside, where the poet finds a tiny icicle clinging to the grass; by the end of the poem he finds comfort in the thought that it is the frozen tear-drop of an <u>Angel of kindness</u> (**15**). The poem ends with the message that <u>if Angels can weep, surely</u> the poet is permitted to <u>repine</u> over the <u>Sister of Snow</u> (i.e., a dead woman, stone cold in her grave).

Does PBS mean to imply that these two dead women are one and the same? This is possible only in PBS's revised version, because in the earlier, letter version of ***On an Icicle*** (see Supplement), the occupant of the grave is not necessarily a <u>Sister of Snow</u>, but could be a military man "his country defending" or a patriot who kills "a dread Tyrant" (Supplement 8, 10–12). The final stanza of the Supplement implies that the poet had once pledged at "the Altar of Glory" to entwine "the loveliest flowers" (presumably those of poesy, such as PBS offers to HWS in the dedication), but now he regrets that decision and would "yield" to "fame all thy glories" for "a tear | To shed on the grave of an heart so sincere" (34–35).

As the texts of the two poems were reshaped for ***Esd,*** the <u>Sister of Snow</u> in the grave may be thought of as the Danish woman who died with a beloved in her arms under Nelson's bombardment of Copenhagen; or she could be the young woman of the ***[Poems about Mary],*** with a sincere heart filled with love, but perhaps denied burial in holy ground because she was a suicide; or she might be the woman named Louisa in ***1808 ("Cold are the blasts")*** (***Esd*** #45), who with her baby is abandoned by her "remorseless betrayer"—a seducer who laughs as he sends them away from his door into a howling storm, driving her to her death. Or, in the context of the military references found in the Supplement version of ***On an Icicle,*** the dead woman (like Louisa in ***Henry and Louisa, Esd*** #46) may have watched her lover go off to seek glory in the British foreign wars, but, instead of following him (as Louisa does), she died at home while her suitor or husband was far away, trying to kill or maim other women's lovers.

Poems with these intertwining themes of love, glory, and death, though foreshadowed as far back as *A retrospect of Times of Old* (#31), begin in earnest with *[Poems about Mary]* and continue through *Zeinab and Kathema* (#49). As a group they recount the stories and bemoan the fates of different kinds of innocent victims of a cruel world: some are betrayed by friends or lovers who abandon them out of prudence or to seek glory; some are killed by the seekers of glory from other countries; some are driven to thoughts of suicide by religious bigotry or the coldness and insensitivity of friends and family; and some are hounded to death within their own societies for trying to disseminate truth and assure justice for others. But this bleak picture of human existence is, in almost every case, relieved by a compensation either of hope for a better existence beyond the grave, or by the sympathy of those few who can empathize and commiserate with their feelings. As time passed, PBS obviously came to feel relief from his own mental anguish through his artistic expression of the tribulations of other persons, real or imagined. He came to believe that through his poetic gift his outcry would strike responsive chords in the heartstrings of compatible souls, if not in his lifetime, then in later times and other places.

Supplement: Version in Letter to Hogg, 6 January 1811

PBS's letter to Hogg (written 6 January 1811) contains a particularly wintery theme appropriate for the season of its composition. When he transformed the text in Pfz 129 (*SC* II, 688–89; *Letters* I, 36–40) into *Esd* #44, his changes were drastic, sharpening the formal and thematic relationships between this poem and *Esd* #43. Again, PBS pruned before he grafted, deleting stanzas 2 and 5 of the Supplement, while slightly rewriting the fourth stanza to create a personal meditation on grief that complements but does not resemble the almost Gothic vision in *Fragment . . . bombardment of Copenhagen.*

line 20. After writing "And" as the first word in the line, PBS then wrote "Say" above it, as a possible replacement; but after considering this change, he rejected it, underlining "And" to indicate his final choice (as it later appears in *Esd* #44).

lines 26–27. PBS underscored <u>thee</u>, <u>Angels</u>, and <u>Man</u>, presumably to emphasize these words in the rhythmic pattern of the line.

line 32. Here, as he often does in the *Esd,* PBS wrote what is apparently "shine" rather than "shrine." We give him the benefit of the doubt, since the word appears particularly ambiguous.

1808 ("Cold are the Blasts")   *[Esd #45]*

PBS earlier published this poem, under the title **Song**, as his first contribution to **Original Poetry** by **Victor and Cazire,** following two verse letters by his sister Elizabeth (see **CPPBS** I, 11–13 for the text; 166–69 for Commentary on that version). After **V&C** was suppressed, PBS wrote out a copy of this poem for Hogg (to whom he seems never to have mentioned **V&C**) along with fragments of two others, telling him that the verses were the work of Elizabeth Shelley. Hogg later published them together as such in Chapter 5 of his *Life of Percy Bysshe Shelley* (ed. Wolfe, 1933) I, 124–27. When Cameron first edited the manuscript for *SC* (II, 625–32), he accepted Hogg's attribution of authorship (just as Hogg had accepted PBS's), but he later corrected the record when editing **Esd** (*1964,* 258–60). Cameron also established then that Hogg's memory was correct when he said that PBS wrote out the poem for him at Oxford (rather than sent it later from home), for the watermarks show that the paper used was from PBS's supply at college, not the stationery at Field Place.

PBS obviously knew this poem by memory because he, not Elizabeth, had written it. He told Hogg that it was written by his sister possibly to arouse Hogg's interest in her (as Cameron suggests), but perhaps also to shield himself from any sarcastic remarks about the quality of the verses in case his new friend did not find them appealing. That PBS himself was proud of the poem is proved by his placing it at the beginning of his contributions to **V&C** in 1810, by his memorization of it, and above all by his inclusion of it again in **Esd** years after its composition. (Though the title/date **1808** cannot be verified as totally accurate, the poem is an early one.) Indeed, there are places in it where some may find that pathos occasionally gives way to bathos because of faults in the poet's choice of words. PBS's handling of the prosody (eight-line stanzas in anapestic tetrameter rhymed *ababcccb*) is, however, skillful enough for one of his earliest experiments in a complex stanzaic form.

As mentioned in the Commentary to **On an Icicle** (**Esd** #44), the poem's theme parallels that of neighboring poems as it explores the misery wrought by the exploitative cruelty of men in PBS's social class toward the poor and weak, especially women. By the time PBS wrote these poems, he was old enough and sensitive enough to realize that as older bullies had picked on him at school because of his attitudes and opinions, others in the society were constantly persecuted simply because they were defenseless and that entire nations were persecuted either by their own tyrannical rulers or by greedy, blood-thirsty, or glory-seeking aggressors from other nations. Thus he transformed the psychological pains that he often felt as a lonely and tormented "atheist" or pariah into a passion for reforming the world.

PBS wrote out the Supplement to *1808 ("Cold are the Blasts")* along with other scraps of poetry from memory while Hogg watched him early in their friendship at Oxford, in late October or November 1810 (*SC* II, 625–27; Hogg, *Life,* ed. Wolfe I, 124–27). Lines 1–40 of that melange had earlier appeared as the third poem in *Original Poetry by Victor and Cazire,* with some other lines and line fragments that appear in *V&C* (see *CPPBS* I, 20 for the full text of that poem; 175–76 for Commentary). See the discussion of *1808* above for its history and relationship to other poems of *Esd.*

The changes that PBS made to this poem when he copied it into **EN** are mostly cosmetic but, like the changes made in the other earlier versions presented here as Supplements, they reveal his growth as an artist, especially in regard to rhythm and diction. **Line 8,** which here reads "Which mixed with groans, anguish & wild madness flow," becomes in *1808* <u>That, envenomed by wildest delirium, flow</u>. PBS further displays here his developing ability to particularize what were before jejune generalities, as in **line 16,** which he changed from "Crossed the dark mountain side tho the hour it was late" to <u>Took the rough mountain path, tho' the hour was late</u>, improving the imagery, sounds, and the meter.

On the same sheet of paper, PBS copied two other fragments from the twelfth and thirteenth poems found in *V&C*—the opening quatrain and the next four words from his *Song: To* ————— *("Ah! Sweet is the moonbeam"),* written for Harriet Grove, and lines 9–15, 17–18 of *Song: To* ————— *("Stern, stern is the voice of fates's fearfull command")* (*CPPBS* I, 20–21; Commentary, I, 175–78). These poems were also written by PBS, but he had not, apparently, bothered to memorize either one completely.

1809 | *Henry and Louisa* | *a Poem in two parts*   *[Esd #46]*

Though it remains unclear exactly when PBS began writing *Henry and Louisa (H&L),* an anti-war narrative apparently intended to be in Spenserian stanzas, both its date/title and its position in *Esd* among poems known to have been circulated before his elopement indicate that it preceded his expulsion from Oxford. Here the date can probably be taken literally, as Cameron does when he calls it "Shelley's first attempt at a long poem" (*1964,* 260), putting it earlier than *The Wandering Jew* (the editors of *1989* place *H&L* seventh in their overall chronology and *WJ* eleventh). Cameron believed that PBS would have been too young to remember the campaign in 1801 by an expeditionary force of the British army under Sir Ralph Abercromby (1734–1801, *DNB;* sometimes spelled Abercrombie in contemporary sources) that ousted the French army left by Napoleon in Egypt, and he argued that PBS must be referring to a British incursion into Egypt in 1807 that ended in their defeat by the Turks (*1964,* 266). But as *1964* and *1989* note, Napoleon is the <u>Tyrant of the World</u> referred to here and his French Revolutionary army is the irreligious enemy to whom Henry alludes in **lines 72 ff.**

Although PBS may not have followed the course of the 1801 campaign (which a nine-year-old *can* do) and although the newspapers had gone on to other topics, one of those was the heroism, death, and subsequent glorification of Sir John Moore (1761–1809), one of Abercromby's leading officers in Egypt, who died in the early stage of the Peninsular Campaign at Corunna, Spain, on 16 January 1809 during the embarkation of his troops under the fire of a larger French army (the Dunkirk of the Napoleonic wars). Furthermore, William Lisle Bowles, the clergyman-poet friend of the Grove family who had hymned Cwm Elan (see ***Esd*** #18 Commentary) also wrote a "Dirge of Nelson" and celebrated Sir John Moore and his army at Corunna in his *Poems (Never Before Published),* which appeared in 1809 as "printed for Cadell and Davies, Strand, London; and Cuttwell, Bath." PBS's uncle Captain John Pilfold, though no friend to religion and PBS's staunchest ally in his struggles with his father after the expulsion, owed both his fame and his fortune to having been—almost by accident—captain of one of Nelson's ships of the line at Trafalgar (see Desmond Hawkins, *Pilfold: The Life and Times of Captain John Pilfold* [Horsham: Horsham Museum Society, 1998]). He would have been aware, either personally or from naval colleagues, of Abercromby's complex amphibious landing near Alexandria, which might be classed as the Iwo Jima, if not the D-Day, of that era. (See Piers Macksey's *British Victory in Egypt, 1801: The End of Napoleon's Conquest* [London: Routledge, 1995]).

Several of PBS's known classmates and friends at Eton were from strongly Tory families (see *SC* IX, 81–84), and part of the isolation and persecution that he experienced in his later years there, leading to his conversion experience (***Esd*** #42 Commentary), would have involved the politics of war. Many Whigs, including Shelley's family, who had opposed the Walcheren Campaign against the French in the Netherlands, still opposed the Peninsular Campaign (***CPPBS*** I, 163–64 and 316). Moreover, though Timothy Shelley and other Whig M.P.s may have opposed the Tory military strategy, PBS's father was a devoted patriot, with a military command as a lieutenant in the Sussex Volunteers from 1804, when they were organized to repel a French invasion, until October 1813, when Wellington's expulsion of the French from Spain after the Battle of Salamanca removed that threat and led to the disbandment of the Volunteers (see *The Letters of Bysshe and Timothy Shelley . . . ,* ed. Susan C. Djabri and Jeremy Knight [Horsham: Horsham Museum Society, 2000], 114). Timothy Shelley's support of the military may have led to dinner-table quarrels because of his son's more pacific idealism. But beyond all other sources or personal experience, PBS's reading of *The Battle of Alexan-*

dria in James Montgomery's *The Wanderer of Switzerland and Other Poems* (three British editions in 1806), which glorifies the victories of Abercromby's army, was probably what stimulated him to draft **H&L.**

The British campaign of 1801 began with an elaborate amphibious landing near Alexandria in the face of seemingly insuperable obstacles, and the British army subsequently won a series of victories, even after Abercromby was killed at the crucial battle, which began as a surprise night attack by the French army (veterans whom Napoleon had led in both Italy and Egypt). This campaign, though disregarded in most modern histories, was a turning point in the French Revolutionary and Napoleonic Wars because it was the first wholly successful campaign by the British army since its humiliation at Yorktown in 1781. Memoirs and diaries of Wellington and his officers, several of whom served under Abercromby, show that they used the Egyptian campaign as an example of how British troops—carefully trained and intelligently led—could fight the French successfully (see Macksey, *British Victory in Egypt, 1801*, passim).

When PBS, however, read the laudatory account of the Battle of Alexandria by Montgomery (1771–1854), a liberal, humanitarian journalist who as editor of the *Sheffield Iris* had been imprisoned twice in the 1790s for attacking government corruption and malfeasance, he may have felt that Montgomery was betraying his beliefs by memorializing a general who had led an army in a foreign campaign that not only killed and maimed many Britons and French but brought death and misery to thousands of innocent Egyptians as well. Montgomery's *The Battle of Alexandria* shows his awareness of the sufferings of individual soldiers and their families: in stanzas after the battle, the poet speaks of a widow who hears of the death of her husband: "In imagination wild | She shall wander o'er this plain; | Rave,—and bid her orphan child | Seek his sire among the slain" (first ed., 1806, 110), thereby outlining the plot that PBS dramatizes. Yet immediately thereafter Montgomery asks the "Harp of MEMNON" to "Breathe enchantment to our ears"; "While the Hero's dirge is sung," he concludes his poem with "tones triumphant," with which he tries to find compensation for the human suffering: "Life's tumultuous battle o'er, | O how sweetly sleep the brave! | . . . Glory's temple is the tomb! | Death is immortality!" (112).

Such glorification of those whom Godwin and his followers thought of as <u>legal murderers</u> (**line 4**) provoked PBS to plan a response on a grand scale, as appears in the second stanza of Part 2: the tutelary <u>Genius of the south</u> (**166**), enthroned upon the cloud-belted Atlas Mountains across the straits from Gibralter (later to be the birthplace of PBS's Witch of Atlas), bemoans the fate of Africa and especially the crime of slavery and the <u>groans</u> of Egypt, <u>his most dear-beloved</u> nation. But, as with his abortive poem **Fragment . . . bombardment of Copenhagen,** PBS failed to expand the text of his poem to epic proportions, for—unlike such prolific poets as Scott and Southey—PBS did not enjoy developing plots with many incidents, but wrote more in the manner of Wordsworth's *Lyrical Ballads* and *Poems; in Two Volumes* or Byron's *The Giaour,* focusing on a single incident or relationship and then commenting on its psychological and moral implications. Thus, he could tell in a few stanzas all the story he needed to illustrate the conflict between love and war: Henry, a young Englishman of good family, takes leave of his sweetheart to seek glory in the Egyptian military campaign. His beloved Louisa, like other heroines before and after her, follows him, disguised as a man, and finds him mortally wounded on an Egyptian battlefield. When he dies, she commits suicide to be with him forever (**285–303**), after which their ghosts haunt the battlefield, causing the <u>pomp-fed despot's sceptered hand</u> . . . to shake <u>as if death were near</u>, while giving <u>comfort</u> to the tyrant's <u>lone captive</u>. PBS supplies dialogue suggested by the plot inherent in Montgomery's lines quoted above, and by adding moral commentary he swells the fragment to 315 lines. As Appendix A shows, PBS tallied additional lines by counting as complete stanzas 3–5 of Part 1, which remain mostly blank in **EN:** either he had lost a sheet of his earlier draft; forgotten those lines—if he had undertaken memorial reconstruction of the poem; or left blanks in his text, as he did in some other poems, to be filled when his inspiration revived.

In *Zeinab and Kathema* (*Esd* #49), PBS inverts this plot and expands it, by narrating the search of a man from Cashmere for his beloved, kidnaped and carried off to England; in *Laon and Cythna* he would further expand the same personal theme by both allegorizing and idealizing the early years of the French Revolution, but he continues to center upon the story of the lovers who try (unsuccessfully) to steer historical action in a moral direction and die together. These romances all involve a search and attempt to rescue a beloved who has been lured or spirited away by evil forces, and each ends in the lovers' deaths, leaving only the hope that their story and example will influence others in the future to ameliorate conditions in a corrupted world.

We cannot know how much PBS revised his lost early text of *H&L* while transferring it into *Esd,* or even where he found that version of *H&L.* Had that source-text been given to Hogg, he would likely have mentioned it in his *Life of PBS* or in his much earlier series of articles "Shelley at Oxford," both of which aim to tell how much Hogg knew about PBS that others did not know. *H&L* and the two poems that follow it—*Translation of The Marsellois Hymn* and *Written in very early youth*—are among the early poems in *Esd* for which we can discover or posit no source-text on which PBS based the version in **EN.** PBS could have recovered the *ur*-texts of such poems in three ways: (1) He may have had access to their originals in one or more earlier notebooks (designated "Notebook X" for discussion purposes) that he carried away with him when he left Field Place to visit Cwm Elan (after which he eloped with HWS) or had shipped to him at York—possibilities that we explore in detail in our introduction to "Poems in the Hand of Harriet W. Shelley" and in the Commentary to the final five poems in **EN** (#54–#58), where we provide the available evidence on the subject. If there was such a Notebook X (with, possibly, Notebooks Y and Z), then the following speculations are superfluous. (2) PBS may have given copies of these poems to other friends before his elopement. (3) He may have memorized enough of them so that he was able to reconstruct them from his capacious memory. As we consider the other early poems in **Esd** that lack identified source texts, we could imagine that one might have been returned to PBS by the Rev. Evan ("Taffy") Edwards, the Vicar of Warnham Church and PBS's first teacher, for we know that in October or November 1812 PBS had been in touch with Edwards (see Commentary to *Written in very early youth, Esd* #48), but PBS was unlikely to have confided such an unfinished start of an abandoned love-epic as *H&L* to Edwards, an Oxford contemporary of his father. By 1813 PBS was totally alienated from both Graham and Hitchener; he would not have shared his anti-war poems with his uncle John Pilfold, the naval captain, retired because of his battle wounds, and two of his Grove cousins (William and George) were also in the British navy.

PBS might have drawn upon his great gift for memorizing poetry to reconstruct the vital parts of *H&L,* or, given his later facility with the Spenserian stanza, he should have been able to reconstitute and even improve his early effort. But neither the opening of the poem nor its final stanzas are regularly Spenserian; though a majority are, the first stanza has twelve lines, that numbered <u>VI</u> has ten lines, and so forth. In his note on the verse form keyed to the poem's opening, PBS speaks of the Spenserian stanza and attributes his abandonment of it at the end to his desire that the public receive a candid picture of the poet's mind and artistic skill at the age when he was first inspired to draft the poem. Yet it may be no accident that the verse form breaks down beginning at **line 258,** just as Louisa goes to pieces upon finding that Henry is dying, for PBS's excuse may be another way of saying that form ought to follow function in the emotionally charged ending of *H&L.* Here again PBS could have found an example in the poems of Wordsworth, who prefaced stanzaic sections to the originally inspired parts of both *'Tis said that some have died for love* and *Laodamia*—the first of which PBS could have seen in *Lyrical Ballads.* In addition to the possible literary sources or analogues that we note, *1989* cites the general influence of, or points out specific echoes from, Scott's *The Maid of Toro,* Bowles's *The Battle of the Nile,* and Gray's *Elegy Written in a Country Churchyard,* that favorite poem by one of PBS's favorite poets.

What does the early date tell us about the place of *H&L* in PBS's poetic development? If this fragment was drafted in 1809, about the time at which he was also composing *I will kneel at thine altar (Esd* #42) and love lyrics addressed to Harriet Grove that he sent to Fergus Graham to set to music (*CPPBS* I, 302), PBS's career as a poet was shaped from its beginnings by four central orientations: (1) a belief in personal autonomy, or "liberty," with an attendant aversion to tyranny; (2) a need for ideal love, his summum bonum; (3) a detestation of the glory attached to war, which he depicts, along with money and libertine passions, as embodiments of the most basic evil, human selfishness; and (4) an aversion to organized religion for the role it played both as a brake upon the natural expression of love and as a supporter of military glory. Many poems in *Esd*, like his early released poems included in the first volume of *CPPBS*, center upon these related themes, but the poems in *Esd, QM*, and most of the later poems that he meant for publication clothe such personal feelings in ideological arguments, in representations of inter- actions among human characters, mythic deities, or elements of nature, or in complex narratives and dramas based on or alluding to historical events.

line 1. *1989* notes (I, 14) that PBS's opening query is likely an echo of Henry Kirke White's *Time*, published in his *Remains* (1807 II, 147–69): "Where are the heroes of the ages past? . . . All to the grave gone down" (lines 134, 137). White's poem may also have suggested *A retrospect of Times of Old* (*Esd* #31) and foreshadows the famous "I want a hero" that opens *Don Juan* by Byron, who in his early years also read and admired Kirke White.

line 9. <u>blood-boltered eyes</u>: In this context, PBS's compound adjective means blood-splattered or bloodshot. As Crook points out to us, it both al- ludes to the appearance of "blood-bolter'd Banquo" (*Macbeth* IV.i.123) and anticipates Beatrice's declaration, "My eyes are full of blood; just wipe them for me" as she enters after her rape in *The Cenci* (III.i.2).

line 21. Following this line, PBS left space for two complete stanzas and the first six lines of a third stanza (a total of twenty-four lines), while heading these empty spaces with the stanza markers <u>III</u>, <u>IV</u>, and <u>V</u> (see the facsimile in *MYR: Shelley* I, 135–36). We do not number these lines, but PBS, appar- ently intending to complete these three stanzas before publishing the frag- ment, added the missing lines to his line count. Through an error—either a miscalculation of the number of lines left blank or an error in his addition— he actually increased his line count by twenty-six, thus adding unwritten lines to the total at the number 2155 (which he includes in **EN** at the end of *Henry and Louisa,* Part 1). Both *1964* and *1989* believe that these lines were left blank because PBS had misplaced a page of his copy-text, but if PBS was try- ing to reconstruct the poetic fragment from memory, he may simply not have been as clear on the contents of those stanzas as he was about the other parts that he did transcribe in **EN** and wished to think over what was needed there.

line 124. <u>In all the pangs</u>: The word that we (following *1964*) read as <u>In</u> ap- pears in Rogers's two texts as "No" and in *1989* as "For." In his transcription, Dowden first wrote "For," with the marginal note, "No? might be In"; but after another hand—presumably Garnett's—wrote "No" in the margin,

Dowden changed his reading to "No." Given the shape of the ambiguously formed word, <u>In</u> still seems to us the most likely reading, here meaning "[Within] all the pangs . . ." that Louisa tried to hide there was "a deeper soulpang" that Henry had trouble resisting—but did, by hurrying away.

line 153. <u>deep</u>: The rhyme word in **EN** is clearly <u>deep</u>, not "sleep" as *1989* gives it. Crook, believing that PBS's syntax is imperfect here, suggests to us that Matthews conjectured "sleep" in order to create two parallel clauses introduced by "that": "wrongs that sleep . . ." and "that dry."

line 170. <u>his most dear beloved nation's groan</u>: *1989* reads "nations groan" (as does **EN**), but in the context of the poem and of history (as taught in 1810), Egypt stands alone as the <u>most beloved</u> nation of the <u>Genius of the south</u> (**166**).

line 172. *1989* emends <u>northern world</u> (**EN**) to "southern world" but while PBS indeed says that the <u>Boreal whirlwinds</u> (**171**) of war are sweeping southward (from England and France, in their strategic struggle to control the shortest route to India), he remembers that Egypt, being north of the Equator, is still part of the <u>northern world</u>. The part of *1989*'s note about the Nile delta being <u>the veined bosom of the . . . world</u> still makes sense, when using PBS's own words, for there is no other place in the classical world that could receive that appellation by combining both the veined, breast-like appearance (on the map) and a reputation as a rich source of food.

line 226. Dowden initially transcribed the first word "There" (as we give it) and later wrote "Thus?" (adopted by *1989*) above it in smaller letters, but never canceled <u>There</u>. Looking at the badly written word again, we believe it more likely to be <u>There</u>, syntactically related to <u>where</u> both in **221** (the first line of the stanza) and later in **226.**

line 227. <u>Thy dear, deserted love?</u>: The tone of the poet's question is changed by the reading in *1966* and *1972*, where <u>deserted</u> is read as "devoted." Either reading may be seen in **EN,** for Dowden first wrote "devoted" and then canceled it and wrote <u>deserted</u> above it. If PBS intended "devoted," the omniscient voice of the poet would be indulging in sarcasm, asking Henry, "Where is the affection and care of your dear army [or Glory]?" This is possible, but given the sentimental concluding stanzas, it is more in keeping with the overall tone of the poem to assume that PBS intended Henry to think about his <u>deserted</u> love just as she finds him.

line 255. <u>Another moment's pain</u>: Dowden originally forgot to transcribe this line; when he wrote it on the facing verso page of MS ED-TCD (in which he transcribed only on the rectos), he was unsure whether the third word was "pause" (his original reading) or <u>pain</u>, which he wrote above it followed by a question mark, but later initialed "ED." While Cameron's and Rogers's editions also chose <u>pain</u>, *1989* preferred "pause," though its justification required a complicated argument and the addition of punctuation in this line. We believe the word looks more like <u>pain</u>.

line 260. <u>More sweet than Memnon's plainings wild</u>: *1989* notes that the ruins of the statue of Memnon at Luxor supposedly emitted music when struck by the morning sun. Montgomery's *The Battle of Alexandria* makes direct reference to the "Harp of Memnon" (line 1) as does Bowles's *The Battle of the Nile*. For other possible sources of PBS's references to the Memnon statue in the writings of Herodotus and Erasmus Darwin, see the Commentary to *A retrospect of Times of Old* (*Esd* #31), PBS's later rendering of the themes found in *H&L*.

line 291. <u>Sacred to Love a deed is done!—</u>: PBS's fascination with suicide appears here in a rather muted moment that leaves the reader to assume, from the understated narrative, that Louisa's <u>triumphant deed</u> is the taking of her own life beside her dead lover.

lines 300, 302. The initial word in these lines can be read as either *Where* or *When*. But the former word may accord better with the context, in which the lovers flee (305) to a better world.

A Translation of The Marsellois Hymn   [Esd #47]

Both *1964* and *1989* date PBS's translation of what is now called *La Marseillaise* according to Cameron's identification of the watermark of the letterpaper on which PBS sent Graham the stanza here printed as a Supplement. That paper was from the supply which PBS used while he was at Field Place, rather than that which he had used earlier in London. But his evidence proves only that PBS had translated the poem sometime *before* he copied this stanza into his letter to Graham, a fact that is also clear from its context in that letter, which indicates that Graham had prior knowledge of the entire translation.

PBS apparently translated six (of seven) stanzas of the *La Marseillaise* sometime between his expulsion from Oxford and his elopement, and since Hogg did not have a copy of it, PBS probably did so after Hogg was reconciled with his father and returned to the North, leaving PBS in London with John and Charles Grove and Edward Fergus Graham as his closest confidants. By the time Hogg, then at the Inner Temple, returned to London from the summer holiday in October 1812 (according to Chap. 19 of Hogg's *Life of PBS* I, 364), Graham was no longer in London and Charles Grove had moved to Edinburgh to study medicine, but Hogg found John Grove still residing at 49 Lincoln's Inn Fields. PBS also reappeared in London in October and November 1812, trying to raise money for the Tremadoc Embankment and for himself, so that he could take possession of Tan-yr-allt. If PBS had lacked the text of his translation of the French war-song by that time, just before he bought the notebook that became **EN** and began to copy his poems into it, John Grove may have been able to provide PBS with a copy. Grove (two of whose younger brothers were in the British navy) would not have agreed with all of its sentiments, even though his defense of PBS to Timothy Shelley and within the Grove family councils and his courting of Elizabeth Shelley after PBS's expulsion show that he was more advanced in his political thinking than most members of the two landed families (see Hawkins, *Shelley's First Love*).

Besides the six-stanza version in *Esd,* we reproduce in our Supplement the fourth stanza as PBS copied it on the cover sheet of his letter to Graham in which he discusses the infamous fête staged by the Prince Regent at Carlton House on 19 June 1811. The letter's sarcastic praise of the monarchy instructs Graham to "magnify, if magnification be possible, our noble Royal Family," and to "let them soar, high as the expanse of the empyrean & may no invidious louse dare to interrupt the reveries of pensive enthusiasm" (*Letters* I, 106; the phrase "invidious louse" alludes to *The Lousiad,* Peter Pindar's mock-epic satire on George III; see *CPPBS* I, 314). The Prince Regent's celebration also inspired a fifty-line poem by PBS, now lost, which he distributed, according to the recollection of Charles Grove, by "throwing copies into the carriages of persons going to Carlton House after the fête" (Hogg, *Life,* ed. Wolfe II, 158). Later Charles Grove recited four lines of the poem from memory to Richard Garnett, who gave his transcript to W. M. Rossetti to publish in *1870* (see *CPPBS* I, 448–51).

La Marseillaise, as it is now known, when written by Rouget de Lisle (1760–1836) at Strasbourg on 26 April 1792, was first called *War Song of the Rhine Army.* After the second revolution, 10 August 1792, a Jacobin leader from Montpellier went to Marseille and taught the song to a group of volunteers gathering there, who then marched to Paris in support of the *sans-culottes,* singing the stirring song along the way. In 1795, it became the French national anthem under the name *L'Hymne Marseillois.* PBS's source for the French text is unknown and perhaps unknowable, for the French words undoubtedly appeared in many contemporary periodicals and historical works and possibly in musical collections brought back from France either during the Peace of Amiens (1802–4), or smuggled into Britain and surreptitiously printed there by radical groups. PBS certainly does not seem to have written his translation to be sung with Rouget de Lisle's music, because his words—especially those of the Chorus—just do not fit it. He treated the French text as a poem, not a song, and replaced Lisle's eight-line stanzas, rhymed *ababcddc* with stanzas of nine lines in iambic tetrameter, rhymed *ababccddb.*

Here is a modern French text of the sixth stanza that is unrepresented in PBS's translation:

Nous entrerons dans la carrière
Quand nos aînés n'y seront plus
Nous y trouverons leur poussière
Et la trace de leurs vertus
Bien moins jaloux de leur survivre
Que de partager leur cercueil
Nous aurons le sublime orgueil
De les venger ou de les suivre!

(A literal translation on a French educational Web site renders this stanza: "We shall enter into the pit | When our elders will no longer be there | There we shall find their ashes | And the mark of their virtues | We are much less jealous of surviving them | Than of sharing their coffins | We shall have the sublime pride | Of avenging or joining them.") It is unclear why PBS did not translate this stanza, unless it was missing from his source. Alternatively, since he was then in a struggle of wills with his father, he may not have wished to endorse the idea of emulating his elders to the death.

PBS's extended translation in **EN** was first published as the initial appendix to André Koszul's book *La jeunesse de Shelley* (Paris: Libraire Bloud, 1910), 401–4. A short headnote to the appendix cites a mention of the existence of **Translation . . . Hymn** in Dowden's *Life* (I, 137) and notes Forman's publication of the stanza in the letter to Graham in his *Shelley Library* (25). Then follows an acknowledgment to Charles Esdaile for permission to publish the entire text: "Hâtons-nous de dire qu'elle n'ajoute rien à la gloire du poète; mais si un lecteur anglais serait excusable de s'irriter qu'on vînt encore grossir la part des *Juvenilia* de Shelley, il sera permis au lecteur français de remercier M. Ch. W. Esdaile, á qui nous devons de pouvoir publier ce qui suit, avec une sorte de patriotique émotion" (401). Koszul similarly thanked Esdaile in his acknowledgments in the front matter (p. xvii), but in the body of his book the poem is never discussed, though it is briefly alluded to on page 391. This suggests that Koszul first saw the poem and received Esdaile's permission to publish it only after *La jeunesse de Shelley* was completed and in the press.

Both *1964* and *1989* find PBS's translation to be "rather free" (*1989*, 158), a treatment consonant with PBS's mature theory of translation, as analyzed by Timothy Webb in *The Violet in the Crucible* (Oxford: Clarendon Press, 1976). PBS's diction not only universalizes the poem's nationality (as *1989* notes, in **line 38** PBS translates *"La France"* as <u>Our Mother Earth</u>), but he also broadens the range of its attack on tyranny. Cameron finds it an appropriate poem to follow **Henry & Louisa,** and we agree that the relationship between these two poems is closer than might first appear. By juxtaposing them PBS expressed his persistent skepticism, as each poem places limits on the message of the other: **H&L** warns against the worship of military glory, but **Translation . . . Hymn** makes an exception when the war is against a perfidious tyrant and his minions. Note that the end of **H&L** condemns a "pomp-fed despot" (line 312), just as *Translation . . . Hymn* indicts <u>pomp-fed Kings</u> (**30**).

Title. Though the form <u>Marsellois</u> may seem strange to those used to referring to *La Marseillaise,* the official designation of the national anthem was then *L'Hymne Marseillois* with the adjective spelled "Marsellois" in some contemporary printings. In eighteenth-century French texts, the forms *Anglois* and *François* appear where the proper forms now are *Anglais* and *Français.*

line 4. <u>bloodred</u>: PBS wrote this compound adjective clearly as a single word, in a transcription that is carefully written, without crowding at either margin of the page. Since, as we noted earlier, PBS's pattern of hyphenation is not yet understood, we leave the word as he wrote it, if only to alert students of PBS's poetry that this issue has not been fully addressed.

line 28. The meaning and therefore the punctuation of the phrase <u>their own alarms</u> has become a debated crux. Cameron, reading the phrase as being in apposition to <u>despots</u>, adds commas before and after it so that **lines 27–29** would mean: "<u>despots</u>, [who are] <u>their own alarms</u> [i.e., warnings], <u>Shall</u> . . . <u>Pass neath the yoke</u> that they prepared for us." A note in *1989* argues that no commas are necessary, glossing the lines as meaning, "their own terrors shall place despots under the yoke intended for us" (*1989* I, 159). We think that Cameron's reading accords better with PBS's English text, which here as elsewhere strays from the literal French.

line 36. In **EN** the comma that ends this line is attached to the terminal <u>t</u>.

lines 41–44. Matthews and Everest (*1989*) believe that PBS misunderstood these lines; on the contrary, his translation here accords perfectly with the spirit of the French text—"Français, en guerriers magnanimes, | Portez ou retenez vos coups! | Épargnez ces tristes victimes | A regret s'armant contre nous"—which may be rendered literally, "Frenchmen, as magnanimous warriors, | Strike or forbear your blows: | Spare those sad victims | Who reluctantly arm themselves against us."

line 46. This, the most dated and particularized reference in Lisle's lyrics, excoriates François Claude Amour, Marquis de <u>Bouillé</u>, an associate of Lafayette in the early days of the Revolution, who in August 1790 suppressed an uprising by the garrison at Nancy "in a pitched battle, had several insurgents executed, and sent forty-one Swiss . . . to the galleys." In June 1791, when King Louis XVI resolved to flee from France, he "ordered the marquis de Bouillé, conqueror of Nancy and commander at Metz, to make preparations for receiving him," but the plan failed when the King and his party were seized at Varennes by peasants and disaffected soldiers and returned to Paris under guard (Georges Lefebvre, *The French Revolution* [New York: Columbia UP, 1962], I, 144, 193, 207).

The final Supplement to the poems in *Esd* is the stanza of ***A Translation of The Marsellois Hymn*** that PBS copied into his letter to Edward Fergus Graham written ca. 19 June 1811 (***Letters*** I, 106), the original of which is in the Berg Collection, New York Public Library (MS Berg). On the fourth and final page of the letter, which sarcastically praises the "noble Royal family" after the Prince Regent's grand fête at Carlton House on 19 June (which purportedly cost £120,000 [***Letters*** I, 105, 110]), PBS wrote, mainly in large block letters, this translation of the fourth stanza of *La Marseillaise,* so placing it that when the letter was folded, sealed, and addressed it appeared on the normally blank back panel. As Elizabeth Denlinger informed us: "if Graham had left it lying with the wrong side up, anyone with reasonable vision would have been able to read it from, say, five or six feet away" (personal communication, 9 July 2002).

We attempt to reproduce the lines exactly as they appear in MS Berg, including a few apparent slips of the pen—the misspelling of <u>NIGT</u> (**37**), and the lowercase letters in **lines 36, 38,** and **40.** All of the letters that are rendered as lowercase (the *i* in **line 36,** the *ll, e,* and *ye* in **line 38;** and the *or* in **line 40**) are about the same size as the adjacent capital letters. Furthermore, in MS Berg the words represented in italics ("*FIGHT*" in **36** and the phrase "*DEATH or VICTORY*" in **40**) have clearly been italicized, rather than underlined, as if PBS was simulating a printed text, perhaps from the broadside that he planned to throw into passing carriages. The four periods after **line 35** and the two that follow **40** (all of which float in the middle of their respective lines) are PBS's only punctuation besides the exclamation marks at the ends of the first and final lines. In **EN,** the four periods become a single one and the last two are omitted (as is the final exclamation mark).

lines 1–3. "TREMBLE": PBS adapted the rhetoric of these powerful lines in lines 39 and 44 of ***To Death*** (***Esd*** #19).

"DESPISED": MS Berg has undergone enough stress to make some of the large letters quite faint; the concluding *D* here is difficult to make out and almost appears to be an *r.*

line 6. "NIGT": In ***Letters,*** Jones inserted a bracketed "H", but we leave the word as PBS wrote it in MS Berg.

Written in very early youth   [Esd #48]

What *is* "very early youth"? For Cameron, pointing especially to "the anti-war implications" of <u>No votarist I at Glory's shrine</u> (**18**), the poem seems less juvenile than PBS's title suggests, and he dates it 1809 (*1964,* 275). Matthews and Everest are willing to move back the date as early as April–May 1808

(*1989*, 4). But for a twenty-year-old man who had assigned the dates 1808 and 1809 to several poems in **EN** that he described as his "younger poems," very early youth would have a different meaning from that assumed by mature scholars. We cannot know how early PBS developed his aversion to "Glory's shrine," but as we have noted in the Commentary to the last few poems, this mind-set did not depend upon his reading of Godwin's *Political Justice* and may have started soon after more athletic boys with militaristic ambitions began harassing him at Eton in 1804, when he was twelve. In allegorizing his life in **Una Favola** (in Italian prose, 1821–22) PBS, as Crook points out to us, speaks of the youth as being awakened to love in his fifteenth year—that is, after his fourteenth birthday in August 1806. In any case, of all the poems in **Esd, Written in very early youth** seems to us the most juvenile in theme and tone, for the simplistic message of its tetrameter couplets (with an unrhymed final line) can be summarized by a saying once used to shame adolescents who complained too much about their hard fate: "Nobody loves me, everybody hates me: Guess I'll go eat worms!"

Lying under English yew trees and bathing in "the poison dew | That falls from yonder deadly yew" (**3–4**) was believed to be suicidal (as PBS also depicts it in **To the Lover of Mary** (**Esd** #40). The fifth "Letter" of Gilbert White's "The Antiquities of Selborne" (the second part of his *Natural History and Antiquities of Selborne*, 1789) mentions pigs, cattle, and horses who died because they ate yew berries or browsed upon the leaves of this low-branching but long-lived tree. (White speculates that a decree by King Edward I in 1307 forbidding the cutting down of yew trees in church yards, which were generally walled to keep out livestock, was related to the needs of English archers during the Hundred Years War, who used longbows made of yew.) *1989* cites Erasmus Darwin on the "umbrageous Yews" that "shed . . . their cold unwholesome dews" (*Temple of Nature* [1803]; Canto II, 189–90). Earlier mentions of the yew's poisonous quality by Caesar, Livy, and Virgil were reinforced by such contemporary warnings, and those old poets' tales and the observations of early naturalists have been confirmed by modern science: the "wood, bark, seeds, and leaves" of most varieties of yew are poisonous, due to the presence of an "alkaloid, taxine, a heart depressant"; and the English yew, *Taxus baccata L.*, is more lethal than its American counterparts (Walter Conrad Muenscher, *Poisonous Plants of the United States* [New York: Collier Books, 1975], 31; see also the article on yew in *Encyclopædia Britannica*).

If PBS did not have a draft of this poem in "Notebook X," we imagine that the Rev. Evan ("Taffy") Edwards, a Welshman who was Vicar of Warnham Church and PBS's first teacher, might have been a recipient of this poem who could have supplied PBS with a copy. In his letter of ?10 December 1811 to Elizabeth Hitchener, who apparently also knew Edwards, PBS wrote, "Do you agree to my definition of Virtue—Disinterestedness? . . . —I am as little inclined as you are to quarrel with Taffy, I am as much obliged to him for the complex idea 'tyranny'"; PBS then goes on to speak of Locke's theory of complex ideas (*Letters* I, 200). In October or November 1812 PBS was in communication with him (possibly even visiting him when he accompanied Hitchener back to her Sussex home?), for Edwards later supplied PBS with a copy of the poet's birth records, presumably to aid his efforts to raise money (*Letters* I, 329 and fn. 4). Mark Antony Lower's short biography of PBS in *The Worthies of Sussex* (Lewes, Sussex: published for subscribers only, 1865, 65), identifies Evan "Taffy" Edwards (1753–1839) as PBS's teacher, educated at Jesus College, Oxford, when Timothy Shelley was also at Oxford (*Alumni Oxoniensis*, 1887–91).

line 11. That PBS includes <u>Lust</u>, along with <u>Avarice, Envy</u>, and <u>Revenge</u>, in this list of particularly heinous sins may support the idea that the poem dates from *very* early youth, before PBS felt comfortable admitting that he had sexual desires, unless he was able from early youth to idealize all of his sexual attractions into true love.

lines 13–14. <u>All that grandeur ever gave</u> | <u>Moulders in the silent grave.</u> These lines compress the famous stanza in Gray's *Elegy*, "The boast of heraldry, the pomp of power, | And all that beauty, all that wealth e'er gave, | Awaits alike the inevitable hour. | The paths of glory lead but to the grave" (33–36). Gray was a very strong influence on PBS throughout his poetic apprenticeship, and PBS himself, while at Eton, more than once visited the churchyard at Stoke Poges where Gray was inspired to write his *Elegy* (White, *Shelley* I, 44). In 1759, as General James Wolfe and his troops were embarking on the Saint Lawrence River before the Battle of Quebec in which Wolfe and Montcalm (the French commander) would both die, Wolfe is said to have told his companions that he would rather have written those lines by Gray than take Quebec (or words to that effect). This story, transmitted orally and first published in 1804, would have been known to PBS and may have impressed itself on him when he rejected military glory and began to commit himself to poetry. (Not all biographies of Wolfe accept this story as literally accurate. W. T. Waugh discussed the issues in the Appendix to *James Wolfe: Man and Soldier* [Toronto: Macmillan, 1928], 311–14.)

lines 19–20. <u>The sacred gift for which I sigh</u> | <u>Is not to live to feel alone;</u> Here PBS identifies the root cause of his depression: isolation and loneliness. His hoped-for cure is, as always, community with at least one understanding person (see his essay ***On Love*** [2002, 503–4]). Another juvenile aspect of this poem appears in the fact that PBS does not specify his preference for a *female* friend, as he did by the time he turned sixteen or so.

lines 22–23. <u>That the tomb might melt this heart of stone</u> | <u>To love beyond the grave.</u> If PBS's hoped-for community with a kindred spirit failed, his alternative was to leap through the gates of death into a better world beyond. The crucial phrase in these final lines is _this_ heart of stone (emphasis added), phrasing that indicates PBS's fear that his own heart is unable to feel or to express love in this life. By the time he wrote the **Esd** poems that he dated 1808 and 1809, his perspective had changed: he usually did not doubt his capacity to love and to give himself to others but worried about finding someone who could reciprocate with equal ardor. **Alastor** is the chief exception, as Crook observes. There he perceives—perhaps in elegiac reflection on his loss of empathy for HWS—that his cosmic perspective may sometimes lead him to overlook the good within the imperfect world.

Zeinab and Kathema   [Esd #49]

PBS composed this narrative poem in thirty carefully wrought six-line stanzas rhymed _ababcC,_ with the first five lines of each stanza written in iambic pentameter and the sixth an Alexandrine. As earlier editors have stated, this poem's date of composition is "unknown" (_1989,_ 171), but PBS had clearly saved for last this poem and **The Retrospect** (#50) so as to end his collection of "Minor Poems" with a bang, rather than with the whimper of youthful fragments and churchyard laments. It therefore probably underwent its final polishing, if not its initial draft, during the summer of 1813, after the poet had met John Frank Newton, Harriet Collins de Boinville, and their circle— liberal in their politics and sentimental in their literary tastes—who would surely have appreciated this poem.

By juxtaposing **Zeinab and Kathema** (**Z&K**)—an outward-looking, socio-ideological poem and one of his strongest indictments of the evils of British society—with both his early lament about his isolation from others in **Esd** #48 and the happier personal history found in **The Retrospect** (#50), PBS highlights his reason for interspersing throughout the volume his personal poems with those centered on social critiques and reformist themes. For PBS, neither focus can be healthy without its complement; the value of the self depends upon its understanding of the needs of others, but an easy acquiescence to established social norms tends to limit the self, which must achieve a higher vantage point from which to discover values beyond the idols of the cave, marketplace, theater, and tribe. Thus, as in Wordsworth's thought, the good of both the Self and the Other depends upon a constant interchange of perspectives between them.

Z&K records the penalties of British imperialism that PBS had earlier tried to portray in his fragmentary **Henry and Louisa.** After evoking the mythical Edenic peace and happiness supposed to be found in the Vale of <u>Cashmire</u> (**92**), the poem confronts aspects of <u>England's varied woe</u> (**119**): its crimes of overseas imperialism, perpetrated by <u>Christian murderers</u> (**1–42**); its lust for riches, <u>the Christian's God!</u> (**68**); its climate of <u>changeful skies and</u>

chilling wind (**91**), matched by the coldness of its people toward strangers in need, amid a scene of famine, disease and crime (**102**), Madness and passion (**107**). Kathema, a young man from Cashmire (his religion is not specified, but as *1989* observes, his name suggests that he may be a Hindu) travels to England in search of his betrothed, Zeinab, who was kidnaped during a raid by British marauders. Her name—that of the widowed mother of the Arab protagonist of Southey's *Thalaba the Destroyer,* 1801, and given as "Zeineb" in a list of Arabian women's names in Sir William Jones's *Essay on the Poetry of the Eastern Nations*—would identify her to English readers as a Moslem. Kathema's search for Zeinab in England ends much as Louisa's search for Henry in Egypt did, when he finds Zeinab swinging on a gibbet, having been hanged as a criminal. Kathema then, like Louisa, joins his beloved in death, in this case by hanging himself on the gibbet.

The Cashmire connection has led scholars to connect this poem with PBS's reading in June 1811 of *The Missionary* (3 vols., 1811) by Sydney Owenson (later Lady Morgan). Though editors have found few direct parallels between the plot of that work and **Z&K,** Hiroshi Harata's careful analysis "Shelley and Lady Morgan's *The Missionary: An Indian Tale*" (in *Centre and Circumference: Essays in English Romanticism* [Tokyo: Kirihara Shoten, 1995], 499–517) points out that Luxima, a Brahmin high-priestess who was the subject of PBS's adoration in his letters to Hitchener and Hogg of June 1811 (see **Letters** I, 101, 107, 112, 130), has little relation to Zeinab. On the other hand, Hilarion, the Portuguese Franciscan missionary who wishes to purify religion ("to exclude the leaven of mortality from the religious perfection" [*The Missionary* I, 16] and then convert Luxima to his faith as a co-worker), was a character with whom PBS strongly identified himself. He planned, argues Harata, to convert HWS to his pure faith of love and service to others, joining their efforts in his missionary work for a new religion of love, of which **QM** was to have been the bible. Harata goes on to find elements of Luxima in the "veiled maid" in **Alastor** and later beautiful incarnations of the "other" from the spiritual world with whom PBS's protagonists rendezvous.

Earlier, Cameron had noted the similarity between the plots and characters of **Z&K** and PBS's expansion of its elements in **Laon and Cythna** (*1964,* 279), but Matthews and Everest (*1989* I, 171), because of the discrepancy between Luxima and Zeinab, suggested a different literary model for **Z&K:** *The Poor Negro Sadi* in Charlotte Dacre's *Hours of Solitude* (2 vols., London: Hughes; and Ridgeway, 1805), I, 117–22. Dacre's eighty-line piece against the slave trade and for the humanitarian treatment of blacks has many plot elements that parallel the cruelties which Zeinab and Kathema experience in England, but it lacks **Z&K**'s larger positive themes of love and loyalty to the death and—above all—the dramatic and poetic presentation that make PBS's effort a work of art instead of sociological propaganda. PBS may have read Dacre's poems and would have sympathized with this story of suffering, but we find nothing in Sadi's story useful to PBS's poem that he could not just as easily have taken from a newspaper article or an anti-slavery tract. Given the wealth of anti-slavery literature and public discussion in England from the late eighteenth-century onward, it would have taken little creativity to imagine the fate of someone of a different race carried to England by bloody freebooters. And PBS's poem dwells not on the process of Zeinab's degradation but rather on how her abduction and death affect her lover Kathema. This story of loss is the same one that PBS rehearses throughout his early poems—almost all of those in Volume I of **CPPBS** and many of those in **Esd,** though there are plenty of literary analogues throughout the contemporary literature of Britain, France, and Germany. Because all Europe was shaken by the loss of kings, religious faith, natal countries (many of which were swept up into pieces of the French Empire), as well as fathers, brothers, husbands, sons, lovers, and friends who were killed, maimed, or lost to new lives in faraway places during twenty years of warfare, the personal feelings of the English Romantic poets who lost their parents through either death (both parents of Wordsworth, Byron, and Keats, and Coleridge's supportive father) or alienation (Coleridge's mother, Shelley's parents) came to embody and express the fate of their contemporaries. The poet's experiences, therefore, internalized these universal losses and gave voice to both the mourning and the rebuilding of hope that those troubled times required. PBS's concern as a poet was to balance his personal sense of loss with a recognition of social upheavals that affected others more unfortunate than he, thereby warning those who had lost their religious faith not to give vent to their natural egoism and selfishness or to use the breakdown of traditional communal values as an excuse to deny their sympathy to others.

lines 13–36. PBS's skill in changing the pace of his six-line stanzas to support the changing moods of his protagonist through different parts of the poem can be seen in these opening six stanzas. The first two, which find Kathema on the beach in despair, are closed stanzas, but the third, fourth, and fifth are enjambed as Kathema drifts into reverie, recalling his happy days with Zeinab, up through **line 31.** When he remembers the <u>Christian murderers</u>— a roving band of marauders killing, raping, and plundering in the name of European "civilization"—who had carried Zeinab away <u>to grace the robbers' land</u> (**35**), the stanzas again are closed, each ending in an unpleasant word, such as <u>brand</u> (i.e., a sword, **36**), <u>gore</u> (**42, 54**), and <u>spurn</u> (**48**), as opposed to <u>sun</u> (**18**), <u>bliss and care</u> (**24**), and <u>entwine</u> (**30**) in the stanzas that flowed into one another during his reverie.

line 25. <u>Superstition's</u>: PBS intended this word to signify any dogmatic religion, including Christianity as practiced by those he knew in England.

line 35. <u>reft</u> is the past tense of the verb reave, meaning to seize or "to take by stealth or violence" (*Entick's Dictionary,* 1805).

line 46. <u>glance</u>: This word is squeezed down the edge of the page in **EN.**

line 48. <u>emprize</u>: an undertaking, especially one of adventure or chivalry.
  <u>spurn</u>: squeezed down edge of page in **EN.**

line 63. <u>wind</u>: Shelley rhymes the noun "wind" three times with "mind" and once with "kind"—accepted contemporary poetic rhymes.

line 64. <u>gave its sail</u>: lowered on, furled its sail; cf. **line 66:** <u>gave some stranger men to land</u>

line 65. <u>o'er</u> ("oer" in **EN**) appears as "on" in *1966* and *1972.*

line 68. <u>Thine is this heap—the Christian's God!</u>": In **EN** this line, which is a foot short, contains no punctuation except the double quotation marks at the end of Kathema's words to the British sailors, nor is there any space between <u>heap</u> and <u>the</u>, where 1989 inserts the bracketed phrase "[of gold]" as an emendation to fill out meter and meaning. We, instead, supply a dash there, assuming that PBS was using the anomaly to characterize Kathema as one who was so contemptuous of gold (or jewels, spices, or anything of material exchange value) that he refrained from naming the nature of the <u>heap</u> he offers, which as the <u>God</u> of every <u>Christian</u>, required no formal introduction. We insert the apostrophe to produce the generic singular <u>Christian's</u>, rather than the plural, which might suggest that there are exceptions to the rule of Christian avidity, and we add an exclamation point to suggest Kathema's disgust at involving himself in any transaction with those of the nationality and religious affiliation that had destroyed his loved ones and his happiness. If the same words were attributed to PBS's omniscient narrator, rather than to Kathema, who is portrayed as more than willing to sacrifice everything he has for love, we would have punctuated differently.

line 83. <u>Albion's</u>: that is, England's; Albion was the name given to England by the Romans when they encountered the white (Latin: *albus*) cliffs near what is now Dover.

line 90. <u>motes</u>: particles of dust, especially the innumerable minute specks seen in a sunbeam.

line 95. <u>zone</u>: the temperate zone, with its change of seasons and periods of cold weather, as opposed to the (mythic) eternal spring of Cashmire.

line 104. Though PBS could certainly have seen <u>Youth tottering on the crutches of old age</u> in England (or any other country), it is not clear that he is alluding to a particular person as the victim of such bad health or to a single disease (such as polio or rickets) as its cause. Clearly his comparisons to the advantage of Cashmire over England are tendentiously ideological, perhaps in an effort to prick the bubble of British self-satisfaction, much as Byron was later to do, in a lighter tone, in lines 321–92 of *Beppo.*

line 111. dark: Though the *r* is strangely formed, dark is correct, "dank" (*2000*) an error.

meteors: here any luminous optical phenomena in the Earth's atmosphere.

line 123. came to a wild heath.: The words came to a are superimposed on earlier words canceled by smearing the wet ink. Cameron reads these words as "thro a city of" (*SC* IV, 1045), and he speculates that PBS may have omitted some text, either intentionally or through eye-skip, during the process of revision.

line 128. deathy: PBS uses this word also in ***Falshood and Vice*** (***Esd*** #6), line 57, and ***September 23, 1809*** (***Esd*** #36), line 11; see gloss of the former. Tokoo's *Concordance* lists two other occurrences, in Bodleian MS Shelley adds. e.12, as found in *BSM* XVIII, 45 (canceled) and 201.

line 132. gibbet: A special kind of gallows, with an upright post and a projecting arm from which the body of a criminal executed for a particularly heinous crime was, by the order of the sentencing judge, chained within an iron frame (to prevent the body from being removed) near the scene of the crime, as a warning to others, until the flesh rotted or was eaten by scavenging birds. Use of the gibbet was legal in England only from 1752 to 1834.

storm: No punctuation follows this line in **EN,** perhaps because the word is cramped and turns downward into the gutter of the Notebook. Cameron added no punctuation in *1964*, though later editors did ("storm!" *1966*, *1972*; "storm," *1989*; "storm." *2000*). But since the next stanza begins with And, a case can be made for following PBS's MS here, because the poet may well have intended Kathema's state of mind as he awakens and suddenly realizes the tragic implications of the scene before him to carry his thoughts rapidly ahead, once again breaking through the norm of closed stanzas with an enjambment reflecting deep emotion.

line 133. its: Rogers's two editions (both based on a photocopy, rather than **EN** itself) read this word as "her." But as a footnote to *SC* IV (1045) explains, PBS first wrote her but then crossed out *er,* inserted *i* before the *h,* crossed the riser of the *h* to form a *t,* and then inserted an apostrophe and *s* following the new *t.* PBS changed the pronoun to emphasize that Zeinab was no longer a living person, but a corpse, lacking all personhood except in Kathema's mind.

line 137. ghastlily: This seems to be PBS's only use of this unpronounceable adverb (with only four examples in *OED*—all between 1829 and 1882, two of them in *Blackwood's Magazine*). At **QM** VII.192, PBS honed down the word to "ghastily," but "ghastly" (which Byron used as both adjective and adverb) was a favorite of PBS, appearing thirteen times in **Laon and Cythna**—three times in the comparative and once in the superlative.

line 162. Night: In *1966* and *1972*, Rogers capitalized "Night" and read deed, rather than "dead"—the word found in *1964*, *SC* IV, and *1989*. When we first prepared our Text, we were much inclined to follow Cameron and Matthews and Everest, rather than Rogers, but so far as the word in PBS's handwriting in **EN** is concerned, the choice between the two words seemed moot. (Night indeed seemed to begin with a capital letter, though a fairly small one.)

The context of "the dead" or "the deed" could support either "dead" (referring to both Zeinab and Kathema following Kathema's suicide) or "deed" (referring to the suicide itself). Turning back to MS ED-TCD, to which neither Cameron nor Rogers had access before they fixed their texts in *1964* and *1966*, we found that Dowden's highly accurate transcription gave "Night" or "night" as ambiguously as it appeared in **EN** (apparently mimicking PBS to keep the options open), but gave deed very precisely. Finally, we consulted the end of **Henry and Louisa,** an earlier composition which seems in some ways the prototype of **Z&K:** there the suicide of Louisa to join her dead lover is expressed in these words: "Sacred to Love a deed is done!—" (line 291). After checking the form of the word and syllable "deed" in its five other poetic appearances in **Esd** (#2, line 46; #6, 76; #23, 16; #31, 3; and #46, 291), we concluded that deed is more probable than "dead."

line 164. shriven: Confessed and absolved; used ironically here. The penance for Zeinab's innocent habits (164) was prostitution, crime and woe (166). Though the word in **EN** is clearly shriven, both Rogers's texts read "riven."

line 167. weal: well-being or happiness.

line 172. matin-prime: Public morning prayers in the Church of England include matins, lauds, and prime: matin-prime would be morning prayers generally, but (as in the "matin lay" of **Triumph of Life** line 8) PBS turns the religious reference into natural piety, here under the morning star.

line 174. careers: moves at full speed.

The Retrospect. | Cwm Elan 1812   [Esd #50]

The Wordsworthian influence on the poems that PBS planned to publish in **Esd** reaches its apogee in this brilliant autobiographical poem, written (all agree) in the period from mid-May to mid-June 1812, during the Shelleys' sojourn in Wales between their first Irish campaign and their departure for Devonshire. Whether or not PBS hoped to make the "Poems" that he assembled in **EN** a counterpart to Wordsworth's untitled poem on his early life, which became *The Prelude,* in **The Retrospect** PBS consciously emulated aspects of *Lines written a Few Miles above Tintern Abbey,* which was the crowning achievement of *Lyrical Ballads*—especially in its two-volume editions (one of which PBS probably owned), from which the *Ancient Mariner* and Coleridge's other contributions had been removed. Dowden, an editor and admirer of Wordsworth, published most of **The Retrospect** in his *Life of Percy Bysshe Shelley* (I, 270–74), emphasizing the relationship of PBS to Wordsworth by omitting its opening lines (**1–14**). PBS's poem alludes to Wordsworth in several passages, and HWS assumes the part "played by Dorothy Wordsworth in the earlier poem"; but when read as a whole, **The Retrospect** proves to be, in theme, prosodic form and structure, language, and tone, related to *Tintern Abbey* more by contrasts than by similarities. PBS used impassioned tetrameter couplets instead of Wordsworth's meditative blank verse, and whereas Wordsworth's message is that memories of a stable past under the tutelage of Nature sustained him through the trials of his disappointment with the French Revolution, PBS declared that "only the joy of the present moment can redeem the scenes of his despairing past" (Reiman, *Romantic Texts and Contexts,* 349).

PBS follows *Tintern Abbey* in focusing on how the poet's feelings had changed since his last visit to a place—five years in Wordsworth's poem, a single year in PBS's. Wordsworth's earlier despair is associated, however, not with the natural scene in the Wye Valley (as PBS associates his with the scenery of Cwm Elan), but with his years involved in human society in London and France. After explaining how his memory of such natural beauty as that of the Welsh hills helped him to resist and eventually to recover from the despair brought on by his disappointment at the corruption of the French Revolution, Wordsworth turns to teach his sister how to protect herself from similar despair through his example. In **The Retrospect,** on the other hand, PBS had been in suicidal despair the last time he had visited Cwm Elan, but afterward, buoyed by HWS's love and companionship, as well as their joint efforts to help others, he overcame that dark mood, brought on largely by his realization that not only were the people in his <u>narrow sphere</u> (**57**) unable to sympathize with his ideals and aspirations, but the natural phenomena through which he sought to escape from that uncongenial society were also totally indifferent to his needs (cf. **Mont Blanc**). PBS's view of Nature as a place to escape from unwanted human interactions has, however, some affinity for Wordsworth's early veneration of Nature as the surrogate for his lost parents, for at the depth of his despair PBS (exiled from home, though not bereaved), falls asleep pressed against the <u>breast</u> of maternal <u>Meadows</u> (**124–27**).

Other poems suggested as literary models for **The Retrospect** are less relevant. Though *1989* notes Southey's poem entitled *The Retrospect* (1794), in which the poet is disappointed as he revisits scenes of his childhood only to find that their commonplace reality contrasts with his fond memories (expressed in some of the most puerile verses that Southey ever wrote), and though *1989* finds Bowles's *Coombe-Ellen* to be a closer parallel, PBS's **Retrospect** also avoids Bowles's religious moralizing of the landscape, such as that we noted in the Commentary on **Written at Cwm Ellan** (*Esd* #18).

PBS sets the tone in the first verse paragraph by telling how emotionally difficult it is for him to look back before the time when peaceful love vivified the natural world with rapture's colour (**1–22**). In describing his behavior during his visit to Cwm Elan, just before his elopement a year earlier (**23–48**), he declares that not unrequited love, nor his spiritual pride, nor his sense of intellectual and emotional isolation taken by itself was enough to break his spirit, but the combination of the three drove him to despair (**49–64**). He then provides specification of each of the three issues in the two verse paragraphs that follow (**65–111**). Next, in a series of short rhetorical stanzas, the poet calls upon each element of the natural world (as Demogorgon does at the end of **Prom**) and asks them collectively if they have not recognized the great change that has come over him since their last encounter. There follows his exultant description of that transformation, comparing it favorably with the transformation of a caterpillar (the loathesome worm) into a multicolored butterfly (**132–43**). The poem's final paragraph addresses HWS, the latest person whose virtues PBS has known but who is the First to claim a throne in his heart (**153–54**), where she along with virtue reigns gently with a downy sceptre. They are bound together in ardent friendship by a flowery band that will outlive any ties (such as legal marriage) added by duty's hard and cold control (**158–61**). He closes with a backward glance at the gloomiest retrospects of his earlier experience that still bind his bleeding mind like crowns of thorn and at prospects of the future troubles that his Fancy presents, but all are gilded with the reviving ray of sunshine that she brings to him.

Though the meter of **The Retrospect** remains iambic tetrameter throughout, PBS did vary the couplet rhyme pattern in a few places to signal changes of thought and tone. As has been noted, he later, in **Lines written among the Euganean Hills,** employed regular iambic tetrameter couplets with masculine endings to underscore the power of Necessity over human action, loosening the rhythms and rhymes in that poem (breaking the monotony of the normal seven-syllable couplets with feminine rhymes and rhymed triplets) in passages suggesting that the human will can break that relentless march of action and reaction. In a similar manner, the opening of **The Retrospect,** which reflects on his past, signals his effort To check the chariot of the year with four lines in which couplets yield to alternate rhymes (**lines 5–8**); this effect is repeated at **39–46,** as the poet tells how he sometimes longed to escape his loneliness and psychic pain through death, and the lock-step rhymes are varied again at **148–51** and **156–60,** where he celebrates his freedom from sadness through the union with his loving wife.

Title. Note the relation between PBS's title of this poem, about how his feelings for HWS in the present time redeem the dark *retrospect* of his personal past, and that of *A retrospect of Times of Old* (#31)—a poem about the murderous ambition of would-be world conquerors throughout human history, which he hopes to redeem through his poetry, especially **QM.**

line 1. PBS used <u>Duration</u> for the years of his recent past both for its sound and for its connotations; deriving from its late Latin and French roots, the word implies hardness and durability, and thus, here, a resistance to the human will-for-good. The opening of the poem suggests that the period before he and HWS eloped had been such a "hard time" that he can scarcely bear to remember it.

line 2. The image of the chariot of Being, Time, or Destiny, which exists in variant forms in the biblical Book of Ezekiel, in Dante's *Purgatorio,* and in Milton's *Paradise Lost,* appears repeatedly in Shelley's poetry, here as the <u>chariot of the year</u> and in line 2 of the next poem, *The wandering Jew's soliloquy,* as "the wheels of destiny." (See also **QM** I.82–83 and Commentary.)

lines 5–7. Kronos (Saturn) devoured his children, and through confusion of his name with Chronos, he was also identified with <u>Time</u>. But note that here PBS alters the Greek mythology by using feminine pronouns for <u>Time the monster</u>.

line 15. <u>wildered</u>: lost, straying.

line 19. PBS's invocation of <u>mountain, meadow, wood and stream</u> echoes "meadow, grove, and stream" in the opening line of Wordsworth's *Ode: Intimations of Immortality* . . . , as well as a number of similar poetic catalogues by several earlier poets found in Chadwyck-Healey's *LION* database, including "mountain, meadow, streamlet, grove, or cell" in Tobias Smollett's "Ode to Independence" (*Plays and Poems Written by T. Smollett . . . With Memoirs of the Life and Writings of the Author,* 1777) and "meadow, vale, and grove" in Robert Anderson's "Song XXXII Summer" (*Poems on various subjects,* 1798). None of these poems seems likely to have impressed PBS as Wordsworth's *Ode* did.

lines 25–28. The <u>wild brook's</u> . . . <u>unremitting roar</u> and the poet's reverie while caught up in its <u>ideal flow</u> anticipate the opening verse paragraph of ***Mont Blanc.***

line 30. <u>heathy</u>: covered with heather or other low herbage.

lines 65–70. The <u>broken vows</u> allude directly to the breaking off of Harriet Grove's engagement to PBS, the <u>envenomed arrow</u> being the letter (perhaps written by her father) that brought that news to PBS's <u>faithful bosom</u> and <u>quelled</u> his <u>stainless spirit's vestal flame</u>, while the Groves (and, perhaps, PBS's own family) <u>Beamed</u> apathetic <u>coldness</u> on his hurt feelings. The word <u>vestal</u> (from Vesta, the Roman goddess of the hearthfire that was kept burning by the vestal virgins, who served in her temple in Rome) specifies that PBS's love for Harriet Grove remained unconsummated.

lines 72–74. The phrase <u>wings of morn</u> echoes Psalm 139:9 ("If I take the wings of the morning and dwell in the uttermost parts of the sea"), but PBS reverses the meaning of that verse, for his <u>soul</u> hopes to flee successfully from earth *toward* the divine, here imaged as the sun, thereby foreshadowing his figure of "the sacred few" (Jesus and Socrates presumably prominent among them) who were not conquered by Life, but "Fled back like eagles to their native noon" (*Triumph of Life,* 128–31). The addition of "eagles" shows that PBS in both poems was drawing also upon the conception, alluded to in Psalm 103:5 and Isaiah 40:31 and elaborated in later bestiary tradition, that the eagle renewed its youthful vision by flying directly toward the sun, which burned the scales of old age from its eyes and renewed its keen vision. As Bryan Shelley notes in connection with these and similar references in PBS's poetry, in Christian iconography the eagle also became a symbol of Christ (*Shelley and Scripture* [Oxford: Oxford UP, 1994], 64).

lines 78 ff. Many <u>friends</u> were attracted to PBS simply because of his <u>unmeaning name</u>, "Shelley," the grandson of a wealthy baronet and son of a Member of Parliament, but failed to comprehend the <u>unknown mind</u> of PBS, who aspired to be <u>saviour of a sinking land</u>. Therefore, *They* (**92, 98**) could never be his true friends (**111**). The word <u>saviour</u> prepares for the <u>crowns of thorn</u> metaphor in **line 164.**

line 89. Many of those supposed friends were content to <u>fatten upon freedom's grave</u>, that is, to support the authoritarian government so that they could continue to enjoy the material benefits and prerogatives of the aristocracy. PBS, on the contrary, would rather suffer martyrdom, be a <u>captive</u> who <u>clasps abhorred despair</u> (**91**).

lines 112–13. <u>jagged peaks . . . | Mocking the blunted scythe of Time</u>: Compare this figure with similar ones in **Dark Spirit** (***Esd*** #20), line 9, and ***"Death-spurning rocks!"*** (***Esd*** #22), 1–5, and see the Commentary on those poems.

lines 150–52. <u>Whilst the mild glances of her eye | Pierce the thin veil of flesh that shrouds | The spirit's radiant sanctuary</u>: Shelley here represents the inner sanctum of his soul as being pierced by the looks of his beloved as the hymen is broken during first intercourse.

This meaning of the image must have made a strong impression on either Edward Dowden or the compositor who set type for the section of Dowden's biography of PBS, where most of *The Retrospect* was first published, for although Dowden correctly transcribed "spirit's radiant sanctuary" in MS ED-TCD, the phrase appears in his *Life of PBS* (*1886*) as "spirit's inmost sanctuary"—an error that persisted unchallenged in all collective editions through *1970* (after *1964* had corrected the text).

The wandering Jew's soliloquy   [Esd #51]

As we implied in our discussion of *The Wandering Jew* (*WJ*) in Volume I of *CPPBS*, PBS came to think of that outcast—miserable in life, but unable to die—as a kind of personal totem or symbol of the poet himself. This embattled figure was appropriate enough for the desperately unhappy youth and young man, whose early poems show him at odds with British society, smarting from the pain of rejection after his engagement to Harriet Grove was broken off, expelled from University College, betrayed by his college friend, and alienated from his family as well. But the full meaning of this poem depends upon exactly when PBS wrote *The wandering Jew's soliloquy* and why he placed a bitterly anti-religious poem as the emphatic finale for the fifty poems that he had chosen to tell the story of his early life and aspirations. This poem seems unrelated to his earlier poem featuring the Wandering Jew, both in subject and style and does not, at first, seem to follow naturally from the poems that immediately precede it, especially *The Retrospect,* which shows how HWS had rescued him from his life of misery.

The date of the poem's composition is unknown. Cameron calls its style more mature than *WJ* itself, and after associating it with *St. Irvyne* in November 1810 (though without specifying for what part of that sentimental romance it might have been intended), he concludes that, since the conception of the title character is closer to that found in *WJ* than in *QM* and its prosody (irregularly rhymed iambic pentameter) does not match that of either long poem, *The wandering Jew's soliloquy* was probably drafted as an independent composition sometime between November 1809 and late 1810 (*1964*, 284–87). Matthews and Everest suggest that PBS added this poem to *Esd* after *The Retrospect* as an afterthought—threw it in for good measure— after he recovered a manuscript that he had composed in December 1810 or January 1811 (*1989* I, 147–48), the time when he wrote bitter letters to Hogg about the injustice of Christianity's coming between him and Harriet Grove. But we find these guesses questionable. In the first place, PBS did not give this strong rhetorical poem an early date, as he did to those that he recovered late from Hogg to pad out the length of his volume, and the language, allusions, and rhymed iambic pentameter of this *soliloquy* exhibit the mature style of several poems that he wrote especially for *Esd* (e.g., *On leav-*

ing London for Wales [#10]). Moreover, the poem's allusions to obscure incidents from the Pentateuch and the histories of Israel and Judea suggest that PBS probably wrote it after a careful search for the least edifying passages in the Old Testament, a quest that he most likely undertook while preparing his attack on Moses in **QM**, VII. Even if PBS had drafted a similar poem years earlier and drawn on that earlier version from memory or a surviving draft, he clearly revised it before copying it into **EN** as the capstone of the volume that tells the story of his early years and his relationship with HWS. Given the jarring note that *soliloquy* introduces after the blissfully triumphant ending of **The Retrospect** and just before he turned back to copy into the front of **EN** his dedication of the volume, **To Harriet,** we think it unlikely that PBS, who had carefully arranged the poems in **Esd** to develop a thematic progression throughout the entire volume, would have added this poem unless its presence said something important about his mood at that time, even if its sentiments were voiced by a fictional surrogate.

The mythic speaker, a figure forced to live through innumerable hardships and continual mental anguish, without hope of respite, opens the poem with a question that for the Wandering Jew would be rhetorical but for a mortal with PBS's perspective may be seen as skeptical: Who is torturing him? Is it <u>the Eternal Triune</u>, the Christian God, who plunges him into <u>this lowest Hell of Hells?</u> If so, he calls upon an opposing trinity to bring him relief: he will <u>rouse</u> . . . <u>dark Destruction</u> (**6**), <u>Oblivion</u> (**9**), and <u>Annihilation</u> (**10**) to let him find peace in death. Next, the Wandering Jew, who—unlike the poet—knows that his attempt at suicide would be unavailing as long as God prevents it, insults and provokes the deity in the hope of making the Power of the Universe angry enough to destroy him.

One way to interpret the poem and rationalize its placement at the end of **Esd,** immediately following the glowing tribute to HWS in **The Retrospect,** is to see it as PBS's reaffirmation of his chosen struggle on behalf of "Love or Virtue," rather than "Prejudice, Priestcraft, Opinion, and Gold," as he declared in **I will kneel at thine altar** (**Esd** #42, lines 2 and 30), though his declarations here are a bit heavily weighted against "Priestcraft." But the operative clue to the poem's meaning is found in PBS's title itself: the poem is a *soliloquy,* for immediately after telling how much HWS has done to inspire him and how she causes a rebirth of his spirit, he here stands, not with her by his side, but bitterly alone against the wide universe.

Considering what we know about PBS's life experiences and mood from the latter half of 1813 into early 1814, the importance of this poem and its placement can, therefore, be read as a counter-piece to **The Retrospect,** which was written in May 1812 when he returned to visit the Grove family at Cwm Elan with an innocent, glowing, and amiable bride whom none of his relatives had met before. Then he displayed not only his happiness at having at last found his true soul-mate and a sense of triumph because HWS favorably impressed the Groves, who had rejected him as not good enough for *their* Harriet. But when late in the summer of 1813 he chose to add to the sequence ***The wandering Jew's soliloquy,*** a poem reminiscent of his earlier mood of despair, at the very end of the intended autobiographical volume that celebrates his close relationship with HWS and the importance of her love to his very will to live, we may suspect that PBS was, through this poem, venting anger upon his fate (symbolically projected as the biblical God) because he once more felt forsaken and alone in the world. The act of adding this poem may thus foreshadow the deterioration of his marriage, his infatuation with Cornelia Boinville Turner (declared at least by March 1814, when he had addressed to her ***"Thy dewy looks sink in my breast";*** see ***CPPBS*** I, 145 and 328–29), and his elopement with Mary W. Godwin in late July 1814. The causes of the alienation between PBS and HWS are too uncertain (or at least too complex) to analyze here in detail, but this final poem, ventriloquized in the persona of the tortured, suicidal figure with whom PBS identified himself during his most painful reflections of his youth, indicates to us that near the end of the summer of 1813, much sooner than scholars have realized, he recognized and admitted to himself that his marriage with HWS had failed to assuage his thirst for kindred love.

The bulk of the eye-witness evidence about PBS's behavior and mood at this period appears in Hogg's *Life of PBS* (*1858*) and Peacock's corrective review essays for *Fraser's Magazine* (1858–62), later collected as his *Memoirs of Shelley,* both representing their authors' recollections after nearly fifty years. Though their accounts and their opinions of HWS's merits as a wife for PBS differ in tone, Hogg and Peacock both provide evidence that PBS grew apart from his wife partly because of his involvement with the liberal intellectual coterie centered around the vegetarian John Frank Newton, his wife Cornelia Collins Newton, and her sister Harriet Collins de Boinville. Hogg alludes to several women in that circle who flattered or flirted with PBS, while Peacock claims to have often joined HWS in laughing at the foibles of that circle of liberal faddists. Godwin's manuscript Journal indicates that PBS was seeing the Newtons frequently in London early in the summer of 1813, that he later went to Bracknell (presumably with HWS), from which he returned to London to see Godwin on 18 August 1813. Amid a flurry of letters to PBS in the autumn, Godwin wrote cryptically in his diary for Saturday, 9 October 1813, "Setting off for Bracknel," alluding to the departure of the Shelleys and Peacock from London to avoid their creditors; they stopped at Bracknell (near the present location of Heathrow Airport) before turning north toward the Lake Country and Scotland (see Cornelia Newton's letter to Hogg and Commentary, *SC* III, 252–59).

The summer of 1813 saw the birth of Ianthe Shelley on 23 June. Peacock testified from his knowledge as an eye-witness that PBS "was extremely fond of it, and would walk" with Ianthe in his arms, singing "a monotonous melody of his own making. . . . It did not please me, but, what was more important, it pleased the child, and lulled it when it was fretful" ("it" then being the proper pronoun for referring to infants). Peacock goes on to say: "He was pre-eminently an affectionate father. But to the first-born there were accompaniments that did not please him. The child had a wet-nurse whom he did not like, and was much looked after by his wife's sister, whom he intensely disliked. I have often thought that if Harriet had nursed her own child, and if this sister had not lived with them, the link of their married love would not have been so readily broken" (Peacock, *Memoirs,* 323). Peacock thought the nursing issue was important because of another scene he had witnessed, but refrained from relating in print, though he had described it to Lady Shelley, who told the anecdote to Stopford Brooke, who recorded it in his diary (from which it was published by L. P. Jacks in his *Life and Letters of Stopford Brooke* [London: John Murray; New York: Scribner, 1917], II, 506). Shelley was "horrified" by Harriet's "unnatural" conduct, believing from accounts in contemporary medical books that the "nurse's soul would enter the child. All day he tried to persuade Harriet to do her duty, walking up and down the room, crooning old songs to the child in his arms. At last, in his despair, and thinking that the passion in him would make a miracle, he pulled his shirt away and tried himself to suckle the child" (White, *Shelley* I, 326 and 666, n. 143; Barbara Charlesworth Gelpi, *Shelley's Goddess* [New York: Oxford UP, 1992], 3 and 31, n.1).

Moderns reading this story may focus upon either PBS's merit as a devoted father or his demerit as a controlling husband, but the birth of a first child affects the lives of its parents in different ways and may distance them from each other for any number of reasons. In **To Harriet ("Harriet! thy kiss to my soul is dear") (Esd #29)** PBS had indicated that he would love HWS more if she tried to empathize with the needs of others. There is no being for whom people have more responsibility than their infant child, and HWS's behavior in this instance—whatever her stated reasons for wishing not to nurse Ianthe—would likely have diminished PBS's respect and love for her. (On PBS's efforts to overcome his own natural egoism and self-centeredness, as well as analyses of his relations with the various women he idealized, see Teddi Chichester Bonca, *Shelley's Mirrors of Love: Narcissism, Sacrifice, and Sorority* [Albany: SUNY Press, 1999].)

line 11. jackall: This spelling is found in the first edition of *Encyclopædia Britannica* (1771), II, 24 and 825.

lines 16–17. As *1989* points out, PBS alludes here to Chapter 24 of II Samuel: King David, at the height of his power, orders his generals (contrary to their advice) to conduct a census, enumerating the number of fighting men in his realm. When he receives the total ("eight hundred thousand valiant men" in Israel and five hundred thousand in Judah), he realizes that he has sinned against God—presumably because it was vainglorious to count the people as his, rather than God's. When David asks his official prophet, Gad, what punishment he must endure, Gad gives him three choices, and David chooses the one easiest for himself—three days of pestilence throughout the land, during which "there died of the people from Dan to Beersheba seventy thousand men" (II Samuel 24:15).

lines 18–20. The invasion of Judah by the Assyrian army of Sennacherib (701 B.C.) and the divine intervention that lifted the siege of Jerusalem appear both in II Kings, Chapters 18–19, and in Isaiah, Chapters 36–37. The crucial relevance of this account to *soliloquy* is that, like PBS's surrogate the Wandering Jew, the Assyrian spokesman who demands the surrender of Jerusalem belittles and insults the God of the Hebrews, and in response "the angel of the LORD went forth, and smote a hundred and fourscore and five thousand: and when they arose in the morning, behold, they were all dead corpses" (Isaiah 37:36). The retribution was completed when two of Sennacherib's sons killed him as he was worshiping at a temple in Ninevah and the murderers escaped safely to Armenia. (Byron's quite different treatment of the story was not even conceived until after June 1814, when Isaac Nathan first proposed *Hebrew Melodies* to Byron, who wrote *The Destruction of Sennacherib* in February 1815; see Thomas L. Ashton, *Byron's Hebrew Melodies* [London: Routledge & Kegan Paul, 1972], 9–10, 27).

lines 21–22. <u>Korah's unconscious crew</u>: While the Israelites wandered in the Sinai desert after their escape from Egypt, Korah led a group of Levites to challenge Moses and his brother Aaron by attempting to perform the duties of the priestly office. First the earth swallowed up their leaders and shortly thereafter the rest of the rebellious Levites were consumed by fire when they, unauthorized persons, attempted to perform a sacrifice (Numbers 16:1–49; according to a twentieth-century authority, the priestly code of the Hebrews distinguished as priests only those—including Moses and Aaron—who descended in a direct male line from Levi, while all other members of the tribe of Levi were to act as servants to the priests). By using the word <u>unconscious</u>, however, PBS asserts that Korah's <u>crew</u>, unlike the Assyrians, did not know that they were opposing the God of Israel, but thought that they, as Levites, were entitled to preside at sacrifices and that Moses and Aaron were the usurpers.

lines 23–26. Whereas <u>Korah's crew</u> were relatively innocent compared with Sennacherib, Adam and Eve were accounted by PBS to be simply victims of God's careless maliciousness, since God had placed them in Eden with dangerous trees and foreknew their behavior. PBS gives Eden Spenserian overtones as <u>their bower of bliss</u> (**24**), suggesting that sexual passion, which he warned about in *Esd* #4, was the trap that had locked him into marriage with a wife of "fair form" and "pure mind" but who no longer seemed to him the fulfillment of his dreams of a union of colleagues in a war on behalf of virtue and reform.

lines 27–29. remit: *Entick's Dictionary* (1805) defines this verb as "to forgive, give up, restore, send money from a distant place, relax, slacken, abate"; the OED gives an even wider range of definitions. In the context of the last line that PBS intended to publish in *Esd,* its most likely signification aligns with *OED* II.5: "To give up, lay aside (anger, displeasure, etc.)." PBS used the word in this sense in 1820 in *Swellfoot the Tyrant:* "Remit, O Queen! Thy accustomed rage!" (II.ii.99).

In *The wandering Jew's soliloquy* the object of remit is not explicit and possibly ambiguous. The Wandering Jew says: Yes! I would court a ruin such as this, | Almighty Tyrant! and give thanks to thee.— | Drink deeply—drain the cup of hate—remit; then I may die. This leaves room for doubt whether it is the Wandering Jew himself, or God, who will drain the cup of hate and then remit hatred, allowing the Jew to die. One may see in PBS's final ambiguous line of his projected volume a glance ahead not only to *Alastor* but even to the basic conflict in *Prom,* where Jupiter is at least partially a creation of Prometheus's own vengeful thoughts. Can it be that PBS is here suggesting that his quarrel with God is at least partly a struggle within himself between his lofty hopes and expectations and his awareness of the impossibility of their fulfillment in the real world?

To Ianthe. ~~Oct~~ Sepr 1813   [Esd #52]

The rhyme scheme of this sonnet hovers between the Shakespearian and Italian forms (*abbacdcdefefgg*), but its *volta* appears at the end of **line 8,** exactly where the ideal Italian sonnet would place it. At its most obvious level, that turn of thought seems to introduce a compliment to HWS, for after saying in the octave that he loves his Baby for her own sweet sake (1), PBS declares that he loves the infant More when he can see in her some feeble lineaments of her Mother's loveliness (9, 14). The sonnet actually contains two turns-of-thought, one within the octave: the first quatrain states that the father loves the infant because of her own qualities, whereas the second quatrain declares that he loves the baby more when . . . Thy mother folds thee to her wakeful heart (i.e., in the nursing position) and with love and pity in her glances, impart[s] to the child's passive eyes all that they can absorb of the mother's loving feelings.

PBS did not want his child nursed by a stranger (see *Esd* #51, Commentary) because it was a current medical opinion (derived from Locke's *tabla rasa* psychology) that only genuine maternal feelings expressed in such sustained processes as nursing her infant could impress upon the child the sense of emotional well-being necessary to jump-start the passive intellect and assure its positive development (see Part I: The Nurse's Soul of Gelpi's *Shelley's Goddess*). Thus, PBS's message to HWS in the sonnet is that his love for the qualities that he sees in the infant Ianthe depends, in large part, on the mother having enough <u>love and pity</u> to instill these social prerequisites in her child through the love and attention with which she nourishes it.

As Cameron notes (*1964,* 287–89), there is a dispute about whether PBS's first child's official name was "Ianthe Eliza" or "Eliza Ianthe." The confusion can be clarified by noting the parallel example of Allegra Byron's name: though she was supposed to be named (and was always called) Allegra, she was christened "Clara Allegra"—probably because Allegra was not a saint's name recognized by the Church of England (see *SC* V, 365). Neither was the Greek name Ianthe (on which, see our Commentary to *QM* I, 27), and at Ianthe's baptism the ministering cleric would have asked the parents to preface it with a christening name, such as "Eliza" or "Elizabeth," even though the Shelleys planned to call her Ianthe.

In **EN,** PBS changed the date that he wrote at the head of this poem as a virtual part of the title. Immediately after <u>To Ianthe</u> he first wrote "Oct" before crossing that out and writing <u>Sept^r</u> <u>1813</u> (***To Ianthe. ~~Oct~~ Sepr 1813***). Combining this evidence with the dual dates that appear on the next sonnet (occupying the Notebook's facing page), which has on its title-line ***Evening—to Harriet. Sep. 1813*** and is followed by the date "July 31st 1813," we deduce that PBS prepared these two poems to commemorate two distinct moments, one at the end of July and the other near the end of September 1813. The latter date may also mark either the day on which he copied the two sonnets into **EN** or the time at which he presented the Notebook to HWS—something that he may first have planned to do on 1 October. The date at the end of the second sonnet (the last words PBS wrote in **EN**) refers to the date some four and a half weeks after the birth of Ianthe on which he may have composed the poem to Harriet, or (just as likely in our view) it may commemorate an <u>Evening</u> that PBS believed to be especially significant because it was the occasion of a serious discussion between HWS and himself (see the following Commentary).

Evening—to Harriet. Sep. 1813   *[Esd #53]*

As indicated above, this sonnet is a companion piece to the preceding one, and it also exhibits a hybrid rhyme scheme (*ababcddcefefgg*), with the *volta* once again after **line 8,** as the poet turns from viewing a glorious sunset to speak of a problem in his marriage. PBS probably copied both sonnets into **EN** at the same time to convey a message to HWS as he abandoned his plans to publish these poems that tell the story of his own early life and the course of their married life together. Though the poem, like many personal ones occasioned by specific private situations, is partially opaque to outsiders, its public message is clear. The poet, witnessing a beautiful sunset (**lines 1–8**), says that such a <u>vision of a beauteous dream</u> should not be viewed through the eye of a scientist <u>with astronomic eye</u> (**9**), who might <u>coldly count</u> the sun's spots and blotches. Using this instance of the critical tendency of knowing intellectuals who "murder to dissect" (as Wordsworth put it), spoiling the natural beauties of life for themselves and others, PBS says that he will not find fault with HWS over trivial matters, which would make him ungrateful for <u>all</u> in her <u>that makes his passion dear,</u> nor will he <u>turn</u> <u>senseless</u> (i.e., insensitively) from her <u>warm caress</u> to <u>Pick flaws</u> in their <u>close-woven happiness</u> (**14**). Clearly, after a disagreement in which PBS found fault with HWS, either to her face or in his own thoughts, he wrote the poem to tell her that he still loved her in spite of her flaws.

The date following the sonnet, <u>July 31st 1813</u>, marks either that quarrel or this composition that commemorates it. The end of July, between five and six weeks after Ianthe's birth on 23 June, was likely a time for PBS to have presented the young mother, recovered to an extent from the strains of childbirth, with his strongest arguments on the virtues of breast-feeding her baby. And if Peacock was correct in finding that issue as a leading cause of the deterioration of PBS's love for his wife (see ***Esd*** #51, Commentary), PBS's copying of these two sonnets into **EN,** just before giving it to HWS, renders them almost epitaphs for PBS's efforts to publish the volume of poems through which he had intended to tell the world how HWS's love had rescued him from loneliness and despair and also for his belief that she was the right person to be his life-companion. By presenting to HWS a collection that now ended with the angry and despairing cry of ***The wandering Jew's soliloquy*** and these two personal sonnets, he may thus have been issuing to her a cry for help, an oblique warning that her husband was still seeing sunspots, or even as a premonitory farewell to their years together.

Poems Transcribed by Harriet Westbrook Shelley   *[Esd #54–#58]*

To Harriett and the remaining four poems in **EN** were copied into the Notebook by HWS rather than PBS. The first scholars who studied these poems— Edward Dowden, Richard Garnett, and William Michael Rossetti in the 1880s and Louise Schutz Boas, Kenneth Neill Cameron, and Neville Rogers in the 1960s—were not sure quite what to do with them, thinking that at least some of them must have been written by HWS herself. Cameron asserted that ***"Full many a mind"*** (#54) was written by HWS in 1815, after she and PBS were separated (*1964*, 300–301), while Rogers in his edition *The Esdaile Poems (1966)*, placed both that poem and ***"Late was the night"*** (#57), along with ***Fragment . . . bombardment of Copenhagen*** (#48) and ***"Cold are the***

Blasts" (#45), which PBS had told Hogg were by his sister Elizabeth, in an Appendix of "Poems not by Shelley or of Doubtful Authorship."

The honor of establishing the probability that all of the poems in **EN** were drafted by PBS belongs to G. M. Matthews, whose essay "Whose Little Footsteps? Three Shelley Pieces Re-Addressed" appeared in the *Festschrift* for Cameron entitled *The Evidence of the Imagination,* (ed. Reiman, Jaye, and Bennett [1978]), 236–63. There Matthews argues convincingly that because HWS was characterized by both Hogg and Peacock as being neat and flawlessly groomed and "well educated" (she translated Sophie Cottin's French novel *Claire d'Albe* into English "exactly and correctly, . . . without blot or blemish"), she would not have been the author of difficult or incoherent poems or fragments but would have written simpler but clearer poems. Matthews, like all those who have contended with PBS's draft MSS, knew that everyone produces some solecisms simply by trying to copy PBS's hand literally. C. D. Locock spoke for us all when he wrote in *An Examination of the Shelley Manuscripts in the Bodleian Library* (Oxford: Clarendon Press, 1903): "Some [words] are practically illegible: in such cases the sight of the word is only confusing, and it is often best to conjecture at night and verify the conjecture afterwards."

While we do not fully subscribe to Matthews's premise that a neat, well-educated person is incapable of writing an incomprehensible poem, his paper does persuade us that HWS likely transcribed only PBS's own poetry into **EN,** while adding a few brief notations of her own relating to her ideas of their occasions and recipients and her own feelings while copying them. After analyzing the evidence contained in the texts of the five poems, with their titles, dates, and place names as recorded by HWS, and the comments on them by earlier scholars, we reached the conclusion that the first one, ***To Harriett ("Thy look of love"),*** is a polished personal poem that PBS gave to HWS, probably sometime early in 1814 during the painful period after his flirtation with Cornelia Boinville Turner, but that the other four poems copied by HWS were all written earlier by PBS, perhaps between the period when he drafted ***Written in very early youth*** (*Esd* #48) in 1808 to late 1810. They were thus contemporaneous with the poems in ***Esd*** that were written before he eloped with HWS. All of these poems might, therefore, have been found in a notebook that PBS had used in his early years to draft or copy poetry. The existence of such a notebook (which for clarity of reference we call "Notebook X") is, we admit, merely a hypothesis, based on the evidence cited below and some unanswered questions about the poems that HWS copied into **EN** and some of the poems in ***Esd*** already analyzed above. The few facts from contemporary documents that we cite are insufficient to *prove* the existence of Notebook X, much less to ascertain the details or nature and its contents, but they allow for such a hypothesis.

Early in October 1811 PBS wrote to his father from York, asking him to send "the Clothes which I left at Field Place . . . as also the books & papers, which can be of little use to any other" and on 12 October wrote again to his father, "The waggoner has written to inform me that my property is sent" (*Letters* I, 143, 146). These references tell when and how PBS recovered his personal books and papers from Field Place. If Notebook X was among these papers and contained drafts of his early poetry, it could have remained in his possession throughout the time that he and Harriet were together. After they returned to London in 1813, PBS could have returned to it or to other such notebooks ("Y" and "Z") to rework the drafts of the poems of early date that he added to *Esd* at the same time that he drew upon the versions that he had given or sent to Hogg in 1810–11. Such notebooks may have been the sources of *"I will kneel at thine altar"* (#42), *Henry and Louisa* (#46), *Written in very early youth* (#48), and *Zeinab and Kathema* (#49). Indeed, they may have included drafts for all of the poems in *Esd* that date from before the beginning of PBS's residence at Oxford late in 1810, including earlier versions of some of the poems now extant in the manuscripts given and letters sent to Hogg at Oxford and over the vacation in December 1810 and January 1811. Notebook X, or another lost early notebook that might have accompanied it, may also have been the source of the *[Poems about Mary]* that PBS wrote in response to Hogg's story of 1810. One bit of evidence favoring the hypothesis that one or more lost notebooks of this kind were in Shelley's possession during his travels is that *To Mary who died in this opinion,* which PBS sent to Hitchener in a letter dated 23 November 1811, was apparently copied from a rough draft MS (*CPPBS* I, 138–39, 307–10) in which at least the original drafts of the other four *[Poems about Mary]* (*Esd* #37–#40) may also have been found, though PBS later revised them into a more polished state.

If PBS did have such a Notebook X—or even Notebooks Y and Z—once he had revised and copied into **EN** the poems through *The Retrospect* (#50), he had probably extracted from them all the poems that he considered worthy of being included in *Esd*—that is, those that illustrated the growth of a very young poet's mind. Thus, having turned **EN** over to HWS, he would likely have put such notebooks and other papers into storage when he and HWS resumed their wandering evasion of creditors with their tour of the Lake Country (accompanied by Peacock) and made later moves to temporary residences at Windsor and Bracknell (see White, *Shelley* I, 317–33). The most likely places for the Shelleys to leave private papers at that time would have been either the Westbrook family home on Chapel Street or in the care of Thomas Hookham, the bookseller. After PBS and MWS eloped to France, HWS could have gained possession of papers left in either location, and there is at least one reference to her likely possession of PBS's early poetic manuscripts, in his letter to her of 5 October 1814, near the end of which he wrote: "If you could copy for me & send one poem called an Indian Tale I wish to have it—will you send also the Wandering Jew if it is with you?" (*Letters* I, 405). The "Indian Tale," probably ***Zeinab and Kathema*** (as F. L. Jones speculated), was clearly in HWS's hands in **EN,** but PBS's question about the manuscript of *WJ* may either have been motivated by his plan to use materials from that work to revise and continue *The Assassins* (see *CPPBS* I, 195) or been an attempt to learn whether HWS had taken his early poetic manuscripts from their place of safekeeping.

We have edited the poems in the hand of HWS more conservatively than those that PBS himself copied into **EN.** His holograph transcriptions of poems that we know he hoped to make public, but which survive only in preliminary or safekeeping copies, require editorial correction of palpable errors and the addition of some punctuation to render them readable to the public for whom he intended them. The copies HWS made, on the other hand, derive from either rough drafts or privately released manuscripts not intended for publication, and we transmit them virtually as HWS copied them, lest we inadvertently take the reader farther from the original text in PBS's lost holograph manuscripts.

HWS seems to have tried to copy the original MSS literally, with little overt punctuation, and though some of her flourishes at the ends of words can be interpreted to hint at periods, dashes, and commas (see p. 673), these markings are usually so ambiguous that it is hard to decide whether they represent punctuation. Moreover, her flowing handwriting, seen as well in her Commonplace Book (MS WSU), stretches out words to occupy more lateral space than does PBS's writing of the same words; since **EN** is a notebook of smaller dimensions (MS WSU is 20.3 centimeters wide, while the width of **EN** is 11.2 cm.), many of her lines crowd to the edge of the recto pages and deep into the gutter of verso pages, producing spill-over lines and leaving little or no room for end punctuation in those lines that do not spill over.

To Harriett ("Thy look of love")   [Esd #54]

Both PBS and HWS usually spelled her Christian name with a single terminal *t* (like Harriet Grove's name), and the appearance here of the doubled final letter (*tt*) requires explanation. Cameron (*1964, 293* fn.) deduced that this was the legal form of HWS's given name, citing a letter from PBS to Thomas Charles Medwin (a lawyer and the father of PBS's second cousin and biographer) that asks him to draw up a legal document for HWS's benefit and specifies that her maiden name was "Harriett Westbrook with two ts to Harriett" (*Letters* I, 154). That should settle the question of where the form originated, but why did PBS use it to head this poem, after spelling her name "Harriet" throughout the poems intended for publication in *Esd?*

We have observed that PBS often made distinctions in spelling homonyms that represent different parts of speech; though he did not follow this penchant consistently, he frequently used the spelling *desert* for the adjective and *desart* for the noun, and *show* for the noun and *shew* for the verb. In a similar vein, he did not like to double the names of his intimate friends. For example, when Elizabeth Hitchener was invited to join his ménage in Devonshire, he asked Hitchener to adopt a new name while she lived with them, since HWS's sister was also named Elizabeth (Eliza) (see ***Letters*** I, 291, 292–93 fn; White, *Shelley* I, 239). Hitchener chose the name Portia, which HWS did not like (***Letters*** I, 275), and when Hitchener arrived, they called her Bessy (***Letters*** I, 321, fn. 6). During the time PBS and HWS were together, both PBS and their correspondents spelled HWS's name with one *t*, but he learned that her legal spelling was Harriett when they remarried (to assure the legality of their Scottish elopement). He used the latter form sometimes during their estrangement; "Harriett" appears at least twice in letters he wrote to HWS after he returned to London in the autumn of 1814 (***Letters*** I, 400 and 406), perhaps at that point to distinguish between the Harriet (Grove) and Harriett (Westbrook) of his emotional past.

PBS's poem ***To Harriett*** contains thirty lines in five six-line stanzas, rhymed *ababcc*, each stanza containing five lines in iambic tetrameter, while its fourth line is in iambic trimeter (the same stanza form he used in a gracious compliment to HWS in ***To November, Esd*** #8). In addition, two notations by either PBS or HWS also appear: following the third stanza, which appears on folio 92 verso of **EN,** are the words "Cook's Hotel" (suggesting that she associated the poem with Cooke's Hotel in London) and at the end of the poem she wrote "May 1814" (perhaps copying PBS's dateline, recalling the date that she received it, or recording the date that she copied it into **EN**). Matthews's "Whose Little Footsteps?" (*Evidence of the Imagination,* 244–54) and the headnote of ***To Harriett*** in *1989* (I, 427–29) argue that the poem was *written* in May *1813*. Matthews does so in an attempt to refute earlier interpretations of the poem's meaning and significance put forward by scholars who believed (with variations) that PBS wrote this poem to urge HWS to show him affection after their initial alienation in the spring of 1814 over his flirtation with Cornelia Boinville Turner. Instead, by redating the poem to May 1813, Matthews relates it to PBS's efforts, after the Shelleys returned to London, to have Harriet accept Hogg's friendship in spite of her revulsion towards him. Matthews's theory of the date "May 1814" depends on the assumption that "May 1814" was not its date of composition, but the date on which HWS copied PBS's poem, for neither she nor PBS was likely to have confused May 1813 with May 1814. In 1813 the Shelleys had just returned to London from Ireland, shortly before the birth of their first child, while May 1814 came in the midst of growing alienation between HWS and PBS, shortly after his flirtation with Cornelia Turner, when Harriet de Boinville had banned PBS from her house at Bracknell, ordered her daughter and Thomas Turner (Cornelia's husband) to move out of PBS's reach, and summoned HWS to collect her husband, less than three months before PBS eloped to the Continent with Mary Godwin. But though Matthews argues that "1814" has no significance for the poem's occasion, he does credit "May" in 1813 as its likely month, even though PBS kept a room at Cooke's Hotel from which to conduct business with his father and others till at least 9 July 1813.

Matthews's acknowledged *reason* for choosing 1813 for the composition of the poem was, however, because he believed that two of its lines that had never been satisfactorily explicated could be explained if the poem had been written in May 1813, rather than May 1814. The crux appears in **lines 5–6:** "No grief is mine but that alone | These choicest blessings I have known." William Michael Rossetti, Dowden, Newman Ivey White (*Shelley* I, 330–31), Boas, and Cameron (all of whom accepted May 1814 as the date of the poem's composition) read the poem as PBS's plea to HWS to show him affection once more, rather than making him pay a <u>price beyond all pain</u> . . . <u>Beneath</u> [her] <u>scorn to die</u> (**9–10**). They saw the poem's occasion as a moment when PBS was conflicted between his affection for HWS, with his sense of his duty to her and their child, and his incipient love for Mary W. Godwin (MWS); they read **To Harriett** as a poem begging HWS to signal him that she forgave his recent infatuation with Cornelia Turner and wanted him to stay with her, rather than rejecting his love. In the final stanza, PBS asks HWS to stop trusting her <u>erring guide</u> (**25**),—presumably her older sister Eliza Westbrook, who may have advised her to take a hard line with her wayward spouse—and instead to show him <u>pity</u>, if she could not immediately <u>love</u> him again (**30**). These scholars believed, with various levels of sympathy for the two parties, that HWS chose not to renew her emotional support for PBS, responding coldly to his plea, and they therefore partially exonerate PBS for soon afterwards consummating his love for MWS and eloping with her in July 1814.

As Matthews says, however, those previous readings do not satisfactorily explain the meaning of the word <u>alone</u> in **line 5.** Deducing from the difficulty of reading this word that the other scholars' dating of the poem must be erroneous, he develops a different scenario out of the different situation in May 1813: While the Shelleys, soon after returning to London from Ireland in the spring of 1813, stayed at Cooke's Hotel for undetermined periods in 1813 (and where PBS may also have stayed at undetermined times in 1814), PBS urged his wife, Matthews argues, to share her <u>look of love</u>, which had <u>power to calm</u> | <u>The stormiest passion of</u> [his] <u>Soul</u> (**1–2**), not only with her husband but also with another <u>fellow being</u> (**18**)—namely, Thomas Jefferson Hogg. Matthews does not accuse PBS of asking HWS to sleep with Hogg (she being about eight months pregnant in May 1813), but he assumes that PBS—perhaps chagrined that his wife had humiliated his old friend Hogg by refusing to meet him in Dublin after PBS invited Hogg to travel there—was trying to work out a reconciliation in which HWS would be kind to Hogg and thus, <u>by a slight endurance</u> (**17**), help to rebuild the self-esteem (and thus the <u>lasting weal</u>) of a <u>fellow being</u>. Consequently, Matthews interprets **lines 5** and **6** to mean that PBS's only stated grief is that he <u>alone</u> (i.e., *only* he) had basked in <u>the warm sunshine</u> of HWS's <u>eye</u> (**8**), and if the <u>price</u> for his wishing that Hogg could share the <u>sunshine</u> arouses her <u>scorn</u> (**10**), PBS (her <u>chosen</u> one) also deserves Hogg's fate. Matthews's own stanza-by-stanza paraphrases (*1989* I, 429) are totally coherent, *if* one accepts his two premises: (1) that the poem was written in May 1813, and (2) that PBS was intent on bringing Hogg back into his family circle.

Whatever one thinks about Matthews's solution of the problem of explicating a single word in a thirty-line poem, it does not meet the test of Occam's Razor ("Entities should not be multiplied beyond necessity"), if only because it requires us to believe that PBS felt so passionately that HWS should be nice to Hogg that he told her that she must do so in order to complete his own marital happiness. The first premise, regarding the date, is weak, simply because there is no evidence to prove the hypothesis of an 1813 date. So little is known about PBS's place(s) of residence during the many times he visited London in 1814 that Cooke's Hotel may have been the mail-drop address he placed on it when sending it to HWS, and she may have also taken the subscribed date from PBS's holograph from which she was copying or (as Crook suggests) from a May 1814 postmark on the letter containing it. Matthews's second premise, however, goes against everything we have learned about PBS's attitude toward Hogg from the poems in **Esd**—especially from those that PBS copied into **EN** after he returned to London in 1813. Some of them contain angry moralizing about Hogg's treatment of women—judgments that PBS carried over into his anonymous public review of Hogg's novel *Memoirs of Prince Alexy Haimatoff* in 1815. On 13 November 1814, after PBS returned to London with MWS and finally arranged for Hogg to meet his new love, PBS wrote in the Journal that they were then keeping jointly, "In the evening Hogg calls. . . . Perhaps he may still be my friend: in spite of the radical defici[e]ncies of sympathy between us. He was pleased with Mary.— this was the test by which I had previously determined to judge his character" (MWS, *Journals* I, 45).

Later, in the spring of 1815, PBS did, it seems, engineer a sexual *ménage à quatre* that ostensibly involved MWS, Claire Clairmont, Hogg, and himself, though since MWS was then advanced in pregnancy (as HWS was in May 1813), she did not have physical relations with either PBS or Hogg (leaving PBS and Claire free to exploit the interim period, while using Hogg's desires as their excuse). Given that strange episode, we might accept Matthews's reading of **To Harriett** in order to parse the sentence in **lines 5–6,** if there were no simpler explanations. We must, first, remember that <u>alone</u>, being a rhyme word, may (like <u>state</u> in **line 13**) have been employed as much for its utility to PBS's rhyme scheme as for its contribution to his meaning. Second, drawing upon what we have learned by tracing the progression of PBS's feelings for HWS throughout his carefully arranged poems of *Esd,* a preferable alternative solution to the crux appears in PBS's repeated advice to HWS to think less about her own desires and more about her <u>fellow being</u>(s), among them one about whom PBS was vitally concerned after 23 June 1813, his daughter Ianthe, whose <u>lasting weal</u> he seems to have believed literally depended upon the child's receiving milk together with love from her own mother while nursing.

PBS probably did not expect HWS to be still nursing her child in May 1814, and the masculine pronouns in the fourth stanza of *To Harriett* (19–24) make clear that PBS is not talking about Ianthe as the only <u>fellow being</u> who requires HWS's sympathy; but from PBS's early days of writing and collecting poems for *Esd,* he had been urging HWS to have more feeling for other people in general—the poor and the oppressed, as well as their friends and social equals. According to Peacock, what PBS saw as her lack of maternal affection and responsibility for Ianthe may have seemed to PBS a troubling and epitomizing example of her lack of empathy for others. The idiom of the age, especially in the Enlightenment-oriented circles of the Godwins, Newtons, and Boinvilles (with whom PBS had been spending much time), favored the use of the abstract generic singular, such as "the philanthropist's" love of his "fellow creature" or "fellow being," and we might do well to remember that when PBS had recently become infatuated with Cornelia Turner they had been reading together the Marchese di Beccaria's treatise on prison reform (see *Letters* I, 384; *CPPBS* I, 328–29) and that he was soon to be won over by Mary Godwin during discussions of the ameliorist philosophical and social ideas of her father and mother. In *To Harriett,* therefore, PBS may simply be reiterating in condensed form the concerns that he had frequently expressed about his wife's lack of a shared interest in the well-being of others, noted as early as his poem *To Harriet ("Harriet! thy kiss to my soul is dear");* see *Esd* #29, Commentary.

Thomas Jefferson Hogg, whom MWS, Peacock, and a few other friends tolerated for various periods but nobody much liked, was certainly <u>a fellow being</u> who would have qualified (like others) for empathy and fair treatment under PBS's dream of universal benevolence, and to this extent Matthews may be correct in saying that PBS hoped that HWS would be more accepting of Hogg. PBS may even have urged her to forgive her would-be seducer, and some argue that he even asked HWS to "love" Hogg, as he later apparently asked MWS to do. But likely in *To Harriett* (May 1814), as certainly in *To Harriet ("Harriet! thy kiss to my soul is dear"),* he might just as likely be signaling his passionate hope that she would strengthen their marital happiness by showing herself to be more altruistic and more accepting of Hogg's oddities and those of all other fellow beings as (he believed) were the other women whom he knew in the Newton-Boinville circle.

Thus—as with several other poems in *Esd*—we are left with distinctly different interpretations of **To Harriett,** according with different surmises about the occasion for which the poem was written and, even more, about what kind of person PBS was. Let us examine briefly the possible views of PBS that the uncertainties about the meaning of **To Harriett** can generate. First, there is the contrite, isolated PBS of May 1814 portrayed by Dowden, White, Cameron, and Boas, begging his young wife to forgive him for a marital indiscretion during her pregnancy and being rebuffed on the advice of her older sister. Second, there is Matthews's reading, based on the notion of Cooke's Hotel and an 1813 date, that PBS urged HWS to be especially nice to Hogg—perhaps even to the extent of eventually fulfilling his college friend's fantasy of sleeping with her—in order to restore the Oxonians' close friendship. Third, a scenario that might fit a date of composition in either the second half of 1813 or the spring of 1814, would have PBS, a doctrinaire reformer, believing that he and HWS are drifting apart because, rather than caring about the needs of a suffering world, she concentrates on pleasing herself and her family (to cite an example fitting the later period, persuading PBS that she needed a fine carriage [see *SC* IV, 153 ff.). Therefore— either just before or after his infatuation with Cornelia Turner—he urges his wife to be more giving of herself (perhaps beginning with her own infant daughter, whom she refused to breast feed). Those who find PBS to be either an emotionally unstable, self-deluded, or calculating person beneath a humanitarian veneer might see a darker, more convoluted combination of these scenarios, in which in 1813 PBS—tiring of HWS after he has been flattered and fawned over by more intellectual women in the Godwin-Newton-Boinville circle and still angry with Hogg for his betrayal in October 1811— urged HWS to accept Hogg's advances as a way of putting both of them in the wrong so that he would be justified in breaking with them both. Choose one—or none—of the above.

line 14. <u>Whose heart is harder not for state—</u>: Of the forty-some principal meanings of the noun *state* discussed in the *OED,* the two that would seem most appropriate to the traditional interpretation of the poem are 5a and 15a. With definition 5a, "a state of affairs," the stanza can be paraphrased thus: "Be then one among all people whose heart is not harder because of the current situation" (i.e., PBS's flirtation with Cornelia Boinville Turner). "In a world of hate, you alone are virtuous, gentle, and kind, and so with little effort on your part (<u>slight endurance</u>) please seal my happiness. Instead of being vindictive about my flirtation, let your kindness and gentleness rise above the world of hate, to endure the situation by making me feel wanted, benefit me lastingly by giving me no reason to seek other companionship."

Reading <u>state</u> with usage 15a, "a person's condition or position in life; a person's natural, social or legal status, profession or calling, rank or degree," the line can be paraphrased: "Be then one among all people whose heart is not harder because of your status as my wife. Don't follow the socially prescribed behavior expected of a married woman when her husband has flirted with another woman, but rather use your kindness and gentleness to rise above the world of hate, endure the situation, and make me happy."

As we suggest above, PBS may have chosen the word state—like alone—primarily for its utility in maintaining his rhyme scheme.

line 18. Below this line, which comes in **EN** at the bottom of the verso page upon which HWS copied the first three stanzas of **To Harriett,** she wrote the phrase "Cook's Hotel." At the end of the fifth and final stanza on the facing recto page she wrote (or copied) the date "May 1814."

line 29. pride is not clear, because the *d* lacks a riser, making the word look as much like "price" with one extra minim as it does like pride.

"Full many a mind"   *[Esd #55]*

Boas in *Harriet Shelley* (*1962BOAS*, 179–80), Cameron, and Rogers agreed that HWS might have written **"Full many a mind,"** but only Cameron went on to supply "her" poem with a putative date, place of composition, and a scenario to explain its significance. Matthews, however, in the admittedly speculative first section of his "Whose Little Footsteps?" (in *The Evidence of the Imagination*, 238–44), argued cogently for PBS's authorship, discussed the difficulty of trying to decipher his drafts, speculated on some of HWS's errors in transcription, and proposed a different occasion for PBS's composition of it. Again, Matthews (whose views are repeated in *1989* I, 187–88) argued that the date following the poem in **EN** ("1815") was HWS's addition and was the date, not of the poem's composition, but of her copying it into the Notebook. Instead, he believed, it might have been written in November 1811, just after PBS, HWS, and Eliza Westbrook slipped out of York following PBS's remonstrance to Hogg about his attempt to seduce HWS. Thus for Matthews this poem, like **To Harriett,** turns out to be about "the Hogg-Harriet situation" ("Whose Little Footsteps?" 242), and in *1989* he punctuates the text and explicates it accordingly. Matthews bases his dating upon his identification of the place-name Stanmore (as recorded by HWS) with an area that he describes as "an impressively desolate region known as Stanemore" (or "Stainmore" or "Stainmoor") located "on the road" to the Lake Country where "this road crosses from Yorkshire into Westmorland" (241), near the Rokeby estate, whose name Walter Scott used as the title of one his poems, "one of Harriet's favorite books." The book uses the spelling "Stanmore" for the Yorkshire site, though (as Matthews himself notes) Scott's poem was published more than a year after Matthews's putative date for the composition of **"Full many a mind."**

Cameron's earlier commentary (*1964*, 300–301) was less speculative, noting only that Stanmore was the name of a village (spelled the same way HWS wrote it into **EN**) ten miles out of London on the Edgware Road—a main coach road toward the Midlands that began at Hyde Park, not far from the Westbrook family home on Chapel Street. After commenting on the textual status and possible meaning of the poem (which he believed to be by HWS), Cameron concludes: "The implication in the poem seems to be that Harriet was at Stanmore sometime in 1815 and that either Shelley visited her there or she there wrote down sentiments which seemed appropriate to a previous meeting in London" (301).

When we return to the text of *"Full many a mind"* itself, we can agree with Matthews that the poem was written by PBS earlier than 1815 and that HWS's placement of the poem's two quatrains on a recto page of **EN,** after leaving the facing verso page blank, could suggest that she extracted only eight lines of what may have been a longer draft, leaving herself space to copy some additional lines on the blank page if she found them worth deciphering. But, judging the quality of the thought and versification as far as these are revealed in HWS's labored transcription, we believe that it was written earlier even than 1811, and we doubt that it relates to HWS in any way other than in her having transcribed it. Of all PBS's poems in **EN,** it seems most closely related, both in concept and quality of execution, to *Written in very early youth* (#48), the earliest poem in the *Esd* sequence. The first quatrain aligns the poet with other <u>mind</u>s laden with <u>radiant genius</u>, making him one of the <u>great souls</u> who had <u>to bear</u> misery and struggle against <u>wild despair</u>. Yet, he argues in the second stanza, it is not the function of <u>Earth's laws</u> to separate <u>Man</u> from <u>God & Heaven</u>, but rather <u>To teach him where to</u> . . . <u>find peace of mind</u>.

One crux appears in **lines 5–6,** which produce the meaning above if we insert an (understood) relative "that" before <u>Earth's laws</u>, but the meaning of <u>Earth's laws</u> is ambiguous. If we assume that this is a late poetic draft, <u>Earth's laws</u> could mean "Nature's laws" (as the phrase might appear in **QM**). The poet is then saying that, in seeking to live with the person he really loves (now MWS?), he is asserting his right to "first follow Nature" and thereby to find <u>peace of mind</u>. If, on the other hand, <u>Earth's laws</u> are the laws of men-of-the-world, or the King and the Church, then the poet may be saying that those <u>laws</u> are unjust to <u>stand between</u> him and his <u>Heaven</u> (union with MWS), which could <u>teach him</u> to find his <u>lasting comfort</u>. Of these two readings, we think that the first would follow better from the rhetoric of the poem as a whole. The burden of the two quatrains would thus be: "We great souls suffer because we don't follow the laws of human society, made for lesser beings. We are taught by <u>Earth's law</u>, which (thinking of the Earth that mediates between Prometheus and the powers of the universe in **Prom**) should not so stand between <u>Man</u> and <u>Heaven</u>, but guide us to <u>peace of mind</u>."

But whatever efficacy these lines might have had for a youthful PBS in venting his frustrations, the two quatrains are so general in their language and so weak poetically that we believe it unlikely that he would have composed them *after* he wrote the poems that he dates 1809 and 1810 in *Esd* (i.e., #15, #16, #33, #34, #36, #41, #42, #44, and #46). And when we compare *"Full many a mind"* with the three poems that follow it, at least one of which was composed during the earliest puppy-love phase of PBS's relationship with Harriet Grove, we have reason to suspect that the blank verso page between the poem *To Harriett* and the other four poems copied by HWS was a space of demarcation, separating those poems that PBS had revised and arranged during his years with HWS from a few early drafts or interim copies that, sometime in 1815, HWS found in one or more poetic notebooks that PBS had left in her possession. Her reason for copying them into **EN**—and adding 1815 to this one, as the year in which she did so—would be much the same as her reason for copying passages from other poets into her Commonplace Book: to collect where she could find them again poems or fragments of poetry that moved her in her abandoned state. One reason why these poems affected her was simply that they were by PBS and reminded her of former happiness or sorrow, or of recalled roads not taken. In 1815 *"Full many a mind"* could have spoken to her about her current situation of loneliness and despair. HWS may have associated these lines with the Stanmore in Yorkshire, suggests Nora Crook, because her reading of *Rokeby* would have reinforced the memory of PBS's dark mood there after he, perhaps at the insistence of the Westbrook sisters, fled from York to put distance between himself and the college friend whose betrayal had been one of the most harrowing experiences in his young lifetime. If HWS did copy the lines from a hypothetical Notebook X containing other youthful laments by PBS, she may even have begun to realize how lonely and vulnerable her poor little rich boy husband had always been and how badly she had underestimated his neediness.

lines 1–2. Note that PBS ends the first line with fraught and then creates an unusual kind of internal rhyme by using taught as the second word in **line 2.** We would consider this occurrence as accidental, did not a similar juxtaposition appear in the previous poem, where the rhyme word "speak" ending line 21 is followed immediately, at the beginning of the next line, by the words "Weak is each" (22), in which not only is the rhyme word repeated but the next two accented words are assonant with that previous rhyme. We do not recall such occurrences in PBS's other poems (though perhaps because we had never before been aware of this possible reinforcement of rhymes); if he experimented with this technique only in his youth, he may have abandoned it as being too *précieuse,* like *rime riche.*

line 5. Though there is no definite apostrophe after Earth, the *s* following Earth is separated from that word by a space.

This, the third poem in the hand of HWS, presents a logical discrepancy between the date given in the title and the place given at the end; one task is to determine whether HWS was copying PBS's notes, or whether she added these herself. The placename written at the end, <u>Cum Elam</u>, is probably HWS's misspelling of Cwm Elan, which she seems to have added along with her responsive comment to the poem, <u>Adieu my love good night</u>. Both the substitution of the English *u* in place of the Welsh *w* and concluding the name of the Groves' Welsh estate with *m* rather than *n* are mistakes that PBS, who spelled the name as "Cwm Ellan" in the title of *Esd* #18, was less likely to make, for he had often heard, spoken, and written the name of his uncle's estate in his frequent communications, oral and written, with his Grove relatives (especially Harriet, John, and Charles) and had also spent more time in Wales than had HWS. Moreover, if *To Harriet* . . . . was composed in May 1813, this poem would not have been written at Cwm Elan but in London. If the poem were written at the Grove estate, the only occasion when PBS and HWS were there together was from April into June 1812, when PBS was trying to lease the nearby property called Nantgwillt. However, the Harriet being addressed in the poem seems to be absent, not present, to the poet (at least most of the time), and we should consider the possibility that PBS could have addressed some poetry to HWS while he was there in 1811, awaiting his chance to elope with her.

Though we cannot prove that PBS did not draft some failed attempts to express his joy either in 1811 while anticipating his union with HWS, or in 1812 to mark the time that he introduced her to his near relations who had rejected him as a suitor for the hand of *their* Harriet, we believe that this poem was more likely an earlier effort. When the structure, prosody, and literal meaning of *To Harriet* . . . . are analyzed, neither the implied situation of the poetic speaker and the Harriet he addresses, nor the mood of the poem, nor the level of poetic sophistication exhibited in the diction, rhythms, or rhyme scheme of this poem comes near to that of the bold metrical experiments in many of the Cwm Elan poems in *Esd* of either 1811 or 1812. On the contrary, the language in general and rhyme words in particular are trite, there is no uniform stanza pattern, and the only metrical scheme to gain any traction as the poem proceeds is a simple, sing-song quatrain, in anapestic tetrameter rhymed *abab*, which appears only in the third, fourth, sixth, and seventh of the poem's eight stanzas. The poet's message in the first two stanzas (a quatrain rhymed *abac,* followed by a six-line stanza in which only the first and third lines rhyme precisely) is that <u>rolling years</u> cannot destroy love like his, which is so strong that he lacks the <u>power</u> | <u>Of words</u> to talk about it, and that it is not a love of momentary <u>delight</u> (**9**), even though such a moment, he says, <u>Would pay me for an age of pain</u> (**10**). In these stanzas and throughout the poem's thirty-six lines (six quatrains and two six-line stanzas in all) there are verbal repetitions, logical contradictions, and non sequiturs of the kind characteristic of amateur poets, young and old, who have not composed enough poetry to master the craft. In short, *To Harriet . . . .* appears to us to be a juvenile work, written before PBS met HWS and, therefore, probably addressed to Harriet Grove.

Desmond Hawkins (*Shelley's First Love*, 5–7) believes that the final poem in **EN** (#58), which HWS labeled as being about "H Grove," could actually have been composed as early as 28 February 1805 (or 1806—see our Commentary below), when PBS would have been twelve or thirteen, an unhappy student at Eton, and certainly old enough and sufficiently motivated to experience epistolary puppy-love cum poetry. There is no evidence that PBS sent this (or any other) poem to Harriet Grove at such an early date, but we strongly believe that *To Harriet . . . .* was written before 1813 and thus very likely expresses PBS's early adolescent longings for an enduring, spiritualized love of the kind that he wrote about in some poems to Harriet Grove found in **CPPBS** I. In 1811–12, on the other hand, he felt sure that he had found such a relationship with HWS, and by 1814 he felt equally certain that he had achieved that bliss with MWS.

The third stanza denies that the poet's love is primarily sensual, like that of <u>the Libertine</u>, and the fourth says that he would gladly die to save Harriet from any unstated danger. The fifth and sixth stanzas say that before he loved Harriet he had no bosom friend and was in such mental anguish that he considered suicide; the next continues that since his love for her began, their separation leaves him <u>nothing but death and despair</u> (**30**); and the final stanza sets forth the idea that even after <u>the charms</u> of his beloved's <u>form</u> . . . <u>decay with the swift rolling years</u> (**33–34**), their love will continue in <u>Heaven</u>, for just being with Harriet creates an <u>Elysium</u>. Though these themes appear in his poems to HWS, they are more consistently present in his poems to Harriet Grove—which probably include *Esd* #34, #35, and #36; the final poem in **EN** (#58); two poems in *V&C*, each entitled simply *To —————* (*CPPBS* I, 20–22; 175–78); possibly all three elegiac laments in *PF* (*CPPBS* I, 99–104; 255–59); and the last three poems in *St.Irv*, each entitled *Song* (114–17; 273–79)—all written before the influence of Godwin and, especially, the materialist French *philosophes* had dampened, if not quenched, PBS's hopes for immortality.

PBS's critical judgment was certainly correct in rejecting this early effort and, instead, including in the *Esd* collection itself much better statements on these perennial themes. But HWS, experiencing her own lonely separation, was less critical and, seeing a poem addressed to "Harriet," she presumed it had been written for her and she adopted it, so far as to imagine that PBS had written it to her at <u>Cum Elam</u>, and responding, <u>Adieu my love good night</u>.

Title. That <u>Harriet</u> is here spelled with a single *t,* in contrast to the spelling of the name in ***Esd*** #54, ***To Harriett (“Thy look of love”),*** supports the thesis that this poem was addressed to Harriet Grove, with HWS copying each poem literally from a MS by PBS. Crook suggests to us, however, that the nine spaced periods following the name could represent the nine letters of “Westbrook.” Did HWS insert them all, or did she add some periods to others that PBS had written following <u>Harriet</u>?

line 27. <u>death’s</u>: Though there is no apostrophe in **EN,** there is a definite space between the word <u>death</u> and the *s* that follows it.

line 28. <u>miseries</u>: Either PBS in composing by the sound of the words or HWS in her copying has unwittingly substituted the plural form for the possessive case that was intended.

“Late was the night”   *[Esd #57]*

Though both Cameron (*1964, 1973*) and Rogers (*1966, 1972*) assigned this poem to HWS, Matthews recaptured it for PBS in “Whose Little Footsteps?” Since then, students of PBS’s early poetry can recognize ***“Late was the night”*** as probably an earlier, Gothicized draft treating the plight of a seduced and abandoned woman—a forerunner of ***1808 (“Cold are the Blasts”)*** (#45), which PBS had first published in ***Original Poetry*** “by Victor and Cazire” (***V&C***) as ***Song (“Cold, cold is the blast”)*** (***CPPBS*** I, 11–13). Nora Crook suggests to us that PBS may have modeled ***“Late was the night”*** on *Edwin and Emma* (1760) by David Mallet (?1705–65; *DNB*).

Whereas ***“Cold, cold is the blast”*** is written in relatively complicated eight-line stanzas rhymed *ababcccb,* the verse form of ***“Late was the night”*** is quasi-anapestic quatrains, the first two of which are rhymed *aabb,* the next two *abab,* the fifth probably an incomplete *abab* (see Commentary to **line 17**), and the final one again *abab.* This is clearly juvenilia, written by a bright schoolboy, probably for his own amusement, which PBS had not thought worth publishing even in 1810, when ***V&C*** appeared. The Gothic <u>murderes</u> in the second stanza, together with the <u>Alpine summits</u> in the third (**line 9**) might suggest that PBS began this poem for possible inclusion in ***St. Irvyne.*** But the later stanzas about the plight of <u>Poor Emma</u>, said to be <u>The victim of misery’s own sad child</u> (**21–22**), make it more likely that it was an earlier effort which PBS abandoned after his thought moved in another direction— one that he may then have stopped to develop into a poem devoted to winning sympathy for the victims of the kind of “Libertine” he mentions in lines 11–14 of ***To Harriet* . . . .** (#56)—a poem such as ***“Cold are the Blasts”*** (***Esd*** #45). Thus this draft of ***“Late was the night”*** remained uncorrected and was abandoned by PBS simply because it was poetically unsalvageable verbal doodling.

HWS, however, may have copied the pastiche of phrases from the schools of Gothicism and Sensibility in ***"Late was the night"*** because its warnings of danger and lamentations about betrayal spoke directly to her condition in 1815 (the date that she appended to it when she copied it into **EN**). Having herself felt the pains of being abandoned, as Poor Emma was, she was unlikely to concern herself with the poem's simplistic logic, phrasing, or prosody.

line 17. See that fair form that [?] [?]: The final words in this line seemed virtually illegible to those involved with the editing of *1964, 1966, SCIV,* and *1972.* In both *1964A* and *1964B,* Cameron's reading was "he can save" but in *1973* (170) the phrase reads "leans ore" (*SC* IV, 1061). When Neville Rogers sent his original transcription to Don and Mary Reiman in June 1962, the end of this line read "passes on" and they replaced it with "?bears on"; but in an accompanying note they also suggested that perhaps the second that in the line was a demonstrative (not a relative) pronoun and that the end of the line was, therefore, a phrase in apposition to "that fair form": See that fair form, that [adjective] [noun]. Rogers's two editions both contain another solution involving emendation, his texts reading the end of this line: "[?none] <?can save>;" this reading attempts to repair the meaning, the meter, and the rhyme scheme. Matthews and Everest took up Rogers's solution for the problem of the missing rhyme, while proposing a different reading for the words visible in **EN**: *1989* completes the line thus: "that leans o'er [the wave];". While we find *1989*'s emendation to be more probable than any of the other suggested solutions, we have not emended our text but simply deciphered the characters in **EN** as well as we can, leaving the incompleteness of the line as evidence supporting the hypothesis that this is a poem by **PBS** that HWS copied from a ragged and uncompleted draft.

line 24. The date written after this line, 1815, is marked just above by an *x*. The nature of this mark is unknown, though it may indicate the cancellation of an illegible word over which cold-striken is written.

14
Feb^ry 28th 1806—To St Irvyne   [Esd #58]

Because this poem's title included the date that **PBS** had given it, HWS could not think that *this* poem about "Harriet" related to herself. Either **PBS** or she wrote below it that the poem was written To H Grove. The "St. Irvyne" of the title was a ruined manor house called Hill Place, near the Shelley home Field Place, that had been the residence of Lady Irvine, a political rival of the Duke of Norfolk for control of the two parliamentary seats allotted to the moderately rotten Borough of Horsham until the duke purchased her estate in 1788. Hill Place was apparently in ruins by the time **PBS** and Harriet Grove walked there under an August Moon (**7**) the summer before **PBS** wrote these six quatrains, which he did, according to its headline, on either 14 or 28 February 1806 (not 1805 as previous editors have read it). Though the versification is simple, in PBS's early style (mixed iambic and anapestic tetrameter, rhymed *abab*), there seems to be real feeling behind this poem. PBS missed Harriet Grove during the months since she sat with him high on the ruined building and they gazed at the stars together. In the absence of her sympathetic companionship, he wrote during the Easter vacation of what in 1806 would have been his second year at Eton, amid an unpleasant season and thoughts of more-unpleasant companions awaiting his return to school, focusing his thoughts on death (though suicide is not specified).

Cameron (*1964*, 305–9) deemed the date of "1805" (as he read HWS's unfamiliar hand) to be too early for PBS to have written such a poem, and he was seconded in this opinion by *1989* (I, 84), both editions positing the date of composition as 1810. But Hawkins, finding the tone of the poem "adolescent, in pursuit of powerful emotions that the poet would like to feel but is not yet able to do so" (*Shelley's First Love*, 6), believed that the verses were likely to have been written about 1805. After correcting the reading of the date to February 1806, we feel that it would have been quite feasible for PBS (then thirteen and a half) to have written this poem and possibly even to have mailed a copy to Harriet Grove (though we have no evidence of that).

The poems that HWS copied may have been in "Notebook X," which perhaps contained drafts of other early poems that PBS copied out for Hogg in 1810–11 and later revised to include in **Esd** proper. This hypothesized notebook (or notebooks) that he either carried when he went to Wales in the summer of 1811 or received in the wagon that brought his books and papers from Field Place in September of that year (**Letters** I, 143, 146) may thus have displayed a conspectus of his poetry from about the time he entered Eton (September 1804) until he gave the first version of his "Minor Poems" to John Stockdale in Dublin to be printed early in 1812. From PBS's later practice of drafting his creative writings in several notebooks and copying the better completed poems into a special copybook (like the larger Harvard Shelley Notebook—*MYR: Shelley* V), we suspect that PBS left with John Stockdale at Dublin another notebook or sheaf of more polished transcriptions that he never recovered but most of which he was able to replace, either by borrowing fair copies that he had earlier given to Hogg or by recreating the poems from drafts in Notebook X. But he still left there some unpublished poetry to which HWS had access as late as 1815. Whether or not this scenario is valid, the level of technical competence of most of the poems or fragments in her hand marks them as juvenilia, and #55 through #58 were, we believe, composed before PBS and his sister Elizabeth put together the best of their early efforts in *V&C*.

Queen Mab; A Philosophical Poem: with Notes.

Textual History

Scholars have suggested various dates for the composition of **Queen Mab** (**QM**) and its prose notes. Part of the uncertainty stems from PBS's apparently misleading letter to *The Examiner* (published 15 June 1821) in response to the 1821 pirating of the poem: "A poem, entitled 'Queen Mab,' was written by me at the age of eighteen, I dare say in a sufficiently intemperate spirit—but even then was not intended for publication, and a few copies only were struck off, to be distributed among my personal friends" (**Letters** II, 304). In attempting to distance **QM** from his more mature productions, PBS thus led both MWS and Thomas Medwin, neither of whom was present to know otherwise, to claim that **QM** was written when he was eighteen. This would have placed composition in 1810, except that Medwin further erred by calculating that PBS was eighteen in 1809, the date he provides for the commencement of the poem (*Life,* ed. Forman, 62). The testimony submitted to Chancery Court by PBS's solicitor, Longdill, in the child custody proceedings following the death of Harriet Westbrook Shelley, however, claimed that the poem was written when PBS "was only 19" (White, *Shelley* II, 515), which seems somewhat closer to the facts we do have from his contemporaneous letters and the diary of William Godwin.

Dowden (*Life* I, 110–11), Hughes (*Nascent Mind,* 174–75), and *1989* (I, 266) have speculated that PBS's lost **Poetical Essay on the Existing State of Things** (see **CPPBS** I, 444–48), which was first advertised in the *Oxford Herald* for 9 March 1811, may have been an early start on **QM**. But, without further evidence, there is no way to confirm a relationship between the two poems. Of PBS's known poems, the contemporaneous ones closest to **QM** are **A retrospect of Times of Old** (**Esd** #31), which shares similar concerns with **QM**, including a generalized critique of monarchy, religion, and war, and **The Voyage** (**Esd** #32), which contains a similar—if more disjointed—critique and which experiments with the same kind of blank unrhymed verse that PBS used in **QM** (see below). Both of these poems may have been connected to, or generated from, early drafts for **QM** (see Commentary for each, pp. 398–99, pp. 402–5).

PBS's letters suggest that he first conceived **QM** in early December 1811, when he wrote to Elizabeth Hitchener from Keswick: "I have now my dear friend in contemplation a Poem. I intend it to be by anticipation a picture of the manners, simplicity and delights of a perfect state of society; tho still earthly.—Will you assist me. I only thought of it last night.—I design to accomplish it and publish" (***Letters*** I, 201). But on 26 December, after intensive conversations with Robert Southey, he explained to Hitchener: "I do not proceed with my poem, the subject is not now to my mind" (***Letters*** I, 213–14). He turned instead to the lyrics of ***Esd,*** the preparation of a volume of metaphysical and moral prose essays, and his novel, since lost, on the failure of the French Revolution, ***Hubert Cauvin*** (see ***Letters*** I, 218).

Actual composition on ***QM*** seems to have been postponed for at least four months, following PBS's return from a short, politically active trip to Ireland, which he began in early February 1812. In a letter to Thomas Hookham on 18 August 1812, PBS wrote: "I enclose also by way of specimen all that I have written of a little poem begun *since my arrival in England* [our italics]. I conceive I have matter enough for 6 more cantos. . . . The Past, the Present, & the Future are the grand & comprehensive topics of this Poem. I have not yet exhausted the second of them" (***Letters*** I, 324). PBS returned from Ireland to Wales in early April 1812 and from Wales to England in late June 1812, establishing a *terminus a quo* for the composition of ***QM*** of either April or June, depending on how literally one takes his phrase "since my arrival in England."

From his description of the MS on 18 August 1812, with its progress halfway through "the Present," PBS appears to have drafted approximately four of a projected ten cantos; in the completed poem, the second half of **Canto II** details the past, **Cantos III–VII,** the present, and **Cantos VIII–IX,** the future). But then his progress seems to have stalled. Matthews and Everest in *1989* speculate that there was a hiatus in composition between mid-August and mid-December 1812, during which PBS's scarce time for writing was given over to ***Esd*** (I, 267). This hypothesis can be further confirmed and newly understood through the following evidence: on 31 October 1812, William Godwin recorded in his diary having read forty-four pages of ***QM*** in manuscript—presumably all he was given (Bod, Abinger, Dep. e.212, f. 17v)—which to judge from the number of pages, was about four cantos, the same size as the "specimen" sent to Hookham. Cameron suggests persuasively that Godwin returned this MS via Hookham in a parcel that PBS received sometime between 3 and 17 December (see *YS,* 382, 386). There is no mention of how Godwin got the MS of ***QM,*** but we believe it likely that he read the *same* "specimen" that PBS had sent to Hookham in mid-August, perhaps receiving it from PBS during his stay in London through October and early November 1812, and returning it thereafter.

Because the period of time this "specimen" was out of PBS's hands—mid-August to mid-December—corresponds with the period that PBS appears to have paused in composing ***QM,*** the following conclusions seem likely. After drafting approximately four cantos by mid-August 1812, PBS made a fair copy of his initial work on the poem—perhaps after his first burst of inspiration ran out—to have it reviewed by his potential publisher and critiqued by his philosophic mentor (and, possibly, others). He then resumed composition in December, shortly after this fair copy was returned to him. Such a hiatus in the midst of composing a long poem was to become characteristic for PBS and is evident in the composition of such poems as **Rosalind and Helen, Prometheus Unbound, Adonais,** and **Hellas** (see, for instance, Fraistat, *Prometheus* [1991], lxiii–lxxv).

By 26 January 1813, however, PBS had written more. He informed Hookham: "I expect to have Queen Mab, & the other Poems finished by March. Queen Mab will be in ten cantos & contain about 2800 lines. The other poems probably contain as much more. The notes to Q. M. will be long and philosophical. . . . A poem very didactic is I think very stupid" (**Letters** I, 350). By 7 February, according to PBS, the "rough sketch" of **QM** was complete; and the poem was "finished & transcribed," with the notes in preparation, by mid-February 1813 (**Letters** I, 352, 354). At this point, PBS suggested to Hookham that **QM** and the **Esd** poems "should form one volume, but of that we can speak hereafter.—" (**Letters** I, 354). Sometime before **QM** actually was in print, PBS gave up altogether trying to publish **Esd,** at which point he transferred from **Esd** to **QM** the dedicatory poem to Harriet Shelley, some lines from **To Harriet** (*"Dark flood of time"*), and the lyric **Falshood and Vice: a Dialogue.**

However "completed" it may have been by mid-February, **QM** probably underwent further revision, because PBS took the manuscript with him to Dublin and did not send it to Hookham until sometime in March 1813, remarking then: "If you do not dread the arm of the law, or any exasperation of public opinion against yourself, I wish that it should be printed & published immediately. The notes are preparing & shall be forwarded before the completion of the printing of the Poem" (**Letters** I, 361). Further revisions were, of course, possible until the poem appeared in print (for possible revisions of the manuscript, see Cameron in *YS*, 388–90). Henrietta Hussey, the niece of Harriet Grove, claimed that her father, John Grove, "once possessed [and lost] a manuscript copy of Queen Mab—in Bysshe Shelley's handwriting," but the reliability of Hussey's memory is questionable and no such manuscript has ever come to light (see Irving Massey, *KSMB* 19 [1968]: 15).

The presence of distinctively Shelleyan spellings throughout *1813* suggests that PBS played a major role in preparing the transcript of the poem and notes for the press and that the printer(s) made no consistent attempt to impose a house style upon his copy. The inconsistencies in spelling, such as "honour" ("honor"), "gulph" ("gulf"), "falshood" ("falsehood"), and "desart" ("desert"), however, do not fall into a clear enough pattern to allow more specific conclusions about the production of the press transcript and its passage into print, partly because PBS himself spelled these words inconsistently. There is a strong possibility that the long quotation in French from Holbach's *Système* in **Note 13** was produced through dictation, perhaps by PBS reading aloud to Harriet Shelley or vice versa (see the Commentary for **Note 13,** pp. 623–35).

PBS specifically instructed Hookham in March 1813: "Do not let the title page be printed before the body of the Poem. I have a motto to introduce from Shakespeare, & a Preface." He added: "Let only 250 Copies be printed. A small neat Quarto, on fine paper & so as to catch the aristocrats: They will not read it, but their sons & daughters may" (**Letters** I, 361). The title of the poem was thus part of a larger strategy aimed at "catching" the children of aristocrats that perhaps included choosing as a publisher Hookham, who was well known for publishing and selling children's stories. Queen Mab, originally a Celtic goddess of sovereignty (see below), had become by the fifteenth century in Welsh and English legend the queen of the fairies described by Ben Jonson (*The Althorp Entertainment* [1603]), Drayton (*Nymphidia* [1627]), and, perhaps most memorably, Shakespeare in *Romeo and Juliet* (I.iv.50–94), from which PBS was planning to draw his original "motto" for the volume. In the eighteenth century, Queen Mab, like Mother Goose or Mother Bunch, was the titular character of such fairy tale collections as *Queen Mab: Containing a Select Collection of Only the Best, Most Instructive, and Entertaining Tales of the Fairies . . . to which is Added, a Fairy Tale in the Ancient English Style by Dr. Parnell: and Queen Mab's Song* (3rd ed., London: J. Dodsley, 1782), which had been published in 1759 and 1770 (see *SCV*, 283–84), and *Queen Mab, or Fairy Adventures; Being a Series of Incidents Wonderful and Surprising: In Which Are Painted the Happiness Attendant on Virtue, and the Punishment that necessarily follows Vice* (London: William Lane, 1795).

But PBS was also well aware of what Stuart Curran has described as the "transgressive potentiality of the realm of fairy," which was being exploited especially by women writers (*The Cambridge Companion to British Romanticism* [Cambridge: Cambridge UP, 1993], 188n). In this regard, Charlotte Dacre's "Queen Mab and Her Fays," which appeared in her *Hours of Solitude* volume (1805), might have influenced PBS's choice of title. Moreover, PBS would have found suggestive Mab's origin as the Celtic goddess of sovereignty (Maeave, Medb) to whom Irish kings needed to be ritually married in order to legitimize their reign. In addition to sovereignty, Mab presided over war, sexuality, and intoxication. All of these associations are pertinent to PBS's *QM,* from its formal use of Mab's association with intoxication and dreams to its thematic preoccupation with issues of legitimate sovereignty, war, and sexuality. Although we cannot be sure that PBS knew of Mab's legendary origins, he could easily have learned of them during his stays in Ireland and Wales.

Whereas the title of PBS's volume remained unchanged, circumstances arose that complicated other aspects of his original plan for publishing it: Thomas Hookham refused to have his name put on it or to distribute it, and the (still unidentified) printer refused to allow PBS to use *his* name. To judge from Harriet Shelley's letter to Catherine Nugent of 21 May 1813, which indicates that presswork on *QM* had just begun, Hookham had the poem in his possession for approximately two months before sending it to the printer. During the interim, Hookham must have decided to withdraw as publisher, impressing the Shelleys with the dangers posed by publication. Hence, PBS's initial assertion to Hookham in August 1812 that "a Poem is safe, the iron-souled Attorney general would scarcely dare to attack 'genus irritabile vatum'" (**Letters** I, 324) gave way to the alarm that Harriet Shelley expressed to Catherine Nugent in May 1813: "Queen Mab . . . must not be published under pain of death, because it is too much against every existing establishment. It is to be privately distributed to his [PBS's] friends, and some copies sent over to America." "Do you [know] any one that would wish for so dangerous a gift?" she asked Nugent; "If you do, tell me of them, and they shall not be forgotten" (**Letters** I, 368). Hookham's nephew later reported that the publisher and PBS quarreled over *QM,* presumably about the publisher's withdrawal of his name, but perhaps over money or other arrangements for the poem's production (see *1927* VIII, xxxiii). PBS may also have had words with the printer, who apparently was not willing to put himself at risk by including his name on the first and last leaf in the volume containing text, as required by British law. As a result of these problems, PBS was forced to declare himself the printer of *QM* and to distribute the volume privately among those he trusted, rather than to have it formally published.

Once PBS realized how much potential legal danger accompanied the publication, he may have decided to forgo the motto from Shakespeare and, possibly, the Preface for a different kind of paratext that might better protect him from prosecution while nonetheless maintaining the integrity of his radical politics. That is, his choice of the subtitle "A Philosophical Poem," as well as the reference on the title page to his lengthy and learned notes, and the printing of epigraphs in three foreign languages from Voltaire, Lucretius, and Archimedes may have been designed to show that the volume was *not* intended to corrupt children or lower-class readers, but was instead for an adult, learned audience. This impression would have been reinforced by the fact that none of the lengthy quotations in foreign languages among the notes was translated into English.

The printed volume was handsomely turned out, although as a crown octavo rather than the quarto PBS had first requested. If, as appears likely from the number of volumes now extant, PBS's instructions to Hookham were followed and only 250 copies of *QM* were printed, then PBS could not have distributed more than some 70 copies himself: Richard Carlile in *The Republican* for 27 December 1822 advertised that he had purchased for sale all of the 180 remaining copies of the original 1813 edition (*Shelley Library*, 49). In all but one known copy of the remaining books, PBS's name appears on the title page as the author and printer, with the address "23, Chapel Street, Grosvenor Square," the home of his father-in-law, John Westbrook, with whom PBS stayed briefly at the beginning of May 1813. The colophon on the final page similarly gives PBS's name as printer and John Westbrook's address.

The one anomalous title page we have discovered, which appears in Fanny Imlay's copy of **QM**—now located at the John Work Garrett Library of Johns Hopkins University—gives PBS as the publisher, not the printer, and has no subtitle or epigraphs. Bibliographical analysis, however, has revealed this page to be a twentieth-century substitution for the missing original title page, which PBS had, no doubt, removed from the volume, along with the colophon. Indeed, even though PBS chose as recipients those likely to sympathize with his politics, he customarily removed from the copies he distributed the title page, colophon, and the dedicatory poem to Harriet Shelley (**To Harriet *******), the first two of which, in particular, could have identified him as legally responsible for the volume. (For a partial list of known recipients, none of whom was in America, or as later rumored, Germany, see White, *Shelley* I, 653 n.11.) That the publisher, printer, and other friends of PBS who must have counseled this prudence were correct in their warnings about the dangers of publishing the work is evident from the Lord Chancellor's later judgment against PBS in the case for custody of his motherless children, which set legal precedents in English law (for the text of the relevant Chancery Papers, see Medwin, *Life*, ed. Forman, 463–86). The outcome of that case, in turn, acted as a deterrent to PBS's publisher Charles Ollier and printer Buchanan McMillan—and probably to PBS himself—when it came time to publish **Laon and Cythna.**

Because **QM** was in press by the end of May 1813, Shelleyans widely—and perhaps incorrectly—have assumed that the volume appeared by June or July 1813. But there is no concrete evidence of this. Thomas Jefferson Hogg's account of **QM,** which characteristically blurs chronology, seems to place the appearance of the volume in the fall of 1812—while Shelley was living in London—months before the poem was even completed. Writing more than forty years after the events he describes, Hogg could easily be mistaking that fall for the fall of 1813, during which PBS returned to London in early December. Shortly thereafter, William Godwin recorded the first known reading of the printed volume on 26 December 1813 (Bod, Abinger, Dep. e.212, f. 11r). Godwin would almost certainly have received a copy of the poem as soon as one was ready, for he was in constant communication with PBS between June and December 1813 (see **Letters** I, 381). A further piece of evidence indicates a later date for the printed volume: upon PBS's return to London in early December 1813, his emotional estrangement from Harriet

Shelley was evident. The removal of the dedicatory poem to her in most of the copies PBS distributed may have been partly to obscure his identity, but it also suggests, as Ingpen remarks, that the **QM** volume "was put into circulation at the end of 1813, or possibly the beginning of 1814, when Shelley and Harriet were drifting apart, or that the copies so treated by him were distributed during, or after, that painful period of his life" (*Shelley in England,* II, 406).

Several reasons, either separately or in combination, could explain why **QM** may have been delayed in the press. First, PBS may not have completed the notes as quickly as he originally hoped. Second, PBS may have had trouble convincing Hookham's printer to proceed with the poem, given the legal dangers, and may even have been forced to engage a new printer. Third, once it was decided that **QM** would not be formally published and sold, PBS would have had to bear the entire cost of the printing. As Harriet Shelley noted to Catherine Nugent, the Dublin printer of **Esd** had refused in the summer of 1812 to continue printing the poems until he was fully paid. Harriet Shelley commented: "Now such a demand is seldom made, as printers are never paid till the profits arising from the sale of the work come in . . ." (**Letters** I, 320), but in the case of **QM,** there were to be no sales from which profits could be garnered. In 1813, PBS was chronically short of cash from spring to fall. A post-obit loan that raised £500 early in October 1813 apparently lasted less than two months, and part of that may have gone towards paying the printer's bill. According to White, Hookham seems to have been concerned in PBS's sale of the post-obit (*Shelley* I, 664; see also PBS's letter to Hookham on the subject, **Letters** I, 377). Thus, although we can be certain only that the volume appeared from the press between the beginning of June and Godwin's reading of it on 26 December 1813, there is reason to suppose that it did not appear before the fall of 1813.

Rather than consisting of the ten cantos and 2,800 lines that PBS initially projected, **QM** as published contains nearly 2,300 lines organized into nine cantos. This structure allowed him to capitalize on the symbolic resonance of the gestational cycle for a poem about human rebirth and renewal, just as Edward Young in *Night Thoughts* and William Blake in *The Four Zoas* had earlier used the form of the nine book epic. (Harriet Shelley was, in fact, pregnant with Ianthe [b. 23 June 1813] during most of the time PBS composed **QM.**) Added to the nine cantos of the poem proper are seventeen prose notes, of which eleven comment relatively briefly upon the text of the poem, while six extensively discuss political economy (**Note 7**), marriage and free love (**Note 9**), Necessity (**Note 12**), religion (two long critiques: **Notes 13** and **15**), and vegetarianism (**Note 17**), respectively. For some of these notes, PBS drew on material he had previously written: *The Necessity of Atheism* (1811; **Note 13**), *Letter to Lord Ellenborough* (1812, **Note 15**), and two poems originally intended for **Esd** (*Falshood and Vice: a Dialogue* [**Note 3**] and *To*

Harriet, **lines 58–69** [**Note 16**]). He may also have used material from his unpublished and subsequently lost collection of "moral and metaphysical essays" on which he worked from 1811 to 1812 (see *Letters* I, 130, 324; *YS,* 402–3). And, if we are correct in dating the publication of *Natural Diet* (see the Commentary for **Note 17**), virtually the entire text of that pamphlet was reprinted in *QM,* with some minor revisions and deletions.

PBS began readying the notes for the press in February 1813 (*Letters* I, 354) and may have continued to work on them until shortly before the volume appeared. Whereas the first four cantos, which he drafted before the hiatus in composition, contain only three short notes, there are six notes alone for **Canto V** (in which PBS attacks "Commerce") and eight more for the following four cantos. It was already commonplace for long poems to be accompanied by notes; they are, for instance, in several of PBS's favorite works by Erasmus Darwin and Robert Southey, as well as Thomas Love Peacock's *Genius of the Thames.* Such a composite production of texts and notes as *QM* provides families, as Marilyn Butler remarks, "for their money a book that works for several family members at once—a story, a serious textbook, even an anthology of materialist thinking, for the footnotes employ antireligious matter culled from natural science and infidel mythography" (*Poet and Legislator,* 162). PBS, moreover, clearly felt that the addition of notes to *QM* would provide him with a "safe" opportunity of "propagating my principles, which I decline to do syllogistically in a poem"; or, as he phrases it in a following letter, "The notes will be long philosophical, & Anti Christian.—this will be unnoticed in a Note" (*Letters* I, 350, 361).

As documented in the Commentary, PBS created in the notes a compendium of eighteenth-century radical thought, along with some of its most prominent sources in the Renaissance and in classical antiquity. These notes, printed in the same size typeface as the poem and taking up almost half of the volume, were more incendiary than the poem itself, which they served to radicalize further, as an indignant Hogg observed:

It was unwise, injudicious, imprudent, unfortunate, and injurious to have appended notes, so-called philosophical. The notes have little to recommend them—little that is original; they consist chiefly of excerpts from the writings of Paine, Godwin, and others. Whatever was startling in these is rendered more offensive by being set out in detached fragments, without the modifications, qualifications, conditions, and softenings, which are found in the works from whence they were taken. . . . But when harsh paradoxes were brought out strongly in separate, segregated passages, the implied adoption of the sentiments and dogmas of their several authors becomes in its nakedness indecent and shocking; and the violent opinions promulgated in the commentary seem to give a meaning to the poem itself which does not in reality belong to it, and could never have been fairly deduced from it. The common proceeding of modern times, that the poet should be at once, and in his own person, both poet and commentator—that he should compose not only verses, but annotations upon his own verses, is preposterous. (*Life,* ed. Wolfe, II, 46)

Perhaps part of Hogg's outrage at the notes can be attributed to the fact that *The Necessity of Atheism,* a tract for which he and PBS were expelled from Oxford and which continued to be a source of embarrassment to him in later life, was reprinted virtually in its entirety in **Note 13.** While Hogg was, no doubt, relieved not to be named as co-author in the note, he clearly saw other reasons to question PBS's originality in the notes as a whole. But PBS was not so much interested in originality as he was in engaging the reader in radical dialectics. He often closely paraphrases or outright copies his sources without acknowledgment, or he misleadingly cites sources as though he had consulted them firsthand when he has merely copied a footnote or a passage indirectly from another source (see Commentary below). If this method permitted PBS to display an erudition he had not fully earned, it enabled him, while only a fledgling, twenty-something poet, to launch a comprehensive "philosophical" critique of British society.

PBS presumably had both strategic and aesthetic reasons for placing the notes in a separate section at the back of the book, rather than as footnotes at the bottom of the page. Such an arrangement was not only cheaper to print, but also permitted him to continue composing the notes while the poem was in press. Moreover, the long footnotes in a volume of poetry, such as the first edition of Southey's *Thalaba,* sometimes overwhelm the text of the poem proper (which is perhaps why they were moved to the back of the book in later editions of *Thalaba* that we have seen), and clearly PBS wanted *QM* to be understood first and primarily as a poem in its own right. He was, on the other hand, also hopeful that much subversive material might go "unnoticed" by the authorities if it were tucked away in the radical primer at the back of the book. His decision to quote in the notes extensive passages in foreign languages without giving translations demonstrates that PBS was not trying to incite the lower classes directly, although they later effectively became part of the audience when pirated editions provided the notes in translation—in which form the notes gradually grew in overall significance. Within ten years of PBS's death, a pirated edition of *QM* by Jane Carlile, the estranged wife of the printer Richard Carlile, actually altered the balance that PBS had tried to create between the poem and the notes by printing the notes at the bottom of the page, placing a premium on the notes themselves. It was in this form that *QM* was subsequently reproduced by most radical pirates and read by working-class audiences (see "Textual Transmission," below).

An important question about the notes concerns their authorship. Rumors that Byron, Leigh Hunt, or some unknown collaborator helped PBS prepare the notes, or was responsible for them all, were rife in the early 1820s when the first pirated editions made *QM* widely available. Byron, in fact, felt compelled to deny this rumor in the Appendix to *The Two Foscari* (1821): "Another charge made, I am told, in the 'Literary Gazette' is, that I wrote the notes to 'Queen Mab;' a work which I never saw till some time after its publication. . . . I never wrote a line of the notes, nor ever saw them except in their published form" (Byron, *CPW* VI, 222). William Bengo Collyer in a review of *QM* in *The Investigator, or Quarterly Magazine* (1822) went so far as to claim that the notes "have been attributed to his early and constant friend, Lord Byron; but we are satisfied that rumour does the noble Lord some wrong, as they are the production of a much less able, and an obscurer man. We saw him once some years ago, but whether he is still to be seen, or is no more, we know not" (*RR*, Part B, III, 366). And a copy of *QM* owned by Forman contained a note by a William Ellis Wallis (unidentified; not in *DNB*) stating, "this was written by Shelley at the age of 19," and "the notes at the end are by Leigh Hunt" (Sales Catalogue of Forman's Library, Sale Part II, lot 931, p. 136).

These rumors ultimately can be traced to one main piece of evidence: the presence of eight indicator hands (☞) placed in the right-hand margins amidst **Notes 3, 7, 9, 10, 12, 13** (2), and **15.** Such signs commonly distinguished the work of otherwise anonymous contributors to radical periodicals and were also used as recognized signatures for more "legitimate" journalists. Leigh Hunt, for example, used the indicator hand to mark his personal contributions to *The Examiner,* a fact that no doubt suggested the rumor that he had authored the notes, as reported by Wallis. The hands are mentioned, moreover, in both *The Literary Gazette* and *The Investigator* as distinguishing, respectively, Byron's contributions and those of the "much less able and obscurer man." PBS's contemporaries, in other words, attached significance to the hands, even if they could not decipher their meaning: even Godwin, the first known reader of *QM,* recorded in his journal for 26 December 1813 a note to query PBS about the meaning of the hands. More recently, this issue has been reopened by William St. Clair, who notes that all the principal pirated editions (except Galignani's) reproduced the hands in their text, as did MWS, and that Richard Carlile retained the hands in the passages he quoted from *QM* in *The Republican* (6 May 1825). St. Clair suggests that the hands may have been included simply for decoration or for emphasis, but "if the latter they were curiously chosen and they point out to the margin of the page instead of inwards." Instead, he offers up the possibility that PBS, "who was not yet fully familiar with the works of his philosophical predecessors, did employ an assistant from the radical underworld to compile these learned notes on his behalf," adding that Erasmus Perkins (pseudonym for George Cannon), the ultraradical behind the articles on *QM* in the *Theological Inquirer* in 1815 and at least one of the early piracies (see below) would be an obvious candidate, along with Perkins's friend R. C. Fair (*The Godwins and the Shelleys,* 517–18).

We see no evidence in style or rhetoric, however, to attribute the notes to anyone other than PBS himself. Nor is there any consistent pattern in the placement of the hands to suggest the interpolation of material from others. Moreover, those closest to PBS never questioned his authorship of the notes. For example, in denying that he authored the notes, Byron, who probably discussed the subject with PBS, wrote: "No one knows better than their real author, that his opinions and mine differ materially upon the metaphysical portion of that work; though in common with all who are not blinded by baseness and bigotry, I highly admire the poetry of that and his other publications" (Byron, *CPW* VI, 222–23). When Edward Williams read *QM* in June 1822, he also understood PBS to be the author of the notes: "the notes are [as] subtle and elegant as he could now write—" (*Maria Gisborne and Edward E. Williams, Shelley's Friends: Their Journals and Letters*, ed. Frederick L. Jones [Norman: U of Oklahoma P, 1951], 156). And, finally, MWS wrote in *1840*, "The notes also are reprinted entire; not because they are models of reasoning or lessons of truth; but because Shelley wrote them." Because MWS proceeds to say how much PBS had changed his opinions and because she included his letter to *The Examiner* distancing himself from *QM*, there is reason to assume that she, an early recipient of *QM*, had talked with him about the notes at some point.

If the hands do not suggest that others authored the notes, there is little evidence in the way they are placed to suggest that they are for emphasis or for decoration, St. Clair's other two alternatives. Whereas we can offer no decisive answer on the function of the hands, we believe it possible that PBS placed them in the text (mostly next to notes actionable at law) so as to be able to blame someone else for their content, just as he claimed that the salacious part of **Epithalamium** in **PF** was written by "a friend's mistress." He may have wanted, in effect, to create the illusion of a contributor, perhaps partly as a prank and partly for legal protection. If so, to judge from contemporary evidence, he was wildly successful. For the significance of the hands in light of PBS's career-long paratextual practices, see Fraistat, "The Material Shelley: Who Gets the Finger in *Queen Mab?*" *The Wordsworth Circle* 33.1 (winter 2002): 33–36. Whatever the ultimate meaning of the indicator hands, we believe that they are a significant part of *QM*, and we have reproduced them in our text of the notes.

Sources and Influences

Within the Commentary we have attempted to document the most important sources and influences on particular ideas, lines, and passages from the extraordinary range of resources PBS tapped to produce *QM;* and, where possible, we have identified the particular edition he used. The extensive scope of these resources becomes apparent in, for instance, the virtual crash course in the classics and in history that PBS undertook in December 1812. Largely under the guidance of two important new friends—Godwin and

Peacock—he placed orders with Thomas Hookham and with Thomas "Clio" Rickman for a total of more than sixty books, almost half of which were classical works (**Letters** I, 342, 344–45; see **Letters** I, 316–18 for PBS's prior resistance to renewed study of classics). The tenor of this reading can be indicated by PBS's comment to Hookham that "any works except those absolutely cosmopolitical or anti-Christian I shall not want unless I write for.—" (**Letters** I, 340).

However reluctantly, PBS turned to history as a necessary prerequisite for informed social critique: "I am determined to apply myself to a study that is hateful & disgusting to my very soul, but which is above all studies necessary for him who would be listened to as a mender of antiquated abuses.—I mean that record of crimes & miseries—History" (**Letters** I, 340). Among the histories he ordered were those by Thucydides, Plutarch, Gibbon, Hume, Vertot, and Robertson (on Scotland, America, and India). PBS also turned to such classical-minded critics of contemporary society as Lord Monboddo, Sir William Drummond, and John Horne Tooke—perhaps at the recommendation of Peacock, as Marilyn Butler suggests (*Peacock Displayed: A Satirist in His Context* [London: Routledge & Kegan Paul, 1971], 38). Other authors of books PBS ordered during this time that may have influenced **QM** include Spinoza, Cabanis, Erasmus Darwin, Diderot, Condorcet, and Thomas Trotter.

However, the three primary intellectual influences on **QM** have long been recognized to be Godwin's philosophical anarchism, particularly as espoused in *Enquiry Concerning Political Justice* but also in *The Enquirer;* Paine's republicanism, especially as articulated in the various parts of *The Rights of Man* and *The Age of Reason;* and the materialist atheism of Holbach, particularly in *Système de la nature* but also in *Le bon sens,* and (perhaps) *Histoire critique de Jésus Christ* (known to English radicals as *Ecce Homo*). In all three of these writers, and especially in Paine, PBS found a powerful negative critique of state religion and monarchy; in Godwin, he found additionally both a critique of early industrial capitalism and a utopian discourse that he would revise to his own purposes; and in Holbach he found not only the most rigorously materialist critique of Christianity perhaps ever to be written but also a general distillation of eighteenth-century French materialist thought that drew heavily on such *philosophes* as Helvétius, Diderot, D'Alembert, and La Mettrie.

PBS apparently was first introduced to Godwin's *Pol. Justice* by his friend and mentor, Dr. James Lind, who served as physician to the royal family at Windsor (Hogg, *Life,* ed. Wolfe, I, 313–14). And it is fairly certain that PBS knew Paine's writings well by the time he was at Oxford: within a year after his expulsion, he was planning to publish selected extracts from Paine's works (**Letters** I, 255). As Cameron notes, PBS must have read about Holbach's *Système* in Barruel's *Memoirs Illustrating the History of Jacobinism* while he was at Oxford, where, Hogg claimed, Barruel's book was one of PBS's favorites (*YS*, 409 n137; *Life* I, 376). However, there is no record that PBS read *Système* itself until 3 June 1812, when in a letter to Godwin he wrote that he had just finished the book and thought it "a work of uncommon powers" (***Letters*** I, 303), a judgment with which Godwin—whose own religious faith was apparently rocked and transformed by Holbach—would no doubt have agreed (see *YS*, 192). Within two months, an admiring PBS had already begun translating *Système* into English (***Letters*** I, 325).

Holbach's influence on **QM** needs some clarification because Shelley scholars have not recognized how deeply indebted Holbach himself was to the tradition of eighteenth-century French clandestine texts circulated only in manuscript. Like PBS himself, Holbach sometimes skirted the line between compiling and plagiarizing the thought of others. Sometimes he stepped over the line: Holbach's *Histoire critique de Jésus Christ* has often been connected to **QM**, but never with the recognition that Holbach himself plagiarized virtually the entire text from an anonymous clandestine manuscript of a similar name, purportedly written by "Salvador, a Jew" (see *Ecce Homo*, 13–17). To understand and examine fully Shelley's relationship to "Holbach," then, is to understand a much larger and more complicated network of texts, most of which were published anonymously or pseudonymously and many of which borrowed generously from the others.

Holbach, indeed, published his own work under pseudonyms. Thus, contemporary French editions of Holbach's *Système* gave as its author "M. Mirabaud." Although Shelley knew this to be a pseudonym, he believed the real author to be Helvétius, a fact scholars sometimes explain by noting that Shelley probably received this information from Godwin, who believed the same thing. However, there were at least two English translations of *Système* with subtitles indicating that they are from the French of Helvétius: one published by J. Murdoch in 1799 and one by Daniel Isaac Eaton that is advertised in the back of the *Trial of Daniel Isaac Eaton* (London: Eaton, 1812), a book PBS appears to have read. Hence, it seems likely that among the English radical community Helvétius was widely thought to have written *Système* and that it was consequently being read and discussed in relation to his known works.

PBS, of course, resists as well as deploys his sources, and his use of Godwin, Paine, and Holbach is further leavened and tempered by elements of Hume's skepticism, Volney's attacks on empire, Newton's physics, Wollstonecraft's feminism, Monboddo's naturist counterculturalism, and John Frank Newton's vegetarianism—all brought into an original synthesis that constitutes the cosmopolitical and anti-Christian revolutionary discourse of **QM**. The large role that science—from astronomy to biology to geology— plays in **QM** can be understood largely in terms of the revolutionary possibilities offered by scientific discourse of the eighteenth century. As Alan Bewell notes, "prior to the events that took place in America and France during the latter part of the eighteenth century, 'revolution,' both in word and concept, was less frequently encountered in political theory than in astronomy, geometry, geography, and especially geology. By the 1790s, geology had assumed the status of *the* preeminent science of revolution" (*Wordsworth and the Enlightenment: Nature, Man, and Society in the Experimental Poetry* [New Haven: Yale UP, 1989], 246). Through such important early influences as Dr. James Lind and Adam Walker (who gave stirring lectures on science at both Syon House and Eton), as well as the works of Erasmus Darwin, and extensive other reading that included frequent resort to William Nicholson's *The British Encyclopedia* and Abraham Rees's *Cyclopædia*, PBS was well acquainted with the revolutionary potential of eighteenth-century scientific discourse.

The major influences on the structure and style of **QM** are also well known. For its epic survey of past, present, and future, the poem is indebted to Constantin Volney's *Les ruines, ou méditations sur les révolutions des empires* (1791), Jean Antoine Condorcet's *Esquisse d'un tableau historique des progrès de l'esprit humain* (published in London in 1795 as *Outline of an Historical View of the Progress of the Human Mind*), and, perhaps, as Stuart Curran has suggested, Joel Barlow's visionary epic *The Columbiad* (*Poetic Form and British Romanticism* [New York: Oxford UP, 1986], 172). *The Columbiad* (published in America in 1807 and England in 1809) is a ten-book epic, the form that PBS had originally planned for **QM;** however, it was originally published as *The Vision of Columbus* (1787, both in America and England), an epic in nine books, which is precisely the form **QM** eventually took. Whereas there is no direct evidence that PBS read Barlow, there is reason to believe that he may have known *The Columbiad* in either one or both of its forms, given its kindred politics and poetic ambitions, as well as the public attention it received in London, which included a long review by Francis Jeffrey in the *Edinburgh Review* (15 [1809]: 24–40). Even without directly influencing PBS, Barlow's *The Vision of Columbus,* with its historical survey and its creation of a world federation that discards all outworn superstitions was, as Curran argues, quite likely an important influence on Volney's *Ruines,* through which its influence would have extended to **QM.**

Cameron describes Volney's *Ruines* as "one of the revolutionary handbooks of the age" (*YS,* 243), and PBS seems to have put his young wife to school on it, according to Hogg, who recounts that it was "one of Harriet's textbooks, which she used to read aloud for our instruction and edification" (*Life,* ed. Wolfe, I, 373). An intellectual leader of the French Revolution and member of the States-General, Volney advocated a Holbachian atheism aimed at unseating established governments and religion of any kind. In so doing, he offered PBS what Marilyn Butler has called "a powerful, proto-Foucauldian critique of discourse as yet another agency of existing power, one that includes but is not identical with religion" (*Poet and Legislator,* 160), but so, for that matter, had Holbach. Perhaps more importantly, Volney offered PBS a successful model of infidel mythography that was quintessentially both cosmopolitical and anti-Christian.

In the framework of Volney's work, a "Genius of Tombs and Ruins" separates the soul from the body of a "Traveller" who has been meditating over the ruins of past empires. The Genius then bears the Traveller's soul into the heavens for a celestial overview and a radical interrogation of the past and the present, ending with the vision of a general assembly of nations, under the guidance of a "Lawgiver," who, after allowing representatives of all human religions to present their mutually contradicting and hence self-defeating arguments, proclaims to the assembled people of the Earth the banishment of religion from the world and announces in triumph: "O kings and priests! you may suspend, yet for a while, the solemn publication of the laws of nature; but it is no longer in your power to annihilate or to subvert them" (*Ruins* II, 227). Almost certainly, PBS derived from *Ruines* the dream-vision framework of **QM,** in which the sleeping Ianthe's soul is separated from her body and taken to the heavenly Hall of Spells by Queen Mab for a cosmic, Volneyan perspective on human history. In **QM,** unlike in *Ruines,* both the nominal protagonist, Ianthe, and her teacher are female, a fact that, along with a few other differences, suggests the additional influence of Sir William Jones's *The Palace of Fortune, An Indian Tale,* in which a young woman named Maia is taken by the Goddess Fortune to a heavenly palace in a golden chariot "By two fair yokes of starry peacocks drawn . . ." (*Poems, Consisting Chiefly of Translations from the Asiatick Languages* . . . [Oxford: Clarendon Press, 1772], 11). However, there are few other salient resemblances between **QM** and Jones's Orientalist fantasy.

PBS's letter of 28 October 1811 to Elizabeth Hitchener provides an interesting biographical gloss on the scene of instruction shaping the narrative framework of **QM:** "If Harriet be not at sixteen all that you are at a more advanced age, assist me to mould a really noble soul into all that can make it[s] nobleness useful and lovely.—Lovely it is now, or I am the weakest slave of error—" (**Letters** I, 163). There is also, of course, a long literary history of women being on the receiving end of the scene of instruction, a particularly interesting and apposite example of which is the Marquise of G**** in Fontenelle's *Entretiens sur la pluralité des mondes* (1686), who is taught over the course of the book the radical tenets of new science. And goddesses of one form or another have conventionally served as instructors, especially in the genre of dream visions, though PBS's didactic Queen Mab bears more than a little resemblance to Erasmus Darwin's Botanic Goddess, the similarly portentous narrator and interpreter of history in *The Botanic Garden* (1791). For the use and mechanics of dream vision, PBS may also be partially indebted to Cicero's "Somnium Scipionis" ("Scipio's Dream") from Book VI of *De re publica,* a staple in the texts for schoolboys of Shelley's day.

In taking Ianthe heavenward for a cosmic view of human history, PBS may also have had in mind the vision of human history from the mountaintop that Michael gives to Adam in the last two books of *Paradise Lost,* the mountaintop Pisgah vision through which Moses sees the promised land, and the Lucretian pinnacle described at the beginning of *De rerum natura,* II, from which the delusions of humanity become apparent. PBS would have found the Lucretian pinnacle dramatically revisited in an important passage of Mary Wollstonecraft's *A Vindication of the Rights of Woman* (1792) that begins: "Let me now as from an eminence survey the world stripped of all its false delusive charms. The clear atmosphere enables me to see each object in its true point of view, while my heart is still" (Chap. 5, sec. v; *WMWV,* 179). Similarly, there is a passage in *Pol. Justice* that, although previously unmentioned in this connection, may have contributed to the framework of **QM:** "We are able in imagination to go out of ourselves, and become impartial spectators of the system of which we are a part. We can then make an estimate of our intrinsic and absolute value; and detect the imposition of that self-regard, which would represent our own interest as of as much value as that of all the world beside. The delusion being thus sapped, we can, from time to time at least, fall back in idea into our proper post, and cultivate those views and affections which must be most familiar to the most perfect intelligence" (*Pol. Justice,* ed. Priestley IV.x; I, 427–28). One further possible influence, as *1989* points out, is Southey's *The Vision of the Maid of Orleans,* originally a part of Book IX of *Joan of Arc* that was removed after the first edition (1795) and published as a separate poem. In a dream, Joan encounters a Spenserean vision of Despair, to which she does not yield, and is subsequently comforted by the spirit of her beloved Theodore, now an angel, who takes her into space and eventually leads her to a vision of an equalitarian futurity much like the one predicted in **Cantos VIII** and **IX** of **QM** (see the Commentary to **VIII.50–52**).

The versification of **QM,** with its irregular blank verse, has long been credited to Southey's metrical experiment in *Thalaba the Destroyer* (1801), but Southey himself credits his friend Frank Sayers, a Norwich physician and man of letters: "The reason why the irregular, rhymeless lyrics of Dr. Sayers were preferred for 'Thalaba' was that the freedom and variety of such verse were suited to the story" (Preface to the *Curse of Kehama, 1838,* in *The Poetical Works of Robert Southey,* 10 vols. [Boston: Little, Brown, 1860], VIII, 6; hereafter *PW*). Sayers authored several gothic verse dramas based on "Nothern Mythology," four of which are collected in *Poems* (1792), along with several miscellaneous lyrics. Most relevant to the meter of Southey's *Thalaba* is the drama *Starno,* in which all of the chorus's dialogue is unrhymed and in varied meter, a principle for which Sayers argues in the essay "Of English Metres" in *Disquisitions Metaphysical and Literary* (1793): "It appears then that the English language is not incapable of receiving forms of metre which are sufficiently harmonious without the repetition of similar sounds; if the example of the poets whom I have mentioned were followed by others, our attachment to rime might at length be diminished, and a greater ease and variety might be introduced into our poetical compositions" (137). Chief among the few examples cited by Sayers is Milton's choruses in *Samson Agonistes,* the model to which PBS ultimately pointed in justifying his own metrical experiments in **QM**. PBS wrote to Hogg, with whom he had been discussing the versification of **QM:** "With some restrictions I have taken your advice, tho I have not been able to bring myself to rhyme. The didactic is in blank heroic verse, & the descriptive in blank lyrical measure. If authority is of any weight in support of this singularity, Miltons Samson Agonistes, the Greek Choruses, & (you will laugh) Southeys Thalaba may be adduced.—" (**Letters** I, 352).

Southey himself claimed that "of all the laudatory criticisms with which I have been favored during a long literary life, none ever gratified me more than that of Henry Kirke White upon this occasion, when he observed, that, if any other known measure had been adopted, the poem [*Thalaba*] would have been deprived of half its beauty, and all its propriety" (*PW* VIII, 6). Given Southey's pride in Kirke White's praise and PBS's own interest in both Kirke White and *Thalaba,* it is quite possible that the two poets discussed the subject of metrical experimentation at Keswick during the winter of 1811–1812, with perhaps some mention of Dr. Sayers himself. Throughout **QM** there are also significant echoes of Pope, Thomson, and Gray, but always reworked in a distinctively Shelleyan manner. In its style and structure, its bold mix of revolutionary discourses, its sharp attacks on the established political, religious, economic, and moral order, its attention to the body and to everyday life in such matters as love, marriage, and diet, and its utopian hopes for social renovation, **QM** is a work beholden to many sources but, remarkably, unlike any other.

Textual Transmission

Harry Buxton Forman has memorably described **QM** as "a receptacle wherein he [PBS] enshrined earlier poetical efforts, a mine wherein he dug for later poetical efforts, a work which he did not abandon readily after getting it into print as he did many a better work, and finally a creation which, when he had abandoned *it,* he found by no means disposed to abandon him" (*The Vicissitudes of Shelley's "Queen Mab"* [London: privately printed, 1887], 10). Indeed, **QM** stands at the center of a network of PBS's efforts in poetry and prose, not only incorporating several of his earlier works, as discussed above, but also providing material for later ones. Much of *A **Refutation of Deism*** (1814) was drawn from the notes (see Commentary, *passim*), and PBS heavily revised two copies of **1813,** with the intention of carving up the unpublished poem for a series of subsequent publications, two of which appeared in the *Alastor* volume—*Superstition* and *Dæmon*—and a few of which were abandoned in draft. (The Commentary in Volume III of *CPPBS* will address the *Alastor* volume and *Dæmon*.) Meanwhile, though unpublished, *QM* began to take on a textual life of its own. In 1813, a young Brazilian medical student in Edinburgh, J. Bernardino (corrected from Peacock's erroneous "Baptisto" by Crook and Guiton, *Shelley's Venomed Melody*, 241n) Pereira, whom Shelley knew, began a translation of *QM* into Portuguese, which was to be prefaced by a sonnet celebrating PBS as "Sublime Shelley, cantor di verdade." Unlike the sonnet, the translation was apparently never completed (White, *Shelley* I, 321; *Letters* I, 431).

In 1815, a glowing review of *QM* quoting substantial portions of the poem, accompanied by an "Ode to the Author of Queen Mab" appeared in installments from March through July in the short-lived *Theological Inquirer; or, Polemical Magazine* (*TI*, 1815) produced by the now notorious ultraradical George Cannon ("Erasmus Perkins") and the shoemaker-poet Robert Charles Fair, who appears to have edited the selections (signed "F.") and written the "Ode" (signed "R. C. F."). Some six years later, the team of Cannon and Fair, along with radical pressman William Benbow, produced one of the first piracies of *QM* itself, the so-called "New York" edition (see below). The quotations from *QM* used in *TI* were apparently taken from a copy of the volume that PBS had given to Cannon and/or Fair in 1815, although, in the review, "F." uses the ruse that "the celebrated Kotzebue" had shown *QM* to him in Germany, doubting that "I had seen [it] in my own country, as he considered it too bold a production to issue from the British press" (*TI*, 34). "F." claims to have bought six copies in Berlin shortly thereafter. Evidence suggests that PBS actively collaborated with Cannon and Fair on the selections from his works in *TI*, including the fact that the journal also reprinted *Refutation*, with emendations from PBS's errata list. However, there are no substantive textual changes in the *QM* excerpts. The first installment of the *TI* review itself was substantially reprinted by Benbow in his *John Bull's British Journal* for 11 March 1821, in response to the Clark piracy, perhaps to prepare the ground for Benbow's own piracy (see *UH*, 52).

QM was next brought to public attention, and PBS was first publicly identified as its blasphemous author, during the Chancery custody proceedings in 1817, when the volume was used as damaging evidence against him (although no prosecution was initiated). At about this time, the radical printer Richard Carlile, then in King's Bench Prison awaiting his first trial for blasphemy and seditious libel (for republishing three political parodies by Hone), was impressed enough by *QM* to copy it twice by hand (see *The Republican* for 1 February 1822, *UH*, 96). Carlile subsequently asked PBS for permission to reprint the volume in the summer of 1819, a request that PBS denied. While Carlile at that time deferred to PBS's wishes—"although advised to [publish] it by many of the Author's friends and intimate acquaintance" (*UH*, 97)—a few of his colleagues nevertheless forged ahead. *QM* was, in fact, pirated at least fourteen times in the years between 1821 and 1840, appearing also in larger pirated collections of PBS's poetry, including, in expurgated form, the various *Beauties of Percy Bysshe Shelley*. Of these unauthorized reproductions of the poem, we have focused for our collations on the two important initial piracies in 1821—which laid the groundwork for all of the subsequent ones—and the two later piracies, by John Brooks (1829) and by John Ascham (1834), upon which MWS ultimately depended for her text of *QM*.

QM was first published in an unauthorized edition produced by William Clark (sometimes spelled "Clarke") in 1821. Clark was a longtime shopman in Carlile's shop (both men had worked earlier for the radical William Sherwin's *Political Register*), where perhaps he first became aware of *QM*. Clark apparently approached Leigh Hunt and other of PBS's friends for a copy of *1813* to prepare his piracy. Hunt wrote to the Shelleys on 10–11 July 1821: "Shelley has heard, I suppose, by this time, that the young bookseller who published his *Queen Mab* without leave has been prosecuted by the Society for the Suppression of Vice (SSV). We all told him he would, and I was doubly glad that I had refused him the use of a copy for his purpose; for I had no right, of course, to do such a thing without Shelley's leave, and concluded, upon the whole, he would not like. Indeed, when I found that the work was out, I felt remorse at not having interfered more actively" (*The Correspondence of Leigh Hunt*, ed. [Thornton Hunt] [London: Smith, Elder and Co., 1862], I, 166). The Clark edition, which exists in several states, presents a complicated publication history, but the facts appear to be as follows: Clark published sometime between January and early March 1821 an "elegant octavo" edition of *QM* (reviewed in William Benbow's *John Bull's British Journal* on 11 March), which was intended to be uniform in appearance with PBS's other published works, and priced high enough (at 12*s*. 6*d*. in boards) for the unnamed author of *Reply to the Anti-Matrimonial Hypothesis and Supposed Atheism of Percy Byssche [sic] Shelley as Laid Down in Queen Mab* (London: Clark, 1821) to claim justifiably that the edition was intended for the "literary world; . . . the splendid edition you have published, plainly indicates you did not intend to circulate it among those whom a certain portion of the press would call the 'rabble readers'" (p. iii). Nonetheless, shortly after publishing this volume, Clark was indicted by the SSV and convicted by a jury for publishing an "Atheistical libel." He was subsequently sentenced, on 19 November 1822, to four months in Cold Bath Fields Prison, despite his abject behavior throughout his ordeal: in an affidavit put before the court at his sentencing hearing, Clark stated that he had published *QM* "as a literary or poetical curiousity [sic]" for pecuniary reasons only; that he had printed and published *A Reply to the Anti-Matrimonial Hypothesis of Queen Mab* so as to answer the doctrines of the poem; and that as soon as the SSV initiated his prosecution "he offered to Mr. Pritchard, the agent of the Society, to give up the whole impression; that he wrote to Mr. Wilberforce, one of the members of the same Society, making the same offer, and entreating his merciful consideration of the case, but received from Mr. Wilberforce only the verbal answer, that deponent was not a person to be treated with, and must go to trial; . . ." (see the account in *The Monthly Repository* [*MR*] for November 1822, p. 717).

Although Shelley scholars have always assumed that Clark was both printer and publisher of the piracy—as is indicated on the title page of his edition—no one notes that Clark himself testified otherwise at his sentencing hearing. When asked to remand to the court all of his remaining copies of *QM*, Clark replied that "he was prepared to give up the only two copies which were in his own possession but that all the remaining copies had been detained by the printer for a debt of £50, which he [Clark] owed him, and which were now selling at the *machine*, of which his Lordship was no doubt aware, for the benefit of the printer, and not for his benefit" (*MR*, 717). When pressed by the court to reveal the identity of the printer, Clark refused, maintaining that "under the agreement into which they originally entered, he could not fairly give him up to prosecution. He would rather suffer any punishment himself than be guilty of such a breach of faith" (*MR*, 717). One week later, Clark returned to court with twenty-five copies of *QM*, claiming that they were the only ones that remained unsold. Although Clark was practicing some form of subterfuge on the court (much of his unsold stock actually wound up in the hands of Richard Carlile, for which see below), his claim that he was not the actual printer of the volume rings true and coincides with other evidence.

In an article in *The Republican* for 1 February 1822, Richard Carlile makes clear that the financial risk for Clark's piracy was not undertaken by Clark himself but by others (*UH*, 96), chief among whom was probably Thomas Moser, a printer identified by William St. Clair as providing Carlile himself with credit and as helping Carlile's wife run his shop when Carlile was imprisoned (*The Godwins and the Shelleys*, 515). Moser's initials, are, in fact, set in Gothic type above the colophon of the Clark piracy, suggesting in light of Clark's testimony that Moser was not only a financial backer of the edition, but also the actual printer. Carlile probably took over Clark's unsold sheets at least in part for Moser's financial relief; he sold them them under his own imprint by tipping in a new title page and pasting in a new colophon (*UH*, 96). Forman claims that about twenty-five of such copies were issued by Carlile without the notes (*Shelley Library*, 49). As Carlile was to discover to his disgust, however, the Clark edition came in many different forms: at some point Clark began producing an inexpensive octavo version of *QM* and he attempted to cut his losses after the prosecution by further reissuing *QM* "at little better than waste paper price," according to Carlile, who noted that these copies—including those he had inadvertently sold under his own name—though advertised as "perfect," had been expurgated, with "all those words and sentences which some simpleton considered libellous" excised from the text of the poem and notes (*UH*, 98).

As our collation indicates, the Clark edition (collated as *1821.CLA*) is a fairly careful attempt to reprint *1813*, with few substantive conjectural emendations aimed at correcting errors of the press or at "improving" PBS's meaning or style, although it does frequently alter the punctuation in small ways (e.g., adding a second or third comma in a series of three parallel elements). The Clark edition omits on its title page both the subtitle and the epigraphs; it sometimes omits the dedicatory poem to Harriet (as in the copy of Clark described to PBS), which in other copies appears in the front, and in still others, just after the notes; and it provides translations in footnotes for the passages in French, Latin, and Greek in the notes, an important change that opened the text up for what Clark refers to as "the general reader" (91). While the author of these translations is unknown, a penciled note in a copy of the Clark piracy at the British Library (shelf number: C.39.e.7) states: "The Greek, Latin, French &c. Notes, [were] translated by a Learned Linguist & scholar a Mr. Fleming," who we believe to be the same "Mr. Fleming" who debated at the British Forum the question: "Ought the conduct of Mr. Carlile [in publishing Paine's writings] . . . be censured . . . or approved . . . ." Fleming's opening speech and reply in this debate were published in pamphlet form by Carlile himself in 1819.

The expurgated Clark edition (collated as *1821.CLAX* when it varies from *1821.CLA*) appears in a few different states, but most commonly deletes text from fifteen pages of the poem and notes, sometimes silently and sometimes indicating the cuts with dashes (see Collations and Commentary for **Cantos IV, VI, VII, VIII, IX,** and **Notes 2, 9, 15,** and **17**). In its unexpurgated form, the Clark piracy established the basic text of the poem, notes, and translations for the several succeeding piracies by the Carlile family, and through them, the later Chartist piracies by Watson (who also worked for Carlile in the early 1820s) and Hetherington. The Clark piracy also had a more important influence than has been previously known on the text of the notorious "New York" edition of **QM.**

Sometime in 1821, Cannon, Fair, and Benbow produced their own piracy of **QM,** supposedly printed and sold in New York, a subterfuge that was not penetrated by their contemporaries and that occasionally still misleads our own. Harry Buxton Forman in 1886 was the first Shelley scholar to suspect that the New York imprint was a ruse intended to evade the kind of prosecution faced by Clark: "I am wholly skeptical about the bona fides of the imprint, and, judging from the general appearance, should think the book was printed in England . . ." (*The Shelley Library*, 51). In 1939 George T. Goodspeed identified William Benbow as the printer of the volume ("The 'First American' *Queen Mab*" in *The Colophon,* New Graphic Series 1). Like the Clark piracy, the "New York" edition appears in several different states: some copies contain both an engraved and a printed title page, others have only one or the other. The copies we have examined that include the printed title page, whether by itself or with the engraved title page, also contain a three-page Preface signed "A Pantheist" and dated "New York, 27th October 1821" as well as PBS's letter to *The Examiner* disavowing Clark's piracy ("out of justice" to PBS); the "Ode to the Author of 'Queen Mab,'" signed "R. C. F." (first published in *TI*); and a sketch outlining the argument of *QM,* acknowledged as taken from the "Theological Enquirer, by Erasmus Perkins" (Cannon's pseudonym). Like the Clark edition, the Benbow/Cannon/Fair edition does not mention the notes on either title page (though it includes them), and it omits both the epigraphs and the dedicatory poem, while retaining the subtitle "A Philosophical Poem," which Clark's edition omits.

After examining two copies of the "New York" edition in his private collection, William St. Clair concluded that the volume consisted originally "only of [the engraved] title page and text . . . When the Preface was added a new printed title page was prepared" (*The Godwins and the Shelleys,* 515). Some copies, however, contain the printed title page but not the engraved title page; and in the copies that we have examined, the engraved title page is always tipped in afterwards whenever it appears with the printed title page. Moreover, the printed title page was itself reset sometime in production (e.g., the subtitle "A Philosophical Poem" appears in Gothic type in some copies and in roman in others). We cannot, therefore, determine exactly how the volume was originally constituted, or even if all "original" copies were uniform because the engraved title page may actually have been produced after the printed title page, the differences among copies being attributable to the way the individual elements of the book were gathered as they were bound or sold, as the Dedication in the Clark piracy appears in different places (or not at all) in various copies. Both the engraved and printed title pages give the printer's address as the "Corner of Chatham Street," but they differ in naming the printer/bookseller: the engraved title page reads, "Printed & Sold by J. Baldwin" (giving the price as "75 cents," as well as the initials of "Erasmus Perkins" in Greek at the bottom of the page), while the printed title page reads "Printed by William Baldwin and Co." There was a printer named Baldwin in New York active at this time, located at 1 Chambers Street, at the corner of Chatham Street (see Goodspeed, "The 'First American' *Queen Mab*"); and although his name was Charles N. Baldwin, the Benbow edition clearly is referring to his shop on the corner of Chatham Street, rather than inventing a location (and perhaps substituting Benbow's own first name for "Charles" on the printed title page). From what is known of Charles Baldwin's list of publications and from the fact that in 1831 he published "attacks on the sociological views of both Frances Wright and Robert Dale Owen, who together published two editions of *Queen Mab*," Goodspeed concluded that Baldwin was an unlikely printer and publisher of the radical *QM*. Goodspeed was not aware that Benbow himself, after being released from jail in 1818, went to New York to join William Cobbett (see Hugh J. Luke, Jr., "An Overlooked Obituary Notice of Shelley," *Papers on Language and Literature* 2 [1966], 39), where Benbow might well have encountered Charles Baldwin. If Baldwin was indeed politically conservative (which is by no means proven by the fact that he published some conservative books), then Benbow and his cohorts might have enjoyed a further in-joke by implicating him as the pirate printer of *QM*.

Benbow's "New York" edition was produced in an inexpensive duodecimo format, as an alternative to the elegant Clark piracy. According to the Preface, apparently written by Cannon (it bears the reversed "P" that Cannon—"Erasmus Perkins"—habitually used to mark his work): "The object of the projectors of this edition, was cheapness and portability, in order that it might come into the hands of all classes of society," adding that "gentlemen" who already possessed copies of PBS's other works in octavo format would find the Clark edition "more suitable to bind for their libraries, the present one being got up merely with a view to give extensive circulation to the principles contained both in the poem and the notes . . . ." The actual roles of the main "projectors" of the "New York" edition can now be clarified. In a presentation copy of the volume at the University of Kentucky Library, R. C. Fair identifies himself as the editor. Benbow was the printer, and Cannon, who appears to be referring to himself as "the Editor . . . superintend[ing] the present edition" within the fictional framework of the Preface, took the main financial risk and was learned enough to have been able to translate the foreign languages in the notes. The three projectors of the fake New York edition may have left a clue to their handiwork in the ads placed at the back of the volume: following ads for an edition of Paine's *Age of Reason* and Moore's *Irish Melodies*—both piracies actually available from Benbow's shop—the final ad is for "That ancient and curious book, 'THE THREE IMPOSTERS,'" an actual notorious French clandestine text with an extremely apropos title. (For an excellent discussion of the *Traitée des trois imposteurs*—the three imposters of the title being Moses, Jesus, and Mohammed—see Margaret C. Jacob, *The Radical Enlightenment: Pantheists, Freemasons and Republicans* [London: George Allen & Unwin, 1981], 215–24).

William St. Clair has questioned the received opinion that the Clark piracy preceded the Benbow, suggesting instead that, whereas the version of the Benbow that contains the Preface referring to Clark obviously came afterward, the earlier issue without prefatory material may have preceded the Clark and consequently would have been the first piracy of *QM* (*The Godwins and the Shelleys,* 515). This hypothesis is, however, wrong, because our collation indicates that the text of the Benbow edition (collated as *1821.BEN*), excepting the translations, is based directly upon the Clark: six clear stanza breaks in *1813* that come at page breaks in Clark (and hence are imperceptible) are missing from Benbow (I.104, V.52, VII.48, VIII.197, and IX.137). Moreover, the expurgated Clark silently omits the word "fiend" in VII.97 and portions of Note 2, all of which are missing from Benbow apparently by mistake, since the Benbow edition makes no other expurgations and is, in fact, ideologically opposed to such omissions, protecting itself from prosecution for printing the entire text through its false imprint. Finally, the Benbow edition mistakenly follows the Clark in mistranslating "cœteris paribus" (in Note 7) as "Making allowances on both sides." These facts, along with all the other similarities in the texts of the two editions (see Collation), provide strong evidence not only that the Clark piracy preceded the Benbow piracy but that the Benbow was based on the text of the expurgated Clark piracy, imperfectly corrected by checks against *1813*.

Collation also shows that the Benbow edition is quicker to emend the text when critical scrutiny suggests a change of word or punctuation, but it is somewhat more carelessly printed, including such howlers as "undeceased" for <u>undiseased</u> and the "brutal pleasures of the chaste" for <u>brutal pleasures of the chase</u> (**Note 17, lines 166** and **393**). Six substantive emendations never before noted—including the change of <u>maiden's sleep</u> to "sleeping maid" (**I.78**) and <u>lore</u> to "store" (**VIII.204**)—were initiated in Benbow's edition and are particularly significant because, although they were not followed in any intervening text, they reappear in MWS's editions (see Commentary for **I.78, IV.7, IV.101, VII.180, VII.192, VIII.204**). Whereas it is remotely possible that all six of these changes were made independently by both Fair and MWS, a far more credible explanation is that MWS, who probably did not acquire a copy of *1813* against which to check her text until after the *1839* text was published, used the Benbow edition to do so and adopted these readings (see the discussion of *1839* below).

As mentioned above, the translations in the Benbow edition are mostly independent of those in Clark (see Commentary, *passim*). Like the translations in Clark, most are placed in footnotes to the text. Unlike those in Clark, however, four long passages in French and Greek are simply replaced in the Benbow with English translations, "with a view to render the book less expensive." Subsequent pirates frequently followed Benbow's precedent and replaced passages in foreign languages in the text proper with English translations, a practice that further radicalized the volume for readers of the lower classes. Two of the more prolific later pirates of **QM**, Charles Daly and William Dugdale (the latter of whom had earlier worked for Benbow), used the translations found in the Benbow edition rather than those in the Clark. Indeed, in its pointed translations, cheap format, and its entire paratextual apparatus, the Benbow edition not only stands as the first piracy to announce openly its use of *QM* for ideological warfare but also remains the most radical of the early piracies.

Our collations confirm and document in greater detail Charles Taylor's conclusion that MWS depended for her *1839* text of *QM* on John Ascham's 1834 pirated edition *The Works of Percy Bysshe Shelley, with His Life*, rather than on the 1829 unauthorized Galignani edition of *The Poetical Works of Coleridge, Shelley, and Keats* (which we therefore do not include in the foot-of-the-page collations), the other work that she generally used as a base text for *1839* (see Taylor, *The Early Collected Editions of Shelley's Poems* [New Haven: Yale UP, 1958], 51). However, the Ascham piracy took its text from John Brooks's elegantly produced piracy of *QM,* in 1829. Brooks, an Owenite publisher, produced a "very handsome edition," priced at 9s. (see ad reproduced in *Shelley Library,* 55). Its engraved title page omits the subtitle and mention of the notes and includes only the epigraph from Archimedes. It does, however, contain a striking vignette depicting Queen Mab calling forth the sleeping Ianthe's spirit (for a reproduction, see p. 314), which was drawn by Charles Landseer (son of the engraver John Landseer and elder brother of the more famous painter Edwin Landseer) and engraved by Edward James Portbury (who did much engraving for the gift books of the 1820s and 1830s). Brooks, who includes the dedicatory poem to Harriet (in the copies we have seen) and does not provide translation of the notes, took his text directly from *1813,* a unique copy of which he had obtained from Robert Madocks, PBS's handyman and the agent for his landlord in Marlow (see *SC* V, 516n), who had confiscated it years earlier in addition to other of the Shelleys' belongings left behind along with an unpaid balance. This copy contains PBS's draft revisions of *QM* into *Dæmon* and other shorter pieces, which are mentioned above and which ended up in the hands of Forman and ultimately Pfz (see *SC* IV, 489–93).

Brooks's edition (collated as *1829.BRO*) follows *1813* closely but not uncritically: rarely emending the text of the poem proper, it is somewhat freer with the notes, especially in revising PBS's grammar and in correcting errors in the foreign language passages (once in **Note 17** even "correcting" back to the original an intentional change PBS made in Horace's Latin). Several of these changes were transmitted through Ascham to MWS's editions. Perhaps Brooks's most significant textual gaffe in editing the poem comes in **VIII.232–33,** where, misunderstanding PBS's grammar, he initiates three misguided emendations ("extends | Its . . . wields" for "extend | Their . . . wield") that were also transmitted through Ascham to MWS. Beyond this textually important edition, Brooks's influence on the transmission of *QM* extended in 1833 to his acquiring the stock and stereotyped plates of Mrs. Carlile's 1832 piracy, which first printed the notes as footnotes to the poem, at the bottom of the page. Brooks published this pocket-sized edition under his own name for the price of 1 *s.* 6*d.*, and from him the plates seem to have passed on to Hetherington and Watson, who continued to make *QM* widely available to the lower classes.

Following Brooks, the next important pirate in the textual transmission of *QM* is John Ascham, a minor printer-pornographer, who may have had some connection to the Benbow/Cannon/Fair team, as St. Clair surmises, given the similarities in the design and typeface of the title page of his two-volume piracy of PBS's poetry to that of the Benbow piracy of *QM* (*The Godwins and the Shelleys,* 517; title pages reproduced on 288). Moreover, as St. Clair points out, not only does the Ascham edition sometimes have both an engraved and a printed title page like the Benbow *QM,* but also, although "the engraving is executed with the perfection of a banknote, the first letter of the word 'Holborn' at the foot of the page is not an H but a capital of the Greek letter P," a symbol possibly indicating the presence of "Erasmus Perkins" (Cannon) as the main financial backer (516).

Ascham's text of *QM* contains a separate title page, indicating that he may have intended to sell it also as a discrete volume. The title itself mentions the notes, but omits "A Philosophical Poem." The title page also claims "VERBA-TIM FROM THE ORIGINAL EDITION," a deceptive statement that might well have misled MWS. Indeed, whatever the connection of Ascham's edition to Cannon, Ascham's text of *QM* (II, 185–351) is less carefully printed than either the Benbow or the Brooks edition, Ascham's real base text. Ascham ac-cepted uncritically into his text virtually all of the errors in the Brooks edi-tion, including such mistakes as "perpetual" for <u>purpureal</u> (**I.102**) and the transposition of two lines in a quotation from Lucretius in **Note 6,** and added to these errors many more. His text of *QM* (collated as *1834*) is, in fact, the most carelessly executed of any we have collated: letters, words, phrases, and even whole lines (e.g., **III.236** and **VII.173**) are mistakenly altered or dropped completely. Ascham sometimes intervened critically in the text, usu-ally to break up PBS's longer verse sentences into smaller units, sometimes al-tering a word to avoid repetition or to "improve" PBS's style. While MWS was able to catch most of Ascham's errors, several slipped into her own text of *QM* (see Commentary, *passim*).

MWS's dependence on Ascham's text in *1839* increased because, as men-tioned above, she was not able to locate a copy of *1813* against which to check the proofs, which were sent to her from the press sometime before mid-December 1838. Her own copy (now at Htn) had been left behind at Mar-low and was confiscated by Madocks, along with the rest of Shelley's copies of the volume. MWS's series of desperate and unsuccessful appeals to friends for their own copies (see *LMWS* II, 301–6) was capped by the following let-ter to an unknown correspondent (identified by Betty T. Bennett as possibly Charles Ollier): "The press has been waiting some days—and I know not what to do—. . . . Who is <u>Brookes</u> The press is waiting & all delay is too tiresome rending success in the end of no avail—Do tell me who & what Brookes is that I may apply. . . . I <u>must</u> send the proofs back <u>early</u> on Monday Morning—I would give any thing to see the original tomorrow—It is <u>too bad</u>. . . . If I cannot get the book tomorrow—it will be welcome at any time to correct the later proofs or for our errata—but the sooner the better" (*LMWS* II, 306). Clearly, MWS's correspondent had suggested that Brooks, who had acquired the stock of some of PBS's original editions (reissuing them with new title pages) and had pirated *QM* itself, might be able to help her.

In the end, however, there is no evidence that MWS received a copy of *1813* until about six weeks later, when Harriet de Boinville sent her own copy from Paris on 26 January 1839 (*SC* VIII, 988), too late to influence MWS's text of *QM,* which appears as the first poem in Volume I (1–106), published at the end of January 1839. Without a copy of *1813* in her possession to check her text, set from the Ascham piracy, MWS seems to have resorted to the Benbow piracy (rather than the Galignani) to make her check, accepting several readings initiated in the Benbow (see above), without even knowing whether at any given point Ascham or Benbow more accurately reflected *1813.* Having helped the editor of Galignani's edition, Cyrus Redding, she knew he had no specific knowledge about the poem. MWS may have turned to Benbow's "New York" edition because she had learned that it was a product of Cannon and Fair, who knew the text well: Godwin records in his diary meeting Cannon twice towards the end of 1820 (25 October and 18 December) and may well have known about the planned subterfuge, or learned about it thereafter. Perhaps MWS also resorted to the Galignani for a quick additional check, because in **I.269** both editions, unlike all others, read "slightest" for <u>lightest</u> (a reading she corrects back to "lightest" in *1840*).

Beyond the shaky textual base of her *1839* text of **QM,** MWS's problems were further exacerbated by her publisher, Edward Moxon, who urged her to cut out all passages of the poem and notes that might be judged under the law as blasphemous and thus might void the copyright of the entire edition, which MWS had convinced him to buy for £500 (paid in installments of £125 for each of the four volumes). Although MWS had great qualms about making such cuts, she had good reason to believe that PBS would not have wanted *QM* published in its original form; she was also concerned about getting a sympathetic reception for his poetry. Most important, she had promised Moxon that she would "take pains to render [the copyright] as valuable as I can" (*LMWS* II, 300), and she felt ethically bound to honor her promise. As a result, beyond omitting the subtitle, epigraphs, and dedicatory poem (because PBS had made an issue about the latter in the Clark piracy), MWS deleted the following portions of the poem in *1839:* **IV.203–20, VI.54** to the end of **Canto VII, VIII.165,** and **IX.48.** She further omitted eight of the notes in their entirety (**Notes 2, 3, 9,** and **11** through **15**) and two sentences from

Note 17 (lines 221–29). All of these cuts concern passages attacking religion, or—as in the case of **Note 9,** which advocates free love—Christian morality. These cuts probably were made *after* the complete text had first been run in proof, as indicated by MWS's letter to Leigh Hunt on 14 December 1838, in which she expresses uncertainty over whether she should "mutilate" **QM** (*LMWS* II, 305) and at which time the proofs of **QM** were already in her possession.

Because some of PBS's friends and the reviewers of *1839* expressed indignation about the cuts MWS had made in **QM,** she convinced Moxon to restore the complete text of **QM** in *1840,* for which the hapless Moxon was indeed convicted for blasphemous libel, although he was merely bound over in his own recognizance and received no actual penalty. (For the interesting details of this case, brought not by the government but by the pirate Hetherington, see Donald Thomas, *The Library,* 5th ser., 33 [December 1978]: 329–34.) Collations show that the text of the restored cuts is still based on Ascham and hence was probably taken from MWS's copy for the press, or the original proofs. However, in restoring the full text of the poem (including the dedication) and notes, MWS continued to omit **IX.48** and the two sentences from **Note 17,** errors she did not catch in Ascham's text and that still remain in her one-volume 1847 edition and in the three-volume edition she published the same year, the last editions to appear during her lifetime. And although she was able after its publication to check her *1839* text against the Boinville copy of *1813,* MWS made relatively few substantive changes in *1840:* she may not have given much fresh critical thought to the text of **QM** either then or in her one-volume 1847 edition, which contains no evidence of her renewed intervention.

As Nora Crook first pointed out to us, however, the three-volume *1847* treats **QM** quite differently. Referring readers who want to read all of **QM** to the one-volume 1847 edition, MWS says in her note on *Queen Mab* that in the three-volume *1847*

it is deemed advisable only to reprint the first two cantos, which he himself appended to "Alastor.". . . The opening of "Queen Mab" is the most striking part of the poem. It is the boy's dream of beauty and love. The gentle loveliness of the sleeping Ianthe, the fairy elegance of Queen Mab, the sublime description of the voyage through the universe, with the final view from the battlements of the skiey palace, form a poem in themselves of surpassing beauty. They hear the impress of earnest, daring, fearless youth. Shelley's angelic nature breathes in every line, and these cantos must always be pre-eminently valued by those happy few who understand and love him.

Although MWS's description suggests that she is presenting **Dæmon,** Shelley's revision of the opening two cantos of **QM,** published as the concluding poem of the **Alastor** volume, she in fact provided the text of the original two cantos along with the dedicatory poem to HWS, taken from *1840,* omitting the notes.

Overall, given the obstacles MWS faced in editing *QM,* she was unable to contribute much of importance to our understanding of the text. Most of her critical acumen was absorbed in ridding her base text, taken from Ascham, of detectable errors and in lightening the punctuation she found throughout Ascham's text, punctuation that she further lightens in *1840.* Ultimately, all of the substantive variants from *1813* in her text need to be evaluated in light of the readings in Ascham and Benbow. Nonetheless, beyond *1813* itself, her text of *QM* has had the most influence on later editors, as a consideration of William Michael Rossetti's edition of the poem helps to demonstrate.

Later Editions

In producing the first major critical edition of PBS's poetry after MWS's, William Michael Rossetti took as his base text an 1853 reprint of the one-volume 1847 edition, cutting out the pages and making corrections for the press directly on them (see Reiman, *Romantic Texts and Contexts* [Columbia: U of Missouri P, 1987], 50), thus introducing into his text of *QM* readings and errors from MWS. For instance, although Rossetti restored **IX.48** to the poem, he did not catch MWS's omission of the two sentences in **Note 17** and consequently omitted them himself in both *1870* and his second and final edition, *1878* (as did Dowden in his editions). However, Rossetti was also the most aggressive critical editor of *QM.* He heavily revised the first two cantos of the poem, arguing that PBS at "a less immature age . . . published a modified extract from the poem [**Dæmon**]. The alterations of diction which he introduced with no sparing hand manifestly represent his own deliberate preference, and ought so far to be respected and adopted in any republication: but then they are alterations introduced into a mere extract of the entire poem, and one cannot be quite sure that, if Shelley had been re-printing the complete and not the abridged version, he would have made all the changes given in the latter" (*1870* I, 464). Consequently, Rossetti decided to emend his text of *QM* when he found readings in **Dæmon** to be "decided improvements" over *1813.* Between such conflations and other verbal alterations to "improve" the text, as well as a constant repunctuating of the poem that alters its rhythms, Rossetti—of all the later editors—most nearly made *QM* his own creation. We collate only those portions of his text of the first two cantos that correspond closely to *1813.*

Beyond the frequent practice of capitalizing words that PBS seems to have intentionally lowercased in *1813* (see, e.g., Reiman, *Romantic Texts and Contexts,* 49), the treatment of *QM* in editions later than *1870* is distinguished not so much by any marked critical revisions of or contributions to the establishment of the text itself (see our Historical Collations) as by the wide discrepancy in how these editions handle the paratextual material and the placement of *QM* within the corpus of PBS's poetry. Rossetti, who omitted both the subtitle and epigraphs, placed his text of *QM* at the beginning of his editions, *1870* and *1878*. Forman, on the other hand, provides a facsimile of the title page in *1876*, but breaks importantly with MWS and Rossetti by separating *QM* from PBS's canon proper and relegating it to a section of juvenilia at the end of Volume IV. Thus two quite different traditions were established, even though Forman himself placed *QM* as the opening poem of his five-volume Aldine edition (*1892F*), explaining in his introduction that he did so "in view of the persistent vogue and historical importance" of the poem.

Dowden's edition, *1927, 1972,* and *1989* all follow MWS and Rossetti in treating *QM* as a part of the main canon. Although Woodberry in *1892W* also followed suit, he separated the poem from the notes, placing the latter at the back of Volume I, following the text of ***The Revolt of Islam*** and directly preceding his own textual notes. A selection of PBS's poetry and prose, *2002,* gives the full text of the poem but only brief quotations from the notes, as footnotes to the text.

On the other hand, Hutchinson's OSA editions (*1904* and *1970*) follow *1876* in relegating *QM* to the juvenilia at the back of the book. The Locock (*1911*) also claims Forman's work as a precedent for treating *QM* as "a kind of Appendix, instead of forcing it on the reader's attention by giving it the leading place among Shelley's poems" (II, 548). Accordingly, Locock placed *QM* as the very last poem in his edition, which contains an opening section, "Principal Poems," from which it is excluded. Locock, moreover, consigned *QM* to the badlands of PBS's canon by omitting its notes, except for the text of the two PBS poems contained therein. Every major edition from *1876* on gives the full title, the epigraphs, and the dedicatory poem. And, with the exception of *1876* and *1989,* the collective editions from *1870* on provide the text of MWS's note on *QM* from *1840* (which itself contains the full text of PBS's letter to *The Examiner* disavowing Clark's piracy). Of all the collective editions, only those of Forman and Woodberry include the indicator hands in their text of the notes, and none until the present edition provides translations of the long passages of the notes in foreign languages.

After *QM* was pirated by Clark in 1821, it was met with a wave of partisan and primarily hostile reviews, ranging from panegyric in Benbow's *John Bull's British Journal* to utter vituperation in *The Literary Gazette and Journal of Belle Lettres.* PBS's friends Horace Smith and Leigh Hunt were justifiably concerned about the effect that the piracy and Clark's trial would have on PBS's already battered reputation. PBS's own ambivalence about the piracy and circulation of *QM* by "low booksellers" is clear in his private letters on the subject (**Letters** II, 298, 300–301), as well as in his public repudiation of the poem, published in *The Examiner* for 15 July 1821 (**Letters** II, 304–5; see Appendix B). Nonetheless, and despite PBS's own preference for more literate readers, **QM** became a fixture in nineteenth-century working-class culture through the pirated editions (see Fraistat, *PMLA* 110 [May 1994]: 409–23): the "Chartist's Bible," according to Shaw (*The Collected Works of Bernard Shaw* [New York: Wise, 1932]: XXIX, 257); the "gospel" of the Owenites, according to Forman (*Shelley Library*, 37); and a general influence on socialist thought throughout the nineteenth century, so inspiring the young Engels that he began his own translation into German (see Ernest Rose, *JEGP* 26 [1927]: 141). What such readers were likely to find in **QM** is explained well by Richard Carlile, who wrote in *Newgate Monthly Magazine* for 1 May 1826:

Of all the writings of Shelly [*sic*], Queen Mab has been the most extensively read, and will always be the most highly appreciated. Its subject comes home to the bosom of an immense portion of mankind; all indeed who feel the weight of civil or religious oppression; and from its strength of declamation it is admired even by those who are the least susceptable [*sic*] of poetic impressions, or the least predisposed of their general utility. If it be not the very best poem in existence, it has the merit of standing without a competitor; for no one has dared to display existing abuses so nakedly and unconditionably [*sic*] as has the one under consideration. (415)

Collation

To illustrate the main lines of the textual transmission of **QM,** we provide collations at the foot of the page for *1813* (our copy-text), MWS's *1839* and *1840* editions, and the most important pirated editions leading to MWS's texts: *1821.CLA, 1821.BEN, 1829.BRO,* and *1834.* To illustrate the later transmission of the poem proper, we provide historical collations at the back of the book of the following significant editions: *1870, 1876, 1904, 1911, 1927, 1989,* and *2002.* For the notes, however, in order to conserve space and because most of these editions contain little by way of critical rethinking of the text, we collate at the back of the book only *1876* and *1989,* two representative critical editions of nineteenth- and twentieth-century textual scholarship.

In 1968, George David Richards edited **QM** as his dissertation at Duke University: although his edition has nothing substantive to offer textually and is therefore not included in the collations, its notes are occasionally mentioned in the Commentary, where the edition is cited as *1968.*

Epigraph I. PBS introduces the anti-Christian theme of **QM** by repeating a favorite slogan from Voltaire's letters that had served as a rallying cry for the *philosophes:* "Crush the Demon!" For Voltaire, "Every sensible man, every honorable man, must hold the Christian sect in horror" (*Examen important de Milord Bolingbroke;* quoted in Peter Gay, *The Enlightenment: An Interpretation* [New York: Knopf, 1967]: I, 391). PBS twice used Voltaire's slogan in his own letters to Hogg. First on 20 December 1810: "On *one* subject I am cool, (religion) yet that coolness alone possesses me that I may with more certainty guide the spear to the breast of my adversary, with more certainty ensanguine it with the hearts blood of Xt's hated name. Adieu.—Ecrasez l'infame ecrasez l'impie in which endeavour your most sincere friend will join his every power, his every feeble resourse [*sic*]—Adieu" (***Letters*** I, 29). About two weeks later, even more melodramatically, he vowed: "I swear that never will I forgive Christianity! . . . I am convinced too that it is of great disservice to society that it encourages prejudice which strikes at the root of the dearest the tenderest of its ties. Oh how I wish I *were* the Antichrist, that it were *mine* to crush the Demon, to hurl him to his native Hell never to rise again——— I expect to gratify some of this insatiable feeling in Poetry" (***Letters*** I, 35). For the lost "*Satirical Poem* on L'infame" in which PBS might have gratified some of that insatiable feeling, see ***CPPBS*** I, 443–44. See also ***1810 ("Dares the Lama, most fleet")*** (***Esd*** #41) for PBS's vehement expression in poetry of the devastating role he sees Christianity playing both in his personal life and in the world at large, especially lines 32–36: "For in vain from the grasp of Religion I flee. | The most tenderly loved of my soul | Are slaves to its chilling control . . . | It pursues me. It blasts me. Oh! where shall I fly? | What remains but to curse it, to curse it and die?"

Epigraph II. Taken from the opening of the fourth book of Lucretius's *De rerum natura* (*Of the Nature of Things*), this Latin passage may be translated as "I blaze a trail through the pathless tracks of poetry, where no foot has ever trod before. What joy it is to discover virgin springs and drink their waters, and what joy to gather new flowers . . . never before wreathed by the Muses around anyone's head! First, I teach of great matters; and I go on to free men's minds from the crippling bonds of superstition." In **line 3, *1813*** erroneously gives "juratque" for <u>juvatque</u>; and PBS omits from **line 4:** "and to seek from there a distinguished crown for my head." The gathering of flowers for a garland here is echoed in **lines 11–12** of the dedicatory poem ***To Harriet * * * * ***. Lucretius's poetry, a favorite among the *philosophes* for its use of scientific materialism to critique religious dogma, was similarly valued by PBS, who considered Book IV of *De rerum natura*, from which the epigraph is taken, "perhaps the finest" in the poem (***Letters*** I, 545). For more on *De rerum natura*, see the Commentary to PBS's note for **V.58** (**Note 6**), below. For PBS's abiding debt to Lucretius, see "Shelley's Lucretian Imagination," in Hugh Roberts, *Shelley and the Chaos of History: A New Politics of Poetry* (University Park: Pennsylvania State UP, 1997), 411–86.

Epigraph III. "Give me a place to stand upon, and I will move the earth." This quotation, attributed to Archimedes (287–212 B.C.) about the power of the lever, was used by radicals of PBS's day to connect mechanical forces with revolutionary actions. By invoking Archimedes here, PBS was situating his poem politically for its readers. As *1989* points out, for example, Paine began the second part of the *Rights of Man* by declaring "What Archimedes said of the mechanical powers, may be applied to Reason and Liberty. . . . The revolution of America presented in politics what was only theory in mechanics" (Paine, *Writings* II, 401). An apposite passage occurs in PBS's meditation on power and Necessity in the note to *QM* VI.198: "In the only true sense of the word power, it applies with equal force to the loadstone as to the human will. Do you think these motives, which I shall present, are powerful enough to rouse him? is a question just as common as, Do you think this lever has the power of raising this weight?" (**Note 12, lines 68–71**). PBS found this epigraph from Archimedes important enough to use again on the title page of his next attempt at a radical epic, **Laon and Cythna**. We have corrected errors in breathing and accent marks.

Dedicatory Poem. TO HARRIET * * * * *. A version of this lyric, written in PBS's hand but titled "To Harriet," opens *Esd* (see p. 7 and the related Commentary). The poem may have originally been written as a dedication for the joint *QM* and *Esd* volume that PBS had hoped to publish with Hookham. After it became clear that he was not going to be able to publish *Esd*, PBS perhaps hurriedly prepared it for publication with *QM*, without altering **lines 11** or **15,** whose reference to these early wilding flowers and flowrets clearly allude to the *Esd* poems rather than to *QM*. Without question, as printed in *1813*, the poem, which PBS years later referred to as the "foolish dedication to my late wife" (**Letters** II, 298), is addressed to Harriet Shelley. The five asterisks following HARRIET in the title, however, have been the source of some confusion because they might be read as indicating the name Harriet Grove, PBS's first love—a claim maintained in Grove family tradition and made by Medwin (*Life* I, 48), who gives the title as "To Harriet G—." It might be added that this same tradition held mistakenly that *QM* led Harriet Grove's father to decide against her marriage to PBS (see Massey, *KSMB* 19 [1968]: 15). Perhaps an early version of the poem was written for Harriet Grove and revised later for Harriet Shelley, but there is no evidence for this. Without the press copy, we do not even know whether the five asterisks were introduced by PBS or by the compositor, the latter of which is more likely. Five asterisks are, in fact, similarly used to signal the omissions in the quotation from Pliny on page 183 of *1813*.

The dedicatory poem did not appear consistently in textual reproductions of *QM*. As noted above, PBS removed it from most of the copies of *QM* that he distributed himself. It is also absent from *1821.BEN, 1829,* and *1839* (reinstated in *1840*). PBS was relieved to think that the dedication—"the only part of the business that could seriously have annoyed me" (**Letters** II,

298)—had been omitted from *1821.CLA,* but that was true in only some copies. In other copies of that piracy it appears after the title page and in still others at the back of the book. John Linnell's copy of **QM** at Harvard University Library contains the reading "winding" for <u>wilding</u> in **line 11,** an error apparently caught early in the print run and rectified by a stop-press correction. That the variant "winding" also appears in a Bodleian copy of *1821.CLA* containing the dedication suggests that the Clark piracy may have been set from another such copy of **1813.**

line 11. <u>wilding</u>: uncultured or wild.

line 12. <u>garlanded</u>: both the act of weaving flowers into a wreath or crown and gathering poems together into a collection.

line 13. <u>unto</u>: i.e., "against" (*OED* 4). The variant "into" was introduced—perhaps through compositorial error—by *1829.BRO,* which was followed by *1834* and *1840,* and by most later editors. We see no reason to alter **1813.**

line 15. <u>flowret</u>: poeticism for a small flower; an accepted variant spelling of "floweret" in PBS's day.

I.1–2. The pairing of Death and Sleep as the infant children of Night was a common classical topos, but PBS specifically may have had in mind Pope's translation of the *Iliad:* "Then *Sleep* and *Death,* two *Twins* of winged Race . . ." (XVI.831–34), of which he would have been reminded by an engraving with this caption in John Flaxman's *The Iliad of Homer Engraved from the Compositions of John Flaxman* (1805), Plate XXV. PBS could well have had this book in his possession while he was composing **QM.** See *SC* III, 202, where Cameron also points out the analogy between Plate XXII, depicting a four-horse chariot (through which Neptune arises from the sea), and **QM I.59ff.**

PBS had earlier described sleep as "that *morbid suspension of every energy*" (**Letters** I, 22), a sentiment that echoes the distaste for sleep that Godwin expressed in the first edition of *Pol. Justice:* "before death can be banished, we must banish sleep, death's image" (see the apparatus in *Pol. Justice,* ed. Priestley III, 226). In **QM,** however, PBS would explore the visionary possibilities of sleep. For the further convergence of death and sleep, see the Commentary to **IX.57–61.**

I.1–8. The stylistic resemblance to the opening lines of Robert Southey's *Thalaba the Destroyer* (1801) was noted by MWS in her note to **QM.**

> How beautiful is night!
> A dewy freshness fills the silent air,
> No mist obscures, no little cloud
> Breaks the whole serene of heaven:
> In full-orbed glory the majestic moon
> Rolls thro the dark blue depths.

> Beneath her steady ray
> The desert circle spreads,
> Like the round ocean, girdled with the sky.
> How beautiful is night!

I.27. <u>Ianthe</u>: In reference to the naming of PBS's daughter Ianthe (b. 23 June 1813), Hogg points out that Ianthe, "violet flower, or violet, is a name of Greek origin, fetched immediately from Ovid's *Metamorphoses,* being the name of a girl, to possess whom another girl, Iphis, was transformed into a youth: potiturque sua puer Iphis Ianthe" (*Life,* ed. Wolfe, II, 107). The radically transformative powers implied by her name and by her role within **QM** make Ianthe a forerunner of such Shelleyan protagonists as Cythna in **Laon and Cythna** and Asia in **Prometheus Unbound.** PBS may have been influenced in his choice of a name for his protagonist by Walter Savage Landor's poems addressed to Ianthe in *Simonidea* (1806). Ianthe may also have been a staple name for heroines of the Sentimental school, as suggested by Ann Batten Cristall's "The Triumph of Superstition: Raphael and Ianthe," which appeared in her *Poetical Sketches* (1795). For other possible sources of the name, including William Thompson (*Sickness* [1745]) and Hesiod, see Carlos Baker (*Shelley's Major Poetry: The Fabric of a Vision* [Princeton: Princeton UP, 1948], 26), who notes that although Byron's stanzas to Ianthe (Lady Charlotte Harley) were written in 1812, they did not appear in print until 1814, when they served as the dedication to the seventh edition of *Childe Harold* I and II. The name Ianthe also appears as the title of a song in John Gay's *The Beggar's Opera* (1728) and of a popular song by William Jackson (first published by Longman in 1768), which begins, "Ianthe the lovely . . . ."

I.28. <u>that faithful bosom</u>: The <u>faithful bosom</u> belongs to Ianthe's lover Henry, as is made clear in **IX.237.** For PBS's use of the name Henry (sometimes autobiographically) for several of his characters, see the headnote to **Henry and Louisa** (**Esd** #46) above. In considering the autobiographical implications of the narrative framework, Stuart Sperry expands upon the observation made in *1977* that Ianthe is modeled upon Harriet Shelley, commenting that PBS is presented in the person of a "rapturous and expectant Henry [kneeling] by the side of Ianthe's couch. . . . assisting, with the help of his celestial midwife Mab, at the birth of his own intellectual offspring, the child bride he had recently married" (*Shelley's Major Verse* [Cambridge: Harvard UP, 1988], 5–6). It is, of course, unclear in the poem whether Ianthe and Henry are actually married.

I.43. <u>parasite</u>: The *OED* cites this unpejorative use of the word by PBS as one of its examples of how *parasite* could be applied "loosely or poetically" to a plant that climbs upon something else for support (2b). *1989* suggests that the popular contemporary use of the word ultimately derives from

"Rousseau's description of the famous 'bosquet' in *Julie, ou la Nouvelle Héloise* (1761) Part IV Letter xi: 'ces ombrages verds et touffus . . . n'étoient formés que de ces plantes rampantes et parasites. . . .'"

I.49. <u>enthusiast</u>: "one carried away by ardent imagination" (*Shelley Concordance*). The *OED* makes clear the equivocal contemporary valences of *enthusiasm* and *enthusiast*, which PBS here uses in the unambiguously positive manner of Joseph Warton's *The Enthusiast; or, The Lover of Nature* (1744), a probable influence on **lines 45–58.** Cf. also his letter of 20 December 1810 to Hogg, in which PBS asked "am not I the wildest, most delirious of enthusiasm's offspring.—" (***Letters*** I, 29).

I.52. <u>strange lyre</u>: the first of many references PBS would make during his career to the Aeolian lyre or harp, a stringed instrument designed to be placed in an open window and "played" by the movement of the wind over its strings, much like wind chimes. The Aeolian harp was a stock figure in the 1790s, used, for instance, by Erasmus Darwin (in *The Botanic Garden*) and by Godwin (in *Pol. Justice*) before most famously crossing over, in Coleridge's "The Æolian Harp," (1795) into Romantic poetry, where it is sometimes used to figure the inspired poetic imagination.

I.53. <u>genii</u>: "spirits fabled as moving powers of nature" (*Shelley Concordance*). The word was originally derived by French translators from the Arab *djinn*, or *jinn*, a class of spirits who, some for good and others for ill, intervene powerfully in human affairs (*OED*).

I.54. <u>lines of rainbow light</u>: *1911* points out that these are the <u>reins of light</u> mentioned in **I.62.**

I.56. <u>teints</u>: purposefully used obsolescent form of *tints*, meaning "colors."

I.59. <u>Behold the chariot of the Fairy Queen!</u>: Queen Mab's chariot is one of the earliest such visionary vehicles in Shelley's poetry, which include the "chariot of the year" in ***The Retrospect*** (***Esd*** #50), the apocalyptic chariots carrying Demogorgon and Asia in ***Prometheus Unbound,*** and the moonlike chariot in ***The Triumph of Life.*** Whereas such vehicles may ultimately derive from Milton's Chariot of Paternal Deity in *Paradise Lost* (VI.749–72) and to the throne of the Ancient of Days (Daniel 7:9), they may also have been influenced by the chariots in Sir William Jones's *Palace of Fortune* (1772) and Southey's *Thalaba* and *The Curse of Kehama* (1810). For a visual analogue to the chariot, see the Commentary for **lines 1–2** above.

I.61. <u>pennons</u>: pinions or wings; first used in this way by Milton in *Paradise Lost* II.933 and VII.441, according to the *OED*, which also adduces Coleridge's *Ode to the Departing Year*, epode ii. PBS had previously used the word in ***The Devil's Walk,*** line 43.

I.70. <u>of lovely, wild and grand</u>: <u>lovely</u>, <u>wild</u>, and <u>grand</u> are used somewhat unconventionally here as nouns in a triadic pattern that becomes common in PBS's poetic rhetoric (see Commentary to line 283 of *The Voyage* [*Esd* #32], p. 408).

I.78. <u>maiden's sleep</u>: "sleeping maid" is one of several emendations made in both *1821.BEN* and *1839* (retained in *1840*) that are discussed above (see "Textual Transmission") and that MWS may have originally made without direct access to *1813* itself. The alteration in *1821.BEN* may have been made because the appropriate object of <u>gaze</u> (**I.77**) is not <u>sleep</u>—which, of course, cannot be seen—but rather the maid, who is sleeping. However, the reading in *1813* is plausible, and there is no evidence that PBS himself initiated such a change.

I.82–83. <u>pellucid . . . line</u>: The chariot is so translucent ("pellucid") that it does not refract light. For PBS's understanding of refraction, see his **Note 1.**

I.98. <u>fair star</u>: the planet Venus as the morning star.

I.102. <u>purpureal</u>: derived from the Latin word *purpureus*, which can mean either purple-colored (an appropriately regal hue of light for Queen Mab) or "brilliant, beautiful," a poeticism used by Horace, Ovid, and Virgil, among others whom PBS would have read. The erroneous reading "perpetual"—introduced by *1829.BRO* and followed by *1834*—was corrected by MWS in her editions.

I.104. The stanza break is missing in *1821.BEN*. This is probably because that edition used as a copy-text *1821.CLA*, which has a page break here.

I.108. <u>amaranth</u>: a fabled flower that never fades; see the Commentary introducing *1810 ("Hopes that bud in youthful breasts")* (*Esd* #35), p. 417.

I.120. <u>restless gossamer</u>: echoing Coleridge's *The Rime of the Ancyent Marinere*: "Are those *her* Sails that glance in the Sun | Like restless gossameres?" (175–76). PBS, in effect, transmutes the horrifying approach of Coleridge's "Spectre-ship" into the transcendent (but equally uncanny) peacefulness arising from the descent of Mab's <u>celestial car</u>. For the literary vogue of *gossamer*, see the Commentary in *CPPBS* I, 181 for *Revenge*, l.42.

I.128. <u>day-stars</u>: These stars, so bright that they are visible during the day, are considered harbingers of future good. Milton—among other poets, including Wordsworth—used the phrase to refer to the sun (see *Lycidas*, 168). Ultimately, the image can be traced back to 2 Peter 1:19: ". . . as unto a light that shineth in a dark place, until the day dawn, and the day star arise in your hearts." Brian Shelley points out that the image "accords with the metaphor of Christ as a morning star (Rev. 22:16)" and concludes that "Shelley appears to be humanizing the messianic emblem by applying it to a select group of people of which Ianthe is a representative" (*Shelley and Scripture* [Oxford: Clarendon Press, 1994], 40).

I.130–38. <u>Sudden</u> . . . <u>ruin.</u>: The apparent contradictions introduced into this avowedly materialist poem by the splitting of its protagonist into body and soul or spirit, with, moreover, primary agency given to the *spirit* throughout the framing narrative, are discussed in Reiman, *Intervals of Inspiration*, 232–34. In so dividing Ianthe, PBS is following Volney in *Ruines*, where a Genius separates the soul from the body of a "Traveller," bearing the soul into the heavens for a celestial overview and radical interrogation of the past and the present. For the ambiguities within French materialism itself concerning the spirituality of matter, see the Commentary to **II.231–43**, below. See also PBS's claim in **IV.140** that <u>Soul is the only element</u> and the Commentary to **I.145–56.**

I.133–38. <u>frame. . . . ruin.</u>: As was first recognized in *1834,* the period following <u>frame</u> in *1813* creates a grammatical crux in the next sentence concerning the referent of the clause "Instinct . . . grace, . . ." (**134**). In *1834,* replacing the period after <u>frame</u> with a comma and inserting a period after <u>grace</u>, clearly indicates that this phrase modifies <u>it stood</u> in **line 131,** a conclusion similarly arrived at by several later editors. We do not agree, however, with Locock's claim that the *1813* punctuation "evidently yields no sense," since **line 134** could be modifying <u>it</u> in **line 136:** <u>Instinct with inexpressible beauty and grace,</u> | . . . | . . . <u>it</u> [i.e., Ianthe's Soul] <u>reassumed</u> | <u>Its native dignity, . . .</u>" Given that possibility, we have kept the punctuation of *1813,* with its grammatical tensions, intact.

I.134. <u>Instinct</u>: animated or filled. As *2002* points out, Milton similarly uses *instinct* in depicting the Chariot of Paternal Deity, which influenced PBS's descriptions of chariots, as discussed in the note to **I.59,** above. See also Southey's analogous usage in *The Curse of Kehama* (London: Longman, Hurst, Rees, Orme, and Brown, 1810) describing the "Ship of Heaven, instinct with thought" that bears the "Maiden," Kailyal aloft to a bower of bliss (Section VIII, p. 57). In a note, Southey explains that he has "converted the *Vimana,* or self-moving Car of the Gods, into a Ship" (p. 294). *Instinct* appears again in *QM* **I.271** and **IX.153.**

I.145–56. <u>body and soul. . . . perishes, and passes.</u>: The general topos of the different destinies of body and soul descends from antiquity. PBS's speculations about the soul in his letters to Elizabeth Hitchener range from materialist positions to those ultimately derived from Plato and Pythagorean metempsychosis: e.g., "When we speak of the soul of man, we mean that unknown cause which produces the observable effect evinced by his intelligence & bodily animation which are in their nature conjoined, and as we suppose, as we observe, inseparable" (**Letters** I, 100); "Shall we sink into the nothing from whence we have arisen? But could we have arisen from nothing— . . . . as I conceive, & as is certainly capable of demonstration that nothing can be annihilated, but that everything appertaining to nature, consisting of constituent parts infinitely divisible, is in a continu[al] change, then do I suppose . . . that neither will soul perish; that in a future existence it will lose all consciousness of having formerly lived elsewhere, will begin life anew, possibly under a shape of which we have now no idea" (**Letters** I, 110); "I then explain [to Southey]—'I think reason and analogy seem to countenance the opinion that life is infinite—that as the soul which now animates this frame was once the vivifying principle of the *infinitely* lowest link in the Chain of existence, so is it ultimately destined to attain the highest—that every thing is animation . . . and in consequence being infinite we can never arrive at its termination'" (**Letters** I, 215).

Cf. also the description of metempsychosis in *Rees's Cyclopædia* under "Pythagoreans": ". . . after the rational mind is freed from the chains of the body, it assumes an ethereal vehicle, and passes into the regions of the dead, where it remains till it is sent back to this world, to be the inhabitant of some other body, brutal or human; and that after suffering successive purgations, when it is sufficiently purified, it is received among the gods, and returns to the eternal source from which it first proceeded." Medwin, who notes that the doctrine of metempsychosis was "introduced by Pythagoras," traces PBS's interest in the concept back through his delight at Oxford "in finding it unfolded in Plato's *Phædo*" to an earlier time "long before . . . Oxford" when it "had taken deep root in his mind" from reading Coleridge (*Life*, ed. Forman, 79). When Catherine Nugent met PBS in March 1812 he talked "as a man believing in the metempsychosis" (*YS*, 374n.155). Although there are no extant works by Pythagoras, his name is on the list of authors copies of whose work PBS attempted to purchase from Thomas "Clio" Rickman on 24 December 1812 (**Letters** I, 344).

I.149. <u>sempiternal</u>: everlasting, eternal.

I.176. <u>extatic</u>: an alternative, less frequently used, contemporary spelling. Its presence in the text is an early indication that the printer was not trying to make PBS's text conform to a rigid house style (cf. <u>extacy</u> in the Commentary to **II.245**).

I.180. <u>yet</u>: probably "in addition to this," as Locock suggests.

I.188. <u>immurement</u>: imprisonment; *Shelley Concordance* records PBS's only use of *immurement* and *immured* as being in **QM** (see **II.61** and **III.90**).

I.190. <u>brake</u>: archaic form of *broke*. *1821.CLA* and *1821.BEN* mistakenly "correct" the word to "break."

I.200. <u>disparted</u>: flew apart.

I.220. <u>Andes</u>: "esteemed the highest [mountain range] in the world," according to the *Encyc. Brit.* (1771; I, 312). According to *Rees's Cyclopædia,* Chimboraco, the highest summit of the Andes, was second in height only to "the highest summit of the mountains of Tibet," perhaps the "rival" peaks over which the chariot flies. Rising 20,702 feet, Chimborazo (as it is now known) is the highest peak in Ecuador, but not the highest in the Andes (as it was long thought to be)—that honor goes to Aconcagua at the border of Argentina and Chile, which is 22,834 feet high. In Anna Letitia Barbauld's "Eighteen Hundred and Eleven," the "Genius" attendant on commerce and empire (quite possibly inspired by Volney's similar figure in *Ruines*) "turns from Europe's desolated shores; . . . | And . . . | On Andes' heights he shrouds his awful form; | On Chimborazo's summits treads sublime, | . . . [Crying] "'Tis now the hour! . . . | . . . and bids the nations rise" (lines 322–28; *The Poems of Anna Letitia Barbauld,* ed. William McCarthy and Elizabeth Kraft [Athens: U of Georgia P, 1994]). There is no record that PBS read this poem, but given the notoriously antagonistic reception accorded its liberal politics by the reviews, he likely knew it. As noted in the Commentary for **To the Republicans of North America,** PBS would have known about Chimborazo from Alexander von Humboldt's *Voyages aux régions équinoxiales du nouveau continent* (1805); see Commentary, pp. 370–71.

I.242–43. <u>The sun's</u> . . . <u>concave</u>: See PBS's **Note 1** for these lines.

I.252–53. <u>Whilst round</u> . . . <u>rolled</u>: See PBS's **Note 2** for these lines.

I.259. <u>Hesperus</u>: Venus as the evening star, sometimes also called Vesper by PBS (e.g., *QM* **IV.24**). The planet appears as the morning star in **I.98–99** (see Commentary, above).

I.260. <u>athwart</u>: across. The track of comets in space is described here.

I.264–68. <u>Spirit of Nature</u> . . . <u>fitting temple</u>: perhaps modeled on the following description from Erasmus Darwin:

> Here, high in air, unconscious of the storm,
> Thy temple, Nature, rears it's mystic form;
> From earth to heav'n, unwrought by mortal toil,
> Towers the vast fabric on the desert soil;
> O'er many a league the ponderous domes extend,
> And deep in earth the ribbed vaults descend;
> (*The Temple of Nature; or, the Origin of Society:*
> *A Poem, with Philosophical Notes* [1803], I.65–70)

I.264. <u>Spirit of Nature</u>: identified with <u>Necessity</u> in **VI.197–98.** In **I.264–77** PBS may have drawn on Pope's *Essay on Man,* I.267–80 (purged of its theism), which begins: "All are but parts of one stupendous whole, | Whose body, Nature is, and God the soul; | That, chang'd thro' all, and yet in all the same,

| . . . | Lives thro' all life, extends thro' all extent, . . ." (*The Poems of Alexander Pope*, ed. John Butt [New Haven: Yale UP, 1963]). PBS described the opening line of this passage as "something more than Poetry, it has ever been my favourite theory" (**Letters** I, 35). On the other hand, Holbach describes nature in terms even more congenial to PBS: "Nature is an active, living whole, whose parts necessarily concur, and that without their own knowledge, to maintain activity, life, and existence. Nature acts and exists necessarily; all that she contains necessarily conspires to perpetuate her active existence" (*System*, 33).

Cf. **The Voyage** (**Esd** #32), lines 108–11, for a similar invocation of the "soul of Nature."

I.269. <u>lightest</u>: "slightest" appears in *1829* and *1839* through what seem to be unrelated errors. MWS corrected "slightest" to "lightest" in *1840*. On 3 January 1811, PBS wrote to Hogg: "I may not be able to adduce proofs, but I think that the leaf of a tree, the meanest insect on wh. we trample are in themselves arguments more conclusive than any which can be adduced that some vast intellect animates Infinity—" (**Letters** I, 35).

I.273. <u>fattens on the dead</u>: PBS may have written "battens" (i.e., feeds) in his manuscript, which could easily have been misread by a transcriber or the compositor as "fattens," given his handwriting. However, because <u>fattens</u> was retained in **Dæmon,** we have refrained from making a conjectural emendation here. Cf. also *Hamlet* IV.iii.21–23: "Your worm is your only emperor for diet: We fat all creatures else to fat us, and we fat ourselves for maggots."

II.1–12. <u>If solitude</u> . . . <u>wreath</u>: Just as at the beginning of **Canto I**, PBS echoes Southey's poetry at the start of **Canto II**, as *1989* points out, turning to "Madoc in Wales," *Madoc* (1805) Part I.iii.276–81:

> When evening came, toward the echoing shore
> I and Cadwallon walked together forth:
> Bright with dilated glory shone the west;
> But brighter lay the ocean-flood below,
> The burnished silver sea, that heaved and flashed
> Its restless rays, intolerably bright.

PBS's use of Southey's popular verse epics as a model for beginning both cantos may be strategic: easing readers gently into the more serious political concerns to come.

II.21. <u>fane</u>: temple, a poeticism that PBS used throughout his career.

II.30. <u>faery</u>: enchanted; as the spelling indicates, this word is ultimately drawn from Spenser, for whom it was already obsolete. Cf. the opening of the second book of the *Faerie Queene:* "Sith none, that breatheth liuing aire, does know, | Where is that happy land of Faery," (II.6–7). Cf. also Wordsworth's *To* *the Cuckoo:* "the earth we pace | Again appears to be | An unsubstantial, faery place" (29–31). Although "faery" was usually read as trisyllabic ("faëry"), the meter of the line suggests two syllables.

II.31–35. As Heaven, . . . Floating on a silver sea: PBS may be echoing Coleridge's "Kubla Khan" here and in the phrase mazy motion in **line 74** below. "Kubla Khan" was written in 1798 but not published until 1816; PBS may have seen a manuscript copy, possibly in the hands of Godwin or Southey. The poetic adjective *mazy* appears in the poetry of Spenser, Milton, and Pope—and, through them, was not uncommon in later poetry.

II.37. circumambient: encompassing. This Latin borrowing is absent from the concordances to Spenser, Shakespeare, Milton, Pope, and Cowper; and though it appears in contemporary English dictionaries (e.g., Bailey's, 1783), it rarely appears in poetry before this use by PBS, who once again employs scientific/materialist diction to achieve a spiritual effect. W. H. Haywood uses the word similarly in a poem that might well have caught Shelley's eye: *A Poetical Essay on the Existence of God* (1774), III.45.

II.39. immense: immeasurable space, as in Milton's "void immense" in *Paradise Lost,* II.829.

II.46. footsteps,: After adding a comma to canopy at the end of **line 45,** MWS was the first editor to delete the potentially confusing comma after footsteps—which nonetheless does not appear to be an error in the text of *1813.* We retain the comma in our text as PBS's indication of a rhetorical pause in the line.

II.51. passive swell: The substitution of "pensive spell" in *1829* may be an attempt to correct a perceived error in *1813.*

II.51–54. Upon their passive swell . . . virtue and wisdom: This difficult sentence partly parallels Asia's Song in **Prometheus Unbound** II.v. Ianthe's spirit gives itself up to the passive swell of mists and melody (**47–48**), which are controlled by the will (**50**). Much of the difficulty stems from the meaning of for (**52**), which Locock in *1911* understood to mean "on account of," explaining, "The 'privilege' is that of resisting 'pleasurable impulses'" (II, 549). Matthews and Everest argue somewhat more persuasively in *1989* that "virtue's reward (though not its only reward: lines 59–64) is to enjoy the beauties of the Fairy's palace, so it seems more natural to take *for* as meaning 'for all,' 'despite' (*OED* vii 4a; cp. *TL* 214) and to interpret: 'Despite the blisses at her command, Ianthe did not immerse herself in them as she was entitled'" (I, 281). However, we believe that for means simply "in order to obtain" (*OED* 9; e.g., "he worked for money") and that the passage may be interpreted best as meaning, "In order to obtain the bliss that pressed around her, the spirit refrained from breaking the spell by raising moral or intellectual concerns." Later in the poem, of course, these concerns will be brought relentlessly into play and the ensuing bliss will be keener and more substantial.

II.59. meed: reward.

II.64. Learn to make others happy: In this line and in the above discussion of virtue, PBS aligns himself with Godwinian "disinterestedness" against Helvétian and Holbachian self-interest. Cf. PBS's May 1811 letter to Janetta Philipps: "What does man exist for? surely not for his own happiness, but as a more perfect instrument of that of others" (***Letters*** I, 89). Cf. also the many disquisitions on selfishness and self-interest in the correspondence between PBS and Elizabeth Hitchener from June 1811 to February 1812.

Godwin identified distinct national traditions on the question of whether benevolent disinterestedness is possible (such British thinkers as Shaftesbury, Butler, Hutcheson, and Hume argued for this possibility), whereas "Among the French, not a single writer upon the nature of the human mind, is to be found, who does not, with more or less explicitness, declare for" the centrality of self-love to all human motives (*Pol. Justice,* ed. Priestley IV.x; I, 422). For Godwin's discussion of these issues and of how benevolent intention is necessary for virtue, see the chapter "Of Self-Love and Benevolence" in *Pol. Justice* (ed. Priestley IV.x; I, 421–38). In a letter to Godwin written 29 July 1812, PBS attempts to separate Godwin's attack on self-love in *Système* from that work's materialism: "Altho' like you an irreconcileable enemy to the system of self love, both from a feeling of its deformity & a conviction of its falsehood, I can by no means conceive how the loftiest disinterestedness is incompatible with the strictest materialism" (***Letters*** I, 316).

William Hazlitt entered the debate powerfully on the side of English disinterestedness, in the anonymously published *An Essay on the Principles of Human Action: Being an Argument in favour of the Natural Disinterestedness of the Human Mind* (1805). A portion of Hazlitt's argument anticipates PBS's own position years later in ***A Defence of Poetry:*** "The imagination, by means of which alone I can anticipate future objects, or be interested in them, must carry me out of myself into the feelings of others by one and the same process by which I am thrown forward as it were into my future being, and interested in it. I could not love myself, if I were not capable of loving others. Self-love, used in this sense, is in its fundamental principle the same with disinterested benevolence" (*The Complete Works of William Hazlitt,* ed. P. P. Howe [London: J. M. Dent and Sons, 1930]: I, 1–2).

II.98. intellectual eye: "mental," as opposed to "corporeal," eye; a not uncommon locution that PBS used earlier in ***WJ***.III.232 (see Commentary in ***CPPBS*** I, 223). He would have seen the phrase, for instance, in Godwin's *The Enquirer: Reflections on Education, Manners, and Literature. In a Series of Essays*

(London: G. G. and J. Robinson: 1797, vi). The crucial difference is that the intellectual eye in **QM** is focused on the big picture, abstracting and theorizing, whereas in *Enquirer* it is trained on local details and experiential knowledge. In disputing Godwin's stand in *Enquirer* on the value of a classical education, PBS reassured him, "the picture of you *in the retina of my intellect,* is a standing proof to me that its original is capable of extending to opinions the most unlimited toleration . . ." (our italics) (**Letters** I, 316–17). Cf. *Hamlet:* "In my mind's eye, Horatio" (I.ii.186).

PBS praises *Enquirer* in a letter to Elizabeth Hitchener of 26 November 1811, in which he advises her to read it first of Godwin's works (**Letters** I, 195).

II.108. <u>great chain of nature</u>: The notion of a "great chain" of being originated in antiquity and was common from the Renaissance onward, receiving a powerful restatement in Pope's *An Essay on Man,* I.237–46:

> Vast chain of being, which from God began,
> Natures æthereal, human, angel, man,
> Beast, bird, fish, insect! what no eye can see,
> No glass can reach! from Infinite to thee,
> From thee to Nothing!—On superior pow'rs
> Were we to press, inferior might on ours:
> Or in the full creation leave a void,
> Where, one step broken, the great scale's destroy'd:
> From Nature's chain whatever link you strike,
> Tenth or ten thousandth, breaks the chain alike.

However, PBS reformulated this hierarchical concept through the necessitarian thought of Holbach (*Système*) and Godwin (*Pol. Justice*) in which the "great chain" is rather one of endless causes and effects within a unified, but always changing, natural world. In the words of Holbach: "L'univers, ce vaste assemblage de tout ce qui existe, ne nous offre par-tout que de la matiere & du mouvement: son ensemble ne nous montre qu'une chaîne immense & non interrompue de causes & d'effets" (*Système* I, 8).

II.110. <u>Palmyra</u>: This once prosperous desert trading city (now in Syria), which challenged Roman power under its queen Zenobia (reigned A.D. 266–75), was besieged and destroyed by Aurelian (Roman Emperor, A.D. 270–75), becoming famous for the ruins that marked its rapid rise and fall. After being described memorably by Volney in *Ruines* (Chaps. 1 and 2), Palmyra also appeared as a monument to the transience of human glory in such works as Erasmus Darwin's *Botanic Garden* (Part 2: II.197–204) and Peacock's *Palmyra* (1806; read by an appreciative PBS in its second edition, published with *The Genius of the Thames* in 1812). In Volney, the "stupendous ruins" of Palmyra appear as "a countless multitude of superb columns, stretching in avenues beyond the reach of sight. Among these were magnificent edifices, some entire, some in ruins; the earth every where strewed with fragments of cornishes, capitals, shafts, entablatures, pilasters, all of white marble, and of the most exquisite workmanship" (*Ruins* I, 3–4). The contemplation of these ruins triggers the narrator's larger meditation on history and change: "I sought the ancient inhabitants, and their works; and I found nothing but a trace, like that of the foot of a traveller over the sand. The temples are fallen, the palaces overthrown, the ports filled up, the cities destroyed; and the earth, stripped of inhabitants, is become a place of sepulchres. . . . Great God! whence proceed these fatal revolutions? From what causes are changed the fortunes of these countries? Wherefore so many cities destroyed? Why has not this ancient population been reproduced and perpetuated?" (I, 10). PBS's treatment of the city in **lines 109–25** is sociological and political, emphasizing Palmyra as an emblem of tyrannical pride and oppression (foreshadowing here and in the next stanza on the pyramids, his sonnet *Ozymandias*).

II.132. <u>scite</u>: The orthography of *1813* provides an alternative, though increasingly obsolescent, spelling for *site* (i.e., the situation or position of a place, building, etc.) that—as the *OED* makes clear—was still in use at the beginning of the nineteenth century.

II.137–48. <u>Salem's haughty fane</u> . . . <u>dotard's vanity</u>: The opulent Temple at Jerusalem was built during the reign of King Solomon (ca. 961–922 B.C.), the <u>dotard</u> of **II.148.** As the consolidation and symbol of a fully integrated religious and political order, the Temple represents one of PBS's primary targets in *QM*. As PBS indicates, Solomon forced his subjects to serve (along with Canaanites) in labor battalions in order to realize his ambitious building program, of which the Temple was but a part and which also included numerous impressive buildings as well as a large fleet of ships and a port. According to *Rees's Cyclopædia*, "The completion of this magnificent edifice [the Temple] conferred singular celebrity on the reign of Solomon. . . . In the various departments of this great work, he employed no less than 183,600 persons." The building of the Temple is described in I Kings 5–8 and II Chronicles 2–5. Solomon's combination of forced labor and oppressive taxation led to internal rebellions within the kingdom during the latter years of his reign and helped lead to the ultimate division of Israel into two countries (Judah and Israel) shortly after his death.

Rees's indicates why Solomon might be called a dotard: "Solomon, however, notwithstanding the wisdom which rendered him so famous, had not sufficient fortitude for resisting the temptations that accompanied his prosperity. He was betrayed, in the most culpable and disgraceful manner, into the vices attendant on luxury and sensuality. Besides 700 wives, he had 300 concubines; and in his declining age, though he had erected a temple to

Jehovah the true God, and was thus implicitly pledged to preserve the religion of the Jews pure and uncorrupted, their influence caused him to degenerate into the most inexcusable idolatry."

II.149–61. <u>an inhuman</u> . . . <u>forgetfulness</u>: The anti-Semitism of this passage was an unsavory strategic feature of much radical writing, from Voltaire and Holbach to Paine and beyond, intended to discredit not simply the Jewish faith, its ostensible target, but also the underpinnings of Christianity. See, for example, PBS's *A Refutation of Deism* (1814), in which a Deist, Theosophus, confronts a Christian, Eusebes, asking "if there exist a record of such groveling absurdities and enormities so atrocious, a picture of the Deity so characteristic of a demon as that which the sacred writings of the Jews contain. I demand of you, whether as a conscientious Theist you can reconcile the conduct which is attributed to God of the Jews with your conceptions of the purity and benevolence of the divine nature" (*Prose/EBM* I, 101). In footnotes, PBS adduces so many passages from the Old Testament to document Theosophus's continued argument about the invidious nature of Old Testament Jews that Murray speculates he had compiled not only a selection of moral extracts from the Bible, which he wanted Hookham to publish as *Biblical Extracts,* but also "a selection of immoral extracts from the same source" (*Prose/EBM* I, 376; for PBS's citations from Hosea, Samuel, Exodus, Numbers, Deuteronomy, and Joshua, see *Prose/EBM* I, 102–3).

II.149. <u>inhuman and uncultured race</u>: Old Testament Jews.

II.153. <u>Promiscuous</u>: indiscriminately.

II.155. <u>he</u>: Moses. In *Refutation,* PBS wrote: "But it is blasphemy of a more hideous and unexampled nature to maintain that the Almighty God expressly commanded Moses to invade an unoffending nation, and on account of the difference of their worship utterly to destroy every human being it contained, to murder every infant and unarmed man in cold blood, to massacre the captives, to rip up the matrons, and to retain the maidens alone for concubinage and violation" (*Prose/EBM* I, 102).

II.156. <u>had</u>: *1876* initiated the variant "hath," either as a mistake or in an unnecessary attempt at emendation that has nonetheless been followed by most later editors.

II.159–60. <u>imposture</u> . . . <u>credits</u>: the fraudulent teaching of clerics, which preys upon human fears to gain acceptance.

II.171. <u>Which, . . . hear,</u>: The commas following each of these words illustrate PBS's rhetorical pointing.

II.176. <u>a tyrant's slave</u>: In *1870*, Rossetti speculates that the reading should be "'a tyrant slave'—*i.e.,* a tyrant who is a 'slave | Even to the basest appetites . . . .'" (I, 470). The passage, however, appears to be a generic condemnation of the brigand-servitors—local strongmen called *ayans*—who, in the name of the Ottoman Empire, ruled in the manner of feudal lords the various parts of what we now call Greece. The most powerful and well-known *ayan* was Ali Pasha, who was visited by Lord Byron. These local warlords represented an unhealthy decentralization of power to the Ottoman Empire, which later, under the leadership of Mahmud II (1785–1839; Sultan, 1808–39), reasserted its control, often by killing them. The character of Mahmud himself (whose two immediate predecessors were themselves deposed and killed) was to be dramatically central to PBS's *Hellas* (1821).

PBS was most likely describing a generic, rather than a particular, *ayan*. One that might have proved influential to his formulation, however, was Mehmet Pasha, who ruled parts of northern Albania rather than Greece proper between between 1757 and 1775; when he attempted to widen his territory and refused to forward taxes, the Sultan had him poisoned. Ali Pasha himself, still very much alive at the time *QM* was written, lived on to play a part in the Greek uprising of 1821 and in *Hellas.* Cf. Volney's general and quite extensive attack on the paschas as the epitome of tyrannical governors in *Ruins* I, 112–16.

II.179–81. <u>Where Cicero</u> . . . <u>deceives</u>: The Pope now rules a Rome once governed by the benevolent emperor Marcus Aurelius Antoninus (A.D. 121–180) and graced by the republican orator Marcus Tullius Cicero (106–43 B.C.), both accomplished philosophers. The Antoninus PBS refers to may be, rather, the emperor Antoninus Pius (A.D. 88–161), the immediate predecessor of Marcus Aurelius Antoninus, who was also famed for his benevolence. PBS, however, ordered the writings of "Marcus Antoninus" from Hookham in mid-December 1812. He had an especially high regard for Cicero's rigorous Skepticism and political courage, commenting in a letter of 26 November 1813 to Hogg that Cicero "is, in my estimation, one of the most admirable characters the world ever produced" (*Letters* I, 380).

II.182–210. <u>ten thousand years</u> . . . <u>with eternity</u>: The reference in this passage to a <u>stately city</u> in the Americas <u>ten thousand years</u> old and undone by its own wealth may be to the ruin of Mayan cities, as *2002* speculates, or to the Inca ruins in the Cuzco settlement, as *1968* suggests. Given the reference to current human sacrifice or cannibalism, however, PBS may well have loosely based his description on Tenochtitlán (Mexico City), the fourteenth-century Aztec capital that, as *1989* points out, was described in D. F. S. Clavigero's *History of Mexico* (trans. Charles Cullen [London: G.G. & J. Robinson, 1787) and of which he would have read a composite description in Southey's *Madoc:* I.vi.107–63 (pp. 61–62), and Notes, pp. 468–69.

If any of these suppositions is correct, the clue to understanding PBS's claim for the antiquity of the city may reside in the usage of other rhetorical poets: Laura Lockwood's *Lexicon to the English Poetical Works of John Milton* (1907) introduces Milton's use of the word *Thousand* by noting that adjectivally it "usually" refers to "an indefinitely large number" and that the noun phrase "ten thousand" is "used for any great number" (citing examples from *Paradise Lost* I.545, I.760, VI.373, VI.836, VII.559; and *Paradise Regained* III.304). See also Pope, *Dunciad* III.160 and IV.172, *Epilogue to the Satires* I.166. These and other poets also use "twenty thousand," "fifty thousand," and even "a thousand thousand," in the same manner. The Bible itself is full of such usages, perhaps most memorably in Revelation 5:11: "And I beheld, and I heard the voice of many angels round about the throne and the beasts and the elders: and the number of them was ten thousand times ten thousand, and thousands of thousands; . . ." Cf. **Ode to Heaven,** line 53.

II.183. <u>past</u>: alternative spelling for *passed*.

II.211–15. <u>There's not one atom</u> . . . <u>human veins</u>: a common formulation of eighteenth-century materialism, expressed by one of Volney's speakers: "the successive movement of the elements, of bodies which perish not, but, having composed one body, pass, when that is dissolved, into other mediums, and form other combinations. . . . All that man can comprehend with certainty is, that matter does not perish . . ." (*Ruins*, II, 53–54). Holbach described it as "the eternal circle of mutation, which all that exists is obliged to describe." "Animals, plants, and minerals, after a lapse of time, give back to nature—that is to say, to the general mass of things, to the universal magazine—the elements or principles which they have borrowed" (*System*, 26). The interconvertibility of water, rocks, and living creatures was also a central tenet of James Hutton's *The Theory of the Earth, with proofs and illustrations* (1795). Hutton's influential geological theories had an important impact on such an immediate Shelleyan source as Erasmus Darwin, who rendered the transformations over time of organic and nonorganic bodies poetically in *The Temple of Nature* IV.383–462. In a note to his text, Darwin speculated that the empirical observation of "the perpetual transmigration of matter from one body to another" led Pythagoras to his theory of the transmigration of souls and "from this doctrine he inculcated a system of morality and benevolence, as all creatures thus became related to each other" (Note to IV.417). For PBS as a Pythagorean, see Commentary to **I.145–56,** above.

II.216–24. <u>And from</u> . . . <u>city stood</u>: Alan Bewell remarks that to eighteenth-century geologists, "the earth was a silent 'archive,' its various land forms, as [Jean André] Deluc had argued, '*the monuments of its revolutions.*'" PBS's abiding interest in geology was undoubtedly provoked because, as Bewell notes, geology also "constituted an extensive and developed *theory* of revolution." During the 1790s, Bewell observes, French and British geologists developed competing theories along the lines of their own immediate national experience of the French Revolution and its aftermath, with French theories emphasizing abrupt and violent change, in which "the history of the world was a history of the supersession and extinction of worlds." British geological theory, on the other hand, was split between what Bewell calls "Hutton's Burkean view, that what we call geological revolutions are . . . slow changes occurring over vast periods of time," and the views of scriptural geologists, that the Bible provided an accurate scientific account of creation and deluge (*Wordsworth and the Enlightenment*, 247).

Georges Cuvier became the chief theoretician of the catastrophic theory of history with the publication in 1812 of *Recherches sur les ossemens fossils,* the important Preface to which was reprinted separately in numerous editions as *Discours sur les révolutions de la surface du globe.* Prominent British catastrophists include Erasmus Darwin (also influenced by James Hutton) and James Parkinson. Geological theory, whether in the Huttonian or the catastrophist form, in emphasizing the long cycles of time and change through which the earth had passed, provided PBS with yet another tool with which to dispute the accounts of orthodox Christianity. By the time of **QM** a counterreaction against theory and for strict empiricism was already taking place within British geological studies (see Roy Porter, *The Making of Geology: Earth Science in Britain, 1660–1815* [Cambridge: Cambridge UP, 1977], 204–8).

In both this passage from **QM** and, especially, in a letter of 23 November 1811 to Elizabeth Hitchener which contains a similar account, PBS reversed a common Enlightenment historical narrative in which wildernesses give way to cities, with a vision of cities predating wildernesses:

—Still, still further!—strain thy reverted Fancy when no rocks, no lakes no cloud-soaring mountains were here, but a vast populous and licentious city stood in the midst of an immense plain, myriads flocked towards it; London itself scarcely exceeds it in the variety, the extensiveness of [or?] consummateness of its corruption! Perhaps ere Man had lost reason, and lived an happy happy race.—No Tyranny, no Priestcraft, no War.—Adieu to the dazzling picture.— (**Letters** I, 189)

Cf. also the Dedication to **Peter Bell the Third,** in which PBS foresees a time when "London shall be an habitation of bitterns, when St. Paul's and Westminster Abbey shall stand, shapeless and nameless ruins in the midst of an unpeopled marsh; when the piers of Waterloo bridge shall become the nuclei of islets of reeds and osiers and cast the jagged shadows of their broken arches on the solitary stream . . . ."

II.216–17. <u>burning plains</u> . . . <u>Lybian monsters</u>: We retain from *1813* PBS's spelling of *Libyan.* Lucan describes Libya as "a land entirely uncultivated and fully exposed to sky and sun; the sun's path is directly above it and burns up the soil." After the blood from Medusa's head soaked into the burning sand, various monstrous snakes and dragons arose, though none but the dragon could be said to "yell" (*Pharsalia* IX.689ff.; trans. J. D. Duff [1928]).

II.219. <u>Greenland's</u>: The work of Hans P. Egede, first published in 1741 and translated into English in 1745 as *A Description of Greenland,* brought Greenland and the Eskimos to the fore of European attention. Egede served for fifteen years as a missionary among the Eskimos of West Greenland, attempting to convert them to Protestantism and to recolonize the old Norse settlement; he produced the first major study of their culture.

II.226–30. <u>I tell thee</u> . . . <u>unbounded world</u>: a commonplace of eighteenth-century microbiology, which, led by the late-seventeenth-century invention of the microscope and Antony van Leeuwenhoek's observation of animalcules, fostered what Desmond King-Hele has called "the eighteenth-century vogue for microbes" (*Shelley: His Thought and Work* [3rd ed.; Rutherford, N.J.: Fairleigh Dickinson UP, 1984], 38). Cf. Paine, *Age of Reason,* Part 1: "If we take a survey of our own world . . . we find every part of it—the earth, the waters, and the air that surrounds it—filled, and, as it were, crowded with life, down from the largest animals that we know of to the smallest insects the naked eye can behold, and from thence to others still smaller, and totally invisible without the assistance of the microscope. Every tree, every plant, every leaf serves not only as a habitation but as a world to some numerous race, till animal existence becomes so exceedingly refined that the effluvia of a blade of grass would be food for thousands" (*Works* VIII, 76–77).

As Marjorie Hope Nicolson has pointed out, microbiology was breaking down the boundaries between organic and inorganic life, as in the following apposite quotation she provides from Bernard de Fontenelle's influential *Entretiens sur la pluralité des mondes* (1686), appearing in a new English translation in 1760 as *Conversations on the Plurality of Worlds:* "A great many bodies which appear solid are scarce any thing, but a mass of those imperceptible animals. . . . A leaf of a tree is a little world inhabited by invisible worms, who there know mountains and abysses. . . . We even find in some kinds of very hard stone innumerable little worms which are there lodged in all parts in insensible voids, and who nourish themselves on these stones which they eat. . . . In short, all is full of life, all is animated" (*Mountain Gloom and Mountain Glory* [1959; rpt., New York: Norton, 1963], 163–64). Fontenelle's book—especially interesting because it is staged as an attempt on the part of a male savant to explain the basic tenets of the new science to a woman (a marquise)—was translated into English by Aphra Behn in 1688.

Thomas Medwin claims that a course of Adam Walker's lectures at Syon House ended on the subject of the solar microscope, after which "The mites in cheese, where the whole active population was in motion—the wing of a fly—the vermicular *animalculæ* in vinegar, and other minute creations still smaller, and even invisible to the naked eye, formed . . . the subjects of many of our conversations; and that he [PBS] had not forgotten the subject is proved by his making a solar microscope his constant companion . . ." (*Life,* ed. Forman, 28–29).

PBS asks for his solar microscope, which he had left behind at Field Place, in a letter to his mother in November 1812 (**Letters** I, 328). As analyzed by Nora Crook, Hogg's well-known anecdote about how PBS's beloved solar microscope was pawned and subsequently redeemed suggests that it was still in his possession in 1814 (see Crook, "Shelley and the Solar Microscope," *K-SR* I [1986]: 49–59, and Crook's letter, *K-SR* 4 [1989]: 112–13). Crook notes that in the solar microscope "the specimen was not merely enlarged, but that the enlarged image could also be thrown onto a screen or wall opposite the light-source," and she observes that perhaps "the solar microscope should be placed in the company of the magic lantern as a source for the 'mirrors of the gigantic shadows which futurity casts upon the present'" (113).

II.231–43. <u>I tell thee . . . rolling orbs</u>: There are numerous possible sources for PBS's description of sentient atoms and microbes as parts of highly organized living matter. Cameron, for example, suggests the work of Lord Monboddo (*Antient Metaphysics* [1789], I, 244) and William Drummond (*Academical Questions*, 252) (*YS*, 246–47). However, French materialist thought presents even more exact analogues, as *1989* recognizes. See, for example, Diderot's *Pensées sur l'Interprétation de la nature* (1754), which extrapolates from the work of Pierre-Louis Moreau de Maupertuis (*Essai sur la fonction des corps organisés*, 1754) the following argument: "all those qualities which we recognise in animals, and which the Ancients comprehended under the name of the *sensitive soul*, . . . [exist] as much in the smallest particle of matter as in the largest animal" (as quoted in H. W. Piper, *The Active Universe* [London: Athlone Press, 1962], 20). Piper illuminates the potentially useful contradictions within such materialist thought: "it made the universe altogether material and, since matter had the qualities of spirit, wholly spiritual. By changes of emphasis it could be made to appear one or the other" (21). For instance, a strong influence on PBS's thought in this passage was Holbach, whose strenuous materialism eschews the spiritual, but nonetheless proposes that—as Piper notes—all action, on whatever atomic scale, is prompted by the internal properties of matter responding to "attraction and repulsion, sympathy and antipathy, affinity or relationship, and, in men, love or hate" (21). See also Commentary for **IV.140** and **IV.143–50**.

II.233. <u>impassive</u>: without feeling or sensation.

II.252–57. <u>The Spirit . . . unchanging harmony</u>: Cf. the passage opening Book II of Lucretius, *De rerum natura* that PBS quotes in Latin in his note to **V.58** (**Note 6**). See the Commentary to this note for an English translation.

In a letter written 14 March 1812, Godwin expressed his wish to perch PBS on a Lucretian pinnacle: "It behoves [*sic*] the friend of man to search into the hidden seeds of things, and to view events in their causes. . . . Oh, that I could place you on the pinnacle of ages, from which these twenty years would shrink to an invisible point!" (**Letters** I, 269n).

III.7–8. past . . . future: Volney's *Ruines* and Condorcet's *Progrès* were PBS's models for such an historical survey.

III.25. centinels: alternative spelling for "sentinels," already somewhat archaic.

III.30–106. The King, . . . from his throne: Although in this extended portrait, PBS is generalizing about kings, he almost certainly had the Prince Regent specifically in mind and was risking government prosecution in making such an attack. Radical attacks on monarchy were, of course, widespread in the second half of the eighteenth century, and PBS would have been influenced especially by Holbach, Volney, Paine, Southey, and Godwin, the last of whom wrote about Books XIII and XIV of Fénelon's *Aventures de Télémaque* (1699), "More forcible and impressive description is scarcely any where to be found, than that of the evils inseparable from monarchical government, contained [in these chapters]" (*Pol. Justice*, ed. Priestley V.iii; II, 26n). There is no record that PBS himself read Fénelon before 1816.

III.30–33. The King, . . . appetites: Cf. Volney's *Ruins:* "And despots, considering empires as their private domains, and the people as their property, gave themselves up to depredations, and to all the licentiousness of the most arbitrary authority" (Chap. 11; I, 84).

III.37–40. thousands groan . . . famine: Cf. Paine, *Rights of Man,* Part II: "It is inhuman to talk of a million sterling a year, paid out of the public taxes of any country, for the support of any individual, whilst thousands who are forced to contribute thereto, are pining with want, and struggling with misery" (*Writings* II, 448).

III.53. fulfills: a less frequently used but alternative contemporary spelling. We have not regularized the inconsistency with which the word is spelled in *1813;* see fulfils in **VI.171.**

III.66–73. Not one moment . . . withered soul: PBS comments similarly on the sleeplessness of tyrants in **To the Emperors of Russia and Austria** (*Esd* #7), lines 35–40 (pp. 21–22, above). Cf. II *Henry IV,* III.i.5–17, especially "O thou dull god [Sleep], why li'st thou with the vile | In loathsome beds, and leavest the kingly couch | A watch-case or a common 'larum-bell?" (III.i.15–17). Cf. Southey's *Madoc:* "My days were days of fear, my hours of rest | Were like a tyrant's slumber" (I.iv, p. 39).

III.70. shun'st: To judge from the *OED* and from the correction to "shunn'st" in most nearly contemporary editions, this spelling was largely obsolescent in PBS's day.

III.72. but once, but pitying: The change in *1834* to "and pitying" in order to avoid the repetition of but in the line is a good example of how Ascham felt free to "improve" PBS's style—and how MWS, who included this reading in *1839*, but reverted to "but pitying" in *1840*, was not able to catch all of Ascham's textual changes. Both *1870* and *1927* follow *1839*.

III.74. In *1813*, the speech of the King ends at the bottom of page 34 (**line 73**); through what is almost certainly an oversight caused by the page break, *1813* does not designate the change of speaker at the top of page 35 (preceding **line 74**), though the following lines are spoken presumably by Queen Mab herself. We have emended the text accordingly.

III.78. <u>They prey like scorpions</u> . . . <u>springs of life</u>: As the entry in *Chambers's Cyclopædia* under "Venereal" makes clear, the sting of the scorpion was still in PBS's day believed to be one of the causes of syphilis (see *Shelley's Venomed Melody*, 126), hence preying upon the springs of life. See *QM* **IX.87–88:** "No longer prostitution's venomed bane | Poisoned the springs of happiness and life; . . ." PBS also may have known from his research into Eastern religions and his friendship with John Frank Newton that in the Mithraic creation myth a scorpion tries to suck from the genitals of the sacrificial white bull the holy seed ("springs of life") from which all creatures of earth arise. See the Commentary to lines 26–27 of *A winter's day* (*Esd* #11) for the use of "springs of life" instead to refer to the roots of spiritual well-being.

The guilty conscience of Macbeth may have helped suggest the image of the scorpion: "O, full of scorpions is my mind, dear wife!" (III.ii.36). But PBS's main point also appears in Holbach: "Envy, if thou darest, the sleep of the murderer, the iniquitous judge, or the oppressor, whose couches are surrounded by the torches of the furies!" (*System*, 362).

III.79–85. <u>There needeth not</u> . . . <u>merits</u>: Holbach's Nature, which works through the necessity of cause and effect, proclaims: "It is I who punish the crimes of this world. The wicked man may escape human laws, but mine he can never fly from. . . . virtue shall never go unrewarded, but crime be ever its own punishment" (*System*, 362).

III.80–83. <u>To punish</u> . . . <u>law</u>: PBS quoted these lines in a footnote to *A Dialogue—1809* (*Esd* #33).

III.90–91. <u>immured</u> | <u>Within a splendid prison</u>: Godwin: a king "is surrounded with an atmosphere, through which it is impossible for him to discover the true colours and figure of things. The persons that are near him, are in a cabal and conspiracy of their own. . . . The man, who is not accessible to every comer, who delivers up his person into the custody of another, and may, for any thing that he can tell, be precluded from that very intercourse and knowledge it is most important for him to possess, whatever name he may bear, is, in reality, a prisoner" (*Pol. Justice*, ed. Priestley V.iii; II, 25).

III.99. <u>Between a *king* and virtue</u>: Godwin: "Royalty inevitably allies itself to vice. Virtue, in proportion as it has taken possession of any character, is just, consistent and sincere. But kings, debauched from their birth, and ruined by their situation, cannot endure an intercourse with these attributes" (*Pol. Justice,* ed. Priestley V.iii; II, 26).

III.102–6. <u>not one slave</u> . . . <u>dash him from his throne</u>: Godwin quotes Fénelon (*Télémaque,* Bk. XIII): "'Render your subjects prosperous, and they will speedily refuse to labour; they will become stubborn, proud, unsubmissive to the yoke, and ripe for revolt. It is impotence and penury alone, that will render them supple, and prevent them from rebelling against the dictates of authority'" (*Pol. Justice,* ed. Priestley V.iii; II, 29). Godwin further comments, "It is the business of the governors to persuade the governed, that it is their interest to be slaves" (V.v; II, 44). Cf. also Richard Price's famous speech at the Old Jewry, *A Discourse on the Love of our Country* (1789): "Why are the nations of the world so patient under despotism?—Why do they crouch to tyrants, and submit to be treated as if they were a herd of cattle? Is it not because they are kept in darkness, and want knowledge? Enlighten them and you will elevate them" (12).

III.105. <u>Is earth's unpitying bosom</u>: The erroneous reading "In" for <u>Is</u> in *1821.CLA* (possibly a conjectural emendation) is carried over into *1821.BEN*, further evidence of the connection between the two editions.

III.106–17. <u>Those gilded flies</u> . . . <u>woe of sloth</u>: *2002* points to the attack on "Sporus" in Pope's *Epistle to Dr. Arbuthnot* (305–33) as a literary influence on PBS's condemnation of courtiers, especially lines 309–11: "Yet let me flap this Bug with gilded wings, | This painted Child of Dirt that stinks and stings." There is perhaps, too, an echo of *King Lear,* in which Lear associates laughing at "gilded butterflies" with "talk of court news" (V.iii.12–14). PBS wrote to Elizabeth Hitchener about such aristocratic <u>gilded flies</u> (see Commentary to **III.110–11**):

But what can be worse than the present aristocratical system? here are in England ten millions only 500,000 of whom live in a state of ease; the rest earn their livelihood with toil & care.—If therefore these 500,000 aristocrats who possess resources of various degrees of immensity were to permit these resources to be resolved into their original stock; that is, entirely to destroy it, if each earned his own living, which I do not see is at all incompatible with the *height* of intellectual refinement, then I affirm that each would be happy & contented, that crime & the temptation to crime wd. scarcely exist.— (*Letters* I, 127)

III.109–11. <u>The drones</u> . . . <u>glebe to yield</u>: Aristocrats are <u>drones</u>, who feed on the fruits of the manual laborer (the <u>mechanic</u>) and the rustic worker (the <u>hind</u>), who ploughs the soil (<u>glebe</u>). The Virgilian trope of the social hive was notably reproduced in Bernard de Mandeville's *The Fable of the Bees*

(1714) and became pervasive in radical discourse in the late eighteenth and early nineteenth century. Paine's *Rights of Man,* Part II, charges that the aristocracy "when compared with the active world are the drones, a seraglio of males, who neither collect the honey nor form the hive, but exist only for lazy enjoyment" (*Writings* II, 471). PBS continued to use the metaphor in both his prose and his poetry as, for example, in ***Song to the Men of England*** (1819): "Wherefore, Bees of England, forge | Many a weapon, chain, and scourge, | That these stingless drones may spoil | The forced produce of your toil?" (lines 9–12). Similarly, ***A Philosophical View of Reform*** (1819–20) claims: "The effect of the financial impostures of the modern rulers of England has been to increase the numbers of the drones. Instead of one aristocracy . . . they have supplied us with two aristocracies (i.e., one consisting of great landowners and merchants; the other of attornies, usurers, country bankers, government pensioners, and stock jobbers)" (*SC* VI, 1016).

Godwin described Mandeville's *The Fable of the Bees* as "highly worthy the attention of every man, who would learn profoundly to philosophise upon human affairs. No author has displayed, in stronger terms, the deformity of existing abuses, or proved more satisfactorily how inseparably these abuses are connected together" (*Pol. Justice,* ed. Priestley VIII.vii; II, 490n).

III.111–17. <u>stubborn glebe</u> . . . <u>woe of sloth</u>: The echoed phrase "stubborn glebe" from Gray's "Elegy Written in a Country Churchyard," line 26, as well as "starved hind" in the line above, create a certain conventional literary tone that is in tension with the scathing indictment of contemporary social conditions contained in these lines: several bad harvests in a row, combined with the ongoing war with France and the recently begun war with America, made for low wages, unemployment, and starvation for the poor. E. P. Thompson recounts a Nottingham action in September 1812 that began with several women "sticking a half penny loaf on the top of a fishing rod, after having streaked it with red ochre, and tied around it a shred of black crape, emblematic . . . of 'bleeding famine decked in Sackecloth'" (*The Making of the English Working Class* [1963; rpt., New York: Vintage Press, 1966], 65). For prior literary expression of similar sentiments, see the peasants' song in Southey's *Wat Tyler* (1794; first published, 1817):

> While the peasant works—to sleep;
> What the peasant sows—to reap;
> On the couch of ease to lie,
> Rioting in revelry;
> Be he villain, be he fool,
> Still to hold despotic rule,
> Trampling on his slaves with scorn;
> This is to be nobly born.
>
> (Act II.13–20)

III.118. <u>kings and parasites arose?</u>: Paine, *Rights of Man,* Part II: "What is called the splendor of a throne is no other than the corruption of the state. It is made up of a band of parasites, living in luxurious indolence, out of the public taxes" (*Writings* II, 448). Earlier, in Part I, Paine wrote about the origin of aristocracy: "That, then, which is called aristocracy in some countries and nobility in others arose out of the governments founded upon conquest. It was originally a military order for the purpose of supporting military government (for such were all governments founded in conquest) . . ." (*Writings* II, 321). Cf. also Charlotte Smith's *The Emigrants* (1793): "Ye venal, worthless hirelings of a Court! | Ye pamper'd Parasites! whom Britons pay | For forging fetters for them . . ." (I.329–31; *The Poems of Charlotte Smith,* ed. Stuart Curran [New York: Oxford UP, 1993]).

III.124. <u>genders</u>: engenders, creates.

III.126. <u>murder. . . . . . And</u>: We retain unaltered the ellipsis marks of *1813* for their rhetorical value.

III.131–32. <u>When man's maturer . . . of its childhood</u>: Cf. Paine, Part I of *Rights of Man,* on the aristocracy: "A certain writer, of some antiquity, says: 'When I was a child, I thought as a child; but when I became a man, I put away childish things' [i.e., I Corinthians 13:11]. It is, properly, from the elevated mind of France that the folly of titles has fallen. It has outgrown the baby clothes of *Count* and *Duke,* and breeched itself in manhood" (*Writings* II, 319–20). Nobility and titles were abolished in France by the Constituent Assembly in June 1790.

III.132–36. <u>kingly glare . . . decay</u>: These lines depict a bloodless revolution, perhaps based on the Godwinian conviction that a general change in human consciousness can transform the social order. See also Paine's rejoinder to Burke in Part I of *Rights of Man:* although the French Revolution "has apparently burst forth like a creation from a chaos, . . . it is no more than the consequence of a mental revolution priorily existing in France. The mind of the nation had changed beforehand, and the new order of things has naturally followed the new order of thoughts" (*Writings* II, 333). Cf. **Prometheus Unbound** III.i, where Jupiter is deposed in a scene far less tranquil than that which PBS imagines here.

III.145–46. <u>strong . . . multitudes</u>: perhaps a reference to the placement of military barracks in the industrial centers of the north to suppress the protests and riots of industrial workers, such as the Luddites. For PBS's sympathies with the plight of such workers, see his 26 December 1811 letter to Elizabeth Hitchener: "The manufacture[r]s [i.e., industrial workers] are reduced to starvation. My friend, the military are gone to Nottingham— Curses light on them for their motives if they destroy *one* of its famine-wasted inhabitants.—" (**Letters** I, 213).

III.150–55. <u>The virtuous man</u> . . . <u>trembling judge</u>: As Cameron points out, PBS may specifically have had in mind such "virtuous" political prisoners as Daniel Isaac Eaton and the Hunt brothers, Leigh and John (*YS*, 250). PBS wrote **Letter to Lord Ellenborough** (1812) in defense of Eaton, who was imprisoned for publishing the so-called third part of Paine's *Age of Reason* (see the Commentary below for **Note 15, lines 66–69**). As editors of *The Examiner* (begun in 1808), a weekly liberal journal, the Hunts had already been unsuccessfully prosecuted for libel three times by the government and were finally convicted of libeling the Prince Regent in an article published 22 March 1812. On 4 February 1813, Lord Ellenborough sentenced the Hunts to a two-year term of imprisonment each, a joint fine of £1000, and an additional £1500 as security for good behavior in the five years following their release. An incensed PBS attempted to start a subscription to help pay these fines. He wrote to Hookham in mid-February 1813: "I am boiling with indignation at the horrible injustice & tyranny of the sentence pronounced on Hunt & his brother, & it is on this subject that I write to you. Surely the seal of abjectness & slavery is indelibly stamped upon the character of England.—" (*Letters* I, 353). The prosecution and sentencing of Eaton and the Hunts provoked a widespread liberal backlash against the government.

III.151. <u>Who, great in his humility, as kings</u>: The alteration of <u>Who,</u> to "As" in *1870* is an example of how Rossetti felt free to "correct" or polish PBS's grammar. In this case, he justifies the choice by claiming "I have also not the least doubt that he [PBS] would have altered it if the blunder had caught his far from punctilious eye" (I, 470). However punctilious PBS's eye, there appears to be no blunder here: <u>Who</u> begins the first of two succeeding clauses that modify <u>The virtuous man</u> in **line 150**.

III.157. <u>impassive</u>: unbending, not susceptible to suffering or pain.

III.170–71. <u>Nature rejects</u> . . . <u>the citizen</u>: Cf. Paine, *Rights of Man,* Part I: "When men are spoken of as kings and subjects . . . what is it that *reasoning* man is to understand by the terms? . . . The romantic and barbarous distinction of men into Kings and subjects, though it may suit the condition of courtiers, cannot that of citizens; . . . Every citizen is a member of the Sovereignty, and, as such, can acknowledge no personal subjection; and his obedience can be only to the laws" (*Writings* II, 384–86).

III.174–80. <u>The man</u> . . . <u>A mechanized automaton</u>: In *Enquirer,* Godwin for similar reasons argues that the "first constituent" of the military character is "obedience"; hence, "A soldier is of all descriptions of men the most completely a machine" (236).

III.180–92. <u>When Nero</u> . . . <u>Nature's suggestions?</u>: In its entry on Nero (emperor, A.D. 54–68), *Rees's Cyclopædia* comments: "Pliny calls him the common enemy of mankind, and in this he has been followed by all writers, who exhibit the savage tyrant as a pattern of the most execrable barbarity and unpardonable wantonness." PBS used Nero as the prototypical tyrant twice more in *QM* (**Notes 14** and **17**). About Nero's behavior during the great fire, *Rees's* makes clear that PBS is diverging from historical sources:

The terrible conflagration of Rome in the year 64, is by Suetonius and Dio possitively [*sic*] charged upon the emperor, but Tacitus expresses a doubt concerning its origin, and the probability is, that the fire was accidental. Nero was at Antium when it happened, but returned in time to see the palace in flames. He now opened his gardens, and caused sheds to be erected for the multitudes who were deprived of a home, and took measures to prevent a scarcity, and supply the most pressing wants of the people. The emperor might have gained credit upon the whole by this disaster, had not the suspicion of his being its author still maintained its grounds in the minds of the people. The method which he took to divert it has, perhaps, excited greater detestation of his memory than all his other enormities. He caused the Christians to be accused as the incendiaries, and, without trial or inquiry, apprehended all whom he could discover in the city, and put them to death in the most horrible manner.

III.196–203. <u>The universe . . . in his agony</u>: The topos of human self-destructiveness over and against a benign and harmonious natural world was commonplace. Cf. Charlotte Smith's *The Emigrants:* "Ah! while I adore | That goodness, which design'd to all that lives | Some taste of happiness, my soul is pain'd | By the variety of woes that Man | For Man creates—. . ." (II.410–14), which is echoed in the second stanza of Wordsworth's "Lines Written in Early Spring": "To her fair works did nature link | The human soul that through me ran; | And much it griev'd my heart to think | What man has made of man" (*Wordsworth and Coleridge: "Lyrical Ballads,"* 1798, ed. W. J. B. Owen. 2nd ed. [Oxford: Oxford UP, 1969]). And, in a tone closer to PBS's, there is Thomas Campbell's *The Pleasures of Hope,* I.435–38: "Man! can thy doom no brighter soul allow? | Still must thou live a blot on Nature's brow? | Shall War's polluted banner ne'er be furled | Shall crimes and tyrants cease but with the world?" (*The Pleasures of Hope; with Other Poems* [1799]). Although it does not invoke Nature, Mary Wollstonecraft's rejoinder to Edmund Burke's *Reflections on the Revolution in France* is also worth noting: "Man preys on man; and you mourn for the idle tapestry that decorated a gothic pile, and the dronish bell that summoned the fat priest to prayer" (*A Vindication of the Rights of Men,* WMWV, 58).

III.199. <u>outcast man</u>: Neither the comma that MWS first inserted between <u>outcast</u> and <u>man</u> nor her capitalization of "Man" is necessary for indicating that the passage refers to humankind in general rather than a particular outcast. *1989* points to the possible influence of stanzas I.ix–xi in James Thomson's *Castle of Indolence* (1748), especially the line: "Outcast of Nature, man!" (I.xi.1).

III.214–40. <u>Spirit of Nature!</u> . . . <u>its perfect symmetry</u>: This hymn to the Spirit of Nature concluding **Canto III** is thoroughly Holbachian in both thought and diction (see Commentary for **I.264, III.78,** and **III.79–85**).

III.235–37. <u>his age of endless peace</u> . . . <u>Will swiftly, surely come</u>: For the relative speed of this change looked at from another perspective, see Mab's later charge to Ianthe: "Let virtue teach thee firmly to pursue | The gradual paths of an aspiring change . . ." (**IX.147–48**).

III.236. <u>Which . . . maturing,</u>: *1834* mistakenly omits the entire line.

IV.1. Although no speaker is specified at the beginning of **Canto IV,** presumably Mab continues her discourse.

IV.7. <u>had</u>: The reading "has" in both *1839* and *1840* appears to have originated in *1821.BEN* and been transmitted to *1870* (see "Textual Transmission," above). We find nothing demonstrably wrong with <u>had</u>, the reading of *1813*.

IV.10. <u>depend</u>: i.e., hang down: a usage the *OED* cites as by then chiefly literary.

IV.33–70. <u>Ah! whence yon glare</u> . . . <u>o'er a warrior's tomb</u>: There has been some confusion concerning the events to which this passage refers. Carl Grabo first saw in them an allusion to the burning of Moscow and Napoleon's retreat (*The Magic Plant: The Growth of Shelley's Thought* [Chapel Hill: U of North Carolina P, 1936], 109), a claim echoed and developed by Cameron, who states: "Canto IV opens with a vivid depiction of the burning of Moscow (the first news of the Russian disaster . . . reached London during Shelley's stay there in the late fall of 1812) . . . and Napoleon's subsequent decimating retreat" (*YS,* 251). *1989* likewise asserts that the passage is "based on the occupation and burning of Moscow . . . and on Bonaparte's subsequent costly retreat." However, a careful look at the passage will not sustain this analysis, except perhaps in the most abstract of terms.

Moscow was set on fire by the Russians between 11 and 12 August 1812, and the fire was not contained by the French until 15 August (the first mention in London of the burning that we have located is in *The Times* for 12 October 1812). The scene of battle described in PBS's passage appears to take place over a single night against a background of snow (**line 36**) and mountains (**line 39**). There was no snow in Moscow during August and there are no mountains to speak of surrounding the city—nor do the contemporary accounts that we have checked give any such misleading information. And there is certainly no indication that the fire described by PBS is set by the *defenders* of the city, rather than by the artillery of the attackers. Nor is there any substantive evidence that PBS is compressing Napoleon's disastrous retreat

into the next passage, **lines 58–70,** which appears to be set on the morning
immediately following the battle and to concern its aftermath.

However much the burning of Moscow may have been recalled by these
lines depicting the carnage of war, then, the description PBS actually pro-
vides seems to be generic rather than particular, much like a passage in
Chapter 12 of Volney's *Ruins,* which, as John Warner Taylor points out, pres-
ents a similar scene (*Sewanee Review* 14 [July 1906]: 337):

Do you see, said the Genius, those flames which spread over the earth, and do you
comprehend their causes and effects?—O Genius! I answered, I see those columns of
flame and smoke, and something like insects which accompany them. . . . Ah!
wretches, cried I, pierced with grief, these columns of flame; these insects; oh! Ge-
nius, they are men! these are the ravages of war! . . . These torrents of flame rise from
towns and villages! I see the squadrons who kindle them, and spread with drawn
swords over the fields!—Before them move the crowds of old men, women, and chil-
dren, fugitive and desolate. (I, 94–95)

Another similar scene appears in Thomas Campbell's *Hohenlinden* (1801), in
which a pure snowy mountainous landscape becomes a battlefield for a night
while the snow and the clear sky are polluted by blood and battlesmoke. Any
number of such descriptions may have contributed to PBS's depiction of war
here.

IV.76–79. <u>Man's evil nature</u> . . . <u>land</u>: PBS and Southey had discussed and
agreed upon these points of Enlightenment doctrine, held by thinkers as di-
verse as Rousseau and Godwin. On 2 January 1812, PBS wrote to Elizabeth
Hitchener: "Southey {is} no believer in original sin: he thinks that which ap-
pears to be a taint of our nature is in effect the result of unnatural political
institutions—there we agree—he thinks the prejudices of education and
sinister influence of political institution[s] adequate to account for all the
Specimens of vice which have fallen within his observations.—" (**Letters** I,
216). Cf. also Paine, *Rights of Man,* Part II: "man, were he not corrupted by
governments, is naturally the friend of man, and . . . human nature is not of
itself vicious" (*Writings* II, 453).

IV.79. <u>land.</u>: The period after <u>land</u> was mistakenly omitted in *1840.*

IV.80. <u>From kings</u> . . . <u>war arose</u>: Godwin, *Enquirer:* "War strikes not at the
offender, but the innocent. . . . Kings and ministers of state, the real authors
of the calamity, sit unmolested in their cabinet" (235–36). For Godwin, all
war originated from "those two great political monopolies, monarchy and
aristocracy" and was motivated by the pursuit of wealth and territory (*Pol.
Justice,* ed. Priestley V.xvi; II, 143). Moreover, he felt European governments
had grown to depend for their own existence upon the very inequalities built
into their economic systems; this stratified social order was easily manipu-
lated for military purposes: "It is by means of a certain distribution of in-

come, that the present governments of the world are retained in existence. Nothing more easy than to plunge nations, so organised, into war" (*Pol. Justice,* ed. Priestley VIII.ii; II, 465). Paine proclaimed that it was the "intrigue of Courts, by which the system of war is kept up . . . ," noting that war "from its productiveness, as it easily furnishes the pretence of necessity for taxes and appointments to places and offices, becomes a principal part of the system of old Governments; . . ." (*Writings* II, 389, 387).

Like many radicals of the eighteenth century (including, for instance, Holbach, Paine, and Volney), PBS further insisted on the fundamental interrelation between religion and monarchy (state religion) and hence a shared responsibility and guilt. See, for instance, his 26 July 1811 letter to Hitchener: "It is this empire of terror which is established by Religion, Monarchy is it's prototype, Aristocracy may be regarded as symbolising with [*sic*] its very essence. They are mixed—one can now scarce be distinguished from the other . . ." (**Letters** I, 126). Cf. Holbach: "*kingcraft* and *priestcraft,* in uniting their forces, always keep men in a state of degrading slavery . . ." (*System,* 285n). By the 1790s, the connection of religion to monarchy and war was already commonplace. See, for example, John Aikin's trenchant essay for January 1799 in *The Monthly Magazine,* an installment in "The Enquirer" series subtitled: "In what Degree is the Future Melioration of the State of Mankind Probable": "[religion's] ministers have long been, and are at the present day, some of the most active promoters of the horrid spirit of mutual enmity. The banner is consecrated at the altar before it is dipped in blood; and prayers are solemnly offered up in every church in Christendom for success in every act of public violence that the sovereign of each country shall please to engage in" (12).

IV.81. unbettered: i.e., "unrelieved"; *1834* reads "embittered," an alteration MWS did not follow.

IV.82–83. Let the axe . . . root: by PBS's day, a radical cliché based on John the Baptist's speech to the Pharisees and Sadducees who had come to him for baptism: "And now also the axe is laid unto the root of the trees: therefore every tree which bringeth not forth good fruit is hewn down, and cast into the fire" (Matthew 3:10). Among the many radicals who appropriated the image to represent the destruction of the old order and the initiation of the new were Voltaire (*Le dîner du comte de Boulainvilliers*), Holbach (*Système*), Condorcet (*Progrès*), and Paine (*Age of Reason*). In fact, the attorney general, in prosecuting Daniel Isaac Eaton for publishing the so-called third part of Paine's *Age of Reason,* proclaimed "let none dare to put the axe to the root of the tree; and, having subverted it, leave us without any hope of happiness here, or prospect of felicity hereafter" (*Trial,* 14).

Cf. also Godwin's analysis in the first edition of *Pol. Justice* of the shortcomings of republicanism: "Republicanism is not a remedy that strikes at the root of the evil. Injustice, oppression and misery can find an abode in those seeming happy seats. But what shall stop the progress of ardour and improvement, where the monopoly of property is unknown?" (VIII.iv; II, 821). For Godwin's fundamental rift with republican analysis of social ills, see also his earlier statement in the first edition of *Pol. Justice:* ". . . however great and extensive are the evils that are produced by monarchies and courts, by the imposture of priests and the iniquity of criminal laws, all these are imbecil [*sic*] and impotent, compared with the evils that arise out of the established administration of property" (VIII.ii; II, 799). A landed aristocrat himself, PBS in **QM** does not similarly attack property as the "root" of social ills, although he does launch a Godwinian critique of property, labor, and luxury in **Note 7;** overall he identifies "commerce" rather than landed property as the greater underlying economic problem.

IV.83–89. poison-tree . . . Eden: Erasmus Darwin's *The Botanic Garden:* "Fell UPAS sits, the HYDRA-TREE of death" (II.iii.238). We quote Darwin's note to the text at length to illustrate why PBS and others would have found the image compelling:

There is a poison-tree in the island of Java, which is said by its effluvia to have depopulated the country for 12 or 14 miles round the place of its growth. It is called, in the Malayan language, Bohon-Upas; with the juice of it the most poisonous arrows are prepared; and, to gain this, the condemned criminals are sent to the tree with proper direction both to get the juice and to secure themselves from the malignant exhalations of the tree; and are pardoned if they bring back a certain quantity of the poison. But by the registers there kept, not one in four are said to return. Not only animals of all kinds, both quadrupeds, fish, and birds, but all kinds of vegetables also are destroyed by the effluvia of the noxious tree; so that, in a district of 12 or 14 miles round it, the face of the earth is quite barren and rocky, intermixed only with the skeletons of men and animals; affording a scene of melancholy beyond what poets have described or painters delineated. Two younger trees of its own species are said to grow near it. See London Magazine for 1784, or 1783. Translated from a description of the poison-tree of the island of Java, written in Dutch by N. P. Foereh. (Vol. II, p. 115)

As the *OED* points out, the account in the *London Magazine* from which Darwin drew his information was apparently the invention of George Steevens, the Shakespeare scholar, literary art forger, and friend of Samuel Johnson. PBS may have derived his reference to the poisonous Upas tree from Darwin, but contemporary references were common (e.g., Wollstonecraft's *Rights of Woman,* Chap. 8, Southey's *Thalaba* IX, and Godwin's *St. Leon,* Chap. 28), especially since the Upas became conflated with the "axe-root" metaphor with which PBS introduces it here. For Sir Francis Burdett's famous allusion to this figure in a speech attacking the corruption of Parliament, see **CPPBS** I, 164. For further references within **QM** to the Upas tree as representing the poisonous British social order, see **IV.260–65** (where it represents the tools of tyranny), **V.44–52** (where it represents commerce) and **VI.207–8** (where it represents religion).

IV.92. Strung . . . unison: two or more strings tuned to identical pitches. The *OED* cites the following quotation from *Chambers's Cyclopædia:* "The most simple Perception the Soul can have of true Sounds, is that of Unison."

IV.98. partial: unjust.

IV.101. meteor-happiness: *1821.BEN* omits the hyphen between these words, an alteration followed by MWS in both *1839* and *1840*. We retain the compounding of the words in *1813*, which appropriately describes the brilliant promise but unattainability of the happiness that the passage invokes.

IV.102. But: merely.

IV.115. sanctifies: In *1878*, Rossetti suggests that sanctifies is a misprint for *sanctify* because "the word 'names' (rather than manhood) appears to be the right nominative" (I, 432). Locock agrees in *1911* that the proper subject of sanctifies is names, adding that PBS probably "had in his thoughts one name only" (II, 550). Neither Rossetti nor Locock emended his text, but their position is not persuasive: manhood is quite clearly the appropriate subject of sanctifies (as *1989* also agrees); the passage traces a form of ideological indoctrination through which names learned in early childhood become the means by which manhood sanctifies war. *Beachy Head* (1807), by Charlotte Smith, explores a similar process in the figure of the young boy, "who his mimic drum | Beats" until "While yet a stripling, [he] finds the sound he lov'd | Has led him on, till he has given up | His freedom, and his happiness together" (lines 274–81).

IV.133. longings: Because the larger passage (**lines 121–38**) concerns the material realities that constrain or defeat the human potential of the stranger-soul as it begins life, a strong case can be made for a conjectural emendation of longings to "lodgings," as first suggested by Reiman (see *Romantic Texts and Contexts*, 50) and emended in *2002*. *1989* identifies an important source for the passage in Southey's *Letters from England "by Don Manuel Alvarez Espriella. Translated from the Spanish"* (1807), in which Southey describes the conditions of child laborers in Manchester factories: "The dwellings of the labouring manufacturers are in narrow streets and lanes, blocked up from light and air . . . crowded together because every inch of land is of such value, that room for light and air cannot be afforded them" (II, 146). Insofar as PBS literally may be invoking these airless and dark dwellings, longings would appear to be a typo for "lodgings." However, insofar as the stranger-soul trapped in such a situation vainly longs for the un-

<u>tainting light of day</u>, the reading in *1813* also makes good sense, and we leave it unemended.

Earlier in his description of the factory conditions for children, "Don Espriella" observes: "when [I learned] that there was no rest in these walls, day nor night, I thought that if Dante had peopled one of his hells with children, here was a scene worthy to have supplied him with new images of torment. . . . They are deprived in childhood of all instruction and all enjoyment; . . . of fresh air by day and of natural sleep by night. Their health physical and moral is alike destroyed; they die of diseases induced by unremitting task work, by confinement in the impure atmosphere of crowded rooms . . . or they live to grow up without decency, without comfort, and without hope, . . . and bring forth slaves like themselves to tread in the same path of misery" (II, 145–46). The entirety of "Letter XXXVIII," from which these passages are excerpted, comprises an indictment of the British manufacturing system, which made an "ineffaceable impression" on PBS, who read Southey's *Letters from England* in 1810 or 1811, according to Thomas Medwin, who describes the whole as "one of the most frightful, faithful pictures ever drawn of the wretchedness, vice, and immorality that seem necessary concomitants of an overproduction of manufactures," and claims that it directly influenced the attack on commerce in **QM** (*Life*, ed. Forman, 190–91). Cf. PBS's letter of 26 December 1811 to Hitchener: "I gasp when I think of plate & balls & tables & kings.—I have beheld scenes of misery.—The manufacture[r]s are reduced to starvation" (**Letters** I, 213).

IV.140. <u>Soul is the only element</u>: For PBS's conception of the soul as the essence of all material things, see his letter of ?19 August 1811 to Hitchener: "Soul may be proved to be not that which changes it's first principles in every new recipient, but an elementary essence, an essence of first principles which bears the mark of casual of [or] intended impressions" (**Letters** I, 136). Cf. also PBS's letter of 24 November 1811 to Hitchener: "What is the Soul? Look at yonder flower; the blast of the North sweeps it from the earth, . . . Yet that flower hath a soul, for what is soul but that which makes an organized being to be what it is, without which it would not be so. . . . I will say then, that all nature is animated, that miscroscopic [*sic*] vision as it hath discovered to us millions of animated beings whose pursuits and passions are as eagerly followed as our own, so might it if extended find that Nature itself was but a mass of organized animation; . . ." (**Letters** I, 192–93).

IV.140–41. <u>element, . . . remained</u>: *1821.BEN* was the first to remove the full stop after <u>remained</u> that appeared in *1813,* a persuasive emendation that was independently arrived at and subsequently argued for by J. R. Tutin (*Notebook of the Shelley Society* [1888], 21) and accepted by most editors as correcting an uncaught error in *1813.* A few editors have also altered the comma after <u>element</u> in *1813* to a semicolon in order to further clarify the syntax of this problematic passage, an emendation that unnecessarily alters PBS's rhetorical pointing of the appositive.

IV.143–50. Every grain . . . eternal universe: For the basis in French materialist thought of PBS's claims about the sentient qualities of matter, see the Commentary for **II.231–43.** Piper notes that, in response to Maupertuis's theory that each molecule is sentient, Diderot proclaimed in *Pensées sur l'interprétation de la nature:* "I ask if the universe, or the whole collection of feeling and thinking molecules, forms a whole or not. If he replies that it does not, he shakes with that word the foundations of belief in the existence of God, by introducing disorder into nature. . . . If he agrees that it is a whole . . . he must admit that in consequence of this universal amalgamation, the world, like a huge animal, has a soul; and that, as the world may be infinite, this soul of the world, I do not say is, but may be an infinite system of perceptions, and the world may be God . . . ." Piper adds: "This theory in which the 'soul of the world' is a system of individual perceptions and sensibilities in matter is very different from Newton's 'ubiquitous God constituting duration and space' who appears as the world-soul of Pope and Thomson . . ." (*The Active Universe,* 20–21). PBS in these lines is closer to Maupertuis than to Pope or to Thomson.

The debate over whether matter had sentient qualities was hotly contested throughout the seventeenth and eighteenth centuries in England, beginning with Locke's claim that God could superadd thought to matter (*An Essay Concerning Human Understanding,* Bk. IV, Chap. 3, pp. 540–41), despite Ralph Cudworth's denial of any such possibility in *The True Intellectual System of the Universe: Wherein, All the Reason and Philosophy of Atheism Is Confuted; and Its Impossibility Demonstrated* (1678). Cudworth and others argued that such claims as PBS made for the sentience of matter were deistical or atheistical attempts to subvert the foundation of Christianity. A common response to the notion of thinking matter was an attempt to reduce it to absurdity; in the words of Richard Bentley's *Matter and Motion Cannot Think* (1692): If it were true, "every single Atom of our Bodies would be a distinct Animal, endued with self consciousness and personal Sensation of its own" (as quoted in John W. Yolton, *Thinking Matter: Materialism in Eighteenth-Century Britain* [Minneapolis: U of Minnesota P, 1989], 21; see Yolton, 3–13, for the broad outline of this debate, in which Hume and Priestley also participated).

IV.168. War is the statesman's game: Cf. the pamphlet entitled *Letters on the Impolicy of a Standing Army in Time of Peace . . .,* which was published by Daniel Isaac Eaton in 1793, and in which David Stewart Erskine (Earl of Buchan) declares: ". . . it is a notorious fact, that having a large Standing Army, has ever proved in all countries, a strong stimulus and incentive to the Ruling Powers of the State possessing it, to go to War, that inhuman, bloody and destructive vortex, whose devouring and insatiable maw, never knows when to be glutted with the lives and treasure of the unfortunate and unhappy people, who are drawn or forced into it. Nothing can more clearly prove the truth of the philanthropic Paine's assertion, that 'war is the Pharaoh [i.e., faro] Table of Governments, and nations the *dupes* of the Game'" (54; quoted in Paine, *Rights of Man,* Part II; *Writings* II, 413).

IV.174. participate: take part in; used here as a transitive verb.

IV.176. Secure: The verb Secure has as its subject Guards (**line 173**); "Secures" in *1813* is an uncaught grammatical error.

IV.178–79. These are the hired bravos . . . throne: See PBS's **Note 3.**

IV.181. refuse: *1839* and *1840* give refuse as "refuge," a typographical error.

IV.184. villainous: The alternative spelling "villanous" is a good example of how features of the early unauthorized editions were transmitted into modern editions. This spelling was initiated in *1829.BRO,* passed through *1834* to *1839, 1840,* and *1847*—and ultimately to *1870,* which was sent to press on cut-and-pasted leaves of the one-volume 1853 reprint of MWS's 1847 edition of the poetry. From *1870,* it entered into Hutchinson's OSA edition (*1904* and, still uncaught, *1970*) which apparently relied on *1870* as its copy-text for **QM.**

IV.190–95. They cajole . . . gold and blood: Soldiers and sailors were recruited from the lower classes into service for the Crown either by the offer of bounties or through the practice of "crimping" or "impressment," in which "press gangs" would, in effect, abduct men into military service—a practice that continued even after the Impress Service was created in 1793 to provide more orderly induction into the military. Few government practices were as bitterly hated and protested. In *Letters on the Impolicy of a Standing Army in Time of Peace . . . ,* David Stewart Erskine protested: "In arbitrary monarchies, where the Despot who reigns can say to his wretched subjects, 'Eat straw, and they eat straw,' accordingly, no wonder that they can raise Armies of human Butchers, to destroy their fellow creatures; but in a country like Great-Britain, which at least is *pretended to be free,* it becomes a matter of no small surprize [*sic*] that so many thousands of men should deliberately renounce the privileges and blessings attendant on Freemen, and voluntarily sell themselves to the most humiliating and degrading *Slavery,* for the miserable pittance of Sixpence a day, and the pitiful pride of strutting about in the mock trumpery and finery of a Soldier's Habiliments" (71). In *The Peripatetic* (1793), John Thelwall attacks press gangs as "these *British Slave merchants,* these *wholesale dealers in their brethren's blood*" (III, 143–44).

The yoking of gold and blood (**195**) is one of the most abiding tropes in PBS's poetry, beginning in **QM** and ending with **The Triumph of Life,** in which the line of Roman emperors from Caesar to Constantine "Had founded many a sceptre bearing line | And spread the plague of blood and gold abroad" (286–87); see Timothy Morton, "*Queen Mab* as Topological Repertoire" in *The Early Shelley: Vulgarisms, Politics, and Fractals,* ed. Neil Fraistat (*Romantic Circles Praxis Series,* August 1997, *Romantic Circles* Web site).

IV.196–220. Those too the tyrant serve . . . earthly power: In these sections, PBS attacks the judicial system (**IV.196–202**) and the Anglican clergy (**IV.203–20**) as tools of tyranny. MWS omitted the latter attack in *1839,* but restored it in *1840.* In fact, **IV.208–20** was one of four passages in **QM** specified in the indictment for blasphemous libel both against Clark's original piracy and *1840.*

IV.199. And, right or wrong,: As *1989* notes, right and wrong are not nouns but adjectives modifying tyrant (**IV.196**), whom they will vindicate for money whether he is right or wrong. The commas bracketing the phrase are therefore necessary and not "misleading" as claimed by *1911,* which follows *1892W* and *1904* in removing them.

IV.240. thy master: Jesus Christ.

IV.252. manhood blighted with unripe disease: This unripe, that is, *premature,* disease is venereal. See Commentary for **III.78** and **V.189–96.**

IV.255. nerveless: weak or inert.

IV.262–65. the bane . . . eat and die: another reference to the Upas tree, this time figured as the potentially enduring legacy of the priest, conqueror, or prince. For the Upas tree, see the Commentary above, **IV.83–89.**

V.1–2. Thus do the generations of the earth . . . issue from the womb: See PBS's **Note 4.**

V.4–6. even as the leaves . . . on the forest soil: See PBS's **Note 5.**

V.9. promise.: *1870* first altered the full stop after promise, an unnecessary emendation of the text.

V.26. name—: The lack of punctuation after "name" in *1813* is an error that all editors have recognized and emended.

V.34. impassive by: unmoved by (*OED* 3: "not susceptible to mental impressions"). There is no need for the emendation "impassive to" as in *1972* and *1977.*

V.38. commerce: In most Enlightenment thought, including the radicalism of Paine, commerce was seen as an important and benevolent element of progress. There were, however, frequent and vehement attacks on commerce by British radicals of the 1790s, who viewed it as a source of war and imperialism abroad and, in the words of John Thelwall, a "rank-poluted" [*sic*], "monopolizing fiend" at home, increasing the wealth of the already wealthy and exploiting the laboring poor (see Thelwall's *The Peripatetic* I, 39). Such attacks are common, for instance, throughout Blake's poetry, which includes child labor and the slave trade as among the woes of commerce.

In 1807, William Cobbett reversed his original pro-commerce position in a powerful series of articles in the *Political Register* for November and December, entitled "Perish Commerce." PBS, who clearly accepted the full range of attacks on commerce, would also have been quite receptive to Cobbett's agrarian arguments against the "upstart class" of industrialists, merchants, and financiers enfranchised by commerce at the expense of the ancient country gentry and the people at large. See, for instance, PBS's letter of 7 February 1813 to Hogg: "My republicanism it is true would bear with an aristocracy of chivalry, & refinement, before an aristocracy of commerce & vulgarity, not however from pride but because the one I consider as approaching most nearly to what man ought to be.—" (***Letters*** I, 352).

For PBS's identification of commerce with <u>vice, selfishness and corruption</u> and for a good example of his attack on commerce as <u>a foe to every thing of real worth and excellence in the human character</u>, see the final prose note of **QM** (p. 306). The suspicion with which commerce continued to be viewed by some English liberals is a notable element in Anna Barbauld's "Eighteen Hundred and Eleven, A Poem." PBS remained consistent in his stand against commerce from his early criticism of Peacock's *Genius of the Thames* ("Mr Peacock conceives that Commerce is prosperity; . . . To me it appears otherwise" [***Letters*** I, 325]) to the later ***A Philosophical View of Reform*** (1819–20). Though Peacock was sympathetic to commerce, he was able to voice the counterarguments with satiric ease. See Peacock's letter to Hookham for 6 June 1809, which supposes what a satirist might say on the subject of maritime commercialism: "It were to be wished, after all, that the crime of *water-sucking* [making navigable canals] were the worst that could be laid to the charge of commercial navigation: but we have only to advert to the conduct of the Spanish Christians in South America, of the English Christians in the East Indies, and of the Christians of all nations on the coast of Africa, to discover the deeper die of its *blood-sucking* atrocities.——" (*The Letters of Thomas Love Peacock*, ed. Nicholas A. Joukovsky [Oxford: Clarendon Press, 2001], I, 35).

V.40–43. <u>Which wealth</u> . . . <u>want demand</u>: For Godwin, the wealthy held their property only provisionally, as a kind of trust; the moral duty of the rich person "calls upon him maturely to consider in what manner it may be employed for the increase of liberty, knowledge and virtue. He has no right to dispose of a shilling of it at the suggestion of his caprice. So far from being entitled to well earned applause, for having employed some scanty pittance in the service of philanthropy, he is in the eye of justice a delinquent, if he withhold any portion from that service" (*Pol. Justice,* ed. Priestley II.ii; I, 134).

V.44. <u>poison-breathing shade</u>: another reference to the Upas tree; see Commentary to **IV.83–89.**

V.49. <u>pining famine and full-fed disease</u>: Commerce mutually involves the poor and the rich within a physically and psychologically destructive system. Lord Monboddo had similarly argued that "such is the effect of wealth in a nation, that (however paradoxical it may appear,) it does at last make all men poor and indigent; the lower sort through idleness and debauchery, the better sort through luxury, vanity, and extravagant expence" (*Antient Metaphysics* III, 195). The famine of the rural poor was the detailed subject of Samuel Jackson Pratt's *Bread; or The Poor* (1801), a work cited in the final prose note to **QM.** Pratt implies that the conditions of the poor will lead to violence if left unremedied. In that same note, PBS considers the subject of <u>full-fed disease</u>, claiming that only the wealthy "can, to any great degree, even now, indulge the unnatural craving for dead flesh, and they pay for the greater licence of the privilege by subjection to supernumerary diseases" (**Note 17, lines 286–88**).

V.51–52. <u>Which poisoned . . . clanks behind</u>: *1911* first compared these lines to ***Julian and Maddalo,*** lines 302–3: "To drag life on, which like a heavy chain | Lengthens behind with many a link of pain!—"

V.53–55. <u>Commerce . . . gold</u>: Southey, *Letters from England:* "here Commerce is the queen witch, and I had no talisman strong enough to disenchant those who were daily drinking of the golden cup of her charms" (II, 144). For the attack throughout this stanza on gold as the ruling principle of society, see Volney, *Ruins:* "the favour of the sovereign has been sold to his Visir, and the Visir has sold the empire. The law has been sold to the Cadi, and the Cadi has made sale of justice. The altar has been sold to the priest, and the priest has sold the kingdom of heaven: and gold obtaining every thing, they have sacrificed every thing to gold. For gold, friend has betrayed friend, the child his parent, the servant his master, the wife her honour, the merchant his conscience; and good faith, morals, concord, and strength, have been banished from the state" (Chap. 12; I,112). Cf. also Peacock's letter of 28 November 1808 to Hookham: "England is the modern Carthage: the love of gold, 'the last corruption of man,' pervades the whole state, from the centre to the extremities" (*Letters,* ed. Joukovsky, I, 25).

V.58. <u>The mob of peasants, nobles, priests, and kings</u>: See PBS's **Note 6.**

V.64–68. <u>Since tyrants . . . woe of war</u>: Whereas we agree with *1989* that this passage includes reference to the West Indies slave trade and the production of sugar as a luxury item, it also invokes a broader international context of oppression, war (for the acquisition and protection of markets), and commerce, as implied in the final prose note to *QM:* "we should require no spices from India; no wines from Portugal, Spain, France, or Madeira; none of those multitudinous articles of luxury, for which every corner of the globe is rifled, and which are the causes of so much individual rivalship, such calamitous and sanguinary national disputes" (**Note 17, lines 300–304**). The tyrant's <u>sale of human life</u> thus refers to slaves, both literal and metaphoric, including <u>his hosts of blind and unresisting dupes</u>, from wage-earners (**V.72**) to the tyrant's ministers (**V.70**). Cf. Volney's *Ruins:* "And those nations which call themselves polished, are they not the same that for the last three centuries have filled the earth with their injustice? Are they not those who, under the guise of commerce, have desolated India, dispeopled a new continent, and subject Africa at present to the most barbarous slavery? Can liberty be born from the bosom of despots? and shall justice be rendered by the hands of piracy and avarice?" (Chap. 14; II, 140–41).

The extent to which the connections between war, slavery, and commerce were already commonplace by the late 1790s is suggested by John Aikin's essay for January 1799 in *The Monthly Magazine.* Aikin asks, "Can luxury ever be separated from refinement, avarice from commerce, or rapacity from power?" He goes on to say: "The spirit of commerce too, which so much distinguishes the present age . . . seems only to have given additional motives for war. Each state aims at a monopoly only to be established by an armed force; . . . . Further, the present system of trade can only be maintained by the slavery or subjugation of great numbers of mankind; and while the East and West Indies compose links in the chain of European commerce, cruelty and injustice must be the means by which they are made to hold together" (11, 12). See, too, William Cobbett's lament in "Perish Commerce": "to support commerce, the wars in Egypt were undertaken; the wars in India are carried on without ceasing, the war in South America, and in Africa are now undertaken. Oh! What English blood and English labour and English happiness and English honour has not this commerce cost!" (*Political Register,* 21 November 1807, 821).

V.72. <u>slaves</u>: As in **V.128,** below, the reference to slaves is to the laboring poor. The equation of the working poor to black slaves was commonplace, as Southey remarks in reviewing the second edition of Malthus's *An Essay on the Principles of Population* (*Annual Review* II [1804]: 301). See also, Southey's Spanish persona, Don Espriella, who in *Letters from England* comments: ". . . Heaven forbid that the clamour of philosophizing commercialists should prevail, and that the Spaniard should ever be brutalized by unremitting taskwork, like the negroes in America and the labouring manufacturers in England!" Through the manufacturing system, says Don Espriella, the British have become "the white slaves of the rest of the world" (II, 149–50).

V.80. Yields: We retain the singular verb form used in *1813* because PBS treats harmony and pleasure in the line above as a single compound subject. The emendation "Yield" was transmitted from *1829.BRO* through *1834* to MWS's editions and *1870*.

V.80. wealth of nations: Whereas the phrase "wealth of nations" had cultural currency due to Adam Smith's *An Inquiry into the Nature and Causes of the Wealth of Nations* (1776), there is no reason to take this as a substantive reference to Smith's work. In a letter of 6 February 1811 that is part of an epistolary debate with his father about Christianity, PBS mentioned Smith's name among a list of Deists that included Voltaire, Kames, Hume, Rousseau, and Franklin, "the life of all of whom was characterised by the strictest morality; all of whom whilst they lived were the subjects of panegyric, were the directors of literature & morality" (*Letters* I, 51). This is the only direct reference to Smith or his works in PBS's known letters. However much a derisive echo of Smith's title, the phrase invokes what was already a commonplace reformist reference to the rapaciousness of governments at the expense of the people; see for instance, Volney's *Ruins:* "And all the strength and wealth of nations were diverted to private [e.g., the monarch's] expence and personal caprice" (Chap. 11; I, 84), and Burdett's statement quoted in the Commentary to **V.93–94,** below.

V.93–94. And statesmen boast | Of wealth!: See PBS's **Note 7.** This phrase echoes a well-known speech by Sir Francis Burdett in an important 1797 debate over parliamentary reform: "Indeed, with all our boast of wealth, the mean and hard lot of poverty falls to the share of the mass of the people; and that comfort which ought to be the reward of honest labour, is seized by the griping [*sic*] hand of a rapacious government. . . . What was the cause of the revolution in France? The progress of reason and philosophy? Alas! reason and philosophy can boast of no such influence over the conduct of mankind" (*Hansard's Parliamentary Debates*, [1797–98]: Vol. XXXIII, 683). As Cameron points out, PBS's "reform pamphlets often echo the type of phrasing used" by prominent Whigs in the parliamentary debates of the 1790s (*YS*, 314 n.27). Also, cf. Southey, *Letters from England:* "The wealth of this nation is their own boast, and the envy of all the rest of Europe; yet in no other country is there so much poverty—nor is poverty any where else attended with such actual suffering" (I, 303).

See PBS's own note and the annotation to it, which elucidates the Godwinian roots underlying his argument. In *On leaving London for Wales* (*Esd* #10), a poem that deplores the huge divide between the wealthy and the poor, PBS declares, "I am the friend of the unfriended poor" (line 62; see p. 27).

V.99–101. trampled . . . field: The reference is to the procession of the Juggernaut, for which see Commentary for **VII.33–36.**

V.112–13. <u>or religion</u> . . . <u>raving mad</u>: See PBS's **Note 8.**

V.116. <u>offsprings scream</u>: Although <u>offsprings</u> has usually been made possessive by the addition of an apostrophe to either the possessive singular or plural ("offspring's" or "offsprings'"), there is no need to emend *1813*: <u>scream</u> serves as a verb, not a noun; and, as <u>their</u> in **line 117** indicates, the plural form "offsprings" (*OED* 1b) is the correct subject of the verb.

V.127–46. <u>The iron rod</u> . . . <u>native town</u>: This entire verse paragraph is strongly influenced by Gray's "Elegy Written in a Country Churchyard," previously echoed in **III.111.** In particular, for **V.127–28,** see Gray's "Chill Penury repressed their noble rage, | And froze the genial current of the soul" (51–52); and for **V.137–46,** see Gray's lines 57–60: PBS replaced Gray's examples of Hampden, Milton, and Cromwell with Milton, Cato, and Sir Isaac Newton. Marcus Porcius Cato Uticensis (95–46 B.C.), famed both for his energy and for his stalwart defense of the Roman republic, was the hero of Lucan's *Pharsalia* and Addison's poetic drama, *Cato.* PBS's introduction of Newton into this list accords with the premium placed on science throughout **QM.** On PBS's youthful fondness for Gray's poetry, see Baker, *Shelley's Major Poetry,* 26–27.

For a comparable thought, see John Ball's speech in Southey's *Wat Tyler:* "our nobles level down their vassals— | Keep them at endless labour like their brutes, | Degrading every faculty by servitude: | Repressing all the energy of mind" (III.4–7). PBS would not yet have known this work: although written during the summer of 1794, *Wat Tyler* remained unpublished until 1817.

V.127–31. <u>The iron rod</u> . . . <u>his doom</u>: See Paine, Part II of *Rights of Man:* "the resources of a country are lavished upon kings, upon courts, upon hirelings, impostors and prostitutes; and even the poor themselves, with all their wants upon them, are compelled to support the fraud that oppresses them" (*Writings* II, 462). PBS encouraged his sister-in-law, Eliza Westbrook, to "employ herself in collecting the usefu[l] passages [in Paine's works] which we shall publish" (**Letters** I, 255), a project that never reached the public.

V.130. <u>solace</u>: The comma first placed after <u>solace</u> in *1870* is unnecessary, although it does help clarify the grammatical structure of the sentence.

V.135. <u>plastic</u>: easily molded; the *OED* records the first similar use of the word as being by Erasmus Darwin in *Botanic Garden* (1791), though it was not uncommon in earlier verse of the seventeenth and eighteenth centuries. PBS would also have seen it both in Godwin's *Enquirer,* in a passage discussing a newborn infant: "How unformed and plastic is his body; how simple the features of his mind" (12) and in Wollstonecraft's *The Wrongs of Woman* (1798):

"He was then plastic in her impassioned hand—and reflected all the sentiments which animated and warmed her" (Chap. 15; *WMW* I, 173). Notopoulos traces the Platonic idea of "plastic Nature" invoked in **V.132–35,** from the Neo-Platonic writing of Cudworth, through Pope, Coleridge, and Wordsworth (*The Platonism of Shelley* [Durham: Duke UP, 1949], 183). Cf. also, Campbell's *The Pleasures of Hope* (1799): "Eternal Nature! . . . | When life sprung startling at thy plastic call" (I.489, 491).

V.147. <u>perfection's germ</u>: Like Godwin, PBS believed that human beings were infinitely perfectible; that is, capable of perpetual improvement without actually ever being brought to perfection, a state that would obviate such improvements (see *Pol. Justice,* ed. Priestley I.v; I, 93). Cf. PBS's 25 July 1811 letter to Elizabeth Hitchener: "You say that equality is unattainable, so will I observe is perfection; yet they both symbolize in their nature, they both demand that an unremitting tendency towards themselves should be made, & the nearer Society approaches towards this point the happier will it be." (***Letters*** I, 125). In *Pol. Justice* Godwin states that the most important implication of Perfectibility is that "every perfection or excellence that human beings are competent to conceive, human beings, unless in cases that are palpably and unequivocally excluded by the structure of their frame, are competent to attain" (ed. Priestley I.v; I, 93). And whereas PBS would have agreed with this claim, the final cantos of **QM** surpass in utopian bravado the vision of the future that *Pol. Justice* offers.

PBS notes approvingly in late 1811 that Southey, too, "looks forward to a state when all shall be perfected . . ." (***Letters*** I, 211–12), a statement that was later confirmed by a letter Southey wrote to Dr. Gooch on 30 November 1814: "I am fully convinced that a gradual improvement is going on in the world, has been going on from its commencement, and will continue till the human race shall attain all the perfection of which it is capable in the mortal state. This belief grows out of knowledge; that is, it is a corollary deduced from the whole history of mankind" (quoted in ***Letters*** I, 212 n.2). Southey's rendering of Perfectibility is transitional from its eighteenth-century formulations in the work of Condorcet and Godwin to a form closer to the "Progress" that was to become a prevalent nineteenth-century ideology.

V.167. <u>around</u>: "about" in *1840* is probably an uncaught compositorial error; it was followed by Rossetti in *1870* and Woodberry in *1892W*. There is no persuasive reason to alter the reading in *1813*.

V.177–78. <u>the very light of heaven | Is venal</u>: a possible reference, as *1989* indicates, to the tax on windows, first significantly levied by William Pitt the Younger in 1784: windows were taxed at a graduated rate starting at 1 shilling per window and rising rapidly in rate for any number of windows

beyond ten. According to the *Encyc. Brit.*, Pitt's added taxes had two aims—
to pay off debts from the war against the American colonies and to encour-
age foreign trade by reducing duties on such items as tea and textiles. Al-
though Pitt in *1792* subsequently revoked the tax for houses with fewer than
seven windows, financial strains brought on by the war with France led him
to triple the tax in *1797*.

V.189–96. <u>Even love is sold</u> . . . <u>with hydra-headed woes</u>: See PBS's **Note 9.**
The anonymous *Reply to the Anti-Matrimonial Hypothesis . . . in Queen Mab*
(*1821*) suggests that PBS's use of the phrase "Even love is sold" is a response
to a couplet from "A better reasoner than Mr. Shelley . . ." (9):

> Judges and senates may be bought for gold;
> Esteem, and *love*, were *never* to be *sold!*

Although unidentified in the pamphlet, the couplet is from Pope's *An Essay
on Man*, IV.177.

Crook and Guiton point out that in the eighteenth century *commerce* was a
synonym for prostitution, a meaning that in this passage blends with its more
general meaning of "any sort of venal transaction" and "intercourse, chiefly
immoral, between the sexes" (See *Shelley's Venomed Melody*, 143). The <u>pesti-
lence</u> of **V.194** is venereal disease, a subject to which the poem returns in
VIII.229–31 and **IX.87–91.**

V.197–204. <u>Falshood demands</u> . . . <u>minister to tyranny</u>: The general mean-
ing of this passage seems clear enough: the bought priest serves the ends of
the tyrannical state by keeping his pastoral flock in line, preying upon their
fear, greed, and apathy. Locock, however, in *1911* questions the pronoun ref-
erence in <u>their languid zeal</u> (**V.203**), claiming that <u>their</u> "must refer to Cow-
ardice and Avarice; but it seems much simpler to take 'their' as a slip for 'his'
(the priest's), adding perhaps a comma at bribe" (II, 551). Neither of these
options is persuasive: <u>their</u> would seem rather to refer to those <u>servile souls</u>
(**V.200**), the less than zealous followers of the priest. The punctuation needs
no emendation.

V.206–13. <u>Without a shudder</u> . . . <u>viler still!</u>: See the quotation about sol-
diers from Godwin's *Enquirer* in PBS's note to **IV.178–79.**

V.211. <u>a patriot mob</u>: "the patriot mob" in *1839* and *1840*. There is no tex-
tual warrant for MWS's change of the indefinite to the definite article, which
is followed by *1870*, *1892W*, and *1927*.

V.214–20. <u>There is a nobler glory</u> . . . <u>with dauntlessness</u>: The confusing
pronouns in these lines led Rossetti in *1870* to emend <u>Its</u> in **line 219** to "His."
However, <u>Its</u> in both **line 219** and **line 222** refers to <u>virtue</u> in **line 217**; <u>his</u> in
line 220 refers to the <u>good man</u> mentioned in **line 237** of the next stanza.

V.232. <u>mediative</u>: The rarity of this adjective ("mediating" or "intervening") led both *1829* and *1892W* mistakenly to emend it to "meditative."

VI.4. <u>periods painted . . . changing glows</u>: Although <u>periods</u> is glossed by *Shelley Concordance* as "recurring times," it clearly means "sentences," as *1911* points out. The reference is to the <u>Fairy's burning speech</u> (**VI.2**), the rhetoric of which is replete with varying and glowing colors, <u>changing glows</u> (with <u>glows</u> used as a noun). Although the addition of a comma after <u>painted</u> in *1840* would seem to be an error, perhaps by the compositor, it is followed in MWS's one-volume 1847 edition and in *1927*.

VI.18–19. <u>illuming . . . night</u>: In *1911*, Locock notes the irregular meter of these two lines, suggesting that PBS might have written "illumining" and "midnight" (II, 551).

VI.36–38. <u>scorpion . . . death</u>: The fabled suicide of the scorpion when surrounded by a ring of fire had passed into folklore and psuedo-scientific "fact" from Classical reports by Pliny and other natural historians. PBS had not only read Pliny's *Natural History* but also translated several of its books while at Eton (Medwin, *Life* I, 49–50). Oliver Goldsmith in *A History of the Earth and Animated Nature* (8 vols.; 1774), perhaps the most popular such compilation of the day, explains that although Maupertuis ineffectually tried the following experiment, Goldsmith himself was "so well assured of it by many eye-witnesses, who have seen it both in Italy and America, that I have no doubt remaining of its veracity. A scorpion, newly caught, is placed in the midst of a circle of burning charcoal, and thus an egress prevented on every side: the scorpion . . . runs about for a minute round the circle, in hopes of escaping; but finding that impossible, it stings itself on the back of the head, and in this manner the undaunted suicide instantly expires" (VII, 299). PBS would have been aware of other contemporary uses of the trope, such as, perhaps, Southey's description of Malthus in the *Annual Review* for 1803: "The latter part of his book [*An Essay on the Principles of Population*] therefore palpably confutes the former, and he perishes by a stupid suicide, like the scorpion who strikes his tail into his own head" (299). Byron's *The Giaour* alludes to the suicide of the scorpion both in the text proper (a long passage beginning: "The Mind, that broods o'er guilty woes, I Is like the Scorpion girt by fire" [lines 422–38]) and in a note explaining that his text refers to the

dubious suicide of the scorpion, so placed for experiment by gentle philosophers. Some maintain that the position of the sting, when turned towards the head, is merely a convulsive movement; but others have actually brought in the verdict 'Felo de se'. The scorpions are surely interested in a speedy decision of the question; as, if once established as insect Catos, they will probably be allowed to live as long as they think proper, without being martyred for the sake of an hypothesis. (Byron, *CPW* III, 418)

The first edition of *The Giaour* appeared in June 1813, almost certainly too late to have influenced PBS's text. PBS reuses this image in **QM IX.43–45** and, to great effect, in **The Cenci** II.ii.70–71.

VI.41. <u>Symphonious . . . planetary spheres</u>: a reference to the music of the spheres, a widespread Classical and Renaissance notion, probably initiated by the Pythagoreans, that the planets made harmonious music as they turned in their orbits around the earth (e.g., Plato, *The Republic* X.616d–617c; Aristotle, *De caelo* ii.9). Cf. Milton, *Paradise Lost:* "And in thir motions harmony Divine | So smooths her charming tones, that God's own ear | Listens delighted" (V.625–27). Holbach discussed the music of the spheres in relation to Pan's pipe, which "composed of seven unequal tubes [representing the "seven planets of our solar system"], but calculated to produce the nicest and most perfect concord" is a symbol intended to represent the "harmony of the universe" (*System,* 179). PBS first referred to the music of the spheres in **Fragment. Supposed to be an Epithalamium of Francis Ravaillac and Charlotte Cordé** (30).

VI.45–46. <u>To the red</u> . . . <u>twinkles there</u>: See PBS's **Note 10.**

VI.53. Fall . . . <u>upon the world</u>: *1839* deletes all text between the end of this line and the beginning of **Canto 8.**

VI.72–102. <u>Thou taintest</u> . . . <u>and called it God</u>!: With some alterations, PBS published these lines as a separate poem entitled **Superstition** in the **Alastor** volume. For a collation of *1813* and **Superstition,** see the foot-of-the-page collation for **Superstition** in **CPPBS** III.

VI.74. <u>distempered</u>: unrestrained.

VI.79. <u>thou becamest, a boy,</u>: <u>boy</u> is appositive of <u>thou</u>.

VI.101–2. <u>And all</u> . . . <u>God</u>!: Although, as collations make clear, this passage has been repunctuated a number of different ways by editors (as well as revised and repunctuated in *1816*), the original punctuation in *1813* makes perfect sense as is. The <u>thou</u> addressed in **line 102** is <u>Religion</u> (**line 69**), which assigns to all phenomena a single abstract cause that it calls God and to which it then bends in worship. The process of abstraction described here was already a radical commonplace, used, for instance, by Blake in *The Marriage of Heaven and Hell* (Plate 11), Volney (*Ruins,* Chap. 22), and articulated as follows by Holbach: "Man originally worshipped nature. All things were spoken of allegorically, and every part of nature was personified. Hence a Saturn, Jupiter, Apollo; &c. The vulgar did not perceive that it was nature and her parts which were thus allegorized. The source from which Gods were taken was soon forgotten. An incomprehensible being was formed from the power of nature, and called its mover. Thus nature was separated from herself" (*System*, 350). Hume likened this process to "*prosopopœia* in poetry, where trees, mountains and streams are personified, and the inanimate parts of nature acquire sentiment and passion" (*The Natural History of Religion*, ed. A. Wayne Colver [Oxford: Clarendon Press, 1976], 34).

For Joseph Ritson, who influenced PBS's writings on vegetarianism (see Commentary to **Note 17**), this process of abstraction was the ultimate source of human sacrifice: "Superstition is the mother of Ignorance and Barbarity. Priests began by persuadeing people of the existence of certain invisible beings, which they pretended to be the creatours of the world, and the dispenseërs of good and evil; and of whose wils, in fine, they were the sole interpreters. Hence arose the necessity of sacrificeës to appease the wrath or procure the favour of imaginary gods, but, in reality, to gratify the gluttonous and unnatural appetites of real daemons" (*Abstinence*, 102).

See also the beginning of the long passage that PBS quotes from Holbach in his note to **VII.13** (**Note 13, lines 121–31**).

VI.120. <u>maniac gladness</u>: The conjectural emendation in *1821.BEN* to "maniac madness" is a good example of how that edition more freely than *1821.CLA* intentionally modifies PBS's text when critical scrutiny suggests a possible change.

VI.123–25. <u>one God</u> . . . <u>dotage</u>: In its <u>senile puerility</u>, <u>Religion</u> takes the form of Christianity, with its Trinity, its tale of Christ's miraculous birth and resurrection, and its concept of eternal punishment (dramatized in **Canto VII** through the story of the Wandering Jew). The incredibility of these elements of Christianity was a favorite point of the *philosophes* and Paine.

VI.126. <u>the mad fiend</u>: Although glossed in *1911* as "religious persecution" (II, 552), the phrase clearly refers to the God created by <u>Religion</u> through the process described in the surrounding passage.

VI.131–34. <u>flames</u> . . . <u>paths</u>: The *auto-da-fé*, described here as an instrument intended to frighten children into avowing Christianity, was unsuccessful against Ianthe, who, at the beginning of the next canto, reports witnessing one as a child.

VI.132. <u>horrent</u>: "shuddering; feeling or expressing horror" (*OED* 2). See the Commentary to line 2 of **The Voyage** (**Esd** #32).

VI.156. <u>stedfast</u>: an older spelling, but still in contemporary use.

VI.167. <u>uprooted ocean-fords</u>: i.e., waterspouts.

VI.171–73. <u>No atom</u> . . . <u>act.</u>: See PBS's **Note 11**.

VI.188. <u>virtue</u>: Whereas *Shelley Concordance* incorrectly glosses this use of *virtue* as meaning "rectitude, moral excellence," it also notes PBS's use of *virtue* in other passages to mean "efficacy, power"—the definition appropriate here.

VI.192–96. phantasmal scene . . . cannot see: This description—with its shadowy images, prison, chains, and massy walls—ultimately derives from Plato's allegory of the Cave in *The Republic* VII.514A–21B, a passage influential throughout PBS's works.

VI.196. feel,: "feel" in *1840* is one of many places where MWS lightens the punctuation of *1813* by removing commas, a practice which may have its roots in her knowledge of PBS's unhappiness while he was in Italy with the way the punctuation of his press transcripts was often increased by English printers.

VI.197. Power,: The change of the comma to a period in *1840* obscures the appositive relationship between Power and Necessity in the following line.

VI.198. Necessity! . . . world!: See PBS's **Note 12.** PBS probably derived this line from Holbach, who wrote in a footnote: "This was the decided opinion of Plato, who says, *'Matter and necessity are the same thing; this necessity is the mother of the world'*" (*System*, 33n). Holbach's own source in Plato is unclear. Notopoulos suggests two possible connections. The first is to *The Republic* X.616c–617c, where "Necessity is the mother of the Fates; the orbits of the universe turn on the spindle of Necessity." In this sense, Necessity is the mother and overseer of the entire material universe. The second, and less likely, possibility is that Holbach is referring to *Timaeus* 48A: "Mind, the ruling power, persuaded necessity to bring the greater part of created things to perfection" (*The Platonism of Shelley*, 176). Cf. **Refutation:** "The necessity of matter is the ruler of the world" (***Prose/EBM*** I, 116).

VI.226–31. A shrine . . . sensitive extension of the world.: a difficult passage, variously glossed by editors, who differ especially on the meaning of sensitive extension. For instance, Locock in *1911* favors interpreting the phrase as "'extended body or space,' in the sense used by Locke and Hume" (II, 552); *1989*, as "sentient life, evolved from matter by Necessity and culminating in Man with his moral sense . . ." (I, 330). Both readings are possible, but neither solves the syntactical difficulties of the passage as a whole. The syntax indicates that the shrine raised to Necessity *is* the sensitive extension of the world, which the following line makes clear is a wonderous and eternal fane. In identifying shrine with world and fane, PBS draws on seventeenth- and eighteenth-century philosophical discourse for the phrase sensitive extension, with sensitive meaning "perceptible by the senses" (*OED* 1b). In this context, of the world means "*which is* the world"; and the shrine raised to Necessity is thus the constantly evolving world itself, as apprehended by the senses. Because the period after world in *1813* blurs somewhat the appositive relationship between world and That wonderous and eternal fane . . . , Rossetti first emended it in *1870* to a colon, and several editors have similarly lightened the punctuation—an arguable but unnecessary alteration of the rhetorical movement of the passage.

VI.232. wonderous: As Forman in *1876* notes, PBS spells the word "wondrous" elsewhere in *1813,* but varies the spelling here for metrical reasons.

VI.236. term: ending.

VI.238. Curls round . . . its strength: The subject of Curls is life (**VI.235**); its refers to fane (**VI.232**).

VII. *1839* omits this canto entirely.

VII.1–13. It is unclear precisely what *auto-da-fé* Ianthe would have been able to witness. The last actual burning of a heretic by the Portuguese Inquisition was in 1761, by the Spanish Inquisition in 1781, although heretics continued to be killed in Spain by other means until 1826. Nonetheless, PBS's general concern about vehement contemporary religious persecution is well articulated in **Letter to Lord Ellenborough** (1812): "If the law 'de heretico comburendo' has not been formally repealed, I conceive that from the promise held out by your Lordship's zeal, we need not despair of beholding the flames of persecution rekindled in Smithfield. Even now the lash that drove Descartes and Voltaire from their native country, the chains which bound Galileo, the flames which burned Vanini, again resound:— . . ." (**Prose/EBM** I, 65). Of these names, the most apposite is Lucilio Vanini (1585–1619, known in his works as "Giulio Cesare"), an Italian atheist who was imprisoned in London for freethinking, before being strangled and burnt at the stake at Toulouse on 9 February 1619 for his religious convictions. *The Life of Lucilio Vanini (alias Julius Caesar), Burnt for Atheism at Thoulouse* was translated from the French and published in London in 1730. PBS may also have been thinking of Spinoza, who is incorrectly discussed in the *Nicholson's Encyclopedia* entry "Atheism" as having been burned to death "for having avowed his adherence to the opinion of atheism" (*SC* II, 709n.1).

1927 suggests that this passage in **QM** was based on Volney's *Ruines*. The relevant section in Chapter 21 describes the attempt of a group of Christian divines to burn a rabbi who challenges the validity of their beliefs: a troop of monks advance upon him bearing a banner on which is painted "pincers, gridirons, lighted faggots, and the words *justice, charity, mercy;* It is necessary, said they, to make an example of these impious wretches, and burn them for the glory of God." The attempted burning is stopped when a "Mussulman" confronts the Christians with their own hypocrisy. The contemporary relevance of the scene is brought home, however, in a footnote mentioning that the banner "answers exactly to the banner of the Inquisition of Spanish Jacobins" (*Ruins* II, 22–23).

Cf. the description of a Spanish *auto-da-fé* in *Chambers's Cyclopædia* (rev. by Rees):

... the professed [heretics] mount their stakes by a ladder; and the Jesuits, after several repeated exhortations to be reconciled with the church, part with them, telling them they leave them to the devil. . . . On this a great shout is raised, and the cry is let the dogs' *beards be made,* which is done by thrusting flaming furze, fastened to long poles, against their faces, till their faces are burnt to a coal, which is accompanied with the loudest acclamations of joy. At last, fire is set to the furze at the bottom of the stake, over which the professed are chained so high, that the top of the flame seldom touches higher, than the seat they sit on, so that they rather seem roasted than burnt. There cannot be a more lamentable spectacle; the sufferers continuously crying out, while they are able, *misericordia por amor de Dios*: yet it is beheld by all sexes and ages, with transports of joy and satisfaction; this joy is not the effect of natural cruelty, but the spirit of their religion; . . . .

For a discussion of the various editions of the *Cyclopædia,* see Commentary for **Note 17, lines 127–30, footnote 3,** pp. 659–60.

In Horsham, the county seat near PBS's home, was a county court town where both quarter sessions and assizes were held. It was apparently the last place in England where the *peine forte et dure,* the torturing of arrested felons who refused to plead either guilty or not guilty, was used (1735), and its executions were great public spectacles, attracting as many as 3,000 people at a time to what was morbidly known as the "Horsham Hang Fair." The last public burning at the stake held at Horsham was in 1776, just sixteen years before PBS's birth; see *History of Horsham,* ed. T. P. Hudson (Chichester: West Sussex County Council, 1988), 133–34 (abstracted and reprinted from *The Victoria County History of Sussex,* Vol. VI, Pt. 2, published for the University of London Institute of Historical Research by Oxford University Press, 1986). The sentence would not have been for heresy; in eighteenth-century Britain, death by strangulation normally preceded a judicial burning. After the Quaker John Howard in 1774 issued a report on the barbarous conditions at the Horsham town jail, the town was shamed into building "the first model prison in England" and the first with single cells (see *History of Horsham,* 133–34).

VII.13. <u>There is no God!</u>: See PBS's **Note 13.** Cf. Psalms: "The fool hath said in his heart, 'There is no God'" (14:1). Holbach observes: "we find many very rational men have said, There is no God. Those who think this proposition hideous and irrational, . . . do they not tell us at the same time that they have never seen him, and therefore know nothing of him? Theology is a science, where every thing is built upon laws inverted from those common to the globe we inhabit" (*System,* 208).

A sonnet beginning "'There is no God,' the atheist cried:" was published in *The Literary Gazette* for 2 June 1821 (no. 228) as a response to *The Literary*

Gazette's earlier review of **QM**. The anonymous author, writing as "C.," ponders why God has not blasted PBS with lightning for such a statement, concluding that the "impious wretch" is better punished by remaining alive: "For well the Almighty Father knew, | Who pierces Nature with his view, | In all creation's ample round, | So fierce a hell could not be found, | As glowed within his breast" (348).

VII.17–26. <u>Let every part</u> . . . <u>its ignorance</u>: The passage argues that, given an infinite chain of cause and effect, no first cause, such as God, can be established. Cf. Sir William Drummond, *Academical Questions:* "We cannot go from any cause, which we know, directly to that, which we assume to be the first. Man cannot count the links in a chain, which infinity alone can measure. He cannot trace the series of events to the origin of time. He may think, that a God exists, and had being before nature and the world; but he can place no second cause after the first" ([1805], 39). Hogg notes that Harriet Shelley was reading *Academical Questions* aloud in November 1812 (*Life*, ed. Wolfe, II, 3). For PBS's early ambivalence about Drummond's work and later acceptance of his arguments against materialism, see Cameron, *YS*, 392–93; and for the seminal statement of the influence of Drummond's *Academical Questions* on PBS, see C. E. Pulos, *The Deep Truth: A Study of Shelley's Skepticism* (Lincoln: U of Nebraska P, 1962), 24–41. Drummond was a contributor to the radical and freethinking *Theological Inquirer* (1815), edited by George Cannon ("Erasmus Perkins"), the first journal to review **QM** (see McCalman, *Radical Underground* [Oxford: Clarendon Press, 1993], 82).

Cf. also PBS's letter to Elizabeth Hitchener on 2 January 1812, in which he reports on a discussion with Southey: "I tell him I believe that God is another signification for the Universe.—I then explain—'I think reason and analogy seem to countenance the opinion that life is infinite— . . . and in consequence of being infinite we can never arrive at its termination. How, on this hypothesis are we to arrive at a first cause?—'" (**Letters** I, 215).

VII.20. <u>silent eloquence</u>: a phrase used earlier, in **III.197**.

VII.23–24. <u>exterminable spirit</u> . . . <u>nature's only God</u>: <u>exterminable</u> seems to mean "without limits," a possible Shelleyan coinage that plays off the use of <u>term</u> ("limit" or "end") above in **line 19** (and **VI.236**), perhaps constructed by analogy with <u>interminable</u> used above in **VI.228**. Locock gives it as "ex-terminable" in *1911* to emphasize this construction of the word, for which the *OED* cites **VII.23** of **QM** as its only example. The other meaning given for *exterminable* by the *OED*, "That may be exterminated," bears an opposite and more customary sense of the word. In **VII.47** below, PBS uses <u>exterminating</u> in precisely this more usual sense.

The claim that this <u>exterminable spirit</u> is <u>nature's only God</u> accords with PBS's note to this passage, which begins by denying a God who created the universe, but affirming "The hypothesis of a pervading Spirit coeternal with the universe" (**Note 13, lines 1–3**).

VII.24–26. but human pride . . . ignorance: Diderot, "Conversation Between the Abbé Barthélemy and Diderot": "What is God but a word, a simple vocable to explain the existence of the world? And note well that after all, this word explains nothing; . . ." (*Interpreter,* 202). See, too, Holbach's comment, "The word God, will rarely be found to designate more than the unknown cause of those effects which man has either admired or dreaded" (*System,* 207), which is echoed in an 11 June 1811 letter from PBS to Elizabeth Hitchener: "What then is a God, it is a name which expresses the unknown cause, the supposititious [*sic*] origin of all existence" (***Letters*** I, 100).

VII.28. Himself . . . worshippers: The notion of God as an anthropomorphic projection permeates the works of the *philosophes*. Cf. Holbach's observation, "Indeed, it is very difficult, if not impossible to prevent man from making himself the sole model of his divinity," to which Holbach attaches a witty footnote: "It was said to a very celebrated man that 'God made man after his own image;' 'Man has returned the compliment,' replied the philosopher" (*System,* 181).

VII.30. Seeva, Buddh, Foh, Jehovah, God, or Lord: This catalogue of deities employs the comparatist technique strategically wielded by the *philosophes* to undercut the "truth" of any one notion of God, perhaps best dramatized in Chapters 20 and 21 of Volney's *Ruins,* where the Lawgiver points out that the doctrinal accounts provided by the various "Chiefs and doctors of mankind" have contradicted each other and proved that at least some are erroneous: "If then such vast numbers of us are in the wrong, who shall dare to say, I am in the right?" (*Ruins* II, 1). Seeva (Shiva) is described by Volney under the name "Chiven" as the Hindu "God of desolation and destruction . . . the most wicked" of the trinity that includes "Brama" and "Vichenou," and the one with the "most followers" (I, 192). Robert Southey in the Preface to *The Curse of Kehama* explains that "Seeva . . . is the same God whose name is variously written Seeb, Sieven and Siva, Chiven by the French, Xiven by the Portugueze . . . ." "Foh" ("Fo," "Fout," or "Fot") is the Chinese name for the Buddha (Buddh), worshipped throughout the East under various names, as Volney takes pains to point out: "At Thibet they call it Budd. . . . The Chinese having neither *b* nor *d,* have supplied their place by *f* and *t,* and have therefore said *Fout*" (*Ruins* I, 194n). Holbach notes, "Among the Chinese, the god Fo was generated by a virgin, made prolific by a ray of the sun" (*Ecce Homo,* 75).

Volney also explains that the true Hebrew pronunciation of Jehovah is "Yahouh" (Yahweh) "since it is evident that the ancients, particularly the eastern Syrians and Phœnecians, were acquainted neither with the *J* nor the *V,* which are of Tartar origin" (*Ruins* II, 161n). Cf. also the first stanza of "The Universal Prayer," in which Alexander Pope calls in quite a different spirit upon the "Father of All! in every Age, | In every Clime ador'd," as "Jehovah, Jove, or Lord!"

VII.33–36. <u>whether hosts</u> . . . <u>groans</u>: These lines depict the Hindu procession of the Juggernaut, a huge statue named for and representing Krishna (as an avatar of Vishnu, "lord of the world" or "Jagganatha," which was mounted on a car under whose wheels worshippers are said to have immolated themselves. The Juggernaut was accompanied by Brahmins, members of the highest Hindu caste, originally composed of priests. This procession is memorably described in Southey's *The Curse of Kehama* (Section XIV.5, p. 147 and its attendant prose notes), a work PBS described in June 1811 as "my most favorite poem" (**Letters** I, 101).

Arm, shoulder, breast, and thigh, with might and main,
To drag that sacred wain,
And scarce can draw along the enormous load.
Prone fall the frantic votaries in its road,
And, calling on the God,
Their self-devoted bodies there they lay
To pave his chariot-way.
On Jaga-Naut they call,
The ponderous Car rolls on, and crushes all.
Through blood and bones it ploughs its dreadful path.
Groans rise unheard; the dying cry,
And death and agony
Are trodden under foot by yon mad throng,
Who follow close, and thrust the deadly wheels along.

From **QM** to **The Triumph of Life,** the image of the Juggernaut was to haunt PBS's poetic imagination as, in the words of Stuart Curran, "a refined model for every hideous perversion resulting from superstition . . ." (*Shelley's Annus Mirabilis* [San Marino, Calif.: Huntington Library, 1975], 90). The image of the Juggernaut also appears in **QM** V.98–101 and in **Note 15, lines 250–51.**

VII.43–44. <u>religion's iron age</u> . . . <u>God of peace</u>: By invoking the four traditional ages of Classical thought (Gold, Silver, Brass, Iron), PBS indicates that religious thought has reached its nadir in the modern world with the creation of what Holbach calls a "theological God," "the last effort of the human imagination" to salvage belief in God. For Holbach, as for PBS, "The modern religion of Europe has visibly caused more ravages and troubles than any other known superstition; it was in that respect very consistent with its principles. They may well preach tolerance and mildness in the name of a despotic God, who alone has a right to the homage of the earth, who is extremely jealous, who wills that they should admit some doctrines, who pun-

Commentary for Pages 214–215   573

ishes cruelly for erroneous opinions, who demands zeal from his adorers, such a God must make fanatical persecutors of all consistent men" (*System,* 206, 200n).

VII.48. <u>Making the earth a slaughter-house</u>: The indicting of religion through the slaughter done in its name was a frequent radical tactic that PBS took to a memorable extreme in this passage. Cf. Diderot, "Conversation of a Philosopher with the Maréchale de X" (1776): "Think of the most bitter antipathy between nations which it [religion] has created and perpetuated. There is not a Moslem who doesn't imagine doing an action agreeable to God and the Holy Prophet, by exterminating all Christians, who, on their side, are hardly more tolerant. Think of the divisions within a nation which it has created and perpetuated, which are rarely extinguished without bloodshed. Our history offers us examples only too recent and too terrible" (*Interpreter,* 222).

As Carl Grabo notes in *A Newton Among Poets* ([1930; rpt., New York: Cooper Square Publishers, 1968], 23), PBS would have seen in Erasmus Darwin's *The Temple of Nature* IV.66 the following line: "And one great Slaughterhouse the warring world!" (134). However, the immediate context of Darwin's line, which describes a natural world red in tooth and claw, differs markedly from PBS's attack on a world devastated by priests and religion. Albert Elmer Hancock cites a more relevant passage from Chapter 12 of Volney's *Ruins:* "'God blesses your arms,' say the priests; 'continue to fast and fight,' and they sprinkled water on the people. And the people breathed nothing but war and slaughter" (*The French Revolution and the English Poets* [1899; Port Washington, N.Y.: Kennikat Press, 1967], 59). In *Le bon sens* Holbach writes of priests: "What can be more presumptuous, than to arm nations and deluge the world in blood, in order to establish or defend futile conjectures?" (*Good Sense,* 151).

Cf. also Theosophus's speech in **Refutation:** "The steam of slaughter, the dissonance of groans, the flames of a desolated land, are the offerings which he [the God of 'uncivilized' cultures] deems acceptable, and his innumerable votaries throughout the world have made it a point of duty to worship him to his taste. The Phenicians, the Druids and the Mexicans have immolated hundreds at the shrines of their divinity, and the high and holy name of God has been in all ages the watch word of the most unsparing massacres, the sanction of the most atrocious perfidies" (***Prose/EBM*** I, 101). Holbach makes much the same point with similar examples in *System* (265) and in the Preface to *Le bon sens* (which PBS footnotes in **Refutation**).

VII.49–66. <u>O Spirit!</u> . . . <u>thy questioning</u>: This passage anticipates the "two worlds of life and death" in **Prometheus Unbound,** an image of the collective memory, which contains "Dreams and the light imaginings of men | And all that faith creates, or love desires, | Terrible, strange, sublime and beauteous shapes" (I.200–202), and from which the Titan summons the phantasm of Jupiter. Mab is able to summon the phantasm Ahasuerus from a similar cultural archive, the <u>Tablets that never fade</u>, an image for human memory inscribed by sense impressions, dreams, desires, and <u>purblind</u> (i.e., impaired) <u>faith</u>.

VII.60–63. <u>for to me is given</u> . . . <u>and reality</u>: Cf. Sir William Jones, *The Palace of Fortune,* in which the goddess Fortune proclaims: "To me has fate the pleasing task assign'd | To rule the various thoughts of humankind; . . ." (*Poems, Consisting Chiefly of Translations from the Asiatick Languages* [Oxford: Clarendon Press, 1772], 17).

VII.67. <u>Ahasuerus, rise!</u>: See PBS's **Note 14.** For PBS's treatment of the legend of Ahasuerus, the Wandering Jew, see the Commentary for PBS's **Note 14** and for ***The Wandering Jew*** (in ***CPPBS*** I, 200–204). The accounts *QM* provides of Ahasuerus's actual crime vary between the text of the poem and its note. In the poem, Ahasuerus mocks Christ's suffering on the cross and is malignantly cursed by Christ. In the note, Ahasuerus callously drives from his door a Christ who is exhausted from carrying the cross, and whereas Christ himself "utters no complaint," an angel of death curses Ahasuerus. Whether intentional or not, the discrepancy between these accounts highlights their fictionality and the adaptability of the legend. In fact, most critical accounts of the legend emphasize its indefinite origins and its protean form through time, emphasizing what Frank Felsenstein describes as "its ability to adapt in different circumstances to the exigencies of those who employ it" (*Anti-Semitic Stereotypes: A Paradigm of Otherness in English Popular Culture, 1660–1830* [Baltimore: Johns Hopkins UP, 1995], 62). Felsenstein also notes that the Wandering Jew, as an Other, is both a projection of Christian beliefs and values and a means—through his repeated testimony—of validating to the skeptical the historical authenticity of Christ's crucifixion and sacrifice (see 58–89). PBS inverts these two aspects of the legend, using the Wandering Jew as a means of discrediting Christian values and beliefs and insisting upon the fictionality of its central events. These events and the existence of God are true from the perspective of the Wandering Jew only because he is himself <u>a wondrous phantom</u> (**line 64**), part of the larger fiction constructed by Christianity.

VII.85–96. <u>Once his</u> . . . <u>pollute</u>: *1989* points out a possible biblical reference to Numbers 16, in which those who resist the consolidation of power by Moses and Aaron as prince and priest are devastated by God: some swallowed up alive by the earth, some destroyed by fire, and the remainder killed by plague. **Lines 84–96** were cited in the indictments for blasphemous libel against *1821.CLA* and *1840*. See also the Commentary to ***The wandering Jew's soliloquy*** (***Esd*** #51).

VII.97. <u>fiend</u>: Some copies of the otherwise unexpurgated version of *1821.CLA* omit the word *fiend* without indicating with dashes that there has been an omission.

VII.99. <u>pæans</u>: songs of thanks, praise, or joy.

VII.100–103. <u>A murderer</u> . . . <u>Accomplice</u> . . . <u>in crime</u>: For Moses as a murderer, see the Commentary to **II.155,** above, and Exodus 2:12, where he slays an Egyptian and hides him in the sand. For Moses as God's accomplice in crime, see PBS's quotation in **Refutation** of Exodus 32: 26–28: "When Moses stood in the gate of the court and said—Who is of the Lord's side? Let him come unto me. And all the sons of Levi gathered themselves together unto him. *Thus saith the Lord God of Israel,* put every man his sword by his side, and go in and out from gate to gate throughout the camp, and *slay every man his brother, and every man his companion, and every man his neighbor.* And the children of Levi did according to the word of Moses, and there fell of the people on that day about twenty three thousand men. *Exodus,* Chap. XXXII, v. 26" (***Prose/EBM*** I, 102n.4). PBS's quotation from Exodus is notable for its strategic placement of italics and for its alteration of the number killed from three thousand in the Bible to "twenty three thousand."

Moses is described as one of history's "legal murderers" in **A retrospect of Times of Old** (**Esd** #31), in PBS's note to **line 72.** Cf. also Paine, *Age of Reason,* Part II: "Among the detestable villains that in any period of the world have disgraced the name of man, it is impossible to find a greater than Moses . . ." (*Works* VIII, 134).

VII.100–114. <u>A murderer</u> . . . <u>misery to my fame</u>: This was another of the four passages in **QM** specified in the indictment against Clark's *1821* piracy and *1840* for blasphemous libel.

VII.107. <u>seven days' toil</u>: God's—or, at least, Ahasuerus's—memory would seem to be faulty here: as PBS recognizes in the note to **VII.135–36,** "God made the earth in six days," according to the Bible.

VII.114. <u>All misery</u> . . . <u>fame</u>: Holbach: "A theology which assures us that God has been able to create men for the purpose of rendering them eternally miserable, shows us nothing but an evil and malicious genius, whose malice is inconceivable, and infinitely surpasses the cruelty of the most depraved beings of our species. . . . Such is the Divinity which is adored even by those nations who boast of being the most enlightened in this world!" (*System,* 200).

VII.119. <u>Wade</u> . . . <u>woman's blood</u>: In **Refutation,** PBS quotes the following apposite passage from Numbers 31:7–18: "And they warred against the Midianites . . . and the children of Israel took all the women of Midian captives. . . . And Moses said unto them—*Have ye saved all the women alive?*— . . .

Now therefore . . . kill every woman that hath known man by lying with him. And all the women-children that have not known a man by lying with him, keep alive for yourselves" (**Prose**/*EBM* I, 102). This passage, analyzed by Paine in Part II of *Age of Reason* and often cited by radicals, was quoted by Eaton during his trial (to the outrage of Lord Ellenborough) in order to illustrate "the barbarities of the Jews" and the bloodthirstiness of the God they worshipped (*Trial,* 28).

VII.121–26. <u>Yet ever burning . . . their God</u>: In **Refutation,** Theosophus objects to the Christian moral economy in which "the good and wise of all ages, involved in one common fate with the ignorant and wicked, have been tainted by involuntary and inevitable error which torments infinite in duration may not avail to expiate" (**Prose**/*EBM* I, 104). Such a critique is common in radical attacks on Christianity. Holbach comments: "In short, theology invests their God with the incommunicable privilege of acting contrary to all the laws of nature and of reason, whilst it is upon his reason, his justice, his wisdom . . . that they are willing to establish the worship which we owe him and the duties of morality. What an ocean of contradictions!" (*System,* 199).

VII.133. <u>but</u>: *1821.BEN* may have omitted <u>but</u> in the (mistaken) belief that the line was hypermetrical. For the variations of rhythms in PBS's poetry, even within a set metrical norm, see the poems in **Esd** and the chart in Appendix A.

VII.135–36. <u>I will . . . world</u>: See PBS's **Note 15.** In Holbach, *Ecce Homo,* those who question Christianity "aver that God his father, without exposing his son to such cruel torments, might with a single word have pardoned guilty men, conformed them to his views, and forgiven them their sins. They think that the conduct of God would have been more generous had he appeased his wrath by requiring less, in exchange for an apple eaten four thousand years ago" (213).

VII.136–37. <u>he shall arise . . . unnoticed corner of the earth</u>: The mystery of the Incarnation and the obscurity of Palestine as the birthplace of Christ were often attacked in infidel literature, as *1989* mentions, pointing to the following passage in Holbach's *Le bon sens:* "You blush for your fellow-citizens, who allow themselves to be persuaded, that the God of the universe could change himself into a man, and die upon a cross in a corner of Asia" (*Good Sense,* 80). Although *1989* claims that it is not known if PBS read *Le bon sens,* PBS quotes from its Preface in **Refutation** (see **Prose**/*EBM* I, 101).

VII.149. <u>endlessly,</u>: *1989* silently replaces the comma after <u>endlessly</u> in *1813* with a period.

VII.156. <u>Many . . . elect</u>: echoing Matthew 22:14: "For many are called, but few *are* chosen." Holbach, *Ecce Homo:* "The small number of the chosen, the difficulty of salvation, and the danger of exercising a reason are everywhere

Commentary for Pages 216–218   577

announced in the gospel. Everything, in short, seems indeed to demonstrate that God has sent his dear Son to the nations only to ensnare them . . ." (40).

VII.163–67. <u>humbly he came</u> . . . <u>parish demagogue</u>: Cf. Holbach's description of Jesus in *Ecce Homo:* "In fine, we shall behold an artisan, a melancholy enthusiast and unskilful charlatan, emerging from a carpenter's shop, in order to deceive men of his own cast . . ." (44). The character of Jesus is later described as "a fairly constant combination of zeal and trickery . . ." (246).

VII.170–72. <u>sword</u> . . . <u>soul</u>: a reference to Matthew 10:34: "Think not that I am come to send peace on earth: I came not to send peace, but a sword." Whereas PBS's harsh description of Jesus in these lines may seem in tension with his portrayal of Jesus as a social reformer "foremost [in] the list of true heroes who have died in the glorious martyrdom of liberty" in his note to **VII.135–36,** the difference between the two positions can be justified because Ahasuerus, not PBS himself, is here the speaker. And as PBS explains in the note, those who (like Ahasuerus) accept "the pretended character" of Jesus "as the Son of God," rather than as a man, believe in "a hypocritical demon, who announces himself as the God of compassion and peace, even whilst he stretches forth his blood-red hand with the sword of discord to waste the earth" (see **Note 15, lines 35–42**). For PBS's own conflicted feelings about Jesus, see the Commentary on the latter passage and the footnote to it in his note.

Cf. ***Refutation,*** in which Theosophus comments: "I will admit that one prediction of Jesus Christ has been indisputably fulfilled. *I come not to bring peace upon earth, but a sword.* Christianity indeed has equalled Judaism in the atrocities, and exceeded it in the extent of its desolation. Eleven millions of men, women and children have been killed in battle, butchered in their sleep, burned to death at public festivals of sacrifice, poisoned, tortured, assassinated and pillaged in the spirit of the Religion of Peace, and for the glory of the most merciful God" (***Prose**/EBM* I, 104).

VII.173. <u>At</u> . . . <u>death</u>: This entire line was omitted by *1834,* apparently by accident.

VII.176–78. <u>Indignantly I summed</u> . . . <u>in my country</u>: *QM* provides a puzzling motive for Ahasuerus's mockery of Jesus (which was left unexplained in *WJ*). Perhaps Ahasuerus has, as *1989* surmises, "proleptic knowledge of events after the Crucifixion"; he, at least, knows that Christ has come "to bring not peace on earth, but a sword." It is even more likely, however, that because Ahasuerus views Jesus as God "Incarnate . . . | Veiling his horrible Godhead in the shape | Of man" (**VII.163–65**), he deems Jesus responsible with God the Father for past "massacres and miseries" (**VII.177**) undergone (and perpetuated) by the Jews.

VII.180. <u>reillumined</u>: "re-illumed" in *1840* probably derives from *1821.BEN* (see "Textual Transmission," above), though it might have been a "correction" by the compositor.

VII.181–83. <u>I go, . . . Eternally.————</u>: based on John 21:20–23, in which Peter asks the resurrected Jesus about the fate of John; Jesus replies: "If I will that he tarry till I come, what *is that* to thee?" The text continues: "Then went this saying abroad among the brethren, that that disciple [John] should not die . . . ."

VII.185. <u>tranced</u> . . . <u>charmed</u>: For the meter of this line to be regular, the *ed* of <u>charmed</u> would have to be voiced.

VII.192. <u>ghastily</u>: frightfully or horribly. The *OED* gives "ghastily" as a rare adverb that is synonymous with "ghastly" (the reading in both *1821.BEN* and *1840*) and "ghastlily" (the reading in *1834*). PBS himself uses "ghastlily" in **Zeinab and Kethema** (*Esd* #49), line 137.

VII.194–95. <u>had long learned</u> . . . <u>servitude of heaven</u>: The thematic resemblances between PBS's Ahasuerus and Milton's Satan in *Paradise Lost* are further underscored in this first of three direct rhetorical echoes: "Better to reign in Hell, than serve in Heav'n" (*PL* I.263). In **VII.198,** Ahasuerus pledges <u>to wage unweariable war</u> against God, echoing Satan's vow "To wage . . . eternal War | Irreconcilable to our grand Foe . . ." (*PL* I.121). For the third echo, see Commentary to **VII.256–58,** below. The connection between the Wandering Jew and Satan is explicitly drawn in *WJ*, in which Cantos I and III begin with epigraphs based on descriptions of Satan in *Paradise Lost* (IV.73–78, I.591–94, and I.600–602).

VII.205–20. <u>These</u> . . . <u>victory!</u>: The general import of this long sentence is relatively clear: it presents a series of examples concerning the bloodthirstiness of so-called Christians and self-appointed servants of God, who turn from massacring "infidels" to massacring each other. However, the grammatical structure of the sentence is difficult, hinging especially on the meaning of <u>So, when</u> in **line 208,** which could be seen as beginning a long subordinate clause ending in **line 220** that is not connected to an independent clause. However, <u>So</u> should probably be read as meaning "They [the Christians] were such" [bloodthirsty, practicing war] when they turned to killing each other instead of infidels (see *OED* 4, for *So* as "representing a word or phrase already employed: Of that nature or description"). In *1911,* Locock suggests "So also have I seen them when they turned to the massacre of mere strangers" (II, 552). *1989* conjectures "'Unchanged in nature,' i.e., turning merely from the conquest of infidels to wars among themselves." Rossetti speculates in *1878* that <u>So</u> may be an error for "To." The tortured sentence structure is dramatically appropriate, since the Wandering Jew is ranting here.

Cf. Paine, *Age of Reason,* Part II, on the sanguinary spirit of Christianity and its attendant hypocrisy: "Whence arose . . . the bloody persecutions and tortures unto death, and religious wars, that . . . have laid Europe in blood and ashes—. . . . Some Christians pretend that Christianity was not established by the sword; but of what period of time do they speak? It was impossible that twelve men could begin with the sword; they had not the power; but no sooner were the professors of Christianity sufficiently powerful to employ the sword than they did so, and the stake and fagot, too; and Mahomet could not do it sooner" (*Works* VIII, 270).

VII.206–7. power; . . . war,: Rossetti first emended the punctuation of these two lines to "power, . . . war;"—an alteration followed by many subsequent editors. However, given the overall grammatical confusion of the entire sentence (see the note above), we prefer the reading in *1813* to this emendation.

VII.208. but: "only" or "merely."

VII.214. its hopes were dreaming: The pronoun its refers to husband's heart in **line 213:** the hopes of the husband's heart are thus doing the dreaming. Apparently finding the reference confused, *1821.BEN* emended its to "his," so as to refer to the husband proper as the dreamer.

VII.218. winepress . . . Almighty's wrath: a reference to Revelation 14:19–20, where an angel thrust his sickle into the earth "and gathered the vine of the earth, and cast *it* into the great winepress of the wrath of God. And . . . blood came out of the winepress, even unto the horse bridles, by the space of a thousand *and* six hundred furlongs."

VII.219. red cross: *1989* suggests that **VII.208–24** describes the conflicts that arose between the Arian and Donatist heresies during the rule of Constantine's son Constantius, as related by Gibbon in *Decline and Fall* (Chaps. 20–21). Whereas Gibbon includes in Chapter 20 an account of the miracle through which Constantine adopted the cross as his military standard, this attribution seems to us overparticularized. PBS's usual method was to generalize such indictments, and the internecine wars within Christianity described in these lines could refer to any crusade of one group of Christians against another, such as, for instance, the brutal repression of the Albigensian heresy in the thirteenth century, out of which both a crusade (1209) and the Inquisition arose, or the bloody massacre of the Waldensians in 1655, the subject of Milton's sonnet "On the Late Massacre in Piedmont." Ahasuerus's long life makes him the perfect witness to the full history of such violence.

Holbach also condemns the general violence between Christian factions in a chapter (18) of *Ecce Homo* on Christianity from Constantine's day to the present: "We shall not go into details over the quarrels to which the Christian religion has given rise. We shall merely observe that they were continual, and have frequently been accompanied by consequences so deplorable that nations have had reason over a hundred times each century to miss the peace of paganism and the tolerant idolatory of their forebears. The gospel, or glad tidings, constantly provided the signal for committing crimes. The Cross was the banner under which [men] assembled to glut the earth with blood" (267).

VII.228. <u>sanctify</u>: During imposition, type fell out of the chase in *1821.BEN,* leaving "sanc ify" in this line and "o" (for <u>of</u>) in **line 254.**

VII.233. <u>spirits of the Lord</u>: Although *spirits* has sometimes been capitalized by previous editors, these are emphatically not supernatural agents, but rather <u>God's worshippers</u> (**VII.225**) whose actions are being described in detail by PBS. Rossetti, on the other hand, was convinced that the word should read "Spirit."

VII.236–37. <u>crime and misery, . . . flows</u>: Once again, PBS treats a compound subject as singular.

VII.237–49. <u>Which flows . . . torments for the brave</u>: i.e., even <u>God's</u> slaves on earth must now pretend to speak of love and mercy because of the progress of reason, which will eventually make impotent <u>God's</u> rage and malice.

VII.244. <u>freedom's young arm dare . . . chastise</u>: "dares" in *1840* was an error carried over from *1834*—either a typo or a failure to note the subjunctive use of the verb.

VII.256–58. <u>Yet peaceful . . . unalterable will</u>: Cf. Satan, in *Paradise Lost,* whose refusal to surrender to God rests on "the unconquerable Will, | . . . And courage never to submit or yield . . ." (I.106, 108). In claiming serenity and peace for himself in opposition to tyranny, Ahasuerus departs from the traditional Wandering Jew, whose essence, as William Marshall has pointed out, is "eternal and unqualified suffering." Marshall sees PBS as fissuring the character so as to make Ahasuerus resemble the "'virtuous man' appearing earlier in the poem (III.150–61), who, though imprisoned by the evil king, is actually free and happy. Possibly he prefigures Prometheus as a type of hero . . ." (*MLN* 74 [May 1959]: 399).

VII.259–63. <u>Even as a giant oak . . . wintry storm</u>: *1989* notes that these lines may have been drawn originally from Milton's description of the fallen angels in *Paradise Lost* I.612–15: "As when Heaven's Fire | Hath scath'd the Forest Oaks, or Mountain Pines, | With singed top thir stately growth though bare | Stands on the blasted Heath." Medwin pointed out that this passage in *QM* was introduced "but slightly changed, from the original Wandering Jew [*WJ* III.213–23], which he [PBS] took as an epigraph of a chapter in his Rosicrucian [*St. Irv,* Chap. 10]" (*Life,* ed. Forman, 2). See our Commentary to *WJ* III.213, 215–23 (*CPPBS* I, 223). The "shattered oak" at Cwm Elan plays an important symbolic role in the "Graveyard Group" of poems in *Esd*—all written before this passage in *QM;* see the Commentary introducing *Dark Spirit of the desert rude* (*Esd* #20).

VII.272. <u>The matter</u> . . . <u>dreams are made</u>: echoing Prospero in Shakespeare's *The Tempest:* "We are such stuff | As dreams are made on . . ." (IV.i.156–57). The final stanza of **Canto VII,** with the disappearance of the phantasmal Ahasuerus, recalls the ending of the masque staged in *The Tempest* (the occasion for Prospero's remarks), in which "These our actors, | . . . were all spirits and | Are melted into air . . ." (IV.i.148–50). Cf. the speeches of Ahasuerus in **Hellas** 762–85, 792ff.

VIII.3–5. <u>Time!</u> . . . <u>thy half-devoured babes</u>: Because Kronus (also Kronos or Cronos), King of the Titans, had been warned that he would be overthrown by his own child, he swallowed each child as soon as it was born, until his wife Rhea tricked him into swallowing a stone instead of Zeus. After Zeus had grown, he forced Kronus into disgorging his <u>half-devoured</u> siblings, who ruled with Zeus thereafter. During the Renaissance, Kronus the Titan was conflated with Chronos, God of <u>Time</u>.

VIII.12–30. <u>Through the wide rent</u> . . . <u>calmly flowed</u>: This long sentence has been broken up at various points by previous editors. The editors of *1989* do not discuss their period after <u>prime</u> (**16**), which may be a typo. *1821.BEN* adds a period (or poorly inked colon) after <u>spheres</u> (**18**) and *1839/40* add a period and dash after <u>death</u> (**22**), both justifiable stopping points. The text of *1813*, however, requires no emendation. The intricate syntax of these lines and their metaphoric linkages among music, water, feeling, and paradise reappear in **Prometheus Unbound,** Acts II and IV: they form a distinctively Shelleyan rhetoric of paradise, far removed, for instance, from the rational registers of Godwin and PBS's other rationalistic and materialistic mentors.

VIII.18. <u>Symphonious</u> . . . <u>planetary spheres</u>: Rossetti in *1878* first noted that this line echoes **VI.41.**

VIII.28. <u>sprung</u>: *1834* altered the reading in *1813* from "sprung" to "sprang." After returning in *1839* to "sprung," MWS (or her compositor) gave "sprang" in *1840*, a reading followed by Rossetti in *1870*. However, because "sprung" and "sprang" were both acceptable alternatives for the preterit in PBS's day, we retain the *1813* reading.

VIII.37. <u>Glow mantling</u>: flushing with color.

VIII.48–49. <u>To me is given</u> . . . <u>to keep</u>: These lines echo **VII.60–61.**

VIII.50–52. <u>Futurity</u> . . . <u>failing hope</u>: Cf. Volney's *Ruins,* where the speaker's Spirit comes to a point of despair after a view of the past and present that ends with the pernicious effects of religion. At this point, the "Genius," Volney's equivalent to Queen Mab, whispers to himself: "Let us revive the hope of this man; for if he who loves his fellow creatures be suffered to despair, what will become of nations? The past is perhaps too discouraging; let us then disclose to the eye of virtue the astonishing age that is ready to begin; that, on viewing the object she desires, she may be animated with new ardour, and redouble her efforts to attain it" (Chap. 14; I, 144).

Similarly, the dreaming Joan of Arc in Southey's *The Vision of the Maid of Orleans,* after her encounter with Despair, is given a vision of futurity that resembles in its tenor much of Cantos VIII and IX of **QM,** particularly in its vision of "The reign of Love":

> For by experience rous'd shall man at length
> Dash down his Moloch-Idols, Samson-like,
> And burst his fetters, only strong whilst strong
> Believed. Then in the bottomless abyss
> Oppression shall be chain'd, and Poverty
> Die, and, with her, her brood of Miseries;
> And Virtue and Equality preserve
> The reign of Love, and Earth shall once again
> Be Paradise, whilst Wisdom shall secure
> The state of bliss which Ignorance betrayed.
> (Bk. III; *Poems* [London: T. N. Longman
> and O. Rees, 1799], II, 64–65)

Joan responds to this vision by exclaiming: "Oh age of happiness! . . . I Roll fast thy current, Time, till that blest age I Arrive!" (II, 65).

VIII.56. <u>Shew</u>: an imperative. Rossetti argues unpersuasively for emending to "Shows," on the supposition that the verb has <u>virtue</u> (**VIII.54**) as its subject rather than the <u>human Spirit</u> (which he reads specifically as the Spirit of Ianthe).

As Locock observed in *1911,* although every word of **VIII.56** begins with a sibilant, "the effect is by no means unpleasing" (II, 552)—veritable virtuoso versifying by PBS.

VIII.58. In the copy of *1813* later owned by John Brooks, PBS began revisions here for the second part of **Dæmon.**

VIII.61. <u>or</u>: The variant "nor" in MWS's editions was initiated in *1834.*

VIII.70–87. <u>Those deserts</u> . . . <u>his feet</u>: The chief underlying sources of this stanza are Virgil's fourth *Eclogue* and Isaiah, especially Chapters 11, 35, 41, 43, and 51: e.g., "The wilderness and the solitary place shall be glad for them; and the desert shall rejoice, and blossom like the rose" (Isaiah 35:1) and "For the LORD shall comfort Zion; he will comfort all her waste places, and he will make her wilderness like Eden, and her desert like the garden of the LORD; joy and gladness shall be found in it, thanksgiving, and the voice of melody" (Isaiah 51:3). Also from Isaiah is the image of the child playing with the basilisk (**line 86**) or cockatrice, as it was alternatively known: "And the sucking child shall play on the hole of the asp, and the weaned child shall put his hand on the cockatrice' den" (11:8). The basilisk (*basilikos* means "kinglet") is a legendary reptile or small snake with the power of destroying animal and vegetable life by its glance or breath, as in the following lines from Southey's *Vision of the Maid of Orleans:* ". . . with eye more dangerous | Than fancied basilisk to wound whoe'er | Too bold approached" (III.271–73, p. 67). As first suggested by the anonymous author of *Reply to the Anti-Matrimonial Hypothesis . . . Queen Mab* (p. 3), PBS may have been influenced by Pope's redaction of Isaiah and Virgil in "Messiah": "The smiling Infant in his Hand shall take | The crested Basilisk and speckled Snake; | Pleas'd, the green Lustre of the Scales survey, | And with their forky Tongue shall innocently play" (lines 81–84).

VIII.70.   deserts: The spelling of deserts here (as opposed to PBS's usual "desarts") and in **lines 81** and **96,** as well as the spelling honor (as opposed to PBS's usual "honour") may indicate that either someone else prepared this part of the press transcript (perhaps Harriet Shelley) or that a different compositor was typesetting this part of the poem.

VIII.80.   unnatural famine . . . toothless cubs: Rather than drinking their mother's milk, the cubs have been unnaturally habituated to meat eating, like the horses, sheep, goats, and woodpigeons that Joseph Ritson claimed can be unnaturally brought to eat meat (*An Essay on Abstinence,* 45).

VIII.81.   Whilst: The change to "While" in MWS's editions was initiated by *1829.BRO* and transmitted through *1834.*

VIII.101–6.   Those lonely realms . . . flowrets there: The surfacing of islands in the ocean as a trope for paradise regained is later used by PBS in **Prometheus Unbound** III.ii, in which Atlantis reemerges from the ocean's depths. In the midst of a detailed geological explanation of the formation of islands, Goldsmith points to a passage in Pliny that might well have captured PBS's imagination: "Pliny assures us, that thirteen islands in the Mediterranean appeared at once emerging from the water . . ." (*A History of the Earth and Animated Nature* I, 126). PBS would also have known from Southey's *Madoc,* about the enchanted and evanescent "Green Islands of the Ocean" from Irish legend, in which "the souls of the virtuous Druids, who, not having been Christians, cannot enter the Christian heaven, but enjoy this heaven of their own" (*Madoc,* Notes, p. 488). The paradisal "garden-isle" was to haunt PBS's poetic imagination, appearing later in such works as *Lines written among the Euganean Hills* and *Epipsychidion.*

VIII.108. <u>consentaneous</u>: reciprocated, harmonious.

VIII.114. <u>Health floats . . . atmosphere</u>: As Alan Bewell has argued, during the eighteenth and through most of the nineteenth century, the dominant medical model of disease transmission was not contagion but contamination: people were thought to become sick from the disease-bearing aspects of their physical environments; "bad" air, once breathed in, would breed infection. Disease was thus a function of ecology, and the world was geographically mapped in terms of its "healthy" and "unhealthy" places (see, for instance, Leonhard Ludwig Finke's landmark study, *An Attempt at a General Medical-Practical Geography,* the first two volumes of which were published in 1792). Medical theorists consequently believed that it was possible to make an unhealthy place healthy by taking concrete steps to alter the local ecology (as in the case of malaria). PBS was thus able to foresee a time when science would triumph over geography, producing abundant food and health even in the harshest climates.

Bewell points out that whereas PBS in *QM* followed the conventional Enlightenment practice of dividing the world into three environmental zones—the polar (**VIII.145–65**), the tropical (**VIII.166–86**), and the temperate (**VIII.187–97**)—he not only represented the pathogenic effects of the first two ecologies but, far more unexpectedly, insisted that the temperate or <u>favoured clime</u> (**VIII.193**) of England is also diseased. That is, PBS inverted the models derived from Montesquieu (e.g., those of Cabanis and Jean Sylvain Bailly) that privilege the role of climate in the development of moral character and political institutions, claiming instead that physical environments are themselves socially constructed. For PBS, then, social relations and economics had an even more fundamental effect on disease and moral character than did climate and geography (see *Romanticism and Colonial Disease* [Baltimore: Johns Hopkins UP, 1999], 205–41).

VIII.115. <u>mantles</u>: spreads or foams (similarly used in **VIII.132**).

VIII.116. <u>storms deform</u>: The change to "storm deforms" in *1821.CLA* was preserved in *1821.BEN,* as was the change from <u>scatter</u> to "scatters" in **line 117.**

VIII.120–21. <u>And autumn . . . spring</u>: The elimination of winter through the precession of the equinoxes is discussed in PBS's note to **VI. 45–46;** see also the Commentary to this note.

VIII.123. <u>Reflects . . . love</u>: After this line, Rossetti inserted three lines into the text: "The buds unfold more brightly, till no more | Or frost or shower or change of seasons mars | The freshness of their amaranthine leaves." Rossetti found these lines in Charles Middleton's *Shelley and His Writings* ([London: T. C. Newby, 1858], I, 256), which contains a description of the alterations made in the Brooks copy of *1813* (later owned by Forman and now in Pfz), as PBS converted sections of *QM* into *Dæmon* and shorter set pieces. (Middleton actually copied these changes into his own copy of *QM,* which is also now located in Pfz.) Rossetti, who did not have direct access to the Brooks copy itself, noted that although Middleton located these three lines at the end of **Canto IV,** "The context makes it impossible," and because "the lines are not of the kind one is better pleased to find unplaceable," he had introduced them into "the *most* appropriate" place in the poem, with some modification: "altering the ungrammatical word 'mar' into 'mars,' and 'its' into 'their'" (II, 471). After seeing the full context of these lines in *1876* and discovering— too late to change the text proper of *1878*—that they were actually revisions PBS had sketched for the beginning of **Canto V** (**lines 12–16**), Rossetti acknowledged his mistake in the textual notes (I, 432).

VIII.124–28. <u>The lion</u> . . . <u>lamb</u>: In *QM,* the vegetarianism that will help transform the world into paradise also results from that transformation, extending from humanity to all animals, who no longer prey upon each other. A similar transformation of carnivores to herbivores occurs in *Prometheus Unbound* III.iv.78–83, where it is represented by the normally meat-eating halcyons (kingfishers) eating the no-longer poisonous berries of the nightshade (see the next note below). The ultimate source for PBS's imagery in this passage is Isaiah: "The wolf and the lamb shall feed together, and the lion shall eat straw like the bullock, and dust *shall be* the serpent's meat. They shall not hurt nor destroy in all my holy mountain, saith the LORD" (65:25). Cf. also Isaiah 11:6: "The wolf also shall dwell with the lamb, and the leopard shall lie down with the kid; and the calf and the young lion and the fatling together, and a little child shall lead them"; and Virgil, *Eclogues* IV.22: "nec magnos metuent armenta leones" ("the herds shall fear not huge lions"). PBS quotes from Isaiah in a letter written 19 October 1811 to Elizabeth Hitchener ". . . *my* golden age is when the present potence [of mind] will become omnipotence: this will be the millenium of Xtians 'when the lion shall lay down with the lamb' . . ." (*Letters* I, 152). He reuses the image in *Proposals for an Association of Philanthropists* (1812; *Prose/EBM* I, 42).

VIII.129–30. <u>nightshade's tempting bane</u> . . . <u>pleasure it bestows</u>: As Crook and Guiton point out, the poisonous woody nightshade (*solanum dulcamara,* or "Bittersweet"), with its striking blue flowers and red and amber berries, appears several times in PBS's poetry, including perhaps the lyric *Passion* (*Esd* #4), the emotion with which PBS often metonymically connects it (see *Shelley's Venomed Melody,* 137–45). In *QM,* as in *Prometheus Unbound* III.iv.78–83, the transformation of the nightshade into a harmless source of pleasure is a Shelleyan revision of Virgil's "et fallax herba veneni | occidet" ("and the false poison plant will wither"; *Eclogue* IV.24–25), standing for a natural world now purely benevolent.

VIII.145–65. <u>Man, where the gloom . . . name of God</u>: Carlos Baker first suggested that PBS's description of life in the far north was influenced by James Thomson's description of Siberia in "Winter" (*Shelley's Major Poetry,* 28n): "Here human nature wears its rudest form. . . . | . . . immersed in furs | Doze the gross race—nor sprightly jest, nor song, | Nor tenderness they know, nor aught of life | Beyond the kindred bears that stalk without—" (940–46). However, both Thomson and PBS are probably indebted to another source, or other sources, as yet unidentified. See, for instance, the description of Eskimos from the journal of James King, who served as a lieutenant on Cook's ship *The Resolution:* "The general appearance of the People seem to denote some Physical evil in their Origin, for their small size, dirty figure, sad countenance, & whining address, demands your commiseration . . ." (*The Journals of Captain James Cook on his Voyages of Discovery,* ed. J. C. Beaglehole [Cambridge: Hakluyt Society, 1955–67], III.ii, 1440). In commenting on the problem of trusting our natural tastes to lead us to a "natural diet," PBS's friend John Frank Newton says about the Eskimo diet: "The Eskimaux delight in train oil and rotten flesh; prefer them to roast beef; and I am not disposed to contend very eagerly for the reasonableness of our choice in opposition to theirs" (*Return,* 82–83).

VIII.154. <u>Fit compeer of the bears that roamed around</u>: Cook's *Voyages,* among other sources, emphasizes the interrelations between humans and bears in the Siberian Northeast, albeit without PBS's scorn: "The Kamschadales acknowledge infinite obligations to the bears, for all the little progress they have hitherto made, as well in the sciences as the polite arts. They confess themselves indebted wholly to those animals for all their knowledge in physic and surgery; that, by observing what herbs they have applied to the wounds they have received, and what methods they have pursued when they were languid and out of order, they have now acquired a knowledge of most of those simples which they have recourse to, either as external or internal applications. But, the most singular circumstance of all is, that they admit the bears to be their dancing-masters; . . ." (James Cook and James King, *Voyage to the Pacific Ocean* [1784], III, 100).

VIII.165. <u>One curse . . . name of God</u>: The atheism or lack of organized religion of Eskimos and Northern Indians was prominently discussed in such eighteenth-century studies as Hans Egede's *A Description of Greenland* (1745), David Cranz's *The History of Greenland* (1767), and Samuel Hearne's *A Journey from Prince of Wales's Fort in Hudson's Bay to the Northern Ocean In the Years 1769, 1770, 1771, and 1772* (1795).

   MWS intentionally omitted this line from *1839* but restored it in *1840.*

VIII.166–72. <u>Nor where the tropics</u> . . . <u>a nobler being</u>: *1989* suggests a source in Thomson's description of the tropics in *The Seasons: Summer:* "The parent Sun himself | Seems o'er this world of slaves to tyrannize" and "Where putrefaction into life ferments | And breathes destructive myriads, or from woods . . . | In vapours rank and blue corruption wrapt | . . . then wasteful forth | Walks the dire power of pestilent disease" (lines 884–85, 1029–35). PBS's sense of the health hazards of the tropics was probably informed by Dr. James Lind's highly influential monograph *An Essay on Disease Incidental to Europeans, in Hot Climates, With the Method of Preventing their Fatal Consequences* (1768), which by 1811 was in its sixth London edition and its first American edition. This James Lind (1716–94), who was best known in his day for his seminal work on the cause of scurvy, was the cousin of Shelley's early mentor James Lind (1736–1812).

VIII.177. <u>changed with Christians</u>: The Christians in Volney's *Ruins* are asked "whether it be gospel charity . . . which makes you continue to dis-people Africa and sell its inhabitants like cattle . . ." (Chap. 23; II, 205). Slav-ery was not abolished in the British colonies until 1833, although the slave trade was outlawed in 1807 under the coalition "Ministry of All the Talents."

VIII.182. <u>fulness of their woe</u>: In *1878*, Rossetti introduced the reading "his woe," arguing that the "true antecedent [of the pronoun] seems to be 'man,' and 'he,' in which case the only correct possessive pronoun must be 'his'" (I, 434). Such an emendation supposes that PBS did not understand his own "true" meaning, but that Rossetti did—an assumption that underlies Ros-setti's editorial methodology. The pronoun <u>their</u> clearly refers to <u>tyrants</u> in the line above, whose <u>woe</u> will come in the retribution ultimately exacted by the oppressed natives of the tropics.

VIII.183–86. <u>legal butchery</u> . . . <u>name of God</u>: The reference is to the fight-ing during Napoleon's Egyptian campaigns (1798–1807). ***Henry and Louisa*** (***Esd*** #46) describes the troops on their way to Egypt as "Britannia's hired as-sassins" (line 186) and dramatizes a particularly savage battle in which a mis-guided Henry dies fighting against the French, the desert sands his "bloody bed" (line 272).

Volney identifies Egypt as "the cradle" of all theological systems and attri-butes this largely to the "idle curiosity" of their priests, who, having "no other food, in the retirement of the temples, but the enigma of the universe, always present to their minds; and because in the political districts into which that country was for a long time divided, every state had its college of priests, who, being by turns auxiliaries or rivals, hastened by their disputes the progress of science and discovery" (*Ruins,* Chap. XXII; II, 156). For Volney, Egypt first consolidates religion and politics into that destructive amalgam, state reli-gion.

VIII.190–91. late . . . create: an unintentional rhyme.

VIII.194. train-bearer of slaves: i.e., obsequious follower of tyrants (cf. the description of a king as a monarch-slave in **IX.94**).

VIII.197. religion's: The most radical of the piracies, *1821.BEN* not only capitalizes the word, to mark the personification, but also sets it in small caps to emphasize the indictment.

VIII.200. bland: gentle, mild.

VIII.203–7. Him, still . . . eternity: See PBS's **Note 16.** These lines pose a significant textual problem primarily because the text keying the note in *1813* differs from the text of the poem proper: first, and most important, Draws in **line 205** appears as "Dawns"; second, everything following Him appears within parentheses (an emendation MWS made to her text of VIII.203–5 in *1840*). Given these differences, it is likely that PBS was working from memory when producing the passage for the notes. Because *Draws* and *Dawns* could look sufficiently alike in PBS's handwriting, either of the two words might have resulted from a compositor's error. However, it is probable that PBS gave more attention to the text of the poem proper than to the citation in the notes. Moreover, the larger passage seems to be less about how bliss awakens (Dawns) in the virtuous mind than about the mental work that bliss performs—impelling (drawing on) the mind from hope to hope. Given these points, we retain the text of the poem proper.

The other significant textual problem arises in **line 204,** where MWS emended lore to "store" in both *1839* and *1840*. However, MWS seems to have taken this reading from *1821.BEN*, without necessarily knowing which word was actually in *1813* (see "Textual Transmission," above), and even though she retains "store" in *1840*, there is little textual authority for the change. To be sure, both *lore* and *store* make sense in this context, and it is even possible that PBS's handwritten "store" (with an uncrossed "t" and a small initial "s") could have looked like *lore* to the compositor. We retain the reading in *1813,* however, first because PBS presumably wrote lore twice without changing it, once here and once in the notes. Second, it is the exhaustless knowledge (lore) of human weal rather than its "store" that appears to be operative here. That is, insofar as lore means "knowledge, learning, or information," the passage is about pursuing a body of cultural knowledge that leads to human happiness and welfare. In fact, precisely when such lore is learned (**IX.141**) by Ianthe, Queen Mab accounts her task as done.

To paraphrase, then, the entire difficult passage from **line 203** to **line 208:** "Moving from hope to hope, the virtuous mind pursues the bliss that— arising from the inexhaustible knowledge of human happiness and welfare—impels it to thoughts that gift it with a feeling of immortality mocking old age."

VIII.211–12. <u>no longer now</u> . . . <u>face</u>: See PBS's **Note 17**.

VIII.222. <u>prune</u>: archaic usage for *preen,* to trim or dress feathers with the beak.

VIII.226–27. <u>His terrible prerogative</u> . . . <u>equals</u>: Marilyn Butler locates the interspecies egalitarianism of this passage in what she terms "the French Revolutionary vision of a new transcendental republicanism," citing Coleridge's exuberant letter to Francis Wrangham in 1794: "I call even my Cat Sister in the fraternity of universal Nature. Owls I respect & Jack Asses I love: for Aldermen & Hogs, Bishops & Royston Crows I have not particular partiality—; they are my Cousins, however, at least by Courtesy" (*Poet and Legislator,* 165). Hogg noted that Joseph Ritson (see Commentary for **Note 17**) called "sheep, oxen and pigs 'our fellow creatures'" (*Life,* ed. Wolfe, II, 87). Cf. also Wollstonecraft, who wrote in *Rights of Woman:* "Humanity to animals should be particularly inculcated as a part of national education, for it is not at present one of our national virtues" (Chap. 12; *WMW* V, 243).

Such transcendental republicanism is memorably satirized in the concluding lines of *The Golden Age: A Poetical Epistle* (London: F. and C. Rivington, 1794, p. 15), which pretends to be written by Erasmus Darwin and addressed to Thomas Beddoes:

> Ye lovely Lambkins, strain your feeble voice,
> And with your Dams in loudest Baas rejoice!
> Calves, join your notes to swell the gladdening sound!
> Cows, let your lowings from the skies rebound!
> Prolific Ducks, quack mid the mighty noise!
> Hens, more prolific, cackle out your joys!
> And ye, oh! Swine, lift up your little Eyes,
> With rapture riot round your rotten Styes!
> Stretch your triumphant throats, and strive to make
> The frighten'd welkin with your Gruntings shake!

For a book-length study of the subject, see David Perkins, *Romanticism and Animal Rights* (Cambridge: Cambridge UP, 2003).

VIII.232–33. <u>extend</u> . . . <u>Their</u> . . . <u>wield</u>: Based on a grammatical misunderstanding of these lines, *1829.BRO* initiated three emendations that were adopted by *1834* and MWS (see foot-of-the-page collation). As *1989* notes, however, the subject of <u>extend</u> and <u>wield</u> is <u>energies</u>; <u>each unfettered</u> is a parenthetic absolute (i.e., <u>Reason and passion</u> are each <u>unfettered</u>).

VIII.236. <u>omnipotence of mind</u>: Cf. PBS's letter quoted in the Commentary to **VIII.124–28,** above: "*my* golden age is when the present potence [of mind]

will become omnipotence . . ." Medwin writes that the young PBS was a be-
liever "in the *Panacea*. He used to cite the opinion of Dr. Franklin, whom he
swore by, that 'a time would come, when mind will be predominant over mat-
ter, or in other words, when a thorough knowledge of the human frame, and
the perfection of medical science, will counteract the decay of Nature'" (*Life*,
ed. Forman, 50). As Cameron points out, Godwin twice in *Pol. Justice* quoted
Benjamin Franklin as conjecturing that "mind will one day become omnipo-
tent over matter" (*YS*, 320–21n.98; *Pol. Justice*, ed. Priestly VIII.viii, ix; II, 503,
520). The second quotation elaborates as follows: "The sense which he
[Franklin] annexed to this expression, seems to have related to the improve-
ments of human invention, in relation to machines and the compendium of
labour. But, if the power of intellect can be established over all other matter,
are we not inevitably led to ask, why not over the matter of our own bodies?"

PBS probably found Franklin's statement in *Pol. Justice*, in which Godwin
cites only the conversation of Richard Price as his source (ed. Priestley
VIII.viii; II, 503n). Though the statement may not appear in any of Franklin's
works, Leo Lemay informs us that Franklin and Price were close friends and
saw one another frequently. Both belonged to the Club of Honest Whigs,
which met on alternate Thursdays, before 1772 at St. Paul's Coffeehouse and
after 1772 at the London Coffeehouse (see Verner W. Crane, *William and
Mary Quarterly* 23 [1966]: 210–33). Franklin was in London from late 1757
to early 1762 and from late 1764 to 1775. Medwin's statement that PBS
"swore by" Franklin suggests that he also had a more direct knowledge of
Franklin's thought, perhaps from his early mentor Dr. James Lind, who had
corresponded with Franklin himself (see W. G. Bebbington, *Notes and Queries*
205 [March 1960]: 83–93, and Desmond King-Hele, *KSMB* 18 [1967]: 1–6).

IX.1–22. O HAPPY Earth! . . . fabric of thy perfectness: This passage marks
the high point of PBS's millennial (Godwinian) hopes for the gradual trans-
formation of human society into a perfect world. Cf. his remark to Elizabeth
Hitchener in a letter of mid-February 1812: "You see I look forward to the
period in which pain and evil the consequences or concomitants of *selfish*
passion shall cease.—" (*Letters* I, 252). Later in his career, PBS returned to
his early apocalyptic imagery, seeing an escape from "pain and evil" in flight
from society to an island refuge or through a catastrophic revolution, with its
own attendant pain.

IX.19. an aspiring change: The slow but progressive change *QM* foresees is
underscored below in **IX.38** (gradual dawned the morn of love) and **IX.148**
(The gradual paths of an aspiring change).

IX.23–37. Even Time . . . prepared his fall: These lines are a reworking of a
passage of poetic prose PBS sent to Hitchener in a letter written 14 February
1812 (*Letters* I, 251): see *"The Ocean Rolls Between Us"* (*CPPBS* I, 438–41).

On the apparent vanishing of time, see *Prometheus Unbound* IV.14, where "Time [is borne] to his tomb in eternity."

IX.27. milleniums: i.e., thousands of years; the spelling of the word with only one "n" was an alternative that was already becoming outdated in PBS's day. The word is also spelled with one "n" in the penultimate paragraph of **Note 14,** about the Wandering Jew (**Note 14, line 57**).

IX.29–30. Across that desert . . . heaped them there: Cf. the later rendering of these lines in *Ozymandias*.

IX.31–32. Yon monarch . . . mushroom: This clause appropriates and politicizes Darwin's coupling of monarch and mushroom in *Temple of Nature* IV.383–84: "Hence when a Monarch or a mushroom dies, | Awhile extinct the organic matter lies . . . ."

IX.38. gradual: an unusual adverbial use of the word, also found in Thomson and Keats, as *1911* points out (II, 553).

IX.50–56. Reason . . . passion . . . broken rod: On the realignment of reason and passion depicted in these lines, PBS wrote in a letter to Hogg of 7 February 1813, upon completing the draft of *QM:* "Reason is only an assemblage of our better feelings, passion considered under a peculiar mode of its operation.—" A "more elevated spirit" has started to make itself felt in "the nineteenth century," PBS added, "which without deducting from the warmth of love or the constancy of friendship reconciles all private feelings to public utility, & scarce suffers true Passion & true Reason to continue at war" (*Letters* I, 352).

IX.48. Nor . . . God: Omitted in *1839,* this line was not restored in *1840,* presumably due to an oversight.

IX.51. meads: meadows.

IX.53–54. Yet like the bee . . . her sister's brow: The worker bee, who is analogous to Passion in this complex metaphor, is a neuter female.

IX.57–61. Mild was the slow . . . full of hope as he: Lord Monboddo's influential contention that the reward of a life lived in accordance with Nature is a natural death, which he represents as "rather sleep than death: Whereas the death produced by intemperance and by an unnatural life, is commonly both painful and lingering. Men in that way are nine years a-killing, as Othello wished that Cassio should be." Monboddo goes on to describe an island mentioned by Homer "where, it seems, the people were more temperate, and lived more in the natural way: And there, he says, nobody died of disease, but only of old age; and even then so easily, that, he says, they were killed with the *gentle* darts" of Apollo and Diana (*Antient Metaphysics* III, 119,

184). Hesiod also describes the golden age under Kronus as a time when there was no such thing as helpless old age and death was like sleep (*Works and Days,* lines 110–117), a passage to which PBS refers directly in **Note 17.**

IX.58. grasp,: The period after grasp in MWS's editions is an uncaught compositor's error.

IX.67. or: "nor" in MWS's editions was initiated by *1829.BRO* and transmitted through *1834.*

IX.71. Which: "With" in *1834* is either a compositor's error (for others of which see **lines 94** and **108** below) or a misguided emendation.

IX.74. life's phantasmal scene: See **VI.192,** where the phrase is first used. PBS similarly describes life as a "phantasmal scene" in **Alastor,** line 697.

IX.82. undoubting: *1876* mistakenly initiated the reading "undoubted"; this variant was transmitted through Hutchinson's edition to *1972.*

IX.83. love: Based on an apparent alteration in the Brooks copy of *1813,* Forman suggested the reading "lore" for love; although he did not make the emendation in his editions, his argument claims (unpersuasively) that it makes better sense.

IX.84. dull and selfish chastity: Insofar as chastity is conditioned by the institution of marriage, PBS consistently challenged it in his work as a "fictitious merit" (**Letters** I, 323); insofar, however, as it reflects the temperance of a mature individual mind, he approved of it (e.g., **Discourse on the Manners of the Ancient Greeks,** David Lee Clark, *Shelley's Prose* [Albuquerque: U of New Mexico P, 1954], 221). Cf. James H. Lawrence, *Nairs,* which attacks enforced chastity but approves of "natural chastity," which "may be compared . . . to temperance . . . . Natural chastity is a duty to one's self and to one's country; it is moderate in natural enjoyment, and abstains from every indulgence that nature reproves" (I, xxxiii–xxxiv). See also PBS's note (9) to **QM V.189** ("Even love is sold") and the Commentary to it.

IX.86. senselessness: absence of sensuousness and sexual feelings.

IX.93–129. Then, where, through distant ages . . . resonant around: Cf. the similar change described in **Prometheus Unbound** III.iv.164–204.

IX.99–102. old thorn . . . whirlwind's ear: In starkly setting the old thorn, with its "strange tales" against the forces of the storm, PBS may have had in mind Wordsworth's "The Thorn" (*Lyrical Ballads,* 1798).

IX.107. withal: i.e., nevertheless. John Warner Taylor claimed that *withal* was a "seventeenth century word"; whereas Pope does not use it at all, "Shakespeare employs it twenty times, seventeen at the end of the clause," as in **QM**

(*Sewanee Review* 14 [July 1906]: 350). In using <u>withal</u> at the end of the line, PBS unintentionally created a rhymed couplet, but as *1977* points out when revising this section of **QM** he moved <u>withal</u> between <u>yet</u> and <u>so</u> to correct his mistake.

IX.116. <u>chaplets</u>: garlands woven to be worn on the head.

IX.130. <u>wreck</u>: vestige or trace.

IX.139. <u>the past</u>: With characteristic force, Rossetti defended his emendation, "the future": "Nothing, I conceive, can be more unquestionable than that Shelley wrote, or meant to write, 'the future'" (I, *472*). Insofar as Mab has just finished recounting a vision of the future, Rossetti's point has validity; but insofar as her entire narrative has itself now become a part of Ianthe's past (**IX.143**), as *1989* points out, the reading of *1813* should stand. Moreover, as Forman noted in *1876,* although PBS heavily revised this section of **QM** for **Dæmon,** he made no change here.

IX.152–54. <u>The restless wheels</u> . . . <u>destined goal</u>: For the chariot imagery, see Commentary to **I.59.**

IX.149–63. <u>For birth and life and death</u> . . . <u>eternal hope</u>: PBS's early letters are laced with speculation about a future state after death. On the one hand, he acknowledged that "All that natural reason enables us to discover, is that *we* now *are,* that there was a time when we were not, that the moment even when now we are reasoning, is a point before & after which is *eternity*" (**Letters** I, 110; see also his essay **On a Future State,** cited and quoted in Reiman, *Intervals of Inspiration,* 242–44). On the other hand, he felt compelled to move beyond the bounds of reason: "I have considered it in every possible light & reason tells me that death is the boundary of the life of man. Yet I feel, I believe the direct contrary" (**Letters** I, 150). See Commentary to **I.145–56,** above, for how PBS turned to the rhetoric of Pythagorean metempsychosis— the transmigration of souls—to imagine a future state beyond death.

IX.175. <u>gulph-dream</u>: "a dream of drowning in, or falling into, a gulf" (*OED*). The "gulph" described here is figurative, "a mental abyss."

IX.190. <u>eternal war</u>: <u>eternal</u> functions rhetorically to signify "things to which endless continuance is ascribed hyperbolically or in relative sense" (*OED* 4).

IX.216–17. <u>Again the enchanted steeds</u> . . . <u>Again the burning wheels</u>: As the repetition of <u>Again</u> in these lines signals, the poem is rounding out upon itself, gaining closure through a return to its opening scene, in which the sleeping Ianthe, watched over by Henry, is first visited by Queen Mab in her chariot. The circular return is a closural device favored by PBS, who used it later in such poems as **Laon and Cythna** and **Ode to Liberty.**

Shelley's Notes to Queen Mab

Note 1 (I.242–43)

In December 1812, PBS asked his friend and publisher Thomas Hookham to send him William Nicholson's *The British Encyclopedia, or Dictionary of Arts and Sciences; Comprising an Accurate and Popular View of the Present Improved State of Human Knowledge* (6 vols. London: Longman, Hurst, Rees, & Orme, 1809) (**Letters** I, 343). As Cameron has pointed out (*YS*, 400), **Note 1** is partly paraphrased from the entry "Light" in *Nicholson's*, which PBS cites only in **Note 2**. Nicholson himself—well known for his erudition, particularly in science—was a close friend of Godwin, who wrote a memorial upon Nicholson's death in 1815.

lines 6–8. Light consists . . . luminous body: The nature of light was the subject of a theoretical debate described in *Nicholson's* between those who followed Malebranche's position—summarized in the first clause of PBS's sentence—and those who followed Newton's—summarized in the second. In language echoed in PBS's first clause, *Nicholson's* remarks: "It must be acknowledged, however, that many philosophers, both English and foreigners, have recurred to the opinion, *that light consists of vibrations propagated from the luminous body, through a subtle ethereal medium*" [our italics].

lines 8–11. Its velocity . . . a distance of 95,000,000 miles: The *Nicholson's* entry "Light" describes how the astronomer Ole Roemer (1644–1710) first derived the speed of light by comparing the calculated and observed times of the eclipses of Jupiter's moons. It then goes on to state what subsequently has been discovered about the velocity of light, in language PBS appropriates here: "Our excellent astronomer, Dr. Bradley . . . ingeniously found, that . . . the velocity of light, is at the rate of about 195,000 miles in a second; *a motion according to which it will require just 8' 7" to move from the sun to the earth, or about 95,000,000 of miles*" [our italics].

lines 11–15. Some idea . . . from the earth: PBS again adapts the *Nicholson's* entry "Light," which comments that with the speed of light understood, "it is easy to know the time in which light travels to the earth, from the moon, or any of the other planets, or even from the fixed stars, when their distances shall be known; *these distances are, however, so immensely great, that from the near-*

est of them, supposed to be Sirius, the dog-star, light takes up many years to travel to the earth: and it is even suspected, that there are many stars whose light has not yet arrived at us since their creation" [our italics]. The actual calculations in PBS's note are not in *Nicholson's* and may have been made by PBS himself. The first of these seems to assume that light travels at slightly less than 172,000 miles per second, a figure much lower than the 195,000 miles per second given in *Nicholson's;* PBS may have made an error in his math, unless he found the calculation for a light year in another source. (See below, **Note 2, Footnote 1,** for how this lower estimate of the speed of light correlates with PBS's calculation of the distance between earth and Sirius.) The second calculation is correct, assuming that the sun is 95,000,000 miles distant from the earth, as given in *Nicholson's.*

Note 2 *(I.252–53)*

White suggests that PBS's notions about the "plurality of worlds" were heavily influenced by Adam Walker's lectures at Syon House and Eton (*Shelley* I, 23). See, for instance, the conclusion of Walker's *Analysis of a Course of Lectures on Natural and Experimental Philosophy* (9th ed.; London, 1800): "Let us on the wings of imagination then launch into the immensity of space, and behold *system* beyond *system, above us, below us,* to the *east,* the *west,* the *north,* the *south!* Let us go so far as to see our sun but a *star* among the rest, and our system itself as a point, and we shall but even then find ourselves on the *confines of creation!* How inadequate then must be the utmost stretch of human faculties, to a conception of the amazing *Deity* who made and governs the whole! Should not the narrow prejudices, the littleness of human pride, soften into humility at this thought" (86). Medwin claims that after hearing Walker lecture, PBS was "delighted at the idea of a plurality of worlds" (*Life,* ed. Forman, 28). However, despite Walker's real influence, most of the information in this note is based directly on two other entries in *Nicholson's,* "Star" and "Astronomy." PBS nonetheless cited only the entry "Light," which he did not actually use for this note. Cf. Thomas Paine, *Age of Reason,* Part 1: ". . . to believe that God created a plurality of worlds, at least as numerous as what we call stars, renders the Christian system of faith at once little and ridiculous, and scatters it in the mind like feathers in the air" (*Works* VIII, 74).

The entire first paragraph of this note was one of four passages in *QM* specified in the indictment for blasphemous libel against both Clark's original piracy and *1840.* MWS entirely omitted **Note 2** in *1839.* The offending passages were deleted in Clark's expurgated version of *1821.CLA* (*1821.CLAX*). Moreover, *1821.BEN* omits the same passages as the expurgated Clark edition, apparently by mistake, since it makes no other similar expurgations. These deletions, given all the other similarities between the two piracies, provide strong evidence that the Clark piracy preceded the Benbow piracy, and that the latter was based on the text of the expurgated Clark piracy, imperfectly corrected by checks against *1813*. For a more extensive discussion of the relationship between the two piracies, see pp. 509–15.

lines 9–11. <u>All that miserable tale</u> . . . <u>knowledge of the stars</u>: Cf. PBS's claim, below, that the "consistent Newtonian is necessarily an atheist" (**Note 13, line 284**). See also Sir William Drummond, *Academical Questions:* "What can be denied to the atomist and the atheist, if it be once confessed, that, without the guidance of mind, all the mighty orbs of the universe methodically move in various courses, still restoring the harmony which they frequently seem to break, and still resuming the order from which they are often known to swerve?" (196).

lines 11–12. <u>The works</u> . . . <u>against him</u>: As *1989* notes, PBS uses scripture to bear witness against God (<u>him</u>), alluding ironically to Psalms 8:3–9, which begins: "When I consider thy heavens, the work of thy fingers . . . ."

lines 13–14. <u>The nearest</u> . . . <u>from each other</u>: The entry "Star" in *Nicholson's* notes that "the Dog-star [Sirius] must be distant from our Earth 2,000,000,000,000, or above two millions of millions of English miles; which is so very great, that a cannon-ball continuing in the same velocity it acquires when immediately discharged at the mouth of the cannon, would spend almost seven hundred thousand years in passing through it: and it is very probable, that the fixed stars are equally distant from each other, as the nearest of them is from our Sun . . . ."

Footnote 1. <u>See Nicholson's Encyclopedia, art. Light</u>: *Nicholson's* does not give the distance between Sirius and the earth in its article "Light," and its article "Star"—as cited above—states the distance as 2,000,000,000,000 miles. Consequently, as Cameron recognized, PBS derived his figure from another source (*YS*, 400), which according to Desmond King-Hele was "by chance ahead of the professional astronomers. Until Bessel first measured stellar parallax in 1838, only a lower limit, much less than the real distance of a star, could reliably be assigned" (*Shelley: His Thought and Work*, 39). PBS's figure is near the correct 51 billion miles. It is also exactly ten times the distance, he believes, that light travels in a year (see **Note 1, lines 11–15**).

lines 16–19. <u>That which appears</u> . . . <u>around them</u>: taken from the *Nicholson's* entry "Astronomy": "If the telescope be directed to these nebulæ, they are resolvable into clusters of stars, which appear as white clouds in instruments of less force. . . . we may deduce, that the universe consists of nebulæ or distinct systems of stars: that each nebula is composed of a prodigious number of suns or bodies that shine by their own native splendour; and that each individual sun is destined to give light to numbers of worlds that revolve about it." For PBS's reaction to Herschel's work on nebulæ, see below, **Note 13, lines 103–9.**

lines 19–21. <u>Millions and millions</u> . . . <u>immutable necessity</u>: PBS uses the
Nicholson's entry "Astronomy" almost verbatim (changing "thousands" to <u>millions</u>) but alters its praise of the Creator to an acknowledgment of the power
of "immutable necessity." *Nicholson's* reads: "What an august, what an amazing conception does this give of the works of the Creator! Instead of one
world and one sun, *we find thousands and thousands of suns, ranged around us
at immense distances, all attended by innumerable worlds, all in rapid motion, yet
calm, regular, and harmonious, invariably keeping the paths prescribed them; . . .*"
[our italics].

Note 3 (IV.178–9)

PBS took the text for **lines 3–36** of this note from Godwin's *Enquirer* (1797),
Part II, Essay V, entitled "Of Trades and Professions" (collated as *Enq*). PBS's
text begins with the third sentence of the first full paragraph on p. 234 of *Enquirer* and continues through the fifth sentence of the bottom paragraph of
p. 236, omitting two-and-a-half paragraphs on pp. 234–35. The elision immediately follows **line 14** of our Text. There are several minor variants in
punctuation and words between the two texts, recorded in our apparatus,
suggesting that PBS copied closely but somewhat freely, and did not care to
check his transcript against the original for accuracy.

The three sentences that immediately precede PBS's text begin Godwin's
discussion of soldiers and read as follows:

> A soldier who will never fight but in a cause that he shall conscientiously and
> scrupulously adjudge to be good, can scarcely be a soldier by profession.
>
> But, to dismiss this consideration, it is no enviable circumstance that a man should
> be destined to maintain the good cause by blows and fighting. In this respect, assuming the propriety of corporal punishments, he is upon a par with the beadle and
> the executioner (233–34).

MWS omitted **Note 3** from *1839*.

lines 12–14. <u>It surely requires</u> . . . <u>maintenance of justice</u>: After this sentence, PBS omitted two-and-a-half paragraphs concerning mercenaries and
the futility of supposing "that a man can be in the right, who is attempted to
be made so through the medium of compulsion" (235).

line 17. <u>trepanned</u>: i.e., trapped or ensnared.

lines 25–32. <u>Its first constituent</u> . . . <u>his exhibitor</u>: Godwin's discussion of soldiers continues for three sentences past the ending of PBS's text: "This singular situation gives to the military a correspondent singularity of manner.
The lofty port of a generous spirit, flowing from a consciousness of merit and
independence, has always something in it of grand and impressive. But the

swagger of a soldier, which it costs him an incessant effort to support, is better calculated, in a discerning spectator, to produce laughter, than to excite awe" (236–37).

lines 33–36. *Falshood and Vice* was originally intended for publication with *Esd,* among which it also appears in this volume. See pp. 14–20 for the Text and pp. 343–46 for the Commentary. PBS moved the poem to the notes of *QM* after it became clear that he was not going to be able to publish *Esd* at the same time as *QM.* Although it does not provide *Falshood and Vice* within the body of the *QM* note, *1989* does base its text on the *QM* version, and therefore we include it in the Historical Collations.

Note 4 (V.1–2)

This quotation from Ecclesiastes 1:4–7, contains two verbal changes in the last sentence: <u>whence</u> for "from whence" and <u>thither shall they</u> for "thither they." Through such a note, PBS is trying to demonstrate his genuine command of the Bible, for which, see Bryan Shelley, *Scripture,* 17–33. He had already put together a selection of quotations from the Bible, **Biblical Extracts,** for which he was unable to find a publisher.

line 2. <u>grave,</u>: We have restored the comma following <u>grave</u>, which appears in the text of the poem proper in *1813;* PBS is more likely to have paid closer attention to the text of his poem than to the lines cuing a note.

Note 5 (V.4–6)

PBS quotes without substantive errors Homer's *Iliad* VI.146–49; we have corrected minor errors in breathing, accent marks, and the accidental compounding of two words in **lines 4** and **7.** *1821.CLA* glosses the Greek with the following translation by Pope:

> Like leaves on trees the race of man is found,
> Now green in youth, now withering on the ground;
> Another race the following spring supplies;
> They fall successive, and successive rise:
> So generations in their course decay;
> So flourish these, when those are past away.
>
> *Pope's Homer.*

1821.BEN replaces the Greek text with an English translation "as being more acceptable [*sic*] to the generality of readers." In an apparent response to Clark's choice of translation, *1821.BEN* remarks: "That of Cowper is chosen as more correct, though not so agreeable as Pope's."

Without errors, PBS quotes from Lucretius, *De rerum natura* II.1–14. Both the Clark and the Benbow editions provide English translations in footnotes, Clark's edition reading as follows:

> When the wide ocean maddening whirlwinds sweep,
> And heave the billows of the boiling deep,
> Pleased we from land the reeling bark survey,
> And rolling mountains of the watery way.
> Not that we joy another's woes to see,
> But to reflect that we ourselves are free.
> So, the dread battle ranged in distant fields,
> Ourselves secure, a secret pleasure yields.
> But what more charming than to gain the height
> Of true philosophy? What pure delight
> From Wisdom's citadel to view below,
> Deluded mortals, as they wandering go
> In quest of happiness! ah, blindly weak!
> For fame, for vain nobility they seek;
> Labour for heapy treasures, night and day,
> And pant for power and magisterial sway.
>   Oh, wretched mortals! souls devoid of light,
> Lost in the shades of intellectual light!
>
>   *Dr. Busby's Lucretius*

The translation in Benbow's edition is from *Good's Lucretius*. According to Eaton's *Trial,* of the three generally available translations of Lucretius—by Creech, Good, and Dr. Busby—that of Thomas Busby (published 1813) was considered the most elegant and was subscribed to by "some of the most learned and enlightened men of the country," including the Prince Regent, Perceval, Muzio Clementi, and Lord Grenville, the chancellor of Oxford University. Busby's translation and his behavior concerning it, however, were ridiculed by many, as attested to by Thomas Rees: "Dr. Busby . . . later in life made himself very conspicuous, and amenable to severe public criticism, by translating 'Lucretius,' and 'giving living recitations of the translation, with tea and bread and butter,' at his house in Queen Anne Street, to select parties of friends, who were invited to endure the one and relish the other. I was among the number, and must own that the display of poetry, oratory, and coxcombry was lamentably ludicrous" (*Reminiscences of Literary London from 1779 to 1853* [London: Suckling and Galloway, 1896], 23).

Also among the subscribers of Busby's *Lucretius* was Byron, who earlier had pilloried Busby's notorious rejected Drury Lane Address in "Parenthetical Address, by Dr. Plagiary" (as did James and Horace Smith in *Rejected Addresses; or, The New Theatrum Poetarum* [1812]), and who memorably wrote in an unpublished MS of *1813* ("On Southey's Laureateship"): "Who gains the bays and annual Malmsey barrel— | Busby the bright—or Southey the sublime?" (1–2). For a humorous account of the fiasco at Drury Lane on 14 October 1812, when Busby's son tried to force his way onto the stage to recite his father's fatuous rejected address commemorating the reopening of the theater, see Rees, *Reminiscences*, 23–24.

See **CPPBS** I, 251–52, for PBS's ownership of *Good's Lucretius* in 1815 and the possibility that it was known to him as early as his days at Eton. Of Lucretius's poem itself, Eaton wrote that "a publication of more atheistical principles cannot be conceived. It is indeed the source from which all those who deny the immortality of the soul have drawn all their arguments . . ." (78, 79n).

Brooks mistakenly transposed lines 5 and 6 of the quotation in *1829.BRO*, an error transmitted through *1834* to MWS's editions.

Note 7 (V.93–94)

The primary influence on this note was the work of Godwin, especially the essay "Of Avarice and Profusion" in *Enquirer* and Book VIII of the first edition of *Pol. Justice* (1793).

line 3. <u>There is no real wealth</u> . . . <u>labour of man</u>: paraphrased from the essay on "Of Avarice and Profusion" in Godwin's *Enquirer:* "There is no wealth in the world except this, the labour of man." Godwin went on to argue: "What is misnamed wealth, is merely a power vested in certain individuals by the institutions of society, to compel others to labour for their benefit" (177).

lines 9–27. <u>A speculator takes pride</u> . . . <u>the hundredth part of society</u>: an elaboration of Godwin's argument against those who propose that luxury is "the rich and generous soil that brought to perfection the true prosperity of mankind" (*Pol. Justice* VIII.iii; II, 815; revised subsequently).

line 14. *jam pauca* . . . *relinquunt*: As *1989* notes, in this quotation from Horace, *Odes* II.xv.1–2, PBS altered the future tense of the verb *relinquent* to the present tense <u>relinquunt</u> in order to emphasize its application to contemporary England: "Now princely mansions leave but few acres for the plow." Rogers in *1972* writes that this quotation "relates the short-sighted effects of Regency magnificence to the situation in Italy around 27 B.C., when the number of small holdings had declined and the yeoman class, which had formed the strength of the Roman legions, was threatened with extinction" (I, 392). The change in tense was ignored in the translations provided by *1821.CLA:* "These piles of royal structure, will soon leave but few acres for the plough"; and *1821.BEN*, which similarly reads: "These royal piles will soon leave but few acres for the plough." In *1829.BRO*, Brooks mistakenly emends the *1813* text back to the reading in Horace, a change that was transmitted through Ascham to MWS's editions.

lines 16–17. <u>The shew and pomp of courts</u> . . . <u>and many a fête</u>: As Cameron suggests, PBS may here indict the Prince Regent's extravagant fête of 19 June 1811, which an outraged PBS attacked in letters to both Edward Fergus Graham (along with a stanza of his translation of the *Marseillaise,* the full version of which appears as ***Esd*** #47) and Elizabeth Hitchener (***Letters*** I, 105–6, 110)—and about which he may have written a satirical poem that has subsequently been lost (see ***CPPBS*** I, 448–51).

<u>adduces</u> . . . <u>its</u>: PBS often treated a compound subject as singular. MWS's alteration of the verb and the following pronoun to plural forms changes the meaning of the sentence. Forman inconsistently emended the verb, but not the pronoun.

line 30, Footnote 1. <u>See Rousseau, "De l'Inegalité parmi les Hommes," note 7</u>: Cameron claims that "Rousseau's note 7 to his essay on inequality has nothing to do with this subject [the relation between how lucrative an occupation is and its general usefulness to society] but deals with the life span of the horse." Hence, he concludes that PBS's "source is really, once again, Godwin's essay [*Enquirer,* "Of Avarice and Profusion"]" (*YS,* 403). Whereas *1972* cites Cameron's conclusion, *1989* claims that they are both "mistaken in saying that S.'s reference is wrong."

This confusion arose because PBS did not note which edition of Rousseau he was citing. In the 1755 first edition of *Discours sur l'origine et les fondemens de l'inégalité parmi les hommes* (Amsterdam: Marc Michel Rey), note 7 is precisely relevant to PBS's point: Rousseau argues in the eighth paragraph of the note that because the products of agriculture are so necessary for all people, their price must be proportionate to the abilities of the poorest to pay, and hence agriculture is the least lucrative of occupations. He concludes that, in general, arts are lucrative in the inverse ratio of their usefulness, so that the most essential come to be the most neglected (*"Du même principe on peut tirer cette règle, qu'en général les Arts sont lucratifs en raison inverse de leur utilité que les plus nécessaires doivent enfin devenir les plus négligés"* [214]).

The notes in the 1755 edition are ordered as follows: 1, 2, 3, a, 4, 5, d, 6, 7. Some later editions, such as the one Cameron consulted, alter the two alphabetically keyed notes into numbers, creating a sequence in which note 7 indeed concerns the life span of the horse and the original number 7 becomes number 9.

lines 36–73. <u>I will not insult common sense</u> . . . <u>more exquisite sources of enjoyment</u>: Cf., Godwin, *Pol. Justice:* "Every man is entitled, so far as the general stock will suffice, not only to the means of being, but of well being. It is unjust, if one man labour to the destruction of his health or his life, that another man may abound in luxuries. It is unjust, if one man be deprived of leisure to cultivate his rational powers, while another man contributes not a single effort to add to the common stock. The faculties of one man are like the faculties of another man. Justice directs that each man, unless perhaps he be employed more beneficially to the public, should contribute to the cultivation of the common harvest, of which each man consumes a share. This reciprocity indeed, . . . is of the very essence of justice" (VIII.i; II, 791).

lines 40–43. <u>so long . . . members</u>: Godwin: "The nobleman, who should for the first time let his imagination loose to conceive the style in which he would live, if he had nobody to observe, and no eye to please but his own, would no doubt be surprised to find that vanity had been the first mover in all his actions" (*Pol. Justice* VIII.i; II, 792–93).

line 40. *cœteris paribus*: "other things being equal"; mistranslated in both *1821.BEN* and *1821.CLA* as "Making allowances on both sides." Cf. Godwin, "But the mischief of aristocracy is, that it inexpressibly aggravates and embitters an evil, which, in its mildest form, is deeply to be deplored. The first sentiment of an uncorrupted mind, when it enters upon the theatre of human life, is, Remove from me and my fellows all arbitrary hindrances; let us start fair; render all the advantages and honours of social institution accessible to every man, in proportion to his talents and exertions" (*Pol. Justice*, ed. Priestley V.xi; II, 93–94).

lines 45–47. <u>Labour is required</u> . . . <u>are precluded</u>: Cf. Godwin: "Hereditary wealth is in reality a premium paid to idleness, an immense annuity expended to retain mankind in brutality and ignorance. The poor are kept in ignorance by the want of leisure. The rich are furnished indeed with the means of cultivation and literature, but they are paid for being dissipated and indolent. The most powerful means that malignity could have invented, are employed to prevent them from improving their talents, and becoming useful to the public" (*Pol. Justice*, ed. Priestley VIII.ii; II, 804–5).

line 51. <u>depriving</u>: The change to "to deprive" in *1829.BRO* is the first of four grammatical emendations here and two paragraphs below that were initiated by Brooks and transmitted through *1834* to MWS's two editions.

lines 55–57. <u>English reformers</u> . . . <u>for their benefit</u>: taken from *Pol. Justice:* "But the rent roll of the lands of England is a much more formidable pension list, than that which is supposed to be employed in the purchase of ministerial majorities [i.e., sinecures]" (ed. Priestley VIII.ii; II, 804).

lines 61–80. <u>The commodities</u> . . . <u>a state of barbarism</u>: These paragraphs are taken, with only small changes in punctuation, from *Enquirer,* 174–76. PBS omits a concessive sentence at the end of paragraph six: "It is not necessary that all our hours of leisure should be dedicated to intellectual pursuits;

it is probable that the well-being of man would be best promoted by the production of some superfluities and luxuries, though certainly not of such as an ill-imagined and exclusive vanity now teaches us to admire; but there is no reason in the system of the universe or the nature of man, why any individual should be deprived of the means of intellectual cultivation" (175).

lines 64–67. <u>If the labour</u> . . . <u>leisure would be ample</u>: Godwin's estimate was lower: twice he claims that if all manual labor were shared by every member of the community, each would have to labor only for half-an-hour per day to provide sufficiently for everyone (*Pol. Justice,* ed. Priestley VIII.vi; II, 484, 493).

lines 70–73. <u>Those hours</u> . . . <u>sources of enjoyment</u>: Three grammatical emendations to this sentence were initiated by Brooks and repeated by Ascham and MWS. They are inappropriate because PBS was quoting Godwin verbatim.

lines 74–80. <u>It was perhaps necessary</u> . . . <u>state of barbarism</u>: "Force grew out of monopoly. It might accidentally have occurred among savages whose appetites exceeded their supply, or whose passions were inflamed by the presence of the object of their desire; but it would gradually have died away, as reason and civilisation advanced. Accumulated property has fixed its empire . . ." (*Pol. Justice* VIII.ii; II, 809).

line 81. *chap.* II: The citation in **1813** to *Pol. Justice* is mistakenly to Chapter 11 rather than Chapter II, most likely due to an error by the compositor. Book VIII of *Pol. Justice* does not have a Chapter 11 (XI).

Note 8 (V.112–13)

If PBS was indeed personally acquainted with such a woman, her identity remains unknown. However, a note on religious mania in Erasmus Darwin's *The Temple of Nature* provides the context for PBS's comments: "Many theatric preachers among the Methodists successfully inculcate the fear of death and of Hell, and live luxuriously on the folly of their hearers: those who suffer under this insanity, are generally most innocent and harmless people, who are then liable to accuse themselves of the greatest imaginary crimes; and have so much intellectual cowardice, that they dare not reason about those things, which they are directed by their priests to believe. Where this intellectual cowardice is great, the voice of reason is ineffectual; but that of ridicule may save many from these mad-making doctors . . ." (note to IV.87). This position on Methodism was widely held. A review by Southey of *Myles's History of the Methodists* in the *Annual Review* for 1803 succinctly claims: "Positively and knowingly we assert, that the increase of madness, melancholy madness, religious madness, the worst form of the worst calamity which flesh is heir to, has been proportioned to, and occasioned by the growth of methodism" (211).

The translation in *1821.CLA* of Lucretius (*De rerum natura* III.85–86) is once again taken from Busby's edition: "For some, the approach of Death and Hell to stay, | Their parents, friends, and country, will betray." The translation in *1821.BEN* is uncredited and in prose: "For now, men, desiring to avoid the infernal regions, will frequently betray their country and dearest parents."

Note 9 (V.189)

As the annotation below makes clear, the theoretical basis for PBS's antimatrimonial note was laid principally by Godwin, Wollstonecraft, and James Henry Lawrence, although PBS would have been aware of similar arguments circulating in contemporary freelove and feminist circles, as Cameron points out (see *YS*, 266–70). Godwin's incisive attack on matrimony in the first edition of *Pol. Justice* as "the worst of all laws" was somewhat moderated in the subsequent two editions, which nonetheless insistently maintained the right of two people freely to choose and change partners. Godwin added in the second edition the suggestion that freelove would not lead to promiscuity. Whereas Wollstonecraft was not an advocate of freelove in her writing, she provided in *A Vindication of the Rights of Woman* (1792) a powerful critique of marriage under the contemporary state of vastly unequal gender relations. More powerful still was the sustained dramatization of the oppressive machinery that matrimonial law placed in the hands of men in Wollstonecraft's novel *The Wrongs of Woman, or Maria* (posthumously published in 1798), in which the protagonist Maria Venable exclaims: "Marriage had bastilled me for life. I discovered in myself a capacity for the enjoyment of the various pleasures existence affords; yet, fettered by the partial laws of society, this fair globe was to me an universal blank" (Chap. X; *WMWI*, 146).

PBS wrote to James Henry Lawrence on 17 August 1812: "Your 'Empire of the Nairs,' which I read this Spring, succeeded in making me a perfect convert to its doctrines. I then retained no doubts of the evils of marriage,—Mrs. Wollstonecraft reasons too well for that; but I had been dull enough not to perceive the greatest argument against it, until developed in the 'Nairs,' viz., prostitution both *legal* and *illegal*" (**Letters** I, 323). Lawrence's *The Empire of the Nairs* concerns the Nairs (or Nayars), a Hindu caste living on the tropical Malabar coast of Kerala in Southwest India that, through the sixteenth to eighteenth centuries, practiced matrilineal inheritance and freelove. Lawrence, an Etonian like PBS, first wrote about the Nair "system of gallantry and inheritance" in 1793, while he was living in Germany. Building upon the work of both Godwin and Wollstonecraft, Lawrence later extrapolated from the essay a full-blown "System of the Nairs," which he fictionalized in his four-volume "Utopian Romance" and explained in his Preface. *Nairs* first appeared in Germany in 1801 under the title *Das Paradies der Liebe* (later changed to *Das Reich der Nairen*). After moving to France, Lawrence produced a French translation in 1803, entitled *L'empire des nairs,* which was followed eight years later by the English translation, issued by PBS's own publisher and friend Thomas Hookham (see Walter Graham, *PMLA* 40 [Dec. 1925]: 881–91).

PBS found congenial Lawrence's attacks on the despotism of matrimonial law in Europe; his advocacy of free, but not necessarily promiscuous, choice of sexual partners; and, especially, his analysis that chastity and marriage lead to prostitution. On the other hand, PBS ignored several of Lawrence's other points, such as his championing of the greater population growth that freelove would presumably create and his argument that matrilineal descent would abolish the problems of illegitimacy. Moreover, both Lawrence and Wollstonecraft considered in far greater detail the interrelated ways that British matrimonial laws and gender inequalities victimized women than did PBS, who focused in this respect primarily on "fallen women." Sometime after receiving PBS's letter praising both *Nairs* and Lawrence's poem "Love: An Allegory" (another work advocating freelove and attacking chastity), Lawrence appears to have sought and made PBS's acquaintance (Hogg, *Life,* ed. Wolfe, 28, 116).

PBS's agenda throughout this note corresponds more closely with what Annette Wheeler Cafarelli has characterized as the "male" radical agenda of "diminishing the risks of perpetual marriage," as opposed to the "female" radical agenda focusing on greater "rights within marriage, educational equality, and destigmatizing female transgressors" (see *Poet and Legislator,* 98–100). As the anonymous contemporary *Reply to the Anti-Matrimonial Hypothesis . . . in Queen Mab* (1821) takes pains to point out, PBS's theoretical position in the note leaves women especially vulnerable to desertion, social marginalization, and destitution.

1839 omits the entire note.

lines 2–3. <u>Not even . . . positive institution</u>: Cf. *Pol. Justice:* "Marriage is law, and the worst of all laws. . . . marriage is an affair of property, and the worst of all properties. So long as two human beings are forbidden by positive institution to follow the dictates of their own mind, prejudice is alive and vigorous" (VIII.vi; II, 850; revised subsequently). PBS indignantly challenged Hogg's position that "it is a duty to comply with the established laws of yr. country," arguing that the truly virtuous person acts in "noble violation of the laws of a prejudiced society" and that matrimonial law precisely calls for such defiance: "For God's sake if you want more argument read the marriage service before you *think* of allowing an amiable beloved female to submit to such degradation—" (*Letters* I, 80–81). Here PBS is following the logic laid out by Darnford in Wollstonecraft's *Wrongs of Woman:* "Ties of this nature [i.e., matrimonial ties] could not bind minds governed by superior principles; and such beings were privileged to act above the dictates of laws they had no voice in framing, if they had sufficient strength of mind to endure the natural consequence" (Chap. XV; *WMW* I, 172).

Nonetheless, PBS recognized the potentially devastating consequences of such defiance and had seen them dramatized at great length in Amelia Opie's *Adeline Mowbray; or, The Mother and Daughter* ([1804; London: Longman, Hurst, Rees & Orme, 1805] itself partly based on Wollstonecraft's life and thought and on Godwin's antimatrimonialism), which he read in 1811. As PBS informed Lawrence, he had himself married "whilst convinced of the unholiness of the act . . . [because] in the present state of society, if love is not thus villainously treated, she, who is most loved, will be treated worse by a misjudging world. . . . If there is any enormous and desolating crime, of which I should shudder to be accused, it is seduction.—" (*Letters* I, 323). He and MWS were to discover first-hand just how devastating flouting matrimonial law and convention could be.

lines 11–18. <u>A husband and wife . . . improvement of the human mind</u>: In *Pol. Justice,* Godwin argues: "It is absurd to expect that the inclinations and wishes of two human beings should coincide through any long period of time. To oblige them to act and to live together, is to subject them to some inevitable portion of thwarting, bickering and unhappiness" (VIII.vi; II, 849; slightly revised in 3rd ed.). Unlike PBS, however, Godwin argued against cohabitation altogether and downplayed the importance of sexuality in human relationships.

In a stinging letter written to PBS in September 1820, Southey reckons the death of Harriet Shelley as the cost of PBS's acting upon his antimatrimonial opinions:

At length you forsook your wife, because you were tired of her, and had found another woman more suited to your taste. . . . I have heard that she followed your example as faithfully as your lessons, and that the catastrophe was produced by shame. Be this as it may, ask your own heart, whether you have not been the whole, sole, and direct cause of her destruction. You corrupted her opinions; you robbed her of her moral and religious principles; you debauched her mind. . . . I will do you justice, sir. While you were at Keswick you told your bride that you regarded marriage as a mere ceremony, and would live with her no longer than you liked her. I dare say you told her this before the ceremony, and that you persuaded her that there was nothing sacred in the tie. But that she should have considered this as the condition upon which she was married, or that you yourself at that time looked forward to a breach of the connexion, I do not believe. (*Letters* II, 232)

lines 12–14. <u>any law which should bind them . . . a most intolerable tyranny</u>: Cf. Wollstonecraft, *Wrongs of Woman:* "surely those laws are much more inhuman, which forge adamantine fetters to bind minds together, that never can mingle in social communion!" (Chap. XI; *WMW* I, 54). Cf. also Lawrence, *Nairs:* "Marriage is a prison that confines both man and wife; but, as, in a jail, one prisoner may exercise over an other the functions of a turnkey, so the husband is the most favored of the two: but would they not be happy in making their escape together? Can the authority of a turnkey reconcile any prisoner to his detention?" (I, viii).

Footnote 1. <u>The first Christian emperor</u> . . . <u>page 210</u>: PBS redacts the quotation of Constantine's edict in Gibbon (*Decline and Fall* II, 252–53). Gibbon explains that Constantine established severe penalties for rape, but made no distinctions between rape and seduction, a category that included all sex outside of marriage (II, 252). Gibbon also describes at some length "the chaste severity" of the early Christians leaders, who believed "that if Adam had preserved his obedience to the Creator, he would have lived for ever in a state of virgin purity. . . . The use of marriage was permitted only to his fallen posterity, as a necessary expedient to continue the human species, and as a restraint, however imperfect, on the natural licentiousness of desire" (II, 323; but see II, 323–25 for the entire passage). In **Refutation,** Theosophus exclaims: "The penalties inflicted by that monster Constantine, the first Christian Emperor, on the pleasures of unlicenced love are so iniquitously severe, that no modern legislator could have affixed them to the most atrocious crimes" (**Prose/EBM** I, 105). As Cameron has observed, PBS took particular pleasure in Gibbon's notorious Chapter XV, which provides a sharply critical account of the establishment of the early Church (see *YS*, 404n.107).

In a letter of 26 September 1815, PBS indicates that he has lost "the 6th vol. of Gibbons Decline & Fall an edition in foolscap 8vo, published in 1807" (**Letters** I, 433). This edition, published by T. Cadell in twelve volumes was probably what he received from Hookham, when he first ordered the work in December 1812 (**Letters** I, 342).

<u>were confiscated</u>: The accidental omission of "were" in both *1834* and *1840* exemplifies how hard it was for MWS to catch all the errors in her base text.

lines 31–36. <u>But if happiness</u> . . . <u>nothing immoral in this separation</u>: According to Godwin, in a passage deleted from the third edition of *Pol. Justice:* "We ought to dismiss our mistake as soon as it is detected; but we are taught to cherish it. We ought to be incessant in our search after virtue and worth; but we are taught to check our enquiry, and shut our eyes upon the most attractive and admirable objects" (VIII.vi; II, 850). Lawrence: "The Nairs maintain that there is no more reason, in enacting that a man should love a woman to-morrow because he may love her to-day, than there would be in compelling a man to dance at the next ball with his partner at the last" (*Nairs* I, viii).

line 31. <u>But if happiness be the object of morality</u>: PBS, like Godwin, used the French materialist rhetoric of pleasure and utility to discuss morals. Like Godwin, he broke with the more purely hedonistic tendencies of Helvétius to follow Shaftesbury, Hume, and other writers of the Moral Sense school, who, in F. E. L. Priestley's words, "insist on the pleasures of self-approbation and disinterestedness, and deny the supremacy of sensual pleasures. He [Godwin] further modifies the doctrine that pleasure is the supreme good by broadening it to mean that the pleasure of others is 'an object which, for its own sake, could, and ought to be pursued'" (*Pol. Justice,* ed. Priestley III, 15–16).

line 36. <u>Constancy has nothing virtuous in itself</u>: Godwin argued similarly, though conversely, that inconstancy is not "incompatible with a character of uncommon excellence. What, at present, renders it, in many instances, peculiarly loathsome, is its being practised in a clandestine manner. It leads to a train of falshood and a concerted hypocrisy, than which there is scarcely any thing that more eminently depraves and degrades the human mind" (*Pol. Justice,* ed. Priestley VIII.viii; II, 510). Cf. also Lawrence's *Nairs,* in which a character argues: "Know ye not, that though constancy is no merit, it is a source of happiness; and that, though inconstancy is no crime, it is no blessing, much less a boast? O ye Europeans! ye children of vanity and prejudice!" (III, 130).

lines 39–41. <u>Love is free</u> . . . <u>excludes us from all enquiry</u>: Lawrence similarly argues: "Experience is the prerogative of age, and every day may bring its portion of wisdom. . . . However great one's sagacity, every addition of wisdom may set one's actions in so new a light, that one may doubt of their propriety; no mortal, therefore, should subject himself to an eternal obligation" (*Nairs* I, v).

lines 50–51. <u>to one</u> . . . <u>their life</u>: A change from <u>one</u> to "those" in *1829.BRO* appears to be a deliberate grammatical emendation and was carried through *1834* to *1840*. On the other hand, the change in *1834* of <u>their children</u> to "the children" in the next sentence may be a compositor's mistake uncorrected by MWS in *1840*.

lines 64–67. <u>The conviction that wedlock is indissoluble</u> . . . <u>all the little tyrannies of domestic life</u>: In *Rights of Woman,* Wollstonecraft argues: "I may be told that a number of women are not slaves in the marriage state. True, but they then become tyrants; for it is not rational freedom, but a lawless kind of power resembling the authority exercised by the favourites of absolute monarchs, which they obtain by debasing means" (Chap. XI; *WMW* V, 226).

line 71. <u>Prostitution is the legitimate offspring of marriage</u>: See the headnote to **Note 9** for PBS's acknowledgment that Lawrence's *Nairs* convinced him of the connection between marriage and prostitution. In *Nairs,* Lawrence claims that "in a country where there were no wives, there would be no courtesans. . . . So long as Hymen continues a monopolist, Love will continue a smuggler" (I, xvi). In *Rights of Woman*, Wollstonecraft argues from a different perspective that the prevailing inequality between the sexes undermined the institution of marriage and engendered prostitution: only after this injustice was redressed would "The father of a family . . . not then weaken his constitution and debase his sentiments, by visiting the harlot . . ." ("Dedication to Talleyrand"; *WMW* V, 68). She also claims that because women of the middle rank were blocked from the professions, "To rise in the world, and have the liberty of running from pleasure to pleasure, they must marry advantageously, and to this object their time is sacrificed, and their persons often legally prostituted" (Chap. IV; *WMW* V, 129). She had first used the phrase "legal prostitution" in a similar analysis appearing in *A Vindication of the Rights of Men* (1790), a phrase that Janet Todd and Marilyn Butler note had been used earlier by Defoe in *Conjugal Lewdness, or, Matrimonial Whoredom* (1727; *WMW* V, 22).

Leigh Hunt observes in *Lord Byron and Some of his Contemporaries*, the "unhappy mass of prostitution which exists in England, contrasted with something which seems to despise it [i.e., marriage], and which, in more opinions than his [PBS's], is a main cause of it, was always one of the subjects that at a moment's notice would overshadow the liveliest of his moods" (1828; rpt., New York: AMS, 1966, 213).

lines 72–73. <u>Women . . . dictates of a natural appetite</u>: Cf. Lawrence, who ascribed to the "preposterous estimation" in which chastity was held in Britain "the number of involuntary courtesans who infest the metropolis; some of whom, women of family and education, and free from every crime, though unable to resist the dictates of nature, have been banished from the protection and endearments of their home, and obliged to seek a precarious livelihood by a loathsome profession" (*Nairs* I, xxv). In *Rights of Woman*, Wollstonecraft had argued: "Still, highly as I respect marriage, as the foundation of almost every social virtue, I cannot avoid feeling the most lively compassion for those unfortunate females who are broken off from society, and by one error torn from all those affections and relationships that improve the heart and mind. It does not frequently even deserve the name of error; for many innocent girls become the dupes of a sincere, affectionate heart, and still more are, as it may emphatically be termed, *ruined* before they know the difference between virtue and vice . . ." (Chap. IV; *WMW* V, 140). Beyond their arguments for destigmatizing such sexual transgressions, contemporary feminists attempted to shift the focus away from women's sexual desire and onto their economic plight, as men usurped jobs formerly done by women, who were left with few satisfactory alternatives for earning a living (see Cafarelli, in *Poet and Legislator*, 100–102).

lines 86–87. <u>one tenth of the population of London</u>: London at the beginning of the nineteenth century had a total population of about one million people. Contemporary estimates of the number of prostitutes in the city varied widely: for example, in 1783 Charles Horne estimated 30,000 (*Serious Thoughts on the Miseries of Seduction and Prostitution,* 14); in 1804, Thomas Holcroft expressed the fear that the number of prostitutes in London "much exceeds" 30,000 (*Travels from Hamburg, Through Westphalia, Holland, and the Netherlands, to Paris,* 125); and, at about the same time, Patrick Colquhoun estimated 50,000 (*A Treatise on the Police of the Metropolis,* 7th ed. [1806], 340), a figure repeated in a letter about prostitution published in *The Examiner* for 5 January 1812 (12). Clearly, PBS accepted by far the largest of such estimates. In a canceled passage of her journal for 7 April 1820, Claire Clairmont similarly claimed that there were 100,000 prostitutes in London (Clairmont, *Journals,* 139).

lines 87–92. <u>Young men</u> . . . <u>excess of generosity and devotedness</u>: Cf. Lawrence, in *Nairs:* "From the chastity which the married woman and every creditable female is forced to maintain, the young Briton is driven into low intrigues and vulgar connections" (I, xxv).

lines 93–94. <u>idiotcy and disease become perpetuated</u>: Cf. Wollstonecraft, *Rights of Woman:* ". . . the rich sensualist, who has rioted among women, spreading depravity and misery, when he wishes to perpetuate his name, receives from his wife only an half-formed being that inherits both its father's and mother's weakness" (Chap. VIII; *WMW* V, 209).

lines 95–97. <u>Chastity is a monkish</u> . . . <u>unintellectual sensuality</u>: Lawrence similarly distinguished between a "monastic chastity" and a "natural chastity": "The first may be compared to starvation, the second to temperance . . . ." While he condemned the former, the latter he praised as a "duty to one's self and to one's country" (I, xxxiii). In adhering to the notion of chastity as a form of temperance, both Lawrence and PBS (see Commentary for **IX.84**) were influenced by Wollstonecraft, who argued in *Rights of Woman* for men especially to practice this form of natural chastity. In *The Wrongs of Woman,* Wollstonecraft attacked the way matrimonial law engendered a "false morality . . . which makes all the virtue of woman consist in chastity, submission, and the forgiveness of injuries" (Chap. XVII; *WMW* I, 180).

line 99. <u>monopolize according to law</u>: Opie's narrator in *Adeline Mowbray* observes, "The true and delicate lover is always a monopolizer, always desirous of calling the woman of his affections his own: it is not only because he considers marriage as a holy institution that the lover leads his mistress to the altar; but because it gives him a right to appropriate the fair treasure to himself,—because it sanctions and perpetuates the dearest of all monopolies, and erects a sacred barrier to guard his rights,—around which, all that is respectable in society, all that is most powerful and effectual in its organization, is proud and eager to rally" (*Adeline Mowbray* I, 103–4). Earlier, in the second edition of *Pol. Justice* (1796), Godwin had objected to marriage as "a monopoly, and the worst of monopolies" (ed. Priestley VIII.viii; II, 508). Cf. PBS's letter of 26 November 1811 to Elizabeth Hitchener: "Marriage is monopolizing, exclusive jealous— . . ." (*Letters* I, 194), and his later prose fragment **On Marriage** (1817): "The same dread of insecurity which gave birth to those laws or opinions which defend the security of property suggested also the institution of marriage: that is a contrivance to prevent others from deriving advantage from that which any individual has succeeded in preoccupying" (*Prose/EBM* I, 274).

lines 102–3. <u>I by no means assert . . . promiscuous</u>: Godwin added a passage in the second edition of *Pol. Justice* that similarly addressed the issue of promiscuity, which was slightly revised in the third edition to read as follows: "It is a question of some moment, whether the intercourse of the sexes, in a reasonable state of society, would be promiscuous, or whether each man would select for himself a partner, to whom he will adhere, as long as that adherence shall continue to be the choice of both parties. Probability seems to be greatly in favour of the latter" (ed. Priestley VIII.viii; II, 508–9). In *Adeline Mowbray*, a chastened Adeline repents her original stand on freelove: "I am convinced, that if the ties of marriage were dissolved, or it were no longer to be judged infamous to act in contempt of them, unbridled licentiousness would soon be in general practice" (III, 209).

Although *1989* claims that PBS on the issue of promiscuity "diverges from Lawrence to follow Godwin and Mary Wollstonecraft" (I, 372), there is evidence to the contrary in Lawrence's praise of natural temperance and in his representation in the novel proper of several unmarried couples who have remained together for many years. See also the discussion of constancy by Lawrence's character, the Preceptor:

But think not, because in this country we change [partners] when we please, that we are less constant in our affections than other nations. Strike out from the list of constant couples in your country, or any other country, where marriage is tolerated, all those who are constant from hypocrisy, avarice, fear of shame or death, ignorance . . . from superstition, and so forth; and count the remaining couples, who are constant from inclination, and you will find that the number of constant couples in Calicut will exceed their number in any city on the globe. (*Nairs* I, 130–31)

PBS's lifelong stand against promiscuity is registered vividly in his anonymous review, published in the *Critical Review* for 1814, of Hogg's novel *Memoirs of Prince Alexy Haimatoff*. PBS objects with "horror and detestation" to the advice of Bruhle, Alexy's tutor, that his pupil should "indulge in promiscuous concubinage. . . . The author [i.e., Hogg] . . . asserts that a transient connection with a cultivated female, may contribute to form the heart without essentially vitiating the sensibilities. It is our duty to protest against so pernicious and disgusting an opinion. No man can rise pure from the poisonous embraces of a prostitute, or sinless from the desolated hopes of a confiding heart. Whatever may be the claims of chastity, whatever the advantages of simple and pure affections, these ties, these benefits are of equal obligation to either sex" (***Prose/EBM*** I, 142).

line 112. <u>dressed up in stiff stays and finery</u>: PBS's figurative use of <u>stays</u> and <u>finery</u> aptly draws upon contemporary feminist protests against the wearing of whalebone stays and tight-fitting clothes, both of which were meant to discipline mind and body. Hogg, who noted that stays "had many enemies at that period" and that he "listened patiently to many a fierce, angry diatribe against them," recounted how he attended a feminist lecture against stays during which a deceased rabbit—who for the purposes of scientific research, had been forced to wear stays—was displayed as evidence of the physical harm stays could cause to women's bodies. Upon being asked by the lecturer (whom he describes as "a first-rate, scientific Blue") whether he had been convinced by her presentation, Hogg supposedly replied: "To say the truth, madam, I do not very well know how to answer you: with respect to women, I am not competent to decide; but I am fully convinced, and you demonstrated it completely, that Providence never meant that a buck rabbit should wear stays!" (*Life*, ed. Wolfe, II, 19–20.)

See also the reprinted "Edict Against the Use of Stays" in *The Lady's Monthly Museum* for May 1800 for concern about the effects of stays on the physical development of girls, which includes the following: "Whereas the dangerous consequences arising from the use of stays, are universally acknowledged to impair the health, and impede the growth of the fair sex; when, on the contrary, the suppression of that part of their dress cannot but be effectual in strengthening their constitutions, and, above all, in rendering them more fruitful in the marriage state: we hereby strictly enjoin, that in all orphan-houses, nunneries, and other places set apart for the public education of young girls, no stays, of any kind whatever, shall be made use of, or encouraged from henceforth, and from this instant; . . ." (393).

Note 10 (VI.45–46)

There is a long history of speculation about the interrelations between the state of humanity's physical environment and its intellectual and moral health. As Israel James Kapstein has surmised, PBS could have read about the idea that earth's climate had changed at the end of the Golden Age or after the Fall in such sources as Thomas Burnet's *Sacred Theory of the Earth*, Milton's *Paradise Lost* X.668ff., and in James Thomson's *The Seasons:* "Spring"

300ff. (*PMLA* 52 [1937]: 242). Whatever general reading PBS found useful for the note, it is questionable that he took any of his three actual citations (to Laplace, Cabanis, and Bailly) directly from their sources: two of the three citations do not give chapter or page numbers and the one citation to a specific page is incorrect (see below).

In early 1813, PBS ordered from Hookham "all possible documents on the Precession of the Equinoxes; as also anything that may throw light upon the question whether or no the position of the Earth on its poles is not yearly becoming less oblique" (***Letters*** I, 349). He may at this point have received Pierre-Simon Laplace's *Exposition du système du monde* (1796), in which Book IV, Chapter XIII is headed: "De la précession des équinoxes, et de la nutation de l'axe de la terre" (II, 164–81). However, he does not actually appear to have read Laplace in earnest until the end of November 1813 (***Letters*** I, 380), perhaps in time for this note, if the ***QM*** notes were not printed until sometime in December. PBS would have seen many contemporary discussions of the precession of the equinoxes, in sources such as Drummond's *Oedipus Judaicus*, Paine's *Age of Reason*, Nicholson's *British Encyclopedia*, Adam Walker's *A System of Familiar Philosophy* (1802), and John Frank Newton's *Return to Nature* (1811). The scientific consensus, as noted in Laplace and in the *Nicholson's* entry "Precession," was that before reaching a perpendicularity in which the sun would shine equally throughout the planet, the poles would oscillate back to their original positions in repeated cycles that, according to *Nicholson's,* would each take 25,791 years. The earth would, therefore, never enjoy the perpetual spring and equal length of night and day anticipated by those such as John Frank Newton, who believed that the poles would achieve and maintain perpendicularity to the earth's orbit. PBS here specifically denies that the precession is "merely an oscillation," choosing perhaps for ideological purposes to follow Newton, whose conversation and work were probably the major influences on this note and from whom he could have learned about the work of Laplace, Cabanis, and Bailly. For Newton's claims about the effects of the perpendicularity of the earth's poles, see the Commentary for **Note 17, lines 8–16.**

line 18. <u>oscillation</u>: The misspelling "occillation" in ***1813*** probably stemmed from PBS, since a compositor would have had a dictionary at hand.

Footnotes 2 and 3. <u>Cabanis, . . . Bailly</u>: Although PBS ordered Pierre Jean George Cabanis's *Rapports du physique et du moral de l'homme* (1802) from Hookham in December 1812 (***Letters*** I, 342), there is no evidence that he read the book before writing this note—and good reason to suppose that he did not. He incorrectly cites Cabanis for information actually provided by J. S. Bailly, suggesting that he cribbed the erroneous citation from another source. Bailly's *Lettres sur l'origine des sciences, et sur celle des peuples de l'asie: Adressées à M. de Voltaire par M. Bailly, & précédées de quelque lettres de M. de*

Voltaire à l'auteur (London: M. Elmesley, 1777) reports on Liebnitz's discovery in Germany of fossils of plants grown in India: *"Un fait plus singulier & plus démonstratif, ce sont les vestiges de ces plantes étrangeres que l'on trouve sur les pierres. . . . Liebnitz avait déjà reconnu quelques feuilles de plantes des Indes, imprimées sur des pierres d'Allemagne"* (314–15). PBS could have found out about the discovery of elephant bones either from Bailly (320–23) or from Newton, who explains how the discovery of such bones in "once genial climates" helps confirm the hypothesis that "the axis of our globe was perpendicular to the plane of the ecliptic" (*Return,* 13; but see 13–15 for his entire argument).

Footnote 3. The specific reference is to Bailly's argument in the eighth letter to Voltaire, which is dated "À Paris le 14 Septembre 1776" and is headed with a summation of the argument: *"Cet ancien peuple paraît avoir habité dans l'Asie, vers le parallèle de 49°. Il semble que la lumiere des sciences & la population se soient étendues sur la terre du nord au midi"* (224). Bailly's discussion of this ancient people can be found on pp. 224–25.

line 27. <u>annually</u>: Some copies of *1813* that we have checked contain the error "anuually": either this was rectified by a stop-press correction or the press was stopped for another reason, at which time a correctly set <u>n</u> turned upside down in the chase.

Note 11 (VI.171–73)

PBS took this quotation from the 1781 edition of Holbach's *Système de la nature,* pp. 44–45 (collated as *1781.HOL*). *1813* contains various errors in agreement, accents, spelling, and tense, which we have corrected (for which, see the collation proper). We do not record as variants the consistent use in *1781* of ampersands for *and*. *1839* omits the entire note. *1821.BEN* replaces all of the French with an English translation that is similar to, but probably independent of, the translation that appears in a footnote in *1821.CLA*. The latter reads as follows:

Two instances will serve to render more sensible to us the principle here laid down; we will borrow one from natural, the other from moral philosophy. In a whirlwind of dust raised by an impetuous wind, however confused it may appear to our eyes; in the most dreadful tempest excited by opposing winds, which convulse the waves, there is not a single particle of dust or of water that is placed by *chance* that has not its sufficient cause for occupying the situation in which it is, and which does not rigorously act in the mode it should act. A geometrician who knew equally the different powers which operate in both cases, and the properties of the particles which are propelled, would shew that according to the given causes, each particle acts precisely as it should act, and cannot act otherwise than it does.

In those terrible convulsions which sometimes agitate political societies, and which frequently bring on the overthrow of an empire, there is not a single action, a single word, a single thought, a single volition, a single passion in the agents, which concur in the revolution as destroyers, or as victims, which is not necessary, which does not act as it should act, which does not infallibly produce the effects which it should produce, according to the place occupied by these agents in the moral whirlwind.

This would appear evident to an intelligence which would be in a state to seize and appreciate all the actions and re-actions of the minds and bodies of those who contribute to this revolution.

Note 12 (VI.198)

Whereas PBS's arguments for Necessity in this note are partially derived from Holbach (*Système*) and, even more so, Godwin (*Pol. Justice*, ed. Priestley IV.vii–viii; I, 361–97), ultimately the single most important influence on its conceptual structure as well as much of its local phrasing is Hume's *Enquiry Concerning Human Understanding*, Sections IV–VIII (esp. Section VIII), the immediate source of much of Godwin's own related discussion in *Pol. Justice.* Two other possible sources or analogues, neither of which has been previously noted, are worth mentioning: PBS seems to have drawn on the discussion of Necessity by the materialist "Hylus" in Chapter IV of William Drummond's *Academical Questions* (228–78); and in the article "Necessity, philosophical" in Nicholson's *British Encyclopedia* there are many resemblances in structure and phrasing to PBS's note, perhaps only because the article drew on the same sources as PBS.

For the general influence of Hume and Godwin on the note, see Frank B. Evans III, *Studia Philologica* 37 (1940): 632–40, and Cameron, *YS,* 270–73. PBS ordered a copy of Hume's *Essays* from Hookham on 17 December 1812 (**Letters** I, 342). Evans points out that Hume's subtle argument, which asserts that the "necessity of causal connection is not in nature, but in the constitution of our intellects," implies that there is no fundamentally rational ground for any science, a more rigorously skeptical position than that taken by either Godwin or PBS—or, we might add, Holbach. Accordingly, Evans concludes that though PBS "borrowed his arguments from Hume," he "interpreted them through the mind of Godwin" (639–40). PBS describes Necessity as "Blind, changeless, and eternal in her paths" in line 109 of **The Voyage** (**Esd** #32), which might contain an early draft for **QM**.

1839 omits this note, and *1821.CLAX,* the expurgated Clark piracy, deletes a phrase attacking God (**lines 136–37;** see collation). We have emended the reading of the cue line "Necessity," in **1813** back to the reading of the poetic text in **1813** for which it is a cue: <u>Necessity!</u>

lines 4–5. <u>no one of which</u> . . . <u>acts</u>: In the early editions, beginning with *1821.BEN,* the phrase *no one of which* was interpreted as calling for the plural verb *act.*

lines 6–9. <u>The idea of necessity</u> . . . <u>inference of one from the other</u>: paraphrased from Hume, "Our idea, therefore, of necessity and causation arises entirely from the uniformity observable in the operations of nature, where similar objects are constantly conjoined together, and the mind is determined by custom to infer the one from the appearance of the other." Unlike PBS, however, Hume went on to stress the tenuous foundation of necessity: "These two circumstances form the whole of that necessity, which we ascribe to matter. Beyond the constant *conjunction* of similar objects, and the consequent *inference* from one to the other, we have no notion of any necessity or connexion" (*Enquiry* VIII.i, 82).

lines 9–10. <u>Mankind are therefore agreed</u> . . . <u>voluntary action</u>: Cf. Hume, "If it appear, therefore, that all mankind have ever allowed . . . that these two circumstances take place in the voluntary actions of men, and in the operations of mind; it must follow, that all mankind have ever agreed in the doctrine of necessity, and that they have hitherto disputed, merely for not understanding each other" (*Enquiry* VIII.i, 83).

lines 12–14. <u>The word liberty</u> . . . <u>the word chance</u> . . . <u>antecedents and consequents</u>: Godwin made the same point about Necessity and liberty: "Where all is constant and invariable, and the events that arise, uniformly correspond to the circumstances in which they originate, there can be no liberty" (*Pol. Justice,* ed. Priestley IV.vii; I, 364). Hume, who claimed, "there be no such thing as *Chance* in the world . . . ," like PBS, described chance as arising from "our ignorance of the real cause of any event . . ." (*Enquiry* VI, 56).

lines 15–18. <u>Every human being</u> . . . <u>otherwise than it is</u>: taken from Godwin: "In the life of every human being there is a chain of events, generated in the lapse of ages which preceded his birth, and going on in regular procession through the whole period of his existence, in consequence of which it was impossible for him to act in any instance otherwise than he has acted" (*Pol. Justice,* ed. Priestley IV.viii; I, 384).

lines 19–22. <u>Were the doctrine of Necessity false</u> . . . <u>all knowledge would be vague and undeterminate</u>: A similar point is made by Hume (*Enquiry* VIII.i, 85), Godwin (*Pol. Justice,* ed. Priestley IV.vii; I, 369), and, in language even closer to PBS's, in *Nicholson's:* "This principle [the cause and effect of necessity] lies at the foundation of all clear reasoning and legitimate conclusion. Its denial would subvert all the forms and degrees of human knowledge."

line 24. <u>with whom we have parted</u>: Brooks (*1829.BRO*) initiated the change from <u>with whom</u> to "from whom" that is transmitted through *1834* to *1840.*

lines 26–27. <u>Similar circumstances produce the same unvariable effects</u>: Once again, Brooks sought to improve PBS's style, this time by substituting "unvariably similar" in *1829.BRO* for PBS's <u>same unvariable</u>. Whereas *1834* accepted the change, MWS revised Brooks's alteration by substituting "invariably similar" in *1840*.

Cf. Hume, "The same motives always produce the same actions: The same events follow from the same causes" (*Enquiry* VIII.i, 83).

lines 27–31. <u>The precise character</u> . . . <u>chemical substances</u>: PBS would have found in Hume the analogy between the moral philosopher and the natural philosopher, along with the underlying claim that Necessity provides a scientific basis for understanding the human mind, a point also made by Godwin (*Enquiry* VIII.i, 83–85; *Pol. Justice,* ed. Priestley IV.vii; I, 369–70). The actual language of PBS's sentence closely parallels Godwin: "He who affirms that all actions are necessary, means that the man, who is acquainted with all the circumstances under which a living or intelligent being is placed upon any given occasion, is qualified to predict the conduct he will hold, with as much certainty, as he can predict any of the phenomena of inanimate nature" (*Pol. Justice,* ed. Priestley IV.vii; I, 363).

lines 31–33. <u>Why is the aged husbandman</u> . . . <u>material universe</u>: taken from Hume: "Why is the aged husbandman more skilful in his calling than the young beginner but because there is a certain uniformity in the operation of the sun, rain, and earth towards the production of vegetables; and experience teaches the old practitioner the rules by which this operation is governed and directed" (*Enquiry* VIII.i, 85).

lines 36–38. <u>Some actions may be found</u> . . . <u>are unacquainted</u>: This point is elaborated both in Hume (*Enquiry* VIII.i, 86–88) and in *Nicholson's,* which states: "Now, though we predict the acts of moral agents with less certainty, and expect them with more hesitation than mingle in our calculations on natural phenomena, this difference is attributable merely to our ignorance of the tempers, characters, and situations of those agents, to the difficulty, and frequently the impossibility, which we experience of exploring the labyrinth of the human heart, and not in the slightest degree to any doubt, that volitions will always be precisely determined by preceding states of mind, and that certain volitions will inevitably be productive of certain acts."

lines 38–40. <u>Hence the relation</u> . . . <u>philosophical dispute</u>: paraphrased from Hume: "Thus it appears, not only that the conjunction between motives and voluntary actions is as regular and uniform as that between the cause and effect in any part of nature; but also that this regular conjunction has been universally acknowledged among mankind, and has never been the subject of dispute, either in philosophy or common life" (*Enquiry* VIII.i, 88).

lines 40–44. <u>None but the few fanatics</u> . . . <u>without a motive</u>: Cf. Holbach, "It is evident that the system of liberty, or free will, has been invented to exonerate God from the evil that is done in this world" (*System,* 102n).

lines 44–45. <u>History, politics, morals, criticism . . . doctrine of Necessity</u>: PBS's catalogue of disciplines dependent on Necessity is drawn directly from Hume (*Enquiry* VIII.i, 90).

lines 45–49. <u>No farmer . . . master of a manufactory . . . to act</u>: The example of the farmer ultimately derives by way of Godwin from Hume's "poorest artificer, who . . . . expects that when he carries his goods to market, and offers them at a reasonable price, he shall find purchasers . . . ." (*Enquiry* VIII.i, 89). Godwin took this passage from Hume and replaced the "poorest artificer" with the "farmer" selling his corn (*Pol. Justice*, ed. Priestley IV.vii; I, 375). The example of the manufacturer is taken directly from Hume (*Enquiry* VIII.i, 89).

line 48. <u>machinery</u>: The emendation to "machines" in the editions of Brooks, Ascham, and MWS (*1840*) is intended to correct a possible agreement problem with the following pronoun (<u>they</u>); *1821.BEN* instead emends <u>they have</u> to "it has." PBS appears to have thought of *machinery* as a collective noun requiring the plural pronoun.

lines 50–63. <u>But, whilst none have scrupled to admit necessity as influencing matter . . . necessity is clearly established</u>: This entire paragraph, excepting its reference to religion, is a compressed redaction of Hume's more pointedly skeptical argument (*Enquiry* VIII.i, 92–94), which speculates that the reason most people are willing to credit the operation of Necessity in matter but not in mind is that

all our faculties can never carry us farther in our knowledge of this relation [between cause and effect] than barely to observe that particular objects are *constantly conjoined* together, and that the mind is carried, by a *customary transition,* from the appearance of one to the belief of the other. But though this conclusion concerning human ignorance be the result of the strictest scrutiny of this subject, men still entertain a strong propensity to believe that they penetrate farther into the powers of nature, and perceive something like a necessary connexion between the cause and the effect. When again they turn their reflections towards the operations of their own minds, and *feel* no such connexion of the motive and the action; they are thence apt to suppose [mistakenly], that there is a difference between the effects which result from material force, and those which arise from thought and intelligence. . . . It may only, perhaps, be pretended that the mind can perceive, in the operations of matter, some farther connexion between the cause and effect; and a connexion that has not place in the voluntary actions of intelligent beings.

In a footnote, Hume added that the "prevalence of the doctrine of liberty may be accounted for, from another cause, viz. a false sensation or seeming experience which we have, or may have, of liberty or indifference, in many of our actions" (94).

The phrase in **lines 54–58** that PBS put into quotation marks is actually paraphrased from later in the same paragraph from Hume that we quote above.

line 50. <u>none have</u>: An emendation to the singular "none has" was initiated by Brooks and transmitted to Ascham, but MWS returned to the plural "have."

line 60. <u>the only idea we can form</u>: MWS in *1839* made a syntactical revision by adding "that" to this clause: "the only idea that we can form."

lines 65–66. <u>What is power?</u> . . . <u>produce any given effect</u>: Hume writes at length on the meaning of power in *Enquiry* VII, and concludes that power can be conceived of only within the context of causes and effects as perceived by the senses, beyond which "we have no idea of it" (77). Closer to PBS's own phrasing is William Drummond's claim in *Academical Questions*: ". . . it would be difficult to show, that we understand any thing else by it [power], than that which may, or does, produce change. . . . [Power] is the indispensable link, which unites every efficient cause with its effect" (176). The central thought of PBS's sentence is restated in **Refutation:** "The word power expresses the capability of any thing to be or act" (**Prose/EBM** I, 121). Whereas PBS's discussion of freewill focuses on the definition of *power,* Hume's focuses on the definition of *liberty,* which, when understood in terms of Necessity, turns out to have no real meaning (*Enquiry* VIII.i, 95–96).

Although PBS glosses the Latin *id quo potest* within his own text, *1821.CLA* provides the following translation in a footnote: "That which can do any thing."

lines 71–75. <u>The advocates of free-will</u> . . . <u>which is absurd</u>: a tenet maintained by Hume, Holbach, and Godwin and articulated by Drummond's speaker Hylus: "Even man . . . obeys the motive which is strongest in his mind, while he vainly vaunts the triumphs of his will, and the sweets and the pleasures of liberty" (*Academical Questions*, 263).

lines 78–79. <u>The doctrine of Necessity</u> . . . <u>change</u> . . . <u>morality, and</u> . . . <u>destroy religion</u>: Hume attempted to defend his position from these implications by stating: "There is no method of reasoning more common, and yet none more blameable, than, in philosophical disputes, to endeavour the refutation of any hypothesis, by a pretence of its dangerous consequences to religion and morality" (*Enquiry* VIII.ii, 96). Whereas he proceeded to argue that Necessity is an essential support to morality (also argued by Holbach [*Système*, Chap. XII] and Godwin [*Pol. Justice*, ed. Priestley IV.vii; I, 383]), he was more evasive about its implications for religion, declaring that there can be no possible way of explaining "how the Deity can be the mediate cause of all the actions of men, without being the author of sin and moral turpitude," but consigning the problem to the realm of "sublime mysteries . . . which mere natural and unassisted reason is very unfit to handle" (VIII.ii, 103). Godwin steered completely clear of the implications of Necessity for religion, but his discussion of its effects on the concept of virtue begins with language that PBS echoed: "But, if the doctrine of necessity do not annihilate virtue, it tends to introduce a great change into our ideas respecting it" (IV.viii; I, 389).

lines 79–82. <u>Reward and punishment</u> . . . <u>conduct</u>: Whereas Necessity's effects on conceptions of punishment are discussed by Hume (briefly in *Enquiry* VIII.ii, 98–99) and by Holbach (*Système*, Chap. XII), PBS's own discussion most closely parallels Godwin (*Pol. Justice*, ed. Priestley IV.viii; I, 393–94) and *Nicholson's*, the latter of which explains in the entry "Necessity": "Punishment upon this system proceeds not from revenge, but from benevolence. The offender is considered as having been urged to the act of guilt . . . not more by voluntary determination than by necessitating motive. He is considered as requiring, indeed, inflictions of a description highly impressive and penal, to enable him to break the bands of vicious habits; but the indispensibleness of these inflictions is perceived with extreme regret, and yielded to with extreme reluctance."

For PBS's reference to the crime and punishment of Robert-François Damiens (1715–57) (**line 89**), cf. Godwin: "When Damiens, the maniac, was arraigned for his abortive attempt on the life of Louis XV of France, a council of anatomists was summoned, to deliberate how a human being might be destroyed with the longest protracted and most diversified agony" (*Pol. Justice*, ed. Priestley I.ii; I, 13). The creativity of the council may be judged by the following details: during the four hours before he was drawn and quartered by horses, Damiens was tortured with red-hot pincers while boiling oil and molten wax and lead were poured into his wounds. Nor did the punishment stop with Damiens himself. His house was razed to the ground, his parents and wife were banished from France, and his siblings were compelled to change their names. Godwin also lists Damiens as among the most determined of political assassins, along with Clement, Ravaillac (the protagonist of PBS's ***Epithalamium*** in ***PF***), and Gerard (*Pol. Justice*, ed. Priestley II.iv; I, 153). Damiens's stabbing of Louis XV in 1757 (as the King was entering his carriage) would find an almost parodic English echo in Margaret Nicholson's attack with a dessert knife on George III in 1786 (see Commentary to ***PF*** in ***CPPBS*** I).

line 88. <u>But utility is morality</u>: Cf. Godwin: "But all approbation or preference is relative to utility or general good" (*Pol. Justice*, ed. Priestley IV.viii; I, 388), and Holbach: "It is not upon the caprices of political society that depend the true notions of justice and injustice, the right ideas of moral good and evil . . . [but] upon *utility* . . . " (*System*, Chap. XII, 108).

lines 109–10. <u>relation</u> . . . <u>is absolutely none</u>: The problem of agreement in *1813* ("are" for <u>is</u>) was first caught and corrected in the 1821 piracies.

lines 114–21. <u>It is probable that the word God</u> . . . <u>supplicate his favour</u>: For the Holbachian roots of PBS's discussion of God in this passage and in the following paragraph, see the Commentary for **VI.101–2,** and for **Note 13** below.

lines 122–24. <u>But the doctrine of Necessity teaches us,</u> . . . <u>God</u> . . . <u>author of</u> <u>evil</u>: a point explored by Hume (*Enquiry* VIII.ii, 100–103) and articulated as follows in the entry "Necessity" in *Nicholson's:* "Finally, upon the principles of necessity, God is undoubtedly the author of evil: a statement which, to the minds of some, may carry the appearance of the most irreverent, and even impious imputation, and excite against the system, which not only thus maintains, but avows it, a repulsion amounting to antipathy."

lines 132–34. <u>But we are taught,</u> . . . <u>mode of being</u>: perhaps taken from Drummond, *Academical Questions,* in which Hylus claims, ". . . if there be an universal necessity, there can neither be good nor evil, nor order nor disorder, in the nature of things, but only as they are so fancied to be by us" (263).

lines 136–39. <u>God made man</u> . . . <u>man made the incongruity</u>: PBS almost certainly took this paraphrase of Hobbes (*Leviathan* [1651] IV.xlvi, 376) directly from Drummond:

If a man do an act of injustice, that is, an act contrary to the law, God, you say, is the prime cause of the law, as well as of all actions whatever, but no cause at all of the injustice, which is the inconformity of the action to the law. This is vain philosophy. You might as well say, (continues Hobbes, in whose language I am now speaking,) that one man makes a straight line and a crooked one, and that another makes their incongruity. . . . What can be more absurd, than for these men to talk of contingencies, and of the operation of occasional causes, while they attribute prescience, and omnipotence to God?" (*Academical Questions,* 275–76)

PBS repeats the parable and the citation to Hobbes in **Refutation.** Murray notes that Montesquieu had also used it in *Persian Letters* (**Prose**/*EBM* I, 375). The original passage in Hobbes reads as follows:

And for their Moral, and Civil Philosophy, it hath the same, or greater absurditie If a man do an action of Injustice, that is to say, an action contrary to the Law, God they say is the prime cause of the Law, and also the prime cause of that, and all other Actions; but no cause at all of the Injustice; which is the Inconformity of the Action to the Law. This is *Vain Philosophy*. A man might as well say, that one man maketh both a streight a [*sic*] line and a crooked, and another maketh their Incongruity. And such is the Philosophy of all men that resolve of their Conclusions, before they know their Premises; pretending to comprehend, that which is Incomprehensible; and of Attributes of Honour to make Attributes of Nature; as this distinction was made to maintain this Doctrine of Free-Will, that is of a Will of man, not subject to the Will of God.

lines 140–54. PBS took, without verbal changes, this story from George Sale, *The Koran, Commonly called The Alcoran of Mohammed, Translated into English immediately from the Original Arabic; with Explanatory Notes, taken from the most approved Commentators. To which is prefixed A Preliminary Discourse* (1734). Sale used the story, purported to be a saying of Mohammed's, to illustrate the difficulty of fixing Mohammed's own opinion on predestination. It appears in Section VIII of the "Preliminary Discourse" and can be found on pages 163–64 of the 1734 edition (although PBS himself used a later edition, perhaps from 1801, for which the page number supplied is correct, according to *1989*). Sale follows the story by commenting: "In the conclusion of which dispute *Mohammed* declared that *Adam* had the better of *Moses*" (164). Sale's *Koran* was a popular text with radicals and is advertised at the back of William Clark's 1821 piracy of **QM.**

Note 13 (VII. 13)

This note derives primarily from two sources: **Lines 5–90** comprise a slightly revised version of **The Necessity of Atheism** (collated as *1811.NA*), pp. 8–13, consisting of the text of the pamphlet in its entirety, with the exception of the Advertisement. **Lines 121–268** are quoted from Holbach, *Système de la nature* II, 13–15, 22, 249–54, with modifications by PBS (see the Commentary to **lines 121–269,** below).

The Necessity of Atheism was composed by PBS and Hogg between mid-December 1810 and the end of January 1811 and privately distributed between February and March 1811. Whereas it remains unclear how much each of the co-authors contributed individually to the work, it is clear from PBS's appropriation of various portions of the text in his **Declaration of Rights, Letter to Lord Ellenborough, Refutation,** and this note to **QM** that he was, as Murray has argued, willing "to accept, and even require, complete responsibility for the piece" (**Prose/EBM** I, 322). The most significant revision of *1811.NA* that PBS made in **1813** is in his opening disclaimer, which asserts that "There is no God!" refers only to those notions of deity that assume the presence of a "creative" God (as in Christianity). PBS is willing to posit rather the existence of "a pervading Spirit coeternal with the universe." In a letter to Elizabeth Hitchener he analogizes the relationship of this Spirit to the universe as being similar to the relationship between soul and body (**Letters** I, 100). For an excellent discussion of PBS's lifelong atheism, see Timothy Webb, *KSMB* 35 (1984): 1–39.

Locke's *Essay Concerning Human Understanding* and, especially, Hume's *An Enquiry Concerning Human Understanding* are the major influences on **The Necessity of Atheism;** and in the other significant alteration of the text in **1813,** PBS strengthens the Humean base of his argument by including a critique of causality as a means of proving the existence of God, since, as he argues below, "The only idea which we can form of causation is derivable from the constant conjunction of objects . . . ." In August 1810, PBS had asked Graham to purchase for him "the cheapest edition of Locke on the Human Understanding . . . " (*Letters* I, 13).

1839 omits this note entirely; *1821.BEN* substitutes an English translation for the French.

line 20. <u>belief</u> . . . <u>volition</u>: PBS often repeated this claim that belief is involuntary, beginning in a letter of 6 February 1811 to his father (*Letters* I, 61) and reiterated in *The Necessity of Atheism, An Address to the Irish People* and below in **QM Note 15, lines 110–23.** He further elaborates it in **Refutation:** "Belief is not an act of volition, nor can it be regulated by the mind: it is manifestly incapable therefore of either merit or criminality. The system which assumes a false criterion of moral virtue, must be as pernicious as it is absurd. Above all, it cannot be divine, as it is impossible that the Creator of the human mind should be ignorant of its primary powers" (**Prose**/*EBM* I, 106).

That Daniel Isaac Eaton used the same argument about the involuntary nature of belief in his own defense in 1812 suggests that it was a common contemporary strategy of religious freethinkers. Eaton grounds his claim in Locke's *An Essay Concerning Human Understanding:* "Faith and belief is not in our power nor under our controul; for, as Mr. Locke very justly observes, 'our will hath no power to determine the knowledge of the mind one way or the other. No more than in objects of sight it depends on the will to see that black which appears yellow, or in feeling to persuade ourselves that what scalds us feels cold.' Essay on the Human Understanding, vol. ii. ch. 13.—This being really the case respecting belief, wherein doth the merit of faith consist? or how can we justly be blame-worthy or punishable for the want of it?" (*Trial,* 58).

It should be noted that in the passage cited by Eaton (from Book IV, Chapter 13), Locke is considering the effect of Will on perception, not on faith and belief. When Locke does take up the subject of faith in Book IV, Chapter 18, "Of Faith and Reason, and their distinct Provinces," the closest he comes to claiming that belief is involuntary is that reason "can never require or enable me to believe that, which is contrary to it self: It being impossible for Reason, ever to procure any Assent to that, which to it self appears unreasonable" (*An Essay Concerning Human Understanding,* ed. Peter H. Nidditch [Oxford: Clarendon Press, 1975], 693). For PBS's own early evaluation of Locke and his dissatisfaction that Locke "affirms in a Chap of whose reasoning I leave your reason to judge, that there is a God; . . . ," see *Letters* I, 100. PBS would have found a stronger argument for the involuntary nature of belief in Hume, *Enquiry Concerning Human Understanding,* Section V, Part II: "It follows, therefore, that the difference between *fiction* and *belief* lies in some sentiment or feeling, which is annexed to the latter, not to the former, and which depends not on the will, nor can be commanded at pleasure" (*Enquiry,* 48); or in Drummond, "There is no power, by which men can create, or destroy their feelings. . . . Belief cannot be forced, nor can conviction be coerced . . ." (*Academical Questions,* 21).

line 34. <u>to the test</u>: Brooks dropped <u>to</u>, either by accident or as an attempt to improve PBS's style: "the test" was transmitted by *1834* to *1840*.

lines 44–45. <u>But the God of Theologians</u> . . . <u>local visibility</u>: PBS added this Holbachian tenet, which is not in *1811.NA,* from his later reading of *Système.*

lines 51–53. <u>The only idea</u> . . . <u>the other</u>: Absent from the text of *1811.NA,* this formulation about causality is from Hume, who took it one step further in *Enquiry,* Section XI: "It is only when two *species* of objects are found to be constantly conjoined, that we can infer the one from the other; and were an effect presented, which was entirely singular, and could not be comprehended under any known *species,* I do not see, that we could form any conjecture or inference at all concerning its cause." Thus, the existence of God, a cause "singular and unparalleled" cannot be rationally inferred from the evidence of the physical universe (148).

lines 59–70. <u>The other argument,</u> . . . <u>but renders it more incomprehensible</u>: The argument of this entire paragraph is restated in **Refutation:** "A man knows, not only that he now is, but that there was a time when he did not exist; consequently there must have been a cause. But we can only infer, from effects, causes exactly adequate to those effects. There certainly is a generative power which is effected by particular instruments; we cannot prove that it is inherent in these instruments, nor is the contrary hypothesis capable of demonstration. We admit that the generative power is incomprehensible, but to suppose that the same effects are produced by an eternal Omnipotent and Omniscient Being, leaves the cause in the same obscurity, but renders it more incomprehensible" (**Prose**/*EBM* I, 114).

lines 61–64. <u>But our idea of causation</u> . . . <u>adequate to those effects</u>: Cf. the discussion of the argument from design in Hume's *Enquiry,* Section XI: "The knowledge of the cause being derived solely from the effect, they must be exactly adjusted to each other; and the one can never refer to anything farther, or be the foundation of any new inference and conclusion" (137).

line 68. <u>but to suppose that the same effect</u>: *1811.NA* omits <u>same</u>, an apparent oversight uncorrected in proofreading.

lines 72–75. <u>The testimony</u> . . . <u>Deity should have appeared to them</u>: Cf. Hume, "Of Miracles," *Enquiry,* Section X, Part I: "When anyone tells me, that he saw a dead man restored to life, I immediately consider with myself, whether it be more probable, that this person should either deceive or be deceived, or that the fact, which he relates, should really have happened" (116).

lines 77–78. <u>for he commanded</u> . . . <u>eternal punishments for disbelief</u>: There are several similar statements in the New Testament, e.g., "He that believeth and is baptized shall be saved; but he that believeth not shall be damned" (Mark 16:16; see also John 3:18 and 3:36).

lines 84–89. <u>Hence it is evident</u> . . . <u>subject of discussion</u>: Following this sentence in *1811.NA* there is a paragraph break and an additional sentence that reads: "It is almost unnecessary to observe, that the general knowledge of the deficiency of such proof, cannot be prejudicial to society: Truth has always been found to promote the best interests of mankind.—"

lines 89–90. <u>Every reflecting mind</u> . . . <u>existence of a Deity</u>: In *1811.NA* this sentence concludes the pamphlet and is followed by "Q. E. D." ("Quod Erat Demonstrandum"), shorthand indicating that a truth has been proven and a term familiar to all students studying Euclidean geometry. Spinoza appears to be the first well-known writer to have applied "Q. E. D." to demonstrations of ethical truths; Isaac Newton uses it recurrently in the *Philosophiae naturalis principia mathematica* (1687).

lines 92–95. *Hypotheses non fingo,* . . . *non habent*: The quotation of this important axiom, used again in **Refutation** (**Prose**/EBM I, 73), is from the penultimate paragraph of the conclusion of Newton's *Principia,* in which Newton attempts to explain the cause of gravity. PBS actually starts quoting toward the end of a sentence that begins: "Rationem verò harum gravitatis proprietatum ex phænomenis nondùm potui deducere" ("For whatever is not deduced from phenomena is to be called an hypothesis"). *1821.BEN* and *1821.CLA* provide nearly identical English translations in footnotes, the latter of which reads as follows: "I do not invent hypothesis; for whatever is not deduced from phœnomena, is to be called an hypothesis; and hypotheses, either metaphysical or physical, or grounded on occult qualities, should not be allowed any room in philosophy."

The compositor seems to have misread PBS's "æ" for "œ" throughout the quotation and elsewhere in the notes (e.g., "nebulœ" for <u>nebulæ</u> in **line 109** below). Similarly, a compositorial error is probably responsible for the mistaken use in *1813* of the singular "hypothesis" rather than the plural in "et hypothesis." In the text of **Refutation,** the errors with "œ" are corrected; although the erroneous "hypothesis" remains, it is corrected in a list of errata PBS wrote into the margins of **Refutation.** In both **QM** and **Refutation,** PBS uses the conjunction <u>vel</u> as an alternative to "seu," the word used in the two editions of Newton's works that we have checked (1742 and 1782). Either PBS was following his still unknown source (which might not be Newton's text directly but rather a quotation of it by someone else), or he was supplying the text from memory.

In ***Refutation,*** the quotation is preceded by the claim: "The system of the Universe then is upheld solely by physical powers. The necessity of matter is the ruler of the world. It is vain philosophy which supposes more causes than are exactly adequate to explain the phenomena of things" (***Prose***/*EBM* I, 115–16). Cf. Drummond, *Academical Questions,* which makes clear how materialists could deploy Newton's dictum about hypotheses: "The Newtonian, who is an atheist, will observe, that the supposition of a prime intellectual mover is not only unnecessary to the system of Newton, but seems even to contradict it. *Hypothesis non fingo* ought to be the common saying of every Newtonian; and the introduction of a spiritual being as the principle of motion is a mere *hypothesis*" (201).

lines 96–113. <u>We see</u> . . . *lui-même*: The general logic of this passage derives from Holbach, from whom PBS also took the line of French poetry (*Système* II, 247n). Holbach attributes the line only to an unnamed "Poëte moderne," who produced a piece of poetry upon the attributes of God that received the sanction of the French Academy, particularly the line that Holbach quotes, which received the most applause. Although the identity of the French poet remains unknown, Rogers in *1972* mentions that the line is quoted as part of a complete quatrain "in a letter to Rousseau dated August 1763 and attributed to 'un savant professeur'" (I, 400). This line is translated exactly the same way in footnotes to both *1821.CLA* and *1821.BEN*: "To tell what he is, you must be himself."

lines 107–9. <u>Words</u> . . . <u>the occult qualities of the peripatetics</u> . . . *effluvium* <u>of Boyle</u> . . . *crinities* or *nebulæ* <u>of Herschel</u>: PBS is critiquing a class of scientific and quasi-scientific terms that give the appearance of representing positive knowledge while masking underlying uncertainties or ignorance even from those who coined the terms. *Occult qualities,* a key term in the physics developed by the Peripatetics (Aristotle's school of philosophy), is used to describe phenomena such as gravity that are hidden, or "occult" to the senses but "apparent" to reason. Likewise, Robert Boyle (1627–91), in *New Experiments Physico-Mechanical touching the spring of the air and its effects,* describes a stream of particles not directly discernible by the senses that he calls "Magnetical Effluvia" passing through a vacuum ([1660; Oxford: Thomas Robinson, 1662], 61). Boyle, who endowed through his will the Boyle Lectures for proving the truth of Christianity against atheists, theists, and Jews, was probably not a great favorite with PBS, however much he may have valued Boyle's scientific achievements. In *The Botanic Garden,* Erasmus Darwin describes Sir William Herschel's (1738–1822) "very sublime and curious account of the construction of the heavens with his discovery of some thousand nebulæ, or clouds of stars; some of which are much larger collections of stars, than all those put together, which are visible to our naked eyes, added to those which form the galaxy, or milky zone, which surrounds us" (I, 9). Herschel, who continually modified his theory about the composition and function of nebulae throughout his career, characterized nebulae as composed of luminous milky white matter, radiating "*chevelure*" (French for "hair"). Both *crinis* and *crinitus,* also meaning "hair," were Latin terms for the long tail of a comet; <u>*crinities*</u>, would seem to be derived from those words, whatever PBS's ultimate source. He would later rework the metaphor in his description of "swift stars with flashing tresses" in **Ode to Heaven** (line 15) and a "comet's flashing hair" in **Prometheus Unbound** (II.iv.139).

PBS's attack on the Peripatetics may come from Hume, *Dialogues Concerning Natural Religion,* Part IV: "it was usual with the *Peripatetics* . . . when the Cause of any Phænomenon was demanded, to have Recourse to their *Faculties* or *occult Qualities* . . . But it has been discover'd, that this Subterfuge was nothing but the Disguise of Ignorance; and that these Philosophers . . . knew not the Cause of these Phænomena" (ed. John Valdimir Price [Oxford: Clarendon Press, 1976], 186).

lines 114–19. <u>Lord Bacon says</u> . . . <u>present life</u>: In "Of Superstition," Bacon actually writes: "Atheism leaves a man to sense, to philosophy, to natural piety, to laws, to reputation; all which may be guides to an outward moral virtue, though religion were not: but superstition dismounts all these, and erecteth an absolute monarchy in the minds of men. Therefore atheism did never perturb states, for it makes men wary of themselves, as looking no farther, and we see the times inclined to atheism (as the time of Augustus Cæsar) were civil times" (*Essays, Moral, Economical, and Political by Francis Bacon* [London: "Printed for 23 booksellers," 1813], 76–77).

PBS appropriated and translated directly from Holbach (*Système* II, 298) a redaction of Bacon more flattering to atheism, as W. O. Scott suggests (*PMLA* 73 [1958]: 230). In "On Atheism," Bacon's estimate of atheism would have been far less suitable to PBS's purposes: "It is true, that a little philosophy inclineth man's mind to atheism; but depth in philosophy bringeth men's minds about to religion" (71–72). The difference between PBS's text and Bacon's was recognized in both 1821 editions, which substitute a more extensive version of Bacon's actual text for that of *1813.* It is likely that the text in *1821.BEN* is drawn directly from *1821.CLA.* Bacon's "Of Superstition" apparently remained in PBS's repertoire of arguments in favor of atheism at least as late as 1817, when he cited it in conversation with Horace Smith (see Arthur H. Beavan, *James and Horace Smith* [London: Hurst and Blackett, 1899], 172–73). Bacon's phrase "natural piety" appears in line 3 of **Alastor**, quite possibly by way of Wordsworth's earlier use of the phrase in "My Heart Leaps Up" (line 9).

lines 121–268. This passage begins with a long quotation from Part II, Chapter 1 (II, 13–15, 22) of Holbach's *Système,* entitled "Origine de nos ideés sur la Divinité." Spliced onto this is a lengthy selection from Chapter 10 (II, 249–54), entitled "Que les hommes ne peuvent rien conclure des idées qu'on leur donne de la Divinité: de l'inconséquence & de l'inutilité de leur conduite à son égard" ("That mankind can form no conclusion from the ideas which are given them of the Divinity: of the inconsequence and the inutility of their conduct toward him"). In effect, PBS fashioned from parts of Holbach's text and his own small alterations a powerful essay attacking belief in a Christian deity.

David Lee Clark claims that PBS quotes Holbach "verbatim, errors and all" from the 1771 London edition of *Système* (*Shelley's Prose* [1954; Albuquerque: U of New Mexico P, 1966], 102), apparently believing that the citation of the 1781 edition in *1813* is erroneous. However, collation indicates that *1813* is somewhat closer to the text of the 1781 edition than to that of 1771—neither of which is quoted verbatim. Moreover, PBS's earlier quotation from *Système* in **Note 11** is clearly from the 1781 edition (which begins the two-paragraph passage on I, 44, as cited in *1813*) rather than from the 1771 edition (which has only a footnote to another passage on I, 44). There is, therefore, no reason to doubt that PBS took his text from the 1781 edition, just as he claims in the text of *1813.*

A collation of *1813* with the 1781 edition suggests the following conclusions: (1) The compositor did not know French well or at all: he probably made errors such as reading the handwritten *aux* as *ceux* and *qui* as *que;* (2) The text for the printer was almost certainly produced by dictation: there are numerous errors in agreement and spelling, as well as confusion of such words as *la* with *leur* and *qu'embrouilles* with *qu'embrouiller* that are far more likely to be produced by hearing the words wrong than by copying directly from the book. Since these errors were not corrected by PBS, they provide additional evidence about both the state of his French and, perhaps, the speed with which he was readying the note.

Using the 1781 edition of Holbach's *Système* (collated as *1781.HOL*), we emend errors in words, agreement, and accents in *1813,* allowing for PBS's own revisions and for accepted contemporary variations in orthography. Our text retains PBS's punctuation and capitalizations. Though ampersands rather than *and* are used throughout *1781.HOL,* this variant is not included in the collation, which is otherwise complete.

In *1821.BEN,* an English translation is substituted for the French text. A note explains to the reader: "The passages brought together in this extract do not follow each other in the original, but are selected from different parts of the second volume." In *1821.CLA,* an English translation at the foot of the page parallels the French text, which is unemended from *1813.* This English translation compensates in literal accuracy for what it may lack in eloquence, and we provide it in full:

The primary theology of man made him first fear and worship even the elements gross and material objects, he then paid his adorations to the presiding agents of the elements, to inferior genii, to heroes, or to men endowed with great qualities. By continuing to reflect he thought to simplify things, by submitting all nature to a single agent, to a spirit, to an universal soul, which put this nature, and its parts into motion. In ascending from cause, to cause, mankind have ended, by seeing nothing, and it is in the midst of this obscurity, that they have placed their God; it is in this dark abyss, that their restless imagination is always labouring to form chimeras, which will afflict them, until a knowledge of nature shall dissipate the phantoms which they have always so vainly adored.

If we wish to render an account to ourselves, of our ideas respecting the Deity, we shall be obliged to confess that by the word *God*, men have never been able to designate any thing else but the most hidden, the most remote, the most unknown cause of the effects which they perceive; they only make use of this word, when the springs of natural and known causes cease to be visible to them; the instant they lose the thread, or their understanding can no longer follow the chain of these causes, they cut the knot of their difficulty and terminate their researches by calling God the last of these causes, that is to say, that which is beyond all the causes with which they are acquainted. Thus they merely assign a vague denomination to an unknown cause, at which their indolence or the limits of their information compels them to stop.

Whenever we are told, that God is the author of any phenomenon, that signifies that we are ignorant how such a phenomenon can be produced, with the assistance only of the natural powers or causes with which we are acquainted. It is thus that the generality of mankind, whose lot is ignorance, attribute to the Deity, not only the uncommon effects which strike them, but even the most simple events, whose causes are the most easily discoverable, to all who have had the opportunity of reflecting on them. In a word man has always respected the unknown causes of those surprising effects, which his ignorance prevented him from unravelling. It was upon the ruins of nature that men first raised the imaginary colossus of a Deity. If the ignorance of nature gave birth to the gods, a knowledge of nature is calculated to destroy them.

In proportion as man becomes informed, his powers and resources increase with his knowledge, the sciences, the conservative arts, and industry furnish him with assistance, experience inspires him with confidence, or procures him the means of resisting the efforts of many causes, which cease to alarm him, as soon as he becomes acquainted with them. In a word, his terrors are dissipated in the same proportion as his mind is enlightened. A well informed man ceases to be superstitious.

It is never but on trust, that whole nations worship the God of their fathers, and their priests; authority, confidence, submission, and custom, to them supply the place of proofs and conviction; they prostrate themselves and pray, because their fathers have taught them to prostrate themselves and pray, but wherefore did the latter kneel? Because in remote periods, their guides and regulators, taught them it was a duty. "Worship and believe," said they "gods which you cannot comprehend, rely on our profound wisdom, we know more than you concerning the Deity." "But why should I rely on you?" "Because it is the will of God, because he will punish you if you dare to resist." "But is not this God the thing in question?" Thus men have always been satisfied with this vicious circle, the indolence of their minds led them to believe the shorter mode was to rely upon the opinions of others. All religious notions, are founded upon authority alone, all the religions of the world forbid investigation, and will not permit reasoning; it is authority which requires us to believe in God, this God himself is only founded upon the authority of some men, who pretend to know him, and to be sent by him to announce him to the world. A God made by men has doubtless need of men to make him known to men.

Is it then only, for the priests of the inspired, for metaphysicians, that a conviction of the existence of a God is reserved, and which is nevertheless said to be necessary to all mankind. But do we find a harmony of theological opinion among the inspired, or the reflective, in the different parts of the world? Are those even who profess to worship the same God agreed respecting him? Are they satisfied with the proofs of his existence which their colleagues bring forward? Do they unanimously subscribe to the ideas which they adduce respecting his nature, his conduct, and the mode of understanding his pretended oracles? Is there a country, throughout the earth in which the knowledge of God is really perfected. Has it assumed in any quarter the consistency, and uniformity, which we perceive human knowledge to have assumed, in the most trifling arts, in trades the most despised. The words *spirit, immateriality, creation, predestination, grace*, this crowd of subtile distinctions with which theology, in some countries, is universally filled, these ingenious inventions, imagined by the successive reasoners of ages, have, alas! only embroiled the question, and never has the science, the most important to mankind, been able to acquire the least stability. For thousands of years, have these idle dreamers transmitted to each other, the task of meditating on the Deity, of discovering his secret paths, of inventing hypotheses calculated to solve this important enigma. The little success they have met with, has not discouraged theological vanity. God has always been talked of, mankind have cut each others throats for him, and this great being still continues, to be the most unknown, and the most sought after.

Fortunate would it have been for mankind if confining themselves to the visible objects in which they are interested, they had employed in perfecting true science, laws, morals, and education, half the exertions they have made in their researches after a Deity. They would have been still wiser and more fortunate, could they have resolved to leave their blind guides to quarrel among themselves and to sound the depths calculated only to turn their brains without meddling with their senseless disputes. But it is the very essence of ignorance to attach importance to what it does not understand. Human vanity is such that the mind became irritated by difficulty. In proportion as an object fades from our sight do we exert ourselves to seize it, because it then stimulates our pride, it excites our curiosity and becomes interesting. In contending for his God every one in fact is only contending for the interests of his own vanity, which of all the passions, produced by the mal-organization of society, is the most prompt to take alarm, and the most calculated to give birth, to great absurdities.

If laying aside for a moment the gloomy ideas which theology gives us of a capricious God, whose partial and despotic decrees decide the fates of men, we fix our eyes upon the pretended goodness which all men, even whilst trembling before this God, agree in giving to him, if we suppose him to be actuated by the project which is attributed to him, of having only laboured for his own glory, of exacting the adoration of intelligent beings, of seeking only in his works, the welfare of the human race; how can we reconcile his views and dispositions with the truly invincible ignorance in which this God so good and glorious leaves the greater part of mankind respecting himself? If God wishes to be known, beloved, and praised, why does he not reveal himself under some favourable features, to all those intelligent beings by whom he wishes to be loved and worshipped! Why does he not manifest to all the earth in an unequivocal manner, much more calculated to convince us, than by these particular revelations which seem to accuse the Deity of an unjust partiality for some of his creatures. Would not the Omnipotent possess more convincing means of revealing himself to mankind than these ridiculous metamorphoses, these pretended incarnations, which are attested to us by writers who so little agree among themselves in the recitals they give of them? Instead of so many miracles invented to prove the divine mission of so many legislators revered by the different nations of the world, could not the Supreme Being convince in an instant the human mind of the things which he chose to make known to it? Instead of suspending the sun in the vault of the firmament, instead of dispersing the stars and the constellations, which occupy space without order, would it not have been more conformable to the views of a God so jealous of his glory, and so well disposed to man, to write in a mode not liable to be disputed, his name, his attributes, and his unchangeable will, in everlasting characters, equally legible to all the inhabitants of the earth? No one could then have doubted the existence of a God, his manifest will, his visible intentions. Under the eye of this terrible Deity, no one would have had the audacity to violate his ordinances, no mortal would have dared to place himself in the situation of drawing down his wrath; and, lastly, no man would have had the effrontery to impose on his fellow creatures, in the name of the Deity, or to interpret his will according to his own fancy.

In fact, even should the existence of the theological God be admitted, and the reality of the discordant attributes which are given to him, nothing could be inferred from it, to authorise the conduct or the modes of worship, which we are told to observe towards him. Theology is truly the *tub of the Danaides.* By dint of contradictory qualities and rash assertions, it has so tramelled, as it were, its God, that it has made it impossible for him to act. If he is infinitely good, what reason have we to fear him? If he is infinitely wise, why should we be uneasy for our future state? If he knows all, why inform him of our wants, and tease him with our prayers? If he is omnipresent, why raise temples to him? If he is master of all, why sacrifice and make offerings to him? If he is just, how can we believe that he punishes creatures whom he has afflicted with weaknesses? If grace does all in them, for what reason should he reward them? If he is omnipotent how can we offend, how resist him? If he is reasonable, how could he be incensed against his blind creatures, to whom he has only left the liberty of falling into error? If he is immutable, by what right do we pretend to make him change his decrees? If he is incomprehensible, why do we busy ourselves in endeavouring to understand him? IF HE HAS SPOKEN, WHY IS NOT THE UNIVERSE CONVINCED? If the knowledge of a God is the most necessary, why is it not the clearest and most evident?—*System of Nature,* London, 1781

lines 121–27. La première théologie . . . en mouvement: PBS deleted phrases from *1781.HOL* in both of these long sentences, almost certainly to prune them of redundancy.

line 150. démêler: After this final word of the sentence, PBS's text jumps in *1781.HOL* from p. 15 to p. 22 (the end of Chapter 1), omitting the opening phrase of the next sentence, "En un mot," because it was used in the previous sentence of his text.

line 159. superstitieux: After this word, which marks the end of the first chapter of Part II in *1781.HOL,* PBS skips ahead to Chapter 10 (II, 249).

lines 199–201. Leur peu de succès . . . le plus discuté: The omission in *1813* of the phrase "disputé, on s'est" in *1781.HOL* may be due to an eye-skip on the part of PBS or the compositor.

lines 210–12. Plus un objet . . . il nous paroît intéressant: PBS omitted the next two sentences in *1781.HOL,* which can be translated as follows: "On the other hand, the longer and more laborious our researches have been, the more importance we attach to our discoveries, real or pretended; we do not wish to have wasted our time, and we are always ready to defend warmly the soundness of our judgment. Do not let us, then, be surprised at the interest that the ignorant masses have always taken in the debates of their priests, nor at the stubbornness which these have always demonstrated in their disputes." Given that the "debates of their priests" probably refers to the contentions between the orthodox Catholics and the semi-Puritan Jansenists in the French Catholic Church of the seventeenth and eighteenth centuries, PBS would have seen little to his point in retaining these sentences.

line 212. excite: one of the few verbal changes PBS clearly made on purpose; he seems to have preferred the connotation of *excite* to that of *irrite,* the word in *1781.HOL.*

lines 214–15. produites . . . société: PBS inserted this clause into Holbach's text, and thereby significantly altered the meaning of the passage by declaring that the selfish vanity productive of social ills and follies of the worst sort is itself an effect of contemporary social institutions on human minds. Indeed, in attempting to stress the pernicious effects of such social institutions, PBS appears to have coined an ungrammatical phrase: mal organization, in which an adverb modifies a noun so as to make nonsense (i.e., "badly organization"). The phrase he adds was probably intended to be translated as "produced by the evil structure of society."

line 241. si jaloux: si was accidentally omitted in *1840.*

line 246. terrible: PBS's alteration of Holbach's "sensible" (acute) to terrible indicates his own gothicized investment in Holbach's argument.

line 247. <u>osé se mettre</u> . . . <u>homme n'eût eu</u>: omitted from *1840*, due to an eye-skip.

lines 250–55. <u>En effet, quand</u> . . . <u>l'impossibilité d'agir</u>: PBS reordered the first three sentences of this paragraph so that sentences 1, 2, and 3 in Holbach's text appear as sentences 2, 3, and 1 in *1813*.

line 250. <u>admettroit</u>: PBS altered "supposeroit" in *1781.HOL* to a misspelled "admetteroit" in *1813*.

lines 264–65. <u>S'il est immuable</u> . . . <u>changer ses décrets?</u>: This sentence was accidentally omitted in *1834*.

lines 271–82. In this passage from Pliny, *Naturalis historia* Vol. II, Chap. V, pp. 14, 27 (the introduction and conclusion of Chapter V), we correct the erroneous "viginta" for <u>viginti</u> ("twenty"). The text is independently translated and placed in footnotes in both *1821.BEN* and *1821.CLA*, the latter of which reads as follows:

For which reason, I consider that the inquiry after the form and figure of the Deity, must be attributed to human weakness. Whatever God may be (if indeed there be one) and wherever he may exist, he must be all sense, all sight, all hearing, all life, all mind, self-existent. * * * * But it is a great consolation to man with all his infirmities to reflect that God himself cannot do all things: for he cannot inflict on himself death, even if he should wish to die, that best of gifts to man amidst the cares and sufferings of life; neither can he make men eternal, nor raise the dead, nor prevent those who have lived from living, nor those who have borne honours from wearing them; he has no power over the past, except that of oblivion, and (to relax our gravity awhile and indulge in a joke) he cannot prevent twice ten from being twenty, and many other things of a similar nature. From these observations, it is clearly apparent that the powers of nature are what we call God.

Medwin claims that Pliny's *De Deo* "was the first germ of his [PBS's] ideas respecting the Nature of God" (*Life*, ed. Forman, 37).

lines 277–80. <u>vitae</u> . . . <u>(ut</u>: *1813* mistakenly gives "vita" for <u>vitae</u> and omits the opening parenthesis.

lines 284–85. <u>*Sir W. Drummond's Academical Questions, chap.* iii.—</u> : In Book II, Chapter 3 of *Academical Questions,* Drummond stages a hypothetical dialogue between a Newtonian atheist and a Newtonian theist to demonstrate that whereas the materiality of Newton's system contradicts Newton's own professed belief in a deity, it is consistent with atheism. See Commentary to **Note 2, lines 9–11** and the following from Drummond: "We are taught by our rules of philosophising to seek for no more causes, than are sufficient to explain the *phænomena*. We find all necessary causes in the properties of matter; and there is no reason to believe, that what now sustains, has not always preserved, the existence of nature and the world. Such are the arguments, which, I think, an atheist might plausibly maintain, if the physical doctrines of the Newtonians be true" (211).

Drummond's own sympathies are with the religious idealism of his speaker Theophilus who, in a dialogue with the materialist Hylus, protests: "To what direful conclusions do the doctrines of *Hylus* lead? I shudder at the thought. They leave the soul without the hope of futurity, the universe without a plan devised by wisdom, man without a judge, and nature without a God" (278). Theophilus then develops his attack on atheism in a manner clearly supported by Drummond himself.

lines 293–98. *1813* contains several errors in this quotation from the first chapter of Spinoza's *Tractatus theologico-politicus*—none of which (including *artem* for *certum*, *catemus* for *eatenus*, *quatemos* for *quatenus*, and, even, *sive* for *hoc*) appears in PBS's copy of Spinoza, now at Pfz. Most of these errors almost certainly occurred because the compositor misread PBS's handwriting and no one checked the proof carefully. These errors, which have been corrected in our Text, remained uncorrected in **A Refutation of Deism,** in which the quotation is used again.

Both *1821.BEN* and *1821.CLA* contain independent translations in footnotes. The translation in the Clark edition reads as follows: "All things are made by the power of God, yet, doubtless, because the power of nature is the power of God: besides we are unable to understand the power of God, so far as we are ignorant of natural causes; therefore we foolishly recur to the power of God whenever we are unacquainted with the natural cause of any thing, or in other words, with the power of God." In the entry "Religion, or Theology" in the 1771 edition of the *Encyclopædia Britannica*, the subsection "Of Polemic Theology" notes that "the theologian will have to combat principally with" twenty-one categories of opponents, led by "The Atheists, with Spinosa at their head" (III, 542). Spinoza's historicizing, anti-supernaturalist hermeneutic attracted PBS, who ordered the philosopher's works from Hookham on 17 December 1812, and—after clarifying his request (**Letters** I, 342, 347–48)—received the 1670 edition of the *Tractatus* (Hamburg: H. Künraht), which he annotated heavily and which is now located in Pfz (see *SC* VIII, 730–43). One of these annotations appears in the margin of the passage quoted in *1813:* "God & Nature the Same" (14). For PBS's continued interest in, and later translation of, parts of the *Tractatus*, see *SC* VIII, 737–43. As pointed out in *SC*, PBS's spelling of the name, "Spinosa," is the correct spelling in Latin—and, we might add, the one used by the *Encyclopædia Britannica*.

PBS produced three prose versions of the Wandering Jew's story: first, in a footnote to his poem, **The Wandering Jew** III.197 (**CPPBS** I, 66–67); second, in a manuscript given to and later published by Thomas Jefferson Hogg in 1858, now at Pfz (*SC* 123); third, in the note to **QM**. All three of these versions ultimately stem from the German poet Christian Friedrich Daniel Schubart's *Der ewige Jude. Eine lyrische Rhapsodie* (1783). In 1801, an English translation entitled "The Wandering Jew. By Schubart" and signed by "P. W." appeared in *The German Museum* 3 (January, 1801): 424–26. Eight years later, a new version of the translation closely following the text in *The German Museum* (hereafter cited and collated as *GrM*) appeared in *La Belle Assemblée; or, Bell's Court and Fashionable Magazine. Addressed Particularly to the Ladies* 6 (January 1809): 19–20 (hereafter cited and collated as *BA*). The text of *BA* is unsigned and is prefaced by the following comments: *"Our Readers are acquainted with the uses to which Mr. Lewis, in his Novel of the Monk, has converted the ancient legend of the Wandering Jew.— The original story was the invention of the celebrated Schubart, and is as follows."*

Collation indicates that all three of PBS's prose versions probably derive from the text in *BA*, although none is a straight transcription and both PBS and Thomas Medwin have provided sufficient misinformation to obfuscate thoroughly an already murky set of issues (see **CPPBS** I, 200–202). The footnote to **WJ** strays far enough from the actual text of *BA* possibly to have been produced from another source (as Cameron believed [*SC* II, 655–56]). PBS's comments imply that he translated the footnote text himself directly from his German source, endeavoring "to deviate as little as possible from the extreme sublimity of idea which the *style* of the German author . . . so forcibly impresses" (**CPPBS** I, 67). Whereas past editors have dismissed this claim out of hand, believing that PBS did not know German at this time (on the basis of Hogg's biography, *Life* I, 122), Leland R. Phelps has argued that Hogg was wrong, and that by 1809 PBS was already producing rudimentary translations (see *Wege der Worte*, ed. Donald C. Riechel [Böhlau Verlag, 1978], 304–12). Hence, PBS's account might be credible. On the other hand, Medwin indicates that the translation may have been performed by his own German master (*Life*, ed. Forman, 489 [Appendix]). More likely than either of these conflicting explanations is that PBS took (possibly from memory) the "sublime" lineaments of the account in *BA*—the one version we can be reasonably certain he did see—and adapted them freely into the narrative provided in the footnote.

Such a supposition fits well with the fact that PBS's two other prose versions are based closely on the text of *BA*, as our collation demonstrates. From bibliographical evidence, Cameron has established that MS Pfz was almost certainly written at Field Place, the Shelley family home, during the Oxford

holidays between 10 December 1810 and 22 January 1811 (*SC* II, 659). It is
probable that during this vacation PBS's attention was drawn, perhaps by his
sister Elizabeth Shelley, to the translation of "The Wandering Jew" in a fairly
recent issue of *BA,* a magazine precisely and effectively targeted at readers
such as their mother and quite likely received at Field Place (see Gelpi, *Shel-
ley's Goddess* [New York: Oxford UP, 1993], 30). "The Wandering Jew" is pre-
ceded in *BA* by "Laurenstein Castle; or, The Ghost of the Nun" (15–19) and
followed by "Milton's Italian Sonnets," both of which would similarly have
caught the eyes of Elizabeth Shelley and PBS. (For the relation of "Lauren-
stein Castle" to the Ghost of the Bleeding Nun subplot in Lewis's *The Monk*
and to *WJ,* see *CPPBS* I, 203–4.)

Beginning in the fourth paragraph, with the words "did the Elephant
trample . . . ," MS Pfz contains approximately the final third of the *BA* text,
but as Cameron speculates, it may originally have also contained another
sheet (now lost) which included the first two-thirds of the text (*SC* II, 659).
Frequently omitting punctuation and—less frequently—words, MS Pfz gives
every appearance of having been written quickly rather than carefully, pre-
sumably as a copy of the Wandering Jew's story for Hogg, to whom it was
given at some point, perhaps shortly thereafter. Collation shows that *1813*
and MS Pfz agree in verbal variants from the text of *BA* slightly more often
than MS Pfz and *BA* agree in verbal variants from *1813;* rarely do *1813* and
BA agree against MS Pfz. Moreover, *1813* could not have been directly tran-
scribed from MS Pfz (even assuming that the MS once contained the full text
and that PBS retained it as late as 1813) because an entire clause present in
BA but missing in MS Pfz is supplied in *1813* (**line 47**: <u>the tyger's tooth could
not pierce me</u>).

The best explanation for these facts is that both MS Pfz and *1813* are de-
rived from a transcription of *BA* that PBS made at Field Place during Christ-
mas vacation 1810–11, and subsequently retained. The existence of this
transcript would explain how, as late as 1813, PBS still had access to the text
of a translation published in a magazine four years earlier. It would also ex-
plain why MS Pfz and *1813* share, for instance, such features as the same er-
roneous reading "hold" for <u>behold</u> in *BA* (**line 57**). Presumably, the original
transcript was carefully made (perhaps by Elizabeth Shelley), preserving
most features of *BA;* the variants between MS Pfz and *1813,* then, would have
arisen from local modifications (both intentional and unintentional) that
PBS introduced as he made each version.

Thus, although dubious, PBS's story in *1813* about finding the unidenti-
fied <u>fragment</u> of a <u>dirty and torn</u> translation in Lincoln's-Inn Fields did, in
fact, provide the useful function of allowing him both to revise freely and to
provide a fragmented version of *BA,* omitting the final paragraph, which,
much against his wishes, depicted God's reconciliation with Ahasuerus. He
was, of course, aware of this paragraph, which as well as appearing in *GrM*

and *BA,* is written in MS Pfz as follows: "And Ahasuerus dropped down Night covered his bristly eyelids. The Angel bore me back to the cavern Sleep here said the Angel, sleep in peace, the wrath of thy Judge is appeased, when thou shalt awake he will be arrived he whose blod [*sic*] thou sawest flow upon Golgotha whose mercy is extended even to thee" (*SC* II, 650). MS Pfz was first published in Hogg's biography of PBS, which is collated here as *1858.* In *GrM* and *BA* there are new paragraphs at "I cohabited . . ." (**line 48**) and "I now provoked . . ." (**line 50**).

   1839 omits the entire note.

line 42. <u>loins::</u> In *1813* the colon after <u>loins</u> is in italics, probably a printer's error from a mixed typecase.

lines 51–52. <u>Nero</u> . . . <u>Christiern</u> . . . <u>Muley Ismail</u>: Nero, Christiern, and Muley Ismail remained for PBS an unholy trinity, the prototypes of tyrants (see ***A Philosophical View of Reform,*** *SC* VI, 983). Christiern, or King Christian II of Denmark and Norway (1481–1559), was nicknamed "The Cruel": in conquering Sweden, he bloodily suppressed Swedish nationalists in what became known as The Stockholm Blood-Bath. Muley Ismail was the last sharifian emperor of Morocco, ruling 1672–1727. Ismail, who died in 1727, was deservedly known as "The Bloodthirsty": as pointed out by Reiman, he not only violently kept his people in check with an elite corps of black slaves, similar to the Janissaries of the Turkish Empire, but even tortured one of his own sons to death (*SC* VI, 983). His son might have seemed expendable because, according to *The Guinness Book of World Records,* Ismail is supposed to be the most prolific parent in history, fathering more than 1,000 children.

line 57. <u>behold</u>: "hold" in *1813* and MS Pfz is an error for "behold," the reading both in *BA* and in Schubart's German, which reads: "*Sehen* müssen dursch Jahrtausende" (line 98; our italics). The Wandering Jew is thus forced not "to hold" but to <u>behold</u> for <u>milleniums that yawning monster Sameness, and Time, that hungry hyena</u> . . . ." None of the editions collated has emended this error.

line 66. <u>Fields.</u>: The compositor of *1813* did not supply a necessary period after *Fields,* perhaps because it was missing in the press transcript (as it is in MS Pfz).

Note 15 (VII.135–36)

This note was omitted in *1839* and, as indicated in the collation proper, three sentences were deleted from the expurgated Clark piracy, *1821.CLAX.* **Lines 46–120** draw closely on material PBS had earlier included in his defense of Daniel Isaac Eaton, ***Letter to Lord Ellenborough*** (1812; collated as *1812.LdEl*), primarily pages 14–21, with insertions from pages 4, 6, 7, and 8. The principal influences on this note are Holbach (*Système* and, perhaps, *Histoire critique de Jésus-Christ*), Paine (*Age of Reason*), and Hume (*Enquiry,* especially "Of Miracles").

line 1. <u>son,</u>: We emend the capitalized "Son" in *1813* to <u>son</u> so as to make the citation keying the prose note conform with the poetic text proper. MWS made a similar emendation, but probably with PBS's ideological position in mind, since she lowercased the same word in **line 36.**

lines 3–16. <u>A book</u> . . . <u>proxy</u>: Such debunking (and often facetious) summary accounts of the Bible and Christian dogma were widespread in radical writings, used influentially, for instance, by Holbach (*Le christianisme dévoilée*), Volney (*Ruines*), Paine (*The Age of Reason*), and memorably by Diderot: "And even your dogmas, obligatory to faith, your God in three people, your wicked angels who revolt against their Creator and try to dethrone Him, your Eve drawn out of Adam's side, your Virgin who receives the visit of a young man and a bird and who becomes pregnant, not by the young man, but by the bird; this virgin who bears a child and remains a virgin; this God who dies on the cross to appease God, then comes to life again and ascends into heaven . . . all that is mythology . . ." ("Conversation between the Abbé Barthélemy and Diderot," in *Interpreter,* 201).

lines 16–17. <u>this sacrifice</u>: altered to "his sacrifice" in *1821.CLA* and unchanged in *1821.BEN.*

Footnote 1. <u>Jesus</u> . . . <u>throne of Judea</u>: PBS's treatment in the text proper of Jesus as a social reformer but not a deity was common Enlightenment practice and can be found in such writers as Voltaire and Paine, as well as in the trial testimony of Eaton (a friend and follower of Paine), who argued that "the first Christians and fathers of the church only looked upon Jesus Christ as an exceedingly virtuous good man, but nothing supernatural or divine. . . . And it appears that he was esteemed a mere man by his family and neighbours" (*Trial,* 36). The title page of Eaton's *Trial* contains an epigraph taken from Jesus: "Why judge ye not of yourselves that which is right" (a paraphrase of Luke 12:57).

PBS's footnote reveals that he had not yet reconciled his early ambivalence about Jesus. Perhaps, as Cameron has suggested, PBS's recent reading or rereading of Holbach's *Histoire critique de Jésus-Christ* (*Ecce Homo*), in which Jesus's political ambitions were attacked, was responsible for the vacillation (*YS,* 259). The relevant passage, which is not given in *YS,* reads as follows: "If nature had given Jesus a[n] inalienable right to the throne of Judæa, we might judge that such claims were, for him, a motive for not putting himself in the power of a prince who was the usurper of his crown. But Jesus could not dissemble that his birth were not well established; he knew that for a long time the family of David had lost the sovereign power" (*Ecce Homo,* 179). PBS also may have recently come across the unflattering depiction of Jesus as the most politically cunning and Machiavellian of the "three imposters" (i.e., Moses, Jesus, and Mohammed) in the eighteenth-century French clandestine classic *Traité des trois imposteurs* (see "Textual Transmission," above, for the advertisement for this book in *1821.BEN*).

PBS's depiction of Jesus was always tailored for the audience he addressed. Nonetheless, certain general tendencies are apparent. For PBS's earlier vitriolic comments on Christ and Christianity, see, for example, his 24 April 1811 letter to Hogg: "The Galilean is not a favorite of mine. . . . let this horrid Galilean rule {t}he Canaille then" (*Letters* I, 66). Not long thereafter, however, and for the rest of his career, PBS attempted to construct a sympathetic and politically useful Jesus, a picture of whom was hung in PBS's room in Field Place (*Letters* I, 102), and whom PBS eventually appropriated as a potent ego-ideal. His lost **Biblical Extracts** was intended to use Jesus's own sayings against established Christianity. As he explains in a letter of 27 February 1812: "I have often thought that the moral sayings of Jesus Christ might be very useful if selected from the mystery and immorality which surrounds them—it is a little work I have in contemplation" (*Letters* I, 265). And if **QM** shows PBS's attitude toward Jesus as still in transition, by the time of **On Christianity** (1817) the transition was complete, and thereafter PBS was able to present a persuasive depiction of Jesus as a martyr to all of PBS's own revolutionary goals. See Teddi Chichester Bonca's chapter "Shelley, Christ, and Narcissus" for a good discussion of the role that Jesus played in the development of PBS's sense of selfhood (*Shelley's Mirrors of Love: Narcissism, Sacrifice, and Sorority* [Albany: SUNY Press, 1999], 11–44).

lines 47–48. Testimonies of miracles . . . something divine: Cf. Holbach, *Ecce Homo:* "Our clever operator [Jesus] also took care to choose his ground for performing miracles; he constantly refused to operate before those whom he supposed inclined to criticize his wonders. He may sometimes have performed them in the synagogues, and in presence of the doctors, but it was in the certainty that the less exacting populace, who believed in his miracles, would take his part, and defend him against the evil designs of the more acute spectators" (247).

line 49. reveries of Plato: phrase taken from Holbach, who claimed, "our European religions, have visibly been infected with the reveries of the Platonists." For Holbach, "all the doctrines and metaphysical subtilties of the *Christian Theology*" originated in Plato's teaching (*System*, 219, 220n).

lines 66–69. Even under a government . . . a man is pilloried and imprisoned . . . outraged humanity: At this point, *1821.BEN* has a footnote correctly explaining that the text is "Alluding to the case of Daniel Isaac Eaton." A bookseller and radical, Eaton was sentenced by Lord Ellenborough on 15

May 1812 to eighteen month's imprisonment in Newgate (with two hours in
the stocks each month) for publishing the so-called third part of Paine's *Age
of Reason* (actually a pamphlet Paine published in New York in 1807, entitled
"An Examination of the Passages in the New Testament . . . called Prophecies
concerning Jesus Christ," which was a conflation of parts of Paine's unpub-
lished manuscript for Part III and his answer to the Bishop of Llandaff). By
the time of his trial in 1812, Eaton had "already undergone six prosecutions"
and been expatriated from England for more than three years, according to
his address to the jury (*Trial,* 38). In a letter to William Godwin, PBS wrote:
"What do you think of *Eaton's* trial & sentence. I mean not to insinuate that
this poor bookseller has any characteristics in common with Socrates or Jesus
Christ, still the spirit which pillories & imprisons him, is the same which
brought them to an untimely end. Still, even in this enlightened age, the
moralist & reformer may expect coercion analogous to that used with the
humble yet zealous imitator of their endeavours" (**Letters** I, 307–8). Late in
1812, PBS had Eaton in mind as a potential publisher for his lost **Biblical Ex-
tracts** (see **Letters** I, 340).

This entire sentence is spliced into *1813* from earlier in *1812.LdEl* (7), in
slightly altered form.

lines 69–71. <u>But it . . . admission</u>: also spliced in with revisions from earlier
in *1812.LdEl* (4).

lines 71–77. <u>and a dispassionate . . . command</u>: taken from *1812.LdEl* (8).

lines 77–87. There is no break between **lines 77** and **78** in *1812.LdEl;* a new
paragraph begins in *1813* after insertions from earlier in *1812.LdEl.*

lines 83–84. <u>Milton's poem alone will give permanency . . . its absurdities</u>:
This praise of *Paradise Lost* (similar to PBS's later statements in **On the Devil**
and **Defence**) is not in *1812.LdEl.* Cf. Godwin's *Enquirer:* "Milton has written a
sublime poem upon a ridiculous story of eating an apple, and of the eternal
vengeance decreed by the Almighty against the whole human race, because
their progenitor was guilty of this black and detestable offence" (135).

lines 105–9. <u>Either the power or the goodness of God . . . irreconcileable</u>
<u>hatred</u>: Cf. *1812.LdEl:* "If, lastly, its truth *cannot* be demonstrated, wherefore
impotently attempt to snatch from God the government of his creation, and
impiously assert that the Spirit of Benevolence has left that knowledge most
essential to the well being of man, the only one which, since its promulga-
tion, has been the subject of unceasing cavil, the cause of irreconcileable ha-
tred?—" (20). Some of the phrasing from this sentence is picked up also in
lines 142–45.

line 109. <u>*If God . . . convinced?*</u>: PBS clearly believed in the rhetorical power
of this question, translated into English from Holbach's *Système.* The same

question appears in French, all in capital letters, as the penultimate sentence of the long quotation from Holbach in **Note 13** ("There is no God") above. In **_Refutation,_** PBS reused the slogan yet again, along with an English translation of the sentence that follows it in **Note 13:** "If the Almighty has spoken, would not the Universe have been convinced? If he had judged the knowledge of his will to have been more important than any other science to mankind, would he not have rendered it more evident and more clear?" (**_Prose/EBM_** I, 109).

lines 110–23. <u>There is this</u> . . .<u>their being</u>: For PBS's views on the involuntary nature of belief, see **Note 13, lines 20–23.**

lines 110–12. <u>There is this passage</u> . . . <u>everlasting destruction</u>: II Thessalonians 1:7–9: ". . . the Lord Jesus shall be revealed . . . in flaming fire taking vengeance on them that know not God, and that obey not the gospel of our Lord Jesus Christ: who shall be punished with everlasting destruction . . . ."

lines 115–21. <u>But belief</u> . . . <u>demerit</u>: These sentences, with small changes, were spliced in from an earlier section of _1812.LdEl_ (6).

line 136. <u>prophesies</u>: Though the _OED_ records the latest use of this alternative spelling for the noun _prophecies_ as being in 1709, after which time it appears confined to the verb (a distinction maintained, e.g., in Johnson's _Dictionary_), the dual use of this form for substantive as well as verb appears in an edition of Bailey's _Dictionary_ of 1733. We retain what may be an intentionally archaic spelling, also used below to speak of "forged prophesies of things long past" (**line 242**); elsewhere in the notes, the conventional spelling for the noun is used.

Footnote 2. <u>Hume's Essay</u>: a reference to "Of Miracles," Section X, Part I of David Hume's _An Enquiry Concerning Human Understanding_ (1748); the pagination of PBS's citation corresponds to an edition of Hume's essays published in 1804: _Essays and Treatises on Several Subjects. In Two Volumes._ Edinburgh: Bell & Bradfute; and London: Cadell & Davies. PBS's general treatment of miracles follows the logic of Hume's essay, especially in its critique of testimony as evidence for miracles. In "Of Miracles," Hume concludes: "the _Christian Religion_ not only was at first attended with miracles, but even at this day cannot be believed by any reasonable person without one" (131). However, because a "miracle is a violation of the laws of nature. . . . no testimony is sufficient to establish a miracle, unless the testimony be of such a kind, that its falsehood would be more miraculous, than the fact, which it endeavours to establish . . ." and "it is nothing strange, . . . that men should lie in all ages" (_Essays and Treatises_ I, 114, 115–16, 120).

Although PBS followed Hume's general critique, his language, as David Lee Clark has pointed out, directly echoes Paine, who wrote in the _Age of Rea-_

son, Part I: ". . . is it more probable that nature should go out of her course or that a man should tell a lie? We have never seen, in our time, nature go out of her course; but we have good reason to believe that millions of lies have been told in the same time; it is, therefore, at least millions to one that the reporter of a miracle tells a lie" (*Works* VIII, 95).

lines 162–63. <u>appearance of a ghost</u>: Paine made a similar point about ghosts and credulity in *Age of Reason*, Part I: "There is now an exhibition in Paris of ghosts or spectres, which, though it is not imposed upon the spectators as a fact, has an astonishing appearance" (*Works* VIII, 93).

lines 165–67. <u>our . . . because</u>: *1834* makes two unnecessary emendations in this sentence ("your . . . as") that remain in the text of *1840*. The entire sentence was restated in **Refutation:** "The humane society restores drowned persons; every empiric can cure every disease; drowning pigs is no very difficult matter, and driving out devils was far from being either an original or an unusual occupation in Judea. Do not recite these stale absurdities as proofs of the Divine origin of Christianity" (**Prose/EBM** I, 109). Cf. Paine, *Age of Reason*, Part 1: "The restoring of persons to life who are to appearance dead, as is practised upon drowned persons, would also be a miracle if it were not known that animation is capable of being suspended without being extinct" (*Works* VIII, 92).

In 1812, PBS ordered Robert Thornton's compilation *The Philosophy of Medicine*, in which there is a long section titled "Of the Institution of the Humane Society for the Recovery of Persons Apparently Dead," which contains a detailed account of the methods of resuscitation advocated by the Humane Society and others.

line 171. <u>cannon of the Spaniards</u>: Cf. Holbach: "The Americans took the Spaniards for Gods, because they made use of gunpowder, rode on horseback, and had vessels which sailed quite alone" (*System*, 233n).

lines 174–75. <u>An author . . . second-hand"</u>: PBS may have been paraphrasing from memory Thomas Paine (literally, the author of *Common Sense*), who wrote in *Age of Reason*, Part I: "But admitting . . . that something has been revealed to a certain person, and not revealed to any other person, it is revelation to that person only. When he tells it to a second person, a second to a third, . . . it ceases to be a revelation to all those persons. . . . *It is a contradiction in terms and ideas, to call anything a revelation that comes to us at second-hand, either verbally or in writing*" (our italics; *Works* VIII, 7). Hume made a similar point in "Of Miracles," Part I.

lines 175–77. <u>he might . . . imagine others</u>: Cf. Paine's remarks upon miracles and natural causes in *Age of Reason*, Part I: "but unless we know the whole extent of those [Nature's] laws, and of what are commonly called the powers of nature, we are not able to judge whether anything that may appear to us wonderful or miraculous be within, or be beyond, or be contrary to, her natural power of acting" (*Works* VIII, 91–92).

lines 178–202. <u>There remains to be considered . . . far from being clear and circumstantial</u>: Arguments throughout the eighteenth century concerning the truth of revealed religion often hinged on whether biblical prophecy had been historically fulfilled, with Christian apologists frequently using the historical truth of prophecy as a foundation for confirming the existence of miracles (see James E. Force, in *Philosophy, Religion and Science in the Seventeenth and Eighteenth Centuries,* ed. J. W. Yolton [Rochester, N.Y.: U of Rochester P, 1990], 127–39). Consequently, in "Of Miracles," Hume's attack on miracles ends by turning to prophecy (see Commentary for **Note 15, line 203,** below). In *Age of Reason,* Part I, Paine similarly moved from critiquing miracles to critiquing prophecy (*Works* VIII, 98–100). PBS's own more extensive attack subsumes within it Paine's general argument that the obscurity of biblical prophecies moots their truth claims. For Paine, Christianity was built upon the triad of mystery, miracles, and prophecy: "As mystery and miracle took charge of the past and the present, prophecy took charge of the future and rounded the tenses of faith" (*Works* VIII, 97); PBS, however, did not specifically rehearse Paine's argument against mystery.

lines 181–83. <u>The greatest stress . . . coming of the Messiah</u>: It was standard fare for Christian writers to quote the prophecies in Isaiah (3:4–5) and Deuteronomy concerning the dispersion of the Jews. See, for instance, Samuel Clarke's *A Discourse concerning the Being and Attributes of God, The Obligations of Natural Religion, and the Truth and Certainty of the Christian Revelation* (1705; 8th ed. London, 1732), which not only cites Hosea but stresses Deuteronomy as providing a type of prophecy whose truth is "obvious to the consideration of the *Whole World*":

It was foretold by *Moses,* that when the Jews forsook the True God, they should be (1) *removed into all the Kingdoms of the Earth;* should be (2) *scattered among the Heathen,* (3) *among the Nations,* (4) *among all people from the one end of the Earth even unto the other.* . . . Had any thing like This, in *Moses*'s time, *ever happened* to Any Nation? Or was there in Nature any Probability, that any such thing *should ever happen* to any People? that, when they were conquered by their Enemies, and led into captivity, they should neither continue in the place of their captivity, nor be swallowed up and lost among their Conquerours, but be scattered among all the Nations of the World, and hated by all Nations for many Ages, and yet *continue* a People? Or could Any description of the Jews, written at this day, possibly be a more exact and lively Picture of the State they have *Now* been in for many Ages; than this Prophetick description given by *Moses,* more than 3000 Years ago? (433)

Clarke, whose metaphysics accommodated Newtonian theory, was an extremely controversial figure, attacked by more-orthodox theologians as well as by atheists, such as Holbach, who devoted an entire chapter of *System* to an "Examination of the Proofs of the Existence of the Divinity, as given by Clarke" (205–25).

line 193. <u>curses</u>: An uncaught compositor's error in reading PBS's handwriting almost certainly produced the reading "causes" in *1813*.

line 194. <u>wilt</u>: An error by either PBS or the compositor (perhaps again in deciphering PBS's handwriting) produced the reading "will" in *1813*. The passage is quoted, with small changes in wording, from Deuteronomy 28:15: "But it shall come to pass, if thou wilt not hearken unto the voice of the LORD thy God, to observe to do all his commandments and his statutes which I command thee this day; that all these curses shall come upon thee, and overtake thee."

lines 196–98. <u>The third, fourth and fifth chapters of Hosea . . . hundred things</u>: These three chapters analogize Israel to a harlot for its lack of faithfulness to God and, in highly metaphoric and sexually charged language, threaten retribution. Hosea begins the third chapter by describing his divinely ordered purchase of "a woman beloved of her friend, yet an adulteress . . ." (3:1), an example of the <u>immodest confession</u> of which PBS complains.

lines 200–201. <u>Moses, Isaiah and Hosea</u>: In Part II of the *Age of Reason*, Paine argues at great length that Moses was not, as was widely believed, the author of the first five books of the Bible and that they were actually written several hundred years after Moses died (*Works* VIII, 118–39). Paine also contends that a portion of the Book of Isaiah "could only have been written by some person who lived at least a hundred and fifty years after Isaiah was dead" (*Works* VIII, 181). Whereas Paine does not comment on Hosea directly, he does state about the books of the "lesser prophets": ". . . as I have already shown that the greater are impostors, it would be cowardice to disturb the repose of the little ones. Let them sleep, then, in the arms of their nurses, the priests, and both be forgotten together" (*Works* VIII, 215). In a letter written 2 January 1811, PBS commented about Moses's supposed authorship: ". . . besides Moses writes the history of his own death whic{h} is almost as extraordinary a thing to do as to describe the creation of the World.—" (***Letters*** I, 216).

line 203. <u>But prophecy . . . miracle</u>: PBS is using Hume's logic from the ending of "Of Miracles": "What we have said of miracles may be applied, without any variation, to prophecies; and indeed, all prophecies are real miracles, and as such only, can be admitted as proofs of any revelation. If it did not exceed the capacity of human nature to foretell future events, it would be absurd to employ any prophecy as an argument for a divine mission or authority from heaven" (*Enquiry*, 130–31).

lines 218–21. <u>Lord Chesterfield . . . radical and sanguinary."</u>: In a letter of 25 December 1753, Lord Chesterfield advises his son to pay close attention to "the affairs of France; they grow serious, and, in my opinion, will grow more and more so every day." He then proceeds to analyze at length France's internal rifts and political instabilities, ending by claiming: "all the symptoms which I have ever met with in history, previous to great changes and revolutions in Government, now exist, and daily increase in France" (*The Letters of Philip Dormer Stanhope, 4th Earl of Chesterfield,* ed. Bonamy Dobrée [London: Eyre & Spottiswoode, 1932], V, 2065, 2066). Chesterfield did not here comment that the revolution would be sanguinary; PBS was either deliberately embellishing or misremembering the text.

lines 229–39. <u>The last proof of the Christian religion . . . founded on their experience</u>: For the ordinary influence of the Holy Spirit through the reading of the Bible, see, for instance, the argument made by the anonymous author of *The Inward Testimony of the Spirit of Christ* (London, 1701): "He who is acquainted with the Sacred Scriptures, and with the inward Operation of the divine Spirit, producing a suitable disposition to Believe and Obey what is reveal'd therein, he is the real Christian, and the true Witness for Religion. . . . Don't we daily see that those, who in their religious Education have been train'd up in the notional knowledge of outward Revelation, have afterward departed from the Faith for want of the Divine Spirit's inward concurring Testimony, disposing their Frames to obey Duties, as well as to believe what notionally they knew?" (vii, xii).

line 234. <u>those whose mind is fitted</u>: a contemporary usage, not uncommon in PBS's works, which treats those who share a common attribute as a single subject. Brooks converts <u>mind is</u> to "minds are"—an emendation followed by Ascham and MWS.

lines 240–50. <u>Admitting . . . superfluous</u>: As PBS claims in his footnote, the argument in this sentence is drawn from the chapter "Enthusiasm" in Locke, *An Essay Concerning Human Understanding:*

. . . he that takes away *Reason,* to make way for *Revelation,* puts out the Light of both. . . . And if they believe it to be true, because it is a *Revelation,* and have no other reason for its being a *Revelation,* but because they are fully perswaded without any other reason that it is true, they believe it to be a Revelation only because they strongly believe it to be a Revelation, which is a very unsafe ground to proceed on, either in our Tenets, or Actions: And what readier way can there be to run our selves into the most extravagant Errors and Miscarriages than thus to set up phancy for our supreme and sole Guide, and to believe any Proposition to be true, any Action to be right, only because we believe it to be so? The strength of our Perswasions are no Evidence at all of their own rectitude: . . ." (Bk. IV, Chap. XIX; 698, 702–3)

lines 251–52. <u>Hottentot</u> . . . <u>an insect</u> . . . <u>Negro</u> . . . <u>feathers</u>: For the Hottentot's worship of an insect, cf. *Rees's Cyclopædia:* "Some have said that they worship a genus of insects called 'Mantis'. . . ." In PBS's copy of *The Poems of Ossian* (at Pfz, and inscribed "Percy B. Shelley, 1810"), he penciled in a note contradicting the assertion in the introduction that "amongst the most barbarous nations, the very populace themselves had some faint notion, at least, of divinity" (I, 10). PBS wrote: "Neither the Hottentots, the Society Islanders, nor the inhabitants of New Holland have any idea of any supernatural being." Linda E. Merians points out that the "question of whether or not the 'Hottentots' had a religion proved to be a significant issue in the eighteenth century," with most English accounts insisting that they did not, though this position was often used to buttress arguments that they were thus beyond being "civilized" by missionaries (*Envisioning the Worst: Representations of "Hottentots" in Early Modern England* [Newark: U of Delaware P, 2001], 128). Nonetheless, missionaries did attempt to recuperate the Hottentots, as is illustrated in an 1818 London Missionary Society pamphlet, *Mantis, the Soothsayer; Or, The Hottentots' God. A Conversation between a Missionary and a Hottentot; With an Account of the Insect,* in which a grateful Hottentot, converted to Christianity, imagines "Almighty God" as saying to the English: "The poor Hottentots in Africa know nothing of me, the true God; they worship a poor insect, that even they themselves can tread to death with their naked feet" (cited in Merians, *Envisioning the Worst,* 223–24).

For the <u>Negro</u> worshipping a <u>bunch of feathers</u>, PBS probably had in mind the practice of Obeah or Obi, described by *Rees's* as "a superstitious practice, or a kind of sorcery or witchcraft . . . the professors of Obi are, and always were, natives of Africa, and none other; and they have brought the science with them from thence to Jamaica, where it is so universally practised, that there are few of the large estates possessing native Africans, which have not one or more of them." The main instrument of this practice is the Obi itself, composed, as *Rees's* describes, "of a farrago of materials," a chief component of which is feathers. PBS explicitly refers to Obi in **Peter Bell the Third,** where Peter (Wordsworth) is described, both in the Preface and in line 552, as having converted to "*White Obi*" (Christianity). For more on the practice of Obi, as well as popular entertainment concerning it during the Romantic period, see *Obi,* ed. Charles Rzepka (August 2002) in the Praxis Series of the *Romantic Circles* Website.

lines 253–54. <u>degree of conviction</u> . . . <u>arise from conviction</u>: *1870* tried to avoid the repetition of <u>conviction</u> by emending to "arise from reasoning." But, as *1989* points out, *conviction* may have two different meanings here: "settled persuasion" and "formal proof," respectively.

lines 263–69. <u>Mox numine</u> . . . *Carmen Paschale*: Claudian, a court poet who lived at the end of the fourth and beginning of the fifth century, was so well known in his own day as an obstinate pagan (with only two references to Christianity in his entire canon) that some scholars have doubted his authorship of "Carmen Paschale" ("Easter Hymn"), better known as "De Salvatore" ("Of the Saviour"). This poem is a twenty-one line Easter hymn that asks Christ to bless the Christian emperor Honorius. O. A. W. Dilke has described the passage quoted by PBS as "a pagan's attempt to be clever and analyse the background of what to him was a fanatical belief" (*Claudian: Poet of Declining Empire and Morals* [Leeds: Leeds UP, 1969], 13). It is quite likely that PBS, who appears to have been ignorant about Claudian's canon, lifted this quotation from another source that obscured his own affinities with the pagan poet.

Claudian's poem begins with six and a half lines that precede PBS's quotation and concludes with eight lines that follow it. Within the quotation itself, *1813* omits two half-lines between the words "poli" and "latuitque" in the penultimate line of its text: "mundique repertor | Pars fuit humani generis" ("the creator of the world | became a part of humankind"). Whether any or all of these omissions were already a part of PBS's source is unclear. Nor is it clear whether the spelling in the fourth line of <u>peritura</u> for *paritura* was a feature of this source or a misreading of PBS's handwriting.

As translated into prose in *1821.CLA,* these lines read: "Upon seeing the Divinity, the Virgin's womb soon swelled, and the unmarried mother was amazed to find herself filled with a mysterious progeny, and that she was to bring forth to the world her own Creator. A mortal frame veiled the Framer of the Heavens, and he who embraces the wide surrounding circle of the world, lay himself concealed in the recesses of the womb." The two errors in *1813* ascribing the quotation to "*Claudiam, Carmen Paschali*" probably resulted from the compositor's misreading of PBS's "Claudian [or, possibly, 'Claudiani'], Carmen Paschale."

PBS's scorn for the notion of the virgin birth resembles Holbach's in a note to *Ecce Homo:* "Nothing is more indecent and ridiculous than the theological questions to which the birth of Jesus Christ has given rise. . . . We may see, therefore, how in the prolific minds of theologians, one absurdity may lead to others" (296–98).

Note 16 (VIII.203–7)

The concept of the subjective nature of time goes back at least as far as Augustine's seminal account in *Confessions* (Book XI, Sections 10–28), which denies the objective nature of time and locates time in terms of human memories (the past) and human expectations (the future). But PBS's most immediate influence was Godwin, whose *Pol. Justice* is cited at the end of PBS's note. The relevant passage reads as follows: "Consciousness . . . appears to be one of the departments of memory. . . . It seems to be consciousness, rather than the succession of ideas, that measures time to the mind. . . . Of thought, may be said, in a practical sense, what has been affirmed of matter, that it is infinitely divisible. Yet time seems, to our apprehension, to follow, now with a precipitated, and now with a tardy course. The indolent man reclines for hours in the shade; and, though his mind be perpetually at work, the silent progress of time is unobserved. But, when acute pain, or uneasy expectation, obliges consciousness to recur with unusual force, the time appears insupportably long" (ed. Priestley IV.ix; I, 411–12).

The two most important influences on Godwin's discussion of the relativity of time (and hence ultimately on PBS's note) were William Watson, Jr., *A Treatise on Time* (London: Joseph Johnson, 1785)—which Godwin cited— and Condillac, *Traité des sensations* (1754), which was cited in turn by Watson. Like Condillac, Watson started from Lockean premises to build an argument that "Time, as applied to any particular subject, is itself nothing more than the train of instants observed to co-exist with that subject." Hence, "if a person, whose life we may suppose to endure many years, as estimated by others, should be so constituted as to apprehend but one invariable perception only . . . his existence, though it should appear to endure half a century as estimated by others, must appear to himself to pass away like a flash of lightning, and be conceived as an instant only" (43–44). Conversely, a mind intensely thinking and feeling would find, in Condillac's words, "its days of surprising shortness. . . . [but its] year would seem to be long, because it would be retraced as the succession of a multitude of days distinguished by varied events" (*Condillac's Treatise on the Sensations,* trans. Geraldine Carr [Los Angeles: University of Southern California School of Philosophy, 1930], 184). Watson rehearsed Condillac's point (112). For Condillac's main arguments about the subjective duration of time, see *Traité des sensations* I.iv.11–18 and III.vii).

In an appendix to the third edition of *Pol. Justice* entitled "Of Health, and the Prolongation of Human Life," Godwin speculates upon the power of mind to extend the term of human life, both in terms of actual life span and in terms of the mind's subjective experience of time, beyond "any limits which we are able to assign," although "It would be idle to talk of the absolute immortality of man. Eternity and immortality are phrases to which it is impossible for us to annex any distinct ideas, and the more we attempt to explain them, the more we shall find ourselves involved in contradiction" (ed. Priestley VIII, ix; II, 527). A footnote to this appendix cites Condorcet's *Outlines of a History of the Progress of the Human Mind* (*Esquisse d'un tableau historique des progrès de l'esprit humain*) as the most recent work to conjecture on "the possibility of extending the terms of human life" (VIII, ix; II, 520n).

Whether or not PBS first learned of Condorcet's work through Godwin's citation, as Cameron suggests (*YS,* 321n.98), he apparently was impressed by the following passage from *Outlines,* which he read aloud to Thomas Medwin: "Is it absurd to suppose . . . that a period must one day arrive, when death will be nothing more than the effect either of extraordinary accident, or of the slow and gradual decay of the vital powers; and that the duration of the middle space, of the interval between the birth of man and his decay, will have no assignable limit?" (*Life,* ed. Forman, 50). This passage and the surrounding paragraphs, taken from the rhapsodic closing section of *Outlines,* "The Tenth Stage" or "Epoque X," were no doubt what PBS had in mind when he mistakenly cited from memory *Epoque* ix at the end of his prose note (see **Note 16, lines 41–43**). Unlike PBS, Condorcet is not concerned with the subjective experience of time; rather, he stresses how the improvement of medical practice and physical environments will increase human well-being and extend the actual human life span indefinitely, a subject PBS explores, with his own utopian slant, in **IX.57–75.**

lines 1–3. <u>Him</u> . . . <u>mind,</u>: In its use of parenthesis and the word "Dawns" (rather than <u>Draws</u>), the text keying the prose note in *1813* differs from the text of the poem proper, which it is meant to reflect. We have consequently emended the text within the prose to match our text of the poem. For the rationale governing our textual emendations, see the Commentary for **VIII.203–7.**

lines 29–40. <u>Dark flood of time</u> . . . <u>feeling unredeemed</u>: This section from *To Harriet ("It is not blasphemy to hope")* (*Esd* #24), lines 58–69, comprises the second of two such borrowings from *Esd* within the *QM* notes. For Commentary, see p. 390.

line 38. <u>veteran's</u>: As recognized in *1821.BEN* and *1989,* the possessive plural reading in *1813* is almost certainly a mistake, perhaps instituted by the compositor, who may have found the word unpunctuated (as it appears in **EN**) or the position of the apostrophe hard to determine (as it often is in PBS's manuscripts).

Note 17 (VIII.211–12)

PBS began practicing vegetarianism regularly at the beginning of March 1812 (*Letters* I, 274–75), and he followed the regimen in principle, if not always in practice, for the rest of his life. This note borrows heavily in conception and phrasing from two sources: John Frank Newton's *The Return to Nature, or, A Defence of the Vegetable Regimen; with Some Account of an Experiment Made During the Last Three or Four Years in the Author's Family* (London: T. Cadell and W. Davies, 1811) and Joseph Ritson's *An Essay on Abstinence from Animal Food, as a Moral Duty* (London: Richard Phillips, 1802). Whereas both Newton and Ritson were interested in the medical, moral, and political implications of vegetarianism, Newton tended to emphasize the medical and

Ritson the moral. For Newton, vegetarianism, along with such practices as temperance and nudism, represented a return to a healthy, "natural" state. For Ritson, the killing of animals and the eating of meat represented a brutal and brutalizing process that affected all species, but especially human beings, and led to such practices as human sacrifice and war. Both Newton and Ritson were deeply influenced by the vegetarian writings of Plutarch (*On the Eating of Flesh*) and Monboddo (*Antient Metaphysics; or, The Science of Universals* [1789] and *On the Origin and Progress of Language* [1773–76]). PBS attempted to fashion from these various sources a vegetarianism that is uniquely his own: a utopian discourse that renders vegetarianism as a vehicle of medical, moral, political, and economic progress—a crucial means of social change for British society as a whole (for a study of which, see Timothy Morton, *Shelley and the Revolution in Taste* [Cambridge: Cambridge UP, 1994]; hereafter *Taste*). PBS's three other extended attempts to make a case for vegetarianism are in **Natural Diet, On the Vegetable System of Diet** (unpublished in his lifetime), and a section in **Refutation.**

Newton was a friend of Godwin, who introduced him to PBS on 5 November 1812, several months after PBS had begun his vegetarian regimen, though he might already have read *Return* by then. Until his elopement with MWS, PBS frequented the radical set of vegetarians that formed in London and at Bracknell around the Newtons and Mrs. Newton's sister, Harriet de Boinville. Soon after meeting Newton, and probably at his suggestion, PBS ordered the works of Monboddo, Trotter, and Ritson that were to make important contributions to the **QM** note. Newton almost certainly also introduced PBS to the work of the clinical physician William Lambe (esp. *Reports of the Effects of a Peculiar Regimen on Scirrhous Tumors and Cancerous Ulcers* [1809]), friend and doctor to Newton, whose findings about the effects of diet and water drinking on health cured Newton's asthmatic condition and influenced his theories (see the letter from Newton to Lambe published as "Case XI" in Lambe's *Reports,* 180–84) and to whom Newton dedicated *Return*. PBS apparently knew Lambe personally, judging from a letter Hogg wrote to PBS in Italy several years later, in which is conveyed news of the Newton-Boinville circle: "Newton I have not seen for a long time, he is still at Weymouth enjoying bloodless feasts. . . . Dr. Lambe has turned his back upon this sanguinary city, and now lives at Kentish Town, on herbs and other country messes, which some Phillis, less neat-handed than Newton's, rudely dresses" (**Letters** II, 187–88).

Although PBS openly acknowledged the influence of Newton's *Return* on his note, he seems to have obscured intentionally any direct debt to Joseph Ritson's *Abstinence*. Ritson was a well-known radical in the 1790s and an accomplished scholar and antiquarian, who liked to be called "Citizen Ritson." Beyond any blatantly self-aggrandizing motives PBS may have had for silently appropriating Ritson's work, it remains unclear precisely why he disguised all his direct borrowings from Ritson, never citing *Abstinence* and even taking citations to other works directly from Ritson's notes, as if he had consulted them himself. E. B. Murray suggests that PBS may have been reluctant to mention Ritson because the dedicated vegetarian had died in 1803 from a nervous condition that degenerated into what was termed "brain paralysis," thus becoming something less than an advertisement for the salubrity of a vegetarian diet, the healthful effects of which PBS illustrates through the splendid condition of the Newton family (see **Prose/EBM** I, 396). One other possibility is that, according to Hogg, Ritson was so extreme in his vegetarian theories that he was "[s]tigmatized, perhaps unjustly, as a wretched maniac" (*Life,* ed. Wolfe, II, 87). PBS may thus have wanted to steer clear of an open dependence on Ritson's work. Whatever his original motives, by the time PBS composed ***On the Vegetable System of Diet*** (?1814–15, though most probably 1815, according to both Murray and Morton [see Morton's *Taste,* 141], he was ready to credit Ritson's *Abstinence* in a footnote (**Prose/EBM** I, 152).

The text of the **QM** note closely parallels the text of **Natural Diet,** which PBS composed sometime between October 1812 and November 1813, perhaps as early as October or November 1812, to judge from his declaration, in the concluding sentence of the Appendix, that "the author and his wife have lived on vegetables for eight months." Published by J. Callow, the printed pamphlet bears the date "1813" and contains the subtitle: "Being One in a Series of Notes to Queen Mab. A Philosophical Poem." For this reason, it had been assumed that the pamphlet was published *after* **QM** until D. L. Clark's "The Date and Sources of Shelley's *A Vindication of Natural Diet,*" *Studies in Philology* 36 (1939): 70–76. Clark argues that the pamphlet preceded the note on the basis of (1) the pamphlet's reference to how long PBS had been a vegetarian, (2) Hogg's later impression that the pamphlet was published prior to **QM,** (3) the fact that many of the notes in **QM** were reworked from material already on hand, and (4) the presence in the note of a paragraph absent from the pamphlet, acknowledging that diet is not solely responsible for mental and physical health, a concession that Clark believed demonstrates PBS's further reading on the subject.

Until quite recently Clark's position stood unchallenged. For instance, Cameron not only agrees with him but also points out several significant stylistic and grammatical differences between the two texts, in which the note consistently corrects the pamphlet, never vice versa. Cameron therefore reasons that the text of the pamphlet must have already been set in type before PBS completed the text of the note, or he would have incorporated the revisions into it. He remarks, moreover, that PBS must have assumed that the pamphlet would soon be followed by the published note "as he would hardly have referred to *Queen Mab* on its title page if he had anticipated a very long time lapse between the two" (*YS,* 376–77). Murray, who concurs that the pamphlet preceded the note, points out, however, that another internal reference in *Natural Diet* implies a spring *1813* rather than a fall *1812* date of composition: more than two years had already elapsed in a study of the effects of vegetarianism on sixty practitioners that, the pamphlet explains, will have lasted more than three years by April *1814* (**Prose/EBM** I, 360). Murray further cautions that the pamphlet was issued in several different bindings, "perhaps at different times" (**Prose/EBM** I, 361). The most important challenge to the general consensus, however, comes in *1989*. Writing before Murray's edition appeared, but too late for Murray to have been able to take their position into account, Matthews and Everest characterize the position of Clark and Cameron as "dubious: the internal evidence which suggests revision of *A Vindication* for *Q Mab* more plausibly indicates modification and corruption of the *Q Mab* text in printing *A Vindication* from it" (I, 265).

Because evidence within the pamphlet suggests conflicting dates of composition, and in the absence of any decisive evidence, the question of whether PBS first composed his argument in the form of a pamphlet or a note is not completely resolvable. Moreover, PBS might even have derived the press transcripts for each text from the *same* safekeeping manuscript, making local changes in texts that, at least initially, might have been scheduled for publication at around the same time. If, however, as seems most probable, one of the texts was typeset directly from a corrected printed copy of the other, the collations below unequivocally indicate, *pace 1989,* that the note is the later version. These collations substantiate and enlarge the context for Cameron's findings about the relative state of the two texts, demonstrating that the note corrects errors in *Natural Diet* involving spelling, grammar, repetition, and sense, whereas the pamphlet makes no such corrections of the note. It is simply not plausible to explain all of these differences as modifications and corruptions of the **QM** text when *Natural Diet* was printed from it. Moreover, whether or not, as Clark believes, the concessive statement in the note about other factors beyond diet affecting health reflects PBS's subsequent reading after he concluded the pamphlet, its presence clearly increases the overall sophistication and persuasiveness of PBS's position. In sum, then, it is likely that, despite the pamphlet's subtitle, it was printed before the note.

Two sentences that MWS omitted from *1839* (**lines 221–29**) because of their attack on Christianity were not restored in *1840,* probably due to an oversight. *1821.CLAX* similarly deletes part of **lines 223–25.**

lines 3–4. <u>I hold . . . unnatural habits of life</u>: PBS's general claim should be compared with that of John Frank Newton, who, in *Return,* desired to "lay before the public what shall constitute a strong presumption that all diseases, including deformity, are artificial, as much so as any production can be artificial; that the existence of poverty is our choice, not our necessity; and finally, that this heated and furious condition of things which we see around us, this infinite scene of toil and contest without any competent purpose, is produced by the dire effects on the human frame of animal food, co-operating with that baneful habit, the use of water, or of something more pernicious, to allay the thirst which that food occasions" (2).

lines 4–8. <u>The origin of man</u> . . . <u>unimportant to the present argument which is assumed</u>: PBS declines to take a position on the unresolved issue of whether human beings existed on the earth immediately after the creation or appeared later in earth's history. Ritson summarizes the classical debate on the subject through the account of Diodorus the Sicilian: "there are two opinions amongst the most famous and authentick naturalists and historians. Some of these are of opinion that the world had neither begining [*sic*] nor ever shal [*sic*] have end; and likewise say, that mankind was from eternity, and that there was never a time when he first began to be. Others, on the contrary, conceive both the world to be made, and to be corruptible, and that there was a certain time when men had first a being." Ritson's argument, however, concludes that since "it is absolutely impossible to demonstrate the origin of these things by fact or argument, reason or science, we must, of necessity, be content to embrace the sensible opinion reported by Diodorus: 'that mankind was from eternity; and that there never was a time when he first began to be'" (*Abstinence*, 6, 11–12).

lines 8–16. <u>The language spoken</u> . . . <u>have flowed from unnatural diet</u>: PBS followed Newton in mining the Bible and mythology for proof of his argument and in his reading of the Fall (see, esp., Newton's reading of the Fall, *Return*, 3–8, wherein the tree of life and the tree of the knowledge of good and evil are allegorized as "the two kinds of food which Adam and Eve had before them in Paradise, viz. the vegetables and the animals" [5]). Newton's conclusion that "the fall of Adam . . . brought diseases into the world" (6) is developed graphically by PBS in the quotation from *Paradise Lost*, for which see the Commentary to **lines 19–30,** below. This position was sympathetically satirized by an anonymous piece in the *London Magazine and Theatrical Inquisitor* for July 1821, sparked by the pirated editions of **QM** and entitled "Dinner by the Amateurs of Vegetable Diet (Extracted from an Old Paper)": "The apple of the fatal tree was nothing, gentleman, but a well-dressed beefsteak, whether plain or with oyster-sauce is doubtful." The speaker later adds: "As in Adam all eat meat, so in Newton shall all eat cabbage" (White, *UH*, 268), which, as Anne Whitmore pointed out to us, is a more or less witty reworking of I Corinthians 15:22: "For as in Adam all die, even so in Christ shall all be made alive."

Newton not only yokes the fall into meat eating with the Fall from Paradise but also finds an attendant change in the earth's climate, which is encoded in the myth of Phaeton, as "invented by the vegetable eaters of old, the Pythagoreans": "It is an astronomical fact which cannot easily be disputed, that the poles of the earth were at some distant period perpendicular to its orbit, as those of the planet Jupiter now are, whose inhabitants must therefore enjoy a perpetual spring. We can scarcely look around us without being struck by the proofs of violence and convulsion which prevailed throughout this our ruined planet at the great catastrophe of which the fable of Phaeton was intended to perpetuate the memory" (*Return*, 13, 15). For PBS's own statements on the perpendicularity of the poles to the earth, see the Commentary to **Note 10,** above.

lines 19–30. <u>Immediately a place . . . joint-racking rheums</u>: PBS seems to have taken these lines of *Paradise Lost* (XI.477–88) directly from Ritson (39–40), with minor changes in punctuation and in Ritson's highly idiosyncratic spelling. He mistakenly identifies Raphael (rather than Michael) as Adam's interlocutor probably because Ritson does not identify the archangel by name, writing only that "an ample and shocking catalogue" is "exhibited to Adam by the favourite archangel of the allmighty power, soon after the creation" (39). Hume also quotes a portion of this same passage from Milton in *Dialogues Concerning Natural Religion,* Part X, 223.

lines 33–77. <u>The story of Prometheus . . . no longer descended slowly to his grave</u>: PBS's use of Prometheus follows closely Newton's *Return*, 6–13, including the references to Horace, Hesiod, and Pliny. Newton's interpretation of Prometheus as the first meat eater is preceded by a quotation from Bacon's account of the Prometheus myth. But Newton disagreed vehemently with Bacon's ultimate interpretation, which is—as quoted by Newton—that "the voyage of Hercules, made in a pitcher, to release Prometheus, bears an allusion to the wisdom of God coming in the frail vessel of the flesh to redeem mankind" (*Return*, 8). PBS would also have been aware of Erasmus Darwin's reading of the story of Prometheus as an "allegory for the effects of drinking spirituous liquors. . . . The swallowing drams cannot be better represented in hieroglyphic language than by taking fire into one's bosom; and certain it is, that the general effect of drinking fermented or spirituous liquors is an inflamed, schirrous, or paralytic liver, with its various critical or consequential diseases" (*The Botanic Garden,* Part II, note to III.369).

lines 33–49. During the printing of *1813,* a few letters in this paragraph slipped loose in the chase (213): *r* in <u>never</u> (**line 34**), final *t* of first <u>that</u> (**line 36**), and *t* in <u>corripuit</u> (**line 49**).

lines 37–39. <u>Hesiod says . . . closed their eyes</u>: This sentence is taken virtually verbatim from Newton (*Return*, 13), who quotes Hesiod's *Works and Days* (lines 110–23). Jupiter's speech to Prometheus (lines 54–58), which describes the consequences of Prometheus's actions, is translated by Newton as follows: "You rejoice, O crafty son of Iapetus, that you have stolen fire and deceived Jupiter; but great will thence be the evil both to yourself and to your posterity. To them this gift of fire shall be a gift of woe; in which, while they delight and pride themselves, they shall cherish their own wretchedness" (*Return,* 12). These same lines from Hesiod are given as the epigraph to *Natural Diet.*

lines 41–49. <u>Audax omnia</u> . . . <u>corripuit gradum</u>: The quotation from Horace's *Odes* (I.iii.25–33) is taken directly from Newton, with small changes in punctuation (*Return,* 12). However, *1813* mistakenly runs together *macies* and *et* in **line 46,** probably an uncaught compositor's error (not in Newton or in *Natural Diet*). The circumflex appearing above "a" in <u>malâ</u> (**line 44**) is in Newton, but not in the pamphlet. Both *1821.BEN* and *1821.CLA* derive their translations (placed in footnotes) from *Francis's Horace (The Odes, Epodes and Carmen Seculare of Horace. In Latin and English With Critical Notes Collected from His Best Latin and French Commentators,* ed. Phillip Francis, 4 vols. [London: A. Millar, 1743]):

> Thus, from the sun's ethereal beam
> When bold Prometheus stole th' enlivening flame,
> Of fevers dire a ghastly brood,
> Till then unknown, th' unhappy fraud pursu'd;
> On earth their horrors baleful spread,
> And the pale monarch of the dead,
> Till then slow-moving to his prey,
> Precipitately rapid swept his way.

line 42. <u>vetitum</u>: The erroneous "vetetum" in *Natural Diet* suggests that its text was printed earlier than *1813:* such a mistake could easily have occurred by the compositor's misreading of a handwritten press transcript.

lines 50–51. <u>Prometheus</u> . . . <u>human race</u>: Newton writes that Prometheus is "pretty generally admitted" to represent the "human race" (*Return,* 8).

line 60. <u>Mr. Newton's</u>: The error in *1829.BRO* of "Mr Newland's" for <u>Mr. Newton's</u> went uncaught in *1834,* but was corrected by MWS in her editions.

lines 62–77. <u>"Making allowance</u> . . . <u>descended slowly to his grave"</u>: The quotation from Newton is without verbal changes from *Return,* 8–9, except for the two parenthetical interpolations. The first of these (in **line 69**) is from Pliny (*Historia naturalis* VII.lvi.209) and was taken directly from *Return,* 10, with part of Newton's text elided: "'Animal occidit primus Hyperbius, Martis filius, Prometheus bovem.' Hyperbius, the son of Mars, first killed an animal, Prometheus first slew an ox." Newton concludes: "it was the same man, Prometheus, who first preserved fire to human uses, and who likewise set the example of slaughtering an ox; a coincidence on which it will be quite unnecessary to comment" (*Return,* 10). Both *1821.CLA* and *1821.BEN* provide the same brief translation: "Prometheus first killed an ox."

PBS's footnote citation to Pliny's *Historia naturalis* is also taken directly from Newton. Later in *Return,* Newton reads the freeing of Prometheus by Hercules as allegorizing a return to a natural diet, through which the body is once again rendered sound and human beings are restored "to their moral and intellectual liberty" (76).

lines 78–81. <u>But just disease . . . man.</u>: These lines are from Pope, *Essay on Man* (III.165–68). Not himself a vegetarian, Pope nonetheless depicts humanity in an original state of nature as vegetarian: "Man walk'd with beast," not preying on other species for food or clothing. This passage from Pope may well have been brought to PBS's attention by—or even taken directly from—Ritson, who quotes it at the end of his second chapter (*Abstinence,* 56). There are small differences in punctuation and spelling between *1813* and Ritson.

lines 82–88. <u>Man, and the animals . . . upon their miseries</u>: Cf. Newton, "The domestication of animals which are rendered useful to us in our civilized state, entails upon them many disorders and much misery. Sheep suffer in a way to call forth the most ordinary compassion" (*Return,* 20). Newton discusses the "subversive" changes introduced into the domesticated hog on pages 28–29. He also claims, "The wild animals, on the contrary, escape the evils above enumerated, as far as we are permitted to judge" (*Return,* 30). Cf. also Monboddo's claim that "wild animals . . . have no disease, . . . except such wild animals as feed upon the food of Men, that is, herbs and fruits raised from dung" (*Antient Metaphysics* III, 119).

line 83. <u>mouflon</u>: a wild mountain sheep of Sardinia and Corsica, discussed by Newton at length (*Return,* 27–28).

line 88. <u>a supereminence</u>: emended to "the supereminence" in *1840,* making it grammatically parallel to the opening of the sentence: "The supereminence of man . . . ."

lines 99–107. <u>It is true . . . human evil</u>: The absence of this important concessive paragraph in **Natural Diet** and its presence in *1813* is another piece of evidence that *1813* is the later text. PBS's general argument is certainly improved by the admission that diet is not solely responsible for mental and physical health.

lines 104–5. <u>muffling . . . apparel</u>: Newton, whose family practiced nudism, remarks: "The custom of flesh eating, as much as that of covering our persons with clothes, appears to have arisen from the migration of man into the northern climates, and the reaction of that circumstance, conjoined with the increasing ill effects of an unnatural diet" (*Return*, 81–82).

lines 108–24. <u>Comparative anatomy teaches</u> ... <u>would he be consistent</u>: The general argument from comparative anatomy that begins here descends from Plutarch and Monboddo, but it is most immediately influenced in its structure and content by Newton, who writes, "That man is wholly adapted to vegetable sustenance is evident from his anatomy" (*Return*, 17). Newton proceeds to adduce evidence from Lambe and Cuvier on the intestinal tract and shape of the teeth, with special attention to the ourang-outang (*Return*, 17–18). Another important influence is Ritson, who argues, "It seems, therefor, that, the teeth and intestines of man being like those of frugivorous animals, he should, naturally, be range'd [*sic*] in this class" (*Abstinence*, 41). Ritson's second chapter, entitled "Animal Food Not Natural to Man," develops this argument (41–56).

The entry "Man" in *Rees's Cyclopædia*, which PBS cites in **footnote 3,** agrees with some of his local claims; for instance: "The teeth of man have not the slightest resemblance to those of the carnivorous animals . . . he possesses, indeed, teeth called canine, but they . . . are obviously unsuited to the purposes which the corresponding teeth execute in carnivorous animals. . . . [and], in short, very closely resemble the teeth of monkies, except that the canine are much longer and stronger in the latter animals." After similarly analyzing the human jaw and the alimentary canal, *Rees's* concludes: "In general, then, the human teeth and joint of the jaw resemble most those of herbivorous animals: and man approaches most nearly in these, as well as in other points, to the monkey race, which are, in their natural state, completely herbivorous."

However, on the larger implications of this data, *Rees's* and PBS part company, the former advising, "In stating these circumstances, we do not wish our readers to draw the inference, that man is designed by nature to feed on vegetables." *Rees's* claims that because human hands and arts can procure food that other animals must "earn by their teeth" and because humans can cook their food, comparative anatomy creates an "analogy . . . too loose for us to place much confidence [in]," concluding that until empirical studies are done of individuals of "different habits" who are solely on the animal diet and solely on the vegetable diet, no inferences should be ventured "on a subject, beset with so many obstacles."

lines 108–12. <u>Comparative anatomy</u> ... <u>even a hare</u>: Cf. Ritson quoting Plutarch (*On the Eating of Flesh*, Essay I): "That it is not natural to mankind to feed on flesh, we first of all demonstrate from the very shape and figure of the body: for a human body no way resembles those that are born for rapine: it hath no hawk-bil; no sharp talon; no roughness of teeth" (*Abstinence*, 47–

48). PBS uses more from this passage in Plutarch below and quotes from it at length in Greek to conclude the notes to **QM.** At the end of November 1813, he completed a translation of Plutarch's entire essay (**Letters** I, 380).

lines 115–23. <u>It is only by softening . . . for such work as this</u>: based on a passage from Plutarch that PBS would have found in Ritson (who cites *On the Eating of Flesh,* Essay I): "Rend an ox with thy teeth; worry a hog with thy mouth; tear a lamb in pieceës; and fall on and eat it alive as they do: but, if thou had'st rather stay until what thou eatest is become dead, and art loth to force a soul out of its body, why, then, do'st thou, against nature, eat an animate thing? Nay, there is no one that is willing to eat even a lifeless and a dead thing as it is, but they boil it, and roast it, and alter it by fire and medicines, that the palate, being thereby deceive'd, may admit of such uncouth fare" (*Abstinence,* 48).

lines 123–24. <u>Then, and then only</u>: *1840* mistakenly drops the second *then.*

lines 125–26. <u>Man resembles . . . cellulated colons</u>: Cf. Newton, who incorrectly cites page 27 of Lambe's *Reports on Cancer* (instead of page 30) to the effect that "all carnivorous animals have a smooth and uniform colon, and all herbivorous animals a cellulated one" (*Return,* 17).

line 125. <u>unless</u>: It would appear that "except" in **Natural Diet** was changed in *1813* to <u>unless</u> in order to avoid "There is no exception, except . . . ."

lines 127–30. <u>The orang-outang . . . this analogy exists</u>: Newton writes: "Dr. Lambe's opponents are called upon to shew, either that classification in the natural sciences means nothing, or that the human teeth and intestines do not resemble those of the Orang Outang, so as to mark us as *the first link in the same chain of animals.* This is the grievous truth from which, though God himself be the author of it, man turns aside with shame or with scorn" (*Return,* 18). Ritson had earlier argued similarly, citing extensively from eighteenth-century accounts of the humanlike qualities of orang-outangs (13–23). PBS did not pursue the resemblance between orang-outangs and humans to Newton's radical conclusion. For Monboddo, the orang-outang represented "the first stage of the human progression" and stood as a noble contrast to the degraded state of contemporary, civilized humanity (*Of the Origin and Progress of Language,* 2nd ed. [Edinburgh: J. Balfour, 1774], 269, 289–90), a position satirized by the character "Sir Oran Haut-ton," Baronet, the best friend of Sylvan Forester, the Shelleyan hero of Peacock's *Melincourt* (1817).

Footnote 3. <u>Cuvier, Leçons d'Anat. Comp. . . . Rees's Cyclopædia, article Man</u>: PBS, who used these same citations to Cuvier's *Leçons* in **Natural Diet** and **Refutation,** apparently took them directly from Lambe without reference to Cuvier's text, which would have shown him that the citation to III, 169 (Lambe, *Reports,* 28)—which begins a discussion of the teeth of reptiles—is mistaken. More apposite material in Cuvier can be found on pages 144–53, in which a table compares the teeth of mammals: on page 144, men and monkeys follow each other as the first and second entries and are shown to be identical in number and type of teeth. The column for *"Remarques"* is left blank for both *Hommes* and *Singes.* On pages 156–58, Cuvier discusses the differences between the canine teeth in humans and monkeys.

However, *pace 1989,* the reference to page 448 in Cuvier (Lambe, 30) is not also mistaken: the footnote is to a table comparing the length of alimentary canals in different simians, which is also reproduced in *Rees's* entry "Man" at a similar point in its discussion of comparative anatomy and correctly cited as III, 448. Lambe does not cite *Rees's,* which PBS consulted independently.

Some confusion exists about exactly which edition of *Rees's Cyclopædia* PBS used in annotating **QM,** prompted largely by Cameron's claim that *"Rees Cyclopaedia* was not published until 1819; Shelley must be referring to Rees's edition of *Chambers's Cyclopaedia"* (*YS,* 390n.29). This publication history, however, is more complicated than Cameron allows. First edited by Ephraim Chambers and published in two folio volumes by Longman in 1728, *Chambers's Cyclopædia* was immensely popular and influential, undergoing a second edition in 1738 and a final reprinting in 1739 under the guidance of Chambers, who died in 1740. After the death of Chambers, the *Cyclopædia* underwent several reprints and one substantial update, culminating in an edition fully revised by Abraham Rees, which was published in weekly numbers beginning in 1778 and which eventually comprised four folio volumes. This is the edition Cameron calls "Rees's edition of *Chambers's Cyclopaedia.*" In 1802, Rees began editing an entirely new encyclopedia under the title *Rees's Cyclopædia,* which was published in parts or half volumes until it was completed in forty volumes some sixteen years later (see Thomas Rees, *Reminiscences of Literary London from 1779 to 1853* [London: Suckling & Galloway, 1896], 49–51). Thus, at the time of writing the notes for **QM,** PBS would have had available to him all of the new *Rees's Cyclopædia* that had been published to date. In fact, the article "Man" in the new *Rees's* edition exactly parallels PBS's discussion above, whereas "Man" in Rees's edition of *Chambers's Cyclopædia* contains no related information. Clearly, then, PBS was working from a partial edition of the new *Rees's* while composing this note for **QM** and may have had available the volumes up to at least the letter "M" (Volume 23) for his reference. An advertisement in *The Oxford University and County Herald* for 21 September 1811 announced that "Thirty-six Parts" (about half of the work) were already printed.

Footnote 3. <u>Cyclopædia</u>: The misreading "œ" for "æ" appears to have originated in the text of **Natural Diet.**

line 136. <u>cæcum</u>: "cœcum" in *1813* is another error that may have originated in *Natural Diet*. Murray suggests that PBS took the erroneous spelling directly from Newton, who made the same mistake, although Newton's own probable source, William Lambe, got it right (see *Prose/EBM* I, 540–41). However, Lambe himself is inconsistent, spelling it "cœcum" on page 26 of his *Reports,* suggesting the possibility that the typesetters rather than the authors may be behind this problem. There is no paragraph break in *Natural Diet* between **lines 137** and **138** in *1813.*

lines 142–44. <u>A lamb</u> . . . <u>the voyage</u>: taken from Newton, who cites Gassendi's "celebrated letter to Van Helmont," in which it is "stated that a lamb which had been fed on flesh until it was nine months old, on board a vessel sailing among the Greek Islands, refused the pasture that was before it when it was sent on shore, and eagerly sought the hand which held out to it its accustomed food" (*Return,* 106, 111).

lines 144–46. <u>There are numerous</u> . . . <u>natural aliment</u>: taken from Ritson: "Horseës, sheep, and oxen, are universally allow'd to be herbivorous animals; and yet there are instanceës of their gradually quiting their usual aliment, and learning to live upon flesh. A young wood-pigeon, even, a species of bird, which is universally known to feed upon any thing rather than flesh, has, by dint of hunger, been brought to relish flesh so as to refuse every other kind of sustenance, even grain, of which it is naturally so fond." Ritson supplied a long footnote further documenting his claim (*Abstinence,* 45–47). Lambe seems to be paraphrasing Ritson's first sentence, adding that questions need to be asked about whether such transformations of diet are healthy (*Reports,* 9).

In *Natural Diet,* PBS appears to have made an error in paraphrasing Ritson: instead of Ritson's phrase "usual aliment," he writes "accustomed aliment," but because PBS's syntax is different from Ritson's, the phrase actually makes nonsense of the argument. PBS's point is that these herbivorous animals have grown accustomed to eating flesh and have thus come to loathe, not their "accustomed aliment," but their <u>natural aliment</u>, a correction he made in *1813*—providing further evidence that *1813* is the later text.

PBS reused this passage in the manuscript of *On the Vegetable System of Diet,* which credits Ritson openly in a footnote (see *Prose/EBM* I, 152).

lines 146–54. <u>Young children evidently prefer pastry</u> . . . <u>the present system</u>: On this point, Ritson cites Rousseau (*Emile* I, 286): "One proof, says Rousseau, that the taste of meat is not natural to the human palate, is the indifference which children have for that kind of food, and the preference they give to vegetable aliments, such as milk-meats, pastry, fruit, &c.," which, Ritson adds, "certainly, agree with them better." As proof of this claim, he cites infant mortality rates from 1800–1801, which he interprets as demonstrating that "near 7,500 of these tender infants perish in the first five years of their life; most likely in consequence of their being stuf'd with flesh-meat, which is unnatural to them, and cannot be digested at so early an age" (*Abstinence,* 42–43, 43n).

Lambe paraphrases the same argument about the taste of children from Rousseau, but without any citation (*Reports,* 9–10). Newton writes, "Of all the children whom I have known or heard of, none has disliked fruit, but several have refused to eat meat. Some have been made sick with it" (*Return,* 62–63).

line 153. not one in fifty possesses: a grammatical correction in *1813* of "not one in fifty possess" in **Natural Diet.**

lines 158–59. in his own cause: it is even worse, it: Ascham emended in his to "of his," and worse, to "worse;" both passed into MWS's editions. She further polished PBS's style, however, by adding a word in *1840,* altering it to "for it."

Footnote 4. The necessity of resorting . . . capable of occasioning disease: Unlike Lambe, who claimed that it is unnatural for human beings to drink water at all (*Reports,* 2–3), PBS took a more moderate position that recognized the potential health risks of drinking polluted water. Newton asserts about water that "Neither the Holy Well, nor the spring at Malvern, nor even the golden water of the kings of Persia, could serve as a substitute for that which has undergone distillation" (*Return,* 38), and he spends considerable time discussing the dangers of drinking water (38–62).

the disease which arises . . . is: Brooks's unnecessary change of disease to "diseases" occasioned the further changes to "arise" and "are" that appear as well in Ascham's; MWS's texts contain these emendations.

lines 195–97. How many groundless opinions and absurd institutions have not received a general sanction from the sottishness and intemperance of individuals!: Ascham "polished" this sentence, omitting not from have not and placing "the" before intemperance; MWS's texts retain his emendations.

lines 197–214. Who will assert that . . . throne of the Bourbons: The brutalizing effects of a carnivorous diet are treated at length in Ritson, especially Chapters IV, "Animal Food the Cause of Cruelty and Ferocity," V, "Animal Food the Cause of Human Sacrificeës," and VI, "Human Flesh the Consequence of Animal Food" (*Abstinence,* 86–145). However, the particular examples PBS provides, from Parisian support for the Reign of Terror to Napoleon's physique and career, would seem to be his own—or, at least, taken from another source.

lines 211–12. It is impossible, had . . . that: In omitting a redundant "that" following "impossible," the reading in *1813,* impossible, had . . . that is clearly superior to "impossible that had . . . that" in **Natural Diet,** providing evidence that the note to **QM** may have been printed after the pamphlet.

lines 221–29. <u>Who can wonder</u> . . . <u>universal sin</u>: These two sentences, omitted from *1839* because of their attack on Christians, were not restored in *1840* and were likewise omitted from the editions of Rossetti and Dowden.

line 228. <u>love</u>: *1829* and *1834* first placed an unnecessary question mark after <u>love</u>.

lines 237–42. <u>On a natural system of diet</u> . . . <u>favoured moments of our youth</u>: Newton discusses the protraction of human life on a vegetable diet, citing the example of Old Thomas Parr of Shropshire, who lived to be 150 years old (*Return*, 63–64). Parr was reputedly a vegetarian who died only after altering his simple diet to that of the Court (see *Return*, 97). In the appendix of **Natural Diet,** PBS provides a chart of vegetarians who had lived until old age, including Parr—all of which, including supporting citations— he extracted from Ritson (*Abstinence*, 156–57) without acknowledgment.

line 253. <u>nine</u> . . . <u>one</u>: The transposition of "nine" and "one" in *1829.BRO* carries over to *1834, 1839,* and *1840.*

lines 256–60. <u>Hopes are entertained</u> . . . <u>taken at random</u>: Newton's text, written in 1811, states:

The number of persons whom I know to be at this time living on the diet is at least twenty five; and of these I have to state, that their health is so good that they have no occasion for the use of medicine, and that, without an exception, their indispositions, where they happen at all, are so trifling as scarcely to deserve the name; although they have not yet relinquished meat, fish, and common water, long enough to derive all the advantages which may be thence expected. These persons are of various ages and constitutions; some of them previously in good health, some otherwise; yet with them all the result has been uniform, that is (for I wish to be perfectly moderate and entirely borne out in my assertions) *No ill effects have in any instance been felt from the adoption of this regimen.* (*Return*, 71)

Either the number of longlasting vegetarians known to the Newton circle had increased to sixty by 1813, or PBS thought that twenty-five was too unimpressive a number and decided to increase it.

lines 260–67. <u>Seventeen persons</u> . . . <u>eloquent essay</u>: In 1811, Newton's own household contained seven people, including the asthmatic nurse to whom PBS refers, who, writes Newton, "entirely got rid of her disorder" (*Return,* 72).

lines 274–86. <u>The change</u> . . . <u>incapable of calculation</u>: PBS's logic is influenced by Ritson and Newton. Ritson—citing Paley's *Principles of Moral and Political Philosophy* II, 361, writes: "Many ranks of people, whose ordinary diet was, in the last century, prepare'd allmost entirely from milk, roots and vegetables, now require, every day, a considerable portion of the flesh of animals.

Hence a great part of the richest lands of the country are converted to pasturage. Much, allso, of the bread-corn, which went directly to the nourishment of human bodys, now onely contributes to it, by fatening the flesh of sheep and oxen. The mass and volume of provisions are hereby diminish'd; and what is gain'd in the melioration of the soil is lost in the quality of the produce" (*Abstinence*, 84–85).

lines 280–83. <u>The quantity . . . bosom of the earth</u>: PBS's estimate that the food supply would increase tenfold if it were consumed directly by humans appears to be taken from a section in Newton that directly attacks Malthus (a strategy PBS himself avoids here): "A writer on population of some celebrity has contended that the destructive operations of whatever sort by which men are killed off or got rid of, are so many blessings and benefits, and he has the triumph of seeing his doctrines pretty widely disseminated and embraced; although no point can be more clearly demonstrable than that the earth might contain and support at least ten times the number of inhabitants that are now upon it." Newton made clear in a footnote that he had much more to say on this subject (which he may have discussed with PBS) and that he intended to write a subsequent pamphlet on poverty and war that would serve as the second part of his present book (*Return*, 67). For PBS's own direct engagement with Malthus, from the early **Proposals for An Association** (1812) to the later poetry, see the note to *SC* VI, 1023–24.

lines 288–322. <u>Again, the spirit of the nation . . . for the general benefit</u>: This passage reveals PBS's agrarian biases, for which see Reiman, *Romantic Texts and Contexts* (Columbia: U of Missouri P, 1987), 260–74. For PBS's attack on commerce—and its connection to imperialism and war—see the Commentary to **V.38**.

line 318. <u>out</u>: The mistaken omission of <u>out</u> in *1834* was carried over to MWS's editions.

Footnote 7. <u>It has come under the author's experience . . . sterile ground by moonlight</u>: PBS took part in a project led by William Alexander Madocks to complete an embankment that would reclaim the model town of Tremadoc, North Wales, from the sea. He twice stayed at Tremadoc, the first time in September 1812 and the second time from mid-November 1812 to 27 February 1813. Madocks was a Whig M.P. who belonged to Burdett's circle of reformers. In 1809, he led an unsuccessful movement to impeach for corrupt practices both the prime minister (Perceval) and the foreign minister (Castlereagh). However, Madocks did realize his strategic goal of using these charges as a means of reinvigorating a parliamentary reform movement that had been all but dormant since 1797. By September 1812, when PBS arrived at Tremadoc, Madocks was financially distressed, hence the unpaid workers mentioned in PBS's note and PBS's subsequent efforts to raise money for the project.

In the notes to Pratt's Poem . . . state of independence: The reference is to Note (k) of Samuel Jackson Pratt's *Bread; or, The Poor* (1801; retitled *Cottage Pictures; or, The Poor: A Poem*, 4th ed., 1805), in which Pratt relates an account provided to him by "Mr. Swan of Wolvercot" concerning Joseph Smith, a laborer who for twenty years rented from Swan an acre of meadow without which "he probably would have been as pennyless and as burthensome as most of the neighboring labourers. He has reared eight children, and buried three, has never received the smallest parochial assistance, and is now possessed of live stock worth at least 70£ and has lately purchased the cottage he lives in, and the one adjoining it." Swan offers Smith as an example "of the incalculable advantages that would arise from the allotment of a small portion of ground to every cottage."

Pratt (1749–1814), a failed actor turned dramatist and poet, wrote voluminously, at first under the Della Cruscan pseudonym "Courtney Melmouth." His antislavery poem *Humanity; or, The Rights of Nature* (1788), like *QM*, uses vegetarian rhetoric for purposes of social critique. *Bread; or, The Poor* was treated derisively in the first number of the *Edinburgh Review* (October 1802) in a review that opened: "The author of this poem professes to instruct, as well as amuse the public; to interest their humanity, by an account of the sufferings of the poor, and enlighten their understandings by this profound lesson of political economy, That scarcity is occasioned entirely by monopoly, and lately took place after most plentiful harvests" (108–9).

lines 338–43. The healthiest among us . . . the physiological critic: Newton similarly claims: "Real men have never been seen that we are aware of, nor has history, nor even poetry, depictured them. It is not man we have before us, but the wreck of man" (*Return*, 66).

lines 346–50. All that I contend for . . . vegetables and pure water: Cf. Newton's statement that the "consolation to the self-denying invalid is this, that after a steady perseverance in the plan we are speaking of for two or three years, he will no longer have to struggle with serious illnesses, it being understood that the stamina of the party are not so worn down that the work of death may be said to be already matured" (*Return*, 70). Lambe's apparent success in checking the progress of twenty cases of incipient cancer is also praised by Newton (*Return*, 90).

lines 354–55. Dr. Trotter asserts . . . his dram: In *A View of the Nervous Temperament; Being a Practical Enquiry into the Increasing Prevalence, Prevention, and Treatment of Those Diseases Commonly Called Nervous, Bilious, Stomach and Liver Complaints . . .* (London: Longman, Hurst, Rees & Orme, 1807), Thomas Trotter—who had earlier written *An Essay; Medical, Philosophical, and Chemi-*

cal on Drunkenness and Its Effects on the Human Body (1804)—is most emphatic about the need for an alcoholic to give up alcohol completely and refers to it several times throughout. However, PBS's specific reference to Trotter comes from page 313:

But there are some physicians who contend that it is hurtful for habitual drunkards to leave off the bottle at once. Were the habit of dram-drinking a salutary practice, there might be some truth in this dictatorial precept. But as ardent spirit is a strong poison to both soul and body, and forms no part of that nourishment which can be converted into animal matter, I have never been able, after the most unwearied application in the exercise of my profession, to find a single fact in support of a doctrine so destructive to moral and physical health. Whenever I have known habitual ebriety completely overcome, it has been where all species of liquors were given up *in toto from the first.*

PBS ordered Trotter's *View* from "Clio" Rickman on 24 December 1812 (*Letters* I, 345), not long after he had met Newton, who may have recommended it. Because PBS's citation of Trotter lacks a page number reference, whereas most citations in this note include one, it may have been done from memory.

lines 356–57. <u>similar to the kind</u>: PBS appears to be within acceptable contemporary practice in the use of this phrase rather than "similar in the kind," the alternative phrasing in **Natural Diet** and the emendation made in *1876* and *1989.*

lines 357–58. <u>The proselyte to a pure diet</u>: Ascham appears to have dropped the <u>a</u> accidentally, providing the reading "to pure diet," followed by MWS.

lines 378–81. <u>The pleasures of taste</u> . . . <u>is supposed</u>: Newton gives an example of his family's usual daily fare, which for dinner consisted of "potatoes, with some other vegetables, according as they happen to be in season; macaroni, a tart, or a pudding, with as few eggs in it as possible: to this is sometimes added a dessert" (*Return*, 114).

lines 384–87. <u>Solomon kept a thousand concubines</u> . . . <u>this venerable debauchee</u>: The Bible describes Solomon as having seven hundred wives and three hundred concubines (I Kings 11:3) and as claiming: "Vanity of vanities; all *is* vanity" (Ecclesiastes 1:2). For PBS's prior attack on Solomon, see the Commentary for **II.137–48.**

line 388. <u>only to the young enthusiast</u>: MWS's alteration of this phrase to "to the young enthusiast only" suggests that she may have considered it within her editorial province to "improve" PBS's style when she saw fit, a practice he assented to during his lifetime when she transcribed his work.

line 393. <u>chace</u>: PBS's characteristic spelling <u>chace</u> was still an accepted contemporary spelling for the more common "chase." Its presence in *1813* is one of several pieces of evidence that PBS himself transcribed for the press part, if not all, of the MS of *QM* and its notes. *1821.BEN* contains one of the most memorable textual errors of all the pirated texts, reading for <u>the brutal pleasures of the chace</u>, "the brutal pleasures of the chaste."

line 402. <u>healths</u>: contemporary usage; the plural stresses the individual health of each child.

Footnote 9. <u>See Mr. Newton's book</u> . . . <u>Sir G. Mackenzie's Hist. of Iceland</u> . . . <u>Emile, chap. i. pages 53, 54, 56</u>: Newton describes the "remarkably healthy appearance" of his four children as "so striking, that several medical men who have seen and examined them with a scrutinizing eye, all agreed in the observation that they knew no where a whole family which equals them in robustness" (*Return*, 73–74). One of these "medical men" was Lambe, who, writing some two years earlier than Newton, had offered the Newton family as exemplary: "I am well acquainted with a family of young children, who have scarcely ever touched animal food; and who have now for three years drunk only distilled water. For clearness and beauty of complexion, muscular strength, fulness of habit free from grossness, hardiness, healthiness, and ripeness of intellect, these children are unparalleled" (*Reports*, 18; the identification of the family as Newton's is in a footnote on page 183).

PBS's statistics on the mortality rates of children are extrapolated from Ritson, who in 1802 wrote: "It appears, by the general bil [*sic*] of all the christenings and burials, for the city and suburbs of London, from December 9, 1800, to December 15, 1801, that, of 17,814 children, males and females, christen'd in that or the four preceding years, not less than 5,395 dye'd under the age of two years, nor less than 2,063, between two and five: a destruction, apparently, oweing to, and occasion'd by, the untimely and unnatural use of animal food" (*Abstinence*, 147).

For the effect of meat eating on breast milk, Ritson cites Rousseau (*Emile,* I, 54): "'The milk of those women,' says Rousseau, 'who [nurse children and] live chiefly on vegetables, is more sweet and salutary than that of carnivorous females'" (*Abstinence*, 154). Newton relates an anecdote of a woman who breast-fed her youngest child after turning vegetarian: "This lady accomplished her purpose much better in this instance than in any former attempt. She enjoyed during the period of nursing, and has since enjoyed, excellent health; and as to the child, he is all that one can wish a child to be" (*Return*, 129n).

Sir George Stuart Mackenzie's *Travels in the Island of Iceland during the Summer of the Year MDCCCX* (Edinburgh: Archibald Constable and Company, 1811) provides an account of the island of Heimaey, near the southern coast of Iceland, on which fewer than two hundred inhabitants had no "vegetable food" and "only a few cows and sheep" (413). Children, he reported, were invariably infected with tetanus: the island was "almost entirely supported by migration from the mainland; scarcely a single instance having been known, during the last twenty years, of a child surviving the period of infancy" (413). Although Mackenzie is more tentative than PBS in identifying the cause of the tetanus, he concludes that it "may reasonably be supposed to have some connection with the extraordinary diet of the natives" (415). The mortality statistics documenting the number of infant deaths during the first three weeks of life are displayed in a table (414). It has not been previously noted that within this same chapter discussing the diseases of Iceland, just pages before the passage alluded to in this footnote to *QM*, Mackenzie provides a detailed description of a variety of elephantiasis—the disease that PBS became worried he was suffering from in December 1813 (408–9; for an analysis of this strange episode in Shelley's life, see *Shelley's Venomed Melody*, 85–101).

PBS's closing citations to *Emile* are taken directly from a footnote in Ritson. After a reference to "*Emilius*, I, 54," for the quotation on the milk of nursing mothers, Ritson adds the following two quotations from *Emile:* "'Can it be suppose'd that a vegetable diet should be the best adapted for a child, and animal food for its nurse? There is an evident contradiction in the notion.' *Ibi,* 56. 'Nor is this to be wonder'd at, since animal substanceës, when putrefy'd, are cover'd with worms, in a manner never experience'd in the substance of vegetables.' *Ibi, 53*" (*Abstinence*, 155n). The pagination of Ritson's citations to *Emile* corresponds to a 1767 translation of *Emile* into English (*Emilius and Sophia: or, A New System of Education*, trans. William Kenrick, 4 vols. [London: T. Becket and P. A. de Hondt, 1767]).

are not . . . not: In both 1821 editions and in the editions of MWS, the first *not* in the sentence is omitted as a stylistic improvement preventing repetition of the word.

to be: The "o" has fallen out of the chase, leaving an empty space, in the copies of **Natural Diet** we have seen.

lines 407–33. The *QM* notes conclude with this selection of passages from Plutarch's two essays *On the Eating of Flesh* in *Moralia*. Of the four separate selections divided by asterisks in **1813,** the first selection is taken from near the beginning of the first essay (994A); the following two selections occur close to each other, towards the end of the first essay—994F–995A and 995C; and the last selection is from the second essay (998B–C). PBS later reused much of this material in a footnote to **A Refutation of Deism** (see **Prose/EBM** I, 117).

While the specific edition of Plutarch that PBS used remains unknown, two prominent editions done towards the end of the eighteenth century were the Leipzig edition edited by J. J. Reiske (Leipzig, 1774–82) and an edition by J. G. Hutton (Tubingen, 1791–1804). A more highly regarded text of the *Moralia* was in progress at Oxford and was published at Leipzig 1796–1834 by Daniel Wyttenbach. The *editio princeps* by Demetrius Ducas, was printed at

Venice in Aldine type in 1509 (*Venetiis, in aedibus Aldi et Andreae soceri*) and was still actively in use during PBS's day (owned and used, for example, by Thomas Jefferson). PBS's text is paleographical, resembling a manuscript or an early type rather than a later Greek type, though there are none of the abbreviations characteristic of paleographical texts. Most of the readings PBS uses also appear to be early. At least one of these readings was accepted and used by Reiske. PBS's main textual deviations are minor, primarily in spelling, accents, and punctuation, a few of which may have been errors in transcription or in typesetting.

In the first selection, **lines 407–9,** we have corrected the misspelling in *1813* of "serpents" (δρακώντας) for δράκοντας and "panthers" (παρδελέις) for παρδάλεις. We also emend the use of the pronoun ἡμῖν for ὑμῖν, which would otherwise change the translation from "for you a mere appetizer" to "for us a mere appetizer," a problem finessed by the translation in *1821.CLA,* which instead of translating this phrase, expands the previous phrase from "their slaughter is their living" to "blood shed by them is a matter of necessity, and requisite for their subsistence."

In the second selection, **lines 410–21,** we correct the omission in *1813* of *tau* from the word στόματος—an error either in transcription or of the press—and the misspelling of "cleaver" (κοπίδη for κοπίδι). Perhaps following its unknown source, *1813* omits the Greek word τινὶ, an omission we leave unchanged although it appears in the other texts we have checked; the word is translated in the Loeb Classical Library edition as "cudgel of any kind."

In the third selection, **lines 422–27,** we correct the transcription or press error that breaks into two separate words the word for "spices" or "ointments and perfumes": ἡ δύσμασι for ἡδύσμασι. Otherwise, throughout we have retained the punctuation of *1813* but have corrected misplaced accents and obvious errors of the press as noted in the collations at the foot of the page.

1821.BEN replaces the Greek text with an English translation that is independent of the translation in *1821.CLA* (which is instead provided in a footnote). The translation in *1821.CLA,* which conflates I.995C and II.998B–C (sections 3 and 4 in *1813*), reads as follows:

You apply the term wild to lions, panthers, and serpents, yet in your own savage slaughters, you far surpass them in ferocity, for the blood shed by them is a matter of necessity, and requisite for their subsistence.

*   *   *   *   *   *   *

That man is not by nature destined to devour animal food, is evident from the construction of the human frame, which bears no resemblance to wild beasts, or birds of prey. Man is not provided with claws or talons, with sharpness of fang, or tusk, so well adapted to tear and lacerate; nor is his stomach so well braced and muscular, nor his animal spirits so warm as to enable him to digest this solid mass of animal flesh. On the contrary, nature has made his teeth smooth, his mouth narrow, and his tongue soft; and has contrived, by the slowness of his digestion, to divert him from devouring a species of food so ill adapted to his frame and constitution. But if you still maintain, that such is your natural mode of subsistence, then follow nature in your mode of killing your prey, and employ neither knife, hammer, or hatchet, but like wolves, bears, and lions, seize an ox with your teeth, grasp a boar round the body, or tear asunder a lamb or a hare, and like the savage tribe, devour them still panting in the agonies of death.

*   *   *   *   *   *   *

We carry our luxury still farther, by the variety of sauces and seasonings which we add to our beastly banquets, mixing together oil, wine, honey, pickles, vinegar, and Syrian and Arabian ointments and perfumes, as if we intended to bury and embalm the carcases on which we feed. The difficulty of digesting such a mass of matter reduced in our stomachs to a state of liquefaction and putrefaction, is the source of endless disorders in the human frame.

First of all, the wild mischievous animals were selected for food, and then the birds and fishes were dragged to slaughter; next the human appetite directed itself against the laborious ox, the useful and fleece-bearing sheep, and the cock, the guardian of the house. At last, by this preparatory discipline, man became matured for human massacres, slaughters, and wars.

HISTORICAL COLLATIONS

To Harriett

Thy look of love has power to calm
The stormiest passion of my soul
Thy gentle words are drops of balm
In life's too bitter bowl
No grief is mine but that alone
These choicest blessings I have known

Harriett! if all who long to live
In the warm sunshine of thine eye
That price beyond all pain must give
Beneath thy scorn to die
Then hear thy chosen own too late
His heart most worthy of thy hate

Be thou then one among mankind
Whose heart is harder not for state
Thou only virtuous gentle kind
Amid a world of hate
And by a slight endurance seal
A fellow being's lasting weal
                Corfe Castle

"To Harriett." *The Esdaile Notebook,* folio 92 verso, in HWS's hand

The following Historical Collations have been selected from a broader computer-generated collation of all variants between the Texts in **CPPBS** and the texts of the editions listed at the head of the variants for each individual poem. Our general policy in the edition as a whole is to record only those variants that we judge may have some potential effect on the sound and rhythm of the verse or on its meaning, through either denotation or connotation. We discuss at length our rationale for the Historical Collations in the Editorial Overview.

The siglum *omnia* indicates that all editions being collated agree upon the reading. In lemmas concerning variant titles of Shelley's poems, the reading for our Text is shown as *no title* whenever Shelley himself did not entitle the poem.

The Esdaile Notebook

To Harriet   [Esd #1]

Text collated with *1966, 1972,* and *1989.*

Title.   Harriet]   HARRIET [SHELLEY]   *1966*

                      Harriet [*Shelley*]   *1972*
1   Whose]   WHOSE   *1972*

     that]   that,   *1966 1972*

     thro']   through   *omnia*

     world]   world,   *1966 1972*
7   on]   on,   *1966 1972*
9   thine:—thou]   thine—thou   *1989*

     soul,]   soul;   *1966 1972*
10   song,]   song;   *1966 1972*
12   Tho']   Though   *omnia*
13   brow;]   brow: *omnia*
14   prime.]   prime,—   *1966 1972*

              prime;—   *1989*

A sabbath Walk   [Esd #2]

Text collated with *1886* (lines 5, 43, 45–46), *1927*/III (lines 45–46), *1966,*
1972, and *1989.*

1   Sweet]   SWEET   *1972*
4   smile.]   smile;   *1966 1972 1989*
5   This]   *omitted   1886*
9   Yes,]   Yes!   *1966 1972*
10   wilds.]   wilds: *1966 1972*

              wilds;   *1989*
11   God,]   God   *1966 1972*
19   Christians']   Christian's   *1989*

     blood-stain'd]   bloodstained   *1966 1972 1989*
21   divinity]   Divinity   *1966 1972*
22   love,]   love;   *1966 1972*

23   Who]   Who,   *1966 1972*
      depth]   depth,   *1966 1972*
24   glare]   glare,   *1966 1972 1989*
25   death]   death,   *1966 1972*
28   day.]   day;   *1966 1972*
29   Deity]   Deity,   *1966 1972*
31   loves.]   loves;   *1966 1972*
32   Ah!]   Ah,   *1989*
33   rise.]   rise.—   *1966 1972*
                  rise: *1989*
34   sweet]   sweet,   *1966 1972*
36   hour.]   hour;   *1966 1972*
      The]   the   *1966 1972*
37   sense]   sense,   *1966 1972*
39   half believed, the]   half-believed,—the   *1966 1972*
40   fear—]   fear,   *1966 1972 1989*
43   But to]   *omitted*   *1886*
44   sabbath]   Sabbath   *1966 1972*
      day]   day,   *1966 1972 1989*
45   holiness]   holiness,   *1886 1927/*III *1966 1972*
46   love.]   love: *1966 1972*
                  love;   *1989*
49   priests.]   priests,—   *1966 1972*
50   pineboughs]   pine-boughs   *1966 1972 1989*
52   pervadeth,]   pervadeth   *1966 1972 1989*
53   purity;]   purity;—   *1966 1972*
56   Thanksgivings,]   Thanksgiving,   *1989*

The Crisis   *[Esd #3]*

Text collated with *1886* (lines 13–16), *1927/*III (lines 13–16), *1966, 1972,*
and *1989.*

1   When]   WHEN   *1972*
2   Falshood]   Falsehood   *1966 1972 1989*
3   Corruption]   Corruption,   *1966 1972 1989*
4   fatten—]   fatten,—   *1966 1972 1989*
5   thro']   through   *1966 1972 1989*
8   ruin—]   ruin,—   *1966 1972 1989*
9   securely,]   securely   *1989*
11   Mother's]   mother's   *1966 1972*
12   murder—]   murder;—   *1966 1972*
                  murder,—   *1989*

13 hour]   hour,   *1886 1927*/III

14 sweetly,]   swiftly,   *1886*

    swiftly]   sweetly,   *1886*

    arriving]   arriving,   *1886 1927*/III

15 Darkness,]   darkness,   *1886 1927*/III *1966 1972*|

    desolation]   desolation,   *1886 1927*/III

16 unresisted.]   unresisted,—   *1966 1972 1989*

17 Then]   Then,   *1966 1972*

    mid]   'mid   *1966 1972*

    anguish]   anguish,   *1966 1972*

18 virtue]   Virtue   *1966 1972*

    Heaven]   heaven,   *1966 1972*

                    Heaven,   *1989*

19 day star]   day-star   *1966 1972 1989*

Passion | (to the   [Esd #4]

Text collated with *1966, 1972,* and *1989.*

Title.   Passion]   Passion: *1989*

          (to the]   TO THE [ ]   *1966*

                    To the [ ]   *1972*

                    To the [Woody Nightshade]   *1989*

1   Fair]   FAIR   *1972*

4   there]   there,   *1989*

7   Doth]   Dost   *1989*

8   Ah! no.]   Ah, no!   *1966 1972*

11   tyrant]   tyrant,   *1966 1972*

13   No—thou]   No,—thou   *1966 1972*

    mayst]   may'st   *1966 1972*

    body,]   body: *1966 1972*

14   soul;]   soul,—   *1966 1972*

15   nigh.]   nigh!   *1966 1972*

17   hind]   hind,   *omnia*

21   sword]   sword,   *1966 1972*

22   blood]   blood,   *1966 1972*

23   shews]   shows   *omnia*

25   courage!]   courage?   *omnia*

26   Ah]   Ah,   *1966 1972*

    else]   Else,   *1966 1972*

    bane]   bane,   *1966 1972*

31   fire]   fire,   *1966 1972*

32   glows,]   glows: *1966 1972*
36   virtue's]   Virtue's   *1966 1972*
37   Falshood's]   Falsehood's   *omnia*
38   soul]   soul,   *1966 1972*
40   fast!]   fast,—   *1966 1972*
              fast—   *1989*
41   great,]   great   *1989*
43   streams,]   streams   *1989*
45   heart!]   heart,—   *1966 1972*
              heart—   *1989*
47   Heaven-directed]   heaven-directed   *1966 1972*
      flight]   flight,   *omnia*
48   wouldst]   would'st   *1966 1972*

To Harriet ("Never, O never, Shall yonder Sun")   *[Esd #5]*

Text collated with *1966, 1972,* and *1989.*

Title.   Harriet]   HARRIET [SHELLEY]   *1966*
                Harriet [*Shelley*]   *1972*
1   Never, O]   NEVER, oh,   *1972*
      O]   oh,   *1966*
      never,]   never   *1989*
      Sun]   sun   *1972*
2   Thro']   Through   *omnia*
      diffuse]   diffuse,   *1966 1972*
4   thee;]   thee!—   *1966 1972*
              thee,   *1989*
7   again]   again,   *1966 1972*
10   untrue—fair]   untrue, fair   *omnia*
11   O Ever]   Oh! ever,   *1966 1972*
      Ever]   ever   *1989*
      life]   life,   *1966 1972*
13   gleam]   gleam,   *1966 1972*
14   within.]   within,   *1966 1972*
              within;   *1989*
16   fire]   fire,   *1966 1972*
17   shed]   shed,   *omnia*
20   die]   die,   *omnia*
      lived]   lived,   *omnia*

Text collated with *1911, 1966, 1972,* and *1989.*

Title.   Vice]   Vice: *1989*
1   Whilst]   WHILST   *1911 1972*
     Monarchs]   monarchs   *omnia*
2   groans]   groans,   *omnia*
3   wealth,]   wealth   *omnia*
4   their]   its   *omnia*
     o'erflow,]   o'erflow,—   *omnia*
5   thrones]   thrones,   *omnia*
6   Famine]   famine   *1989*
7   slavery]   Slavery   *1911 1966 1972*
     with]   wields   *omnia*
     iron]   iron,   *1911 1966 1972*
8   Stained in]   Red with   *omnia*
9   war's]   War's   *1911 1966 1972*
     environ]   environ,   *omnia*
10   roar,]   roar,—   *1911 1966 1972*
11   Falshood]   Falsehood   *omnia*
     stand]   stand,   *omnia*
Speaker.   Falshood]   FALSEHOOD   *1911 1966 1989*
                      Falsehood   *1972*
13   fare]   fare,   *1911 1966 1972*
14   toild]   toiled   *omnia*
     bestow—]   bestow;   *omnia*
17   And]   And,   *omnia*
     done]   done,   *1911 1966 1972*
18   compare]   compare,   *omnia*
     pride]   pride,   *omnia*
     me—]   me?   *1911 1989*
19   I,]   Me,   *1966 1972*
     career]   career,   *1911 1966 1972*
     thro']   through   *omnia*
     year]   year,   *1911 1966 1972*
20   marked]   tracked   *omnia*
     ruin]   despair   *omnia*
     misery?]   agony   *1911*
                 agony?   *1966 1972*
                 agony.   *1989*

Speaker. Falshood] FALSEHOOD *1911 1966 1989*
                    Falsehood *1972*
21 done! I've] done!——I have *1911*
                    done!—I have *1966 1972 1989*
22 Truth's] truth's *1989*
    form] form, *omnia*
24 Worn] Borne *omnia*
    charm.] charm: *omnia*
25 dungeon floor] dungeon-floor *omnia*
26 dauntless] fearless *omnia*
28 rent] rent, *omnia*
29 gave . . .] gave. . . . *1911 1966 1972*
30 blood. No] blood!——No *1911*
                    blood!—No *1966 1972*
                    blood!—no *1989*
    more. This] more!—this *1911 1966 1972*
                    more—this *1989*
31 tho'] though *omnia*
32 grave . . .] grave. *omnia*
34 mask] robe *omnia*
    Heaven,] heaven, *1989*
37 know] know, *omnia*
    toil] toil, *omnia*
38 noisome] loathsome *omnia*
    while] while, *omnia*
39 Heaven,] heaven *1989*
40 MONARCHY] MONARCHY, *omnia*
    or] and *omnia*
    MURDER] MURDER, *1911 1966 1972*
    given,] given; *omnia*
44 Falshood,] Falshood! *omnia*
    had] hadst *omnia*
45 But] Yet *omnia*
    dispute . . . we] dispute?—we *omnia*
    tend] tend, *omnia*
46 Fraternal] Fraternal, *omnia*
    end.] end; *omnia*
47 feet] feet, *1911*
48 fears] fears, *omnia*
    labours] labours, *1911 1966 1972*
Speaker. Falshood] FALSEHOOD *1911 1966 1989*
                    Falsehood *1972*

49   daughter]   daughter,   *omnia*
        RELIGION]   Religion,   *omnia*
        Earth.]   earth: *1911 1966 1972*
                    earth;   *1989*
50   its sweetest buds]   Reason's babes   *omnia*
        birth]   birth;   *omnia*
51   Reason's]   their mother's   *omnia*
        severe]   severe,—   *omnia*
52   fear]   fear,   *omnia*
53   den—]   den. . . .   *1911 1966 1972*
                    den . . .   *1989*
54   men]   men,   *omnia*
55   And]   And,   *1911 1966 1972*
        eye]   eye,   *1911 1966 1972*
56   Earth]   earth   *omnia*
        frightfully.]   frightfully: *omnia*
57   deathy]   dreadful   *omnia*
58   air.]   air: *omnia*
60   many mingling]   many-mingling   *omnia*
62   Victory!]   victory!—   *omnia*
64   noonday]   noon-day   *1966 1972 1989*
        sun]   sun,   *1911*
65   carnage smoke]   carnage-smoke   *omnia*
        won;]   won: *omnia*
66   Murder,]   murder,   *1911 1989*
        Hell]   hell   *1911 1989*
        Power]   power   *1911 1989*
67   sated]   glutted   *omnia*
        joyous]   glorious   *omnia*
68   fate]   Fate   *1911 1966 1972*
        stampt]   stamped   *omnia*
69   his]   her   *omnia*
        security.]   security. . . .   *omnia*
                    security . . .   *1989*
70   Wretch]   wretch   *omnia*
71   rise;]   rise.   *1966 1972 1989*
73   Nation's]   nation's   *omnia*
        miseries,]   miseries;   *omnia*
74   Whilst]   While   *omnia*
        even him]   even him   *1911*
        defiled,]   *defiled,*   *1911*

75   extacies]   ecstasies   *omnia*
     smiled . . . .]   smiled: *omnia*
76   theirs!!—but]   theirs,—but   *omnia*
     deed:]   deed!   *omnia*
77   meed.]   meed—   *omnia*
78   bleed;]   bleed.   *omnia*
79   think]   dream   *omnia*
80   air,]   air: *omnia*
81   tyrants]   tyrants,   *omnia*
     thorn]   thorn,   *omnia*
82   in their dreams]   with the thoughts   *omnia*
     fame]   fame,   *omnia*
84   morn.]   morn: *omnia*
85   all.]   all;   *omnia*
     Without]   without   *omnia*
     aid,]   aid   *omnia*
87   deathbed]   death-bed   *omnia*
Speaker. Falshood]   FALSEHOOD   *1911 1966*
                       Falsehood   *1972*
                       omitted   *1989*
89   well.—The]   well:—the   *omnia*
     ours,]   ours;   *omnia*
92   Sun.]   sun.   *omnia*
93   honors]   honours   *omnia*
94   milkwhite]   milk-white   *omnia*
     winding sheet:]   winding-sheet: *omnia*
95   joy,]   hope,   *omnia*
97   curse]   curse,   *omnia*
101   smile]   smile,   *1911 1966 1972*
102   toil.]   toil;   *omnia*
103   And]   And,   *omnia*
      Brother!]   brother,   *omnia*
      Whether]   whether   *omnia*
105   boots.—thy]   boots: thy   *omnia*
      pain]   pain,   *omnia*
106   aid]   aid,   *omnia*
      vain,]   vain;   *omnia*
108   Heaven's]   heaven's   *1989*
      palace gate.]   palace-gate.   *1911*

*To the Emperors of Russia and Austria | who eyed the battle of
Austerlitz from the heights whilst Buonaparte was active in the
thickest of the fight   [Esd #7]*

Text collated with *1966, 1972, 1989,* and *2002.*

Title.   Buonaparte]   BUONAPARTE   *1966*
     fight]   fight.   *1989*
1   Coward]   COWARD   *1972*
     who]   who,   *1966 1972*
2   below]   below,   *1966 1972*
4   brow,]   brow,—   *1966 1972*
6   Thro']   Through   *omnia*
     sleep?]   sleep.   *2002*
7   deep]   deep,   *2002*
11   ye]   Ye   *1966 1972*
     still,]   still—   *1966 1972*
           still.   *1989*
12   bud]   bud,   *1966 1972 2002*
13   kill]   kill,   *1966 1972 1989*
16   hear]   heard   *2002*
     death-shots]   death shots   *2002*
     fly,]   fly   *1966 1972 2002*
17   And]   And,   *1966 1972*
     Victory]   victory   *1966 1972*
18   good,]   good   *1989 2002*
20   game,]   game   *2002*
     lost,]   lost   *2002*
25   Equalizing]   equalizing   *1966 1972 1989*
26   Abase]   Exalt   *1966 1972*
     exalt]   abase   *1966 1972*
     low,]   low   *1966 1972 2002*
27   And]   And,   *1966 1972*
     shock]   shock,   *1966 1972*
28   wield,]   wield,—   *1966 1972*
           wield   *2002*
32   Heath,]   heath,   *1966 1972*
           heath—   *1989*
33   where]   when   *1972 1989 2002*
35   Kings!]   Kings?   *1966 1972 1989*
38   beneath:]   beneath,   *1966 1972 1989*
41   secure.]   secure,—   *1966 1972*

42 Thou] Thou,   *1966 1972 2002*
   Northern] northern   *1966 1972*
   chief,] chief   *1989*
43 Austria, calm] Austria,—calm   *1966 1972*
   fears.] fears!   *1966 1972*
44 you:] you!   *1966 1972*
            you.   *1989 2002*
47 gay] gay,   *1966 1972*
48 woe] woe,   *1966 1972 1989*

To November   *[Esd #8]*

Text collated with *1966, 1972,* and *1989.*

1 month] MONTH   *1972*
   gloom] gloom,   *omnia*
2 beneath,] beneath,—   *1966 1972*
4 draws] draw   *1966*
6 thine.] thine!   *1966 1972*
7 obscurest] obscure'st   *1966 1972*
                  obscur'st   *1989*
10 tomb.] tomb,—   *1966 1972*
                  tomb;   *1989*
11 Yes!] Yes,   *1966 1972*
   tho'] though   *omnia*
   flee] flee,   *1966 1972*
12 me.] me!   *1966 1972*
13 storms,] storms;   *1966 1972*
15 And] And,   *1966 1972*
   Heaven] heaven   *1989*
   deforms] deforms,   *1966 1972*
16 care,] care;   *1966 1972*
19 May.] May;   *omnia*
   The] the   *omnia*
   Month] month   *1966 1972*
   Love] love   *1966 1972*
22 measure,] measure;   *1966 1972*
25 here—come!] here—come,   *1966 1972*
26 warms.] warms!   *1966 1972*
                  warms;   *1989*
27 Month!] month,   *1966 1972*
28 charms] charms,   *1989*

29 And] And, *1966 1972*
    nothing's] nothing 's *1966*
    done] done, *1966 1972*
30 won.] won! *1966 1972*

Written on a beautiful day in Spring   [Esd #9]

Text collated with *1966, 1972,* and *1989.*

1   In] In *1972*
4   satiation's] Satiation's *1966 1972*
5   When] When, *1966 1972*
6   around, the] around—the *omnia*
    Earth] Earth, *omnia*
7   birth,] birth— *omnia*
8   its] it[s] *1972*
    brings] brings, *omnia*
9   recurs—] recurs;— *1966 1972*
                recurs, *1989*
11 stirs,] stirs *1966 1972*
12 And] And, *1966 1972*
13 driven,] driven *1989*
14 eye,] eye *1966 1972*
15 And] And, *1966 1972*
    thro'] through *omnia*
    wide] wide, *1966 1972*
16 die.] die, *omnia*
17 warms] warms, *omnia*

On leaving London for Wales.   [Esd #10]

Text collated with *1886, 1892W, 1927/*III, *1966, 1970* (lines 19–45, 55–63), *1972,* and *1989.*

Title. Wales.] Wales *1966 1972 1989*
                WALES *1892W 1927/*III *1970*
1   Thou] Thou *1972*
    city! where] city!—where *1966 1972*
4   Courage] courage *1966 1972 1989*
    died,] died! *1966 1972*
6   contain] contain!— *1966 1972*
                contain, *1989*

7   extremes]   extremes,   *1966 1972*
    wide]   wide,   *1966 1972*
8   brain,]   brain   *1966 1972 1989*
9   pain.]   pain!   *1966 1972*
10   free]   full   *1966 1972 1989*
13   depart,]   depart;   *1966 1972*
Stanza marker.   *none*]   1   *1927*/III
19   Hail]   HAIL   *1892W 1927*/III *1970*
    Cambria,]   Cambria!   *1886 1892W 1927*/III *1970*
20   feel]   feel,   *1886 1892W 1927*/III *1966 1970 1972*
21   behind]   behind,   *1886 1892W 1927*/III *1966 1970 1972*
22   steel!]   steel;   *1886 1892W 1927*/III *1970*
                steel!—   *1966 1972*
                steel.   *1989*
23   True!]   True   *1886 1892W 1927*/III *1966 1970 1972*
    Mountain]   mountain   *1886 1892W 1966 1970 1972*
24   bring,]   bring!—   *1966 1972*
26   ever-sacred]   ever sacred   *1886 1892W 1927*/III *1966 1970 1972*
27   worldly]   wordly   *1966 1972*
    witnessing.]   witnessing!   *1966 1972*
Stanza marker.   *none*]   2   *1927*/III
28   soul]   soul,   *1886 1892W 1966 1970 1972 1989*
    resigned]   resigned,   *omnia*
30   freeborn]   free-born   *1966 1972*
33   sleep,]   sleep   *1927*/III *1989*
    unhonouring]   unhonoring   *1892W*
35   hall]   hall,   *1886 1892W 1927*/III *1966 1970 1972*
36   Tyranny]   Tyranny,   *1966 1970 1972*
    high-raised]   high raisèd   *1886*
                high raised   *1892W 1927*/III *1989*
                high raised,   *1966 1970 1972*
    over]   on   *1886 1892W 1927*/III *1970*
Stanza marker.   *none*]   3   *1927*/III
37   Cambria!]   Cambria,   *1966 1972*
38   shield,]   shield;   *1886 1892W 1927*/III *1970*
                shield!—   *1966 1972*
40   yield.]   yield!   *1966 1972*
41   me!]   me   *1966 1972*
42   hurled,]   hurled—   *1966 1972*
44   unfurled—]   unfurled,   *1886 1892W 1927*/III *1966 1970 1972*
                unfurled   *1989*

45   world.]   world!   *1966 1972*
                    line break followed by series of dots   *1886 1892W 1970*

46   my]   My   *1966 1972*

47   away]   away,   *1966 1972 1989*

49   day]   day,   *1966 1972*

51   succeed;]   succeed,   *1966 1972*

52   reason's]   Reason's   *1966 1972*
      obey.]   obey: *1966 1972*

53   tyrant's]   tyrants'   *1989*
      murderer's]   murderers'   *1989*
      meed,]   meed,—   *1966 1972*

54   Conscience]   conscience   *1966 1972*

Stanza marker.   *none*]   4   *1927*/III

55   Cambria!]   Cambria,   *omnia*
      thought;]   thought,   *1989*

56   between,]   between   *1989*

58   scene.]   scene;   *1886 1892W 1927*/III *1966 1970 1972*

59   forever]   for ever   *1886 1927*/III

60   forever]   for ever   *1886 1927*/III

61   linger,]   linger   *1886 1892W 1927*/III *1970*
      pale]   pale,   *1886 1927*/III
      lean.]   lean;   *1886 1892W 1927*/III *1966 1970 1972*

62   poor;]   poor,   *1886*
                    poor,—   *1892W 1966 1970 1972*
                    poor: *1989*

64   the]   The   *1966 1972*

65   air]   air,   *1966 1972 1989*

66   light:]   light;   *1966 1972*

68   woe,]   woe   *1966 1972*
      fear,]   fear   *1966 1972*

69   soul,]   soul   *1966 1972*

70   despotism]   despotism,   *1966 1972*

72   passion's]   Passion's   *1966 1972*
      nor]   not   *1966*
      interest's]   Interest's   *1966 1972*

A winter's day   [Esd #11]

Text collated with *1966, 1972,* and *1989.*

1   O!]   O   *1966 1972 1989*

wintry]   WINTRY   *1972*
day!]   day,   *1966 1972*
spring]   Spring   *1966 1972*
2   year—]   year,   *1966 1972 1989*
4   And]   And,   *1966 1972*
cascade's]   cascades   *1966 1972*
murmuring]   murmuring,   *1966 1972*
7   Thro']   Through   *omnia*
atmosphere:]   atmosphere!—   *1966 1972*
atmosphere,—   *1989*
8   o]   O   *omnia*
year!]   year,   *1966 1972*
9   premature,]   premature,—   *1966 1972*
10   incompleted]   uncompleted   *1966 1972*
day]   day?   *1966 1972*
15   Genius's]   Genius'   *1966 1972*
matin bloom,]   matin-bloom,—   *1966 1972*
19   time]   Time   *1966 1972*
21   dream]   dream,   *1966 1972*
25   gone]   gone,   *1966 1972*
26   And]   [And   *1966 1972*
27   alone?]   alone]?   *1966 1972*
30   wreathe]   wreath   *omnia*

To Liberty   *[Esd #12]*

Text collated with *1886* (lines 26–30), *1927*/III (lines 26–30), *1966*, *1972*, and *1989*.

1   O]   Oh,   *1966*
Oh,   *1972*
2   perish;]   perish!—   *1966 1972*
perish,   *1989*
4   cherish]   cherish!   *1966 1972*
cherish,   *1989*
6   high,—]   high,   *1966 1972*
high   *1989*
7   cry—]   cry   *1966 1972 1989*
8   And]   And,   *1966 1972*
9   lone]   lone,   *1966 1972 1989*
12   not]   not?   *1966 1972*
16   free]   pure   *1989*
17   control—]   control,   *1966 1972 1989*

19 Palace] palace *1966 1972*

20 true?] true. *1989*

22 scorning,] scorning: *1966 1972*

24 warning:] warning,— *1966 1972*
          warning; *1989*

25 Revenge!] revenge! *1966 1972*
    stanza break added *1989*

26 And] AND *1927/*III

27 grave] grave, *omnia*

28 Whilst] Whilst, *1966 1972*
    throne] throne, *1966 1972*

30 change.] change— *1886 1927/*III
          change! *1966 1972*

31 Monarch! sure] Monarch!—sure *1966 1972*

33 Conscienceless] conscienceless *omnia*

34 thou!—] thou?— *1966 1972 1989*

35 prison house] prison-house *1966 1972*

37 man] Man *1966 1972*
    built,] built,— *1966 1972*

39 flow] flow, *1966 1972*

40 sky.] sky! *1966 1972*

41 fall . . . . . .] fall— *1966 1972*
          fall . . . *1989*

42 And] And, *1966 1972*
    Monarchs!] Monarchs, *1966 1972*
    ye!] ye, *1989*

44 royalty] royalty! *1966 1972*
          royalty, *1989*

45 arise] arise, *1966 1972*

49 dream] dream, *1966 1972*

On Robert Emmet's tomb   *[Esd #13]*

Text collated with *1886* (lines 21–28), *1892W* (lines 21–28), *1927/*III (lines
21–28), *1966, 1970* (lines 21–28), *1972,* and *1989.*

Title. tomb] Grave *1886*
          GRAVE *1892W 1970*

1 May] MAY *1972*
    Winter] winter *1966 1972*

2 thine;] thine! *1966 1972*

4 shrine.] shrine! *1966 1972*
          shrine; *1989*

5   slave]   slave,   *1966 1972*

6   repose,]   repose!—   *1966 1972*

9   marked]   marked,   *1966 1972*

    among]   among,   *1966 1972 1989*

10   lay]   lay,   *1966 1972 1989*

11   long]   long,   *1966 1972*

12   And]   <And   *1966 1972*

    passed]   passèd   *1989*

    away.]   away.>   *1966 1972*

13   pause]   pause,   *1989*

14   heart:]   heart?—   *1966 1972*

19   dearly loved]   dearly-loved   *1966 1972*

Stanza marker.   *none*]   VI   *1892W 1927*/III *1970*

22   fame]   fame,   *omnia*

23   caresst,]   carest,   *1886 1927*/III

                caressed,   *1892W 1966 1970 1972 1989*

Stanza marker.   *none*]   VII   *1892W 1927*/III *1970*

25   When]   "When   *1886 1892W*

    storm cloud]   storm-cloud   *omnia*

    daybeam]   day-beam   *1886 1892W 1927*/III *1970*

26   lifespring]   life-spring   *1892W 1927*/III *1966 1970 1972 1989*

    shine—]   shine;   *omnia*

27   groan,]   groan   *1966 1972 1989*

28   thro']   through   *1886 1892W 1966 1970 1972 1989*

a Tale of Society as it is \ from facts 1811   [Esd #14]

Text collated with *1870, 1876, 1892W, 1927*/III, *1927*/VIII, *1966, 1970* (lines 1–79), *1972,* and *1989.*

Title.   a . . . 1811]   MOTHER AND SON.   *1870 1876*

                MOTHER AND SON   *1927*/VIII

    is]   IS: *1927*/III *1970*

    facts]   FACTS,   *1966 1892W 1970*

            Facts,   1972

            facts,   *1989*

Stanza marker.   *none*]   I   *1870 1876 1892W 1927*/III *1927*/VIII *1970*

1   She]   SHE   *1870 1876 1892W 1927*/III *1970 1972*

    Aged]   aged   *1870 1892W 1927*/VIII *1989*

            agèd   *1876 1927*/III *1966 1970 1972*

Woman,]   woman;   *1870 1876 1892W 1927/*III *1970*
         woman,   *1927/*VIII *1966 1972 1989*

2 had]   *omitted*   *1927/*III

3 decay.]   decay.—   *1989*

4 Aged]   aged   *1870 1892W 1927/*VIII *1989*
         agèd   *1876 1927/*III *1966 1970 1972*
  Woman,]   woman;   *1870 1876 1892W 1927/*III *1927/*VIII *1966*
        1970 1972
         woman,   *1989*

5 thro']   through   *1870 1876 1892W 1927/*VIII *1966 1970 1972*
   1989
  the]   her   *1870 1876 1892W 1927/*VIII *1970*
  tears,]   tears   *1989*

6 from their beds]   into light   *1870 1876 1892W 1927/*VIII *1970*
  beds]   lids   *1927/*III
  misery,]   misery   *1989*

7 energy.]   energy.—   *1989*

9 golden]   gold-fed   *1870 1876 1892W 1927/*VIII *1970*
  luxury,]   luxury: *1870 1876 1927/*III *1927/*VIII *1970*
        luxury;   *1892W 1966 1972*

10 clearly]   dimly   *1870 1876 1892W 1927/*VIII *1970*

11 Poverty—the]   poverty, the   *1870 1876 1892W 1970*
         Poverty, the   *1927/*III *1927/*VIII *1966 1972 1989*
  stain—]   stain,   *omnia*

12 its]   the   *1966*
  depths]   depths,   *1870 1876 1892W 1927/*III *1927/*VIII *1970*
Stanza marker.   *none*]   II   *1870 1876 1892W 1927/*III *1927/*VIII *1970*

14 infirmity]   infirmity,   *1870 1876 1892W 1927/*III *1927/*VIII *1970*

15 from]   to   *1870 1876 1892W 1927/*III *1927/*VIII *1970*
  lifescenes,]   life-scenes;   *1870 1876 1892W 1927/*III *1966 1970*
         1972
        life scenes;   *1927/*VIII
        life-scenes,   *1989*
  die]   die,   *1870 1876 1892W 1927/*III *1927/*VIII *1966 1970 1972*

16 fate]   Fate   *1966 1972*
  tie]   tie,   *1870 1876 1892W 1927/*III *1927/*VIII *1966 1970 1972*

17 Not]   Would   *1870 1876 1892W 1927/*III *1970*
        [Tha]t   *1927/*VIII
  wish,]   wish   *1966 1972*

18 But]   But,   *1870 1876 1892W 1927/*III *1927/*VIII *1970*
  her]   the   *1870 1876 1892W 1927/*VIII *1970*
  Child]   child   *omnia*

19   tyrant's]   his cursed   *1870 1876 1892W 1970*
                        tyrants'   *1927*/III
                        his curst   *1927*/VIII *1966 1972*
     wield,]   wield—   *1870 1876 1892W 1927*/III *1970*
20   will, become]   will—become   *1870 1876 1892W 1927*/III *1970*
21   battle field,]   battlefield—   *1870 1927*/III *1970*
                        battle field—   *1876 1927*/VIII
                        battle-field—   *1892W*
                        battlefield,   *1966 1972 1989*
22   sting,]   sting;   *1870 1876 1892W 1927*/III *1927*/VIII *1970*
23   past]   passed   *1870 1876 1892W 1927*/III *1927*/VIII *1966 1970*
                1972
     would]   w[oul]d   *1927*/VIII
Stanza marker.   *none*]   III   *1870 1876 1892W 1927*/III *1927*/VIII *1970*
25   solitude:]   solitude.   *omnia*
26   mightst]   might'st   *1966 1972*
     desart]   forest   *1870 1876 1892W 1927*/III *1927*/VIII *1966 1970*
                1972
                desert   *1989*
27   wood;]   wood.   *1870 1876 1892W 1927*/III *1927*/VIII *1970*
28   human,]   human   *1966 1972 1989*
     mightst]   might'st   *1966 1972*
     grieve.]   feel.   *1870 1876 1927*/VIII
30   supply;]   supply.   *1870 1876 1892W 1927*/III *1927*/VIII *1970*
                        supply,   *1966 1972*
32   eye:]   eye;   *1966 1972*
33   Season's]   season's   *1870 1876 1892W 1927*/III *1927*/VIII *1966*
                1970 1972
                        seasons'   *1989*
     felt,]   felt.   *1870 1876 1892W 1927*/III *1927*/VIII *1970*
                felt;   *1966 1972*
34   yearned]   groans,   *1870 1876 1892W 1927*/VIII *1970*
                        yearned,   *1927*/III *1966 1972*
     her]   yet her   *1870 1876 1892W 1927*/VIII *1970*
     sad course]   race   *1870 1876 1892W 1927*/VIII *1970*
     run,]   run—   *1966 1972 1989*
35   hope]   hope: *1870 1876 1892W 1927*/III *1927*/VIII *1970*
     was, once]   was—once   *omnia*
     son.]   Son.   *1927*/VIII
Stanza marker.   *none*]   IV   *1870 1876 1892W 1927*/III *1927*/VIII *1970*
37   Heaven]   heaven.—   *1870 1876*
                        heaven   *1892W*
                        Heaven.   *1927*/VIII

to those on Earth that live.]   *omitted*   *1870 1876 1927*/VIII
Earth]   earth   *1892W 1970*

38   moor . . . .]   moor.   *1870 1876 1892W 1927*/III *1927*/VIII *1966*
                         1970 1972
                  moor . . .   *1989*
     'twas]   'Twas   *1870 1876 1892W 1927*/III *1927*/VIII *1966 1970*
                         1972

39   grieve—]   grieve: *1870 1876 1927*/III *1927*/VIII *1966 1970 1972*
                         1989
                  grieve;   *1892W*

40   here . . . now]   there; now   *1870 1876 1892W*
                         here; now   *1927*/III *1927*/VIII *1970*
                         here—now   *1966 1972*
     far.]   far!   *1927*/VIII

41   freshness]   sweetness   *1870 1876 1892W 1927*/VIII *1970*

42   weary]   aged   *1870 1892W 1927*/VIII
                  agèd   *1876 1970*

43   tear;]   tear: *1870 1876 1927*/III *1927*/VIII *1970 1989*

44   sting:]   sting.   *1870 1876 1892W 1927*/III *1966 1970 1972 1989*
                  sting!   *1927*/VIII

45   aged]   agèd   *1876 1927*/III *1966 1970 1972*
     year,]   year   *omnia*

46   comfort . . . .]   comfort.   *1870 1876 1892W 1927*/III *1927*/VIII
                         1966 1970 1972
                  comfort . . .   *1989*
     she]   She   *1870 1876 1892W 1927*/III *1927*/VIII *1966 1970*
                         1972
     supprest]   suppressed   *1870 1876 1892W 1966 1970 1972*
                         1989

47   sigh, and]   sigh—and,   *1870 1892W 1927*/VIII
                  sigh—and   *1876 1927*/III *1970*
                  sigh and,   *1966 1972*
     round clasp'd]   round, clasped   *1870 1876 1892W 1927*/III
                         1927/VIII *1970*
                  round . . . clasped   *1966 1972*
                  round clasped   *1989*
     breast.]   breast!   *1870 1876 1892W 1927*/III *1927*/VIII *1966 1970*
                         1972

Stanza marker.   *none*]   V   *1870 1876 1892W 1927*/III *1927*/VIII *1970*

48   And]   And,   *1870 1876 1892W 1927*/III *1927*/VIII *1970*
     tho']   though   *1870 1876 1892W 1966 1970 1972 1989*

49   despots]   tyrants   *1870 1876 1892W 1927/VIII 1970*
     victims]   Victims   *1927/VIII*
     wreak—]   wreak,   *omnia*
50   Tho']   Though   *1870 1876 1892W 1966 1970 1972 1989*
     eyeball,]   eyeballs   *1870 1876 1892W 1970*
                  eyeball   *1927/III 1927/VIII 1966 1972 1989*
     cheek,]   cheek   *omnia*
51   slavery,]   slavery's   *1870 1876 1892W 1927/III 1970*
     violence]   violence,   *1927/VIII*
     speak—]   speak,   *omnia*
52   aged]   agèd   *1876 1927/III 1966 1970 1972*
     Woman's]   woman's   *omnia*
     glow;]   glow.   *1870 1876 1892W 1927/III 1970*
                  glow!   *1927/VIII*
                  glow: *1966 1972*
53   reillumed]   re-illumed   *1927/III 1966 1970 1972*
55   O!]   Oh   *1870 1876 1927/VIII*
             Oh,   *1892W 1927/III 1970*
             O   *1966 1972*
56   Fancy's]   fancy's   *1870 1876 1892W*
     dauntless]   wildest   *1870 1876 1892W 1927/VIII 1970*
57   O!]   Oh   *1870 1876*
             Oh,   *1892W 1927/III 1970*
             O   *1927/VIII 1966 1972*
     foundst]   found'st   *1870 1876 1892W 1927/VIII*
58   Prince!]   Prince   *1870 1876 1892W 1927/III 1927/VIII 1970*
                  Prince,   *1966 1972*
     swell upon]   pride thee on   *1870 1876 1892W 1927/VIII 1970*
     sway,]   sway,—   *1966 1972*
59   thou]   *thou*   *1870 1876 1892W 1927/III 1970*
     canst]   cans't   *1966*
     love,]   love   *1966 1972 1989*
     they!]   they.   *1927/VIII 1989*
Stanza marker.   none]   VI   *1870 1876 1892W 1927/III 1927/VIII
                  1970*
60   tyrant's]   country's   *1870 1876 1892W 1927/III 1927/VIII 1970*
61   battle,]   battle;   *1870 1876 1892W 1927/III 1927/VIII 1970*
62   That]   Which   *1870 1876 1892W 1927/VIII 1970*
     soul]   soul,   *1927/III*
63   bowl]   bowl,   *1870 1876 1892W 1927/III 1927/VIII 1966 1970
                  1972*
64   wrought.]   brought.   *1870 1876 1892W 1927/III 1927/VIII
                  1970*

67 For her did earn]   Did earn for her   *1870 1876 1892W 1927/*VIII
                        1970

    honesty]   honesty,   *1870 1876 1892W 1927/*III *1927/*VIII *1966
                1970 1972

69 poverty]   poverty;   *1870 1876 1892W 1927/*III *1927/*VIII *1970*
                poverty,—   *1966 1972*
                poverty,   *1989*

70 power]   Power,   *1870 1876 1892W 1927/*III *1927/*VIII *1966 1970*
                1972
                power,   *1989*
    this, her]   her this   *1870 1876 1892W 1927/*VIII *1970*
                this her   *1927/*III *1966 1972 1989*

Stanza marker.   *none*]   VII   *1870 1876 1892W 1927/*III *1927/*VIII
                1970

72 charity's]   Charity's   *1966 1972*
73 pair,]   pair;   *1870 1876 1892W 1927/*III *1966 1970 1972*
                Pair;   *1927/*VIII

74 would perish rather than]   *set in italic*   *1927/*VIII
    would]   *w[oul]d*   *1927/*VIII
    bear]   *bear*   *1927/*VIII

75 The law's stern]   *set in italic*   *1927/*VIII
    slavery]   slavery,   *1870 1876 1892W 1927/*III *1970*
                slavery,   *1927/*VIII
    and the insolent stare]   *set in italic*   *1927/*VIII

76 soul—]   soul,   *1989*
78 men]   men,   *1870 1876 1927/*III *1927/*VIII *1970*
    boys]   boys,   *1870 1876 1927/*VIII
79 misery . . .]   misery.   *1870 1876 1892W 1927/*III *1927/*VIII *1966*
                1970 1972
80 Oh!]   Oh,   *1966 1972*
81 die.]   die,—   *1966 1972 1989*
83 live.]   live!   *1966 1972*
86 pain]   pain,   *1966 1972 1989*
87 again,]   again.   *1966 1972*
93 crumbs]   crumbs,   *1989*
    share]   share,   *1966 1972*
94 prayer:]   prayer;   *1966 1972*
                prayer.   *1989*
95 thus. Thou]   thus—thou   *1966 1972*
                thus, thou   *1989*

die.]   die: *1966 1972*
              die;   *1989*
96   them.]   them,   *1966 1972 1989*
     The]   the   *1966 1972 1989*
     tyrant,]   tyrant   *1966 1972 1989*
     man,]   man   *1966 1972 1989*
97   Youth's]   youth's   *1966 1972 1989*
98   are]   is   *1966 1972*
     enjoyed—]   enjoyed,—   *1966 1972*
                   enjoyed,   *1989*
100   destroyd,]   destroyed   *1966 1972*
                    destroyed,   *1989*
101   shorn,]   shorn?—   *1966 1972*
                   shorn   *1989*
103   blow,]   blow,—   *1966 1972*
104   soul]   soul,   *1966 1972*
     Heaven]   heaven   *1966 1972*
     arrive—]   arrive,   *1966 1972 1989*
105   low,]   low?—   *1966 1972*
109   Seest]   See'st   *1966 1972*
     oziers]   osiers   *1966 1972 1989*
110   dead.]   dead?   *1966 1972 1989*
111   There]   There,   *1966 1972*
     sped]   sped,   *1966 1972*
112   aged]   agèd   *1966 1972*
114   and]   And   *1966 1972*
     there]   there,   *1966 1972*
     eve]   eve,   *1966 1972*
119   And]   And,   *1966 1972*
     tho']   though   *1966 1972 1989*
     prayer]   prayer,   *1966 1972*

The solitary   1810   *[Esd #15]*

Text collated with *1870, 1876, 1886* (lines 7–9), *1892W, 1927*/III, *1966,
1970, 1972,* and *1989.*

Title.   Solitary]   SOLITARY.   *1870 1876*
        1810]   *omitted*   *1870 1876 1892W 1970 1989*
Stanza marker.   *none*]   I   *1876 1892W 1927*/III *1970*
1   Darest]   DAR'ST   *1870 1876 1892W 1927*/III *1970*
              Dare'st   *1966*
              DARE'ST   *1972*

this]   the   *1870 1876 1892W 1927/*III *1970*

2   thing,]   thing?   *1870 1876 1892W 1927/*III *1966 1970 1972*

3   spring]   spring,   *1870 1876 1892W 1927/*III *1966 1970 1972 1989*

4   none?—in]   none; in   *1870 1876 1892W 1927/*III *1970*

    solitude,]   solitude   *1966 1972 1989*

5   desart]   desert   *1870 1876 1892W 1927/*III *1966 1970 1972 1989*

Stanza marker.   *none*]   II   *1876 1892W 1927/*III *1970*

7   swarth]   swart   *1870 1876 1892W 1927/*III *1970*

    Grove]   grove,   *omnia*

8   lean]   lean,   *omnia*

    brothers']   brother's   *1876 1892W 1927/*III *1970*

9   fate]   fate.   *1886*

10   love.]   love: *1870 1876 1927/*III *1966 1970 1972 1989*

11   remove—]   remove,   *1870 1876 1892W 1927/*III *1966 1970 1972*
       1989

12   killing,]   killing   *1870 1876*

Stanza marker.   *none*]   III   *1876 1892W 1927/*III *1970*

13   smiles . . . 'tis]   smiles—'tis   *1870 1876 1892W 1927/*III *1966 1970*
       1972

14   speaks . . . the]   speaks—the   *1870 1876 1892W 1927/*III *1966*
       1970 1972

15   bowl;]   bowl,—   *1870 1876 1892W 1927/*III *1966 1970 1972*
      bowl,   *1989*

16   longs altho']   longs—although   *1870 1876 1892W 1970*
         longs—altho'   *1927/*III
         longs, although   *1966 1972 1989*

    fears to]   fears—to   *1870 1876 1892W 1927/*III *1970*
       fears, to   *1966 1972 1989*

    die.]   die;   *1870 1876 1892W 1927/*III *1966 1970 1972 1989*

18   Life's]   life's   *1870 1876 1892W 1927/*III *1966 1970 1972*

Dateline.   *none*]   1810.   *1870*

The Monarch's funeral | An Anticipation | *1810*   [Esd #16]

Text collated with *1966, 1972,* and *1989.*

Title.   funeral]   FUNERAL   *1966*
          Funeral   *1972*
          funeral: *1989*
     1810]   *omitted*   *1989*

1   The]   THE   *1972*

2   glow]   glow,   *1966 1972*

5   sight]   sight,—   *1966 1972*
6   funeral]   funeral,   *omnia*
8   pall;]   pall!—   *1966 1972*
9   Arches]   arches   *omnia*
    shew]   show   *omnia*
12   displayed;]   displayed!—   *1966 1972*
14   brood,]   brood,—   *1966 1972*
15   tho']   though   *omnia*
16   multitude]   multitude!—   *1966 1972*
                   multidude;   *1989*
20   away.]   away!   *1966 1972*
21   slain,]   slain   *1966 1972*
22   isle]   isle,   *1966 1972*
24   pile?]   pile?—   *1989*
26   sing]   sing,   *1966 1972*
30   thence]   thence,   *omnia*
31   Dotard]   dotard   *omnia*
32   monarch's]   Monarch's   *1966 1972*
     impotence!]   impotence?   *omnia*
33   —Yet,]   —Yet   *1966 1972*
                   —Yes,   *1989*
38   poor]   poor,   *1966 1972*
43   Who]   Who,   *omnia*
     death]   death,   *omnia*
45   restore! . . .] restore,   *1966 1972*
     Pride,]   Pride!—   *1966 1972*
50   vext]   vexed   *1989*
51   Earthworms]   earthworms   *omnia*
     rest,]   rest,—   *1966 1972*
                   rest—   *1989*
52   feel . . . . and]   feel—and   *1966 1972*
                   feel . . . and   *1989*
     next.]   next!   *1966 1972*
54   fail—]   fail,—   *1966 1972*
                   fail,   *1989*
56   gale.]   gale!   *1966 1972*
                   gale: *1989*
57   dross,]   dross   *omnia*
     King,]   *King*   *omnia*
58   Earth]   earth   *omnia*
     supplies,]   supplies,—   *1966 1972*
                   supplies   *1989*
60   lies:]   lies;   *omnia*

65   Sun]   sun   *1966 1972*

   forever]   for ever   *1966 1972*

67   bourn]   bourne   *1966 1972*

73   Ah!]   Ah,   *1966 1972*

   no—'tis]   no! 'Tis   *1966 1972*

                 no. 'Tis   *1989*

   woe:]   woe,—   *1966 1972*

           woe;   *1989*

75   *People,*]   People   *1966 1972 1989*

76   Majesty.]   Majesty!   *1966 1972*

To the Republicans of North America   [Esd #17]

Text collated with *1870, 1876, 1886* (lines 21–22), *1892W, 1927/*III,
*1927/*VIII, *1966, 1970* (lines 1–30, 41–50), *1972,* and *1989.*

Title.   To . . . America]   THE MEXICAN REVOLUTION.   *1870 1876*
                 1886
             *omitted   1927/*VIII

Stanza marker.   *none*]   I   *1870 1876 1892W 1927/*III *1927/*VIII *1970*

1   Brothers!]   BROTHERS!   *1870 1876 1892W* 1927/III *1970 1972*
   me]   me,   *1927/*VIII

2   roar,]   roar: *1870 1876 1892W 1927/*III *1927/*VIII *1970*

4   the]   thy   *1870 1876 1892W 1927/*III *1927/*VIII *1970*

5   banner]   banners   *1870 1876 1892W 1927/*III *1927/*VIII *1970*
   wave,]   wave,—   *1870 1876 1892W 1927/*III *1966 1970 1972*

7   by]   in   *1870 1876 1892W 1927/*VIII *1970*
   grave,]   grave,—   *1870 1876 1892W 1966 1970 1972*
             grave   *1927/*VIII

8   gore,]   gore,—   *1870 1876 1892W 1966 1970 1972*
             gore   *1927/*III

9   patriot's]   warrior's   *1870 1876 1892W 1927/*VIII *1970*

10   "Liberty"]   "Liberty   *1870 1876 1892W 1927/*VIII *1966 1970 1972*
             Liberty   *1927/*III
   in]   or   *1870 1876 1892W 1927/*III *1927/*VIII *1970*
   death.]   death!"   *1870 1876 1892W 1966 1970 1972*
             "death!"   *1927/*III
             death."   *1927/*VIII

Stanza marker.   *none*]   II   *1870 1876 1892W 1927/*III *1927/*VIII *1970*

11   let]   Let   *1870 1876 1892W 1927/*III *1966 1970 1972*
   slave]   slave,   *1870 1876 1892W 1927/*III *1927/*VIII *1970*

12   corruption's]   Corruption's   *1870 1876 1892W 1927/*VIII *1966*
             1970 1972
   throne]   throne,   *1870 1876 1892W 1927/*III *1927/*VIII *1970*

13 man] man, *1870 1876 1892W 1927/VIII 1966 1970 1972 1989*
14 groan!] groan; *1870 1876 1892W 1970*
            groan: *1927/VIII*
            groan!— *1966 1972*
15 Let] And *1870 1876 1892W 1927/III 1927/VIII 1970*
    glow] glow, *1870 1876 1892W 1927/III 1927/VIII 1970*
16 woe] woe, *1870 1876 1892W 1927/III 1927/VIII 1970*
17 blow,] blow— *1870 1876 1892W 1927/VIII 1970*
18 peep] peep, *1870 1876 1892W 1927/III 1927/VIII 1970*
    gone,] gone; *1870 1876 1892W 1927/VIII*
            gone *1927/III 1970*
            gone!— *1966 1972*
19 Whilst] Whilst, *1870 1876 1892W 1927/III 1927/VIII 1966 1970*
            1972
    misery's] Misery's *1927/VIII*
    risen] risen, *1870 1876 1892W 1927/III 1927/VIII 1966 1970*
            1972
20 Captive's] captive's *1870 1876 1892W 1966 1970 1972*
            Captive *1927/III*
Stanza marker. *none*] III *1870 1876 1892W 1927/III 1927/VIII 1970*
22 Thro'] Through *1870 1876 1886 1892W 1966 1970 1972 1989*
            Thro *1927/VIII*
    ring] ring, *1870 1876 1892W 1927/III 1927/VIII 1966 1970 1972*
            ring. *1886*
24 welcoming.] welcoming! *1870 1876 1892W 1927/VIII 1966 1970*
            1972
            welcoming— *1927/III*
            welcoming, *1989*
25 And] And, *1892W 1927/III 1966 1970 1972*
    o!] O *1870 1876 1892W 1927/III 1966 1970 1972*
        Oh *1927/VIII*
        O! *1989*
    Ocean-deep] Ocean deep, *1870 1876 1892W 1970*
                Ocean—deep, *1927/III*
                ocean deep, *1927/VIII*
                Ocean-deep, *1966 1972*
26 Whose] Thou whose *1870 1876 1892W 1927/VIII 1970*
    eternal] foamy *1870 1876 1892W 1927/VIII 1970*
28 some] a *1870 1876 1892W 1927/III 1927/VIII 1970*
    King,] king, *1870 1876 1892W 1927/VIII 1966 1970 1972*
            King. *1927/III*
29 winds] wings *1927/III*

30   freedom's]   Freedom's   *1870 1876 1892W 1927/*III *1927/*VIII *1966
                    1970 1972
     rest.]   rest!   *1870 1876 1892W 1927/*VIII *1966 1970 1972*
31   start:]   start,   *1966 1972*
                    start;   *1989*
34   Frenzy,]   Frenzy   *1966 1972*
     speak . . . .]   speak;   *1966 1972*
                    speak . . . *1989*
35   fertilize]   fertilise   *1966 1972 1989*
36   new bursting]   new-bursting   *1966 1972*
     Liberty—]   Liberty,—   *1966 1972*
                    Liberty;   *1989*
39   tyrant-brood]   tyrant-brood,   *1966 1972*
                    tyrant brood   *1989*
40   Peace]   peace   *1966 1972*
Stanza marker.   *none*]   IV   *1870 1876 1892W 1927/*III *1927/*VIII *1970*
41   Can]   Ere   *1870 1876*
     daystar]   day-star   *1927/*VIII
     love]   love,   *1870 1876 1892W 1927/*III *1927/*VIII *1970*
44   Such a desolated]   The fabric of a ruined   *1870 1876 1892W*
                    *1927/*VIII *1970*
     world? . . .]   world—   *1870 1876 1927/*VIII
                    world?   *1892W 1927/*III *1970*
                    world?—   *1966 1972*
45   Never!]   Never   *1870 1876 1892W 1927/*III *1970*
     but]   but,   *1966 1972*
     driven]   driven,   *1966 1972*
47   death]   Death   *1927/*VIII
     Heaven—]   heaven!   *1870 1876 1892W*
                    Heaven!   *1927/*III *1927/*VIII *1970*
                    Heaven,   *1966 1972 1989*
48   Then]   There,   *1870 1876 1892W 1927/*VIII *1970*
                    There   *1927/*III
                    Then,   *1966 1972*
     speechless horror]   desolation   *1870 1876 1892W 1927/*VIII *1970*
     hurled]   hurled,   *1870 1876 1892W 1927/*III *1927/*VIII *1966 1970*
                    1972
49   Earth]   love   *1870 1876 1892W 1927/*VIII *1970*
                    earth   *1927/*III
     balm the]   watch thy   *1870 1876 1892W 1927/*III *1927/*VIII *1970*
     bier]   bier,   *1870 1876 1892W 1927/*III *1927/*VIII *1970*

50   Of . . . a]   Balm thee with its dying   *1870 1876 1892 W 1927/III*
                  1927/VIII 1970
Dateline.   *none*]   14 *February* 1812.   *1870*

Written at Cwm Ellan   1811   [Esd #18]

Text collated with *1966, 1972,* and *1989.*

Title.   Ellan]   ELAN   *1966*
                  Elan   1972
                  Elan   *1989*
         1811]   *omitted   1966 1972 1989*
1   When]   WHEN   *1972*
    home,]   home   *1966 1972*
    reposes,]   reposes   *1989*
3   closes]   closes,   *1966 1972*
4   sombre, shrouded]   sombre-shrouded   *1989*
    twilight]   Twilight   *1966 1972*
    Night.]   Night,—   *1966 1972*
                  Night,   *1989*
5   lightness]   lightness,   *1966 1972*
6   daybeam's]   day-beam's   *1966*
    brightness:]   brightness,—   *omnia*
7   tho']   though   *omnia*
    day]   Day   *1966 1972*
10   'mid]   mid   *1989*
     wak'd]   waked   *omnia*
     lay]   lay,   *omnia*
11   numbers,]   numbers   *1989*
12   silence,]   Silence,   *1966 1972*
                  silence   *1989*
     fancy's]   Fancy's   *1966 1972*
     throne,]   throne   *1989*
13   it, hark!]   it—hark!   *1966 1972*
     for]   For   *1966 1972*
     pouring]   pouring,   *omnia*
14   beneath,]   beneath   *1966 1972*
     Ellan]   Elan   *omnia*
     roaring]   roaring,   *1966 1972*
15   Mid tongued]   'Mid tangèd   *1966 1972*
                  Mid tangled   *1989*
     woods,]   woods   *1966 1972*
     soaring]   soaring,   *omnia*

To Death   [Esd #19]

Text collated with *1858* (lines 1–48), *1870* (lines 1–48), *1876* (lines 1–48), *1892W* (lines 1–48), *1927*/III (lines 1–48), *1966, 1970* (lines 1–48), *1972*, and *1989*.

Title.   To Death]   *omitted   1858*
DEATH VANQUISHED.   *1870 1876*

1   Death,]   Death!   *1858 1966 1989*
     DEATH!   *1870 1876 1892W 1927*/III *1970 1972*
 victory!]   victory?   *1858 1876 1892W 1927*/III *1966 1970 1972 1989*
    victory?—   *1870*

2   die,]   die,—   *1870*
    die?—   *1966 1972*

4   Infolds]   Enfolds   *1870 1892W 1927*/III *1966 1970 1972   1989*
 soul,]   soul.   *1858 1876*
   soul!   *1870*
   soul?   *1892W 1927*/III *1966 1970 1972*
   soul—   *1989*

5   O]   Oh,   *1858 1876*
 Death,]   Death!   *1858 1870 1876 1892W 1927*/III *1966 1970 1972*

6   when]   where   *1927*/III

7   Nations]   nations   *1858 1870 1876 1892W 1927*/III *1970*
 groan]   groan,   *1858 1870 1876 1927*/III *1970*
 Kings]   kings   *1858 1870 1876 1892W 1927*/III *1970*
 bliss,]   bliss.   *1858 1870 1876*

8   Death,]   Death!   *1858 1870 1876 1892W 1927*/III *1970*
 couldst]   canst   *1858 1870 1876 1892W 1970*
   could'st   *1927*/III *1966*
 this,—]   this?   *1858 1876*
   this!   *1870*
   this—   *1892W 1927*/III *1970*
   this!—   *1966 1972*

9   When]   When,   *1966 1972*
No break between lines 9 and 10 in 1858 1870 1876 1892W 1927/III *1970*

10   Of]   of   *1858 1870 1876 1892W 1927*/III *1970*
 power]   power,   *1966 1972*

11   Thy slave,]   His blow   *1858 1870 1876 1892W 1970*
 slave,]   slave   *1927*/III
 murderer,]   murders   *1858 1870 1876*
    murderer   *1892W 1927*/III *1970*
 gave]   gave,   *1858 1876 1892W 1927*/III *1970*

12   Mid]   'Mid   *1858 1870 1876 1966 1972*

nature's]   Nature's   *1870 1892W 1927*/III *1966 1970 1972*
cries]   cries,   *1870 1927*/III *1966 1972*
No break between lines 12 and 13 in 1858 1870 1876 1892W 1927/III *1970*
13   The]   the   *1858 1870 1876 1892W 1927*/III *1970*
14   myriads]   millions   *1858 1870 1876 1892W 1970*
grave,—]   grave;   *1858 1876 1970*
       grave—   *1892W*
       grave!   *1927*/III
15   tyrant,]   tyrant   *1858 1870 1876 1892W 1927*/III
       Tyrant   *1970*
sensualism's]   desolation's   *1858 1870 1876 1892W*
       Desolation's   *1970*
slave,]   slave;   *1858 1876 1927*/III *1970*
16   Freedom's]   freedom's   *1870*
life-blood]   lifeblood   *1870*
shrine?]   shrine;   *1858 1876 1927*/III *1970*
       shrine,—   *1870 1892W 1966 1972 1989*
17   despot,]   tyrant,   *1858 1876*
       Tyrant   *1870*
       Tyrant,   *1892W 1970*
couldst]   could'st   *1966*
Victory]   victory   *1858 1870 1876 1892W 1966 1970 1972 1989*
mine?—]   mine?   *1858 1870 1876 1892W 1927*/III *1966 1970 1972*
       mine.   *1989*
18   know,]   know   *1858 1870 1876 1892W 1927*/III *1966 1970 1972*
void]   void,   *1858 1876 1989*
19   Earthly]   earthly   *1927*/III *1966 1972 1989*
Earthly hopes and fears]   mortals baubles sunk   *1858 1876*
       mortals' baubles, sunk,   *1870*
       mortals' baubles sunk   *1892W 1970*
decay,]   decay,—   *1870*
       decay;   *1892W 1927*/III *1970*
20   every sense]   everything,   *1858 1876 1892W 1970*
       everything   *1870*
       every sense,   *1927*/III
Love,]   love,   *1870*
destroyed,]   destroyed   *1858 1892W 1927*/III *1966 1970 1972*
21   clay,—]   clay.   *1858 1876*
       clay;   *1870*
       clay—   *1966 1972 1989*
22   ambition's]   Ambition's   *1858 1870 1876 1892W 1927*/III *1966*
       1970 1972
crown!]   crown,   *omnia*

23   its]   her   *1858 1870 1876 1892W 1970*
     sceptered]   sceptred   *1870 1892W 1927/*III *1966 1970 1972
                   1989*
     sway;]   sway,—   *1966 1972*
               sway,   *1989*
24   fade]   fades   *1858 1876 1892W 1927/*III *1970*
     frown]   frown.   *1858 1876 1927/*III *1970*
               frown;   *1870 1892W*
               frown,   *1966 1972 1989*
25   death's]   Death's   *1858 1870 1876 1892W 1927/*III *1966 1970 1972*
     vault,]   vault   *omnia*
     decay]   decay,   *1858 1876 1892W 1927/*III *1970*
26   Which]   That   *1858 1870 1876 1892W 1970*
     virtue's]   Virtue's   *omnia*
     beam;]   beam—   *1858 1876 1927/*III *1966 1970 1972*
               beam,   *1989*
               stanza break added   *1858*
27   subside]   subside,   *1858 1876 1892W 1927/*III *1970*
29   stream ....]   stream.   *1858 1876*
                    stream;—   *1870 1892W 1927/*III *1970*
                    stream,—   *1966 1972*
                    stream . . .   *1989*
30   Yes!]   Yes;   *1927/*III
     this]   *this*   *1870*
     were]   is   *1858 1870 1876 1892W 1927/*III *1970*
     Victory!]   victory!   *omnia*
31   some]   yon   *1858 1870 1876 1892W 1970*
     rock]   rock,   *1858 1876 1892W 1927/*III *1970*
     sky]   sky,   *1858 1876 1892W 1927/*III *1970*
32   limbs]   limbs,   *1858 1876 1892W 1927/*III *1970*
     when]   where   *1927/*III
     fled,]   fled;   *1858 1876 1892W 1927/*III *1970*
               fled,—   *1870 1966 1972*
33   passions]   Passions   *1870*
     prey,]   prey,—   *1870*
               prey;   *1892W*
34   chambers]   palace   *1858 1870 1876 1892W 1927/*III *1970*
     dead!—]   dead!   *1858 1870 1876 1892W 1927/*III *1970*
35   Oh!]   Oh,   *1966 1972*
     Wretch]   King,   *1858 1876 1892W 1970*
               king   *1870*
               wretch,   *1927/*III *1966 1972*
               wretch   *1989*

36   say,]   say   *1870*

37   bud]   buds   *1870*

     blown,]   blown   *1870 1966 1972 1989*

38   on Death's last pang]   in this cold bed,   *1858 1876 1892W 1927/*III
                              1970
                         in this cold bed   *1870*

     groan.]   groan!   *1858 1870 1876 1892W 1927/*III *1966 1970 1972*

39   Kings]   proud,   *1858 1870 1876 1892W 1970*
                Kings,   *1927/*III *1966 1972*

     luxury]   grandeur   *1858 1870 1876 1892W 1970*

     woe]   woe,   *1858 1876*

40   That]   Which   *1858 1870 1876 1892W 1970*

     thy]   the   *1858 1870 1876 1892W 1927/*III *1966 1970 1972*

     state:]   state,   *1858 1876*
                State!   *1870*
                state!   *1892W 1927/*III *1970*
                state!—   *1966 1972*

41   Ye]   You   *1858 1870 1876 1892W 1970*
            Ye,   *1989*

     curses]   curses,   *1966 1972*

     curses deep tho']   plainings faint and   *1858 1870 1876 1892W*
                          plainings, faint and   *1970*

     tho']   though   *1966 1972 1989*

     low]   low,   *1858 1876 1892W 1927/*III *1966 1970 1972*

42   misery's]   Misery's   *1870 1927/*III *1966 1970 1972*

     breast]   soul   *1858 1870 1876 1892W 1970*

     flow]   flow,   *1858 1876 1892W 1927/*III *1966 1970 1972*

43   fate.—]   fate.   *1858 1870 1876 1892W 1927/*III *1966 1970 1972*
                *stanza break added 1858 1876 1892W 1927/*III *1970*

44   Tremble,]   Tremble   *1927/*III

     conquerors]   conquerors,   *1858 1870 1876 1892W 1927/*III *1966*
                    1970 1972

45   War-fiend]   war-fiend   *1858 1876 1892W 1927/*III *1970 1989*
                   War-Fiend   *1966 1972*

     Riots]   riots   *omnia*

     an]   a   *1927/*III

     an happy]   a peaceful   *1858 1870 1876 1892W 1970*

     land—]   land.   *1858 1876*
               land!   *1870 1892W 1927/*III *1966 1970 1972*
               land: *1989*

46   Ye,]   You   *1858 1870 1876 1892W 1970*
            Ye   *1927/*III *1966 1972*

     desolation's]   Desolation's   *1927/*III *1966 1970 1972*

47   victory]   Victory   *1858 1876 1927*/III   *1970*
48   Death's]   that   *1858 1870 1876 1892*W   *1970*
Dateline.   *none*]   *Oxford,* 1810.   *1870*
49   Hell]   well   *1972*
50   memory]   Memory   *1966 1972*
     gives]   gives,   *1966 1972 1989*
51   Tho']   Though   *1966 1972 1989*
     selfsame]   self-same   *1966 1972*
52   receives . . .]   receives.   *1966 1972*
53   grave—no]   grave,—no   *1966 1972*
54   wreathes]   wreaths   *1966 1972 1989*
55   brow.]   brow,—   *1966 1972*
59   thunder cloud,]   thunder-cloud,—   *1966 1972*
                         thunder cloud   *1989*
60   roar,]   roar   *1966 1972*
61   But]   But,   *1966 1972*
     past]   past,   *1966 1972*
63   lie]   lie,   *1966 1972*
64   power's]   Power's   *1966 1972*
     or]   nor   *1966 1972*
     fame's]   Fame's   *1966 1972*
65   decay.]   decay,—   *1966 1972*
                decay—   *1989*
66   triumph,]   triumph   *1966 1972*
     defeat;]   defeat,   *1966 1972*
     joy,]   joy   *1966 1972*
     shame.]   shame,   *1966 1972*
67   Death,]   Death!   *1966 1972*
     thee—]   thee,—   *1966 1972*
                thee: *1989*
68   Victory.]   Victory!   *1966 1972*

"Dark Spirit of the desart rude"   *[Esd #20]*

Text collated with *1966, 1972,* and *1989.*

1   Dark]   DARK   *1972*
    desart]   desert   *omnia*
    rude]   rude,   *1966 1972*
4   below]   below,   *1966 1972*

6   Whilst]   Whilst,   *1966 1972*
    still,]   still   *omnia*
7   rill;]   rill,—   *1966 1972*
9   time,]   Time,   *1966 1972*
10   Ellan's]   Elan's   *omnia*
    course,]   course   *1966 1972*
11   force—]   force,—   *1966 1972*
                    force,   *1989*
13   oak]   oak—   *1966 1972*
14   scowl]   scowl,   *1989*
15   its]   <its>   *1966 1972*
21   storm:]   storm,—   *1966 1972*
                    storm;   *1989*
23   shot,]   shot   *omnia*
    thro']   through   *omnia*
    air]   air,   *omnia*
26   gloom?..]   gloom?—   *1966 1972*
                    gloom? . . .   *1989*
27   Nature's]   nature's   *1989*
    tomb]   tomb,   *1966 1972*
29   gone!—]   gone!   *1966 1972*
30   Violets]   violets   *omnia*
33   *stanza break added 1972*
34   here,]   here   *omnia*
35   Thou]   Thou,   *1966 1972*
    Oak,]   oak,   *1966 1972*
    scathed]   scathèd   *omnia*
    head]   head,   *1966*
36   trembled,]   tremblèd   *1966*
                        tremblèd,   *1972 1989*
39   spread—]   spread,   *1966 1972*
                    spread,—   *1989*
40   Thou]   thou   *1966 1972*
41   thing,]   thing   *1966*
42   shrub]   shrub,   *1989*
    grass]   grass,   *1989*
43   King]   King,   *omnia*
44   And]   And,   *1966 1972*
    power]   power,   *1966 1972*
45   Suck]   <Suck>,   *1966*
                    <Suck>   *1972*
    race]   race,   *1966 1972*
    away]   away,   *1966 1972*

46   *And yet upon the spoil*]   And yet upon the spoil   *1972*
       decay.]   <decay>.   *1966*
                    [decay].   *1972*

             "The pale, the cold and the moony smile"   [Esd #21]

Text collated with *1886* (lines 1–6), *1966*, *1972*, and *1989*.

Title.   *no title*]   [REALITY]   *1966*
                        Reality   *1972*
Epigraph.   *none*]   There is no work, nor device, nor knowledge, nor
                        wisdom, in the grave, whither thou goest. *Ecclesiastes*
                        ix. 10   *1966 1972*
1   The]   THE   *1972*
     cold]   cold,   *omnia*
2   stormy]   starless   *1966 1972 1989*
3   seagirt]   sea-girt   *omnia*
     isle]   isle,   *1966 1972 1989*
4   Till]   Ere   *1966 1972 1989*
     light]   light,   *1966 1972 1989*
5   taper]   flame   *omnia*
7   Oh! Man,]   O man!   *1966 1972 1989*
     with]   in   *1966 1972 1989*
8   Thro']   Through   *1966 1972 1989*
     long, long night]   stormy shades   *1966 1972 1989*
     doubtful]   wordly   *1966*
                  worldly   *1972 1989*
10   subside]   sleep   *1966 1972 1989*
      calm]   light   *1966 1972 1989*
      eternal]   a wondrous   *1966 1972 1989*
      day:]   day,   *1966 1972 1989*
11   For . . . know]   Where hell and heaven shall leave thee free   *1966*
                        1972 1989
12   Is . . . woe.]   To the universe of destiny.   *1966 1972 1989*
13   All . . . that]   This world is the nurse of all   *1966 1972 1989*
      know—]   know,   *1966 1972 1989*
14   All . . . that]   This world is the mother of all   *1966 1972 1989*
      feel;]   feel,   *1966 1972 1989*
16   by nervestrings]   with nerves   *1966 1972 1989*
      steel,]   steel;   *1966 1972 1989*
17   we]   or   *1966 1972 1989*
      feel]   feel,   *1966 1972 1989*

and we]   or   *1966 1972 1989*
see]   see,   *1966 1972 1989*
18   fleet by]   pass   *1966 1972 1989*
19   there]   there,   *1966 1972*
20   body]   frame   *1966 1972 1989*
21   Tho']   Though   *1966 1972 1989*
23   bright]   great   *1966 1972 1989*
24   gradual path]   boundless realm   *1966 1972 1989*
25   the]   a   *1966 1972 1989*
tales]   tale   *1966 1972 1989*
Death?]   death?   *1966 1972 1989*
27   beings]   shadows   *1966 1972 1989*
28   wide-stretching realms]   wide-winding caves   *1966 1972 1989*
tomb]   tomb?   *1966 1972 1989*
29   And]   Or   *1966 1972 1989*

"Death-spurning rocks!"   [Esd #22]

Text collated with *1966*, *1972*, and *1989*.

1   Death-spurning]   Death-spurning   *1972*
here]   Here   *1966 1972*
2   height]   height,   *1966 1972*
3   climb,]   climb   *1966 1972*
4   night.]   night,—   *1966 1972*
5   Each]   each   *1989*
6   storm]   storm,   *1966 1972*
7   Whilst]   Whilst,   *1966 1972*
there]   there,   *1966 1972*
aged]   agèd   *1966 1972*
Oak]   oak   *1966 1972*
8   stroke.]   stroke;   *1966 1972*
9   fast,]   fast   *1966 1972*
away—]   away,—   *1966 1972*
away,   *1989*
10   Oak]   oak   *1966 1972*
decay.]   decay!   *1966 1972*
13   spot.]   spot . . . *1966 1972*
14   memory]   Memory   *1966 1972*
lay—]   lay,—   *1966 1972*
lay,   *1989*
15   fear]   fear,   *1966 1972*
16   tear—]   tear;   *1966 1972*

20   blood.]   blood!   *1966 1972*

21   moor—]   moor.   *1966 1972*
               moor;   *1989*

22   shew:]   show,—   *1966 1972*
               show,   *1989*

24   woe]   woe.   *omnia*

25   turn]   [turn]   *1966 1972*
     back.]   back?   *omnia*
     The]   the   *1989*

26   thro']   through   *omnia*
     air]   air,   *1966 1972*
               air;   *1989*

27   gulph]   gulf   *omnia*
     yawns.]   yawns,   *1966 1972*
               yawns   *1989*

28   daystar]   day-star   *1966 1972*
     dawns.]   dawns,—   *1966 1972*
               dawns.—   *1989*

29   Chance! remit]   Chance!—Remit   *1966 1972*
     misery—]   misery,—   *1966 1972*
               misery.   *1989*

30   burns!—why]   burns!—Why   *1966 1972*

The Tombs   *[Esd #23]*

Text collated with *1886* (lines 14–15), *1966*, *1972*, and *1989*.

1   These]   THESE   *1972*
     Death,]   Death   *1989*

2   Kingdom]   kingdom   *1966 1972*
     see.]   see!—   *1966 1972*
               see: *1989*

7   sculls]   skulls   *1966 1972 1989*

8   loathsomeness,]   loathsomeness   *1989*

9   flesh]   flesh,   *1966 1972*

10   Say——"thou]   Say: "Thou   *1966 1972*
               Say—"thou   *1989*
     life!"]   life"?   *1966 1972*
               life!   *1989*

12   soul—]   soul,   *1966 1972 1989*

14   truth]   truth,   *1966 1972*

15   devotedness—]   devotedness;   *1966 1972*
               devotedness,   *1886 1989*

20   world:]   world,—   *1966 1972*
                 world"?   *1989*
21   That]   <That   *1966 1972*
                 —That   *1989*
22   victim-patriot's]   victim patriot's   *1966 1972*
      shone,]   shone   *1966 1972 1989*
23   land,]   land   *1966 1972 1989*
25   burn.]   burn>.   *1966*
                 burn.>   *1972*
                 burn?   *1989*
26   Ah,]   Ah   *1989*
      else]   Else,   *1966 1972*
      stand]   stand,   *1966 1972*

To Harriet   *[Esd #24]*

Text collated with *1870* (lines 5–13), *1876* (lines 5–13), *1886*, *1892W*, *1911*
(lines 58–69), *1927*/III, *1962BOAS* (lines 24–27, 29–56, 64–69), *1966*,
1970, *1972*, *1989*.

Title.   Harriet]   HARRIET [SHELLEY]   *1966*
                 Harriet [*Shelley*]   *1972*
1   It]   IT   *1892W 1927*/III *1966 1970 1972*
5   Infuses in the heaven-born soul—]   *omitted*   *1870 1876*
      Soul—O]   soul. O   *1886 1892W 1927*/III *1966 1970 1972*
      Thou]   thou   *1886 1892W 1927*/III *1966 1970 1972*
                 THOU   *1870 1876*
7   cold,]   cold   *1870 1876 1989*
8   Yet]   But   *1870 1876*
9   Time]   time,   *1870 1876*
                 time   *1886 1892W*
10   Time]   time   *1870 1876*
      more: wilt]   more,—wilt   *1870 1876*
                 more; wilt   *1886 1892W 1927*/III *1966 1970 1972*
11   eyes]   eyes,   *1870 1876*
12   Earth]   earth   *1870 1876*
      Heaven]   heaven,   *1870 1876*
                 Heaven,   *1892W 1966 1970 1972*
13   Heaven]   heaven   *1870 1876*
      Earth?—]   earth?   *1870 1876*
14   mine]   mine,   *1886 1892W 1927*/III *1966 1970 1972*
15   thro']   through   *1892W 1966 1970 1972 1989*

16   thro']   through   *1892W 1966 1970 1972 1989*

19   existence,]   existence   *1989*

20   kiss . . .]   kiss *1886 1892W 1927/*III
     oh]   O   *1886 1892W 1927/*III *1966 1970 1972*

21   Heaven]   Heaven,   *1886 1892W 1927/*III *1966 1970 1972 1989*

24   dissolve]   dissolve,   *1886 1892W 1927/*III *1962BOAS 1966 1970*
            1972 1989

25   mortal—the]   mortal! The   *1886 1892W 1927/*III *1962BOAS 1966*
            1970 1972

26   Time]   time   *1962BOAS*
     Earthly]   earthly   *1886 1892W 1927/*III *1962BOAS 1966 1970 1972*
     minds]   minds,   *1989*

27   now,]   now;   *1886 1892W 1927/*III *1966 1970 1972 1989*

28   souls]   souls,   *1927/*III
     day—]   day;   *1886 1892W 1927/*III *1966 1970 1972*
            day,   *1989*

29   dies]   dies,   *1886 1892W 1927/*III *1962BOAS 1966 1970 1972*
     arose]   arose,   *1886 1892W 1927/*III *1962BOAS 1966 1970 1972*
            1989
     Earth:]   earth.   *1886 1892W 1927/*III *1962BOAS 1966 1970 1972*
            Earth,   *1989*

30   oh]   oh,   *1886 1892W 1927/*III *1962BOAS 1966 1970 1972 1989*
     fancy's]   Fancy's   *1962BOAS 1966 1970 1972*

31   now,]   now   *1989*

32   spirit-healing.]   spirit-healing;   *1886 1892W 1927/*III *1970*
     Nor]   nor   *1886 1892W 1927/*III *1970*
            . . . nor   *1962BOAS*

33   extacies,]   extasies,   *1886 1927/*III *1962BOAS*
            ecstasies,   *1892W 1966 1970 1972 1989*

37   reason,]   reason;   *1886 1892W 1927/*III *1962BOAS 1966 1970*
            1972
     æstival]   aestival   *1962BOAS 1966 1970 1972 1989*

38   me,]   me;   *1886 1892W 1927/*III *1962BOAS 1966 1970 1972*

39   judgement's]   judgment's   *1886 1892W 1927/*III *1962BOAS 1970*
            1989

40   sweetness, all]   sweetness—all   *1966 1972*

41   heart,]   heart;   *1886 1892W 1927/*III *1962BOAS 1970*
     heart, not]   heart,—not   *1966 1972 1989*

43   assume?)]   assume?),   *1886 1892W 1927/*III *1970*
     assume?) not]   assume?),—not   *1966 1972*
            assume?)—not   *1989*

44   custom]   Custom   *1966 1970 1972*

45   us]   us,   *1886 1892W 1927/III 1962BOAS 1970*
46   As]   That,   *1966 1972*
            As,   *1989*
47   communion,]   communion   *1966 1972*
48   can we]   we can   *1966 1972*
50   hate]   hate,   *1886 1892W 1927/III 1962BOAS 1966 1970 1972*
      world]   world,   *1886 1892W 1927/III 1962BOAS 1966 1970 1972*
            1989
52   Virtue—can]   Virtue. Can   *1886 1927/III*
                  virtue. Can   *1892W 1962BOAS 1966 1970 1972*
                  Virtue?—can   *1989*
      eyes]   eyes,   *1886 1892W 1927/III 1966 1970 1972 1989*
54   purity]   purity,   *1886 1892W 1962BOAS 1966 1970 1972 1989*
56   self!]   Self!   *1966 1970 1972*
      is]   Is   *1886 1892W 1927/III 1966 1970 1972*
      is confidence]   *omitted   1962BOAS*
58   The mirror even of Truth?—]   *omitted   1911*
      Truth?—Dark]   Truth? Dark   *1886 1892W 1927/III 1966 1970 1972*
      Dark]   DARK   *1911*
      Flood]   flood   *1886 1892W 1911 1927/III 1966 1970 1972*
      Time!]   Time,   *1886 1892W 1927/III 1966 1970 1989*
59   listeth]   listeth;   *1966*
      thee.]   thee;   *1886 1892W 1927/III 1970*
            omitted   1966
      thee. I]   thee—I   *1911 1972*
60   months]   month   *1892W 1970*
61   thy]   the   *1911*
      brink]   brink,   *1892W 1966 1970 1972*
62   ken]   ken,   *1886 1892W 1927/III 1966 1970*
63   Which]   That   *1911 1972*
      feet.—The]   feet. The   *1886 1892W 1911 1966 1970 1972*
                  feet: the   *1927/III*
                  feet—the   *1989*
65   being.]   being;   *1886 1892W 1962BOAS 1966 1970*
                  being: *1911 1972*
      If]   if   *1886 1892W 1911 1962BOAS 1966 1970 1972*
      more]   more,   *1886 1892W 1911 1927/III 1962BOAS 1966 1970*
            1972
67   grey]   gray   *1892W 1962BOAS 1970 1972*
      veteran's]   veterans   *1886 1892W 1927/III*
                  veterans'   *1911*
      school]   school,   *1886 1892W 1911 1927/III 1962BOAS 1966 1970*
            1972

68   roll,]   roll   *1886 1892W 1927/*III *1962BOAS 1966 1970 1972 1989*

69   unredeemed.]   unredeemed,   *1892W 1970*

71   Devotedness]   Devotedness,   *1886 1927/*III

     Purity—]   Purity!   *1886 1892W 1927/*III *1970 1989*

72   spirit]   Spirit   *1886 1966 1970 1972*

     you.]   you!   *1966 1972*

Sonnet: To Harriet | on her birth day, August 1, 1812   *[Esd #25]*

Text collated with *1886* (lines 9–12; two versions A and B), *1892W* (lines 9–12), *1927/*III (lines 9–12), *1966*, *1972*, and *1989*.

Title.   Sonnet:]   SONNET   *1966*

                    Sonnet   *1972*

         Harriet]   HARRIET [SHELLEY]   *1966*

                    Harriet [*Shelley*]   *1972*

         birth day,]   BIRTHDAY   *1966*

                    Birthday   *1972*

                    Birthday,   *1989*

         August 1,]   1 August   *1966 1972*

                    August 1   *1989*

1   thou,]   thou   *1966 1989*

              THOU   *1972*

    smile]   smile,   *1966 1972 1989*

3   guile]   guile,   *1966 1972*

4   bring,]   bring: *1966 1972*

5   thus!]   thus,   *1966 1972*

    day,]   day—   *1989*

6   Tho']   Though   *1966 1972 1989*

    age's]   Age's   *1966 1972*

7   dyes]   dyes,   *1966 1972 1989*

8   grey,]   grey—   *1966 1972 1989*

9   Ever]   EVER   *1892W 1927/*III

    now]   now,   *1886*(B)

    glow]   glow,   *1886*(B)

10 thy]   thine   *1966 1972*

    burn.]   burn,   *1886*(A) *1892W 1927/*III *1989*

             burn;   *1886*(B)

             burn,—   *1966 1972*

12 return,]   return.   *1886 1892W 1927/*III

              return!   *1966 1972*

13 this]   this,   *1966 1972*

14 Thou]   thou   *1966 1972*

Sonnet: To a balloon, laden with <u>Knowledge</u>   [Esd #26]

Text collated with *1886, 1892W, 1927/*III, *1966, 1970, 1972, 1989,* and *2002.*

Title. Sonnet:] SONNET. *1886*
                SONNET *1892W 1927/*III *1966 1970*
                Sonnet *1972*
                Sonnet *2002*
       balloon,] BALLOON *1886 1892W 1927/*III *1966 1970*
                Balloon *1972*
       <u>Knowledge</u>] KNOWLEDGE. *1886*
                KNOWLEDGE *1892W 1927/*III *1970*

1 Bright] BRIGHT *1892W 1927/*III *1970 1972*
  thro'] through *1892W 1966 1970 1972 1989 2002*
  Even] even *omnia*
2 etherial] ethereal *1886 1892W 1927/*III
             aethereal *1966 1970 1972*
  way] way, *1886 1892W 1927/*III *1966 1970 1972*
4 Depths] depths *1886 1892W 1966 1970 1972 1989*
  Heaven,] Heaven,— *1886 1892W 1927/*III *1966 1970 1972*
             Heaven: *2002*
5 Fire] fire *1886 1892W 1966 1970 1972*
6 gloom,] gloom *2002*
7 that] that, *1966 1970 1972 1989 2002*
  unquencheable] unquenchable *1886 1892W 1927/*III
                unquenchable, *1966 1970 1972 1989*
  glow—] glow *1886 1892W 1927/*III *1966 1970 1972 1989*
8 watch light] watch-light *1886 1892W 1927/*III *1966 1970 1972*
              1989
  patriot's] Patriot's *1927/*III
  tomb,] tomb; *1886 1892W 1927/*III *1966 1970 1972*
9 opprest] oppressed *1892W 1966 1970 1972 1989*
  poor,] poor; *1886 1892W 1927/*III *1966 1970 1972*
10 spark,] spark *1927/*III
  tho'] though *1886 1892W 1966 1970 1972 1989 2002*
  on] in *1989*
11 thro'] through *1886 1892W 1966 1970 1972 1989 2002*
  tyrants'] tyrant's *omnia*
  roar,] roar; *1886 1892W 1927/*III *1966 1970 1972*
12 Earth,] Earth; *1886 1892W 1927/*III *1966 1970 1972*
13 Sun] sun *1886 1892W 1927/*III *1966 1970 1972*

which] which, *1886 1892W 1927*/III *1966 1970 1972*
scene] scene, *1886 1892W 1927*/III *1966 1970 1972*
14 truth] Truth *omnia*
Falshood] Falsehood *1886 1892W 1927*/III *1966 1970 1972*
1989

Sonnet: On launching some bottles filled with <u>Knowledge</u> into the Bristol Channel. [Esd #27]

Text collated with *1886, 1892W, 1927*/III, *1966, 1970, 1972,* and *1989.*

Title. Sonnet:] SONNET. *1886*
SONNET *1892*W *1927*/III *1966 1970*
Sonnet 1972
<u>Knowledge</u>] KNOWLEDGE *1886 1892W 1927*/III *1970*
Channel.] CHANNEL *1892W 1927*/III *1966 1970*
Channel 1972
Channel *1989*
1 Vessels] Vessels *1892W 1927*/III *1970 1972*
Heavenly] heavenly *1886 1892W 1927*/III *1966 1970 1972*
may] May *1966 1972*
3 stern] stem *omnia*
4 seas;] seas: *1989*
5 Liberty] liberty *1927*/III
6 brow,] brow *1989*
8 west] West *1966 1970 1972*
blow.] blow, *1966 1972*
10 eyebeam,] eye-beam *1886 1927*/III
eye-beam, *1892W 1966 1970 1972*
11 on] in *1886 1892W 1927*/III *1970*
light] light, *1886 1892W 1927*/III *1966 1970 1972*
12 Its] its *1892W 1927*/III *1966 1970 1972 1989*
pole] pole, *omnia*

Sonnet: On waiting for a wind to cross the Bristol Channel from Devonshire to Wales. [Esd #28]

Text collated with *1886* (lines 5–10), *1892W* (lines 5–10), *1927*/III (lines 5–10), *1966, 1970* (lines 5–10), *1972,* and *1989.*

Title. Sonnet: . . . Wales.] *omitted 1886*
FRAGMENT OF A SONNET: Farewell to
North Devon *1892W*

WRITTEN BEFORE LEAVING LYNMOTH
FOR ILFRACOMBE 1812 |
FRAGMENT   *1927/*III
FRAGMENT OF A SONNET | Farewell to
North Devon   *1970*

Sonnet:]   SONNET   *1966*
            Sonnet   1972
Wales.]   WALES   *1966*
            Wales   1972
            Wales   *1989*

1   Oh!]   Oh,   *1966*
            Oh,   *1972*
2   Come]   Come,   *1966 1972 1989*
    spirit!]   Spirit!   *1966 1972 1989*
    thro']   Through   *1966 1972*
            through   *1989*
    sweep;]   sweep: *1966 1972*
            sweep,   *1989*
4   deep.]   deep!   *1966 1972*
5   These wilds]   *omitted   1886 1892W 1970*
    wilds]   wilds,   *1966 1972*
    where]   Where   *1886 1892W 1970*
            Where   *1927/*III
    Man's]   man's   *1886 1892W 1927/*III *1970*
6   primæval]   primeval   *1886 1892W 1927/*III *1989*
            primaeval   *1966 1970 1972*
    marred]   marred,   *1886 1892W 1970*
8   (Which]   Which   *omnia*
    command)]   command;   *1886 1892W 1970*
            command; | *1927/*III
            command,   *1966 1972 1989*
9   I leave without a sigh. Ye]   *omitted   1886 1892W 1927/*III *1970*
    sigh.]   sigh;   *1966 1972*
    Ye]   ye   *1966 1972*
    mountain]   Mountain   *1886 1927/*III
            . . . mountain   *1892W 1970*
10   vales,]   vales.   *1886 1892W 1927/*III *1970*
11   smiles]   smiles,   *1966 1972 1989*
12   storm cloud]   storm-cloud   *1966 1972*
    sails—]   sails,—   *1966 1972*
            sails,   *1989*
14   fraught]   <fraught>   *1966 1972*
    purity.]   <purity>!   *1966 1972*

To Harriet   [Esd #29]

Text collated with *1966, 1972,* and *1989.*

Title.   Harriet]   HARRIET [SHELLEY]   *1966*
Harriet [Shelley]   *1972*

1   Harriet!]   Harriet!   *1972*
    dear:]   dear,—   *1966 1972*
dear,   *1989*

4   thine.]   thine: *1989*
10   Heaven,]   Heaven—   *1966 1972*
12   even,]   even—   *1966 1972*
14   Tho']   Though   *omnia*
15   light,]   light   *omnia*
    dove!]   dove,   *1966 1972*
17   care:]   care,—   *omnia*
18   Heaven,]   heaven,   *1966 1972*
    world;]   world!   *1966 1972*
20   tho']   though   *omnia*
    hurled.]   hurled: *1966 1972*
22   lover,]   lover   *1966 1972*
24   me]   me,   *1989*
26   Harriet!]   Harriet,   *1966 1972*
    too,]   too;   *1966 1972*
29   Honor,]   Honour   *1966 1972*
Honour,   *1989*

Mary to the Sea-Wind   [Esd #30]

Text collated with *1966, 1972,* and *1989.*

1   implore]   IMPLORE   *1972*
    softly swelling]   softly-swelling   *1966 1972*
    Breeze,]   breeze,   *1966 1972*
2   shore]   shore,   *omnia*
3   darkly-woven]   darkly woven   *1989*
4   him]   him,   *1966 1972*
5   Sea-Wind,]   Sea Wind,   *1989*
6   perfume.]   perfume;   *omnia*
7   wilt]   will   *1972*
    them,]   them   *1966 1972*
    yet]   yet,   *1966 1972*
    Henry's]   Henry's,   *1966 1972*

9   Summer]   summer   *1966 1972*
    inhale—]   inhale,   *1966 1972*
10   kind—thy]   kind thy   *1966*
                  kind, thy   *1972*
    breath;]   breath,   *omnia*
11   fail]   fail,   *1966 1972*
12   heath.]   heath: *1989*
13   bosom—and]   bosom—and,   *1966 1972*
    true,]   true   *1989*
14   there.]   there;   *omnia*
15   it,]   it   *1966 1972*
    Sea-Wind,]   Sea Wind,   *1989*

A retrospect of Times of Old   *[Esd #31]*

Text collated with *1966, 1972,* and *1989.*

1   The]   THE   *1972*
    tenantless . . . .]   tenantless,—   *1966 1972*
                  tenantless . . . *1989*
2   shame.]   shame!   *1966 1972*
3   Deeds]   deeds   *omnia*
    bless,]   bless,—   *1966 1972*
            bless;   *1989*
4   fame,]   fame!   *1966 1972*
            fame;   *1989*
5   gold*]   gold   *1989*
Footnote.   *Gilding]   "Gilding   *1989*
            palace]   palaces   *1966 1972*
            Persepolis—]   Persepolis.   *1966 1972*
                  Persepolis—"   *1989*
7   glow]   glow,   *1966 1972 1989*
8   mid]   'mid   *1966 1972*
    below,]   below   *1989*
11   Their]   (Their   *omnia*
    worship.]   worship,   *omnia*
    Ah]   ah,   *1966 1972*
            ah   *1989*
12   (Yet]   Yet   *omnia*
    multitude.)]   multitude!)—   *1966 1972*
                  multitude),   *1989*
13   dwells!—Where]   dwells. . . . Where   *1966 1972*
    Kings?]   Kings,   *1989*

16 kings] Kings *1966 1972*
    heroes] Heroes *1966 1972*
17 Scrolls] scrolls *omnia*
    hand,] hand *omnia*
18 were.——] were?. . . *1966*
                    were? . . . *1972*
                    were?— *1989*
19 Victory] victory *1966 1972*
    here] here, *1989*
20 Death!—Yet] Death! . . . yet *1966 1972*
                    Death!—Yet *1989*
    cry,] cry *1966 1972 1989*
21 Victory!"] victory!" *1966 1972*
22 Dream] dream *1966 1972*
    the] The *1966 1972*
23 lie . . .] lie; *1966 1972*
24 gate] gate, *omnia*
25 where] where, *1966 1972*
    towers] towers, *1966 1972*
    Simoon's] simoon's *1966 1972*
26 below] below, *omnia*
28 There] Here, *omnia*
    Royal] royal *1966 1972*
    Bloodhound] bloodhound *1966 1972*
    crept] crept, *omnia*
29 lay—] lay *omnia*
30 Which,] Which *omnia*
    memories,] memories *omnia*
    fled—] fled, *omnia*
31 slept,] slept *1966 1972*
32 And] And, *1966 1972*
33 when] when, *omnia*
    betrayed—] betrayed, *omnia*
34 day—] day, *omnia*
36 The] the *1989*
    chaste] chaste, *1966 1972*
37 blade—] blade *omnia*
38 moment!] moment *1966 1972*
    and] and, *1966 1972*
    brightness,] brightness *omnia*
    blood,] blood *1989*
39 flood.] flood! *1966 1972*

40 moon,] moon *omnia*
    shrouded.] shrouded; *1966 1972*
41 triumph;—but] triumph,—but *1966 1972*
42 fear,] fear *1966 1972*
    clouded.] clouded— *1966 1972*
                    clouded; *1989*
43 Destruction ..] Destruction, *1966 1972*
                        Destruction . . . *1989*
    Suicide ..] suicide, *1966 1972*
                    suicide . . . *1989*
    resource . . .] resource!— *1966 1972*
                    resource *1989*
44 Wider] Wide *omnia*
    torrent. The] torrent,—the *1966 1972*
45 tumultuousness . . . the] tumultuousness—the *1966 1972*
46 hoarse.] hoarse: *1966 1972*
                hoarse *1989*
47 moment!] moment, *1966 1972*
    And] and *omnia*
    dies!] dies: *1989*
    Hark] hark *1989*
    dash!*] dash! *omnia*
Footnote. *I] "I *1989*
                unendurable ..] unendurable. *1966 1972*
                        unendurable . . . *1989*
                men,] men *omnia*
                slowly] slowly, *1966 1972*
                and] & *1989*
                former.] former" *1989*
49 gone,] gone *omnia*
50 hid] hid, *omnia*
51 forever] for ever *1966 1972*
    flown.] flown.[1] *1966 1972*
52 tide:] tide, *omnia*
53 grave,] grave *1989*
    stone,] stone *1989*
55 On] In *1966 1972*
    slept! now] slept,—now *1966 1972*
    gone,—] gone *omnia*
56 Passion] Passion, *1989*
    heart] heart, *1989*
    brain] brain, *1989*
    bone!] bone. *1989*

57 bust]   bust, *1966 1972*
60 bier,]   bier,—   *1966 1972*
              bier—   *1989*
62 Gods]   gods   *1972*
    prey,]   prey,—   *1966 1972*
63 echoing]   echoed   *1989*
64 death-pangs,]   death pangs,   *1989*
66 moan—]   moan,—   *1966 1972*
67 away!]   away,   *1989*
68 Gods,]   gods,   *1966 1972*
    men,]   men   *1989*
69 antient]   ancient   *omnia*
    decay,]   decay;   *1989*
70 Heroes,]   Heroes   *1966 1972*
    Kings]   kings   *1966 1972*
              Kings,   *1989*
    woe.]   woe!   *1966 1972*
71 Pizarro come!]   Pizarro,—come!   *1966 1972*
                      Pizarro, come!   *1989*
72 Thou]   Thou,   *omnia*
    Moses!]   Moses,   *1966 1972*
    Mahommed,* leave]   Mahommed,[1]—leave   *1966 1972*
                         Mahommed, leave   *1989*
    gloom!]   gloom;   *1989*
Footnote. *To]   "To   *1989*
              Suwarroff,]   Suvoroff,   *1966 1972*
              and]   &   *1989*
              and]   &   *1989*
              day.——]   day.   *1966 1972*
                         day—"   *1989*
73 Destroyers!]   Destroyers,   *1966 1972*
    die!]   die.   *1989*
74 mould'ring]   mouldering   *omnia*
75 crimes]   crimes,   *1966 1972*
    lie.]   lie!   *1966 1972*
           lie;   *1989*
76 pass't]   pass'st   *1966 1972*
77 Where]   Where,   *1966 1972*
    pride]   pride,   *1966 1972*
79 conqueror]   conqueror,   *omnia*
80 abide,]   abide   *1989*
81 clay,]   clay,—   *1966 1972*
82 bend]   bend,   *1966 1972*

Text collated with *1966, 1972,* and *1989.*

Title.   A Fragment]   *omitted   1966*
                                      A Fragment . . . *1989*
                    Devonshire—August 1812]   August 1812   *1966*
                                                        Devonshire, August 1812   *1972*

1   Quenched]   Quenched   *1972*
      rage;]   rage: *1966 1972*
2   wave]   wave,   *1966 1972*
10   colourings]   colourings;   *1966 1972*
                                colourings,   *1989*
11   wind]   wind,   *1966 1972*
        thro']   through   *omnia*
12   Sail,]   sail,   *omnia*
        prow,]   prow   *1989*
15   O!]   Oh,   *1966 1972*
17   sorrow!]   sorrow?   *1966 1972*
19   loveliness—]   loveliness: *omnia*
23   given.]   given;   *omnia*
31   prest]   pressed,   *1966 1972*
                        pressed   *1989*
41   voyaging—]   voyaging;   *1966 1972*
                            voyaging: *1989*
45   name,]   name—   *1966 1972*
47   shares,]   shares;   *1966 1972*
50   heads;]   heads—   *omnia*
51   *stanza break*]   *omitted   1966 1972*
52   land . . . .]   land,   *1966 1972*
                        land . . . *1989*
      Sea;]   sea,—   *1966 1972*
                  Sea: *1989*
54   scene . .]   scene,   *1966 1972*
                        scene . . . *1989*
58   dream]   dream,   *1966 1972*
59   main,]   main   *1989*
62   Thro']   Through   *omnia*
      wide woven]   wide-woven   *omnia*
      many colour'd]   many-coloured   *omnia*
65   thro']   through   *omnia*
      atmosphere—]   atmosphere,—   *omnia*

67   long—]   long   *1966 1989*
                          long,   *1972*
70   they]   they,   *1966 1972*
72   Till]   Till,   *1966 1972*
       fellowship]   fellowship,   *1966 1972*
73   liberty]   liberty.   *1989*
74   undismayed, aye]   undismayed,—aye,   *1966 1972*
76   deep,]   deep;   *1966 1972*
78   mountain-wave]   mountain-wave,   *omnia*
79   tempest cloud,]   tempest-cloud   *omnia*
80   tinging]   tingeing   *1972*
84   bark:—]   bark,—   *1966 1972*
86   aid!]   aid,   *1966 1972*
87   parched]   parchèd   *omnia*
88   clime.]   clime,   *1966 1972*
90   equality,]   equality;   *1966 1972*
91   And]   And,   *1966 1972*
92   When]   Where   *1989*
       failed . . .] failed,   *1966 1972*
95   waves.]   waves;   *1989*
96   generous.]   generous,—   *1966 1972*
                          generous,   *1989*
98   smil'd]   smiled   *omnia*
99   When]   When,   *1966 1972*
       height]   height,   *1966 1972*
103   friend,]   friend   *1966 1972*
106   rage,]   rage   *1966 1972*
107   Earthly]   earthly   *1966 1972*
108   work—]   work,   *1966 1972*
109   changeless]   changeless,   *1966 1972*
       paths—*]   paths,   *1966 1972*
                          paths—   *1989*
Footnote.   *It]   "It   *1989*
                 necessity]   Necessity   *1966 1972*
                 and]   &   *1989*
                 engaging]   engaging,   *1989*
                 and]   &   *1989*
                 and]   &   *1989*
                 ill-equipped]   ill equipped   *1989*
                 trading vessels]   trading-vessels   *1966 1972*
                 possess]   posess   *1989*
                 habits]   habit   *1966*

and] & *1989*

difference.] difference." *1989*

111 blasphemy?] blasphemy?[1] *1966 1972*

115 lowering] lowering, *1966 1972*

brow] brow, *1966 1972*

116 intervals] intervals, *1989*

117 bent,] bent *1989*

122 villainy . . .] villainy. *1966 1972*

127 Kings] kings *1966 1972*

129 Yes!] Yes, *1966 1972*

life,] life *1989*

133 woman;] woman, *omnia*

136 cank'ring] cankering *1989*

137 thought] thought, *1966 1972*

140 tho'] though *omnia*

142 thriving.] thriving; *1966 1972*

thriving: *1989*

143 him,] him *1966 1972*

146 beneath,] beneath *1966 1972*

147 friends,] friends *1966 1972*

poor,] poor *1966 1972*

149 too . . .] too,— *1966 1972*

150 mould.] mould *1966 1972*

152 Passion,] Passion *1966 1972*

and] and, *1966 1972*

tho'] though *omnia*

155 past] passed *omnia*

157 wrapt] wrapped *1989*

dream.] dream— *1966 1972*

158 love,] love— *1966 1972*

159 And] And, *1966 1972*

gazed] gazèd *omnia*

160 shade,] shade *omnia*

162 dream.] dream: *1989*

167 barren] sullen *1966*

[sullen] *1972*

168 isle . . . no] isle—no *1966 1972*

egg] egg, *1966 1972*

169 sea mews] sea-mews *omnia*

170 isle . . no] isle—no *1966 1972*

isle . . . no *1989*

172 nutriment . . . .] nutriment. *1966 1972*

nutriment . . . *1989*

stanza break]   *page break*   *1989*

173   there]   then   *1989*

174   But]   But,   *1966 1972*

      nerved]   nervèd   *1989*

      tho']   though   *omnia*

176   availed . . .]   availed;   *1966 1972*

177   vanquished.]   vanquished;   *omnia*

178   breast.]   breast,—   *1966 1972*

          breast,   *1989*

179   subdued,]   subdued   *1966 1972*

181   dreaming . . . .]   dreaming;   *1966 1972*

          dreaming . . .   *1989*

183   eye,]   eye.   *1966 1972*

186   And]   And,   *1966 1972*

      malice]   malice,   *1966 1972*

189   gone.]   gone;   *1966 1972*

191   dead]   [the] dead   *1966 1972*

          [a] dead   *1989*

      frame.]   frame;   *1966 1972*

192   Victim]   victim   *1966 1972*

      head]   head;   *1966 1972*

193   insupportable]   insupportable,   *1966 1972*

194   lay,]   lay,—   *1966 1972*

195   Nature]   nature   *1966 1972*

198   him.]   him,   *1966 1972*

          him;   *1989*

199   eye . . . .]   eye,   *1966 1972*

          eye . . .   *1989*

200   lips . . .]   lips.—   *1966 1972*

204   came! . .]   came!—   *1966 1972*

          came! . . .   *1989*

205   love]   love,   *1966 1972*

206   decay]   decay,   *1966 1972*

207   rekindled]   rekindled,   *omnia*

210   Sister]   sister   *1966 1972*

211   pair,]   pair   *1966 1972*

212   He]   he,   *1966 1972*

          He,   *1989*

      soul]   soul,   *omnia*

213   *stanza break*]   *page break*   *1972*

215   the]   The   *1966 1972*

      sight!]   sight   *omnia*

218   town]   town,   *omnia*

221   here]   here,   *1966 1972*
      Town:]   town;   *1966 1972*
              Town   *1989*
223   within]   within,   *1966 1972*
225   town! it]   town?—It   *1966 1972*
226   blood.]   blood,—   *1966 1972*
227   spot.]   spot: *1966 1972*
      Should]   should   *1966 1972*
      one,]   one   *1966 1972*
229   *stanza break*]   omitted   *omnia*
230   tyrants]   tyrants,   *1966 1972*
232   far distant]   far-distant   *1966 1972*
233   quay]   quay,   *1966 1972*
235   tho']   though   *omnia*
236   murders,]   murders   *1966 1972*
237   sailor]   sailor,   *1966 1972*
      years]   years,   *omnia*
238   eyes]   eyes,   *1966 1972*
239   reposes,]   reposes   *1989*
240   joy,]   joy   *1966 1972*
      store,]   store   *1989*
241   Hard earned]   Hard-earned   *1966 1972*
243   Sea]   sea   *1966 1972*
244   quiet . . . such]   quiet,—such   *1966 1972*
246   speeds]   speeds;   *1966 1972*
                  speeds,   *1989*
247   latch . . His]   latch.—His   *1966 1972*
                  latch . . . His   *1989*
248   eagerly.—When]   eagerly,—when   *1966 1972*
249   rapture—no]   rapture. No   *1966 1972*
250   pity! unexpostulating]   pity!—Unexpostulating   *1966 1972*
      power]   Power   *1966 1972*
251   feelings . . . he]   feelings. He   *1966 1972*
      stript]   stripped   *1989*
252   master's]   masters'   *1966 1972*
253   give;]   give!   *1966 1972*
254   toys,]   toys   *1966 1972*
255   These]   (These   *1966 1972*
      gain,]   gain   *1966 1972*
      love,]   love   *omnia*
256   concealed,]   concealed)   *1966 1972*
      away;]   away,—   *1966 1972*
257   gave]   gave,   *1966 1972*

258 wore] wore, *omnia*

259 his] His *1966 1972*

260 tyrant's] tyrants' *1966 1972*

261 arm;] arm: *1966 1972*
Wife?] wife? *1966 1972*

262 Where] "Where *1966 1972*
Children?"—close] children?" Close *1966 1972*

263 town's man—"oh!] townsman: "Oh! *1966 1972*
townsman—"Oh! *1989*

264 this time] last *1966 1972*
Industry—] Industry; *omnia*

266 you—Parish] you—parish *1966 1972*

268 happiness, but] happiness,—but *1966 1972*

269 nice balanced] nice-balanced *omnia*

270 expedient] expedient, *1966 1972*

272 Earth] earth *1966 1972*

273 all.—But] all,—but *1966 1972*
all—but *1989*

275 Liberty] liberty *1966 1972*

277 selfishness.—The] selfishness,—the *1966 1972*
hills,] hills *1966 1972*

278 vallies] valleys *omnia*

279 seashore,] sea-shore, *1966 1972*

280 mountain peaks,] mountain-peaks, *1966 1972*

281 footstep . .] footstep, *omnia*
ravines] ravines, *1966 1972*

282 were,] were,— *1966 1972*

284 out . . . some] out.—Some *1966 1972*
Lord] Lord, *1966 1972*

285 pilferer,] pilferer *1966 1972*

287 heart,] heart *1966 1972*

288 *Mine*—in] *Mine,* in *1966 1972*
pride.] pride! *1966 1972*
pride; *1989*

291 cries,] cries: *1966 1972*
cries *1989*

292 them—resign] them,—resign *1966 1972*

293 Brilliant] "Brilliant *1966 1972*

294 Loaded] "Loaded *1966 1972*

295 Which] "Which *1966 1972*
bring] buy *omnia*

296 And] "And *1966 1972*
man, then] man,—then *1966 1972*

297 One] "One *1966 1972*
298 Into] "Into *1966 1972*
        misdeeds!"] misdeeds!" *omnia*

A Dialogue—1809 *[Esd #33]*

Text collated with *1858* (lines 1–10, 13–30, 33–44), *1870* (lines 1–10, 13–30, 33–44), *1876* (lines 1–10, 13–30, 33–44), *1892W* (lines 1–10, 13–30, 33–44), *1927/*III (lines 1–30, 33–44), *1966, 1970* (lines 1–10, 13–30, 33–44), *1972, 1989.*

Title. A Dialogue—1809] *omitted 1858*
                          DEATH:—A DIALOGUE. *1870*
                          DEATH: A DIALOGUE. *1876*
                          A DIALOGUE *1892W 1970*
                          A DIALOGUE | 1809 *1927/*III *1966*
                          A Dialogue | 1809 *1972*
                          A Dialogue *1989*

1 Yes!] For *1858*
          FOR *1870 1876 1892W 1970*
          YES, *1927/*III
          YES! *1972*
   drenched with] bathed in *1858 1870 1876 1892W 1970*
   brave.] brave, *1858 1876 1892W 1927/*III *1966 1970 1972 1989*
2 have sped with Love's wings] come, care-worn tenant of life, *1858
                          1876 1970*
                          come, careworn tenant of life, *1870
                          1892W*
   Love's] love's *1927/*III
   battlefield] *omitted 1858 1870 1876 1892W 1970*
          battle-fields' *1927/*III
   grave] grave, *1858 1870 1876 1892W 1927/*III *1966 1970 1972*
3 Ambition] ambition *1927/*III
   Ambition is hushed] Innocence sleeps *1858 1876 1892W 1970*
                          innocence sleeps *1870*
   neath] 'neath *1858 1870 1876 1892W 1927/*III *1966 1972*
   peacegiving] peace-giving *1858 1870 1876 1892W 1927/*III *1966
          1970 1972*
   sod] sod, *1858 1870 1876 1892W 1966 1970 1972*
4 slaves] the good *1858 1870 1876 1892W 1970*
   Tyranny's] tyranny's *1870*
   nod.] nod; *1858 1876 1892W 1966 1970 1972 1989*

5 thee,]   thee: *1870 1989*
              thee,—   *1927*/III *1966 1970 1972*

6 Victim]   Say, victim   *1858 1870 1876 1892W 1927*/III *1970*
   grief,]   grief   *1927*/III

7 Drear . . . Judge]   My mansion is damp, cold silence   *1858 1870 1876*
              1892W 1970

   damp]   cold   *1927*/III
   Judge]   judge   *1927*/III
   there]   there,   *1858 1876 1892W 1927*/III *1966 1970 1972*
              there;   *1870*

8 Who steeps]   But it lulls   *1858 1870 1876 1892W 1970*
   brands]   fiends   *1858 1870 1876 1892W 1970*
   Despair.]   despair,   *1858 1876*
              despair.   *1870*
              despair;   *1892W 1970*
              Despair;   *1927*/III *1966 1972*

9 Nor]   Not   *1858 1870 1876 1892W 1970*
   nor]   not   *1858 1870 1876 1892W 1970*
   nor]   not   *1858 1870 1876 1892W 1970*
   breath]   breath,   *1858 1870 1876 1892W 1927*/III *1970*

10 Silence]   silence   *1858 1870 1876*
    Death;]   Death.   *1858 1870 1876 1892W 1970*
              Death   *1927*/III
              Death,   *1966 1972 1989*

11 thro']   through   *1966 1972 1989*

12 tomb.]   tomb;   *1966 1972*

13 thee;]   thee,   *1858 1876 1892W*
              thee:—   *1870*
              thee,—   *1927*/III *1966 1970 1972*
              thee: *1989*

14 Victim]   victim   *1858 1870 1876 1892W 1927*/III *1966 1970 1972*
              1989

15 heavy,]   heavy;   *1858 1876 1892W 1927*/III *1970*
    repose—]   repose,   *1858 1870 1876 1927*/III *1966 1970 1972*
              1989
              repose;   *1892W*

16 arms]   cells   *1858 1870 1876 1892W 1970*
    woes,]   woes;   *1870 1892W*

17 that realm]   thy cells   *1858 1870 1876 1892W 1970*
    load]   load,   *1858 1870 1876 1892W 1927*/III *1966 1970 1972*

18 perfidy] Perfidy *1858 1876 1892W 1927/*III *1966 1970 1972*
    goad,] goad; *1858 1876*
                goad,— *1927/*III *1966 1970 1972*
19 Prejudice] prejudice *1870*
    away] away, *1858 1870 1876 1892W 1927/*III *1966 1970 1972*
20 Bigotry's] bigotry's *1870*
    prey.] prey; *1858 1876 1966 1972*
21 Death, when] Death—when *1870*
                Death: when *1966 1972*
    Empire] empire *1858 1870 1876 1892W 1966 1970 1972*
    o'er] o'er, *1858 1870 1876 1892W 1966 1970 1972*
22 futurity's] Futurity's *1858 1876 1892W 1927/*III *1966 1970 1972*
    mist-circled] mist-covered *1858 1870 1876 1892W 1927/*III *1970*
23 mortal!] Mortal! *1858 1876 1892W 1927/*III *1966 1970 1972*
24 oer] on *1858 1870 1876*
            o'er *1892W 1927/*III *1966 1970 1972 1989*
    eternity's] Eternity's *1858 1876 1892W 1927/*III *1966 1970 1972*
    vale.] vale; *1858 1876 1892W 1966 1970 1972*
            vale: *1870*
25 What . . . A] Nought waits for the good, but a *1858 1876*
                Nought waits for the good but a *1870 1892W 1970*
    thinkest] think'st *1927/*III *1966 1972*
    *Spirit] spirit *1858 1876 1892W 1927/*III *1970*
            Spirit *1870 1966 1972 1989*
    Love] Love, *1858 1876 1927/*III *1970*
            Love[1] *1966 1972*
Footnote. *The . . . law."] *omitted* *1858 1870 1876 1892W 1927/*III
                1970
            *The] "The *1989*
            Universe,] Universe *1966 1972*
            Deity.—When] Deity. When *1966 1972*
            thus,] thus: *1966 1972 1989*
            transcription,] transcription *1966 1972*
            because] because, *1966 1972*
            Happiness,] happiness, *1966 1972*
            Justice,] justice, *1966 1972 1989*
            reason] reason, *1989*
            another:] another. *1966 1972 1989*
            "Earth] . . . earth *1966 1972*
                    Earth *1989*
            "Contains] Contains *1966 1972 1989*
            and] & *1989*

cure]   cure;   *1966 1972*

"And]   And   *1966 1972 1989*

all sufficing]   all-sufficing   *1966 1972*

chastize]   chastise   *1966 1972*

"Those]   Those   *1966 1972 1989*

law."]   law . . . *1966 1972*

26   thy blest]   their blest   *1858 1876*
                            their blessed   *1870 1892W 1970*

mansions]   regions   *1858 1870 1876 1892W 1970*

above?]   above.   *1858 1876 1892W 1927/*III *1970 1989*
          above: *1870*
          above;   *1966 1972*

27   mortal!]   Mortal,   *1858 1876 1892W 1927/*III *1966 1970 1972*
              mortal,   *1870*

thro']   through   *1870 1892W 1927/*III *1966 1970 1972 1989*

sway]   sway,   *1858 1870 1876 1892W 1927/*III *1966 1970 1972*

28   clouds that]   shades which   *1858 1870 1876 1892W 1970*
              stanza break added   *1966 1972*

29   *loved?—then*]   loved?—Then   *1858 1876 1892W 1970*
              loved? Then   *1870*
              loved?—Then   *1927/*III *1966 1972*

hate]   hate,   *1858 1870 1876 1892W 1927/*III *1966 1970 1972*

30   quench]   blunt   *1858 1870 1876 1892W 1970*

fate]   fate.   *1858 1876 1892W 1927/*III *1970*
          Fate.   *1870*
          fate,   *1966 1972*

32   depart.]   depart;   *1966 1972*

33   thee;]   thee,   *1858 1876 1892W*
          thee:—   *1870*
          thee,—   *1927/*III *1966 1970 1972*
          thee: *1989*

34   Victim]   victim   *1858 1870 1876 1892W 1927/*III *1966 1970 1972*
              1989

35   Oh]   Oh!   *1858 1876 1892W 1927/*III *1970*
          Oh,   *1966 1972 1989*

slumber,]   slumber!   *1858 1870 1876 1892W 1927/*III *1966 1970*
              1972

and]   oh!   *1858 1876 1892W 1927/*III *1970*
          oh   *1870*

sweeter]   sweet is   *1858 1870 1876 1892W 1927/*III *1970*

36   day!]   day;   *1858 1876 1892W 1966 1970 1972*
          day.   *1927/*III *1989*

37   soft,]   concealed,   *1858 1870 1876 1892W 1927/*III *1970*
     persuasive,]   persuasive   *1989*
     self-interest's]   Self-interest's   *1972*
     breath]   breath,   *1858 1870 1876 1892W 1927/*III *1966 1970 1972*
38   Tho']   Though   *1870 1892W 1966 1970 1972 1989*
     Death!]   Death.   *1858 1876 1989*
                    Death   *1927/*III
39   all,]   all:—   *1870*
40   may]   might   *1858 1870 1876 1892W 1970*
     fall,]   fall;   *1870*
41   Virtue]   duty   *1858 1870 1876 1892W 1970 1989*
     tho']   though   *1870 1892W 1927/*III *1966 1970 1972 1989*
     languish]   languish,   *1966 1972 1989*
     die,]   die   *1927/*III *1989*
42   Departure]   departure   *1858 1870 1876 1892W 1966 1970 1972*
                    1989
     Virtue's]   virtue's   *1858 1870 1876*
43   Yet]   Oh,   *1858 1876 1892W*
               O   *1870 1927/*III *1970*
               Yet,   *1966 1972 1989*
     Death! oh!]   Death! oh,   *1858 1876 1892W*
                       Death! O   *1870 1927/*III *1970*
                       Death!—oh,   *1966 1972*
     friend,]   friend!   *1858 1870 1876 1892W 1927/*III *1966 1970 1972*
     shrine]   shrine,   *1858 1870 1876 1892W 1927/*III *1966 1970 1972*
               1989
44   repine.]   repine!   *1870*
                    repine   *1927/*III
Dateline.   *none*]   1810.   *1870*

1810 ("How eloquent are eyes!")   *[Esd #34]*

Text collated with *1858* (lines 33–39), *1870* (lines 1–13, 33–39), *1876*
(lines 1–13, 33–39), *1892W* (lines 1–13, 33–39), *1927/*III (lines 1–13, 33–
39), *1927/*VIII (lines 33–39), *1966, 1970* (lines 1–13, 33–39), *1972,* and
1989.

Title.   1810]   *omitted*   *1858 1927/*VIII *1989*
                  EYES.   *1870 1876*
                  EYES   *1892W*
                  EYES: A FRAGMENT | 1810   *1927/*III
                  [EYES] | 1810   *1966*

EYES: A FRAGMENT   *1970*

Eyes | 1810   *1972*

1   How]   How   *1870 1876 1892W 1927/*III *1970 1972*

2   Poet's]   poet's   *1870 1876 1892W 1970*

4   *page break*   *1927/*III *1966*
    stanza break added   *1972*

6   music's]   Music's   *1927/*III
    note]   note,   *1927/*III

7   love's]   Love's   *1927/*III *1966 1970 1972*
    fervours]   fervors   *1892W*
    float]   float,   *1927/*III

8   they]   them   *1870 1876 1892W 1927/*III *1966 1970 1972*
    bid]   bids   *1870 1876 1892W 1966 1970 1972*
    stanza break]   *omitted*   *1870 1876*

9   Love!]   Love,   *1870 1876 1892W 1966 1970 1972*
                Love   *1927/*III
    again,]   again,—   *1870 1876 1892W 1927/*III *1970*
                again!—   *1966 1972*

10   light]   lighten   *1870 1876*
     years]   years,   *1870 1876 1892W 1966 1970 1972 1989*
                years.   *1927/*III

12   Thro']   Through   *1870 1876 1892W 1966 1970 1972 1989*
     tears!]   tears.   *1870 1876 1892W 1970*
                tears   *1927/*III
     stanza break]   *page break*   *1972*

13   Love!]   Love,   *1870 1876 1892W 1927/*III *1966 1970 1972*
     again,]   again! | 1812.   *1870*
                again!   *1876 1892W 1927/*III *1970*
                again!—   *1966 1972*

14   victor]   victor,   *1966 1972*
     flies]   flies,   *1966 1972*

15   eyes,]   eyes,—   *1966 1972*

16   vain!—]   vain!   *1966 1972 1989*

17   no! arrest]   no!—Arrest   *1966 1972*
     Time,]   Time!   *1966 1972*
                Time.   *1989*

18   spurn,]   spurn;   *1966 1972 1989*

19   burn]   burn,   *1966 1972 1989*

21   Ah]   Ah,   *1966 1972*
     no! arrest]   no!—Arrest   *1966 1972*
     Time.]   Time!—   *1966 1972*
                Time,   *1989*

22   wing,]   wing   *1989*

26   fire,]   fire!   *1966 1972*

29   gaze]   gaze!—   *1966 1972*
                 gaze,   *1989*

30   joy;]   joy,   *1966 1972 1989*

31   destroy.]   destroy,—   *1966 1972*

33   love]   Love   *1858 1876 1892W 1927*/III *1927*/VIII *1970*
       destroy.]   destroy,   *1858 1876 1892W 1927*/III *1927*/VIII *1970*
                 destroy: *1870*
                 destroy!—   *1966 1972*

34   Can]   But   *1858 1870 1876 1892W 1927*/III *1927*/VIII *1970*
       perfidy]   perfidy,   *1989*
       then]   can   *1858 1870 1876 1892W 1927*/III *1927*/VIII *1970*
                 then,   *1989*
       blight its]   blast the   *1858 1870 1876 1892W 1927*/III *1927*/VIII
                 1970
       flower]   flower,   *1858 1870 1876 1892W 1927*/III *1927*/VIII *1966*
                 1970 1972

35   when]   when,   *1870 1966 1972*
       hour]   hour,   *1870 1966 1972*

36   fancy's]   Fancy's   *1858 1876 1892W 1927*/III *1927*/VIII *1966 1970*
                 1972
       bower?]   bower.   *1858 1870 1876 1892W 1927*/III *1927*/VIII *1970*
                 page break   *1966*
                 stanza break added   *1972*

37   love]   Love   *1858 1876 1892W 1927*/III *1927*/VIII *1970*
       destroy.]   destroy,   *1858 1876 1892W 1927*/III *1927*/VIII *1970*
                 destroy: *1870*
                 destroy!—   *1966 1972*

38   Can slighted vows then]   But perfidy can   *1858 1870 1876 1892W*
                                 1927/III *1927*/VIII *1970*
       vows]   vows,   *1989*
       then]   then,   *1989*

39   On]   In   *1858 1870 1876 1892W 1927*/III *1927*/VIII *1970*
       chastened]   vermeil   *1858 1870 1876 1892W 1927*/III *1927*/VIII
                 1970
       splendours]   splendors   *1892W*
       shine]   shine.   *1858 1870 1876 1892W 1927*/III *1927*/VIII *1970*
       Dateline. *none*]   1811.   *1870*

1810 ("Hopes that bud in youthful breasts")   *[Esd #35]*

Text collated with *1858* (lines 1–14), *1870* (lines 1–14), *1876* (lines 1–14), *1892W* (lines 1–14), *1927/*III (lines 1–14), *1927/*VIII (lines 1–14), *1966*, *1970* (lines 1–14), *1972*, and *1989*.

Title.   1810]   *omitted   1858* 1927/VIII *1989*
                 LOVE'S ROSE.   *1870 1876*
                 LOVE'S ROSE   *1892W 1970*
                 LOVE'S ROSE | 1810   *1927/*III

Stanza marker.   *none*]   I   *1876 1892W* 1927/III *1970*

1   Hopes]   Hopes,   *1858* 1927/VIII
                 HOPES   *1870 1972*
                 HOPES,   *1876 1892W* 1927/III *1970*
    bud]   swell   *1858 1870 1876 1892W* 1927/VIII *1970*
    breasts]   breasts,   *1858 1870 1876 1892W* 1927/III 1927/VIII
                 1970

2   Live]   Leave   *1927/*VIII
    not thro' the lapse]   they this, the waste   *1858 1870 1876* 1927/VIII
    thro']   through   *1892W 1966 1970 1972 1989*
    lapse]   waste   *1892W* 1927/III *1970*
    time:]   time?   *1858 1870 1876 1892W* 1927/VIII
                 time!   *1927/*III *1970*
                 time;   *1966 1972*

3   invest]   invests;   *1858 1876 1892W* 1927/III 1927/VIII *1970*
                 invests: *1870*
                 invests,   *1966 1972*
                 invests   *1989*

4   And]   Cold,   *1858 1870 1876 1892W* 1927/VIII *1970*
    ungenial]   ungenial,   *1870*
    clime]   clime,   *1858 1876 1892W* 1927/III 1927/VIII *1970*

5   blossoms]   honours   *1858 1870 1876* 1927/VIII *1970*
                 honors   *1892W*

6   says—the]   says, The   *1858 1876* 1927/VIII
                 says: "The   *1870*
                 says, "The   *1892W* 1927/III *1966 1970 1972*
                 says—"The   *1989*
    mine]   mine,   *1858 1876*
                 mine"—   *1870*
                 mine,"   *1892W* 1927/III *1966 1970 1972*

7   That fade]   Which die   *1858 1870 1876 1892W* 1927/VIII *1970*
    glow.]   glow."   *1989*

Stanza marker.   *none*]   II   *1876 1892W* 1927/III *1970*

8   Fancy]   fancy   *1870*

9   while]   whilst   *1858 1876 1892W 1927/*VIII *1970*
    'tis]   it's   *1858 1870 1876 1892W 1927/*VIII *1970*
    granted.]   granted: *1858 1870 1876 1892W 1927/*III *1927/*VIII
            1970
            granted;   *1966 1972*

10   that breathes]   which lives   *1858 1876 1892W 1927/*VIII
                which lives,   *1870 1970*
    Heaven]   heaven,   *1858 1876 1892W 1927/*VIII
            heaven   *1870*
            Heaven,   *1927/*III *1966 1970 1972 1989*

11   Altho']   Although   *1858 1876 1892W 1927/*VIII *1966 1970 1972*
            1989
                (Although   *1870*
    Earth]   earth   *1858 1870 1876 1892W 1927/*VIII *1970*
    planted,]   planted);   *1870*
            planted   *1966 1972 1989*

12   Where]   While   *1927/*III
    blossoms]   honours   *1858 1870 1876 1927/*III *1927/*VIII *1970*
            honors   *1892W*

13   Where]   While   *1858 1870 1876 1892W 1927/*III *1927/*VIII *1970*
    the frosts its]   earth's slaves the   *1858 1870 1876 1892W 1927/*VIII
            1970

14   That fade]   Which die   *1858 1870 1876 1892W 1927/*VIII *1970*

17   sin,]   sin,   *1966 1972*

18   love]   love,   *1966 1972*

19   blow,]   blow,—   *1966 1972*

20   shrine,]   shrine   *1989*

September 23, 1809
("Moonbeam! leave the shadowy dale")   *[Esd #36]*

Text collated with *1858, 1870, 1876, 1892W, 1927/*III, *1927/*VIII, *1966,
1970, 1972,* and *1989.*

Title.   September 23, 1809]   TO THE MOONBEAM.   *1858 1870 1876*
                TO THE MOONBEAM   *1892W*
                    *1927/*VIII *1970*
                TO THE MOONBEAM | 1809   *1927/*III
                TO THE MOONBEAM | 23 September
                    1809   *1966*
                To the Moonbeam | 23 September 1809
                    1972
                To the Moonbeam   *1989*

Stanza marker.   *none*]   I   *1876 1892W 1927*/III *1970*

1   Moonbeam!]   Moonbeam,   *1858 1927*/VIII *1966 1989*
                            MOONBEAM,   *1870 1876 1892W 1927*/III *1970 1972*
    dale]   vale,   *1858 1870 1876 1892W 1927*/III *1927*/VIII *1970*
                dale,   *1966 1972*
                vale   *1989*

2   cool]   bathe   *1858 1870 1876 1892W 1927*/III *1927*/VIII *1970*
                1989
    brow—]   brow.   *1858 1876 1892W 1927*/VIII *1970*
                brow!   *1870 1966 1972*
                brow: *1989*

3   Moonbeam,]   Moonbeam cool,   *1927*/III
    pale]   pale,   *1858 1870 1876 1892W 1927*/III *1927*/VIII *1966 1970*
                1972

4   glidest . . . midnight]   walkest o'er the dewy   *1858 1870 1876 1892W*
                            1927/VIII *1970 1989*
    vale]   dale,   *1858 1876 1892W 1927*/VIII *1970*
                dale   *1870 1989*
                vale,   *1927*/III *1966 1972*

5   dewy]   humble   *1858 1870 1876 1892W 1927*/VIII *1970*
    flowrets]   wild flowers   *1858 1876 1892W 1927*/VIII *1989*
                wildflowers   *1870*
                flowerets   *1927*/III
                wild-flowers   *1970*

7   Ah,]   But   *1858 1870 1876 1892W 1927*/III *1927*/VIII *1970 1989*
    be;]   be,—   *1870*
                be,   *1989*

8   thy path]   thine orb   *1858 1870 1876 1892W 1927*/VIII *1970 1989*
    bright]   bright,   *1858 1870 1876 1892W 1927*/III *1927*/VIII *1966*
                1970 1972

9   light]   light,   *1858 1876 1892W 1927*/III *1927*/VIII *1966 1970*
                1972

10   shadow]   show   *1870*

Stanza marker.   *none*]   II   *1876 1892W 1927*/III *1970*

11   Earth,]   earth,   *1858 1870 1876 1927*/VIII
                earth;   *1892W 1966 1970 1972*
                Earth: *1989*

12   reposes;]   reposes,   *1858 1876 1927*/III *1927*/VIII

13   Yet]   And   *1858 1876 1927*/VIII *1989*
                And,   *1870 1892W 1970*
                Yet,   *1966 1972*
    ere]   in   *1927*/III

14   gates]   hues   *1858 1870 1876 1892W 1927/III 1927/VIII 1970*
             1989

     uncloses,]   discloses,   *1858 1870 1876 1892W 1927/VIII 1970*
                   discloses   *1989*

15   her]   its   *1858 1870 1876 1892W 1927/VIII 1970*
     breath;]   breath.   *1858 1870 1876 1892W 1927/III 1927/VIII 1966*
                   1970 1972
                   breath,   *1989*

16   death,]   Death,   *1858 1876 1892W 1927/III 1927/VIII 1970*
                   death;   *1870*

17   Nature's]   nature's   *1927/VIII*
     morn]   morn,   *1858 1876 1927/III 1927/VIII*

18   forlorn]   forlorn,   *1858 1876 1927/III 1927/VIII*

19   thorn.]   thorn!   *1870*
                   thorn   *1876*

Stanza marker.   *none*]   III   *1876 1892W 1927/III 1970*

20   Wretch!]   Wretch,   *1966 1972*
     suppress]   Suppress   *1858 1876 1892W 1927/III 1927/VIII 1970*

21   eye,]   eye!   *1870 1966 1972*

23   despair's]   Despair's   *1858 1876 1892W 1927/III 1927/VIII 1970*

24   me.]   me;   *1858 1876 1892W 1927/VIII 1970*
             me!   *1927/III*
             me,   *1989*

25   But]   And   *1858 1870 1876 1892W 1927/III 1927/VIII 1970 1989*
     that]   this   *1858 1870 1876 1892W 1927/III 1927/VIII 1970 1989*
     can]   must   *1858 1870 1876 1892W 1927/VIII 1970 1989*
     never]   ever   *1858 1870 1876 1892W 1927/III 1927/VIII 1970*
                   1989
     be]   be,   *1858 1876 1892W 1927/III 1927/VIII 1966 1970 1972*

26   darkness]   twilight   *1858 1870 1876 1892W 1927/VIII 1970 1989*
     care]   care,   *1858 1876 1892W 1927/III 1927/VIII 1970*

27   death]   night   *1858 1870 1876 1892W 1927/VIII 1970 1989*
     despair]   despair,   *1858 1876 1892W 1927/III 1927/VIII 1970*

28   joys]   joys,   *1870*
     pangs]   pangs,   *1858 1876 1927/III*
     rankle]   wake   *1858 1870 1876 1927/III 1927/VIII 1989*
     there.]   there!   *1870*

Dateline.   *none*]   May 1811.   *1870*

[Poems about Mary]

Advertisement

Text collated with *1966, 1972,* and *1989.*

Heading.　[Poems about Mary]]　[FOUR POEMS TO MARY]　*1966*
　　　　　　　　　　　　　　　　Four Poems to Mary　*1972*
　　　　　　　　　　　　　　　　omitted　*1989*
Title.　Advertisement]　[SHELLEY'S] ADVERTISEMENT　*1966 1972*
2　story——I]　story. I　*1966 1972*
3　and]　&　*1989*
4　me]　me,　*1989*
　　heart-breaking]　heart breaking　*1989*
5　Leonora.—For]　"Leonora". For　*1966 1972*
　　myself]　myself,　*1966 1972*
　　time:]　time,　*1966 1972*
　　　　　　time　*1989*
　　nondum,]　"nondum　*1966 1972*
　　　　　　nondum　*1989*
　　amabum,]　amabam,　*omnia*
6　amerem,]　amarem,　*omnia*
　　amare.*]　amare".　*1966 1972*
　　　　　　amare*　*1989*
7　before]　[~~after~~] before　*1989*
　　tale.—]　tale.　*1966 1972*
Footnote.　*Confess. St. Augustin.]　*omitted*　*1966 1972*

To Mary I　[Esd #37]

Text collated with *1966, 1972,* and *1989.*

Title.　To Mary I]　TO MARY I | November 1810　*1966*
　　　　　　　　　To Mary—I | November 1810　*1989*
1　Dear]　DEAR　*1972*
　　girl!]　girl,　*1966 1972*
　　madness,]　madness!　*1966 1972*
2　sweet.]　sweet,—　*1966 1972*
　　　　　　sweet,　*1989*
3　sadness,]　sadness;　*1966 1972*
5　sincerely.]　sincerely,　*1966 1972*

6   Yes!]   Yes,   *1966 1972*
    mine;]   mine—   *1966 1972*
9   Oh!]   Oh,   *1966 1972*
10   past;]   past,—   *1966 1972*
                 past: *1989*
12   Virtues]   virtues   *omnia*
Footnote.   *This]   "This   *1989*
              is]   is,   *1966 1972*
              others]   others,   *1966 1972*
              blasphemy.—Mary,]   a blasphemy—Mary   *1966 1972*
                            a blasphemy.—Mary,   *1989*
              alone.—Nor]   alone—Nor   *1989*
              summer's]   summer   *1989*
              side.—whilst]   side, whilst   *1966 1972*
                            side,—whilst   *1989*
              table,]   table   *1966 1972*
              and]   &   *1989*
              extasies]   ecstasies   *1966 1972*
              and]   &   *1989*
              despair!—(What]   despair! What   *1966 1972*
                            despair! [What   *1989*
              life?)]   life?   *1966 1972*
                            life?]   *1989*
14   thee.]   thee;   *1966 1972*
                 thee,   *1989*
19   anguish.]   anguish,—   *1966 1972*
                 anguish;   *1989*
20   Love!]   Love,   *1966 1972*
21   thee,]   thee   *omnia*
22   alone.]   alone,—   *1966 1972*
23   together.]   together,   *1966 1972*
                 together;   *1989*
24   Mary!]   Mary,   *1966 1972*
     begone.]   begone!   *1966 1972*
26   Death . . . .]   Death,—   *1966 1972*
                 Death . . .   *1989*

To Mary II   [Esd #38]

Text collated with *1966, 1972,* and *1989.*

Title.   To Mary II]   To Mary—II   *1989*
1   Fair]   Fair   *1972*

one!]   one,   *1966 1972*
heart . . . .]   heart!   *1966 1972*
     heart . . .   *1989*

3 art?]   art—   *1966 1972*
4 Tho']   Though   *omnia*
 me,]   me?   *1966 1972*
    me.   *1989*

5 tear;]   tear,—   *1966 1972*
9 Tho']   Though   *omnia*
 hill . . .]   hill,—   *1966 1972*
11 chill;]   chill!   *1966 1972*
15 low,]   low   *1989*
16 dread.]   dread,—   *1966 1972*
     dread;   *1989*
18 head . . .] head.   *1966 1972*
21 devotion]   devotion[1]   *1966 1972*
 holy day]   holy-day   *omnia*
 keep.*]   keep.   *omnia*
Footnote. *The]   "The   *1989*
   devotion,]   *devotion*   *1966 1972*
   sense;]   sense,   *1989*
   word,]   word   *1966 1972*
   Author.]   Author"   *1989*

To Mary III *[Esd #39]*

Text collated with *1966, 1972,* and *1989.*

Title. To Mary III]   To Mary—III   *1989*
1 Mary,]   MARY,   *1972*
 Mary!]   Mary,   *1966 1972*
3 stone?]   stone,   *1966 1972*
4 groan,]   groan   *1989*
5 alone]   alone,   *omnia*
9 Tho']   Though   *omnia*
10 And]   And,   *1966 1972*
 blast]   blast,   *1966 1972*
15 Thine,]   Thine   *omnia*
 despair]   despair,   *1966 1972*
16 love—more]   love, more   *1966 1972*
     love more   *1989*
 bear . . .]   bear.   *1966 1972*

17   I—wretch!—weep]   I, wretch, weep   *1966 1972*
                              I, wretch! weep   *1989*
     were,]   were   *1989*
18   I . . . . still]   I—still   *1966 1972*
                    I . . . still   *1989*
20   tie—]   tie,   *1966 1972 1989*
21   pityless]   pitiless   *omnia*
22   hurl'd]   hurled,   *1966 1972*
                    hurled   *1989*
23   storm.]   storm,—   *1966 1972*
                    storm;   *1989*
25   misery,]   misery   *omnia*
29   magic]   magic,   *1966 1972*
30   wrapt]   wrapped   *1989*
     ethereal]   etherial   *1989*
32   doom . . . .]   doom: *1966 1972*
                    doom . . .   *1989*
33   wait]   wait,   *1966 1972*
34   gate]   gate,   *omnia*
35   tomb.]   tomb,—   *omnia*
36   flower!]   flower,   *1966 1972*
37   dank]   rank   *omnia*
     serpent,]   serpent   *1966 1972*
     interest,]   Interest   *1966 1972*
     feeds!]   feeds.   *1989*

To the Lover of Mary   *[Esd #40]*

Text collated with *1966, 1972,* and *1989.*

1   Drink]   Dʀɪɴᴋ   *1972*
     moonbeam]   moonbeam,   *1966 1972*
4   flare . . . . .]   flare!—   *1966 1972*
                    flare . . .   *1989*
5   Wretch,]   wretch,   *omnia*
6   tenantless—]   tenantless,   *omnia*
7   caress—]   caress,   *omnia*
8   dew.]   dew!   *1966 1972*
                    dew;   *1989*
9   moon-ray]   moonray   *1966 1972*
12   Spirit]   spirit   *1966 1972*
14   Angel]   angel   *1966 1972*
17   stain]   stain,   *1966 1972*

22   Love,]   Love   *1966 1972*
     purity]   purity,   *1966 1972*
23   O]   Oh,   *1966 1972*
     joy!]   joy,   *1966 1972*
24   woe,]   woe!—   *1966 1972*
27   live—for]   live,—for   *1966 1972*
28   shew]   show   *omnia*
     Virtue]   virtue   *1966 1972*
29   tears:]   tears!   *1966 1972*
30   Paradise,]   Paradise   *omnia*
31   And]   And,   *1966 1972*
     joy]   joy,   *1966 1972*
32   ever]   even   *1966 1972*
     *love]   Love,   *1966 1972*
                  love,   *1989*
33   *Virtue]   Virtue[1]   *1966 1972*
                  Virtue   *1989*
     prove.]   prove!   *1966 1972*
Footnote.   *As]   "as   *1989*
             synonimous!]   synonymous!   *1966 1972*
                            synonimous!"   *1989*

1810 ("Dares the Lama, most fleet")   *[Esd #41]*

Text collated with *1858, 1870, 1876, 1892W, 1927*/III, *1927*/VIII, *1966, 1970, 1972,* and *1989.*

Title.   1810]   *omitted*   *1858 1927*/VIII *1989*
                  BIGOTRY'S VICTIM.   *1870 1876*
                  BIGOTRY'S VICTIM   *1892W 1970*
                  BIGOTRY'S VICTIM | 1811   *1927*/III
                  [BIGOTRY'S VICTIM] | 1810   *1966*
                  Bigotry's Victim | 1810   *1972*
Stanza marker.   *none*]   I   *1870 1876 1892W 1927*/III *1970*
1   Dares]   Dares   *1870 1876 1892W 1927*/III *1970 1972*
     Lama,]   lama,   *1858 1876 1892W 1927*/VIII *1970*
                  llama,   *1870 1966 1972 1989*
     Sons]   sons   *omnia*
     Wind,]   wind,   *omnia*
2   Lion]   lion   *1858 1870 1876 1892W 1927*/VIII *1966 1970 1972
                  1989*
     lair?]   skull-covered lair?   *1858 1870 1876 1892W 1927*/III
                  1927/VIII *1970*

3   tyger]   tiger   *1858 1870 1876 1892W 1927/*VIII *1966 1970 1972 1989*
    awakes,]   approaches   *1858 1876 1892W 1927/*VIII *1970*
                approaches,   *1870*
                awakes   *1927/*III *1966 1972*
4   air?]   air!   *1870*
5   No—abandoned]   No? Abandon'd   *1858*
                No! abandoned   *1870 1966 1972*
                No! Abandon'd   *1876 1927/*VIII
                No! Abandoned   *1892W 1927/*III *1970*
    it]   he   *1858 1870 1876 1892W 1927/*VIII *1970*
    helpless]   a trance of   *1858 1870 1876 1892W 1927/*VIII *1970*
    despair;]   despair,   *1858 1876 1892W 1927/*III *1927/*VIII *1966 1970
                1972*
                despair: *1870 1989*
6   prey,]   prey: *1870*
7   its]   his   *1858 1870 1876 1892W 1927/*III *1927/*VIII *1970*
    away,]   away;   *1858 1876 1892W 1927/*III *1927/*VIII *1966 1970 1972*
8   And the rocks and the]   Whilst India's rocks to his   *1858 1870 1876
                *1892W 1927/*VIII *1970*
    reply]   reply,   *omnia*
Stanza marker.   *none*]   II   *1870 1876 1892W 1927/*III *1970*
10   desart]   desert,   *1858 1870 1876 1892W 1927/*III *1927/*VIII *1966
                1970 1972*
                desert   *1989*
    encroaches]   encroaches,   *1858 1870 1876 1892W 1927/*III
                *1927/*VIII *1966 1970 1972*
11   dreadless]   fearless   *1858 1870 1876 1892W 1927/*VIII *1970*
    perish,]   perish   *1858 1876 1892W 1927/*III *1927/*VIII *1970*
    brood,]   brood   *1989*
12   Tho']   Though   *1858 1870 1876 1892W 1927/*VIII *1966 1970 1972
                1989*
    approaches,]   approaches   *1927/*III *1970 1989*
13   Thirsting—aye,]   Thirsting—ay,   *1870 1892W 1927/*III *1970*
    thirsting for]   thirsting—for   *1870*
    blood—]   blood;   *1858 1876 1892W 1927/*III *1927/*VIII *1970*
                blood,   *1870 1966 1972 1989*
14   food,]   food;   *1858 1876 1892W 1927/*III *1927/*VIII *1966 1970
                1972 1989*
                food:—   *1870*
15   gentle,]   gentle   *1858 1876 1892W 1927/*III *1927/*VIII *1966 1970
                1972 1989*
    they;]   they,—   *1870*
                they,   *1989*

16   glory,]   glory   *1927*/III
17   perish—revenge]   perish. Revenge   *1858 1870 1876 1892W*
                    1927/VIII *1966 1970 1972*
     o'er]   in   *1858 1876 1892W 1927*/VIII *1970*
     dead,]   dead.   *1927*/III *1970*
18   bind]   crown   *1858 1870 1876 1892W 1927*/VIII *1970*
Stanza marker.   *none*]   III   *1870 1876 1892W 1927*/III *1970*
19   Tho']   Though   *1858 1870 1876 1892W 1927*/VIII *1966 1970 1972*
              1989
     weak]   weak,   *1858 1876 1927*/VIII
     Lama]   lama,   *1858 1876 1927*/VIII
              llama   *1870 1966 1972 1989*
              lama   *1892W 1927*/III *1970*
     Mountains]   mountains,   *1858 1870 1876 1892W 1927*/III
              1927/VIII *1966 1970 1972*
                  mountains   *1989*
20   air,]   air   *1927*/III *1989*
22   Tho']   Though   *1858 1870 1876 1892W 1927*/VIII *1966 1970 1972*
              1989
     tygers]   tiger   *1858 1870 1876 1892W 1927*/VIII *1970*
                  tigers   *1966 1972 1989*
     there,]   there.   *1858 1876 1892W 1927*/III *1927*/VIII *1966 1970*
              1972
                  there;   *1870*
23   Tho']   Though   *1858 1870 1876 1892W 1927*/VIII *1989*
                  Though,   *1966 1970 1972*
     frightful]   dreadful   *1858 1870 1876 1892W 1927*/III *1927*/VIII
              1970
     death]   death,   *1858 1876 1892W 1927*/III *1927*/VIII *1966 1970*
              1972
24   And]   Though   *1858 1870 1876 1892W 1927*/VIII *1970*
     shadow,]   shadow   *1858 1870 1876 1892W 1927*/III *1927*/VIII
              1970 1989
     eclipsing]   eclipses   *1858 1870 1876 1892W 1927*/VIII *1970*
     day,]   day   *1989*
25   Spreads]   And   *1858 1870 1876 1892W 1927*/VIII *1970*
26   O'er]   Spreads   *1858 1870 1876 1892W 1927*/VIII *1970*
                  On   *1966*
     withered . . . nations]   influence of soul-chilling terror   *1858 1870*
                    1876 1892W 1927/VIII *1970*
     around]   around,   *omnia*

27   the war-mangled]   lowers on the   *1858 1876 1892W 1927/VIII*
                                1970
                        lours on the   *1870*
      corpses]   corpses,   *1858 1876 1892W 1927/VIII 1970*
Stanza marker.   *none*]   IV   *1870 1876 1892W 1927/III 1970*
28   They]   *They   1870*
      fountain]   fountain,   *1870*
      stream]   stream,   *1858 1876 1892W 1927/VIII*
29   poisonously lovely]   pure, too celestial,   *1858 1870 1876 1892W*
                                1927/VIII 1970
30   basked]   bathed   *1858 1870 1876 1892W 1927/III 1927/VIII 1970*
      awhile]   a while   *1858 1876 1892W 1927/VIII 1966 1972*
      the]   its   *1927/III*
      the love-darting]   its silvery   *1858 1870 1876 1892W 1927/VIII*
                                1970
      beam]   beam,   *1858 1870 1876 1892W 1927/VIII 1966 1970 1972*
                1989
31   perished—and]   perish'd, and   *1858 1876 1927/VIII*
                        perished, and   *1892W 1927/III 1970*
                        perished,—and   *1966 1972*
      me,]   me.   *1858 1870 1876 1892W 1927/III 1927/VIII 1966 1970*
                1972 1989
32   Religion]   the Bigot   *1858 1870 1876 1892W 1927/VIII 1970*
      flee:]   flee;   *1858 1876 1892W 1927/III 1927/VIII 1966 1970 1972*
                1989
34   its chilling]   his hated   *1858 1870 1876 1892W 1927/VIII 1970*
      control . . .]   control.   *1858 1870 1876 1892W 1927/III 1927/VIII*
                1966 1970 1972
35   It]   He   *1858 1870 1876 1892W 1927/VIII 1970*
      me. It]   me, he   *1858 1876 1892W 1927/VIII 1970*
                me—he   *1870*
                me, it   *1927/III 1966 1972*
      me.]   me!   *1858 1870 1876 1892W 1927/III 1927/VIII 1966 1970*
                1972
      Oh!]   Oh,   *1966 1972*
      Oh! where shall]   'Tis in vain that   *1858 1870 1876 1892W*
                        1927/VIII 1970
      fly?]   fly: *1858 1876 1927/VIII 1970*
                fly!   *1870*
                fly;—   *1892W*
                fly,   *1989*
36   remains]   remains,   *1858 1876 1892W 1927/VIII 1970*

it, to curse it]   him,—to curse him   *1858 1876 1892W 1927*/VIII
1970
him—to curse him,   *1870*
it, to]   it—to   *1927*/III
Dateline.   *none*]   28 *April,* 1811.   *1870*

1809 ("*I will kneel at thine altar*")   *[Esd #42]*

Text collated with *1966, 1972,* and *1989*.

Title.   1809]   [LOVE AND TYRANNY] | 1809   *1966*
Love and Tyranny | 1809   *1972*
omitted   *1989*

1   will]   WILL   *1972*
bays.]   bays,   *omnia*
2   Love]   Love,   *1989*
art,]   art!   *1966 1972*
art   *1989*
3   live . . . aye!]   live,—aye,   *1966 1972*
live—aye!   *1989*
lays]   lays: *1966 1972*
lays—   *1989*
4   heart.]   heart!   *1966 1972*
heart;   *1989*
5   love!]   Love!   *omnia*
life-strings]   life-springs   *1966 1972*
shalt]   shall   *1989*
part,]   part   *1989*
6   Tho']   Though   *omnia*
Prejudice]   Prejudice,   *1966 1972*
7   Tho']   Though   *omnia*
Interest]   Interest,   *1966 1972*
13   thee.]   thee;   *1966 1972*
14   free.]   free,—   *1966 1972*
15   nay,]   Nay   *1966 1972*
16   not,]   not?   *1966 1972*
adore]   Adore   *1966 1972*
adore?   *1989*
17   What]   What,   *1966 1972*
existing]   existing,   *omnia*
18   live.—]   live?—   *omnia*
19   Religion]   Religion,   *1966 1972*
North]   North,   *1966 1972*

20   thro']   through   *omnia*
21   forth;]   forth,—   *1966 1972*
              forth: *1989*
23   control.]   control;   *omnia*
26   war-drowned]   war-drownèd   *omnia*
     cry]   cry,   *1966 1972*
27   selfishness,]   selfishness   *1966 1972*
     conquering,]   conquering   *1966 1972*
     Victory!]   "Victory"!   *1966 1972*
              "Victory!"   *1989*
28   we]   we,   *1989*
     then]   then,   *omnia*
     impassive]   impassive,   *omnia*
29   springs]   springs,   *1989*
30   Opinion]   Opinion,   *1989*
     Gold—]   Gold,   *omnia*
31   passion]   Passion   *1966 1972*
     alloyed—]   alloyed,   *omnia*
32   reign,]   reign   *1989*
34   totters, its]   totters,—its   *1966 1972*
35   nations.—It]   nations—it   *1966 1972*
     falls,]   falls;   *1989*
     love]   Love   *omnia*
     sway;]   sway,   *1989*

Fragment of a Poem, | *the original idea of which was suggested by the*
cowardly and infamous bombardment of Copenhagen   *[Esd #43]*

Text collated with *1858* (lines 1–14), *1927*/VIII (lines 1–14), *1966, 1972,*
and *1989.*

Title.   Fragment . . . Copenhagen]   *omitted*   *1858 1927*/VIII
1   The]   THE   *1972*
    ice mountains]   ice-mountains   *1966 1972 1989*
    Ocean]   Ocean,   *1858 1927*/VIII *1966 1972*
2   cold]   Cold   *1858 1927*/VIII *1989*
    its]   his   *1858 1927*/VIII *1989*
    solium]   column   *1858 1927*/VIII
    snow:]   snows,   *1858 1927*/VIII
              snow;   *1966 1972 1989*
3   Even]   E'en   *1989*
    commotion.]   commotion,   *omnia*

4 whirlwinds]   whirlwind   *1858 1927*/VIII
    sleet]   sleet,   *1858 1927*/VIII
    they]   this   *1858 1927*/VIII
    blow,]   blows   *1858 1927*/VIII
                 blow;   *1966 1972*
                 blow—   *1989*
5 clots with]   tinges   *1858 1927*/VIII *1989*
    half frozen]   half-frozen   *1858 1927*/VIII *1966 1972*
6 Lurid . . . war]   The meteors of war lurid flame thro' the air,   *1858*
                 1927/VIII
                 The meteors of War lurid flame through the air,
                 1989
    war]   war,   *1966 1972*
7 And]   They   *1858 1927*/VIII *1989*
    deep]   bright   *1858 1927*/VIII *1989*
    bright]   red   *1858 1927*/VIII *1989*
    polar]   Polar   *1989*
    glare.]   star.   *1858 1927*/VIII
9 triumph]   triumph,   *1858 1927*/VIII *1966 1972*
                 Triumph   *1989*
    terror]   glory,   *1858 1927*/VIII
                 Glory   *1989*
    spread.]   speed,   *1858 1927*/VIII
                 spread;   *1966 1972*
                 spread,   *1989*
10 rearing,]   rearing.   *1858 1927*/VIII
                 rearing,—   *1966 1972*
                 rearing: *1989*
11 Ruin]   Ruin,   *1927*/VIII
    follows . . . it]   follows, it   *1858 1927*/VIII
                 follows—it   *1966 1972*
                 follows! it   *1989*
    dead . . .]   dead,   *1858 1927*/VIII
                 dead.   *1966 1972*
                 dead;   *1989*
12 But her]   Thy   *1858 1927*/VIII *1989*
    fall . . . the]   fall, the   *1858 1927*/VIII *1989*
                 fall—the   *1966 1972*
    bloodreeking]   blood-reeking   *omnia*
13 sigh;]   sigh,   *1858 1927*/VIII
                 sigh: *1966 1972 1989*

14   victory.]   Victory.   *1858 1927*/VIII
                            Victory!   *1989*
15   female. The]   female,—the   *1966 1972*
       descending—]   descending,   *1966 1972 1989*
16   glare.]   glare,—   *1966 1972*
                            glare,   *1989*
17   blending]   blending,   *1966 1972 1989*
18   stare.]   stare,—   *1966 1972*
                            stare: *1989*
19   death shrieks]   death-shrieks   *1989*
20   prest,]   pressed,   *1989*

1809 | *On an Icicle that clung to the grass of a grave*   *[Esd #44]*

Text collated with *1858, 1870, 1876, 1892W, 1927*/III, *1927*/VIII, *1970, 1966, 1972,* and *1989.*

Title.   1809 . . . grave]   *omitted*   *1858 1927*/VIII
                            THE TEAR.   *1870 1876*
       1809]   *omitted*   *1892W 1970 1989*
                 1811   *1927*/III
Stanza marker.   *none*]   I   *1870 1876 1892W 1927*/III *1970*
1   O]   Oh!   *1858 1927*/VIII *1966 1989*
       Он!   *1870 1876 1892W 1927*/III *1970 1972*
    Southernly]   southerly   *1858 1870 1876 1892W 1927*/VIII *1970*
                            Southerly   *1927*/III
                            southernly   *1966 1972 1989*
    Breezes]   breezes,   *1858 1876 1927*/III *1927*/VIII *1970*
                 breezes   *1870 1892W 1966 1972 1989*
3   love]   Love   *1989*
    freezes]   freezes,   *1858 1870 1876 1892W 1927*/III *1927*/VIII *1966*
                 1970 1972
4   As it]   *omitted*   *1927*/III
    circulates]   Circulates   *1927*/III
    circulates . . . shamelessly]   rises unmingled with selfishness   *1858*
                            1870 1876 1892W 1927/VIII *1970 1989*
5   Which]   Which,   *1858 1870 1876 1892W 1927*/III *1927*/VIII *1966*
                 1970 1972
    crime,]   pride,   *1858 1870 1876 1892W 1927*/VIII *1970*
                 Pride,   *1989*
6   this]   the   *1858 1870 1876 1892W 1927*/III *1927*/VIII *1970 1989*
    dear]   dim   *1858 1870 1876 1892W 1927*/III *1927*/VIII *1966 1970*
                 1972

ice-drop,] icedrop, *1858 1870 1876 1927/*III *1927/*VIII *1966 1970 1972*

7 skies.] skies; *1989*

Stanza marker. *none*] III *1870 1876 1892*W *1927/*III *1970*

8 gem] gem, *1858 1876 1892*W *1927/*III *1927/*VIII *1966 1970 1972*

daybeam] day-beam *1989*

returning] returning, *1858 1876 1927/*III *1927/*VIII *1966 1970 1972*

9 snow-spangled] snow-covered *1858 1870 1876 1892*W *1927/*III *1927/*VIII *1970 1989*

10 others] *others* *1989*

longed-for] wished-for *1858 1870 1876 1892*W *1927/*VIII *1970 1989*

11 night-dreams] visions *1858 1870 1876 1892*W *1927/*VIII *1970 1989*

pain.] pain; *1858 1876 1892*W *1927/*III *1927/*VIII *1966 1970 1972 1989*

12 insult. To] insult—to *omnia*

vain.] vain: *omnia*

13 spirit] Spirit *1870*

14 Sought] Seeks *1858 1870 1876 1892*W *1927/*III *1927/*VIII *1970 1989*

Heaven] heaven *1870*

meet] mix *1858 1870 1876 1892*W *1927/*VIII *1970 1989*

kindred] own kindred *1858 1870 1876 1892*W *1927/*III *1927/*VIII *1970*

Stanza marker. *none*] IV *1870 1876 1892*W *1927/*III *1970*

15 Yet] But still *1858 1870 1876 1892*W *1927/*VIII *1970 1989*

Angel] spirit *1858 1876 1892*W *1927/*VIII

Spirit *1870 1970 1989*

angel *1966 1972*

kindness] kindness, *1870 1966 1972*

16 Mortality's] mortality's *1858 1870 1876 1892*W *1927/*VIII *1966 1970 1972 1989*

woe,] woe *1989*

17 Who,] Who *1858 1870 1876 1892*W *1927/*III *1927/*VIII *1970 1989*

bending,] bending *1858 1876 1892*W *1927/*III *1927/*VIII *1970 1989*

18 tear-drops] tear-drop *1858 1870 1876 1892*W *1927/*VIII *1989*

teardrop *1927/*III *1970*

teardrops *1966 1972*

flow]   flow.   *1858 1870 1876 1892W 1927/*III *1927/*VIII *1970 1989*
                flow,   *1966 1972*
19   And . . . Snow;]   Not for *thee*, soft compassion, celestials did know,
                    *1858 1876 1927/*VIII
                Not for *thee* soft compassion celestials did know:
                    1870
                Not for *thee* soft compassion celestials did know,
                    1892W 1970 1989
    Sister]   sisters   *1927/*III
            sister   *1966 1972*
    Snow;]   snow.   *1927/*III
            snow;   *1966 1972*
20   And]   But   *1858 1876 1892W 1927/*VIII *1970 1989*
            But,   *1870*
    Angels]   *angels*   *1858 1876 1892W 1927/*III *1927/*VIII *1970*
            angels   *1870 1966 1972*
            Angels   *1989*
    I]   *man*   *1858 1876 1892W 1927/*VIII *1970*
        man   *1870*
        Man   *1989*
    repine]   repine,   *1858 1876 1892W 1927/*III *1927/*VIII *1966 1970*
            1972 1989
            repine —   *1870*
21   And . . . shrine.]   May weep in mute grief o'er thy low-laid shrine.
                    *1858 1870 1876 1892W 1927/*VIII *1970 1989*
    tear-drops,]   tear drops   *1927/*III
                teardrops,   *1966 1972*
    tho']   though   *1966 1972*
    ice,]   ice   *1927/*III

1808 ("Cold are the Blasts")   [Esd #45]

Text collated with *1858, 1966, 1972,* and *1989.*

Title.   1808]   *omitted*   *1858 1989*
1   Cold]   Cold, cold   *1858*
            COLD   *1972*
    are]   is   *1858*
    Blasts]   blast,   *1858*
            blasts   *1966 1972 1989*
2   Chill]   Cold   *1858*
    friend's]   man's   *1858*

brow,]   brow.   *1858*
   brow,—   *1966 1972*
3 is]   are   *1858*
 Ocean]   seas,   *1858*
 tempests]   the wild waves   *1858*
4 Sad is]   And sad   *1858*
 brother]   loved one   *1858*
 low,]   low.   *1858*
   low;   *1966 1972*
   low,—   *1989*
5 chillier]   colder   *1858*
 false one that]   being who   *1858*
 lov'd]   loved   *omnia*
6 that]   who   *1858*
7 thee]   thee,   *1858 1966 1972*
8 That, . . . delirium,]   Which mixed with groans, anguish, and wild
      madness   *1858*
 That,]   That   *1966 1972 1989*
 delirium,]   delirium   *1966 1972 1989*
9 And]   And,   *1858*
 alas! thou,]   ah! poor   *1858*
 Louisa,]   Louisa   *1858*
 hast]   has   *1858*
 horror! . .]   horror;   *1858*
   horror,—   *1966 1972*
   horror! . . .   *1989*
10 Victim]   victim   *omnia*
 fate]   fate,   *omnia*
11 Till—a]   Till a   *1858*
   Till, a   *1966 1972 1989*
 outcast]   outcast,   *1858 1966 1972*
 sorrow—]   sorrow,   *omnia*
13 betrayer;]   betrayer,   *omnia*
14 laughing away]   callous aside   *1858*
 anguish-fraught]   moan and her   *1858*
 prayer,]   prayer,—   *1858 1966 1972*
   prayer;   *1989*
15 spoke not,]   said nothing,   *1858*
 not,]   not   *1966 1972*
 but]   but,   *1966 1972*
 rain]   wet   *1858*
 hair,]   hair   *1989*

16   Took]   Crossed   *1858*
rough]   dark   *1858*
mountain]   mountain's   *1858*
path,]   side,   *1858*
              path   *1966 1972*
tho']   though   *1966 1972 1989*
was]   it was   *1858*

17   On the cloud-shrouded]   'Twas on the dark   *1858*
dark]   huge   *1858*
Penmanmawr]   Penmanmauer   *1858*

18   The]   That the   *1858*
reclined,]   reclined;   *omnia*

19   loud croaking]   that croaked from   *1858*
                        loud-croaking   *1966 1972*

20   She]   And she   *1858*
wild sweeping]   wild-sweeping   *1858 1966 1972*
wind.—]   wind.   *1858*
              wind:—   *1966 1972 1989*

21   "Ye . . . soaring,]   "I call not yon clouds, where the thunder-peals
                        rattle,   *1858*

22   Ye . . . lowering,]   I call not yon rocks, where the elements battle,
                        1858

23   Thou . . . pouring,]   *omitted*   *1858*

24   cruel]   perjured   *1858*
unkind."]   unkind!"   *1858 1966 1972*

25   a wild crown from the]   in her hair the wild   *1858*
flow'rs]   flowers   *omnia*

26   And]   And,   *1858*
laughing]   laughing,   *1858 1989*
the heath twigs]   a garland   *1858*
heath twigs]   heath-twigs   *1966 1972 1989*
entwined.]   entwined,   *1858 1966 1972*
              entwined;   *1989*

27   tear-drops,]   tears,   *1858*
                  tear drops,   *1966 1972*
leaned]   she hung   *1858*
fountain]   fountain,   *1858 1966 1972*

28   And . . . wind.]   And, laving it, cast it a prey to the wind.   *1858*
wild sweeping]   wild-sweeping   *1966 1972*

29   "Ah! go,"]   "Ah, go!"   *1858 1966 1972*
              "Ah, go,"   *1989*

yelling.]   yelling;   *1858 1989*
                            yelling,   *1966 1972*
30   swelling—]   swelling;   *1858*
                                swelling,   *1966 1972*
31   pityless]   pitiless   *omnia*
     dwelling.]   dwelling;   *1858 1966 1972*
                                dwelling,   *1989*
32   torn—so]   torn—so,   *1858 1966 1972*
     say]   say,   *1858 1966 1972*
33   Louisa.—And]   Louisa—but   *1858*
                                Louisa, and   *1966 1972*
                                Louisa;—and   *1989*
34   Waved]   Wave   *1966 1972*
     limbs]   form   *1858*
     yew.]   yew,   *1858*
                    yew;   *1966 1972 1989*
35   demons]   demon   *1966 1972*
     rave,]   rave   *1989*
36   love]   Peace   *1858*
     dew;]   dew.   *omnia*
37   mid]   'mid   *1858 1966 1972*
     heather,]   heather   *1858*
38   Tho']   Though   *1966 1972 1989*
     bleak be the scene]   chill blow the wind   *1858*
39   perfidy,]   Perfidy,   *1858*
40   due.]   due!   *1858*

1809 | Henry and Louisa | a Poem in two parts   [Esd #46]

Text collated with *1966, 1972,* and *1989.*

Title.   1809 | Henry and Louisa*]   HENRY AND LOUISA[1] | 1809   *1966*
                                Henry and Louisa[1] | 1809   *1972*
                                Henry and Louisa   *1989*
Footnote.   Poem]   poem   *1966 1972*
                    Spencer]   Spenser   *1966 1972*
                    altho']   although   *1966 1972*
                                altho   *1989*
                    mind;]   mind,   *1966 1972*
                    pronounced.]   pronounced"   *1989*
Heading.   The Parting | Part the First.]   PART THE FIRST | The Parting
                                1966

Scene—England]   *Scene: England*   *1966*
Scene: England   *1972*
Scene: England   *1989*

1   Where]   WHERE   *1972*
Heroes?]   heroes?   *1966 1972*
sunk]   Sunk   *1966 1972*
2   titles]   Titles   *1966 1972*
3   Heaven]   heaven   *1966 1972*
4   legal]   "legal   *1966 1972*
murderers]   murderers"   *1966 1972*
6   tho']   though   *omnia*
see?]   see?—   *1966 1972*
7   tho']   though   *omnia*
8   selfishness]   selfishness,   *omnia*
ay]   aye   *omnia*
enscrolled,]   enscrolled   *1989*
10   misery?]   misery?—   *1966 1972*
misery;   *1989*
11   give,]   give?   *1966 1972*
can]   Can   *1966 1972*
12   love . . .]   love?   *omnia*
13   darest]   dar'st   *1989*
superior.—Thou!]   superior thou,   *1966 1972*
superior. Thou!   *1989*
14   worm!]   worm,   *1966 1972*
bless,]   bless?—   *1966 1972*
15   And,]   And   *1989*
19   Oh!]   Oh,   *1966 1972*
started'st]   startedst   *1989*
20   Glory]   glory   *1966 1972*
21   resigned'st,]   resignedst,   *1989*
line break * * * * *   *added*   *1989*
22   And]   [And,   *1966 1972*
affection's]   Affection's   *1966 1972*
wing]   wing,   *1966 1972*
24   dead.]   dead.]   *1966 1972*
25   Glory's]   glory's   *1966 1972*
26   Heaven-aspiring]   heaven-aspiring   *1966 1972*
27   voice,]   voice   *1989*

28   resolve]   resolve,   *1966 1972*

29   flood,]   flood   *omnia*

     roll,]   roll,—   *1966 1972*

31   felt—]   felt,—   *omnia*

32   battle thirst,]   battle-thirst?   *1966 1972*

                      battle-thirst,   *1989*

33   melt,]   melt,—   *1966 1972*

35   Yes!]   Yes,   *1966 1972*

     vibrated . . . a]   vibrated. A   *1966 1972*

36   stood.]   stood;   *1966 1972*

37   Virtue,]   virtue,   *omnia*

     grace,]   grace   *omnia*

38   rights . . . . in]   rights,—in   *1966 1972*

                      rights . . . in   *1989*

39   stood]   stood,   *omnia*

40   Glory's]   glory's   *1966 1972*

     eye]   eye,   *1966 1972*

42   death,]   Death,   *1989*

     Victory,]   victory   *1966 1972*

44   She]   she   *omnia*

     exclaimed]   exclaimed,   *omnia*

45   "Go . . mingle]   "Go!—Mingle   *1966 1972*

                      "Go . . . mingle   *1989*

     battle tide . . .]   battle-tide!   *1966 1972*

                      battle-tide . . .   *1989*

46   burned.]   burned   *1966 1972*

47   meet'est]   meet'st   *omnia*

     Victor-pride]   victor-pride;   *1966 1972*

48   thee . . .] thee!   *1966 1972*

     far]   Far   *1966 1972*

50   seek . . but]   seek!—But   *1966 1972*

                seek . . . but   *1989*

     abide—]   abide   *1966 1972*

                abide,   *1989*

51   Here in]   Here—in   *1989*

     breast—thou]   breast thou   *1966 1972*

     alone.]   alone,—   *1966 1972*

                alone,   *1989*

53   Princes]   princes   *1966 1972*

54   Virtue's]   virtue's   *1966 1972*

56   indeed;]   indeed: *1989*

58   away.]   away;   *1989*

59   love,]   love,—   *1966 1972*

60 day,] day,—   *1966 1972*
62 spoke] spoke, *omnia*
    tear,] tear: *1966 1972*
63 thee] thee, *1966 1972*
    ever] ever, *1966 1972*
67 cause,] cause: *1966 1972*
68 vengeance.] vengeance; *1989*
69 foe.] foe: *1966 1972*
72 Say,] "Say, *omnia*
    World] World. *1966*
                World? *1972*
                World, *1989*
74 unfurled,] unfurled *1989*
75 Wing] wing *omnia*
76 wave,] wave?—   *1966 1972*
77 arm,] arm *1966 1972*
81 Even] "Even *omnia*
84 heart.] heart; *omnia*
85 start] start, *1966 1972*
86 wills)] wills), *1989*
    thine.] thine, *omnia*
88 mine,] mine— *1966 1972*
89 thee . . round] thee—round *1989*
90 cheek . . . .] cheek: *1966 1972*
                cheek . . . *1989*
92 speak.] speak,—   *1966 1972*
93 may] May *1966 1972*
94 enthrall.] enthral! *1966 1972*
                enthral. *1989*
95 Heaven] heaven *1966 1972*
    above,] above: *1966 1972*
                above; *1989*
96 Soul] soul *1966 1972*
    Saviour] saviour *1966 1972*
    call.] call, *1966*
                call,—   *1972*
97 thine . . my] thine—my *1966 1972*
                thine . . . my *1989*
    heaven,] heaven *omnia*
    love;] love, *omnia*
98 Hell,] hell *1966 1972*
    fates] Fates *1966 1972*

99   Farewell". . . she]   "Farewell." She   *1966 1972*
                                 "Farewell". . . she   *1989*

     breast,]   breast   *1989*
100   agonized]   agonised   *1966 1972*
      excess,]   excess   *1989*
103   caress.]   caress,   *1966 1972*
104   glades;]   glades,   *1966 1972*
      spring]   spring,   *1966 1972*
105   recess,]   recess   *1989*
106   seem'd]   seemed   *omnia*
      sing]   sing,   *omnia*
107   woe]   Woe   *1966 1972*
      string;]   string.   *1966 1972*
108   Ivied]   ivied   *omnia*
      Thorn]   thorn,   *1966 1972*
                       thorn   *1989*
112   East]   east   *1966 1972*
114   flower]   flower,   *omnia*
115   eyebeam,]   eyebeam   *1989*
      thrilling,]   thrilling   *omnia*
      warm,]   warm   *1989*
116   charm;]   charm,—   *1966 1972*
                       charm;—   *1989*
120   memory.]   memory;   *1989*
121   extacy,]   ecstasy   *omnia*
122   adieu,]   adieu   *omnia*
123   sigh;]   sigh: *1966 1972*
                sigh,   *1989*
124   In]   No,   *1966 1972*
                For   *1989*
128   spring-flowers,]   spring-flowers   *1966 1972*
                            spring flowers   *1989*
      lawn]   lawn,   *omnia*
129   awake.]   awake;   *omnia*
130   reproach,]   reproach;   *1966 1972*
131   war-steed's]   war steed's   *1989*
      prance,]   prance;   *1966 1972*
                   prance.   *1989*
132   take,]   take   *omnia*
136   gale]   gale,   *omnia*
138   tale—]   tale!—   *1966 1972*
                 tale,   *1989*

139   wail,] wail   *1966*
140   Tho'] [That   *1966*
                Though   *1972 1989*
      prized,] prized   *omnia*
141   vale,] vale   *1989*
142   sacrifized,] sacrificed,   *omnia*
143   disguised.] disguised.]   *1966*
      stanza break] omitted   *1972*
144   Religion!] Religion,   *1966 1972*
      woe] woe .   *1972*
145   wilderness.] wilderness!   *1966 1972*
146   flow,] flow!—   *1966 1972*
149   Love! thy] Love,—thy   *1966 1972*
152   succeed? . . oh] succeed? Oh,   *1966 1972*
                      succeed?—oh   *1989*
      no,] no!   *1966 1972*
      whilst] Whilst   *1966 1972*
              while   *1989*
      never!] never.   *1989*
153   For] For,   *1966 1972*
      deep] sleep   *1989*
154   agony,] agony . . .   *1966 1972*
155   weep,—] weep,   *1989*
156   die!] die.   *1966 1972 1989*
Heading.   Henry and Louisa]   *omitted   omnia*
           The . . . Second]   PART THE SECOND | The Meeting | *Scene:*
                               Africa   1966
                               PART THE SECOND | *The Meeting* | Scene:
                               Africa   *1972*
                               PART THE SECOND: THE MEETING. |
                               Scene: Egypt   *1989*
157   'Tis] 'Tɪs   *1972*
      night . . No] night.—No   *1966 1972*
      night . . . No]   *1989*
158   scenery,] scenery;   *omnia*
160   War's] war's   *1966 1972*
161   And,] And   *1989*
      sky,] sky   *1989*
162   War,] war,   *1966 1972*
163   harmony] harmony,   *omnia*
164   vultures] vultures,   *1966 1972*
      afar] afar,   *1966 1972*

166   Now]   [Now   *1966*
       south,]   South,   *omnia*
169   moan]   moan: *1989*
170   dear-beloved]   dear-belovèd   *1966 1972*
                     dear beloved   *1989*

       nation's]   nations   *1989*
       groan.]   groan   *1966 1989*
172   veined]   varied   *1966 1972*
              veinèd   *1989*

       northern]   southern   *1989*
173   deep,]   deep   *1966 1972*
175   groan]   groan,   *1989*
       hurled.]   hurled.]   *1966*
176   this]   [this]   *1966 1972*
179   No—the]   No,—the   *1966 1972*
180   blow,]   blow   *1989*
181   despair;]   despair,   *omnia*
183   love,]   love   *1966 1972*
       glare]   glare,   *1966 1972*
184   star.]   star!   *1966 1972*
185   her—Ocean's]   her. Ocean's   *1966 1972*
                   her.—Ocean's   *1989*

       wave,]   wave   *1989*
186   asassins]   assassins   *omnia*
187   unhonored]   unhonoured   *omnia*
       grave,]   grave   *1989*
188   mid]   'mid   *1966 1972*
       alone.]   alone;   *1966 1972*
              alone: *1989*

189   form is]   form's   *1989*
190   eye,]   eye;   *1989*
191   stone;]   stone: *1966 1972*
192   modesty,]   modesty   *omnia*
194   love—my]   love, my   *1966 1972*
              love!—my   *1989*

195   Half-drowned]   Half drowned   *omnia*
196   lips—"is]   lips—"Is   *omnia*
       ador'd]   adored   *omnia*
197   accurst]   accursed   *1989*
198   immerst,]   immersed,   *omnia*
201   Warrior,]   warrior,   *omnia*
202   Death]   death   *1966 1972*
       fling."]   fling?"   *1989*

203   Warrior's]   warrior's   *omnia*
      gaze.]   gaze;   *1966 1972*
206   ought]   aught   *1966 1972*
208   dear loved]   dear-loved   *omnia*
      begun.]   begun—   *1966 1972*
211   Sun.]   sun.   *1966 1972*
213   glow,]   glow   *1989*
215   vow:]   vow.   *1966 1972*
216   mid]   'mid   *1966 1972*
      blew,]   blew   *1989*
217   men]   men,   *omnia*
218   sympathized]   sympathised   *1966 1972*
      woe.]   woe;   *omnia*
220   New-nerved]   New nerved   *1989*
      hope]   hope,   *1966 1972*
221   again! . . . a]   again!—A   *1966 1972*
222   lineaments,]   lineaments;   *1966 1972*
      cheek]   cheek,   *1966 1972*
223   pourtrayed]   portrayed,   *1966 1972*
                     portrayed   *1989*
224   Glares,]   Glares   *omnia*
      ghastly.]   ghastly;   *1966 1972*
      Utterings]   utterings   *1966 1972*
      break—]   break,   *omnia*
225   unformed—his]   unformed, his   *1966 1972*
226   There]   Thus   *1989*
      lies!]   lies,   *1966 1972*
      where]   Where   *1966 1972*
227   deserted]   devoted   *1966 1972*
228   brow,]   brow—   *1966 1972*
229   lend,]   lend   *1989*
231   Yes!]   Yes,   *1966 1972*
      flame]   flame,   *1989*
232   When,]   When   *1989*
      dismay,]   dismay   *1989*
233   deer]   deer,   *1966 1972*
      came,]   came   *1989*
234   distraction.—A]   distraction. A   *1966 1972*
235   day.]   day;   *omnia*
236   breast.]   breast,   *1966 1972*
238   prest]   pressed   *1966 1972*
                  pressed,   *1989*

239 And] And, *1966 1972*
hope] hope, *1966 1972*
exprest.] expressed. *omnia*
240 wavering . . .] wavering: *1966 1972*
242 thro'] through *1966 1972 1989*
243 Tho'] Though *1966 1972 1989*
245 exclaimed—"Love,] exclaimed, "Love, *1966 1972*
246 sea gales] sea-gales *1966 1972*
247 war;] war,— *1966 1972*
248 Thro'] Through *omnia*
249 Live] "Live *1972 1989*
and] And *1966 1972*
251 away—] away. *1966 1972*
              away:— *1989*
252 pale.] pale; *1966 1972*
Death's] death's *1966 1972*
cheek.] cheek!— *1966 1972*
253 Oh!] Oh, *1966 1972*
fate] Fate *1966 1972*
254 mine:] mine! *omnia*
255 pain] pause . . . *1989*
wreak.] wreak; *1966 1972*
             wreak— *1989*
256 moment . . . . . I] moment—I *1966 1972*
                moment . . . I *1989*
thine!] thine,— *1966 1972*
257 ah,] Ah, *1966 1972*
shine."] shine!" *1966 1972*
258 voice.] voice; *1966 1972*
The] the *1966 1972*
259 away.] away; *1966 1972*
           away, *1989*
261 ray] ray. *1989*
262 sound . . save] sound,—save *1966 1972*
sound . . . save] *1989*
when] when, *1966 1972*
263 plain] plain, *1966 1972*
264 legions] legions, *1966 1972*
sweeping,] sweeping *1966 1972*
267 ruins,] ruins *1989*
nigh,] nigh *1989*
270 faint] faint, *omnia*

271 groan,] groan; *omnia*
273 agonized] agonised *1966 1972*
     laid] laid, *omnia*
274 alone . . .] alone. *1966 1972*
276 tie,] tie *1989*
277 death;] death, *omnia*
278 contempt] contempt, *1989*
281 Why? ask] Why?—Ask *1966 1972*
                    Why? Ask *1989*
     pallid,] pallid *1966 1972*
     griefworn] grief-worn *1966 1972*
282 speak:] speak. *1966 1972*
285 dies! his] dies!—his *1966 1972*
     breath,] breath *omnia*
286 bears.] bears; *omnia*
287 death,] death *omnia*
291 done!—] done, *1966 1972*
292 thro'] through *omnia*
     battle clouds] battle-clouds *omnia*
     Sun,] sun! *1966 1972*
293 fair] fair, *1966 1972*
294 Earth] earth *1966 1972*
     there.] there! *1966 1972*
295 Virtue] virtue *1966 1972*
     No;] No! *1966 1972*
300 Where] When *omnia*
301 ray,] ray,— *1966 1972*
302 rod] rod, *1966 1972*
303 nod.] nod! *1966 1972*
304 There] There, *1966 1972*
305 fled] fled, *1966 1972*
306 blood] blood, *1966 1972*
307 dread.] dread; *omnia*
309 Tho'] Though *omnia*
311 command] command, *1966 1972*
312 sceptered] sceptred *omnia*

Text collated with *1876* (lines 32–40), *1892W* (lines 32–40), *1910K*, *1927*/III (lines 32–40), *1927*/IV, *1927*/VIII (lines 32–40), *1966*, *1970* (lines 32–40), *1972*, and *1989*.

Title.   Marsellois]   MARSEILLAISE   *1892W 1910K 1927*/III *1927*/IV
                                     1966 1970
                                   Marseillaise   1972
                                   Marseillaise   *1989*

Stanza marker.   1]   *omitted   1989*

1   Haste]   HASTE   *1927*/IV *1972*
   battle,]   battle   *1910K*
   Patriot Band!]   Patriot-Band   *1910K*
                      Patriot-Band!   *1927*/IV
                      Patriot-Band,   *1966 1972*
                      Patriot Band,   *1989*

2   Glory]   glory   *1910K 1927*/IV *1966 1972*
   thee!]   thee   *1910K*
         thee,   *1927*/IV

3   hand:—]   hand—   *1910K 1927*/IV *1989*
             hand,   *1966 1972*

4   bloodred]   blood red   *1910K*
             blood-red   *1927*/IV *1966 1972 1989*

5   See!]   See   *1910K 1927*/IV
         See,   *1966 1972*

6   wasted]   vasted   *1910K*
   scour]   scour,   *1927*/IV *1966 1972*

8   joy—]   joy.   *1910K*
         joy,   *1927*/IV *1966 1972 1989*

9   family!]   family   *1910K 1927*/IV *1989*

10   citizens,]   citizens   *1910K 1927*/IV *1966 1972*
   array,]   array   *1910K 1927*/IV

11   day.]   day   *1910K*
       day—   *1927*/IV
       day!—   *1966 1972*
       day;   *1989*

12   march,]   March,   *1910K*
   toil,]   toil   *1910K*
       toil—   *1927*/IV

13   soil!]   soil.   *1910K 1927*/IV *1989*

15   Kings,]   Kings   *1927*/IV

16   chain,]   chain   *1910K*

18   you. On]   you, on   *1910K 1927/IV*
                    you!—On   *1966 1972*
     rests . . .] rests,—   *1966 1972*
19   breasts!]   breasts   *1910K*
20   train]   train,   *1927/IV*
22   free!]   free.   *1910K 1927/IV 1989*
Chorus.   &c.]   Then citizens etc. . . .   *1910K 1927/IV 1966 1972*
                    etc.   *1989*
23   shall]   Shall   *1966 1972*
24   tyranny?]   tyranny   *1910K*
                    tyranny!   *1927/IV*
26   upraised]   up-raised   *1910K 1927/IV*
     liberty?]   liberty!   *1927/IV*
27   God! by]   God!—By   *1966 1972*
28   despots,]   despots   *1910K 1927/IV 1966 1972 1989*
     their]   in their   *1910K 1927/IV*
                [in] their   *1966 1972*
     alarms,]   alarms   *1910K 1927/IV 1966 1972 1989*
29   neath]   'neath   *1966 1972*
     head!]   head   *1910K*
                head.   *1927/IV*
                head;   *1989*
30   Yea!]   Yes!   *1927/IV*
          Yea,   *1966 1972*
     dread—]   dread   *1910K*
                dread,   *1927/IV 1966 1972 1989*
Chorus.   &c.]   Then citizens etc. . . .   *1910K 1927/IV 1966 1972*
                    etc.   *1989*
32   Tremble,]   TREMBLE   *1876 1892W*
                Tremble   *1910K 1927/VIII 1966 1972*
                TREMBLE,   *1927/III 1970*
     Kings!]   Kings   *1876 1892W 1927/III 1927/VIII 1970*
                Kings,   *1966 1972 1989*
     Man!]   man!   *1876 1892W 1927/IV 1927/VIII 1970*
                man   *1910K 1927/III*
                Man,   *1966 1972*
33   country,]   Country   *1876 1892W 1927/VIII*
                country   *1910K 1989*
                Country,   *1927/III 1970*
                country!   *1966 1972*
34   your]   Your   *1876 1892W 1927/VIII 1966 1970 1972*
35   destiny.]   destiny . . .   *1876 1892W 1927/III 1927/IV 1927/VIII 1970*
                destiny!   *1966 1972*

36   all are]   are all   *1966 1972*
       for]   to   *1876 1892W 1927*/III *1927*/VIII *1970*
       fight,]   fight   *1876 1892W 1910K 1927*/VIII
38   Mother]   mother   *1876 1892W 1927*/III *1927*/VIII *1970*
       Earth]   EARTH   *1876 1927*/VIII
40   That]   Which   *1876 1892W 1927*/III *1927*/VIII *1970*
       Death]   DEATH   *1876 1927*/VIII
                   death   *1966 1972*
       Victory!]   VICTORY . . .   *1876*
                      Victory. . . .   *1927*/III
                      Victory . . .   *1892W 1927*/IV *1970*
                      Victory.   *1910K 1989*
                      VICTORY.   *1927*/VIII
                      victory!   *1966 1972*
Chorus.   &c.]   Then citizens etc. . . .   *1910K 1927*/IV *1966 1972*
                      etc.   1989
41   on]   On   *1966 1972*
42   energy.—]   energy   *1910K*
                      energy,   *1927*/IV
                      energy!—   *1966 1972*
                      energy—   *1989*
43   Yet]   Yet,   *1966 1972*
       triumph,]   triumph   *1966 1972 1989*
       pitying]   pitying,   *1966 1972*
44   unwilling]   un-willing   *1910K*
       tyranny;]   tyranny   *1910K*
45   bleed,]   bleed   *1910K*
46   Bouillé's]   Bouilli's   *1910K 1927*/IV
       bloodhound-meed;]   blood-hound-meed   *1910K*
                                  blood-hound-meed,   *1927*/IV
                                  bloodhound-meed,   *1966 1972 1989*
48   mothers']   mother's   *1910K 1927*/IV *1966 1972 1989*
49   tyger]   tiger   *1910K 1927*/IV *1966 1972 1989*
       cruelty!]   cruelty.   *1910K 1927*/IV *1989*
Chorus.   &c.]   Then citizens etc. . . .   *1910K 1927*/IV *1966 1972*
                      etc.   1989
50   uphold]   Uphold   *1910K 1927*/IV *1966 1972*
51   thee;]   thee   *1910K*
                   thee,   *1927*/IV
                   thee!   *1966 1972*
52   thou,]   thou   *1910K 1989*
       gold,]   gold   *1910K*
53   efforts,]   efforts   *1910K*

54 conquest's] Conquest's   *1966 1972*
    wave,]   wave   *1910K 1966 1972 1989*
                wave;   *1927/*IV
55 brave,] brave   *1910K 1927/*IV
57 See] See,   *1966 1972*
    unclose] unclose,   *1966 1972*
58 Victory!] Victory.   *1910K 1927/*IV *1989*
                victory!   *1966 1972*
    Chorus. | Then citizens etc. . . .   *added*   *1910K 1927/*IV

Written in very early youth   *[Esd #48]*

Text collated with *1966, 1972,* and *1989.*

1   I'll]   I'll   *1972*
    church-yard]   churchyard   *1966 1972*
4   yew,]   yew;   *1966 1972*
5   And]   And,   *1966 1972*
    away]   away,   *1966 1972*
10 death;]   death: *1966 1972*
11 Revenge] Revenge,   *1989*
12 change;]   change,—   *1966 1972*
14 grave.]   grave;   *omnia*
15 Oh!]   Oh,   *1966 1972*
20 live]   live,   *1966 1972*
    alone—]   alone;   *1966 1972*
                alone,   *1989*
21 die,]   die   *1989*

Zeinab and Kathema   *[Esd #49]*

Text collated with *1886* (lines 79–84), *1927/*III (lines 79–84), *1966, 1972, 1989,* and *2002.*

1   Upon]   Upon   *1972*
    lay;]   lay,   *1966 1972 1989*
2   fast.]   fast;   *1966 1972 1989*
3   Thro']   Through   *omnia*
    Sun's]   sun's   *1966 1972 1989*
4   past,]   passed,   *1966 1972 1989*
                past   *2002*
5   And]   And,   *1966 1972*
    unfelt]   unfelt,   *1966 1972*

7   "Oh!"]   "Oh",   *1966 1972*
8   "But]   But   *omnia*
    Sun]   sun   *1966 1972 1989*
    dawn."]   dawn!"   *1966 1972*
9   roll;]   roll,   *1989*
10   on,]   on,—   *1966 1972*
13   And]   And,   *1966 1972*
14   sea;]   sea,   *1966 1972*
16   semicircled]   semi-circled   *1966 1972*
17   betrothed]   betrothèd   *1966 1972 1989*
19   betrothed . . . for]   betrothèd. For   *1966 1972*
                              betrothèd . . . for   *1989*
20   grew.]   grew;   *1966 1972*
21   love,]   love   *1966 1972*
     truth]   truth,   *1989 2002*
24   care.]   care,   *1989*
25   O]   A   *1966 1972 1989*
     Superstition's]   superstition's   *1966 1972*
     spell—]   spell,   *1966 1972 2002*
                 spell: *1989*
26   gave;]   gave,   *1966 1972*
                 gave—   *2002*
28   Passion]   Passion,   *2002*
     save]   save,   *omnia*
30   entwine,]   entwine.   *omnia*
31   pain.]   pain   *omnia*
33   plain,]   plain   *1966 1972 1989*
34   burning]   burning,   *1966 1972*
     all.]   all.—   *1966 1972*
37   bring,]   bring   *1989 2002*
39   peace,]   peace   *1966 1972 1989*
40   defiled,]   defiled.   *1966 1972*
44   expanse.]   expanse;   *1966 1972 1989*
46   glance;]   glance,—   *1966 1972*
                 glance,   *1989*
50   above.]   above;   *1966 1972 1989*
54   ties,]   ties   *1966 1972*
     stain'd]   stained   *1966 1972 1989*
55   Sun]   sun   *1966 1972 1989*
58   before,]   before,—   *1966 1972*
                 before;   *1989 2002*
59   be,]   be   *1989*
60   bent,]   bent   *1966 1972*

61 mind.]   mind;   *1966 1972 1989*
62 fail,]   fail;   *1966 1972*
63 When]   When,   *1966 1972*
    wind]   wind,   *1966 1972*
65 o'er]   on   *1966 1972*
    slow-raised]   slow raised   *2002*
67 shore]   shore,   *1966 1972*
68 Thine]   "Thine   *1966*
    heap—the Christian's]   heap [of gold], the Christians'   *1989*
    God!"]   God."   *1966 1972 1989*
69 ore]   ore,   *1966 1972 1989*
70 nod.]   nod;   *1966 1972*
71 fresh'ning]   freshening   *1966 1972 1989*
    rise]   rise,   *1966 1972 1989*
74 hope]   hope,   *1966 1972*
76 scope,]   scope?   *1966 1972*
77 appeared]   appeared,   *1966 1972*
78 ever-present]   ever present   *2002*
    endeared?]   endeared.   *1966 1972*
79 Meanwhile]   Meanwhile   *1927/III*
    thro']   through   *1966 1972 1989 2002*
    thro']   through   *1966 1972 1989 2002*
80 went]   went,   *1886 1927/III 1966 1972*
82 intent,]   intent   *2002*
83 bow]   bow,   *1886 1927/III 1966 1972 1989*
84 river-floods]   river floods   *2002*
85 leaped]   leaped,   *1966 1972*
86 sown—]   sown;   *2002*
88 on,]   on   *2002*
89 past]   passed   *1966 1972 1989*
90 prest]   pressed   *1966 1972 1989*
    charmed]   charmèd   *1966 1972 1989*
92 Cashmire's]   Kashmire's   *1989*
    denote:]   denote.   *2002*
93 There,]   There   *omnia*
    kind;]   kind,   *1966 1972 1989*
94 Here,]   Here   *1966 1972 1989*
    forever]   for ever   *1966 1972*
    float,]   float   *2002*
95 zone—]   zone,—   *1966 1972*
              zone,   *1989*
96 own.]   own;   *1989*

97   ripe;]   ripe,   *1966 1972 1989*

98   spring]   spring,   *1966 1972 1989*

100   fling;]   fling,—   *1966 1972*
                        fling,   *1989*

101   Here,]   Here   *1966 1972*
         foot.]   foot,   *1966 1972*
                        foot: *1989*

102   wealth's]   Wealth's   *1966 1972*

105   And]   And,   *1966 1972 2002*
         day,]   day   *1989*

107   passion]   passion,   *1966 1972 2002*
         flames,]   flames,—   *2002*

109   given]   given,   *1966 1972*

110   sway.]   sway: *1966 1972 1989*

111   dark]   dank   *2002*
         Heaven]   Heav'n   *2002*

112   day]   day,   *1966 1972*

113   shew]   show   *1966 1972 1989*

116   wide-altered]   wide altered   *2002*

118   been.]   been;   *1966 1972*

119   woe]   woe,   *1966 1972 2002*

120   mid]   'mid   *1966 1972*

123   came to]   [came to]   *1966 1972*

124   staid]   stayed   *1966 1972 1989*
         long;]   long,   *1989*

125   cold,]   cold   *1966 1972*
         unappeased]   unappeasèd   *1972 1989*
         hunger]   hunger,   *1989*

127   horror]   horrors   *1966 1972*

130   started . . . lo!]   started—lo,   *1966 1972*

132   storm]   storm!   *1966 1972*
                        storm,   *1989*
                        storm.   *2002*

133   its]   her   *1966 1972*
         swung,]   swung   *1989*

134   clangor]   clangour   *1966 1972 1989*
         chain,]   chain   *2002*

138   thro']   to   *1966 1972*
                        through   *1989 2002*

140   filled.]   filled;   *1966 1972*
         He]   he   *1966 1972*

142   avail'd]   availed   *1966 1972 1989*

143 chain,] chain *1966 1972*

when] when, *1966 1972*

gleam] gleam, *1966 1972*

145 Yes! in] Yes!—in *1966 1972*

148 blight,] blight *1989*

152 Calmly.—In] Calmly—in *1966 1972*

153 paused,] paused *1989*

154 spoke—"My] spoke: "My *1966 1972*

thee,] thee,— *1966 1972*

155 carcase] carcase, *1989*

blest,] blest,— *1966 1972*

156 prey,] prey *1966 1972*

guest."] guest!" *1966 1972*

157 leaped] leapt *1966 1972*

158 Forward, in] Forward,—in *1966 1972*

come.] come . . . *1966 1972*

160 doom] doom, *1966 1972 1989*

161 death-scene] death scene *2002*

frowned] frowned. *1966*

frowned, *1972*

162 Night] night *1966 1972*

deed] dead *1989 2002*

163 home,] home,— *1966 1972*

home; *1989*

home— *2002*

164 shriven;] riven *1966 1972*

shriven, *1989*

shriven— *2002*

165 And,] And *1989 2002*

tomb,] tomb *1989 2002*

166 driven.] driven; *1966 1972 1989*

167 weal,] weal *1966 1972 2002*

170 crime,—] crime; *1966 1972*

crime, *1989*

172 matin-prime] matin prime *1989 2002*

173 comet,] comet *1989*

bright,] bright *1989*

175 pityless,] pitiless, *1966 1972 1989*

176 Man,] Man.— *1966*

Man. *1972*

man, *1989 2002*

177 heart,] heart *1966 1972 1989*

178 man's,] Man's *1966 1972*

God's,]   God's   *1966 1972*

plan—]   plan,—   *1966 1972*

plan?—   *1989*

180 disease,]   disease   *1966 1972*

wars]   wars,   *1989*

they.]   they?   *1966 1972*

The Retrospect. | *Cwm Elan 1812   [Esd #50]*

Text collated with *1886* (lines 15–168), *1892W* (lines 15–168), *1927*/III (lines 15–168), *1962BOAS* (lines 98–103, 144–68), *1966*, *1970* (lines 15–168), *1972*, *1989*, and *2002*.

Title.   Retrospect.]   Retrospect: *1886 1989*

RETROSPECT: *1892W 1927*/III *1970*

RETROSPECT   *1966*

Retrospect   *1989*

Elan]   Elan,   *1886*

ELAN,   *1892W 1966 1970*

Elan,   *1972*

1   To]   To   *1972*

2   year]   year,   *1966 1972*

4   deep ....]   deep—   *1989*

deep....   *2002*

deep,—   *1966 1972*

5   Time]   Time,   *2002*

monster's]   monster's,   *2002*

6   borne]   borne,   *1989*

7   And,]   And   *1989*

maw,]   maw   *1989*

8   morn]   morn,   *1966 1972*

10   scrutiny ....]   scrutiny! ...   *1966 1972*

scrutiny—   *1989*

scrutiny....   *2002*

12   steel;]   steel,   *omnia*

14   feeling]   feeling,   *1966 1972*

compare;]   compare   *1966 1972*

compare: *1989*

15   scene]   SCENE,   *1892W 1970*

SCENE   *1927*/III

wildered]   'wildered   *1927*/III *1970*

16   solitude;]   solitude,   *1886 1892W 1927/*III *1966 1970 1972 2002*
                 solitude   *1989*
18   colour]   color   *1892W*
                 colours   *1989*
     grove,]   grove   *1927/*III *2002*
19   wood]   wood,   *1886*
20   gleam]   gleam,   *1886 1892W 1927/*III *1966 1970 1972*
22   *stanza break*]   *omitted*   *1886 1892W 1970*
23   day:—]   day;   *1886 1892W 1927/*III *1966 1970 1972*
24   away]   away,   *1886 1892W 1927/*III *1966 1970 1972 1989*
25   And]   And,   *1886 1892W 1966 1970 1972*
26   roar,]   roar   *1989*
29   night]   night,   *2002*
30   height]   height,   *1886 1892W 1927/*III *1966 1970 1972*
34   decay]   decay,   *1886 1892W 1927/*III *1966 1970 1972 1989*
36   night;]   night,   *1989*
37   me,]   me   *1886 1892W 1927/*III *1966 1970 1972 1989*
40   wild-wood's]   wild woods'   *1886 1892W 1970*
                 wild-woods'   *1927/*III *2002*
     shade]   shade,   *1886 1892W 1927/*III *1966 1970 1972*
42   preyed;]   preyed;—   *1989*
44   plain,]   plain   *2002*
45   there]   there,   *1886 1892W 1927/*III *1966 1970 1972*
50   wildered]   'wildered   *1892W 1927/*III *1970*
51   'Twas]   'T was   *2002*
     pride]   pride,   *1989 2002*
54   impotence,]   impotence   *1927/*III
55   weep,]   weep   *1886 1892W 1966 1970 1972*
56   Heaven;]   Heaven.   *1886 1892W 1927/*III *1966 1972 2002*
57   'Twas]   Twas   *1970*
                 'T was   *2002*
     not,]   not   *1886 1892W 1927/*III *1966 1970 1972 1989*
58   Nature]   nature   *1886 1892W*
60   mate,]   mate   *1989*
61   Which]   Which,   *omnia*
     pinion]   pinion,   *omnia*
62   around . . . .]   around;   *1886 1892W 1927/*III *1966 1970 1972*
                 around . . .   *1989*
                 around. . . .   *2002*
63   Ah]   Oh   *1886*
         Oh,   *1892W 1970*
         Ah,   *1927/*III *1966 1972*

64   grave:]   grave.   *1886 1892W 1927/III 1966 1970 1972 1989*
     stanza break]   omitted   *1927/III 1970*
66   flame.]   flame: *1886*
                 flame;   *1892W 1927/III 1966 1970 1972*
67   swelled]   swelled,   *1886 1892W 1927/III 1966 1970 1972 2002*
68   came]   came,   *1886 1892W 1927/III 1966 1970 1972 1989*
69   apathy's]   Apathy's   *1966 1970 1972*
70   misery;]   misery,   *1989*
75   soar]   soar,   *omnia*
     spurn]   spur   *1892W 1927/III 1970*
77   its]   it   *1892W 1970*
                 stanza break added   *1886 1892W 1927/III 1970*
78   O]   Oh,   *1892W 1927/III 1966 1970 1972*
                 O,   *2002*
79   name]   name,   *1886 1892W 1927/III 1970*
84   sought. It]   sought, it   *1886*
                 sought—it   *1892W 1927/III 1966 1970 1972*
85   around.—]   around.   *1886 1892W 1927/III 1966 1970 1972*
86   who,]   who   *1886 1892W 1966 1970 1972*
     stand]   stand,   *1886 1892W 1966 1970 1972*
87   saviour]   savior   *1892W*
88   crawl]   crawl,   *omnia*
     slave]   slave,   *omnia*
89   freedom's]   Freedom's   *1886 1892W 1927/III 1966 1970 1972*
90   Tho']   Though   *1892W 1966 1970 1972 1989 2002*
91   despair.]   despair?   *1989*
92   *They*]   They   *1886 1892W 1970*
     feeling,]   feeling   *1989*
93   Which]   Which,   *omnia*
     revealing]   revealing,   *omnia*
96   ray,]   ray,—   *2002*
97   day!]   day!—   *1966 1972*
98   *They*]   They   *1886 1892W 1970*
                 . . .   *1962BOAS*
99   talk]   talk,   *1886 1892W 1962BOAS 1966 1970 1972*
100   spirit]   spirits   *1886 1892W 1927/III 1970*
103   little]   little,   *1886*
108   learned,]   learnèd,   *1927/III 1966 1970 1972*
110   emblazoned]   unblazoned   *1927/III*
115   vale!]   vale: *1886 1892W 1927/III 1966 1970 1972 1989*
116   rock,]   rock   *1989*
     vast]   vast,   *1892W 1966 1970 1972 1989*

119   below!]   below: *1886 1892W 1927/III 1966 1970 1972*
       stanza break]   *omitted   1972*
120   Woods,]   Woods   *1989*
       depth]   depths   *1892W 1970*
121   echo's]   Echo's   *1966 1970 1972*
123   footstep]   footsteps   *1927/III*
       intent—]   intent: *1886 1892W 1966 1970 1972*
124   Meadows!]   Meadows   *1927/III*
                            Meadows,   *1966 1972*
       whose]   Whose   *2002*
125   pressed]   pressed,   *1886 1892W 1966 1970 1972*
126   Despair]   despair   *1989 2002*
127   there!]   there!—   *1966 1972*
                   stanza break added   1989
131   brain?]   brain.   *1886 1892W 1927/III 1970*
       stanza break]   *page break   1892W*
                            omitted   1970
132   nature's]   Nature's   *1892W 1966 1970 1972*
133   charm,]   charm   *2002*
134   sadness—]   sadness   *1886 1892W 1927/III*
                            sadness,   *1966 1970 1972 1989*
136   Changed!—not]   Changed?—not   *1966 1972*
137   dead,]   dead   *1886 1892W 1927/III*
138   thro']   through   *1892W 1966 1970 1972 1989 2002*
       air]   air,   *1886 1892W 1927/III 1966 1970 1972*
140   butterfly]   butterfly,   *1886 1892W 1927/III 1966 1970 1972*
       hues]   hues,   *1927/III*
141   views,]   views   *1989*
143   change!]   change.   *1886 1892W 1970*
       stanza break]   *omitted   1970*
146   gone,]   gone   *1989*
147   alone,]   alone;   *1886 1892W 1927/III 1962BOAS 1966 1970 1972*
                            2002
152   radiant]   inmost   *1886 1892W 1927/III 1962BOAS 1970*
153   virtues]   virtues,   *1962BOAS*
154   throne;]   throne,—   *1966 1972*
                            throne,   *1989*
156   there;]   there,—   *1966 1972*
                            there,   *1989*
157   form]   form,   *1886 1892W 1927/III 1962BOAS 1966 1970 1972*
159   bind,]   bind   *1989*
162   Had]   Has   *1962BOAS 1970*

soul;]   soul,—   *1892W 1962BOAS 1966 1970 1972*
              soul—   *1989*
163   retrospects]   retrospects,   *1886 1927/*III
164   mind,]   mind;   *1886 1927/*III
165   hue]   hue,   *1886*
166   view,]   view;   *1886 1927/*III
              view,—   *1892W 1962BOAS 1970*
              view   *1966 1972 1989*

The wandering Jew's soliloquy   [Esd #51]

Text collated with *1892W, 1927/*III*, 1966, 1970, 1972,* and *1989.*

1   Is]   Is   *1892W 1927/*III *1970 1972*
3   this]   the   *1892W 1927/*III *1970*
5   blood-life]   life-blood   *1927/*III
6   Destruction]   destruction   *1989 1927/*III
      dwells,]   dwells   *1989*
7   deeply-caverned]   deeply caverned   *1892W 1927/*III *1970*
      lair]   lair,   *1892W 1966 1970 1972 1989*
8   And,]   And   *1892W 1927/*III *1989*
      curst]   cursed   *1892W 1966 1970 1989*
      ire,]   ire   *1892W 1927/*III *1989*
9   death-torch]   death torch   *1892W 1927/*III
10   *stanza break*]   *omitted*   *1927/*III *1970*
11   misery's]   Misery's   *1966 1970 1972*
      jackall]   jackal *omnia*
      thou!]   Thou!   *1966 1970 1972*
13   thy]   Thy   *1966 1970 1972*
14   thy]   the   *1892W 1927/*III *1970*
              Thy   *1966 1972*
15   thee]   Thee   *1966 1970 1972*
16   pestilence]   Pestilence   *1966 1970 1972*
17   favoured]   favored   *1892W*
18   minister]   Minister   *1966 1970 1972*
21   Earthquake demon]   Earthquake-daemon   *1966 1970 1972*
                              Earthquake-demon   *1989*
      ingorged]   ignored   *1927/*III
              engorged   *1966 1970 1972 1989*
22   thy]   the   *1892W 1927/*III *1970*
      crew?]   crew,   *1989*
25   thine]   Thine   *1966 1970 1972*
      own,]   own   *omnia*

26   thine]   Thine   *1892W 1966 1970 1972*
28   Tyrant!]   Tyrant,   *1966 1972*
      thee.—]   Thee—   *1892W 1970*
                  thee—   *1927/*III
                  Thee!—   *1966 1972*
29   deeply—drain]   deeply, drain   *1966 1972*
      hate—remit;]   hate—remit   *1892W 1927/*III
                  hate, remit! . . .   *1966 1972*
                  hate; remit   *1970*
                  hate—remit,   *1989*
      then I]   this I   *1892W 1927/*III
                  Then I   *1966 1972*
                  this—I   *1970*
      die.]   die!   *1966 1972*

To Ianthe. ~~Oct~~ Septr 1813   [Esd #52]

Text collated with *1886, 1892W, 1927/*III, *1966, 1972,* and *1989.*

Title.   Ianthe.]   Ianthe: *1886*
                  IANTHE   *1892W 1927/*III
                  IANTHE [SHELLEY]   1966
                  Ianthe [*Shelley*]   *1972*
                  Ianthe   *1989*
~~Oct~~ Septr 1813]   *omitted*   *1892W 1989*
                  September, 1813.   *1886*
                  september 1813   *1927/*III
                  September 1813   *1966 1972*
1   love]   love   *1892W 1927/*III *1972*
      Baby!]   baby!   *1966 1972*
      sake:]   sake;   *1892W 1966 1972*
3   frame]   frame,   *1892W*
      weak,]   weak   *1989*
5   more,]   more   *1886 1892W 1966 1972*
7   pity]   pity,   *1892W 1966 1972*
8   feel,]   feel   *1886 1892W 1966 1972*
      impart;]   impart: *1886 1892W*
9   her]   her,   *1892W*
10   bosom,]   bosom   *1989*
11   recur,]   recur;   *1886*
                  recur,—   *1892W 1966 1972*
12   blossom,]   blossom;   *1886 1892W 1966 1972*
                  blossom   *1927/*III

13   Dearest,]   Dearest   *1886 1892W 1966 1972*
14   Mother's]   mother's   *1886 1892W 1966 1972 1989*
        loveliness.—]   loveliness.   *1886 1892W 1966 1972*

Evening—to Harriet. Sep. 1813   [Esd #53]

Text collated with *1886, 1892W, 1927*/III, *1966, 1970, 1972,* and *1989.*

Title.   Evening—to Harriet.]   Evening. To Harriet.   *1886*
                                              Evening. To Harriet   *1927*/III
                                              EVENING — TO HARRIET [SHELLEY]
                                                 1966
                                              EVENING | to harriet   *1970*
                                              Evening—to Harriet [*Shelley*]   *1892W 1972*
                                              Evening: To Harriet   *1989*
        Sep. 1813]   *omitted*   *1886 1892W 1970 1989*
                              1813   *1927*/III
                              September 1813   *1966 1972*
1   thou]   thou   *1892W 1927*/III *1970 1972*
     Sun!]   Sun,   *1966 1972*
3   And]   And,   *1892W 1966 1970 1972*
     decline,]   decline   *1989*
4   vapour]   vapor   *1892W*
5   And]   And,   *1892W 1970*
7   Earth]   Earth,   *1886 1892W 1966 1970 1972*
     splendor]   splendour   *1886 1927*/III *1966 1970 1972 1989*
     bright]   bright,   *1886 1892W 1927*/III *1966 1970 1972*
8   Shews]   Shows   *omnia*
     the]   a   *1927*/III
     dream;]   dream,   *1927*/III *1989*
                     dream!—   *1966 1972*
12   dear,]   dear   *1989*
13   And]   And,   *1892W 1966 1970 1972*
     caress,]   caress   *1886 1927*/III *1989*
Dateline.   July 31ˢᵗ 1813.]   *omitted*   *1892W 1966 1970 1972 1989*
                     31ˢᵗ]   31st,   *1886 1927*/III

To Harriett ("Thy look of love")   [Esd #54]

Text collated with *1886, 1892W, 1911, 1927*/III, *1962BOAS, 1966, 1970, 1972,* and *1989.*

Title.   Harriett]   Harriett: May, 1814.   *1886*
                           HARRIET   *1892W 1970*

HARRIET | (May 1814)   *1911*
HARRIETT | MAY 1814   *1927/III*
HARRIET [SHELLEY] | May 1814   *1966*
Harriet [Shelley] | May 1814   *1972*
Harriet   *1962*BOAS *1989*

Stanza marker.   *none*]   I   *1911 1927/III*

1   Thy]   THY   *1892W 1911 1927/III 1970 1972*

2   Soul]   soul;   *1886 1892W 1911 1927/III 1962*BOAS *1966 1970 1972*
     Soul,   *1989*

3   balm—]   balm   *omnia*

4   lifes]   life's   *1886 1892W 1927/III 1962*BOAS *1966 1970 1972 1989*
     Life's   *1911*

  bowl.]   bowl;   *omnia*

5   mine]   mine,   *1886 1892W 1911 1927/III 1962*BOAS *1966 1970 1972*

Stanza marker.   *none*]   II   *1911 1927/III*

7   Harriett!]   Harriet!   *1892W 1911 1927/III 1962*BOAS *1966 1970*
     1972 1989

8   eye]   eye,   *1886 1892W 1911 1927/III 1962*BOAS *1966 1970 1972*

9   give]   give,—   *1892W 1911 1927/III 1962*BOAS *1970*

10   die]   die—   *1886 1966 1972*
     die;   *1892W 1911 1927/III 1962*BOAS *1970*
     die,   *1989*

Stanza marker.   *none*]   III   *1911 1927/III*

13   thou]   thou,   *1886 1892W 1911 1927/III 1962*BOAS *1966 1970*
     1972
  then]   then,   *1886 1892W 1911 1927/III 1962*BOAS *1966 1970 1972*
  mankind]   Mankind   *1927/III*

14   state—]   state,   *1886 1892W 1927/III 1962*BOAS *1966 1970 1972*
     1989
     state,—   *1911*

15   virtuous]   virtuous,   *omnia*
  kind]   kind,   *1886 1892W 1911 1927/III 1962*BOAS *1970*

16   hate]   hate;   *1886 1892W 1911 1927/III 1962*BOAS *1966 1970 1972*
     hate,   *1989*

18   fellow beings]   fellow-being's   *omnia*

Comment.   *Cook's Hotel*]   *appears in dateline below*   *1886*
     omitted   *1892W 1911 1927/III 1962*BOAS *1970*

Stanza marker.   *none*]   IV   *1911 1927/III*

19   cheek]   cheek,   *omnia*

20   fast]   fast,   *omnia*
  dim]   dim,   *omnia*

22   limb.]   limb;   *omnia*

Stanza marker.   *none*]   V   *1911 1927*/III

25   O]   Oh,   *1892W 1911 1927*/III *1962BOAS 1966 1970 1972*
       guide]   guide!   *1886 1892W 1911 1927*/III *1962BOAS 1966 1970
                  1972*
                guide,   *1989*
26   flee]   flee;   *1886 1892W 1911 1927*/III *1962BOAS 1966 1970 1972*
              flee: *1989*
27   Tis]   'Tis   *omnia*
     malice]   malice,   *omnia*
     tis]   'tis   *omnia*
     revenge]   revenge,   *omnia*
     tis]   'tis   *omnia*
     pride]   pride,   *omnia*
28   Tis]   'Tis   *omnia*
     any thing]   anything   *omnia*
     thee.]   thee;   *omnia*
29   O]   Oh,   *1892W 1911 1927*/III *1962BOAS 1966 1970 1972*
     prove]   prove,   *omnia*
Dateline.   *May 1814*]   *Cook's Hotel.*   *1886*
                  omitted   *1892W 1911 1927*/III *1962BOAS 1966*
                  1970 1972 1989

"Full many a mind"   *[Esd #55]*

Text collated with *1962BOAS, 1966, 1972,* and *1989.*

1   Full]   Full   *1972*
2   bear]   bear,—   *1962BOAS 1966 1972*
            bear;   *1989*
4   despair]   despair!   *1962BOAS 1966 1972*
               despair: *1989*
     stanza break]   *page break*   *1962BOAS*
5   T'would]   'Twould   *1962BOAS*
                It would   *1966 1972*
                "It could   *1989*
6   &]   and   *1966 1972 1989*
     Heaven]   Heaven,—   *1962BOAS 1966 1972*
                Heaven—   *1989*
7   &]   and   *omnia*
8   comfort]   comfort,   *omnia*
     mind.]   mind."   *1989*
Dateline.   Stanmore.   1815]   Stanmore, 1815   *1962BOAS*
                          Stanmore 1815   *1966 1972*

Text collated with *1966*, *1972*, and *1989*.

Title.   May 1813: To Harriet . . . .]   TO HARRIET [?GROVE]
1966
To Harriet [? *Grove*]   *1972*
To Harriet * * * * * * * * *
1989

1   Oh]   Oh, *1966*
         Oh,   *1972*
    Harriet]   Harriet,   *omnia*
2   destroy]   destroy? *omnia*
3   woes,]   woes?   *omnia*
4   grief?]   joy?   *1989*
5   no—past]   no,—past   *1966 1972*
              no, past   *1989*
6   mine.]   mine;   *omnia*
8   attains]   attain   *1966 1972*
    prime]   prime: *1966 1972*
              prime.   *1989*
10   pain]   pain.   *omnia*
11   Rapture]   rapture   *1966 1972*
    Joy]   joy   *1966 1972*
12   swells]   swell   *1966 1972*
    thro']   through   *omnia*
    Libertine's]   libertine's   *1966 1972*
    frame]   frame;   *omnia*
14   flame]   flame.   *omnia*
15   love]   love,   *omnia*
17   prove]   prove,   *omnia*
19   gloom]   gloom,   *1989*
20   joy.]   joy;   *omnia*
21   thee]   thee,   *omnia*
    Harriet]   Harriet,   *omnia*
22   away]   away,—   *1966 1972*
              away;   *1989*
23   dear]   dear,   *omnia*
27   death's]   Death's   *1966 1972*
28   miseries]   misery's   *omnia*
30   despair]   despair,   *omnia*
31   that]   that,   *omnia*
    Harriet]   Harriet,   *omnia*

33   Tis]   'Tis   *omnia*
34   swift rolling]   swift-rolling   *1966 1972*
      year]   year,—   *1966 1972*
                years—   *1989*
35   Ah no]   Ah, no!   *1966 1972*
                Ah no,   *1989*
      sight]   sight—   *1966 1972*
                sight,   *1989*
36   be.]   be!   *1966 1972*
Comment.   Cum Elam]   Cwm Elan   *1966 1972*
                          omitted   *1989*
          Adieu]   Adieu,   *1989*
          love]   love,   *1989*
          night]   night.   *omnia*

"Late was the night"   [Esd #57]

Text collated with *1966, 1972,* and *1989.*

1   Late]   LATE   *1972*
     night]   night,   *omnia*
     bright]   bright;   *1966 1972*
               bright,   *1989*
2   teinted]   tinted   *omnia*
     wals]   walls   *1966 1972*
              vale   *1989*
     light]   light,   *omnia*
3   wide]   wide,   *1966 1972*
              wide   *1989*
4   its]   <?its>   *1966*
             <?the>   *1972*
                  the   *1989*
     mountains]   mountain   *omnia*
     stream]   stream.   *omnia*
6   been dyed by]   heard yelling   *1989*
     dyed]   <?dyed>   *1966 1972*
     murderes]   <murderers'>   *1966*
                  murderers'   *1972 1989*
     song]   song,   *omnia*
7   wave]   staves   *1989*
8   murderes]   <murderers>   *1966*
                  murderers   *1972 1989*

braved]   braved.   *1966 1972*
                    braves.   *1989*
9   which]   which,   *omnia*
    high]   high,   *omnia*
10   Valley]   valley   *omnia*
11   Huge]   huge   *omnia*
    Sky]   sky   *1966 1972*
                    sky,   *1989*
12   death]   death.   *omnia*
13   air]   air,   *1966 1972*
14   torrents]   torrent's   *omnia*
    tide]   tide,   *1966 1972*
                    tide;   *1989*
15   fair]   fair,   *omnia*
16   Shade]   shade   *omnia*
    glide]   glide.   *omnia*
17   See]   See,   *1966 1972*
    [?] [?]]   [?none] <?can save>;   *1966 1972*
                    leans o'er [the wave];   *1989*
18   tattered]   tattered,   *1989*
    so]   is   *1989*
    bare]   bare,—   *1966 1972*
                    bare;   *1989*
19   yawning]   yawning,   *1966 1972*
    grave]   grave,   *omnia*
20   And]   And,   *1966 1972*
    shivering]   shivering,   *omnia*
    hair]   hair.   *omnia*
21   oer]   o'er   *omnia*
    mile]   mile,   *omnia*
22   child]   child,   *1966 1972*
                    child;   *1989*
23   cheek]   cheek,   *1966 1972*
                    cheek;   *1989*
    awhile]   awhile,   *omnia*
24   &]   and   *omnia*
    cold-striken]   cold-stricken   *omnia*
Dateline. 1815]   *omitted   omnia*

14
Feb^{ry} 28th 1816— To St Irvyne   [Esd #58]

Text collated with *1966, 1972,* and *1989.*

Title. Feb^{ry} . . . Irvyne]   TO ST. IRVYNE—TO HARRIET [GROVE] |
                28 February 1805   *1966*
                To St. Irvyne—to Harriet [Grove] | 28 February
                    1805   *1972*
                February 28th 1805: To St Irvyne   *1989*

1   Oer]   O'er   *1966 1989*
            O'ER   *1972*
    turrets]   turrets,   *omnia*
    St]   St.   *omnia*
    Irvyne]   Irvyne,   *omnia*
    roar]   roar,   *omnia*
2   Towers]   towers   *omnia*
    blast]   blast;   *omnia*
3   never]   never,   *omnia*
    St]   St.   *omnia*
    Irvyne]   Irvyne,   *omnia*
    more]   more?   *omnia*
4   past]   past?   *1966 1972*
            past.   *1989*
5   height]   height,   *omnia*
6   star spangled]   star-spangled   *omnia*
    sky]   sky,   *1966 1972*
7   Moon]   moon   *omnia*
    thro']   through   *omnia*
    night]   night,—   *1966 1972*
            night?   *1989*
8   moments]   moment   *1989*
    by.]   by!   *1966 1972*
10   breast]   breast,   *omnia*
    sorrow torn]   sorrow-torn   *omnia*
    confess]   confess;   *omnia*
11   Harriet]   Harriet,   *omnia*
    tho']   though   *omnia*
    nigh]   nigh,   *1966 1972*
12   less.]   less!   *1966 1972*
13   roamed]   roamed,   *omnia*
    thro']   through   *omnia*
    Eve]   eve,   *omnia*

14 St] St. *omnia*

away] away! *1966 1972*

away; *1989*

15 pleasure winged] pleasure-winged *omnia*

grieve] grieve: *1966 1972*

grieve, *1989*

16 Soul] soul *omnia*

decay] decay. *omnia*

17 fled] fled, *1966 1972*

fast fading] fast-fading *omnia*

dream] dream, *1966 1972*

18 mind] mind, *omnia*

19 &] and *omnia*

20 Soul] soul *omnia*

bind] bind. *omnia*

21 cold] cold, *1966 1972*

grave] grave, *omnia*

22 oer] o'er *omnia*

Stroods] Strood's *omnia*

Lea] lea, *1966 1972*

lea *1989*

23 Tomb] tomb *omnia*

night tempests] night-tempests *1966 1972*

rave] rave, *omnia*

24 Then] Then, *omnia*

Harriet] Harriet, *omnia*

Dedication. To H Grove] *omitted 1966 1972 1989*

Queen Mab;

A Philosophical Poem: with Notes.

Text collated with *1870, 1876, 1904, 1911, 1927, 1989,* and *2002.* Greek Text in epigraph III collated with *1876* and *1989.*

Title.   MAB;]   MAB.   *1870*

                MAB   *1904 1911*

                Mab   *1989*

Subtitle.   A . . . NOTES.]   *omitted   1870 1989*

         POEM:]   POEM,   *1904*

             POEM | (1813)   *1911*

             Poem   *2002*

         WITH NOTES.]   *omitted   1911 2002*

         NOTES.]   NOTES   *1904*

Epigraph I.   ECRASEZ . . . *Voltaire.*]   *omitted   1870*

             L'INFAME!]   L'INFAME!—   *1904*

Epigraph II.   Avia . . . *Lucret.* lib. iv.]   *omitted   1870*

           juvatque]   juratque   *1927*

           musæ.]   musae.   *1904 1989*

              Musæ.   *1911*

           pergo. | *Lucret.* lib. iv.]   pergo.—*Lucret.* lib   *1904*

Epigraph III.   Δὸς . . . *Archimedes.*]   *omitted   1870*

             Δὸς]   Δος   *1876*

             που]   ποῦ   *1989*

             στῶ,]   ςῶ,   *1876*

             κόσμον]   κοσμον   *1876*

             κινήσω.]   κινησω.   *1876*

Dedication.   TO HARRIET * * * * *]   TO HARRIET SHELLEY.   *1870*

                         TO | HARRIET * * * * *.   *1876*

                         To Harriet * * * * *.   *1989*

1   that,]   that   *1876 1904 1927*

9   Harriet!]   HARRIET!   *1904 1927*

13   unto]   into   *1870 1876 1904 1927 1989*

    love,]   love;   *1870 1876 1904 1927*

15   flowret]   floweret   *1870 1876 1904 1927*
Title.   QUEEN MAB.]   *omitted   1989 2002*
        MAB.]   MAB   *1904 1911 1927*

Canto I

1   Death,]   Death—   *1870*
2   Death]   Death,   *1870*
3   moon]   moon,   *1870*
6   When]   When,   *1870*
     wave]   wave,   *1870*
12   then]   *omitted   1870*
     peerless]   divinest   *1870*
     form]   form,   *1870*
21   theme,]   theme   *1870*
30   life]   life,   *1870*
     rapture]   rapture,   *1870*
34   eloquence,]   eloquence   *1870 1989*
35   tyger's]   tiger's   *1870 1876 1904 1911 1989*
39   dark blue]   dark-blue   *1870 1911*
56   teints]   tints   *1904 1989*
62   light:]   light.   *1870*
63   spells]   Spells   *1870 1904 1911 1927*
     in,]   in;   *1870*
64   spot,]   spot;   *1870*
65   And]   And,   *1870*
     etherial]   aethereal   *1904*
                  ethereal   *1927*
66   gaze,]   gaze   *1870*
     silently,]   silently   *1870*
69   wildered]   'wildered   *1904 2002*
70   grand]   grand,   *1927*
72   fancy]   Fancy   *1911*
73   wondrous]   wond'rous   *1927*
83   line:]   line.   *1870*
84   pageant:]   pageant.   *1870*
                  pageant;   *1911 1927*
88   scene,]   scene,—   *1870*
90   sound,]   sound;   *1870*
91   pageant,]   pageant,—   *1870*
94   slight,]   slight;   *1927*
     slight, yon]   slight,—yon   *1911*

103 Yet]   Yet,   *1911*
110 air,]   air;   *1870*
114 Stars!]   "Stars!   *1904*
123 boon,]   boon   *1989*
127 custom,]   Custom,   *1911*
129 arise!]   arise!"   *1904*
133 frame.]   frame,   *1911 1989 2002*
134 grace,]   grace;   *1911 2002*
            grace.   *1989*
136 away,]   away;   *1870*
     reassumed]   re-assumed   *1911*
139 lay]   lay,   *1870*
140 Wrapt]   Wrapped   *1870 1904 1989*
141 meaningless,]   meaningless;   *1870*
            meaningless.   *2002*
144 functions:]   functions.   *1870*
     'twas]   'Twas   *1870*
145 soul.]   Soul.   *1870*
147 identity]   identity,   *1870*
     there:]   there;   *1870*
148 Yet,]   Yet   *1870*
     oh,]   oh   *1870 1927*
     Heaven,]   heaven,   *1870*
150 And]   And,   *1870*
     ever changing,]   ever-changing,   *1870 1876 1904*
     ever rising]   ever-rising   *1870 1876 1904*
154 rapidly;]   rapidly: *1876 1904 1989*
155 Then]   Then,   *1870 1904 2002*
     an]   a   *1870*
157 Spirit!]   Spirit   *1870*
          "Spirit!   *1904*
     deep;]   deep,   *1870*
158 Spirit!]   Spirit   *1870*
     soared]   soar'd   *1927*
     high;]   high,   *1870*
160 earned,]   earned,—   *1870*
161 me.]   me."   *1904*
162 Do]   "Do   *1904*
     is]   Is   *1870 1876 1904 1927*
164 soul,]   Soul,   *1870*
165 soul,]   Soul,   *1870*
166 me.]   me."   *1904*

167 I]   "I   *1904*
     Mab: to]   Mab. To   *1870*
168 keep:]   keep.   *1870*
169 past,]   past   *1870*
171 stern,]   stern   *1870*
     find:]   find.   *1870*
173 gather: not]   gather. Not   *1870*
175 man;]   man,   *1870*
176 extatic]   ecstatic   *1870 1904 1911 1989*
178 day,]   day   *1876*
180 me,]   me   *1870 1911*
181 spirit]   spirit,   *1870 1904 1927*
185 peace,]   peace   *1870*
187 me!]   me!"   *1904*
189 spirit;]   Spirit;   *1870 1911*
193 uncontrolled]   uncontrouled   *1911*
198 *stanza break*]   *omitted*   *1870 1911 1927*
201 And]   And,   *1870*
204 Queen]   Queen,   *1870*
205 reins]   reins,   *1870 1927*
209 heaven's]   Heaven's   *1904 1911*
     dark blue]   dark-blue   *1870 1911*
212 on—]   on.   *1870*
214 flew,]   flew;   *1870*
215 And]   And,   *1870*
218 it . . . rock,]   far above a rock, the utmost verge   *1870*
219 The . . . earth,]   Of the wide earth, it flew—   *1870*
     earth,]   earth—   *1911*
220 Andes, whose]   Andes,—whose   *1911*
221 Lowered]   Loured   *1870*
222 Far,]   Far   *1870*
225 shewed]   showed   *1870 1904 1927 1989*
228 grey]   gray   *1904*
231 Seemed . . . way]   The chariot seemed to fly   *1870*
232 Lay]   *omitted*   *1870*
     through]   Through   *1870*
     midst]   abyss   *1870*
235 semicircled]   semi-circled   *1989*
238 goal]   goal,   *1870 1927*
239 speed;]   speed.   *1870*
241 Appeared]   Appear'd   *1927*
246 fell,]   fell   *1870*

251 heaven;] heavens   *1870*
                    Heaven;   *1911*
257 horned] hornèd   *1870 1876 1904 1911 1989*
260 dash'd] dashed   *1870 1904 1911 1989*
262 suns,] stars,   *1870*
     and] and,   *1870 1904*
263 Eclipsed] Bedimmed   *1870*
264 here!] here,   *1870*
266 worlds,] worlds   *1870*
275 thou!] thou   *1870 1911*
276 scene,] glorious scene!   *1870*
                    scene!   *1911*
277 temple.] temple!   *1870*

Canto II

2   ocean's] Ocean's   *1904*
3   there,] there   *1870*
5   wave,] wave,—   *1870*
9   clouds] mountain-clouds   *1870*
10 radiancy] radiancy,   *1870*
13 moment,] moment—   *1870 1911*
15 ocean's] Ocean's   *1904*
     edge,] edge—   *1870 1911*
18 dark blue] dark-blue   *1911*
21 *stanza break*] *page break*   *1911*
                    omitted   *1870*
23 Gleaming in] That gleam amid   *1870*
     light,] purple light   *1870*
25 Stretching o'er] That canopy   *1870*
     bright] resplendent   *1870*
26 ocean] Ocean   *1904*
     ocean waves] ocean-waves   *1870 1911*
     waves] waves,   *1927*
29 etherial] aethereal   *1904*
                    ethereal   *1927*
30 faery] fairy   *1870*
                    faëry   *1911*
     Hall!] hall.   *1870*
31 Heaven,] heaven   *1870*
33 dome,] dome;   *1870*
42 Hall] hall   *1870*
     Spells:] spells.   *1870*

46   etherial]   aethereal   *1904*
     footsteps,]   footsteps   *1870 1904 1911 1989 2002*
47   mists,]   mists   *1870*
55   Spirit!]   "Spirit,"   *1870*
                 "Spirit!"   *1904 1911 2002*
57   This]   "This   *1870 1904 1911 2002*
     sight]   sight,   *1870*
59   meed,]   meed   *1870*
63   nature]   Nature   *1870 1904 1911*
67   future.]   future."   *1870 1904 1911 2002*
70   universe!]   universe.   *1870*
76   nature's]   Nature's   *1870 1904 1911*
77   around]   around,   *1870 1904 1911 2002*
84   distance:]   distance.   *1870*
90   earth's]   Earth's   *1870 1911*
91   space]   space,   *1870*
     time]   time,   *1870*
92   aërial]   aëreal   *1904*
95   obstacles,]   obstacles   *1870*
97   earth.]   Earth.   *1911*
101   anthill's]   ant-hill's   *1870 1904*
102   wonderful!]   wonderful   *1870*
108   nature.]   nature!   *1870*
                 Nature.   *1904 1911*
109   Behold,]   "Behold,"   *1870 1904 1911 2002*
110   Palmyra's]   "Palmyra's   *1870 1904 1911 2002*
111   Behold!]   Behold   *1870*
112   Behold!]   Behold   *1870*
     smiled;]   smiled.   *1870*
114   shame—]   shame.   *1870 1911*
116   Nothing—it]   Nothing.—It   *1870*
123   race;]   race,—   *1870*
126   Beside]   "Beside   *1870 1904 1911 2002*
     Nile,]   Nile   *1870*
128   way:]   way;   *1870*
129   pyramids]   Pyramids   *1870 1904 1911*
130   Yea!]   Yea,   *1870*
131   stood;]   stood!   *1876 1904 2002*
132   scite]   site   *omnia*
133   name!]   name.   *1870*
134   Behold]   "Behold   *1870 1904 1911 2002*
     spot;]   spot,   *1870*

136   desart-blast.]   desert-blast.   *1870 1904 1989*
                               desert-blast   *1911*
138   heaven]   Heaven   *1904 1911*
141   orphan]   orphan,   *1870*
150   Demon-God;]   Demon-God.   *1870*
154   fiends:]   fiends!   *1870*
156   nature]   Nature   *1911*
       had]   hath   *1876 1904 1911*
158   fading,]   fading;   *1870*
162   Where]   "Where   *1870 1904 1911 2002*
163   desart]   desert   *1870 1904 1911 1989*
       now:]   now.   *1870*
                       now   *1911*
166   antient]   ancient   *1870 1904 1989*
       fanes,]   fanes   *1870 1989*
169   stalks,]   stalks;   *1870 1911*
171   Which,]   Which   *1870 1904 1911 1989*
173   But,]   But   *1870*
181   curses]   curses,   *1870 1927*
182   Spirit!]   "Spirit!   *1870 1911 2002*
                        "Spirit,   *1904*
183   past]   passed   *1870 1904 1927 1989*
       away,]   away   *1870*
185   and]   and,   *1870*
188   continent:]   continent.   *1870*
189   There,]   There   *1870*
       now,]   now   *1870*
190   time's]   Time's   *1870 1904 1911*
192   All,]   All   *1870*
196   sojourner,]   sojourner   *1870*
197   desart]   desert   *1870 1904 1911 1989*
198   earth]   Earth   *1911*
199   haunt,]   haunt   *1870*
201   merchandize:]   merchandise: *1904 1911 1989*
202   blest]   blessed   *1870 1904 1989*
203   plain:]   plain.   *1870*
207   not,]   not   *1870*
210   eternity.]   Eternity.   *1911*
211   There's]   "There's   *1870 1911 2002*
213   rain,]   rain   *1870*
217   Lybian]   Libyan   *1870 1904 1911 1989 2002*
225   How]   "How   *1870 1904 1911 2002*

226   things,] things   *1870*
227   grass,] grass   *1870*
229   noon,] noon   *1870*
230   world;] world,—   *1870*
231   beings,] beings   *1870*
233   atmosphere,] atmosphere,—   *1870*
234   feel] feel,   *1870*
      live] live,   *1870*
243   orbs.] orbs."   *1870 1904 1911 2002*
245   extacy] ecstacy   *1870 1989*
                ecstasy   *1904 1911*
246   revived; the] revived. The   *1870*
250   view;] view,   *1870*

Canto III

1   FAIRY!] "FAIRY!"   *1870 1904 1911 2002*
2   spells] Spells   *1870 1904 1911 1927*
3   etherial] aethereal   *1904*
4   I] "I   *1870 1904 1911 2002*
13   heaven.] Heaven."   *1904 1911 2002*
Speaker. MAB.] FAIRY.   *1870*
14   Turn] "Turn   *1904*
16   knowest] know'st   *1870*
17   knowest] know'st   *1870*
      imbecility:] imbecility:—   *1870*
18   is;] is: *1904*
20   time] Time   *1870 1911*
22   Behold] "Behold   *1904*
      palace,] palace   *1870*
      that,] that   *1870 2002*
23   city,] city   *1870*
      towers] towers,   *1870*
25   centinels,] sentinels,   *1870 1904 1911 1927 1989 2002*
26   around: the] around. The   *1870*
27   hearest] hear'st   *1870*
29   on:] on.   *1870*
              on—   *1911*
33   appetites—that] appetites:—that   *1911*
40   famine: when] famine. When   *1870*
43   shame,] shame   *1870*
46   gold,] gold   *1870*

51 Unfeeling,] Unfeeling *1870*
53 fulfills] fulfils *1870 1876 1904 1911 1927 1989 2002*
64 visage.] visage." *1904*
     No] "No *1904*
65 for ever!] forever! *1911*
     ever!] ever? *1870 1904 2002*
     death,] Death, *1870 1904 1911*
66 wish,] wish *1870*
     thee!—Not] thee! Not *1870*
67 blessed] blessèd *1876 1904 1911*
     peace!] Peace! *1870 1911*
69 wherefore] Wherefore *1870*
70 solitude;] solitude, *1870*
     shun'st] shunn'st *1870 1904 1911 1927 1989 2002*
71 peace!] Peace! *1870 1911*
72 but pitying] and pitying *1870 1927*
73 soul.] soul! *1870*
             soul." *1904*
Speaker. MAB.] *omitted* *1876 1927*
                     FAIRY. *1870*
                 THE FAIRY. *1904 2002*
74 Vain] "Vain *1904*
75 peace] Peace *1870 1904 1911*
76 mutters;] mutters;— *1870*
77 agonies,] agonies; *1870*
80 earth] Earth *1911*
82 nature] Nature *1870 1904 1911*
86 woe?] woe, *1870*
95 strange.] strange: *1870*
96 acts] acts, *1870*
     lives] lives, *1870*
99 *king*] king *1870*
     yet,] yet *1870*
100 To] (To *1870*
     nature,] Nature, *1904 1911*
101 present,] present) *1870*
     seem,] seem *1870*
102 slave,] slave *1870*
103 being;] being, *1870*
     wretch,] wretch *1870*
105 earth's] Earth's *1911*
108 corruption!—what] corruption—what *1870*
     they?] they?— *1911*

109   —The]   The   *1870 1911*
      community;]   community.   *1870*
      they]   They   *1870*
110   labour:]   labour;   *1870*
115   death,]   death   *1870*
118   Whence,]   Whence   *1870*
                  "Whence,   *1904*
      thinkest]   think'st   *1870 1904 1911*
      thou,]   thou   *1870*
124   genders]   'genders   *1904*
125   earth]   Earth   *1911*
126   murder. . . . . . And]   murder.—And,   *1870*
                              murder. . . . And   *1904 2002*
                              murder. . . . . And   *1911*
                              murder . . . And   *1989*
      reason's]   Reason's   *1870 1904 1911*
127   nature,]   Nature,   *1870 1904 1911*
129   misery; that]   misery—that   *1870*
130   happiness]   happiness,   *1870*
132   childhood;—kingly]   childhood; kingly   *1870*
139   vain-glorious]   vainglorious   *1870 1904 2002*
141   time's]   Time's   *1870 1904 1911*
143   bubble.]   bubble!   *1870*
      Aye!]   Ay!   *1870 1904 1911*
146   comes!]   comes: *1870*
149   closed,]   closed;   *1870*
150   man,]   man   *1927*
151   Who,]   As   *1870*
      humility,]   humility   *1870*
155   judge,]   judge   *1870 1911*
158   more:]   more;   *1870*
160   reason's]   Reason's   *1904 1911 2002*
161   Yes!]   Yes,   *1870*
162   death's]   Death's   *1904*
164   virtue]   Virtue   *1904*
165   man,]   man   *1870*
170   Nature]   "Nature   *1904*
172   for ever]   forever   *1904 1911*
179   and,]   and   *1870*
      frame,]   frame   *1870*
180   Nero,]   Nero   *1870*
181   Rome,]   Rome   *1870*
182   Lowered]   Loured   *1870*

185   new created]   new-created   *1870 1904 1911 2002*
187   Thinkest]   Think'st   *1870 1904 1911*
188   Rome,]   Rome   *1870*
189   blow,]   blow   *1870*
192   earth:]   Earth: *1911*
196   universe,]   Universe,   *1870*
197   nature's]   Nature's   *1904 1911*
199   outcast]   outcast,   *1870 1904 1927 1989*
       man.]   Man.   *1870 1904 1911*
202   tyrant,]   tyrant   *1870*
205   thatch,]   thatch   *1870 1904*
206   earth]   Earth   *1870 1904 1911*
207   sons,]   sons   *1870*
212   self-important]   self important   *1989*
       that]   the   *1870*
214   Spirit]   "Spirit   *1904*
       no.]   no!   *1870*
217   Thou,]   Thou   *1870*
       aye,]   aye   *1870*
222   by.]   by: *1870*
224   shew]   show   *1870 1904 1927 1989*
       justice,]   justice   *1870*
226   Spirit]   "Spirit   *1904*
229   thro']   through   *1870 1904 1911 1989 2002*
       Heaven's]   heaven's   *1870*
230   being,]   being   *1870*
236   time]   Time   *1911*
237   surely]   surely,   *1870*
238   frame,]   frame   *1870 1911*
       pervadest,]   pervadest   *1870*

Canto IV

Speaker.   *none*]   [THE FAIRY CONTINUES:]   *2002*
1   How]   "How   *1904*
     the]   The   *1870*
     sigh,]   sigh   *1870*
2   zephyrs]   Zephyrs   *1870*
     evening's]   Evening's   *1870*
     ear,]   ear   *1870*
7   love]   Love   *1870 1911*
     had]   has   *1870*
8   hills,]   hills   *1870*

10   rocks,]   rocks   *1870*

11   stainless,]   stainless   *1870 1927*

12   steep,]   steep   *1870*

14   idly,]   idly   *1870*

16   solitude]   Solitude   *1870 1904 1911*

17   earthliness;]   earthliness,   *1870*

18   silence]   Silence   *1870 1904 1911*

     alone,]   alone,—   *1870*
                      alone: *1911*

24   vesper's]   Vesper's   *1911*

30   pityless]   pitiless   *1870 1904 1911 1989*

33   jagged]   jaggèd   *1876 1904 1911*

     gulf.]   gulph.   *1876 1911 2002*

34   heaven?—that]   Heaven?—that   *1904 1911*
                      heaven!—that   *1927*

     dark red]   dark-red   *1870 1911*

37   round!]   round.   *1870*

38   roar,]   roar   *1870*

     deaf'ning]   deafening   *1870 1911*

40   midnight]   Midnight   *1870 1904 1911*

44   clangor,]   clangour,   *1904*

45   rage:—loud,]   rage:—loud   *1870*
                      rage;—loud,   *1989*

46   death]   Death   *1870 1904 1911*

49   there,]   there   *1870 1927*

51   sun-set]   sunset   *1870 1904 1911*

58   Wrapt]   Wrapped   *1870 1904 1989*

     grey]   gray   *1904*

64   warriors,]   warriors   *1870*

69   day,]   day   *1870 1911*

75   uncaused,]   uncaused   *1870*

79   land.]   land: *1870*

84   And]   And,   *1870*

85   Ruin,]   Ruin   *1870*

     death,]   death   *1870*

89   soul,]   soul,—   *1870*

97   love; on]   love,—on   *1870*

99   slavery;]   slavery?   *1870*

101   meteor-happiness,]   meteor happiness,   *1870 1911*

102   gulph]   gulf   *1870 1904 1927 1989*

104   statesmen,]   statesmen   *1927*

     flower]   flower,   *1870 1927*

111   infant-arm]   infant arm   *1870 1911*

112   earth;]   Earth;   *1911*

113   Learnt]   Learned   *1904*

115   reason's]   Reason's   *1904 1911*

118   force]   Force   *1870 1904*

119   falshood]   Falsehood   *1870 1904*
          falsehood   *1876 1911 1927 1989*

120   *stanza break*]   *omitted*   *1904*

121   Ah!]   "Ah!   *1904*

127   pityless]   pitiless   *1870 1904 1911 1927 1989*
    frame,]   frame—   *1870*

129   sprung]   sprung,   *1870 1911*

130   custom, the]   custom,—the   *1870*

131   heaven,]   Heaven,   *1904 1911*

133   longings.]   lodgings.   *2002*

136   defencelessness;]   defencelessness   *1911*

139   Throughout]   "Throughout   *1904*

140   element,]   element: *1904*
       element;   *1911 2002*

141   remained]   remained.   *1870 1876 1927*

143   active,]   active   *1870*

146   hatreds; these]   hatreds. These   *1870*

147   falsehood]   falshood   *2002*

148   will]   will,   *1870 1927*
    thought]   thought,   *1870 1927*

152   heaven's]   Heaven's   *1904 1911*
    orb,]   orb   *1870*

154   Man]   "Man   *1904*
    body,]   body   *1911*

155   resolve,]   resolve;   *1870 1911*

163   blest]   blessed   *1870 1904 1989*

164   death]   Death   *1870 1904 1911*

168   War]   "War   *1904*

169   trade,]   trade;   *1870*

170   murderers,]   murderers   *1870*

176   crown,]   crown   *1870*

177   woe]   woe,   *1870*
    penury]   penury,   *1870*

184   villainous,]   villanous   *1870*
       villanous,   *1904*
       villainous   *1911*

185   good,]   good   *1870*
    self-contempt,]   self-contempt   *1870*

186   kindle; they]   kindle. They   *1870*

187 Honour] Honour, *1870*

power,] power; *1870*

197 justice] Justice *1870 1904 1911*

198 Stand,] Stand *1870*

199 And,] And *1870 1904 1911*

wrong,] wrong *1870 1904 1911*

200 public] Public *1870*

virtue,] Virtue, *1870*

201 pityless] pitiless *1870 1904 1911 1989*

203 Then] "Then *1904*

207 flow. . . .] flow. *1870*

flow . . . *1911 1989*

208 words:—well] words (well *1870*

210 world!—God,] world)—God, *1870*

Hell,] Hell *1927*

211 pityless,] pitiless, *1870 1904 1911 1989*

212 nick-name] nickname *1870 1904 2002*

213 tygers] tigers *1870 1876 1904 1911 1989*

blood.] blood: *1870*

214 gulf] gulph *1876 1911 2002*

217 crimes.] crimes: *1870*

221 These] "These *1904*

222 and] and, *1870*

wills] wills, *1870 1927*

226 *stanza break*] *omitted* *1870*

page break *1911*

227 They] "They *1904*

comes] comes, *1870*

228 destruction's] Destruction's *1911*

237 Look] "Look *1904*

238 falsehood,] falshood, *2002*

240 master] Master *1870 1904 1911*

was:—or] was; or *1870*

delightst] delight'st *1870 1904 1911 2002*

243 fame:] fame; *1870*

246 Aye,] Ay, *1870 1904 1911*

250 When] "When *1870 1904 1911 1989 2002*

come?] come?" *1870 1904 1911 1989 2002*

256 judgment,] judgement, *1904*

260 holdst] hold'st *1870 1904 1911 2002*

Speaker.   *none*]   [THE FAIRY CONTINUES:]   *2002*
1   THUS]   "THUS   *1904*
4   world; even]   world. Even   *1870*
7   there, though]   there—though   *1904*
     choke,]   choke   *1870*
8   Loading]   (Loading   *1870*
     land,]   land)   *1870*
9   promise. Yet]   promise, yet,   *1870*
                     promise, yet   *1904 1989*
15   die.]   die:—   *1870*
16   selfishness,]   Selfishness,   *1870 1911*
20   judgment]   judgement   *1904*
21   *stanza break*]   *omitted*   *1870 1876 1904 1911*
22   religion,]   Religion,   *1870 1911*
     selfishness!]   Selfishness,—   *1870*
                     Selfishness!   *1911*
23   falshood,]   falsehood,   *1870 1876 1904 1911 1927 1989*
26   name—]   name;   *1870 2002*
                 name,   *1876 1904 1911 1927*
                 name: *1989*
27   Compelled, . . . deformity,]   Compelled . . . deformity   *1870*
28   right,]   right   *1870*
29   lineaments,]   lineaments   *1870*
30   All,]   All   *1870*
     ignorance:]   ignorance;   *1870*
                   Ignorance: *1911*
35   fame;]   fame: *1870*
37   fears]   fears,   *1870 1927*
38   Hence]   "Hence   *1904*
     commerce]   Commerce   *1911*
39   nature]   Nature   *1911*
43   For ever]   Forever   *1911*
44   Commerce!]   Commerce,   *1870*
45   spring,]   spring;   *1870 1927*
46   poverty]   Poverty   *1870 1904 1911*
     wealth]   Wealth   *1870 1904 1911*
48   death,]   death   *1870 1911 1989*
50   life,]   life;   *1870*
51   Which poisoned]   Which—poisoned,   *1870*
                       Which poisoned,   *1904 2002*
                       Which, poisoned   *1911 1989*

soul, scarce]   soul—scarce   *1870*

chain,]   chain   *1870 1989*

52   goes]   goes,   *1870*

53   Commerce]   "Commerce   *1904*

selfishness,]   Selfishness,   *1911*

54   power]   power,   *1870*

55   gold:]   gold;   *1870*

64   Since]   "Since   *1904*

68   woe]   woe,   *1870*

71   will,]   will   *1870*

72   Even]   (Even   *1870*

driven,]   driven   *1870*

73   master,]   master)   *1870*

76   Scarce living]   Scarce-living   *1911*

pullies]   pulleys   *1870 1904 1911 1989*

79   The]   "The   *1904*

80   Yields]   Yield   *1870*

81   heaven]   Heaven   *1911*

pride,]   pride   *1870*

82   soul;]   soul,   *1870*

83   hopes,]   hopes;   *1870*

87   enterprize]   enterprise   *1870 1904 1911 1989*

daring, even]   daring. Even   *1870*

91   groveling]   grovelling   *1870 1904 1911 1927 1989*

94   eloquence]   eloquence,   *1870 1904 2002*

96   woe,]   woe;   *1870*

98   idol]   idol,   *1870 1904 2002*

fame,]   Fame,   *1870 1904 1911*

99   virtue,]   Virtue,   *1870 1904*

tread,]   tread,—   *1870 1911*

103   fire-side,]   fireside,   *1870 1904*

104   intercourse]   intercourse,   *1870 1904*

114   misery,]   misery   *1870*

fear,]   fear   *1870*

116   offsprings]   offspring's   *1870 1876 1904 1911 1927 1989*

scream,]   scream;   *1870 1911*

118   For ever]   Forever   *1911*

121   tyranny; his]   tyranny. His   *1870*

125   power,]   Power,   *1911*

127   The]   "The   *1904*

penury]   Penury   *1870 1904 1911*

129   poison,]   poison   *1870*

toil,]   toil   *1870*

130   solace]   solace,   *1870 1911 1989*

133   will.]   will: *1870 1927*

137   past]   passed   *1870 1904 1927 1989*

145   tinsel,]   tinsel   *1870*
      heaven]   Heaven   *1904 1911*

147   Yet]   "Yet   *1904*

148   earth,]   earth   *1870*

150   Science]   Science,   *1870*

151   boy,]   boy—   *1870*

153   love,]   love—   *1870*

156   death]   Death   *1870 1904 1911*

158   eyebeam)]   eye-beam)   *1870*
                  eyebeam,)   *1876*
                  eye-beam,)   *1911*
                  eyebeam),   *1927*

159   Him,]   Him   *1870*

164   crime,]   crime   *1870*

165   soul,—]   soul,   *1870*

167   around]   about   *1870*
      earth,]   earth   *1870*

169   venal: gold]   venal. Gold   *1870*

170   selfishness,]   Selfishness,   *1911*

172   Whom,]   Whom   *1870*

175   tyranny]   Tyranny   *1870 1904 1911*
      falshood,]   Falsehood,   *1870 1904 1911*
                  falsehood,   *1876 1927 1989*

177   All]   "All   *1904*
      sold: the]   sold. The   *1870*
      heaven]   Heaven   *1904 1911*

178   venal;]   venal: *1870*
      earth's]   Earth's   *1911*

183   liberty, the]   liberty,—the   *1870 1911*

185   instinctively,]   instinctively,—   *1870*

187   selfishness,]   Selfishness,   *1870 1911*

189   sold; the]   sold. The   *1870*

190   agony,]   agony: *1870*

193   horror]   horror,   *1870 1911 1989*

194   commerce;]   commerce: *1927*

195   sensualism,]   sensualism   *1870*

197   Falshood]   Falsehood   *1870 1876 1911 1927 1989*
                  "Falsehood   *1904*

200   souls,]   souls   *1870*

201   cowardice]   Cowardice   *1911*

202   avarice]   Avarice   *1911*
      bribe]   bribe,   *1870*
204   him]   *him*   *1870*
206   shudder,]   shudder   *1870 1927*
207   heart,]   heart   *1870 1989*
210   nature,]   nature   *1870*
211   a]   the   *1870 1927*
214   There]   "There   *1904*
      glory,]   glory   *1870 1927*
217   virtue]   Virtue   *1911*
219   Its]   His   *1870*
221   when,]   when   *1870*
      power's]   Power's   *1904 1911*
      hand,]   hand   *1870*
222   last]   last,   *1870*
      title—death;]   title—death;—   *1911*
223   —The]   The   *1911*
224   bliss,]   bliss   *1904 2002*
228   brain,]   brain   *1870*
229   ever wakeful]   ever-wakeful   *1870 1911*
231   This]   "This   *1904*
      commerce]   "commerce"   *1870*
234   long;]   long:—   *1870*
235   weighed,]   weighed;   *1870*
239   hardened,]   hardened   *1870*
      they,]   they   *1870 1927*
242   give,—]   give!   *1870*
245   virtue]   Virtue   *1911*
249   But]   "But   *1904*
      selfishness]   Selfishness   *1870 1904 1911*
250   grave:]   grave.   *1870*
251   day,]   day;   *1870*
252   earth's]   Earth's   *1911*
256   hell]   hell,   *1870*
257   time,]   Time,   *1870 1904 1911*
258   libertine,]   libertine   *1927*
259   years.]   years."   *1904*

Canto VI

3   frame,]   frame   *1870*
4   painted]   painted,   *1927*
    glows,]   glows;   *1870 1927*

12   It]   "It   *1870 1904 1911 2002*
     world!]   world,   *1870*
15   years,]   years   *1870*
21   universal]   Universal   *1870 1911*
22   Heaven?]   heaven?"   *1870*
                 Heaven?"   *1904 1911 2002*
26   Oh!]   "Oh!   *1870 1904 1911 2002*
27   soul,]   soul   *1870*
30   Falshood,]   Falsehood,   *1870 1876 1904 1911 1927 1989*
36   falshood]   falsehood   *1870 1876 1904 1927 1989*
                 Falsehood   *1911*
39   How]   "How   *1870 1904 1911 2002*
     earth]   Earth   *1911*
     become!]   become—   *1870*
40   spirits,]   spirits   *1870 1904 1911 1989*
41   spheres;]   spheres—   *1870*
42   man,]   Man,   *1911*
     nature]   Nature   *1870 1904 1911 2002*
43   work,]   work!   *1870*
46   there.]   there!   *1870*
47   Spirit!]   "Spirit,   *1870*
                 "Spirit!   *1904 1911 2002*
                 Spirit,   *1927*
     earth,]   earth   *1870*
                 Earth,   *1911*
48   Falshood]   Falsehood   *1870 1876 1904 1911 1927 1989*
     power]   Power   *1870 1911*
49   truth!]   Truth.   *1870*
                 Truth!   *1911*
50   there!]   there: *1870*
51   wretched!]   wretched.   *1870*
     confide,]   confide—   *1870*
52   health-drops,]   health-drops   *1870*
     joy,]   joy   *1870*
53   *stanza break added*   *1911*
54   Now,]   Now   *1870*
                 "Now,   *1911*
     shew,]   show   *1870*
                 show,   *1904 1989*
56   nature]   Nature   *1870 1904 1911*
     recreating]   re-creating   *1870 1904 1911*
57   earth.]   Earth.   *1911*
58   passion's]   Passion's   *1870 1904 1911*

59   reason's]   Reason's   *1870 1904 1911*
61   grave!]   grave,—   *1870*
                 grave—   *1911*
63   frown!]   frown,—   *1870*
                 frown,   *1911*
64   roar!]   roar,   *1870 1911*
65   curse,]   curse   *1870 1904 1911*
66   light! and]   light, and   *1870*
                 light,—and   *1911*
68   deceit!—but]   deceit—but   *1870 1911*
70   hell]   Hell   *1904*
71   heaven]   Heaven   *1904 1911*
72   Thou]   "Thou   *1870 1904 1911 2002*
      lookest]   look'st   *1870 1904 1911 1927*
      upon!—the]   upon!—The   *1870*
      stars,]   stars   *1870*
73   sweet,]   sweet   *1870*
79   worshipper.]   worshiper.   *1870*
      becamest,]   becam'st,   *1870 1904 1911 1989*
                 becamest   *1927*
81   vast,]   vast   *1870*
82   Which,]   Which   *1870*
      relics,]   relics   *1870*
85   give]   gave   *1870*
      nature's]   Nature's   *1904 1911*
89   brain;]   brain.   *1870*
93   stoodst]   stood'st   *1870 1911*
94   gloomy; then]   gloomy. Then   *1870*
95   know;]   know,—   *1870*
96   winter's]   Winter's   *1911*
97   heaven-breathing]   Heaven-breathing   *1904 1911*
99   sun-rise,]   sunrise,   *1870 1904 1911*
100   disease,]   disease;   *1870 1911*
101   causes,]   causes   *1870 1989*
      point,]   point   *1870 1904 1911 1989 2002*
102   bend, and]   bend and   *1876 1904 1911*
                 bend,—and   *1989*
      called]   call   *1870*
      God!]   God!   *1870 1876 1904 1927*
104   God!]   God,—   *1870*
106   heaven's]   Heaven's   *1904 1911*
108   forever]   for ever   *1870 1876 1904 1989 2002*

109 he] He *1904*
     created] created, *1876 1904 1989 2002*
110 fell!] fell. *1870*
111 earth] Earth *1870 1904 1911*
112 his] His *1904*
     heaven,] Heaven, *1904 1911*
114 millions,] millions *1870 1927*
117 his] His *1904*
120 gladness,] gladness *1870*
122 Religion!] "Religion! *1870 1904 1911 2002*
     prime:] prime. *1870*
124 puerility; thou] puerility. Thou *1870*
     framedst] framed'st *1870*
126 soul,] soul; *1870*
127 pictured,] pictured *1870 1904*
131 heardst] heard'st *1870 1911*
     fate;—that] Fate; that *1870*
                  Fate;—that *1904 1911*
137 thine] thy *1870*
139 But] "But *1870 1904 1911 2002*
     grey] gray *1904*
141 Unhonored] Unhonoured *omnia*
     unpitied,] unpitied *1870*
144 truth,] Truth, *1911*
145 lowered] loured *1870*
146 Throughout] "Throughout *1870 1904 1911 2002*
147 earth] Earth *1911*
148 spirit] Spirit *1870 1904 1911*
155 sense:] sense; *1870*
156 stedfast,] steadfast, *1870 1904 1911 1989*
164 fill;] fill;— *1870*
165 that,] that *1876 1904*
167 ocean-fords,] ocean-fords *1870 1927*
168 Whilst,] (Whilst, *1870*
     mariner,] mariner *1870*
170 chance:] chance) *1870*
                  chance,— *1911*
173 act.] act *1927*
174 light,] light *1870*
176 Fulfills] Fulfils *1870 1904 1911 1927 1989 2002*
     destined,] destined *1870*
     work,] work *1870*

178   ambition,]   ambition   *1870*
         zeal,]   zeal   *1870*
180   That,]   That   *1870*
         blind,]   blind   *1870*
         graves,]   graves   *1927*
182   passions: not]   passions. Not   *1870*
189   Unrecognised,]   Unrecognized   *1870*
                              Unrecognized,   *1876 1904 1911 1989*
                              Unrecognised   *1927*
196   feel,]   feel   *1870 1927*
         see.]   see!   *1870*
197   Spirit]   "Spirit   *1870 1904 1911 2002*
         Power,]   Power!   *1870*
198   Necessity!]   Necessity,   *1870*
200   Requirest]   Requir'st   *1870 1904*
         praises; the]   praises. The   *1870*
203   harmony: the]   harmony. The   *1870*
         slave,]   slave   *1870*
205   man,]   man   *1870*
         lifts,]   lifts   *1870*
         pride,]   pride   *1870*
206   happiness,]   happiness   *1870 1989*
207   poison-tree,]   poison-tree   *1870*
209   oak,]   oak   *1870*
211   sight:]   sight.   *1870*
212   hate]   hate,   *1870*
         revenge]   revenge,   *1870*
213   favoritism,]   favouritism,   *1870 1904 1911 1927 1989*
         fame]   fame,   *1870*
214   knowest]   know'st   *1870 1904*
                      knowst   *2002*
         not: all]   not. All   *1870*
216   Regardst]   Regard'st   *1870 1904 1911*
         eye,]   eye: *1870 1911*
                      eye   *1927*
220   Yes!]   "Yes!   *1870 1904 1911 2002*
222   fiend,]   fiend   *1870 1989*
                      Fiend   *1904*
223   honors,]   honours,   *1870 1904 1911 1989*
         blood]   blood,   *1870*
226   thee,]   thee   *1870*
227   Which,]   Which   *1870*

tempest breath]   tempest-breath   *1904 1911 2002*

time,]   Time,   *1911*

228   flood,]   flood   *1870 1989*

229   Over]   O'er   *1911*

earth's]   Earth's   *1911*

231   world.]   world: *1870 1911*

world,   *1989*

232   wonderous]   wondrous   *1870 1904 1911 1989*

fane,]   fane   *1870*

233   evil]   evil,   *1870*

join,]   join   *1870*

234   necessity,]   Necessity,—   *1870*

Necessity,   *1911*

235   life,]   life   *1870*

238   strength.]   strength."   *1870 1904 1911 2002*

Canto VII

1   I]   "I   *1904*

2   there:]   there.   *1870*

5   And]   And,   *1870*

7   forth:]   forth.   *1870*

10   the]   The   *1870*

12   Weep]   "Weep   *1870 1904 1911 2002*

child!]   child!"   *1870 1904 1911 2002*

for]   "for   *1870 1904 1911 2002*

13   said,]   said   *1870*

There]   'There   *1870 1911 2002*

"There   *1904*

is]   *is*   *1870*

God.]   God.'"   *1870 1904 1911 2002*

14   sealed:]   sealed.   *1870*

15   heaven]   Heaven   *1911*

earth,]   Earth,   *1911*

16   generations]   generations,   *1870 1927*

18   whole,]   whole   *1870*

19   let]   Let   *1870*

falls]   falls,   *1870 1927*

20   eloquence]   eloquence,   *1870*

21   argument:]   argument.   *1870*

argument;   *1904*

infinity]   Infinity   *1870*

23 exterminable] ex-terminable *1911*
24 nature's] Nature's *1911*
27 holiness,] holiness; *1870 1911*
28 his] His *1904*
    worshippers,] worshipers; *1870*
                    worshippers; *1911*
29 change,] change— *1870 1911*
30 Lord,] Lord— *1870 1911*
31 his] His *1904*
    shrines,] shrines; *1911*
33 desolation's] Desolation's *1911*
    watch-word;] watch-word: *1870*
                   watchword; *1904*
34 his] His *1904*
    chariot wheels,] chariot-wheels, *1870 1876 1904 1911 1989*
35 roll,] roll *1870*
37 his] His *1904*
41 heaven] Heaven *1904 1911*
42 honor] honour *1870 1876 1904 1911 1927 1989*
    his] His *1904*
43 religion's] Religion's *1911*
44 peace,] peace *1870*
45 blood,] blood,— *1870*
49 O] "O *1904*
51 shews,] shows, *1870 1904 1989*
55 sky,] sky,— *1870*
59 earth.] earth *1927*
60 These] "These *1904*
62 fancy's] Fancy's *1904*
64 dreams] dream *1870*
67 rise!] rise!" *1904*
74 ancientness] antientness *1911 2002*
77 vigor] vigour *1870 1904 1911 1927 1989*
79 primæval] primaeval *1904 1989*
83 Is] "Is *1904*
    God?] God?" *1904*
84 Is] "Is *1904*
    God!—aye,] God?—ay, *1870*
                 God!—ay, *1904 1911*
85 his] His *1904*
88 Abhorrence,] Abhorrence; *1870*
    nature] Nature *1904 1911*
90 his] His *1904*

97   fiend,]   Fiend,   *1904*

99   pæans]   paeans   *1904 1989*

102   power,]   power,—   *1870 1911*

105   words.]   words:—   *1870 1904*
      words: *1989*

106   From]   "From   *1870 1904 1911 2002*

107   earth]   Earth   *1911*

108   man:]   man.   *1870*

109   paradise,]   Paradise,   *1904*

110   evil,]   evil;   *1870*

111   my]   My   *1904*

114   my]   My   *1904*

115   my]   My   *1904*
 honor,]   honour   *1870*
   honour,   *1876 1904 1911 1927 1989*

120   my]   My   *1904*

121   ever burning]   ever-burning   *1870 1904 1911 2002*

125   fulfill]   fulfil   *1870 1904 1911 1927 1989 2002*

126   justice)]   'justice')   *1870*
 God.]   God."   *1870 1904 1911 2002*

128   God]   "God   *1870 1904 1911 2002*

131   thou]   Thou   *1904*

133   just:]   just!   *1870 1927*

134   save.]   save!"   *1870*
   save."   *1904 1911 2002*
 One]   "One   *1870 1904 1911 2002*
 remains:]   remains.   *1870*

135   son,]   Son,   *1904*
 he]   He   *1904*

136   world; he]   world. He   *1870*
 he]   He   *1904*

140   my]   My   *1904*

141   honor]   honour   *1870 1904 1911 1927 1989*

143   alive: millions]   alive. Millions   *1870*
 die,]   die   *1870*

144   Saviour's]   saviour's   *1870*

145   But,]   But   *1870*
 unredeemed,]   unredeemed   *1870*

148   gulph]   gulf   *1870 1904 1989*

149   endlessly,]   endlessly;   *1870*
   endlessly.   *1989*

151   torment,]   torment   *1870*

152   honor,]   honour,   *1870 1904 1911 1989*

155   ray?]   ray!   *1927*
157   my]   My   *1904*
      Moses!]   Moses."   *1870*
              Moses!"   *1904 1911 2002*
159   uttered—O]   uttered—"O   *1870 1904 1911 2002*
      one,]   One,   *1904*
160   obey!]   obey!"   *1870 1904 1911 2002*
161   O]   "O   *1904*
163   came: humbly]   came. Humbly   *1870*
      he]   He   *1904*
164   his]   His   *1904*
165   his]   His   *1904*
      unheard,]   unheard   *1870*
166   his]   His   *1904*
168   he]   He   *1904*
169   he]   He   *1904*
170   blest]   blessed   *1870 1904 1989*
172   his]   His   *1904*
173   his]   His   *1904*
174   him:]   Him: *1904*
175   his]   His   *1904*
176   he]   He   *1904*
177   his]   His   *1904*
178   cried,]   cried   *1870*
179   Go! go!]   "Go! go!"   *1870 1911 2002*
              "Go! Go!"   *1904*
180   reillumined]   reillumed   *1870 1904*
              re-illumined   *1911*
181   lineaments.—I]   lineaments. "I   *1870*
              lineaments.—"I   *1904 1911 2002*
      go,]   go,"   *1870 1904 1911 2002*
      he]   He   *1904*
      cried,]   cried;   *1870*
182   But]   "But   *1870 1904 1911 2002*
183   Eternally.———The]   Eternally."———The   *1870 1904 2002*
              Eternally."———The   *1911*
              Eternally.——The   *1927*
              Eternally.————The   *1989*
185   charmed]   charmèd   *1870 1876 1904 1911 1989*
186   awoke]   awoke,   *1870*
      hell]   Hell   *1904*
189   them,]   them,—   *1870*

191   sculls]   skulls   *1870 1904 1911 1989*

192   ghastily]   ghastlily   *1870*

195   heaven.]   Heaven.   *1904 1911*

197   pilgrimage,]   pilgrimage;   *1870*

199   tyrant,]   Tyrant,   *1904*

200   his]   His   *1904*

204   his]   His   *1904*

206   unstable]   unstable,   *1870*
       power;]   power,   *1870 1904 1989 2002*

207   war,]   war;   *1870 1904 1911 1989 2002*

211   veins, and]   veins,—and   *1870*
       pityless]   pitiless   *1870 1904 1911 1927 1989*

215   to brothers]   to brothers,   *1870*

216   war,]   war   *1870 1989*

217   Scarce]   (Scarce   *1870*
       fate's]   Fate's   *1911*
       death-draught]   death-draught)   *1870*
                           death-draught,   *1904 1911 2002*

218   winepress]   wine-press   *1870 1927*

225   Yes!]   "Yes!   *1904*
       worshippers]   worshipers   *1870*
       unsheathe]   unsheath   *1870 1927*

226   his]   His   *1904*

233   spirits]   Spirit   *1870*
                   Spirits   *1904 1911*
       Lord,]   Lord,—   *1870*

235   Spirit!]   "Spirit,   *1904*

236   misery,]   misery   *1870*

237   his]   His   *1904*
       slaves]   slaves,   *1870 1989*

239   red]   red,   *1927*

241   peace; and]   peace. And   *1870*

242   mercy,]   mercy   *1870*
       whilst]   (whilst   *1870*

244   freedom's]   Freedom's   *1870 1904 1911*
       dare]   dares   *1870*
       chastise,]   chastise)   *1870*

245   now]   now,   *1870*

247   truth,]   truth   *1870*

248   foe,]   foe;   *1870*
                   Foe,   *1904*

251   his]   His   *1904*

254 Thus] "Thus   *1904*
     stood,—through] stood—through   *1989*
256 peaceful,] peaceful   *1870*
     serene,] serene   *1870*
257 tyrant's] Tyrant's   *1904*
258 will,] will;   *1870*
259 heaven's] Heaven's   *1904 1911*
260 scathed] scathèd   *1870 1876 1904 1911 1989*
261 there;] there,—   *1870*
264 sun-light's] sunlight's   *1870 1904 1911 1989*
266 noon.] noon."   *1904*
267 wand:] wand   *1911*
269 mist,] mist   *1870*
270 grove,] grove   *1870*

Canto VIII

Speaker.   *none*]   THE FAIRY.   *1904 2002*
1   THE] "THE   *1870 1904 1911*
    present] Present   *1870 1904*
    past] Past   *1870 1904*
2   Now,] Now   *1927*
    learn] learn,   *1870*
3   future.—Time!] Future.—Time!   *1870 1904*
                     Future.————Time!   *1911*
5   half-devoured] half-devourèd   *1870*
6   eternity,] Eternity,   *1911*
8   deep murmuring] deep-murmuring   *1911*
10 destiny!] destiny!"   *1870 1904 1911*
13 fear:] fear.   *1870*
14 hell;] Hell;   *1904*
16 prime,] prime.   *1989*
22 death,—] death.—   *1870*
                death;—   *1911*
24 sea] sea,   *1870*
26 swells] swells,   *1870*
    fits:] fits,   *1870 1911 1989*
28 sprung] sprang   *1870*
35 death,] death;   *1870*
41 Queen:] Queen.   *1870*
42 I] "I   *1870 1904 1911 2002*
43 lore;] lore.   *1870*
44 past,] past;   *1870*

55   And] And, *1927*
     midst] 'midst *1870*
     things,] things *1870*
56   Shew] Shows *1870*
             Show *1904 1927 1989*
             Shews *1911*
57   lighthouse] light-house *1870*
58   The] "The *1870 1904 1911 2002*
     bliss;] bliss. *1870*
60   snow-storms] snowstorms *1904 1911*
61   or] nor *1870*
66   broad,] broad *1870*
68   heaven-breathing] Heaven-breathing *1904 1911*
     groves] groves, *1870 1927*
69   blest] blessed *1870 1989*
70   Those] "Those *1870 1904 1911 2002*
     deserts] desarts *2002*
     sand,] sand *1870*
71   fervors] fervours *1870 1904 1911 1927 1989*
72   spring,] spring,— *1911*
76   Corn-fields] Cornfields *1870 1904*
     cottages;] cottages. *1870*
79   tygress] tigress *1870 1876 1904 1911 1989*
     lambs,] lambs *1870 1904 1911 1927 1989 2002*
81   Whilst] While *1870*
     desert] desart *2002*
     rang,] rang,— *1870 1911*
83   sun-rise,] sunrise, *1870 1904 1911 1989*
84   door,] door *1870*
88   Those] "Those *1870 1904 1911 2002*
     deeps,] deeps *1870*
89   plain,] plain *1870 1989*
90   morning] morning, *1870*
96   desert] desart *2002*
     solitudes,] solitudes *1870*
99   many mingling] many-mingling *1870 1876 1904 1911 1989*
103 vallies,] valleys *1870*
             valleys, *1904 1911 1989*
106 flowrets] flowerets *1870*
             flow'rets *1904*
107 All] "All *1870 1904 1911 2002*
     recreated,] re-created, *1870 1911*
108 life:] life. *1870*

109 earth] Earth *1870 1911*

110 care,] care *1870*

111 perfectness:] perfectness. *1870*

115 stream:] stream. *1870*

116 heaven,] Heaven, *1904 1911*

118 ever verdant] ever-verdant *1870 1904 1911*

119 fair,] fair; *1870*

120 autumn] Autumn *1870 1904 1911*

121 spring,] Spring, *1870 1904 1911*

123 tint] tint, *1870 1904 1927*

124 The] "The *1870 1904 1911 2002*

130 bestows:] bestows. *1870*

134 But] "But *1870 1904 1911 2002*
     man, he] man,—he *1870*
                Man, he *1904*
                Man,—he *1911*

135 joy] joy, *1870*

139 refining] refining, *1870*

142 change,] change: *1870*
               change; *1927*

145 Man, where] "Man—where *1870*
               "Man, where *1904 1911 2002*

146 Lowers] Lours *1870*

148 glow,] glow— *1870*
          glow,— *1911*

150 heart,] heart *1870*

155 own:] own; *1927*

157 wants,] wants *1876*

160 cold] cold, *1870 1927*
     toil] toil, *1870 1927 2002*

161 mind, whilst] mind—whilst *1911*

162 stubbornly, had] stubbornly—had *1911*
     brought:] brought. *1870*

163 earth's] Earth's *1870 1904 1911*

166 Nor] "Nor *1870 1904 1911 2002*
          Nor, *1927*

171 tempest] tempest, *1870 1927*

172 man] Man *1904*
     being; slavery] being. Slavery *1870*

173 bloodstained] blood-stained *1870 1904 1911*

175 Which] Which, *1870*

178 where] where, *1870*

182 fulness] fullness *1870*

184   sun,] sun   *1870 1989*
187   Even] "Even   *1870 1904 1911 2002*
      man] Man   *1904*
190   truth] Truth   *1911*
193   clime:] clime.   *1870*
196   ambition's] Ambition's   *1911*
197   religion's] Religion's   *1911*
198   Here] "Here   *1870 1904 1911 2002*
200   Blest] Blessed   *1870 1904 1989*
203   Him, still] Him (still   *1870 1989*
                    Him,—still   *1911*
      pursuing,] pursuing   *1870 1904 2002*
204   lore] store   *1870*
205   Draws] Dawns   *1870 1904 1911*
      mind, the] mind) the   *1870 1989*
                    mind,—the   *1911*
206   infiniteness,] infiniteness   *1870*
208   age,] age;   *1870*
211   earth: no] earth. No   *1870*
214   Which] Which,   *1870 1904 1927*
      nature's] Nature's   *1904 1911*
217   loathing] loathing,   *1870*
219   winged] wingèd   *1870 1876 1904 1911 1989*
      habitants,] habitants   *1870*
220   away,] away   *1870*
225   terror: man] terror. Man   *1870*
      man] Man   *1904*
227   equals: happiness] equals. Happiness   *1870*
228   dawn] dawn,   *1870 1927*
      late] late,   *1870*
232   extend] extends   *1870*
233   Their] Its   *1870*
      wield] wields   *1870*
236   mind,] Mind,   *1911*
238   paradise] Paradise   *1904*
      peace.] peace."   *1904 2002*

Canto IX

Speaker. *none*] [THE FAIRY CONTINUES:]   *2002*
3   universe,] universe   *1870*
    aspire;] aspire!   *1870*
5   will!] will,   *1870*

7   point]   point,   *1870*
     forever]   for ever   *omnia*
     there:]   there!   *1870*
8   dwelling-place!]   dwelling-place,   *1870*
10   ignorance]   ignorance,   *1870 1927*
     come:]   come!   *1870*
12   Genius]   "Genius   *1870 1904 1911 2002*
     dreams,]   dreams;   *1870 1927*
13   loveliness]   loveliness,   *1870*
20   peace,]   peace   *1870*
23   Even]   "Even   *1870 1904 1911 2002*
24   giant,]   giant   *1870*
     who,]   who   *1870*
     pride,]   pride   *1870*
25   world,]   world   *1870*
27   milleniums]   millenniums   *omnia*
29   desert]   desart   *2002*
32   day,]   day   *1870*
33   his]   *his*   *1870*
     light-winged]   light-wingèd   *1870 1876 1904 1911 1989*
37   fury]   fury,   *1870*
38   Yet]   "Yet   *1870 1904 1911 2002*
40   heaven]   Heaven   *1904 1911*
     away:]   away.   *1870*
41   crime]   Crime   *1870 1904 1911*
     careered]   careered,   *1870*
43   falshood,]   Falsehood,   *1870 1904 1911*
                   falsehood,   *1876 1927 1989*
     virtue's]   Virtue's   *1870 1904 1911*
45   Till]   Till,   *1870 1911 1927*
     death,]   death   *1989*
46   law,]   law,—   *1870*
47   passion's]   Passion's   *1870 1904 1911*
48   reason]   Reason   *1870 1904 1911*
50   and]   and,   *1870*
     passion]   Passion   *1870 1904 1911*
53   Yet]   Yet,   *1870*
55   Who]   Who,   *1870*
     sober]   sober,   *1870*
     child,]   child   *1870*
57   Mild]   "Mild   *1870 1904 1911 2002*
58   Spirit]   spirit   *1870 1876 1904 1911 1989 2002*
     grasp,]   grasp   *2002*

59   fear,] fear,— *1870*

61   hope] hope, *1870*

63   purity] Purity *1904*

64   Blest] Blessed *1870 1904 1989*
     worshippers.] worshipers. *1870*

66   brow!] brow, *1870*

67   or] nor *1870 1904 1927*

68   grey] gray *1904*

69   time.] time! *1870*

70   youth!] youth *1870*

71   grace;] grace! *1870*

72   soul,] soul *1870*

73   will,] will *1870*

75   pleasure,] pleasure *1911*
     stanza break] *omitted 1870 1927*

76   Then,] "Then, *1904 1911 2002*
     freedom's] Freedom's *1904*

79   law:] law. *1870*

81   nature's] Nature's *1904 1911*

82   undoubting] undoubted *1876 1904*

85   virtuous,] virtuous *1870*

88   life;] life. *1870*

90   pure] pure, *1870 1911*

93   Then,] "Then *1870*
             "Then, *1904 1911 2002*
     where,] where *1870*
     ages,] ages *1870*

95   groan,] groan *1870*
     penury's] Penury's *1904 1911*

101   tower] tower, *1870*

102   whirlwind's] Whirlwind's *1904*
      stanza break] *omitted 1870 1927*

103   Low] "Low *1904 1911 2002*

104   sung:] sung. *1870*

107   withal!] withal,— *1870*

114   Within] "Within *1870 1904 1911 2002*

117   wall-flower,] wall-flower *1870*

118   gloom;] gloom. *1870*

123   captivity] Captivity *1904 1911*

125   playfulness:] playfulness. *1870*

126   despair] Despair *1904 1911*

127   vaults,] vaults; *1870*

129   *stanza break*] *omitted 1870 1927*

130   These] "These   *1904 1911 2002*
131   wide scattered]   wide-scattered   *1911*
133   impulses:]   impulses.   *1870*
134   perfected,]   perfected;   *1870*
      earth,]   Earth,   *1911*
138   Now]   "Now   *1870 1904 1911 2002*
139   stedfast]   steadfast   *1870 1904 1911 1927 1989*
      past]   future   *1870*
140   charmed]   charmèd   *1870 1876 1904 1911 1989*
143   past:]   passed: *1904*
146   Yet,]   "Yet,   *1870 1904 1911 2002*
      Spirit,]   Spirit!   *1927*
      course,]   course.   *1870 1911*
154   goal:]   goal.   *1870*
156   shews,]   shows,   *1870 1904 1927 1989*
162   skies]   skies,   *1870 1927*
167   spring's]   Spring's   *1870 1904 1911*
      earth,]   earth   *1870 2002*
168   favorite]   favourite   *1870 1904 1911 1989*
170   green wood]   greenwood   *1870 1904 1911 1927*
171   Fear]   "Fear   *1870 1904 1911 2002*
      death's]   Death's   *1870 1904 1911*
      hand,]   hand—   *1870*
175   gulph-dream]   gulf-dream   *1870 1904 1927 1989*
176   virtue:]   Virtue: *1904*
178   freedom's]   Freedom's   *1904 1911*
179   bliss.]   bliss.—   *1870*
180   thee,]   thee   *1870*
181   confirmed?]   confirmed—   *1870*
183   When]   When,   *1870 1904 1911*
      walk]   walk,   *1927*
189   but]   but,   *1870*
191   falshood,]   falsehood,   *1870 1876 1904 1911 1927 1989*
194   crime,]   crime   *1870*
                crime—   *1911*
195   Whose]   (Whose   *1870*
      gains,]   gains),   *1870*
                gains—   *1911*
199   power]   power,   *1870 1911*
201   custom's]   Custom's   *1911*
      control,]   controul,   *1911*
202   pure]   pure,   *1870*
203   thee,]   thee;   *1870*

205   received:] received.   *1870*

virtue]   Virtue   *1870 1904*

209   one,]   one!   *1870*

211   life]   life,   *1870*

rapture]   rapture,   *1870*

smile.]   smile."   *1870 1904 1911 2002*

212   fairy]   Fairy   *omnia*

213   bliss]   bliss,   *1870*

214   battlement,]   battlement,—   *1870*

218   heaven's]   Heaven's   *1904 1911*

219   flew:]   flew.   *1870*

222   degrees,]   degrees   *1876 1904*

226   below:]   below.   *1870*

228   descended:]   descended.   *1870*

231   heaven.]   Heaven.   *1904 1911*

232   then,]   then.   *1870*

then;   *1927*

233   frame:]   frame;   *1870*

234   unclosed;]   unclosed.   *1870*

235   dark blue]   dark-blue   *1911*

236   wonder and]   wonder—and   *1870*

wonder, and   *1927*

Shelley's Notes to Queen Mab

Text collated with *1876* and *1989*.

Note 1 (I.242–43)

3   BEYOND]   Beyond   *1989*
10   8 minutes and 7 seconds]   8′ 7″   *omnia*

Note 2 (I.252–53)

5   falshoods]   falsehoods   *omnia*
9   synonime]   synonym   *omnia*
15   Syrius]   Sirius   *omnia*

Note 3 (IV.178–79)

34   falshood,]   falsehood,   *omnia*
37   VICE:]   VICE.   *1989*
45   iron,]   iron   *1989*
49   Falshood]   Falsehood   *omnia*
52   fare,]   fare   *1989*
53   bestow;]   bestow   *1876*
57   done,]   done   *1989*
59   career,]   career   *1989*
     year,]   year   *1989*
62   done!——I]   done!—I   *1989*
70   gave. . . . .]   gave . . .   *1989*
75   heaven,]   heaven   *1989*
82   MURDER,]   MURDER   *1989*
86   Falshood!]   Falsehood!   *omnia*
89   feet,]   feet   *1989*
90   labours,]   labours   *1989*
92   earth:]   earth;   *1989*

96 den. . . .] den . . . *1989*
98 And,] And *1989*
    eye,] eye *1989*
108 sun,] sun *1989*
113 security. . . . .] security . . . *1989*
118 even him] *even him* *1989*
    defiled,] defiled, *1989*
119 ecstacies] ecstasies *1989*
127 name.] name *omnia*
132 *stanza break*] *omitted* *1989*
133 FALSHOOD.] *omitted* *1989*
136 lowers] lours *1876*
138 honors] honours *1989*
146 smile,] smile *1989*
154 ☞] *omitted* *1989*

Note 4 (V. 1–2)

2 grave,] grave *omnia*

Note 5 (V. 4–6)

4 γενεή,] γενεή, *1876*
           γευεή, *1989*
   τοίη δὲ] τοιήδε *omnia*
   ἀνδρῶν,] ανδρῶν. *1876*
           αυδρῶυ. *1989*
5 μέν] μέυ *1989*
   δὲ] δέ *omnia*
6 ὥρη·] ὥρη *1989*
7 ἀνδρῶν] ἀυδρῶυ *1989*
   μὲν] μὲυ *1989*
   ἡ δ᾽] ἡδ᾽ *1876*
           ἡδ᾽ *1989*
   ἀπολήγει.] ἄπολήγει. *omnia*

Note 6 (V. 58)

5 suave'st.] suave 'st. *1876*

Note 7 (V.93–94)

4   vallies]   valleys   *1989*
7   expence]   expense   *1989*
9   characterise]   characterize   *omnia*
16   shew]   show   *1989*
    adduces]   adduce   *1876*
28   mistakes]   mistake   *1989*
60   ☞]   *omitted*   *1989*
81   *chap.* II.]   *chap.* 11.   *omnia*

Note 8 (V.112–13)

No variants appear.

Note 9 (V.189)

58   falshood.]   falsehood.   *omnia*
78   pityless]   pitiless   *1989*
95   bigotted]   bigoted   *1989*
107   right,]   right;   *1876*
113   ☞]   *omitted*   *1989*

Note 10 (VI.45–46)

26   antient]   ancient   *1989*
29   ☞]   *omitted*   *1989*

Note 11 (VI.171–73)

5   l'un]   l'une   *omnia*
6   qu'élève]   qu'éleve   *omnia*
    impétueux,]   impetueux,   *omnia*
7   excitée]   excité   *omnia*
9   placée]   placé   *omnia*
10   où]   oû   *omnia*
11   Un]   Une   *omnia*
12   démontreroit]   demontreroit   *omnia*
13   données,]   donnés,   *omnia*
20   infailliblement]   infalliblement   *omnia*
22   seroit]   sera   *omnia*
23   réactions]   reactions   *omnia*

Note 12 (VI.198)

1   Necessity!]   Necessity, *omnia*
13   chance,]   chance *1876*
36   shewn]   shown *omnia*
44   reasoning,]   reasonings, *1876*
95   tyger]   tiger *omnia*
98   desart]   desert *1989*
110 is]   are *omnia*
139 ☞]   *omitted   1989*

Note 13 (VII.13)

15   remove,]   remove *1876*
20   belief,—that]   belief—that *1989*
80   active:]   active; *omnia*
82   shewn]   shown *omnia*
93   *phænomenis*]   *phænomenis   omnia*
     hypotheses]   *hypothesis   omnia*
     meta physicæ,]   *metaphysicæ,   omnia*
94   *vel physicæ,*]   *vel physicæ,   omnia*
     mechanicæ,]   *mechanicæ,   omnia*
109 *nebulæ*]   *nebulæ   omnia*
     incomprehensible;]   incomprehensible, *1989*
113 ☞]   *omitted   1989*
120 *Essays.*]   *Essays   1989*
122 éléments]   élémens *omnia*
     mêmes,]   même, *omnia*
123 agents]   agens *omnia*
     présidans]   présidens *omnia*
124 grandes]   grands *omnia*
127 de]   des *1876*
     des [de] *1989*
128 cet]   cette *omnia*
130 qui]   que *1876*
     que [qui] *1989*
133 hommes]   homme *1876*
137 fil]   fit [fil] *1989*
138 la difficulté]   leur difficulté   *omnia*
144 secours]   sécours *1876*
146 le]   la *omnia*
147 qui]   que *omnia*

événemens] évènemens *1989*

150 débris] debus *1876*

debus [débris] *1989*

153 détruire.] detruire. *omnia*

mesure] mésure *omnia*

156 bien] biens *1876*

162 l'habitude,] l'habitude *omnia*

165 législateurs] legislateurs *omnia*

167 Divinité."] divinité." *omnia*

168 rapporterois-je] rapporterai-je *1876*

174 croie] crire [croie] *1989*

175 fondé] fonde *omnia*

176 l'annoncer] l'anoncer *1989*

177 doute] doutes *1876*

179 prêtres] prêtres, *1989*

métaphysiciens] metaphysiciens *omnia*

180 réservée] reservée *omnia*

néanmoins] neanmoins *omnia*

181 nécessaire] necessaire *omnia*

182 differens] différens *1876*

183 répandus] repandus *omnia*

qui] que *1876*

que [qui] *1989*

188 perfectionnée?] perfectionné? *1989*

190 Les] des *1876*

les *1989*

d'esprits,] *d'esprit* *1876*

d'esprit, *1989*

193 des] ces *omnia*

qui] que *omnia*

194 qu'embrouiller] qu'embrouilles *1876*

qu'embrouilles [qu'embrouiller] *1989*

la science] le science *omnia*

195 la plus] le plus *omnia*

196 rêveurs] reveurs *omnia*

198 énigme] enigme *omnia*

199 succès] succés *omnia*

210 les] des *omnia*

dérobe] derobe *omnia*

212 orgueil,] orgueil *1876*

paroît] paroit *1989*

214 produites] produits *omnia*

organisation] organization *omnia*

215 société,] societé, *omnia*
    de] des *omnia*
216 très] tres *omnia*
    grandes folies.] grands follies. *omnia*
217 fâcheuses] facheuses *omnia*
218 partiaux] partaux [partiaux] *1989*
224 ses vues] ces vues *1876*
    ses dispositions] ces dispositions *1876*
225 laquelle] lequelle *1989*
230 particulieres] particuliers *omnia*
231 fâcheuse] facheuse *omnia*
    quelques-unes] quelqu'uns *omnia*
232 aux] ceux [aux] *1989*
239 répandre] repandre *omnia*
240 n'eût-il] n'eut-il *omnia*
249 fantaisies.] phantasies. *omnia*
250 admettroit] admetteroit *omnia*
    théologique,] théologique *1876*
252 autoriser] autorizer *omnia*
254 garoté] garroté *omnia*
255 l'a] a [l'a] *1989*
256 qu'elle] quelle *1876*
                qu'elle [quelle] *1989*
257 inquiéter] inquieter *1989*
    besoins,] besoins *1989*
261 récompenser?] recompenser? *omnia*
262 résister?] resister? *omnia*
263 raisonnable,] raisonnable *omnia*
265 décrets?] decrets? *omnia*
267 nécessaire,] necessaire, *omnia*
277 vitae] vita *omnia*
281 viginti] viginta *omnia*
286 falshood] falsehood *omnia*
291 falshood,] falsehood, *omnia*
292 ☞] *omitted 1989*
293 naturæ] natura *1876*
                natura [naturae] *1989*
294 certum] artem *1876*
                artem [certum] *1989*
    eatenus] catemus *1876*
                catemus [eatanus] *1989*
295 quatenus] quatemus *1876*
                quatemus [quatenus] *1989*

296   hoc]   sive   *omnia*

Note 14 (VII.67)

12   country:]   country;   *1876*
15   sculls]   skulls   *1989*
17   sculls]   skulls   *1989*
19   scull]   skull   *1989*
20   scull,]   skull,   *1989*
41   scull:]   skull: *1989*
47   tyger's]   tiger's   *omnia*
49   dragon.]   dragon.—   *1876*
     me.—]   me.   *1876*
51   tyrants.]   tyrants: *1876*
53   —————Ha!]   ——Ha!   *1989*
57   behold]   hold   *omnia*
     milleniums]   millenniums   *omnia*

Note 15 (VII.135–36)

1   son,]   Son,   *omnia*
11   mean while]   meanwhile   *omnia*
41   hand]   hands   *1989*
Footnote 1   seen]   some   *1876*
56   divinity,]   divinity   *1989*
60   falshood;]   falsehood;   *omnia*
69   falshood]   falsehood   *omnia*
126   inutility]   inutillity   *1876*
136   prophesies,]   prophecies,   *omnia*
180   inspiration?]   inspiration;   *omnia*
193   pass,]   pass   *omnia*
213   prophesies]   prophecies   *omnia*
235   any thing]   anything   *omnia*
269   *Paschale.*]   *Paschali.*   *omnia*
271   ☞]   *omitted*   *1989*

Note 16 (VIII.203–7)

1   still]   (still   *omnia*
3   Draws]   Dawns   *1876*
     mind,]   mind,)   *omnia*
38   veteran's]   veterans'   *1876*

15   God,]   God   *1876*

18   disobedience.]   disobedience:—   *1876*

19   ————————————Immediately]   Immediately   *1989*

26   ulcer,]   ulcer;   *1876*

60   Mr.]   Mr   *1989*

109   every thing,]   everything,   *1876*

Footnote 3   448,]   443,   *1989*

136   cæcum]   cœcum   *omnia*

179   blood-shot]   bloodshot   *1989*

195   feelings.]   feelings?   *1876*

201   auto da fé?]   auto da fè?   *omnia*

209   brow,]   brow   *1989*

226   habits,]   habits   *1876*

260   Dr.]   Dr   *1989*

261   Mr.]   Mr   *1989*

266   Mr.]   Mr   *1989*

271   evidence;]   evidence: *omnia*

298   views?]   views.   *1876*

322   liquors,]   liquors   *1876*

338   much]   much,   *omnia*
       however]   however,   *omnia*

354   Dr.]   Dr   *1989*

357   to]   in   *omnia*

393   chace]   chase   *1989*
       horror]   horror,   *1876*

Footnote 9   Mr.]   Mr   *1989*

405   implacable,]   implacable   *omnia*

407   δράκοντας]   δρακώντας   *omnia*
       ἀγρίους]   ἀγριούς   *1876*
       καλεῖτε]   καλῆιτε   *omnia*
       παρδάλεις]   παρδελέις   *omnia*
       αὐτοὶ δὲ]   αὐτοὶδέ   *omnia*

408   ὠμότητα]   ὠμοτητα   *omnia*
       ἐκείνοις]   ἐκέινοις   *omnia*
       ἐκείνοις]   ἐκέινοις   *omnia*
       μὲν]   μέν   *omnia*
       τροφή,]   τροφὴ,   *omnia*

409   ὑμῖν]   ἡμῖν   *omnia*
       ἐστίν.]   ἐστίν.   *omnia*

410   γὰρ]   γάρ   *omnia*

ἀνθρώπῳ] ανθρώπω *omnia*
φύσιν] φὐσιν *omnia*

411 τῶν] των *omnia*
σωμάτων] σωμὰτων *1876*
σωμοτων *1989*
κατασκευῆς.] κατασκεῦης. *omnia*
ἀνθρώπου] ἀνθρὠπου *omnia*

412 τῶν] των *omnia*
ἐπὶ] επὶ *omnia*

413 κοιλίας] κοιλίας *omnia*
εὐτονία,] ευτονία, *omnia*
πνεύματος] πνέυματος *omnia*
θερμότης,] θερμὸτης, *omnia*

414 τὸ] τό *omnia*
βαρὺ] βαρὺ *omnia*
ἀλλ’] ἀλλ’ *omnia*

415 τῶν] των *omnia*
στόματος,] σοματος, *omnia*

416 γλώσσης,] γλὼσσης, *omnia*
πρὸς] πρὸος *omnia*
ἀμβλύτητι] ἀμβλὺτητι *omnia*
τοῦ] του *1876*
πνεύματος,] πνέυματος, *omnia*
ἐξόμνυται] εξόμνυται *omnia*

417 σαρκοφαγίαν.] σαρκοφαγιὰν. *omnia*
Εἰ] Ει *omnia*
λέγεις] λεγείς *omnia*
τοιαύτην] τοιὰυτην *omnia*
ἐδωδήν,] ἐδώδην, *omnia*
ὅ] ὅ *omnia*

418 ἀπόκτεινον.] απόκτεινον. *omnia*
αὐτὸς,] αὐτός, *omnia*

419 κοπίδι,] κοπίδη, *omnia*
μηδὲ] μὴδὲ *omnia*
τυμπάνῳ] τυμπανω *omnia*
μηδὲ] μὴδὲ *omnia*
ἀλλά] ἀλλὰ *omnia*

420 αὐτοὶ] αὐτόι *omnia*
ἐσθίουσι] ἐσθιούσι *omnia*
φονεύουσιν,] φὸνευοὺσιν, *1876*
φὸνευουσιν, *1989*
ἢ] ἤ *omnia*

ἦ] ἤ *omnia*
ἦ] ἤ *omnia*

421 λαγωὸν] λαγῶον *omnia*
φάγε] φὰγε *omnia*
ζῶντος] ξῶντος *omnia*

422 Ἡμεῖς] Ημεῖς *omnia*
τῷ] τῷ *omnia*
μιαιφόνῳ] μιαιφŏνῳ *omnia*
ὄψον] ὤψον *1989*

423 προσαγορεύομεν,] προσαγορέυομεν, *omnia*
πρὸς] προς *omnia*
αὐτὸ] αὑτὸ *omnia*
δεόμεθα,] δέομεθα, *omnia*

424 οἶνον,] οἶνον, *omnia*
μέλι,] μὲλι, *omnia*
γάρον,] γὰρον, *omnia*
ὄξος,] ὄξος. *1989*
ἡδύσμασι] ἡ δύσμασι *omnia*

425 νεκρὸν,] νεκρὸν, *omnia*
ἐνταφιάζοντες.] ἐνταφίαξοντες. *omnia*
αὐτῶν] αὐτων *omnia*
διαλυθέντων] διαλυθέντων *omnia*

426 τινὰ] τινὰ *omnia*

427 βαρύτητας] βαρύτητας *omnia*
νοσώδεις] νοσῶδεις *omnia*
ἀπεψίας.] απεψιάς. *omnia*

428 ζῷον] ξῶον *omnia*
ἦ] ἤ *omnia*
ἰχθὺς] ἰχθύς *omnia*

429 εἴλκυστο·] ἔιλκυστο· *1876*
              ἔιλκυστο *1989*
ἐν] εν *omnia*
ἐκείνοις] ἐκεὶνοις *omnia*
ἐπὶ] ἐπι *omnia*

430 πρόβατον] πρὸβατον *omnia*
οἰκουρὸν] οἰκουρον *omnia*
ἀλεκτρυόνα·] ἀλεκτρὺονα· *1876*
              ἀλεκτρὺονα. *1989*

431 ἀπληστίαν] ἀπληστιάν *omnia*
ἀνθρώπων,] ανθρώπων, *omnia*
φόνους] φονους *omnia*

432 πολέμους] πολὲμους *omnia*

APPENDIXES

Upon the leagued Assyrian's attempt?
Where the dark Earthquake demon who ingorged
At thy dread word Korahs unconscious crew
Or the Angels two edged sword of fire that urged
Our primal parents from their bower of bliss
(Reared by thine hand) for errors not their own
By thine omniscient mind foredoomed foreknown
Yes! I would court a ruin such as this
Almighty Tyrant! & give thanks to thee —
Drink deeply — drain the cup of hate — emit thou
may die
279⅔
7⅔
2322

"The wandering Jew's soliloquy," The Esdaile Notebook, folio 91 recto,
with PBS's line count

In Appendix A, we provide a table enumerating the poetic forms used by PBS in ***The Esdaile Notebook.*** Appendix B provides texts of the editorial notes on ***Queen Mab*** in MWS's 1839 and 1840 editions of *The Poetical Works of Percy Bysshe Shelley.*

Appendix A. Poetic Forms in *The Esdaile Notebook*

Esd # and Title	Lines in Poem	Line Count in Text	PBS's Line Count	PBS's Line Count, Revised	Stanzas	Lines per Stanza	Length of Lines	Rhyme Scheme
1	To Harriet ("Whose is the love")	16	16	NA	NA	4	4	5-4-4-3	unrhymed
2	A sabbath Walk	56	72	NA	NA	4	14-13-15-14	4-4-4-3-5-5-5-5-4-4-4-4-3-3	unrhymed
3	The Crisis	20	92	NA	NA	5	4	5-5-5-3[1]	unrhymed
4	Passion	50	142	NA	NA	10	5	5-5-3-3-3	unrhymed
5	To Harriet ("Never, O never")	20	162	NA	NA	2	10	4-3-4-3-2-2-4-2-2-3[2]	unrhymed
6	Falshood and Vice	108	270	256[3]	254	8	varied	tetrameter	rhymed couplets and *abab* quatrains
7	To the Emperors of Russia and Austria	50	320	306	304	5	10	tetrameter	*ababcccbdd*
8	To November	30	350	336	334	5	6	4-4-4-3-4-4	*ababcc*
9	Written on a beautiful day in Spring	18	368	354	352	1	18	5-5-5-5-5-5-5-5-5-3-4-4-3-5-5-5-5-6	*ababcddc-efegfhghiI[4]*
10	On leaving London for Wales	72	440	427[5]	424	8	9	5-5-5-5-5-5-5-5-6	*ababbcbcC*
11	A winter's day	34	474	461	458	5	7-7-6-7-7	varied	*abaabab[6]*
12	To Liberty	50	524	511	508	5	10	3-3-3-3-5-3-3-3-3-5[7]	*ababcddeec*
13	On Robert Emmet's tomb	28	552	540[8]	536	7	4	tetrameter	*abab*
14	a Tale of Society as it is from facts 1811	120	672	661[9]	656	10	12-11-12-12-12-12-12-13-12-12	pentameter	varied; often *abbbaccd-cdeE[10]*

[1] The number of metrical feet in the lines of the last stanza are 5-6-6-3.
[2] Possibly in quantitative verse, as gauged by number of syllables.
[3] PBS's first line count is ahead of the actual line count by two lines.
[4] The last line of stanza is an Alexandrine.
[5] PBS's line count has increased by one, putting it three lines ahead of the revised line count.
[6] Stanza 3 is rhymed *abaaba*.
[7] For the line-length patterns, see the Commentary.
[8] PBS's line count gains an additional line, making it four more than the actual total.
[9] PBS's line count gains another line, bringing the extra lines to five.
[10] See the Commentary for additional notes on the rhyme scheme.

Esd # and Title	Lines in Poem	Line Count in Text	PBS's Line Count	PBS's Line Count, Revised	Stanzas	Lines per Stanza	Length of Lines	Rhyme Scheme
15 The solitary 1810	18	690	679	674	3	6	6-5-5-5-5-3	*abbaab*
16 The Monarch's funeral	76	766	755	750	19	4	tetrameter	*abab*
17 To the Republicans of North America	50	816	805	800	5	10	tetrameter	*ababcccbdd*
18 Written at Cwm Ellan 1811	16	832	821	816	2	8	heptameter	*ababcccb*
19 To Death	68	900	889	884	3	17-20-29	varied	varied; often rhymed couplets or *abab* quatrains
20 "Dark Spirit of the desart rude"	46	946	935	930	3	15-10-21	varied; mostly tetrameter	varied; often rhymed couplets or *abab* quatrains
21 "The pale, the cold and the moony smile"	30	976	965	960	5	6	tetrameter	*ababcc*
22 "Death-spurning rocks!"	30	1006	NA	990	3	10	5-5-5-5-4-4-4-4-5-6[11]	*ababccddee*
23 The Tombs	30	1036	1025	1020	6	5	5-5-4-4-3	unrhymed
24 To Harriet ("It is not blasphemy")	72	1108	1100[12]	1092	1	72	pentameter	blank verse
25 To Harriet on her birth day	14	1122	NA	1106	1	14	pentameter	*ababcddcefefgG*[13]
26 To a balloon, laden with <u>Knowledge</u>	14	1136	NA	1120	1	14	pentameter	*abbacdcdefefgg*
27 On launching some bottles	14	1150	NA	1134	1	14	pentameter	*abbacdcdeffegg*
28 On waiting for a wind	14	1164	1156	1148	1	14	pentameter	*ababcddcefefgG*
29 To Harriet ("Harriet! thy kiss to my soul is dear")	32	1196	1188	1180	4	8	tetrameter	*ababcdcd*
30 Mary to the Sea-Wind	16	1212	1204	1196	4	4	basically anapestic tetrameter with variations	*abab*
31 A retrospect of Times of Old	83	1295	1287	1279	6	varied	pentameter	varied; often rhymed couplets and *abab* quatrains
32 The Voyage	298	1593	1588[14]	1577	16	varied	varied	unrhymed
33 A Dialogue	44	1637	1632	1621	4	varied	mostly anapestic tetrameter	rhymed couplets

[11] The final line is heptameter.
[12] PBS increases his line count by three extra lines, eight lines more than the revised total.
[13] The sonnet ends in an Alexandrine.
[14] PBS's line count gains three more lines, and thus eleven lines ahead of the revised total.

Esd # and Title	Lines in Poem	Line Count in Text	PBS's Line Count	PBS's Line Count, Revised	Stanzas	Lines per Stanza	Length of Lines	Rhyme Scheme
34 1810 ("How eloquent are eyes!")	40	1677	1672	1661	5	8	3-4-4-3-3-4-4-3[15]	_abbbacca_[16]
35 1810 ("Hopes that bud in youthful breasts")	21	1698	1693	1682	3	7	4-3-4-3-3-4-3	stanza 1: _ababcbc_ stanzas 2 & 3: _ababcac_
36 September 23, 1809 ("Moonbeam! leave the shadowy dale")	28	1726	1723[17]	1710	3	10-9-9	stanza 1: 4-3-4-4-3-3-3-3-3-4 stanza 2: 4-4-4-3-3-3-2-2-6 stanza 3: 4-4-4-4-3-3-2-2-6	stanza 1: _abaabccddd_ stanzas 2 & 3: _ababccddd_
37 To Mary I	28	1754	1751	1738	7	4	trimeter	_abab_
38 To Mary II	21	1775	1772	1759	3	7	varied	_ababccc_
39 To Mary III	37	1812	1809	1796	5	varied	varied	varied
40 To the Lover of Mary	33	1845	~~1831~~[18]	1818	3	11	5-5-5-3-5-5-5-3-6	_abbacddceee_
41 1810 ("Dares the Lama, most fleet")	36	1881	1867[19]	1854	4	9	4-3-4-3-4-3-3-4-4	_ababbccdd_
42 1809 ("I will kneel at thine altar")	36	1917	1903	1890	4	9	4-3-4-3-4-3-3-4-4	_ababbccdd_
43 Fragment . . . suggested by the . . . bombardment of Copenhagen	21	1938	1924	1911	3	7	tetrameter	_ababbcc_
44 1809 ("On an Icicle")	21	1959	1945	1932	3	7	tetrameter	_ababbcc_
45 1808 ("Cold are the Blasts")	40	1999	1985	1972	5	8	tetrameter	_ababcccb_
46 Henry and Louisa | a Poem in two parts	I: 156[20] (180) II: 159	2155 2314	2167 2326	2152 2311	35	varied; mostly 9	varied; mostly pentameter	varied; mostly _ababbcbcC_ (PBS's stated attempt at Spenserian stanzas)

[15] Line 10 is pentameter rather than tetrameter.

[16] The fifth line of every stanza echoes the stanza's first line.

[17] PBS's line count gains two more extra lines, thirteen lines ahead of the revised count.

[18] After line 22 of _Esd_ #40, PBS records the line count as 1831 but later cancels it when he adds another stanza (11 lines) and fails to write a new line count. Because PBS will compensate for this stanza later when he revises his count after removing the poetry written between _Esd_ #47 and #48, we do not add the 11 lines of the additional stanza to our revised total, but instead add the 22 lines as PBS did (correctly) to the previous total of 1796. PBS is still, technically speaking, ahead by only 13 lines.

[19] PBS still does not include the 11 lines added after the canceled line count in _Esd_ #40 to the line count following _Esd_ #41, maintaining an excess of 13 lines in his line count.

[20] Our total of 156 lines for the first part of _Esd_ #46 does not include the blank spaces with stanza numbers that PBS left in the Notebook, labeling spaces for stanzas III and IV and writing only three lines of stanza V (24 missing lines, assuming the unwritten stanzas to be Spenserian). For these projected lines, he added 26 (rather than 24) lines, arriving at a total of 2167 through the end of part one. We add 24 lines to our revised total, charging the two additional lines to PBS's faulty addition. His total is now 15 lines greater than the actual count.

Esd # and Title	Lines in Poem	Line Count in Text	PBS's Line Count	PBS's Line Count, Revised	Stanzas	Lines per Stanza	Length of Lines	Rhyme Scheme
47 A Translation of The Marsellois Hymn	58	2372	2384	2369	6[21]	9	tetrameter	_ababccddb_
48 Written in very early youth	23	2395	2467[22]	2452	3	8-8-7	tetrameter; last line of third stanza is trimeter	stanzas 1 & 2: rhymed couplets; stanza 3: _aabcbcd_
49 Zeinab and Kathema	180	2575	2648 2600[23]	2632 2583	30	6	5-5-5-5-5-6	_ababcC_
50 The Retrospect. | Cwm Elan 1812	168	2743	2767[24]	2751	12	varied	tetrameter	rhymed couplets and _abab_ quatrains
51 The wandering Jew's soliloquy	29	2772[25]	2796[26] 2822	2780 2796	2	10-19	pentameter; last line is heptameter	varied
52 To Ianthe	14	2786	NA	NA	1	14	pentameter	_abbacdcdefefgg_
53 Evening— To Harriet	14	2800	NA	NA	1	14	pentameter	_ababcddcefefgg_
54 To Harriett ("Thy look of love")[27]	30	2830	NA	NA	5	6	4-4-4-3-4-4	_ababcc_
55 "Full many a mind"	8	2838	NA	NA	2	4	5-5-5-5-4-4-5-4	stanza 1: _abab_ stanza 2: _aabb_
56 To Harriet ("Oh Harriet love like mine")	36	2874	NA	NA	8	4-6-4-4- 6-4-4-4	stanzas 1 & 2: tetrameter; stanzas 3–8: trimeter	varied; mostly _abab_ quatrains
57 "Late was the night"	24	2898	NA	NA	6	4	tetrameter	varied
58 To St Irvyne	24	2922	NA	NA	6	4	tetrameter	_abab_ quatrains

[21] Six stanzas (of the seven in the French original) plus the four-line Chorus.

[22] PBS's line count (2467) here registers the presence of the poems on leaves 78 and 79 (pages that PBS removed from the Notebook just before _Esd_ #48). His line count suggests that the missing poem or poems totaled 60 lines and his total is off from the revised total by 75 lines. We therefore give our revised total as 2452, adding the 60 lines from the discarded poem(s) and the 23 lines of _Esd_ #48. PBS's count is still off by 15 lines.

[23] PBS writes two line counts following this poem—2648, followed by 2600 beneath it—due to the removal of leaves 78 and 79 and the addition of another stanza to _Esd_ #40. "2648," uncanceled in the MS, is exactly 181 lines off from his line count for _Esd_ #48—PBS thus having added 181 lines rather than 180, the actual number of lines in _Esd_ #49. By subtracting 48 lines from his total, PBS attempted to account for the two leaves preceding _Esd_ #48 that he removed from the Notebook, while adding the 11 lines of the third stanza of _Esd_ #40. PBS, we infer, compensated in terms of stanzas (60 lines equals 5 stanzas of 12 lines each), deleting the equivalent of four stanzas, having thus removed five stanzas from one part of the Notebook while adding another stanza to his earlier poem. But the stanza that he added to _Esd_ #40 is 11 lines, not 12 lines long. We maintain our revised total of 2583, registering the amount PBS would have arrived at had his math been correct (the addition of 180 lines from _Esd_ #49 minus a 49-line correction). PBS is now ahead by 17 lines due to the extra line he added to _Esd_ #49's total and the extra line he calculated for _Esd_ #40's third stanza.

[24] PBS here adds 167 lines (rather than the correct 168) to his previous total of 2600, leaving him 16 lines ahead of our revised total.

[25] The actual number of lines of poetry printed in our Text up to this point is 2772. The difference between our lines reproduced and our revised total of PBS's line count (2796) is 24—the 24 unwritten lines that PBS intended to add to _Esd_ #46.

[26] After PBS correctly added the 29 lines of _Esd_ #51 to his previous total and arrived at 2796, he added 16 lines (the number of lines in the dedication poem _Esd_ #1—**_To Harriet_**) to his line count and arrived at the incorrect total of 2822 because he accidently carried an extra one into the tens column. Now his line count exceeds the revised total by 26 lines instead of the 16 lines that he had earlier accumulated through small miscalculations.

[27] This and the remaining four poems are written in the hand of HWS, who was not keeping score.

Appendix B. Mary W. Shelley's "Note on *Queen Mab*"

I. From the 1839 Edition of
The Poetical Works of Percy Bysshe Shelley, *Volume I,*
Edited by Mary W. Shelley

SHELLEY was eighteen when "Queen Mab" was written: he never published it. When he wrote it, he had come to the decision that he was too young to be a "judge of controversies;" and he was desirous of acquiring "that sobriety of spirit which is the characteristic of true heroism." But he never doubted the truth or utility of his opinions; and in printing and privately distributing "Queen Mab" he believed that he should further their dissemination, without occasioning the mischief either to others or himself that might arise from publication. The poem has since been frequently reprinted; and it is too well known, and the poetry is too beautiful, to allow of its being omitted, although it is doubtful whether he would himself have admitted it into a collection of his works. His severe classical taste, refined by the constant study of the Greek poets, might have discovered defects that escape the ordinary reader, and the change his opinions underwent in many points, would have prevented him from putting forth the speculations of his boyish days. To a certain extent, the same motives influence me. Were the poem still in manuscript, even less might be given;—as it is, such portions are omitted as support, in intemperate language, opinions to which at that age he was passionately attached.

A series of articles was published in the "New Monthly Magazine" during the autumn of the year 1832, written by a man of great talent, a fellow collegian and warm friend of Shelley: they describe admirably the state of his mind during his collegiate life. Inspired with ardour for the acquisition of knowledge; endowed with the keenest sensibility, and with the fortitude of a martyr, Shelley came among his fellow-creatures, congregated for the purposes of education, like a spirit from another sphere, too delicately organised for the rough treatment man uses towards man, especially in the season of youth; and too resolute in carrying out his own sense of good and justice not to become a victim. To a devoted attachment to those he loved, he added a determined resistance to oppression. Refusing to fag at Eton, he was treated with revolting cruelty by masters and boys: this roused, instead of taming his spirit, and he rejected the duty of obedience, when it was enforced by menaces and punishment. To aversion to the society of his fellow-creatures, such as he found them when collected together in societies, where one egged on the other to acts of tyranny, was joined the deepest sympathy and compassion; while the attachment he felt for individuals and the admiration with which he regarded their powers and their virtues, led him to entertain a high opinion of the perfectibility of human nature, and he believed that all could reach the highest grade of moral improvement, did not the customs and prejudices of society foster evil passions, and excuse evil actions.

The oppression which, trembling at every nerve yet resolute to heroism, it was his ill fortune to encounter at school and at college, led him to dissent in all things from those whose arguments were blows, whose faith appeared to engender blame and hatred. "During my existence," he wrote to a friend in 1812, "I have incessantly speculated, thought, and read." His readings were not always well chosen, among them were the works of the French philosophers; as far as metaphysical argument went, he temporarily became a convert. At the same time, it was the cardinal article of his faith, that if men were but taught and induced to treat their fellows with love, charity, and equal rights, this earth would realise Paradise. He looked upon religion as it is professed, and, above all, practised, as hostile, instead of friendly, to the cultivation of those virtues, which would make men brothers.

Can this be wondered at? At the age of seventeen, fragile in health and frame, of the purest habits in morals, full of devoted generosity and universal kindness, glowing with ardour to attain wisdom, resolved at every personal sacrifice to do right, burning with a desire for affection and sympathy,—he was treated as a reprobate, cast forth as a criminal.

The cause was, that he was sincere; that he believed the opinions which he entertained to be true; and he loved truth with a martyr's love: he was ready to sacrifice station and fortune, and his dearest affections, at its shrine. The sacrifice was demanded from, and made by, a youth of seventeen. It is a singular fact in the history of society in the civilised nations of modern times, that no false step is so irretrievable as one made in early youth. Older men, it is true, when they oppose their fellows, and transgress ordinary rules, carry a certain prudence or hypocrisy as a shield along with them. But youth is rash; nor can it imagine, while asserting what it believes to be true, and doing what it believes to be right, that it should be denounced as vicious, and pursued as a criminal.

Shelley possessed a quality of mind which experience has shown me no other human being as participating, in more than a very slight degree: this was his *unworldliness.* The usual motives that rule men, prospects of present or future advantage, the rank and fortune of those around, the taunts and censures, or the praise of those who were hostile to him, had no influence whatever over his actions, and apparently none over his thoughts. It is difficult even to express the simplicity and directness of purpose that adorned him. The world's brightest gauds, and its most solid advantages, were of no worth in his eyes, when compared to the cause of what he considered truth, and the good of his fellow-creatures. Born in a position which, to his inexperienced mind, afforded the greatest facilities to practise the tenets he espoused, he boldly declared the use he would make of fortune and station, and enjoyed the belief that he should materially benefit his fellow-creatures by his actions; while, conscious of surpassing powers of reason and imagination, it is not strange that he should, even while so young, have believed that his written thoughts would tend to disseminate opinions, which he believed conducive to the happiness of the human race.

If man were a creature devoid of passion, he might have said and done all this with quietness. But he was too enthusiastic, and too full of hatred of all the ills he witnessed, not to scorn danger. Various disappointments tortured, but could not tame, his soul. The more enmity he met, the more earnestly he became attached to his peculiar views, and hostile to those of the men who persecuted him.

He was animated to greater zeal by compassion for his fellow-creatures. His sympathy was excited by the misery with which the world is bursting. He witnessed the sufferings of the poor, and was aware of the evils of ignorance. He desired to induce every rich man to despoil himself of superfluity, and to create a brotherhood of property and service, and was ready to be the first to lay down the advantages of his birth. He was of too uncompromising a disposition to join any party. He did not in his youth look forward to gradual improvement: nay, in those days of intolerance, now almost forgotten, it seemed as easy to look forward to the sort of millennium of freedom and brotherhood, which he thought the proper state of mankind, as to the present reign of moderation and improvement. Ill health made him believe that his race would soon be run; that a year or two was all he had of life. He desired that these years should be useful and illustrious. He saw, in a fervent call on his fellow-creatures to share alike the blessings of the creation, to love and serve each other, the noblest work that life and time permitted him. In this spirit he composed Queen Mab.

He was a lover of the wonderful and wild in literature; but had not fostered these tastes at their genuine sources—the romances and chivalry of the middle ages; but in the perusal of such German works as were current in those days. Under the influence of these, he, at the age of fifteen, wrote two short prose romances of slender merit. The sentiments and language were exaggerated, the composition imitative and poor. He wrote also a poem on the subject of Ahasuerus—being led to it by a German fragment he picked up, dirty and torn, in Lincoln's-inn-Fields. This fell afterwards into other hands—and was considerably altered before it was printed. Our earlier English poetry was almost unknown to him. The love and knowledge of nature developed by Wordsworth—the lofty melody and mysterious beauty of Coleridge's poetry—and the wild fantastic machinery and gorgeous scenery adopted by Southey, composed his favourite reading; the rhythm of Queen Mab was founded on that of Thalaba, and the first few lines bear a striking resemblance in spirit, though not in idea, to the opening of that poem. His fertile imagination, and ear, tuned to the finest sense of harmony, preserved him from imitation. From his boyhood he had a wonderful facility of versification which he carried into another language, and his Latin school verses were composed with an ease and correctness that procured for him prizes— and caused him to be resorted to by all his friends for help. He was, at the period of writing Queen Mab, a great traveller within the limits of England, Scotland, and Ireland. His time was spent among the loveliest scenes of these countries. Mountain and lake and forest were his home; the phenomena of nature were his favourite study. He loved to inquire into their causes, and was addicted to pursuits of natural philosophy and chemistry, as far as they could be carried on as an amusement. These tastes gave truth and vivacity to his descriptions, and warmed his soul with that deep admiration for the wonders of nature which constant association with her inspired.

He never intended to publish Queen Mab as it stands; but a few years after, when printing Alastor, he extracted a small portion which he entitled "The Dæmon of the World;" in this he changed somewhat the versification—and made other alterations scarcely to be called improvements.

I extract the invocation of Queen Mab to the Soul of Ianthe, as altered in "The Dæmon of the World." I give it as a specimen of the alterations made. It well characterises his own state of mind:

> Maiden, the world's supremest spirit
> Beneath the shadow of her wings
> Folds all thy memory doth inherit
> From ruin of divinest things,
> Feelings that lure thee to betray,
> And light of thoughts that pass away.
>
> For thou hast earned a mighty boon;
> The truths which wisest poets see
> Dimly, thy mind may make its own,
> Rewarding its own majesty,
> Entranced in some diviner mood
> Of self-oblivious solitude.
>
> Custom and faith and power thou spurnest,
> From hate and fear thy heart is free;
> Ardent and pure as day thou burnest

> For dark and cold mortality;
>   A living light to cheer it long,
>   The watch-fires of the world among.
>
>   Therefore, from nature's inner shrine,
>   Where gods and fiends in worship bend,
>   Majestic Spirit, be it thine
>   The flame to seize, the veil to rend,
>   Where the vast snake Eternity
>   In charmed sleep doth ever lie.
>
>   All that inspires thy voice of love,
>   Or speaks in thy unclosing eyes,
>   Or through thy frame doth burn and move,
>   Or think, or feel, awake, arise!
>   Spirit, leave for mine and me
>   Earth's unsubstantial mimicry!

Some years after, when in Italy, a bookseller published an edition of Queen Mab as it originally stood. Shelley was hastily written to by his friends, under the idea that, deeply injurious as the mere distribution of the poem had proved, the publication might awaken fresh persecutions. At the suggestion of these friends he wrote a letter on the subject, printed in "The Examiner" newspaper—with which I close this history of his earliest work.

TO THE EDITOR OF "THE EXAMINER."

"Sir,

"Having heard that a poem, entitled 'Queen Mab,' has been surreptitiously published in London, and that legal proceedings have been instituted against the publisher, I request the favour of your insertion of the following explanation of the affair, as it relates to me.

"A poem, entitled 'Queen Mab,' was written by me, at the age of eighteen, I dare say in a sufficiently intemperate spirit—but even then was not intended for publication, and a few copies only were struck off, to be distributed among my personal friends. I have not seen this production for several years; I doubt not but that it is perfectly worthless in point of literary composition; and that in all that concerns moral and political speculation, as well as in the subtler discriminations of metaphysical and religious doctrine, it is still more crude and immature. I am a devoted enemy to religious, political, and domestic oppression; and I regret this publication not so much from literary vanity, as because I fear it is better fitted to injure than to serve the sacred cause of freedom. I have directed my solicitor to apply to Chancery for an injunction to restrain the sale; but after the precedent of Mr. Southey's 'Wat Tyler,' (a

poem, written, I believe, at the same age, and with the same unreflecting enthusi-
asm,) with little hope of success.

"Whilst I exonerate myself from all share in having divulged opinions hostile to existing sanctions, under the form, whatever it may be, which they assume in this poem; it is scarcely necessary for me to protest against the system of inculcating the truth of Christianity or the excellence of Monarchy, however true or however excellent they may be, by such equivocal arguments as confiscation and imprisonment, and invective and slander, and the insolent violation of the most sacred ties of nature and society.

"Sir,

"I am your obliged and obedient servant,

"PERCY B. SHELLEY.

"Pisa, June 22, 1821."

II. *From the 1840 Revised Edition of*
The Poetical Works of Percy Bysshe Shelley,
Edited by Mary W. Shelley

SHELLEY was eighteen when he wrote "Queen Mab:" he never published it. When it was written, he had come to the decision that he was too young to be a "judge of controversies;" and he was desirous of acquiring "that sobriety of spirit which is the characteristic of true heroism." But he never doubted the truth or utility of his opinions; and in printing and privately distributing "Queen Mab" he believed that he should further their dissemination, without occasioning the mischief either to others or himself that might arise from publication. It is doubtful whether he would himself have admitted it into a collection of his works. His severe classical taste, refined by the constant study of the Greek poets, might have discovered defects that escape the ordinary reader, and the change his opinions underwent in many points, would have prevented him from putting forth the speculations of his boyish days. But the poem is too beautiful in itself, and far too remarkable as the production of a boy of eighteen, to allow of its being passed over: besides that having been frequently reprinted, the omission would be vain. In the former edition certain portions were left out, as shocking the general reader from the violence of their attack on religion. I myself had a painful feeling that such erasures might be looked upon as a mark of disrespect towards the author, and am glad to have the opportunity of restoring them. The notes also are reprinted entire; not because they are models of reasoning or lessons of truth; but because Shelley wrote them. And that all that a man, at once so distinguished and so excellent, ever did, deserves to be preserved. The alterations his opinions underwent ought to be recorded, for they form his history.

A series of articles was published in the "New Monthly Magazine," during the autumn of the year 1832, written by a man of great talent, a fellow collegian and warm friend of Shelley: they describe admirably the state of his mind during his collegiate life. Inspired with ardour for the acquisition of knowledge; endowed with the keenest sensibility, and with the fortitude of a martyr, Shelley came among his fellow-creatures, congregated for the purposes of education, like a spirit from another sphere, too delicately organised for the rough treatment man uses towards man, especially in the season of youth; and too resolute in carrying out his own sense of good and justice not to become a victim. To a devoted attachment to those he loved, he added a determined resistance to oppression. Refusing to fag at Eton, he was treated with revolting cruelty by masters and boys: this roused, instead of taming his spirit, and he rejected the duty of obedience, when it was enforced by menaces and punishment. To aversion to the society of his fellow-creatures, such as he found them when collected together in societies, where one egged on the other to acts of tyranny, was joined the deepest sympathy and compassion; while the attachment he felt for individuals and the admiration with which he regarded their powers and their virtues, led him to entertain a high opinion of the perfectibility of human nature, and he believed that all could reach the highest grade of moral improvement, did not the customs and prejudices of society foster evil passions, and excuse evil actions.

The oppression which, trembling at every nerve yet resolute to heroism, it was his ill fortune to encounter at school and at college, led him to dissent in all things from those whose arguments were blows, whose faith appeared to engender blame and hatred. "During my existence," he wrote to a friend in 1812, "I have incessantly speculated, thought, and read." His readings were not always well chosen; among them were the works of the French philosophers; as far as metaphysical argument went, he temporarily became a convert. At the same time, it was the cardinal article of his faith, that if men were but taught and induced to treat their fellows with love, charity, and equal rights, this earth would realise Paradise. He looked upon religion as it is professed, and, above all, practised, as hostile, instead of friendly, to the cultivation of those virtues, which would make men brothers.

Can this be wondered at? At the age of seventeen, fragile in health and frame, of the purest habits in morals, full of devoted generosity and universal kindness, glowing with ardour to attain wisdom, resolved at every personal sacrifice to do right, burning with a desire for affection and sympathy,—he was treated as a reprobate, cast forth as a criminal.

The cause was, that he was sincere; that he believed the opinions which he entertained, to be true; and he loved truth with a martyr's love: he was ready to sacrifice station and fortune, and his dearest affections, at its shrine. The sacrifice was demanded from, and made by, a youth of seventeen. It is a singular fact in the history of society in the civilised nations of modern times, that no false step is so irretrievable as one made in early youth. Older men, it is true, when they oppose their fellows, and transgress ordinary rules, carry a certain prudence or hypocrisy as a shield along with them. But youth is rash; nor can it imagine, while asserting what it believes to be true, and doing what it believes to be right, that it should be denounced as vicious, and pursued as a criminal.

Shelley possessed a quality of mind which experience has shown me to be of the rarest occurrence among human beings: this was his *unworldliness*. The usual motives that rule men, prospects of present or future advantage, the rank and fortune of those around, the taunts and censures, or the praise of those who were hostile to him, had no influence whatever over his actions, and apparently none over his thoughts. It is difficult even to express the simplicity and directness of purpose that adorned him. Some few might be found in the history of mankind, and some one at least among his own friends, equally disinterested and scornful, even to severe personal sacrifices, of every baser motive. But no one, I believe, ever joined this noble but passive virtue to equal active endeavours, for the benefit of his friends and mankind in general, and to equal power to produce the advantages he desired. The world's brightest gauds, and its most solid advantages, were of no worth in his eyes, when compared to the cause of what he considered truth, and the good of his fellow-creatures. Born in a position which, to his inexperienced mind, afforded the greatest facilities to practise the tenets he espoused, he boldly declared the use he would make of fortune and station, and enjoyed the belief that he should materially benefit his fellow-creatures by his actions; while, conscious of surpassing powers of reason and imagination, it is not strange that he should, even while so young, have believed that his written thoughts would tend to disseminate opinions, which he believed conducive to the happiness of the human race.

If man were a creature devoid of passion, he might have said and done all this with quietness. But he was too enthusiastic, and too full of hatred of all the ills he witnessed, not to scorn danger. Various disappointments tortured, but could not tame, his soul. The more enmity he met, the more earnestly he became attached to his peculiar views, and hostile to those of the men who persecuted him.

He was animated to greater zeal by compassion for his fellow-creatures. His sympathy was excited by the misery with which the world is bursting. He witnessed the sufferings of the poor, and was aware of the evils of ignorance. He desired to induce every rich man to despoil himself of superfluity, and to create a brotherhood of property and service, and was ready to be the first to lay down the advantages of his birth. He was of too uncompromising a disposition to join any party. He did not in his youth look forward to gradual improvement: nay, in those days of intolerance, now almost forgotten, it seemed as easy to look forward to the sort of millennium of freedom and brotherhood, which he thought the proper state of mankind, as to the present reign of moderation and improvement. Ill health made him believe that his race would soon be run; that a year or two was all he had of life. He desired that these years should be useful and illustrious. He saw, in a fervent call on his fellow-creatures to share alike the blessings of the creation, to love and serve each other, the noblest work that life and time permitted him. In this spirit he composed QUEEN MAB.

He was a lover of the wonderful and wild in literature; but had not fostered these tastes at their genuine sources—the romances and chivalry of the middle ages; but in the perusal of such German works as were current in those days. Under the influence of these, he, at the age of fifteen, wrote two short prose romances of slender merit. The sentiments and language were exaggerated, the composition imitative and poor. He wrote also a poem on the subject of Ahasuerus—being led to it by a German fragment he picked up, dirty and torn, in Lincoln's-inn-Fields. This fell afterwards into other hands—and was considerably altered before it was printed. Our earlier English poetry was almost unknown to him. The love and knowledge of nature developed by Wordsworth—the lofty melody and mysterious beauty of Coleridge's poetry—and the wild fantastic machinery and gorgeous scenery adopted by Southey, composed his favourite reading; the rhythm of Queen Mab was founded on that of Thalaba, and the first few lines bear a striking resemblance in spirit, though not in idea, to the opening of that poem. His fertile imagination, and ear, tuned to the finest sense of harmony, preserved him from imitation. Another of his favourite books was the poem of Gebir, by Walter Savage Landor. From his boyhood he had a wonderful facility of versification which he carried into another language, and his Latin school verses were composed with an ease and correctness that procured for him prizes—and caused him to be resorted to by all his friends for help. He was, at the period of writing Queen Mab, a great traveller within the limits of England, Scotland, and Ireland. His time was spent among the loveliest scenes of these countries. Mountain and lake and forest were his home; the phenomena of nature were his favourite study. He loved to inquire into their causes, and was addicted to pursuits of natural philosophy and chemistry, as far as they could be carried on, as an amusement. These tastes gave truth and vivacity to his descriptions, and warmed his soul with that deep admiration for the wonders of Nature which constant association with her inspired.

He never intended to publish Queen Mab as it stands; but a few years after, when printing Alastor, he extracted a small portion which he entitled "The Dæmon of the World;" in this he changed somewhat the versification—and made other alterations scarcely to be called improvements.

I extract the invocation of Queen Mab to the Soul of Ianthe, as altered in "The Dæmon of the World." I give it as a specimen of the alterations made. It well characterises his own state of mind:

INVOCATION.

———

Maiden, the world's supremest spirit
  Beneath the shadow of her wings
Folds all thy memory doth inherit
  From ruin of divinest things,
    Feelings that lure thee to betray,
    And light of thoughts that pass away.

For thou hast earned a mighty boon;
  The truths which wisest poets see
Dimly, thy mind may make its own,
  Rewarding its own majesty,
    Entranced in some diviner mood
    Of self-oblivious solitude.

Custom and faith and power thou spurnest,
  From hate and fear thy heart is free;
Ardent and pure as day thou burnest
  For dark and cold mortality;
    A living light to cheer it long,
    The watch-fires of the world among.

Therefore, from nature's inner shrine,
  Where gods and fiends in worship bend,
Majestic Spirit, be it thine
  The flame to seize, the veil to rend,
    Where the vast snake Eternity
    In charmed sleep doth ever lie.

All that inspires thy voice of love,
  Or speaks in thy unclosing eyes,
Or through thy frame doth burn and move,
  Or think, or feel, awake, arise!
    Spirit, leave for mine and me
    Earth's unsubstantial mimicry!

Some years after, when in Italy, a bookseller published an edition of Queen Mab as it originally stood. Shelley was hastily written to by his friends, under the idea that, deeply injurious as the mere distribution of the poem had proved, the publication might awaken fresh persecutions. At the suggestion of these friends he wrote a letter on the subject, printed in "The Examiner" newspaper—with which I close this history of his earliest work.

TO THE EDITOR OF "THE EXAMINER."

"Sir,

"Having heard that a poem, entitled 'Queen Mab,' has been surreptitiously published in London, and that legal proceedings have been instituted against the publisher, I request the favour of your insertion of the following explanation of the affair, as it relates to me.

"A poem, entitled 'Queen Mab,' was written by me, at the age of eighteen, I dare say in a sufficiently intemperate spirit—but even then was not intended for publication, and a few copies only were struck off, to be distributed among my personal friends. I have not seen this production for several years; I doubt not but that it is perfectly worthless in point of literary composition; and that in all that concerns moral and political speculation, as well as in the subtler discriminations of metaphysical and religious doctrine, it is still more crude and immature. I am a devoted enemy to religious, political, and domestic oppression; and I regret this publication not so much from literary vanity, as because I fear it is better fitted to injure than to serve the sacred cause of freedom. I have directed my solicitor to apply to Chancery for an injunction to restrain the sale; but after the precedent of Mr. Southey's 'Wat Tyler,' (a poem, written, I believe, at the same age, and with the same unreflecting enthusiasm,) with little hope of success.

"Whilst I exonerate myself from all share in having divulged opinions hostile to existing sanctions, under the form, whatever it may be, which they assume in this poem; it is scarcely necessary for me to protest against the system of inculcating the truth of Christianity or the excellence of Monarchy, however true or however excellent they may be, by such equivocal arguments as confiscation and imprisonment, and invective and slander, and the insolent violation of the most sacred ties of nature and society.

"Sir,

"I am your obliged and obedient servant,

"PERCY B. SHELLEY.

"*Pisa, June 22, 1821.*"

DONALD H. REIMAN, Adjunct Professor of English at the University of Delaware, has since 1965 been editor (later co-editor with Doucet Devin Fischer) of *Shelley and his Circle,* a catalogue-edition of the relevant manuscripts through 1824 in the Carl H. Pforzheimer Collection of Shelley and His Circle at the New York Public Library. He has co-edited *Shelley's Poetry and Prose,* the second edition with Neil Fraistat, compiled *The Romantics Reviewed* (9 volumes) and *The Romantic Context: Poetry* (128 volumes), and was general editor of *Manuscripts of the Younger Romantics* (29 volumes) and *The Bodleian Shelley Manuscripts* (23 volumes), editing or co-editing eight volumes in those series. His other books include *Shelley's "The Triumph of Life," Percy Bysshe Shelley, Byron on the Continent* (with D. D. Fischer), *English Romantic Poetry, 1800–1835, Intervals of Inspiration: The Skeptical Tradition and the Psychology of Romanticism, Romantic Texts and Contexts,* and *The Study of Modern Manuscripts* (the Lyell Lectures in Bibliography for 1989). He also co-edited *The Evidence of the Imagination: Studies of Interactions between Life and Art in English Romantic Literature* and has contributed 140 essays and reviews to encyclopedias, other multiauthored books, and professional periodicals on subjects ranging from *Beowulf* and Chaucer to Yeats and Ammons.

Since earning degrees at the College of Wooster (1956) and the University of Illinois (1957, 1960), Reiman has taught the Romantics at eight universities and lectured at colleges and universities in the United States, Canada, and the United Kingdom. He has served on the editorial board of the University of Delaware Press, the advisory boards of several periodicals, was a founding director of the Wordsworth-Coleridge Association, the Society for Textual Scholarship, and the Byron Society of America, and has been an officer of the Keats-Shelley Association of America since 1973.

NEIL FRAISTAT, Professor of English at the University of Maryland and a founder and general editor of the *Romantic Circles* Web site, received his Ph.D. from the University of Pennsylvania in 1979. He has published *The Poem and the Book: Interpreting Collections of Romantic Poetry, Poems in Their Place: The Intertextuality and Order of Poetic Collections,* and *The "Prometheus Unbound" Notebooks.* He has edited with Donald H. Reiman the second edition of *Shelley's Poetry and Prose,* with Elizabeth B. Loizeaux a collection of essays entitled *Reimagining Textuality: Textual Studies in the Late Age of Print,* and with Susan S. Lanser an edition of Helen Maria Williams's *Letters Written in France.*

Fraistat's online editions of Percy Bysshe Shelley's *The Devil's Walk,* co-edited with Reiman, and *The Medusa of Leonardo da Vinci,* co-edited with Melissa J. Sites, can be found on *Romantic Circles,* as can the collection of essays he edited, *The Young Shelley: Vulgarisms, Politics, and Fractals.* His articles on Romantic period literature and culture have been published widely, in such journals as *PMLA, JEGP, Studies in Romanticism, Keats-Shelley Journal, The Wordsworth Circle, TEXT,* and *Publications of the Bibliographical Society of America.* He currently serves on the editorial boards of *Studies in Romanticism, Keats-Shelley Journal, Romanticism, Romanticism on the Net,* the *Emily Dickinson Electronic Archive,* and the University Press of Virginia's Electronic Imprint. He has been awarded the Society for Textual Scholarship's Fredson Bowers Memorial Prize for Most Distinguished Essay on Textual Scholarship, the Keats-Shelley Association Prize, and the Keats-Shelley Association's Distinguished Scholar Award.

Library of Congress Cataloging-in-Publication Data

Shelley, Percy Bysshe, 1792–1822.
    [Poems]
    The complete poetry of Percy Bysshe Shelley / edited by Donald H.
Reiman and Neil Fraistat.
        p.   cm.
    Includes index.
    I. Reiman, Donald H.   II. Fraistat, Neil, 1952–   III. Title.
PR5402   2000
8219.7—dc21

                                                        99-15163
                                                          CIP

VOL 1. 0-8018-6119-5   •   VOL 2. 0-8018-7874-8

Library of Congress Cataloging-in-Publication Data

Shelley, Percy Bysshe, 1792–1822.
    [Poems]
    The complete poetry of Percy Bysshe Shelley / edited by Donald H.
Reiman and Neil Fraistat.
        p. cm.
    Includes index.
    I. Reiman, Donald H.   II. Fraistat, Neil, 1952–   III. Title.
PR5402   2000
8219.7—dc21

                                                                99-15163
                                                                    CIP

VOL 1. 0-8018-6119-5 • VOL 2. 0-8018-7874-8